COUNTRY
MUSIC USA

Brad and Michele Moore
Roots Music Series

COUNTRY MUSIC USA

Bill C. Malone & Tracey E. W. Laird

UNIVERSITY OF TEXAS PRESS 〽 AUSTIN

Fiftieth anniversary edition, 2018

Requests for permission to reproduce material from this work should be
sent to:
    Permissions
    University of Texas Press
    P.O. Box 7819
    Austin, TX 78713-7819
    utpress.utexas.edu/rp-form

♾ The paper used in this book meets the minimum requirements of
ANSI/NISO Z39.48-1992 (R1997) (Permanence of Paper).

LIBRARY OF CONGRESS CATALOGING-IN-PUBLICATION DATA

Names: Malone, Bill C., author. | Laird, Tracey E. W., author.
Title: Country music USA / Bill C. Malone and Tracey E. W. Laird.
Description: Fiftieth anniversary edition. | Austin : University of Texas
    Press, 2018. | Includes bibliographical references and index.
Identifiers: LCCN 2017046039| ISBN 978-1-4773-1534-7
    (cloth : alk. paper) | ISBN 978-1-4773-1535-4 (pbk. : alk. paper) |
    ISBN 978-1-4773-1536-1 (library e-book) | ISBN 978-1-4773-1537-8
    (nonlibrary e-book)
Subjects: LCSH: Country music—History and criticism.
Classification: LCC ML3524.M34 2018 | DDC 781.6420973—dc23
LC record available at https://lccn.loc.gov/2017046039

doi:10.7560/315347

Contents

LIST OF ILLUSTRATIONS   vii

FOREWORD by Henry Sapoznik   ix

PREFACE   xiii

1. The Folk Background before Commercialism   1
2. The Early Period of Commercial Hillbilly Music   37
3. The First Country Singing Star: Jimmie Rodgers   91
4. Country Music during the Depression   111
5. The Cowboy Image and the Growth of Western Music   160
6. The War Years: The National Expansion of Country Music   208
7. The Boom Period: The Emergence of a Big Business, 1946–1953   233
8. The Development of Country-Pop Music and the Nashville Sound   287
9. The Reinvigoration of Modern Country Music, 1960–1972   314
10. Bluegrass   380
11. Country Music, 1972–1984   433
12. Tradition and Change: Country Music, 1985–2000   489
13. A New Century   545

NOTES   573

BIBLIOGRAPHICAL ESSAYS   592

INDEX   679

INDEX OF SONG TITLES   733

Illustrations

1. Eck Robertson   28
2. Al Hopkins, John Hopkins, Tony Alderman, John Rector, Uncle Am Stuart, and Fiddlin' John Carson   36
3. Carson Robison   53
4. Charlie Poole and the North Carolina Ramblers   60
5. Bradley Kincaid   65
6. Vernon Dalhart   72
7. The Carter Family   77
8. Uncle Dave Macon and Dorris Macon   87
9. Jimmie Rodgers   92
10. The Callahan Brothers   131
11. The Cumberland Ridge Runners   134
12. The Blue Sky Boys   135
13. The Monroe Brothers   138
14. The Coon Creek Girls   140
15. Floyd Tillman   161
16. Carl T. Sprague   164
17. Gene Autry   169
18. The Girls of the Golden West   174
19. The Prairie Ramblers and Patsy Montana   175
20. Ernest Tubb   185
21. The Light Crust Doughboys   191
22. Milton Brown and His Musical Brownies   192
23. Bob Wills and the Texas Playboys   203
24. Roy Acuff and the Louvin Brothers   222
25. Merle Travis   237
26. The Bailes Brothers   253
27. Molly O'Day and Lynn Davis   259
28. Kitty Wells   260

29. Hank Thompson   267

30. Lefty Frizzell   272

31. Hank Williams   281

32. Johnny Cash   297

33. Jim Reeves   304

34. George Jones   336

35. Merle Haggard   344

36. Tammy Wynette   363

37. Dolly Parton   365

38. Bill Malone and Kinky Friedman   368

39. Charley Pride   371

40. Bill Monroe   381

41. The Blue Grass Boys   385

42. Ralph and Carter Stanley   389

43. Lester Flatt and Earl Scruggs   390

44. Conway Twitty and Loretta Lynn   448

45. Willie Nelson   466

46. Waylon Jennings   469

47. George Strait   481

48. Emmylou Harris   484

49. Ricky Skaggs   487

50. Garth Brooks   503

51. Earl Scruggs and Marty Stuart   514

52. Tim O'Brien   527

53. Bill Monroe and Doc Watson   532

54. Del McCoury Band   533

55. Alison Krauss   536

56. Rhonda Vincent   538

57. Chris Thile   540

58. New Grass Revival   541

59. Luke Bryan   546

60. Beyoncé and the Dixie Chicks   549

61. Miranda Lambert   555

62. Brad Paisley and Carrie Underwood   558

63. Sturgill Simpson   563

Foreword

Henry Sapoznik

The history of country music is awash in a seemingly limitless supply of memorable "firsts": the first commercial recording (1922), the first broadcast of the *Grand Ole Opry* (1925), the first singing cowboy movie (1930), among many others. But the first *book* to bring together the full panoramic sweep of country music in a well-written and closely observed unimpeachable work is in your hands. *Country Music USA* originated as a dissertation penned in 1965 by thirty-one-year-old Bill C. Malone in fulfillment of his doctorate in American History at the University of Texas, Austin.

Malone was born in 1934 on his family's tenant farm, a lonely, hardscrabble outpost in rural Smith County—then East Texas cotton country—about twenty miles west of Tyler. Malone's early and easygoing ownership of the received raft of traditional music came from his mother, Maude Owens Malone, who seamlessly rendered offerings from church hymnody as easily as those rescued from old songbooks and fragile, yellowed sheet music. This patchwork quilt of repertory—rendered in a stripped-down and practical style—placed the emerging historian of his southern folk culture immediately into the sturdy musical continuity of the traditional transmission of generations. Because the amenities of the Malone household differed little from a similar farm of the mid-nineteenth century, the arrival in 1939 of a Philco battery radio overnight introduced the family to the outside world and to the radio hillbillies who helped them survive the exigencies of hard times. A flood of programs both day and night made passionate fans of his parents and older brothers, with young Bill soaking up the sound of dozens of earnest influences.

Malone's homegrown smooth and reliable singing style won him some local notoriety after he arrived at UT-Austin to pursue his studies. He even took up the guitar, not in any kind of hot licks plectrum style but with the traditional thumb/index strum, reminiscent of what was played in countless parlors, at parties, and on porches, a style he still resolutely plays today. But, had Malone not built upon a dissertation topic suggested by his professor, this cornerstone work may never have been written. The release of *Country Music USA* in 1968 came when Nashville, as the citadel of country music, was being challenged by new and growing grassroots audiences for bluegrass and old-time music and by other revivals such as Cajun and western swing. Evidence of this rise of interest in older forms of country music could also be found in the cottage industries of reissue LPs, specialty magazines, instruction books, and new traditional music festivals and contests. Lacking, however, was a unifying vision that brought all these styles—and their fascinating backstories—between two covers. Construction of an overarching ingathering of this confluence of movements called for a well-observed, well-analyzed, well-described, and compelling narrative. Such a work could best be accomplished by a disciplined scholar of cultural history, who just happened to be a product of that society.

What makes this book so resilient is Malone's equity as what anthropologists accurately, though inelegantly, refer to as a "participant-observer." As a participant, he is first and foremost a fan: a passionate carrier and conveyor of key moments in the life of country music. His own ironclad possession of the music is a living representation of the generation of fans who honed and internalized it before him. Yet, as the observer, he is also a diligent digger-outer of knowledge with a historical researcher's penchant for detail and documentation. The industrial-strength academic training he received in his doctoral work—in concert with his native curiosity and smarts—is always evident in thoughtfully crafted and compellingly articulate books. If Stetson made a mortarboard, it would be the "Bill C. Malone" model.

Despite *Country Music USA* having started life as a doctoral dissertation, its tone and equitable inclusive narrative allowed even the most casual reader to fully grasp the rather miraculous emergence of a national music from the outcroppings of regional and local traditions. For scholars and researchers, it was an unimpeachably thorough and groundbreaking work. Malone's book effortlessly tapped into the bulletproof discipline of a university tome with the lively effervescence of an enthusiastic fan. So why, in the subsequent years with a dependable outpouring of new books, biographies, and country music cable networks, has the importance and relevance of this book remained powerful and undimmed? *Country Music USA*, an evergreen, has been revised but never out of print since its first publication. It is not merely that Malone is the only country music author to have seen Uncle Dave Macon perform in a *Grand Old Opry* tent show in 1949, but it certainly doesn't hurt. Malone is an in-the-bone adherent of the "three chords and the truth" school of country music, a kind of straight-ahead simplicity that has found a fresh revival among the new generation of alt. country/Americana fans. Malone might say that today's mainstream music would sound better if the people from the end of his book knew more about the music of the people from the beginning.

To add depth to the sweep of such an ambitious overview, Malone continues to create a definitive library of books, essays, and liner notes on a satisfyingly wide spectrum of topics and subjects designed to offer a wider and more vibrant platform from which to understand country music in its myriad forms. Away from his writer's desk, he has even taken a star turn on *A Prairie Home Companion* in 2013 and is the featured historian in Ken Burns's forthcoming docuseries on country music, which is based on the narrative within these covers.

Together with his wife, the author, historian, singer, and mandolinist Bobbie, Bill is a ubiquitous presence in Madison, Wisconsin, giving audiences an invaluable visceral connectivity to the old-time country songs and sound he grew up with. Since his arrival in the city in 1997, Malone has hosted *Back to the Country*, a weekly three-hour thematic program on community radio station WORT, an expansive and personal guided tour of country music delivered in his evocative and mellifluous Texas drawl. It might seem that as Bill C. Malone was moved, inspired, and shaped by the great country music coming over his family's old Philco radio, *Back to the Country* is his way of offering a parallel experience to his own eager and fiercely loyal broadcast audience.

And finally, what also makes *Country Music USA* a truly great book *to me* is the role it played in my own life. In the early 1970s, I received a copy when I was just beginning to discover and play old-time music. Malone's book became a vivid cultural passport for a child of Holocaust refugees, who turned to traditional music as a way of accelerating and underscoring a desire to be part of the deep cultural continuity of my family's new adopted American home. When it came time for me to write my book, *Klezmer! Jewish Music from Old World to New*—also a first serious history of a musical genre composed by a community-based "participant/observer"—I used Malone's work as a road map, because I, too, hoped to produce something representative and timeless. Only when I arrived in Madison in 2009 to further my work in Yiddish culture did I first meet and get to know Bill and Bobbie Malone, and it is where we have become friends and brought to full circle my connection to the man whose work inspired my own.

Happy birthday, *Country Music USA!* Here's to yet another first: its first fifty years.

Preface

I am pleased that as a product of my initial foray into scholarship and a lifetime of devotion to the sounds I love, *Country Music USA* has endured for fifty years as a chronicle of country music's history and evolution. And I am also pleased to have been given the opportunity to revise it once again—the last chance that I will probably have. Consequently, I have tried meticulously to correct mistakes, clarify my language, update tenses, add new information, and take advantage of new insights. I have also been joined in the enterprise by a gifted young scholar, Tracey Laird, who has written a new concluding chapter.

My romance with country music began long before this book was conceived. It has been about eighty years since the little Philco battery radio came into our farmhouse in East Texas (a little community, now vanished, called Galena—about twenty miles west of Tyler), bringing a touch of the outside world, along with the music of the Carter Family, the Chuck Wagon Gang, the Stamps Quartet, the Shelton Brothers, the Callahan Brothers, Cowboy Slim Rinehart, and the many performers of the *National Barn Dance* and the *Grand Ole Opry*. For me, it was the beginning of a love affair that has never ceased. It has been even longer than that since I first heard my mother singing old-fashioned sentimental songs like "The Eastbound Train" and "Prisoner at the

Bar," or pouring out her soul in religious tunes like "Farther Along" and "Leave It There." My older brothers, Wylie and Kelly, began trying out their voices on what we then called hillbilly music when they were about fourteen or fifteen years old, strumming on a cheap guitar that Wylie had obtained in a trade with our neighbor Thomas Starr, plowing for him for about a week. Through my brothers, and through the voices that sang to us over the battery radio, songs like "The Last Letter" and "It Makes No Difference Now" moved into my consciousness alongside the gospel and sentimental parlor pieces learned from my mother.

I sang country music all my life but made no serious attempts to learn the guitar until my graduate days at the University of Texas in Austin. Until I learned my first chords, such friends as Tom Crouch and Willie Benson wore out their fingers accompanying me as I sang at parties and beer busts in the Austin area. I eventually discovered Threadgill's, a now-famous bar and restaurant in North Austin, where I sang a couple of times a week in the informal jam sessions that prevailed around the big circular wooden tables. It was my notoriety as an amateur country singer that led to the writing of this book. In December 1960, I traveled to Houston with a few graduate student friends and my supervising professor, Joe B. Frantz, to see the Texas Longhorn football team play in the Bluebonnet Bowl. We sang songs all the way to Houston, with Dr. Frantz requesting song after song, and that evening during dinner he suggested that I choose as a doctoral dissertation a business history of Nashville music publishing. Once the work was begun, I expanded the topic to its present limits with his blessing. I will always be thankful that in history, a conservative discipline, Dr. Frantz exhibited such tolerance for an unorthodox subject—the first academic study of country music. The dissertation eventually became *Country Music USA*, bearing a title suggested by the folklorist John Greenway.

When I began my research, Austin had not yet become a hotbed of live music performance. I was far removed from the few people who did serious collecting or scholarship in the field of country music and was largely unaware of their existence. The two major country music repositories—the Country Music Foundation in Nashville and the Southern Folklife Collection at the University of North Carolina in Chapel Hill—did not exist when I began my research in 1961 and were still in their infancy by the time the book was published in 1968.

The resources for studying the phenomenon of country music were sketchy and widely scattered. In the decades that have passed since the original publication, an explosion of scholarship has occurred, and many writers, both academic and popular, have entered the field, unearthing new information and fresh perspectives. In addition to the archival resources that now exist in Nashville and Chapel Hill, a wealth of musical material also awaits the scholar on the web—in websites, blogs, published books and articles, iTunes, YouTube offerings, and related items that can no longer be found anywhere else. Country music itself, as a dynamic and ever-changing facet of American popular culture, has burgeoned and metamorphosed since the late sixties. The careers of many musicians have faded, while others have blossomed; others will have bloomed and withered by the time this new edition appears.

I believe that *Country Music USA* has done its part to tell country music's story around the world while also lending some respectability to its serious academic treatment. Country music courses are now taught in many colleges and universities; theses and dissertations assay the field in a variety of scholarly disciplines—even in music departments where they were once rare—and academic papers dealing with country music are annually presented at conventions and symposia. The International Country Music Conference (ICMC) has now been meeting annually in Nashville for over thirty years, giving scholars opportunities to share their insights. Almost a decade elapsed, however, before my own discipline, history, paid any serious attention to the study of country music. A milestone of sorts was reached in November 1977, when I gave a lecture-concert on country music, accompanied by a bluegrass band, at the opening session of the Southern Historical Association convention in New Orleans. Thirty years later, I gave another solo presentation, at the meeting of the same organization and in the same city, on the occasion of this book's fortieth anniversary. This was a considerable advance, indeed, for an association that had previously ignored country music at its convention sessions and in its journal, and that had once had as a president an eminent historian of the South—Thomas D. Clark—who referred to the "hillbilly rabble" of radio in one of his books.[1]

I hope that my perspective as both a historian and a fan of country music has worked to assure balance in my study, although my biases have no doubt affected my perceptions and interpretations. Still, I have striven for objectivity and have attempted to be fair to those styles that I do not like. My personal preferences clearly lean toward hard-core country, and to singers with individuality whose sounds and styles reflect their rural or working-class origins—whether they are "down-home" stylists like the Blue Sky Boys, Molly O'Day, the Bailes Brothers, and Ralph Stanley, or honky-tonk performers like Ernest Tubb, George Jones, Merle Haggard, and Dale Watson. To purists like me, country music has been inundated by musicians whose sounds suggest neither regional, rustic, nor blue-collar nativity, but are instead rooted in the homogenizing and mass-consumption-oriented media establishment. On the other hand, the continued emergence of musicians—such as the Carolina Chocolate Drops, the Quebe Sisters, Sturgill Simpson, and Jason Isbell, who effectively fuse modernity and tradition—and the remarkable growth of interest in old-time string band music indicate the existence of a large audience hungry for more "authentic" fare and therefore grateful to find something palpable rather than plastic. May there always be such a public to keep these impulses alive.

My debts are many, and I have tried to acknowledge them in the bibliographical essays. As noted in the first edition, the real sources of this book are the many musicians, professional and amateur, who have captivated my interest since I was a child. While I can neither name nor repay all of them, I can at least acknowledge the profound impact they have had on my life. Among the many nonmusicians who have provided both friendship and research support, I still feel the need to single out three individuals: Jo Walker-Meador and the late Bob Pinson and Archie Green. Bob Pinson, onetime Director of Acquisitions for the Country Music Foundation Library, sought me out during the early stages of my dissertation research (when he was a private collector in Southern California) and never ceased to be unselfish in his aid and encouragement. Archie Green was known and revered by every student of American vernacular music. One of our greatest folklorists, Green was a model of indefatigability, limitless ideas, and insatiable curiosity. He was an inspiration to all who knew him. Jo Walker-Meador, who served for many years as the Executive Director of the Country Music Association, was with that organization at its beginnings and was a prime force in its remarkable expansion. Without her help back in 1961 in arranging interviews and providing contacts, my first research trip to Nashville might very well have proved fruitless.

Finally, I wish to dedicate this book to the memory of my mother and father, Maude and Cleburne Malone, and to my wife, Bobbie. My parents bequeathed to me the culture of which country music is a part as well as a special love and respect for that music's primacy in their lives. Bobbie came to me with little knowledge of or experience with country music, but in the years since our marriage began she has become an accomplished mandolin player and a good country singer. Above all, she has given me a special love that I never believed possible. In the words of the Ricky Skaggs song, "I wouldn't change a single thing."

BCM

1985, 2010, 2018

★ ★ ★

Bill Malone's original publication of *Country Music USA* launched an entire field of study. His work definitively surveyed country music's territory, asserting a scope and range of style wide and deep enough to inspire scholars of music, language, geography, history, sociology, anthropology, and philosophy for decades afterward. His work canvasses country's varied sounds and underscores concerns about its production, artistry, audiences, and expressive culture; in a spirit of exhaustive exploration, *Country Music USA* engages far-reaching questions about media, race, gender, region, and identity.

It is hard to find a scholar working on country music today who cannot point to something in Malone's original book that planted a seed for future work. My own career constitutes a case in point. In his encyclopedic grasp of country music history, Bill mentions the radio barn dance *Louisiana Hayride* and describes the distinctive music scene in Austin, Texas. These became the focal points for two decades of my scholarly research and writing. That said, my contributions to this project have been circumscribed in comparison to the sweeping impact the first-edition *Country Music USA* had on me as a scholar.

Country Music USA was not my first encounter with Bill's work. That came more by accident or, it seems with hindsight, kismet. I recall laboring in the music library as a graduate student at the University of Michigan. I had burned out on reading and listening assignments in preparation for a class about the music of Tchaikovsky, and so my attention wandered to materials on the shelves all around me. I grabbed a boxed set—the *Smithsonian Collection of Classic Country Music*—and lowered the phonograph needle onto the first spinning disc.

The sounds pouring forth from the record player sparked a surge of joy, and I kept listening until the library closed its doors that night. Perhaps it was a sense of comfort and familiarity derived from music that took me back to my grandparents' kitchen in Shreveport, Louisiana, not far from Bill's hometown of Galena. Pampaw and Micmaw tuned their set to Shreveport's clear-channel 50,000-watt station KWKH for the better part of each day. The musical sounds also sparked my curiosity. I opened the Smithsonian Collection's liner notes for my first encounter with Bill Malone, who had also curated the music.

Bill's scholarly apprehension of the story of country music has shaped me as a student, teacher, and writer. His feedback, critique, and encouragement throughout my scholarly undertakings likewise have been invaluable. I'm honored to contribute my perspective on country music during the twenty-first century to this fiftieth anniversary edition. In doing so, I do not attempt to mirror Bill's exhaustive approach. Instead, I plumb a handful of significant examples that in some way address country music's meaning, identity, and relationship with its multiple audiences. Essentially I address how a twenty-first-century listener might answer the question, "What is *real* country music?"

For my part, I wish to acknowledge my gratitude and love for Brandon, the source for never-ending inspiration and support, both editorial and, more broadly speaking, lifewise. Henry and Zoey equally amaze, encourage, humble, and fill me with pride and joy every day. Family, loved ones, friends, and colleagues in Georgia, Louisiana, Colorado, Texas, Oklahoma, Indiana, and elsewhere keep me going in ways of which they are likely unaware. I dedicate this project to Big Annie, who invariably "just can't wait to get on the road again."

TEWL
2018

COUNTRY MUSIC USA

CHAPTER I
The Folk Background before Commercialism

Country music long ago ceased to be simply an American cultural expression; it is now a phenomenon of worldwide appeal. Nevertheless, the music defies precise definition, and no term (not even "country") has ever successfully encapsulated its essence. A vigorous hybrid form of music, it constantly changes and grows in complexity, just as the society in which it thrives also matures and evolves. Introduced to the world as a southern phenomenon, in the almost one hundred years since it was first commercialized, the music has preserved, to a remarkable degree, the marks of that origin. While the roots of country music predate the American South itself, the massive commercialization it has undergone is merely one facet of that larger and ongoing technological and communications revolution that has radically transformed American popular tastes, pulling the rural, socially conservative South into the homogenizing mainstream of American life.

Hillbilly music—a once universal designation for country music— drew originally from a great reservoir of folk songs, ballads, dances, and instrumental pieces brought to North America by Anglo-Celtic immigrants. Gradually absorbing influences from other musical sources, particularly from the culture of Afro-Americans, it eventually emerged as a force strong enough to survive, and even thrive, in an urban-industrial society. British folk culture, of course, came to all regions of English-speaking North America, and pockets of tradition still persist in such places as rural New England and Canada's Maritime Provinces. Only in the southern United States, though, did dynamic folk cultural expressions, black and white, evolve into viable commercial forms. The interrelationship of black and white musical styles, or what Mike Seeger called "Music from the True Vine," set southern music apart from other American styles while underpinning many of the commercial genres that later appeared.[1]

The social conservatism that encouraged the preservation of older values and institutions in the South was a product of geography, economics, religion, and politics. Climate and topography conspired to create an environment favorable to productive agriculture, or one where white people could live in relative freedom and security, as did the herders and stock drovers, by exploiting the abundant resources of the public domain. While some people accumulated great wealth from agriculture, the majority embraced such a livelihood, or professed to do so, because it provided self-subsistence as well as the supposed nonmaterial blessings that came from cultivation of the soil: independence, self-fulfillment, health, and virtue. This beneficent vision of agriculture and the rural life that surrounded it did not really begin to dim until after the Civil War. When tenantry and sharecropping became fastened upon the land, and as farmers of all kinds became enmeshed in an impersonal system of credit and marketing demands, much of the old sense of freedom began to diminish, and people began to feel imprisoned by agriculture.[2] It is only then that we begin to see the first stirrings of what would become a mass exodus from the farms.

Whether rural life promoted independence and virtue is an arguable point, but that it fostered isolation would seem to be a certainty. In the South, people were separated, not only by social class but also by great distances and by rugged terrain that hindered easy communication. Until the late nineteenth century, cities grew slowly, while most villages and small towns remained mere appendages of the surrounding agricultural areas. European immigration, for the most part, flowed into the northern states, forsaking the South because of the lack of cities, the scarcity of jobs, and the competition of slavery. Slavery, which lay at the base of the South's socioeconomic system, contributed even more virulently to the region's isolation as white southerners from all social classes banded in defense of white supremacy and in opposition to the growing chorus of worldwide hostile criticism. Thus, the defense of slavery and the racial hierarchy that derived from it lay at the core of the South's belief system, a system militantly dedicated to the preservation of the status quo. Increasingly cut off from the currents of change in a nation rapidly succumbing to the blandishment of urbanism and industrialization, responding to the rhythms of agriculture, and clinging to an evangelical Protestantism that encouraged Bible literalism and orthodoxy, southerners adhered to that which was familiar and comfortable, and to the maintaining of traditions once the common property of Americans everywhere.

The South, then, was a folk culture. And while the reliance on the familiar was a trait that cut across social and economic lines, it was strongest among the poorer classes, black and white. The plantation owners might know ballads like "Barbara Allen" or "Lord Lovel," and they very well might have fond memories of kicking up their heels at a country dance, but their yeomen and poor white cousins *preserved* these kinds of musical diversions. Regardless of where they lived, in mountains or flatlands, the common people of the South shared a passionate commitment to music. Furthermore, since they shared similar cultural traditions, they knew and performed the same songs and styles. Arthur Palmer Hudson, a distinguished folklorist from Mississippi, argued that "not only was the singing habit a widely and perhaps equally diffused one in the South as a whole; the songs sung over the South are much the same, irrespective of locality."[3]

The socially ingrown rural South, from the tidewater of Virginia to the pine barrens of East Texas, encompassed a population that, in its commitment to and maintenance of traditional cultural values, should be considered a distinct family unit. This immense region, so incredibly diverse in its topography, is what two scholars have called "the fertile crescent of country music."[4] Following the lure of King Cotton, which forever demanded fresh land and a suitably long growing season, or otherwise seeking a temperate climate similar to that which they had left, southern migrants moved southwestward across the mountains and toward the potential cotton-producing regions of Arkansas, Louisiana, and Texas. As the frontier receded steadily westward, the southern musical culture moved with it. A poor Georgian entering a small farmer's cabin in East Texas would have felt very much at home. The architecture of the house, the food on the table, the dress and speech patterns of the hosts, and even the theology of the local church would have been reassuringly familiar. And more than likely one would have found a fiddle over the mantel, and in the general area, a multitude of musical reminders of the old homestead: a shape-note singing school, a Sacred Harp convention, fiddle contests, and house parties galore.

Of course, the folk music heard in East Texas would not have been precisely identical to that heard in North Georgia, just as the music cherished on the southern frontier was not exactly like that found in the British Isles. British immigrants to the United States brought a great storehouse of lore and song, but three thousand miles of ocean and radically different historical experiences wrought a similar divergence in musical expression. It is now next to impossible to determine the exact ethnic origin of a particular song or style dating from the British experience. English, Highland Scots, Scotch-Irish, Catholic Irish, and Welsh elements intermingled on the southern frontier, as they had previously done in the British Isles. The backcountry South may very well have been Celtic, as two eminent historians have argued,[5] but cultural intermixing had occurred so frequently and for such a long period of time that white folk culture should most appropriately be called "British" (that is, it was a composite of ethnic elements drawn principally from the British Isles and Ireland).

Whatever the specific source of the British tunes, rural southerners did not rely exclusively upon them. As soon as the American experience began, colonists began creating songs based upon their new lives here, and they borrowed songs from other cultural groups with whom they came in contact. With the passage of time, the country people built up a body of songs of American origin that sang, not of knights and fair English damsels, but of scenes and events in their own purview. Similarly, the ancient British ballads underwent, in terms of structure, subject matter, and melodic contour, a strong measure of Americanization. American names and places sometimes replaced those of British origin, and words from the American vocabulary replaced the sixteenth- and seventeenth-century terms that no longer had meaning. American ballads still spoke of "wee pen knives," "milk white steeds," and fair maidens with "lily-white hands," but the Robin Hood ballads and songs of witchcraft rarely survived the Atlantic transit. British folk culture remained most dramatically evident in the most inaccessible areas, such as the Appalachian and Ozark Mountains. Many of the songs discovered by the English folk song and dance authority Cecil Sharp and other collectors in the early twentieth century were in the modal scale of an older musical culture, that is, restricted to five or six tones and characterized by melodies that sound incomplete to modern ears.

British folk culture did not survive intact in the southern wilderness, nor should one expect it to have done so. The folk music of the South was a blending of cultural strains, British at its core but overlaid and intermingled with the musical contributions of other ethnic and racial groups who inhabited the vast southern region. As they inched their way across the southern frontier, British migrants came in contact with other peoples, whom they often fought with, traded with, and worked with; made love to; and sang and danced with: the Germans of the Great Valley of Virginia; the Indians of the backcountry; Spanish, French, and mixed-breed elements in the Mississippi Valley; the Mexicans of South Texas; and, of course, blacks everywhere. Southern folk music was touched and energized by the contributions of all these people, and country music still bears the marks of these influences. Of all the southern ethnic groups, none has played a more important role in providing songs and styles for the white country musician than that forced migrant from Africa, the black. Nowhere is the peculiar love-hate relationship that has prevailed among the southern races more evidenced than in country music. Country music—seemingly the most "pure white" of all American musical forms—has borrowed heavily from African Americans. White southerners, many of whom would have been horrified at the idea of mixing socially with blacks, have nonetheless enthusiastically accepted their musical offerings: the spirituals, the blues, ragtime, jazz, rhythm-and-blues, hip-hop, and a whole host of dance steps, vocal shadings, and instrumental techniques.

Black-white contact began so early and was so omnipresent in American life that it is virtually impossible to know who profited most from the resulting musical exchange. From the time they first saw them on slave ships, white observers have commented frequently on blacks' alleged penchant for music. In the four hundred years that have passed, white musicians have continually drawn on black sources for rejuvenation and sustenance. Anywhere that blacks and whites mingled in the United States—in field, factory, or mine; on railroad section gangs; in juke joints or taverns; at camp meetings or in church; at county fairs or on street corners—the potential existed for mutual cultural transmission. The mountains were no more immune to this kind of musical interchange than were the flatland regions. Blues records, of course, began making their way into the mountains in the mid-1920s, but even before then black folk musicians had been seen and heard on street corners or in work camps. Both the guitar and the blues form may have ventured into the mountains with black laborers who followed the highways and railroads as they gradually inched their way up the Appalachian ridges. Such early country singers as Dock Boggs from Virginia and Frank Hutchison and Dick Justice from the West Virginia coal fields performed both songs and styles learned from local black musicians. A long list of country musicians, from Jimmie Rodgers through Bob Wills and Hank Williams to Charlie Rich and Willie Nelson, provide testimony of the unending appeal of black music. Unfortunately, the black musicians who performed country music, even during its early commercial period, have not been properly acknowledged.[6]

If southern white folk music was neither pure white nor "Anglo" in origin or manifestations, neither was it exclusively rural or noncommercial. Though touted by romanticists of varying stripes, "folk isolation" has been largely fictional. No area in America, North or South, has ever been totally isolated from the world at large. The currents of change that have swept over the United States, making it the most advanced, industrially oriented nation in the world, have also moved across the South. The South, though changing slowly, and often with dogged resistance, has nevertheless changed.

The southern pockets of rural folk culture—whether mountain, hill country, delta, bayou, or flatland—have never been completely immune to the forces of technological or social change. Scarcely a rural community in the decades before 1920 remained unvisited at one time or another by some kind of peripatetic agent of the world outside who brought news, business, religion, education, or amusement. It might be the Methodist circuit rider braving the flooded streams or frozen wilderness to deliver not only the gospel but gossip from the towns and cities. It might be the singing-school teacher boarding with farm families until the entire community had mastered the shape-note method. Or it might be any number of salesmen or agents of mercantile houses, the "rider" sent out by the general store to see if the farmers' crops would enable them to meet their credit obligations, or the Yankee or Jewish peddler in a horse-drawn wagon carrying a valuable cargo of needed items—which might even include a musical instrument.

Rural America—prior to the coming of radio, television, and rural electrification—never totally resisted the musical trends emanating from the cities. The popular music originating in Tin Pan Alley (the colloquial term once used to describe the music produced by commercial songwriters in New York City) or on the vaudeville stages of northern cities moved into the hinterlands in a variety of ways. The city could most effectively transport its musical ideas to the country through the traveling show. Circuses with their singing clowns and brass bands, puppet shows with their fiddlers, and the brown chautauqua tents with a variety of entertainment that might include anything from Swiss yodelers to Hawaiian string bands—all did their part to broaden the horizons of isolated rural dwellers. Perhaps the most common of the traveling shows, but one as yet inadequately documented, was the medicine show. The "physick" wagon, with its glib-talking "doctor" and cargo of patent medicines, became a familiar phenomenon to rural Americans as late as the 1930s. Even as late as 1984 "Doc" Tommy Scott (best known to country music fans for his 1950s recording of "Rosebuds and You") was still touring throughout the United States and Canada, performing variety entertainment and selling a bottled liniment that was appropriately named "Snake Oil." Nearly all of the medicine shows employed an entertainer—often in blackface—to warm up the crowd by singing, cracking jokes, or playing an instrument. Not only were songs introduced to rural America in this manner, but the medicine shows also provided an early commercial outlet for country musicians, who were often employed by the traveling shows. On the "physick" wagons, country entertainers gained invaluable show business experience that served them well when they set out on their professional careers. The extensive list of country entertainers who learned in this manner includes Uncle Dave Macon, Jimmie Rodgers, Roy Acuff, Gene Autry, Lew Childre, Clarence Ashley, and Hank Williams.

On a larger scale and almost as common as the medicine show through the 1930s, was the traveling tent phenomenon—generally known as the "tent repertory" show. Often described as "Toby Shows," so-called because of the hillbilly comic characters who inhabited them, the tent-rep shows brought to rural America a touch of vaudeville, including everything from magicians, acrobats, and trained bears to Irish tenors, Swiss yodelers, and dancing girls. Transported by horse-drawn wagons in the early days, the tent-rep shows would move into a rural community, stake out their tents, hold nightly shows that might run as long as a week, and then move on to another excited community. The communities visited, it is clear, often included the smallest villages imaginable. My father remembered a tent show that, just before World War I, lingered for a week in his rural home community of Galena, an East Texas village near Tyler so small that it could not be located on the map. Practically every man, woman, and child attended the show—night after night—spending money if they had it, but just as often bartering eggs, vegetables, or canned goods for the price of admission.

Although the traveling shows were important vehicles for transmitting urban culture to the rural regions, a more common, and obvious, means was the movement of country people to and from the town. As long as the city has existed, it has beckoned the rural dweller. Often pictured in American myth, story, and song as the center of vice, corruption, and lost innocence, the city has more often exerted a contrary pull on the rural mind. Country youth have traditionally seen the city in many different lights: as a place of employment, a means of escape, and a source of amusement. More accurately, then, country people have responded ambivalently to the city and its charms. They have often sought the city's advantages while at the same time attacking its values and longing for the rural life that they readily extol but to which they would rather not return. The catalogue of country music is filled with songs extolling the farmer and the whole scheme of rural values (from "The Farmer Is the Man" to "Blackland Farmer" to "Thank God I'm a Country Boy"), and with scores of others describing the innocent ruralite lost in the big city and at the mercy of the city slicker (the classic piece in this genre is "Stay in the Wagon Yard"). But, attacked and ridiculed as the city may have been, the statistics of the past two hundred years or more reveal its irresistible appeal for rural Americans.

Burdened by the rigors of farmwork and by the social isolation of country life, southern country boys and girls have traditionally longed for the bright lights of the city that lay somewhere down the road or beyond the mountains. By the thousands they have ventured into such cities as Louisville, Memphis, Nashville, Knoxville, Atlanta, Baltimore, New Orleans, and Houston or, eventually, into Chicago, Detroit, Akron, Cincinnati, Los Angeles, and other industrial centers throughout the nation. Many went only for temporary employment, later going back to the farm, but the great majority remained as part of the swelling ranks of the urban lower-middle class. In the decades before 1920, the city was never too far away for the country boy whose dreams and longings were sufficiently intense. By foot, by wagon, by horseback, by flatboat or steamboat, the trip to the city was made.

Increasingly after the Civil War another agent of industrial change—the railroad—played its powerful role in uniting city and farm. The railroad was among the earliest, and certainly the most dramatic, examples of the industrial process that ultimately transformed the rural South, shattered its façade of isolation, and weakened the hegemony of agriculture over its people. No other industrial phenomenon has held such a magnetic and romantic fascination for Americans,[7] and it is doubtful that any ever will again, even though the automobile has had a greater impact on the breaking down of regional barriers. The railroad provided employment apart from agriculture; it offered the means of escape from unpleasant or unwanted responsibilities; and it, in fact, could and did transport people to alternative, and presumably better, economic opportunities. Even those people who were bound to the land and who had no realistic expectations of leaving it could experience a vicarious satisfaction in identifying with this great symbol of industrial energy and with the tough, unfettered men who had mastered it. No one can document the number of people who have lain awake in quiet and darkened farmhouses listening to the lonesome wail of a distant freight train or have seen it belching smoke as it thundered down the mountainside and longed for the exciting world that the iron monster seemed to symbolize.

So off they went to the textile mills of the Carolina piedmont, the coal mines of eastern Kentucky, the dockyards of New Orleans and Galveston, the railroad shops of Atlanta and Richmond, and, in the twentieth century, to service installations, oil fields, defense plants, and industrial and clerical jobs all over the United States. Many of those who roamed had no particular destination in mind but were part of that nameless throng of drifters and homeless men that has always been such a visible part of American life. Whether they came to visit or stay, in the city they were exposed to a multitude of musical influences that in time would be taken back to their rural homes.

In the mid-nineteenth century, one of the more popular urban musical sources was the blackface minstrel show, which contributed a brand of humor and stage patter, banjo styles, and very popular songs and instrumental pieces—such as "Old Zip Coon," "Blue-Tailed Fly," "Yellow Rose of Texas," and "Old Dan Tucker"—that have endured in the rural tradition. The minstrel troupes were made up primarily of northern-born song-and-dance men who were skillful interpreters of folk-derived or folk-like material. While there may be some doubts about the authentic folk origins of this material, there is no question that songs, dance steps, instrumental styles, and jokes performed by minstrels made their way freely among the southern folk, where they have remained ever since. Blackface humor, for instance, remained a staple of country music stage shows up to the 1950s. A blackface duo called Jamup and Honey (Lee Roy "Lasses" White and Lee David Wilds) headlined a popular *Grand Ole Opry* tent show as late as the early post–World War II years, and J. E. Mainer and his Mountaineers performed a skit for their Carolina audiences called "Sambo and Liza" right into the days of racial integration in 1965.

Following in the wake of the minstrel performance was the vaudeville show, a variety extravaganza that began to assume a national identity in the last decades of the nineteenth century and that flourished until the burgeoning popularity of motion pictures in the 1920s. Like the earlier minstrel show, to which it was much indebted, vaudeville inspired the emergence of a professional songwriting class, and it developed highly sophisticated means of circulating songs around the nation. Vaudeville troupes played in most of the southern cities, but the songs they introduced made their way into the smaller towns and villages on sheet music, in stereopticon slide shows, on piano rolls and cylinder recordings, and in the performances of tent-rep actors. Northern-composed "pop" tunes were not the only items utilized and circulated by the vaudeville shows. The shows occasionally employed rural talent. Long before the coming of radio, several country entertainers—one of them Uncle Dave Macon—toured the southern theater circuits: Loew's, RKO-Pathe, Keith-Orpheum. During the 1930s, Al Hopkins and his band, Asa Martin, Jimmie Rodgers, Otto Gray, the Weaver Brothers and Elviry, and a host of other country performers continued to travel the vaudeville circuits.

The city held a thousand attractions, and not all of them were of the "legitimate" vaudeville variety.[8] Nearly every southern city had its "sin street"—Beale Street in Memphis, Basin Street in New Orleans, Fannin Street in Shreveport, Elm Street in Dallas, for example—a thoroughfare where gambling, drink, and prostitution thrived and where blues, ragtime, and jazz were learned. Sounds heard there eventually found their way into the repertories of almost all country musicians, from Jimmie Rodgers and Milton Brown to the Delmore Brothers and Hank Williams. Arguably, the most famous of these vice-ridden streets was "Deep Elm" (pronounced by country folk as "Ellum"), Dallas's notorious red-light district, which lured East Texas farm boys at least through the 1930s. Here one could find amusement in the white taverns or black juke joints, or listen to street singers—both white and black—who could be heard with frequency in any southern city in those days before ordinances drove them from the streets.

If what was heard was appealing, the country folk were sure to take the song or style back home. It might be a song learned from a Tyrolean yodeler (one of many Swiss musicians who came to the United States in the mid-nineteenth century), the latest tune from the pen of a Tin Pan Alley songwriter, a sentimental melody introduced by a touring Hawaiian string band, a rousing march played by a brass band in the city park on the Fourth of July, maybe even an exotic "oriental" piece danced to by some Little Egypt at a state fair, or a ragtime, blues, or jazz melody learned from black performers. Regardless of the origin or style, once a song was introduced into a rural community, the folk esthetic began to assert its process of natural selection and the song or style was either widely accepted or rejected. More important, through some kind of musical chemistry, even the most urban songs and styles were radically transformed into country songs. That is, melodies were altered to fit the tastes of an audience with little formal musical training and accustomed to learning songs orally rather than from printed scores. Complex chords were eliminated, melodies were flattened, and words were often misremembered or unconsciously changed. As the years passed, the social conservatism of the rural South not only influenced the modification of urban song structure, it also encouraged the preservation of such songs and styles long after they were forgotten or scorned elsewhere. Few country music fans know or care that such beloved songs as "Little Rosewood Casket," "I'll Be All Smiles Tonight," "Letter Edged in Black," and "Wildwood Flower" were composed by professional songwriters who had originally aimed them at a northern, urban, middle-class audience. As far as the casual observer can tell, the songs not only are "country" but always have been.

It is difficult to unearth the precise models used by southern folksingers when they reshaped borrowed songs to fit their community esthetic standards. The sentimental songs of Tin Pan Alley origin bear little resemblance to the Old World ballads and love songs that were part of the singers' cultural inheritance. Religious music, on the other hand, so central to rural southerners' existence, may very well have been a source for both the shaping and the performance of secular songs. Country music has been subjected to no greater influence than southern religious life, which affected both the nature of songs and the manner in which they were performed. Country music evolved in a society where religion was pervasive and where the church and its related functions touched the individual's life in a hundred different ways. Rural southerners generally learned to sing in church, or in a milieu that stressed religious music, and they absorbed values in the same settings that colored the lyrics and the performance of even the secular songs they sang.

Rural southerners were heirs to the great tradition of British religious dissent. While the Church of England became established along the Atlantic Coast, the conservative and dissenting sects pushed into the backcountry. Even before the American Revolution, Scotch-Irish Presbyterians moved down the Appalachian valleys as far as Georgia, while German Lutherans and pietistic groups paralleled their movements only a few miles to the east. Meanwhile, Baptist and Methodist congregations, who would soon conquer the whole interior South, steadily made their way from the east into the Piedmont areas and from there into the trans-Appalachian regions.

The phenomenon that did most to deliver the South into the hands of the Methodists and Baptists was also the vehicle that served mightily to transform the music of southern Protestants: the Great Revival of the early 1800s.[9] Beginning with the Kentucky camp meetings of 1799–1800, the fire of evangelical revivalism swept across the South spreading its democratic message of the availability of universal salvation for those who would seek it. Once the fires had cooled, Methodist and Baptist congregations became the main beneficiaries of the mass wave of conversions, along with such new sects as the Cumberland Presbyterians and Disciples of Christ who rose to prominence in the wake of the revivals. The simplicity of the evangelists' message and the emotional urgency with which it was delivered were powerful sources of the revivalists' appeal. But music may have been even more important. The stirring congregational music that swept across the old campgrounds, belted out by farmers and frontier people who felt the rapturous relief from the release of sin, must have been one of the most dramatic spectacles of the whole camp meeting experience. Throughout the colonial era, psalm singing had been the norm in the churches of Protestant America, but during the years of the American Revolution, the hymns of Isaac Watts and the songs of British Methodism began to compete for the favor of American religious singers.

Camp meeting music, then, built upon a tradition of musical change that had begun many years earlier. Camp meeting song leaders usually chose song texts that were familiar to the singers and set them to folk or popular melodies that were equally familiar (responding to the popular dictum: "Why should the Devil have all the good tunes?"). Since few songbooks were available, the leader often resorted to a time-honored practice well known by British Americans: lining the hymn, a procedure in which the verses are declaimed, usually two lines at a time, to the congregation, which then sings them. Other methods were devised to encourage rapid memorization and to lend variety to old hymns. Choruses were added to venerable hymns: after the verses of a song such as "On Jordan's Stormy Banks," people were encouraged to sing "I am bound for the promised land," etc. Repetitive phrases were incorporated into songs ("Say, brother, will you meet me?" "Say, sister . . ." "Say, mother . . .") to the point that even the most illiterate participant could sing with gusto. Camp meeting songs or songs inspired by them began to appear in books soon after the earliest Kentucky revivals, and both their theology and their structure have endured as part of the fabric of southern religious music and country music. Simple, singable melodies and song texts characterized by choruses, refrains, and repetitive phrases have always been obvious characteristics of country music.

As the southern frontier gave way to a more settled, agricultural existence, the drama and emotional fervor of the camp meetings subsided. Camp meeting ritual became institutionalized and, in fact, became largely identified with the Methodist Church. Nevertheless, the revival became a permanent and venerated feature of most southern Protestant churches. All rural and small-town southerners grew up accustomed to the "protracted meetings" (services that might stretch out for several weeks) that individual churches held, usually on an annual basis, and generally when crops were "laid by." In rural areas, church people often moved out of their hot, steaming churches and held their services under a protective canopy of brush and limbs. These "brush arbor meetings," marked by the emotion of the service and by the swarms of insects that gathered around the kerosene lanterns, are bittersweet memories that many southerners can warmly recall.

The music that flowed into the southern country churches in the middle and last years of the nineteenth century, then, flowered from many roots: from traditional British hymnody, from American revivalism, from anonymous folk composers, from African American sources, and, most important, from the gospel composers of post–Civil War America. Gospel music—so-called for the first time in Ira Sankey and P. P. Bliss's *Gospel Hymns*, published in 1875—obviously owed an indebtedness to the camp meeting music that had preceded it. Gospel music, though, profited from a vigorous interchange between British and American revivalists and songwriters and was disseminated largely through the big-city revivals of the late nineteenth century. Famous evangelists such as Dwight L. Moody, Gypsy Smith, Billy Sunday, and Sam Jones all had songleaders such as Ira Sankey, Charles Alexander, and Homer Rodeheaver who soothed or cajoled the crowds, or whipped them into an emotional euphoria much the way a contemporary cheerleader works the fans at a football game. The urban revivals, along with such organizations as the YMCA, the Sunday School Union, and the Salvation Army, provided a huge market for religious songs that a large body of commercial writers were ready to provide. Such writers as George F. Root, P. P. Bliss, Charles Gabriel, and Fanny Crosby contributed an immense number of songs that even yet appear in American songbooks and still reside in the repertories of gospel and country singers.

This was a music strongly allied with the popular music of the day, and several writers wrote for both genres. Although at times filled with the martial imagery of missionary Protestantism ("Onward Christian Soldiers," "Keep on the Firing Line," and the like), the music was more often gentle, bucolic, nostalgic, and sentimental, reflective of trends in the popular music of the late nineteenth century. The Savior was perceived as a shepherd tending his flock or as a loving father watching over his sometimes-erring family. Heaven was sometimes described as a city of gold but more often as an abundant Beulah Land traversed by flowing rivers and fragrant with the aroma of eternally blooming flowers. In keeping with an urbanizing society that was becoming more prosperous and secure, the songs tended to be more optimistic and complacent than older religious songs. Nevertheless, blood still stained "The Old Rugged Cross," and the vision of a suffering Jesus remained as a central image. And as a rural American society slowly gave way to an urban society of fragile family and human relationships, songs equating rural life with Christian virtue proliferated, as did the number of songs evoking the memory of mother and the old home place or bewailing the fate of the son or daughter who had ventured into the big city and never returned.

Circulated by the thousands in the little paperback hymnals published by the southern shape-note publishing houses, these songs moved with great frequency into the repertories of southern singers. The themes favored by the northern composers also found acceptance in the South, but the southern writers seemed more informed by the folk theology that underlay the religion of their region and by a tragic vision of life that had only been reinforced by Civil War defeat and by the poverty that followed it. As in the case of earlier camp meeting song theology, southern gospel songs perceived heaven as a land devoid of earth's limitations—a land "Where We'll Never Grow Old" and "Where the Roses Never Fade."

Song after song described the Christian as a pilgrim in an unfriendly world, and the world as a dying, unchangeable, but temporary abode. Death could not be ignored, and the soul's combat with it did not always have a happy ending, as described in "Conversation with Death" (more often called "Oh Death"). Although a folk fatalism that their British ancestors had shared colored the lyrics of southern gospel songs, influencing the popular view of reform and political change, a strong strain of antimaterialism, and even inchoate class consciousness, appeared in many songs like "This World Is Not My Home," "Farther Along," and "What Would You Give in Exchange for Your Soul?" Above all, the nostalgic evocation of home as a bastion of virtue and security in a world of ceaseless change is arguably the central theme of southern gospel music. A song like J. B. F. Wright's "Precious Memories," for example, which recalls "precious father, loving mother, fly across the lonely years," has long been cherished by white and black southerners alike.

The "folkness" of southern religious music was reinforced by the Holiness-Pentecostal revival at the turn of the century. This movement, which was begun principally by dissident Methodists in the 1870s as an effort to restore a sense of piety and emotional urgency to their church, led directly to the emergence of sects and denominations that responded to the call of "holiness." The Holiness movement in turn gave rise to groups that stressed the need for a gift beyond sanctification, the baptism of the Holy Spirit as first witnessed on the Day of Pentecost and evidenced by "speaking in tongues" (glossolalia). Pentecostalism was not exclusively a southern phenomenon, but it flourished in the South among both poor whites and blacks, and its most bizarre offshoot, the snakehandlers, reside in the southern mountains. Pentecostalism was a genuine folk religious movement, with mostly untrained, itinerant ministers who preached to poor people like themselves.

The Pentecostal groups and the Holiness bands that preceded them restored an emotional vitality to a southern Protestantism that had become lukewarm and respectable. They also reinvigorated congregational singing (as opposed to choirs) and, ironically, they seized upon the Devil's music with great passion and converted it to heavenly uses. Giving vent to a freedom that was not always open to them in secular society, Pentecostal singers tended to be freewheeling in style, with open-throated, expressive voices. Instrumentally, they were even more liberated. In the over one hundred years since the Pentecostal faith first began to spread, its adherents have utilized virtually every secular music style available, from folk tunes to ragtime and jazz. Furthermore, no instrument has been taboo in Pentecostal churches, and anything from a tambourine and rhythm guitar to an electric steel guitar or a retinue of horns can be heard in their joyous services. The Pentecostal and Holiness evangelists, along with their brethren in other evangelistic sects, were receptive to the songs of the paperback hymnals and to other songs of popular origin. But they also produced their own songs. Itinerant evangelists, street preachers, ballad hawkers, and other anonymous balladeers contributed such songs as "When the Saints Go Marching In," "That Old-Time Religion," "This World Is Not My Home," "The Great Speckled Bird," "Something Got a Hold of Me," and "Tramp on the Street" to the southern song bag. The singing of such songs has been virtually mandatory for country singers ever since.

When country music began its commercial development in the 1920s, a large and diverse repertory of songs, religious and secular, southern and nonsouthern, folk and popular, was available to musicians. The Columbia Record Company, in fact, labeled the first country songs in its catalogues as "Old Familiar Tunes." At the core of the country repertory, however, lay the store of traditional songs, both British and American. Love songs, children's songs, nonsense songs, and even a few bawdy songs endured in the repertory of the southern folk. Many of the traditional items were ballads, that is, narrative, impersonal songs that told a story. A large store of British ballads survived the trek across the Atlantic, some in long, extended versions, but many in only fragmentary form. Some verses floated freely from song to song just as did "the mournful dove that flies from pine to pine." Some ballad fragments even took on a life of their own. The beautiful verse beginning with "Who's gonna shoe your pretty little feet" originally came from the Scottish ballad "The Lass of Roch Royal." It is now universally sung as a lyrical love song in one of several versions that have no relation whatsoever to the original ballad.

The old songs were neither consciously preserved nor consciously discarded; they were merely maintained as part of a familiar and comfortable inheritance, and they were forgotten when they no longer had meaning or when alternative entertainment forms became available. In a sense, with their tales of seduction, rape, murder, retribution, and revenge, the old ballads served as the soap operas of their day. Although many were based on actual historical events, they did not document the news of the time, but instead brought emotional release in the same way that fairy tales do. Rural southerners loved the drama and excitement of such ballads as "The House Carpenter," "Little Matty Groves," or "Lord Randall," and they could easily identify with the suffering or romance of the protagonists. But they could not easily accept the overt sexuality conveyed in many of the old British songs. The Puritanism fed by southern revivalism encouraged a bowdlerization of texts. Consequently, graphic or explicit details were sometimes omitted, and moral injunctions were often tacked on at the end of the song. American listeners were generally left to wonder why Willie had killed his sweetheart with "the dark and roving eye," and they were almost always warned to avoid a similar fate.

While southerners gradually forgot the ballads of their ancestors, they did not soon abandon the ballad form. They adopted songs from other regions such as cowboy ballads or political assassination songs like "The Ballad of Charles Guiteau," and they also composed their own story-songs like "The Wreck of the Old 97" and "Omie Wise." Train wrecks, murders, mountain feuds, fires, mine disasters, labor disputes, bad men, lovers' quarrels, and war experiences were only a few of the topics that appealed to the ballad makers. The identities of most of these bards must forever remain unknown, but a few were still actively performing as late as the early commercial period in the 1920s. Blind men, for example, sometimes hawked ballads—the trade that had been open to them since the Middle Ages. A few of them, such as J. W. Day, Charlie Oaks, and Dick Burnett (all from Kentucky), made the transition to commercial country music. Day wrote "Rowan County Troubles" about a famous feud in eastern Kentucky and later found himself immortalized as Jilson Setters of Lost Hope Hollow by the festival promoter Jean Thomas. Oaks and Burnett made phonograph recordings in the 1920s, and both had toured through the Upper South in the early years of the twentieth century circulating broadsides of their own compositions. Anyone who visited a county fair, county court day, religious revival, or public hanging, or who traveled by railway in the days before World War I, was likely to see a lonesome blind fiddler or banjo player hawking songsheets or small pocket songbooks.

The subject matter of southern ballads and songs ran the gamut from the ridiculous to the tragic—from "Froggie Went a-Courtin'" to the "Fatal Flower Garden" (an American adaptation of "Sir Hugh, or the Jew's Daughter"). No one has ever tried to document the precise percentage of themes and moods favored by the southern folk in their music, but the predilection for the mournful would certainly rank very high. In part, this inclination was another legacy from the British tradition, because many of the British songs dealt with somber themes and were cast in modal patterns that evoked melancholy responses in the minds of the singer and the listener. The religion of the southern backwoods, with its otherworldly stance and depiction of the world as a vale of sorrow, also contributed to the mood of sadness. The average rural dweller needed few reminders from the Bible or any other source to know that life was indeed tragic—a brief period filled with unrewarded labor, sadness, and disappointment, at last ending in death.

As filled with death as the old ballads might be, a major difference nevertheless existed between them and the sentimental songs that predominated in the nineteenth century. The ballads were usually tragic rather than pathetic and were seldom deliberately contrived to evoke sadness in the listener. The sentimental songs, on the other hand, repeatedly sought sadness for its own sake. Often described as "parlor songs" because they were designed for performance in such a setting and because they commemorated the virtues of domesticity, these items were written primarily by northern composers who aimed them at an urban-middle-class audience. The rapidly urbanizing America of the late nineteenth century still contained a population that had not yet come to terms with city life and still yearned nostalgically for the departed farm and village. Improved material comfort brought not only a piano and sheet music into the parlor but also a heightened awareness of what death could do to shatter such a tenuous hold on security. The Civil War had touched thousands of American homes, where a "vacant chair" was the most poignant memorial to that tragic struggle. Bernard Weisberger notes of late-nineteenth-century Americans that "parting and death were real terrors to that generation. The sentimentality which overflowed in the short stories of both the popular and religious presses, however mawkish it might be, had a foundation in real anguish."[10]

Although some parlor songs were so genteel in tone and rhetoric that they never had a life beyond polite upper-middle-class soirées, many of them received a wide hearing throughout America, and a very large percentage found a seemingly permanent home in the rural regions of the nation. These songs moved into the repertories of folksingers right alongside the venerable ballads, and they constituted one of the single largest categories of songs found on country records in the early 1920s. Many of the writers were obscure even in their own day, but a few achieved fame as composers or publishers: Henry Clay Work ("The Ship That Never Returned," "Father, Dear Father, Come Home," "Grandfather's Clock"), Gussie Davis ("The Fatal Wedding," "Maple on the Hill," "The Baggage Coach Ahead"), Edward B. Marks ("My Mother Was a Lady"), Paul Dresser ("Just Tell Them That You Saw Me," "I Believe It For My Mother Told Me So"), Will S. Hays ("Molly Darling," "We Parted by the Riverside," "The Little Old Log Cabin in the Lane," "Nobody's Darling on Earth," "I'll Remember You, Love, in My Prayers"). Hays, a Louisville newspaperman and riverboat pilot, may have been the quintessential "southern" writer with his songs of rural nostalgia, gentle—but often broken—love, and pastoral retreats. Rural southerners responded affectionately to songs that reaffirmed the values of home, family, mother, and God, and they took to their hearts songs about dying orphans, neglected mothers, blind children, maidens who died of broken hearts, and eastbound trains that carried penniless children to see their poor blind convict fathers.

Although the sad, lonesome tunes may have been preferred, the more joyful, boisterous tunes also remained a cherished part of the rural musician's repertory. The frolic traditions of "Merrie Olde England" had endured despite the Puritan Revolution, and a large body of dance tunes, instrumental pieces, and bawdy songs had survived the journey to America. From the southerners' Celtic forebears and from their black neighbors came a legacy of jigs, reels, hoedowns, and frolic pieces. Much material that might ultimately have had a folk origin actually came from professional song-and-dance men, blackface minstrels who re-created steps or tunes picked up from grassroots sources, vaudeville performers, nimble equestrian entertainers, to mention only a few. Today, all country fiddlers play hornpipes, but probably few now know that a hornpipe originated as a solo quickstep dance and that the tunes were devised to accompany it. Probably only a few performers know, too, that such presumed country folk dances as the Virginia reel and the square dance were originally upper-class dances that somehow made their way out among the rural poor, who made them their own.

The instrument most favored by rural folk, and for a long time virtually the defining instrument of country music, was the fiddle. The fiddle came to America as early as 1619 and was taken to the farthest reaches of the frontier. The instrument was soon mastered by nearly every folk group in North America, from the French *habitants* of Acadia to the blacks of the South. Inheriting an old British folk myth that the fiddle was the Devil's instrument, many southern Christians, black and white, repudiated both the instrument and the tunes it played. But even the most devout Christians could scarcely keep their feet still when the fiddle began its work, an indication perhaps that the Devil works in insidious ways! Nowhere does one find the moral dichotomy of the rural South—what W. J. Cash describes as the contest between hedonism and Puritanism[11]—more strongly displayed than in the controversies swirling around religion and music. The rural South's reputation as both the home of corn whiskey *and* Prohibition, and the land of hell-raising good old boys *and* God-fearing fundamentalists, is reflected in the music of the region.

The fiddle appeared at all social, and even political, occasions, but it was most favored at the rural house party, one of the great seedbeds of country music. The description that A. B. Longstreet gives of a country dance in Georgia in 1835 is remarkably similar to that given of other dances in other states almost one hundred years later.[12] Once neighbors learned that a dance was to be held in some farmer's house, a room or two was stripped of furniture, and a fiddler was hired to keep the dancers moving. Often a fiddler worked alone for hours with no rhythmic accompaniment, but on occasion someone might beat the straws against the fingerboard of the instrument to achieve a kind of percussive effect. Sometimes two or more fiddlers might alternate or even play a tune together. Depending on the place and time, other instruments might join in to form a rudimentary string band: a harmonica (usually called a French harp) or even a piano or parlor organ, but more often a five-string banjo or guitar.

Most fiddlers had to be content with playing part-time at house parties or community social functions, and a fiddler was generally nothing more than a farmer or laborer who made music when his neighbors called upon his services. But in the activities of the fiddlers, probably to a greater degree than the street musicians or the ballad hawkers, we begin to see the first faint traces of the professionalism that gradually evolved into country music. Fiddlers often played at political events, and some politicians, such as Thomas Jefferson, Henry Clay, the Taylor Brothers (Bob and Alf) in Tennessee, and Tom Watson in Georgia, were fiddlers themselves. Fiddlers also took their talents to county fairs and other public gatherings, and into medicine shows, showboats, carnivals, minstrel shows, circuses, and Punch and Judy shows. Music has no doubt always been associated with advertising, and fiddlers were sometimes employed to drum up business. The eccentric Mason "Parson" Weems, the inventor of the George Washington cherry-tree myth, roamed up and down the Atlantic seaboard in the early 1800s, selling books from his horse-drawn wagon and playing his fiddle to attract an audience. He was probably not unique.

Many of the formats available to fiddlers in the eighteenth and nineteenth centuries, such as the medicine show, have, of course, disappeared. One venerable institution, though, that has not only survived but has shown a remarkable resurgence since the 1950s, is the fiddlers' contest. Fiddle contests have been documented in what is now the United States as early as 1736, when fiddlers competed for prizes in Hanover County, Virginia. The early contests appear to have been held in conjunction with county fairs or similar events. In the late nineteenth and early twentieth centuries, the contests became increasingly associated with Old Settlers' Days and Confederate reunions.

Even at this early date, then, there seemed to be a recognition of fiddling as both an "old-time" art and a southern phenomenon, as well as a community enterprise through which the "New South" justified itself as an act of reverence for the old society that was passing away. Atlanta, the capital of the banking and business interests that were struggling to dominate the region, was the site of a large fiddlers' convention annually from 1913 to 1935. City officials and local business leaders well understood the powerful political and economic potential of nostalgia, and everyone smiled as thousands of people poured into the city each year to experience the old-time rural art.

Though their art might be a very old one, fiddlers in general did not confine themselves to hoary and age-encrusted melodies. "Old-time" fiddlers were indeed eclectic in their song preferences. Many of the fiddle tunes, of course, were genuine folk melodies whose authorship had been lost or forgotten many years before. Some of them, such as "Soldier's Joy," "Irish Washerwoman," "Patty on the Turnpike," "Old Molly Hare," or "Molly, Put the Kettle On," were of British origin. Others, presumed to be American, such as "Flop-Eared Mule," "Fire on the Mountain," and "Leather Breeches," probably drew on British airs. Many tunes also grew out of the frontier experience, referring to specific places such as "Cumberland Gap," "Cripple Creek," "Sourwood Mountain," or "Natchez Under the Hill," or referring to occupations like "Mississippi Sawyer" or "Tennessee Wagoner." A few fiddle tunes commemorated historical events, such as "Bonaparte's Retreat" or "Eighth of January" (a celebration of Andrew Jackson's victory over the British at New Orleans in 1815).

Fiddle tunes, though, did not come solely from the white folk experience. Black fiddlers, for example, were omnipresent in the South in the nineteenth century. Slave fiddlers were mentioned often in the literature of the antebellum period, and their presence could not have been unknown to white rural musicians. Unfortunately, the precise debts to black fiddlers have not been documented, and some tunes ascribed to black sources may in fact have been derived from minstrel or "coon-song" performers. Blackface minstrelsy contributed some of the most venerated fiddle tunes, such as "Old Dan Tucker," "Listen to the Mockingbird," "Old Zip Coon" (better known as "Turkey in the Straw"), and "Cotton-Eyed Joe" (a much-recorded tune that was at the center of the urban cowboy craze), while tunes like "Whistling Rufus" and "Bully of the Town" probably came from the "coon-song" era at the end of the nineteenth century. Other tunes came from the broad panoply of popular and vaudeville styles available to musicians, with some, like "Arkansas Traveler," dating to the antebellum period, but most coming from the period dated roughly between 1890 and 1915: "Ragtime Annie," "Dill Pickle Rag," "Chicken Reel," "Red Wing," "Snow Deer," "Rainbow, My Pretty Rainbow," and many others. If the country fiddler heard a good tune, he made it his own, whether it came from his own immediate experience, was a legacy from his ancestors, or moved into his consciousness from a foreign source. "Over the Waves," which is still probably the most popular country waltz, was originally written as "Sobre las olas" by the Mexican composer Juventino Rosas. "Fisher's Hornpipe" was the brainchild of the German composer Johann Christian Fischer (1733–1800), while "Under the Double Eagle," long one of the most popular instrumentals among country musicians, was originally a march tune commemorating the ruling house of Austria-Hungary, by the Austrian composer J. H. Wagner.

Through the contributions of collectors and historians such as Guthrie (Gus) Meade, we are gradually gaining an understanding of where early country music found its songs, but we are not nearly so knowledgeable about the styles in which they were performed. We have a storehouse of old 78 rpm records from the 1920s and a cache of field recordings from that period and the mid-1930s, but we cannot know how much earlier history is represented in those collections. Our speculations about "Celtic" or "Anglo" origins, or about "black" influences, are frankly guesses based upon severely limited data. The recording of the first southern voices and instrumental sounds in the 1920s came about two hundred years after the first white immigrants had pushed into the southern backcountry, and even longer after their shifting ethnic strains had begun to mix with one another and with the black elements that moved in their midst. If Old World traits were blunted by centuries of American existence, they were not totally obliterated, and neither was southern folk culture molded into one homogeneous whole. Musically, not one southern folk style, but many, exist simultaneously. Southern fiddlers share a common repertory, but they differ markedly from state to state, and even within states, in the way they note with their left hands and the way they move their bows. Southern singers betray their regional origins in their drawls, dialects, vocal inflections, and pronunciations, even as they reveal a strong social kinship in their attitudes toward religion, politics, and life itself. Nevertheless, they do not all move from note to note in a song in precisely the same way.

In folk societies, where contacts with outsiders are limited, and where audiences tend to be small and socially ingrown, performance styles change slowly. But they *do* change, often unconsciously and imperceptibly. A folk style is in fact more tenacious in its persistence than is a song. Songs may be forgotten, but the manner in which they are performed can persist through time and societal changes. The great folklorist and musicologist Alan Lomax argued that a musical style is "one of the most conservative of culture traits" because it is so deeply interwoven in the security framework of the community, symbolizing for the singer "the place where he was born, his earliest childhood satisfactions, his religious experience, his pleasure in community doings, his courtship and his work." And, adds Lomax, "an entirely new set of tunes or rhythms or harmonic patterns may be introduced; but, in its overall character, a musical style will remain intact."[13]

In the days before radio and recording made it possible for folk musicians to professionalize their art, most performances were carried on in rather restricted, localized formats. D. K. Wilgus and Norm and Anne Cohen referred to a "domestic tradition" (music performed at home and usually vocal oriented) and an "assembly tradition" (music performed at public gatherings, which generally had an instrumental component).[14] The music of the home, it has been suggested, was usually performed by women either as part of their normal workaday activities (while sewing, cooking, cleaning, rocking the baby, etc.) or during quiet periods for the edification of the family or for a few guests. The predominance of women in home singing may help explain why some male singers sang in a "womanish" tone, that is, in a high register with a rigidly pitched and constricted voice. Of necessity, much home singing was performed without the benefit of instrumental accompaniment; consequently, the voice set its own pitch, pace, and rhythm, altering melody and time to fit the words of the song. Our knowledge of the "pure" folk style is actually limited, because most early descriptions of it came from outside observers who usually saw performances in unnatural settings. The folklorist with pad and pencil in hand, or armed with recording apparatus, saw stiff, often embarrassed performances and thought they were the norm. Among their own kind, and not under the scrutiny of an outsider, the singers may very well have cut loose with a natural flair that would have astounded the observer.

Folksinging was often characterized by group performance but only rarely by harmony embellishments. Country singers are now famous for their harmony singing, and it is virtually taken for granted that this is an art as natural with family singers as is eating and drinking. Close, precise harmony, though, is something that developed only gradually in the years after country music was first commercialized. Harmony-singing models, of course, were sometimes available to American audiences in the nineteenth century. In 1839, the Tyrolese Rainer Family, a group of "Alpine" Swiss singers, toured the United States, thrilling large audiences with their "close harmony and clear enunciation." Their paths were soon followed by a number of American disciples who stressed close harmony: the Bakers, Ordway's Aeolians, Father Kemp's Old Folks, and, most famous of all, the Hutchinson Family Singers of New Hampshire. Minstrel troupes also occasionally featured singing by two or more people, as did vaudeville acts toward the end of the nineteenth century. Southern country people could not have been totally unaware of such singers, nor of the barbershop and popular quartets that began to appear on recordings at about the same time.

A more immediate inspiration for harmony singing, though, came from the world of religion. Country church singing, well into the twentieth century, was not necessarily harmonized. Singers sang in unison or just let their voices follow their own undisciplined routes. When harmony did exist among both church and secular singers, it was probably a product of the southern gospel quartets and of the four-part emphasis of the shape-note singing schools. Pioneered by James D. Vaughan, a successful publisher of shape-note hymnals in Lawrenceburg, Tennessee, the publishing-house quartets toured widely through the rural South in the early twentieth century. Hawking songbooks as they toured, the Vaughan quartets—along with those employed by the Hartford Music Company in Arkansas; the Trio Music Company in Waco, Texas; and the Stamps-Baxter Music Company in Dallas—popularized their style of harmony (usually first tenor, second tenor, baritone, and bass) in country churches, at singing schools, at schoolhouse concerts, and at the famous all-day singings with dinner on the grounds. The latter were usually held at the county courthouse or some other central meeting place and were described as "singing conventions." People thronged to the conventions as much to gorge themselves on the sumptuous feasts laid out on the ground or on picnic tables as they did to sing gospel songs with their neighbors.

The gospel quartets were much influenced by the popular music currents surrounding them, but they were intimately associated with, and were often instructors in, the shape-note singing schools. In the early twentieth century, the schools became progressively identified with the shape-note publishing houses, but they grew out of the activities of the indefatigable singing masters who had earlier roamed through the backwoods of America taking their brand of culture to the masses. The itinerant singing-school master played a profound role in the shaping of southern musical style and in the enlargement of the southern song bag. The masters taught a method known as the "shape-note" system, in which the pitch of musical notes was indicated by their shapes independently of the lines and spaces of the staff. Originating in New England in about 1800, the shape-note singing school entered the South from Philadelphia and eastern Pennsylvania. From the Shenandoah Valley of Virginia, where Joseph Funk initiated the first shape-note activity at the little community of Singer's Glen (near Harrisonburg, Virginia), the method eventually penetrated as far west as Texas and Oklahoma and included both black and white singers. This style of musical instruction, along with religious songs that embodied it, were popularized in such books as William Walker's *Southern Harmony* and B. F. White's *Sacred Harp*. It was a rare southerner indeed whose life was not at some point touched by shape-note activity in the long period from the mid-nineteenth century virtually to the beginning of World War II, and those who went to the ten-day or two-week singing schools learned the rudiments of part singing and were introduced to the beauties of harmony by their instructors or by the professional gospel singers who sometimes appeared at closing ceremonies.

Public performances of *all* kinds, religious and secular, were dominated by men. The physically aggressive skills of fiddling, banjo playing, and the like were generally felt best confined to male participants, particularly when displayed at such rowdy events as country dances or fiddle contests. Although women did occasionally participate, and win, in musical contests, they more often played banjos, fiddles, and other instruments at home. Some of them, such as Samantha Bumgarner and Eva Davis, also appeared as instrumentalists on early commercial recordings, but few men were eager to compete against the ladies in any kind of public arena, and the women were encouraged to keep their talents noncompetitive and at home. These facts help explain why men almost monopolized early commercial country music, and why male-dominated string band music prevailed on early records, radio, and barn dances.

Like the vocal arts, folk instrumentation exhibited a peculiar blend of conservatism and receptivity to innovation. Fiddlers, for example, were conservative in that they generally tried to re-create a song the way they first heard it. But few fiddlers resisted innovation, and change often came unconsciously. As in the case of songs, styles were picked up from nonrural musicians: minstrel fiddlers, traveling show entertainers, vaudevillians, and even brass band musicians. We know that from the 1920s on, country fiddlers have borrowed extensively from blues, ragtime, and jazz musicians, particularly from the stylings of Stéphane Grappelli, Django Reinhardt, and the Quintet of the Hot Club of France.

Fiddling was not an exclusive Celtic art, even though some modern aficionados strain to establish a direct relationship between Celtic styles and southern renditions. Richard Nevins, for example, asserts that "it is likely that all the countless variations in southern fiddling are traceable to seven or eight different styles brought over to America by predominantly Celticly cultured immigrants from various sections of northern Ireland, southern Scotland, and to a lesser degree parts of England." Nevins describes Eck Robertson's famous 1922 rendition of "Sallie Gooden" as an "example of a particular American style that most likely was unchanged by even a hair from the time it got off the boat." It is, he says, "probably the oldest extant Celtic fiddle style preserved anywhere."[15]

While some listeners insist that they hear the echoes of Irish or Scottish pipe players in Robertson's music, others hear only the superb improvisations of a fiddler who learned from his American experiences. Robertson played about fourteen separate melodic variations of this basically simple tune, a practice encouraged, some say, by his constant appearances at fiddle contests where the fierce competition inspired novel, and winning, techniques. Public performances of any kind, including the house parties where the repetition of tunes was necessary, encouraged improvisation and melodic variation. Popular fiddlers also resorted to physical and instrumental tricks to win the favor of their audiences. Long before the commercial period began, fiddlers had begun transforming the sentimental minstrel tune "Listen to the Mockingbird" into a novelty piece complete with bird imitations and woodpecker rappings.

Fiddle styles varied from state to state and even within states.

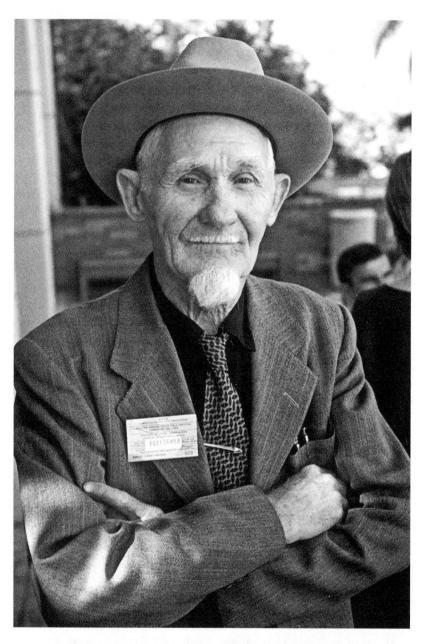

Eck Robertson. Courtesy of Peter Feldmann, BlueGrass West!

Individual fiddlers differed in the ways they held the instrument, the emphases they devoted to noting, and the manner in which they bowed. A few fiddlers accompanied their own singing, playing a unison response to the vocal lines. Some fiddlers stuck resolutely to the melody, while others improvised freely or employed syncopated techniques. Some musicians played single-string style; others used double stops, the simultaneous playing of two strings. Some shuffled their bows, while others used a long, flowing bow movement and depended on their left hands to produce intricate note changes. Fiddlers in close geographical proximity learned from each other; consequently, one hears a North Georgia style, a Mississippi style, a Texas style, and so on. The generalizations are sometimes confounded, however, because fiddlers occasionally journeyed to other states or communities where they picked up ideas, and they appeared in contests against each other. The long-bow technique, to cite one example, is identified with the fiddlers of Texas but is certainly not confined to musicians from that state.

Fiddlers of necessity often played alone, but they were joined by other musicians when they were available. The minstrel format of banjo, fiddle, and such rhythm instruments as tambourine and bones provided a model for country musicians to follow, but we do not know when the first country string bands took shape. They did, however, precede the era of radio and recording. From visual evidence, we encounter examples of the combining of instruments by folk musicians at least as early as the 1870s. *Scribner's Monthly*, for example, carried an engraving in 1873 of a fiddler and a guitarist playing for a boisterous dance in Denison, Texas. The fiddle and guitar combination appears to have been the most common coupling of instruments in the South as a whole and was the immediate ancestor of many of the most important commercial bands of the 1920s and 1930s. Although present in America since the colonial period, the guitar was originally perceived mainly as a polite upper-class instrument. It seems to have moved into the hinterlands very slowly. Virginia mountain folksinger Hobart Smith told Alan Lomax that he saw his first guitar about the time of World War I when a black construction gang laid rails into Saltville, Virginia. Cajun musicians tell similar stories about their region of the country, asserting that guitars did not appear in southwestern Louisiana until about World War I. The guitar seems to have been a flatland phenomenon long before it ventured into the mountains or other less accessible regions of the nation. The "classical" styles favored by urbane guitar lovers seem to have been rejected everywhere in the rural South. Instead, the most crucial innovations in rural guitar playing came from black musicians who contributed a retinue of fingerpicking or slide styles that have forever intrigued white musicians.

The basic instrumental combination of the southern mountains seems to have been the fiddle and five-string banjo. The banjo's identification as a rural white instrument is rather curious, since its "ancestor" arrived in this country from Africa and was long associated with slaves. Its earliest appearance cannot be documented, but the instrument that Thomas Jefferson referred to in 1781 as a "banjar" resembled the gourdlike device found much earlier in West Africa. Blackface minstrels introduced their modified version of the banjo to an international public in the three decades before the Civil War. Originally a four-stringed, fretless instrument, the banjo was "revolutionized" in the early 1830s by the addition of a shorter fifth, or drone, string that made it more adaptable and flexible. The invention of the five-string banjo is generally attributed, without proof, to a minstrel entertainer from Virginia, Joel (Joe) Walker Sweeney. While Sweeney's claim cannot be authenticated, he at least did popularize the instrument on tours in this country and in the British Isles.

Banjos remained fretless until the 1880s, when important manufacturers such as the S. S. Stewart Company began producing their special lines. Thereafter, rural musicians played both homemade banjos and those purchased from the manufacturers. Rural styles were also a mixture of folk and city-bred traits. A few banjoists, particularly in the Piedmont South, experimented with the "classical" style popularized by Fred Van Eps and others (a finger-style technique borrowed from parlor guitar playing), but more learned from the blackface minstrels who traveled extensively through the South. Uncle Dave Macon, the first star of the *Grand Ole Opry*, featured a variety of techniques presumably learned from old-time song-and-dance men, while frailing (sometimes called the stroke style) is believed to have been a product of the minstrel entertainers, who in turn picked up the essentials of the style from black musicians. The banjo circulated widely in nineteenth-century America, from the popular stage to the cow camps of the Southwest, and its four-string version became a central feature of early Dixieland and jazz music and early western swing. The five-string banjo, on the other hand, became almost synonymous with the mountain music of the Southeast, and in the hands of skillful rural musicians, this highly adaptable instrument could lend pathos to a lonely lament or give driving excitement to the wild hoedown and breakdown. The banjo was destined to play a leading and crucial role in the country music history that was soon to unfold.

Although the fiddle, banjo, and guitar were the dominant instruments of southern rural music, other instruments made frequent appearances among folk musicians. Dulcimers have become common and widely desired since Kentucky-born Jean Ritchie popularized them during the folk music revival of the 1950s, but they never played a very prominent role in rural string bands. The instrument's origins are clouded in mystery. It may have come into the South with the German immigrants from Pennsylvania, or it may have ventured into the southern hills with English settlers who moved in from the East. Principally a solo instrument, the dulcimer beautifully complemented the singing of the lonesome ballads and love songs, but its delicate, fragile sound made it unsuitable for inclusion in hard-driving string bands.

Other instruments were borrowed from other forms of music or were obtained through mail-order catalogues. As the frontier South gave way to a society dotted with settled farms and stable towns and villages, rural southerners began to acquire the trappings of middle-class civilization. Like Americans elsewhere in the nineteenth century, southerners bought, when they could afford it, that visible and audible symbol of middle-class culture and respectability, the piano. Stationed prominently in the front room (or parlor if there was one) and decorated with the newest, brightly illustrated sheet music, the piano lent dignity to a household and brought enjoyment to family gatherings. Many pianos, of course, were merely decorative or displayed for status; others provided instruction for future musicians who went into church or pop music, while still others provided accompaniment for dances at country house parties. When country music began its commercial existence in the 1920s, one often heard pianos on radio barn dances or on commercial hillbilly recordings.

In households where pianos were financially prohibitive, the little parlor organ made a most appealing substitute. Farm families could much more readily afford it, and they could more easily move it, even by wagon, if necessity forced a move to another homestead. Actually, those who wanted to make instrumental music found no real deterrents. French harps could easily be found at the general store or purchased through mail-order catalogues, along with racks that permitted the player to strap the instrument around his neck, and they were easily transportable when families moved or when a young man decided to hit the road. Comb and paper, kazoos, or Jew's harps would suffice if nothing else could be found.

For those who had only minimal musical talent, an autoharp could be obtained through the same sources. Invented by Karl August Gutter in the early 1880s, the autoharp became a popular parlor instrument in late Victorian America. Designed for children, who merely had to press a lettered key bar and then strum the strings to obtain a musical sound, it was soon taken up by adults and pressed into the services of musical home entertainment. Eventually, though, ingenious musicians, such as Ernest Stoneman, Maybelle Carter, Kilby Snow, and Bryan Bowers, learned how to "pick" the instrument (that is, to play melodies note for note with finger picks), and the autoharp evolved into a complex instrument of great subtlety.

Finally, some instruments became known to folk musicians through their appearances in chautauqua or vaudeville performances or in urban music clubs that flourished at the turn of the twentieth century. Some of these instruments had a foreign, and therefore exotic, aura about them. Hawaiian musicians began appearing in the United States shortly after the Islands became part of the American Empire. In 1915, troupes of Hawaiian musicians, including Joseph Kekuku—who claimed to have invented the style of fretting the guitar with a steel bar—appeared to great acclaim at the Panama Pacific World Exposition in San Francisco. After World War I, such troupes took the country by storm, popularizing Hawaiian melodies and introducing the ukulele and steel guitar to American audiences. Fretted with a steel bar, the Hawaiian steel guitar emitted a melodious but crying sound that has thrilled generations of country listeners. Southern rural audiences may have been preconditioned to enjoy the whining sounds of the steel guitar, having heard similar sounds produced by black guitarists using knife blades, bottle necks, and similar devices.

The mandolin seems to have been brought to this country by both Italian immigrants and concert musicians. Virtuoso musicians introduced it at polite middle-class soirées, and by 1900, the mandolin had become the rage throughout urban America. Everywhere, but particularly on college campuses, mandolin, banjo, and guitar clubs flourished. Entire mandolin orchestras gave concerts composed of popular and semiclassical airs, and smaller string combos performed the equivalent of chamber music or specialized in ragtime or syncopated pop music. The mandolin made its way out into the rural areas by a variety of methods, but most often, one would assume, through the Sears Roebuck and Montgomery Ward catalogues that also offered easy instruction manuals. The mandolin's early "tater bug" construction (a bulging, striped back) may have inhibited both its sound and the ability of musicians to hold it comfortably, but when Lloyd Loar fashioned his slim, finely crafted F5 for the Gibson Company in 1919, he devised an instrument that fit readily into the string bands of the day. Although it appeared earlier in rural string bands, the heyday of the mandolin in country music did not come until the 1930s.

At the dawn of the 1920s, southern folk music remained largely unknown to the outside world. Generally ignored and unobserved by others, it was left to develop on its own. The songs of the South, however, were gradually being presented to Americans at large through the publication of various folk-song compilations such as those by John Lomax and Cecil Sharp. Sharp's collection of English folk songs found in the southern mountains, *English Folk Songs from the Southern Appalachians* (1917), constituted the first attempt to include the musical notation as well as the lyrics for the South's traditional store of songs. But nothing had been done as yet to publicize the singers themselves, and since Sharp ignored some of the basic categories of musical expression (such as religious and instrumental music), little was known of the total musical culture that folk southerners had created.

A thorough understanding of southern rural music was also hampered by the reluctance of both folk scholars and high-art exponents to see it as it really was: that is, a thoroughly hybrid form of music that shared Old World and American traits and that revealed itself as both a commercial and a folk expression. More significantly, it was difficult for such observers to see southern rural culture as it really existed: a culture that was neither static nor pure. Folk music, for example, was too often perceived as nothing more than a survival of British culture, or as a static or rarefied expression of a dying peasantry, an art form that could not survive the industrializing process. Consequently, folklorists collected specimens of it before it vanished, high-art people such as Aaron Copland sometimes utilized its songs for artistic purposes, and commercial-music people generally ignored it on the mistaken assumption that it would not sell. African American ragtime, jazz, and blues musicians had been knocking down the color walls of

American entertainment since the early years of the twentieth century, and the Fisk Jubilee Singers from Nashville had been circulating their versions of the spirituals even earlier. But no one yet saw any apparent commercial or artistic merit in the musical performances made by rural white entertainers.

Rural music remained an inchoate phenomenon, existing in a thousand different communities and performed by fiddlers, banjoists, balladeers, songsheet hawkers, family gospel groups, and occasional string bands. Performed usually at home or at a community social function—but occasionally in a paying situation, such as on the medicine show stage—the music was as commercial as its socioeconomic context would permit it to be.

Now that our discussion has reached the period of commercialization, it might be useful to suggest a social profile of a "typical" southern folk musician in, say, 1920. Such composite theorizing has its obvious pitfalls, but a hypothetical case might tell us much about the folk music that prevailed at the end of World War I and about the "hillbilly music" that was soon to be presented to the world at large.

First of all, our hypothetical folk musician who was just about to become a hillbilly was more than likely a man. He and other men predominated in the early commercial era because women in southern folk culture had been discouraged from assuming the role of public entertainer (even though one finds many examples of women who *did* play fiddles and banjos at country dances). Our "typical" hillbilly, though, was a man whose musical perceptions had been shaped by women, first by the mother who had lullabied him to sleep and who, perhaps, had taught him his first musical instrument. Furthermore, his songs often revealed the insecurities that plagued his life as a poor, unfulfilled worker or farmer, and they often worked themselves out in expressions of unrequited love, guilt, or self-pity, or in macho songs such as "Black Jack David."

He was also white—but probably not the "Anglo-Saxon" about whom romanticists often theorize. He may have been "Celtic," or German, but most likely was a composite of forgotten European groups, with a bit of Indian thrown in (at least he liked to romanticize himself as part Indian). His music was just as eclectic, being a composite of instrumental and vocal styles and songs, heavily indebted to the various ethnic groups of the South and particularly to the blacks from whom his ancestors had borrowed since the beginning of American life.

He was Protestant Christian but, more than likely, only in a very general, almost cultural, sense. He was much influenced, if unconsciously, by the dissenting, evangelical Protestantism of his British forebears. He was nominally an adherent of one of the distinctive southern churches (Baptist, Methodist, Campbellite, or Holiness) but was not necessarily a churchgoer or church member. His outlook on life, or worldview, was strongly shaped by the God-centered fatalism of his religious conditioning, and his music was influenced crucially by that of the camp meeting, all-day singings, and shape-note schools. Intellectually and emotionally, he was torn by the conflicting impulses of Puritanism and hedonism. His was a rowdy but God-fearing existence.

Our hypothetical folk/hillbilly musician was also rural. His ruralism, however, did not necessarily connote an agricultural existence. He may have been a timber cutter, a sawmill worker, a coal miner, a textile worker, a railroad man, a farmer, or some other kind of wage worker. If he was a farmer, he was no doubt conscious of the declining status of his work and of the economic penury from which he and so many of his fellow southern agriculturalists suffered in the years after World War I. The impulse or deep-seated anxieties that perhaps lured him away from farming and into such areas as railroading and coal mining may also have made music all the more attractive to him.

He was also folk, that is, tradition oriented, and dependent on inherited aural/oral resources. His "folkness," though, was not a conscious posture, for it is essential to understand that the folk are never aware that they are folk until someone tells them so. He was strongly marked by the culture of his ancestors and by the social conservatism of his society, but he was not consciously committed to their preservation. Neither he nor his society had ever been totally isolated from the world outside. There was a good chance that he had served in the recent Great War or perhaps even earlier in the Spanish-American War. He had also roamed around considerably, as many southern men had done, and a little bit of that larger world had rubbed off on him. He still sang traditional songs (after all, they represented the world of his parents even if they did not quite represent his own), but he and his society had changed them, lyrically, structurally, and melodically, to the point that his Old World forebears could scarcely recognize them.

Finally, he was southern. The soon-to-emerge hillbilly music world would have its quota of midwesterners, westerners, New Englanders, and even Canadians, but the genre would be dominated by southerners

Left to right: *Al Hopkins, John Hopkins, Tony Alderman, John Rector, Uncle Am Stuart, Fiddlin' John Carson. Photographed at old-time fiddlers' convention, Mountain City, Tennessee, 1925. Bill Malone personal collection; courtesy of Bob Pinson.*

such as our hypothetical character. Whether they came from East Texas, North Georgia, Kentucky, or any number of other southern locales, they would share a musical culture that each could readily understand. Our composite character's southernism was strongly displayed in his speech, values, and attitudes, and in the presumptions that colored the lyrics of his songs. The presumed southernness of his music would also affect public attitudes toward it for years to come. Both the negative and the positive images that clung to southern rural life would always affect public perceptions of country music. Nevertheless, much of his music came from *nonsouthern* sources, a very large percentage, in fact, from the North: from blackface minstrelsy, vaudeville, Tin Pan Alley, and evangelical hymnody. Very soon, that same northern society, represented by recording company talent scouts and broadcasting executives, would contribute powerfully to the exploitation and national dissemination of southern rural music, simultaneously shaping and transforming its character forever.

CHAPTER 2

The Early Period of Commercial Hillbilly Music

n the early years of the twentieth century, American popular entertainment was urban based and urban oriented. Before World War I,
the music industry—then represented chiefly by vaudeville, the
sheet music business, and the phonograph interests—concentrated
on urban America because of its population density and easy accessibility. Musicians, however, did not shun the rural hinterlands and
were pleased to see their songs embraced by rural people. They also
marketed musical material that came from older musical traditions,
such as ballads or minstrel tunes, and they frequently contributed
songs that exploited the national and recurring hunger for the rural
past, real or imagined. Country music itself did not exist as a commercially marketed product. In fact, the word "country" was not used to
define the music until well after World War II. Of course, rural people
made music all over North America, but they performed usually for
local audiences: at home, in church, or at other community social
settings such as fiddle contests, only rarely winning exposure outside
their home areas. Uncle Dave Macon, for example, a Middle Tennessee
native who joined the *Grand Ole Opry* in 1925, had performed in a few
southern vaudeville houses before his "country music" career began.

The recording companies, on the other hand, showed little awareness of either a rural market or a body of entertainment that might

exist among country people. The phonograph industry, in fact, became aware of the commercial potential of *city* ethnic subcultures more quickly than it did that of the native rural cultures of the nation. The recognition of an ethnic buying population—among Italians, Greeks, Jews, and so on—who were eager to buy music made by their compatriots, may have made record industry people cognizant that similar markets existed out in the hinterlands.[1]

The rural market was not totally neglected, but it received the same entertainment material that was directed to the cities. Rustic characters were staples of American entertainment, but these tended to be sophisticated entertainers, such as Josh Denman and Cal Stewart, who merely acted the parts of hayseeds or rubes. Folk or rural songs likewise were not absent from either the stage or phonograph records, but they were generally performed by urbane song-and-dance men like Billy Golden, Harry Browne, or the Edison Male Quartet. The first recorded cowboy song, for example—"The Dying Cowboy"—was performed in 1919 on a Columbia recording by Bentley Ball, a vaudeville entertainer who "interpreted" various types of folk songs. Entertainers like Ball were in fact quite common in the early twentieth century and sometimes performed in costumes presumed to be indigenous to the cultures being interpreted. Genuine rural performers, on the other hand, may have been rejected because they sounded strange and primitive to urban music executives, who believed that the urban buyer would be repelled by the raw country sound. The commercial interests, of course, were not displeased when country people bought their products, but the product was usually urban produced and urban performed.

The music industry's neglect of rural music might have persisted had it not been for the emergence of one medium of communication and the temporary submergence of another. In general, the discovery of southern grassroots music was only one consequence of a general communications revolution that has gradually broken down American rural isolation and narrowed the distance between city and farm. Along with electrification and the automobile, the phenomenon that has exerted perhaps the most profound urbanizing influence upon rural areas is the radio, a device that in the 1920s temporarily stifled the growth of the phonograph industry and brought a welcome measure of entertainment and information to the rural population.

Only in the research stage during World War I, and chiefly a diversion for amateur operators, radio became a craze in the 1920s and experienced a phenomenal growth in sales and popularity. In only a few short years, radio was transformed from an expensive toy to a widely popular and inexpensive pastime for millions of Americans. Social observers recognized immediately that radio would revolutionize rural existence. It did that while transforming American popular tastes as a whole.

The financial figures on radio sales during the 1920s are little short of astounding. From a relatively modest figure of $60,000,000 in 1922, sales rose to a total of $842,548,000 in 1929, and some observers estimated that radio had penetrated every third home in the country. According to the federal census of 1930, 12,078,345 families owned radio sets. Of this number, the smallest percentage of ownership was in the South, a fact attributable in part to the existence of a large low-income black population that could not afford the purchase of radio sets.[2] One report maintained that "the ownership ratios among the white populations of southern states would doubtless be much higher than general state ratios indicate."[3] Broadcasting stations, the majority of them small and low-powered, made early appearances in the South. Of 510 active broadcasting stations operating on 360 meters at the end of 1922, 89 were in the South. The numbers ranged from Texas's 25 to Mississippi's 1.

The development of southern radio broadcasting was important in the discovery, refinement, modification, and eventual standardization of southern country music. Southern folk musicians found radio to be an irresistible attraction and an indispensable outlet for their entertainment energies. Rural musicians saw in radio the first real opportunity to build a broad and ever-widening audience outside their home locales. Radio promoters, on the other hand, quickly recognized the utility of this cheap and abundant source of entertainment.

Many southern broadcasting stations featured live country entertainment almost from the day they opened their doors. In the years following 1920, radio remained the most important means of country music dissemination, eventually in the form of disc-jockey programs. The first high-powered radio station in the South, and possibly the first to feature country music, was WSB in Atlanta. It was only fitting that Atlanta should play this role. Breathing an aura of Old South romance and charm, the city simultaneously suggested the spirit of urbanity and industrial growth that would soon overshadow the old image. Country music, after all, was a fusion of these conflicting impulses. The WSB officials surely also recognized the large rural and working-class audience that lay within the station's range and the fact that many of these people lived within Atlanta itself.

Owned by the *Atlanta Journal*, WSB went on the air on March 16, 1922, with a 100-watt transmitter, which was subsequently increased to 500 watts on June 13. Less than three months later, on September 9, 1922, Fiddlin' John Carson, well known because of his musical performances in fiddle contests and in political campaigns, appeared on a station broadcast. He was soon followed by a wide variety of other folk performers. For approximately one year before the first recording expedition went to Atlanta searching for folk talent, singers and string bands had been appearing on WSB, providing a reservoir of talent for any recording scout who might venture into the city.

With WSB probably leading the way, radio stations all over the South and Midwest began featuring country talent in the early 1920s. Although exhaustive research on the relationship between broadcasting and early country music has not yet been completed, the collector and folklorist Guthrie T. Meade, who was the most knowledgeable authority on this particular subject, pointed to the very significant role played by WBAP in Fort Worth.[4] WBAP can justly lay claim to having produced one of the first, if not the first, radio barn dances in the United States—about a year and a half before the WLS (Chicago) *National Barn Dance*, and about three years before the WSM (Nashville) *Grand Ole Opry*.

In the first several months of its existence, WBAP—as was true of almost all early radio stations—programmed nothing but popular, jazz, sacred, and semiclassical music. But on the night of January 4, 1923, WBAP featured an hour-and-a-half program of square-dance music directed by an old-time fiddler and Confederate veteran, Captain M. J. Bonner. The music was performed by a string band that normally played only Hawaiian music (Fred Wagner's Hilo Five Hawaiian Orchestra), and Captain Bonner's was the only fiddle music provided. The program provoked the largest audience response—in the form of telegrams and telephone calls—that the station had experienced in its short history. Touching an unexploited but eager audience, WBAP thus inaugurated the hillbilly radio barn dance. In those early unregulated days of American broadcasting, WBAP programs were picked up by listeners as far away as New York, Canada, Hawaii, and Haiti, and the square-dance shows that followed periodically—featuring such groups as the Peacock Fiddle Band from Cleburne, Texas—may have triggered the entire wave of hillbilly barn dances that began appearing on radio stations throughout the United States. After the striking success of the first program, WBAP presented the country-music shows on a rather unplanned, periodic basis, usually two or three times a month, but by 1927 a regularly scheduled Friday night program was broadcast. Broadcasting executives at stations like WBAP, WSB, WLS, and WSM were the first members of the commercial fraternity to devote any consideration to the musical interests of America's rural and working-class population.

The phonograph industry was only a step behind the broadcasting business in the commercial exploitation of southern folk music. This thrust came at the precise moment when recording as a whole was experiencing a sharp downturn in volume of sales, due largely to the competition of radio, which lured listeners away and gave them a greater variety of entertainment. Business declined tremendously in 1923 and 1924 as radio became an established facet of American entertainment. People preferred to sit in comfort and listen to an entire program of music without having to crank up the Victrola or change records every few minutes. The public discovered, too, that the better-grade radio sets were superior in tone and quality to the then-existent phonographs. The peak in record sales had been reached in 1922, when the figure neared 100 million; the market diminished during the next ten years under the combined assaults of radio and the national Depression. In the period between 1927 and 1932, record sales declined to one-fortieth of what they had previously been.

Although radio competition forced the phonograph industry to search for new marketing outlets, it had already moved in this direction before radio made such terrific inroads. At least a few of the recording executives had recognized earlier that a market might exist among America's rural population. This recognition came first as a result of the newfound buying habits of African Americans in the post–World War I period. Lured by wartime prosperity and fleeing a century or more of racial oppression, blacks by the thousands migrated to northern urban centers in pursuit of employment in shipyards and mills.

In the spring of 1920, a young African American vaudeville singer, Mamie Smith, recorded for two Okeh recording scouts, Fred Hagar and his assistant, Ralph Peer. Miss Smith was neither a blues singer nor a southerner (she was from Ohio), but her recording of Perry Bradford's "Crazy Blues" set off a boom for blues music and launched the General Phonograph Corporation (owner of the Okeh label) into a leading position as a record company. Although a market for African American music was found to exist among blacks themselves, this was a body of music produced in the cities and by city people. As yet, the record companies had not seen fit to concentrate on the rural or "country blues" performers, and when the recording executives learned that rural southern blacks, whether back home or in Chicago, desired to purchase recordings by members of their own race, such enterprising recording men as Ralph Peer resolved to venture into the South to find native singers in their own habitats. Through this kind of scouting activity, the white hillbilly recording industry also came into existence.[5]

The recording of early hillbilly talent was, in part, accidental and unexpected; it was also partly a by-product of the recording of African American talent. The identity of country music's "earliest" recording performer is still being debated. Nevertheless, no one seems to have a stronger claim than Eck Robertson, champion old-time fiddler from Amarillo, Texas, and Henry Gilliland, another active contestant in fiddle matches from Altus, Oklahoma. Alexander Campbell "Eck" Robertson, born in Arkansas on November 20, 1887, and named for a famous Disciples of Christ minister, was a legendary fiddler in the Southwest long before he made any phonograph recordings. He sometimes played in silent movie houses for early western films, and was a professional piano tuner, but was best known for his constant and winning performances in fiddle contests. In June 1922, he and Gilliland traveled to Virginia to play for a civil war veterans' reunion. Apparently, on the spur of the moment, both fiddlers decided to go to New York to make some records. The Victor recording people, who up to this point had shown no interest in rural talent, must have been taken aback when Gilliland and Robertson, dressed in Confederate uniform and cowboy suit respectively, marched into the Victor offices and asked for auditions. We do not know what went on in the minds of the Victor directors—they may very well have been charmed by the music they heard (or by the romantic symbols of the Old South and Old West being displayed before them)—but they did permit the tests and subsequently released several selections. Robertson recorded a few tunes with Gilliland, but his solo version of "Sallie Gooden" is one of the most justly famous renditions in country music; after more than ninety years of history, Robertson's virtuosity still dramatically commands the attention of the listener.

Although Victor released a publicity blurb describing the records, and although sales were reasonably good, the company did not immediately follow through in its exploitation of the untapped folk reservoir. In fact, Robertson himself was not recorded again until 1930, when Ralph Peer (by then a Victor talent scout) arranged another session for the Texas fiddler and his family. On March 29, 1923, about a year after his unsolicited New York recording session, Robertson performed on WBAP the two numbers that he had earlier recorded, "Sallie Gooden" and "Arkansas Traveler." These radio performances may have been the first by a folk musician who had earlier recorded for commercial records. In doing these numbers, in fact, Robertson—termed a "Victor artist" by the *Fort Worth Star-Telegram*—may have been the first country performer to "plug" his recordings on a radio broadcast. This important Texas folk musician thus played significant roles in two important commercial media whose dual exploitation of folk talent coincidentally converged in the early 1920s to produce that brand of music that we now call country music.

Almost a year after Robertson's first trip to New York, a similar incident occurred: Henry Whitter, a textile worker, singer, and multi-instrumentalist from near Fries, Virginia, traveled uninvited to New York in March 1923 and made some test recordings for the General Phonograph Corporation. The recordings were shelved away and remained unevaluated until Fiddlin' John Carson's successful recording in June 1923. Whitter was invited back to New York in December 1923, when he recorded nine numbers, including "Lonesome Road Blues" and a famous song for which he claimed partial authorship: "The Wreck of the Old 97." Whitter was a good harmonica player (he was one of the first country musicians to use a harmonica rack around his head), a passable guitarist, but a mediocre singer at best. Probably his greatest claim to fame, apart from his association with "Wreck of the Old 97," lay in his recordings with the blind fiddler and singer Gilliam Banmon Grayson. Several of Grayson's and Whitter's songs, such as "Lee Highway Blues," "Handsome Molly," "Little Maggie," "Tom Dooley," and "Omie Wise," were destined to become standards in country music. By the time Whitter's own solo records were released in January 1924, Ralph Peer's field trips were reaping a rich harvest of old-time performers.

Ralph Peer played a crucial role in the recording of much early country talent (including Jimmie Rodgers and the Carter Family), but strangely enough was not elected to the Country Music Hall of Fame until 1984. His involvement in the record business began as a teenager with Columbia, but by the early 1920s, he had joined the General Phonograph Corporation as an assistant to Fred Hagar. Born in Kansas City, Missouri, Peer had no intimate association with either rural people or rural music. He was, however, a brilliant businessman and, like many Americans, had preconceptions about the South's alleged richness in music. His most significant innovation in recording, perhaps, was the field trip that took him directly to wherever the talent resided. Peer generally traveled by automobile, with two engineers, to such cities as Asheville, North Carolina; Bristol and Johnson City, Tennessee; St. Louis; Dallas; and, most important because of its strategic location, Atlanta. Peer rarely advertised his visits but instead sometimes managed to get himself interviewed by area newspapers or, more often, collaborated with someone who had an intimate knowledge of local talent.

Although Peer was the agent who first presented country music to the American public, thereby inaugurating its development as a commercial force, Polk Brockman was the catalyst. As director of the phonograph department of his grandfather's furniture store, James K. Polk, Inc., in Atlanta, Brockman had, by 1921, built up a flourishing business selling "race" records (the term generally used to describe all black popular music) and had made his firm the largest regional distributor of Okeh records in the country. A business trip to New York in June 1923 kindled in Brockman an idea that led directly to Ralph Peer's historic 1923 trip to Atlanta and the subsequent birth of the hillbilly industry. During Brockman's stay in New York he visited the Palace Theatre on Times Square, where he saw a newsreel of a Virginia fiddlers' contest. The astute Brockman, who was well acquainted with the country talent of his own Georgia area and particularly with those who had been performing on WSB the preceding year, immediately recognized the commercial possibilities of recorded hillbilly music. He instantly thought of one person, Fiddlin' John Carson, who had built up a wide popularity performing over Station WSB. As he thought of Carson, Brockman picked up a memorandum pad and wrote the following words: "Let's record."

Brockman could scarcely have avoided some kind of contact with

Carson. Fiddlin' John (born March 23, 1868, on a hill country farm in Fannin County, Georgia) had been a vital presence in North Georgia folk music for nearly forty years before his first recordings, playing his fiddle in political campaigns, at a multitude of social functions, and at the annual Georgia Old-Time Fiddlers' Association convention held in Atlanta after 1913. Between 1913 and 1922 he won the Old-Time Fiddlers' championship at least seven times. And since 1922 he had been winning an even larger audience through his performances on WSB.

When Peer came to Atlanta in mid-June 1923, he was searching for black talent, but Brockman persuaded him to listen also to Fiddlin' John. Brockman rented an empty lot on Nassau Street where Okeh engineers Charles Hibbard and Peter Decker installed their acoustical equipment. Peer listened to and recorded several performers, mostly in the blues and popular categories: Warner's Seven Aces; Eddy Heywood, a black pianist; Bob White's syncopating band, and others. But with the recording of Fiddlin' John Carson on June 13 or 14, Peer made his initial venture into the unexploited field of country music. When Peer listened to the two songs that Carson chose to record—"The Little Old Log Cabin in the Lane" and "The Old Hen Cackled and the Rooster's Going to Crow"—he responded with disbelief. He thought the singing was awful and insisted that only Carson's fiddle tunes be recorded. Brockman, however, understood the Georgia entertainment market and realized that the small farmers and mill workers enjoyed Fiddlin' John's vocalizing as much as his instrumental virtuosity. Brockman offered to buy five hundred copies of Carson's unpressed numbers immediately. Unable to conceive of a regional or national market for such items, Peer issued the record uncatalogued, unadvertised, unlabeled, and for circulation solely in the Atlanta area. By late July, when the first shipment of five hundred records had been sold, and after Brockman had ordered another shipment, Peer acknowledged his early mistake and gave the recording the label number 4890, a move that placed the songs in Okeh's popular catalogue and gave them national publicity. In November, as sales continued to mount, Carson was asked to come to New York, where he recorded twelve more songs and signed an exclusive Okeh contract. Needless to say, while Ralph Peer's appreciation of the aesthetics of country music may not have been improved by the incident, Fiddlin' John nonetheless made him a believer in the commercial value of the medium.

With the recording of Fiddlin' John, the first southern white folk musician to have his songs recorded and marketed on a commercial basis, the hillbilly music industry began its real existence. Peer now remembered the recorded but unreleased tunes of Henry Whitter, and after Brockman gave these a favorable review, Whitter was invited back to New York for further recordings. The popularity shown by Carson's, Robertson's, and Whitter's records encouraged other record companies to enter the virgin hillbilly territory to bolster their lagging sales capacities. In the years leading up to the Great Depression, such companies as Brunswick, Gennett, Paramount, Victor (hesitantly), and Columbia began emulating the successful tactics used earlier by Ralph Peer and Okeh. Recording directors and engineers took their portable equipment all over the South and Southwest, converting available building space into temporary recording studios and implanting the music they heard on wax discs, which were then shipped in dry ice back to company headquarters. It is difficult to generalize about the talent scouts (now called artists-and-repertoire, or A&R, men), because they went about their work with a variety of conflicting motivations. Essentially, such men as Frank Walker and Dan Hornsby (both with Columbia), James O'Keefe (Brunswick), Eli Oberstein (Victor), Arthur Satherley (American Record Company), and, of course, Ralph Peer were businessmen who had little knowledge of music. They were, on the other hand, unwitting folklorists who collected (and therefore preserved) an immense and valuable body of musical, social, and cultural materials dealing with the rural South. As Charles Wolfe has observed, the old 78 rpm records of the 1920s document more than just the folk music of southern whites; they also tell us much about the dialects, folkways, customs, and lifestyles of the plain people.[6]

The talent scouts used a variety of methods to find folk talent (including newspaper advertisements), but they all relied on local agents to supply them with names. The scouts varied in the kind of control they tried to exercise over the talent that came before them. Ralph Peer, for example, encouraged the use of traditional or old-timey material, while others left the choice of songs to the performers. Some recording sessions were conducted with meticulous care; others were done haphazardly, almost as if the ignorant rubes who presumably bought the records wouldn't know the difference anyway.

As the number of rural bands and musicians proliferated in the mid-1920s, observers, friendly and otherwise, were hard-pressed to find a name that correctly described the kind of music they performed. Record company release sheets and catalogues camouflaged the songs under a variety of headings, most of them evoking a romanticized conception of southern rural music. Interestingly, no one ever described the music as "country," although a term like "hill country tunes" might sometimes be used. The presumed "southernness" of the music was often evoked in accompanying illustrations showing happy "darkeys," doleful or feuding mountaineers, cotton fields, or plantations, and early Brunswick catalogues described their recordings as "songs from Dixie." The folkness of the music was dimly recognized in such labels as "old familiar tunes" (used by Columbia to advertise its 15000-D series) or "old-time music" (favored by the Okeh label and by many fans and musicians).

The word that was destined to crowd most of the romantic terms aside, though, and which has persisted to our own day, was "hillbilly." "Hillbilly," as Archie Green has noted in a discerning *Journal of American Folklore* article, had been used in print since at least 1900 as a catch-all designation for the southern backwoods inhabitants. Not until 1925, however, was the term used in association with the music of the rural South.[7] In that year the word was used to describe the music recorded by a group of musicians led by Al Hopkins. This band was the first to perform before a president (at a press reception for Calvin Coolidge), they were the first to appear in a movie (a fifteen-minute short subject for Warner Brothers), they were the first to use a piano (played by Al), they were among the earliest to perform in New York City (1927), and they were one of the first bands to include a Hawaiian steel guitar (played by Frank Wilson from North Carolina). Most crucially, they were also the first to be described on a record label as "Hill Billies." After recording six songs for Ralph Peer at a January 1925 session, Al Hopkins suggested that Peer find a suitable name for the group. Hopkins said, "Call the band anything you want. We are nothing but a bunch of hillbillies from North Carolina and Virginia anyway." Peer then instructed his secretary to list the six selections on company ledger sheets as performed by the "Hill Billies" (it was also spelled occasionally with a hyphen, but then finally as only one word).

Despite considerable misgivings on the part of some of the band members about the seemingly disreputable name, the group was advertised as such for personal appearances and in Okeh catalogues. Hopkins and his associates became more confident about the use of the title after an old friend and highly respected Virginia musician, Ernest Stoneman, told them he approved of the term. They lived to see "hillbilly" applied widely to the entire field of country music.

The term "hillbilly" has had a curious history within country music. It was seldom used by recording companies or radio stations to describe the down-home musical culture they were so busily disseminating. But it was commonly used by country musicians and by their fans and detractors alike, although no one can document the precise moment when the label began to attain such currency. Country musicians and fans have always reacted ambivalently to the term, sometimes resenting it as a presumed denigration of their music and the way of life it supposedly represents, but often proclaiming it proudly as an accurate description of their musical and cultural tastes. Many country entertainers in modern times, such as Waylon Jennings, Steve Earle, and Dwight Yoakam, privately described themselves as hillbillies but responded bitterly if someone else called them that. Archie Green suggested that the ambivalence Americans have shown toward country music and the terms used to describe it arises largely out of a similar love-hate relationship with rural life: "Out of the long process of American urbanization-industrialization there has evolved a joint pattern of rejection as well as sentimentalization of rural mores. We flee the eroded land with its rotting cabin; at the same time we cover it in rose vines of memory. This national dualism created the need for a handle of laughter and ridicule to unite under one rubric the songs and culture of the yeoman and the varmint, the pioneer and the poor white."[8]

The tension described by Green tells only part of the story. Hillbilly music was not simply rural; it also came before the American public as a southern art form. Like the South itself, hillbilly music suffered and profited from a conflicting set of images held by Americans that ranged from stability and enchantment to decadence and cultural degeneracy. The music took shape as a commercial entity during a decade when the South's reputation seemed at a particularly low ebb. To many people, hillbilly music was just one more example, along with Ku Kluxism, Prohibition, sharecropping, racial violence, and religious bigotry, of the South's retarded and degenerate culture. On the other hand, many people no doubt responded positively to the South as a bastion of traditional values and orthodox religion in a nation given over to rapid and bewildering change. The role that hillbilly, or old-time, music played in the revitalization campaigns of the 1920s may never be realized conclusively. We simply do not know who the audience was or why it was attracted to the music. Recording companies and promoters seemed to assume that the passion for "old familiar" music was strongest among conservative southerners. Consequently, it has been assumed that hillbilly music was little more than a vigorous expression of a regional culture and that such songs as "Why Do You Bob Your Hair, Girls" appealed only to fundamentalist citizens south of the Mason-Dixon line. But how widely did hillbilly records circulate among northerners, and what impulses motivated those Americans, North and South, who bought the records and listened to the radio barn dances?

The most famous example of the political uses to which old-time music could be put was Henry Ford's highly publicized campaign to revive old-time fiddling and the dances of his youth. Ford's mixture of technological curiosity and commitment to tradition was not at all odd; it was in the American grain, and if the efforts made by this technologically innovative industrialist to recover an imagined "American innocence" seem strange, they nonetheless reflected an illusion that many of his compatriots shared. Ford was appalled at the ragtime and jazz rhythms that had engulfed American music since the turn of the century, feeling that it indicated a similar decline in morals. His concern for "pure," white, Christian America spilled over into the nativist and hysterically anti-Semitic feelings expressed by his magazine, the *Dearborn Independent*. Yet this same impulse had its more positive manifestations. Ford sponsored the publication of a book describing old-time dance steps; invited traditional musicians to Dearborn, Michigan; and sponsored fiddle contests throughout the United States. In 1926 he encouraged his dealers, principally in the East and Midwest, to hold a series of local, state, and regional contests to determine the final entries who would compete for the national championship in Detroit. Uncle Bunt Stephens, representing the South, won the championship, playing "The Old Hen Cackled." Uncle Bunt won a new car, $1,000 in cash, and a new suit; Henry Ford received wonderful publicity as the champion of common men and common values; and old-time fiddling gained wide coverage in the national press.

If we do not really know the makeup of the hillbilly audience, we are only a little more knowledgeable about the hillbilly entertainers. The early hillbilly musicians, for the most part, were folk performers who stood in transition between the traditional milieu that had nourished them and the larger popular arena that beckoned. They performed in the only way they knew, according to the dictates of the culture that had shaped their values and musical tastes. And they performed a body of music that was similarly drawn from family or community resources. These musicians absorbed songs and styles from people like themselves, but they had no success models in their own communities on whom to draw. The only known symbols of musical success at the beginning of the 1920s were vaudeville or light-comedy people like Harry Lauder, George M. Cohan, or Al Jolson. Folk musicians did not cease to be folk merely because they stepped in front of a recording or radio microphone, nor did the original audience change instantaneously. But once a career began to blossom and the audience began to expand through radio coverage, record sales, and the like, the temptation to alter a style or freshen one's repertory generally became irresistible. Most of the early hillbillies, though, could be nothing more than what they were. Riley Puckett or Charlie Poole, for example, might experiment with pop songs of recent vintage, and even Uncle Dave Macon might try his hand at a modern sentimental ditty, but the marks of their southern folk cultural origins clung resolutely to them.

The early commercial performers were, by and large, working people who played music in their leisure hours. A rare person like Vernon Dalhart was in full-time show business (but he adopted hillbilly music after a long career as a pop and light-opera singer); most, though, worked as textile mill workers, coal miners, farmers, railroad men, cowboys, carpenters, wagoners, painters, common laborers, barbers, and even an occasional country lawyer, doctor, or preacher. Generally, they were people who had established only local reputations as entertainers, although a few of them, such as Dick Burnett and Charlie Oaks, had traveled widely beyond their homes, playing music and selling song sheets, and a few—like Uncle Dave Macon and Charlie Poole—had appeared regularly in medicine shows or on the vaudeville circuit. Instrumentally, these pioneers encompassed a wide range of approaches. Kelly Harrell, for example, played no instrument and refused to learn one. A few singers, like Blind Alfred Reed and Fiddlin' John Carson, sang to their own fiddle accompaniment, while others sang to their own guitar or banjo backup. String instrumentation predominated on the early records, with the fiddle, five-string banjo, and guitar the favored instruments. Actually, an extraordinarily wide range of instruments can be heard on the old records, including kazoos, whistles, French harps (harmonicas), Jew's harps, zithers, organs, pianos, mandolins, autoharps, Hawaiian steel guitars, ukuleles, accordions, tenor guitars, cellos, trumpets, clarinets, and so on.

Generalizations concerning vocal styles and types of voices are just as difficult to make. Voices were as diverse as instrumental styles, echoing the singer's place of birth and rearing, age, extent of vocal training, religious beliefs, and other related factors. Southernism and ruralism persisted as the two main constants affecting vocal style, but some musicians, such as Carson Robison and Frank Luther, possessed neither conditioning trait (they were Kansans who spent their adult lives in New York City). Some singers sang in a high, strained register or with the pinched-throat style often associated with "classic" folk singing. Riley Puckett, on the other hand, sang with a relaxed baritone, while Bradley Kincaid sang with a soft, sweet tenor voice. Uncle Dave Macon was anything but relaxed and soft, projecting instead a vital, energetic sound made doubly distinctive by his southern-country-gentleman style of enunciation. Some singers sang with noticeable nasal twangs, as in the case of Dock Boggs and Charlie Poole; drifted off into a falsetto, as did Gid Tanner; or yodeled like Jimmie Rodgers. Fiddlin' John Carson sang with a style suggestive of rural hymn singing, while a few singers, such as Lester McFarland and Robert Gardner (Mac and Bob), showed evidence of formal musical instruction. Vernon Dalhart sang with the studied affectation of a trained concert singer.

The song choices favored by early hillbilly performers also resist easy categorization. The music was "traditional" for the most part, but very little of it came over "on the boats" in the forms in which it was presented in the 1920s. Song origin is an admittedly speculative topic, and little hard research has been done on the subject. Anne and Norm Cohen, though, have made some interesting but tentative judgments.[9] In their sampling of 280 recordings made by eighteen different performers between 1922 and 1924, they conclude that surprisingly little material (2 percent) was of British origin. Twenty-six percent came from pre-1900 Tin Pan Alley and 6 percent from post-1900 TPA sources. Fifty-nine percent had pre-1900 "folk" origins (presumably from anonymous grassroots composers). Surveys of titles listed in record and mail-order catalogues from the period, or from Tony Russell's magisterial listing of records made between 1921 and 1942,[10] would seem to bear out the Cohens' conclusions. Such a study as theirs, however, does not sufficiently measure the wealth of material that circulated in fragmentary form, that is, the maverick lines, phrases, and stanzas that survived from earlier British songs.

Virtually all of the material performed in the early period was "anonymous" to the hillbilly musicians, whether it was a seventeenth-century ballad like "Barbara Allen," a play-party song like "Fly Around My Pretty Little Miss," a minstrel tune like Dan Emmett's "Jordan Is a Hard Road to Travel," or a recent urban parlor song such as Charles Harris's "Hello Central Give Me Heaven." These were indeed a body of "old familiar tunes" remembered by many Americans, northern as well as southern, and cherished perhaps as artifacts of an older and simpler society than the one taking shape in the 1920s. Most hillbilly repertories contained little original material, but nearly all musicians made changes, unconscious or otherwise, to the songs they performed. Lyrics were often only half-remembered; melodies were often forgotten; and titles were altered. In a sense, virtually every hillbilly musician was an "arranger," but few bothered to copyright their arrangements until A. P. Carter, through the urging of Ralph Peer, began producing his prolific "compositions" after 1927. Of course, original composers appeared very early among the hillbillies, and people outside the country tradition soon emerged to supply material for the burgeoning field.

As the infant country music industry expanded, the inherited storehouse of songs began to diminish, causing fledgling performers to search for fresh material. As one consequence, individuals emerged who were as well known for their writing as for their performances, or who were known for their writing alone. Carson Robison, for instance, became involved in hillbilly music through his association with Vernon Dalhart. Born in Chetapa, Kansas, in 1890, Robison had a background similar to Dalhart's, that is, he began his career as a popular, vaudeville-style entertainer. He became a professional musician in the Midwest at the age of fifteen, and in the early 1920s he worked briefly in Chicago with Wendell Hall, "the Red-Headed Music Maker." In 1924 he went to New York, where he recorded for Victor, chiefly as a whistler. In the same year he became associated with Vernon Dalhart, in a rather stormy relationship that lasted for three years. His association with hillbilly music, however, was a colorful and influential one that lasted until his death in 1957.

Robison was one of several individuals who successfully wrote

Carson Robison. Courtesy of Tony Russell.

songs that appealed to the hillbilly public. Beginning with his first popular hillbilly composition, "Way Out West in Kansas," Robison wrote many of the favorite songs of the 1920s (such as "Wreck of the Number Nine," "Little Green Valley," "Zeb Turney's Girl," and "Carry Me Back to the Lone Prairie"), many of which were recorded by Vernon Dalhart. Along with writers like Blind Andy Jenkins, Charlie Oaks, and Bob Miller, Robison specialized in a type of song—the "event" song—a throwback to the British broadside and a characteristic genre of hillbilly music in the 1920s. The event-song writers concentrated on the leading news topics of the day, and especially on violent or sensational incidents such as train or plane wrecks, murders, kidnappings, robberies, mine explosions, and related material. Southern folk music had long been filled with such ballads, but Robison developed the practice almost to a science. He supposedly read all the newspaper accounts of an event, then wrote the song according to a formula that began with a happy mood that degenerated into tragedy. The last stanza usually pointed out the moral to be learned.

It is now difficult to know whether Robison's lyrics represented his own feelings, or whether they merely demonstrated what he believed his audiences wanted to hear. Consequently, we do not know whether he wrote with tongue in cheek when he concluded his song about the famous Monkey Trial of 1925, "The John T. Scopes Trial," by saying that "Mr. Scopes will know wherever he may go, that the old religion's better after all." If Robison's songwriting motives are less than clear, those of some of his balladeer contemporaries seem much more certain.

Richard (Dick) Burnett, Charlie Oaks, Alfred Reed, and Andrew Jenkins, to cite examples of a few of the hillbilly bards who happen to be known, were all genuine folk musicians who wrote from within the culture of their birth. They also all happened to be blind, and were therefore forced into a life of music through economic and social necessity. Each of them, of course, had an audience that helped shape his musical perspectives, and Jenkins was particularly affected by commercial considerations. Nevertheless, there seems to be little or no gap between the men and the messages conveyed by their lyrics. Burnett was a banjoist, guitarist, and singer from near Monticello, Kentucky, who made several important recordings with fiddler Leonard Rutherford between 1926 and 1930. He served as a valuable link to country music's folk past and as a repository of material that he had both preserved and rewritten: "Pearl Bryan," "Short Life of Trouble," "Bury Me beneath the Willow," "Little Stream of Whiskey," and a ballad known to all folk revivalists through its inclusion in the famous Harry Smith Folkways anthology, "Willie Moore." Burnett's most famous song, though, documented the tragedy that accompanied much of his early life. He was orphaned by the time he was twelve and blinded in 1907 at the age of twenty-four after being shot in the face during a robbery attempt. Soon thereafter he began his life as a wandering musician, singing and selling his song "ballets" on sheets about the size of a postcard. One of these broadside pamphlets in about 1913 contained his mournful "Farewell Song," known today in altered form as "Man of Constant Sorrow," and first commercially recorded by Emry Arthur in 1929.

Dick Burnett and Charlie Oaks were living reminders to hillbilly audiences in the 1920s of the folk roots from which country music grew, and both easily made the transition from printed broadsheets to phonograph recordings as a means of disseminating their compositions. Oaks came from Richmond, Kentucky, and was well known in the Upper South before World War I for his performances at public gatherings and for the song sheets he sold (two of his compositions even showed up in an issue of the *Journal of American Folklore* in 1909). When Oaks's songs appeared on recordings in the 1920s, he was merely continuing a tradition, albeit in a new media setting, that had characterized his life for several decades. His 1925 tribute to the great Democratic leader William Jennings Bryan not only exemplified the survival of the centuries-old broadside tradition, it also reflected the lingering populist impulse that made Bryan a hero among millions of rural southerners.

Alfred Reed and Andy Jenkins wrote from much the same perspective as Burnett and Oaks, but their songs were also permeated with a moralism that probably came from religious conviction, since both men were preachers who were much influenced by the Holiness impulse that swept across the South at the turn of the century. Reed was born in Virginia but spent much of his life in West Virginia. The twenty-one songs he recorded for Victor, all presumably original, included secular material that was, however, laced with a fundamentalist and moral view of life. He wrote excellent "event songs," such as "The Wreck of the Virginian," but his most interesting compositions dealt with social commentary. "Why Do You Bob Your Hair, Girls" poked jibes at one of the social fashions of the 1920s, with Reed seeing the practice as unscriptural as well as unsettling. "How Can a Poor Man Stand Such Times and Live?" commented on the inflation of the decade, while "There'll Be No Distinction There" projected a kind of social and racial liberalism rare among the hillbilly songs of the era. Although conventional in its depiction of relief beyond the grave, the song went a step beyond this traditional religious fare when it posited a future condition of equality in heaven among gentiles, Jews, blacks, and whites.

A real folk bard of the 1920s and a producer of some of the most popular hillbilly songs was Andrew "Blind Andy" Jenkins. Born in Jenkinsburg, Georgia, in 1885, Jenkins, who became totally blind in middle age, developed a proficiency for several instruments, including the French harp, banjo, guitar, and mandolin. In 1910 he became a Holiness preacher, and except for occasional odd jobs—such as selling newspapers on the streets of Atlanta—he remained a revivalist until his death in 1957.

Jenkins's second marriage, in 1919, brought him into a musical family. When WSB Radio opened its doors in 1922, the Jenkins Family— Andy and two stepdaughters, Irene Spain and Mary Lee Eskew—were well prepared to move into studio entertainment. Their radio debut of August 14, 1922, was followed by recordings about two years later (August 29, 1924). With songs like "If I Could Hear My Mother Pray Again," the Jenkins family became probably the first country music family to be recorded and one of the first groups to do both country and gospel music.

Although Jenkins was an accomplished musician and entertainer, he achieved his greatest fame as a songwriter. He composed well over eight hundred songs, the majority of them sacred. His repertory of compositions includes the murder ballad "Little Marian Parker," "God Put a Rainbow in the Clouds" (much performed by radio quartets), "Ben Dewberry's Final Run" (recorded by Jimmie Rodgers), and "Kinnie Wagner" (about an Alabama badman). His two most famous songs, "Billy the Kid" and "The Death of Floyd Collins," were written at the urging of Polk Brockman who, once again, demonstrated an understanding of the needs and tastes of the country music audience just as he had done in his earlier promotion of Fiddlin' John Carson. "Billy the Kid" sounds like a traditional cowboy ballad, but it was written by Jenkins in 1928 after Walter Noble Burns's biography of the boy outlaw (*The Saga of Billy the Kid*) appeared. "The Death of Floyd Collins," recorded by Vernon Dalhart and others, chronicled the sad story of a young spelunker who became trapped in a sandstone cave near Mammoth Cave in 1925. The incident won national attention because of radio coverage, and Polk Brockman, who at that time was in Jacksonville, Florida, communicated with Jenkins and asked him to write a ballad. Jenkins's composition, arranged by his stepdaughter, Irene Spain, was mailed to Brockman, who paid twenty-five dollars for it. Brockman in turn sold it to Frank Walker of Columbia Records, who gave it to Dalhart for recording purposes. Both songs were typical of the event ballads of the period: highly moralistic in tone, they informed the listener of the dire fate that awaited young men who chose a life of crime or who, like Floyd Collins, disregarded their fathers' warnings.

Country music's expanding popularity inevitably lured writers who had no direct experience with the tradition. Some of the music's greatest writers, such as Fred Rose, have come to it after earlier careers in popular music or jazz. The first outstanding example, Bob Miller, was born in 1895 in Memphis, where he was introduced to some of the great forms of southern music, if not to country music. In the early 1920s, Miller played the piano for a dance band called the Idlewild Orchestra, which performed on the steamer *Idlewild* on the Mississippi River. In 1928 he moved to New York, working as an arranger for the Irving Berlin Company before establishing his own music concern, the Bob Miller Publishing Company. Although he composed numerous blues and popular tunes, his hillbilly compositions were the most important items in his repertory of over seven thousand songs. In the decades following the 1920s, Miller produced scores of lucrative and lastingly popular numbers, including the well-known "Eleven Cent Cotton and Forty Cent Meat"; the prison song that has inspired countless others, "Twenty-One Years"; and the sentimental favorites, "When the White Azaleas Start Blooming" and "Rocking Alone in an Old Rocking Chair." As the event composer par excellence, Miller was always alive to the possibility of exploiting any incident that struck the fancy of the public. In fact, he was sometimes ahead of a story. He supposedly prepared an obituary song for Huey Long two years before his assassination, and even went so far as to predict accurately that the killing would occur in the state capitol.

Regardless of the origins of the songs circulated by the hillbillies in the 1920s, whether taken from "tradition," written by the musicians themselves, or penned by professional composers like Bob Miller, the music quickly began to move into the possession of the "folk." Eventually, when later generations of folklorists moved into the byways and backwaters of the South, promoted by academia or subsidized by the Library of Congress, they collected such songs as "The Death of Floyd Collins" as authentic specimens of the folk-produced songs of the region. Only rarely were the commercial hillbilly origins of such songs either known or recognized, but, as Donald Knight Wilgus has noted, "a commercialized tradition was being established."[11]

When we turn from the writers to the performers themselves, we find that singing was generally incidental to instrumentation. On recordings and on the radio barn dances, the fiddle and its accompanying string instruments predominated. The hillbilly string bands of the early commercial era were the direct descendants of (and in many cases were the same as) the folk entertainers who played for house parties, barn dances, church socials, tent shows, and political gatherings in the decades before 1920. Although the term "string band" did not appear on a record label until about 1925, string musicians had grouped themselves into bands since at least the nineteenth century. As is often the case, the identifying term evolved long after the music had been formed.

The identity of the first recorded string band is a bit shadowy, but if such a band can be considered as consisting of as few as two members, then the early fiddle-and-banjo duos would hold the distinction. Gid Tanner and Riley Puckett recorded with fiddle and banjo on March 7–8, 1924, as did Samantha Bumgarner and Eva Davis on April 22–23, 1924. That same April, Fiddlin' John Carson combined his eccentric, undisciplined solo style of fiddling with a trio of other musicians to create a band called the Virginia Reelers. Other musicians who were sometimes included in the Reelers' roster were Fiddlin' John's daughter, Moonshine Kate, who sang and played the guitar and banjo, and (after 1927) one of the great North Georgia fiddlers, Earl Johnson. Fiddlin' John never permitted other band members to interfere with his style; he stuck resolutely to his own rhythm, time, and meter. Before the end of 1924, other bands with two or more members began swelling the ranks of those who had made records. Henry Whitter recorded in late July 1924 with a group named the Virginia Breakdowners, and in late August, Fiddlin' Powers and his family recorded a few breakdown instrumentals for Victor. In November 1924, William B. Chenoweth, a fiddler and farmer from near Dallas, recorded with his Cornfield Symphony Orchestra in probably the first recording session made by a Texas string band. Ernest Stoneman, performing with a group called the Dixie Mountaineers, made his first recording for Okeh on September 1, 1924. In the course of a long and distinguished career, which took him from Edison cylinder recordings to television, Stoneman introduced some of the most durable, and even legendary, country songs—such as "We Parted by the Riverside" and "The Titanic" (his first recording). He made the autoharp a solo instrument capable of playing melodies, and he sired a large group of children who became outstanding musicians in their own rights. Until his death in June 1968, Stoneman, now universally referred to as Pop Stoneman, continued to appear in concerts with his children in one of the most sensational bluegrass bands of the modern period.[12]

The radio and recording entrepreneurs definitely contributed to the shape and tone of the hillbilly bands by sometimes suggesting band names (as in the case of Ralph Peer and Al Hopkins's Hill Billies), appropriate stage costumes, repertory, or styles of performance. The businessmen sensed the public fascination with rustic types during the 1920s and consequently urged such images upon the musicians. Often the images projected by the promoters coincided with the desires and self-conceptions of the musicians; some hillbillies were pleased to have the opportunity to perform and had no pretensions of being anything other than hillbillies. Others, however, resisted the rube stereotype or otherwise chafed at the presumed limitations placed on their art. Above all, the hillbilly musicians were ambivalent about their status and became increasingly so as the decades passed and as public tastes changed. Consequently, we find within the string bands, and among hillbilly musicians in general, a confusion about who they were, what they wanted to be, and what their audiences expected of them.

The careers of two of the finest bands of the period, Charlie Poole and his North Carolina Ramblers, and the Skillet Lickers, illustrate the conflicting impulses that worked upon hillbilly musicians. The two groups were highly dissimilar in repertory and style, but both had wide and enthusiastic followings. Poole was one of the earliest examples in country music of the hard-living, hard-drinking young man who burns his life away, a type that has appeared periodically and seems endlessly appealing to both country musicians and fans.

Charlie Poole (seated) and the North Carolina Ramblers. Left to right:
Posey Rorer, Charlie Poole, Roy Harvey. Courtesy of David Freeman.

Before his death from a heart attack at the age of thirty-nine, Poole
and the North Carolina Ramblers made some of the most irresistibly
infectious sounds heard in early hillbilly music. The Alamance County
native did a lot of rambling and worked as a doffer at the Haw River
Mills before turning to a career of full-time music. As a singer, Poole
bore the marks of his southern country origins in his dialect and tight

nasal sound and in the traditional songs that he and his group often performed. His musical interests, though, ranged far beyond the rural material of his youth. His singing idol was Al Jolson, and one can hear traces of the great vaudeville singer in Poole's style. Poole and his group also favored songs from the vaudeville and ragtime traditions, tunes like "Goodbye Sweet Liza Jane," "Leaving Home," "Moving Day," and "Milwaukee Blues."

Poole and the other two original Ramblers—fiddler Posey Rorer and guitarist Norman Woodlieff—began entertaining at dances and fiddlers' conventions in the area around Spray and Leaksville, North Carolina, in about 1917. It was not until 1925, however, when they made their first records for Columbia in New York, that they gained enough financial security to free themselves from the textile employment at which they had periodically worked during their earlier musical career. After the success of their first recording in 1925, "Don't Let Your Deal Go Down" (always their most popular song), the Ramblers became much sought after for personal appearances, mostly in the Upper South and in Ohio. In the years before Poole died, the Ramblers' personnel changed, first in 1926 with the addition of an outstanding guitarist and one-time railroad engineer named Roy Harvey, and then in 1928 when fiddler Lonnie Austin replaced Posey Rorer. The group sometimes included a piano and second fiddle, but the trio format was their most popular combination and the sound with which they are always identified. Their predictable signature sound included a bluesy fiddle lead, backed up by long, flowing, melodic guitar runs, and the three-finger-style banjo playing of Poole. Predictable though it might be, it was nonetheless outstanding. No other string band in early country music equaled the Ramblers' controlled, clean, and well-patterned ensemble sound.[13]

The Skillet Lickers, on the other hand, were anything but orderly and well disciplined. They were one of several North Georgia bands who were famous for their rough, hard-driving sound (Earl Johnson and His Dixie Entertainers, Bill Helms and His Upson County Band, Fiddlin' John's Virginia Reelers, Lowe Stokes and His Georgia Potlickers, and, on occasion, the Georgia Yellow Hammers). The original Skillet Lickers had performed extensively in various combinations around Atlanta before 1924, but it was not until March 7 of that year that any of them appeared on recordings. James Gideon (Gid) Tanner, a chicken farmer and old-time fiddler from Dacula, Georgia, combined with George Riley Puckett, a blind guitarist from Alpharetta, Georgia, to become the Columbia label's first hillbilly talent. They, in turn, were joined in Columbia recording sessions in 1926 by two other popular WSB performers and Georgians, the fiddler Clayton McMichen and the five-string banjoist Fate Norris. McMichen and Norris had been members of a group called the Hometown Boys, but McMichen suggested that the new organization be called the Skillet Lickers—after an earlier group that had played at Atlanta conventions, the Lick the Skillet Band. In their Columbia recording period from 1926 to 1931, the Skillet Lickers recorded in a wild, raucous, but highly infectious style everything from traditional ballads, breakdowns, and rural "dramas" (humorous skits) to the latest popular hits from Tin Pan Alley. Much of the band's popularity can be attributed to the energetic personality and showmanship of Tanner, who whooped, sang in falsetto, and in general played the part of a rustic fool. His hoedown fiddle style was just as unrestrained and, according to some observers (including Clayton McMichen), tended to detract from the overall quality of the band.

Several musicians played with the Skillet Lickers from time to time, including Lowe Stokes, one of the outstanding fiddlers of the period who was equally adept at breakdowns or pop tunes. The mainstays of the group were Puckett—as popular for his singing as for his multiple guitar runs—and McMichen, a wonderfully inventive fiddler who resisted being confined to any one style of music. McMichen's career well illustrates the contrasting impulses that tugged at the hearts of some old-time musicians. McMichen grew up in a household of Scotch-Irish fiddlers in Dallas, Georgia, and many of the tunes he knew, such as "Boil Them Cabbage Down," "Nancy Rollin," and "Billy in the Lowground," came directly from his father. No one ever doubted his ability to play breakdowns or other forms of old-time music. He frequently participated at the Atlanta Old-Time Fiddlers' Contest and, in fact, continued to stage contests, many of them on the radio, long after he left the Skillet Lickers. He also participated in their "rural skits" (humorous rural dialogue interspersed with short musical phrases) and even wrote much of the material contained within them. McMichen submitted to the stereotyping of the group as a wild bunch of young country boys who made and drank whiskey and played a little music on the side. Nevertheless, he always resented the narrow hillbilly focus to which he thought the Skillet Lickers were being limited.

McMichen was also drawn to jazz and popular music, and with his own groups, such as the Georgia Wildcats, he tried to create a mixture of sounds that sounded much like the "hot dance" style featured by Bob Wills and similar musicians in the Southwest. The hillbilly image, however, remained with him for the rest of his life. It was always a point of some bitterness to McMichen that later generations of listeners who discovered his music were more interested in what he called "swamp opera" than in his attempted pop fusions.

Much of the vocal music of early country music was merely tangential to the string band emphasis. String band members took turns at doing vocals, but only rarely did someone forge an identity apart from the band of which he was a member. Charlie Poole, of course, was as well known individually as his band was collectively, and a few others, like Fiddlin' John and Ernest Stoneman, attained some reputations as singers. Of all the early musicians, Riley Puckett came closest to achieving both popular and commercial recognition as a singer and instrumentalist. Born in about 1890 in Alpharetta, Georgia, Puckett was accidentally blinded at the age of three months when a lead acetate solution was used to treat a minor eye irritation. He attended the School for the Blind at Macon, Georgia, and turned to a life of music soon after his graduation. Puckett was one of the few pioneer hillbillies who tried to make music a full-time profession, and he was an active participant on WSB well before he made his first records. His recording career began in 1924 with "The Little Old Log Cabin in the Lane" and "Rock All Our Babies to Sleep" (Columbia 107-D). On the second song, he yodeled, becoming probably the first hillbilly singer to do so and preceding Jimmie Rodgers, of "blue yodel" fame, by about three years. Puckett's smooth, clearly articulated baritone singing was a major source of the Skillet Lickers' popularity; Clayton McMichen said, in fact, that Puckett's singing "sold" the group. Puckett remained with the Columbia label until the 1930s and then moved to Decca and Bluebird. Many of his songs came from rural or traditional sources but, like McMichen, he ranged far and wide for his repertory and showed no reluctance to record any song that caught his fancy. He could dip back into the rustic song bag to do a song like "I'm Going to Georgia" or into the vaudeville tradition to perform something like "Ragged but Right" (one of his finest numbers done with the mandolin player Ted Hawkins), or he could draw from turn-of-the-century Tin Pan Alley with songs like "Let Me Call You Sweetheart" and "Red Sails in the Sunset." Puckett was a rural musician, but like most rural singers before and since, he embraced any songs that appealed to him.

Early country singers exhibited an ambivalence toward their profession similar to that which we have observed among instrumentalists. The hillbilly image and label troubled some, while repertory and style of performance bothered others (whether to perform old-time songs or not, and whether to adhere to a "rural" sound or to blunt it in favor of a smoother and presumably more salable sound). Riley Puckett demonstrated a wide-ranging eclecticism and opted for a smooth, well-rounded sound. Bradley Kincaid's voice was even smoother, but he resisted the urge to do modern pop songs. Born in Garrard County, Kentucky, in 1895,[14] Kincaid grew up hearing old-time songs and strumming his own accompaniment on the "hound dog guitar" his father had given him (his dad had traded a hound for the instrument). Kincaid harbored no thoughts about a professional career until he moved to Chicago in 1924 to begin training as a YMCA worker. While attending George Williams College, Kincaid began singing occasionally with the college quartet. A fellow classmate and member of the quartet informed Don Malin, the WLS music director, that Kincaid also knew a lot of folk songs. Malin contacted Kincaid about doing a fifteen-minute show on WLS, and Kincaid, who had not sung folk songs for years, borrowed a guitar and began brushing up on the old songs from back home. His initial show evoked a tremendous audience response, and by the fall of 1926, he had become a regular on the *National Barn Dance*, where he remained for about four years. Kincaid received more than 100,000 letters a year on WLS, but he did not fully understand the impact he made on his radio listeners until he offered a songbook for sale. His first songbook sold over 100,000 copies in six printings, and he had to prepare additional folios (by the time he left WLS, about 400,000 copies had been sold).

No phenomenon of the 1920s provides better evidence of the tremendous appeal of old-time music to Americans in that decade than does Kincaid's popularity. Performing only to the sometimes-unsure accompaniment of his own guitar, and singing with a clear, sweet, uncomplicated tenor, Kincaid won a devoted following in the Midwest and Upper South. The powerful WLS provided him his first audience; several other stations, including WLW in Cincinnati, KDKA in Pittsburgh, WBZ in Boston, WGY in Schenectady, WEAF in New York, and eventually WSM in Nashville, introduced him to additional millions.

Bradley Kincaid. From the John Edwards Memorial Foundation Records, #20001, 1485-01, Southern Folklife Collection, Louis Round Wilson Special Collections Library, University of North Carolina at Chapel Hill.

Kincaid also toured widely, giving concerts throughout the Midwest and in New England. One member of his entourage was a young man named Louis Marshall Jones, who joined him in 1935. While traveling with Kincaid, Jones began playing the role of an old man and singing songs that he picked up from his mentor. During their brief stint in Boston, Kincaid gave Jones the title of "Grandpa" that clung to him for the rest of his career.

From the very beginning of his long tenure in show business, Kincaid bitterly resented being called a "hillbilly," a term that he associated with bums, prisoners, and other disreputable elements. Kincaid seemed to identify his old-fashioned songs with old-fashioned morality, and he appears to have picked up some of his attitudes about music and mountain culture from his settlement-school teachers at Berea College in Kentucky. He often spoke of the pure "Anglo-Saxon" blood of the mountains and seemed to equate that with a similar purity in morality and music. Actually, Kincaid's repertory was much wider than that usually favored by the settlement teachers (who generally preferred the older British or British-derived material). He preferred to call himself a "singer of mountain songs," but, as his repertory demonstrates, a large concentration of nineteenth-century parlor tunes, religious hymns, and modern-composed country items had made their way into his personal song bag. His tastes ran toward sad, beautiful ballads such as "Barbara Allen" and "Fatal Derby Day," sentimental songs from the late nineteenth century such as "Letter Edged in Black," "The Fatal Wedding," and "I'll Be All Smiles Tonight," and religious ballads such as "The Legend of the Robin Red Breast." Through his recordings (first made for the Starr Piano Company's Gennett label in 1927), personal appearances, and radio broadcasts, Kincaid probably did more than any other individual to popularize old-time songs and ballads among Americans.

Kentucky contributed to country music some of its finest traditional singers.[15] Kincaid, Dick Burnett, and Charlie Oaks, as we have seen, made enduring contributions to the country music repertory. Their careers should also tell us, though, that not one but many folk traditions have defined southern music. The choices of songs favored by these men were not radically dissimilar (although one can hardly envision Kincaid doing Burnett's "Little Stream of Whiskey"!). The style of presentation, however, was indeed different.

Another Kentuckian, Buell Kazee, reveals still another approach to traditional music and suggests further ambivalence in the performance of America's newfound rural music. Unlike Kincaid, Kazee was a genuine mountain boy, from Magoffin County, Kentucky, who grew up in a family of traditional singers. He began fooling with the banjo when he was five years old and at an early age became a popular performer at neighborhood social functions. At the age of seventeen, he became a Missionary Baptist minister. He then attended college at Georgetown, Kentucky, where he studied voice and music and majored in English. His study of Elizabethan literature revealed to him the importance of the ballads he had known all his life. As a result, his concerts, usually performed in a college setting, were marked by an erudition rare among country performers. From 1927 to 1929 he recorded fifty-two selections for Brunswick, only forty-six of which were issued. When the Brunswick Company collapsed in 1930 at the onset of the Depression, Kazee terminated his recording career. Like the cowboy singer Carl Sprague, Kazee was never a full-fledged commercial performer, largely because he had committed himself early in life to the Baptist ministry. Kazee alleged that he had two voices, a hillbilly one that his recording promoters encouraged him to use (the voice of his mountain youth), and a more cultivated one that came out of his academic training. He had a genuine respect for the old-time songs of his mountain inheritance, but he seemed to harbor a bit of bitterness for having been expected to perform them in a certain way. Probably the finest ballad singer found on early commercial records, Kazee recorded such songs as "The Lady Gay" (an American variant of "The Wife of Usher's Well"), "The Butcher's Boy," "Faded Coat of Blue," and "The Wagoner's Lad." Under the prodding of his Brunswick directors, Kazee also recorded "Election Day in Kentucky" and "A Mountain Boy Makes His First Record," attempts by his company to compete with the Skillet Lickers' popular rural dramas. Rediscovered by modern folk enthusiasts on the Folkways *Anthology of American Folk Music*, Kazee won another, and probably larger, audience late in life. Before he died on August 31, 1976, a new generation of listeners thrilled to his haunting, loping banjo style and learned that time had not diminished the power of his affecting voice.

Kentucky was not alone in the spawning of traditional ballad singers, but some of the singers from other states, such as the Texan Arnot Jackson "Peg" Moreland, popularly known as the "King of the Ditty Singers," may never be properly documented. The one-legged guitar player probably knew a thousand songs, such as "I Had but Fifty Cents," "I Wish I'd Stayed in the Wagon Yard," and "Prisoner at the Bar," but recorded only a handful of them between 1928 and 1930. His career, however, spent mostly as a radio singer on such Texas stations as WFAA in

Dallas, extended into the 1950s. Other singers, such as Bascom Lamar Lunsford, had only a fleeting relationship with commercial hillbilly music but were prolific singers of folk songs and ballads. Lunsford, a product of Asheville, North Carolina, and a lawyer by trade, made a handful of commercial recordings but was exhaustively recorded by the Library of Congress and by academic folklorists. He was an indefatigable collector and sponsor of folk festivals, which were generally more receptive to hillbilly acts than were other such venues. His life often crossed paths with country music in positive ways. For example, he was a friend and sponsor of Scott Wiseman, one half of the team of Lulu Belle and Scotty, and a longtime member of the *National Barn Dance*. Lunsford also wrote the original verses of "Good Old Mountain Dew," a song that is now one of the standards of country music.

Tennessee made contributions to the performance of old-time music in a number of important instances. Knoxville's strategic location in the Tennessee hills made it a focal point for old-time musicians who congregated there to sing on its street corners, in its railroad depots, and on its radio stations. G. A. Nennstiel, the record manager for Sterchi Brothers in Knoxville, a furniture company that was also the chief southern distributor for Vocalion Records, astutely recognized the folk talent that gathered in the city and set out to attach it to the Vocalion label. Charlie Oaks, Lester McFarland and Robert Gardner (Mac and Bob), and George Reneau, all blind musicians who often frequented Knoxville, became Vocalion recording talent because of Nennstiel's sponsorship. Of the group, Reneau had the most unusual career in that he did not sing on the early records on which he alone was listed! Vocalion seems originally to have been interested only in Reneau's harmonica and guitar playing. Consequently, when Reneau made his first records in 1924, the popular crooner Gene Austin, who was then about three years away from the smashing success of "My Blue Heaven," provided the vocals. Austin's boyhood in Texas and Louisiana may have given him an acquaintanceship with southern rural music and dialect that enabled him to do a convincing imitation, or he may merely have been a skillful mimic. At any rate, few people seemed to discern that a Tennessee mountain boy was not in fact singing "You Will Never Miss Your Mother Until She Is Gone" and "Life's Railway to Heaven."

In 1925 Reneau was finally permitted to do his own singing. For the most part, his songs differed little from those done by other hillbilly singers, and several were in fact "covers" of earlier recordings. But he did record the first version of "Old Rattler," the comic dog song that Grandpa Jones later made famous, as well as a humorous complaint about female assertiveness called "Woman's Suffrage." Reneau made no records after 1927 and, in a sense, it is remarkable that his recording career lasted as long as it did into the Jazz Age. His rough-edged, singular style did not conform well with the search for smooth vocalists that characterized both pop and country music in those years. As Charles Wolfe notes, Reneau was "one of the relatively few traditional musicians to make the transition from the wandering street corner minstrel to recording artist."[16] Unfortunately, his life as a musician ended as it had begun. He contracted pneumonia while working the streets of Knoxville and died in a local hospital a few days later. He was only thirty-two years old.

Clarence "Tom" Ashley's life had a much happier ending. This East Tennessee musician lived long enough to experience, as did Buell Kazee and a few other early hillbilly performers, a second career in music. Born in Bristol, Tennessee, in 1895, as Clarence Earl McCurry, he legally adopted the name of his grandfather, Enoch Ashley, who reared him. He had become an accomplished banjoist and guitarist by the time he reached his early teens and had absorbed an extensive repertory of traditional material from friends and relatives in the Mountain City area of northeastern Tennessee, where his family had moved in 1899. As yet another example of country music's commercial history prior to the coming of radio and recording, Ashley had been a commercial performer for several years before he made records. At the age of sixteen he joined a medicine show in Mountain City as a featured singer and remained on the medicine show circuit, with some exceptions, until World War II. He gained invaluable experience in this type of format and met other performers—including Roy Acuff, the future great star of the 1940s.

Ashley's recording career began in the mid-1920s when he joined with fiddler Clarence Greene, harmonica player Gwen Foster, autoharpist Will Abernathy, and lead guitarist Walter Davis to form the Blue Ridge Mountain Entertainers. In this and other bands, such as the Carolina Tar Heels (originally composed of Gwen Foster and Dock Walsh, and named by Ralph Peer) and Byrd Moore and His Hotshots, Ashley played the guitar. To folk revivalists of the 1960s, though, Ashley was best known as a five-string banjoist, and his renditions of such songs as "The Coo Coo Bird" and "The House Carpenter" were highly valued by young folk musicians who heard them for the first time on the Folkways *Anthology*. These were his "lassy-makin'" tunes, so called because they were learned at molasses-making time back home, and were among the oldest songs he knew.

Virginia also figured prominently in the shaping of early commercial country music. As we have seen, Virginians like Henry Whitter and Ernest Stoneman did much to inaugurate country music's history, and as we shall be reminded in a later portion of this chapter, Virginia's Carter Family bequeathed to the music one of its dominant styles. But many fiddlers, banjoists, string bands, and vocalists hailed from the state. Kelly Harrell, for example, was born in Drapers Valley, Wythe County, Virginia, in 1899. He never learned an instrument, but as a singer with a large storehouse of traditional songs, he was never long without an accompanist. He rambled around the country for several years as a young man but settled down in about 1927 in Fieldale, Virginia, where he went to work for the Fieldcrest Mill as a loom fixer. He was still employed by the mill when he died from asthma in 1942. Even before he took up a permanent life as a mill worker, Harrell had ventured into commercial music, and he continued to combine it with textile work until the Great Depression ended his singing career. He recorded a few songs for Victor in January 1925 (after having traveled to New York for an audition) and several later in the year for Okeh with his friend Henry Whitter. His greatest performances came in 1927, when he returned to the Victor label with an outstanding band composed of Posey Rorer on fiddle, R. D. Hundley on banjo, and Alfred Steagall on guitar. On songs like "Nobody's Darling on Earth," "Charles Guiteau," "Henry Clay Beattie," and "In the Shadow of the Pines," the group created a well-patterned sound very much like that of the North Carolina Ramblers—a fiddle lead with melodious guitar runs and a three-finger-style banjo backup. With his backcountry dialect and nasal timbre, Harrell even sounded a bit like Charlie Poole. But his voice had a resonance and full-bodied quality that Poole's did not always possess, and his enunciation was considerably clearer than that of the North Carolinian. Harrell's recordings made his name a popular one in the southeastern region where he made his home, but they brought him only moderate commercial success. His greatest claim to fame came through the composition of "Away Out on the Mountain," a wonderful hobo song about a mythical land of abundance somewhere in "the land of the sky." Ralph Peer persuaded him to let Jimmie Rodgers have the song, and, coupled with "Blue Yodel No. 1," it brought Harrell $985 in writer's royalties for the first three months of sale. Tradition-oriented performers struggled to survive during the Great Depression, and Harrell made no serious attempts at professional music after 1929, even though his last recordings show him to be at the peak of his vocal powers.

Another Virginian, Moran Lee "Dock" Boggs, took traditional music in a direction radically different from that followed by Harrell. Boggs's repertory was filled with traditional songs, too, but, like his contemporaries in West Virginia, Frank Hutchison and Dick Justice, Boggs also successfully adapted black material to traditional white rural performing styles. All three were coal miners who either worked with black people or heard them play on phonograph recordings, at dances, or as street musicians. But unlike Hutchison and Justice, who became skillful blues guitarists, Boggs concentrated on the five-string banjo and was one of the few old-time banjoists who seemed drawn to the blues idiom. Boggs began playing the five-string banjo as a teenager, not long after he began working as a coal miner. But music was never more than a sideline to him, and he remained a miner until he retired in 1952. Boggs began recording more or less by chance in 1927, when he wandered into a hotel in Norton, Virginia, where two Brunswick scouts were holding auditions. With a borrowed banjo, he won his opportunity to record by playing two of the songs that appeared later in his recorded repertory: "Country Blues" and "Mistreated Mama Blues." Old-time ballads, religious pieces, and love songs predominated in Boggs's music, but blues songs such as "Down South Blues" (which he learned from a phonograph recording) have proved most interesting to collectors and to the fans who rediscovered his music in the 1960s. Boggs's banjo style has been as intriguing to listeners as his song choices. Unlike any other performer, he did not strum or frail but instead picked out the melodies note for note as he sang.

As the fledgling country music industry grew, it inevitably attracted musicians with minimal rural influence who were drawn to the genre either through a genuine love for it or through opportunism. One such individual, and probably the most important, was Vernon Dalhart (Marion Try Slaughter). Although Dalhart was an urban man with urbane musical tastes, his biographer Walter Haden argues that his subject was intimately familiar with southern rural life and singing.

Vernon Dalhart. From the John Edwards Memorial Foundation Records, #20001, 0515-01, Southern Folklife Collection, Louis Round Wilson Special Collections Library, University of North Carolina at Chapel Hill; photo by Marion Hoffman.

Dalhart was born in Jefferson, Texas, a once-thriving port city on Big Cypress Creek in northeastern Texas, and was the son of a prominent rancher whose fortunes, however, were on the skids by the time Dalhart reached young manhood. Dalhart worked as a cowboy in the region between Vernon and Dalhart, Texas, the towns that he drew upon for his stage name. Dalhart, then, was not unfamiliar with cowboy songs and other types of folk material when he enrolled at the Dallas Conservatory of Music. Fired with the ambition to be a grand opera singer, he moved to New York after his graduation and became part of that city's active music scene. He gained employment as a popular and light-opera singer, spent several years with the Century Opera Company, and later appeared at the New York Hippodrome in Gilbert and Sullivan's *H.M.S. Pinafore* in 1913–1914.

Dalhart began recording for Edison in 1916 and later freelanced for practically every recording company in the United States. He recorded under his stage name and also under innumerable other pseudonyms (Haden counted at least 110). Prior to 1924, he was listed in the record catalogues as a "tenor." Few of his songs were even remotely close to the hillbilly category, but he did do many songs with southern themes, including some, like "Can't Yo' Heah Me Callin', Caroline," that featured a heavy black dialect. As a popular singer, however, Dalhart was only moderately successful. In fact, by 1924, his popularity with the Victor label was waning, and he desperately needed something to reinvigorate his career. He recognized the growing popularity of hillbilly songs and asked the directors of the Victor company to permit him to record a hillbilly number. Although Dalhart's financial woes were shared by the company, Victor was hesitant to allow one of their popular artists to record a song of questionable artistic quality. Their eventual affirmative decision, however, gave hillbilly music a national boost, bolstered the sagging Victor sales capacity, and made Vernon Dalhart one of the best-known recording stars of the 1920s.

Two songs served to convert Dalhart to the status of "hillbilly singer" and catapulted him to national attention. These were "The Wreck of the Old 97" and "The Prisoner's Song." "The Wreck of the Old 97," probably the most seminal hillbilly event song, tells of the fatal crash of the Fast Mail of the Southern Railway on its run between Monroe and Spencer, Virginia, on September 27, 1903. Engineer Joseph A. (Steve) Broady and twelve others died in the tragedy. Several ballads, including one by Fred Lewey and another by Charlie Noell, were composed about the wreck. In 1927 a Virginia farmer named David Graves George, seeing the great commercial success that the song enjoyed, filed a claim for compensation asserting that he was the real author of the song that Dalhart and others had recorded. Although the Circuit Court of Appeals concluded in 1934 that Graves was not the composer and had, in fact, copied his version from the Dalhart recording, the song's legitimate authorship has never been conclusively ascertained. "The Wreck of the Old 97" had been subjected to the molding influence of oral tradition for over twenty years before it was recorded in 1923; the "finished" product, therefore, was probably the work of several people, including Lewey and Noell. One individual who contributed to the song's structure and popularity was the well-known Virginia hillbilly musician Henry Whitter, who had kept the ballad alive through local performances in the Fries, Virginia, area. Using a melody inspired by "The Ship That Never Returned," he recorded the great railroad ballad in 1923 on Okeh 40015. Not only was his recording one of the very earliest in the commercial hillbilly field, but its popularity also directly inspired the entrance of Vernon Dalhart (and others) into hillbilly music.

Whatever Dalhart's motives may have been, he persuaded the Victor people to allow him to record the number, which he had already recorded on Edison Diamond disc no. 51361. He used the lyrics from the Whitter recording and sang them in an exaggerated rural dialect similar to Whitter's, even repeating Whitter's mistakes. The Victor directors asked Dalhart to find something to go on the other side of the record, and he produced the manuscript of a song supposedly written by a cousin, Guy Massey. Nathaniel Shilkret, Victor's staff accompanist, added a few words to the song and thought up a melody. Based on fragments that had floated around for many years, "The Prisoner's Song"—best known by the lines "If I had the wings of an angel, over these prison walls I would fly"—became the biggest-selling record in Victor's pre-electric recording history. It sold a little over one million copies and appeared on eighteen masters and over sixty labels. While the exact number of total record sales is unknown, both songs made their way into the repertory of all country singers and into the consciousness of most Americans of that and future generations. After the smashing success of these two numbers, Dalhart remained firmly in the hillbilly field forever, thereafter recording only rural and folk-flavored melodies.

Vernon Dalhart therefore became the first recording artist "to attain an international following for himself and commercial country music."[17] At a time when popular record sales in general were declining, hillbilly records, because of the low budget required to produce them and because of the small but reliable audience for them, were considered to be a profitable investment. Although coming out of a light-opera background, Dalhart knew how to perform rural songs in a sincere, plaintive style that hillbilly fans loved. In his first Edison hillbilly recording, he was accompanied by his own French harp and the Hawaiian guitar of Frank Ferera. As a Hawaiian of Portuguese descent who came to the United States in 1915 as an entertainer at the Panama Pacific Exhibition in San Francisco, Ferera claimed to have introduced the Hawaiian guitar to Americans.

From 1925 to 1931, Dalhart enjoyed a commercial success in hillbilly music that was second only to that of Jimmie Rodgers. While "The Prisoner's Song" alone accounted for the vast majority of his sales, he also recorded other widely circulated songs such as "The Death of Floyd Collins." His repertory, recorded by practically every recording company of even the slightest importance in the United States, appeared on literally thousands of records and included both traditional numbers and newly written ones. His prodigious output includes nearly every type of song with which rural southerners were familiar: comical songs that evoked the Gaslight Era like "The Little Black Mustache"; pathetic songs like Gussie Davis's "The Fatal Wedding"; badman ballads like "Sydney Allen"; train songs like "The Wreck of the Old 97"; sentimental-religious tunes like "The Dying Girl's Message"; unrequited love ballads like "I'll Be All Smiles Tonight"; and newly composed topical ballads like "The Death of Floyd Collins."

Not only did Dalhart enjoy commercial dominance for a few years, he also influenced the entry of a few other individuals into the newly emerging hillbilly field. Carson Robison and Frank Luther, for example, both born in Kansas, were performing as vaudeville entertainers in New York when Dalhart made his transition to hillbilly music. Both of them recorded often with Dalhart, as vocalists and instrumentalists, and Robison spent the rest of his entertainment life as a hillbilly. But even some pure country types, like the cowboy singer Carl Sprague, sometimes used a kind of stilted or overly formal studio sound reminiscent of that of Dalhart. Dalhart, however, bequeathed no permanent style to country music, although he did contribute to the popularity of singing. While string bands continued to flourish into the 1940s, the outlines of the singer's future dominance in country music had become clear by the end of the 1920s.

In one of the great coincidences of country music history, two of its most influential vocal acts, Jimmie Rodgers and the Carter Family, made their initial records for the same company—Victor—in the first four days of August 1927 in Bristol, Tennessee. The recording of Rodgers and the Carter Family was the work of the indefatigable commercialist-folklorist Ralph Peer. In late July 1927, Peer and his Victor recording crew set out for a tour of the South with Atlanta, Savannah, Memphis, and Bristol, Tennessee, scheduled as their main stops. He already knew about the wealth of country talent in the Bristol area, because Ernest Stoneman had earlier recorded for him and had reputedly earned $3,600 from his Victor recordings of the previous year.

Lying astride the Tennessee-Virginia border, Bristol was destined to be the site of Peer's most successful talent excursion and the scene of one of country music's most seminal events. Bristol hardly deserves the title of "the Birthplace of Country Music," which local promoters have affixed to it, because country acts had been recorded since at least 1922. But the Bristol sessions of late July and early August 1927 may justly deserve the description given by Nolan Porterfield who called them "the Big Bang of Country Music."[18] No recording event has been more important in the music's long history. Working in a makeshift studio on the third floor of the Taylor-Christian Hat Company on the Tennessee side of the state line, Peer brought a wonderfully diverse array of old-time musicians before his microphones. Ernest Stoneman provided him a list of possible recording talent, but Peer found others by persuading the editor of the *Bristol News Bulletin* to run a short story about the sessions on the front page of the July 27 issue. This was the "advertisement" that lured Jimmie Rodgers, the Carter Family, and a host of other old-time musicians to Bristol.

The sessions began on July 27 with recordings by Ernest Stoneman and his wife, Hattie, and by Ernest Phipps (a Holiness preacher and singer of religious songs). In subsequent days running through early August, some of country music's most interesting and powerful acts made their first recordings. These include Alfred Karnes, a Baptist preacher and powerful gospel singer from Corbin, Kentucky; the Tenneva Ramblers, who had earlier performed in and around Asheville, North Carolina, as an independent act and with Jimmie Rodgers;

The Carter Family: left to right, A.P., Sara, and Maybelle. Courtesy of Tony Russell.

Blind Alfred Reed from West Virginia; and B. F. Shelton, a Kentuckian whose haunting renditions of such ballads as "Pretty Polly" and "Darling Cory" are among the finest on early country records. While all of these musicians brought vital and distinctive styles to the emerging country genre, none of them demonstrated the kind of artistic and commercial potential exhibited by the Carter Family and Jimmie Rodgers. Both acts were recorded within two days of each other—the Carter Family on August 1 and 2, and Rodgers on August 4.

Rodgers and the Carters endowed country music with two of its most imitated styles and two of its most appealing impulses. Rodgers brought into clear focus the tradition of the rambling man, an idea that long had been attractive to country music's folk ancestors and which has ever since fascinated much of the country music audience. This ex-railroad man conveyed the impression that he had been everywhere and had experienced life to the fullest. His music suggested a similar openness of spirit, a willingness to experiment, and a receptivity to alternative styles. The Carter Family, in contrast, represented the impulse toward veneration of home and stability, a theme as perennially attractive as that of the rambler. When the Carters sang, they evoked images of the old country church, Mama and Daddy, the family fireside, and "the green fields of Virginia far away." Theirs was a music that might borrow from other forms but would only reluctantly move away from its roots.

The Carter Family endured as significant country performers until the early 1940s.[19] Although the original group ceased to make commercial records in 1941, they did not actually retire from radio work until two years later. Coming as it did at the beginning of World War II, their retirement assumed symbolic significance to many people: the war seemed to be a great watershed, marking the end of country music's golden age. The Carter Family, which in many respects dominated that era, was composed of A.P. Carter, his wife, Sara, and his sister-in-law, Maybelle Addington Carter.

Alvin Pleasant Carter was born at Maces Spring, Scott County, Virginia, in 1891. Reared in a strict Christian environment, A.P. learned to love religious songs but was nonetheless attracted also by the sound of the fiddle. His religious parents rejected the fiddle as the devil's instrument, so A.P. had to wait until he had earned enough money as a fruit-tree salesman to acquire one. While visiting relatives on Copper Creek in Scott County, he met Sara Dougherty (born in 1898 in Wise County, Virginia), an accomplished young singer and instrumentalist. After their marriage on June 18, 1915, they settled at Maces Spring, where their home became a neighborhood attraction because of A.P.'s and Sara's singing. Maybelle Addington, born in 1909 at Nickelsville, Virginia, married A.P.'s brother Ezra in 1926. She brought to the Carter Family an exceptional talent for the autoharp, banjo, and guitar. When Ralph Peer arrived in Bristol, the Carter Family was well prepared to record.

The Carter Family recorded over three hundred sides for several companies: Victor (1927–1934); American Record Company (1935); Decca (1936–1938); Columbia (1940); Victor (1941). At the first Bristol session, the Family led off with "Bury Me Under the Weeping Willow" and then followed that with five more songs, all of which were subsequently released. The sound established on these initial recordings never varied substantially in the sixteen years that followed. The Carters did not change; they merely got better. Ralph Peer was most impressed with Sara's singing, and though he did not interfere with their choice of songs, he insisted that she be the centerpiece of all of the Carters' records. Sara almost always led the singing with her clear, strong soprano voice; Maybelle countered with a gentler alto harmony; and A.P., always an idiosyncratic singer, sang bass or baritone when he felt like it. Sara often sang solos, and even reluctantly attempted a bit of yodeling at Peer's urging. A.P. sang an occasional solo, such as "I Found You among the Roses," with a rather tentative, tremulous voice, which was peculiarly affecting in its gentle shyness. The highpoint of the Carter vocal sound, however, was the duet singing of Sara and Maybelle, most strongly displayed in their Decca recordings of 1936–1938.

The Carters' instrumental sound was as distinctive and recognizable as their vocal approach. Maybelle played a much-copied guitar lead on all of their records, while Sara seconded with autoharp chords or a second guitar. Maybelle sometimes picked finger-style blues guitar licks, and on occasion even played a steel guitar. The style that attracted generations of guitar pickers, though, was her thumb-brush technique (in which the thumb picks the melody on the bass strings while the fingers provide rhythm with a downward stroke of the treble strings). Featured on her big Gibson L-5 cello model guitar, which she played from 1928 on, Maybelle produced an infectiously rhythmic and melodic sound that captured the interests of guitar players everywhere. In the decades after 1927, it became the height of accomplishment for southern country guitarists to learn the Maybelle Carter guitar style; her rendition of "Wildwood Flower," for example, became the model used by most subsequent fledgling guitarists when they did their first solo guitar piece.

The Carter Family never made extensive tours; most of their appearances were arranged personally by A.P. and confined largely to schoolhouses, churches, and little movie houses in the Upper South.

They won their popularity mostly through phonograph recordings and through radio broadcasts made after 1938 over the powerful Mexican border stations. They sang mostly traditional songs but also a few of their own compositions, and even an occasional "modern hit" like "The Last Letter." Most of their songs were arranged or written ("worked up," as A.P. called it) by A.P., who was one of the first individuals in country music to protect his repertory by securing copyrights on the music—even on that very large percentage that was in the public domain. Ralph Peer insisted on this practice, as he did with Jimmie Rodgers. Peer then published the songs through his own Southern Music Company and shared the profits fifty-fifty. Carter readily admitted that he took many of his songs from traditional sources, but, as Archie Green has said, "every time A.P. Carter recorded a song or published it in a folio, he 'collected' a variant as does any folklorist in the field with his notebook, acetate disc, or tape."[20] The Carters, of course, absorbed many songs as they were growing up, but after their commercial career began, A.P. periodically went on song-hunting trips, collecting sheet music or gospel hymnals, or writing down lyrics as his informants sang to him. One known Carter informant was Lesley Riddle from Burnsville, North Carolina, a black guitarist and singer, who taught the family "Cannonball Blues" and other songs and sometimes accompanied A.P. on collecting trips.

Given his song-collecting habits, it should not be surprising to find A.P. Carter listed as author of songs that he could not possibly have written, such as "I'll Be All Smiles Tonight," "Wildwood Flower," and "The Wabash Cannonball." Nevertheless, modern country and folk music enthusiasts owe A.P. and the Carter Family a great debt because they preserved and disseminated such a large body of old-time material that might otherwise have been lost forever. Carter Family records were never million sellers, and no single record of theirs seems to have experienced any great commercial success, but "Carter Family songs" (as they are generally described) have circulated widely and have become the staples of the repertories of a multitude of country, bluegrass, and urban folksingers. And there is no way to count the number of plain folk who faithfully listened to their broadcasts and transcriptions over XERF in Del Rio, Texas, after 1938, or who bought their records and then bequeathed their songs to children and grandchildren. "I'm Thinking Tonight of My Blue Eyes," "Little Darling Pal of Mine," "Jimmie Brown the Newsboy," "Keep on the Sunny Side" (their radio theme), "Engine 143," "Worried Man Blues," and "Will the Circle Be Unbroken" are only a few of the Carter songs that yet endure.

The Carter Family sang of an America that was gradually disappearing, an America whose values had seemed inextricably interrelated with rural or small-town life. That America had been fading since even before the Carters were children, though its vision may have continued to burn brighter in the rural South or Midwest than anywhere else in the nation. Songs about wandering boys, abandoned mothers, dying orphans, and forsaken lovers had a special poignancy for people who saw the stable world of their parents disintegrating around them. The paeans to "The Homestead on the Farm," the "Little Village Churchyard," or the "Little Poplar Log House on the Hill" became increasingly meaningful as such nostalgic symbols of rural innocence and security receded further and further into memory. The Carters themselves surely knew the pangs of parting and family dissolution; A.P. and Sara separated in 1932 and divorced in 1933. They sang together for ten years after they parted as husband and wife.

The emphasis on home, mother, and old-fashioned morality lived in country music long after the Carter Family dissolved their commercial partnership. It is a self-image that the country music industry has carefully cultivated and resolutely clung to, albeit with increasing difficulty. The radio barn dances, to cite one example, were designed to re-create the atmosphere of wholesome family fun and entertainment associated with village or rural life. Radio, as a matter of fact, reached more Americans than did phonograph recording, and hillbilly entertainers won a much wider public through broadcasting than through any other forum. Rural-flavored variety shows seemed peculiarly appropriate for those radio stations located in farm states or that reached out to far-flung rural areas: WSB, which covered a large portion of the deep rural South; WBAP, which could be heard far outside its home base in Fort Worth; and various farm-town stations like WNAX in Yankton, South Dakota, and KMA in Shenandoah, Iowa, both owned by seed companies that recognized the commercial potential of homespun music.

The barn dance name, if not the explicit format, was introduced to radio by WBAP as early as 1923. The first barn dance show to experience any kind of longevity or national recognition, however, was the one broadcast by WLS in Chicago. WLS inaugurated a hillbilly show on about April 19, 1924, only one week after the station went on the air. WLS (World's Largest Store) was a Sears-Roebuck station from its beginning until September 1928, when it was purchased by the *Prairie Farmer* newspaper. From the very first it aimed many of its broadcasting features at rural and small-town listeners in the Midwest. The first WLS barn dance show got off to a rather inauspicious beginning on the small mezzanine of the Sherman Hotel in Chicago where a group of country-style fiddlers alternated with the popular Isham Jones dance band from the College Inn. The identities of the country musicians are not recalled, although it is believed that fiddler Tommy Dandurand from Kankakee, Illinois, was accompanied by banjoist Jesse Doolittle. The music, made doubly realistic by the square dance calls of Tom Owens, elicited hundreds of requests for fiddle tunes over the course of the next few days. This humble beginning on April 19 ultimately led to the development of the popular *National Barn Dance*.

Throughout its long history (it did not really come to an end until 1968, after having been broadcast on WGN in Chicago for about seven years), the *National Barn Dance*[21] had a broader musical perspective than most country shows. From the time of its inception in 1924, the *National Barn Dance* featured a high proportion of sentimental pop tunes and "heart songs" along with country and folk music. Although criticized by some observers, the inclusion of old-fashioned pop music made sense to most midwesterners. Such songs as "Down by the Old Mill Stream" and "When You Wore a Tulip" were the closest approximations of folk music that they knew. These were the songs of their youth, and they remained basic ingredients of the *National Barn Dance* long after performers from the South and West brought their mountain and cowboy tunes to the Chicago radio show. Fiddle bands and balladeers appeared from the very beginning but often in conjunction with performers of old-time pop and standard melodies. The organist Ralph Waldo Emerson played such songs as "Silver Threads among the Gold," while Ford and Glenn (Ford Rush and Glenn Rowell), the Maple City Four quartet, and Bill O'Connor (the Irish Tenor) sang sentimental melodies and novelty tunes from earlier years. The two most famous singers of "heart songs" ever to appear on the *Barn Dance* were Henry Burr and Grace Wilson. Burr did not join the *Barn Dance* until 1934, but he came with a well-established reputation as a tenor who had performed extensively on the theater and concert circuits since World War I.

Grace Wilson, a popular contralto, was born in Owosso, Michigan, on April 10, 1890. She became a professional singer in 1906 in musical comedy and vaudeville. Between this time and her radio debut in 1922 on WTAS in Elgin, Illinois, she introduced such songs as "In the Shade of the Old Apple Tree" and "I'd Love to Live in Loveland with a Girl Like You." She already had a wide following, therefore, when she joined the *Barn Dance* in 1924. From then until her retirement in 1960, Grace Wilson remained one of the best-loved *Barn Dance* stars, with her most popular rendition being "Bringing Home the Bacon."

Hillbilly entertainers gradually moved onto the show after 1925, although the noncountry performers—as evidenced by Grace Wilson's career—never left the program. Tommy Dandurand and his Barn Dance Fiddlers were there from the very beginning, and southern performers began to appear in 1925, when Chubby Parker, a singer and banjoist from Kentucky, brought such songs as "Stern Old Bachelor" and "My Little Old Sod Shanty on My Claim" to the show. Bradley Kincaid brought his hound-dog guitar and storehouse of old-time songs to the *Barn Dance* in 1926. Missouri-born Luther Ossenbrink, who billed himself as Arkie the Woodchopper, came up from KMBC in Kansas City in 1929. He was still appearing on the *National Barn Dance*, singing his mountain, country, and cowboy ballads, when the show was dropped from WLS in 1960. His tenure on the show was second only to that of Grace Wilson.

The modern-day giant among country music radio shows, the *Grand Ole Opry*, had a slightly later beginning than the WLS program and, for a number of years, exerted a lesser influence and popularity. The *Grand Ole Opry* was the brainchild of George D. Hay, a native of Attica, Indiana. Hay became involved in radio in Memphis in 1923, after having been a popular columnist for the Memphis *Commercial Appeal*. Within a year he had moved to WLS in Chicago, where he became one of the most popular announcers in America (according to a *Radio Digest* poll). Calling himself the "Solemn Old Judge" and blowing blasts from a steamboat whistle, Hay helped give the new *Barn Dance* show an authentic, homey atmosphere. By November 9, 1925, he had moved once more, this time to the brand-new station in Nashville, Tennessee, WSM, which was owned by the National Life and Accident Insurance Company. As its new station director, Hay soon began trying to steer WSM toward the successful rural format he had witnessed earlier in Chicago. Although he confronted resistance from WSM's directors, who held a rather strong distaste for rural music, and from Nashville's upper crust, who gloried in the city's reputation as "the Athens of the South," Hay nevertheless won acceptance for his experiments. The National Life and Accident Insurance Company sold inexpensive weekly policies to working-class people, and its managers eventually recognized the commercial possibilities of old-time music even if they could not always see its artistic qualities.

On November 28, 1925, Hay launched a hillbilly radio show, the *WSM Barn Dance*, with only two entertainers, a seventy-seven-year-old fiddler named Uncle Jimmy Thompson and his niece, Eva Thompson Jones, who accompanied him on piano. Uncle Jimmy was a hard-living, hard-drinking man from LaGuardo, Tennessee, whose repertory of tunes extended back to the antebellum era. He had spent some time in vaudeville and had participated in fiddle contests all over the South, particularly in Texas, where he had lived for ten years and had picked up the long-bow style associated with that state. At his WSM debut, Uncle Jimmy was seated in a comfortable chair in front of an old carbon microphone. At the end of an hour, Hay asked the old fiddler if he was tired of playing, and Uncle Jimmy replied: "Why, shucks, a man don't get warmed up in an hour. I just won an eight-day fiddling contest down in Dallas, Texas, and here's my blue ribbon to prove it."[22] Uncle Jimmy claimed to know a thousand tunes, and he evidently wanted to be given a chance to play all of them.

The fiddle playing brought an immediately favorable response, and telegrams and letters requesting tunes poured into the station. As a result, Uncle Jimmy, his niece, and Hay carried on for an hour each Saturday night for several weeks. This small group did not long remain the total personnel of the *WSM Barn Dance* show. As George Hay later recalled, "After three or four weeks of this fiddle solo business, we were besieged with other fiddlers, banjo pickers, guitar players, and a lady who played an old zither."[23] Most anyone who could perform was accepted; the entertainers (mostly from the Middle Tennessee region) performed without pay, and the performances were given without commercials. The musicians for the most part were amateurs who worked as farmers and laborers during the week and then performed at WSM on Saturday night. Hay zealously worked to preserve the informal, down-home atmosphere of the shows, and he constantly admonished the musicians to keep things "down to earth," while he also gave the string bands names like the Possum Hunters, Clodhoppers, and Fruit Jar Drinkers that seemed appropriate to the rustic image.

As was common on nearly all early radio stations, the early WSM shows emphasized instrumental music. The first old-time string band featured was that of Dr. Humphrey Bate and the Possum Hunters. Dr. Bate, a well-educated physician, surgeon, and harmonica player from Sumner County, Tennessee, led a group that included his thirteen-year-old daughter, Alcyone, who played the piano. Dr. Bate was no stranger to radio when he joined WSM on October 24, 1925; he had appeared on WDAD in Nashville over a year previously.

Shortly after the arrival of Bate's group, three similar string bands joined the regular Saturday night broadcast. These were the Crook Brothers, the Gully Jumpers, and the Fruit Jar Drinkers. Following not far behind these groups was a brother team from the rural area around Franklin, Tennessee, Kirk and Sam McGee. Sam was one of the finest finger-style guitarists of the early period, known especially for his renditions of songs like "Railroad Blues" and "Buck Dancer's Choice." Although the McGee boys were raised in a family that often played string music (their father was an old-time fiddler), Sam did not become interested in the guitar until shortly before World War I, when he heard it being played by black street musicians in Perry, Tennessee. From that time forward, although he also played the five-string banjo competently, McGee's chief instrument was the guitar, which he put to proficient use in 1923 when he began touring with Uncle Dave Macon. By 1925 the two McGees were playing on *Grand Ole Opry* broadcasts and touring along with Dr. Bate and the Possum Hunters on *Opry*-sponsored shows on the RKO vaudeville circuit in the Midwest and Upper South.

Although the early *Grand Ole Opry* string bands did vocal numbers as well as instrumentals, none of them had a featured vocalist. Obed "Dad" Pickard came as close as anyone to being a star singer. Pickard was a master of many instruments who eventually became the leader of the Pickard Family, a group that played on radio stations all over the United States (including WJR in Detroit, 1928). On WSM, he specialized in such sentimental parlor tunes as "Kitty Wells" and "Bury Me Not on the Lone Prairie." The chief singing star of the *Grand Ole Opry*, before the coming of Roy Acuff, was a colorful five-string banjoist named Uncle Dave Macon. David Harrison Macon, a superbly gifted musician and comedian, was born in Smart Station near McMinnville in Warren County, Tennessee, on October 7, 1870. The musical education that would one day make him such a versatile performer began when his parents moved to Nashville in 1873 and opened a boardinghouse that catered to theatrical people. At an early age he learned songs, stories, and instrumental techniques from the colorful vaudeville and circus personalities who passed through the city. One performer to whom he paid special tribute was Joel Davidson, a circus comedian and banjoist who fired young Dave's resolve to become an entertainer. After Macon's marriage to Mathilda Richardson, he moved to a small farm in Kittrell, not far from Readyville, Tennessee, where, in 1900, he established the Macon Midway Mule and Wagon Transportation Company, which hauled material from Woodbury to Murfreesboro for the next twenty years. Uncle Dave frequently sang as he and his team slowly plodded toward their destination. (The company is immortalized in Uncle Dave's recording of "From Earth to Heaven.")

Before 1918, music was no more than an amusing but constant diversion for Uncle Dave. Known for miles around as a first-rate comic, an extraordinary finger-style banjoist, and a thorough professional in his approach to audiences and musical skills, he had never performed for money. His performances at picnics and social functions had been strictly for fun. The commercial world of show business beckoned, however, in 1918, when he demanded fifteen dollars to play at a large party given by a farmer whom he believed to be a bit pompous. To Uncle Dave's great surprise, the farmer accepted. A talent scout for Loew's Theatre Circuit, who happened to be present at the party, approached Macon after the performance and booked him for a concert at a leading theater in Birmingham. From there he went on to bookings all over the South.

When Uncle Dave Macon joined the *Grand Ole Opry* in 1926, he was fifty-six years old; he had been a professional entertainer for eight years and a semiprofessional for much longer. He brought to the *Grand Ole Opry* both the versatile skills of a seasoned vaudeville and minstrel entertainer and a storehouse of folk material garnered from a host of southern sources. He also knew a wide variety of complex picking and frailing styles—some of minstrel origin—which modern banjoists might well envy. In his commitment to traditional styles he certainly deserves the praise given to him by Ralph Rinzler: "With the exception of the Carter Family, Uncle Dave preserved more valuable American folklore through his recordings than any other folk or country music performer."[24] Many of his songs also came from minstrel, vaudeville,

*Uncle Dave Macon and his son, Dorris. Bill Malone
personal collection; courtesy of Ralph Rinzler.*

and nineteenth-century Tin Pan Alley sources or from the vast reservoir of southern gospel music. Others had been picked up through
the years from friends, relatives, or other folksingers, both black and
white. Uncle Dave's recordings are important repositories of social
commentary about politics, fashions, and the industrial revolution
that steadily moved across the South in the decades following the
Civil War. They include songs about life on a Georgia chain gang ("Way
Down the Old Plank Road"); bitter labor upheavals in Tennessee in the
1880s occasioned by the use of convict labor in the coal mines ("Buddy,
Won't You Roll Down the Line"); Henry Ford's car and his Muscle
Shoals project ("On the Dixie Bee Line"); political corruption in Ten-
nessee ("Wreck of the Tennessee Gravy Train"); presidential politics
("Governor Al Smith"); evolution ("The Bible's True"); agricultural
distress ("Farm Relief"); the Great Depression ("All In and Down and
Out Blues").

Uncle Dave's recording career began in 1924, when he and the fiddler Sid Harkreader (his vaudeville companion for the previous two years) recorded fourteen sides for the Vocalion label in New York. His first session included some of his most popular songs, such as "Keep My Skillet Good and Greasy," as well as the first song to carry "hillbilly" in its title: "Hill Billie Blues." In later sessions beginning in 1926, he was generally supported by those talented brothers from Tennessee, Sam and Kirk McGee, and by the old-time fiddler Mazy Todd. Their 1927 sessions resulted in some of the most exciting string band sounds heard on records; Uncle Dave's delight is clearly evident in his whoops, hollers, and shouted words of encouragement.

Until his death at the age of eighty-three, Uncle Dave Macon played with a zest and enthusiasm that few, if any, modern country entertainers can equal. He continued to record off and on up through 1938, being accompanied by his son Dorris, the McGees, the Delmore Brothers, and Smoky Mountain Glenn. His radio work and his appearances in tent shows and the like continued almost to his death in 1952. Although thoroughly professional in his approach to show business and in his musical skills, Macon was totally unaffected and unpretentious, and he never lost the zest to perform for the pure personal enjoyment of it. When the *Grand Ole Opry* began sending out tours in the late 1920s and early 1930s, Uncle Dave was a source of considerable consternation to the show's directors. Harry Stone, a former manager of the *Grand Ole Opry*, said that Macon sometimes had to be restrained from giving the whole show away through his willingness to perform in hotel lobbies, free of charge, before the main program got under way. He cut a striking figure in his double-breasted waistcoat, high wing collar, bright red tie, and broad-brimmed hat of black felt. He looked the part of a merry country gentleman of the 1890s, and with his old-time songs, homey sayings, shouted enthusiasms, and boundless vitality, he captivated his audiences and recaptured the spirit of rural, small-town America that was about to be submerged by the sophistication and glamor of urban twentieth-century America.

The popularity of the WSM show necessitated its gradual enlargement. The program's cast had grown to about twenty-five when Uncle Dave Macon joined it, so WSM decided to build a much larger studio, Studio B, with a large plate-glass window through which spectators could watch. Soon the WSM executives decided to allow about fifty or sixty people to listen from within the studio. From this small beginning

WSM gradually expanded the facilities for the show, first building an auditorium studio with a seating capacity of five hundred, and later renting the Hillsboro Theatre, which also proved to be too small for the program's fans. The show moved next to a large tabernacle in East Nashville, then on to the War Memorial Auditorium before finding a suitable location. In 1941 the show relocated to a converted tabernacle replete with church pews and a balcony dedicated as a Confederate memorial, the historic Ryman Auditorium. This "mother church of country music," originally built by Captain Thomas Ryman, a riverboat man, as a memorial to his religious conversion by the great evangelist Sam Jones, remained the home of the *Grand Ole Opry* until 1974, when the show moved to a new and ornate location at Opryland Park.[25]

In 1927 the announcer George D. Hay gave the *WSM Barn Dance* its present title of *Grand Ole Opry*. The program, then three hours long, followed NBC's *Music Appreciation Hour,* conducted by Dr. Walter Damrosch. While introducing a number on one of his evening programs, Damrosch remarked that "while most artists realize that there is no place in the classics for realism, I am going to break one of my rules and present a composition by a young composer from Iowa. This young man has sent us his latest number, which depicts the onrush of a locomotive . . ." When the WSM country music show came on the air, Hay announced that while there was no room for realism in the classics, the following three hours would be devoted to nothing but realism. Then, in an obvious good-natured jibe at Damrosch, Hay introduced one of the show's most popular performers, DeFord Bailey, a black harmonica player, who played a train song, "Pan American Blues," which had been inspired by the famous southern train that ran near Bailey's home. When the performance was over, Hay said, "For the past hour we have been listening to music taken largely from grand opera, but from now on we will present 'The Grand Ole Opry.'"[26] The name proved to be popular with the listeners and came to be the official title of the show.

In the years that followed, Hay introduced the show each Saturday night with his steamboat whistle and his warm command, "Let her go, boys." DeFord Bailey did his country harmonica blues; Uncle Dave regaled the audiences with his wit and zestful songs; and Dr. Bate and the other old-time string bands kept the mood close to that of the hoedowns of rural America. But the mood of spontaneous simplicity could not last, because the barn dances had demonstrated that country music could sell. Judge Hay lived long enough to see his "down-to-earth" show become a national institution and the longest-lasting program on American radio. The popularity of the *Grand Ole Opry* and other barn dance shows presaged country music's coming commercial success—and its incorporation into the American popular culture mainstream.

CHAPTER 3

The First Country Singing Star: Jimmie Rodgers

C ountry music's evolution as a star-oriented phenomenon, with traits increasingly national rather than local, is largely the legacy of Jimmie Rodgers. One of the top Victor record sellers of the 1920s, and acknowledged as the "father of modern country music," Rodgers introduced new techniques and styles to the music and inspired a legion of followers who sought to emulate their master. In his repertory of 111 recorded songs,[1] Jimmie Rodgers exhibited his debt to the diverse strains that made up the South's musical culture. He recorded almost every type of song with which the rural southerner was familiar, but strangely only one religious piece. He may be most famous for the novel fusion that he introduced to country music, the "blue yodel," but neither the blues nor yodeling constituted the whole of his musical approach. Similarly, to concentrate primarily on his debt to black music, as is often done, would create a highly incomplete picture of Rodgers.

Jimmie Rodgers was a small-town southern boy who wanted very much to be a popular singer. As he reached manhood in the World War I years, the entertainers associated with vaudeville and Tin Pan Alley provided the only show-business models available. As recordings became available to him, they certainly included black performers, and like most young people of the time, he could not have been

Jimmie Rodgers. Bill Malone personal collection.

unaffected by the jazz rhythms and blues music that flowed into the public consciousness. But as a singer, he probably made few distinctions between musical forms, and he gravitated toward the types of songs favored by Al Jolson, Harry Lauder, and other stage singers. When Rodgers ventured into professional entertainment, the enthusiasm for hillbilly music had begun, and he was fated—because of his background and deep southern dialect—to be drawn into the new rural music business. He could easily follow that route, and probably with no reluctance, because the vast panoply of American popular music on which he drew included the sentimental, blues, and bum songs that appealed to the hillbilly audience.

James Charles Rodgers was born in the rural Pine Springs community just north of Meridian, Mississippi, on September 8, 1897.[2] He was the son of Eliza Bozeman Rodgers and Aaron W. Rodgers, an extra gang foreman on the Mobile and Ohio Railroad. His mother died when he was about five or six years old, and his father was left with the prime responsibility of rearing him to manhood. Jimmie verbalized his debt to his father in his great sentimental song "Daddy and Home." The young Rodgers had only an occasional encounter with formal schooling and learned what he knew in the "school of hard knocks," while following his father from place to place as he pursued his railroad duties. Aaron Rodgers's work as an extra gang foreman took him for extended periods to different cities in the South, including New Orleans, because it was the duty of the extra gang to travel by railroad car to those sections of the line that needed repairing. This kind of life, plus the experience of growing up in a succession of relatives' homes, introduced to Jimmie Rodgers a broader knowledge of life's varieties—both the exciting and the sordid—than most small-town southern boys had known.

Rodgers also grew up faster than the average youth. He went off on his own occasionally but always penned scrawled postcards to let his relatives know where he was. He joined a medicine show at the age of thirteen, and at fourteen began working with his dad's railroad crews. He stumbled into an early, unfortunate marriage on May 1, 1917, but was separated by fall. The marriage, though, resulted in a child and, eventually, an embarrassing and costly lawsuit over child-support payments. He knew very well the world of ramblers and rounders of which he sang.

Rodgers's association with railroading has always lent an air of romance to his life, and it contributed greatly to his later commercial success as a singer. The public found the image of "the singing brakeman" irresistibly appealing, particularly during the Great Depression when millions of Americans could identify with an allegedly liberated and rambling life that they personally could not enjoy. Railroad work, however, was something that Rodgers did only by necessity and not by choice. Even before tuberculosis robbed him of much of the strength necessary to do outside work, Rodgers sought the means—preferably through music—to escape that "romantic" profession. From the time he joined his father's extra gang until he retired from railroad work in 1925, Rodgers worked sporadically as a railroad man, though often unemployed, living a hardscrabble life with his second wife, Carrie (whom he married in 1920), and often roaming throughout much of the United States looking for work. During his career he worked on lines all over the Southwest, usually as a flagman or brakeman, but the line he worked most was the New Orleans and Northeastern on the run between Meridian and New Orleans. Rodgers became thoroughly conversant with the vocabulary and music of the railroad workers, a hardy breed of men that he later commemorated so well in his bestselling Victor records. As a wandering railroad man, he had the opportunity to sample many kinds of music, including the fragments of songs shouted out by black workers who traveled on the extra gang. We do not know where the song originated, but a line from his well-known "Muleskinner Blues"—"Hey, little water boy, bring that water 'round"—may very well have been inspired by the times when, as a teenager, he carried water to the black workers.

Through all his years as a railroad worker, Rodgers's thoughts never strayed far away from music. Among the many contributions made by biographer Nolan Porterfield is his demonstration that Rodgers tried hard to be a professional entertainer long before he made his first Victor records. He learned to play the banjo and guitar at a very early age and often entertained his fellow workers during lunch and rest breaks. In his off hours, he occasionally played with black musicians down around Tenth Street in Meridian or for his favorite southern belles, who would gather in their well-chaperoned parlors to hear him play. In 1923 he spent a few weeks with a tent-repertory show, Terrell's Comedians, playing the small towns between Hattiesburg, Mississippi, and New Orleans. Before he left the railroad permanently in 1925, his most sustained activity as a professional musician was with a trio composed of Slim Rozell (violin), Rodgers's sister-in-law, Elsie McWilliams (piano), and Rodgers on banjo, guitar, or mandolin. The trio played dance music and pop standards at fairs, picnics, and political rallies, and at Lauderdale Springs, a resort area north of Meridian. Rodgers apparently sang very little at these functions, but he obtained a touch of the show-business experience that would later prove to be invaluable; the experience also introduced him to a repertory of pop music that would one day appear with great frequency in his "hillbilly-oriented" concerts and recordings.

Rodgers's most intensive experience as a professional entertainer came in 1925 just as he was making the transition from railroad work to full-time music performance. In April of that year he became part of a "world tour" in New Orleans designed to raise money for disabled soldiers. He joined a small group of would-be musicians that included Lucien "Piggy" Parks, a fellow guitarist and street singer in the Crescent City, and Goebel Reeves, who had just driven in from California in a Model T truck with a specially built body that permitted very rough sleeping accommodations for about five people. The ambitious young musicians did not take their music around the world, as they sometimes claimed in tales told to newspaper reporters, but they did venture as far as Canada and covered much of the United States, playing for hundreds of customers in bars, barber shops, and on street corners in places like Topeka, Kansas; Lincoln, Nebraska; Cleveland, Ohio; Chattanooga, Tennessee; and Miami, Florida. They also apparently played at least a couple of days at radio station WDOD in Chattanooga, only a few months after that station went on the air. We do not know what songs Jimmie was performing at this time, but he probably sang the blues and popular songs of the day, and he may have begun experimenting with the blue yodels that later became his trademark.[3]

By September of 1925, Jimmie had left the show in Miami and had taken a temporary position with the Florida East Coast Railroad. Soon he was back on the road as a blackface entertainer with a medicine show that toured the mountain and hill-country districts of the Upper South as well as southern Ohio and Indiana. This kind of show-business experience—shared by so many other early big-time country stars—helped give him ease and confidence in front of audiences and further kindled his desire for stardom as he heard the people applaud and saw their delighted faces. After spending a brief period on the medicine-show circuit, he and Carrie went back to Geiger, Alabama, where they briefly operated a roadside café. He tried one last fling at railroading and then moved to the mountain resort city of Asheville, North Carolina, in search of a more healthful climate and outlets for his entertainment ambitions. In Asheville, sometime in April 1927, he met a group of string musicians who called themselves the Tenneva Ramblers (Jack Pierce and the Grant Brothers, Jack and Claude). Jimmie was already appearing occasionally on WWNC in Asheville, and he won the boys over with his visions of a radio career. They reconstituted themselves as the Jimmie Rodgers Entertainers and began making scattered personal appearances, as well as singing occasionally on WWNC. The connection with WWNC did not last long, and by June 1927 Rodgers had gone to work as a city detective, working at that job and performing locally until Ralph Peer came south on his historic recording expedition in late July.

Peer had gone into business for himself as a music publisher, but had worked out a relationship with Victor that permitted him to select artists and supervise hillbilly recordings for the company. In return, his publishing firm was permitted to own the copyrights, and Peer was compensated by the royalties resulting from the compositions he had selected for recording (the basis for the Peer-Southern complex). Under this new arrangement he made a survey of various southern cities and decided to produce initial recordings for Victor in Atlanta, Savannah, Memphis, and Bristol. As noted in the previous chapter, newspaper publicity generated extensive excitement about Peer's visit to Bristol. In Peer's words, "This worked like dynamite and the very next day I was deluged with long-distance calls from the surrounding mountain regions. Groups of singers who had not visited Bristol during their entire lifetime arrived by bus, horse and buggy, trains, or on foot."[4]

One of those singers who made a hopeful long-distance call was Jimmie Rodgers, who came down from Asheville with the little string band that he called his "hillbilly ork." After reaching Bristol, Rodgers was disappointed to learn that the Jimmie Rodgers Entertainers had decided to try their luck at recording without him. Disagreeing over proper billing, and probably chafing at the loss of identity caused by the association with Rodgers, the group resurrected their old name, the Tenneva Ramblers, and made a number of important recordings, including an interesting variant of "In the Pines" called "The Longest Train."

When Rodgers appeared before Peer, it was "just him and his guitar," and he nervously sang a couple of old songs that he had earlier tried out on his WWNC audiences. In most of his Asheville performances, Rodgers's song choices had usually been the current hits, the compositions of New York publishers. But in this initial recording session he chose two deeply sentimental old-time tunes for his first renditions: "The Soldier's Sweetheart," a Spanish-American War–era song that had been updated to refer to that "awful German war," and an old lullaby, recorded earlier by Riley Puckett, called "Sleep, Baby, Sleep." He yodeled on "Sleep, Baby, Sleep," thus inaugurating a fashion that was to endure in country music for at least a decade.

Rodgers's first quarterly royalty check achieved only the discouraging total of twenty-seven dollars, and the fame he had long sought still seemed to be very far away. By the end of 1927, however, his popularity had begun to mount, and the Victor people realized that they had signed a potential star. Rodgers was soon permitted another recording session, this time at the Victor headquarters in Camden, New Jersey. At this second session he recorded the first of his twelve blue yodels (popularly known as "T for Texas" but listed by Victor as simply "Blue Yodel"). Backed with Kelly Harrell's composition "Away Out on the Mountain," it became the hillbilly hit of the year, and fame and success seemed finally near at hand. In its structure, the song resembled the typical blues form, but at the conclusion of the third line, Rodgers lifted his voice to a higher octave and uttered the blue yodel that made him the most famous hillbilly star in history.

Between 1927 and 1933, Jimmie Rodgers became a household name in thousands of rural and small-town American homes, particularly in his native Southland. His recording popularity was augmented by vaudeville and tent-show appearances and by radio performances throughout the southern region. Unfortunately, Rodgers's barnstorming potential was greatly hindered by his affliction with tuberculosis, the grim disease that drained his strength and forced him to seek a permanent home in the drier regions of Central Texas.

He made no tours in the northern United States, although schedules for such appearances were sometimes planned. Concerts in Washington, DC, in August 1928—at the Earle Theatre, on WTFF, and at local social functions—were about as close as he ever got to the Mason-Dixon line. WTFF announcer Ray McCreath became Rodgers's manager for a short time but was never able to secure the national bookings that he sometimes talked about.

By the time he began his first southern vaudeville tour on November 5, 1928, Rodgers was sporting at least two images, that of the Singing Brakeman and that of the Blue Yodeler. He no doubt thought of himself as a vaudevillian, or as a popular singer in the broadest sense of the term (an eclectic musician who was wedded to no one style), but his song material was closest to the hearts of working-class people and not to the urban middle class who set the standards of pop music. His vaudeville tour carried him into Norfolk, Atlanta, Memphis, New Orleans, and Houston, where he generally received top billing and appeared to favorable reviews. When he completed his tour of the circuit in December, he joined a tent-repertory show, the Paul English Players, working out of Mobile, Alabama. The employment of a "name attraction" for limited engagements was said to be something new in the tent-rep line, and Rodgers's appearances doubled the company's business. Rodgers remained with the English Players until March 1929 and traveled with them from Mobile to Texas. Working only as a concert feature, about fifteen to twenty minutes a night, he earned $600 a week. His performances greatly increased the company's receipts and stimulated the sale of Victor records, since the show had tie-ups with Victor dealers in all of the towns visited.

Rodgers made still another vaudeville tour, for RKO Interstate, from May to July 1929 in theaters extending from Atlanta to Oklahoma. In the years that followed, he made occasional solo performances, usually in lodge halls, schoolhouses, or auditoriums, and occasionally on radio, and traveled with assorted tent-show groups similar to the Paul English organization. He appeared regularly with such groups unless his health interfered, or until Ralph Peer called him away for another recording session. Each show typically featured Rodgers as the major attraction. During the spring and summer of 1930, he traveled with the W. I. Swain show, Hollywood Follies, through Louisiana and Texas. The show carried a number of acts, including an Irish comedian, a Hawaiian group, and a blues singer, but according to *Billboard*, Jimmie Rodgers was the "outstanding hit of the show." The Swain show drew capacity crowds during its one-night stands in Texas, but attendance declined sharply in Kansas and Oklahoma. By this time, though, Rodgers had become ill and had left the show in mid-May.

During the last few years of his life, Rodgers made most of his appearances in Texas. In May 1929 at Kerrville, in the heart of the Texas Hill Country, he built a $25,000 home, which he called "Blue Yodeler's Paradise." He lived there with his wife, Carrie, and daughter, Anita, until mounting medical costs and extravagant living necessitated the sale of the house. Thereafter, until his death in 1933, he and his family lived in a much more modest cottage in San Antonio.

In the spring of 1931, he and Will Rogers conducted a benefit tour in northeast Texas for the victims of a recent Red River flood. The pair also gave a number of charity performances throughout the Southwest for the unemployed. In March of that year, he journeyed to Austin, where he was appointed an honorary Texas Ranger; he took great pride in this honor and eventually composed a song called "The Yodeling Ranger." When the Texas Rotary Club held its statewide meeting in Austin in March 1931, Rodgers appeared as the featured attraction. Upon receiving an invitation from the chairman of the program committee, Adjutant General William W. Sterling, Rodgers responded with these words: "I am ready and happy to obey any order from my superior officer."[5] The audience gave his performance an enthusiastic reception, and at the conclusion he presented Ranger chief Sterling with one of his fabulous Weymann guitars, worth an estimated $1,500.

The last year and a half of Rodgers's life was filled with recording dates, radio shows, tent theater appearances, costly medical treatments, a lawsuit with his first wife, and never-realized plans for nationwide tours. During the winter of 1931–1932, he appeared with Leslie E. Kell's tent theater company in an extended engagement in Houston and a shorter one in San Antonio. The Kell Company was a variety show that featured, in addition to Rodgers, a fan dancer named Holly Desmond.

Rodgers and Kell made elaborate plans for an extensive tour that would carry them through the Northwest, British Columbia, eastward through Canada to New York, and finally back to Texas. The plan was never completed, however, because Rodgers left Kell in March 1932 to join the J. Doug Morgan show for its spring and summer tent tour in East Texas. During his off months, Rodgers remained in San Antonio, where he became a twice-weekly feature on station KMAC. Here he remained until an intensification of his disease necessitated his entry into the Baptist Hospital in Houston in January 1933. He remained in the Houston hospital for about a month, charming the nurses and keeping Mickey, his Boston terrier, beside his bed despite the hospital restriction banning dogs. He returned to San Antonio in the following month, partially recuperated and with orders to remain in the Alamo City for at least a six-month rest. But, despite the doctors' orders and despite a prediction made two years earlier by Dr. I. W. Cooper that he could not live longer than two years, Rodgers decided to make a recording trip to New York that May, probably knowing that it would be his last.

His last recording session is one of the most heart-rending episodes in show-business history. He had become so weak that the Victor company provided him a special cot in a room near the studio. At the conclusion of each recorded take, he lay down until he regained adequate strength for another performance. He recorded almost to the very end; his last session was on May 24, two days before he succumbed in the Taft Hotel. On the day of his death, he went to Coney Island on a sight-seeing tour with his private nurse, Cora Bedell, and while there suffered an attack of spasms. He died that night in his hotel room, far from his native home and family. When his death train pulled into Meridian, Mississippi, late at night, the engineer, Homer Jenkins, blew the whistle in a long moaning wail that grew in intensity as the train rolled toward the terminal station. This was the train crew's tribute to the "Singing Brakeman," who now lay in a coffin in one of the baggage cars. Many years later, this tribute was beautifully commemorated in "The Train Carrying Jimmie Rodgers Home," a song written by Greg Brown and performed by the Nashville Bluegrass Band.

In assessing Jimmie Rodgers's influence on American folk music and on a later generation of commercial performers, one can safely use the adjective "phenomenal." Indeed, one would be hard-pressed to find a performer in the whole broad field of pop music—whether it be Al Jolson, Bing Crosby, or Frank Sinatra—who has exerted a more profound and recognizable influence on later generations of entertainers. No one as yet has made a full-scale attempt to determine how many of his songs have gone into popular or folk tradition, and there is no way to measure the number of people, amateur and professional, whom he may have inspired to take up the guitar or try their luck at singing. With the emergence of Jimmie Rodgers, country folk finally had one of their own to use as a model—a personification of the success that might be possible in the world of music, and the possessor of a magnetic style and personality that might be emulated to attain that success. Rodgers singlehandedly originated a new tradition in country music and inspired a host of followers—most of whom heard him only on records—to become country musicians. The center of country music activity shifted more heavily toward the Southwest, and a new generation of hillbilly entertainers, captivated by Rodgers's blue yodels, his unorthodox guitar style, and his intriguing songs, began to dominate the country music scene. The new group of performers arising in the late 1920s and early 1930s would have repertories significantly different from those of the earlier hillbillies and would perform them in styles that were often direct imitations of Jimmie Rodgers. The record companies, of course, searched for Rodgers sound-alikes who could be competitive with him, and Victor immediately looked for successors when Rodgers died. Ernest Tubb estimated that perhaps 75 percent of modern country music performers were directly or indirectly influenced to become entertainers either through hearing Rodgers in person or through his recordings. Rodgers's popularity and influence, moreover, were not confined to this country. His records sold widely in various parts of the British Empire, where they were introduced and favorably reviewed as early as 1928, and the folklorist John Greenway found that in Australia, "all contemporary country singing is clearly attributable to Rodgers's compositions, themes and styles." Greenway found, too, that Rodgers's popularity reached beyond the confines of the English-speaking world—one of his correspondents reported seeing a large collection of the "Blue Yodeler's" records in an Eskimo's hut near Point Barrow. The most bizarre manifestation of Rodgers's worldwide appeal came right after World War II in Kenya, after a British missionary played some of Jimmie's records for members of the Kipsigis tribe. Apparently, some of the tribesmen were so fascinated by Rodgers's tenor yodeling sound that they thought of him as a deity, and they made up a song about him called "Chemirocha" that they sang at religious ceremonies for many years.[6]

No other hillbilly star of the 1920s rivaled Rodgers in popularity. He was one of the few country performers to receive any notice in the major trade publications, and his records, which sold more widely than those of any other hillbilly, exceeded the sales of most pop performers in the Victor catalogue. The actual sales figures of Rodgers's records remain unknown, and as a result, "guesses" have ranged as high as twenty million. Writing in 1979, Nolan Porterfield estimated that the figure (from the issuance of Rodgers's first record to then) was closer to twelve million. He further asserted that the Blue Yodeler had only one million seller, "Blue Yodel No. 1," and that the second-highest seller, "Waiting for a Train," sold in the neighborhood of 365,000 copies. Most crucially, Porterfield pointed out that total record sales are irrelevant and are an imprecise measure of Rodgers's popularity. Rodgers's records were played repeatedly until their labels were bare and scratchiness obscured their sound, and they were lent to neighbors and friends and made the center of neighborhood gatherings.

Rodgers's lifestyle, or public perceptions of it, was almost as important to his success as was his music. He spent money freely, before his career ever began and after his record sales declined during the Depression. Big cars, jewelry, guitars, expensive clothes, and the "mansion" in Kerrville were all lavishly consumed even as his medical expenses mounted. His extravagant tastes made him all the more alluring to his fans; such behavior, after all, was expected of a "star" and especially condoned when one was deemed to be as generous and free-hearted as Jimmie was with friends and down-and-outers. The light-hearted demeanor he displayed in the face of what was then terminal illness brought only admiration. Rodgers sang "TB Blues" and "Whipping That Old TB" even as he succumbed to its effects. His fans marveled at his ability to hit those high-yodeling notes despite his affliction, or they theorized that, somehow, his lung-crippling disease contributed to the making of his yodels. Jimmie's well-known taste for good whiskey was also magnified by his fans, and many people still have favorite stories about the time he visited the local bootlegger. People did not always appreciate that alcohol helped numb the pain he constantly had to endure, or that he could not possibly have consumed the amounts of liquor attributed to him. Jimmie had neither the health nor the stamina to be the kind of rounder that his personal image suggested or that public myth would have him be. Nor did his songs necessarily mirror the reality of his life, even though he liked to give the impression that they did—an affectation that his fans heartily endorsed. If he sang "I've Ranged, I've Roamed and I've Travelled," his listeners were sure he had done just that. When he sang "Lullaby Yodel," many people were convinced that he was singing to an estranged wife who had taken their child with her (even though his wife's sister wrote the song!). "High Powered Mama," of course, just had to be about that same wife who "just wouldn't leave other daddies alone." Humble, adoring fans were not the only people who succumbed to romantic myths about Rodgers. Many years later, the famous British blues scholar, Paul Oliver, while spelling his name as "Jimmy," wrote that Rodgers had played to "packed houses" in Canada, Mexico, and England, and had built a mansion "within sight of the Mexican border"![7] Rodgers would not be the last country singer whose public image and personal music style were strongly intermeshed—and certainly not the last one to capitalize on that impression.

Any discussion of Jimmie Rodgers's remarkable popularity would be incomplete without at least some attempt to analyze his distinctive performing style. Although he recorded with a diverse assortment of instrumental accompaniment—violins, banjos, ukuleles, Hawaiian steel guitars, and jazz bands—his personal appearances were almost always made in solo fashion: just Jimmie and his guitar. For his stage appearances, he generally dressed in a white or tan lightweight suit and sported a jauntily cocked straw sailor hat (he often posed for publicity pictures in a cowboy costume or railroad brakeman's attire but seldom dressed this way during a performance). He looked and acted the part of a young man-about-town out for an evening of pleasure. He would put his foot on a chair, cradle his guitar across his knee, and captivate his audiences with a selection of both rakish and sentimental tunes that generally consumed no more than twenty minutes. In a voice unmistakably southern, he kidded his audiences in a whimsical fashion and beguiled them with songs that seemed to catalogue the varied memories, yearnings, and experiences of small-town and rural Americans: nostalgia for the departed mother or "the old southern town" of childhood; pathos for the homeless hobo dying in a boxcar or trying to bum a southbound freight train; unrequited love; laughter for the rakes and rogues who "loved and left them" in every town; and a variety of other emotions with which most people could identify.

As he sang and recorded, he amused himself and teased his accompanying musicians with a running patter of commentary. As an accompanist took an instrumental break, Rodgers would occasionally say something like "Play that thing, boy," or he would say to himself or no one in particular, "Sing them blues, boy," "Hey, hey, it won't be long now," or "Hey, sweet mama." The total effect of his performances was an air of effortless informality, marked by a very personal approach that insinuated its way into the hearts of listeners, making them feel that the song was meant just for them. His voice—a nasal tenor distinguished by the lazy drawl of the Mississippi Black Belt—was capable of adjusting itself to almost any kind of song—a spirited railroad piece, a rollicking blues number, or a tender, plaintive lullaby. He sang them all with sincerity and in the particular spirit in which they were written. When his audiences of railroad workers, truck drivers, laborers, farmers, and small-town people heard his songs, they recognized him as one of their own, and the deadening, bleak years of the Depression were thereby made more endurable.

Jimmie's records popularized a number of sounds and styles, both ephemeral and permanent, that made their way into country music. He did not introduce the steel guitar to country music, but with recordings like "Treasures Untold," written and performed by Ellsworth T. Cozzens, his records certainly popularized the instrument. Cozzens played what was then called a Hawaiian steel guitar on Rodgers's second session of February 1928, and it appeared periodically in other sessions, played by such men as Cliff Carlisle, John Westbrook, and Joe Kaipo. Kaipo was an authentic Hawaiian and only one of many who toured the United States in the wake of the Panama-Pacific International Exposition of 1915. Jazz sounds also appeared in Rodgers's recording sessions as early as October 1928, and he was joined in a historic session in Hollywood in July 1930 by Louis Armstrong on trumpet and Lillian Armstrong on piano. The result was a recording of "Blue Yodel No. 9" (also known as "Standing on the Corner"). The jazz style did not immediately win the day in country music, but such sounds heard on Rodgers's records may very well have influenced the styles of young musicians who idolized the Blue Yodeler.

Rodgers himself influenced the style and content of country music through his singing and choice of songs. His unique contribution to American folk song, the blue yodel, had the most immediate impact on country music. Blues singers and yodelers had preceded Rodgers in American entertainment. Hawaiian musicians, who were heirs to the *paniolo* (cowboy) tradition of the islands, had typically featured falsetto or vocal breaks in their music. But nothing corresponding exactly to the blue yodel song had been collected in American folklore. As a Mississippian, Rodgers could not have avoided contact with the blues in some form. He worked as a railroad man during the years when the blues form was originating, and, as a water boy for black construction groups, he accumulated maverick blues fragments and work-song stanzas that he eventually incorporated into his own songs. As an inveterate record buyer, the young Rodgers would have had ample opportunities to sample the blues records that began to appear in great profusion after 1920. We do not know how much Rodgers borrowed or how much he created (song fragments from his records apparently moved with some frequency into the repertories of black musicians),[8] but one thing is certain: he did much to inspire an interest in the blues in at least a generation or more of country musicians.

If Rodgers's introduction to the blues can be readily understood, the antecedents of his yodeling cannot so easily be discerned. One can posit the existence of a number of possible folk ancestors of the yodel, any one of which might have influenced him. Hollering, for example, has a venerable history in the South as an accompaniment of work, as a means of communication, and as an emotional release. Street cries would have been familiar to Rodgers through his residence in New Orleans, and even the Mexican *grito* and the lonesome cowboy wail might have wafted into his consciousness during his wanderings in the Southwest. As a railroad man, too, Rodgers might have been inspired to re-create vocally the distinctive locomotive whistles that reverberated across America in those prediesel days. Yodeling, though, had been quite common in American entertainment before Rodgers combined the practice with the blues. Blackface minstrels experimented with yodeling from at least 1847, when Tom Christian introduced the technique into a minstrel routine. The minstrels may have borrowed the yodel from indigenous folk sources or, as appears more likely, they may have picked it up from Tyrolese minstrels who toured widely in the United States during the mid-nineteenth century. As noted earlier, Hawaiian musicians had also introduced their style of falsetto singing, as well as their guitar styles, to the American public during the World War I era. Yodelers began to appear on recordings in the 1890s and were fairly common in vaudeville before World War I. Rodgers was even preceded as a yodeler in country music by Riley Puckett, who recorded, complete with yodel, "Rock All Our Babies to Sleep" (Columbia 107-D) as early as 1924.[9]

Regardless of its origin, Jimmie Rodgers fashioned his blue yodel into a distinct form that captivated his listeners and stimulated a new generation of hillbilly performers. As Alan Lomax has said, "Jimmie's yodeling songs sounded as if they might have been composed by a lonesome Texas cowboy or a hobo kicked off a freight in Tucson or Albuquerque."[10] Rodgers's yodels expressed a variety of emotions, ranging from the nostalgic moan of "Daddy and Home" to the blue lament of "Never No Mo' Blues" and the spritely yodel of "My Little Lady." The popularity of the Rodgers yodel and of his blues renditions should not tempt us to forget his multifaceted repertory. He recorded almost every conceivable type of song—serious, humorous, maudlin, religious, risqué, and rowdy. There were railroad songs like "The Southern Cannonball" and "Waiting for a Train"; "rounder" tunes like "Frankie and Johnny" and "My Rough and Rowdy Ways"; risqué numbers like "Pistol Packin' Papa"; lullabies like "Sleep, Baby, Sleep"; cowboy songs like "When the Cactus Is in Bloom"; hobo melodies like "Hobo Bill's Last Ride"; and a large number of sentimental songs depicting semireligious, nostalgic, and romantic themes. Sentimental love tunes were quite popular in the 1920s, and in his recording of such songs as "My Carolina Sunshine Girl" and "Old Pal of My Heart," Rodgers performed the same type of item that his friend Gene Austin was recording for the American popular-music audience. In fact, Jimmie Rodgers was the first person to record and publicly perform "The One Rose," a song that has gained its most lasting fame in popular music. Rodgers's own tastes seemed to run toward such sentimental and melancholy tunes as "Daddy and Home," which evoked memories of "an old southern town" and the only parent he had ever known. His sentimental songs have had a more lasting effect on country entertainers than have his other offerings. Blue yodels, or songs similar to them, were performed for a few years after his death but are a rarity in country music today. Many of his other songs, however, have made an enduring impression. Love songs have since dominated in country music, and even Rodgers's very sentimental and seemingly dated "Miss the Mississippi and You" was a major hit for country-pop singer Crystal Gayle in 1981.

Like many of the country performers who followed him, Rodgers wrote or arranged—usually in conjunction with his sister-in-law, Elsie McWilliams—a substantial number of the songs he recorded (his name, at least, appears on them). After he completed his third recording session in February 1928, Rodgers felt the need for fresh material. He contacted Elsie, his wife Carrie's oldest sister, who was then teaching in a Meridian business college. Elsie played the piano and had had musical training, and she already had acquired the reputation of local poet and songwriter with her writings for church and club periodicals. She contributed several songs to his June session that year, and according to her own memory, she wrote or helped write altogether thirty-eight songs recorded by her brother-in-law (some of which do not bear her name on the composer credits). These include the beautiful sentimental ballads "Sailor's Plea," "I'm Lonely and Blue," and "Mississippi Moon," and novelty tunes like "My Little Lady" and "Everybody Does It in Hawaii." Elsie McWilliams, however, was only one of several individuals who either wrote songs for Rodgers or collaborated on songs with him. The list includes Kelly Harrell ("Away Out on the Mountain"), Clayton McMichen ("Peach Picking Time in Georgia"), Shelly Lee Alley ("Traveling Blues"), Waldo O'Neal ("Hobo Bill's Last Ride"), Carey D. Harvey ("Down the Old Road to Home"), and Andrew Jenkins, of "The Death of Floyd Collins" fame, who wrote such songs as "A Drunkard's Child" and "Ben Dewberry's Final Run." The most interesting of the writers, if not the best known, was Raymond Hall, a convict serving a life sentence in the Huntsville, Texas, state prison in 1929, when he sent Rodgers his first song, "Moonlight and Skies." Hall eventually contributed such songs as "Ninety-Nine Year Blues," "Gambling Polka Dot Blues," "TB Blues," and "The Southern Cannonball." As late as 1980, Hall, who had received a parole, was still trying to peddle his songs.

During his lifetime, Rodgers's popularity was greatest in the Southwest, particularly in his adopted state of Texas. His popularity there can be attributed in part to his residence and to his tours and radio broadcasts in that state. He became so closely identified with Texas that many people believed him to be a native, and even Alan Lomax referred to him as a Texas brakeman. Rodgers took great pride in the Texas heritage, especially its romantic cowboy past. He must be given much of the credit for starting the trend toward the "singing cowboy" and the association of country music with the romantic "western" image. In the lyrics of his Texas songs, Rodgers conveyed a conception of the American West typical of that held by many people around the world, that is, the depiction of the cowboy as a self-reliant, unselfish individual, free from the shackles and restraints of society, who whiled away the lonely hours with song. This attitude was expressed in "Yodeling Cowboy," which asserts that "My cowboy life is so happy and free, out west where the laws don't bother me," and again in "The Yodeling Ranger," which describes "that old ranger band" singing carefree songs as it rides into dangerous situations. The Rangers were no doubt a courageous group, but it is doubtful that any of them went into a critical confrontation in as lighthearted a manner as that described in the song. Indeed, if Rodgers's philosophy had been the accepted one of the Texas lawmen, "that old ranger band" might well have vanished.

Rodgers's reverential and romantic concept of the West colored a variety of songs—such as "When the Cactus Is in Bloom"—that were the progenitors of a spate of Hollywood and Tin Pan Alley cowboy songs that flourished in the United States during the 1930s. It is significant that the man who did most to inaugurate the era of romantic cowboy songs in the coming years was Billy Hill, who wrote "Prairie Lullaby" for Rodgers in 1932 under the name of George Brown.

Whatever the source of his popularity, Rodgers made a profound impression on most of the young country boys and girls who heard him. Some of them went on to found country music traditions of their own. Bill Bruner, a seventeen-year-old Western Union messenger boy in Meridian, Mississippi, substituted for Rodgers one night when the Blue Yodeler became too ill to fill an engagement with the Paul English Players. After this appearance in February 1929, Bruner began touring with tent shows as "The Singing Messenger Boy," and singing Jimmie Rodgers's songs in a yodeling style that was almost a carbon copy of Rodgers's. Until the mid-1930s, scores of other country singers, partly through their own inclinations and partly through the prodding of record producers, made records that bore strongly the imprint of the Rodgers style. Frankie Marvin appears to have been the first to "cover" a Rodgers song, but he was soon followed by Gene Autry, Jimmie Davis, Cliff Carlisle, Billy Cox, Rex Griffin, Jerry Behrens (who was called the "Dixie Blue Yodeler"), Dwight Butcher, Leon Huff, Roy Rogers, Tommy Duncan, Tex Morton (in Australia), and a host of others. These singers used a style that not only employed the Rodgers repertory and yodel technique but borrowed his "hey hey hey" style of spoken commentary as well.

The Rodgers influence was so pervasive in the period running roughly from 1928 to 1935 that not even the Carter Family was immune to it. Encouraged by Ralph Peer, Sara Carter yodeled on a few songs, and the entire Carter Family joined in at least two recording sessions with Rodgers. Gene Autry, known to most Americans today as the singer of "Rudolph the Red-Nosed Reindeer," or otherwise remembered as a corporate executive and baseball magnate, got his initial start as a singer of Jimmie Rodgers songs. Equally important, because of his longevity within the country music field, was Ernest Tubb, who idolized Rodgers, and in his early performing years tried to re-create the identical sound of the Blue Yodeler. Although Tubb never met Rodgers personally, he can almost be considered his protégé because of the personal encouragement he received from Carrie Rodgers. In many of his earliest professional engagements, Tubb proudly played one of Jimmie's guitars, a cherished gift from the Blue Yodeler's widow.

The Rodgers appeal was even felt in far-off Canada. Motivated by reports of Rodgers's commercial success, the RCA Victor offices in Montreal decided to branch out into country music. The Canadian country music industry dates, therefore, from the 1932 signing by Victor of a young yodeler named Wilf Carter (known in this country as Montana Slim), a native of Nova Scotia, who gained his first musical inspiration from hearing a vaudeville yodeler who was an "added attraction" at a performance of *Uncle Tom's Cabin.*

The Rodgers influence was exerted more directly in the case of a young Nova Scotia farm boy who became so enthralled with Rodgers's recording of "Moonlight and Skies" that he resolved to become a country entertainer. He taught himself the guitar and sat by the phonograph for hours trying to master the Rodgers technique. This was Clarence E. "Hank" Snow, one of the few country singers who continued the train-song tradition of Jimmie Rodgers. Snow's recording career began with Victor in 1936 when he recorded two of his own compositions, "Lonesome Blue Yodel" and "Prisoned Cowboy." Calling himself the "Yodeling Ranger," by the end of the 1930s he rivaled Wilf Carter for the title of Canada's most popular country performer. After his voice deepened, his yodeling facility began to vanish. He then changed his performing title to the "Singing Ranger" and went on to become one of the greatest country stars in the United States.

Although the continuing careers of people like Hank Snow and Ernest Tubb served as lasting memorials to the greatness of Jimmie Rodgers, more immediate expressions of affection came in the songs of tribute recorded at the time of his death by such singers as Gene Autry, Bradley Kincaid, Dwight Butcher, and Leon Huff of the W. Lee O'Daniel and Light Crust Doughboys organization. Even more important, perhaps, as testimonies of his popularity are his recordings, which have continued to enjoy robust sales in the many years since his death. In 1949 and 1950, after years of intensive lobbying by people like Ernest Tubb and Jim Evans, head of the Jimmie Rodgers Society, RCA Victor issued two collections of Rodgers's songs (selected 78 rpm records that were packaged in albums). Their healthy sales revealed the enduring appeal of the Blue Yodeler and introduced his music to still another generation of listeners. Since that time, tribute LPs have periodically reintroduced his name and music to still-younger legions of fans. One of the greatest of these tributes, released in 1951, was by William Orville "Lefty" Frizzell, a Texas singer who knew of Rodgers only through the old 78s that his parents had saved through the years. The Frizzell recordings eventually caught the ear of Merle Haggard, who produced in 1969 his own influential tribute to Rodgers, a double LP: *Same Train, A Different Time.*

The bulk of Jimmie Rodgers's career came during the bleak years of the greatest depression the United States has experienced. And his performances were concentrated in the area of the most intense regional poverty, the South. Nevertheless, farmers and workers attended his concerts and bought his records when they became available. The notes to one of his memorial albums relate a legend concerning his popularity among hard-pressed Depression-era folk: "Legend has it that in his heyday, general-store customers would approach the counter and say: 'Let me have a pound of butter, a dozen eggs, and the latest Jimmie Rodgers record.'"[11] His records, of course, did not sell quite that universally, but his songs were widely known and cherished. When he died in 1933, at the age of thirty-six, he was unknown to the great majority of the American people, but in the South, where hillbilly music has always gained its most devoted following, Rodgers had already become a hero to millions.

CHAPTER 4

Country Music during the Depression

W hen Jimmie Rodgers died in 1933, one decade had elapsed since Fiddlin' John Carson made his first Okeh record and inaugurated country music's commercial history. In that relatively brief period of time, the music had secured a solid niche in American entertainment and gave every indication of expanding both in popularity and in personnel.

In this one decade of commercial life, however, country music had already changed significantly in content and style. Traditional songs still appeared frequently in the radio and recording repertories of people like the Carter Family, and would continue to do so in the performances of newer musicians such as J. E. Mainer's Mountaineers, the Monroe Brothers, and the Blue Sky Boys. Increasingly, though, musicians learned the old-time songs from earlier commercial hillbilly performances, not from folk sources. A singer might learn a song like "The Fatal Wedding" from Mama, but Mama probably learned it from a Bradley Kincaid recording. Newly written compositions or arrangements of older songs gradually edged the traditional ballads aside. In a quest for fresh material or the means to supplement the meager royalties awarded to recording artists, performers began writing many of their own songs. Led by Ralph Peer, the founder of both Peer-International and the Southern Music Company, and soon joined by other organizations such as M. M. Cole of Chicago, publishers appeared who concentrated heavily on the hillbilly market. Hillbillies in the 1930s routinely advertised their picture songbooks on radio broadcasts and sold them by mail or at personal appearances. Some performers made a fairly good living just from the sale of their books.

Perhaps the most remarkable fact of country music's history during the Great Depression is that the music not only survived but expanded. The once-modest hillbilly business began to take shape as an industry with booking agents, promoters, advertising firms, publishers, music-licensing agencies, and motion picture representatives who recognized the gold that might be mined from this new territory. The music also took great strides toward national dissemination and eventual national homogenization during the Depression years: Sears-Roebuck catalogues advertised the same records in all regions of the country; powerful radio stations boomed the music out to city and farm alike; advertising agencies linked the music with such brand names as Alka-Seltzer and won new consumers for each; radio transcriptions permitted musicians to popularize themselves on stations far beyond their own geographical areas; touring units took the music to all sections of the country; and Hollywood films made many of the performers visible while also introducing their music to millions of Americans who would not have heard it in any other format.

The record industry did not succumb to hard times, but it was forced into a massive reorganization. Only 6 million records were sold in 1932, a striking contrast to the 104 million that had been sold in 1927. A few of the pioneer hillbilly performers who had exhibited little commercial appeal were not permitted to record again. Some record companies followed the precedent of Victor, which established a cheaper subsidiary line, Bluebird, for its race and white country artists. The Okeh label—originally owned by the General Phonograph Corporation, but bought by Columbia in 1926—was reestablished in 1940 (after a six-year submergence) as Columbia's country and race subsidiary. Brunswick, one of the traditional leaders of the record business, had been taken over by the American Record Company, a producer of cheap discs sold by chain stores under such labels as Melotone, Perfect, Banner, Oriole, and Romeo. Gennett, another old-time label owned by the Starr Piano Company, went out of business and sold its catalogues and labels to the newly formed American Decca Company. Sears-Roebuck and Montgomery Ward continued to issue their low-priced records (dubbed from the big companies' masters) aimed at the rural population.

American Decca was organized in 1934 and, with its thirty-five-cent records, immediately became one of the dominant phonograph companies. The issuance of Decca's inexpensive records encouraged other companies, which had generally charged seventy-five cents, to lower their prices, and a "platter war" began. Decca made a successful "raid" on the major companies and emerged with some of their leading performers; its most important acquisition was Bing Crosby.

Led by their talent scout David Kapp, who traveled through America with a portable recording crew, Decca sought aggressively to build a hillbilly catalogue. Although his travels ranged far and wide, Kapp's most productive efforts came in the Southwest: Louisiana, Oklahoma, Texas, and California. The 1930s definitely saw a shift in the recording of hillbilly personnel from the Southeast to the Southwest, with a corresponding shift in the character of the music. The newer performers were more influenced by "western" styles, that is, by cowboy songs, ersatz and real, and by the eclectic "hot dance" music that evolved in southwestern dance halls. The fiddle was as central to the music of the Southwest as it was to that of country music elsewhere, but some southeastern-based instruments, such as the five-string banjo, did not thrive among musicians in the West.

Significantly, hillbillies continued to record despite the economic woes of the phonograph industry. Hillbilly record sales were low during the Depression; Paul Cohen, the former director of Decca's country music division, estimated that a "hillbilly hit" during those years was one that sold a total of ten thousand copies. Nevertheless, hillbilly music was still considered to be a profitable venture for the companies because of the low expense of recording.

Whatever the appeal of recording—and hillbillies certainly enjoyed the prestige of being "recording artists" even if they made no money from the venture—radio probably proved much more important to the budding country music industry. The 1930s marked the heyday of live radio entertainment in the United States. The typical hillbilly musician of that decade was an itinerant entertainer, moving from station to station, seeking sponsors and working a territory until it provided no further dividends. No region of the United States was alien to the country musician, but the greatest concentration of such performers could be found in the South, in the Midwest, and on the

West Coast. Musicians played on the smallest stations imaginable, usually at times presumed to be "farmers' hours," that is, early in the morning or at noon—but the prize plums were the fifty-thousand-watt stations that blanketed many states with their coverage. The hillbillies performed their music, put on comic skits, read religious recitations, hawked their sponsors' wares, and sold their picture songbooks or records. Personal appearances were generally limited to the area covered by the broadcast and were negotiated through listener contacts. The hillbillies were sincere when they asked their audience to "Keep them cards and letters coming in." Furthermore, when the hillbilly musicians signed off their programs by saying, "That old clock on the wall says it's time to be getting out of here," they probably meant that literally, too. Quite often, they had to pack up their instruments hastily, tie the bass fiddle on top of their car, and drive immediately to their next personal appearance.

Musicians played wherever they could get a hearing, but the Saturday-night barn dances broadcast on the high-powered stations provided the most security and exposure. The *Grand Ole Opry* expanded beyond its Middle Tennessee base during the Depression years and became an institution of wide significance in rural America. Indeed, the acquisition of a thirty-minute time slot on NBC, sponsored by the R. J. Reynolds Tobacco Company, in 1939 put the *Opry* well on the way to becoming a national phenomenon. The first step in the *Opry*'s elevation came in 1932, when WSM became a fifty-thousand-watt clear-channel station. The show could be heard distinctly all over the southeastern United States and, on most nights, at least as far west as Texas. Then in 1934, Harry Stone, named station manager four years earlier, established an Artists' Service Bureau designed to promote bookings for *Opry* performers, a decision that advertised WSM and the *Opry* while also furthering the professionalization of the musicians. Along with Vito Pellettieri, WSM's music librarian, who dealt with the problems of publishing and performance rights, Stone actively campaigned to increase the number of sponsors supporting the country show. As the *Grand Ole Opry* became increasingly commercially attractive to musicians, performers began to join the show from areas outside the Middle Tennessee region. The Delmore Brothers (Alton and Rabon) did not have far to travel when they left their North Alabama home to join the *Opry* in 1933, but the Vagabonds, who came in 1931, relocated from Chicago, where they had performed both pop and country music.

This smooth-singing trio (Herald Goodman, Curt Poulton, and Dean Upson) were probably the first true "professionals" (entertainers who did nothing but perform music) to join the *Grand Ole Opry*. Their arrival on the show, along with that of the Delmores, Roy Acuff (1938), and Bill Monroe (1939), greatly broadened the horizons of the *Opry* and put it well on the road toward being a haven for "stars."

As the *Grand Ole Opry* solidified its popularity in the South, the *National Barn Dance* built a similar reputation in the Midwest. By the late 1930s, hillbilly music had become one of the staples of midwestern small-town entertainment, and WLS entertainers were making personal appearances all over the region. In a later discussion of the phenomenon, Lewis Atherton argued that hillbilly music was "surpassing even the minstrel show in popularity" and had become "the favorite of Main Street."[1] The *Barn Dance* experienced its greatest development in the seven or eight years immediately following 1930. In that period, the show's cast expanded and the program's listening range increased to take in a broad swath of the United States. Some of the entertainers—like Gene Autry—stayed for only a couple of years, but others—like Lulu Belle and Scotty (Myrtle Cooper and Scott Wiseman)—remained for twenty years and more. One of the most important of the early groups was the Cumberland Ridge Runners, an assemblage of musicians who came to the *Barn Dance* in 1930 from the areas around Mount Vernon and Berea, Kentucky. The creator and leader of the Ridge Runners was John Lair, an authority on and collector of old-time music, who eventually founded, at his home in Kentucky, the popular *Renfro Valley Barn Dance*. Several fine musicians, including Clyde "Red" Foley and Hugh Cross, appeared periodically with the Ridge Runners. The most tradition-oriented members, perhaps, were Slim Miller, an old-time fiddler and comedian; Howard "Doc" Hopkins, who sang traditional ballads; Kentucky-born Linda Parker (born Jeanne Muenich), an alumna of the Chicago pop music scene who nonetheless sang old sentimental favorites like "I'll Be All Smiles Tonight"; and Karl Davis and Harty Taylor, a mandolin and guitar duo, who introduced such well-known favorites as "I'm Just Here to Get My Baby Out of Jail."

Spurred by the *Barn Dance*'s popularity, WLS became the first radio station to construct a studio theater. By 1932, with reservations being made seven months in advance for the show, WLS began looking for larger audience accommodations and, as a result, took over the Eighth

Street Theatre, broadcast the program in two complete shows, and charged admission. The Eighth Street Theatre remained the home of the *National Barn Dance* for the next twenty-five years. Only one year after moving into the theater, the *Barn Dance* moved well beyond its midwestern scope when Alka-Seltzer, in 1933, began the sponsorship of a one-hour Saturday night segment on NBC. This coast-to-coast radio coverage, augmented by the road-show units that traveled from WLS in an ever-widening arc after 1932, made the *National Barn Dance* the nation's leading country music show in the years before the *Grand Ole Opry* became predominant.

The *Opry* and the *National Barn Dance* may have been the most important hillbilly radio shows, but they were far from being the only ones. Some were clearly spinoffs from the *National Barn Dance* and featured the same kind of variety entertainment heard on the Chicago show. The *Iowa Barn Dance Frolic*, for example, heard after 1932 on WHO in Des Moines, was a highly eclectic mixture of old-fashioned pop music, barbershop singing, novelty tunes, and folk music. Like the WLS show, the *Iowa Barn Dance Frolic* had a high percentage of nonsouthern performers, but it also included in the 1930s occasional southern country musicians such as Texas Ruby (Owens) and Zeke Clements.

Other barn dances were obviously inspired by the success enjoyed by the *Opry* and the *National Barn Dance* or were organized by men who had been affiliated with these shows. The *Boone County Jamboree*, broadcast on WLW in Cincinnati after 1938, was the brainchild of George Biggar, a former Farm and Market editor at WLS and a producer-announcer for Sears-Roebuck Farm, Home, and Musical Programs on several stations. The famous *Renfro Valley* show was conceived by John Lair while he was working at WLS with the Cumberland Ridge Runners. The show went on the air in Cincinnati in 1937, but by November 4, 1939, had moved to Renfro Valley itself, a little village near Mount Vernon, Kentucky, where its cast played to an audience of five thousand or more each Saturday night. The *Crazy Barn Dance* in Charlotte, North Carolina, was an example of a radio variety show organized by a business for merchandising purposes. Making its debut on WBT in Charlotte in 1934, the show was created and named by J. W. Fincher, the southeastern representative of the Crazy Water Crystals Company of Mineral Wells, Texas.

All of these barn dances played important roles in presenting country music to an ever-widening audience; none, however, was more instrumental in introducing the music to the Northeast than the *Wheeling Jamboree* in Wheeling, West Virginia. Inaugurated on WWVA on January 7, 1933, the show became a forum for the talents of some of country music's major entertainers during the following decades: Harry McAuliffe (Big Slim, the Lone Cowboy), Jimmy Dickens, Wilma Lee and Stoney Cooper, Hank Snow, Hawkshaw Hawkins, and a balladeer from Pennsylvania, Doc Williams, who joined the show in 1937 and remained there for over forty years. WWVA's powerful directional signal beamed north and east, easily blanketing much of Pennsylvania, New York, rural New England, and eastern Canada. Many northeasterners who later tried their hands at country music first became attracted to the music through the broadcasts of the *Wheeling Jamboree.*

In the dissemination of country music throughout the United States, no stations were more important than those along the Mexican border.[2] These powerful X stations (so-called because of their call letters) operated just across the border in Mexico, and could be heard quite clearly throughout much of the United States and even occasionally in Canada. The border stations operated on wattage as much as two or three times in excess of the maximum limit in the United States. This practice was condoned by the Mexican authorities presumably because of a prior snubbing of Mexico by its northern neighbors. The American and Canadian governments had divided between themselves the entire AM broadcast band, leaving neither Cuba nor Mexico any clear channels at all. Therefore, for many years Mexico rejected American protests about the border stations.

Often leased to American entrepreneurs, these stations aimed their transmitters toward the United States and, operating on 100,000–150,000 watts, cut in on wavelengths used by US and Canadian stations. With this powerful means of transmission, American advertisers were able to exploit their products throughout much of the United States. The border station era was inaugurated in October 1931, when Dr. John R. Brinkley's XER (changed to XERA in 1935) began operations with about 100,000 watts at Villa Acuña, Mexico. Born in North Carolina about 1885, Brinkley moved to Kansas in 1916 armed with a shrewd business wit and what many people considered to be a bogus medical license. He opened radio station KFKB in 1923 in Milford, Kansas, and made himself a political power in the state while also making the station one of the most popular in the nation. Brinkley's ticket to fame and wealth was his goat-gland operation, designed to restore sexual potency to men, which was advertised on his station and performed in his hospital. In Kansas, Brinkley had employed the services of hillbilly performers such as the fiddler Uncle Bob Larkin. Brinkley's use of a hillbilly band in his races for governor of Kansas in 1930 and 1932 made him the predecessor of such famous hillbilly politicians as Texas's W. Lee O'Daniel and Louisiana's Jimmie Davis.

When the Federal Radio Commission refused to renew his license, Brinkley moved to Del Rio, Texas, and became the first of the X-station entrepreneurs. Not only did he advertise his own medical remedies and the hospital that he built in Del Rio, he also pushed products of other US businesses. In addition to the almost incessant advertising, the radio listener was given a steady diet of religious evangelists, hillbilly singers (mostly by transcription), and, on many occasions, right-wing politicians. Brinkley, on XERA and later acquisitions XEPN and XEAW, set a pattern that was closely followed by later border entrepreneurs: eleven border stations operated by 1938, several of which had more than 50,000 watts. His success inspired numerous other individuals in the following decades—some of them, like Brinkley or Norman Baker, of a not-too-savory reputation. Baker plugged his cancer-cure over XENT, across from Laredo, before he was convicted of using the mails to defraud. Brinkley sold XEAW, his station at Reynosa, to Carr Collins, who made himself a millionaire through the selling of Crazy Water Crystals. XEAW, like most of the other border stations, sold commercial time to a motley assortment of patent-medicine proprietors, evangelists, and small business establishments, such as chick farms. Collins felt that in his programming he was giving listeners the unsophisticated material that the major networks neglected. The merchandising habits of the border stations moved directly into the nation's folklore. Long-winded announcers talked incessantly about such products as Resurrection Plants, portraits of Jesus that glowed in the dark, autographed pictures of Jesus Christ (they didn't always explain whose autograph it was), prayer cloths, baby chicks, "genuine simulated" diamonds, and, of course, hillbilly and gospel songbooks.

If one could endure the seemingly never-ending advertising, one might occasionally hear a hillbilly song of the best quality. Eventually, phonograph recordings dominated border programming, but in the mid- and late 1930s, hillbilly music was disseminated through live performances and transcriptions. Several singers who did not have nationally established reputations nevertheless built loyal followings through border broadcasts. Cowboy singers thrived on border radio, just as they did elsewhere in the America of the decade. Jesse Rodgers (Jimmie's cousin from Waynesboro, Mississippi), Nolan "Cowboy Slim" Rinehart (from Brady, Texas), and J. R. Hall (the "Utah Cowboy," who actually hailed from Crowley, Texas) were just a few of the cowboy balladeers who popularized their songs on the border stations. The cowboy singers were joined by close-harmony duet singers, string bands, gospel quartets, yodelers, folk balladeers, and family groups. The most famous of the latter, the Pickard Family, came to San Antonio in 1936, and the Carter Family followed them there two years later. Both groups came to Texas through the sponsorship of the Royal Chemical Corporation of Chicago, maker of such products as Kolorbak hair dye and Peruna tonic, and an early and major advertiser on border radio stations. The Pickards and Carters made live broadcasts, as all early hillbillies did, but they also made numerous transcriptions so that their performances could continue when they were unable to do them in person or when they were on the road. Studio broadcasts were often transcribed and rebroadcast at a later time, but, increasingly, transcriptions were made through an independent service, such as Don Baxter's in San Antonio or Sellers in Dallas, and then sold to radio stations. Transcriptions obviously made it easier for hillbilly musicians to popularize their songs and talents on more than a regional basis, and, disseminated on Mexican border broadcasts, the music actually made its way throughout North America.

As country music circulated around the nation, it demonstrated its power to sell, whether the product was politics, religion, or commerce. In the realm of commerce, products identified with hillbilly music ranged from work clothes and farm implements to flour (to make those good biscuits that every farmer and worker ate) to patent medicines. The percentage of drugs and medicinal products ranged so high among hillbilly advertisers that it almost seemed as if the format of the old-time medicine show had been transferred to hillbilly radio broadcasts. Advertising concerns, such as the William Wade Agency of Chicago, evidently perceived the country audience to be made up of rural and small-town Americans who clung to a folk fear of doctors or who had no money to invest in proper medical care. Alka-Seltzer, for example, was a new and unknown product until it was advertised on the *National Barn Dance* in 1933. Wine of Cardui, designed to ease the discomforts of "women's complaints," and Black Draught, a laxative, were well known in southern rural homes in the late nineteenth century (chiefly because of the famous wall calendars distributed by their manufacturer, the Chattanooga Medicine Company). But their commercial lives were no doubt extended through their association with hillbilly music after the 1920s.

Black Draught was only one of several laxatives aimed at the rural public and popularized by hillbilly advertising. The most ubiquitous of the laxatives, though, and the one most identified with country music, was Crazy Water Crystals. This product was a white concentrate of mineral water taken from the Crazy Well in Mineral Wells, Texas. Although the well was discovered in 1885, the company did not embark on a national campaign of radio exploitation until 1930. Originally claiming grandiose curative qualities for their product, the company's directors eventually settled on the claim that it would facilitate proper elimination (which was probably true). Crazy Water sponsored various types of entertainment on radio stations all over the United States, in Canada, and on the Mexican border stations, but country music was the medium most often favored by the company. The company's general manager in the region of the two Carolinas and Georgia, J. W. Fincher, began utilizing hillbilly talent soon after he was transferred to the territory in 1933. Capitalizing on the local availability and popularity of hillbilly music, Fincher soon established Crazy Water sponsorship on fourteen stations in the three-state area. The capstone of the coverage was the establishment of the *Crazy Barn Dance* on WBT in Charlotte, March 17, 1934. Several of the bands who worked under Crazy Water sponsorship carried "crazy" in their performing titles (Crazy Hickory Nuts, Crazy Mountaineers, etc.). Country musicians profited from the relationship with the Crazy Water Company (if only through radio exposure), but probably not nearly as much as the company gained from the association. At the peak of Crazy Water Crystals radio involvement in the Southeast, the company sold an estimated refrigerated carload of crystals per day.

One of the most pervasive methods used by radio stations to link advertising and country music in the 1930s was the P.I. account—a system in which royalties were paid to a station "per inquiry" for an advertised product. The 50,000-watt, clear-channel stations, with their broad rural coverage, made particularly effective use of this system because it brought them revenue with only a minimal outlay for talent. Even the powerful station in New Orleans, WWL—owned by the Jesuit-run Loyola University—specialized in P.I. accounts for several years after 1932. Though located in the heart of a city that had few discernible leanings toward country music, WWL catered to the tastes of the rural population living in northern Louisiana and in surrounding southern states. Therefore, for several years during the 1930s, such musicians as the Pickard Family, Hank Penny, the Shelton Brothers, Curly Fox, and, above all, Lew Childre performed live on WWL, hawking their sponsors' products and disseminating the best in hillbilly music. Many entertainers, or their announcers, were famous for the warm, convincing manner in which they presented commercials. Of course, an entertainer who sold the music effectively would have little trouble selling the merchandise described on the show; hillbilly audiences were acutely loyal to their favorite musicians' sponsors. The spectacle of a Catholic-owned station disseminating music to a rural, Protestant audience was surely lost on few people, but the Jesuit fathers were more embarrassed by the nickname their station acquired: "the ache and pill station of the South." It was hard to quarrel with the increasing royalties that flowed into the station, though, and so the hillbillies remained at WWL through much of the 1930s.

With a few exceptions, the hillbilly musician of the 1930s was a radio performer. The popular gospel group, the Chuck Wagon Gang, based in Fort Worth, Texas, recorded for Columbia throughout the 1930s and 1940s, but made their living as radio performers on WBAP in their home city.[3] Some musicians were permanent members of barn dance casts, and a few, like Bob Wills at KVOO in Tulsa, remained at the same radio station for several years. Others, though, moved from station to station and from state to state, always looking for a better financial deal. A large percentage of them never made phonograph recordings, depending instead on the sale of songbooks or on personal appearances for economic sustenance. But once these generalizations are made, we find that these musicians had little else in common. Their choice of songs and styles of performance were so radically dissimilar that it is difficult to discuss them in any systematic way. Some singers accompanied themselves on guitar and sang ballads in styles reminiscent of Bradley Kincaid or Doc Hopkins. Many musicians were eclectic in their absorption of songs and styles, but few were the complete "entertainers" that Lew Childre was (a singer, instrumentalist, comedian, dancer). Some singers were carbon copies of Jimmie Rodgers, imitating his guitar runs, his yodel, and every vocal nuance. Others specialized in the blues, drawing their style from black singers rather than Rodgers. Many paraded before the public as cowboy singers, an affectation favored by easterners and westerners alike; still others sang only gospel or "moral" material. Duets and family groups abounded, but with harmony styles that differed greatly and instrumental styles and combinations that varied just as widely. Some string bands sounded little different from the bands of the 1920s, reflecting the hoedown tradition from which the music evolved, while others borrowed substantially from pop and jazz music. Fiddlers abounded as always, but they too differed both in style and in approach to tradition; mandolin-and-guitar groups arose in profusion, and the steel guitar made its way into more and more bands. By the end of the 1930s, musicians were learning how to electrify the steel guitar and other instruments as well, an innovation that radically changed the nature of country music. While these traits were discernible throughout the South, measurable differences nevertheless existed between musical styles in the Southeast and Southwest. The discussion that follows concentrates, primarily, on musicians from east of the Mississippi River. ("Western" musicians will be discussed in chapter 5.)

For much of the decade of the 1930s, Jimmie Rodgers's influence could be heard everywhere, from Daddy John Love in North Carolina to Jerry Behrens in New Orleans. Not every yodel, of course, sounded like Rodgers's; some were very primitive, and some were in the sophisticated Swiss style favored by Montana Slim (Wilf Carter) and Patsy Montana. Singers also went a step beyond Rodgers when they fashioned duet yodeling (or even multiple yodeling, as in the case of the Sons of the Pioneers). Reese Fleming and Respers Townsend of Memphis are said to have been the first to introduce duet yodeling, in their recordings of the early 1930s, but Alton and Rabon Delmore, the Callahan Brothers, and the Girls of the Golden West (Millie and Dolly Good) took the art to greater harmonic heights.

Blues singing remained popular among country singers, but only part of it came from the Rodgers tradition; much of the feel for the blues style came directly from black singers (either in the flesh or on records). The fascination with the blues had been exhibited by country singers ever since the country music industry began. Out of ten songs recorded by Henry Whitter at his December 1923 session for Okeh, five had "blues" in the title. Excellent blues performances by men like Frank Hutchison, Dick Justice, Jimmie Tarlton, and the Allen Brothers had been recorded in the late 1920s; Tarlton and the Allens were still recording blues songs, along with other types of traditional material, well into the 1930s.

Johnny James Rimbert Tarlton, who came out of a South Carolina family of textile workers and folksingers, is one of the most interesting figures in the rich history of country music. He possessed a penetratingly clear tenor voice and an individualistic instrumental and vocal style that placed him in the front rank of country singers of that or any other era. Beginning with the banjo, but capable of playing almost all the stringed instruments, he eventually settled on the steel guitar, which he played bottleneck style until he learned the steel technique from Hawaiians whom he met in California at about the time of World War I. By the time of his first recording session in 1927, he had already hoboed around the country, working in everything from cotton mills to oil fields and singing his way as far north as New York and as far west as California. He met Tom Darby, a singer and guitar player, in Columbus, Georgia, sometime in 1927. The two made their first records in April of that year, but they did not make history until their second session on November 10, 1927. They recorded two numbers arranged by Tarlton: "Columbus Stockade Blues" and "Birmingham Jail" (both released on Columbia 15212). These two songs, known by country music fans around the world, earned Darby and Tarlton seventy-five dollars, the only remuneration they ever received for the songs. Darby and Tarlton knew and recorded all kinds of songs, including old standards like "Where the River Shannon Flows" and British ballads like "Lowe Bonnie," but they were both much influenced by black music. The guitar style of each suggests a black influence, Tarlton's a modification of bottleneck playing, and Darby's an adaptation of fingerpicking. It is in Tarlton's singing, however—especially in a song like "Slow Wicked Blues"—that we find the greatest infusion of the "soul" usually attributed to black people. Country music provides no better example of the "white blues."

None of the "hillbilly blues" singers of the 1930s sang blues exclusively; scattered through their repertories one can hear ballads, love songs, religious pieces, and virtually every other kind of song favored by hillbilly singers. One duo, however, the Allen Brothers, was so

competent at performing the blues that their recordings were sometimes erroneously catalogued as "race" performances. The Allens
reportedly left the Columbia label (for whom they first recorded in
April 1927) because of this mix-up. Whatever their larger racial views
may have been, Austin and Lee Allen undoubtedly listened to a lot of
black music. Between 1927 and 1934, the Sewanee, Tennessee, natives
recorded a body of songs for Columbia, Victor, and Vocalion that has
no analogue in the recorded repertory of any other white musician.
Their songs were, for the most part, original compositions or adaptations of older blues tunes such as "A New Salty Dog." Although their
vocals were strong (with Austin doing most of the singing and Lee
sometimes joining in on tenor harmony), the Allens' instrumentation was the most interesting facet of their performances. There was
nothing extraordinary about their banjo and guitar work, but Lee's
kazoo playing was little short of sensational. He took this child's toy
of presumed limited range and converted it to a lead instrument of
exceptional flexibility. On Allen Brothers recordings, the kazoo is used
like a trumpet; the result is a sound not unlike that heard on Charlie
Poole's string band recordings, a syncopated but structured swing.

The singers who experimented with the blues idiom also, as a matter of course, ventured into the rowdy underworld of sex, sin, and
bawdiness that was absent from much of the standard hillbilly fare.
Puritanical Protestantism, though, had not eliminated from southern
folk culture the Elizabethan-derived penchant for bawdy and earthy
song material. The blues genre, as the product of an allegedly uninhibited people, did seem to give license to sample rowdy and risqué songs.
Many of the hillbilly songs dealing with drink and drugs, masculine
boastfulness, and sexual high jinks, were couched in the blues form.
Jimmie Rodgers was not alone among southern singers in growing up
with the blues; everywhere, in mountains and flatlands alike, white
people heard black singers either in person or on records. Some of this
material made its way onto hillbilly records in relatively unaltered
form, but much of it provided the inspiration for original compositions
by hillbilly writers.

Prohibition, of course, evoked ambivalent responses among hillbilly
singers—reflecting a similar ambivalence in the culture that produced
them—but blues tunes generally commented negatively on the phenomenon and welcomed its demise when repeal came in 1933. Singers
often mentioned the unfortunate personal consequences of drinking

(headaches, hangovers, fights, love complications, etc.), but only rarely did they denounce the habit in general terms. The Allen Brothers endorsed the art of moonshining in "Fruit Jar Blues," and David McCarn commented on one of the cheapest substitutes for whiskey in "Bay Rum Blues" (Bay Rum was a hair tonic with a high alcoholic content). The Allens, however, responded cynically to one of the most tragic consequences of illicit drinking when they recorded "Jake Walk Blues," one of at least seven hillbilly songs recorded between 1928 and 1934 that dealt with the affliction that came from drinking Jamaica Ginger ("Jake").

The only addiction to which hillbillies readily admitted was that of alcohol; nevertheless, mention of drugs was not totally absent from recordings. Riley Puckett and the Skillet Lickers had spoken approvingly of morphine in "Soldier's Joy." The few overt references to hard drugs seem to have come from black sources. One of the greatest early "hillbilly blues" performances, in fact—Dick Justice's "Cocaine"—was a 1928 "cover" of Luke Jordan's "Cocaine Blues," recorded the previous year. Another cocaine song, "Take a Whiff on Me," also moved into hillbilly music, but in a modified form that more readily reflected the habits of southern country folk. Charlie Poole and the North Carolina Ramblers did it as "Take a Drink on Me." Many southerners would neither knowingly take hard drugs nor imbibe alcohol, but they did consume both in the form of patent medicines, which were staples in southern homes and in hillbilly radio commercials.

Much more common than drinking and drug references in the hillbilly blues were the assertions of male ego and sexual prowess, preoccupations that were important to many men who were otherwise socially and economically emasculated during the Depression era. The blues provided yet another mode of expression for the omnipresent macho impulse that lay deeply embedded in southern rural culture. Of course, black blues singers in the previous decade had proven that "naughty" lyrics could be commercially viable, and Jimmie Rodgers had demonstrated that a white market existed for such material. Rodgers's rounder songs and risqué tunes (such as "Ground Hog Rootin' in My Back Yard") were actually rather mild compared to the songs that came out in the early 1930s. The young Gene Autry recorded a body of songs that were populated with "high stepping mamas," "low down mamas," "bear cat papas," and "do right daddies." "Do Right Daddy Blues," one of his most affecting songs, was filled with assertions of boasting and some of the sexiest lines in hillbilly music: "You can feel of my legs, you can feel of my thighs," etc.

The three greatest "imitators" of Jimmie Rodgers—Gene Autry, Cliff Carlisle, and Jimmie Davis—all had racy repertories that were considerably spicier than that of the Blue Yodeler. Clifford Raymond Carlisle was born at Mount Eden, Kentucky, in 1904. Although he grew up in a family permeated by traditional music, he was drawn to a career in music through an early fascination with the Hawaiian guitar and black blues styles, both of which he heard as a teenager. Both influences remained with him until he retired as an entertainer in 1947. He was one of the first country musicians to play a Dobro steel guitar, and his yodeling blues remain unsurpassed in the hillbilly field. Jimmie Rodgers's partisans would no doubt find such an assertion sacrilegious, but there are those who think that Carlisle, while less original than Rodgers, was a better singer and yodeler. Carlisle sang with unusual clarity of tone and featured an effortless yodel that combined a Jimmie Rodgers sound coupled with Swiss techniques. Carlisle began his recording career with Gennett in 1930, and during the next seventeen years, he recorded sometimes alone but most often with a partner, such as guitarist Wilbur Ball, Fred Kirby, or his brother Bill (as "the Carlisle Brothers"). His repertory was diverse, but his prison, hobo, and "rowdy" songs are probably the most interesting items he recorded. "Pan American Man," one of his finest songs, asserts two themes: the movement of a famous train across the southern landscape and the prowess of a free-born man who equates his own freedom with that of the train he rides. The theme of masculine boasting is more aggressively asserted in songs like "Shanghai Rooster Yodel," "Tom Cat Blues," and "Black Jack David," the hillbilly version of "The Gypsy Laddie" (Child 200).

James Houston "Jimmie" Davis was born in a sharecropper's cabin at Beech Springs, Louisiana, in 1902. He probably enjoyed the longest career in country music (commencing as a radio entertainer in Shreveport in 1928) and also had one of the most richly diverse repertories. A number of factors have unfortunately obscured his importance for modern country music fans. His association with "You Are My Sunshine," the theme of his Louisiana gubernatorial campaigns and one of the most-performed songs in country music, made him seem as hackneyed as the song. His absorption with gospel music at the end of his life, and his marriage to Anna Carter of Chuck Wagon Gang fame, tended to make people forget that he ever did any other kind of music, while his notoriety as a segregationist governor in the early 1960s inhibited the appreciation that should be due him as a performer. Davis himself, of course, was largely responsible for the limited view of his career. In speaking to interviewers, he invariably talked only of his association with Decca after 1934 and neglected the very important records made for Victor from 1929 to 1933. By the time he signed his Decca contract, he had already lived a very full and active life, and one very unlike that of the typical hillbilly. He earned a bachelor's degree from Louisiana College (Pineville) and a master's degree from Louisiana State University, taught history at Dodd College, and somehow found time to sing regularly on Shreveport's KWKH, make records, and give occasional concerts. His popularity as an entertainer, along with his interest in public affairs, combined to give him an exposure that proved invaluable in politics. His election as Public Service Commissioner was merely the first step in a career that ultimately led him to the Louisiana governorship in 1944 and again in 1960.

Davis's stylistic diversity and his long association with such Texas performers as Moon Mullican, Cliff Bruner, and the Shelton Brothers make it difficult to place him in any category. His early stylistic preferences drew him firmly toward the country blues camp, a genre in which he excelled. Davis was an excellent Jimmie Rodgers–style yodeler, with a repertory strongly reminiscent of his Mississippi mentor. In "Where the Old Red River Flows," for example, Davis wrote a sentimental evocation of his northwest Louisiana home, redolent of plantation imagery and singing "darkeys." Black musicians were indeed important in his career. In contradistinction to the racist political views he later expressed as governor, he was one of the few hillbilly performers to be accompanied on records by black musicians, having been joined on his 1932 Victor recordings by guitarists Oscar Woods and Ed Schaffer, two bluesmen who came from the area around Shreveport. Many of his songs from this period likewise show a strong black influence, and, like the music of Autry and Carlisle, they are much more openly sexual than those of Rodgers. "Down at the Old Country Church" is a heavy-handed monologue/song, done in Negro dialect, suggestive of a blackface minstrel routine. But in songs like "Tom Cat and Pussy Blues," "High Behind Blues," "Red Nightgown Blues," and "Do-Do-Daddling Thing," Davis recorded some of the most risqué numbers found in the country repertory.

Blues of the type fashioned by Carlisle, Davis, and others did not endure past the mid-1930s, but fascination with the style, and with other black-derived forms, survived into the following decades. It even surfaced frequently in duet singing, a style usually associated with gentle parlor or gospel songs. The duet teams, like most country singers of the period, performed a mixed bag of songs, and some of them sought a commercial formula that would permit the performance of both traditional and innovative material. Several duets, such as North Carolina's Callahan Brothers, Texas's Shelton Brothers, and Alabama's Delmore Brothers, were especially versatile, with rowdy blues, old-time ballads, and sentimental parlor songs.

Of all the eclectic duet groups, none exerted a stronger or more lasting impact than the Delmore Brothers.[4] Alton and Rabon Delmore were born in Elkmont, Alabama, in the hilly Tennessee River region that produced such great country musicians as Rex Griffin, the Anglin Brothers, and the Louvin Brothers. The Delmores began performing for community gatherings at an extremely early age—Rabon was only ten and Alton eighteen—but their boldest step toward a commercial career came when they won first prize in 1930 at the old-time fiddlers' contest in Athens, Alabama. In 1931 they recorded two songs for Columbia (the only ones they ever made for that label), and in 1932 they successfully auditioned for the *Grand Ole Opry*. Their first session for Victor's Bluebird label in December 1933 yielded two of their most famous songs, the slightly risqué "Brown's Ferry Blues" and "Big River Blues" (now widely known as "Deep River Blues" because of Doc Watson's performances), both inspired by the Tennessee River. Blues tunes thus figured prominently in the Delmore Brothers' repertory from the very beginning of their career (their first recording for Columbia in 1931 had been "I've Got the Kansas City Blues"). As might be expected, they were much impressed by Jimmie Rodgers and even wrote a song especially for him, "Blue Railroad Train," although he died before receiving it. Rodgers was far from being the only blues influence in their lives, for they learned from black musicians who worked in the fields in the Tennessee Valley bottoms or who recorded during the brothers' formative years. The Delmores picked up a fondness for ragtime and eight-to-the-bar rhythms that surfaced repeatedly in their music, although the boogie beat did not figure prominently until they recorded "Hillbilly Boogie" for King in 1945. Both Delmores were excellent guitarists, but Rabon did most of the lead instrumental work on his tenor guitar, an instrument that rarely appears in country music.

While blues music was always attractive to the brothers, they did not by any means confine themselves to that form. Their vocal harmony was dramatically different from their instrumentation, but was just as influential. They sang in a soft, gentle style, with clearly enunciated diction and a carefully worked-out harmony. Placid love songs (such as Alton's own compositions "Southern Moon" and "When It's Time for the Whippoorwill to Sing"), gospel songs, and nineteenth-century parlor pieces figured just as prominently in their repertory as did blues tunes. Still, although they influenced them all, the Delmore Brothers did not sound like other "brother duets." Their unusual blending of lively, syncopated guitar work and soft, close harmony set them apart from most other musicians and made them a much-admired act. The greatest tribute to their work is the large number of "Delmore Brothers songs" still found in the repertories of modern country singers such as Doc Watson.

The brother duets of the pre–World War II era favored a diverse assortment of songs and performed them with a variety of instrumental combinations. Of course, they also differed greatly in vocal sound and quality and in their ability to harmonize. Howard and Dorsey Dixon, from Darlington, South Carolina, featured Howard's steel guitar and Dorsey's fingerpicking style of rhythm guitar. Vocally, their rough and sometimes-strident harmony was far removed from that of the smooth Delmores.

The Dixon Brothers came from the same type of textile-mill environment that spawned a long line of important country musicians, from Henry Whitter, Kelly Harrell, and Jimmie Tarlton to Lester Flatt. Although music was always an integral part of their lives, the Dixon Brothers were never permanently away from the mills. Howard went to work there as a child of ten and died on the job at the age of fifty-eight; Dorsey went to work at twelve and remained there until he retired in 1951. Fortunately, Dorsey enjoyed a second career after his rediscovery during the folk revival of the 1960s.

The two brothers played music as children but made no serious attempt at a professional career until the early 1930s. In 1931, Jimmie Tarlton, in one of his frequent forays through the country, stopped in East Rockingham, North Carolina, where he worked temporarily at the same mill where the Dixons were employed. Because of this chance encounter, Dorsey was inspired to develop a fingerpicking style on the guitar, and Howard began playing the steel guitar. In 1934 the Dixon Brothers inaugurated their professional career with a performance on J. W. Fincher's *Crazy Barn Dance*. Although their recorded repertory of over sixty songs for Victor over a two-year period never earned them enough money to free them from textile employment, they introduced several songs (most of them written or arranged by Dorsey) that have endured in country music: "Intoxicated Rat," the widely circulated "Weave Room Blues," and Roy Acuff's great hit "Wreck on the Highway," which the Dixons entitled "I Didn't Hear Nobody Pray." Dorsey Dixon continued to write long after his professional music career ended. One of his most compelling songs, "Babies in the Mill"—a recollection of the textile child labor that he and his brother had known—was written in the sixties after his music experienced a temporary resurgence.

Unlike the Dixon Brothers, the Callahan Brothers made music their full-time career. Many of the brother groups had little name recognition outside of the southeastern states. Homer and Walter Callahan, on the other hand, roamed from radio station to radio station in the South and Midwest before finally settling down in Dallas, where they built a large territorial following. Radio transcriptions broadcast over the Mexican border stations contributed further to their wide appeal. They also maintained a commercial viability in the years after the 1930s because they successfully adapted their style to the electric-based country and western fusion that became ascendant in the 1940s.

The Callahans hailed from Madison County, North Carolina, one of the richest storehouses of traditional music in the United States. They learned gospel songs and such old ballads as "Katie Dear" and "Banks of the Ohio" from their mother but were swept away by the music of Jimmie Rodgers in the late 1920s. They experimented with duet yodeling for the first time in 1933 at the Rhododendron Festival in Asheville, North Carolina. The delighted audience response was enough to kindle the young men's dreams of a professional entertainment career. Soon thereafter they landed their first radio job in Knoxville for the JFG Coffee company, and in 1934 they recorded fourteen songs for the American Record Company in New York. The Callahans demonstrated their penchant for the blues at this first session by doing songs like "Corn Licker Rag," "Gonna Quit My Rowdy Ways," and "St. Louis Blues." In the following years, they continued to do songs like

The Callahan Brothers. Bill Malone personal collection.

"Rounder's Luck" (better known today as "House of the Rising Sun"), "Step It Up and Go," and "Rattlesnake Daddy" (a hillbilly blues much unlike the black song of the same title). Gospel songs, traditional ballads, and modern-composed country songs always competed with the blues tunes, however, and a song called "She's My Curly Headed Baby," made up of old verse fragments, appeared in their first recording session of 1934 and always remained the song most identified with them.

The Callahans' career as hillbilly singers took them as far east as Wheeling, West Virginia, as far north as Cincinnati, as far west as Springfield, Missouri, and Tulsa, Oklahoma, before reaching Texas. During those years (1935–1941), they worked with the famous vaudeville hillbillies the Weaver Brothers and Elviry and with Red Foley. In 1941 they were associated with the hillbilly promoter and announcer Gus Foster ("who could sell anything") and had radio shows on KRLD in Dallas and KWFT in Wichita Falls. In Texas, the Callahans acquired the radio names of "Bill and Joe" and became one of the most popular bands of the Southwest.

In Texas, "Bill and Joe" ceased to be just a simple mountain duet. They progressively absorbed modern country songs into their repertory and added a growing retinue of musicians, including a much-admired fiddler named Georgia Slim Rutland and the superb mandolin player Paul Buskirk, who was one of the first "modern" (i.e., jazz-influenced) exponents of that instrument in country music. The brothers adopted electric instruments and devised a variety stage show built around their harmony and Bill's (Homer's) zany comedy. By the time of their last recording session in 1951, little distinguished their music from the dominant honky-tonk sound of that era. By this time as well, Bill Callahan had become a bass player and, briefly, manager for the young Lefty Frizzell and was identified largely as a comedian.

One of the most common instrumental combinations supporting the duet vocal sound was the mandolin and guitar. The mandolin had been a popular middle-class instrument before World War I, much favored by chamber musicians and college students. Precisely how and when it moved into rural music is unknown, but it was widely advertised in the mail-order catalogues during the 1920s. It has become one of the most versatile instruments in country music, capable of supporting anything from a mournful dirge to a progressive jazz tune. In the 1930s it was sometimes heard as a ragtime instrument—as played by Ted Hawkins on Riley Puckett's 1934 recording of "Ragged but Right"—but its proper domain seemed to be the music of the brother duets.

Interestingly, the "brother" duet that may have done most to popularize the instrument was not composed of brothers. Lester McFarland and Robert A. Gardner came from Gray, Kentucky, and Oliver Springs, Tennessee, respectively. They first joined their musical interests in 1915 at the Kentucky School for the Blind, where both were enrolled as students. McFarland usually sang tenor on their duet performances and picked the instrumental leads on his mandolin. His mandolin playing on their Brunswick recordings after 1927, and on *National Barn Dance* broadcasts after 1931, did much to stimulate the general popularity of the instrument among country musicians. Along with Gardner, who played guitar and sang lead, McFarland began entertaining in schoolhouses, at county fairs, and on the Keith vaudeville circuit in 1922. From 1925 to 1931, they performed over WNOX in Knoxville, and in 1931 they moved to Chicago as part of the *National Barn Dance* cast, where they were generally advertised only as "Mac and Bob." On radio shows and recordings made for Brunswick and the American Record Company after 1927, the duet introduced some of the classics of country music: for example, "When the Roses Bloom

Again" (their first recording), "'Tis Sweet to Be Remembered" (later done by bluegrass musicians in a much-modified form), "Twenty-One Years" (the great prison song written by Bob Miller), and "That Little Boy of Mine." Mac and Bob actually had one of the most wide-ranging repertories in country music, including everything from "I'm Forever Blowing Bubbles" to "Midnight on the Stormy Deep" and "The East Bound Train." Their sound was not necessarily rural but instead had an old-fashioned, cultivated flavor, suggestive of the music hall or barbershop singing. It was a rather formal style, much like that sometimes used by Buell Kazee; the McCravy Brothers (Frank and James); and a Texas duo, (Jerry) Sloan and (Frank) Threadgill—but it conveyed a charming, if sometimes stilted, sound.

Karl and Harty formed yet another nonbrother duet that profoundly influenced the sound of those who *were* brothers. Karl Davis and Hartford Connecticut Taylor came to the *National Barn Dance* in 1931 as part of John Lair's Cumberland Ridge Runners. Both men grew up in the vicinity of Mount Vernon, Kentucky, and received part of their grade-school instruction from Lair, the man who would eventually accompany them to the WLS country show and then back again in the late 1930s to the *Renfro Valley* show in Kentucky. Although they often performed as part of a larger group, Karl and Harty made their most distinctive mark on country music through their duet harmonies, mandolin and guitar instrumentation, and influential songs. Karl learned to play the mandolin at the age of twelve after hearing the instrument played by Doc Hopkins, the well-known mountain balladeer and later member of the Ridge Runners. Along with Harty, who had taught himself to play the guitar, Karl began playing for local parties in Mount Vernon. In their later recording and performing career, the duo featured a somewhat formal style of singing, probably much influenced by Mac and Bob, who were their contemporaries on the *Barn Dance*. More important than their performance style was the body of songs they introduced to country music. Beginning with "I'm Just Here to Get My Baby Out of Jail," a song that Davis set to the melody of "Old Reuben," and continuing with others like "Prisoner's Dream," "The House Where We Were Wed," "They're All Going Home but One," and "Kentucky" (Davis's most beautiful composition), Karl and Harty bequeathed a large number of songs that have moved into the repertories of entertainers as diverse as the Blue Sky Boys and the Everly Brothers.

The Cumberland Ridge Runners: standing, left to right, *Slim Miller,
Karl Davis, Red Foley, Harty Taylor;* seated, *John Lair, Linda Parker.
Bill Malone personal collection; courtesy of George Biggar.*

Among the bona fide brother acts who performed with mandolin
and guitar, two stand out because of the lasting contributions they
made to country music: the Bolick Brothers and the Monroe Brothers.
Popularly known as the Blue Sky Boys, Bill and Earl Bolick uncom-
promisingly adhered to traditional patterns in their style of singing
and instrumentation and in their selection of old-time songs. The
student of American folk song could begin in no better place than
the Blue Sky Boys' repertory, for there one can find myriad examples
of the song types that found their way into the hearts and homes of
southern country people. However, one will encounter few examples
of the raw, rowdy, or sexy side of human experience, for, like Bradley
Kincaid before them, the Bolicks believed that music should serve a
moral purpose.

As Bill and Earl grew up on a small farm near Hickory, North Carolina, on the edge of the mountain region known as the "Land of the
Sky," they were exposed to a set of moral values and a variety of song

The Blue Sky Boys, Bill and Earl Bolick.
Courtesy of Peter Feldmann, BlueGrass West!

sources that would one day affect both their performing style and their repertory. They learned from friends and relatives in the mountains, from *Reformation Glory* and other Church of God hymnals (Anderson, Indiana, branch), and from the recordings of such singers as Bradley Kincaid, Riley Puckett, and Karl and Harty. Both young men had a passionate commitment to traditional songs and styles, and Bill Bolick, in particular, viewed his songmaking role as a folkloristic one of collecting and preserving the ballads and gospel songs of earlier years.

Bill Bolick sang briefly in 1935 for a group called the East Hickory String Band (renamed the Crazy Hickory Nuts after they gained sponsorship by the Crazy Water Crystals Company), and in that same year he and Earl teamed up with the fiddler Homer Sherrill as the Good Coffee Boys (JFG Coffee) on WWNC in Asheville. The Bolicks were immediately popular there, and on WGST, Atlanta, where they performed for a few months in early 1936 as the Blue Ridge Entertainers. Their recording career began in June 1936, for Victor's Bluebird label; at this time, it is said that Eli Oberstein, the Victor talent scout, gave them their permanent performing title, the Blue Sky Boys, which was a composite of "Land of the Sky" and "Blue Ridge."

From the date of their first recording until they retired in 1951, the Blue Sky Boys made little substantial change in either their material or style of performance, although their harmony got higher; newly composed songs moved into their repertory; and, after 1946, they added a string bass and fiddle to the original mandolin and guitar format. But their sound remained close to what it had been in 1936: both characteristically distinctive and predictable. Their carefully contrived harmony flowed from the skillful blending of Earl's resonant baritone voice with Bill's smooth tenor. Their instrumentation was just as unique. Bill Bolick never chorded the mandolin, but instead played tremolo passages, and even produced a third harmony to his own tenor harmony. Set against the background of deep, rhythmic guitar tones supplied by Earl Bolick, the instrumentation created a mood similar to that evoked by their singing.

And it was truly mood that really set the Blue Sky Boys apart from other singers during the Depression years. When one recalls that "hot dance" rhythms were winning the day at that precise moment in the Southwest, the Bolicks' commitment to a serious and moralistic body of songs assumes an even more singular significance. They did occasionally sing a novelty song like "Cindy," or a high-stepping vaudeville tune like "Are You from Dixie?" (their radio theme), and comedy (though strained) was not absent from their performances. Earl created a character, replete with whiskers and old-man's gait, called Uncle Josh. Nevertheless, the dominant theme of their music was the "tragic side of life." In plaintive, close harmony, they sang tales of death, sorrow, and unrequited love, and they approached each number with a compassion and tenderness seldom equaled in country music.

In making selections for recording, the Bolicks sometimes chose numbers that had already demonstrated popularity when recorded by earlier performers.[5] In other cases, they merely recorded those songs often requested by their large and loyal radio audience. The Blue Sky Boys' inclination toward somber and sentimental melodies was evidently shared by their listeners. The bulk of their recorded numbers included traditional songs like the American murder ballad "Banks of the Ohio" and the British broadside "The Butcher's Boy," sentimental Tin Pan Alley melodies like "There'll Come a Time" and "I Believe It for My Mother Told Me So," unrequited-love songs like "Why Not Confess," and religious songs like "Only One Step More."

The Blue Sky Boys' harmony has been often imitated by modern country singers (one even hears a touch of it in the Everly Brothers), and their songs have been widely preserved, particularly in bluegrass music.[6] Still, their influence has not been as profound as that of the Monroe Brothers. Originally composed of brothers Birch, Charlie, and Bill (and finally only Charlie and Bill), the Monroes contributed a style and repertory of songs that have inspired thousands of rural and urban musicians. As a duo, Charlie and Bill touched the lives of many aspiring performers, such as Lester Flatt, Ira and Charlie Louvin, Ralph and Carter Stanley, and Everett and Mitchell Lilly, igniting within them the flames of musical ambition. As separate acts, Charlie and Bill provided employment for scores of musicians who later went on to forge important careers of their own.

The Monroe Brothers, in existence only from 1934 to 1938, featured Bill's inventive mandolin style and high harmony singing and Charlie's lead singing and dynamic, run-filled guitar playing. Through his independent work after the 1940s, Bill Monroe became famous as a solo singer of great power and range, but with the Monroe Brothers, he never sang anything but tenor harmony. He and Charlie became a full-time duet in 1934, working on a series of radio stations in Gary, Indiana; Shenandoah, Iowa; Omaha, Nebraska; and finally, in 1935, in Greenville, South Carolina; and Charlotte, North Carolina, all under the sponsorship of Texas Crystals (not to be confused with the Crazy Water Company). In February 1936, they recorded the first of what would eventually be sixty songs for Bluebird, including their best-selling song, "What Would You Give in Exchange for Your Soul?" From

The Monroe Brothers: left to right, *Charlie Monroe,*
Byron Parker, Bill Monroe. Courtesy of Pat Ahrens.

1936 to 1938, they and their popular announcer, the Old Hired Hand,
Byron Parker (a native of Hastings, Iowa), worked the Carolinas under
the sponsorship of Crazy Water Crystals, becoming probably the most
popular hillbilly act in the southeastern United States. Superficially
similar in style and repertory to other mandolin-and-guitar duets,
they were nonetheless crucially different. In songs like "Nine Pound
Hammer," "Feast Here Tonight," "Roll in My Sweet Baby's Arms," and
"My Long Journey Home," all of which have become country standards, Charlie and Bill impressed listeners with the high vocal pitch
of their singing, the aggressiveness of their instrumentation, and the
breakneck speed of their tempos.

When we leave the blues singers and the duets, we find an almost-
bewildering array of entertainers who tried to make country music
their profession during the 1930s. The broadening coverage of radio
encouraged what Bob Coltman has called a cross-fertilization of styles
as well as a softening of sound among country musicians.[7] Once-local

styles moved across the country and became intermeshed with those found elsewhere to the point that it becomes dangerous indeed to speak precisely of "southeastern" or "southwestern" traits. Furthermore, as Coltman argues, country music became smoother and more polished, with much of its wild, tangy backwoods flavor removed, as broadcasting executives discovered that women and children composed the bulk of the audience that daily listened to the radio sets. This same perception of woman's gentleness and refinement may have encouraged the search for and greater cultivation of women entertainers.

Women had played important, if often unseen, roles since the beginning of country music; their visibility became much more pronounced, and their influence stronger, in the decade of the 1930s. Myrtle Eleanor Cooper, popularly known as Lulu Belle, made one of the most important breakthroughs for women entertainers. She joined the *National Barn Dance* in 1932 as a comedienne and singer, working first with Red Foley, and then with Skyland Scotty Wiseman, a versatile singer, writer, and banjoist from North Carolina, whom she married in 1934. As Lulu Belle and Scotty, they became one of the most popular acts on the *Barn Dance*, known for their comic repartee, novelty songs, and sentimental numbers (such as "Remember Me When the Candle Lights Are Gleaming" and "Have I Told You Lately That I Love You?"—both written by Scotty). Both entertainers were immensely talented, but Lulu Belle won an enormous audience for them with her vivacious personality, attractive looks, and saucy singing style. She even won a *Radio Digest* poll in 1936 as the most popular radio entertainer in America.

Women also began to create identities apart from their husbands, families, or supportive instrumental groups. Cynthia May Carver, a Kentucky girl discovered by John Lair, broke into show business at the end of the 1930s as Cousin Emmy, a madcap but versatile entertainer. She sang, played the banjo (she claimed to be the master of fifteen instruments), danced, acted the fool, but also found the time to do hymns and sweet love songs. She was seldom recorded, but she left as part of her legacy a rollicking tune called "Ruby Are You Mad at Your Man?," a song now deeply ensconced in the repertory of bluegrass music through the performances of the Osborne Brothers.

Kentucky was also the birthplace of Lily May Ledford, another five-string banjoist and balladeer, who became the founder of the first all-female string band, the Coon Creek Girls.[8] Lily May joined the

The Coon Creek Girls: left to right, Rosie Ledford, Violet Koehler, Lily May Ledford, Daisy Lange. Bill Malone personal collection; courtesy of Bob Pinson.

National Barn Dance in 1936 at the age of nineteen but spent only one year in Chicago before journeying on to Cincinnati to become part of John Lair's new *Renfro Valley Barn Dance.* Lair, who played a leading role in the encouragement of women entertainers, organized and named the Coon Creek Girls, a band built around Lily May (banjo), her sister Rosie (guitar), Esther "Violet" Koehler (mandolin), and Evelyn "Daisy" Lange (fiddle and bass). The Girls became a trio in 1939 when Susie Ledford joined her sisters after Daisy and Violet departed to become members of the Callahan Brothers' Blue Ridge Mountain Folk in Dallas. The Coon Creek Girls excelled as both singers and instrumentalists and were known both for their gospel and sentimental pieces and for hard-driving mountain songs such as "Pretty Polly" and "How Many Biscuits Can You Eat?"

Although women made important breakthroughs in the 1930s, they still had very far to go. Negative images still clung to women who dared to forsake their "traditional" roles and venture into an area formerly reserved for men. It may be significant that though many of the leading women entertainers were of southern origin, most of them made their mark outside the Deep South—in the border states, on the *National Barn Dance*, and as western cowgirls. Women still found it difficult to go before the public without at least giving the impression that they were related, by blood or marriage, to the musicians with whom they played. The story has often been told of how Rachel Veach, a comedienne and banjo player for Roy Acuff after April 1939, was depicted as the Dobro player Beecher Kirby's sister to discourage censure of an unmarried woman traveling with a group of male musicians. Even the pioneering sister acts of the 1930s, such as Millie and Dolly Good (the Girls of the Golden West) and Maryjane and Caroline Dezurik (known as the Cackle Sisters because of the "clucking" style of harmony they developed), had the advantage of traveling together so that each sister could be considered a chaperone for the other. The real "liberation" of women country singers would not come until decades later.

Innovation reared its head repeatedly in the country music of the 1930s, but singers still appeared everywhere who adhered to traditional forms of music or who promoted a down-home or family ambience. Whenever hillbilly singers who lived during the 1930s reminisce about those days, talk will invariably turn at some point to a father-and-son team called Asher Sizemore and Little Jimmie. Few radio entertainers from that era seem to have been more popular. Sizemore was born in Manchester, Kentucky, and began his radio career on WSAZ in Huntington, West Virginia, in 1931. By 1932 he was joined on WSM by four-year-old Jimmie in a "home and hearth"–type show that lasted until 1942 (they were on other stations after this date). Audiences were sufficiently impressed with the Sizemores to send in an enormous amount of fan mail—up to forty thousand pieces in a single week—and if impressionistic evidence garnered from antique shops can be trusted, their songbooks were widely circulated.

Many entertainers of the period were like the Sizemores in that they built their reputations almost exclusively on radio or by personal appearances. Grandpa Jones, one of the major talents of country music history, made no records until 1943, although he had been a radio entertainer since 1929. Another extraordinarily versatile entertainer, Lew Childre, did make some obscure recordings in the 1930s (for Gennett and the American Record Company), but his public name recognition came principally as an itinerant radio performer. The Opp, Alabama, native was basically a country vaudeville performer whose skills as a buck dancer, steel guitarist, comedian, and singer had been perfected on the tent-rep circuit in the 1920s and 1930s. Regrettably, neither a phonograph recording nor a radio broadcast could effectively communicate the exuberant personality or performing genius of the man. Childre was meant to be seen as well as heard.

Some singers had only regional radio followings. Two WWVA performers, Big Slim (the Lone Cowboy) and Doc Williams, were immensely popular in the Northeast because of the powerful signal transmitted by the station. Big Slim (Harry McAuliffe) did make some recordings in the 1930s, and one of his compositions—"Sunny Side of the Mountain"—eventually became one of the classics of country music. Slim's reputation, however, was made principally through his thirty-plus years of performance on the big West Virginia station. His colleague Doc Williams (an ex-coal miner from Pennsylvania named Andrew J. Smik) did not record until 1947, but he had been a popular emcee and balladeer since he joined the station in 1937, and he was still there in the 1970s.

Buddy Starcher, on the other hand, worked on not one but many stations. He made no records either until 1946 but had a following in the 1930s that was surpassed by few country entertainers. This Ripley, West Virginia, native began his radio career on WFBR in Baltimore in 1928 (he was only eighteen), but he moved to a succession of stations, mostly in Virginia and West Virginia, during the next several years. Starcher was a true radio personality, with a warm, reassuring voice that easily won the confidence of his listeners, selling them songbooks, commercial products, and himself. He sang songs to his own Carter-style guitar accompaniment and saw several of them (such as "Those Brown Eyes," "I'll Still Write Your Name in the Sand," and "Sweet Thing") become standards in the repertories of country singers everywhere.

One can hear in the instrumental music of the 1930s the same type of "cross-fertilization" observable in singing. Musicians learned at home or from local community resources, but also absorbed new techniques as they traveled from one region to another or as they listened to radio broadcasts and phonograph recordings. The sounds of pop music, jazz, and even the Hot Club of France (Django Reinhardt, Stéphane Grappelli) seeped into the consciousness of "traditional" musicians. Music in the Southeast tended to be more conservative than that of the Southwest, preserving much of the tangy flavor and repertory of the hoedown bands. Nevertheless, musicians there had always exhibited a fascination with pop sounds, too, and many of them filtered into the performances of the most traditional entertainers. Clayton McMichen, as we have seen, had leaned toward "modern" material even when playing with the Skillet Lickers. In 1931 he organized the kind of band he had always wanted, the Georgia Wildcats, which had an ultraeclectic repertory ranging from "Farewell Blues" (from the Benny Goodman collection) to hoedowns like "Boil Them Cabbage Down." The band left Atlanta and relocated for several years to Louisville, where it included some of the most progressive musicians in country music: Hoyt "Slim" Bryant, who began playing single-string solos and "sock" rhythm (a percussive, closed-chord style) long before most guitarists; Carl Cotner, a "hot" violinist who later became Gene Autry's musical director; and the young Merle Travis, who joined the band in 1937 with his seminal "thumb style" of guitar playing. McMichen, however, made little money from his new sound, and he had to resort to promoting fiddling contests or to participating in the contests staged by Larry Sunbrock. The Sunbrock contests usually involved McMichen and Natchee the Indian (backed by Cowboy Copas) and were resolved by audience vote.

McMichen, then, was experimenting with hot and swinging rhythms well before Bob Wills made them popular out in the Southwest. However, McMichen's innovations never caught fire as he envisioned them, and when the hot sounds caught on among southeastern musicians, they usually came through the influence of the Texas and Oklahoma musicians. The Kentucky Ramblers, the Tennessee Ramblers, and Hank Penny's Radio Cowboys were among the earliest of the southeastern bands to adopt songs and styles from their southwestern contemporaries. The Kentucky Ramblers, organized in 1932, were composed of Charles Hurt, Jack Taylor, Shelby "Tex" Atchison, and Floyd "Salty" Holmes. By 1934 the western image had exerted its irresistible attraction, and the boys changed their title to Prairie Ramblers. In their long tenure on the *National Barn Dance*, from 1933 to 1948, the Ramblers performed a repertory that reflected the appeal of both the cowboy and the southwestern swing bands. The Tennessee Ramblers (led by Dick Hartman and later by Cecil Campbell) popularized themselves on the *Crazy Barn Dance* in Charlotte, and by 1937 were recording their swing sounds on the Bluebird label. Herbert Clayton "Hank" Penny, of Birmingham, Alabama, was the musician most directly influenced by what he called "Texas fiddle music." Penny had never cared for hoedown music, and though virtually living at its back door, he was contemptuous of the music he heard on the *Grand Ole Opry*. The Texas sounds, therefore, swept him away when he heard them for the first time in New Orleans where he was playing on WWL. He returned to Birmingham with the hot fiddler Sheldon Bennett and the banjoist Louis Dumont and organized the Radio Cowboys, a band closely modeled on Milton Brown's Musical Brownies. Performing on WSB's *Crossroad Follies* in Atlanta, and recording for Arthur Satherley and Okeh records after 1938, Hank Penny popularized "western swing" throughout the South. Many innovative musicians played for Penny during the following decades, including the violinist Boudleaux Bryant (who would become one of country music's greatest songwriters) and the pioneering steel guitarists Noel Boggs and Eddie Duncan, both of whom borrowed freely from jazz trombonists and saxophonists.

While Penny and the Radio Cowboys were doing their country-jazz versions of "Hesitation Blues," "Hot Time Mama," and their signature song, "Won't You Ride in My Little Red Wagon," most other southeastern bands were clinging to a more traditional repertory of hoedowns and country tunes. The most influential of the old-time string bands was a group from Buncombe County, North Carolina, Mainer's Mountaineers. Headed by the fiddler Joseph Emmett (J.E.) Mainer and his banjo-playing brother Wade, the Mainer's were an important transitional organization: they preserved much of the heritage of traditional country material—breakdowns, reels, ballads, folk songs—while at the same time anticipating many of the stylistic features of modern bluegrass music. The Mainers experimented with harmony sounds that later showed up among bluegrass singers, popularized a large body of songs that appeared in the repertories of many later singers, and featured the full retinue of instruments now associated with bluegrass music—fiddle, five-string banjo, mandolin, guitar, and string bass.

Most of the original musicians in the Mainer group came out of a cotton mill background, with J.E. himself going to work in such an environment at age twelve. Music was never more than an amateur diversion for J.E., except for the fiddle conventions that he often entered. Then, in 1932, he began playing on a station in Gastonia, North Carolina, and two years later, along with brother Wade, an old friend and guitarist called Daddy John Love, and Claude "Zeke" Morris, began performing over WBT in Charlotte, North Carolina. They were known as J.E. Mainer's Crazy Mountaineers, a name inspired by their first sponsor, the Crazy Water Crystals Company. The Mainer's eventually played on radio stations as far west and south as New Orleans and the Mexican border, but their longest tenure was at stations in the Upper South. The group's personnel changed many times before J.E.'s death in 1972, but it included many of the most important musicians of the Southeast, such as Homer Sherrill, Steve Ledford, Dewitt "Snuffy" Jenkins, and two of Zeke Morris's brothers, Wiley and George.

The Mainer's repertory, first recorded on Bluebird in August 1935, was filled with traditional songs, including many fiddle pieces such as "Run Mountain" and J.E.'s wonderful version of "Johnson's Old Grey Mule"; religious songs such as the very popular "Take Me in the Lifeboat"; sentimental parlor duets like "Maple on the Hill" (sung by Wade and Zeke); ballads such as "John Henry"; and yodeling blues songs (done by Daddy John Love). Performing with great verve and abandon, the Mainer's created a tangy backwoods atmosphere, reminiscent of the Skillet Lickers, that lay a vast cultural distance from the music of the Georgia Wildcats and the Radio Cowboys.

Mainer's Mountaineers influenced the styles of other musicians and also spawned other bands that flourished in the Upper South in the late 1930s and early 1940s. By 1937 Wade Mainer had organized his own band,[9] the Sons of the Mountaineers, which included such musicians as Jay Hugh Hall, Steve Ledford, and Clyde Moody. Hall and Moody in turn later worked as a duet called the Happy-Go-Lucky Boys. The fiddler Homer Sherrill and the banjoist Snuffy Jenkins began one of the longest partnerships in country music in 1937 when they joined with the announcer Byron Parker at WIS in Columbia, South Carolina, to form the WIS Hillbillies. Through this medium Snuffy Jenkins became the first five-string banjoist to popularize the three-finger roll before a large audience. Many young musicians listened in awe to Jenkins's syncopated sound; two of them, Don Reno and Earl Scruggs, later introduced it to the world. Musicianship was a major factor in building the Hillbillies' audience, but the announcer Byron Parker, the self-styled "Old Hired Hand"—who had earlier been associated with the Monroe Brothers—contributed mightily to their success. Widely recognized as a supersalesman, Parker was as well known as the musicians with whom he worked, and many people all over the Southeast can still recall his closing lines: "Goodbye, good luck, and may God bless you, everyone."

Band personnel shifted constantly among hillbilly musicians in the 1930s. Homer Sherrill, for example, found time to play with other groups while serving as a member of the WIS Hillbillies. He appeared on Wiley and Zeke Morris's first recording session for Bluebird in January 1938. Wiley and Zeke performed in typical brothers fashion with guitar and mandolin, and at their second session in September 1938 recorded their famous and influential version of "Let Me Be Your Salty Dog" (later recorded as "Salty Dog Blues"). Not only did they introduce one of the great warhorses of bluegrass music, they also were the first employers of the seminal bluegrass banjoists Earl Scruggs and Don Reno.

Among the several southeastern bands that shared the radio audience at the end of the 1930s, few were as popular as Roy Hall and his Blue Ridge Entertainers. Hall was a textile worker from Waynesville, North Carolina, who inaugurated his career as a professional musician in February 1937 with a dozen recordings he made with his brother Jay Hugh Hall. The Hall Brothers had two more sessions in 1938, before Roy formed the larger band—the Blue Ridge Entertainers—which became one of the most popular regional bands in the years before Roy Hall's death in an automobile accident on May 16, 1943. Hall and his musicians were undistinguished as singers, but they popularized songs such as "Come Back Little Pal," "Can You Forgive," and "Don't Let Your Sweet Love Die," which have endured in country music, and they introduced to southeastern audiences some songs identified with western musicians, such as Bob Wills's "New San Antonio Rose" and Johnny Bond's "I Wonder Where You Are Tonight." Like Mainer's Mountaineers, the Blue Ridge Entertainers functioned as a transitional band, performing both old-time and modern material, providing a bridge between the mountain hoedown bands and the country and western bands of the 1940s.

By the end of the 1930s, both individual singers, like Roy Acuff, and individual musicians had begun to achieve identities apart from specific bands. With an occasional exception, such as Charlie Poole or Clayton McMichen, the old-time string bands generally had neither "stars" nor individual soloists who were distinguished from the other band members. But by the beginning of World War II, specific musicians were being recruited by various bands, and some instrumentalists traveled widely across the country, either giving shows of their own or finding employment in one band or another. A number of southeastern fiddlers in the 1930s were prized for their individual contributions. Roy Hall's fiddler, Tommy Magness, was an old-time fiddler in the J.E. Mainer mold, but he had a smoothness and individual verve that few hoedown fiddlers possessed. Magness was sufficiently prized to be lured away by other prominent band leaders, first by Bill Monroe (with whom he became one of the first bluegrass fiddlers) and later by Roy Acuff.

Magness seems to have been one of the few prominent fiddlers who never traveled outside his native region to find employment. Some southeastern fiddlers, such as Clifford Gross and Carl Cotner, left permanently to be closer to the kind of jazzy or popular-based country music that they really preferred. Others, like Georgia Slim Rutland, Howard "Howdy" Forrester, Arnim Leroy "Curly" Fox, and Arthur Smith, left their homes to become barnstorming entertainers. Georgia Slim and Howdy Forrester went to Tulsa as part of Herald Goodman's Tennessee Valley Boys, and then on down to Dallas, where they were associated for several years with the Callahan Brothers and other local entertainers. Curly Fox, from Graysville, Tennessee, was probably the greatest showman of all the fiddlers. He led his own band on WSB in 1932 but spent most of the decade winning fiddle contests throughout the South and playing on various radio stations with his wife, Texas Ruby Owens, and with other entertainers such as the Shelton Brothers. He was an outstanding hoedown fiddler, and he excelled at trick tunes on which he could assert his personality and showmanship: "Listen to the Mockingbird" (replete with bird imitations and woodpecker rappings), "Orange Blossom Special," and "Johnson's Old Grey Mule" (in which the voice and scraped fiddle strings combine to simulate the braying of a mule).

Of all the southeastern fiddlers, Arthur Smith was generally acknowledged to be the best. Born in Humphreys County, Tennessee, Smith worked as a railroad man for several years on the North Carolina and St. Louis Railroad; this was the Dixie Line, the inspiration for his first band, the Dixieliners. He appeared on the *WSM Barn Dance* as early as December 1927 but did not become a regular until 1932, when he teamed with Sam and Kirk McGee. Smith was often associated with outstanding musicians, including the Delmore Brothers, with whom he toured and recorded in 1935 and 1936; the Shelton Brothers, with whom he played at KWKH in 1940; and the cowboy singer Jimmy Wakely, with whom he made movies from 1945 to 1947. He was also a singer and songwriter, having written or arranged such well-known songs as "Beautiful Brown Eyes" and "There's More Pretty Girls Than One." But it was as a fiddler that he touched the lives of musicians everywhere. With his rapid fingering and cleanly noted style of playing, Smith moved fiddling dramatically away from the shuffling hoedown style, and he left a host of songs, such as "Red Apple Rag," "Blackberry Blossom," and "Dickson County Blues," that have attracted fiddlers ever since.

The fiddle preserved its dominance in country bands in the 1930s, but other instruments rapidly challenged its hegemony, and in so doing, radically changed the nature of the country sound. The mandolin, as we have seen, flourished during the decade, but its gentle parlor sound did not survive the wholesale introduction of electrical amplification into country music. Instead, in the hands of men like Bill Monroe and Red Rector, it became an aggressive, and even percussive, instrument capable of holding its own in a large ensemble and in a high-powered strident style such as bluegrass. In Knoxville at the end of the 1930s, a teenage musician named Kenneth Burns was already beginning to make the mandolin a jazz instrument; in later years he would be best known as Jethro (of Homer and Jethro). In the Southwest, such musicians as Joe Shelton, Leo Raley (probably the first person to electrify the instrument), and, preeminently, Paul Buskirk (a North Carolinian who relocated to Texas), demonstrated that the mandolin could not be confined to any one type of music.

The five-string banjo had declined as the mandolin-and-guitar combos proliferated. Uncle Dave Macon, of course, remained active during the decade, and a few musicians, such as Lily May Ledford, Cousin Emmy, and David "Stringbean" Akeman, used it to accompany old ballads and mountain breakdowns. The instrument came to be perceived as old-fashioned or comic and was presumed to have little value in a band other than as a rhythm instrument. Nevertheless, men like Wade Mainer, with his distinctive two-finger style, kept the instrument alive, and Snuffy Jenkins popularized the syncopated, three-finger technique that was common in his part of western North Carolina. As the 1930s ended, the five-string banjo was only a few years away from a sensational resurgence that only a few instruments have enjoyed.

Guitars were common in all country bands, as were string basses. Only the expense involved in purchasing the instrument and the inconvenience of finding space in a touring car to transport it had deterred the acquisition of string basses (also known as bass fiddles, bull fiddles, or stand-up basses). But country musicians had long desired some kind of "bottom" for the sounds of the fiddle bands (which may be one reason why accompanying guitarists often favored bass runs), and bowed cellos were sometimes used to achieve a bass sound. String basses were easily observable in jazz or popular dance bands, but when country bands adopted them, there seemed so little for the bass player to do that he was often given the extra duty of being a rube comic dressed in hillbilly clown clothing.

Most guitar players played a simple open-chord backup style, marked by occasional bass runs between chords. Although guitarists bought expensive, finely crafted Martin or Gibson guitars as soon as they could afford them, most beginning instrumentalists had to be content with cheap, low-volume, hard-to-play brands. Thumb picks, rather than flat picks or finger picks, were favored because they required less exertion and fit readily into the kind of "claw-hammer" style of strumming favored by many players. A few guitarists, such as Sam McGee, Maybelle Carter, Roy Harvey, and Dick Justice, had earlier excelled as solo musicians, but it was not until the mid- and late 1930s that major breakthroughs were made in the art of guitar playing. Most of the advances in guitar picking came in the West, largely under the influence of such blues and jazz men as Charlie Christian, Eddie Durham, and Aaron "T-Bone" Walker, and with the help of electrical amplification, which came after 1934. Still, the portent of the guitar's distinctive future could already be heard in the playing of such southeastern musicians as Slim Bryant and Merle Travis, through whose innovations the guitar began to move out of the shadow of the fiddle and banjo to become an instrument of melodic and improvisatory capabilities.

Even more prophetic of country music's future was the sound heard at the end of the 1930s in bands like Roy Hall's Blue Ridge Entertainers and Roy Acuff's Smoky Mountain Boys, that of the steel guitar. This was the instrument that did the most to set such groups apart from earlier string bands and which, in the 1940s, would come to be virtually the defining feature of country music. The steel guitar, or its equivalent, appeared early in country music. Frank Hutchison used a knife style on his October 1926 recording of "Worried Blues," and the Johnson Brothers (Paul and Charles) and Jimmie Tarlton made similar steel recordings by the end of 1927. Such early steel guitarists as Hutchison and Tarlton seem to have been more influenced by black bottleneck styles than they were by Hawaiian styles, although Tarlton picked up some of the latter in his travels, too. The steel guitarists who popularized the instrument on Jimmie Rodgers's recordings were either real Hawaiians like Joe Kaipo or men like Ellsworth Cozzens, John Westbrook, and Cliff Carlisle, who learned directly from Hawaiian musicians either on the chautauqua, vaudeville, and tent-rep circuits before World War I or in special courses on the style taught by "real" Hawaiians.

In the days before electrical amplification, the American enthusiast either converted a conventional guitar by elevating the strings or bought one of the specially constructed amplified guitars that the manufacturers began placing on the market. Two brand names predominated among these manufactured guitars: National, which appears to have been the first, and Dobro, which was the most popular. Both were equipped with metal vibrating discs or cones called resonators—the National had three and the Dobro one—that amplified the instrument without benefit of electrification. The Dobro was the creation of the Dopyera Brothers (Ed, Robert, and Rudy) of California. The brothers had been partners in the National Musical Instrument Company, the manufacturer of a metal-bodied tricone resophonic guitar, but in 1928 they formed a new organization that introduced the Dobro, a single-resonator instrument whose wooden body permitted a much more melodious sound than the tinny quality conveyed by the Nationals. Cliff Carlisle was one of the first musicians to play a Dobro, but its real popularization in American life came through the recordings of Roy Acuff in the late 1930s and early 1940s. Acuff's rise to fame as a *Grand Ole Opry* artist permitted the Dobro, played in his band first by James Clell "Cousin Jody" Summey and later by Beecher "Oswald" Kirby, to receive a similar recognition. Acuff had many great musicians, but the Dobro was the distinctive feature of his instrumentation.

Although the Dobro (the brand name became a generic term) appeared periodically in country bands throughout the nation, it was fated to carry an old-time and southeastern identification (and after its temporary eclipse after World War II, it was reintroduced to country music as a bluegrass instrument). The real wave of the future in steel guitar playing came in its electrification and in its emergence as a flexible instrument capable of playing either country music or jazz. Most of the innovative developments in steel guitar style came from musicians west of the Mississippi River, but southeasterners sometimes played crucial roles, as in the case of Noel Boggs, who was applying jazz-derived techniques to the instrument as early as 1939. Above all, in the playing of Jerry Byrd one could hear the sound of country music's future.

Byrd grew up in Lima, Ohio, where, as a boy, he developed an enthusiasm for Hawaiian music that never left him. He in fact eventually became a resident of Hawaii and an active member of the Hawaiian Music Foundation. As a fledgling musician, he played songs of the Hawaiian Islands, but he gravitated toward country music in the late 1930s, a time when the music was receptive to the melodious and full-chorded sound of the steel guitar. He began playing on WLW in Cincinnati in 1939 and joined the *Renfro Valley Barn Dance* in the early 1940s. He later became a member of Red Foley's band and was one of the first session musicians in Nashville. Probably more than any other musician, he made the electric steel guitar the dominant and defining instrument of the mainstream country music that began to concentrate in Nashville in the 1940s.

Before ending this discussion of the 1930s and the transformations affecting the traditional music of the Southeast during that period, it is appropriate to explore further the economic context in which those changes occurred: the Great Depression. The Depression inspired the rediscovery and consequent romanticization of "the folk." Southern farmers and workers, "ill clad, ill housed, and ill nourished," commanded the attention of social workers, politicians, artists and intellectuals, reformers, radicals, and folklorists. In this new age of the "common man," the southern folk, once dismissed as cultural degenerates and snakehandlers—H. L. Mencken's "booboisie"—now emerged as a people whose folkways deserved commemoration, if not preservation. The photographic division of the Farm Security Administration (FSA), the WPA's cultural projects (for writers, artists, actors, and musicians), and the Library of Congress's Archive of American Folk Song all contributed to the documentation of southern folk culture. Under the leadership of Robert Winslow Gordon from 1928 to 1933, and John and Alan Lomax after 1933, the Archive of American Folk Song (now the American Folklife Center) embarked on a massive campaign to collect, on field recordings, folk material from all over the United States.

In the meantime, the plain folk were making themselves dramatically visible as never before. Unemployed people haunted the relief offices, and hobo jungles appeared on the edges of every American city, luring the homeless and jobless who rode the rails or merely wandered across the country. The hoboes were generally individuals who acted alone; the Okies, on the other hand, migrated as families. Dispossessed southwestern farmers, made homeless by automation, hard times, and dust storms, trekked westward toward the fabled land of California, seeking the illusory promise of jobs and material abundance that the Golden State supposedly possessed. Most Americans, however, did not migrate but instead remained at home to deal with hard times as best they could. Tenant farmers and sharecroppers in the Arkansas and Tennessee delta region roused themselves briefly against their landlords and organized the Southern Tenant Farmers' Union. Their brothers and sisters in the Appalachian coalfields and Piedmont textile mills marched into the national headlines with a series of strikes that gave the lie to the images of fatalism and docility that surrounded southern workers.

The labor uprisings that spread across the South between 1929 and 1933 were largely spontaneous affairs, generated by declining wages, the uncertainty of labor, and harsh working conditions (the most notorious being the textile industry's "stretch-out system"). Indigenous protest, though, soon attracted the support of northern labor organizers, reformers, radicals, and the liberal intelligentsia. The northerners who came south to promote the cause of social justice, whether at Marion or Gastonia, North Carolina, among the "lintheads" (a term that "polite" southerners had affixed to the cotton mill workers), or in "Bloody Harlan County," Kentucky, among the coal miners, found themselves among a people who sang and made ballads. Archie Green has described well the musical phenomenon that resulted from the mating of radical and intellectual ideas from the North with the conservative and rural tradition of ballad making in the South: "From this setting came a group of topical songs using old melodies to set off intensely stark and militant texts. In a sense, Piedmont mill villages and Cumberland mine camps became meeting grounds for the ideologies of Andrew Jackson and Karl Marx, Abraham Lincoln and Mikhail Bakunin."[10]

Every struggling social group had its balladeers: Aunt Molly Jackson, Sarah Ogan Gunning, Jim Garland, and Florence Reece, in the Kentucky coalfields; Ella May Wiggins, who was shot to death near Gastonia because of her activism; John Handcox, the song poet of the Arkansas sharecroppers; and, most famous of all, Woody Guthrie, the bard of the Okies. When the northern liberal/radical coterie went back home, they took a body of songs, such as Florence Reece's great labor hymn "Which Side Are You On?" and John Handcox's "Roll the Union On," which have ever since served the cause of human justice in the United States. Northern social activists soon saw people like Aunt Molly and Jim Garland in the flesh, because these mountain balladeers moved north when the movement for which they fought was defeated. But when Woody Guthrie took his Okie songs to New York in 1940, the radical community felt they had discovered a "new Joe Hill," a proletarian who wrote and sang protest material. Thus, the seeds of what would later be called "the urban folk revival" were planted. Young people like Pete Seeger and Cisco Houston passionately attached themselves to Guthrie, sang his songs, and passed them on to a later generation of "folksingers." The urban folk movement's radical origins have always affected public perceptions of it, and the linking of "protest" and "folk song" has contributed to false impressions about the nature of the folk and the music they have made. Furthermore, a regrettable distinction between "folk" and "hillbilly" music developed in the popular mind, where it remained lodged and unexamined. "Folk" music, which had become largely the province of intellectuals and reformers, became increasingly removed from the folk, while "hillbilly" music, the creation of the folk, developed in its own independent fashion.

Hillbilly music's response to the Great Depression reflected the varied, and often conflicting, impulses of the society that gave it birth. Despite the efforts made by its friends and foes alike, country music revealed no clear-cut, consistent ideology, just as none had existed in southern rural culture. Rural southerners have been socially conservative in their personal habits, but, historically, they have veered radically in their patriotism (the 250,000 Confederate deaths in the Civil War should suggest that national allegiance has not always been a cardinal virtue among southerners), and they have sometimes responded explosively to public injustice, as in the wave of strikes that dotted the southern landscape in the early 1930s. Furthermore, neither the strong strain of populism that erupted in the 1890s nor the religious-bred suspicion of materialism has ever totally vanished from southern rural life. Woody Guthrie, whose stylistic debt to hillbilly music was profound, represented one political posture. Merle Haggard in our day, with his "conservative" songs, seemed to come from a different perspective. But neither man reveals the whole of country music's history nor of its sociopolitical outlook.

If country music has had no clear-cut political stance, it has nonetheless been a music of social commentary, and scarcely any phenomenon in American life has escaped being brought into its purview. The reaction to hard times made by hillbilly musicians and their audiences ranged from outright indifference to passionate activism. The 1930s, after all, were marked by a popular culture of escapism; many Americans sought relief from the Depression through detective movies and Busby Berkeley musicals, marathon dancing and big band swing. Country music audiences sought similar escape or cathartic release through western swing dance music, cowboy songs, gospel music, and parlor songs of old-fashioned love and morality. In commenting directly on the Depression, some songs adopted the Hoover view that economic decline was basically a product of public doubt and that prosperity would accompany a revival of confidence. The Light Crust Doughboys, for example, took the idea to an extreme when they talked of putting Depression on the run in Pappy O'Daniel's "My Million Dollar Smile." In "No Hard Times," Jimmie Rodgers exuded the confidence of a man who had "chickens in my back yard . . . and corn in my crib"; Jimmie, though, spoke from a position of economic security that few of his listeners shared.

Religion, as always, colored the responses of some singers to economic distress. In "No Depression in Heaven," the Carter Family saw the disaster as merely one more trial that humanity had to suffer and opined that the only true relief lay beyond the grave. Most religious songs, of course, made no references to public events, but instead brought their traditional messages of private hope and salvation to millions of poor people who found little solace this side of heaven. Such songs as "Farther Along," which consoled troubled hearts by saying that someday "we'll know all about it," and Charles Tindley's "We'll Understand It Better By and By" did not explain the world's problems, but they did promise eventual release from them. Tindley, the great black gospel composer from earlier in the century, contributed several songs such as "Stand By Me" and "Leave It There" that seemed peculiarly suited to the needs of poor or oppressed people. They entered the white gospel hymnals in the 1930s, along with those of the younger black writer Thomas A. Dorsey, whose 1932 composition "Precious

Lord, Take My Hand" was destined to become the cherished possession of whites and blacks alike. Oklahoma-born Albert E. Brumley,[11]
the most popular of the white gospel composers, found his first receptive audiences among rural southerners in the 1930s. His visions of
a caring, personal Savior and of an abundant, pastoral heaven where
old acquaintances would be renewed were images especially satisfying in a world of deprivation. Brumley's 1931 composition "I'll Fly
Away"—one of the most performed gospel songs in the world—entered
the repertories of country and gospel singers alike, and his nostalgic
songs, such as "Dreaming of a Little Cabin" and "Did You Ever Go
Sailing? (Down the River of Memories)" poignantly evoke recurrent
longings universal to his audience.

Some country songs expressed compassion for the victims of suffering but drew no social lesson and made no political statement about
them. Elton Britt's "New London Texas School Tragedy," recorded on
March 24, 1937, only six days after a gas explosion took the lives of over
295 students and teachers, exhibited great sympathy for the victims
and their families, but did not speculate about the possible negligence
that caused the disaster. Grady and Hazel Cole's "Tramp on the Street,"
first recorded by them in 1936, was based on a much older poem and
is one of the great pleas for Christian compassion found in country
music. The song's compelling lyrics make an analogy between "the
angel unaware" and the tramp on the street. Hobo songs, of course,
had appeared in country music since the 1920s, but usually as a facet
of the romantic idealization of rambling men. Jimmie Rodgers, on
the other hand, recorded two songs identifying with the misfortunes
of hoboes: "Hobo Bill's Last Ride," recorded in November 1929, and
"Hobo's Meditation," recorded in 1932. Both of them were very much
in the tradition of sentimental songs, but they probably profited, as
did "Tramp on the Street," from the heightened public awareness of
homeless, wandering men during the Depression. "Hobo's Meditation" refers to "tough cops and brakemen," yet, like "Hobo Bill's Last
Ride," places no blame on society and instead sees its subjects as part
of the natural flotsam and jetsam of life. To find statements of overt
political import dealing with hoboes or migratory workers, one has to
turn to the music of the Industrial Workers of the World, popularly
known as the Wobblies (who are outside the scope of this book), or to
the songs of Woody Guthrie.

Woodrow Wilson "Woody" Guthrie[12] occupies a unique position in

American country and folk music that makes him admittedly difficult to categorize. He began as a hillbilly singer with strong traditional roots and advanced to the position of America's most revered urban folksinger and writer. Born in Okemah, Oklahoma, in 1912, Woody absorbed a wide variety of folk songs and ballads from his parents and from the commercial hillbillies. Plagued by a restlessness that may have been accentuated by the family disease of Huntington's Chorea, Guthrie went out on his own rather early in life and traveled over much of the Southwest doing odd jobs. In Pampa, Texas, where he experienced the dust storms for the first time, he learned a few basic guitar chords from his uncle Jeff, one of the local deputy sheriffs. The two of them formed a hillbilly band and began entertaining at local functions in the Pampa area.

Guthrie's wanderlust led him in 1937 to California, where he became part of the horde of Okies who had already been thronging into the state. On July 19, he and his cousin Leon "Jack" Guthrie began singing on KFVD in Los Angeles; they were joined soon thereafter by a woman called "Lefty Lou" (Maxine Crissman) who often sang duets with Woody. At the beginning of his radio career, Guthrie was very much in the mold of the hillbilly singer. His guitar playing was a proudly admitted modification of that of Maybelle Carter, and his songs came from the Carter Family, Jimmie Rodgers, and other hillbilly singers. And when he wrote his own songs, they were invariably set to older melodies of commercial and noncommercial origin (for example, "Oklahoma Hills" follows the melody of "The Girl I Loved in Sunny Tennessee"; "The Philadelphia Lawyer" is set to the melody of "The Jealous Lover"; "This Land Is Your Land" is set to the melody of "Little Darling Pal of Mine"). Guthrie's hillbilly emphasis, however, was accompanied by a flowering of radicalism. He felt a strong emotional kinship with the homeless and often persecuted migratory workers, especially his fellow Okies, and he began to compose songs that expressed his sympathies as well as his anger at the system that caused their misfortunes. By the end of the 1930s, he had accumulated an extensive collection of original compositions dealing with the dust bowl refugees and other victims of social and economic persecution: "Talking Dust Bowl Blues," "I Ain't Got No Home in This World Anymore," "Pastures of Plenty," "Vigilante Man," and "Do-Re-Mi," a wonderfully sardonic song warning poor people about the perils of migrating to California. When Guthrie moved to New York in 1940, he was no longer simply a singer of hillbilly songs and would never again be identified as such (even though some of his songs, such as "Oklahoma Hills" and "Philadelphia Lawyer," remained permanent and beloved elements of the country repertory). The post-1940 Guthrie would always be known as a protest singer.

Migrant workers were not the only economically oppressed people chronicled in hillbilly songs. One of the richest, but as yet incompletely documented, bodies of industrial and protest songs on hillbilly records consists of those from the textile-mill villages of the southeastern Piedmont region. The existence of the textile factories—with their regimentation, long hours, low pay, and child labor—provides a grim refutation of the idea that the South has had no industrial tradition. The textile mills were brick-and-stone testimonials to those "New South" propagandists who sought to bring progress to the South by ending its economic colonial dependence on the North. They sought to "bring the factory to the field"—and to hire cheaper labor. The textile mills did bring progress to the South, and prosperity to some, but they also brought misery to many. Thousands of mountain and hill-country people willingly left their farms to seek the promise of a better life, only to find that they had merely traded rural deprivation for an industrial poverty that robbed them even of their dignity and independence. Kept close to economic penury, depressed by a burdensome regimentation, and ostracized by middle-class southerners who called them "lintheads" and "factory trash," the textile operatives found solace in old-time religion, protection through the trade-union movement, and comfort in their age-old tradition of ballad making.

The textile mills produced not only an important body of folk songs; they also spawned a high percentage of commercial country singers, a phenomenon that has been insufficiently explored.[13] While many of the textile songs of the period were performed by comparatively well-known entertainers such as the Dixon Brothers (of "Weave Room Blues" fame), some important songs were recorded by individuals who regrettably have had a much more obscure place in country music history. Two interesting protest items, "The Marion Massacre" (about the killing of unarmed strikers in North Carolina) and "The North Carolina Textile Strike," were recorded in October 1929 on the Paramount label by Frank Welling and John McGhee under the name of the Martin Brothers. Welling and McGhee were prolific recording entertainers from West Virginia who usually sang sentimental and religious material. Although both songs clearly expressed sympathy for the strikers, Ivan Tribe asserts that "the ultimate message is of the next world and the joys of Heaven."[14] Wilmer Watts's recording of "Cotton Mill Blues," on the other hand, contains no mixed messages: it is overtly class conscious when it notes that "uptown people call us trash." David McCarn, from Gaston County, North Carolina, similarly did not permit sentimental or religious trappings to cloud his picture of mill work. McCarn went to work in the mills when he was twelve years old, and while working in a series of factories (and somehow also finding enough time to roam around much of the United States) he developed a flair for writing topical songs. In 1930 and 1931 he recorded twelve songs for Victor, six of which deal directly with cotton mill conditions. These include "Poor Man, Rich Man," "Cotton Mill Colic," and the sardonic "Serves 'Em Fine," which poked fun at the mountaineers foolish enough to leave their placid homes for the material allure of the textile mills.

A rather extensive body of songs commented directly on the Depression or on the government's response to it. Uncle Dave Macon, always a perceptive and witty critic of the social scene, recorded a few songs that at least touched the borders of protest. Uncle Dave would no doubt have said "I told you so" when news of the stock market crash appeared. He had campaigned for Hoover's opponent in "Governor Al Smith," which significantly also called for the repeal of Prohibition. "All I've Got's Gone" described what had happened to people who lived beyond their means during the 1920s, and "All In Down and Out Blues" argues that for millions of Americans "Wall Street's propositions were not all roses."

Hoover's handling of the Bonus Bill for World War I veterans also received scathing criticism from hillbilly singers. Buddy Starcher, for example, went to Washington at the time of the 1932 Bonus March; he sang for the marchers and passed out broadsides containing two of his compositions, "Bonus Blues" and "Hoover Blues." Starcher's songs did not enjoy wide circulation, but another song inspired by the suffering of the marchers—"The Forgotten Soldier Boy"—was later recorded by the Monroe Brothers in 1937, and then reintroduced to a new generation of country fans by the Lilly Brothers in the 1960s.

Support for Franklin D. Roosevelt was hardly radical or surprising, given the state of the economy in 1932; therefore, the appearance of pro-FDR and pro–New Deal sentiments on hillbilly records is not at all remarkable. Slim Smith's "Breadline Blues" was partisanly political, castigating the "big-legged elephant" and advising listeners to "vote away those blues" in 1932. Fiddlin' John Carson probably spoke for most southern farmers when he sang "Hurrah for Roosevelt," who was doing all within his power to "bring the farmers through." Much of the political commentary of the period was personal in its preoccupation with Roosevelt, but songs also commented occasionally on New Deal legislation or agencies. Billy Cox, a West Virginia yodeling disciple of Jimmie Rodgers, was also acutely partisan in his Democratic sympathies. Well known for his performances of two of country music's great perennials, "Sparkling Brown Eyes" and "Filipino Baby," he also wrote "NRA Blues," which extolled the effort of one of the major New Deal agencies to alleviate unemployment and to improve working conditions. The Allen Brothers' "New Deal Blues" ardently supported the whole range of relief legislation, including the National Recovery Administration (NRA). Although one hears no overtly anti-Roosevelt sentiments expressed on hillbilly recordings, one does encounter an occasional doubt concerning some of the social movements of the time. Roy Acuff's "Old Age Pension Check," for example, poked good-natured fun at the Townsend Plan movement, the California crusade that lobbied for a monthly $200 pension for Americans above the age of sixty. The song described how "poor old grandma" would suddenly become like a frivolous sixteen-year-old when the monthly payments started rolling in. In the final analysis, Billy Cox probably summed up the feelings of most working-class southerners when, on November 28, 1936, only a few weeks after FDR's stunning reelection, he gleefully recorded "The Democratic Donkey Is in His Stall Again" and "Franklin Roosevelt's Back Again."

By the end of the 1930s, country music, in its myriad forms and impulses, had not only survived the ravages of hard times but had broadened its horizons and moved well beyond the boundaries of its original regional identity. The music, though, had changed substantially since it first took shape as an industry in the early 1920s. Even in the Southeast, where tradition was presumed to be most strongly cherished, novel styles and sounds had moved in alongside the older forms. And while the musicians of the Southeast and Deep South were perpetuating certain styles and modifying others, musical winds were blowing in from the Southwest—particularly from Texas—that would have far-reaching and dynamic effects upon the future course of the music.

CHAPTER 5

The Cowboy Image and the Growth of Western Music

The emergence of the western image in country music was probably inevitable. Long before the process of commercialization began, the cowboy had been the object of unparalleled romantic adulation and interest. Given the pejorative connotations that clung to farming and rural life, the adoption of cowboy clothing and western themes was a logical step for the country singer.

The increased emphasis on western themes and attitudes appeared unsurprisingly in the westernmost southern states—Louisiana, Oklahoma, Texas—and in California. In these areas, country music assumed forms differing from those in the more easterly southern states. Oklahoma, Louisiana, and Texas, although southern in traditional orientation, embodied significantly different elements. All three were touched by the oil boom of the early twentieth century, and each possessed population groups that stood apart culturally while simultaneously influencing the dominant "Anglo" element of the state. Oklahoma and Texas were settled, for the most part, by former residents of the older southern states, who had brought with them their values, traditions, and institutions. Louisiana, on the other hand, can be perceived as a land of at least three great cultures: a Roman Catholic, "Latin" culture in the South; an "Anglo," Protestant culture in the north; and an African American culture whose influence could be felt

Floyd Tillman. Bill Malone personal collection; courtesy of Floyd Tillman.

throughout the state. Immigrants brought slaves and the cotton culture to all parts of the Southwest, making Texas and Louisiana parts of the southern economic and political orbit. They also transported their evangelical Protestantism to southwestern soil and brought with them many features of their folk heritage. Some of the old British ballads survived the westward migration, although they had lost many of their former characteristics. In some Texas communities, such as those found in the Big Thicket, a heavily forested area in the eastern part of the state, old ballads and old styles of singing endured well into the twentieth century.[1] Many of the East Texas communities were, and remain, replicas of the older southern environment. And, in many of them, folk traditions died slowly.

Texas folk music, then, was basically southern derived. Texas rural musicians used instruments common to the rest of the South, sang in styles similar to those of other rural southerners, frequently attended house parties where old-time fiddlers held sway, and learned to read music at the shape-note singing schools. But despite its close cultural affiliation with the South, Texas had a culture all its own—a culture produced by the mingling of diverse ethnic strains: southern "Anglo," black, German and Central European (especially prevalent throughout the southern part of the state), Mexican, and Louisiana Cajun (in the area extending from Beaumont to Houston). A passion for dancing was common among all these groups, and in this heterogeneous society, musical styles and songs flowed freely from one group to another, modifying the old southern rural styles. While rural music was prevalent and pervasive, it differed substantially from that produced in the Southeast or in the Deep South.

The discovery of oil at Spindletop, near Beaumont, in 1901 was the first of a series of finds in southeastern Texas, southwestern Louisiana, Oklahoma, and Arkansas in the years extending up through World War I. The discovery of the great East Texas oil field in the early 1930s, along with the rapid industrialization that began during World War II, further set Texas apart from the other southern states. While these factors contributed to Texas's uniqueness, they are probably less important than the fact that it was also part of the West. In fact, to most Americans, Texas was and *is* the West. And this West was a glorious land peopled by cowboys.

The romantic concept of the West, shared by most Americans, has a history virtually as old as the nation itself. James Fenimore Cooper's early novels describing the restorative qualities of the frontier were not substantially different, nor less romantic, than the themes emphasized later in Bret Harte's stories, in the western "dime novels," or in such books as Owen Wister's *The Virginian*. Thus, the cowboy and the West had been bathed in romance long before Hollywood and the television industry began their exploitations of the theme. The American people also had long demonstrated a general interest in the songs of the cowboy—beginning with Nathan Howard Thorp's *Songs of the Cowboys*, 1908, and John A. Lomax's *Cowboy Songs and Other Frontier Ballads*, 1910 (as a matter of fact, as early as 1907, when "San Antonio" appeared, Tin Pan Alley tunesmiths had experimented with "cowboy" themes). Although a few concert-musicians such as Oscar Fox (from Burnet, Texas) and David Guion (from Ballinger, Texas) made classical arrangements of a few cowboy songs, the western theme did not make any significant impact on American music until the 1930s. Guion's version of "Home on the Range," first performed in 1930 in a New York play called "Prairie Echoes," became the most popular arrangement of the song and was said, perhaps apocryphally, to be President Franklin Roosevelt's favorite song. Such songs became so widely circulated in the 1930s that even Tin Pan Alley reverberated with the melodies of the range. The farther Americans became removed from the cowboy past, the more intense became their interest in cowboy songs and lore. Hillbilly singers and musicians did much to implant the romantic cowboy image in the minds of their American audiences.

Before the 1930s, a few musicians recorded songs that genuinely reflected the cowboy heritage. The concert singer Bentley Ball—who did many programs of patriotic and traditional songs, many of them in colleges—recorded "The Dying Cowboy" and "Jesse James" for Columbia in 1919.[2] Charles Nabell, in November 1924, recorded some cowboy songs for Okeh, along with other types of traditional material. Several of the early cowboy singers came from Texas, and their songs, for the most part, reflected genuine cowboy experience. Carl Sprague, for example, may have done most to generate an immediate interest in the recorded songs of the cowboy. He grew up on a South Texas ranch near Alvin where he learned many of the songs (most of them from his cowboy uncle) that he later recorded for Victor. His 1925 recordings of cowboy songs—topped off by the immensely popular "When the Work's All Done This Fall"—mark him as one of America's first singing cowboys. While attending Texas A&M, Vernon Dalhart's success as a singer of traditional songs convinced Sprague that a similar market for cowboy singers might exist. He traveled to New York and had a successful audition with Victor Records; his earliest recordings had a sound very similar to that of Dalhart, including guitar and studio violin. Singing, however, was never more than a hobby with Sprague, and aside from his recordings, he made few commercial appearances. For many years he was on the coaching

*Carl T. Sprague.
Bill Malone
personal collec-
tion; courtesy of
Carl Sprague.*

staff at Texas A&M, and, in addition, he attained the rank of major in the United States Army.

Jules Verne Allen, on the other hand, had actually experienced the rugged life of a working cowboy before he embarked on his career as a radio singer. Born in Waxahachie, Texas, Allen began working cattle in Jack County, west of Fort Worth, at the age of ten. From 1893 to 1907 he worked as a rough string rider and bronco buster from the Rio Grande to the Montana line. Unlike Sprague, he used cowboy music as the basis for a professional career. During the 1920s and 1930s, Allen sang over numerous radio stations, including WOAI in San Antonio, where he performed as "Longhorn Luke." Like most of the pioneer recording performers of the 1920s, Allen and Sprague drew most of their material from turn-of-the-century cowboy life, although some of their songs were learned directly from the Lomax collection.

Other cowboy singers of the early commercial period varied widely in the amount of actual range experience they possessed. The Cartwright Brothers (Bernard and Jack) grew up in Boerne, Texas, directly on the route of "the long drive" that proceeded on to Kansas. Essentially a fiddle band, the Cartwrights performed a variety of songs. Their version of "Texas Rangers," however—marked by Bernard's haunting fiddle—is one of the greatest performances of a cowboy song heard on early commercial records. Carmen William "Curley" Fletcher, from California, was a rodeo performer and itinerant hawker of songs long before he made any commercial recordings. His greatest claim to fame came through his writing in 1915 of the poem that became the basis for "The Strawberry Roan," which he sold on broadside sheets. The song became one of the most popular western numbers, performed usually with a chorus added by the California radio singers Fred Howard and Nat Vincent. At least a couple of the pioneer cowboy singers, Goebel Reeves and Harry McClintock, were southerners whose wanderlust drew them west, where they worked at a wide variety of occupations. Both men, for example, spent some time in the famous radical labor union the Industrial Workers of the World (IWW, or Wobblies).

Our knowledge of the otherwise shadowy figure of Goebel Reeves comes from the pioneering research done by Fred Hoeptner. Known as "the Texas Drifter," Reeves was born in Sherman, Texas, in 1899. Before his death in California in 1959, he had enjoyed a varied career that led him across the United States and around the world. Although he came from a respectable middle-class family (his father served in the Texas legislature), Reeves deliberately chose the life of a hobo. During the course of his wanderings, he enlisted in the army, saw front-line service in World War I, worked as a merchant seaman, became active in the IWW, toured the vaudeville circuit, performed on radio, and recorded under several names for such companies as Okeh and Brunswick. In his recording career as a singer and yodeler—he claimed to have taught Jimmie Rodgers the yodeling style in the early 1920s while living in New Orleans—Reeves introduced some of the most interesting examples of both cowboy and hobo songs found in American music. These included the well-known "Hobo's Lullaby" (which he claimed to have written), "The Hobo and the Cop," "Railroad Boomer," and the cowboy songs "Bright Sherman Valley" and "The Cowboy's Prayer."

Harry McClintock was as well traveled as Reeves, having also been a merchant seaman, a soldier, and a hobo. Born in Knoxville, Tennessee, he roamed widely throughout the United States and became a member of the IWW in the early twentieth century. Because of his musical talents, McClintock was a welcome addition to the Wobblies, who had a well-known fondness for singing and whose *Little Red Songbook* became virtually the bible for labor/protest singers in America. McClintock's claim that he wrote "Hallelujah, I'm a Bum" and "Big Rock Candy Mountain," two of the world's most famous hobo songs, has never been seriously challenged. Once he settled down from his wanderings, McClintock began a career as a radio cowboy singer as early as 1925 on KFRC in San Francisco. "Haywire Mac," as he was often called, also recorded for Victor from 1927 to 1931. Along with superbly performed cowboy songs such as "Sam Bass," "Jesse James," and "Texas Rangers," McClintock's labor songs make him one of the important progenitors of western music.

John White and Otto Gray contributed to the shaping of western music by presenting it widely to a national audience. White was an unlikely "westerner," hailing from Washington, DC. However, he was the first person to introduce cowboy songs on radio to a New York audience (on NBC from 1927 to 1936). He also recorded cowboy songs, as well as hillbilly material, from 1929 to 1931, under several pseudonyms including "the Lonesome Cowboy." White specialized in the history of cowboy songs, and over the years he did more than any other person to describe the origins of the ballads, and he dispelled much of the romantic claptrap that had gathered around them.

Otto Gray, a prosperous rancher from near Stillwater, Oklahoma, pioneered in the commercialization of cowboy music. In about 1923, he assumed the leadership of a string band that earlier had been composed of real cowboys—the McGinty Cowboys (named for Billy McGinty, an Oklahoma rodeo performer). Gray's group had the distinction of being one of the few country groups publicized in *Billboard,* although Gray paid for most of the advertising. From 1928 to 1932, Gray and his Oklahoma Cowboys made a tour of radio stations throughout the country and performed on the northeastern RKO vaudeville circuit. Momie Gray (Otto's wife) was the featured singer of the organization, specializing in sentimental songs. The Oklahoma Cowboys were a highly professional group that possessed most of the characteristics of slick show-business organizations. A special publicity man traveled in advance of the group, and appearances on radio stations provided further exposure. Two agencies, the Weber-Simon Agency in New York and the William Jacobs Agency in Chicago, handled the group's RKO bookings. The Gray performers, dressed in plain, western-style clothing, traveled in Gray's $20,000 custom-built automobile, which was wired for sound reproduction and had a radio receiver and transmitter.

If Otto Gray contributed significantly to the commercialization of "western" music, Jimmie Rodgers played an equally important role in fusing it with country music. As discussed earlier, Rodgers spent the last few years of his life in Texas and conducted many of his most successful tours there. He took great pride in the Texas heritage and the romantic cowboy past. The modern concepts of the "singing cowboy" and of "western" music may very well date back directly to Rodgers.

Scores of singers who modeled themselves after Jimmie Rodgers emerged in the 1930s, and most of them gave themselves "cowboy" titles and dressed in western attire. Young Hank Snow, for example, in far-off Nova Scotia, dressed in cowboy regalia and called himself "the Yodeling Ranger." In even more remote Australia, Robert William Lane performed under the name of Tex Morton, described himself as "the Boundary Rider," and sang cowboy songs with a bizarre, trilling yodel about both the Australian bush and the Texas Plains. Others, like Ernest Tubb, included few cowboy songs in their repertories but wore cowboy boots and ten-gallon hats. Since the western attraction was irresistible, even young hillbilly singers from the Deep South or from the southeastern mountains, whose associations with cowboys came only through story and song, embraced the western image and imagined themselves "way out west in Texas for the roundup in the spring."

Perhaps because of Rodgers's close association with Texas, many of the successful Texas hillbilly performers—Ernest Tubb, Lefty Frizzell, Floyd Tillman, Bob Wills, Tommy Duncan—credited Jimmie Rodgers as their inspiration. One of the most important of these individuals, and the one who completed the "romantic westernizing" process begun by Rodgers, was Orvon Gene Autry.[3] Autry owed most of his initial success to the fact that he could perform Rodgers's repertory in Rodgers's yodeling style. Autry was born on a horse farm near Tioga, Texas, on September 29, 1907, but moved to Oklahoma with his parents while in his teens. Although his father was a horse trader, one finds that Gene experienced little of the cattle ranch life that his promotional material later stressed. At any rate, he left the "ranching" life as quickly as he could, working as a railroad telegrapher and singing at every opportunity.

According to a much-repeated story, confirmed by Autry himself, Will Rogers inspired his decision to become a professional musician. One day in 1927 the great humorist came to Chelsea, Oklahoma, where Autry was working as a telegrapher for the St. Louis and Frisco Railroad, heard the young man singing and strumming his guitar, and strongly encouraged him to go to New York and become a professional. Autry's first trip to the big city in 1927 was unsuccessful, but he returned to Tulsa and got a job on KVOO as "the Oklahoma Yodeling Cowboy." Returning to New York in 1929, he made his first records for Victor, accompanied by the Marvin Brothers, Johnny and Frankie. In December of the same year, Autry began a crucial association with Arthur Satherley, who recorded him for the American Record Company (ARC), producer of records for chain stores and for Sears. It was through the association with the Sears Conqueror label that Autry made it to WLS and the *National Barn Dance*.

In Chicago after 1931, Autry was an immediate success. His appearances on the *Barn Dance* and on his own radio program, *Conqueror Record Time*, made him one of the most popular performers in WLS history. His records, released on Sears labels, were those most prominently displayed in the Sears-Roebuck catalogue. As a result of his growing popularity, a number of Gene Autry songbooks and guitar instruction books began to appear in the early 1930s. An ad for a Gene Autry "Roundup" Guitar, priced at $9.95, reminded the reader that

Gene Autry. Courtesy of Gene Autry Entertainment and Holly-George Warren.

Autry had become a famous performer "simply because he learned to play a guitar while on the ranch."[4] Autry's promotional mentors, Art Satherley and Ann Williams of the WLS production staff, capitalized on the "western" motif and advertised him as a singing cowboy long before the bulk of his recorded repertory came to include western numbers.

In his early years as a professional singer, and on through the WLS period from 1931 to 1934, Autry remained a hillbilly singer, only rarely singing anything of a western variety. In both song selection and in style of performance, he revealed his indebtedness to the southern rural tradition. His Jimmie Rodgers imitations were among the best in country music, and his own "compositions" (written or cowritten with people like Jimmie Long) included such songs as "A Gangster's Warning," "A Hillbilly Wedding in June," "Gosh, I Miss You All the Time," and "My Old Pal of Yesterday." In 1931, he recorded one of the biggest-selling hits in hillbilly music's then-short history, "That Silver Haired Daddy of Mine," recorded as a duet with the song's co-composer, Jimmie Long. Autry's many and varied recorded selections even included at least one labor song: "The Death of Mother Jones," recorded on at least seven labels, which applauded the life of the famous and radical labor leader. While the song seemed rather remote from the type one would expect from a cowboy singer, it nevertheless reflected the passion for social and economic justice that many people felt during these Depression years.

Autry's success on the Chicago radio stations and on record labels gained him in 1934 the position that made him the best-known cowboy in the United States and one of the most famous hillbilly singers. In that year, he arrived in Hollywood and began his career as the "Nation's Number One Singing Cowboy." Beginning with a small part in Ken Maynard's *In Old Santa Fe*, he then starred for thirteen episodes in a strange cowboy/science-fiction serial called *The Phantom Empire*. Autry went on to a featured role in 1935 in *Tumbling Tumbleweeds*, a film that also included his old sidekick from Chicago days, Lester Alvin "Smiley" Burnette. In the following decades, he made more than ninety movies for Republic, Columbia, and Mascot, eighty-one of which included the multitalented Burnette, who usually played a bumbling character, Frog Millhouse. While becoming one of the most popular and wealthy actors in Hollywood, Autry also created the stereotype of the heroic cowboy who was equally adept with gun and guitar. Autry was not the first individual to sing in a western movie—Ken Maynard had done so as early as 1930—but he was the first to institutionalize the phenomenon. With Autry ensconced as a singing movie cowboy, hillbilly music now had a new medium through which to popularize itself. The silver screen further romanticized the cowboy and helped shape the public idea of western music.

After signing his Hollywood contract, Autry made a radical shift in his repertory from "country" themes to "western" motifs. Instead of singing songs about the mountains, he came increasingly to perform songs with such titles as "Ridin' Down the Canyon," "The Round-up in Cheyenne," and "Empty Cot in the Bunkhouse." Both in Autry's singing and in the instrumentation that accompanied him, one hears a distinctly measurable change in the records he made from 1929 to 1939. As the one-time hillbilly singer reached out to a larger audience, he smoothed out his presentation of material with a lower vocal pitch, well-rounded tones, and honey-coated articulation. Instrumentally, Autry's sound exhibited a similar evolution, particularly after the violinist Carl Cotner became his musical director. Soft guitars, muted violins, a melodious but unobtrusive steel guitar, an accordion, and occasionally even horns could be heard as background instrumentation, as he and his directors sought a sound that would give no offense to America's broad urban middle class. Whatever vocal sound was featured, however, Autry demonstrated a mastery of it. No country singer has ever shown more versatility.

Autry's popularity inspired other movie companies to present their own versions of the singing cowboy. In searching for likely candidates, the companies usually delved into the ranks of country music, acquiring acts that had already established themselves on hillbilly radio shows or on record labels. Following Smiley Burnette, the Light Crust Doughboys became the first country group to join Autry in a movie (*Oh, Susanna!*). Some Autry sidemen went on to become important entertainment personalities in their own right. Johnny Bond, Jimmy Wakely, and Dick Reinhart, for example, came to Hollywood in 1940 (as the Jimmy Wakely Trio) and joined Autry's *Melody Ranch* radio show in September of that year. Reinhart became one of the early exponents of the honky-tonk style, with songs like "Fort Worth Jail" and "Truck Driver's Coffee Stop." Wakely eventually starred in many movies of his own, became one of country music's smoothest singers, and made several seminal recordings, such as "One Has My Name (The Other Has My Heart)" (one of the first successful "cheating" songs in country music). Bond remained on the *Melody Ranch* program until it ended in 1956, playing the role of a comic sidekick and opening the show each Sunday with the bass guitar run introduction to "Back in the Saddle Again." Bond also became one of country music's greatest songwriters, creating such songs as "Cimarron" (a song about a southwestern river, and performed by all western groups), "I'll Step Aside," "Old Love Letters," and "I Wonder Where You Are Tonight" (now a standard in both bluegrass and mainstream country music).

A long line of hillbilly singers made only occasional appearances in western movies, usually as supporting actors for such leading cowboy stars as Charles Starrett and Johnny Mack Brown. The Sons of the Pioneers appeared in numerous movies, while Bob Wills and his Texas Playboys were in about eight. A few singers, such as Ernest Tubb, Jimmie Davis, and Bill Callahan, made only rare appearances.

Other singers, however, became leading men and posed at least modest challenges to Autry's dominance. Atlanta-born Ray Whitley, the writer of "Back in the Saddle Again" and the designer of one of country music's most popular guitars, the Gibson SJ-200, became a movie star in 1936 after an earlier successful career in New York as a cowboy singer. Tex Ritter also began his movie career in 1936, and, in the fifty-six movies that he eventually made, he became the most believable of all the singing cowboys. The most successful challenge to Autry, though, came from Roy Rogers, who signed with Republic in 1937. His visibility in American public life would last, because of television, well into the 1960s. The singing cowboy genre also persisted in American movies on into the 1950s, with Arizona-born Rex Allen being its chief exponent after 1949. In many ways, this last singing cowboy was the best singer of them all. Allen's rich voice ranged from a deep bass to a sweeping tenor—a sound that almost no other country singer could equal.

Largely as a result of Hollywood exploitation, the concept of "western music" became fixed in the public mind. After the heyday of Gene Autry, the term "western" came to be applied even to southern rural music by an increasing number of people, especially by those who were ashamed to use the pejorative term "hillbilly." Not only did the public accept the projection, but even most hillbilly singers became fascinated with the western image and eventually came to believe their own symbols. Autry was the first of a long line of country singers who clothed themselves in tailored cowboy attire; in the following decades, the costuming became increasingly elaborate and gaudy, with the brightly colored, bespangled, and rhinestone-laden uniforms created by Nudie the Tailor (Nudie Cohn, born Nuta Kotlyarenko in the Ukraine in 1902) in Los Angeles being the most favored fare. Eventually, most country performers, whether they hailed from Virginia or Mississippi, adopted cowboy regalia—usually of the gaudy, dude cowboy variety.

Along with the clothing, country bands and singers—particularly in the Southwest and on the West Coast—adopted cowboy titles. Singers with names like Tex, Slim, Hank, Red River Dave, the Utah Cowboy, and Patsy Montana, and groups with such titles as the Cowboy Ramblers, Riders of the Purple Sage, Radio Cowboys, Swift Jewel Cowboys, Lone Star Cowboys, and Girls of the Golden West (Dolly and Millie Good) abounded on radio stations (and record labels) all over the nation. Radio and record promoters, of course, were very much alive to the appeal of the western myth, and they often encouraged musicians to adopt appropriate western monikers. Millie and Dolly Good, for example, were farm girls from Illinois who sang and yodeled in sweet, close harmony. Their agent advised them to dress like cowgirls, gave them the romantic title Girls of the Golden West, and then, after scanning the map of western Texas, attached to their promotional literature the statement that they were born in Muleshoe, Texas. The Girls very carefully preserved this fiction to the end of their performing career.

Patsy Montana's career was similarly shaped by romantic conceptions of the West. She was a singer and a fiddler from Arkansas named Rubye Blevins, but on the West Coast in the early 1930s, Stuart Hamblen renamed her Patsy Montana, and she thereafter cultivated the performing image of the cowgirl. Although much of her career saw her appearing as a "girl singer" with such groups as the Prairie Ramblers, Patsy made dramatic history in 1935 when "I Want to Be a Cowboy's Sweetheart" became the first huge hit by a woman country singer and a virtuoso yodeling piece that still influences the style of women singers (Austin country-rock singer Marcia Ball, for example, made the song and yodel standard parts of her repertory in the late 1970s).

Many of the "western" entertainers performed cowboy songs, usually highly romanticized, but more often their titles and attire were the only ties they had with the "West." Several musicians, however, stayed rather close to the cowboy repertory. Some of them had been performing long before Gene Autry achieved Hollywood fame, and many of them, such as "Haywire Mac" McClintock and the Crockett Family (John H. "Dad" Crockett and his five sons, originally from West Virginia), had performed on California radio stations since at least 1925. Other early California groups included Len Nash and his

The Girls of the Golden West: Dolly (left) and Millie (right) Good.
Bill Malone personal collection; courtesy of Bob Pinson.

Original Country Boys, broadcasting from KFWB, Hollywood, as early as March 1926; Sheriff Loyal Underwood's Arizona Wranglers; Charlie Marshall and his Mavericks; and perhaps the most important (and certainly the most interesting), the Beverly Hillbillies.

The Beverly Hillbillies were the brainchild of Glen Rice, station

The Prairie Ramblers: left to right, *"Happy" Jack Taylor, Charles "Chuck" Hurt,*
Shelby "Tex" Atchison, Floyd "Salty" Holmes—and Patsy Montana (center).
Bill Malone personal collection; courtesy of George Biggar.

manager at KMPC in Los Angeles. Reversing the trend toward adoption of western names during the 1930s, Rice used the eastern moniker Hillbillies for the group of western musicians that he assembled
around the accordion player Leo Mannes (renamed Zeke Manners)
and conducted a ballyhoo campaign alleging that a group of strange
and primitive musicians had been unearthed in the hills of Beverly.
The band made its debut on KMPC on April 6, 1930, and remained a
popular feature throughout the decade. Over the years the Hillbillies
included several fine musicians, such as Manners, who had no background in country music but had been attracted to California because
of the lure of Hollywood. A few Hillbillies were genuine country boys,
such as the sky-high yodeler Elton Britt (James Britt Baker), who came
from Arkansas in 1930, and Stuart Hamblen, who came from Texas in
the same year. Britt went on to become one of country music's most
gifted yodelers (virtually the last of that once-hardy breed) and a leading soloist during the 1940s. Hamblen, the son of a Methodist minister
in Abilene, Texas, was a fixture on West Coast radio from 1930 to the

1950s. He hosted his own shows in Hollywood after 1931, boosted the careers of other performers, wrote many of the most successful songs of the decade (including "My Mary," "Texas Plains," "Golden River," and "My Brown-Eyed Texas Rose"), was the first country performer signed by Decca in 1934, and became sufficiently known to become a candidate for Congress in 1938.

The western group that ultimately became the most famous, and the most frequently emulated, was the Sons of the Pioneers. They sang virtually every type of country song and even ventured into popular music, but the majority of their melodies dealt with western themes. Perhaps more than any other group, they preserved a western repertory and exploited the romantic cowboy image. More "western" stylistically than any other group, they were among the least western in terms of origin. Bob Nolan (Robert Clarence Nobles) was born in New Brunswick, Canada, but he moved with his parents to Tucson at the age of fourteen. In Tucson he found himself fascinated with the desert, a feeling that never left him and eventually inspired some of country music's greatest songs, such as "Cool Water," "Tumbling Tumbleweeds," and "At the Rainbow's End." Tim Spencer, also an outstanding songwriter, was born in Missouri but grew up in Oklahoma, Texas, and New Mexico. Roy Rogers came from southern Ohio.

The three musicians came to California in the early 1930s and soon fell into a pattern common to most country singers during the decade, moving from group to group before they formed their own organization. Roy Rogers, the prime organizer of the trio, was born Leonard Slye in Cincinnati, on November 5, 1911,[5] but grew up on a small farm near Portsmouth, in southern Ohio. Here he garnered his earliest musical training from his Kentucky-born mother and his mandolin-and-guitar-playing father. In 1931 he and his father moved to Tulare, California, and worked as migratory fruit pickers. In the following three years, beginning with a duo called the Slye Brothers (Leonard and a cousin), he worked with several western-style groups until the Pioneer Trio was formed in 1933. Renamed the Sons of the Pioneers the following year, the trio soon became noted for their smooth, inventive harmonies and yodeling, and for the finely crafted songs that Nolan and Spencer created. They became so famous for their harmony that their instrumental accompaniment is often forgotten. Two extraordinarily talented brothers from Llano, Texas, Hugh and Karl Farr, joined them in 1934 and 1935. The Farrs were jazz-influenced country musicians whose progressive styles were sometimes obscured by the vocal emphasis of the Pioneers. Hugh Farr, who also sang a low-down bass with the group, was one of the hottest fiddlers of the period, and his brother, Karl, was a master of both the rhythm and single-string styles of guitar.

The Pioneers won extensive popularity on the West Coast with an early-morning radio program on KFWB in Hollywood, but 1936 proved to be their banner year. By this time their radio transcriptions were being widely circulated, and the group became a featured act, along with Will Rogers, at the Texas Centennial in Dallas. Leonard Slye left the group in 1937 after signing a movie contract with Republic Studios. At this point he changed his name, first to Dick Weston, and later to Roy Rogers. His performances after this time were made on an individual basis, and he eventually rivaled Gene Autry as America's most popular singing cowboy (Rogers was also one of country music's finest yodelers). He was replaced in the Sons of the Pioneers by Lloyd Perryman from Ruth, Arkansas, whose natural tenor was the first the group had ever had, and who gave them an even closer harmony than they had earlier possessed. The Sons of the Pioneers underwent numerous personnel changes after 1937 but have never disbanded. Their songs moved into the repertories of country singers everywhere, and their style of harmony was widely copied, most effectively by Foy Willing (originally Willingham) and the Riders of the Purple Sage, who appeared with Monte Hale and Roy Rogers in Republic Pictures from 1942 to 1952.

The flourishing singing cowboy industry inspired the emergence of songwriters, including two of country music's finest—Fred Rose and Cindy Walker—who made their debuts as country composers in the 1940s when they wrote songs for movies (Rose for Autry, Walker for Bob Wills). The interest in western music in the 1930s, however, was not confined to country performers and their supporters. Writers from Tin Pan Alley also reacted to the western craze, and the entire nation was soon humming western-style tunes such as "Gold Mine in the Sky," "There's a Home in Wyoming," and "I'm an Old Cowhand." Some of these tunes were written by easterners who had never been near a cow, but the Happy Chappies at least lived in California in the midst of the Hollywood industry. The Chappies were a pop-singing duo named Nat Vincent and Fred Howard who wrote or arranged such songs as "When the Bloom Is on the Sage," "Mellow Mountain Moon,"

"My Pretty Quadroon," and "Strawberry Roan" (the last a musical adaptation of Curley Fletcher's earlier poem). The most successful of the western-oriented popular songwriters was a Bostonian, William J. (Billy) Hill. Hill's birth and musical training gave no indication of his future success as a western songwriter. Born in Boston in 1899, he studied violin at the New England Conservatory of Music and performed for a short time with the Boston Symphony Orchestra. In 1916 he traveled west, riding the rails and working at odd jobs until he had seen most of the western states. He returned to New York in the late 1920s after becoming thoroughly acquainted with western life—including everything from camp cooking to cowpunching. In New York he worked as a doorman at a fashionable hotel and composed songs occasionally. Over the years his compositions ranged from popular melodies like "The Glory of Love" to hillbilly songs like "They Cut Down the Old Pine Tree" and "The Old Spinning Wheel." His chief success, however, came with western-style songs like "Call of the Canyon," which were distinguished for their beautiful melodies and for rhythms that suggested the gait of a horse. He experienced his most spectacular success in 1933 with "The Last Roundup," the song that really awakened the general public to the romantic West while becoming the most popular tune in the country. Performed by both hillbilly and popular groups, its appeal may have stimulated a greater interest in the more "authentic" country and western material and ensured a greater national following for country music.

Most of the western bands in California and the Southwest used Billy Hill's material, but his New York songwriting ventures were directed primarily at big-city popular-music audiences. Although country music has always encountered its coolest reception in the Northeast, particularly in the city of New York, country-style entertainers have always achieved some prominence there on local radio stations. Ethel Park Richardson, for example, did much to educate New Yorkers about the beauties of folk culture between 1933 and 1935 with her weekly dramatizations on WOR and the NBC Network. Each week she was assisted by such singers as Frank Luther, Carson Robison, and Tex Ritter as she dramatized a famous folk song. Luther and Robison had been in New York since the 1920s, but Ritter was one of several cowboy singers who kept New Yorkers range conscious during the mid-1930s. Others included Texas Jim Robertson, a deep-bass singer from Batesville, Texas; Zeke Manners and Elton Britt, who had moved from California; Dwight Butcher, a Jimmie Rodgers disciple from Tennessee; Ray Whitley, who sang regularly at the Stork Club and on WMCA; and Wilf Carter, the Nova Scotia yodeler who performed over CBS as Montana Slim.

The most singular of all the cowboy singers in New York, however, was Woodward Maurice "Tex" Ritter. Born in Murvaul, in deep East Texas, January 12, 1905, Ritter grew up far removed from the scene of much cowboy activity. He attended the University of Texas for five years (singing in the university glee club under the direction of Oscar Fox) and then went to Northwestern Law School for one year. Throughout his youth he had collected western and mountain songs, and therefore had a storehouse of interesting songs when he began singing on KPRC in Houston in 1929. In 1930, he joined a musical troupe on a series of one-night stands through the South and Midwest. By 1931, he had gone to New York, where he joined the Theatre Guild and began his acting career with a featured role in *Green Grow the Lilacs* (a short-lived play that eventually became the basis for the musical *Oklahoma*). With his thick Texas accent and storehouse of cowboy lore, Ritter quickly emerged as a New York sensation. He became greatly in demand for lecture recitals in eastern colleges on the cowboy and his song. During the fall of 1932, he was the featured singer with the Madison Square Garden Rodeo and from there went on to a recording contract with ARC and a program slot on WOR entitled *The Lone Star Rangers*, one of the first western radio shows ever featured in New York City. From 1932 to 1936, he appeared on other New York stations, including the *WHN Barn Dance*, where he acted as cohost with Ray Whitley. Then, inevitably, in 1936, he made the first of several movies, *Song of the Gringo*. Ritter, however, was not a cowboy, but was instead a very believable interpreter of cowboy songs. Impressionable easterners were easily convinced that he came, not from a small East Texas community and a college background, but from a working cattle ranch. And Tex very skillfully lived up to the part.

Tex Ritter's exploitation of the western theme was typical of what was happening all over the United States in the mid-1930s. From New York to California, individuals responded to the western myth, and "cowboy" singers and groups sprang up in all sorts of unusual places. "Western" became a rival and often preferred term to "hillbilly" as a proper appellation for country music. It is easy to understand, of course, why "western" would be preferred to the seemingly disreputable backwoods term. "Western," specifically, suggested a music that had been developed by cowboys out on the Texas Plains or in the High Sierras; more generally, it suggested a context that was open, free, and expansive. In short, the term fit the American self-concept.

In reality, except for the fabric of usable symbols that surrounded him, the cowboy contributed virtually nothing to American music. As we've already explored, the "western" music that became fashionable in the mid-1930s, ironically, came from other sources, mostly from Hollywood and New York City. A modification or imitation of older southern rural styles, it was a fusion of the southwestern cultural heritage and of the new social and economic forces that were developing in the region. In the Southwest, the country musician could borrow from an abundance of musical influences. Some, of course, were also available to musicians in the Southeast: southern traditional and gospel music, popular music, commercial recordings of all kinds (including blues and jazz), and, crucially, black music. Southwesterners could draw additionally on Mexican, Cajun, German, and what was generally described as "Bohemian" music (that is, the polka-derived styles of people who immigrated to south-central Texas from what is now Czechoslovakia). Young people who grew up in any of the several ethnic communities that extended from southwest Louisiana to the Texas Hill Country were torn between strong competing loyalties: the "Old Country" music of their parents (from France, Mexico, Germany, Poland, Bohemia), and the fashionable music that drifted in from the outside world. Consequently, musical styles became strongly intermeshed, and often in wonderfully exciting ways. Cajun musicians, for example, freely mixed their traditional forms with country, blues, and jazz, while over in South Texas it was not at all uncommon to find "western" bands composed of musicians with names like Fojtacek or Wolenski who played polkas, schottisches, hoedowns, and the latest country hits. Musicians who hoped to prosper playing for dances in the broad territory extending south, east, and west from Austin, Texas, learned quickly that they must be prepared to play anything from "Allá en el rancho grande" and "Herr Schmidt" to "Jole Blon" and "Cotton-Eyed Joe."

The career of Texas country-band leader Adolph Hofner (June 8, 1916–June 2, 2000) vividly illustrates the cross-cultural matrix that characterized the music of Texas. Hofner's paternal and maternal grandparents came from what is now Czechoslovakia to the area near

Praha, Texas (one of the oldest Czech communities in the United States). He could not speak English when he first went to school, and at home he had heard only "Bohemian" music, usually waltzes and polkas, played by his mother on the accordion, reinforced by the big community dances. Hofner played his parents' music to the end of his days, but as a teenager he was also attracted to Hawaiian music, and then later to the music of the western swing bands. Hofner's music always reflected the richly eclectic culture in which he matured. His band always played songs like "Dreamland Waltz" (a Bohemian tune learned from his mother), as well as "María Elena," "San Antonio Rose," "Cotton-Eyed Joe" (which he helped make famous in south-central Texas), and any other songs his dance-conscious audiences desired. Of course, when he ventured back home to play in one of the few surviving Czech community halls, his repertory became centered more strongly on the music of his youth.

While competing styles of music had filtered into Hofner's little home community, such forms did not become irresistible until his family moved to San Antonio in 1928. Soon after the repeal of Prohibition, he and his brother Emil began playing in local beer joints—a decisive act that was being emulated by thousands of other musicians throughout the South and West. The factors that contributed to the emergence of new forms and styles in country music were in evidence in much of America. It was in Texas, however, that conditions proved to be most fertile for new developments. Since the 1930s, Texas has spawned many of country music's most spectacular stars, and most of them received their basic musical training in a common school. This was a social institution, springing up in the chaotic ferment of the Depression and acutely attuned to the needs of rural dwellers: the honky-tonk.[6]

Saloons and taverns, of course, were not new to the American scene, nor was the relationship between drinking and music a recent thing. But they assumed a new significance in the 1930s. The Texas oil boom had put money in the pockets of a host of people who otherwise would have been destitute during the Depression years. Country musicians found receptive audiences in the oil communities, sometimes playing for nickels and dimes at root beer stands or in the wide-open taverns and dance halls where illegal liquor was consumed by oil workers. With the repeal of Prohibition in 1933, the taverns achieved a confirmed status. For a variety of reasons, these establishments usually lay on the outskirts of town. Tax rates were lower in such locations, police supervision was apt to be more lax, and the establishments were easily reached by both city and rural dwellers. In Texas, with some counties exercising their right of local option to be either "dry" or "wet," both county and state-line taverns emerged. These convenient locations could attract customers from both wet and dry areas. These out-of-the-way clubs were sometimes only small, dingy bars, but many contained dance floors. A few were large and elaborate dance halls that described themselves as "ballrooms" or "night clubs." All were emblazoned with neon lights. Whatever the size, they were generically described as "honky-tonks" by the plain people who frequented them. People went to the honky-tonks for the widest variety of reasons—as both occasional and habitual drinkers—but many working-class folk looked forward to the weekend when they could find relief from their daily jobs by moving from club to club, drinking, dancing, and socializing (this is still described as "honky-tonking").

Music proved indispensable to the honky-tonk's business. Musicians were sometimes hired, or permitted to play for tips, but the jukebox was more reliable. Led by the Wurlitzer Company, which introduced its ornate, gaudily painted model in 1928, the automatic coin-operated phonograph experienced heavy sales after 1934 when Prohibition repeal opened up thousands of beer halls and taverns that needed some kind of musical entertainment. The jukebox, so called because of its popularity in southern roadhouses called "juke joints," could be purchased for about $250 and originally played twelve records. Its popularity was further enhanced by the end of the 1930s, when remote control devices permitted song choices without leaving one's booth or stool. By 1940, more than 300,000 jukeboxes were in operation.

When country music entered the honky-honk, it had to change, both in lyrics and in style. The music's older pastoral or down-home emphasis could not survive in such an atmosphere. Songs about "poor old Mother at home" and "The Old Country Church" definitely seemed out of place in the honky-tonk environment. Instead, songs reflecting the problems and changing social status of the ex–rural dweller became paramount. With lyrics that seldom commented on work, honky-tonk songs instead often addressed family fragility, the insecurities of love, marriage dissolution, drinking, and having a good time. Many songs, beginning with Al Dexter's "Honky Tonk Blues" in 1937, commented on this new milieu in which country music thrived. "Stompin' at the Honky Tonk," "I Ain't Goin' Honky Tonkin' Anymore," "Honky Tonk Mama," "Driving Nails in My Coffin" ("every time I drink a bottle of booze"), and "Headin' Down the Wrong Highway" were just a few of the songs that commented on both the joyful and the depressing side of honky-tonk life. The songs inspired by the honky-tonk world were topical in that they spoke of experiences that were becoming increasingly common, but they were often far from realistic. Country musicians and fans generally sought *escape* from reality, and even the songs about "honky tonk mamas" avoided the realities of women's lives. Fundamentalist Protestant culture still undergirded the world of honky-tonk musicians, coloring the lyrics of even their drinking and cheating songs, with guilt and self-pity at the core of such early classic honky-tonk songs as "The Last Letter," "Born to Lose," and "It Makes No Difference Now."

Country music changed significantly within the honky-tonk, where laughter and merriment, the clinking of glasses, and the shuffling of dancing feet made it imperative that instrumentation change to accommodate the environment. Amid the din and revelry there had to be, for both the dancer and the passive listener, a steady and insistent beat that could be felt even if the lyrics could not be understood. The music became louder: "sock rhythm"—the playing of closed chords, or the striking of all six strings in unison in order to achieve a percussive effect—characterized honky-tonk rhythm playing; the string bass became a fixture in bands; pianos became more common; and in rare cases, drums were used. By the end of the 1930s, hillbilly bands were steadily adopting that bane of traditionalists, the electric guitar.

Honky-tonks of one variety or another became the hard but instructive "schools" in which hundreds of country musicians gained invaluable experience. The entertainer who worked there—and in the early days that might mean working with only a fiddle and a guitar—had to contend with competing noise, fights, and paltry income. The most violent phase of honky-tonk history probably came during the 1940s, when servicemen and defense workers began thronging into these good-time arenas, but even in the 1930s, the honky-tonks had already become what Glen Campbell called "the fightin' and dancin' clubs." In these "joints" musicians quite often had to be just as tough and brawling as the customer, and a smashed guitar might be the least hazard with which a physically endangered musician had to contend.

Most honky-tonk musicians lived obscure lives, working hard at day jobs and then spending much of the night playing music. A few were fortunate enough to receive a fixed salary; most received a percentage of the beer sales or whatever patrons were willing to drop into the tip box ("the kitty"). Very few musicians ever moved far outside the honky-tonk's perimeter. One singer who was lucky enough to move on ultimately became one of the most influential performers in modern country music: Ernest Tubb.[7] Tubb was born on a farm near Crisp, in Ellis County, Texas, in 1914, but lived in a succession of relatives' homes in various parts of Texas after his parents separated in 1926. At the age of fourteen he was inspired to become a country singer when he heard one of his sisters singing Jimmie Rodgers's "In the Jailhouse Now." He bought every Rodgers record that became available and tried to model his style completely after that of the Singing Brakeman. He practiced diligently for months trying to perfect a yodeling style. It was always Tubb's greatest regret that he did not meet his hero, although they lived in the same state (and in 1932 even in the same city, San Antonio!). After a short stay with another sister in West Texas, Tubb returned to San Antonio in 1933 (after Rodgers's death) and began making the rounds of the radio stations, willing to do shows free in order to gain the exposure. Eventually, KONO gave him fifteen minutes twice a week at 5:30 in the morning. He was singing and yodeling at this station and working full-time for the WPA and any other useful job he could find, when he met Carrie (Mrs. Jimmie) Rodgers. She did not think that Tubb sounded like her deceased husband, but she was strongly impressed with the young man's sincerity and devotion and took Tubb under her tutelage, lent him one of Jimmie's valuable guitars, helped him arrange a tour through South Texas, and used whatever influence she had to get him a recording contract with Victor. Two sessions with that company in 1936 and 1937 yielded eight releases (including two tribute songs to Rodgers) but no hits.

For almost five years, from 1936 until he recorded his first great Decca hit, "Walking the Floor over You," in 1941, Tubb struggled to make a breakthrough into the world of professional country music. He maintained that the removal of his tonsils in 1939 destroyed his ability to yodel. While Tubb was bitterly disappointed, the incident was probably a boon to his career; it forced him to abandon imitation in favor of his own unique style. During these years, Tubb roamed from San Antonio to Midland, Texas, and from there to Beaumont, San Angelo

Ernest Tubb. From the John Edwards Memorial Foundation Records,
Southern Folklife Collection, Louis Round Wilson Special Collections
Library, University of North Carolina at Chapel Hill.

(twice), Corpus Christi, and Fort Worth. He sang on radio stations, at
root beer and hamburger drive-ins, and in innumerable clubs. He even
operated his own honky-tonk in San Angelo, the E and E Tavern, for
several months in 1940. Tubb never managed to make music his full-
time profession until the fall of 1940, when he moved to Fort Worth
and commenced a six-day-a-week, fifteen-minute program on KGKO,
receiving a modest weekly salary for about a year.

Tubb's recording career with Decca began on April 3, 1940, under the direction of the veteran talent scout Dave Kapp; it did not end until 1975, when MCA (the new owner of the Decca label) began emphasizing its newer talent to the exclusion of the old-timers.[8] "Walking the Floor over You," released in the fall of 1941, demonstrated his popular appeal and won him his first sponsor: Universal Mills, the maker of Gold Chain Flour. As the Gold Chain Troubadour, Tubb made numerous personal appearances, singing from a stage built on the top of a white Plymouth automobile. After years of frustration, Tubb made a rather rapid ascent to stardom and, by the end of 1942, was appearing on the *Grand Ole Opry*, where he became the inspiration for thousands of young country singers all over the United States.

The evolution of Ernest Tubb's instrumental accompaniment is suggestive of what happened in country music as a whole during the late 1930s and early 1940s. In his earliest appearances, he accompanied himself, à la Jimmie Rodgers, on the guitar. Later, another musician joined him as lead guitarist, playing single-string passages while Tubb supplied a background rhythm. His earliest Decca recording session in 1940 featured a sound that always endured in his music, despite the gradual enlargement and electrification of his band in the following years. Jimmie Short, whom Tubb had first heard in San Angelo as part of the Short Brothers (Jimmie and Leon), played a melody lead on an acoustic guitar. All subsequent Tubb guitarists (even the most jazz-influenced) played a similar style, although it was a later musician, Billy Byrd (a Tubb accompanist for thirteen years), who popularized the ascending four-note run that became virtually the defining feature of Tubb's instrumental sound.

The next phase in Tubb's instrumental evolution—the adoption of electrical amplification—came as a result of country music's entry into the honky-tonks. Not long after Tubb's first Decca recordings began to circulate, a Fort Worth jukebox operator complained to him that it was difficult to hear the acoustic sound of Tubb's recordings once business picked up during the night. At his next recording session, in April 1941, Tubb added an electric guitar in order to increase the volume of his sound. Jimmie Short could not be present at the session, so Tubb was accompanied by Fay "Smitty" Smith, the staff guitarist at KGKO. To preserve the sound heard on his recordings, Tubb instructed Jimmie Short to attach an electric pickup to his conventional Martin guitar. Ernest Tubb was not the first country musician to feature an electric guitar, but as a *Grand Ole Opry* star with national exposure, he lent the instrument a legitimacy that contributed to its rapid dissemination.

Guitar electrification had long been a dream of musicians, and experiments with the process had been made since at least the early 1920s. The pop guitarist Alvino Rey (Albert McBurney) began his own experimentation in 1921, when he was only twelve years old. By 1924, he had invented an electrical amplifier for the guitar that was not, however, patented. Lloyd Loar, of the Gibson Company in Kalamazoo, Michigan, was conducting similar efforts as early as 1924. While other experiments, both amateur and commercial, were no doubt made during the following decade, the electric guitar did not appear in a country band until 1934, when Bob Dunn began playing the instrument with the Musical Brownies. Dunn grew up hearing traditional hoedown music at his home near Braggs, Oklahoma, but he did not become interested in the steel guitar until he heard it used by a group of Hawaiians who played a stage show in the World War I boomtown of Kusa, Oklahoma, in 1917. During the next several years, Dunn obtained a steel guitar, took lessons through correspondence with a native Hawaiian, Walter Kolomoku, and finally, in 1927, became a professional by joining an Oklahoma group called the Panhandle Cowboys and Indians. For seven years (1927–1934), Dunn played with several groups on vaudeville tours and on radio stations in the Midwest and on XEPN on the Mexican border.

His real involvement with country music, however, came in late 1934 as a member of the extremely popular Milton Brown and his Musical Brownies in Fort Worth. Dunn converted a standard roundhole Martin guitar into an electric instrument by magnetizing the strings and raising them high off the box. He then attached an electric pickup to the guitar, which in turn was connected to a Volu-Tone amplifier that Milton Brown had purchased in Mineral Wells, Texas. In January 1935, when Dunn used the electrical amplifier in a recording session in Chicago, he was probably the first country musician to do so. Within the next two or three years, other electric instruments appeared on country recordings and in other performances: Leo Raley, for example, was playing an electric mandolin with Cliff Bruner's Texas Wanderers by 1936; Bobby Simons played an electric standard guitar on recordings with Al Dexter in 1937; and Muryel "Zeke" Campbell was playing his influential, single-string style of electric guitar with the Light Crust Doughboys by 1938. Bob Dunn's innovations on the steel guitar prompted other masters of that instrument—such as Ted Daffan, Leon McAuliffe, Lefty Perkins (who replaced Dunn in the Musical Brownies), Noel Boggs, and Kermit Whalen—to make similar electrical adaptations. Leon McAuliffe's recording of "Steel Guitar Rag" in September 1936 probably did most to popularize the electric guitar among a national audience and foretold that instrument's coming dominance in country music. By 1936 such guitar manufacturers as Gibson had begun to introduce their own electric models, and the mail-order catalogues were advertising guitars that included built-in pickup devices and volume controls.

It is no accident that electrification made its first inroads among the southwestern string bands that played in honky-tonks and in large dance halls and ballrooms. Many of these musicians played a style of music that, after the war, would be described as "western swing." By the end of the 1930s, Americans were becoming well aware of the "hot dance music" or the "Okie jazz" coming out of the Southwest (particularly after Bing Crosby's recording of "San Antonio Rose" took the country by storm in 1941), but few were cognizant of the roots of the music. Western swing was, in part, a stage in the development of the southern string-band tradition and was performed by rural musicians whose ancestors had emigrated from the southeastern cotton states bearing a legacy of fiddling and hoedown music. But western swing also reflected the diverse mingling of musical cultures (Cajun, Tex-Mex, German, Bohemian, black, cowboy, Anglo) that prevailed in the Southwest. Southwestern musicians had eclectic repertories, and they honed their skills at the dances that were common to all of the cultural groups. Fiddlers played at innumerable house parties and at scores of fiddle contests where they learned to improvise.

Despite the obvious cultural divergence demonstrated by southwestern music, one can easily make too much of the remote historical rootedness of western swing. The current preoccupation with hot fiddling and country-jazz fusions unfortunately obscures the fact that Southwesterners also heard and loved more traditional forms of rural music: cowboy music, ballads, sentimental and gospel songs, and breakdown fiddling. One hears no "swing" at all in the gospel songs fashioned by the Chuck Wagon Gang, nor in the cowboy ballads of Carl Sprague or the Cartwright Brothers, nor in the old-time material favored by the balladeer Peg Moreland in his many years of performances on Texas radio stations, nor in the Bradley Kincaid style of singing and repertory featured by Cecil Gill, who maintained a large radio audience for decades in the area around Dallas and Fort Worth, Texas, with only his guitar and sweet-tenor style of singing (he later claimed to have made 6,448 live broadcasts). Western swing musicians did borrow frequently from older and diverse folk resources, but they more often drew upon commercial music forms popular in their own day. Immersed in the popular culture of their time, such powerful music personalities as Milton Brown and Bob Wills forged a highly successful fusion of contemporary popular music and the rural music of their forebears, inspiring a host of other musicians to follow their example.

Brown and Wills received their earliest musical schooling in the most important seedbed of western swing, the fiddle-and-guitar band. A host of such instrumental combinations, playing at barn dances, house parties, and fiddlers' contests, had performed all over the Southwest before and during the 1920s, and several of them made their way onto phonograph recordings after 1922. Some of the groups were famous in their own time and milieu but left only a few recordings by which modern enthusiasts can judge their abilities. At least three units came from the musically rich area around Terrell, about forty miles southeast of Dallas: Oscar and Doc Harper, Ervin Solomon and Jay Hughes, and Prince Albert Hunt, who sometimes played with the Harpers and sometimes with his own group, the Texas Ramblers. While Hunt's fiddling anticipated the melodic variations of western swing, he was no more accomplished as a fiddler than Oscar Harper and Ervin Solomon, both of whom are less well known. Hunt, though, was assured of a kind of immortality when he was shot to death outside a Dallas tavern by a jealous husband on March 21, 1931, and became the subject of a public television documentary in the 1970s, a project inspired as much by his star-crossed, bad-boy image as by his fiddling skills.

Farther south and west in the region around Burnet, Texas, the Humphries Brothers (Jess and Cecil) won a large local following playing for civic functions, at fiddlers' contests, at the annual Old Settlers' Reunion in Round Rock, and on Central Texas radio stations (such as KUT, Austin's first radio station, which was located at the University of Texas). They made only eight recordings for the Okeh label in 1930 (presumably not enough to warrant a modern reissue) and were not widely known outside Central Texas. Their repertory was characterized by the eclecticism generally found among southwestern fiddle bands. Not surprisingly, "Listen to the Mockingbird" was their most-requested tune (it was almost mandatory for fiddlers everywhere to play it), but Jess also knew such tunes as "Beaumont Rag," "Ragtime Annie," "Black and White Rag," and "St. Louis Tickle." He was an unusual old-time fiddler indeed, since he also played trombone in an army band during World War I, was the organizer and "violinist" of one of Central Texas's first Dixieland bands, and was a popular musician at weddings and similar social occasions with his pianist wife, Cynthia.

Even more anticipatory of western swing were the East Texas Serenaders of Lindale, a little community near Tyler. The Serenaders received their name from their practice of going from farmhouse to farmhouse and standing out in the yard entertaining the people. (The custom may have been widespread; the Taylor-Griggs Louisiana Melody Makers, another early recording band, got their start the same way in Bienville Parish, Louisiana.) The center of the band was fiddler Daniel Huggins Williams, a left-handed musician who absorbed both style and repertory from his Tennessee-born father, but he also learned formal technique from a Lindale music teacher named Ellen Cannon. Williams was backed by a strong rhythm section dominated by the guitar of Cloet Hamman, the tenor banjo of John Munnerlyn, and the truly unique cello playing (sometimes plucked, but most often bowed) of Henry Bogan. The Serenaders played at house parties and civic functions throughout East Texas from the Oklahoma line to Houston but never really made music their full-time profession (although Williams played with country and western groups in the 1940s). The twenty-four songs that they recorded for Columbia (1927), Brunswick (1928–1930), and Decca (1936) show a preference for syncopated dance tunes, especially rags from the early twentieth century. Their choice of songs suggested the stylistic directions that the western swing bands would later follow. The fiddler Huggins Williams had an even more direct influence on western swing musicians; at least two of the great modern fiddlers, Buddy Brady and Johnny Gimble, often came over from Tyler to learn directly from the Lindale master.

A crucial step in the development of western swing came in the late 1920s, when Bob Wills and Herman Arnspiger began playing house parties in the Fort Worth area as Wills's Fiddle Band. When Wills, the fiddler, and Arnspiger, the guitarist, were joined by the vocalist Milton

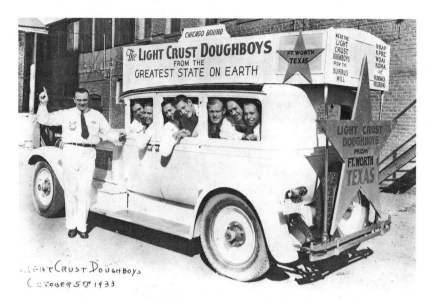

The Light Crust Doughboys, 1933: left to right, *W. Lee "Pappy"*
O'Daniel, Henry Steinbarth (the driver), Sleepy Johnson, Raymond
DeArman, Leon McAuliffe, Leon Huff, Clifford Gross, Herman Arnspiger.
Bill Malone personal collection; courtesy of Bob Pinson.

Brown in 1930, they became known as the Aladdin Laddies (because of
their sponsorship on Fort Worth station WBAP by the Aladdin Mantle
Lamp Company). By 1931, the trio had obtained jobs with Burrus Mills
advertising Light Crust Flour over KFJZ in Fort Worth at 7:00 a.m. and
at noon. During the rest of the day, they worked for the flour company
in other capacities, Brown as a salesman, Arnspiger and Wills as dock
loaders and truck drivers. They also played many nights at the Crystal
Springs Ballroom in Fort Worth. By early 1932, Arnspiger had left the
group and had been replaced by the multitalented Sleepy Johnson,
who could play the guitar, fiddle, tenor guitar, and tenor banjo. Joined
by Brown's younger brother Durwood, this group recorded two songs
for Victor on February 9, 1932. Known first as the Fort Worth Doughboys and later as the Light Crust Doughboys, the organization became
one of the important parent groups of western swing. Their 12:30 p.m.
show on WBAP after 1933 (also carried by WOAI in San Antonio and
KPRC in Houston) made their music known all over the Southwest.

Wilbert Lee "Pappy" O'Daniel, the Burrus Mills general manager
who hired them and served as their master of ceremonies, rode to

Milton Brown and His Musical Brownies, 1935: left to right, *Ocie Stockard, Fred Calhoun, Wanna Coffman, Milton Brown, Cecil Brower, Bob Dunn, Durwood Brown. Bill Malone personal collection; courtesy of Bob Pinson.*

fame and political success through his association with the popular musicians. O'Daniel had little association with country music before he cast his fortunes with the Doughboys. He was born in Malta, Ohio, in 1890, but grew up in Kansas, where he became a flour mill owner. He came to Fort Worth in 1925 to be the sales manager of the Burrus Mill and Elevator Company; by June 1935, when he left to organize his own business, he had served as general manager and president. O'Daniel was indifferent toward the Doughboys until he found out how popular they were, but he then took a very personal interest in their careers, affixing his name to theirs on record labels, serving as their announcer, and writing approximately 150 poems and songs (including the very popular "Put Me in Your Pocket" and "Beautiful Texas"). O'Daniel had a warm, folksy, and appealing radio voice at a time when radio was the most potent political image maker in the nation. By the time he made his first successful race for the governorship in 1938, O'Daniel was known in thousands of Texas homes, where he was perceived as an almost fatherly presence and a quasi-populist champion of common people.

The family aura projected by O'Daniel, however, masked the dissension within the Doughboy ranks, and its founding members, Milton Brown and Bob Wills, had left the band by the time it made its next recordings in October 1933. Brown organized a rival band called the Musical Brownies in September 1932 and began performing on another Fort Worth station, KTAT.[9] Bob Wills left in 1933 over a wage dispute and soon began forming the group that would one day be called the Texas Playboys. O'Daniel himself severed his connections with Burrus Mills and the Doughboys in midsummer of 1935 when he formed his own flour company and began promoting a product called Hillbilly Flour. He also organized a band, the Hillbilly Boys, who helped him sell flour and campaign for political office. The group included a cowgirl singer named Kitty Williamson whom O'Daniel dubbed Texas Rose (he gave nicknames to all of his musicians); Kermit Whalen; O'Daniel's sons, Pat and Mike; and one of the finest singers and yodelers of the 1930s, Leon Huff (the Texas Songbird), who remained until 1940. After the Hillbilly Boys warmed up his audiences, O'Daniel attacked the "professional politicians" and promised the old folks a modest monthly pension. Hillbilly music and folksy rhetoric proved to be an unbeatable combination, and O'Daniel swept into office with landslide votes in both 1938 and 1940; he also won a special election to the United States Senate over Lyndon B. Johnson in 1941 and a full Senate term in 1942. O'Daniel's success was most certainly noted by entertainers elsewhere, and Jimmie Davis would ultimately win two elections to the Louisiana governorship by emulating the Texas politician's campaign tactics (once in office, he would also project a plain-folk image while pursuing an essentially ultraconservative political course).

In the meantime, the Light Crust Doughboys endured as a popular radio and recording group, even while changing personnel frequently. Tommy Duncan brought his warm, fluid vocal style to the group for a brief period in late 1933. Clifford Gross, a hot fiddler from Kentucky, joined the Doughboys in the same year as a replacement for Bob Wills; Gross took the string band more firmly into the parameters of jazz. Sixteen-year-old Leon McAuliffe also joined the group in 1933, but by 1934 had taken his steel guitar into Bob Wills's new and popular band. Muryel "Zeke" Campbell came in 1935, and by 1938 was playing his electric standard guitar on recordings with the organization. By the end of the decade, the Doughboys, who had always been eclectic in their song selections, had become even more oriented toward hot dance music, and an array of talented musicians, who were as comfortable with jazz as they were with country music, had become members of the group. The pianist John W. "Knocky" Parker and the tenor banjoist Marvin Montgomery, for example, were educated musicians who had considerable experience playing in pop and jazz bands.

The organization created by Milton Brown was equally committed to "country jazz." The original members of the band included Jesse Ashlock on fiddle, Ocie Stockard on tenor banjo, Wanna Coffman on bass, Durwood Brown on guitar, and Milton Brown as vocalist. When the fiddler Cecil Brower and the pianist Fred "Papa" Calhoun joined the group, the Musical Brownies gained musicians who were comfortable in any musical idiom. Calhoun was a veteran of jazz bands in the Fort Worth area, and Brower had studied music and violin at Texas Christian University and had also played briefly with the Dallas Symphony Orchestra and with Ted Fio Rito's Orchestra. Brower was one of the most jazz-influenced fiddlers of the era, and he sharpened the jazz perceptions of other fiddlers (such as Jesse Ashlock and Cliff Bruner) who played with him in the Brownie organization. The Brownies' jazz emphasis was further accentuated in late 1934 when the steel guitarist Bob Dunn joined the band. Dunn's style was virtually unique in steel-guitar circles. He played the steel guitar like a horn, with his short, staccato notes resembling the bursts of a trumpet. Dunn, who had played in jazz bands earlier, was involved throughout his life in a personal campaign to make the steel guitar a jazz instrument, or what he termed a "modern instrument."[10]

The Brownies' recorded repertory, found on Bluebird and Decca, only rarely touched conventional country music (as in "Little Betty Brown," "Get Along Home, Cindy," and "My Mary," beautifully sung by Milton Brown). More often, the Brownies' recordings were direct copies of current "popular" hits. The musicians would often gather at Will Ed Kemble's, a Fort Worth furniture store, to hear the latest records as they came in. They would then adapt them to the string band style. In addition to their radio shows on KTAT, the Brownies played regularly at the Crystal Springs Ballroom and frequently at dances throughout North Texas and Oklahoma. Consequently, they played what their dance audiences wanted to hear: pop standards such as "Girl of My Dreams," "The Object of My Affection," and "The Waltz You Saved for Me"; jazz chestnuts such as "Joe Turner Blues," "Hesitation Blues,"

"Black and White Rag," and "St. Louis Blues"; and a few "foreign" tunes such as "Cielito lindo" and "Allá en el rancho grande."

The Brownies were far from being exclusively an instrumental organization. With his husky, virile voice, Milton Brown set a standard that other western swing vocalists found difficult to equal. His version of "St. Louis Blues" is the finest done by any country entertainer. Brown's tragic death on April 18, 1936, as the result of an automobile accident a few days earlier, came at the peak of the Brownies' popularity and was a demoralizing blow from which the band never recovered. Milton's brother Durwood tried to keep the band intact and even arranged one more Decca recording session in March 1937. Musicians, however, had begun to drift away soon after Milton died, either forming their own bands or joining other organizations.

The Brownies permanently shaped the course of country music history, and they did so without ever abandoning the string band format. Milton Brown's singing was greatly admired and widely copied; the fiddlers Cecil Brower and Cliff Bruner featured improvisational styles that still appear in the work of modern instrumentalists; Fred "Papa" Calhoun introduced jazz piano playing to country music; and Bob Dunn pioneered in the electrification of the steel guitar while also moving that instrument dramatically away from the chorded Hawaiian style. More immediately, the Brownies inspired the creation of bands all over the Southwest—even in Cajun country, and as far away as Birmingham, where Hank Penny organized the Radio Cowboys. Several of the bands, of course, were led by erstwhile Brownies: Cliff Bruner, Bob Dunn, and Ocie Stockard each had a band by 1937. Bruner and Dunn both moved to Houston in 1936 and played with musicians who were often interchangeable; therefore, Bruner's Texas Wanderers and Dunn's Vagabonds, for recording purposes at least, were virtually the same band. From 1936 on up into the years of World War II, Bruner's band became the most successful musical organization on the Texas Gulf Coast, or in the region from Houston through the Cajun territory of Southwest Louisiana. Bruner's dazzling fiddle style defined his band's sound, but he was joined from time to time by other versatile musicians, such as Leo Raley, who fashioned an electric mandolin out of a homemade pickup device built in Ted Daffan's radio repair shop; J. R. Chatwell, a hard-driving, jazz-style fiddler, who, however, played piano with Bruner; and Aubrey "Moon" Mullican, a country boogie pianist and singer who joined Bruner in 1937. Musicians moved from band to band frequently in the mid- and late 1930s and in a fashion often bewildering to the researcher. Bands, furthermore, periodically experienced secessions, and new groups came into existence; for example, the Modern Mountaineers and the Village Boys (headed by Bruner vocalist Dickie McBride) were spinoffs from Bruner who performed in the Houston area in the late 1930s.

Houston was, in fact, a very fertile region for hot country dance bands in the 1930s. The Swift Jewel Cowboys (sponsored by Jewel Oil and Shortening) were organized in 1933 but remained in the city for only about a year before relocating to Memphis. The Blue Ridge Playboys, the Bar-X Cowboys, and Shelly Lee Alley's Alley Cats, on the other hand, remained fixtures in the musical life of the city for several years. The Playboys and the Cowboys evolved out of a traditional country string band background, while Shelly Lee Alley began his career as a violinist in a pop dance orchestra. All three groups found themselves irresistibly drawn to the hot dance styles pioneered by Milton Brown and Bob Wills. Alley appeared on radio as early as January 1923, when he played on WFAA in Dallas in a pop dance orchestra called the Dixie Serenaders. Although he appeared on a Jimmie Rodgers recording in 1931 and wrote a couple of songs for Jimmie ("Traveling Blues" and "Gambling Barroom Blues"), he remained a pop musician and vocalist until the mid-1930s, when he met the fiddler Leon Selph in Houston and began turning toward western swing. Along with his brother, Alvin Alley, he organized the Alley Cats and began recording for ARC in November 1937. The Alley Cats stayed close to the mold cast by the Musical Brownies (even employing Cliff Bruner for recording purposes), but they also used horns on occasion. The Bar-X Cowboys (led by brothers Ben and Elmer Christian) did not confine themselves to swing material but also did cowboy songs and country tunes. They performed on such stations as KTRH in Houston and in local clubs and found a particularly receptive audience at the family-oriented dance halls in the German communities near Houston. The Blue Ridge Playboys were also eclectic in style and repertory, as most Texas bands had to be, and they were a seedbed of honky-tonk talent that would dominate country music for years to come. The Playboys were named by Jesse Jones, a Houston oil millionaire and radio station owner (KXYZ), who affixed upon them the name of one of his properties, the Blue Ridge oil patch located between Houston and Stafford. Led by Leon "Pappy" Selph, a fine fiddler in his own right, and drawing upon the floating circle of musicians that populated the western swing bands of the era, the band also enlisted the services of tenor banjoist Chuck Keeshan; bass player Lou Frisby; and a remarkable trio of innovative musicians, Ted Daffan, Floyd Tillman, and Moon Mullican, who remained giants of country music through the 1940s.

Theron Eugene "Ted" Daffan was born in 1912 in Beauregard Parish, Louisiana, but grew up in Houston, where he developed an early and undying fascination with the Hawaiian guitar and electronics. He was drawn to country music through the recordings and broadcasts of the Musical Brownies and played in a succession of Houston bands (including the Blue Ridge Playboys, the Alley Cats, and the Bar-X Cowboys), before forming his own influential Texans in 1940. Daffan pioneered in the electrification of instruments—his radio repair shop was the center of much of the experimentation with homemade pickups and amps that went on in the Houston area—but he made his most enduring contributions to country music through his songwriting. Striving to augment the pitifully low royalties that musicians received from recordings, in the late 1930s Daffan began writing songs that would ultimately make him one of the charter members of the Nashville Songwriters Association Hall of Fame. They included the first truck-driving song, "Truck Driver's Blues" (1939), and three of the classics of honky-tonk music: "Worried Mind" (1940), "Born to Lose" (1943), and "Headin' Down the Wrong Highway" (1945).

Floyd Tillman made significant contributions in three areas of country music—guitar playing, songwriting, and singing—although only the first two were sufficiently exploited during the 1930s. Tillman was born in 1914 in Ryan, Oklahoma, but was brought to Post, Texas, by his parents when he was less than a year old. He began honing his skills as a guitarist backing up fiddlers at innumerable ranch parties in West Texas, but his introduction to the honky-tonk world came in 1933, when he joined Adolph and Emil Hofner at Gus's Palm Garden in San Antonio. At this point in his career, Tillman was playing a single-string style of guitar on an instrument amplified by a metal disc; three years later he was playing an electric guitar with a Volu-Tone amplifier and homemade pickup supplied by Ted Daffan. Like Daffan, Tillman became one of the most respected songwriters in country music, contributing "I'll Keep on Loving You," "They Took the Stars Out of Heaven," "Each Night at Nine," "This Cold War with You," and the perennial favorite "It Makes No Difference Now." He sang regularly with the Blue Ridge Playboys but was fated to see his biggest song of the prewar era, "It Makes No Difference Now," recorded first by Dickie McBride, who sang with Cliff Bruner's Texas Wanderers. Tillman did not really come into his own as a vocalist until after World War II when he recorded his super hits "Slipping Around" and "I Love You So Much It Hurts." He was named to the Country Music Hall of Fame in 1984.

Aubrey "Moon" Mullican, the third member of this stellar Houston fraternity, brought the barrelhouse style of piano playing to country music, a style pioneered by itinerant black juke joint musicians. Mullican was born in 1909 in Corrigan, Polk County, in the heart of the East Texas Piney Woods. While no hard evidence suggests that he ever listened directly to the piano players who entertained the black lumber workers, he did hear black guitar players in Corrigan, and he picked up elements of style from one musician in particular, Joe Jones, who sometimes worked on the Mullicans' sharecrop farm. At about the same time (when he was eight years old), Mullican began applying these blues licks to the little pump organ that his father had bought to encourage his daughters to learn church songs. At the age of sixteen, he hopped a train to Houston, where he began receiving a hard indoctrination in the world of honky-tonk entertainment. He later acknowledged that "the only place a piano playing kid like me could get work in those days wasn't exactly high class. The ladies of the evening, who worked there, would come and set on the piano bench and fan me while I played."[11] Mullican did not introduce the piano to country music, but his earthy, rollicking style was significantly different from that of Fred Calhoun or Al Stricklin (Bob Wills's famous pianist), who played with a more jazz-derived New Orleans style. With the Blue Ridge Playboys and the Texas Wanderers, Mullican featured a melodic-based boogie style of playing that was designed, in his own words, "to make the bottles bounce on the tables." Mullican's piano playing, combined with his zestful singing, made him one of the most colorful personalities of southwestern country music.

San Antonio did not experience quite as much musical activity in the 1930s as did Houston or the Dallas–Fort Worth area, but important musicians thrived there nonetheless. In 1936, Jimmie Revard created a band that was obviously inspired stylistically and commercially by Bob Wills's glittering success. Revard even named his band the Oklahoma Playboys. The Hofner Brothers (Adolph and Emil) constituted the heart of the band, but they went out on their own by the end of the 1930s to form Adolph Hofner's Texans. Another group that was just as popular as the Oklahoma Playboys was the Tune Wranglers, organized in 1935 by the singer and guitarist Buster Coward. The group's repertory and instrumentation was similar to that of other western swing bands and was marked by the hot fiddling of Tom Dickey (who left to form the Show Boys in 1938), the jazzy piano of Eddie Whitley, and the similarly sophisticated steel guitar stylings of Eddie Duncan. The Tune Wranglers played in a freewheeling, exuberant style, replete with spoken asides and shouted commentary that were no doubt borrowed from Bob Wills. None of the San Antonio groups were known very far outside their home area, but the Tune Wranglers did record two songs, "Hawaiian Honeymoon" and "Texas Sand," which moved among a wider audience. "Texas Sand," written by Buster Coward, won a renewed life in the 1950s, when Webb Pierce reintroduced it to country music on a Decca recording.

The Dallas territory was dominated by the bands of Roy Newman and Bill Boyd, whose membership often overlapped, and by a string band headed by the Shelton Brothers (Bob and Joe). Neither Newman nor Boyd spent much time as a touring musician; instead, both were associated for many years with Dallas radio stations—Newman as a studio musician with WRR and WFAA, and Boyd as a longtime announcer and disc jockey on WRR. The two men drew upon a common pool of talent yet were markedly dissimilar in their overall approach to musical style. Newman had been a radio staff pianist since the early 1920s, but in the bands that he began to organize after 1931 he seldom played a lead or solo passage and was instead content to provide a rather unobtrusive, rhythmic background. On the other hand, he demonstrated a remarkable talent for finding superb musicians. Performing as Roy Newman and His Boys on WRR's *Noontime Varieties* after 1933, the band produced an infectious dance music that revealed little indebtedness to country music and much to blues and New Orleans jazz. Although Newman did not consider his music to be country, some of the greatest country performers of the era saw service in his band from 1933 to 1939. Bob Dunn and Cecil Brower sat in on at least one recording session soon after they left the Musical Brownies; Art Davis, Walter Kirkes, and Jim Boyd sometimes came over from Bill Boyd's band to help Newman out (it was in these sessions that Jim Boyd first tried out his electric guitar phrases); and a lengthy retinue of hot fiddlers (such as Art Davis, Thurman Neal, Brower, Jesse Ashlock, and Carroll Hubbard) played with Newman at one time or another. These talented string musicians, along with Holly Horton, a veteran ragtime clarinet player, contributed toward making Newman's band the most genuine country jazz band of the era.

Bill Boyd's Cowboy Ramblers, on the other hand, remained basically a country string band even as they moved progressively toward the performance of jazz and dance music. Bill and Jim Boyd were born on a cattle and cotton farm in Fannin County, Texas, in 1910 and 1914 respectively. The brothers performed country music on radio in Greenville as early as 1926 but were always identified with the music scene in Dallas, where they moved in 1929. Bill immediately became active as a local musician, and even appeared as a guitarist in Jimmie Rodgers's Dallas recording session in February 1932. Bill and Jim organized the Cowboy Ramblers in that same year and in 1934 made the first of their recordings for Victor, an association that lasted until 1951. The Cowboy Ramblers were built around a nucleus of Bill and Jim Boyd (guitar and bass), Art Davis (fiddle), and Walter Kirkes (banjo), all of whom were studio musicians at WRR. This was the group that made the first recordings in 1934, although their number was augmented by other musicians from time to time, such as the fiddler Jesse Ashlock and the steel guitarist Lefty Perkins and, on recordings, by such Light Crust Doughboys members as Knocky Parker, Kenneth Pitts, and Marvin Montgomery. The Cowboy Ramblers were essentially a recording band, for the members often played with other groups, and Bill Boyd remained associated with WRR as a musician and announcer for many years. The Cowboy Ramblers were very influential as recording musicians, and some of their tunes remained country standards long after the 1930s. "Under the Double Eagle," for example—featuring Bill Boyd's guitar lead and Art Davis's bluesy fiddle—was one of the most popular instrumentals in country music and was probably second only to "Wildwood Flower" as the favorite number in the country guitarist's repertory.

As important as Newman's and Boyd's bands may have been, they did not enjoy the popularity of another Dallas-based group, the Shelton Brothers. The music of the Shelton Brothers remains difficult to categorize. It was not western swing, although they shared some of the repertory of the hot fiddle bands. The Sheltons were a brother duet who, with mandolin and guitar, performed songs similar to those of

their duet contemporaries in the Southeast. Nevertheless, their repertory also contained a blues component that most of the mandolin-and-
guitar teams did not possess, and Joe Shelton's mandolin style was
characterized by a syncopation and blues feeling that was rare among
other players of the instrument. The Sheltons thought of themselves
as hillbillies—and many of their songs did reflect a rural impulse—but
they ranged far and wide for their material, demonstrating that none
of the southwestern groups could totally resist the swing and honky-
tonk trends of the period.

Bob and Joe Attlesey, who performed under the name of Shelton
(their mother's maiden name), were born on a cotton farm in Rylie
Springs, Hopkins County, Texas. The poverty of tenantry and the
need to help take care of their eight younger brothers and sisters contributed to their decision to become professional entertainers. They
began singing in Longview, an East Texas oil boomtown, in 1929, for
tips at root-beer and near-beer stands, and at Clint Aycock's café,
where twenty-five cents would buy "all you could eat." In late 1929,
they moved to Tyler, where they played with Leon Chappelear, as the
Lone Star Cowboys, on KGKB. During the 1930s they spent much of
their time in Louisiana, playing on powerful KWKH in Shreveport
(the personal mouthpiece of W. K. Henderson, who promoted his iron-
works and Hello World Coffee and castigated the chain stores), and on
WWL in New Orleans, where they were teamed with Lew Childre and
Curly Fox. In 1934, they became one of the earliest groups to sign with
the new Decca Company (they had made one previous recording with
Victor as the Lone Star Cowboys), an arrangement that resulted in
the issuance the following year of their two most popular songs: "Just
Because" and "Deep Elem Blues."

In the late 1930s, the Shelton Brothers alternated between KWKH
(where they were also billed as the Sunshine Boys) and WFAA in
Dallas, where they became securely ensconced after 1941. They also
maintained a close relationship with Jimmie Davis, both musically
and politically; Joe Shelton, for example, fronted Davis's band from
1943 to 1949 and was prominently involved in his successful race for
the Louisiana governorship in 1944. During their performing career,
the Sheltons maintained a hillbilly image that was unusual in the
Texas musical scene of the 1930s, and Bob Shelton, in fact, continued to play the role of a rube hillbilly comic (complete with overalls
and brown flop hat) on into the seventies. Their repertory always

included "rustic" songs like "Stay in the Wagon Yard" (learned from their hero, the Texas radio singer Peg Moreland) and "Who Wouldn't Be Lonely" (a sentimental parlor-style song written by Leon Chappelear), but blues and hokum jazz tunes also occasionally intruded into their music: "Match Box Blues," "Sittin' on Top of the World," "Four or Five Times," "Knot Hole Blues," and similar songs. Instrumentally, the Sheltons tried to resist some of the swing emphasis of the period, even to the point of forbidding their brother Merle, who often played with them after 1935, to play bar chords on his rhythm guitar. The newer sounds, though, could not long be excluded, and by the time they retired from full-time entertainment in the late 1940s, electrification and hot instrumental licks had all but submerged their original acoustic and hillbilly-based identity.

The man who did the most to make the newer sounds irresistible to country musicians was James Robert (Bob) Wills (born in Kosse, Limestone County, Texas, in 1905).[12] Wills did not invent western swing—men like Milton Brown and Cecil Brower should certainly share much of the credit—but he did the most to popularize it around the United States in a long career that extended from the late 1920s to 1969. Wills could scarcely escape being a fiddler, inheriting the art from his father and from relatives on both sides of the family (the Wills and the Foleys). From about 1915 and on through the 1920s, Wills and his father, John, became locally famous in the area around Memphis, Texas (where the family had moved in 1913), playing in contests and at innumerable house parties. Wills served a musical apprenticeship with a medicine show in 1929 and then, as previously noted, played with Herman Arnspiger as Wills's Fiddle Band, and with Arnspiger and Milton Brown as the Aladdin Laddies and the Light Crust Doughboys. When Wills left the Doughboys in 1933, he moved first to Waco, where the Texas Playboys were born, and then, in 1934, to Oklahoma, where he experienced his most glittering success. From 1934 to 1942, Wills and the Texas Playboys performed daily on KVOO in Tulsa, almost every night at a large ballroom called Cain's Academy, and occasionally at dances in Oklahoma, Arkansas, Kansas, and Texas. These live performances, along with his popular Okeh recordings after 1935, made Wills the most famous southwestern musician and an influence for change that has seldom been equaled in country music history.

Although the Texas Playboys used horns and reeds after 1935 as they became a large, versatile organization that could play big band

Bob Wills and the Texas Playboys, at KVOO (Tulsa), 1937: left to right, *Everett Stover, Zeb McNally, Leon McAuliffe, Al Franklin (announcer), Herman Arnspiger, Al Stricklin, Joe Ferguson, Smokey Dacus, Tiny Mott, Bob Wills, Tommy Duncan, Son Lansford, Sleepy Johnson. Bill Malone personal collection; courtesy of Bob Pinson.*

jazz with skill, they always remained essentially a fiddle band. Wills himself was a hoedown fiddler, and though he had an undoubted affinity for the blues (Bessie Smith and white bluesmen Emmett Miller and Jimmie Rodgers were some of his favorite musicians), he could not play the hot, swinging style that became so characteristic of western swing. Wills's genius lay in his ability to attract musicians who *could* play jazz and other forms of music and in his skill to extract from them every ounce of musicianship they possessed. When Wills pointed at musicians or called on them by name to take an instrumental break, he expected them to play something original and innovative. He employed a long string of fiddlers, such as Jesse Ashlock, Louis Tierney, Joe Holley, and Johnny Gimble, who were adept at jazz, blues, and breakdowns and who possessed technical skills that their employer admired but could not duplicate.

Apart from the dazzling performances made in our own time by the Austin-based Asleep at the Wheel and the Nashville all-star group the Time Jumpers, the Texas Playboys' jazz experiments have seldom been re-created by modern country bands, and horns and reeds only rarely appear in country performances. Other traits pioneered or popularized by Wills, however, have endured in country music. Al Stricklin, described by Wills as "the old piano pounder," further popularized the improvisational style pioneered by Fred Calhoun. Smokey Dacus apparently introduced drums to country music when he joined the Playboys in 1935. Eldon Shamblin, formerly with the Alabama Boys, came to the Playboys in 1937 with his electric standard guitar; he and such contemporaries as Muryel Campbell, Junior Barnard, Jim Boyd, and Floyd Tillman popularized the single-note jazz style that probably came to them from the playing of such black musicians as Charlie Christian and Aaron "T-Bone" Walker. Leon McAuliffe, who electrified his steel guitar not long after Bob Dunn made the innovation, did more than any other musician to make his instrument one of the dominant stylistic forces in country music. His 1936 recording of "Steel Guitar Rag" (adapted from Sylvester Weaver's earlier recording of "Guitar Rag") made that tune a standard in the country repertory and was a vivid forecast of the prominence the instrument would enjoy in the coming decades. As these great musicians demonstrated their instrumental prowess, the vocalist Tommy Duncan (from Whitney, Texas) caressed his audiences with a smooth, liquid, and extraordinarily supple baritone that moved easily from slow, romantic ballads to yodeling blues tunes. This disciple of Jimmie Rodgers and Emmett Miller was singing for tips at a Fort Worth root-beer stand in 1932 when Wills hired him to replace Milton Brown in the Light Crust Doughboys. He remained with Wills until the early 1950s; he was universally admired, frequently emulated, but never surpassed as a singer. And not the least of his accomplishments was his ability to maintain composure as Wills kept up a running fire of silly patter even during the most serious of songs.

Wills's repertory was wide and varied and reflected the broad range of influences that affected the music of Southwesterners. Many of his popular tunes came from his southern rural forebears: fiddle pieces such as "Beaumont Rag," "Lone Star Rag," "Prosperity Special," or tunes that featured both lyrics and breakdown instrumentation such as "Cotton-Eyed Joe," "Ida Red," and "Take Me Back to Tulsa." Wills's extensive debt to traditional country music has not yet been fully measured, and it is somewhat camouflaged by the fact that he and his musicians often gave new names to old melodies.

Traditional rural music, however, was only one source that contributed to the Bob Wills catalogue. His very first recordings, made with Herman Arnspiger in November 1929—two unissued selections for Brunswick—illustrate the two major impulses that always dominated his performances: "Wills Breakdown" and Bessie Smith's "Gulf Coast Blues." Although Wills had been fascinated with the blues since his youth, one finds little hard evidence that he picked up the style through direct contact with black people. Rather, his songs came from the performances of professional musicians, and especially from the recordings to which he and other young western swing partisans avidly listened. Even some of his spoken patter came from the performances of earlier minstrel entertainers such as Al Bernard (e.g., "You're a man after my own heart, with a razor"). Like a host of country musicians who came before him—beginning at least as early as Dock Boggs, Sam McGee, and Frank Hutchison—Wills borrowed heavily from black musicians, an indebtedness that extended on through the days of big band jazz. "Sittin' on Top of the World," "Corrine, Corrina," "Basin Street Blues," "St. Louis Blues," "Trouble in Mind," and "Big Beaver" were only a few of the songs that came to Wills, at least indirectly, from the performances of black artists. Other tunes, such as Emmett Miller's "Right or Wrong" and "I Don't Love Nobody" (sung impeccably by Duncan) and Jimmie Rodgers's "Gambling Polka Dot Blues," "Mississippi Delta Blues," and "Blue Yodel No. 1," came from the repertories of white blues singers.

Along with this extensive catalogue of older borrowed material, Wills and the Playboys also utilized modern compositions—their own or those written by other songwriters. Their most profitable association with a songwriter came during the 1940s, when Cindy Walker began contributing songs to the several movies that Wills made. Such Walker compositions as "Cherokee Maiden" and "Dusty Skies" (inspired by memories of the great dust storms of the late 1930s) and songs that came from the pens of other writers, such as "My Confession," "Whose Heart Are You Breaking Now," "Roly Poly," "Time Changes Everything," "Rose of Old Pawnee," and, most popular of all, "Faded Love," are still known by most country singers and will endure long after Wills's jazz imitations have been forgotten. The majority of Wills's national hits did not come until the war years, but early in 1941, one composition forecast the future popularity that both Wills and country music would attain. This was "San Antonio

Rose," first recorded as a country instrumental on November 28, 1938; on April 16, 1940, it was recorded with the addition of lyrics sung by Tommy Duncan. The Duncan recording achieved wide popularity, but in 1941 Bing Crosby's version sold over eighty-four thousand copies in the month of January alone. The Bob Wills style, if not the Bob Wills name, had now been given national distribution.

Bob Wills left his brand on country music in an uncountable variety of ways. His irresistible personality dominated every performance, and dancers and spectators could scarcely keep their eyes off him as he strutted across the stage, dressed in the attire of a rancher, chomping on a cigar, and pointing toward musicians as they took their instrumental breaks. Certainly, no one could ignore his shouts and hollers that punctuated the performance of virtually every song: "Ahh haa," "Take it away, Leon," "Brother Al Stricklin," "Aw, come in, Tommy," and on and on. While musicians marveled at Wills's energy, they also borrowed permanently the songs and instrumentals that he and his musicians had introduced. Long after the large western swing band had declined in popularity, the Bob Wills "beat" and style of fiddling continued to attract the attention of country musicians. All through the southwestern states, particularly, in literally hundreds of taverns, dance halls, and country night clubs, countless groups—such as Hoyle Nix and his West Texas Cowboys, who for many years after 1946 worked a three-hundred-mile radius around Big Spring, Texas—were living testaments to the Bob Wills influence. And a phenomenon that folklorists should begin to ponder—because it provides clues to the future directions that folk music will follow—is the influence exerted by Bob Wills on participants at the old fiddlers' contests. In these contests, long acknowledged as arenas for authentic old-time music, many of the performers (usually the younger ones) practically duplicate old Bob Wills recordings.

By the end of the 1930s, such southwestern performers as Bob Wills, Gene Autry, Ernest Tubb, Al Dexter, Cliff Bruner, Jimmie Davis, Floyd Tillman, Ted Daffan, and the Shelton Brothers were beginning to dominate the jukeboxes. The eclectic and infectiously improvisatory sounds heard in their performances appealed to country musicians everywhere. By the end of the 1940s, the honky-tonk- and dance-hall-inspired styles of the Southwest had found receptive audiences all over the nation. Traditional "rural" acts still abounded in country music—such as Roy Acuff, the Blue Sky Boys, Grandpa Jones, and

Mainer's Mountaineers—but few performers could resist the temptation to experiment with the dynamic and increasingly electrified sounds then being popularized by the musicians of the Southwest. Although World War II contributed most toward its nationalization, hillbilly music had already made giant strides toward national acceptance by the end of the 1930s. Some songs became so widely popular, and were performed in so many stylistic formats, that they virtually lost their country identities. *Billboard* in 1941 described "You Are My Sunshine" as the "tavern and taproom classic" of the year,[13] but it was destined to be much more than that. First recorded by the Rice Brothers (Paul and Hoke) in 1939, but given its widest hearing through the performances of Gene Autry, Bing Crosby, and Jimmie Davis (who used it as his theme song in his successful race for the Louisiana governorship in 1944), the song eventually became one of the most commercially programmed numbers in American popular music. Sung to death at innumerable parties, hayrides, fraternity bashes, and assorted social functions, it became one of the few country songs that everyone knows. "You Are My Sunshine" represented both the national flowering of country music and its eventual absorption into the mainstream of American popular culture.

CHAPTER 6

The War Years

The National Expansion of Country Music

The Japanese attack on Pearl Harbor abruptly ended American isolation. The war that followed brought full employment and heightened prosperity, but it also quickened the tempo of American life and accentuated social tensions that eventually gave rise to the racial, sexual, and generational conflicts of the late 1950s and early 1960s. The war also encouraged mass population shifts as young men and women marched off to training camps and civilians moved into defense occupation centers. In a very real sense, America's rural population was liberated by the war, especially in the South, where poor white and black tenant farmers, sharecroppers, and mill workers left their meager farms and jobs and trekked to the urban areas in a quest for better economic and social conditions. Except for the significant movement of the Okies, relatively little out-migration from the South had occurred in the 1930s. But during the war, southerners moved often and in great numbers to contiguous cities in their own region (from the Georgia countryside to Atlanta; from rural Alabama to Mobile or Birmingham; from East Texas into Houston, Dallas, or the industrial Gulf Coast, and to industrial-defense centers all over the United States (Baltimore; Washington, DC; Cincinnati; Chicago; Detroit; Los Angeles).

The population movements of World War II brought Americans

into closer contact with one another, intermingled differing cultures, and contributed to the breaking down of regional differences. World War II, and the prosperity it generated, accentuated the inherent American tendencies toward mobility and dynamism. Rural and small-town Americans found themselves subjected to increasingly irresistible pressures to conform to the new society that was taking shape.

Just as the war enlarged the scope and magnitude of American life, it also affected the character and popularity of country music. The music had taken great strides toward national acceptance during the 1930s but was still basically regional at the end of the decade; it would become a national phenomenon during the war. Expanded popularity brought increased commercial attention—from recording companies, promotional and booking agencies, and associated endeavors—whereas augmented incomes, particularly in the years immediately following the war, encouraged increased activity among the performers themselves. Together, these influences exerted terrific pressure on country musicians to modify their styles and performing images in order to attract a potentially new and larger audience while also promising greater material benefits and public gratification than previous country entertainers had enjoyed.

Jukebox expansion, heightened road-show activity, movie exposure, and radio coverage (particularly on the 50,000-watt channels and Mexican border stations) suggest that country music was already achieving a national footing before the war. Events during the 1940s, some of them independent of the military conflict, further served to strengthen the music's public and commercial positions. A major conflict between the American Society of Composers, Authors and Publishers (ASCAP) and the nation's broadcasters over music licensing rights helped open the door to greater protection for country composers. A five-year contract between ASCAP and the radio networks expired on December 31, 1940. In negotiations for a new contract, ASCAP demanded about $9 million a year, or twice what it had been receiving. The National Association of Broadcasters resisted the increased rates and, in anticipation of the difficulty, had established a rival licensing concern on October 14, 1939. The new organization, Broadcast Music, Inc. (BMI), was at a great disadvantage in its competitive struggle with ASCAP, which controlled most of the music written and published in the United States after 1884. The only exceptions were songs in the public domain and a small number held by a noncompetitive performance-rights society, Selected Editions of Standard American Catalogues (SESAC). On January 1, 1941, the broadcasters imposed a ban on all material controlled by ASCAP and determined to use only those songs protected by other licensing organizations. BMI, however, originally had few songs in its musical reservoir. Most music publishers were hesitant about joining the fledgling organization because they believed that it would ultimately collapse. BMI therefore had to rely on new and inexperienced songwriters, but the fortunes of the young organization had begun to rise the year after its founding, when the established publishing firm of Edward B. Marks, with its extensive catalogues of popular and Latin material, became a member. The Marks acquisition established a precedent that other publishing firms followed. Important in the furthering of hillbilly music were Ralph Peer's Southern Music and M. M. Cole of Chicago, both of which had extensive country music catalogues.

During the first ten months of 1941, BMI steadily expanded its catalogue until it included over thirty-six thousand copyrights from fifty-two publishers. As the sole source of music for broadcast purposes during that period, BMI attracted a number of composers who had been thrown out of work because of the ban. Hillbilly music owes much of its success in the 1940s to the protection granted it by BMI (ASCAP traditionally had been reluctant to admit hillbilly composers, and those who did gain admittance often complained about the delays involved in obtaining compensation). During the ten-month ban, hillbilly songs gained increased airplay because of the new catalogue acquisitions and because of the increased reliance on public-domain melodies. When ASCAP and the radio networks resolved their differences in October 1941, BMI had secured a firm footing in the entertainment world and was well on the way to success. It provided a measure of competition for ASCAP and contributed to the economic security of fledgling songwriters. BMI was instrumental, therefore, in breaking New York's, or Tin Pan Alley's, monopoly on songwriting. The American music industry consequently became more decentralized. Songwriters who specialized in so-called grassroots material (country, Latino, and race music) now felt encouraged to be more aggressive in the commercialization and promotion of their art.

Less than a year after the settling of the ASCAP-broadcasters feud, a new controversy erupted in the music industry. This was the strike called by James C. Petrillo and his American Federation of Musicians, a phenomenon that gave a further impetus to the development of country music. Petrillo argued that jukeboxes, which now numbered over four hundred thousand, and broadcasting stations using phonograph records were driving musicians out of work. Asking for the establishment of a fund for unemployed musicians, payable by the recording companies, the American Federation of Musicians went on strike on August 1, 1942, declaring that there would be no more recording. Having been warned on July 25 that such an event was imminent, the record companies had built up a heavy backlog of records by operating their studios on a round-the-clock schedule. By the fall of 1943, however, the companies began to feel the pinch, and they noticed, too, that their reservoir was inadequate in one important respect: it did not contain the new songs that caught the public's fancy in musicals and movies. When customers requested these songs at a record store, they were not available.

Decca was the record company most adversely affected by the strike, because its revenue came almost entirely from popular music. In September 1943, faced with possible bankruptcy, Decca signed a contract with the American Federation of Musicians. Columbia and Victor followed suit in November 1944, when they concluded similar agreements with the musicians' union.

The musicians' strike was a great boon to numerous small and independent record firms. Most of these signed contracts with Petrillo immediately, and the others followed when Decca came to terms. Of the newer firms, Capitol Records, a Los Angeles company headed by Johnny Mercer, proved to be the most durable. Organized shortly before the strike went into effect, Capitol achieved a strong position that it might not have won so quickly had the strike not been in progress. Capitol profited from the great pool of talent associated with the movie industry, and its country music roster drew upon the large number of entertainers who flocked to the West Coast during and right after the war to become part of the region's booming club business. Tex Ritter was one of the first country artists to sign with the label, and his 1942 hit, Frank Loesser's "I've Got Spurs That Jingle, Jangle, Jingle," was the first of many successes for the popular cowboy singer.

The recording strike significantly furthered grassroots music because many of the small record companies specialized in hillbilly and race music. Hillbilly records began to circulate in areas where they formerly had been rare, and their success inspired the major companies to capitalize on the music's popularity. Decca's first release after the resumption of recording in September 1943 was Bing Crosby and the Andrews Sisters' version of "Pistol Packin' Mama," a hillbilly song first written and recorded by Al Dexter. Crosby, in fact, recorded many of the country and western favorites of the period—a phenomenon that some student of country music ought to explore.

While the strike was in progress, BMI suffered because of the lack of depth in its catalogue. Most of the older recordings were songs listed in the ASCAP catalogue. In 1942, however, at the height of the strike, the songwriter Fred Rose withdrew from ASCAP and signed with BMI. He and the country singer Roy Acuff organized the publishing firm of Acuff-Rose, with headquarters in Nashville. This event strengthened BMI and heralded the beginning of Nashville's preeminence as a country music center. The most important publishing house that emerged because of the increased interest in hillbilly music, however, was Hill and Range. The company was organized in 1945 when Julian Aberbach, a naturalized American of German birth, returned to the United States after his army duty determined to capitalize on the widespread popularity of country music. He had heard the music often during his army duty and decided that the country was ripe for a hillbilly music boom. Along with his brother Gene, Aberbach had originally organized two country music firms, Hill Music and Range Music, which eventually merged into one organization and became one of the largest BMI firms.

The phonograph industry, which also suffered from the ASCAP-BMI controversy and the recording strike, languished because of scarcities imposed by the war effort. At the outset of the war, shellac, important in the manufacture of records, was frozen by government order. Although the restrictions were later relaxed, record issues did not regain their prewar levels until after the war's end. Recording studios could not operate at full capacity because new machinery was unobtainable and trained personnel was scarce. Under these pressures, only about 50 percent of previous record quotas could be filled, even though the entertainment-hungry public was eager to obtain anything that could be produced.

Because of shellac rationing, hillbilly record releases were limited. Some hillbilly entertainers temporarily stopped recording either because of the shellac scarcity or because gas and tire shortages curtailed their abilities to tour and advertise their new recordings. Many musicians, of course, were inducted into the armed forces. Companies released an average of only three hillbilly records a week, and at one critical point, only one a week.

But even at the most restricted points of shellac rationing, the companies continued without interruption to release some hillbilly records—an illustration of the importance attached to country music by the recording companies. And the public bought the records or played them on jukeboxes. Although few songs were released, jukebox operators and record-retailing firms found that these new tunes experienced a strong and enduring popularity. Long after a popular song had declined in popularity, melodies like Ted Daffan's "Born to Lose" or Roy Acuff's "The Great Speckled Bird" continued to attract the nickels of jukebox patrons.

By 1942, country music's growing national popularity had become generally apparent. *Billboard*, the leading trade music magazine, after decades of neglect, began to devote some attention to country performers. Country music coverage was initially undertaken with considerable hesitation, for no one was quite certain how permanent the popularity would be. *Billboard*'s first accounts dealt primarily with the astonishing expansion of country music, but it was some time before the periodical devoted an entire column to the music. *Billboard* did not quite know what to do with the music, or even what to call it. In its first cautious ventures into the exploitation of hillbilly music, the periodical lumped the country tunes in a category along with foreign numbers. In January 1942, *Billboard* inaugurated a column entitled "Western and Race," which featured current releases by everyone from Tex Ritter to Louis Armstrong. Then, in February 1942, the designation was changed to "American Folk Records," a title that remained throughout the war years. In 1944, *Billboard* began a brief listing of the most popular hillbilly songs found on jukeboxes and included them along with popular race recordings. It was not uncommon to see a song like Floyd Tillman's "They Took the Stars Out of Heaven" listed alongside Ella Fitzgerald's "When My Sugar Walks down the Street."

Country music flourished in some northern urban areas simply because southern rural people had moved there during the late 1930s and early 1940s in search of defense work or other industrial jobs. Cities such as Baltimore; Washington, DC; Detroit; Cincinnati; and Chicago reported heightened country music activity as southern migrants—particularly from such border states as Kentucky, West Virginia, Virginia, and Tennessee—poured into the areas and demanded a music for their own tastes. The migrants sought out their own kind and frequented the churches, community centers, and taverns that most reflected their socioeconomic and regional backgrounds. The proprietors of the "hillbilly" bars and taverns, as well as the jukebox operators, found it advantageous to feature songs by Jimmie Davis, Ernest Tubb, and other country singers. Hillbilly tunes were said to be especially popular at places patronized by former West Virginians and North and South Carolinians. The demand for country music in Baltimore became so enormous that the jukeboxes were inundated with hillbilly selections. The migration from contiguous rural areas into Baltimore and nearby Washington, DC, and the consequent burgeoning there of country music interest, helped to lay the basis for the future flourishing of the bluegrass style in that region. Detroit jukebox operators reported in 1943 that hillbilly recordings were the most popular single class of music present on their machines. Hillbillies had been migrating to Detroit at least as early as World War I, when Henry Ford and his marvelous machine began attracting the marginal laborers of the South. The second great war inspired an even greater influx of southern workers seeking defense work. The West Coast, which had experienced the Okie migration of the mid-1930s, reported a tremendous growth in country music popularity as southerners and midwesterners—both civilians and military personnel—poured into the area. Working-class cities like Bakersfield began to experience a rapid growth of clubs and dance halls that catered to the needs of the new arrivals. In Los Angeles, as many as five to ten hillbilly songs were appearing on coin machines that formerly had no more than one. California began to attract country musicians in great numbers, and Bob Wills himself had moved to a San Fernando Valley ranch by November 1943. Popular bands in the state that normally featured only swing and jazz music began adding country tunes to their repertories in response to demands from their audiences. Crowds in Southern California insisted particularly that the popular swing bands should add Bob Wills songs to their repertories.

The intermingling of people from different backgrounds in the armed services was an important factor in the spread of country music. Military personnel sought the cheapest possible forms of entertainment and were probably the main source of the jukebox boom of the early 1940s. Young rural southerners, many of whom had scarcely been more than a few miles from the place where they were born, marched off to training centers carrying their musical tastes with them. Barracks reverberated with the sounds of guitars, lonesome rural voices, and the current hillbilly songs. These same spaces often echoed with arguments as to who was the better singer, Roy Acuff or Frank Sinatra. Country music was transported all over the United States by men and women in the military services who listened to the professional singers and by those who formed their own amateur bands. And, ultimately, the music was carried around the world. By 1943, the Special Services Division of the European Theater of Operations included at least twenty-five hillbilly bands. Once the war was over, the Armed Forces Network (AFN) began broadcasting country music to an even larger audience of people in Europe and Asia.

To satisfy the musical hunger of soldiers and sailors, the R. J. Reynolds Tobacco Company and the *Grand Ole Opry* organized in August 1941 a traveling unit of twenty country entertainers called the Camel Caravan. The Nashville-based country group included the comedienne Minnie Pearl, Pee Wee King and his Golden West Cowboys, and the young Eddy Arnold, who was just a few years away from superstardom. Typically giving a concert climaxed by a public square dance, the Caravan by late 1942 had traveled more than fifty thousand miles in nineteen states (as well as Panama) and presented 175 shows in sixty-eight army camps, hospitals, airfields, and naval and marine bases.

The popularity of the Camel Caravan was only one example of the striking success exhibited by traveling hillbilly units during the war. Throughout the United States, country entertainers were drawing larger crowds and larger box-office receipts than ever before. The personal-appearance field, now becoming highly developed, was based primarily on the established radio barn dances such as the *Grand Ole Opry*, the *National Barn Dance*, Cincinnati's *WLW Barn Dance*, the *Wheeling Jamboree* in West Virginia, and the *Renfro Valley Barn Dance* in Kentucky. These programs sent their touring units on an ever-widening arc, depending on the appeal and range of the radio show.

Chicago's WLS *National Barn Dance* continued to be an important source of the personal appearances made in the midwestern and southern border states, featuring such musicians as Kentucky-born Bob Atcher, whose comic, "crying" version of "I'm Thinking Tonight of My Blue Eyes" was a huge hit in 1939. The WLS road shows, which had played more than six thousand personal appearances since 1932, grossed over $500,000 in the period from 1939 to 1942. These performances, like the other hillbilly shows of the period, were conducted with a minimum of initial investment. Profits, thus, tended to be rather substantial. The Hoosier Hot Shots, a small instrumental group utilizing homemade and off-beat instruments and singing comic songs, frequently grossed between $3,000 and $5,000 on one-day stands. Lulu Belle and Scotty, who performed periodically over WLS in Chicago and WLW in Cincinnati, were in constant demand for public appearances, for which they commanded $500 a day plus transportation.

Other barn dances experienced similar financial successes. The WLW *Boone County Jamboree* on occasion grossed as much as $12,000 on one-day stands. The *Renfro Valley Barn Dance*, created and conducted by the folk-music authority John Lair, maintained two tent roadshows that averaged about $5,000 a week. The biggest one-day grosses for the *Renfro Valley* organization were a $5,500 matinee and night show in Indianapolis and a $4,000 gross in Dayton, Ohio. These road shows, along with radio performances, won the *Renfro Valley* show extensive popularity. The show began its existence in Cincinnati in October 1937 and relocated to Dayton in the fall of 1938, before moving on to Renfro Valley (near Mount Vernon, Kentucky) itself in November 1939. Renfro Valley is a small village sixty miles from Lexington and two and a half miles from any railroad station, but the paid attendance at the regular Saturday night show averaged about five thousand and was sometimes as high as ten thousand. The *Renfro Valley* show satisfied a hunger for down-home security that was particularly felt in the chaotic and lonely years of World War II. Audiences that could not attend the live concerts heard the Saturday night broadcasts or the *Sunday Morning Gathering*, a show broadcast nationally. Listeners were alternately left weeping or somber by the old-time ballads and hymns of the Coon Creek Girls or hysterically amused by the antics of Aunt Idy (Margaret Lillie) and her overgrown brat, Little Clifford (played by Harry Mullins). The *Sunday Morning Gathering* gave listeners a heavy dose of nostalgia. The show was heavily scripted and narrated by Lair and based each morning around a common theme (songs of the Civil War, the songs of Stephen Foster, and the like).[1]

Despite the success experienced by the barn dances and their road-show units, it became increasingly evident during the war years that Nashville's *Grand Ole Opry* was becoming the most important country music show. The program, which boomed out all over the South over the clear-channel, 50,000-watt WSM, became nationally known when it gained network status in 1939. For thirty minutes each Saturday night the National Broadcasting Company carried a segment sponsored by Prince Albert Tobacco. The thirty-minute program, representative of the larger four-and-a-half hour show, was hosted by Roy Acuff and featured a variety of "guest" acts, including such comedians as Lazy Jim Day (known for his "Singing News" routines) and Minnie Pearl. Minnie Pearl, a character created by Sarah Ophelia Colley, was as responsible for the *Opry*'s popularity as any of the musicians. Colley's background and culture suggested little of the hayseed naïveté that surrounded Minnie Pearl. Although she came from a rural background in Centerville, Tennessee, her parents were sufficiently prosperous (her father was a lumberman) to send her to the fashionable Ward-Belmont School in Nashville. Colley worked from 1934 to 1940 for the Sewell Production Company, a dramatic troupe that staged plays all over the South by training and using local talent. One night in January 1936 she stayed with a humble rural family in northern Alabama who kindled the idea for Minnie Pearl and her brother. Representatives of the National Life and Accident Insurance Company, the owner of WSM and the *Grand Ole Opry*, heard her at a convention where she played the part of Minnie Pearl and invited her to appear on the Saturday night show. She became a regular member of the NBC segment in early 1942, and audiences thereafter responded enthusiastically to the guileless country girl who wore a straw hat with the price tag hanging prominently from it, greeted each audience with a "How-dee, I'm so proud to be here," and told jokes about Brother, her boyfriend Hezzie, and Uncle Nabob, all of which were perversely appealing in their utter corniness.

As Minnie Pearl's career suggests, the *Grand Ole Opry* was well on the way to becoming a haven for "stars." During the 1940s, the show became famous for its vocalists and featured comedians: Roy Acuff, Bill Monroe, Ernest Tubb, Lloyd "Cowboy" Copas, Eddy Arnold, Minnie Pearl, Lazy Jim Day, the Duke of Paducah (played by Benny Ford, famous for his closing line: "I'm going to the wagon, boys, these shoes are killing me"), and Rod Brasfield. Even before America's entry into the war in 1941, the *Opry* had begun sending its troupes far beyond the bounds of Middle Tennessee. Some *Opry* units performed in huge tents that attracted thousands of fans all over the South. A blackface team, Jamup and Honey, headed one such unit; Bill Monroe traveled with another; and the great fiddler Curly Fox headed another, which included his wife, Texas Ruby, as well as Lazy Jim Day and Uncle Dave Macon.

The *Grand Ole Opry*'s upsurge in popularity was attended, as was true in the case of other country music shows, by the rise of independent promoters who were quick to recognize the financial possibilities of the country music business. At the beginning of the war, the most important promoters were individuals like Earl Kurtze, George Ferguson, and Dick Bergen, who gained success through their associations with the WLS Artists' Bureau. By 1943, they were being rivaled by independent promoters such as Larry Sunbrock and, in the South, Oscar Davis, "Happy" Hal Burns, Tom Parker (the famous "Colonel" who later gained international notoriety through his association with Elvis Presley), and J. L. Frank, who capitalized on the wealth of southern hillbilly talent, particularly that found on the *Grand Ole Opry*. Frank, the father-in-law of Pee Wee King, was instrumental in the careers of Gene Autry, Roy Acuff, and Ernest Tubb (whose first southern tours he arranged), and because of his pioneering efforts on behalf of expanded country road shows, he was called the "Flo Ziegfeld of country music show business." In October 1967, Frank was named, as a deceased nonperformer, to the Country Music Hall of Fame.

In touting hillbilly performances, all of the promoters used similar methods. They placed heavy emphasis on radio saturation instead of billing or newspaper advertising, although many groups continued to tack their placards and posters on posts, windows, and walls. Scores of hillbilly acts still played in schoolhouses or gymnasiums, or between films at movies, yet an increasing number took their performances into city auditoriums or other public arenas. "Folk music parks" also attracted touring country units. These resort areas were concentrated primarily in New England (where they seem to have originated in the early 1930s), New York, Pennsylvania, the Midwest, and such border states as Maryland and Delaware. They were distinguished from regular parks in that they contained large outdoor stages with seating areas where weekly music performances were given. Such parks as Buck Lake Ranch, at Angola, Indiana, and Ravine Park, at Blairsville, Pennsylvania, attracted southeastern migrant musicians long before professional acts began frequenting them.

Country acts booked by such promoters as Oscar Davis and Hal Burns played to large audiences all over the United States. Other entrepreneurs, though, concentrated on more limited areas. Foreman Phillips, for example, a country disc jockey in Los Angeles, made California his sphere of operation. In June 1942, Phillips converted the ballroom on Venice Pier into a country music haven when he opened the *Los Angeles County Barn Dance*. He could draw upon a large storehouse of local talent for the *Barn Dance* and for the dance halls that he established throughout Southern California, but he also brought big-name country performers in from other parts of the country. The two most successful appearances were those by Bob Wills, who attracted 8,600 customers to the pier, and Roy Acuff, who set an attendance record of 11,130.

Foreman Phillips was only one of many individuals who contributed to country music's great wartime surge. By 1944, more than six hundred hillbilly radio programs could be heard on stations ranging from the tiny 100-watt WAGM, at Presque Isle, Maine, to a score or more of powerful 50,000-watt stations such as WSM. The number of recording performers was also extensive. In a list prepared by *Billboard* in 1943, a total of 608 recording artists was led by hillbillies, with a total of 198. The entire aggregate of hillbilly performers, ranging from the professionals to the amateurs who struggled for success in the honky-tonks or on obscure radio barn dances, must have been enormous. Of the total, only a small percentage did well enough financially to warrant independent professional careers; most could not "give up their day jobs." It is impossible to determine and hazardous to guess who the most successful country entertainers of the period were. Certainly, no one has a stronger claim to the distinction—at least at the beginning of the war—than Gene Autry. Autry's movie appearances kept him in the public eye, and shrewd business activities made him a wealthy man. His phonograph records were among the nation's top sellers, and he commanded a greater popularity in northern areas than any other country performer. Autry would have gained even greater success had he not volunteered for military service, at the age of thirty-five, in 1942. He was part of a Special Services unit at first but soon became a flight officer in the Air Transport Command in Burma and India. At the time of his induction, he commanded $1,000 a performance and was said to be a profitable investment at that figure. Autry's popularity suffered a gradual decline after his induction, and he was never able to regain his leadership as a recording star (even though the phenomenal success of "Rudolph the Red Nosed Reindeer" was yet to come). He even lost to Roy Rogers his title of "America's Number One Singing Cowboy."

Texas musicians, in general, won extensive recognition during the war years. Bob Wills was well known far beyond the range of KVOO when he, too, enlisted in the army in December 1942. Upon receiving a medical discharge about a year later, Wills moved to California, re-organized the Texas Playboys, and began playing to turn-away crowds all over the West Coast. Wills never really tried to gain much exposure outside the Southwest and West, but his one guest appearance on the *Grand Ole Opry* in December 1944, when he shocked traditionalists by his use of drums, evoked an enthusiastic response. Wills, Ted Daffan, Al Dexter, Floyd Tillman, Tex Ritter, and Ernest Tubb all produced records that, according to BMI estimates, dominated the jukeboxes during the first half of the 1940s. Tubb was destined to have the great-est longevity and, in many respects, the most widespread influence.

Tubb took his Texas style to the *Grand Ole Opry* in January 1943, and there he popularized such songs as "Walking the Floor over You," "Blue Eyed Elaine," "Our Baby's Book" (inspired by the death of his infant son, Rodger Dale), "Take Me Back and Try Me One More Time," and "When the World Has Turned You Down" (all of which were written by Tubb himself). By this time, Tubb had gone beyond the rather simple accompaniment that characterized his first Decca releases (just two guitars) and had begun devising the full-blown electric honky-tonk sound, complete with steel guitar and takeoff guitar, that would remain an integral part of his style. Tubb's move to Nashville more than symbolized the "West's" growing influence in country music and the mixing of regional styles that occurred in the 1940s; through his popular broadcasts and recordings, he became the direct inspiration of many of country music's future stars, several of whom came from states far removed from Texas (Loretta Lynn from Kentucky; Harold "Hawkshaw" Hawkins from West Virginia; Jack Greene from Tennessee; Hank Williams from Alabama; and even Bobby Osborne, the future bluegrass entertainer, from Kentucky).

Southwestern singers may have dominated the jukeboxes during the war, but they did not monopolize the country field. Southeastern musicians remained active and popular, and one of them, Roy Acuff (who will be discussed later), won unprecedented success as a singer. Some old-time groups, such as Mainer's Mountaineers, although fixtures on the radio barn dances, rarely made records of hit proportions. Roy Hall and the Blue Ridge Entertainers had a few moderately successful records, such as "Don't Let Your Sweet Love Die," but were best known in Virginia and the Carolinas through their radio shows. Before Hall's death in an automobile accident in 1943, few groups surpassed the Blue Ridge Entertainers in popularity in the Upper South. Wartime rationing and restrictions made it difficult for some acts, such as the Delmore Brothers, to remain active, while others, such as the Blue Sky Boys, were called to military service.

The duet tradition ebbed significantly during the war. Martha and James Carson, however—a husband-and-wife team from Kentucky—performed regularly on the *WSB Barn Dance* in Atlanta; Bill and Joe Callahan from North Carolina had settled down in Dallas, where they performed daily on KRLD; and Wiley and Zeke Morris, another North Carolina duo, amassed a large following through their mandolin-and-guitar-backed renditions of such songs as "Salty Dog Blues." Another stellar duet from the 1930s, the Monroe brothers, had gone their separate ways well before the war started, but each had organized bands that achieved prominence during the 1940s. Charlie Monroe's Kentucky Pardners became one of the most popular North Carolina hillbilly bands, and although they stayed close to the older string band format, several musicians who later became identified with the bluegrass style—Lester Flatt, Red Rector, and Curly Sechler—got their start with the group. Bill Monroe's Blue Grass Boys had been a leading act on the *Grand Ole Opry* since 1939, but their collective talents had been subsumed by the sky-high tenor voice of their leader, heard to great advantage on such songs as "Muleskinner Blues" and "Footprints in the Snow." With the addition of the guitarist Lester Flatt and the banjoist Earl Scruggs in 1944 and 1945 respectively—musicians who could command attention equal to that accorded Monroe—the Blue Grass Boys began making the crucial transition from old-time string band music to bluegrass.

Many musicians achieved recognition during the turbulent war years, but none so dominated and symbolized country music as did that mountain boy from East Tennessee, Roy Acuff. With his showmanship and relaxed stage presence, an utterly sincere and believable vocal style, and skill at choosing appropriate songs, Acuff won an immense audience that is all the more remarkable in that it came at a time of growing "western" dominance in country music. Neither

Roy Acuff and the Louvin Brothers. From the John Edwards Memorial
Foundation Records, #20001, 1632-01, Southern Folklife Collection,
Louis Round Wilson Special Collections Library, University of North
Carolina at Chapel Hill; photo by Elmer Williams.

Acuff's singing nor his instrumental accompaniment echoed any of the honky-tonk or "hot dance" traits of the Southwest.

Roy Claxton Acuff was born September 15, 1903, in Maynardville, Tennessee, the son of Neill Acuff, a Missionary Baptist minister and lawyer. A country preacher's income proved insufficient to support the family, so Roy spent his early life in a succession of homes in the foothills of the Smoky Mountains while his father sought additional means of livelihood. When Roy was sixteen, the family moved to a Knoxville suburb, Fountain City. During his attendance at Central High School in Knoxville, Acuff became a star athlete and won a total of thirteen athletic letters. His dream of a professional baseball career did not materialize, even though the New York Yankees invited him to a summer training camp. An almost fatal sunstroke in July 1929 (during a Florida fishing trip) ended his hopes for athletic stardom and, in the long period of recuperation that followed, his interests turned toward music.

Acuff had always shown an aptitude for music and probably received his greatest inspiration from his father, who played the fiddle in the wee hours of the morning before doing the chores. A recurrence of his illness kept Acuff in Knoxville for two years, a period in which he practiced both the fiddle and his singing style. His boyhood experience of singing in Missionary Baptist church services did much to shape the lusty and emotional vocal style for which he became famous, but he also learned from a sister who had taken voice lessons and from the hillbilly records (Fiddlin' John, Gid Tanner, the Carter Family, etc.) to which he often listened. Acuff ventured into the world of show business in the spring of 1932 when he joined Doc Hauer's medicine show that toured eastern Tennessee hawking Moc-A-Tan Compound. Performing in blackface or playing the part of "Toby," the red-haired rube character well known to traveling rural entertainment, Acuff developed the ease and showmanship that remained with him for the rest of his career.

In 1933, Acuff began performing with a group of friends at dances and private parties but soon obtained a spot on WROL in Knoxville. Calling themselves the Tennessee Crackerjacks, the boys had moved by 1934 to rival station WNOX, where they were among the earliest performers on Lowell Blanchard's *Mid-Day Merry-Go-Round*, a show that became a Knoxville institution and a forum for the music of such entertainers as Chet Atkins, Bill Carlisle, Pee Wee King, and Kitty Wells. In 1935, Roy and the Crackerjacks returned to WROL to inaugurate a rival noontime show. Renamed the Crazy Tennesseans by an announcer impressed by their rather casual approach to formal radio entertaining, they remained on the station until Roy joined the *Grand Ole Opry* in 1938.

Acuff began his recording career in 1936, when William R. Calaway of the American Record Company heard him singing "The Great Speckled Bird" (the original record labels, however, spelled it "Speckle," and to many people it will always bear that title). Set to a melody reminiscent of "I'm Thinking Tonight of My Blue Eyes," the song came to Acuff through the performances of another Knoxville radio group, Charlie Swain and the Black Shirts. The authorship of this famous song will probably always remain unknown, although it has been attributed to a Rev. Gant and to a Rev. Guy Smith. (Acuff also wrote four additional verses that became "The Great Speckled Bird No. 2.") The song, which pictures the church as a group of persecuted individuals who ultimately will gain eternal salvation as a reward for their earthly travail, is based on the ninth verse of the twelfth chapter of Jeremiah: "Mine heritage is unto me as a speckled bird, the birds round about are against her." The song was popular not only as a recording hit but as a favorite in some of the Pentecostal Holiness churches as well. Vance Randolph, for example, heard it sung in Pawhuska, Oklahoma, as an official Assembly of God hymn, and W. J. Cash claimed that it was "the official hymn of the Church of God."[2]

After repeated tries, Acuff moved to the *Grand Ole Opry* on February 19, 1938, largely through the influence of J. L. Frank, who urged the show to take the gamble, and as a possible replacement for the fiddler Arthur Smith, who had left the show. Acuff's fiddle debut tunes did not particularly impress either the audience or the *Opry* staff, but his heartfelt performance of "The Great Speckled Bird," done as his third number, elicited a large response of cards and letters. The move to the *Opry* eventually made Acuff one of the most well-known country performers in the nation and the *Opry* the most famous radio barn dance in the United States. Accompanied by his string band, now called the Smoky Mountain Boys, he became the first real singing star of the *Grand Ole Opry*. When NBC began its thirty-minute coverage in 1939, no one but Acuff seems to have been considered for the host position. In the years that followed, "Roy Acuff" and "*Grand Ole Opry*" became almost synonymous.

As the leading star of the *Opry*, Roy Acuff performed a repertory heavily weighted with sacred and traditional-style songs,[3] all rendered in an emotionally earnest and plaintive manner. Like all great country singers, Acuff felt strongly the sentiments he expressed and was able to communicate his feelings to his listeners. On some of his most serious numbers, he became so emotionally involved with the lyrics that he wept openly. His intense delivery and graceful stage presence made him a crowd-pleaser and a great drawing card.

Oddly enough, two songs from his first recording session always remained most strongly identified with him: "The Great Speckled Bird" and "The Wabash Cannonball." "The Wabash Cannonball" is usually attributed to A.P. Carter, but it is actually of traditional derivation, telling of a mythical train that would carry the hobo to the land of fantasy. Acuff's version seems more inspired by a 1929 recording made by fellow East Tennessean Hugh Cross than by that of the Carter Family. Ironically, Acuff did not sing on the first recording of the song—the harmonica player Dynamite Hatcher did—but Roy supplied an imitation train whistle (inspired by his days as a callboy for the Louisville and Nashville [L&N] Railroad) that contributed to the song's great success. He did not record the song with his own vocal until 1947. But in the meantime, he had been singing it constantly on the *Opry* and on his many road shows.

Acuff resisted electrical amplification long after it had become the norm in most country bands and instead adhered to the style and format of the older acoustic string bands. Lacking confidence in his ability to play the fiddle (which he actually played rather well), he left the bulk of the instrumentation to other band members. Acuff always employed outstanding fiddlers, such as Tommy Magness and Howard "Howdy" Forrester, but the center of his instrumentation, and a defining feature of the Roy Acuff sound, was the Dobro steel guitar. On his earliest recordings, the instrument was played by James Clell Summey, who, as Cousin Jody, later became a popular baggy-pants comedian known for his toothless grin. After 1938, Acuff's Dobro player was Beecher Kirby (best known as "Bashful Brother Oswald"), who sang one of the highest and most easily recognized harmonies in country music, frailed the five-string banjo, and did comedy routines, often with Rachel Veach, who was advertised as his sister. Kirby made the unelectrified Dobro the most prominent feature of the Smoky Mountain Boys' instrumentation at the very time when electric instruments were becoming the rage in other country music groups.

Acuff's efforts to keep his music as traditional as possible could be noted not only in his use of acoustic instrumentation but also in his singing style and choice of songs. The influence of church music was particularly apparent. When his entire group joined him on gospel numbers, no attempt was made to achieve close harmony, for Acuff wanted to keep the style similar to that heard in his boyhood Baptist church. The Smoky Mountain Boys were unaffected by the western image. Acuff wore sport clothes during his stage appearances, while his band members dressed in overalls or other casual attire. Acuff's repertory was largely of his own choosing, but it also reflected (at least during the Columbia years) the inclinations of his artists and repertory (A&R) man, Arthur Satherley. The British-born Satherley, who came to the United States as a young man filled with visions of cowboys and romantic isolated mountaineers, tried to keep country music moored to its traditional roots, and he found Acuff to be much more committed to old-time songs than his other two famous "discoveries," Bob Wills and Gene Autry. Although an occasional vintage pop song, such as "Yes Sir, That's My Baby," did appear in his early recording repertory, not a single "cowboy" or western-style song can be found in Roy Acuff's repertory and very little that suggests a western swing influence. Acuff's song catalogue was heavily weighted with sacred numbers like "The Great Judgment Morning," sentimental songs of unrequited love like "Come Back Little Pal" (learned from Roy Hall) and "All the World Is Lonely Now," old-time novelty numbers like "Ida Red," and tragic numbers such as "Unloved and Unclaimed" (about the suicide drowning of an anonymous woman in Nashville).

Acuff seems to have written some of his most popular songs—such as "The Precious Jewel," a song about the death of a young prospective bride—set to the melody of a mournful mountain ballad, "The Hills of Roane County." But most of his repertory came from other composers. Some of them, like Fred Rose, were very well known. Much of his material, though, came from obscure or anonymous writers. Jim Anglin, for example—a one-time member of the Anglin Brothers singing team in the late 1930s—wrote many of Acuff's finest songs: "Lonely Mound of Clay," "Branded Wherever I Go," "Stuck Up Blues," "They Can Only Fill One Grave," "As Long as I Live," "Just a Friend," and "Unloved and Unclaimed."

Acuff succeeded as a "mountain" singer when the majority of country performers seemed to be discarding traditional rural numbers and accepting "western" styles and techniques. His great accomplishments came partly because he presented a musical alternative to the country music fans who were being deluged with the newer musical styles and partly (and this probably helps to explain country music's

overall popularity) because the war "caused people to turn to simpler
and more fundamental things."[4] When Roy Acuff raised his voice in
his mournful, mountain style, he seemed to suggest all the verities for
which Americans believed they were fighting: home, mother, and God.

Regardless of the source of his appeal, Americans packed any place
in which Roy Acuff appeared, whether it was Nashville's Ryman Auditorium for the Saturday night *Grand Ole Opry* or the site of one of his
numerous touring appearances. A capacity crowd at Constitution Hall
in Washington, DC, paid as much as $6.60 each to see him; at Cincin-
nati's Music Hall a country music show starring Acuff and Ernest
Tubb attracted 13,000 people for two performances; and at Venice
Pier, California, Acuff drew the largest crowd that had ever gone to a
Foreman Phillips promotion. The 11,130 paid admissions gave rise to
fears that the pier would fall from the weight.

Acuff's income, which over the years was among the highest in
the country music business, was estimated at well over $200,000 in
1942. Largely through the business acumen of his wife, Mildred, Acuff
built an immense personal fortune through adroit financial dealings,
and particularly through his co-ownership of Acuff-Rose Publishing
House and Hickory Records, both in Nashville.

His popularity was not confined to American audiences. A two-
week popularity contest held on the Armed Forces Network's *Munich
Morning Report* gave Acuff, out of 3,700 votes cast, a lead of 600 votes
over the popular crooner Frank Sinatra. As a result, the AFN instituted
a new show, *Hillbilly Jamboree,* directed from Munich at American
occupation forces in Europe.

An incident that reveals the worldwide significance of Roy Acuff's
name, and is probably the greatest tribute he ever received, occurred
on the remote island of Okinawa. Upon attacking a Marine position, a
Japanese banzai charge used a battle cry that it thought would be the
ultimate in insults: "To hell with Roosevelt; to hell with Babe Ruth; to
hell with Roy Acuff!"

An important figure in Acuff's career, and one of the major forces
behind country music's commercial evolution, was Fred Rose, who
grew up outside the country music world and spent his early career
as a popular music entertainer. Despite his "nonrustic" origins, he became one of the most successful country songwriters of all time and a
major discoverer and promoter of young country talent. He was one of
the first three individuals elected to the Country Music Hall of Fame.

Rose was born in Evansville, Indiana, on August 24, 1897, but grew up in St. Louis. Before the 1940s, he had little association with country music but had pursued a career as a pianist and popular songwriter in Chicago. Elected to ASCAP in 1938, Rose had attained considerable success as the writer of such songs as Sophie Tucker's "Red Hot Mama," as well as "'Deed I Do," and "Honest and Truly."

His first venture into the writing of country-style songs came on the West Coast in 1940, when he wrote sixteen songs for Gene Autry, including the very popular "Be Honest with Me." In the next decade, Rose wrote hundreds of songs that were recorded or otherwise performed by most country performers. When he moved to Nashville and became the staff pianist for station WSM, he became acquainted with Roy Acuff—an association that proved mutually profitable and beneficial. Rose commented that he never truly understood the real meaning or power of country music until he stood backstage one night at the *Grand Ole Opry* and watched Acuff, with tears streaming from his eyes, sing a song about a dying child, "Don't Make Me Go to Bed and I'll Be Good."[5] Writing often under assumed names, such as Floyd Jenkins and Bart Dawson, Rose composed many of the most popular and enduring songs of the 1940s and 1950s. Like Cindy Walker and Boudleaux and Felice Bryant, Rose could easily adapt to any style of country music, from gospel to secular. Songs like "Be Honest with Me," "Pins and Needles (in My Heart)," and "No One Will Ever Know" are known by all country fans. His biggest hit came posthumously: "Blue Eyes Crying in the Rain," though recorded by earlier singers, became a massive success for Willie Nelson in 1975.

In 1942, Rose and Roy Acuff organized the first exclusive country music publishing house in the United States, Acuff-Rose Publications. This firm provided the nucleus for Nashville's later rise to eminence in the music industry and brought further financial success to each of its founders. In December 1945, Fred Rose turned the operation of the business over to his son Wesley and began devoting most of his time to the aid and encouragement of prospective young songwriters, the most famous being Hank Williams.

Country songwriters explored a variety of themes during the 1940s, but nothing attracted their attention more than the war itself. Continuing a tradition set by their ballad-making ancestors centuries earlier, the country singers and writers chronicled the war as they talked of the experiences, sufferings, and death of the departed soldiers, and of the anxieties and sadness of their loved ones. Patriotic songs and related war songs were among the most popular numbers in the hillbilly repertory from 1941 to 1946. Carson Robison's "1942 Turkey in the Straw" was, according to *Billboard*, the most popular hillbilly song during the first year of the war. No song, however, surpassed in popularity Elton Britt's version of "There's a Star Spangled Banner Waving Somewhere." Attributed to the prolific songwriter Bob Miller, but probably merely arranged by him, the song was first released in May 1942 as the "B" side of a Bluebird record. Recounting the story of a crippled mountain boy who yearned to do his part in the war effort, the record gained astounding success because it attracted not only hillbilly enthusiasts but popular music fans as well. Britt's recorded version sold over a million and a half copies, while almost as many copies of the sheet music were sold. Remaining popular well into 1943, the song was eventually recorded by many acts, both popular and hillbilly. In his recorded version, however, Elton Britt, billed as "the highest yodeler in the world," became the first hillbilly singer since Vernon Dalhart to record a song of national-hit proportions that transcended the bounds of most musical categories.

Some of the songs, like Roy Acuff's "Cowards over Pearl Harbor," expressed Americans' shock and anger at their sudden and undesired entry into the war. "Smoke on the Water," recorded by its writer, Zeke Clements, and also by such singers as Red Foley, breathed a defiant tone as it described what would happen "when our army and navy overtake the enemy." "I'll Be Back in a Year, Little Darlin'" was actually written *before* the bombing of Pearl Harbor, but it denoted the growing military preparedness in the United States. It was only one of several country war songs that expressed the promise of faithfulness: Others included "Each Night at Nine," "We'll Meet Again, Sweetheart," "I'll Be True While You're Gone," "When My Blue Moon Turns to Gold Again," "I'll Wait for You," "Silver Dew on the Blue Grass Tonight," "Down Where the River Bends," and "Mother, I Thank You for the Bible You Gave." Some songs, of course—such as "Are You Waiting Just for Me," "At Mail Call Today" (about a "Dear John" letter), and "Have I Stayed Away Too Long" (written by the pop composer Frank Loesser, who admitted a liking for hillbilly music)—discussed unfaithful love or the anxieties felt by servicemen about their loved ones back home.

The most poignant wartime songs dealt with the tragedy of war. Frank Loesser contributed a song about one of America's military heroes, "The Ballad of Rodger Young." Tex Ritter's "Gold Star in the Window" told of "the price a mother paid to keep us free." Songs like "Stars and Stripes on Iwo Jima" and "White Cross on Okinawa," both recorded by Bob Wills, described American sacrifices for the cause of freedom. "Soldier's Last Letter," written by Ernest Tubb and Sergeant Henry "Redd" Stewart (Pee Wee King's longtime vocalist and partner), dealt with a mother's sorrow upon receiving word that her son had been killed in action. Red River Dave McEnery's "The Blind Boy's Dog" was more ludicrous than pathetic, and it probably provoked more laughs than its composer intended, but it no doubt touched a few hearts with its tale of a blind boy who patriotically sent his lead dog off to die in the war. The two most affecting songs about war's tragedies were "Teardrops Falling in the Snow" (written by Mac McCarty and beautifully sung by Molly O'Day) and "Searching for a Soldier's Grave" (written by Jim Anglin and recorded by the Bailes Brothers). "Teardrops Falling in the Snow" tells of a mother's trip to a railroad station to receive the casket "wrapped in red, white, and blue" that bears her son. "Searching for a Soldier's Grave" tells of a person who travels abroad to find the final resting place of a loved one, and it universalizes the individual tragedies produced by the war when it remarks that beneath the white crosses lie buried the hearts of thousands of Americans back home across the ocean.

Apart from the patriotic songs, wartime country music continued to mine the same veins that had attracted earlier writers. Except for the songs composed for motion pictures, however, "cowboy" melodies declined significantly as a part of the hillbilly repertory. The western myth nevertheless remained in the wearing of gaudy cowboy paraphernalia. The honky-tonk had definitely come to exert a powerful and dominating role in country music. Among songs of the honky-tonk variety, those of Texas origin generally predominated: Ernest Tubb's "Walking the Floor Over You"; Ted Daffan's "Worried Mind," "Headin' Down the Wrong Highway," and "Born to Lose"; Jerry Irby's "Driving Nails in My Coffin"; and Floyd Tillman's "They Took the Stars Out of Heaven" and "It Makes No Difference Now." The composers of "The Last Letter" and "When My Blue Moon Turns to Gold Again" were not born in the Lone Star State, but they were strongly identified with Texas because of long residence there, and their songs competed for the nickels of beer hall patrons all over the state. Neither Rex Griffin ("The Last Letter") nor Gene Sullivan ("When My Blue Moon Turns to Gold Again") were honky-tonk musicians; they were instead radio performers who merely happened to write and record songs that made their way into honky-tonks all over the country. Griffin was a Gadsden, Alabama, native who wandered into radio stations all over the South before winding up in Dallas in the early 1940s. His great song of forsaken love, "The Last Letter," has traveled much farther than its creator, entering the repertory of almost every country singer. Gene Sullivan, from Alabama, and his longtime singing partner Wiley Walker, from Florida, traveled separate routes as entertainers before organizing their duet in Texas in 1939. Walker was a fiddler and a singer who performed with Lew Childre for several years and who had been a dancer, singer, musician, and actor with Harley Sadler's West Texas tent show in the late 1930s. Sullivan belonged to several bands, including those headed by Happy Hal Burns in Birmingham, the Shelton Brothers in Shreveport, and Roy Newman in Dallas, before finally teaming up with Walker in Dallas. They made radio transcriptions, performed in Fort Worth and Lubbock, and then moved to Oklahoma City, where they became ensconced on local radio (WKY) for many years. They had settled down in Oklahoma City when their two most famous songs, "When My Blue Moon Turns to Gold Again" and "Live and Let Live," appeared as opposite sides of the same Okeh record. The melancholy lyrics, combined with Walker's and Sullivan's gentle, low-pitched harmony, made the songs extremely popular with country fans everywhere. They captured the mood of loneliness and separation that so many people felt during the war years, and they have never since lost their appeal.

Many songs demonstrated popular appeal in the early 1940s, but few were as commercially successful as "Pistol Packin' Mama." Although released by Okeh in March 1943, the song was inspired by the violence and turbulence of East Texas oilfield days in the 1930s. Its performer and writer, Al Dexter (Albert Poindexter, born in Jacksonville, Texas, in 1905), had been the proprietor of a honky-tonk near Longview, Texas, in about 1933. The idea for the song came to him one day when a gun-toting woman chased her husband's girlfriend (and one of Al's waitresses) through a barbed-wire fence. Some years later, he attached the words to a melody borrowed from Bob Wills's "Take Me Back to Tulsa" and ultimately saw his song become one of the smash hits of American country and popular music. The rollicking novelty tune, which offended some people because of its open reference to drinking beer, succeeded "There's a Star Spangled Banner Waving Somewhere" as the country's most popular hillbilly song and reached even greater commercial heights when that remarkable urban bucolic Bing Crosby and the Andrews Sisters performed it as their first post-strike recording in September 1943. Within six months of its issuance, over a million copies of the record had been sold; the song itself ranks as one of the two or three most popular hits of the war years. The song, however, did not appear on CBS's *Lucky Strike Hit Parade*, then the chief means of denoting America's most popular melodies, until October 1943. The reasons it was rejected earlier were unknown, but *Life* magazine speculated that it might be because of the sponsor's dislike, or because Frank Sinatra, the show's star vocalist, would or could not sing the little ditty. The periodical's editorial staff may have been unaware that Sinatra had actually recorded the number that very year![6] The song sold more than three million records in less than two years, and Dexter was still receiving royalties on it into the 1960s.

Country music emerged from the war years, therefore, exhibiting a remarkable strength, given the context of scarcity and restrictiveness in which it operated. The process of nationalization that had begun in the 1930s accelerated during the war when servicemen, servicewomen, and migrating civilians introduced their musical tastes to new people in distant climes. The names of such entertainers as Jimmie Davis, Ernest Tubb, Gene Autry, Ted Daffan, Bob Wills, and Roy Acuff had become known, in varying degrees, all over the United States. Throughout the late 1930s and the war years, songs had occasionally transcended the bounds of country music to become national favorites. The music industry as a whole certainly took note of country music's great gains during the early 1940s. *Billboard* noted prophetically that the music had "shown by its work against adverse conditions that when the war is over and normalcy returns it will be the field to watch."[7]

CHAPTER 7

The Boom Period

The Emergence of a Big Business, 1946–1953

The uncertain peace that followed World War II ushered in a period of unparalleled prosperity. Freed from wartime restraints, anxious Americans now sought the stability and material abundance that had been denied them in earlier eras. Country music profited as one consequence of the pursuit of pleasure and amusement that followed the war. In many respects, the dawning period should be perceived as the real "golden age" of country music. Later decades would bring greater material rewards to country musicians, but no period would experience a happier fusion of "traditional" sounds and commercial burgeoning than did the immediate postwar era.

As the nation converted successfully to a civilian, domestic economy, the music industry, unhampered by wartime restrictions, geared itself for a highly prosperous period. Records could now be produced in quantities above their prewar levels, and an entertainment-hungry public was ready to buy them. Country music, which had prospered despite (or perhaps because of) defense regulations, was already showing signs of increased national recognition. In 1946, songs like "Oklahoma Hills," performed by Jack Guthrie (soon to die in a veteran's hospital), Tex Williams's "Shame on You," Wesley Tuttle's "Detour," Arthur Smith's "Guitar Boogie," and Merle Travis's "Divorce

Me C.O.D." were jukebox favorites all over the nation. Bing Crosby, moreover, crossed once more into the country field and recorded the biggest song of all, "Sioux City Sue" (done the previous year by Dick Thomas).

At the conclusion of the war, at least sixty-five recording companies, fifteen of them on the West Coast, were releasing country records. Radio continued to be an indispensable means of exploiting hillbilly talent. By 1949, at least 650 radio stations featured live country performers. In the early commercial years, most of the hillbilly shows had been broadcast at noon or during the early morning hours, since program directors felt that only early-rising farmers listened to the programs. But with their newly discovered popularity, country entertainers were scheduled at more advantageous hours and were produced with the same care given to other musical offerings. In addition to established shows like the *Grand Ole Opry*, the period saw the emergence of regional barn dances like the *Wheeling Jamboree* on WWVA in West Virginia; Atlanta's *WSB Barn Dance*; *Farm and Fun Time* (heard each day at noon over a five-state area), from Bristol, Virginia; Dallas's *Big D Jamboree*; Los Angeles's *Town Hall Party* and *Dinner Bell Roundup* (later called the *Hometown Jamboree*); and, most important of all, Shreveport's *Louisiana Hayride*. In addition to providing local entertainment, these shows started many successful country musicians on the road to wider fame.

Country music, therefore, was in the midst of a burgeoning commercial success most evidenced, perhaps, by the growth and development of the personal-appearance field. *Billboard* claimed that country performers were major box-office attractions almost everywhere in the United States, even in "sedate New England."[1] The South, as usual, remained a lucrative area for hillbilly entertainers, but Pennsylvania, Ohio, and Michigan were recognized as important markets for country music. Country music even ventured into historic Carnegie Hall in October 1947, when a *Grand Old Opry* unit headed by Ernest Tubb played two nights for a gross of over $9,000.

The most vigorous region for live country performances may very well have been California,[2] with major emphasis devoted to ballroom performances and the big radio barn dances that began in the mid-1940s. When Bob Wills relocated to California in September 1943, the dance hall business had already begun to thrive, but he soon became a major musical force in the state, breaking attendance records everywhere he went, operating a club in Sacramento called Wills Point, and occasionally making cross-country tours. His Texas Playboys had moved away from their earlier emphasis on horns, once again becoming basically a fiddle band. Wills himself was devoting more attention to fiddle hoedowns, and he acquired two new fiddlers, Johnny Gimble (from Texas) and Keith Coleman (from Oklahoma), both at home in any style. Wills had also added another twist to his band by adding a female vocalist, Laura Lee McBride, the first featured woman singer in the western swing genre. As the daughter of the radio cowboy singer Tex Owens, McBride was well connected in the country field. She was also the niece of Texas Ruby Owens and the wife of the bandleader Dickie McBride.

The era of country ballrooms had begun in 1942 when Foreman Phillips opened the Venice Pier Ballroom, catering to transplanted Okies, defense workers, and servicemen. Before his retirement in 1952, Phillips had opened three other thriving ballrooms in Culver City, Baldwin Park, and Compton, where he had hired such musicians as Ray Whitley, Hank Penny, Ted Daffan, Curley Williams, T. Texas Tyler, and Red Murrell to head his house bands. Phillips also was instrumental in the creation of the band that did the most to give western swing its name: Spade Cooley and His Orchestra.

Donnell Clyde "Spade" Cooley's story is one of success and tragedy. Cooley came to Modesto, California, with his family from Grande, Oklahoma, in the 1930s and soon became a fiddler with various bands in the area around Los Angeles. Foreman Phillips hired him away from the Jimmy Wakely Trio in about 1942 to head a band at Venice Pier. He was joined late that same year by a singer and bass player from Illinois, Sollie Paul "Tex" Williams, who was to have a profitable relationship with Cooley until 1946. In 1943, Cooley took his band to the Riverside Rancho Ballroom, where they played nightly to overflow crowds for the next three years. During this busy and prosperous interlude, and at the Santa Monica Ballroom after 1946, Cooley became known as the "King of Western Swing," apparently the first use of the term to describe the music that Bob Wills and Milton Brown had pioneered. Cooley's music was more heavily orchestrated than that of Wills (whose musicians generally improvised what they felt), but his large band included some remarkably innovative musicians, such as the jazz-style steel guitarist Joaquin Murphy, and an instrument or two, such as a harp, that almost never appeared in other country bands.

Cooley maintained his popularity until one sad night in 1961 when, in a fit of drunken rage, he beat and stomped his wife to death. Tragedy remained with Cooley for the last few short years of his life. He served a prison term for eight years and died of a heart attack in 1969 while on a temporary parole to attend a concert in his honor.

Cooley's former vocalist, Sollie "Tex" Williams, formed his own band, the Western Caravan, in 1946 and went on to become one of the most-admired singers of the period. His smooth, ultradeep voice was first heard on "Shame on You," a big Columbia hit for Spade Cooley in 1945–1946, but Williams had a successful string of recordings on his own for the Capitol label after 1946. One of them not only was financially satisfying to Williams but also was well ahead of its time in the message it conveyed. This was his 1947 hit, "Smoke! Smoke! Smoke!" a half-sung, half-recited complaint about the inconveniences caused by chronic smokers.

"Smoke! Smoke! Smoke!" was the brainchild of Merle Travis, one of country music's most brilliant and multitalented entertainers. When Travis left the Marines and moved to California in 1944, he became part of a rather large migration of musicians, including Speedy West, Ted Daffan, Adolph Hofner, Hank Thompson, and Lefty Frizzell, who wandered to the West Coast in the late 1940s and early 1950s. Travis had already made a name for himself back east, and had made a few records with his old friend Grandpa Jones. He had also developed his much-admired guitar style by building on tips picked up from such guitarists as Kennedy Jones and Mose Rager in his home county of Muhlenberg in the coal-mining district of western Kentucky. Guitarists everywhere now describe the style as "Travis picking," but Merle himself called it "thumb style" (the use of the thumb to maintain a bass rhythm while the forefinger plays a syncopated melody on the treble strings). When Chet Atkins was growing up in East Tennessee, he heard Travis on the radio and was later amazed to discover that so much music could be made with only two fingers.

In California, Travis was quickly swept into a busy whirl of music as both a soloist and a sideman. He made records of his own for Capitol after 1946, and some of them—such as "Divorce Me C.O.D.," "Kentucky Means Paradise," "Three Times Seven," and "So Round, So Firm, So Fully Packed"—are excellent examples of the West Coast honky-tonk sound. The trumpet, for example, appears with greater frequency on California-made records than it does on those made elsewhere. Travis

Merle Travis (at the Kerrville Folk Festival), 1977. Bill Malone personal collection; photo by Bobbie Malone.

appeared on hundreds of recordings as a supporting musician for other acts; he performed on the *Town Hall Party* and *Dinner Bell Roundup*; he kept friends and audiences amused with his wit and storehouse of tales; he drew cartoons and penned stories; and he crafted some of country music's greatest songs. Travis generally wrote rather happy-go-lucky songs, such as "So Round, So Firm, So Fully Packed," "Sweet Temptation," and his paean of boastful masculinity, "Three Times Seven" ("I'm three times seven, and I do as I doggone please"). But he also demonstrated a flair for writing religious numbers and songs of social commentary. When asked in 1947 to record some folk songs from "back home," he responded by writing some of his own. They included the now well-known religious piece "I Am a Pilgrim" and two famous documents of coal-mining life, "Dark as a Dungeon" and "Sixteen Tons."

Country musicians who flocked to California also found outlets for their talents on the local radio stations, particularly on the barn dances that flourished after the mid-1940s. Along with Foreman Phillips, Cliffie Stone probably did more to popularize country music in the region than any other person. Stone had a daily variety show, the *Dinner Bell Roundup*, on KXLA in Pasadena. Many country entertainers appeared on the program, one of the most notable being the swing fiddler and bandleader Red Murrell, who had one of the most popular bands in California. Other important members included Herman the Hermit (Cliffie Stone's father and a popular banjo player); the ace fiddler Harold Hensley; Tennessee Ernie Ford; and the Armstrong Twins (Lloyd and Floyd), a mandolin and guitar duo who brought a touch of their native Arkansas countryside to the West Coast. In 1949, the show moved to the Legion Stadium in El Monte, California, where it became known as the *Hometown Jamboree*. Another show that endured until the 1960s as a haven for country entertainers was the Saturday night *Town Hall Party* in Compton, broadcast on KFI Radio and KTTV-TV. The show featured a nucleus of established performers such as Tex Ritter, Johnny Bond, Tex Williams, Joe and Rose Maphis, Eddie Kirk, Eddie Dean, Lefty Frizzell, Skeets McDonald, Wesley Tuttle, and Merle Travis, and it also served as a launching ground for such future stars as Freddie Hart and the Collins Kids (Lorrie and Larry). The young Buck Owens, for example, appeared as a sideman on the show, playing his electric guitar for most of the featured acts.

California's vigorous country music scene inspired innovations that eventually affected musicians elsewhere. Country entertainers had long shown a preference for western wear, but the passion for performing in gaudy, bespangled, and sequined attire began in California when Nudie the Tailor started supplying his unique creations to local musicians. Nudie Cohn came to the West Coast from Brooklyn shortly after World War I and, after a brief career as a boxer, began sewing costumes for Warner Brothers. Before Tex Williams hired him to make costumes for his band in the late 1940s, Nudie had also had some experience as a brassiere and G-string manufacturer for the striptease industry back in New York City. The western suits supplied to the Tex Williams organization were tasteful and restrained, but the costumes commissioned thereafter became progressively more outlandish, with their bright colors, ornate decorations, and fringe. Success for country musicians became almost defined by the number of Nudie suits in their wardrobe.

California also provided a context for the flourishing and maturation of electrical amplification. A trio of manufacturers—Rickenbacker, Bigsby, and Fender—supplied electric standard guitars, steel guitars, and basses to the scores of musicians who played in the club bands in the Greater Los Angeles area and in Southern California. The specific origins of solid-body guitars, vibrators, and pedal steel instruments are undetermined, but they were coming into general use by the end of the 1940s. Some special brands were made on demand for certain musicians: Paul Bigsby, for example, made a guitar to Merle Travis's specifications with a solid wood body and all the tuning pegs on one side of the headstock. The neck was cut deeply into the body, allowing the musician's fingers to move easily up and down. In the meantime, from his home in Anaheim, Leo Fender supplied a steady stream of solid-body electric guitars to musicians such as Jimmy Bryant (one of the most respected of the jazz-country guitarists in California) and Arthur Smith, a country guitar wizard in Charlotte, North Carolina (not to be confused with the fiddler or songwriter), whose hit recording of "Guitar Boogie" in 1947 ironically had been made with an acoustic guitar.

Fender introduced his Broadcaster model in 1948, and this popular instrument, whose name was soon changed to Telecaster, became the most favored guitar among country musicians and budding rock-and-roll musicians. The name Fender almost became synonymous with "electric guitar," and in the hands of such musicians as James Burton, Roy Buchanan, Buck Owens, and Roy Nichols (who was just beginning his career in the mid-1940s as a teenage guitarist with the Maddox Brothers and Rose), the Fender guitar contributed crucially to the making of the "California sound." The sharp, staccato bursts of the Fender, combined with the high-pitched, strident, wailing sound of the pedal steel guitar, gave California country music its distinctive flavor. Leo Fender's bass guitar, introduced in 1951, contributed further to the thoroughgoing electrification of country music, while also freeing the bass player to become a more mobile and flexible member of a band. Musicians no longer had to drag the big stand-up acoustic bass across the stage to get close to the microphone to sing, and they found that they could easily transport the electric instrument and amplifier on road-show engagements. When hillbilly bands no longer roamed across the country with the "bass fiddle" tied to the top of their touring car, an era of American music had truly come to an end.

In the immediate postwar era, country music was characterized not only by commercial success and stylistic innovation but also by the entertainers' growing sophistication about the world of show business. Many country performers, like Gene Autry, owned radio stations. A few, like Roy Acuff, owned publishing houses, an activity that increased tremendously in the following decades. Universally, country musicians were learning to manage their own promotional and contractual affairs or were employing skilled managers to do so for them. No longer, as was often true before 1940, was the hillbilly easy prey for the crafty promoter who ventured into an area laden with a portable recording apparatus, made some quick recordings, paid a small sum, and then dashed off again. Hopeful country entertainers everywhere evidenced a growing understanding of contract stipulations. By 1946, performers were demanding from $150 to $200 for each record side, asking for advances against royalties, and exhibiting familiarity with copyright laws and American Federation of Musicians (AFM) regulations. With the rise of BMI, hillbilly songwriters had begun to receive greater protection and profits from the performance rights of their songs. ASCAP had come to recognize the legitimacy of country music and was becoming more favorably disposed to the admission of hillbilly songwriters. Conceding that hillbilly songs had been inadequately covered in previous surveys, ASCAP in 1947 promised to improve its logging surveys of independent radio stations, where the majority of hillbilly songs were played.

As the ranks of professional country musicians increased, along with the availability of entertainment outlets, a new group of personal managers and bookers emerged. Until the end of the war, most country-talent promotions were handled by radio-station talent bureaus, such as those of WSM and WLS. Under this arrangement, the scheduling of personal appearances was often limited to the immediate territory blanketed by the station's transmitter. After the war, a number of major talent offices concerned with cross-country touring became interested in country music. Such booking agencies as Jolly Joyce in Philadelphia, Stan Zucker in New York, American Corporation in Hollywood, and Gene Johnson in Wheeling, West Virginia, by 1949 had expanded their touring operations to the then forty-eight states.

In addition, such personal managers as Oscar Davis, J. L. Frank, and Colonel Tom Parker made huge sums of money through their super-intendence of talent, and their ranks were gradually being joined by such native southern entrepreneurs as Connie B. Gay, Hubert Long, Jim Denny, and Jim Halsey.

If some doubts had existed in previous years, the *Grand Ole Opry* had definitely become "king" of barn-dance radio shows, and Nash-ville had emerged as the leading country music center. The *Opry*, with its wide radio coverage on WSM augmented by the thirty-minute NBC segment, had become universally known as the "hillbilly heaven." Roy Acuff's immense popularity had transformed the *Opry* from a localized barn dance to a national program featuring "star" talent. Regardless of their commercial origins—honky-tonk or small radio show—most hillbilly performers dreamed of someday being invited to become members of the *Opry* cast. The *Opry* paid only the most minimal of fees, but membership on its roster lent prestige to an individual and indispensable aid in obtaining bookings everywhere. Most performers were willing to appear on the *Opry* for a modest fee on Saturday night and then tour with an *Opry* unit during the week in the belief that their overall income would be increased.

By the late 1940s, many country fans had come to look upon the *Grand Ole Opry*, perhaps unfortunately, as synonymous with country music. All rabid country enthusiasts felt that before they died they must make at least one trip to the mecca of country music. As a result, every Saturday night people from all over the United States, and from Canada and other foreign countries, gathered in Nashville to view the program. Those without reserved seats gladly stood in line outside the Ryman Auditorium for hours and then sat inside for hours more to view their favorites. The schedule has since changed radically, but the *Grand Ole Opry* in the late 1940s was carried over WSM from 7:30 p.m. until midnight.

As the *Grand Ole Opry* grew in size and popularity, it lost both its original geographical identity (that of a Middle Tennessee barn dance) and much of its down-home ambience. George D. Hay's dream of an uncommercialized "folk" format had long before been obliter-ated under an avalanche of commercial advertising, and "stars" had proliferated in the show's firmament ever since Roy Acuff joined its cast. Nevertheless, "good old boys and girls" from the South still predominated overwhelmingly on its roster, and they and the *Opry* management strove mightily to preserve the sense of family and informality for which the show was famous. Friends and relatives still sat on benches at the back of the stage, and performers walked in and out while their colleagues performed before the microphones. The whole effect of organized confusion or controlled chaos was held together largely through the patience and planning of Vito Pellettieri, the *Opry*'s longtime stage manager.

By 1950, the *Grand Ole Opry* had a cast of about 120 individuals, including singers, instrumentalists, and comedians. The program was divided into fifteen- and thirty-minute segments, each of which featured a leading performer supported by other acts. Although millions of Americans heard the show on the lengthy WSM broadcasts, many heard only the thirty-minute NBC segment, the "Prince Albert" show, hosted for about eight years after 1946 by Clyde Julian "Red" Foley. Foley was arguably the most versatile singer of the 1950s, and no one since has surpassed him. He came from Blue Lick, Kentucky (not far from Berea), where he was born in 1910. He arrived at the *National Barn Dance* in 1930 as part of John Lair's Cumberland Ridge Runners, and while in Chicago, in 1933, he married Eva Overstake, one of the Three Little Maids and a sister of Jenny Lou Carson, a talented country music songwriter. Foley was one of the Chicago show's most popular entertainers, beloved for his comedy, his duets with Lulu Belle Cooper, and his solo singing. He was a founder and charter member of the *Renfro Valley Barn Dance* and was a regular on that show for about three years. Very early recognized as a person who was at home with any kind of song material, Foley is said to have been asked on occasion to forsake country music for a career as a pop singer.

As a *Grand Ole Opry* host, Foley acted as a genial master of ceremonies, served as a straight man for the antics of comedians Minnie Pearl and Rod Brasfield, introduced guest acts, gave serious recitations, hawked his sponsor's products, and sang a wide variety of songs. Foley could give convincing interpretations of the most sentimental material. His version of "That Little Boy of Mine" was a much-requested song, while "Old Shep"—a song about an aged, dying dog—evoked tears from an array of listeners (including Elvis Presley, according to his own testimony). Foley was just as believable on boogie, blues, and jump tunes. "Chattanooga Shoe Shine Boy" was a giant hit for him, while "Birmingham Bounce," "Tennessee Saturday Night," "Hearts of Stone," and "Pinball Boogie" demonstrated his thorough knowledge of and pleasure in performing black-derived tunes. It is a testimony to his skill that he could so readily move from a slightly raunchy song like "Pinball Boogie" ("you rattle and you shake it till it gets in the hole") to his soulful versions of the spiritual/recitation "Steal Away" and such gospel songs as "Just a Closer Walk with Thee" and "Peace in the Valley." Recorded in March 1951, "Peace in the Valley" (written by the great black gospel composer Thomas A. Dorsey) became one of the first country religious songs to receive wide commercial exposure.

Although Foley did much to make the *Grand Ole Opry* the most famous country radio show in the nation, the program certainly had no monopoly on country broadcasting. Throughout the United States, in small towns and cities alike, scores of shindigs, hoedowns, jamborees, and barn dances commanded the attention of radio listeners on Saturday nights or, as in the cases of Knoxville's *Mid-Day Merry-Go-Round* and Bristol's *Farm and Fun Time*, at lunchtime. Each of the larger shows, such as the *Wheeling* (West Virginia) *Jamboree* or Dallas's *Big D Jamboree*, had its quota of well-known stars, but few could equal Shreveport's *Louisiana Hayride* as a forum for musical exposure or as a launching ground for future stardom.[3] The *Hayride* appears to have been the joint creation of three men associated with powerful KWKH: the station manager Henry Clay, the announcer and program director Horace Logan, and the commercial manager Dean Upson, who had once been a member of the smooth-singing trio the Vagabonds. The three-hour show that debuted on Saturday night, April 3, 1948, built on an earlier tradition of country music on KWKH dating back to the early 1930s. These included at least a couple of variety shows— a Sunday afternoon talent show conducted by the Shelton Brothers in 1936 and a *Saturday Night Roundup* featuring the Rice Brothers Gang and other groups after 1940. The *Hayride* included some musicians who had been present at the station for several years (such as the West Virginian Harmie Smith and the western swing bandleader Pappy Covington), but it also featured some acts, such as the Bailes Brothers (Walter, Johnnie, and Homer) and Johnny Wright and Jack Anglin (along with Johnny's then-unknown wife, Kitty Wells), who had arrived in Shreveport only a few months earlier. Broadcasting each Saturday from the Memorial Auditorium, the show found a large and receptive audience in the three-state area (Louisiana, Texas, Arkansas) contiguous to Shreveport, which, according to a *Hayride* historian, Stephen Ray Tucker, "was experiencing an economic upsurge that was tied to the area's expanding oil and gas industry."[4] The 50,000-watt KWKH, of course, was heard over a much broader swath of territory, but *Hayride* performers typically gave concerts during the week in towns whose proximity would permit them to get back to Shreveport on Saturday night.

On August 7, 1948, only four months after the show got under way, Hank Williams joined its cast and soon became its, and country music's, dominant star. Largely on the strength of his sensational re-cording of "Lovesick Blues," Williams moved to the *Grand Ole Opry* in November 1949, a pattern that was repeated by many performers in the following ten or eleven years. Despite the *Hayride*'s considerable popularity, it never really threatened the *Grand Old Opry*'s leader-ship because as soon as *Hayride* performers gained wider exposure (usually with a hit record or two), they moved on to join the Nashville barn dance. This happened with such frequency—as in the cases of Webb Pierce, Faron Young, Johnny Cash, George Jones, Johnny and Jack, the Wilburn Brothers, and Jim Reeves—that the *Hayride* gained the sobriquet of "the Cradle of the Stars." The *Hayride*'s most famous member, Elvis Presley, who joined in 1954, brought a new audience to the show, but when he left for bigger and better things, much of that audience moved with him. The *Hayride* endured into the 1960s, but its glory days had come earlier, in the years from 1948 to 1955.

Even though live radio performances preserved their potency up into the 1950s, the trend toward the playing of phonograph recordings proved irresistible. Disc jockeys proliferated during the 1950s, and many of them proved to be as popular as the musicians whose records they played (many of the DJs, of course, were also aspiring musicians). They were men and women with distinctive voices, engaging person-alities, and high-powered but homey patter that appealed to country music's working-class audience. Country music had not yet become so concerned with respectability, nor so removed from its rural roots, that it was embarrassed by the hayseed imagery and parlance that some DJs conveyed. And country music had not yet become so pros-perous that it attracted people into its midst with little knowledge of its traditions. Consequently, most of the disc jockeys were people who had a genuine love for the music they played and who had grown up with it or had tried to make a living from it. A few of the announcers, such as Lee Moore at WWVA, Nelson King at WCKY (Cincinnati), Randy Blake at WJJD (Chicago), Rosalie Allen at WOV (New York),

Eddie Hill at WSM, Hugh Cherry at WKDA (Nashville), Biff Collie at KLEE (Houston), Squeakin' Deacon Moore at KXLA (Pasadena), Don "Barkin'" Larkin at WAAT (Newark, New Jersey), Don Owens at WARL (Arlington, Virginia), and Tom Perryman at KSIJ (Gladewater, Texas), were among those who enjoyed national reputations. By the end of the 1950s, Perryman had become probably the nation's first all-night DJ, at WSM in Nashville. He and the hundreds of disc jockeys who appeared on stations large and small, and who were seldom known outside of a rather limited geographical area, all contributed to country music's popularization in the postwar years, and each played a part in preserving much of the music's down-home distinctiveness while simultaneously extending its commercial appeal.

The long-range trend in the recording business, of course, tended toward merger and consolidation. But in the 1950s, scores of small companies specialized in the recording of country, blues, ethnic, and gospel performers. Gold Star in Houston; Four Star and Imperial in Los Angeles; Bullet in Nashville; Starday in Beaumont; Rich-R-Tone in Johnson City, Tennessee; Dot in Gallatin, Tennessee; Sun in Memphis; and King in Cincinnati were only a few of the labels that circulated country music in the postwar years. The most important of these record companies, King, was owned by Sydney Nathan, who began his career in the music business in the 1930s as a record retailer. During World War II, he began buying used records that he then resold, and that experience as a used record dealer introduced Nathan to the large population of southern migrants who lived in Cincinnati and its immediate environs. Recognizing their musical tastes led him, in August 1944, to the recording of both black and white talent. That year Grandpa Jones and Merle Travis, performing as the Sheppard Brothers, made the first recording for King in Dayton, Ohio. After that date, a large number of important musicians, such as Lloyd "Cowboy" Copas, Moon Mullican, Harold "Hawkshaw" Hawkins, Clyde Moody, the York Brothers (George and Leslie), Jimmie Osborne, the Bailes Brothers, Wayne Raney, and the Delmore Brothers, recorded for the King label in its Cincinnati studios. Sydney Nathan took a personal, hands-on interest in each recording and was therefore responsible for much of the distinctive sound heard on his records. The King sound represented a fusion of southeastern and southwestern traits and therefore demonstrated the larger process of stylistic borrowing and blending then going on in country music. Even the most tradition-based entertainers, such as Grandpa Jones and the Bailes Brothers, typically combined electric guitars with the older acoustic instruments on King records. Steel guitars probably would have been used in any case, but Syd Nathan loved to hear a tremolo sound on them, so he often implored his steel guitarists to "put more jelly" into their playing.[5] Nathan also encouraged his black and white performers to use each other's material and, in fact, sometimes to record with each other; consequently, King artists sometimes "covered" each other's records. Although the impulse toward the performance of blues and boogie material had always been strong among white musicians, Nathan's encouragement no doubt proved instrumental in the decision made by such artists as the Delmore Brothers and Moon Mullican to record their classic boogie tunes for the label in the early 1950s.

The kind of field recording pioneered by such men as Ralph Peer and Frank Walker in the 1920s was gradually coming to an end in the 1950s. Nevertheless, the recording industry remained decentralized, and musicians were able to put their songs on wax or tape in a wide variety of cities from Cincinnati to Los Angeles. Many of Columbia's country recordings in the early 1950s, superintended by the veteran producer Don Law, were made in the studios of Jim Beck in Dallas. Such singers as Marty Robbins, Ray Price, and Lefty Frizzell sang to the accompaniment of some of the large group of talented sidemen like Joe Knight and Johnny Gimble who lived in the Dallas–Fort Worth area. Beck's untimely death on May 3, 1956, after inhaling hydrochloride fumes in his studio, ended his opportunity to make Dallas one of the leading recording centers in the nation.

The most significant development in recording, however, came from the emergence of Nashville as a music center. Much of Nashville's evolution toward musical preeminence is directly attributable to Paul Cohen. Cohen, who had been associated with Decca since the 1930s, became that company's country artists-and-repertory (A&R) director in the mid-1940s. Cohen and the Decca company inaugurated the modern era of recording in Nashville in the spring of 1945 when Red Foley recorded in WSM's Studio B. Later that year or early the next, two WSM engineers, Aaron Shelton and Carl Jenkins, organized a commercial recording enterprise called the Castle Recording Company with a studio in the Tulane Hotel. Cohen was the first A&R man to use the Castle facilities extensively, and the recordings of such Decca artists as Red Foley, Ernest Tubb, Webb Pierce, and Kitty Wells were important milestones in Nashville's eventual emergence as one of the four or five music capitals of America.[6] Virtually every recording company that utilized country talent made use of the Castle studios, at least until Owen Bradley opened his barnlike studio in 1953 and until such companies as RCA began operating their own independent studios toward the end of the 1950s.

The growing concentration of recording in Nashville also led to the appearance there of session musicians, that talented group of people—musically uneducated for the most part—who could improvise in any style. For all practical purposes, the first members of this fraternity were Red Foley's band: Zeke Turner, electric guitar; Jerry Byrd, steel guitar; Louis Innis, rhythm guitar; and Tommy Jackson, fiddle. This cadre played on their leader's sessions and on numerous others, including those of the early Hank Williams. In effect, they also became the house band for King records in Cincinnati in late 1948 when they sat in on the first of their many sessions there. By the early 1950s, other musicians had become stationed permanently in Nashville and were beginning to appear on most of the recordings made in the city: electric guitarists Hank Garland and Grady Martin; bass players Ernie Newton, Willie Thall, Hal Smith, and Junior Huskey; rhythm guitarist Ray Edenton; drummers Farris Coursey and Buddy Harman; and pianists Marvin Hughes, Gordon Stoker, Hargus "Pig" Robbins, and Owen Bradley. When Chet Atkins arrived in the city in 1950, as a guitarist for Mother Maybelle and the Carter Sisters, he immediately began to shape and direct the style of music heard in Nashville sessions. Atkins's smooth finger-and-thumb style of playing was admired by every musician in Nashville, and he was soon employed by recording directors to gather appropriate pickers for various recording sessions. Most important of all, in 1952 he became assistant to Steve Sholes, RCA's chief recording man in Nashville, a step that eventually put Atkins at the center of country music's revolutionary stylistic changes in the next decade.

Nashville's rapid growth as a leading music center, evidenced first by the assembling there of top-ranking country talent, was accentuated also by the arrival of the music entrepreneurs—the booking agents, the A&R men, the promoters, and the publishers. Sheet music had ceased to be the most important product of the music industry; the typical music publishing house instead now depended primarily on phonograph recordings for its existence. After a song was copyrighted and published, the publishing house—if it expected a financial return—had to get the song recorded by some performer. In effect, the publishing house became a vehicle for the recording of a written composition. Scores of publishing firms, many of them owned by country performers, eventually appeared in Nashville, but the giant among them was Acuff-Rose.

Acuff-Rose's ticket to commercial supremacy, and a vivid example of country music's great postwar expansion, was "The Tennessee Waltz." Now an international pop standard and one of Tennessee's state songs, "The Tennessee Waltz" was first released in 1948 as a hillbilly song (via Pee Wee King's and Cowboy Copas's recordings) that gained considerable immediate popularity and then was seemingly forgotten. Resurrected in November 1950 by the popular vocalist Patti Page and considered, strangely enough, as the "B" side of her record, the song had become the nation's favorite by December of that year. "The Tennessee Waltz" was written by the bandleader and accordionist Pee Wee King and his vocalist Redd Stewart, who received the inspiration for the song after noting the popularity of Bill Monroe's "Kentucky Waltz" in 1948. "The Tennessee Waltz" was a typical country song in its depiction of a broken romance, but its simplicity and haunting melody quickly made it a national favorite.

"The Tennessee Waltz" alone must be given much of the credit for country music's commercial surge and the future integration of America's popular music forms. By May 1951, 4,800,000 records of the song had been sold, and it had earned its writers and Acuff-Rose a gross of $330,000. These totals did not include foreign-language recordings or rhythm-and-blues and minor country recordings. It was generally believed that "The Tennessee Waltz" was the biggest hit in modern popular music history, and it was certainly the top song ever licensed by BMI. The song brought extensive financial profit to its composers and launched Acuff-Rose on the road to publishing success. The song's popularity actually surprised Acuff-Rose because the company had neglected, or had been unable, to exploit it nationally. The Nashville publishing firm had no contact people or business representation in the three traditionally accepted centers: New York, Los Angeles, and Chicago.

Country music's prosperity also stimulated the further growth of a songwriting industry. Country singers continued to write much of their own material, but the ranks of the professional composers grew as the music demonstrated its permanence and viability. As country music edged closer to pop, the distinctiveness of country songs began to fade somewhat, and some country songwriters, such as Felice and Boudleaux Bryant, even denied that the lyrics of the two musical forms basically differed. Nevertheless, country songs tended to concentrate on the concerns and preoccupations of working people and to employ melodies that the average person could hum or sing. The music was "realistic" in that it sang less and less of mountain cabins, village churchyards, and sunbonnet mothers, and more and more about the everyday concerns of urban-industrial existence. Country songs, however, seldom protested against larger political and social problems, but instead voiced a preoccupation with private sins and worries. Some lyrics responded joyously and affirmatively to life; some exhibited a healthy willingness to combat the world's problems and adversities; while others succumbed to guilt and self-pity or otherwise sought escape through nostalgia or fantasy.

The question of song authorship is often a cloudy and troublesome one. Song credits often reveal only the owner of a piece and not its composer or arranger. Rumors abound in country music that such-and-such individuals did not actually write the songs attributed to them, and the experience of songs sold outright by their writers for twenty-five dollars or so is more than just folklore. It is common knowledge among country musicians, for example, that Arthur Q. Smith of Knoxville (whose real name was James Arthur Pritchett) wrote "I Overlooked an Orchid," "Wedding Bells," "I Wouldn't Change You if I Could," and other hits of the 1950s, and that his name appears on only a few of them. As compensation, Pritchett was usually satisfied with just enough money for a bottle of whiskey. Jim Anglin fared somewhat better. His authorship of such songs as "What about You" and "Ashes of Love" (recorded by Johnny and Jack) is properly recognized, but a much larger body of material, dating back to the early 1940s and appearing on scores of recordings (such as "Branded Wherever I Go" and "Stuck Up Blues"), has too often gone unacknowledged. Mac Odell, on the other hand, popularized his own song creations by performing them on radio stations throughout the South and in Detroit. Odell (whose real name was Odell McLeod) was one of several country-gospel performers in the 1950s who kept alive the spirit of folk simplicity and down-home fundamentalism once characteristic of country music. Such songs as "From the Manger to the Cross,"

"Purple Robe," "Thirty Pieces of Silver," "Life's Elevator," and "The Stone Was Rolled Away," recorded in the 1950s by such singers as Cowboy Copas and Wilma Lee Cooper and since preserved by bluegrass musicians, demonstrated that some country music was indeed different from pop music.

Writers like Anglin and Odell preserved the folksiness of country music but regrettably received little commercial advantage from it. Closer to the commercial mainstream, and consequently better known, were such writers as Johnny Bond, Floyd Tillman, Jenny Lou Carson, Vaughn Horton, Cy Coben, Cindy Walker, and Felice and Boudleaux Bryant. Of all the writers of the 1950s, Walker and the Bryants exhibited the greatest endurance while also showing a remarkable ability to weather, and in fact to prosper from, successive stylistic changes in country music.

Walker's success was a product of luck, pluck, and talent. While on a trip to Los Angeles with her parents in 1942 (her father was a Texas cotton merchant), she impulsively dropped in at Bing Crosby's office and persuaded Bing's manager to accept one of her songs, "Lone Star Trail," for an upcoming Crosby film. Her very profitable association with Bob Wills began also in 1942 when she saw Wills's bus driving down a Los Angeles street on the way to a recording session. She was actually on the way to a post office to mail a sheath of songs to Wills at his headquarters in Tulsa. A subsequent meeting with him and his manager, O. W. Mayo, at their hotel resulted in the successful auditioning of several of her songs. She wrote all of the songs used in Wills's movies, including the great standards "Dusty Skies" and "Cherokee Maiden." From the mid-1940s on, beginning with the songs that she wrote for Al Dexter and Ernest Tubb, Walker skillfully tailored her creations to fit the styles of specific singers. Few writers have equaled her ability to write country-pop love songs such as "Thank You for Calling" and "You Don't Know Me," honky-tonk numbers like "Bubbles in My Beer" and "Warm Red Wine," bluegrass songs like "Flying South to Dixie," cowboy songs such as "Dusty Skies," and teenybopper songs like Roy Orbison's "Dream Baby."

If anyone demonstrated a similar versatility, it would most likely be Felice and Boudleaux Bryant. From the time Jimmy Dickens recorded their composition "Country Boy" in 1947, the Bryants experienced over thirty-five years of commercial songwriting success. Their songs actually always exhibited more of a "rural feel" than those of Cindy

Walker, even though neither of the Bryants grew up with much exposure to country music: Felice was from Milwaukee, and Boudleaux
studied violin at his home in Shellman, Georgia, with hopes of becoming a classical violinist. He played with Hank Penny's western swing
band in Atlanta, however, and had received a thorough grounding in
country music by the time he and Felice married in 1945. They wrote
well over 7,000 songs, and about 1,500 of them have been recorded.
Such Bryant-composed songs as "We Could," "Take Me as I Am," and
"Hey Joe" are known by all country singers, and their "Rocky Top" is
the most famous bluegrass song in the world.

The writers wrote for a wide array of stylists in the late 1940s and
early 1950s, the last such display of stylistic diversity that the homogenizing country field has experienced. "Traditional" is a relative term,
of course, and even the most "old-time" entertainers of the period,
such as the Blue Sky Boys, Grandpa Jones, and Molly O'Day, exhibited certain stylistic traits that set them apart from the performers of
earlier years. The Blue Sky Boys returned from military service with
a style of harmony that was even more precise and clear than that of
the prewar years. Their recordings now featured a bass and fiddle
in addition to the mandolin and guitar, and their repertory included
a greater percentage of modern-composed songs than in the 1930s.
Their beautiful performance of "Kentucky" in 1947 was probably the
most commercially successful of their career. Unfortunately, their retirement in 1951, a product of the brothers' conflicting career choices,
came at the peak of their vocal powers.

The duet tradition persisted into the 1950s, but only a few performers clung to the mandolin-and-guitar format. Martha and James
Carson, known as the Barn Dance Sweethearts at WSB, used such
instrumentation to back up their wonderful duets on such songs as
"Budded on Earth," "Man of Galilee," and "The Sweetest Gift" (one
of the first country recordings of this gospel/mother song). But by
1950, the two had separated as husband and wife, and Martha went
on to become one of the most popular solo performers of the decade.
Other mandolin-and-guitar teams, like Charlie and Danny Bailey or
Jim and Jesse McReynolds, tended to adapt to the bluegrass style or,
like the Bailes Brothers and the Louvin Brothers, to augment their
acoustic sound with an electric standard or steel guitar. The Bailes
Brothers included, in varying combinations, the brothers Johnnie, Walter, Homer, and Kyle, from Charleston, West Virginia. The

brothers performed during the war in Huntington, West Virginia, and at Nashville's WSM, where they were *Grand Ole Opry* regulars and hosts of an early-morning show sponsored by Martha White Flour. In December 1946, they moved with Dean Upson to KWKH in Shreveport, where they became charter members of the *Louisiana Hayride*. Performing first as a duet composed of Johnnie and Walter, and later of Johnnie and Homer, the Bailes Brothers became extremely popular in the Arkansas-Louisiana-Texas region, appearing frequently in churches and schoolhouses and making daily broadcasts marked by an informal, down-home atmosphere. Their repertory was strongly reminiscent of that of the Blue Sky Boys—exclusively sentimental and gospel in nature except for an occasional fiddle or steel guitar instrumental—but their vocal style was radically different from that of the Bolicks. The Bailes Brothers sang in a lusty and emotionally heartfelt style, and with an evangelical zeal that suggested the singing and preaching heard in Pentecostal Holiness churches (Walter, in fact, eventually become an itinerant Pentecostal minister, and Homer became a United Methodist preacher with Pentecostal leanings). Many of their songs were certainly didactic in nature, such as "Whiskey Is the Devil," "Building on the Sand," and "When Heaven Comes Down," but their most commercial and enduring songs were "Dust on the Bible," "Oh So Many Years," "I Want to Be Loved," and "Give Mother My Crown." Instrumentally, the Bailes Brothers always featured a mandolin (played at various times by either Ernest Ferguson or Clyde Baum), but the distinctiveness of their sound came from the Dobro and electric steel guitar work of Shot Jackson, the most respected of the old-time steel guitar players.

With the emergence of the Louvin Brothers, country music found its greatest duet.[7] Ira and Charles Loudermilk came from Henagar, Alabama, in the hill country area that had also spawned the Delmore Brothers. The Loudermilks grew up listening to folk and gospel music at home, and to the records and broadcasts of the Monroe Brothers, Delmore Brothers, and Blue Sky Boys. Ira and Charles had some radio experience before they went into military service, but their first real attempts at a full-time professional career came in 1946. They adopted the stage name Louvin and set out on a grueling schedule that took them to several radio stations in the Upper South before they finally found a position with the *Grand Ole Opry* in 1955 (although they did not become securely ensconced on the show until after 1957). The Louvins

*The Bailes Brothers: Homer (left) and Johnny (right). Bill Malone
personal collection; photo by Bobbie Malone.*

always had ambitions of being mainstream country singers, but their
first big commercial breakthrough came in 1952 with the success of a
gospel song, "The Family Who Prays." They became typecast as gospel
singers for a few years, and they had no trouble playing the role. Such
songs as "Preach the Gospel," "Satan and the Saint," "Satan Lied to
Me," and "Don't Let Them Take the Bible Out of Our Schoolrooms"
breathed with the biblical fundamentalism that they had imbibed
in northeastern Alabama. Shortly after joining the *Grand Ole Opry*,
they recorded for Capitol a "secular" song, "When I Stop Dreaming,"
their most popular number and one of the finest performances of pure
country music ever heard in American music. In 1956 they recorded
an album of old-time country and folk songs called *Tragic Songs of
Life*, a beautiful reminder of their (and country music's) roots. One
song from the album, "The Knoxville Girl" (an American variant of a
British murder ballad dating from at least 1744), received extensive
airplay and has since become a standard in the bluegrass genre.

The Louvins' use of duet harmony and mandolin-and-guitar
instrumentation suggested their old-time origins, but their additional employment of an electric guitar (played on their first Capitol

recordings by Chet Atkins and later by Paul Yandell) pushed them closer to mainstream country music. Although several of their songs have become part of the bluegrass repertory—"Are You Missing Me?," "Childish Love," "I'm Changing the Words to My Love Song," "I Don't Believe You've Met My Baby," "The Family Who Prays"—the Louvins always vehemently resisted their music being categorized as bluegrass. The Louvins actually were in a class by themselves. No one in country music before or since achieved the kind of crisp, precise, and yet ultra-high style of harmony that the duo produced. Before they dissolved their partnership in 1963, the Louvin Brothers had built a body of songs and a style of performance that have ever since influenced the music of American entertainers, some of them as far afield from traditional country music as Gram Parsons and Emmylou Harris.

Johnny and Jack (Johnny Wright and Jack Anglin) provide one of the best examples of the fusion of old-time and modern elements heard in the music of the 1950s. Both men started out on the kerosene circuit in the 1930s, playing in schoolhouses, small-town theaters, and country churches, and arriving bleary-eyed at some radio station at 5:30 in the morning to do a broadcast of sentimental and gospel songs. They possessed genuinely rural voices that reflected their East Tennessee and North Alabama origins. Along with Ira Louvin and Bill Monroe, Jack had one of the highest and most penetrating tenor voices in country music. Soon after leaving the Anglin Brothers group, Jack teamed with his brother-in-law Johnny Wright in 1940 at WBIG in Greensboro, North Carolina. Through the war years and on into the postwar period their repertory remained close to that of the earlier brother duets and to that of Roy Acuff: old-time gospel songs like "The Eastern Gate," sentimental weepers such as "The Little Paper Boy," and some timely songs like "This World Can't Stand Long" and "Jesus Hits Like an Atom Bomb," which reflected the political preoccupations of the day. Their tenure on the *Louisiana Hayride*, from 1948 to 1950, witnessed a significant shift in style and repertory and their first breakthrough into mainstream country music. Performing as Johnny and Jack and the Tennessee Mountain Boys, with Miss Kitty Wells (Johnny's soon-to-be-famous wife), they began turning out a long string of hits such as "What about You," "Ashes of Love," and "Poison Love." On the *Grand Ole Opry* after 1950, Johnny and Jack broke new ground for country duets with their Latin-beat country songs (such as "Down South in New Orleans" and "Poison Love") and with their mixture of traditional acoustic and electric instrumentation. An all-star lineup of supporting musicians, including the fiddler Paul Warren, the mandolin player Clyde Baum, and the steel guitarist Shot Jackson, helped to give them a peculiar, but commercially appealing, blend of church-style and honky-tonk music.

The Maddox Brothers and Rose represented the most eclectic mix of all and were a graphic example of a musical form that still showed its rural roots even as it reached out toward modern stylistic innovations. Few groups could perform so many styles as ably as the Maddoxes: gospel, honky-tonk, sentimental parlor, blues, and incipient rockabilly. They could sound like a mandolin-and-guitar band from the 1930s, or they could sound like a raucous rock-and-roll band of the late 1950s. The family's migration from Boaz, Alabama, to Modesto, California, in 1933 is part of the folklore of country music. Mama and Papa Maddox and five of their children hitchhiked to Meridian, Mississippi, and then hopped a freight train to the San Joaquin Valley, befriended by sympathetic railroad men and fed by Salvation Army workers. They became migratory fruit pickers for a few years, but then the Maddox siblings drifted into radio work in Modesto in 1937. Their early career as hillbilly performers was as migratory as fruit picking had been; they played at rodeos and in honky-tonks all the way up to Oregon. Twelve-year-old Rose sang in honky-tonks where no patron below the age of eighteen was admitted. It was during one of these rambles that she heard Woody and Jack Guthrie singing "Reno Blues." Later, under the title of "The Philadelphia Lawyer," it became her most famous hit.

When her brothers returned from military service in 1946, the siblings regrouped as the Maddox Brothers and Rose and gradually began to take their music outside of California. In California they played for enthusiastic audiences of servicemen, defense workers, and Okies, and they learned to put on a show that their listeners would enjoy. Dressed in bright, gaudy costumes (which earned them the title of "the most colorful hillbilly band in America"), the Maddoxes presented high-energy performances characterized by hollers, spoken asides, and Cal's maniacal laughter. Only a religious song such as "I'd Rather Have Jesus" or "Gathering Flowers for the Master's Bouquet" could dampen their boundless exuberance. On such songs as "Step It Up and Go" and "Hangover Blues," which featured Fred's slapped bass and the hot electric guitar work of men like Roy Nichols (who got his start with the Maddox Brothers), they even foreshadowed the sound of rockabilly music. Although Rose Maddox's career soon surpassed that of her brothers and extended well past their retirement, her deserved success should not obscure for us the considerable achievements made by this family of musicians. They conveyed a spontaneity and zest for life and music rarely displayed among country musicians today.

One country musician, however, who never lost that enthusiasm was Grandpa Jones.[8] Of all the tradition-based performers of the 1950s, none had a career that began earlier nor lasted longer. When Grandpa went into the army in 1945, his career already reached back for about sixteen years, including a valuable apprenticeship with Bradley Kincaid in the mid-1930s. While in the service, he organized the Munich Mountaineers and did much to popularize American country music in Europe through his broadcasts on the Armed Forces Network. During the years from 1946 to 1952, he spent time on several radio stations before finally settling down at WSM and the *Grand Ole Opry*: Jones actually had three stints on the *Opry* before finally taking up permanent residence there in 1959. He had always been a performer of great versatility and irrepressible energy and was the kind of entertainer who needed to be seen as well as heard. Jones was first and foremost a showman, and a living reminder of what minstrelsy and country vaudeville must have been like. His later prominence on the *Hee Haw* show, where audiences could hear and view his droll humor, reinforced public perceptions of him as a comedian. He was indeed a comic—one of the greatest natural wits in country music—but he was also a singer and yodeler of considerable ability, and he possessed one of the largest and most varied repertories in the country field. Best known for his hard-driving, banjo-backed rendition of songs like "Old Rattler," "Mountain Dew," and "Eight More Miles to Louisville," he also ably performed Jimmie Rodgers songs (one of them, "T for Texas," was a hit in 1963), and he wrote and recorded some of the finest sentimental songs in the country genre, such as "The Tragic Romance" and "Fallen Leaves." Between 1945 and 1947, and periodically thereafter, he also recorded gospel songs as part of a quartet called the Brown's Ferry Four, an all-star group that included from time to time such singers as the Delmore Brothers, Merle Travis, Wayne Raney, and Red Foley. While remaining a versatile musician, Jones was also a faithful partisan of old-time country music, and his only real concession to modern tastes had been his use of an electric lead guitar (played by Merle Travis on Grandpa's early recordings). After the 1950s, Jones became even more traditional in approach, and he often performed with his daughters and talented wife, Ramona Riggins Jones, in a program that re-created the family-and-home atmosphere of pre–World War II country music.

Ramona Jones was one of several women who began to gain some recognition in a musical form long dominated by men. Virtually all of the women in the immediate postwar years—Martha Carson, Kitty Wells, Molly O'Day, Texas Ruby, Wilma Lee Cooper, Anita Carter, Rose Maddox—worked with their husbands or family groups, but each eventually began to carve an independent identity. Some of the women, such as Rose Maddox, Molly O'Day, and Wilma Lee Cooper, always overshadowed the groups with whom they worked, but they generally assumed no leadership roles within their respective units. Of the performers named, only Anita Carter anticipated the modulated, pop-country sounds of the 1960s. As Mother Maybelle's youngest daughter, she usually sang as part of the family group with her mother and two sisters, Helen and June. (After the original Carter Family disbanded in 1943, Maybelle went on the road with her three daughters as Mother Maybelle and the Carter Sisters.) But possessing what was often described as an "achingly pure" soprano voice—one of the finest natural voices in country music—Anita soon stood apart from her sisters as a popular solo act.

Most of the other women performers of the period possessed rural and almost rough-hewn voices, and except for Texas Ruby, who sang in a deep vocal register, and Kitty Wells, who performed with a marked physical restraint, they sang in lusty, freewheeling styles. Martha Carson (who was born Irene Amburgey in Neon, Kentucky) made the charts in 1951 with a hand-clapping, Holiness-style song called "Satisfied," a tune she wrote during the emotionally low period following her divorce from James Carson. She eventually took her gospel act onto the nightclub circuit, arguing that Jesus meant for his message to be taken out of the churches and directly into the midst of sinners.[9] Rose Maddox, of course, had never been a stranger to night clubs or honky-tonks. She did not aggressively pursue an independent solo career until the late 1950s, but her performances with her brothers made her one of the most beloved and highly regarded singers of the day. Her energetically emotional, open-throated style strangely suggested the influence of both the honky-tonk and the country church. However, if any religious touches crept into her singing, they probably came from home or some source other than the church. She admitted to no religious influence and said that, while she admired Pentecostal/ Holiness singing, the theology of the movement left her cold.[10]

On the other hand, religious influence permeated the styles and repertory of Wilma Lee Cooper, Molly O'Day, and Kitty Wells. Cooper and O'Day can scarcely be discussed apart, for their vocal styles were similar—they have been called the female equivalents of Roy Acuff—and their repertories often overlapped. One significant difference lay in Cooper's longevity. She was still performing actively in the 1980s, while ill health and religious convictions contributed to O'Day's early retirement from professional music in the mid-1950s. Molly O'Day was the stage name of LaVerne Williamson from Pike County, Kentucky. When she began singing in the late 1930s, she was much influenced by the leading female singers of the day: Texas Ruby, Patsy Montana, and Lulu Belle Wiseman. She called herself Dixie Lee at this stage of her career and clothed herself like a cowgirl, one of the two or three performing images that seemed appropriate for a woman singer. In 1942, after her marriage to Lynn Davis, she adopted the stage name of Molly O'Day and moved more logically toward the mountain style of gospel and ballad singing for which she became famous. O'Day was a good five-string banjo player—just listen to her performance of the old murder ballad, "Poor Ellen Smith"—but her chief forte lay in the singing of ballads with moral messages, such as "Don't Sell Daddy Any More Whiskey," "Drunken Driver," and "Matthew 24," or tender story songs such as "Teardrops Falling in the Snow" and "Tramp on the Street." The last song, which proved crucial to her career, came from Hank Williams, whom she heard singing it in Montgomery, Alabama, in about 1942. Williams in turn had learned it from its authors, Hazel and Grady Cole, who recorded the song, with a substantially different melody, on the Bluebird label in 1939. One of the great songs of compassion in country music, "Tramp on the Street" soon moved into the repertories of country singers everywhere (first through the performances of Wilma Lee Cooper, who heard Molly singing it on the radio). O'Day had a fateful association with Hank Williams. Not only had she learned her most famous song from him, through the encouragement of Fred Rose, she recorded some of his first important compositions in 1946: "Six More Miles to the Graveyard," "The Singing Waterfall," "When God Comes and Gathers His Jewels," and "I Don't Care If Tomorrow Never Comes." No woman country singer

Molly O'Day (right) and husband, Lynn Davis (left), 1950. Courtesy of Ivan Tribe.

enjoyed a greater popularity in the southeastern United States in the late 1940s, and no one sang with a greater emotional urgency or heartfelt sincerity. Many people could easily agree with veteran Columbia talent scouts Arthur Satherley and Don Law, who described Molly O'Day as the greatest woman country singer of all time.[11]

Wilma Lee Cooper began her career as part of the Leary Family Singers from Valley Head, West Virginia: Mom and Dad Leary and four daughters. The Learys represented West Virginia at the National

Kitty Wells. Bill Malone personal collection.

Folk Festival in Washington, DC, in 1938, and managed to record a few songs for the Library of Congress while in the city. They toured widely after that, wandering as far north and west as Chicago and Nebraska. Stoney Cooper joined them as a fiddler in the early 1940s, and by the end of the war he and Wilma Lee had married and organized their own music act. Fred Rose, who had a keen ear for talent, heard them in 1947 while they were recording for Rich-R-Tone in Johnson City, Tennessee. Rose helped them get a contract with Columbia that lasted from 1948 to 1955, and then signed them to his own label, Hickory, after that date. Wilma Lee and Stoney were regulars on WWVA's *Wheeling Jamboree* from 1947 to 1957. During this period they and their band, the Clinch Mountain Clan, kept old-time country music alive and were one of the few groups in country music to preserve the sound of the Dobro steel guitar, played by Bill Carver and Buck Graves. Wilma Lee and Stoney often sang duets—as on the song that became their theme, "The West Virginia Polka," written for them by Ira and Charlie Louvin—but the real strength of the group lay in Wilma Lee's soulful solo singing. She sang a few songs also identified with Molly O'Day, such as "Tramp on the Street" and "Matthew 24," but she also introduced a number of story songs and recitations, such as "Thirty Pieces of Silver," "Legend of the Dogwood Tree," and "Walking My Lord up Calvary's Hill," which remained staples in the country repertory. After Stoney's death on March 22, 1977, Wilma Lee continued to perform as a touring entertainer and became even more traditional than before; she continued to dip into the bag of old-time songs and once again took up the five-string banjo, an instrument that she earlier ignored in deference to the guitar.

The first bona fide female country superstar proved to be the modest and unassuming Kitty Wells. No "Queen of Country Music" ever wore her crown more lightly. Born Muriel Deason in, of all places, Nashville, Tennessee, she was given the stage name "Kitty Wells" by her husband, Johnny Wright, who remembered an old parlor song of the same name that had once been popular on the *Grand Ole Opry*. Kitty appeared regularly with Johnny and Jack and the Tennessee Mountain Boys, sometimes singing solos and often joining in on the choruses of songs. She made a few records for RCA in the late 1940s, but her own career did not catch fire until she signed with Paul Cohen and Decca in 1952. In that year she crossed the threshold to stardom with a song called "It Wasn't God Who Made Honky Tonk Angels," an answer to Hank Thompson's smash success of a few months earlier, "The Wild Side of Life" (known generally by its first line, "I didn't know God made honky tonk angels"). Kitty's recording was number one on *Billboard*'s country chart for six weeks and was, in fact, the first song by a woman to attain the top position since *Billboard* had begun compiling such listings in 1948. Kitty did not have another number one record until 1961—"Heartbreak U.S.A."—but from 1952 to 1963 she recorded nineteen songs that appeared in the top ten. She competed with the men on more than even terms, and such songs as "Paying for

That Back Street Affair," "Making Believe," "I Don't Claim to Be an Angel," and "Whose Shoulder Will You Cry On" moved onto jukeboxes everywhere.

Although she took her songs into the honky-tonks and often sang songs that reflected that tawdry environment, Kitty Wells preserved an image of wholesomeness and domesticity far removed from the world about which she often sang. Kitty was not a "honky-tonk angel," nor was she particularly liberated, even though her commercial success helped make it possible for other women performers to thrive. She always preserved an aura of gentle dignity and conveyed the impression that she was a country housewife who had gotten dressed up to sing at the church social or community pie supper. The aggressively competitive country music world, of course, was much harsher than any church social, but Kitty seems to have been protected from much of its reality by her husband, who handled the details of her career and who generally spoke for her. Revolutions come slowly in country music, and although her first big hit—"It Wasn't God Who Made Honky Tonk Angels"—is often interpreted as a breakthrough for woman's liberation in country music, it would be another ten years or so before women would really begin to stand alone as performers.

The more country music changed, the more it remained the same. Although the music stood on the brink of the rock-and-roll deluge that would sweep away many of the older concepts of popular music, country musicians in the early 1950s still held to preoccupations that had attracted their predecessors. Religious music remained a staple in the country repertory; in fact, no period since that time has seen so many singers committed to the gospel genre nor so many religious songs making their way into the popularity charts. Given the postwar context of uncertainty and fear, it is not surprising that songs of faith and reaffirmation would appear frequently in country music repertories. Although all country singers included such numbers in their performances, some entertainers, such as the Masters Family (Johnny and Lucille) from Florida, the Johnson Family from North Carolina, the Chuck Wagon Gang from Texas, and Mac Odell, performed gospel music exclusively. Other performers, such as the Bailes Brothers, the Blue Sky Boys, the Louvin Brothers, and Martha Carson, either started out as gospel singers or made such songs a basic part of their repertory. The Brown's Ferry Four did as much as any group of entertainers to keep the songs from the old shape-note hymnals alive, but they were a shifting group of musicians (Grandpa Jones, Alton and Rabon Delmore, Wayne Raney, Merle Travis, Red Foley) who got together only for recording purposes. Foley also sang religious material on his own and was one of several singers, such as Cowboy Copas, Johnny Masters, Jimmie Davis, Martha Carson, and Stuart Hamblen, who experienced commercial success with the genre. Foley demonstrated his remarkable versatility as a singer when he moved into the popularity charts with such songs as "Just a Closer Walk with Thee," "Peace in the Valley," and "Steal Away" (the last song also featured an old recitation about a Negro funeral, done in dialect). Stuart Hamblen, a veteran of country music since the 1930s, probably had the greatest success of all the country-religious singers because he both wrote and recorded his material. A longtime problem drinker, Hamblen began writing sacred songs soon after his well-publicized conversion in 1949, in one of Billy Graham's Los Angeles crusades. His "It Is No Secret" became a standard in country music, while "This Old House" went on to become a pop sensation after being recorded by Rosemary Clooney.

Comic songs also figured prominently in country music,[12] and some singers specialized exclusively with such material or made it the most prominent part of their repertory. Little Jimmy Dickens, for example, performed all kinds of songs very effectively but was generally typecast as a novelty singer because of such songs as "Country Boy," "Out Behind the Barn," "Bessie the Heifer," "Sleeping at the Foot of the Bed," and "Take an Old Cold Tater and Wait"—all bittersweet recollections of growing up poor and rural. Dickens was a genuine country boy from Bolt, West Virginia, who acquired the title of "Little Jimmy" because of his diminutive size: 4 feet 11 inches. A dynamo of energy on stage, Dickens began his career in the late 1930s at a radio station in Beckley, West Virginia, where he opened Johnnie Bailes's morning show by crowing like a rooster. Another performer almost as energetic as Little Jimmy was Bill Carlisle, a Kentucky entertainer who had been involved in country music since the 1930s. Carlisle had been the rhythm guitarist and singing partner with his brother Cliff in the 1930s and early 1940s but toured in the 1950s with his own band. Known as Jumping Bill Carlisle because of his stage antics, he introduced some of the most popular comic tunes of the period, such as "Too Old to Cut the Mustard" and "No Help Wanted." The most consistent, and probably most popular, performers of comic music were two duets, Lonzo and Oscar and Homer and Jethro. Of the two groups,

Lonzo and Oscar always maintained the strongest rustic identifica-tion, while Homer and Jethro gradually evolved into a sophisticated night club act. The Lonzo and Oscar team began in the late 1930s when Ken Marvin (Lonzo) and Rollin Sullivan (Oscar) organized a comedy routine on WTJS in Jackson, Tennessee. Another alumnus of WTJS, Eddy Arnold, later gave them their stage names while they were tour-ing with him. Marvin retired in about 1945, and John Sullivan (Rollin's brother) became Lonzo until his death in 1967; David Hooten played the role after that time. Throughout most of their career, Lonzo and Oscar affected a cornball image, wearing rube costumes, engaging in silly repartee, and singing novelty songs in hillbilly harmony style. Two of their earlier songs, "I'm My Own Grandpa" and "Hole in the Bottom of the Sea," remained those with which the duo were most closely identified.

Homer and Jethro (Henry Haynes and Kenneth Burns in real life) also started out as "stage hillbillies," replete with ill-fitting hayseed costumes and droll, backwoods humor, but by the 1950s, they had abandoned rube attire in favor of business suits or casual street dress. They featured deadpan humor as opposed to the rather strident, free-wheeling style employed by Lonzo and Oscar, and they specialized in song parodies. "How Much Is That Doggie in the Window" became "How Much Is That Hound Dog in the Winder" (replete with the memorable line: "You know what a basketball nose is, it dribbles all over the floor"), and "Let Me Go, Lover" became "Let Me Go Blubber." They gradually took their act off the barn dance stage and into supper clubs and night clubs around the country. Their dialogue tended to be considerably more sophisticated than their song lyrics, and their musicianship won support from many people who were normally not attracted to country music. Homer and Jethro performed often on recordings and in concert with their old friend Chet Atkins (all were from Knoxville). When they departed from their song burlesques, they played some of the finest string band jazz heard in country music. Homer was an incomparable rhythm guitarist, and Jethro's mandolin playing made him a much-admired "musician's musician."

Boogie tunes also enjoyed great popularity during country music's postwar commercial surge. Country musicians had long demonstrated an affinity for the blues and for other black-derived forms, but the term "boogie" did not appear on a country record until Johnny Barfield re-corded "Boogie Woogie" in 1939. Other songs appeared periodically that embodied the essence of boogie-woogie, even if they did not bear the label, but the postwar preoccupation with the style began with the Delmore Brothers' recording of "Hillbilly Boogie" for the King company in 1945. Before they ceased recording in 1952, the Delmores did at least eleven songs with "boogie" in the title, including "Freight Train Boogie" (in 1946), which has had the longest life of any in this genre. Between 1945 and the early 1950s, a wide variety of country musicians recorded boogie material, including the Maddox Brothers and Rose, Hardrock Gunter, Jack Guthrie, Wayne Raney, Arthur Smith, Moon Mullican, Tennessee Ernie Ford, and Red Foley. Some of their songs were among the most popular in the entire country field: Arthur Smith's big hit of 1946–1947, "Guitar Boogie"; Moon Mullican's "Cherokee Boogie"; Tennessee Ernie's "Shotgun Boogie"; and Red Foley's "Chattanooga Shoe Shine Boy." The fascination with the boogie form reached its zenith (although some would say "depths") in 1948, when a white gospel group, the Homeland Harmony Quartet, recorded "Gospel Boogie" (also known as "Everybody's Gonna Have a Wonderful Time Up There"). The gospel field has seldom witnessed such a major hit.

Despite the popularity of various kinds of country music, the sounds that predominated during the booming postwar years were those that reflected the honky-tonk and dance hall scene of the Southwest. While the fiddle was universal, the electric steel guitar reigned supreme in almost every band; it and the electric standard guitar (sometimes called a "takeoff" guitar) provided most of the melodic or improvisatory passages heard in country performances. The large western swing bands had declined in national popularity and were now confined largely to the West Coast, Las Vegas, Oklahoma, and Texas. Many of their styles and innovations, however, had become standard features of the smaller bands. A few musicians prospered through their ability to combine honky-tonk vocal and lyric approaches with the instrumental sound of western swing. Leon Rausch, for example, had been one of Bob Wills's best vocalists (surpassed only, perhaps, by Tommy Duncan), but after the mid-1950s, he generally fronted his own smaller bands in the Dallas–Fort Worth area and specialized in songs similar to those of his honky-tonk contemporaries. Similarly, down in the sprawling territory between Waco and Austin, Jimmy Heap led a group called the Melody Masters that played regularly for dances in such well-known night spots as the Skyline Club in Austin and at Dessau

Hall northeast of the state capitol. Like most dance hall bands, the Melody Masters possessed a big repertory of Bob Wills–style songs, but they also featured beer-drinking tunes, then becoming paramount in country music. The Melody Masters, as a matter of fact, introduced to country music two of its classic honky-tonk songs: "Release Me" and "The Wild Side of Life" (both sung by Perk Williams).

No one achieved a more commercial fusion of honky-tonk and western swing than Waco-born Hank Thompson. Before the war, Thompson sang as "the Hired Hand" on local Waco radio stations, but he did not really hit his stride as a professional performer until he returned from military service in 1946. He was encouraged and promoted by a Dallas radio personality, Hal Horton, who featured Thompson on his noontime show, *Cornbread Matinee* (Thompson was even married on the show), and by Tex Ritter, who persuaded the Capitol record company to add Thompson to its roster. Thompson immediately showed a facility for writing clever and engaging lyrics, a talent that appeared in two of his hits of 1947, "Humpty Dumpty Heart" (a pleasant little honky-tonk number) and "Whoa Sailor" (a delightful song, inspired by his recent Navy tenure, about a sailor who was repeatedly rebuffed by a bar girl until he flashed his six months' pay). Thompson became noted for his beer-drinking honky-tonk songs—particularly after his super hit of 1951, "The Wild Side of Life"—but his vocal style never embodied the plaintive or emotionally heart-wrenching sounds featured by most honky-tonk singers. His was a clean and crisply articulated sound that eschewed emotional involvement in favor of a precise narration. While Thompson recorded his hit vocals (mostly for the Capitol label), his band, the Brazos Valley Boys, won poll after poll as the nation's best western swing group.

Several singers of the period often projected a honky-tonk sound or flavor but were not exclusively wedded to the genre. Cowboy Copas, T. Texas Tyler, Carl Smith, and Little Jimmy Dickens, for example, sometimes sang in front of electric instrumental accompaniment that suggested the noisy environs of a Texas beer joint, and their material frequently resembled or came from the western swing and honky-tonk repertories. Copas and Tyler, however (from Ohio and Arkansas respectively), came out of the 1930s and carried the marks of the tent-show–schoolhouse–and–church circuit with them. Copas was best known for "Filipino Baby," a variant of an 1890s Tin Pan Alley song about an American sailor and his South Seas sweetheart that

Hank Thompson. Courtesy of Nathan Gibson.

was updated to fit the context of World War II. He also specialized in waltz tunes and old-style sentimental songs such as "The Tragic Romance." But with a song like "Signed, Sealed and Delivered," he set tears to flowing in a thousand beer glasses around America. T. Texas Tyler, who was born David Myrick near Mena, Arkansas, had also been a barnstorming hillbilly entertainer in the 1930s and was a storehouse of traditional material that he reshaped for modern tastes. One of the big hits of 1948 was his version of a very old British folktale that Tyler renamed "Deck of Cards." Tyler transformed the tale into a story about an American soldier in the North African campaign who used his deck of cards as an almanac, prayer book, and Bible (the Ace representing the One God; the Deuce representing the two divisions of the Bible, the Old and New Testaments; the Trey representing the Holy Trinity; and so on). The recitation has since been recorded many times and has been periodically recast in the context of America's subsequent wars. Although Tyler performed an extensive number of old-fashioned songs such as "Deck of Cards," "Black Jack David," and "Remember Me When the Candle Lights Are Gleaming" (which he spiced with a bizarre and virtually inimitable growl), he sang to the beat and blare of honky-tonk instrumentation, and he was a fixture on the California western ballroom circuit in the mid- and late 1940s.

Carl Smith came from Roy Acuff's hometown of Maynardville, Tennessee, but little in his style suggested the traditional mountain influence that one hears in the singing of Acuff, Wilma Lee Cooper, or Molly O'Day. Smith did have a large repertory of gospel music, and he eventually recorded an album of bluegrass songs; nevertheless, his personal tastes were inclined heavily toward "western" styles. He dressed in western attire; he built a horse farm near Nashville; and he borrowed extensively from the areas of honky-tonk and western swing music. Vocally, his sound veered close to that of the crooner, although there was little sweetness in his lusty and heartfelt style. Smith rose to prominence in country music in 1952 when two of his songs, "Let Old Mother Nature Have Her Way" and "Don't Just Stand There," became successive number one songs on *Billboard*'s country chart. Few of his songs gained such distinction in the following years—other than "Hey Joe" in 1953 and "Loose Talk" in 1955—but several of his recordings appeared in the top ten, and a few, like "I Overlooked an Orchid," "Let's Live a Little," and "Hey Joe," are still known to country fans today through the recordings of other people. It is regrettable that Smith is so seldom remembered today, because few singers enjoyed the commercial prominence that he had in this country and in Canada during the first half of the 1950s.

As noted earlier, Jimmy Dickens became famous for his novelty songs. His skill at comic material, however, should not obscure his excellence as a singer of more serious material. Dickens's voice conveyed great emotional strength (a trait displayed by many West Virginia singers), and he possessed probably the most pronounced vibrato in country music. No one has ever been a better performer of "heart" songs (love songs) or of honky-tonk weepers. Dickens's soulful intensity—displayed in such songs as "Take Me As I Am," "We Could," "Just When I Needed You," "What about You," and "Life Turned Her That Way"—made him a much-admired entertainer among his singing contemporaries and contributed to his success on jukeboxes all over the nation.[13]

Among the pure-and-simple honky-tonk singers of the early 1950s, Texas names still predominated, some of whom had been around since the first stirrings of the style in the mid-1930s. Three of the Grand Old

Masters of the genre were very active and commercially successful in the postwar years: Ernest Tubb, Floyd Tillman, and Moon Mullican. Tubb had become sufficiently institutionalized in country music that he not only exerted great influence on younger singers but also did much to shape the style and tone of the country music industry. He, Kitty Wells, and Red Foley launched the modern era of recording in Nashville with their performances for Decca in the years right after the war; he became one of the first country singers to make records with other established stars, including the pop-singing Andrews Sisters; and he and Red Foley were instrumental in persuading the music industry to replace the word "hillbilly" with the seemingly more respectable "country." Above all, Tubb remained true to the honky-tonk style that he had done so much to create and perfect, and he took it into dance halls and Carnegie Hall alike.

After toiling obscurely for years as a sideman in southwestern bands, Floyd Tillman gradually began to create a solo identity during the war with such songs as "They Took the Stars Out of Heaven." In 1948 and 1949, he recorded his greatest hits, "I Love You So Much It Hurts" and "Slipping Around," both of which were covered and made into even greater successes by Jimmy Wakely. As a singer, Tillman featured a lazy, drawling baritone style replete with peculiar swoops and note bendings that was too irresistibly appealing to avoid imitation. As a writer, he was equally respected, and his songs moved into the repertories of country singers everywhere. "Slipping Around" was one of the first, and probably the best, of a spate of "cheating songs" that began to circulate in country music, evidence perhaps of the social realism that gradually crept into the music as its audience became increasingly urban and working class. However, while country singers and writers might comment on illicit behavior, few could openly condone it. Tillman, for example, soon followed his song with "I'll Never Slip Around Again" (opining that the one he had slipped around with was now slipping around on him).

Tillman's longtime friend and colleague Moon Mullican also rose to prominence as a singer during the 1950s. Mullican, of course, had been singing since he entered professional music in the 1930s, but his identity, if not his voice, had generally been subsumed by the groups with whom he played. Recording for the King label in the late 1940s and early 1950s, however, Mullican revealed a vocal versatility that had scarcely been suspected in the bluesy and swing material in which he had earlier specialized. His piano playing remained his most distinguishing trait, ranging from a rather sedate style appropriate for romantic ballads to the aggressive barrelhouse style that he had perfected in the honky-tonks and sporting houses of Houston and the Gulf Coast. Mullican could still "make the bottles bounce" with an array of blues and boogie tunes that anticipated rock-and-roll, but he could also sing honky-tonk and sentimental tunes as convincingly as any singer of the period. His husky tenor voice showed the effects of a thousand noisy, smoke-filled dance halls, which, ironically, made peculiarly effective such poignant heart songs as "I Was Sorta Wonderin'," "I'll Sail My Ship Alone," and even "Sweeter than the Flowers" (a rather uncharacteristic song for a honky-tonk singer about a family's remembrances of a deceased mother). Mullican also dabbled with Cajun music, a form with which he certainly would have been familiar during his long tenure as a musician in the region between Lafayette, Louisiana, and Houston, Texas. In 1946, Harry Choates recorded on the Gold Star label an old Cajun song called "Jole Blon" and saw it become a hit in the Houston area. Mullican played around with the tune in the King studios in Cincinnati, but not understanding the French lyrics, he substituted his own nonsense words, a potpourri of Louisiana clichés about dirty rice, filé gumbo, and the like, and also of rural metaphors such as "possum up a gum stump" and "turning plow." This rollicking fusion was one of the most commercially successful songs of the era.

Harry Choates was one of the younger breed of honky-tonk musicians and the man most responsible for bringing Cajun sounds and rhythms into country music. Choates was born in Rayne, Louisiana, but grew up in Port Arthur, Texas, and had been a guitarist in a band led by Leo Soileau, a fiddler and singer and one of the pioneer recording performers of Cajun music. Choates probably picked up some of his fiddle style from Soileau and may have even learned "Jole Blon" from him because Soileau had recorded a version of the song in 1935, "La Valse de Gueydan," which was punctuated by the same shouts and high-pitched wail later heard in Choates's version. After "Jole Blon" popularized his name, Choates became a regular on the Texas honky-tonk circuit. He might have gained some national support had his life not ended tragically at a relatively young age. The wild and hard-living twenty-nine-year-old Cajun was arrested in Austin in 1951 for nonpayment of child support. He died in the Austin city jail under clouded circumstances, a victim of delirium tremens or, as many of his friends insisted, of police brutality.

Choates performed in a social milieu shared by many hopeful young entertainers, the honky-tonk and dance hall world of eastern and southeastern Texas. This hard but busy environment molded the styles and careers of many of country music's greatest late-twentieth-century entertainers. George Jones and Ray Price, for example, were just inaugurating their famous careers in the early 1950s but were listening to and learning from men like Mullican, Tillman, Choates, and Tubb. Jones had not yet found his own style, but was instead a composite of all he had heard. Price, too, was searching for a commercial sound, but he gained much encouragement as a protégé of Hank Williams. The two best young honky-tonk singers—with the exception of Williams, whose music spilled across several categories—were Lefty Frizzell and Webb Pierce.

William Orville "Lefty" Frizzell's stature has steadily risen in the years since his death in 1975.[14] He is today recognized as one of the great stylists of country music history, and his influence has been clearly detected in the styles of performers like Stoney Edwards, John Anderson, Randy Travis, Keith Whitley, Mark Chesnutt, and Merle Haggard. Frizzell was born in Corsicana, Texas, in 1928, and as a youngster, lived in a succession of homes in Texas, Oklahoma, and Arkansas, moving frequently as part of the family of an itinerant oil driller. He discovered his parents' Jimmie Rodgers records very early in life, and by the time he was sixteen, was singing frequently in and around El Dorado, Arkansas, where the family lived for several years, and as far away as Dallas. The specific origin of the nickname Lefty is unclear; popular legend attributes it to Frizzell's participation in Golden Gloves contests in El Dorado, but his widow, Alice Frizzell, denied that he was ever involved in that boxing program.[15] Whatever the source of the moniker, Frizzell probably needed a good left hook to survive in some of the places he played in Arkansas and Texas. A honky-tonk in Big Spring, Texas—the Ace of Clubs—inspired his most famous song, "If You Got the Money," while an overnight stay in a county jail in West Texas prompted his first recording, "I Love You a Thousand Ways." Lefty and Alice married when they were teenagers, and in "I Love You a Thousand Ways" he begged her to "please wait until I'm free." This would not be the last song inspired by this enduring but often turbulent relationship.

Lefty Frizzell. Columbia Records; Creative Commons Attribution-ShareAlike 3.0, www.creativecommons.org/licenses/by-sa/3.0/legalcode.

Lefty's rise in country music was meteoric. He made his first records for Columbia in 1950 when he was only twenty-two years old—his association with the company lasted until 1973—and by the time he was twenty-three, he was one of the most successful acts in country music. A Merle Haggard recording, "The Way It Was in '51," asserts that Hank and Lefty ruled every jukebox that year. At one point, for example, Frizzell had four songs simultaneously in *Billboard*'s Top Ten chart (numbers one, two, six, and eight), an unprecedented accomplishment for a country singer. He also recorded the first of his Jimmie Rodgers songs in that year, and one of them, "Traveling Blues," became a popular hit. His Rodgers interpretations, eventually released on an LP called *Lefty Frizzell Sings the Songs of Jimmie Rodgers*, have been among the most highly valued of the performances made by the Blue Yodeler's disciples. Lefty did not try to imitate Rodgers (although he did yodel in a few of the songs recorded in 1953); he instead put his own individual stamp on the songs. At this stage of his career, Lefty sang in a relatively high register (as opposed to the mellifluous baritone of his later years), but even then he was noted for his voice control (his ability to bend notes and stretch musical syllables) and for his habit of modulating from a high note to a low one and then back again.

Lefty worked out of Beaumont, Texas, for a year or two and then moved in 1953 to Los Angeles, where he became a member of the *Town Hall Party*. His hits became fewer after that year—a product of personal problems and of changing musical tastes in America—but he never lost the vocal artistry that he had so precociously displayed. If anything, his style became more intimate and more subtly nuanced as his public identity grew less pronounced. Already he was developing the personal mystique that has ever since clung to his memory.

Webb Pierce, on the other hand, has generated no personal mystique, and he was generally forgotten until 1982, when Willie Nelson recorded an LP with him. For several years previously, Pierce had become largely content with drawing his royalties; overseeing his extensive business holdings; and welcoming tourists to view his mansion, ornately decorated automobile (also a product of Nudie Cohn's ingenious imagination), and guitar-shaped swimming pool in Nashville. Almost forgotten was the dominance he had enjoyed in country music during the 1950s. No one, not even Hank Williams, monopolized the country popularity charts as did Webb Pierce during the first half of that decade. Pierce was born in West Monroe, Louisiana, in 1926, and he remained a rather obscure country singer, combining his music activities with his work as a Sears Roebuck store manager, until he joined the *Louisiana Hayride* in 1950. In 1952, he recorded his first big hit, "Wondering," which had been a Louisiana favorite since Joe Werner and the Riverside Ramblers introduced it in 1936. Pierce thereafter showed a great facility for resurrecting older songs, such as Buster Coward's "Texas Sand," Billy Cox's "Sparkling Brown Eyes" (by way of a Jerry and Sky recording), and Jimmie Rodgers's "In the

Jailhouse Now," and converting them into commercial successes. He demonstrated an even greater skill at selecting modern-composed songs with popular appeal—such as "More and More," "I Don't Care," "Slowly," and "That Heart Belongs to Me"—although his performance of them contributed most to their success. Pierce's vocal and instrumental sounds were quintessentially honky-tonk. His wailing tenor voice easily cut through the din and babble of bars and dance halls, while his instrumental accompaniment set down a hard-to-resist danceable beat. Pierce's band differed little from other honky-tonk combos in its use of fiddle, electric lead guitar, and steel guitar, but it made history in the early 1950s when Bud Isaacs popularized the pedal steel guitar on several of Pierce's recordings. Pioneered by West Coast musicians, but not widely heard until the mid-1950s, the pedal steel guitar became omnipresent in country music and eventually made its way into other kinds of music as well. Pierce's honky-tonk emphasis was also demonstrated in his use of lyrics. His "Back Street Affair" was one of the best of several "cheating" songs that appeared in the late 1940s and early 1950s, and it also inspired Kitty Wells's "Paying for That Back Street Affair." "There Stands the Glass" (1953) became virtually the national anthem of beer drinkers. Its endorsement of drinking as an antidote to the pangs of unsuccessful love was both unique in its realism and controversial. Some radio stations reputedly refused to play the record.

The hard-edged and often rough sound of the honky-tonk singers was paralleled by the smooth, soft sound of another group of singers whose approach eventually won the day in country music. The crooning, or country-pop, impulse goes back at least to the performances of Vernon Dalhart, who was never able to hide his music-hall and light-opera training. Gene Autry also anticipated the modern pop-country sound with his 1935 recording of "You're the Only Star in My Blue Heaven," an effort to reach out to that broader middle-class audience attracted to his films. A few West Coast singers of the early 1950s, such as Eddie Kirk, Wesley Tuttle, and Jimmy Wakely, featured styles that seemed more than a little indebted to Autry. Wakely, in fact, came to California from Oklahoma in 1936 and became part of a trio that backed up Autry on personal appearances. Wakely later became a singing cowboy in his own right and recorded several popular numbers, such as his own composition "Too Late" and Johnny Bond's "I Wonder Where You Are Tonight." In the late 1940s, he recorded

"Slipping Around," one of his greatest successes with the pop vocalist Margaret Whiting. Another of his big hits, "One Has My Name (The Other Has My Heart)," was written and also recorded by another Hollywood cowboy crooner, Eddie Dean.

Texas-born Leon Payne also spent much of his time in California but was also identified with the Nashville scene and with the honky-tonk music of his native state. Payne studied music at the Texas School for the Blind in Austin and began making an attempt at a professional career not long after graduating from the institution. Payne will always be best known for the songs that he wrote: "Lost Highway" and "They'll Never Take Her Love from Me" (both turned into hits by Hank Williams), "You'll Still Have a Place in My Heart," and "I Love You Because." But with his pleasant and smooth tenor voice, he was also one of the better singers of the period. Many performers, from Ernest Tubb to Elvis Presley, have recorded "I Love You Because," but no one has surpassed Payne himself in the vocal interpretation that he gave to the song written for his wife, Myrtie.

The southeastern United States also produced its quota of smooth country crooners: Pete Cassell, Zeke Clements, Hank Locklin, George Morgan, Red Foley, and Eddy Arnold, for example. Cassell was another blind singer and a longtime performer on WSB in Atlanta. People who performed with him remember not only his easy and smooth vocal delivery but also his expertise in handling a microphone—a technical art that many country singers were slow to master. Zeke Clements, from Warrior, Alabama, was a veteran of country music who had appeared on radio stations in the South and Midwest since the late 1920s. He was one of the first singers to dress like a cowboy on the *Grand Ole Opry*, but his songs seldom commented on western themes (his most famous song was the militant anthem of World War II, "Smoke on the Water"). While his versatile style and repertory won him a big following among country fans, Clements achieved a measure of wider fame as the voice of Bashful in the movie *Snow White and the Seven Dwarfs*.

Hank Locklin, from McClellan, Florida, possessed a tenor voice sufficiently pure to make him the most popular country singer in Ireland, but with enough raw edge to also guarantee him a honky-tonk audience in the United States. Locklin's first popular recording, "Same Sweet Girl," was a lovely tribute to faithful love—a rare genre in a music traditionally given over to broken, unrequited, or illicit love. "Let Me Be the One" and "Send Me the Pillow That You Dream On," both major hits for Locklin, were more in the mainstream of country music, and both anticipated the country-pop songs of the late 1950s.

George Morgan, Red Foley (discussed earlier), and Eddy Arnold bore a closer resemblance to the pop singers of the 1950s than did any other country singers. Morgan, who was born in Waverly, Tennessee, but grew up among the large colony of transplanted southerners in Akron, Ohio, seems to have been groomed by the Columbia label as a successor to Eddy Arnold. Morgan, however, never abandoned country music for the sounds of pop or pop-country, and he clung to the use of the Hawaiian-chorded steel guitar (the "ting-a-ling" sound, as he called it) throughout his career. His first big hit, "Candy Kisses," was as trite and bland as its title, but most of his other songs, such as "Almost," had greater emotional depth and textual vigor. Characterized by silken and softly modulated tones, Morgan's vocal style was among the least rural in country music, but he remained a missionary for the more traditional country styles. He even served as president of the Association of Country Entertainers (ACE)—an organization devoted to the preservation of "real" country music—for a brief period in the 1970s.

Eddy Arnold became virtually an institution in American life, with an identity only peripherally related to country music.[16] But in the late 1940s, he dominated the country charts with a sound that lay at the center of mainstream country music. It was neither "mountain" nor "honky-tonk," and it contained few traces of western swing. His music certainly contained little backwoods flavor, yet it was not quite pop either, even as he moved persistently in that direction. His music was somewhat suggestive of that of Gene Autry, but without the hard edge of the early Autry nor the almost affected, pear-shaped phrasing of the later cowboy singer. Arnold's sound was sweet, smooth, pleasant, and plaintive—that of a down-home crooner. On the other hand, he was every bit the "Tennessee Plowboy" he claimed to be, born in 1918 on a sharecropper's farm in Chester County near Madisonville and educated in a one-room school. He performed on WTJS in Jackson, Tennessee, and on WMPS in Memphis, and spent some time in St. Louis with the fiddler Speedy McNatt before joining Pee Wee King and the Golden West Cowboys in the early 1940s. The affiliation with the Golden West Cowboys became his ticket to the *Grand Ole Opry* and to wider fame through appearances with such troupes as the Camel Caravan. He made his first solo recording for Victor in

December 1944, "Mommy, Please Stay Home with Me," a tender song about a neglected, dying child that now seems greatly out of character with the urbane and hip image that he later projected. In his earliest recordings of such songs as "It's a Sin" and "Chained to a Memory," Arnold sang in a simple, unaffected, and thoroughly appealing style. His 1945 recording of "Cattle Call," a somewhat altered version of Tex Owens's earlier song, demonstrated that he was no stranger to yodeling either. It thereafter remained his theme song and was probably his most identifying number. Arnold's accompanying instrumentation brilliantly complemented his singing. To many listeners, the melodious, Hawaiian-chorded steel guitar playing of Roy Wiggins was just as important as Arnold's singing in defining and popularizing the sound heard on his records.

Arnold's style, however, did not long remain down-home. By 1947, when he recorded the very popular "Bouquet of Roses," his voice had become fuller, his register lower pitched, and his words more roundly articulated. The country crooner was well on the way to becoming a mainstream pop singer. By the mid-1950s, he could no longer be described as strictly a hillbilly singer, if indeed he had ever been one. Arnold has since claimed that he listened to and sang all kinds of music while growing up, and that he had been unaware that music was divided into categories. This catholicity of taste led him away from the old-time country repertory and toward an experimentation with sounds that were more compatible with his pop-country blend. According to his own testimony, his 1954 recording of "I Really Don't Want to Know"—a soft, muted sound produced by two acoustical guitars and a bass guitar—came closest to achieving his stylistic ideal.[17]

Arnold left the *Grand Ole Opry* in September 1948, primarily because he had greatly outgrown that forum, having already won national exposure through a daily radio show for Purina Mills carried on at least three hundred Mutual Broadcasting System stations. He also achieved a distinction that, until that time, had seldom been attained by country singers—a series of guest appearances on big-time radio shows. A half-page ad in *Billboard* in 1948[18] announced the following Arnold appearances: *RCA Victor Show, We the People, Spike Jones Show, Hayloft Hoedown, Luncheon at Sardi's, Paul Whiteman Club, Breakfast Club, Sunday Down South,* and *Western Theatre.* Later decades saw him also becoming a fixture on network television shows, first as the summer replacement for Perry Como on CBS in 1952.

Arnold's growing visibility as a popular culture hero, however, should not obscure the overpowering role he played in country music. In the fifteen years after 1948, when *Billboard* began its Top Ten listings, he led all country performers with a total of fifty-three tunes, thirteen of which reached the number one position. His election to the Country Music Hall of Fame in 1966 may not have pleased country traditionalists, but it did indicate the almost unparalleled impact that the Tennessee Plowboy had on the country field.

Eddy Arnold was one of several country singers in the 1950s who defy precise categorization. Hank Snow and Slim Whitman were reminiscent of the cowboy singers of the 1930s, but their repertories were broader than those of their predecessors. Clarence Eugene "Hank" Snow may very well have been the most versatile country entertainer of the mid-1950s.[19] Red Foley, of course, also comes to mind, but Foley showed no particular strength as a guitarist. Snow, on the other hand, was a master of the flat-picking style of guitar playing and could ably sing any kind of material, fast or slow. A native of Brooklyn, Nova Scotia, Snow lived a life that few novelists could imagine or re-create. He grew up in a very poor home, victimized by an abusive stepfather, but sustained in large part by the mother who taught him songs and guitar chords. He left home when he was fourteen and worked for a few years as a cabin boy in the dangerous waters off Nova Scotia. He was won over to country music through the recordings of Vernon Dalhart and Jimmie Rodgers. When he began his radio career in the mid-1930s on CHNS, he fashioned a singing-yodeling style similar to that of Jimmie Rodgers. Recording for Victor after 1936—an association that did not end until the early eighties—first with a song called "Prisoned Cowboy," Snow became one of Canada's favorite entertainers and was second in popularity only to Montana Slim. Snow came to the United States in 1944 and began six rather frustrating years trying to break into big-time country music. He spent some time in Philadelphia, on WWVA in West Virginia, and in California, before finally settling down in 1948 on the *Big D Jamboree*, where his first big American hits began to appear. "Brand on My Heart," a well-written tale of unrequited love that featured the melodious steel-guitar backing of Johnny Beaulieu, became the most popular song for several weeks on Hal Horton's *Hillbilly Hit Parade* on KRLD in Dallas. Continuing with "Marriage Vow" in 1949 and "I'm Moving On" in 1950, Snow became a big favorite in Texas and a popular act on the Dallas *Big D Jamboree*.

Supported by the lobbying of Ernest Tubb, and on the strength of "I'm Moving On," his first nationally charted number one song and only one of several train songs that he featured during his career, Snow joined the *Grand Ole Opry* in 1950. With his distinctive Canadian accent, nasally resonant voice, faultless articulation, and formal stage manner, Snow—who now called himself the Singing Ranger—created one of the most admired and distinctive styles in country music.

Ottis Dewey "Slim" Whitman, from Tampa, Florida, had a high, clear tenor voice and a yodeling style virtually unique in the 1950s. Whitman was unusual in that he rarely recorded a novelty song or one of the raw honky-tonk variety. His specialty was the sentimental or sad love song, and he often delved into the popular field for material. Like many country singers—from Roy Acuff to Charley Pride—Whitman's first love was baseball, and he pitched one year for Plant City, Florida, where he compiled an 11–1 record. He began singing in 1943 while serving in the navy on the USS *Chilton*, but did not record until 1949, when he joined RCA. Several of his RCA recordings, such as "Tears Can Never Drown the Flame," "I'll Never Pass This Way Again," and "Please Paint a Rose on the Garden Wall," were lovely performances distinguished by the instrumental accompaniment of Jethro Burns's mandolin and Chet Atkins's electric guitar. Lovely or not, Whitman's performances remained largely unnoticed until the early 1950s, when he joined the *Louisiana Hayride* and began making records for the Imperial label. Whitman cut a striking figure with his mustache, lean physical frame, and well-tailored cowboy suits, and he enthralled audiences with his easy stage presence and effortless yodeling and falsetto vocal breaks. He originally had a broad-ranging repertory that included folk songs like "Birmingham Jail," old pop tunes such as "When I Grow Too Old to Dream," modern-composed country songs like "Amateur in Love" and "Haunted Hungry Heart," religious numbers like "Sunrise," and romantic cowboy songs such as "Casting My Lasso to the Sky." But after "Indian Love Call" became the nation's number one country song in 1952, Whitman moved more insistently into the field of popular material and recorded with great success such numbers as "Rose Marie" and "Secret Love." Traditionalists might prefer to hear him do songs such as "Bandera Waltz," a cowboy song about the famous Bandera Stampede in Texas, but Whitman from that time on adhered closely to the performance of pop or country-pop tunes, some of them of the most saccharine quality.

Not only was Whitman's style unusual, he was also unique in his own time for the kind of appeal he exerted abroad. After "Rose Marie" became the number one song in England for eleven consecutive weeks, Whitman began making periodic trips to the British Isles and was one of the first American country singers to appear in the London Palladium. British audiences were probably as intrigued by his cowboy persona as they were by his tenor vocalizing. He never lost his appeal in Great Britain. Even during the days of the Beatles' ascendancy—and at a time when neither his name nor his music was heard in the United States—Slim Whitman always found a loyal and receptive audience when he went to England.

Many stars illuminated the firmament of country music in the 1950s, but none shown more brightly than that gifted but troubled boy from Alabama, Hank Williams.[20] Williams, Jimmie Rodgers, and Fred Rose constituted the triumvirate first elected to country music's Hall of Fame. He was the most dramatic symbol of country music's postwar surge, and his sudden death at the beginning of 1953 signaled the ending of the boom period. His early death solidified the legend that had already begun during his lifetime.

It is paradoxical that Hank Williams, whose compositions were more readily accepted by popular-music devotees than any other country writer's, was more firmly grounded in the rural tradition than most other hillbilly performers. King Hiram "Hank" Williams was born on September 17, 1923, in the little community of Mount Olive, Alabama, where he remained until the age of five, when his family moved to Georgiana, near Montgomery. Hank's dad, Lonnie, was a part-time farmer and log train engineer for the W. T. Smith Lumber Company until illness forced him into retirement and, eventually, into a veteran's hospital. Hank had little contact with his father, but he left an affectionate portrait of him in a song called "The Log Train," recorded on a home tape shortly before Hank died. Hank grew up in the care of his strong-willed and almost-smothering mother, Lilly, who tried to preserve a protective control over him well into his adulthood. It is hard to assess the influences, both good and ill, that came from this relationship, but Williams was at least introduced to religious music by his mother. He always loved and performed the hymns and gospel tunes that he heard in the fundamentalist Baptist churches of his childhood, and much of the style of gospel singing always remained in his own professional performances.

Hank Williams. Bill Malone personal collection; courtesy of Bob Pinson.

In many important respects, Williams grew up under no one's care but his own, and he was forced into a life of self-sufficiency much earlier than most children. As a small boy, he helped supplement the family income by selling peanuts and newspapers and by shining shoes. Most important of all, he was fronting his own hillbilly band by the time he was fourteen years old. Like most fledgling country singers of that era, Williams was part of all that he had heard. He absorbed much from the commercial singers of the day, and two of them—Roy Acuff and Ernest Tubb—directly affected his choice of material and delivery. Williams's style and repertory were curious blends of country gospel and honky-tonk, a mixture rare in Hank's own day and almost unknown now. As a product of the rural Deep South, however, Williams could scarcely avoid hearing the music of African Americans, and that, too, affected his style and song choices. When he was about twelve years old, Hank began listening to the music of a black street singer named Rufus Payne (known locally as Tee-Tot) who played for nickels and pennies on the streets of Georgiana and Greenville, Alabama, where the Williams family lived for a few years. Hank followed Tee-Tot around on many of his musical jaunts, sometimes sang with him, and Mrs. Williams occasionally fed the black musician from her kitchen. The extent of Tee-Tot's influence on Williams cannot be determined, but it is believed that he taught the little white boy a few guitar chords, gave him hints about how to please an audience, and bequeathed to him at least one song, "My Bucket's Got a Hole in It."

During the same period of his life, Williams won an amateur-night contest at Montgomery's Empire Theatre, singing his own composition, "The WPA Blues." Encouraged by this recognition of his talents, he began performing at any affair that might be willing to listen. Reflecting the omnipresent western image, Hank in 1937 formed a band called the Drifting Cowboys and began sporting the cowboy attire that he wore for the rest of his career. He and the Drifting Cowboys began appearing on WSFA in Montgomery and in schoolhouses, private homes, medicine shows, or anywhere that an audience might gather. He also began paying his dues in the honky-tonks, particularly at Thigpen's Log Cabin, a rather primitive, barnlike building just a few miles north of Georgiana in Butler County. Butler County was dry, but patrons often brought bootleg whiskey into Thigpen's, where they bought ice and setups. Hank had a fatal attraction to and weakness for alcohol, and he began developing the drinking problem that plagued him the rest of his life.

Williams's early years as a professional singer were fraught with struggle, disappointment, and economic penury, and he temporarily gave up music during the war years. He moved to Mobile in late 1942 and worked in the shipyards as a laborer and welder. Right at the end of the war he began playing regularly again, and did another stint in the honky-tonks, this time in the rough South Alabama clubs that were locally described as "blood buckets." His 1942 marriage to Audrey Sheppard began a tempestuous relationship that eventually ended in a divorce that inspired such famous songs as "Your Cheatin' Heart."

The series of events that made Hank Williams the most famous country singer in the world began in September 1946, when he and Audrey made an unsolicited call on Fred and Wesley Rose in Nashville. Williams auditioned a few of his songs for the Roses and, although this encounter did not immediately lead to the recording contract that he desired, he was signed by the Acuff-Rose company as a writer. Several of his songs, such as "When God Comes and Gathers His Jewels," "Six More Miles to the Graveyard," and "I Don't Care If Tomorrow Never Comes," were subsequently recorded by Molly O'Day, whose career Fred Rose was busily promoting. In December 1946, Williams signed his first recording contract with Sterling, a New York company just branching out into the country field. At this point in his career, Williams still sang with a marked Roy Acuff influence, but he was backed by a trio called the Oklahoma Cowboys (Vic, Guy, and Skeeter Willis) whose music was more reminiscent of western swing. When *Billboard* reviewed "Wealth Won't Save Your Soul" and "When God Comes and Gathers His Jewels," it made the following revealing comments: "It's the backwoods gospel singing—way back in the woods—that Hank Williams sings out for both of these country songs taken at a slow waltz tempo. Both the singing and the songs entirely funereal." The journal further added that the songs were "not for music machines."[21] While the music magazine may not have been impressed with Williams's sound, Fred Rose was bowled over by both Hank's singing and his writing abilities. Rose helped Williams obtain a recording contract with a new company named MGM, where he came in contact with its owner and longtime talent scout, Frank Walker. Williams's first recordings for MGM, in 1947, were "Move It On Over" and "I Heard You Crying in Your Sleep."

Hank Williams's association with Acuff-Rose and MGM served to ensure the commercial success of both organizations. Hank also contributed directly to the fame of Shreveport's *Louisiana Hayride*, which he joined on August 7, 1948, only four months after its founding. Hank became the headliner on the Saturday night show and on its personal appearances throughout the Southwest, and he reached still another audience as the guest host of the *Johnny Fair Syrup Hour* each weekday morning on KWKH. In the four-and-a-half-year period that followed, Hank Williams became the best-known and most emulated country entertainer in the United States. Several of his early recordings were moderately successful, but the one providing his breakthrough to commercial fame was "Lovesick Blues," an old Tin Pan Alley tune recorded at least as early as the 1920s by such singers as Jack Shea and Emmett Miller. Although Hank's version was similar to Miller's recordings of the song in 1925 and 1928 (the second time with the accompaniment of Eddie Lang and the Dorsey Brothers), Hank seems to have shaped his performance after that of fellow Alabamian Rex Griffin, whose earlier yodeling version was almost identical to his. When publicly performed by Williams, the song won encore after encore, establishing him as the most popular country singer in America. It also earned him a position on the *Grand Ole Opry*, which he joined on June 11, 1949, against the misgivings of some of the *Opry*'s directors, who had been warned about the young singer's drinking problems.

After this date, Hank Williams never again had financial problems. He earned an average of $200,000 a year from recordings and personal appearances until his death in 1953; his estate has never since ceased earning money. In October 1951, he signed a five-year movie contract with MGM, which, however, had not resulted in a motion picture before he died. Williams's artistic worth, of course, cannot be measured in dollars, but his recording success indicated his ability to communicate with millions of listeners. And no one communicated as well as Hank Williams. He had a small, light voice capable of all sorts of peculiar twists and turns. He had a remarkably versatile vocal style and could perform fast novelty tunes, blues numbers, religious melodies, and mournful love songs equally well. And in the guise of Luke the Drifter, he also gave competent performances of recitations, a musical subgenre that was very popular with country audiences in the 1950s. Williams sang with the immersive quality that has characterized every great hillbilly singer: utter credibility. He "lived" the songs he sang—he could communicate his feelings to the listener and make each person feel as if the song were being addressed directly to that individual. On one occasion, when asked to explain the success of country music, Williams replied: "It can be explained in just one word: sincerity. When a hillbilly sings a crazy song, he feels crazy. When he sings, 'I Laid My Mother Away,' he sees her a-laying right there in the coffin. He sings more sincere than most entertainers because the hillbilly was raised rougher than most entertainers. You got to know a lot about hard work. You got to have smelt a lot of mule manure before you can sing like a hillbilly. The people who has been raised something like the way the hillbilly has knows what he is singing about and appreciates it."[22]

When a heart attack brought a sudden and tragic end to Hank Williams's glittering career on New Year's Day, 1953, he had won a popular acclaim that no country singer had previously equaled. Neither popularity nor material success, however, had brought peace of mind to the twenty-nine-year-old entertainer. In fact, the last several months of his life were clouded by heartbreak and tragedy. Persistently troubled by a congenital birth defect of the lower spine that forced him to walk in a slightly stooped position and necessitated the periodic employment of drugs and medical attention, Williams lived a tortured physical existence. These sufferings, combined with mental anguish arising from marital problems, produced a singer—often lonely and unhappy—who poured his feelings into his music in a steady stream of melancholy and tragedy. The last few months of his life were materially rewarding but emotionally draining. Fired from the *Grand Ole Opry* in August 1952 because of chronic drunkenness and instability, Williams returned to the scene of his earliest barn-dance triumph, the *Louisiana Hayride*. During this short period, while continuing to record such hit songs as "Jambalaya," he divorced his first wife, Audrey, and quickly married a beautiful model and singer named Billie Jones, the daughter of the Bossier City, Louisiana, police chief, in three ceremonies: once before a justice of the peace and twice before paid-admission audiences at New Orleans's Municipal Auditorium.

Death came to Williams in Oak Hill, West Virginia, while he was en route to a New Year's performance in Canton, Ohio. His funeral, held in Montgomery, Alabama, amid a background of gospel singing performed by Ernest Tubb, Carl Smith, Roy Acuff, Red Foley, and the Statesmen Quartet (a gospel quartet from Georgia), drew one of the largest gatherings in the city's history. An estimated crowd of twenty thousand people gathered in and outside the city auditorium to catch the last glimpse of the young singer. Termed the "greatest emotional orgy" in Montgomery's history,[23] the event provoked an outburst of weeping, wailing, and fainting spells.

On the day of Williams's death and periodically thereafter, country radio shows devoted major segments of their air time to songs that he made famous. (Many radio stations still typically broadcast tributes to Williams on New Year's Day.) Almost immediately after his death, songs describing the event or commemorating his career made their appearances on jukeboxes and radio shows: Jack Cardwell's "The Death of Hank Williams," Jimmie Skinner's "Singing Teacher in Heaven," Johnny and Jack's "Hank Williams Will Live Forever," and, perhaps prophetically for the future of country music, Ernest Tubb's "Hank, It Will Never Be the Same without You."

CHAPTER 8

The Development of Country-Pop Music and the Nashville Sound

The years following Hank Williams's death witnessed a series of far-reaching developments that made country music a more secure commercial entity while threatening its unique identity. Country music would probably have followed such a course even if Williams had lived, but, coming as it did at the beginning of a new era, his death symbolized the closing of country music's "high" period. It is ironic that Williams, whose style was so firmly grounded in rural tradition, did as much as any one individual to broaden the music's base of acceptance, thereby contributing to the dilution of its rural nature. Williams's successful songs contributed to a wider acceptance of country music and, furthering the advances made by "The Tennessee Waltz," served to batter down the tenuous walls between popular and country music. With increasing regularity, country songs made their appearances on the popular song charts. As the number of songs accepted by popular vocalists increased, so did the desires of country performers to be recognized by a wider audience. Country singers hoped to enter the popular music charts along with their songs. "Crossing over," as it would ultimately be called, would be achieved with great frequency in the following years, but not without radical changes in the stylistic structure of both instrumentation and singing. Country musicians and singers adapted their sounds to fit the presumed tastes of popular music devotees who, it was believed, would refuse to accept the traditional country styles. These changes brought grief to many supporters and joy to others, made country music a billion-dollar industry, and completely "revolutionized" the popular music world.

For a brief time following Williams's death, country styles did not change materially. The songs played on radios, on jukeboxes, and at personal appearances still demonstrated the honky-tonk beat and the sounds of the fiddle and steel guitar. New singers continued to appear, many of whom would eventually become major stars in country music. Some of them, like Ray Price and George Jones (both from Texas), received their inspiration from Hank Williams. A few, like Marty Robbins of Arizona, Faron Young and Al Terry from Louisiana, and Jim Reeves from Texas, used crooning and quasi-pop styles somewhat suggestive of Eddy Arnold. Such veteran performers as Ernest Tubb, Red Foley, Kitty Wells, Carl Smith, and Webb Pierce more than held their own against the competition from new singers and new sounds well into the mid-1950s. Hank Snow, in fact, held down the number one position on *Billboard*'s country chart for twenty consecutive weeks beginning in June 1954. The song was a pure country weeper called "I Don't Hurt Anymore."

The year 1954, however, saw the emergence of a new musical force that completely engulfed the other musical forms, dominated American popular music for several years, and shattered the existing conceptions of what a popular song should be. The rock-and-roll phenomenon was, in part, a consequence of the heightened consciousness shown by American youth during World War II and in the immediate postwar years. A self-aware "youth culture," whose outlines had only been dimly perceived in earlier years, became clearly visible during the 1950s as music became an identifying and rallying symbol for many young people who sought to set themselves apart from their elders. Young people searched for alternative role models on the Silver Screen, in the television medium that was becoming so ubiquitous in the mid-1950s, and among musical performers. Rock-and-roll was fueled largely by a revolution in the record-buying habits of America's teenage population. Postwar prosperity had placed more money in the hands of greater numbers of young people, who, in turn, expended an increasing proportion of it for amusement, particularly the buying of records. The teenage market had, in fact, accounted for much of the success of country music after the war. In the mid-1950s this market, taking in the ever-increasing youthful segment of the population, turned toward another product of grassroots America, and one that was scarcely known by their parents. This was a form of music that, in point of ultimate origin, was as old as country music and of an equally hybrid nature. One line of ancestry, of course, ran through African American musical history. The country blues of the 1920s, generally subsumed in record catalogues under the rubric of "race" music, had become metamorphosed by the early 1950s into "rhythm and blues," an aggressive and highly electrified style that effectively mirrored the urbanization of African Americans.

Although rhythm and blues was a music produced for blacks by blacks, the walls dividing the musical genres had never been strong enough to keep individual songs and styles (and even some musicians) from crossing the boundaries. Throughout the late 1940s and early 1950s, young white jukebox devotees became increasingly acquainted with such legendary rhythm-and-blues names as Louis Jordan, Wynonie Harris, Big Joe Turner, Roy Brown, Lloyd Price, Chuck Berry, and Ray Charles. Implanted on the multitude of small record labels that appeared after the war, songs like "Good Rockin' Tonight," "One Mint Julep," "Lawdy Miss Clawdy," and "I Got a Woman" appealed to teenagers as refreshing alternatives to the kinds of songs that then dominated mainstream popular music. When the cultural traditions of black and white America fused their musical chemistries in the mid-1950s, they created an explosion that still reverberates throughout the popular music world.[1]

Rock and roll (the term was popularized by Cleveland disc jockey Alan Freed in 1951) emerged as an intensely controversial musical phenomenon in its earliest years of development. To some listeners, rock and roll was an example of musical barbarism or, worse, a reflection of a degenerate society. The sociologist Vance Packard, for example, asserted that the music had been foisted upon an unwilling public by BMI and was designed to "stir the animal instinct in modern teenagers." Other observers, however, welcomed the innovations introduced by the rock and rollers. Alan Lomax summed up the attitudes of many observers when he termed rock and roll "the healthiest manifestation yet in native American music" and the furthest intrusion made by "Negro styles" into popular music.[2] It was this and much more, however. Rock and roll was a conglomeration of musical forms.

The music did draw much of its content and style from black sources, from both the juke joint and the church. Although black influence was obvious, rock and roll became essentially a music performed by white people for white audiences. Even the wide variety of black performers (such as Chuck Berry, Fats Domino, and the Platters) who worked with the rock-and-roll idiom generally presented smoothed-over or toned-down versions that would be palatable to white audiences. Unfortunately, few black musicians prospered from the rock-and-roll phenomenon.

Country musicians had long demonstrated their affinity for the stepped-up rhythms of African American musicians, as evidenced in the performances of the Allen Brothers in the 1920s, Jimmie Davis and the Delmore Brothers in the 1930s, and Arthur "Guitar Boogie" Smith in the 1940s. The late 1940s and early 1950s proved an especially fruitful period of experimentation with black-derived forms. Black and white performers on the King label, prodded along by owner Syd Nathan, sometimes recorded one another's songs and even sat in on one another's sessions. Beginning with the Delmore Brothers' "Hillbilly Boogie" in 1945, several country singers—including Red Foley, Tennessee Ernie Ford, Hardrock Gunter, Hank Penny, Moon Mullican, and the Maddox Brothers and Rose—recorded songs with "boogie" in their titles or songs that embodied that stylistic form. On songs such as "Hangover Blues," the Maddox Brothers and Rose foreshadowed the later rockabilly style with their interplay of electric guitar licks and slapped-bass techniques, as well as with the high-energy content of their total performances. Much of this music, of course, remained confined to country audiences until the musical deluge foreshadowed by the independent work of black and white musicians cascaded in 1954 when Bill Haley, who had directed a country organization with little success for several years, recorded the extremely popular "Rock around the Clock." Used as the musical background for a violent movie about inner-city youth—*Blackboard Jungle*—the song easily reinforced the popular attitude that rock and roll was the product of rebellious youth. To many critics, this was the real beginning of rock and roll. Bill Haley, with his band the Comets, became the first country entertainer to anticipate the coming spectacular success of the new musical phenomenon. Many others, recognizing alluring new financial possibilities, followed his example.

The performer who most ably illustrated the intermingling of country and rhythm-and-blues music, and the one who achieved the most fabulous success, was Elvis Presley,[3] born in Tupelo, Mississippi, in January 1935, the son of poor, working-class parents. In September 1948, he and his family moved to Memphis, following a dream pursued by many rural southerners in the years after World War II. The family lived in a low-cost government housing project while Elvis attended Humes High School, worked at odd jobs, and quietly nourished his dreams of becoming a singer. On July 6, 1954, Elvis, then working as a truck driver for the Crown Electric Company, made some test records for Sam Phillips and his Sun Record Company. If Phillips was looking for "a white man who could sing like a Negro," as popular legend would have it, then he seems to have found him in the person of Presley. The details concerning his first recording session have been discussed fully elsewhere and will not be retold here,[4] but his first release seemed to embody the two major influences that shaped the developing rock-and-roll genre. One side featured "That's All Right, Mama," an old rhythm-and-blues tune first recorded by Arthur Crudup, while the other consisted of a supercharged version of Bill Monroe's hillbilly waltz "Blue Moon of Kentucky." Dewey Phillips (no relation to Sam) played the record immediately with great success on his local radio show *Red Hot and Blue* on WHBQ. As this record and subsequent releases attracted similar attention throughout the South, country disc jockeys realized that Elvis was a hybrid and a largely undefinable phenomenon. Although his early tours were made with such country singers as Hank Snow, he was generally billed as "the Hillbilly Cat" (a name presumably coined by his first manager, Bob Neal), and his appeal was most intense among teenagers who were not firmly wedded to country or any other brand of popular music.

Presley, in truth, belonged to no precise musical category, and the sources on which he drew were remarkably diverse and eclectic. Like many young people of his generation, Elvis Presley was largely a child of the media. His dress and demeanor were partially shaped by the movies and television, while his musical tastes were affected by the radio. He listened to the country music favored by his parents, but he also heard the gospel music, rhythm and blues, and mainstream pop music that boomed out over Memphis radio stations. The pop singer Dean Martin was just as appealing to Elvis as was country singer Red Foley or blues singer B. B. King. Much has been made of his Pentecostal church background—the Presley family were longtime members of the Assembly of God—and Elvis may very well have picked up some of his theatrical stage presence from the dynamic preachers he had seen. But the most crucial religious ingredients in his style probably came from the white gospel singers who thrived in Memphis. Elvis loved the music of such groups as the Blackwood Brothers, who had their headquarters in the Tennessee city, and the Stamps Quartet, who could be heard in many of the all-night singing conventions that flourished in the 1950s. Elvis particularly resembled the quartet singers when he let his voice fall into the low registers, and he remained fond of religious music until the day he died.

The reasons for Presley's popularity are not difficult to gauge. He certainly capitalized on the newly developing interest in rhythm and blues and, with his extraordinary sense of rhythm, could perform the music more ably than most of his white contemporaries. Presley's appeal, however, did not derive solely from his musical abilities. Several of his competitors were also remarkably talented, and a few of them, such as Charlie Rich, Carl Perkins, and Jerry Lee Lewis, were probably more adept at re-creating black styles than was Elvis. Along with talent and energy, Elvis brought a sexual charisma into the music business that his colleagues did not possess. No country entertainer before him had exhibited such raw masculine appeal. Elvis's unusual combination of little-boy shyness and leering sensuality won him a legion of female followers of all ages. Nicknamed "Elvis the Pelvis" because of his dramatic dance gyrations, Presley awakened feelings among his young women listeners that they may not have fully understood. Only nineteen years old when he made his first Sun recordings, Elvis was the first of a myriad of youthful entertainers who won large followings as much because of their youth and vitality as for their talent.

Rock and roll has gone far beyond the parameters originally established by Elvis and has traveled many stylistic roads, to England, around the world, and back again. But it should never be forgotten that the music first vaulted onto the national scene with a southern accent and was performed by "good old boys" and even a few "good old girls" who were comfortable with both country and black music. Such male performers as Carl Perkins, Johnny Cash, Charlie Rich, Roy Orbison, Warren Smith, Bob Luman, Werly Fairburn, Rudy Grayzell, Sleepy LaBeef, Gene Vincent, Jerry Lee Lewis, Buddy Holly, Conway Twitty, and the Everly Brothers were joined by such women entertainers as Janis Martin (known as "the female Elvis"), Wanda Jackson (best remembered for "Fujiyama Mama" but later a born-again gospel singer), Charlene Arthur (a popular performer on the *Big D Jamboree* in Dallas), and Brenda Lee (whose very successful career as a singer began in 1949 when she was only five years old). These performers were generally described as "rockabillies" because of their successful fusion of "rocking" black music and "hillbilly" music. While their vocal and performing styles could be markedly dissimilar, on the whole they carried southernness further into mainstream popular culture than any musicians before them, with their dialects, drawls, and vocal inflections setting them dramatically apart from other popular musicians of the day. Black music contributed to the "liberation" of southern rural youth, providing a vehicle for uninhibited expression, but the rockabillies actually gave vent to impulses that had long been embedded, if often dormant, in southern culture as a whole—a hell-for-leather hedonism and a swaggering masculinity or, in the case of the women, an uncharacteristic aggressiveness, and, strangely, a visceral emotionalism among both men and women that seemed as reflective of the church as of the beer joint.

Nowhere do these often-conflicting impulses find more vivid expression than in the music and persona of Jerry Lee Lewis, one of the most superbly talented individuals in country music history.[5] Like Elvis, Lewis was reared in the Pentecostal faith (the Assembly of God), but, although he devoted much of his childhood energy to the music of that church, he was very early and irresistibly drawn also to the "music of the world." Born on September 29, 1935, in Ferriday, Louisiana, the precocious Lewis began playing the piano at the age of eight and was performing in a Natchez, Mississippi, night club (across the river from Ferriday) by the time he was a teenager. Lewis was a first cousin of Mickey Gilley and Jimmy Swaggart, and all three learned to play the piano in a similar style. Gilley eventually became a leading mainstream country and western performer, while Swaggart went on to become a successful, if controversial, radio-and-television Pentecostal evangelist, eventually humbled by womanizing. Lewis's parents also had ministerial designs for their son, and they sent him to the Assembly of God Bible college in Waxahachie, Texas, but according to legend, he was dismissed after he played a boogie version of "My God Is Real" in chapel. As with his cousin Jimmy, the demands of the flesh and the spirit have often warred in Jerry. Although the religious indoctrination of his youth permanently influenced him—he could always quote liberally from the Bible, while periodically professing a sense of guilt—he has devoted most of his life and music to the flesh.

Back home in Ferriday, Jerry Lee spent much time at Haney's Big House, a black night spot, and in other clubs there and in Mississippi. Inspired by Elvis's success, he journeyed to Memphis and persuaded Sam Phillips to record him in 1956, his first song a cover of Ray Price's "Crazy Arms." But his first big hit was a song done earlier (in 1955) by the pianist Roy Hall—"Whole Lotta Shakin' Goin' On." Jerry Lee presented his exuberant and hedonistic version to a national audience on Steve Allen's television show, where he kicked over the piano bench and otherwise bowled over the audience. In gratitude, he later named one of his sons Steve Allen. This first hit, along with others such as "Great Balls of Fire" and "High School Confidential," made him one of the leading rock and rollers in the United States and in Europe. A 1958 trip to England, however, proved to be ill-fated. His recent marriage to a thirteen-year-old cousin and his wild behavior drew harsh and hostile criticism. His career eclipsed in the United States, too, although he never stopped performing. In 1968, he reentered the field of country music with a hit version of "Another Place, Another Time" and soon followed that with another, "What's Made Milwaukee Famous." Time revealed that he had lost little of the energy and abandon that had characterized his earlier career.

The impact made by Elvis, Jerry Lee, and the other rockabillies inspired an accent on youth in music generally and in country music specifically. The music business was now well aware of teenage power. Everywhere, teenagers were buying records in great quantities and were forming fan clubs, organizing sock hops and coke parties, and dancing the dirty bop. The record industry had made significant innovations that contributed to its massive expansion: introduction of 45 rpm singles and 33⅓ rpm long-playing albums, all of which were made more appealing by the maturation of high fidelity and stereophonic sound reproduction. The 78 rpm record rapidly became a thing of the past. Radio stations everywhere responded to the teenage audience with shows directed toward them, while television shows such as Dick Clark's *American Bandstand* gave exposure to new performers and songs.

In the wake of Elvis Presley's astounding success, the country music industry began searching for new, youthful talent while also encouraging older and established performers to record rock-and-roll material or peppy songs that would appeal to a young audience. Marty Robbins, for example, did a country version of "That's All Right, Mama" on December 7, 1954, and soon followed that experiment with covers of such rhythm-and-blues tunes as "Long Tall Sally" and "Maybelline." Robbins's versions of such upbeat country songs as "Singing the Blues" also reflected the desire to appeal to teenagers who liked to dance. Few country singers came out of the mid-1950s untouched by the rock-and-roll mania. George Jones, usually remembered and revered for his dedication to hard country sounds, recorded several rock-and-roll songs, such as "Rock It," and even some bluegrass musicians succumbed to pressures to get on the rock bandwagon. Largely through the urging of King Records producer Syd Nathan, the Stanley Brothers, who were famous for their traditional mountain sound, recorded a rock-spiced song called "So Blue" as well as a cover of a rhythm-and-blues song, "Finger Poppin' Time." Even the king of bluegrass music, Bill Monroe, went so far as to speed up the tempo on later versions of "Blue Moon of Kentucky" after Elvis's rollicking adaptation came out. The most commercially successful spinoff from the rock-and-roll interest was Tennessee Ernie Ford's big hit, "Sixteen Tons." This song came from the pen of Merle Travis, who had included it in an excellent, but only moderately successful, album (*Folk Songs of the Hills*) in 1947. Ford's version was presented over a modest, rocking beat and was given immediate national exposure on his television show. It attained the number one position on *Billboard*'s charts in December 1955 and remained there through the spring of 1956.

Although a large number of musicians only dabbled with the rock-and-roll idiom and never really drifted very far from the country mainstream or from traditionally rooted styles, a few performers were permanently affected by their rock-and-roll experiences or by their flirtations with youthful audiences. Don and Phil Everly, whose beautiful and close harmony has influenced musicians around the world, were originally marketed as country singers. They began developing their singing style as children in a family group headed by their father, Ike Everly, a finger-style guitarist who was part of the circle of western Kentucky musicians from whom Merle Travis learned his famous style. The Everlys therefore were heirs to the brother duet tradition of country music, and though they are usually described as rockabillies, their sound and performance styles were very different from those in Sun's stable of musicians. The Everlys' traditional debts are strongly revealed in the superb, but regrettably out-of-print, album *Songs Our Daddy Taught Us*, where with songs like "Barbara Allen," "Down in the Willow Garden," "Long Time Gone," and "Lightning Express," they employed a vocal approach strongly reminiscent of such earlier duos as Karl and Harty, the Blue Sky Boys, and the Bailes Brothers. Since they exuded boyish innocence and vigor, and played guitars—sometimes with a beat borrowed from Bo Diddley—the Everly Brothers were easily identified with other rock and rollers. During their peak years, from 1957 to 1959, the Everlys performed a repertory of songs that easily found favor among both country and rock fans. The Nashville songwriters Felice and Boudleaux Bryant supplied them with a steady stream of hits, including "Bye Bye Love," "Wake Up, Little Susie," "All I Have to Do Is Dream," and "Bird Dog."

Sonny James also brought several years of experience as a country singer to the world of youth-oriented music. Like the Everlys, he came from a musical family, the Lodens from Hackleburg, Alabama. Performing as a regular on such regional country shows as the *Big D Jamboree*, the *Louisiana Hayride*, and the *Saturday Night Shindig* (Dallas), James revealed a versatile style as a singer, flat-top guitarist, and fiddler. Although he was well schooled in country music's rural idioms, James easily made the transition to the rockabilly and country-pop genres in the late 1950s. "Young Love" (1957), a quintessential teenybopper song, became one of the first giant crossovers in country music history, a number one song in both country and pop music, and one of the first examples of a country singer (rather than the song) moving onto the pop charts. This was the first of a long string of hits for James. He was never a rockabilly per se, but his songs often embodied the kind of youth consciousness that was so strong in rock and roll. In his later career, he periodically resurrected songs from the 1950s, succeeding commercially with many of them. He styled himself as the Southern Gentleman, and performed generally with sparse instrumentation, often just his own cleanly played acoustic guitar and bass, but almost always with background voices—an unfortunate, if enduring, legacy of 1950s teen music.

Johnny Cash entered professional music in the mid-1950s as part of Memphis's Sun stable of rockabillies, and he never ventured far from that sound in his later performing years. Born into a family of poor cotton farmers in Kingsland, Arkansas, he moved with his family in 1936 to the New Deal–built community of Dyess (part of the government's

Johnny Cash. Courtesy of Nathan Gibson.

program of resettling farmers on productive land that they had the
option to buy). Cash's childhood experiences of growing up poor in the
1930s were strongly reflected in some of the songs he later wrote and
recorded: "Pickin' Time," for example, which described the improved
family fortunes that would hopefully accompany cotton harvest; and
"Five Feet High and Rising" about the devastating Mississippi River
flood of 1937 that almost wiped out the Cash homestead.

The Cash family loved and sang music, but Johnny also enjoyed the songs he heard on his father's little battery radio. Fresh out of high school in 1950, Johnny joined the horde of hillbillies seeking employment in the mills and factories of the North. But after a brief stay at the Fisher Body Plant in Pontiac, Michigan, in 1950, the bored young man went back home and joined the Air Force. While stationed in Germany, he began perfecting the musical skills he had exhibited since childhood, singing and playing the guitar and trying his hand at song lyrics. Back home once again in 1954, he began jamming with friends Luther Perkins (guitar) and Marshall Grant (bass). In 1955 they recorded two songs for Sam Phillips that reflected the contemporary interest in up-tempo and highly rhythmic music: "Hey, Porter," an infectious, hard-driving train song, written during his military service, and "Cry, Cry, Cry," a song written when Phillips asked for one to accompany "Hey, Porter." Luther Perkins's single-string electric guitar playing, Marshall Grant's slapped bass, and Cash's percussive rhythm accompaniment (enhanced sometimes by a piece of paper placed under the strings of the guitar) neatly complemented Cash's baritone-bass singing and established a sound from which the singer never substantially deviated. His first major hit, "I Walk the Line," recorded in 1958, won him a large audience outside country music and was a good example of the country-rockabilly fusion. Although Cash experienced crippling personal problems throughout much of the 1960s—marital strain, drug dependence—he was never absent very long from the center of country music action. He remained a barometer of country music change, and while basically preserving his original performing style, he was often in the vanguard of innovation and experimentation and consistently lent encouragement to younger talent.

While Johnny Cash and certain other performers made their own individual adjustments to rock and roll, the country industry as a whole responded to the rock threat by trying to create a product that would appeal to the broadest possible audience. The industry also sought to expand on the crossover precedents set by "The Tennessee Waltz" and Hank Williams in the late 1940s and early 1950s. Country songs had periodically made their way into pop repertories, but almost always as performed by musicians like Dean Martin or Frankie Laine who were identified as "pop." In the new period, the chief emphasis was to be on the marketing of the singer as well as the song. A country singer, it was believed, might win a new audience if his instrumental accompaniment was modified sufficiently (no fiddles or steel guitars, for example). The industry believed that the urban pop audience should not be repelled by harsh or "corny" rural accoutrements. The mixing of pop and country sounds, of course, had never been absent from country music, and country entertainers had never been resistant to popular recognition. Indeed, they had actively sought it. Nevertheless, never before had there been such an insistent quest for pop identification as that which came in the late 1950s and early 1960s.

Eddy Arnold, of course, had been making his own compromises since at least 1948, when he tried to shed both the title of "Tennessee Plowboy" and the image that accompanied it. According to Arnold's own testimony, however, his real breakthrough to pop acceptance— and the first real example of the kind of sound that he wanted to project—was "I Really Don't Want to Know" in 1954. Accompanied only by two acoustic guitars, a bass guitar, and background voices, the recording achieved a soft, muted, and romantic supper-club sound that thereafter marked Arnold's performances. The peak period of country-pop fusion, however, came in 1957 and early 1958. Sonny James's "Young Love," Ferlin Husky's "Gone," George Hamilton IV's "A Rose and a Baby Ruth," Johnny Cash's "Ballad of a Teenage Queen," and, preeminently, Marty Robbins's "A White Sport Coat" and "The Story of My Life" (written by Hal David and Burt Bacharach) were leading examples of the songs geared to teenage sock-hop tastes. Recognizing the appeal of the country-pop fusion, merchandisers and chart makers began advertising records without prefixes or labels. To cite one example, the Nashville journalist Charles Lamb, who had been publishing the *Country Music Reporter*, dropped the word "country" from the title and began running the "one big chart" that lumped songs together according to popularity, regardless of style or identification.

Country traditionalists reacted bitterly to the pop trends, but the juggernaut of homogenization relentlessly rolled on. The fiddle and steel guitar seemed on the way to banishment from country recordings and could scarcely be heard on jukeboxes or country radio DJ shows in 1957. A major exception, however, was Bobby Helms's "Fraulein," written by Texas songwriter Lawton Williams, which was the number one country song in September and October 1957. The recording began with a rousing fiddle introduction by Tommy Jackson and was, in fact, the only song in the top ten during that period that featured a fiddle. Significantly, Helms's next big hit was "My Special Angel," a thoroughly poppish, teenage-oriented song that included no fiddle at all. An occasional honky-tonk-style song made its way through the tangle of country-pop offerings to become a hit—Charlie Walker's "Pick Me Up on Your Way Down," for example—but only Ray Price, a Texas-born protégé of Hank Williams, provided a consistent challenge to the pop fraternity. In August and September 1956, Price had warmed the hearts of traditionalists with "Crazy Arms," and he continued to perform such numbers down through the late 1950s and into the early 1960s. Songs like "City Lights," "My Shoes Keep Walking Back to You," and "Heartaches by the Numbers" brought thousands of feet to the dance floor and inspired a resurgence of hard country music.

Country-pop's emergence was paralleled by the hypergrowth of Nashville as a music center. Together, this convergence gave rise to what was soon called the "Nashville sound." As described in chapter 7, the *Grand Ole Opry* was a catalyst that after the war had attracted a pool of talent and an expanding network of promoters, booking agents, publishers, and the like to Nashville. The proliferation of recording studios and publishing houses, which fed off each other, encouraged the arrival of musicians and songwriters who would be permanently based in the city. Session musicians, as they came to be called, rarely toured or acted as members of professional bands; instead, they were on constant call to back up any singer who happened to need them for recording purposes. They became thoroughly familiar, and at ease, with one another's styles, and they developed a "numbering system" that permitted them to adapt easily and transpose keys while learning new songs. These Nashville musicians became famous for their versatility and improvisational skills. The rock singer John Sebastian later paid tribute to them in a song that alleged, "Nashville cats, been playin' since they's babies."[6] Their expertise contributed to Nashville's growing reputation as "Music City, USA," and to the worldwide marketability of the musical product that emerged from there. Unfortunately, their presence on record after record inspired a sameness of sound that inhibited creativity within the country music field.

Chester (Chet) Atkins had become the center, and driving force, of these musicians by the late 1950s. He was as responsible as any person for the Nashville sound, or what would sometimes be called the Chet Atkins compromise. Atkins was born into a musical family in 1924 in Luttrell, Tennessee. His father was a music teacher, and an older brother, Jim, was a guitarist who played professionally as a jazz and pop musician. As a fledgling guitarist, Chet heard Merle Travis over a radio station from Cincinnati and was deeply impressed by what he heard. He did not realize that this unseen radio presence was playing with only his thumb and forefinger, so Chet developed a three-finger style instead. Atkins's style, therefore, though much influenced by Travis, was very much his own. In Nashville after 1950, while playing at the *Grand Ole Opry* and on numerous recording sessions, he came to know most of the musicians in the city. He also began making recordings on his own and did much to make the electric guitar a distinctive solo instrument in country music. In 1952, Steven Sholes, the head of RCA's operations in Nashville, made Atkins his assistant. Five years later, Atkins became chief of RCA's country division in Nashville. Some of the musicians who played on RCA's sessions, as well as on other labels' sessions in the city, were men who often played with Chet at the Carousel Club in Printer's Alley: Floyd Cramer, piano; Buddy Harman, drums; Bob Moore, bass; and Boots Randolph, saxophone. With the exception of Randolph, these musicians played on the majority of recording sessions in Nashville. Along with the guitarists Grady Martin and Hank Garland (badly injured in a 1963 automobile accident that ended his playing career), the pianist Hargus "Pig" Robbins, the rhythm guitarist Ray Edenton, and a host of others, these men contributed mightily to the making of the Nashville sound. Their instrumental licks were complemented by vocal choruses contributed by a one-time gospel quartet, the Jordanaires; the Anita Kerr Singers; and, a little later in the 1960s, the Glaser Brothers.

Chet Atkins deliberately tried to create a middle-of-the-road sound (his "compromise") that would preserve the feel and ambience of "country" music while also being commercially appealing to a broader audience that had no experience with rural life and no liking for the harder sounds. RCA's leadership in the shaping of this sound came, first of all, through its association with Elvis Presley. Floyd Cramer, for example, played on many of Elvis's hits, including "Heartbreak Hotel," and quartets were often present on Elvis's records. Cramer's distinctive style, however—his "slip-note" technique (moving quickly from one note to another in order to bend notes a full tone rather than a half tone—was borrowed from a demo tape made by West Coast pianist/songwriter Don Robertson. Robertson sent his composition "Please Help Me, I'm Falling" to RCA, where it was given to Hank Locklin, who recorded it with the accompaniment of Cramer, who in turn copied

Robertson's style. The commercial success of this record in 1960 encouraged Cramer to use the technique consistently thereafter, and he even recorded a big hit on his own called "Last Date."

The country-pop emphasis was tempting to many singers who recognized the commercial advantages of a larger audience. Only a few, however, were qualified to take advantage of the pop trends. One can scarcely imagine such deep-dyed rural singers as Ernest Tubb, Bill Monroe, and Roy Acuff enjoying much success as pop performers, even had they chosen to make the attempt. But those singers whose vocal equipment was palatable to pop fans, and whose stylistic preferences were sufficiently latitudinarian, were well positioned to prosper within the country-pop format. For example, when a brother and sister team from Sparkman, Arkansas, Jim Ed and Maxine Brown,[7] began singing on the *Barnyard Frolics* over KLRA in Little Rock in 1953, their sweet, smooth harmony was warmly praised. They became a trio, known as the Browns, in 1954, when their sister Bonnie joined them. Their excellent three-part harmony was, in part, church derived, but it also reflected the styles of contemporary pop groups such as the McGuire Sisters. Their pure country repertory, however, ranged from such downright corny tunes as "Looking Back to See" and "Goo Goo Dada" to warmly romantic numbers like "I Take the Chance" (written by the Louvin Brothers) and "Here Today and Gone Tomorrow." Affiliated with RCA after 1956, the Browns gradually moved toward an assemblage of songs compatible with their sound. And under Chet Atkins's tutelage, they recorded one of the premiere country-pop songs of 1959, "The Three Bells," an import from France that held down *Billboard*'s number one slot from August to November.

RCA had at least three other performers who underwent a similar transformation under Atkins's leadership: Skeeter Davis, Don Gibson, and Jim Reeves. Davis, who was born Mary Frances Penick in Dry Ridge, Kentucky, began her music career singing with a schoolmate named Betty Jack Davis in a duo they dubbed the Davis Sisters. They sang throughout central Kentucky and southern Ohio and did a stint on the *Kentucky Barn Dance* in Lexington and the *Wheeling Jamboree* in West Virginia, where they were occasionally associated with the bluegrass team of Flatt and Scruggs. The Davises gave promise of becoming one of the major singing groups in country music after they signed with RCA in 1953. Their version of "I Forgot More Than You'll Ever Know" was one of the best sellers of that year. Tragedy struck, though, in the midst of their newfound success. In August 1953, Betty Jack was killed in an automobile accident that also seriously injured Skeeter and left her physically and psychologically unable to continue her career. When Skeeter returned to professional music in 1959, she had little experience as a solo performer. Nevertheless, she achieved popularity in her new role and also began to carve out a niche in the developing country-pop genre. "Set Him Free," "Optimistic," and "The End of the World" were only a few of the Skeeter Davis songs that made it into the charts, and the latter, in 1962, became a crossover song of considerable popularity that introduced her to an audience far beyond that earlier enjoyed by the Davis Sisters.

Don Gibson was a highly commercial property for RCA as both a singer and a writer. His country credentials were very strong. He was born in Shelby, North Carolina, not far from where the bluegrass banjo wizard Earl Scruggs grew up. Gibson even tried his hand at bluegrass music, and in fact generally adhered to hard country styles while performing on Knoxville's *Mid-Day Merry-Go-Round* before 1954. In that year, he signed a writer's contract with Acuff-Rose, an event that contributed to the emergence of a new breed of writers in Nashville. As a writer, Gibson made his most enduring impact on country music; such songs as "Oh Lonesome Me," "Legend in My Time," and "I Can't Stop Loving You" have become country standards while also representing the growing fusion of country and pop sounds. As a singer, Gibson had a husky, soulful voice that was then unique among country singers, as well as an affinity for rockabilly rhythms that lent to his popularity outside the country field. The year 1958 was a big one for Gibson, with three of his recordings ("Oh Lonesome Me," "I Can't Stop Loving You," and "Blue Blue Day") reaching the number one position on the *Billboard* charts. An inability to cope with his commercial success and a growing addiction to pills seriously hampered the progress of his career, and he sought medical rehabilitation in 1961. Although Gibson soon resumed his professional career, he never regained the stature as a performer that he had enjoyed earlier.

Of all the country-pop singers of the late 1950s and early 1960s, James Travis (Jim) Reeves had probably the greatest ability to appeal to popular audiences while maintaining a country identity. He was born August 20, 1923, in Galloway, Panola County, Texas, the same rural East Texas area that produced Tex Ritter. Since his father, Tom Reeves, died when Jim was only ten months old, his upbringing

Jim Reeves. Courtesy of Nathan Gibson.

became the responsibility of his mother, Beulah Reeves, and his eight older brothers and sisters. Reeves discovered very early, as farm boys have always done, that farm life could be intolerable unless diversions were found. His diversions were baseball and country music.

Although Reeves had played the guitar since he was six and had often played in neighborhood sessions with Bill Price, a guitarist friend from Galloway, baseball initially seemed to hold the most promising future. After a successful athletic career at Carthage High School, he attended the University of Texas for about six weeks in 1942 but then dropped out and went to work in a Houston shipyard. He also began playing semiprofessional baseball and was able to move from that into professional athletics as a pitcher in the St. Louis Cardinal system, playing for Marshall and later Henderson in the East Texas League. His baseball career ended, however, when he injured his leg in July 1947.

Despite his talents as a singer, it was Reeves's fine speaking voice that brought him into show business. He obtained a position as an announcer and hillbilly disc jockey on a Henderson radio station, KGRI, which he later owned jointly with the popular disc jockey Tom Perryman. Between 1947 and 1953, Reeves began singing in the Henderson area and in an ever-widening range of places throughout East Texas, including short stints as a sideman with Moon Mullican in Beaumont and as a singer/bandleader at one of Texas's most famous honky-tonks, the Reo Palm Isle in Longview. As a Henderson disc jockey, and program director at KGRI after 1952, Reeves occasionally picked up his guitar and charmed his listeners with a hymn or vintage sentimental song such as "Have I Told You Lately That I Love You?" His earliest recordings were made in Houston in 1949 and were released on the Macy label. Real success, however, did not come until the early 1950s when he signed a contract with Abbott Records (1952) and joined the *Louisiana Hayride* (1953). His first appearances on the *Hayride* were made, ironically, as an announcer, but his second Abbott release, "Mexican Joe," also in 1953, gave him an identity as a singer that no station or record label could resist. The song was only the beginning of a long string of successful recordings that took him to the *Grand Ole Opry* and earned him a contract with RCA (both in 1955).

When Reeves began his association with RCA, his performing sound was not far removed from the dominant honky-tonk style of the early 1950s. Even as late as 1959 the sounds of the fiddle and steel guitar could be heard on his recordings. His voice, though, had begun to lower into its more natural and pleasing baritone registers, away from the high and rather strident sound heard on such early recordings as "Mexican Joe" and "Bimbo." He and Chet Atkins also began choosing songs well suited for such a voice. "Billy Bayou," composed by Roger Miller and a number one song for Reeves in early 1959, had some echoes of his earlier hillbilly emphasis, but "Four Walls" later in that year and "He'll Have to Go" in early 1960 marked the real development of the style that would soon be described as "a touch of velvet."[8] Singing to the accompaniment of vibes and muted guitars, and backed by the seemingly mandatory chorus of voices, Reeves fashioned a mellow and caressing sound that somehow satisfied his original "hillbilly" listeners while winning him a legion of fans around the world. Reeves's popularity outside the United States may have surpassed that of any other country singer; a series of tours on the European continent, in Scandinavia, and in South Africa (where he made a movie called *Kimberley Jim*) in the late 1950s and early 1960s increased the following that had already been attracted to him through his recordings. Reeves's death in a plane crash on July 31, 1964, did not dim his popularity. Songs like "I Guess I'm Crazy" continued to win posthumous commercial acclaim for several years after his death. RCA has skillfully marketed much of his unreleased material on a periodic basis, and some of these songs have become important hits. The record company received fan material addressed to Jim Reeves long after his death, an indication that for many people the singer had never died, and the Country Music Association made its tribute to Reeves by naming him to the Country Music Hall of Fame in 1967.

While Jim Reeves had an impact on country music that can still be measured many years after his death, Missouri-born Ferlin Husky probably won more immediate national exposure in the late 1950s than any other country entertainer. He did so through a fortuitous combination of singing ability, comedy, and showmanship. He began his singing career on KXLW in St. Louis but spent most of his time in the late 1940s and early 1950s performing in California, in the clubs around Bakersfield and on the *Hometown Jamboree* in Los Angeles. During this period of his life, he styled himself "Terry Preston," and he began recording for the Capitol label under that name. His first big hit, recorded under the name of Ferlin Husky, came in 1953 when he and Jean Shepard did a song inspired by the Korean War separations called "A Dear John Letter." This hillbilly hit was far removed in tone and style from his super commercial recording of 1957, "Gone." This quintessential country-pop song, a slow romantic ballad punctuated by strings and vocal chorus, was the number one song in both country and pop music throughout the spring of 1957. However, he did not have another hit of such magnitude until November 1960, when he recorded the gospel-country-pop song "On the Wings of a Dove."

Husky was a master stage entertainer with a gift of gab and a cornball sense of humor. Much of his popularity was won through his mythical hayseed creation, Simon Crum, who told jokes, did imitations of other country singers, and sang comic songs. Husky managed to maneuver himself onto a wide variety of national television shows, such as *Kraft Television Theatre*, the *Ed Sullivan Show*, the *Steve Allen Show*, the *Rosemary Clooney Show*, the *Arthur Godfrey Show* (as guest host), and the *Tonight Show*. While Husky moved the music away from its rural moorings and into middle-class homes throughout America, his alter ego, the hayseed Simon Crum, told audiences in a song that "Good old country music's here to stay."

Another Capitol artist who flirted with the country-pop idiom, yet never really strayed very far from the mainstream, was Faron Young. Young, who was born on a dairy farm near Shreveport, Louisiana, joined KWKH's *Louisiana Hayride* in the early 1950s, after a short stay at the local Centenary College. He was one of several country musicians, such as Floyd Cramer and Red Sovine, who profited from Webb Pierce's aid and encouragement. Young's first hit came in 1953, with "Going Steady," a tune sufficiently rocking and teenage-oriented to later warrant its inclusion in rockabilly anthologies. Young seems never to have consciously sought pop acceptance and always showed a fondness for twin fiddle accompaniment; nevertheless, his big voice, precise articulation, and pop phrasing made him a likely candidate for country-pop stardom. With songs like "Country Girl" in 1959 and "Hello Walls" in 1961 (one of the first Willie Nelson compositions to be recorded by a major performer), Young became one of the dominant entertainers of country music. "The Young Sheriff," so-called because of his appearance in the movie *Hidden Guns*, became as well known for his outspoken, opinionated personality and profanity-laden speech as for his musical talents.

Marty Robbins was one of the most diversely talented performers in country music, from the time he made his first Columbia recordings in 1951 to his death from massive heart failure in 1983. Born on September 26, 1925, in the desert outside Glendale, Arizona, Robbins drifted from job to job until he entered military service in World War II. Although he had had a childhood fondness for cowboy music, he did not begin to see the value of country music as such until he heard it performed by fellow soldiers from the South. After his return to civilian life, he began singing in local clubs and on radio in Mesa and

Phoenix. On the strength of a recommendation from Jimmy Dickens, who heard him in one of these clubs, Robbins was signed to a Columbia recording contract in 1951. On his early recordings, 1951–1954, Robbins showed the influence of his childhood hero, Gene Autry, in his smooth tone and phrasing. He also demonstrated more than a little touch of the early Eddy Arnold, especially in the plaintive, ting-a-ling steel guitar accompaniment of James Farmer, who appeared on these original Columbia records. A penchant for sad and sentimental songs, such as "I Couldn't Keep from Crying," "The Hands You're Holding Now," and "At the End of a Long Lonely Day," gained Robbins the sobriquet of "Mr. Teardrop."

Robbins soon revealed, however, that he was wedded to no single style and that he was capable of enormous stylistic growth. He made the first country cover of Presley's "That's All Right, Mama," and he followed that with other rockabilly experiments. When the country-pop phase set in, Robbins was supremely qualified to prosper from the impulse; indeed, he often set the directions that the style would follow. After his successful performance of "A White Sport Coat" and "The Story of My Life," Robbins never again strayed very far from the lucrative countrypolitan field. If his heart truly lay with any one area of performance, however, it was the songs of the West. Down deep, Robbins was a singing cowboy who had been born just a few years too late to profit from the phenomenon. He never forgot the open country of his birth, nor the singers like Autry and the Sons of the Pioneers who had fired his childhood imagination. He always made room in his concerts for cowboy songs, and his immensely popular recording of "El Paso" in 1960 did much to move country music back toward its roots.

With the emergence of Patsy Cline, the modern era of women country singers really began.[9] Born in 1932, Cline (whose real name was Virginia Patterson Hensley) had sung since at least the age of fourteen on WINC in her hometown of Winchester, Virginia, but she made no significant breakthrough in commercial country music until the mid-1950s. She made her first records in 1954 for a California company, Four Star, which had also given Hank Locklin and Jimmy Dean their starts. Her career was only moderately successful until she joined the cast of *Town and Country Time,* broadcast each Saturday night from the Capitol Arena in Washington, DC. This show, which featured such performers as Jimmy Dean, Roy Clark, George Hamilton IV, and Mary

Klick, was merely one of many operations promoted by the country music entrepreneur Connie B. Gay. Fifty-two of the shows were filmed and presented in a syndicated TV series by the same name. In January 1957, Patsy appeared as a contestant on the *Arthur Godfrey's Talent Scouts* show on CBS. She won first place with a torch song she had recorded for Decca the previous year, "Walking after Midnight." She appeared on Godfrey's morning show for about two weeks, and this national exposure contributed to the success of the song; it made both the pop and country charts. The year 1960 saw both her admission to the *Grand Old Opry* and her first giant recording: "I Fall to Pieces." Written by Hank Cochran and Harlan Howard, the recording remained on the charts for thirty-nine weeks and climbed as high as the number twelve position on *Billboard*'s pop music charts. The recording marked the beginning of Decca's all-out efforts to market Cline as a pop singer; she was backed by a full and lush retinue of strings and voices.

The ironic feature of Patsy Cline's country-pop orientation is that she did not seek such classification. She dressed in cowgirl attire until 1962; she always expressed a desire to yodel on her records; and she disliked the three songs that gave her national exposure: "Walking after Midnight," "I Fall to Pieces," and "Crazy" (another early songwriting venture by Willie Nelson after he moved to Nashville). Her strong, resilient voice, however, was so well suited for the pop emphasis that was now selling millions of records that her managers could not resist such packaging. She had remarkable vocal control and commanded attention with a number of appealing vocal mannerisms such as growls, sighs, and bent notes. By the time she died on March 5, 1963, in the plane crash that also killed Cowboy Copas and Hawkshaw Hawkins, she had reached out to an audience that had not earlier listened to country music and had taken older country fans into stylistic regions where they had not previously gone. Perhaps most important, she had moved female country singing closer to the pop mainstream and light-years away from the sound projected by Molly O'Day, Rose Maddox, Jean Shepard, and Kitty Wells.

The broad commercial exposure enjoyed by Patsy Cline and other country singers at the beginning of the 1960s indicated that an industry that had faltered and acted indecisively during the rock-and-roll onslaught was now reemerging with unparalleled economic strength. In part, this renewed vitality was a consequence of the work of men like Chet Atkins, Owen Bradley, and Jim Denny, who reached out to win a new audience. The country-pop compromise may have attracted some rock-and-roll fans, but it was no doubt much more appealing to old-time pop fans who could no longer hear the kind of music to which they had been accustomed. Eddy Arnold, Marty Robbins, Jim Reeves, and Patsy Cline, to name only a few members of a much larger fraternity, provided the kind of middle-of-the-road, easy-listening sound that many people were seeking. The Nashville sound, as a whole, soon lost definition and became identified with any kind of recording that came out of the city. The vigorous music activity of Nashville gained the city the title of Music City, USA, an identity and reputation that must have embarrassed the high-culture partisans who lived there. City officials began to pay great attention to the vernacular musical culture that was developing around them, particularly as the big bucks poured in. The almost ceaseless recording activity lured musicians who made the city their permanent home. These session musicians became famous far and wide, and all kinds of singers came to Nashville to take advantage of the ease and informality that characterized recording there.

The recording studios were joined by a vast, and generally interlocking, panoply of music business interests that made their headquarters in the city. Jim Denny, who had headed WSM's booking agency for several years, formed his own independent operation in 1954. Thereafter, virtually all country performers began signing contracts with Denny, Hubert Long, Hal Smith, and the growing retinue of booking and promotional organizations that congregated in Nashville. Recording, of course, spawned a vast network of songwriters and publishing houses. Acuff-Rose's leadership, made possible by the success of "The Tennessee Waltz" and by its ownership of the Hank Williams catalogue, was challenged in the mid-1950s by, first, Jim Denny's Cedarwood Publishing Company (which was lucky enough to control Webb Pierce's long string of hits) and, later, such companies as Pamper, Tree, and Sure-Fire. Now that sheet music had become relatively unimportant, publishing had become inextricably interrelated with the recording business. A publishing house existed, in effect, to market a written composition to a recording company.

Reflective of country music's commercial growth, and largely responsible for it, was a new trade organization founded in 1958, the Country Music Association (CMA), which grew out of the Disc Jockeys Convention. It was conceived as a device by which country music could attain respectability and achieve a wider popularity, in other words, as a facet of the music's counterattack against the threats posed by rock and roll in the late 1950s. For several years, the organization worked out of a small covey of offices in a nondescript building in downtown Nashville and was staffed totally by an executive secretary named Jo Walker (now Jo Walker-Meador). Walker, along with Frances Preston of BMI, was one of the few women who attained executive status in the country music business. She ran the fledgling CMA and did much to keep it afloat during its first tentative years and later became its executive director. The CMA emerged as an aggressive organization unconcerned with definition or stylistic integrity. It frankly perceived its mission in economic and public relations terms, and made no attempts to define what was or was not country music. The CMA argued that all forms of country music would prosper if the industry as a whole was healthy.

One of the most significant tasks undertaken by the CMA was the sponsorship of all-country-music radio stations. The identity of the first all-country station is still not conclusively known, but it has been argued that KXLA in Pasadena, in 1949, and KDAV in Lubbock, Texas, in the early 1950s were the first to program country music on a mass basis. By 1967, at least 328 stations broadcast country music on a full-time basis, while over 2,000 featured some country music during their broadcast hours. Country music was undoubtedly presented to every sector of American life in this way, but critics argued that the music's identity became diluted and clouded through this mass exposure. Radio stations did not have enough personnel who were familiar with the music's traditions to staff their shows, and many of them frankly had little love for the music they were required to play, or, at best, they came from rock-and-roll backgrounds that forever colored their musical choices and selections. Even if the DJs liked traditional forms of country music, they were given little opportunity to play them, because most stations moved rapidly toward the "tight playlist" concept pioneered by rock stations. Only a handful of records, produced almost exclusively by the largest corporations, were played repeatedly during the broadcast day. The old-time disc jockeys—the Eddie Hills, Nelson Kings, Hal Hortons, Paul Kallingers, and Wayne Raneys—were fading from the scene. These were men who had both known and loved the music they played (some of them, in fact, had served apprenticeships as country musicians). While they were often corny, and even grotesquely hayseed in style, they had individuality and warmth, and were replaced too often by jive talkers, or ignoramuses who had no feeling at all for the music they spun.

The Country Music Association deserves much of the credit for country music's great commercial upsurge and worldwide expansion during the 1960s. In its early years, the CMA appeared to be wholly commercially oriented and to be little concerned with the traditions and historical importance of the music. As one CMA brochure noted, "The 'C' in country music means cash."[10] The annual conventions held in Nashville (along with the business meetings held in places like London and San Juan, Puerto Rico) demonstrated just how far removed from the rustic image country music had ventured and how much it had succumbed to the middle-class ethic of respectability and success. The yearly conventions were reminiscent of meetings of businessmen, replete with stockholders' reports, innovative merchandising ideas, fancy banquets, cocktail hours, and a final formal dance with music provided by one of the sophisticated, pop-style country bands such as that headed by Leroy Van Dyke. The organization's growth, in short, paralleled that of the country music industry.

One of the most heartening contributions made by the CMA, and an indication that the organization was trying to at least combine history with promotion, was the establishment of the Country Music Hall of Fame and Museum. Largely through the devoted work of people such as Roy Horton and Steve Sholes, a massive fund-raising campaign resulted in the construction of a multimillion-dollar structure, ultramodern in design, which in addition to museum facilities would also contain the offices of the Country Music Association, the plaques of Hall of Fame honorees, and a center for historical research. The dream, which had been conceived as early as 1961, came to fruition on March 31, 1967, when the doors of the Country Music Hall of Fame and Museum officially opened in Nashville. The gala opening ceremony began when CMA Board Chairman Roy Horton and President Paul Cohen cut the ribbons before NBC television cameras, and continued with speeches by Tennessee Governor Buford Ellington, Congressman Richard Fulton, and Nashville Mayor Beverly Briley.

This beautiful building housed the Hall of Fame until May 2001, when it was replaced by a larger and much more ornate structure that has since become one of the major tourist attractions in the Music City. There one can meander down the Walkway of the Stars, which is embedded with the names of those entertainers who have contributed at least $1,000 to the Hall of Fame, see the instruments, wearing apparel, and mementos of the earlier stars, and top off the visit by watching short films on the history of country music. Those with a scholarly interest can ensconce themselves in the Library and Media Center, the repository for an enormous collection of records, tapes, interviews, magazines, and other assorted material of usefulness to researchers.

The Hall of Fame itself was originally modeled on the one established by professional baseball at Cooperstown, New York, but the plan was modified when it was discovered that such rigid rules allowed admission of only a very few individuals. A special committee of the CMA in 1961 selected Jimmie Rodgers, Fred Rose, and Hank Williams as the first honorees. In November 1962, the CMA abandoned its initial intention to select only deceased entertainers and chose Roy Acuff as the first living member of the Hall of Fame. With the exception of 1963, when no one was chosen, the CMA has yearly added new names to the Hall, and in 1967 adopted a policy to name people from both performing and nonperforming categories. Despite its contributions, the Hall of Fame has been persistently criticized for its seeming bias toward Nashville and contemporary performers. With the exception of Jimmie Rodgers, every honoree up to the selection of Gene Autry in 1969 was a Nashville-based musician or businessman. Furthermore, some of the obvious giants of country music were not named until long after the Hall of Fame had been established, and some, like Carson Robison, Bradley Kincaid, John Lair, and Woody Guthrie, will probably never be named.

At the end of the 1950s, then, country music was beginning to be faced with the debate that has only intensified in the decades that have followed: would the music lose its identity, and its soul, as it gained the world? Had Chet Atkins's compromise saved the music and made it possible for all styles to thrive, or had he and other country-pop people headed it down the road to accommodation, homogenization, and ultimate extinction? Whatever the value of "countrypolitan" music, it and the urge to "cross over" into the lucrative pop field were here to stay. In the years to come, reactions would sometimes come, alternatives would appear, and "back-to-the-roots" movements (such as bluegrass) would periodically manifest themselves, but the pop impulse would remain irresistible.

CHAPTER 9

The Reinvigoration of Modern Country Music, 1960–1972

A lthough the rockabilly obsession and the subsequent country-pop emphasis were relatively short phases of country music history, they must have seemed like eternities to partisans of traditional country music. But as a matter of fact, the rockabilly craze introduced to music a large number of young people who later took their guitars and energy into the country field. In some cases, their styles of country music took on the manifestations of rock; in the music of others such as Conway Twitty and Jerry Lee Lewis, the performers revealed that they could perform hard-core or honky-tonk country as well as any of the old-timers. The country-pop urge, on the other hand, sometimes bred boredom, just as homogenization of any type often does, and the more tradition-based country styles steadily began to reappear.

Commercially, country music continued to prosper. All-country radio stations proliferated. When WHN in New York City adopted the format in 1973, country music had indeed become chic. Perhaps more significant than radio programming was the blossoming of country music on television. Country and cowboy singers had already appeared in early television experiments. Tex Owens, for example, claimed to have appeared on the tube as early as 1935; Bobby Gregory made an appearance on a New York demonstration sometime in the 1930s; Red

River Dave was on a show at the 1939 World's Fair in New York; and he and several other entertainers appeared on local country shows when television stations appeared in their cities. Red River Dave, for example, had a popular show in San Antonio in the late 1940s.

The barn dance format began to appear on television almost as soon as the medium became institutionalized after World War II. The *Midwestern Hayride* debuted on local television in Cincinnati in 1948 and secured an NBC affiliation in 1955. The *Grand Ole Opry* did not permit the televising of its regular programs until the late 1970s, when public television aired a couple of the shows in their entirety, but Al Gannaway did produce an extensive number of thirty-minute shows featuring Opry talent. These were revised and newly syndicated in the 1980s and can still be seen on DVDs. The *Ozark Jubilee*, from Springfield, Missouri, was the king of the televised barn dances. The show had begun in 1946 and acquired network status on ABC on January 22, 1956. It was hosted by Red Foley and featured at one time or another such performers as Brenda Lee (as a child star), Leroy Van Dyke, Sonny James, and Porter Wagoner, as well as the comedy team of Uncle Cyp and Aunt Sap Brasfield (tent vaudeville veterans who took their routines into country music).

Numerous television shows aimed at hard-core country audiences were syndicated and sold to a wide variety of markets around the nation. These shows, of course, were sometimes watched by the casual or curious spectator (sometimes secretly). Among the more important were those of Ernest Tubb (often featuring a neatly dressed and clean-shaven Willie Nelson), Buck Owens, Flatt and Scruggs, the Wilburn Brothers, and Porter Wagoner. The two last-named programs were oases for "traditional" country music, humor, patter, and advertisements. Each show preserved much of the flavor of early stage and radio performances and offered a large sampling of down-home features that country music seemed to be in danger of forgetting. People who watched the *Wilburn Brothers Show* could hear the Wilburns (Teddy and Doyle) sing old-time gospel and country songs such as "Farther Along" and "My Little Home in Tennessee," as well as the modern hits. Born in Hardy, Arkansas, the Wilburn Brothers started out as child singers in their family's band but began to create an identity as a brother duet when they signed with Decca in 1954. Tours with Webb Pierce and Faron Young contributed immeasurably to their wider exposure. The Wilburns, in turn, furthered the careers of other entertainers who appeared on their television segments; Loretta Lynn, for example, began her rise to superstardom while singing on the *Wilburn Brothers Show* in the early 1960s.

The *Porter Wagoner Show* became part of Americana, deeply beloved by those who cherished the rustic imagery it conveyed and ridiculed by those who recoiled from its hayseed trappings. As the most widely syndicated country show in the nation, Wagoner's television program was the most important haven available for the older styles of country music. Wagoner grew up on a farm near West Plains, Missouri, and in 1951 began singing each morning from 5:30 to 6:00 a.m. on a local radio station that could be heard for only five or six miles. After a bus driver heard his program and passed on the word to the station manager, KWTO in nearby Springfield called Wagoner in for an audition. He gained additional exposure on the *Ozark Jubilee* and in 1955 signed a contract with RCA. His successful recording in 1956 of "A Satisfied Mind," one of the most finely crafted songs in country music, was his main ticket to the *Grand Ole Opry*, which he joined in 1957. As a hillbilly in a time of stylistic cloudiness, Wagoner definitely did not fit into RCA's vision of a country-pop compromise. Nevertheless, the company recognized his commercial appeal and kept him on its roster. While resolutely remaining faithful to the hard country sounds and image, Wagoner more than repaid RCA's trust by recording some of the major hits of country music, including the classics "Green, Green Grass of Home" and "The Carroll County Accident."

Wagoner's television show, introduced in 1960, was sponsored by a firm long familiar to rural southerners: the Chattanooga Medicine Company, the maker of Black Draught and Wine of Cardui (for "women's complaints") and the distributor of the famous wall calendars that were once found in nearly all rural homes. The thirty-minute television segment showcased other talented performers, including Norma Jean Beasler (known simply as "Miss Norma Jean"), a sweet-voiced singer from Oklahoma who served as the show's "girl singer" until replaced by Dolly Parton in 1967. Parton, of course, rose to national fame on the strength of her appearances on the show and in concert with Wagoner up to 1975. Parton's and Wagoner's duet recordings for RCA were consistent award winners throughout the late 1960s and early 1970s. The comedian Speck Rhodes provided a light-hearted contrast, with his baggy pants and burlesque style of humor, and Mack Magaha, who previously had been a member of Don Reno and Red

Smiley's Tennessee Cutups, contributed some of the best old-time fiddling heard on any country show in the 1960s. Buck Trent, a gifted instrumentalist who played both electric guitar and five-string banjo, probably made country music history when he successfully converted the banjo into an electric instrument—a development that could only bring dismay to tradition-minded enthusiasts. His innovation had the dubious distinction of making the banjo sound like an electric guitar.

Despite the presence of so many gifted individualists, the dominating presence of the show was Wagoner himself, who cut a striking figure, to say the least, in one of the many brightly colored, rhinestone-studded cowboy suits that Nudie Cohn had begun providing for him in 1953. Along with Hank Snow, Wagoner was one of the few country entertainers who persisted with such costuming at a time when everyone else was adopting business suits or modish attire. Making over two hundred concerts a year, appearing regularly on the *Grand Ole Opry*, and entering millions of homes via his syndicated television show, Porter Wagoner brought renewed strength and vitality to hard-core country music. Neither wealth nor success caused him to forget his rural origins and the people who had nurtured both him and his music.

While shows like Porter Wagoner's were important repositories for old-time country music, other shows did more to introduce the music to the masses, and particularly to the urban middle class who would have listened to it in no other guise. In 1957, CBS put the lanky and affable Jimmy Dean, from Plainview, Texas, opposite NBC's venerable Dave Garroway, and the country show more than held its own for several months. The program came on at 7:00 a.m. (Eastern Standard Time) out of WTOP in Washington, DC, and was part of Connie B. Gay's country music empire. Born in Lizard Lick, North Carolina, Gay had gotten into radio work through the government-sponsored *Farm Hour* in the 1940s. Dean had a remarkably winning personality and a better-than-average singing voice and piano style. His recitations, cornball humor, and country crooning were ably supported by Mary Klick's sweet ballads, Smitty Ervin's five-string banjo, and Buck Ryan's hot old-time fiddling. In short, the show did provide a format for real country music. It also introduced newer entertainers, such as the guitarist/singer Billy Grammer, to a wider public. However, when Dean returned to network television in 1964—this time in a prime nighttime slot on ABC—the show was more fully in the country-pop camp and had about as many pop guests as country.

By and large, the network country shows that followed in the wake
of Jimmy Dean were overproduced, slickly professional, and only
marginally "country." The producers of such shows only reluctantly
gave viewers a strong dose of the real thing. Above all, the proliferation of such shows indicated the "arrival" of country music and its
growing respectability on the American scene. On the strength of his
evident commercial appeal, Roger Miller hosted a show on NBC for
a few months in 1966. After spending several artistically successful
but economically unrewarding years as a sideman, writer, and singer,
Miller made the whole world of American show business sit up and
take notice of his talents in 1964 and 1965. He won eleven Grammy
awards during this two-year period—a feat that no other country entertainer had equaled—and he became an often-seen guest on such
prime-time national programs as the *Tonight Show*, starring Johnny
Carson. Born and reared in Texas and Oklahoma, and a lifelong disciple
of Bob Wills's music, Miller emerged from a hard-core country background to become one of the most sophisticated lyricists in country
music—as witnessed by such songs as "King of the Road" and "Kansas
City Star"—and a clever and witty singer and comedian. The diversely
talented Miller, though, could not save his own show from the bland
packaging that was imposed upon it. Country music received little
emphasis on the show; therefore, many country fans did not mourn
its rather abrupt departure from television programming.

In 1969, three country shows debuted on network programming:
The Glen Campbell Goodtime Hour (CBS), *The Johnny Cash Show*
(ABC), and *Hee Haw* (CBS). Campbell, from Delight, Arkansas, finally
moved from undeserved obscurity when he made his very popular
recording in 1966 of John Hartford's "Gentle on My Mind." Campbell
had spent much of his life as a session musician in Los Angeles, where
he contributed to the fame of other people. In the summer of 1968 he
became the summer replacement for the Smothers Brothers, and he
charmed his viewers with an easy, relaxed personality; a supple tenor
voice (sharply honed through a short stint with the Beach Boys);
and his guitar virtuosity. Campbell's singing was pop oriented, and
he gravitated toward structurally sophisticated songs such as those
written by Jim Webb ("By the Time I Get to Phoenix," "Wichita Lineman," "Galveston"), but he maintained a down-home ambience with
his high-pitched country laugh and patter and through the occasional
guest appearances of his charming parents, who were indeed rural

and folksy. Campbell's own show in 1969 was smooth, fast-paced, and countrypolitan in mood. Whatever the misgivings that some country fans might have had about the style of music heard, most were probably delighted at the success that one of their own had attained.

Country fans had much higher hopes for *The Johnny Cash Show* when it began in 1969.[1] And Johnny tried his best to present a real country show. He performed his own dyed-in-the-wool country songs (such as "Folsom Prison Blues," which he had revived with even greater success than when first released in 1955) and sometimes featured his famous mother-in-law, Maybelle Carter. He gave much exposure to her daughter and his wife, June, and he ran a well-done segment, complete with movie and photo footage, called "Ride This Train," a combination of history and song. Cash was also receptive to young and innovative musicians and to those who came from non-country backgrounds. Louis Armstrong, for example, appeared as part of a reenactment of his famous 1930 session with Jimmie Rodgers. The urban folk hero Bob Dylan also appeared on the show to great fanfare, and Doug Kershaw, the frenetic Cajun/rock fiddler, began a major comeback in American music after a guest appearance on the Cash series. As time went by, though, the show's country flavor gradually became diluted under an avalanche of pop guests and overstylized production numbers.

The third major television show of 1969, *Hee Haw*, was hillbilly to the point of grotesque parody; its commercial success was indeed strange. It presented an image of country music, and of rural life, that most musicians had been resisting for years: that of the hayseed buffoon. Nevertheless, the backwoodsy skits were produced and merchandised through the most sophisticated and urbane of techniques. The show's producer, Sam Lovullo, described it as a "fully computerized" production,[2] in that after enough scenes were shot to compose as many as thirteen shows, the material was fed into a computer that selected the best and most effective groupings of skits. Inspired by the popular comedy series *Laugh-In, Hee Haw* was an hour-long program that interspersed music with comic vignettes and shots of beautiful, scantily clad women. Most of the humor was freshly written by modern gag writers or by the performers themselves (as in the case of Grandpa Jones, who compiled his "country menus" from old cookbooks), but some of it was of hoary vintage: from jokebooks, vaudeville, burlesque, and minstrel sources, and from the early country music tradition.

The show's appeal suggested that the humor of country music was more traditional than its music, even though viewers enjoyed many fine musical moments on the show. The best came each week when the Hee Haw Gospel Quartet—Kenny Price, Grandpa Jones, Roy Clark, and Buck Owens—sang old-time religious songs in Brown's Ferry Four fashion and to the sole accompaniment of Clark's guitar. *Hee Haw* skits took place in barbershops, in cornfields, around pot-bellied stoves at the general store, in the front yards of rickety cabins, and in similar rustic settings. Hosts Buck Owens and Roy Clark did a comic routine with guitar and banjo reminiscent of the venerable "Arkansas Traveler" skit, and Jack Pruitt and Jimmie Riddle did a takeoff on juba patting, keeping a highly rhythmic pattern going by slapping their legs and chests, as they emitted wheezes and hiccough-like sounds that they called "eephing."

The *Hee Haw* cast constituted a "Who's Who" of country comedy. Old-time comedians such as Grandpa Jones, Stringbean (David Akeman), Minnie Pearl, and Archie Campbell gained access to newer and larger audiences through the popular show. Newer performers also won a national exposure through the show that most earlier country comedians had only dreamed of. Junior Samples, a natural, but semiliterate, rural comedian came to the show with virtually no professional experience. Sheb Wooley, a cowboy actor, singer, and songwriter from Oklahoma (who had attained notoriety and wealth as the writer of "Purple People Eater"), performed on the show as a drunken song parodist called Ben Colder. Kenny Price, a fine baritone singer whose rotundity garnered for him the title of "the round mound of sound," showed *Hee Haw* audiences that he was also a very funny man, and Jerry Clower, a former Mississippi fertilizer salesman, gave television audiences a sample of the humor that had been delighting clubs, service organizations, and seed conventions for years. Public visibility, however, carried dangers as well as delight. In November 1973, thugs went to Stringbean Akeman's secluded country home near Nashville and killed the beloved comedian and his wife after ransacking their house in a fruitless search for the large sum of money believed to be sheltered there.[3]

Country music's expanding popularity was not confined to the United States. The music exhibited surprising strength and commercial viability in Europe, Asia, and South Africa. Country entertainers had never been totally unknown in other parts of the world. Even in the 1920s and 1930s American hillbilly records had been reissued rather extensively abroad, and Jimmie Rodgers, particularly, had built up at least a modest international following. Rodgers's reissued recordings contributed directly to the birth of the country music industry in Australia and New Zealand, a phenomenon fashioned primarily by the confluence of local folk music traditions (e.g., that of the Australian Bush) and the vision of American cowboys. The image of the cowboy and its identification with country music do much to explain why some country singers, such as Gene Autry and Slim Whitman, experienced considerable success abroad. When Autry toured the British Isles in 1939, though, he was not the first American country entertainer to do so; Carson Robison had made earlier jaunts in 1932, 1936, and 1938, when he performed throughout the British Isles and on Radio Luxembourg. Although born on a farm in Kansas, Robison projected the persona of a cowboy and fronted a band called the Oxydol Cowboys (named for the then-popular detergent).

Despite the earlier manifestations of interest abroad, World War II was the force that really promoted the internationalization of country music. American military personnel carried all forms of their nation's popular music around the world, but it was the Armed Forces Network (AFN), which grew from a weak GI station using a borrowed transmitter into a mammoth system that proved most instrumental in generating interest in American music among Europeans. By 1960, one report indicated that about fifty million Europeans listened to the AFN,[4] and the network received correspondence from interested listeners in every country in Western Europe, from North Africa, and even from Soviet bloc nations.

Country music experienced a remarkable popularity among American military personnel during the war, a preference that only deepened in the years that followed the conflict. Record purchases even suggested that country music had a wide lead in popularity over other brands of music on American military bases. Throughout 1960 and 1961, for example, country record sales in base PXs accounted for about 65 percent of the entire total, and even reached as high as 72 percent on one occasion. Obviously, the music appealed to many people who had neither southern nor rural backgrounds, an apparent morale builder that seemed to be a powerful reminder of home. A US Army record buyer was quoted as saying: "Country and western strikes the troops as part of the American heritage, and the troops prefer it to sophisticated, schmaltzy music."[5]

Servicemen formed string bands everywhere, and some of them were heard over the AFN. While fulfilling his military obligations in World War II Germany, Grandpa Jones played with a group called the Munich Mountaineers. In Japan, the future recording star Charlie Walker introduced country music to that part of the world as the leader of a band that included the famous fiddler and songwriter Red Hayes ("Satisfied Mind") and other Eighth Army buddies. While live programming was important in the dissemination of country music, DJ shows—following the trend back home—ultimately reached a much larger audience of military personnel and European civilians. One of the more popular postwar programs carried by the AFN was a country record show called *Stickbuddy Jamboree*, conducted by Sergeant Tom Daniels from Texas. The *Jamboree* was said to have the biggest audience of any program on the air in Europe at that time (3:05 p.m.). Daniels also conducted another popular country show, *Hillbilly Reveille*, which was broadcast during the early-morning hours. Other country DJ shows spiced up AFN programming, and at least one show was hosted by a future professional performer, Dick Curless, who broadcast in Korea during the early 1950s as the Rice Paddy Ranger.

One of the most remarkable consequences of country music expansion was the emergence of people in other nations who became musicians, fans, collectors, or promoters. Kitty Prins, who conducted the *Melody Ranch* show from Belgium, and Connie Tex Hat, who ran a similar show in Austria, were only two of a large number of foreigners who began promoting local country music in the late 1950s. Country shows soon abounded in nations around the world, although only a few were as ambitious as the Tokyo *Grand Ole Opry* or England's huge Wembley Festival (1969–1991), an annual event that attracted dozens of American stars each year. Some non-Americans have pursued careers in the country music industry in the United States. It is not unheard-of to find a Japanese fiddler or steel guitarist in an American band, and occasional singers, such as the Englishman Pete Sayers, who went to Nashville in the early 1960s, have competed with American-born entertainers. Country music also profited from the promotion of such people as Richard Weize, who created the Bear Family label in Germany[6] and issued scores of state-of-the-art box sets that featured rereleased recordings of American entertainers. In Dover, England, Dave Barnes, who throughout his life had collected literally thousands of country recordings, founded the British Academy of Country Music (BACM),[7] and began making out-of-print and often forgotten items newly available on his own LP and CD labels.

Some of these musical entrepreneurs moved to the United States. Martin C. Haerle, for example, was a former executive in the export department of a Stuttgart, Germany, refrigerator manufacturing company who became such an active producer of country shows on German radio and television that he was hired in July 1960 to head Starday Records' international sales and exploitation department. By 1961, Haerle had relocated to Starday's Nashville offices; he later remained in the United States as an independent record producer. Dixie Deen was a trick rider for a Wild West show in her native England, but she did not receive an intensive introduction to country music until she came to the United States in 1960 at the urging of Starday Records' Don Pierce. After coming to the United States, she became an award-winning songwriter and an assistant editor and columnist of the *Music City News* (a country music publication that was then owned by Faron Young). Deen's association with country music was further cemented by her marriage to the singer/songwriter Tom T. Hall.

Country musicians now routinely scheduled performances in countries throughout the world, and a few, such as George Hamilton IV, Tennessee Ernie Ford, and Roy Clark, performed in the Soviet Union. Hamilton, a North Carolinian who started his career in 1957 as a rockabilly, became one of country music's most zealous ambassadors abroad. He traveled extensively in the British Isles and on the European continent, giving performances and lecturing on the meaning and history of the music he had made his profession. Hamilton's dedication to the international acceptance of American country music rivaled that of Bill Clifton, a Maryland-born performer of bluegrass and old-time country music. After about eleven years of performance in the United States, Clifton moved to England in 1963 and became an entertainer in the folk clubs there.[8] At first, his audiences had little knowledge or appreciation of the music he performed, but he was such an avid missionary for old-time country music (as well as a competent performer) that by 1966 he was playing six nights a week in the clubs, appearing often on the continent, and hosting *Cellar Full of Folk*, a weekly BBC radio show. Clifton's commitments became so exhausting that he joined the Peace Corps in 1967 for a three-year stint as an administrator in the Philippines. By October 1970, however, he had returned to England and was once again educating folk club audiences in England and on the European continent about the beauties of American country music.

Clifton's success before foreign audiences was evidence that the older varieties of American country music were popular outside the United States. Smooth country-pop-style singers such as Jim Reeves and Don Williams had large followings in various countries, but performers of older styles—bluegrass, honky-tonk, yodeling cowboy, and the like—also exhibited remarkable appeal to foreigners. The Japanese showed great facility in re-creating all kinds of American music, and many of them became both avid fans and performers of bluegrass music. Bluegrass musicians who toured in Japan, such as Bill Clifton and Jim and Jesse McReynolds, testified to the quiet attentiveness and knowledge of Japanese fans. The reasons for the appeal of older forms of music are no doubt many and varied, but visions of American cowboys, mountain individualism, and frontier simplicity probably did much to shape the perceptions of country music. Vernon Oxford, Boxcar Willie, and Slim Whitman, three examples of Americans who achieved considerable popularity in the British Isles, each profited from others' romantic fixations concerning America and its music. Oxford, from Rogers, Arkansas, proved to be "too country" for the tastes of most American top-forty DJs, and he achieved little success until he went to England, where he found his hard country style of singing much appreciated. Boxcar Willie also intrigued English fans with his hobo attire, railroad songs, and rambling man image. Born Lecil Travis Martin in Sterrett, Texas, he came to traditional country music in the early 1970s after a successful background in the Air Force and as a civilian flight engineer. Wearing overalls, a floppy hat, and a smudged face, and performing mostly older songs—from the Roy Acuff, Jimmie Rodgers, and Hank Williams song bags—Boxcar Willie demonstrated conclusively that a considerable hunger existed here and abroad for older country music and for the symbols surrounding it. He went to England for the first time in 1977 and received a tremendous reception, with record sales there only adding to the luster of his growing popularity back home.

Vernon Oxford's and Boxcar Willie's British popularity, however, was preceded by that of Slim Whitman, whose success in England dated to the early 1950s, when the Florida-born yodeler and tenor singer began giving his first concerts in that country. The tall, mustachioed Whitman, who dressed in western-tailored costumes and yodeled an occasional cowboy song like "Cattle Call," was highly regarded in a country where fans often dressed in dude cowboy clothing to listen to country entertainers. When Whitman experienced his American resurgence in 1980–1981—a product of massive television advertising promoted by New York's Suffolk Marketing Company—he could point to almost twenty-five years of unbroken commercial popularity in Great Britain.

Slim Whitman's commercial strength in England, along with his eventual resurgence in the United States, indicates that the older styles of country music had never lost the support of millions of people. Even during the peak period of rock-and-roll ascendancy, the more "traditional" forms of country music did not die, though they sometimes faded from public view or reappeared in modified forms. In 1957, when Elvis reigned supreme in American music, Wilma Lee and Stoney Cooper took their brand of mountain music to the stage of the *Grand Ole Opry*, and the Country Gentlemen, one of the most innovative and popular bluegrass bands, began to create a stir in Washington, DC. And out in Texas, Ray Price and his Cherokee Cowboys were producing some of the most exciting honky-tonk music ever made. During the next few years, and especially after 1960, hard-core country performances became more frequent, and an increasing number of them began to make the popularity charts.

One powerful force that contributed to the revitalization of older musical traditions, while also inspiring a general urge to make music, was the "urban folk revival."[9] The term "revival" is something of a misnomer, since the entire history of folk-music interest in the cities, at that time, was relatively brief. Urban folk interest dates to the Depression years when Library of Congress field-recording units and WPA cultural researchers stimulated an interest in America's grassroots music, and when social activists and labor sympathizers began using folk songs as political weapons. Beginning from this relatively narrow base, and centered primarily among the socially conscious intelligentsia, folk music gradually became more generally popularized as performers such as Huddie "Leadbelly" Ledbetter, Jean Ritchie, Burl Ives, Josh White, and Big Bill Broonzy took the music to college campuses, into night clubs, and onto radio stations. The music's radical identification, however, was preserved by such entertainers as Woody Guthrie, Cisco Houston, Pete Seeger, and the Almanac Singers, who, during World War II, performed at anti-Fascist rallies and on behalf of "progressive" causes. Although its political bias remained left of center, urban folk music moved closer to the pop mainstream in the late 1940s when groups like the Weavers (an offspring of the Almanac Singers) began placing songs like "Goodnight, Irene" and "Kisses Sweeter Than Wine" on the popular music hit charts. Harry Belafonte continued the popularizing trend in the 1950s by making the nation calypso conscious.

The tremors of interest in folk music in the late 1940s became a groundswell in the late 1950s and early 1960s. In 1958, the Kingston Trio (Dave Guard, Bob Shane, and Nick Reynolds) recorded a song called "Tom Dooley," an old North Carolina murder ballad (about a man originally named Tom Dula), which vaulted to the top position in the nation's popular hit charts. Following up this ballad with other very popular songs, both traditional and modern, the Kingston Trio became one of the biggest concert attractions in the United States. More than any single recording, "Tom Dooley" set off the urban folk music boom. Almost immediately, a spate of Kingston Trio imitators bearing such names as the Brothers Four, the Cumberland Trio, the Chad Mitchell Trio, and the Wanderers Three appeared on record labels. The new groups, all quite young, directed their approach toward college and high-school age groups, but before long, people all over the nation, old and young alike, were humming "folk" melodies and buying recordings. The college folk interest at the beginning of the 1960s differed from that generated during the Depression and World War II years in that the latter folk movement was more inclusive and attracted a broad campus spectrum, including the fraternity and sorority groups, while the earlier movement had been identified with the more radical and intellectual segments of college life. Although folksinging by the middle of the 1960s had become deeply intertwined with the movements for peace and civil rights and had spawned an important body of protest material, such as that written by Malvina Reynolds, Phil Ochs, and Bob Dylan, the average folk-song session (usually called a "hootenanny") attracted a wide assortment of Americans: the young and the old, the intellectual and the uneducated, the conservative and the liberal, and the poor and the prosperous.

Despite the name it bore, urban folk music was essentially a facet of pop music. Some people may have been drawn to it in reaction to rock and roll, and some may have seen in it a reflection of a simpler and more manageable society, but most probably gravitated to it because of its freshness or because it represented just one more phase of pop music's ever-changing contours. It gave young people an opportunity to pick and sing and to be creative. And many people, such as Janis Joplin and Gram Parsons, moved easily from rock and roll to folk and then to hard rock or other forms of music. American songwriting was greatly furthered by the folk interest. Led principally by such alumni of the folk movement as Bob Dylan, Joni Mitchell, and Paul Simon, hundreds of people began writing songs, an urge that over the years has also been strongly displayed in the country music made by such people as Nanci Griffith, Iris DeMent, Guy Clark, Steve Earle, and Townes Van Zandt.

Most would-be folksingers—content to perform in the styles of the Kingston Trio or Peter, Paul and Mary—were unconcerned with stylistic authenticity or with the sources of their songs. Many enthusiasts, however, found that pop-folk music merely whetted their appetites for something more real, and they ventured increasingly into the sampling of old-time music: country, blues, gospel, Cajun, Tex-Mex, and other "ethnic" or vernacular forms. This search for "sources" inspired a recognition of the importance of early commercial hillbilly music, and 78 rpm records became vital documents. As a result, such names as Uncle Dave Macon, the Carter Family, the Skillet Lickers, Dock Boggs, and Charlie Poole began to assume great importance for many young "folkniks." A powerful catalyst that worked to stimulate that interest in hillbilly music among urban folk fans was a Folkways recording, *Anthology of American Folk Music*, originally produced in 1952 and widely available in public libraries as well as in record catalogues.[10] Issued as six long-playing 33⅓ rpm discs, the *Anthology* included reissues of both white and black country selections recorded between 1927 and 1933, or from the advent of electrical recordings until the diminution of field recordings during the Depression. Taken from commercial recordings borrowed from the gigantic collection of Harry Smith, the *Anthology* was intended as an introduction to authentic country music from the days before the radio and phonograph had blurred regional distinctions. Marketed as "folk music" and disseminated by the select Folkways Records, the *Anthology* reached the ears of countless individuals who probably would have ignored it had it been dispensed under the label of "country" or "hillbilly" music. Songs from the *Anthology* made their way into the repertories of such urban performers as Joan Baez and the New Lost City Ramblers, who, with their appetites whetted by this initial introduction, resolved to learn more about songs and performers from the early hillbilly era.

The urban folk discovery of early hillbilly music had several happy consequences. Not only did it promote the reissuance of early recordings, as well as the re-creation of old styles, including a revived string band movement, it also inspired a search for still-living pioneer commercial performers. Dedicated researchers discovered that many of the original hillbilly, blues, and gospel musicians were still alive and, better yet, that some of them could still perform as well as they ever could. Bluesmen Mississippi John Hurt and Furry Lewis and country musicians Buell Kazee, Tom Ashley, Jimmie Tarlton, and Dock Boggs were only a few of the individuals who were fortunate enough to have second careers performing at the festivals, clubs, and university concerts spawned by the folk revival.

The relationship between country music and the urban folk scene was often a reciprocal one. Urban musicians such as the New Lost City Ramblers (Mike Seeger, John Cohen, Tom Paley, and, later, Tracy Schwarz)[11] and the Greenbriar Boys (Ralph Rinzler, Bob Yellin, Eric Weissberg, and John Herald) borrowed freely from the hillbilly repertory, with the Ramblers faithfully re-creating early string band styles and the Greenbriar Boys playing in the more recent bluegrass fashion. Country musicians, on the other hand, sometimes borrowed from the urban folk fanciers (both pop and traditional), not always realizing that such material had originally been purloined from their country forebears.

One of the most beneficial consequences of the country–urban folk interrelationship was the discovery of Arthel "Doc" Watson, one of country music's most superb entertainers.[12] Watson was a blind musician and singer from Deep Gap, North Carolina, who had performed locally for years, as both an acoustic and electric guitarist, until 1960, when he was "discovered" by Ralph Rinzler as a by-product of the latter's interest in Clarence "Tom" Ashley. With Rinzler as his manager, Watson began appearing at folk clubs and concerts in the North, first with his Tennessee and North Carolina friends, Ashley, Fred Price, and Clint Howard, and after 1964, as a solo act. Watson amazed his newfound audiences with his storehouse of songs, his skill as a banjoist and French harp player, and, above all, his virtuosity as a flat-picking guitarist. Watson was not the first guitarist to play fiddle tunes on his instrument, or to otherwise play melodies with great rapidity (he freely admitted his indebtedness to such musicians as Don Reno, Grady Martin, Merle Travis, and the Delmore Brothers), but he probably did most to revitalize the acoustic guitar and to encourage the flat-picking technique (the use of a flat pick instead of a thumb pick to play individual notes). His versions of "Black Mountain Rag" and "Deep River Blues" became classics of modern guitar picking. Such brilliant young guitarists as Dan Crary, Norman Blake, Tony Rice, and Clarence White, plus an untold number of bluegrass musicians, can be described as his musical children. Watson gained public exposure through his involvement in the urban folk movement and through his appearances at bluegrass festivals. Nevertheless, he was not a bluegrass musician—as he was quick to point out to interviewers[13]—nor was he exclusively an old-time performer, although he could perform both styles with great proficiency. Watson accumulated an immense repertory of traditional ballads, folk songs, and instrumental pieces as he grew up in the mountains, but he was never totally wedded to such material, and he supplemented it with songs learned from books and modern commercial sources. Launching his professional career in the midst of the urban folk revival and appearing at such events as the Newport Folk Festival in 1963, Watson tailored his repertory to fit the perceived needs of his folkie listeners. He did magnificent versions of traditional songs such as "Matty Groves" and "Omie Wise," but it was only in later years—particularly after his talented son, Merle, joined him as an accompanist in 1966—that audiences learned of his skills as a blues and modern country singer.

Watson was one of several country musicians who appeared at the Newport Folk Festival during the 1960s. Earl Scruggs (backed by Hylo Brown and his band, the Timberliners) was the first to do so, in 1959, and he was followed by such performers as Mac Wiseman, Jim and Jesse McReynolds, Bill Monroe, Wiley and Zeke Morris, and Merle Travis. Johnny Cash, who appeared at the Newport affair in 1964 and 1969, was the first mainstream country and western singer to forge an alliance with the folk revival. Cash had earlier affected a kind of Harry Belafonte style of stage behavior, dressing in black and projecting a dramatic and sensual presence reminiscent of method-school acting. His 1962 performance of "The Legend of John Henry's Hammer," for example, lasted more than eight minutes and was punctuated by grunts and the striking of two steel bars together at periodic intervals. Cash was fond of traditional material, such as Leadbelly's "The Rock Island Line," but he seemed much more in tune with the pop-folk fraternity and their modern-composed songs, and his own writing increasingly showed their influence. He was the first country entertainer to cultivate a relationship with Bob Dylan, and he recorded some of the young poet's material, as well as songs written by such performers as Peter La Farge.

Although no country singer was as thoroughly immersed in the urban folk waters as Johnny Cash, several of his colleagues flirted with the revival and, in so doing, began to win back some of that youthful audience that had moved away from country music in the mid-1950s. George Hamilton IV, for example, abandoned his earlier flirtations with rock and roll and country-pop and began performing such folkish tunes as "Steel Rail Blues," "Abilene," "Break My Mind," and "Gentle on My Mind." Country-rock superstar Waylon Jennings began his career with RCA in 1965, just before the tremors of the urban folk movement faded away. The Littlefield, Texas, native had not yet found the highly commercial sound that later characterized his performances, but even then he exhibited an eclecticism that led him into all areas of popular music. Consequently, in this early stage of his career, Jennings did such folk chestnuts as "The House of the Rising Sun" and "I'm a Man of Constant Sorrow," as well as newer pop-folk offerings such as "Kisses Sweeter Than Wine" and "Four Strong Winds." Jennings's recordings were obviously shaped by the pop fashions of the day.

Jimmy C. Newman, on the other hand, dipped back into his own cultural heritage to revitalize his performing career. Although Newman's first recordings in 1946 had been performed in the French patois of his native Southwest Louisiana—he was a real Cajun boy from Big Mamou—his entry into country music in 1954, via a Dot recording of "Cry, Cry Darling," was pure honky-tonk. In 1957 he made the transition to country-pop with "A Fallen Star," one of the most successful songs in that genre. Newman, however, was never very happy in the role of pop singer, and largely through the influence of the urban folk enthusiasm, he returned to the performance of Cajun-country songs in 1962. An album from that year, *Folk Songs of the Bayou Country*, featured the Dobro steel guitar and the fiddling of Rufus Thibodeaux, one of the best-known Cajun fiddlers of the modern era. After that time, Newman became a major participant in a full-scale Cajun music revival that saw old-time Cajun bands, such as the Balfa Brothers, and country-Cajun fusionists, like Newman and Doug Kershaw, take their music to the Smithsonian Folklife Festival on the Mall and to concerts in Europe.

Of the various country performers who experimented with the urban folk genre in the early 1960s, Bobby Bare was the most successful. With a compelling voice that could be alternately mournful or raucous, the Ironton, Ohio, native became one of the premier "song salesmen" in modern country music. His down-home demeanor and unalloyed rural voice did not deter Bare from being on the cutting edge of country music. He borrowed freely from other fields of music and exhibited an uncanny ability to elicit highly commercial songs from a long string of outstanding songwriters such as Mel Tillis, Paul Craft, Shel Silverstein, Kris Kristofferson, Billy Joe Shaver, Guy Clark, and Tom T. Hall. Above all, Bare was a storyteller, a talent shown with great effectiveness in such songs as "Miller's Cave," "Detroit City," and "Marie Laveau." In recording songs like "500 Miles," a pop version of a traditional mountain song, and "Four Strong Winds," a lonesome love song dealing with Canadian migratory workers, he revealed his affinity for the urban folk style. Songs like these, while commercially advantageous to Bare, also reinvigorated the storytelling tradition in country music and moved the music a bit closer to its roots.

Another offshoot of the urban folk revival, and a phenomenon that contributed to the reinvigoration of country music, was the so-called saga song. Although similar in some ways to the event ballad of the 1920s, the saga song differed greatly because it depicted completely fictional episodes or remote historical events. Only rarely did the saga song describe events of contemporary significance. Such songs were clearly inspired by the success in 1958 of the Kingston Trio's "Tom Dooley." For several months, the airwaves were filled with both pop and country songs about mythical and real heroes who gained fame or notoriety during America's pioneer period.

Columbia Records played a preeminent role in the recording of saga songs in late 1958 and early 1959 when a variety of such songs appeared, most of them on the label. These recordings strongly suggest that someone in the Columbia offices was alive to the immediate commercial advantages of the pseudo-historical song. Johnny Horton's "When It's Springtime in Alaska," a ballad in the Robert Stewart

Service tradition, which related the story of a prospector killed in a tavern brawl in the Klondike, inaugurated the series. To the delight of dyed-in-the-wool country fans, this ballad, performed with simple string accompaniment, attained the number one position on the country music charts and remained for several weeks against the competition of country-pop numbers.

"Springtime in Alaska" was followed soon after by the release of Johnny Cash's "Don't Take Your Guns to Town," an account of a young cowboy who disregarded his mother's warnings and was killed when he ventured into town. Cash followed this best-selling song with several others about cowboys and Indians ("Old Apache Squaw," "The Ballad of Boot Hill," etc.), themes that he returned to again and again in the mid-1960s.

The most notable success won by a country saga song came in 1959 when Johnny Horton recorded "The Battle of New Orleans." The ballad first appeared in a 1958 album recorded by Jimmie Driftwood (James Morris), an Arkansas folklorist and schoolteacher who had written the song as a device to teach history to his students. Driftwood set the lyrics about Andrew Jackson's famous victory to an old hillbilly fiddle tune, "Eighth of January," which had also commemorated the event. Horton's version, considerably shorter than Driftwood's, first appeared on a Columbia record in April 1959, and by June of that year it had vaulted to the position of number one song in the nation.

A native of Los Angeles who grew up in the area around Tyler, Texas, Horton was only a moderately successful honky-tonk singer and barn dance performer (the *Hometown Jamboree* and *Louisiana Hayride*) until he recorded "Honky Tonk Man" in 1956. This dance-hall classic, with a modest rockabilly beat, gave Horton a national reputation, but it was only a dim suggestion of the diversity of his talents. Performing as "the Singing Fisherman" because of his highly acclaimed skill as a professional angler, Horton showed the ability to perform almost any kind of song, from a romantic tune like "All for the Love of a Girl" to a raucous novelty like "Ole Slew Foot." He was also the performer par excellence of the saga song. For a year and a half following the huge success of "The Battle of New Orleans," Horton recorded such songs as "Sink the Bismarck," "Johnny Reb," and "The Battle of Bull Run." Under the tutelage of his manager and bass player, Tillman Franks, who later had similar success with Claude King and David Houston, Horton seemed assured of a long and glittering career. But country music suffered a tragic loss on the night of November 5, 1960, when Horton was killed in an automobile collision near the small town of Milano, Texas. A grimly ironic feature of the tragedy was that Horton's wife was left a widow for the second time; she had been the second wife of Hank Williams.

Several historical, or folkish, songs that had varying degrees of success were issued in 1959, but none approached "The Battle of New Orleans" in popularity. They included Carl Smith's "Ten Thousand Drums" and Hawkshaw Hawkins's "Soldier's Joy," both pseudo–Revolutionary War songs—although the latter was set to the melody of a famous old fiddle tune—and Eddy Arnold's "Tennessee Stud," another classic Jimmie Driftwood composition that became a staple of Doc Watson's repertory. Of all the folkish ballads of the period, "The Long Black Veil," recorded by Lefty Frizzell, demonstrated the strongest durability and most widespread appeal. Written by Marijohn Wilkin and Danny Dill, this ghostly song of death, infidelity, and mistaken identity became a vehicle for Frizzell's return to the popularity charts and was eventually recorded by a diverse group of performers, ranging all the way from the Country Gentlemen, a bluegrass group, to Joan Baez, an urban folk performer, and John Anderson, a modern honky-tonk revivalist.

In late 1959, the saga-song craze subsided somewhat, but the trend continued spasmodically in the following years with the appearance of albums and occasional singles devoted to fictional narratives or historical events. Some of these songs enjoyed extensive popularity. Marty Robbins, for example, in 1959 wrote and recorded a song that rivaled the success gained earlier that year by "The Battle of New Orleans": "El Paso," a meticulously crafted ballad with a Mexican flavor, which tells of a man who was killed fighting for the love of his border-tavern sweetheart. Impeccably sung by Robbins, it was one of many cowboy songs, both old and recently composed, that he recorded and included in his concerts. The television personality Jimmy Dean enjoyed similar success with a couple of songs in 1961 and 1962 that featured dramatic stories. "Big John" depicted the tale of a huge miner who gave his life to save his fellow workers, while "PT 109" chronicled the wartime exploits of John F. Kennedy. At least two other hit songs, Claude King's "Wolverton Mountain" in 1962 and Lefty Frizzell's "Saginaw, Michigan" in 1964, were humorous ballads that dealt with fictional characters and incidents. They were major commercial successes and welcome signs that the narrative impulse had not vanished from country music.

Throughout the early 1960s, other songs and singers periodically appeared that suggested the healthy revitalization of older country music. In 1960, one of the veterans of country music, Lloyd "Cowboy" Copas,[14] recorded for the Starday label an old ragtime-style song that he renamed "Alabam," essentially a reworking of Frank Hutchison's "Coney Isle," but it was made distinctive, and commercially appealing, by Copas's clean and crisp flat-picking, a talent that few fans knew he possessed. The song was number one on *Billboard*'s country charts for twelve consecutive weeks and marked the beginning of renewed popularity for Copas that lasted until his death on March 5, 1963. Fans of "hard country" music, as the older styles were now increasingly called, were also thrilled in early 1963 by Carl and Pearl Butler's "Don't Let Me Cross Over," a pure country song in lyrics and style of performance. Carl Butler's Tennessee mountain roots were strongly displayed in his full-throated, emotional singing, and his stylistic debts to Roy Acuff and the Bailes Brothers were apparent and proudly admitted. Carl and Pearl's duet singing sparked the resurgence of male-female harmonizing, a style that has since become common in country music (as exemplified by the recordings of Porter Wagoner and Dolly Parton, Conway Twitty and Loretta Lynn, David Frizzell and Shelly West, Don Williams and Emmylou Harris, and many others).

Nineteen sixty-three was a good year for hard country music. The popular television situation comedy *The Beverly Hillbillies* gave "The Ballad of Jed Clampett" the exposure it needed to become number one on *Billboard*'s country charts—a rare accomplishment for a bluegrass song. Its performers, Flatt and Scruggs, were richly deserving of the fame and profit they received. Hawkshaw Hawkins's untimely death in March 1963 certainly contributed to the commercial success of his "Lonesome 7–7203," which topped the charts in May and June of that year. But the reward was long overdue for the West Virginia-born Hawkins; his rich, smooth voice had long been one of the best in country music, but superstardom had generally eluded him. For Bobby Bare, on the other hand, 1963 marked the real beginning of his long and successful career. In that year, he recorded one of the great standards of country music, "Detroit City," a song that effectively expressed the loneliness and homesickness felt by rural southerners in the industrial North. Although it contained a few faint echoes of urban folk music—particularly in its melody—the song made few concessions to the pop-country sound. Even less compromising in style was another recording of that year, "We Must Have Been Out of Our Minds." The song combined the talents of two of America's premier hard country singers, George Jones and Melba Montgomery, and featured the interplay of Dobro and pedal steel guitar.

George Jones was at the center of a honky-tonk resurgence in the early 1960s that stretched from his native Texas to California.[15] These years marked the maturing of the vocal style that made him one of the legendary singers of country music. Jones was born on September 12, 1931, in Saratoga, Texas, in the midst of a heavily forested area known as the Big Thicket and very near the sites of some of Texas's earliest oilfields. His working-class parents represented the moral and social dichotomy that often surfaced in rural southern families: his hard-working father (a log truck driver, an oil worker, a shipyard worker) often sought solace from disappointment and poverty in music and the bottle; his mother, on the other hand, found her comfort in sobriety and fundamentalist religion. George absorbed traits from both parents, a love for music from both of them, but, unfortunately, a fatal weakness for whiskey from his father. Though he sang in his mother's church (the Full Gospel Tabernacle Church in Kountze, Texas), he found the songs of the radio much more appealing. He listened faithfully to the *Grand Ole Opry*, where he discovered his first heroes in Bill Monroe and Roy Acuff. Acuff's influence was powerful in the singing of the early George Jones, and to the end of his life one could hear a trace of the Acuff sound, especially in Jones's phrasing on high notes.

The Jones family moved to Beaumont in 1942, following the lure of war-related jobs in that industrial sector of southeast Texas. As thousands of rural Texas families poured into cities like Beaumont, Port Arthur, Texas City, and Houston in search of defense work, the country music honky-tonk culture expanded to exploit their needs and satisfy their desires. Jones was not old enough to be a regular participant in this dance-hall culture, but he learned the songs that issued from it, and he developed an unquenchable desire to be a professional singer. In about 1943, when he was only twelve years old, Jones began singing on the streets of Beaumont, or anywhere that a crowd was willing to listen. A charming photograph from this period shows a serious, tow-headed youngster walking along a Beaumont street strumming a guitar.[16] From this point on, nothing but music could satisfy Jones, and

George Jones. Bill Malone personal collection.

by the time he was fourteen he was performing on radio stations in and near Beaumont. In 1948, he fell under the spell of Hank Williams, and that great singer became the kind of model and inspiration that Bill Monroe and Roy Acuff had earlier been. During a two-year stint in the US Marine Corps, from November 1951 to November 1953, Jones continued to sing as often as he could, particularly at a dance hall in Redwood City, California, near Camp Pendleton. When he returned to Beaumont, he was ready to begin his full-time professional career.

In January 1954, Jones made his first recordings for Starday,[17] a company only recently organized in Beaumont by Jack Starnes and Harold W. "Pappy" Daily. The early Starday records were made at Starnes's residence in Beaumont, and they provided a wonderful means of exposure for the wealth of talent that played in the area from Louisiana through southeast Texas to Houston. In fact, the label's first big hit was "Y'all Come," written and recorded by the former Texas schoolteacher and longtime radio personality Arlie [Arleigh] Duff. Jones's first recordings, "No Money in This Deal" and "You're in My Heart," were rollicking and slow respectively, an accurate prophecy of the alternating styles he featured for the rest of his career. A 1955 release, "Why Baby Why," made the national popularity charts, but Red Sovine and Webb Pierce's duet version was more successful. Nevertheless, Jones became sufficiently known and appreciated to be named to the cast of the *Louisiana Hayride*, where he stayed for three months before moving on to the *Grand Ole Opry* in August 1956. By the following year, he had followed his producer and manager Pappy Daily to the larger Mercury label, where he began carving out his own identity while making the first of his classic honky-tonk recordings. Under Daily's constant admonition to "sing like George Jones," he began casting off most of the vocal mannerisms borrowed from other singers. In turn, he developed the intense and unique style that subsequently enthralled generations of listeners. For the two or three minutes consumed by a song, Jones immersed himself so completely in its lyrics, and in the mood they conveyed, that the listener could scarcely avoid becoming similarly involved.

Although Jones excelled in the performance of novelty songs, such as "White Lightning" (his first number one *Billboard* hit), "Who Shot Sam," and "The Race Is On," he displayed his real strength in slower songs, particularly in the heart-wrenching complaints of unrequited or broken love. Some of his most powerful performances in this vein came in 1957 and 1958 when he recorded "Don't Stop the Music," "Just One More," and "Color of the Blues." Jones's searing emotional singing on these songs was almost undisciplined in its passion, but one could hear the stylistic traits that made him famous: the alternating low moans and high wails, the bending and lengthening of notes to almost incredible lengths, and the enunciation of words either with rounded, open-throated precision or through clenched teeth.

Jones's first real dominance in country music came in the early 1960s. Typically, he now sang in a lower and fuller register, and his managers began adding background voices and lusher instrumental accompaniment to his recordings. But no matter how full and engulfing these accoutrements might become, they could not blunt or hide his distinctiveness. He remained a hard country singer. Beginning with "The Window Up Above" in April 1960 and extending on through the 1960s with an almost unending stream of hits such as "Tender Years," "She Thinks I Still Care," "A Girl I Used to Know," and "Walk through This World with Me," Jones strengthened his popular appeal and solidified his reputation as "a singer's singer," winning the admiration of performers as disparate as Waylon Jennings, Elvis Costello, Emmylou Harris, James Taylor, Carter Stanley, and Merle Haggard.

George Jones's great Texas contemporary Ray Price proved not quite so faithful to hard country styles. From the mid-1960s on, Price increasingly cast his lot with the country-pop fashion that he had earlier so resolutely resisted. Nevertheless, during the rockabilly and early country-pop years, Price almost singlehandedly kept the hard country torch aflame and, in so doing, virtually created an industry of musicians who either wrote or played for him. He and his Cherokee Cowboys also created a highly electrified and infectiously rhythmic honky-tonk style that won them a legion of fans and was the envy of musicians everywhere.

Price was born near the East Texas community of Perryville in 1926, but he grew up in Dallas. He abandoned his intentions of becoming a veterinarian when he left North Texas Agricultural College (now the University of Texas at Arlington) in 1949 to pursue a career in music. He had already combined singing with student life, having sung in local clubs and on a radio barn dance in Abilene, Texas, in 1948. Like so many other American youth, such as George Jones, Price was mesmerized by the music of Hank Williams, which only strengthened his resolve to be a full-time professional. From 1949 to

1950, he appeared regularly on the *Big D Jamboree* and made his first recordings for Bullet, a small label in Nashville. In 1951, he began his association with Columbia Records and became close friends with his hero Hank Williams, a relationship that led to his being signed by the *Grand Ole Opry* in January 1952.

In these early professional years, and virtually up to 1956, Price's performing style remained very close to that of his mentor, Williams, and he recorded at least one song, "Weary Blues," that the Alabama legend had written for him. Price toured briefly with Williams's band, the Drifting Cowboys, before organizing his own group, the Cherokee Cowboys. Although he was never merely a carbon copy of Williams, the first dramatic evidence of a truly original Ray Price sound came with his recording in 1956 of "Crazy Arms." Written by the inventive California steel guitarist Ralph Mooney, the song was a hit of major proportions for Price, a refreshing reassertion of hard-core country music at a time of rockabilly ascendancy and a vehicle for the introduction of Price's shuffle-beat sound into country music.

In song after song—such as "City Lights," "My Shoes Keep Walking Back to You," "I've Got a New Heartache," "The Same Old Me," and "Invitation to the Blues"—Price adhered to an exciting and commercially winning formula. The pedal steel guitar and fiddles (played in the single-string rather than double-stop style) almost always took the lead passages, while a shuffling drum beat and an electric walking bass laid down a rhythm that no dancer could resist.[18] The sound drew some of its inspiration from Bob Wills, but it was made more distinctive through the thorough electrification of instruments, including the fiddles, in the Cherokee Cowboys' band. Vocally, the sound was dominated by Price's expressive singing and by the duet harmony that was almost always heard on the choruses of his songs—an innovation introduced to honky-tonk music by Price and George Jones. The style translated beautifully to phonograph recordings, but its proper milieu was the dance hall where would-be cowboys and cowgirls clung tightly to each other, following the electric, pulsating beat of the music as Price's songs of hurt and disappointment insinuated themselves into their consciousness.

Price's music touched the lives of millions of plain people who knew the singer only through his songs. It also financially enriched the lives of many professionals who developed a working relationship with Price. Virtually every major songwriter from the mid-1950s up to the early 1970s supplied him with songs, and many of them, in fact, began building their reputations through the exposure that he gave their songs. Roger Miller, Bill Anderson, Harlan Howard, Hank Cochran, Mel Tillis, Willie Nelson, and Kris Kristofferson made up only a portion of the roster of songwriters who profited from Price's great popularity. The roster of Cherokee Cowboys alumni also reads like a "Who's Who" of great country musicians. Price was once asked, after leaving the honky-tonk style for the more sedate field of country-pop, why he did not bring the Cherokee Cowboys back together. His reply that he could not afford them[19] becomes more understandable when it is recalled that at one time or another such musicians as Roger Miller, Willie Nelson, Johnny Paycheck (who was then known as Donnie Young), Tommy Jackson, Johnny Bush, Darrell McCall, and Buddy Emmons were employees of Price. There is no way, of course, to document the number of musicians, unsung and otherwise, who were influenced by the Ray Price sound. On occasion, hit records appeared, such as the Wilburn Brothers' "Which One Is to Blame" (1959) and Mel Tillis's "Heart over Mind" (1970), that bore the obvious marks of Price's shuffle beat; in dance halls throughout the country, especially in Price's native Texas, singers like Johnny Bush, Darrell McCall, Justin Trevino, Bobby Flores, Joe Paul Nichols, and Tony Booth even yet perform in fashions reminiscent of the Cherokee Cowboy. The survival of the Ray Price honky-tonk sound among numerous disciples, great and small, is all the more remarkable, given the fact that Price himself had abandoned the style much earlier. Price gradually lowered his singing voice to a more relaxed crooning register—one more appropriate to the supper club atmosphere that he came to favor. Most crucial, the pedal steel guitar and fiddles were replaced with the easy-listening sound of a string section and muted guitars. Price had experimented with the pop approach as early as 1957 in a religious album that featured the accompaniment of the Anita Kerr Singers and seventeen violins. "Burning Memories," in 1964, a good honky-tonk song written by Mel Tillis, aroused the ire of many traditionalists with its choral background and modest use of strings. Price's real transition to pop music, however, came in 1967 when he recorded "Danny Boy" with the backing of a forty-seven-piece orchestra. To the regret of many of his old-time fans, who felt disappointed if not betrayed, Price thereafter remained in the country-pop field. In 1970, he demonstrated his commercial mastery of that genre, too, when he recorded the first of several chart-making country-pop songs, "For the Good Times."

As Ray Price made his own personal and individualistic odyssey, the dynamic honky-tonk style that he had done so much to create and popularize continued to mature and evolve. Out on the West Coast, important young musicians made crucial contributions that helped fuel the hard country revival of the mid-1960s. The "California sound," as it came to be called, was the product of a coterie of musicians who often played together in the large number of clubs that dotted the landscape of the state. Ray Price influenced the musicians of California with his shuffle beat and high-duet choruses, but his style of fiddling had a lesser impact. Instead, California honky-tonk music was distinguished by the clarity and high-decibel sound of its electric and pedal steel guitarists. This was the sound, in fact, that guitarist Joe Maphis was thinking about when he wrote "Dim Lights, Thick Smoke, and Loud, Loud Music." Old-timers like Maphis, Jimmy Bryant, and Speedy West had originally set the standards to which the younger musicians aspired, but in the late 1950s and early 1960s, such guitarists as James Burton, Roy Nichols, Buck Owens, Ralph Mooney, and Tom Brumley, who had grown up listening to both rock-and-roll and country music, set their own special brands upon the developing music. Turning the volume of their Fender Telecaster guitars to an almost ear-splitting pitch, the guitarists played a single-string style that often featured sharp, staccato phrases known as "chicken picking." The overall result was a crisp, sparkling, electronic sound with an infectious beat.

Although Los Angeles played the most important role in the formation of the California sound—because of its powerful radio stations, its active club scene, and the presence there of Capitol Records—its leadership was seriously challenged by Bakersfield.[20] It was only fitting that Bakersfield should exert a strong influence. As an oil and cotton center in the San Joaquin Valley, it had attracted in the 1930s a heavy migration of Okies who had transplanted their love for rural music to California soil. By the early 1950s, a rash of honky-tonks provided a steady supply of country music for the working folk of the city. Musicians like Ferlin Husky, Tommy Collins, and Wynn Stewart worked in and out of the city for short periods, while such bandleaders as Billy Mize and Bill Woods built more permanent bases as house musicians in various clubs during the 1950s. Woods was an employer and father figure for many of the young musicians who congregated in Bakersfield.

It was as a guitarist in the Bill Woods Band that Buck Owens made his entrance into the Bakersfield music scene. Alvis Edgar "Buck" Owens was born in Sherman, Texas, in 1929, and grew up in Mesa, Arizona, where he had his first radio experience as a mandolin and guitar player. Owens moved to Bakersfield in 1951 and began working for Bill Woods and for other country musicians. He also became a busy session musician for Capitol Records, even though such work required frequent trips to Hollywood, about one hundred miles away. Owens remained a sideman during the early 1950s, and he was the lead guitarist on many of Tommy Collins's hit records during that period. Collins, whose real name was Leonard Raymond Sipes, wrote and recorded such successful songs as "You Better Not Do That," "You Gotta Have a License," and "High on a Hilltop."

Not content with his status as a sideman, Owens made his first solo recordings for a small label, Pep, in 1956. Two years later, he joined the prestigious Capitol label and, beginning with "Above and Beyond" (one of Harlan Howard's earliest successful compositions), was soon one of the hottest commercial properties of the period. Owens sang with a pleading tenor voice, and was joined on the choruses of songs by the even higher tenor sound of his fiddler-guitarist, Don Rich. Despite Owens's own background as a guitarist, he delegated most of the lead guitar work to Rich, who became one of the vital ingredients in the shaping of the Buck Owens sound. The steel guitar work on the early Buck Owens recordings was done by Ralph Mooney, an alumnus of Wynn Stewart's popular band and later a member of Waylon Jennings's group, the Waylors. During the peak years of Owens's popularity, however, his steel guitarist was Tom Brumley, a son of the famous gospel composer Albert E. Brumley. Owens and his band, the Buckaroos, created a sound that had the hard edge of honky-tonk combined with the bounce of rockabilly, a remarkably winning composite. Few singers have had the consistent string of hit records that Owens produced in the 1960s. During the decade, nineteen of his songs, including one instrumental, "Buckaroo," reached the number one position on the *Billboard* popularity charts. Although he recorded an occasional sad song, such as "Second Fiddle" or "Excuse Me, I Think I've Got a Heartache," his biggest successes were lively, upbeat numbers like "Act Naturally," novelties like "Who's Gonna Mow Your

Grass," or slow songs expressing affirmative or successful love such as "Together Again."

Owens was highly visible during the 1960s, first on his own syndicated television show, the *Buck Owens Ranch*, and then as cohost of *Hee Haw*, which was seen on over two hundred stations. He was such a dominating presence in American music that, in a euphoric moment in 1965, he took out a full-page ad in the leading music magazines expressing his undying loyalty to country music and pledging to perform no other style.[21] Like most pledges, it was soon broken. But for several years during the 1960s, the music of Buck Owens and the Buckaroos blew like a breath of sparkling fresh air over the country music landscape, reinvigorating hard country enthusiasts with its sharp, clearly delineated string band sound, its vocal harmony sung both high and hard, and the absence of multivoice vocal choruses. Owens's musicianship was so profitable that he branched out into other areas, establishing a publishing house, acquiring radio and television stations and real estate, and assuming the promotion of other acts such as the Hager Twins, his son Buddy Alan, Doyle Holley, and an instrumental group called the Bakersfield Brass. His holdings and investments became so extensive that some people began referring to Bakersfield as "Buckersfield."

It is poetically appropriate that the biggest superstar to emerge from the California firmament should be a product of Bakersfield. Merle Haggard was born near the city in 1937, only two years after his parents migrated from Checotah, Oklahoma.[22] His parents had met at an Oklahoma country dance, but his devout Church of Christ mother soon put a damper on such worldly merriment and on the fiddling that was so appealing to her husband. Haggard always cherished fond memories of the father whose musical gifts he inherited, but, unfortunately, their ties were severed by his father's death in 1946. Haggard grew up in a converted boxcar, a restless, wandering child whose mother had neither the time nor the power to control him. He eventually documented these early experiences in "Hungry Eyes," a testimonial to his hard-working parents and their Okie contemporaries, and in "Mama Tried," a tribute to his mother's love and sacrifice.

Mama's efforts were indeed in vain, and Haggard drifted into a life of petty juvenile delinquency, and from there into detention homes and reform school. He eventually wound up in San Quentin Prison in 1956, only nineteen years old and with a seemingly permanently

Merle Haggard. Bill Malone personal collection.

blighted life. Haggard, however, had not totally wasted his young years; he began perfecting his musical skills as a teenager, and he continued to pick and sing during his prison years. When he was released in 1960, he began trying to support a wife and growing family—one of several unsuccessful marriages—by working at odd jobs and playing at night and on weekends in such Bakersfield honky-tonks as the High Pockets, Blackboard, Lucky Spot, and Barrel House. As with many fledgling singers, Haggard's early sound reflected the styles of older performers, particularly those of his hero Lefty Frizzell and of Wynn Stewart, who was one of the most popular club performers on the West Coast.

Wynn Stewart gave Haggard his first big break as a professional performer. A native of Morrisville, Missouri, Stewart had a very successful stint as singer and bandleader for three years at the Nashville Nevada Club in Las Vegas. An occasional hit record on the Capitol label—such as "Waltz of the Angels," "Keeper of the Key," and "Wishful Thinking"—also contributed to his commercial viability and to his reputation among musicians who sought positions in his very prosperous band. Haggard began playing bass for Stewart in 1962 and also began singing an occasional number when the bandleader took breaks. Although Haggard had signed with Tally (a small California label) in 1961, he achieved only modest success until January of 1963, when he recorded a song written by Stewart called "Sing a Sad Song." It became his first chart-making record. The following year, he had an even bigger hit with Liz Anderson's "All My Friends Are Gonna Be Strangers," a song that named his band—the Strangers—and led to his signing with Capitol Records.[23]

Haggard's commercial progress to 1967 was steady but unspectacular, and his first real recognition came from his West Coast colleagues in the Country and Western Music Academy, who voted him most promising male vocalist in 1966 and best male vocalist the following year. The California-based organization also voted Haggard and Bonnie Owens the best duet act in country music for three consecutive years, 1965–1967. The year 1967 proved to be the beginning of a period of rapid ascent for Haggard, largely because he discovered the commercial potential of his prison record. His convict experience was rarely mentioned in his early promotional literature, but after 1967 it became a central theme in most stories dealing with Haggard, and it began to dominate the story line of many of his songs. The distorted stories dealing with Johnny Cash's alleged prison record—he had actually spent only two days in jail because of minor infractions—may have reminded Haggard of the age-old public fascination with bad men. More likely, the success of one of Haggard's recordings, "I'm a Lonesome Fugitive," convinced him that a market existed for songs about outlaws, convicts, and prison life. The song was written by Liz Anderson and seems to have been inspired by a popular television series called *The Fugitive*. Whatever its source, it became Haggard's first number one recording, and it was followed in the next couple of years by "Branded Man," "Sing Me Back Home," "Legend of Bonnie and Clyde," and "Mama Tried" (the theme of a little-known movie named *Killers Three*), all dealing with prison/bad-guy themes, all number one songs, and all written by Haggard.

Another factor, then, in Haggard's vault toward stardom was the blossoming of his writing abilities. He exhibited great sensitivity and skill in his treatment of a wide variety of topics ranging from prisons and ex-convicts to disappointed lovers and truck drivers. His simple and direct language, homely metaphors, and preoccupation with the lives of plain, everyday folk evoked comparisons with Woody Guthrie and led some observers to describe him as the "poet of the common man." Unlike Woody Guthrie's subjects, though, Haggard's common man was a middle-class worker who, while sometimes unemployed, as in "If We Make It through December," works hard, drinks beer, rejects welfare, takes a dim view of reformers, and supports his country right or wrong. Haggard's compassion came through most strongly in areas that touched upon his own life or upon his family's history. Like Johnny Cash, who seems to have influenced him greatly, Haggard was fascinated with the 1930s, so he frequently invited hoboes, railroad bums, and migratory workers to populate his songs. "Hungry Eyes" presents Haggard at his poetic and compassionate best; it will probably stand the test of time as his greatest song. Unlike the modern workers he also applauded, the characters described in "Hungry Eyes" work hard but do not succeed. In "Grandma Harp" and "The Roots of My Raising," Haggard lovingly discussed people and places central to his youth and to his parents' past, and in "They're Tearing the Labor Camps Down," he commented on the passing of an institution that made life bearable for many of California's Okies, about the closest he ever came to endorsing government social legislation.

Although Haggard was more preoccupied with social and historical topics than most writers, he did not ignore the other subjects that compose the country music repertory. There has been no better statement of unrequited love than "Today I Started Loving You Again," while "Sing Me Back Home," ostensibly a prison song, is really a poignant evocation of the nostalgic power of music. The beer-drinking genre is well represented by such songs as "The Bottle Let Me Down," "Swinging Doors," and "Back to the Barrooms," while alcoholism, the other side of the coin, is the subject matter of the beautiful "I Threw Away the Rose." And even in the often-hackneyed area of truck-driving music, Haggard rose well above the norm: "Movin' On" captures the aggressive excitement of long-distance trucking, while "White Line Fever" portrays its weariness. All in all, Haggard's songs typify country songwriting at its best.

Any emphasis on Haggard's writing should not divert our attention from his superb musicianship. As a singer, he had few peers, and as an instrumentalist and band leader, he exhibited continual growth and inventiveness over a period of fifty years and more. Haggard moved away quickly from the early imitativeness that most young singers display, although a trace of Lefty Frizzell always lingered in his phrasing and in his nasally resonant vibrato. Haggard could sound sweet and smooth, as he did on "Sing a Sad Song" in 1963, but he could also, if the occasion called for it, sound raucous, harsh, or strident. Few singers had such suppleness of voice. Although he forged his own unique style, Haggard remained loyal to his sources. Tribute albums and songs dedicated to Jimmie Rodgers, Bob Wills, and Lefty Frizzell attest to his respect for the giants of country music, while "Bill Woods of Bakersfield" and "Leonard" (about his old friend Tommy Collins) were loving recollections of two men who supported him early in his career. Haggard's admiration for Bob Wills sparked his interest in Emmett Miller, the minstrel-blues singer who influenced both Wills and Tommy Duncan. Most important of all, his interest in Wills affected the total instrumental sound favored by Haggard and the Strangers. The Strangers were best known for their classic California-style honky-tonk music marked by the pedal steel work of Norman Hamlett and the searing, blues-tinged phrasing of electric guitarist Roy Nichols. But the Strangers also went through a phase that included a retinue of horns along with the traditional string instruments, and they played what Haggard described as "country jazz." Haggard himself mastered the fiddle, a rare accomplishment for an adult musician, and he regularly included Bob Wills songs in his concerts. Merle Haggard's emergence in the 1960s was a development of major significance for country music because he contributed to both its economic resurgence and its stylistic revitalization. His creativity as an artist and musician fit solidly within the traditional framework he respected, demonstrating that one could be simultaneously hard country, original, and commercial.

Merle Haggard's career as a man who wrote most of the songs that he sang is not an unusual one. Country music has been blessed with an abundance of singer-songwriters. They, and the writers who have tried to parlay their craft into a full-time profession, were responsible for much of the growth and general acceptance that country music has enjoyed since World War II. With some striking exceptions, the writers have been southern-born men and women from rural or working-class backgrounds who drew upon their own experiences and observations to paint musical portraits of popular and commercial appeal. Increasingly, however, these experiences have come to be much like those known by people elsewhere. Thrown into a common crucible of military service and war, provided with expanded educational opportunities, and exposed to television and other homogenizing aspects of industrial capitalism, Americans everywhere began to exhibit a growing sameness of life. As musicians, country writers have heard and absorbed much from the other musical forms that have swelled around them, and such writers as Bob Dylan and Paul Simon have sometimes served as conscious models. Furthermore, the lure of the crossover record has often tantalized writers into seeking that which is broadly popular and commercial.

Nevertheless, country songwriters have not been merely borrowers; they have had much to say that is fresh and original. Like their contemporaries, the southern novelists, they have retained a sense of place that is refreshing in an age of ceaseless change and dislocation. Although no evidence suggests that William Faulkner ever recognized any kinship with the tunesmiths who proliferated around him, like the great Mississippi novelist, they always showed skill at "teasing the universal out of the particular."[24] They may have written about Carolina cotton fields or long, hot Texas roads, but they touched sensitive chords that rang true in the hearts of everyone. The "Green, Green Grass of Home" and "Harper Valley PTA" could be anywhere in the United States.

These country writers were truly part of the audience for whom they wrote. Although that audience has changed vastly in the more recent past, it remained basically working class with middle-class aspirations. Country song lyrics have been realistic in that they concern themselves with the petty details of human existence. They could therefore be as inconsistent and contradictory as the people whose values they expressed, describing life as it is, not as one might wish it would be.

Country songs, therefore, have demonstrated little consciousness of history, but instead tend to be intensely nostalgic. Private recollections of the past, often distorted by time and colored by romanticism or sentimentality (or put to the service of some present prejudice), appear frequently in country songs. Unpleasant remembrances of the past, as in Dallas Frazier's "California Cotton Fields," Dolly Parton's "In the Good Old Days When Times Were Bad," or Johnny Cash's "Five Feet High and Rising," sometimes compose the subject matter of country songs. One remarkable song written by Bobby Braddock—"I Believe the South's Gonna Rise Again"—ignored the lure of Confederate nostalgia and spoke positively about improved race relations and other signs of improvement in the late-twentieth-century South. Most writers, however, could not resist the temptation to cloak their songs with a veneer of romanticism that stressed the redemptive qualities of love that transcend suffering. In recalling her childhood as the daughter of a Kentucky coal miner, Loretta Lynn reminded her listeners that "We were poor but we had love."[25]

Familial love of this type lay at the center of the traditional scheme of values celebrated in country songs. While such precepts were often violated in both life and lyrics—home is abandoned, church is forsaken, laws are broken, husbands and wives separate, parents are neglected, and so on—the old-time code of conduct is nevertheless endorsed with great fervor. Familiar social relations, especially between men and women and adults and children, are reaffirmed. Male dominance was long taken for granted in country songs, even though men often seem rendered helpless by love unfulfilled or gone wrong. Traditional morality and the belief in the certainty of punishments and rewards are stressed, and even the sins most often discussed in country lyrics—drinking and cheating—were "traditional" transgressions, although the latter did not become a major preoccupation of country lyrics until the late 1940s.

Country lyrics have remained profoundly topical. Event songs, as such, are not as common today as they were in the 1920s, and writers are now more likely to concentrate on reactions to such phenomena as automation or war than on the concrete incidents themselves. Nevertheless, occasional songs such as "PT 109" or "Ballad of the Green Berets" climb into the charts, and ballads commenting on current events, such as the Kennedy assassination and school integration, have appeared with great frequency on small record labels. The grand master of the modern event song, Red River Dave McEnery, who wrote on such subjects as "Amelia Earhart's Last Flight" and "The Ballad of Emmett Till," was still turning out reams of topical material through the 1970s, dealing with everything from Watergate to the kidnapping of Patricia Hearst. Most writers, however, have shunned such explicit data and instead discuss general perceptions of the confusing world that forever seems to crowd around the "common man."

Although topicality has been a major concern of country songs, the songwriters have usually eschewed explicit political identification. Like country musicians as a whole, they tend either to be apolitical or to keep their opinions to themselves. Occasional songs complain about welfare programs or the Internal Revenue Service, and a few songs circulate that criticize political corruption (as in the Watergate affair) or Reaganomics. Both mainstream country and bluegrass writers, however, have generally endorsed establishment political positions, particularly in the realm of foreign affairs, and take a dim view of organized dissent. While country music's identification with national establishment norms reflected the changing political moods of the 1960s and early 1970s and was an indication of the conservatism of its audience and of the urge for "respectability" within the industry, this embracing of the status quo was a recent phenomenon in southern life. The 250,000 southerners who died in rebellion against the United States government from 1861 to 1865 are dramatic reminders that political orthodoxy has not always been considered a virtue in southern culture.

Politics has actually been of minor concern to the country writers. Compassion, on the other hand, and even tolerance for many of the foibles of humanity have been motivating impulses behind a multitude of country songs. Neglected old people, abandoned or mistreated children, and homeless hoboes and derelicts have always figured prominently in country songs. Drunkards are often treated with humor or scorn, but they are also made the objects of pity or sympathy. Some socially peripheral types have received sympathetic treatment in country lyrics. The condemned prisoner of "Sing Me Back Home," the prostitute in "The Son of Hickory Holler's Tramp," the black river tramp of "Catfish John," and the emotionally disturbed woman in "Delta Dawn" are modern examples of antisocial characters who have drawn the compassion of country writers. Clearly, no political intent underscores such concern. "Catfish John," for example, is idealized, not because he is black, but because he is a worldly wise old man who introduces a white boy to the joys of primitive river life. Country songwriters recognize and exploit the poetic appeal of such characters; seldom do they suggest that they be made the objects of public or legislative action.

Country songs, then, while frequently expressing compassion, have rarely been liberal in any conventionally defined sense. Johnny Cash in 1964 recorded a hard-hitting song about the Indian war hero, "The Ballad of Ira Hayes," who was tragically ignored during his postmilitary years, as well as an album devoted to the plight of American Indians that contained both his own compositions and those of other writers such as Peter La Farge; but, despite his reputation as "the Man in Black" (allegedly a sign of mourning for the injustices of the world), Cash gave no meaningful support to any of the other liberal crusades of the decade. Occasional country songs, such as "Harper Valley PTA," defended unconventional lifestyles (but not to the point of homosexuality or, usually, free love), and for five weeks in early 1968 a didactic song called "Skip a Rope" held the number one position on *Billboard's* country charts. This song indicted parents who set bad examples for their children by such acts as cheating on their income taxes and practicing racial discrimination. Country songs did sometimes protest—against job harassment or insecurity, hypocritical churchgoers, the high cost of living, declining moral standards, and a multitude of private ills and frustrations—but they generally remained skeptical of, or indifferent to, organized human solutions.

In country music, individuals are usually left alone to confront life. The failures are many, and some people surrender to become "Driftwood on the River" or rolling stones on the "Lost Highway." In despair or frustration, some turn to the bottle, often finding temporary relief but occasionally becoming a "prisoner to drink" (as in "Warm Red Wine") or finding their lives "Out of Control." Some men are "Almost Persuaded" by the charms of honky-tonk temptresses; others succumb to the lure of "The Other Woman"; while most yearn for the security and permanence of "A Good Woman's Love." The rambling life and the open road continue to be attractive options for country song protagonists. Truck-driving song popularity can be understood, in part, as an identification with a group who are perceived as exercising power (if only over a machine) while also enjoying the freedom of mobility. The related machismo urge, of course, is also strongly displayed in country lyrics. The tough guy pose, or the image of a man who enjoys complete mastery over women (if nothing else), is presumably a motif appealing to both men and women. Another venerable impulse that persists in country music is the desire to go back home—to a place that is comfortable because it is familiar—or to a mythical community like "Rocky Top," or "Luckenbach, Texas," where life and cares are simpler and more manageable. In song lyrics, as well as in the real life they attempt to portray, individuals often discover that their strength and will are feeble weapons in the battle against loneliness and pain; they therefore seek the solace of religion and the fortitude to take "One Day at a Time."

Whatever the emotion or impulse, country lyrics have addressed needs that all people have. But in a society where the open display of emotion is sublimated or considered to be in bad taste, country music has sometimes been denigrated as "soap opera" or worse. Country writers have shown no reluctance to discuss the pain, disappointment, and insecurity that sometimes touch everyone's life. Unselfconscious, rather than unsophisticated, country lyrics act as emotional cathartics and remind the listener that his or her private pain has been felt by other people.

Few writers have shown such skill at converting the private pains and public preoccupations of average people into commercially successful formulas as the men and women who congregated in Nashville in the late 1950s and early 1960s. The modern era of country songwriting began in about 1958 when Bill Anderson and Harlan Howard began supplying songs to Ray Price and other singers resisting the rock-and-roll tide. Anderson always sought a successful singing career, and he achieved it in 1962 and 1963 when his recordings of "Mama Sang a Song" and "Still" became major hits. Sometimes described as "Whispering Bill" because of his soft singing style, Anderson became well recognized because of his work as the host of television game shows, and his writing was sometimes forgotten. Few writers, though, have been so adept at exploiting homely sayings, metaphors, and clichés for commercial purposes (in "When Two Worlds Collide," cowritten with Roger Miller, Anderson borrowed a phrase from science fiction and made it fit into the scheme of lovers' incompatibility), and few have had so many big songs recorded by other singers. Anderson was born in South Carolina, but grew up near Atlanta and graduated from the University of Georgia—a fact that he tried to hide from his early Nashville contemporaries. The first evidence of his ability came in 1958 when Ray Price recorded "City Lights," a song about urban loneliness and anonymity that was *Billboard*'s number one country song for thirteen consecutive weeks. In the years that followed, songs like "The Tip of My Fingers" (for Roy Clark), "Once a Day" (for Connie Smith), and "Saginaw, Michigan" (for Lefty Frizzell) won him commercial acclaim and demonstrated his understanding of popular tastes. Anderson was still writing hit songs into the early 2000s.

Harlan Howard, reared in Detroit by Kentucky-born parents, was the acknowledged "king" of country songwriters, at least until the emergence of Kris Kristofferson in the early 1970s. Although he had written songs since he was twelve years old, none were published until the late 1950s, when he was living in Huntington Park, California, and working as a $90-a-week apprentice bookbinder. Johnny Bond published and recorded his first song, and Howard soon thereafter began writing songs for Wynn Stewart and Buck Owens. His first major hit, "Pick Me Up on Your Way Down," was written for Ray Price, who, however, passed it on to his friend Charlie Walker, a San Antonio singer and disc jockey, who recorded it and saw it become one of country music's honky-tonk classics. The song became popular almost simultaneously with two other Howard songs, "Heartaches by the Number," recorded by Ray Price, and "Mommy for a Day," recorded by Kitty Wells. Howard never seriously pursued a singing career, as did Anderson, but instead supplied a steady stream of songs for other singers such as Ernest Tubb (his boyhood idol), Ray Price, Patsy Cline, and Buck Owens. Owens, in fact, began his rise to fame singing songs written by Howard ("Above and Beyond," "Foolin' Around," and "Excuse Me, I Think I've Got a Heartache"). Howard's most successful song, "Heartaches by the Number," recorded in both popular and country music, grossed well over $50,000 for the writer's share alone. His songwriting earned him ten citations (awards of merit) from BMI in 1961 (a record) and well over $100,000 in that same year.

Howard moved to Nashville in 1960, at about the same time as did an old friend and songwriting buddy from California, Hank Cochran. Cochran was another southern boy, from Isola, Mississippi, who had drifted around from job to job before landing in Belle Gardens, California, in the mid-1950s, when he began writing songs for Pamper, a Nashville publishing house owned by Ray Price and Hal Smith. After his move to Nashville in January 1960, he began writing a series of very personal songs about hurting and loneliness such as Patsy Cline's huge hit "I Fall to Pieces" (cowritten with Howard), "Don't Touch Me," "Don't You Ever Get Tired of Hurting Me," and "A Little Bitty Tear" (recorded by the famous folk balladeer Burl Ives). Early in 1960, Cochran met a young musician fresh from Texas, Willie Nelson, who was almost starving while he tried to pitch his songs to publishers. Cochran, Nelson, and other fledgling musicians such as Mel Tillis met often at Tootsie's Orchid Lounge on Broadway (just back of the Ryman Auditorium), where they drank, commiserated with each other, and tried out their songs on Tootsie and the bar patrons. Cochran secured a staff writer's job at Pamper for Nelson and arranged for the struggling writer/singer to receive royalty advances while waiting for his songs to be published and recorded.

Willie Nelson was born on April 30, 1933, in the little Central Texas town of Abbott.[26] Like most Texas country musicians of his era, Nelson absorbed music from a wide variety of cultural and ethnic sources. He and his sister Bobbie, his longtime pianist, grew up singing gospel songs in the Baptist Church, but he also played in honky-tonks all over the state. Before he was a teenager he began playing guitar in the German/Czech polka bands in the "Bohemian" communities of Central Texas; he listened to the country music of Bob Wills, Ernest Tubb, and Floyd Tillman, and kept his ear glued to the radio, where he heard jazz and vintage pop music. All of these musical forms contributed to the shaping of the Willie Nelson style and repertory.

Despite his skills as a guitarist and unorthodox singer (with his blues inflections, distinctive nasal intonation, and off-the-beat phrasing), Nelson's ticket to Nashville came through his songwriting. While working the honky-tonks of Houston, Nelson wrote and sold outright two songs, "Family Bible" (recorded by Claude Gray) and "Night Life" (a big hit for Ray Price), which made him just enough spending money to finance the trip to Nashville. In Nashville, his lean and struggling period came to an end when singers began to record his songs: Billy Walker, "Funny How Time Slips Away," 1960; Faron Young, "Hello Walls," 1961; and Patsy Cline, "Crazy," 1961. His days as a recognized singer and superstar were still far in the future, but, as a writer, he became valued by every singer in the country music business. The presence of Willie Nelson, Hank Cochran, and Harlan Howard on the Pamper roster made that company one of the most powerful in the country music industry. Its catalogue eventually became the property of the giant Tree Publishing Company.

Nelson, Cochran, Howard, Roger Miller, Bill Anderson, and Mel Tillis all contributed to country music's economic resurgence and stylistic revitalization in the early 1960s. By the middle of the decade, a number of other writers, such as Dallas Frazier, Billy Edd Wheeler, Curly Putman, Sonny Throckmorton, Bobby Braddock, and Tom T. Hall, had moved country music even closer to its roots with their story songs and nostalgic, but often bittersweet, evocations of rural and small-town life. The recollections were sometimes disquieting, as in the case of Bobbie Gentry's superhit "Ode to Billie Joe"; grim, as in John D. Loudermilk's "Tobacco Road"; tongue-in-cheek, as in Wheeler's "Ode to the Little Brown Shack Out Back"; ambivalent, as in Putman's "As Long as the Wind Blows"; but most often affectionate or brutally honest, as in Putman's "Green, Green Grass of Home." Most of the talented new writers were intelligent young men who combined a cultivated sophistication, acquired in college or military experience, with an empathy and understanding of the plain people with whom they grew up and for whom they wrote.

Tom T. Hall was a tall-tale spinner whose mode of communication was music.[27] Born in Olive Hill, Kentucky, Hall began his career as a teenage bluegrass musician and disc jockey. He began writing songs during his military tenure in Germany in the late 1950s, and after he returned to the United States in 1961, he resumed his former life as a musician/radio announcer on a series of radio stations in Kentucky and West Virginia. In 1964, one of his compositions, "DJ for a Day," reached the ears of Jimmy Key of Newkeys Music in Nashville. After Jimmy C. Newman's recording of the song reached number one on the *Billboard* charts, Hall made plans to move to Nashville to pursue the writer's craft. He brought to the profession of songwriting a keen sensitivity to the problems and interests of plain people, a gift for storytelling, and an economical and direct style of writing influenced by his reading of Ernest Hemingway. He was at home in all realms of country expression, and he wrote two of the earliest songs about the Vietnam War ("Hello Vietnam" and "Mama, Tell Them What We're Fighting For"). His genius, though, lay in his almost conversational narratives of everyday life, somehow capturing "the subtlest nuances of the men in southern towns who sit around feed stores and filling stations swapping stories with the county agent and the butane man."[28] His first superhit came in 1968 when Jeannie C. Riley recorded her sassy version of "Harper Valley PTA," a song about small-town hypocrisy.

Now freed to pursue his craft full time, Hall began turning out a steady stream of journalistic and highly commercial songs, mostly about his own experiences or observations—and mostly recorded by himself: "A Week in a Country Jail," "Ballad of Forty Dollars" (about a gravedigger's mixed feelings as he buries a man who owed him money), "Homecoming" (one of the best songs yet written about a musician's days on the road), "Trip to Hyden" (about the bleakness of life in a Kentucky coal community), "Old Dogs, Children, and Watermelon Wine" (about a wise old man he met in a lounge in Miami), "The Year That Clayton Delaney Died" (Hall's personal favorite, about a gifted Kentucky musician who had influenced him), and many others.

Hall captured a new audience for country music and gave the music new economic strength by restoring the old tradition of storytelling. That impulse remained in country music, but it was accompanied increasingly in the late 1960s and early 1970s by a torrent of very personal songs—some in the vein of Hank Cochran's "Don't Touch Me" and some in an almost stream-of-consciousness mode like John Hartford's "Gentle on My Mind")—that dealt with intimate relationships, individual soul-searching, and passionate quests for identity and self-fulfillment. Such writers as Mickey Newbury, Rodney Crowell, John Hartford, Shel Silverstein (a children's poet, cartoonist, and *Playboy* columnist), Bobby Braddock, and Kris Kristofferson were poets whose perceptions were drawn from life and literature and from exposure to other forms of music. Hartford was a wondrous blend of old-time and contemporary influences: schooled in bluegrass music as a fiddler and five-string banjoist, inspired by Uncle Dave Macon, fascinated by the lure of the Mississippi riverboats, and a free spirit whose dress and lifestyle reflected the counterculture of the 1960s. Robert Valentine "Bobby" Braddock, on the other hand, had a much less colorful past, but he contributed songs that covered the full gamut of human emotions and touched upon the most basic themes of country music. The son of a Florida citrus grower and a former piano player in a rock-and-roll band, Braddock brought a cerebral approach and a rare liberal disposition to country songwriting: he was one of the few outspoken Democrats in Nashville. Beginning in the mid-1960s with songs like "D-I-V-O-R-C-E" and "Something to Brag About," Braddock continued to write chart-making songs for the next fifty years.[29]

Kris Kristofferson was also a mixture of seemingly contradictory experiences: a military-trained person with liberal inclinations. As the son of a professional Air Force man—born in Brownsville, Texas, and reared in California—Kristofferson received an introduction to the world that made it difficult for him to identify strongly with any specific region or class. On the other hand, a childhood affection for the music of Hank Williams inspired an undying desire to write songs, while his liberal and worldly education contributed to a tolerance and compassion for plain, working people. No country songwriter had ever been quite like him. He was a Rhodes Scholar who prepared for a career as a professor of English literature, but then changed direction and spent five years in the army, working mainly as a helicopter pilot, with plans for settling down at West Point as an officer and teacher. Two weeks before his assignment to the military academy, in June 1965, he went to Nashville, largely through the encouragement of songwriter Marijohn Wilkin, and decided to try his hand at full-time writing.

Kristofferson went through the "starving years" that seem almost a prerequisite for country songwriters, but in 1969 his first big breakthrough came when Roger Miller recorded his "Me and Bobby McGee"—a song since recorded by many people. He began his own recording career with Monument Records and, in rapid fashion during the next couple of years, saw several of his songs recorded with great success by country singers: Johnny Cash, "Sunday Morning Coming Down"; Ray Price, "For the Good Times"; Bobby Bare, "Come Sundown"; Sammi Smith, "Help Me Make It through the Night." The high point of his career, and almost a turning point for country music, was the selection of "Sunday Morning Coming Down" in 1970 as the CMA's Song of the Year. Wearing shoulder-length hair and bell-bottom suedes, and mumbling his acceptance of the award for a song that seemed clearly about a drug hangover, Kristofferson stunned many viewers and music-industry people, who swore he was stoned (Kristofferson later replied that he was merely tired and nervous when he walked to the stage). Kristofferson's lyrics spoke often of loneliness, alienation, and pain, but they also celebrated freedom and honest relationships, and in intimate, sensuous language that had been rare in country music. The songs of Kristofferson, Hartford, Crowell, and their contemporaries certainly represented a new departure for country music. Sometimes self-consciously poetic, the new writers were probably more important for what they said, rather than for how they said it: they opened up new realms of expression for country singers and writers.

The emergence of a "new breed" of songwriters in country music was paralleled by other significant departures from the traditional norms. The image, if not the outright fact, of a music dominated by adult male white Protestants has been severely shaken since the early 1960s. As will be discussed in chapter 11, young musicians have made major inroads into country music, bringing both innovative ideas and a commitment to older forms. Women have also emerged as superstars with independent identities, while at least one African American, Charley Pride, has achieved great fame and popularity as a country singer. Since Patsy Cline's trailblazing performances in the early 1960s, women have increasingly built solo careers apart from male companions or family groups; they have almost completely cast off the roles thought appropriate for women singers (cow girls, Sunbonnet Sues, rustic comediennes); and they have increasingly sung about subjects once deemed unsuitable for women.

Probably the most important departure taken by women entertainers has been in their growing independence and assertion of artistic control. Gail Davies can be remembered for many important contributions to country music, including the writing and performance of such superbly crafted songs as "Grandma's Song" and "Someone Is Looking for Someone Like You." Her most important gift to her country music sisters, though, was demonstrating that they could shape their own recording sound. Born Patricia Gail Dickerson in Broken Bow, Oklahoma, but reared in Washington State, Davies did a short stint in Los Angeles as a jazz singer, but then moved to Nashville in 1976. Just three years later, after signing with the Warner Brothers label, she began producing her own recordings, and in the process, she became a role model for other young women who were beginning their own careers.

Women singers varied in style and public persona. Connie Smith, for example, was a beautiful woman, but her success flowed from her straight-ahead emotional singing, and not from any stage histrionics or unconventional repertoire. Her pre-professional biography was textbook working class. She was born Constance June Meador in Elkhart, Indiana, on August 14, 1941, but spent much of her growing-up years in West Virginia and Ohio. She suffered from an alcoholic and abusive father and, after her mother's second marriage, grew up surrounded by thirteen brothers and sisters. She understandably sought refuge in music, and, fortunately, was heard singing one day in August

1963 by Bill Anderson at a talent show at the Frontier Ranch Park near Columbus, Ohio. Through Anderson's influence, she appeared about one year later at Ernest Tubb's *Midnight Jamboree* show, broadcast live from his record shop in Nashville, and soon after won a record contract from Chet Atkins at RCA. At a subsequent session on July 16, 1964, she recorded Anderson's "Once a Day" and saw it debut as number one on the country record charts, a distinction that no other first recording has ever achieved in the history of country music.

Distinguished by clear enunciation and a passionate singing style, Smith produced a long string of chart-making songs (such as "Then and Only Then" and "Cincinnati, Ohio") and won admission to the *Grand Ole Opry* in 1965. Though her producers often packaged her as a country-pop performer, Smith's heart always lay with the songs written by Dallas Frazier, Bill Anderson, and other hard country writers, and she took pride in the steel guitar stylings of Weldon Myrick that helped define her sound. The great gospel hymn "How Great Thou Art" was, however, her favorite song, and she always used it as the concluding number in her concerts. The marvel of her career is that she never achieved the superstar status enjoyed by Dolly Parton and other contemporaries, but she did win their respect and admiration, and her artistic contributions eventually won her admission to the Country Music Hall of Fame.

Unlike Connie Smith, some women country singers increasingly seemed emboldened to project a sexiness that their sisters (and brothers) of the past would have found scandalous, and they often sang about the experience, and even joy, of sex with unprecedented openness. Jeannie C. Riley was tough and spunky in her performances of such songs as "Harper Valley PTA" and "The Girl Most Likely," but she raised more eyebrows with the miniskirts and go-go boots that she then wore in her concerts. The honky-tonk angel, it seemed, had become a public performer. Fourteen-year-old Tanya Tucker, though, was even more seductive when she began her career in 1972 as a "country Lolita," combining childish innocence with playful sexuality. Dressed in skintight pantsuits, punctuating her songs with Elvis-like body movements, and singing in a style and voice far beyond her years, Tanya evoked audience responses that the young girl probably did not always understand. It was not until the end of the 1970s, when an attempt was made to market her as a rock singer, that she and her managers began consciously to build the image of a brazen sex queen:

posters showed her standing on six-inch spike heels and standing tightly enveloped in a red Spandex jumpsuit. The rock audience, however, remained unresponsive, and Tucker soon moved away from this sexually aggressive posture. The most open display of sexuality among women country singers appeared in the Las Vegas performances of Barbara Mandrell and Dolly Parton, both marked by suggestive dance routines and revealing costumes, although Parton certainly moved into a bold territory never previously occupied by women singers when she played the role of a madam in the musical *The Best Little Whorehouse in Texas.*

The lyrics sung by women also projected a greater boldness. Sammi Smith, for example, asked her lover to remain with her through the night (in Kristofferson's "Help Me Make It through the Night"), as did Linda Hargrove in "Just Get Up and Close the Door." Hargrove was even more explicit in "Mexican Love Songs" when she spoke of waking up with a hangover next to a big cowboy that she'd only met the night before. Tanya Tucker sang "Would You Lay with Me (in a Field of Stone)," and Barbara Mandrell moved into an even greater forbidden zone when, in "Burning the Midnight Oil," she spoke of cheating on her husband. Hargrove's songs were probably the boldest of those mentioned, because they were her own compositions; the others were written by men. Hargrove was nevertheless not alone as a female writer of songs that expressed a type of womanly independence. Both Loretta Lynn and Dolly Parton often spoke up for the right of women to be free and honestly expressive.

The examples of honesty displayed in some women's country performances should not obscure the fact that "revolutions" proceed slowly in country music. For the most part, women performers still championed traditional male-female relationships and usually endorsed the idea that a man's frailties should be tolerated and his "good woman" should remain faithful to him. Woman's chief domain still seemed to be the home, and her basic roles were presumed to be the preservation of its sanctity and the nurturing of her family. Women could and did admit their need for sexual satisfaction, but implicit in this new honesty was the idea that sexuality was a weapon that a woman should exploit in her relations with men. The presumption of woman as sex object remained largely unchallenged. Women country singers, of course, violated such precepts constantly—they did not "stand by their men" through thick and thin; they did not defer to the leadership of the "stronger sex"; and they certainly did not remain in their homes—but they publicly, and in their songs, generally adhered to the myth of domesticity.

The central fact about women country singers did not lie in the "rebellion" that their songs or performing images occasionally conveyed. Jeannie C. Riley, for example, spent several years—particularly after she "found the Lord"—trying to shed the bad-girl image and memories of miniskirts that became attached to her during her "Harper Valley PTA" days. Their singing was most strongly marked by the influences that came from other areas of American music; very few of them, frankly, sounded country. Such singers as Dottie West (whose greatest success came through her duet performances with Kenny Rogers), Crystal Gayle, Lynn Anderson, Donna Fargo, Barbara Fairchild, or Sylvia (her sole performing title) were virtually indistinguishable from contemporary pop singers. Such older, down-to-earth singers as Kitty Wells, Jean Shepard, and Melba Montgomery were heard infrequently (and almost never on the Top Forty programs), and even those bona fide rural/mountain girls, Loretta Lynn and Dolly Parton, moved progressively toward the smooth countrypolitan sound. Down-home or hard country performances did sometimes appear in the repertories of such singers as Shelly West, Melba Montgomery, Reba McEntire, Lacy J. Dalton, Margo Smith (who occasionally demonstrated that yodeling was not a totally lost art), and Jeanne Pruett (whose version of the pure country "Satin Sheets" topped the charts in 1973). Most young women singers, however, reflected the sounds and phrasing of soul, rock, and pop musicians, except for an occasional singer like Emmylou Harris who seemed more in the mold of Joan Baez and the urban folk singers.

No one was more instructive of the kinds of influences then working on the young women than Loretta Lynn's talented sister, Brenda Gail Webb—better known as Crystal Gayle. Crystal grew up in Wabash, Indiana, after her family had left the coal country of eastern Kentucky. She scarcely knew her country-singing sister until Loretta's first records were released in 1960. By that time, Crystal had spent much time listening to pop singers, such as Barbra Streisand and Lesley Gore, who were active in her own day. She had no real identification with the Kentucky mountains, and one can scarcely imagine her singing or writing a song like "Coal Miner's Daughter." Instead, with such songs as "Don't It Make My Brown Eyes Blue" and "I'll Get Over You,"

Crystal Gayle cast her lot with country-pop music and a style of clear, modulated, and slightly affected phrasing that bears absolutely no similarity to that of her famous sister.

While her singing may have lost some of its rough edges, Loretta Lynn always exhibited the traits of her rural heritage. Along with two other authentic rural-bred girls, Tammy Wynette and Dolly Parton, she achieved a superstardom that no other woman—including her mentor, Patsy Cline, and country's first "queen," Kitty Wells—had ever enjoyed. Because of her best-selling autobiography, *Coal Miner's Daughter*,[30] and the popularly acclaimed movie that came from it, Loretta's story is probably the best known of any country singer's: birth in a bleak coal community called Butcher Holler (near Paintsville, Kentucky); marriage at the age of fourteen; a move to the state of Washington in about 1951; her early days as a singer in the clubs and grange halls of her adopted state; her first recording of "I'm a Honky Tonk Girl" on the Zero label in 1960, and her barnstorming car trip with her husband, Doolittle, from radio station to radio station pushing the song; the early struggling days in Nashville and appearances on the Wilburn Brothers' television show; and, finally, the zooming career that followed her first big Decca hit (the appropriately named "Success") in 1962. Starting out with a honky-tonk sound that bore a strong resemblance to that of Kitty Wells, Loretta gradually developed her own unique style and began honing her talents as a writer. On the road to her selection as the CMA's Entertainer of the Year in 1972—she was the first woman to receive the award—she recorded a number of songs, mostly self-written, that spoke for working-class women in a way that no ardent feminist could ever do. With such "feisty" songs as "Don't Come Home a-Drinkin' (with Lovin' on Your Mind)," "You Ain't Woman Enough (to Take My Man)," "Fist City," "One's on the Way," and "The Pill" (an endorsement of birth control), she became "the spokeswoman for every woman who had gotten married too early, gotten pregnant too often, and felt trapped by the tedium and drudgery of her life."[31] Loretta also became a household word in American popular culture, highly visible because of her frequent appearances on television and in the pages of magazines and newspapers and beloved because of her disarming honesty and simple country charm.

Tammy Wynette became extraordinarily popular with a message radically different from that of Loretta Lynn. One finds few of the feisty, talking-back-to-men songs in her repertory, other than "Your

Tammy Wynette. Bill Malone personal collection.

Good Girl's Gonna Go Bad," which was recorded soon after her career began. Instead, Tammy will always be identified with one powerfully commercial song, "Stand by Your Man," that feminists denounced as an outrageous display of female submission. Tammy always denied that the song counseled such abject surrender to masculine dominance, and, indeed, her three divorces and one annulment suggest that the philosophy exerted no real power over her own life. The title of another one of her hit songs, "D-I-V-O-R-C-E," best summed up the reality of her life, although as a true romanticist, she clung to the philosophy of still another song, "Till I Get It Right."

Born Virginia Wynette Pugh in Itawamba County, Mississippi (near the Alabama line) in 1942,[32] Tammy grew up on her grandparents' cotton farm, working in the fields and dreaming of a career as a singer. After the collapse of her first marriage, she decided to turn her fantasy into reality. She moved with three small children to Birmingham, enrolled in a beauty college, and began singing wherever she could gain a hearing—eventually at a local television station on a very early morning show. In 1966, she moved to Nashville and began making the rounds of the record companies before finally winning a successful audition with Billy Sherrill and Epic Records. Her first recording, "Apartment Number Nine," was moderately successful, but her second release, "Your Good Girl's Gonna Go Bad," climbed into the charts, and a duet recording with David Houston, "My Elusive Dreams," became her first number one song. Her commercial ascent was spectacular, and "Stand by Your Man," recorded in August 1968, became the biggest-selling single ever recorded by a woman. Tammy gained immense public exposure when the song became part of the sound track of the movie *Five Easy Pieces*. Her marriage to George Jones in 1968 brought her even greater publicity, and as "Mr. and Mrs. Country Music," pursuing solo careers and singing duets together, the two singers profited greatly from the association with each other. Artistic compatibility, however, could not save the turbulent marriage, and Jones's acute alcoholism eventually drove a wedge between them that resulted in divorce in 1975. The soap opera qualities of Tammy's life—chronic illness and marital disappointment—seemed only to endear the singer even more to her many fans. Her clear, expressive, pleading voice tore at the emotions and pulled the listeners into her orbit of personal experience, making them feel that her songs of hurt and loneliness, which were somehow tempered by hope, mirrored both their own and the singer's lives.

Dolly Parton's prominence in American popular culture, and indeed throughout the world, should not obscure the facts of her rural-mountain origins and of her thorough immersion in country music culture.[33] She was one of twelve children born to a poor mountain couple in the hills near Sevierville, Tennessee. No ad writer or Hollywood script could create a story more appealing in its rags-to-riches qualities or in its depiction of her transition from folk simplicity to worldly sophistication. Dolly inherited an affinity for music from both sides of her family, and her mother was a singer of ballads and old-time

Dolly Parton. Bill Malone personal collection.

songs. As a very small child, she made up songs that she then dictated to her mother; she sang in her grandfather Owens's local Church of God congregation; and she was appearing on the Cas Walker television show in Knoxville by the time she was ten years old. Through the influence of an uncle who was then stationed in an army camp in Louisiana, she even made a record in 1959, when she was only thirteen:

a song called "Puppy Love" recorded on Eddie Shuler's Goldband label in Lake Charles, Louisiana. Dolly was already a seasoned performer, then, when she set out to Nashville by bus on the day after her high school graduation.

Within a few months after her arrival in 1964, Dolly had secured a recording contract with Fred Foster at Monument Records and had met her future husband, Carl Dean. Monument wasted a couple of years trying to market her as a pop-rock singer, but then in 1967 let her cut a country record called "Dumb Blonde." Its writer, Curly Putman, had also written Tammy Wynette's "My Elusive Dreams." She joined Porter Wagoner in that same year as his "girl singer" but soon moved beyond that subordinate status to become a featured performer on his show and one of the most striking personalities in country music. Through Wagoner's influence, she moved to the RCA label, and though her superhits—such as "Joshua"—did not begin appearing until 1971, she did experience success as a soloist and as an award-winning duet singer with Wagoner.

Parton's appeal was the result of a fortuitous combination of physical attractiveness, singing talent, and a genius for song composition. Dressing extravagantly in blond wigs, heavy makeup, and a profusion of jewelry, and wearing costumes that dramatically displayed her bountiful physical attributes, Parton not only caused people to look at her, she also fulfilled the fantasies of a childhood marked by material deprivation. As a singer, she possessed a flexible soprano voice capable of soaring into the piercing, high-pitched yodel of "Muleskinner Blues" or of descending to the wistful, plaintive sound heard on "Coat of Many Colors." As a songwriter, she has had few peers in country music, bearing a strong comparison with Merle Haggard in her wide range of interests and in her facility with a diverse array of idioms. Her compositions encompass virtually every major theme in country music, and at least three songs—"To Daddy," "Just Because I'm a Woman," and "Down from Dover"—grapple with the problems of contemporary women in sensitive and compelling ways. Her most interesting songs are those that draw upon her mountain folk beginnings—sometimes rhapsodically affectionate like "Tennessee Mountain Home" or rowdy like "Traveling Man," but more often bittersweet like "In the Good Old Days When Times Were Bad" or her masterpiece, "Coat of Many Colors." "Coat of Many Colors" is a tender recollection of a jacket made of rag patches and of the love her "mother sewed in every stitch."

It is no wonder that Porter Wagoner was bitterly disappointed when Dolly left him in 1974 to pursue an independent career, but she had already actually outgrown his show. She won the CMA's Female Vocalist of the Year Award in 1975 and 1976, and in the spring of the latter year she became the first woman country singer to obtain her own syndicated television show, carried in 130 markets. The year 1976 also marked the beginning of her all-out campaign to achieve identity as a pop singer, a move that evoked great controversy within the country music industry and among her fans. Dolly never abandoned the singing of country songs, but her arrangements and repertory shifted heavily toward middle-of-the-road and pop material. Most important of all, her interests expanded well beyond the performance of music and into the realms of television and movie making, taking her into areas of public awareness where few country-derived entertainers have gone.

While women after 1960 were challenging the dominance once enjoyed by men in country music, other "new people" were beginning to trickle into the business as singers, songwriters, and musicians. The music's great commercial expansion lured talented newcomers who whittled away at country music's "Anglo-Protestant" consensus. Catholics, Jews, Mexicans, and other "ethnic" groups began to show up as sidemen and -women in bluegrass and country bands, and particularly in country-rock groups, where a greater tolerance for beliefs and diverse lifestyles existed. At least one Jewish cowboy, Kinky Friedman, pursued a career in country music with an outrageous, irreverent style of humor and a band called the Texas Jewboys. Kinky profited from his involvement in the active Austin musical scene but was particularly popular in New York City, where he performed often at the progressive country bar the Lone Star Café. When he wasn't singing or campaigning for public office in Texas, Kinky also turned out a torrent of detective novels that starred a supersleuth named Kinky.

Cajun musicians, of course, had never been absent from country music as both singers and instrumentalists, but the dynamic singer/fiddler Doug Kershaw, from Tiel Ridge, Louisiana, enjoyed more national exposure than any of his French-American colleagues had ever won. Kershaw had experienced an earlier career in the late 1950s with his brother Rusty (as the team of Rusty and Doug), a frenetic act that combined rockabilly and Cajun music. The duo introduced the song "Louisiana Man," written by Doug Kershaw, which was a richly

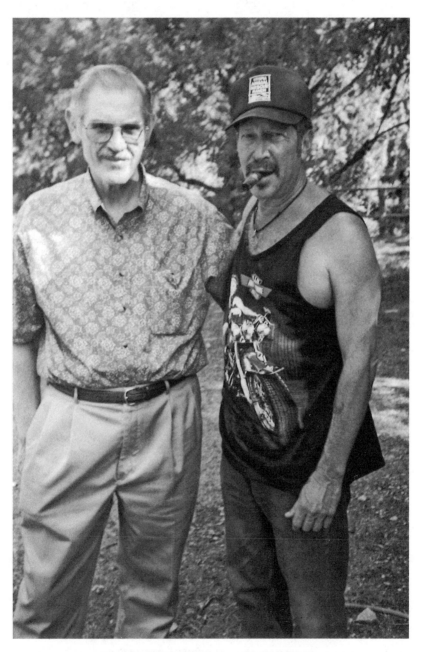

Bill Malone (left) and Kinky Friedman (right). Bill Malone
personal collection; courtesy of Bobby Malone.

evocative song about Cajun swamp life of southwest Louisiana and a tribute to their deceased father. Doug Kershaw returned to music as a solo act in 1970, this time with long hair; a reputation as the "Cajun Hippie"; and an exuberant style and repertory that embodied Cajun, rock, and country forms of music. Buoyed by the support of Johnny Cash, who featured him on his national television show, Kershaw began reaching a horde of young fans all over America.

Probably more significant than the emergence of Doug Kershaw as a quasi-country musician was the rise to commercial prominence of two Mexican American country performers, Freddy Fender and Johnny Rodriguez. Chicano musicians, of course, had sometimes played in country bands ever since the 1930s, but only rarely—and then usually in a local context—did a performer from such a background attempt a career as a solo country performer. Fender and Rodriguez emerged in the context of the increasingly tolerant racial atmosphere of the 1960s and in a region of the country—South Texas—where Mexican and Anglo cultural forms had often intermixed. Obviously, they also profited from the precedent set by the black country star Charley Pride (discussed below). Freddy Fender was really Baldemar Huerta from Weslaco, Texas, and he, like Doug Kershaw, had had an earlier career in the 1950s as a rock-and-roll singer, when his "Wasted Days and Wasted Nights" achieved moderate success. A Louisiana prison term for possession of marijuana destroyed his first career, but he returned to a successful professional career in 1975, this time as a country singer, with a very popular bilingual version of "Before the Next Teardrop Falls."

Fender was preceded by Juan Raul Davis "Johnny" Rodriguez from Sabinal, Texas, whose attachment to country music seemed much firmer and whose loyalty to the form has been more enduring. Rodriguez was a disciple of Merle Haggard, and his early records show a strong trace of the California singer's style. Rodriguez bore virtually no stylistic evidence of Tejano or other Mexican-ethnic forms of music but instead carried the influence of the cowboy-kicker culture of South Texas and of the honky-tonk and western swing bands that thrived in the region. Tom T. Hall heard him singing at Happy Shahan's Alamo Village in Brackettville, Texas, and eventually hired him as a guitarist for his band. Rodriguez's first hit record in 1972, for Mercury, was written by Tom T. Hall's brother, Hillman, and was a dyed-in-the-wool honky-tonk song called "Pass Me By." Rodriguez maintained this hard-edged, beer-drinking style through several releases while also mixing a few Spanish verses with the English lyrics (as in "Jealous Heart"). But by the mid-1970s he had moved toward a smoother, easy-listening sound. It is not hard to see why he and/or his managers made this decision. Rodriguez was strikingly good looking with a boyish Latin charm and was virtually the first potential youth sex symbol that country music had ever had—he was only twenty when his first record was made, and he was often featured with Tanya Tucker in concerts. The promise of a major crossover into pop music was never realized, and Rodriguez survived, first, a bout with drugs in the early 1980s, and then a murder charge on August 29, 1998 (the charge was reduced to manslaughter, and he was declared innocent on the grounds of self-defense). Through periods of personal adversity, most of it self-imposed, Rodriguez somehow managed to keep his career intact, and he edged back somewhat toward the hard country, Texas style of music on which he was nurtured.

The man who did most to open the doors to new ethnic or nonwhite talent was the remarkable Charley Pride. The black contributions to country music are too well known to warrant repetition here, although we should be reminded that Charley Pride was not the first black "star" of the genre. DeFord Bailey, a diminutive and partially crippled harmonica player, was on the *Grand Ole Opry* from 1925 to 1941 and was one of the most popular and frequently scheduled performers on the show.[34] One of the pleasant by-products of Charley Pride's ascendancy was the search for earlier black country musicians and the consequent rediscovery of Bailey.

When Pride made his first RCA recordings in 1965, the rhythm-and-blues legend Ray Charles had already made his groundbreaking LP *Modern Sounds in Country and Western Music,* a collection that introduced country music to a broader middle-class audience. According to their own testimonies, Charles and Pride both listened to the *Grand Ole Opry* when they were growing up, and both expressed an affection for country music. Charles's popular versions of such songs as "Born to Lose" and "I Can't Stop Loving You" were done in the singer's famous soul style. Charley Pride's singing, on the other hand, was so country that no one suspected he was black until they saw his photograph or saw him in concert.

Pride's country legitimacy is all the more remarkable, given the place and context in which he was born. He was born on a sharecropper's

Charley Pride. John Edwards Memorial Foundation Records, #20001,
Southern Folklife Collection, Louis Round Wilson Special Collections
Library, University of North Carolina at Chapel Hill.

farm on March 18, 1938, near Sledge, Mississippi, and in the heart of
the Delta where "the blues was born."[35] Unlike his contemporaries,
and even his brothers and sisters, Pride listened to country music and
began trying to pick and sing it when he was still a teenager. His two
passions were baseball and music, and he hoped that one or the other
would liberate him from "them old cotton fields back home." Between
1954 and 1964, he actively sought a baseball career, beginning with
the Memphis Red Sox in the Negro American League, but a series of

injuries at crucial moments kept him from fulfilling his desire to be a big-leaguer. While working at a zinc smelter in Helena, Montana, in 1963, playing semi-pro baseball, and singing in local clubs at night, he had a fortuitous encounter with Red Foley and Red Sovine. The two men gave a show in Great Falls, and after hearing Pride do a guest performance, Sovine encouraged him to come to Nashville.

Pride made the pilgrimage to Nashville the following year, received the support of Jack Johnson and Jack Clement, who became his first co-managers, and somehow put his tapes into the possession of Chet Atkins. Pride's first RCA recordings, "Snakes Crawl at Night" and "Atlantic Coastal Line," were produced in the fall of 1965 and released in December. No photographs accompanied the first records, nor did the promotional literature mention that he was black. Disc jockeys played his records, and fans bought them for several weeks, without anyone knowing his racial identity. By the time Pride's face became known to people, his music had won them over for life.

Pride's acceptance by the country music public is attributable to many factors. His managers and record producers skillfully marketed him with a low-profile campaign during the crucial early months, and Pride carefully cultivated his audiences with a repertory of solid country songs (many of them standards taken from other singers such as Hank Williams) and with good-natured, self-effacing banter that put people at ease. He talked of his "permanent tan" and of being a person who "didn't sound like he was supposed to," and he built trust among his working-class listeners by talking about baseball and his days in the cotton field. He was the right singer at the right time in history. His singing contained almost none of the vocal inflections identified with black singers, and his stage presence conveyed few of the body movements and postures identified with soul or rhythm-and-blues musicians. He was a handsome man but with little of the overt sexuality projected by many of the younger black singers, and he avoided any references to civil rights or political topics. He was therefore basically unthreatening to white masculinity, civil order, or the identity of country music.

Pride definitely profited from the heightened mood of racial tolerance promoted in the United States by the civil rights movement and from the desires of the country music industry to improve its image and broaden its audience. His appeal, though broad and knowing no regional bounds, was particularly intense in the South and among working-class whites. He was one of the first country singers to receive standing ovations at the end of his concerts, a tribute to his talent, one supposes, but also a means by which audiences rid themselves of racial guilt and announced to the world: "Look, we're not prejudiced after all." Above all, people responded to Charley Pride because he was such a good country singer, with a supple baritone voice that could easily accommodate itself to any style of music. His Grammy nomination in 1966 for "Just between You and Me" was merely the first of an unending stream of awards and accolades that accompanied his rise to commercial music fame. By the time he received the CMA's Entertainer of the Year Award in 1971—a major milestone in country music history—he had already become an institution in American popular culture and had moved far beyond the country audience that originally gave him support.

Although Charley Pride broke down some racial barriers in country music, few black people have followed him across them. There is no way to document the number of black people who like and listen to country music, nor can one determine how many black musicians perform at the local level. Linda Martel from South Carolina, O. B. McClinton from Mississippi, and Big Al Downing and Stoney Edwards from Oklahoma have been among the handful of black singers who have recorded for major labels or who have otherwise gained some kind of national exposure.[36] Of this group, only Stoney Edwards ever gave any indication of achieving major commercial acceptance. Born in Seminole, Oklahoma, of black, Indian, and Irish extraction, Edwards received his first exposure to country music by listening to the music of Tommy Duncan and Bob Wills on the radio. He always had vivid memories of standing along the roadside with his seven brothers and sisters, watching the Bob Wills bus go by and picking up the candy that the Texas Playboys tossed to them. He sang country music all his life but made no major efforts at a professional career until 1969, when an industrial accident took him out of circulation and when Charley Pride's success provided inspiration. Living in California at the time, Edwards made his first records for a major label, Capitol, which was no doubt delighted at the opportunity to compete with RCA and Charley Pride. From 1970, when his first records were made, down to the mid-1970s, Edwards kept his name before the country music public with such songs as "Mississippi, You're on My Mind" (a poignant evocation of life in the rural Deep South) and "Hank and Lefty

Raised My Country Soul" (an affectionate tribute to two of the giants of country music). Since that time, however, Edwards slowly faded from the limelight, and Charley Pride maintained his position as the only African American on a major record label.

Although the entrance into its ranks of women, youth, divergent ethnic groups, and a more relaxed attitude toward sexual expression and alternative lifestyles suggests a broadening vision within the country music industry, one should not interpret such changes to be a bold expression of liberalism. Commercialism, not ideology, has motivated many of country music's bold experiments. While much has been borrowed from urban folk and rock music—songs, instrumental licks, long hair, casual dress, and even relaxed attitudes toward drugs and sexual relations—country musicians have withdrawn from the encounters with a largely unaltered political consciousness. The politics of the urban folk revival, in other words, did not rub off on country music to any substantial degree, nor did the ideologies of such postrevival singers as Bob Dylan, Joan Baez, Phil Ochs, and Bruce Springsteen, who marshaled their protest songs to combat America's growing involvement in the Vietnam War.

Country music's identification with "the silent majority" in the mid-1960s was one consequence of at least twenty years of growing disquietude in the United States about the sweeping and bewildering social changes that occurred in the wake of World War II. The roots of these changes, of course, were much older and were products of the nation's rise to industrial power. In a society swept successively by racial, youth, and sexual revolutions; torn by the tensions arising from long ideological conflict with the Soviet Union; and subjected increasingly to the alienation inherent in postindustrial technology, many Americans sought reassurance that the older, comfortable, and predictable world they once knew was still intact. In the realm of popular culture, country music seemed a safe retreat to many because it suggested the "bedrock" American values of solidity, respect for authority, old-time religion, home-based virtues, and patriotism.

Some anticipations of a conservative political stance surfaced in the songs dealing with the Korean War and with atomic energy in the 1950s. Most of these songs were merely topical items like Harry Choates's "Korea, Here We Come," Bill Monroe's "Rotation Blues" (written by Lieutenant Stewart Powell in Korea), the Louvin Brothers' "From Mother's Arms to Korea," and Fred Kirby's "When That Hell Bomb

Falls," but a few made reference to the larger struggle with communism, and some commented on the domestic consequences of that conflict: Lulu Belle and Scotty's "I'm No Communist," Elton Britt's "The Red That We Want Is the Red We've Got (in the Old Red, White, and Blue)," Roy Acuff's "Doug MacArthur," and Gene Autry's "Old Soldiers Never Die" (a defense of MacArthur after his dismissal by Truman). Nevertheless, such songs were few, and room still existed for an item like the Sons of the Pioneers' "Ole Man Atom" that called for cooperation between world powers in the face of nuclear annihilation.

The civil rights revolution probably did most to politicize some country musicians.[37] The struggles waged by African Americans to attain economic dignity and racial justice provoked one of the ugliest chapters in country music's history, an outpouring of racist records on small labels, mostly from Crowley, Louisiana, which lauded the Ku Klux Klan and attacked blacks in the most vicious, explicitly vulgar, and stereotypical terms. George Wallace also forged an alliance with many country singers, such as Autry Inman, Hank Snow, and the Wilburn Brothers, who often participated in his campaigns for the Alabama governorship and for the presidency. Racism was certainly one factor that contributed to Wallace's popularity, but his southern rural/populist roots also made him appealing to many of the "good old boys and girls" who picked guitars and sang. Not only did Wallace identify with country music, but he also spoke the same language, ate the same food, and responded to the same cultural traditions (both good and bad) that most country musicians understood. He linked his southernness with their own while also tapping vaguely understood, but often legitimate, feelings of alienation that many Americans everywhere felt.

The George Wallace–country music alliance was a major factor that contributed to the music's rediscovery by the media—the belief that at worst the music represented reactionary and racist politics, or that at best it spoke for alienated American working people. The appearance of a rash of songs after 1965 that defended American involvement in the Vietnam War and attacked those who protested against it gave renewed credence to the ideas that country music was either unthinkingly jingoistic or unabashedly patriotic in its sentiments. An indication that country music's response to the war was a bit more complicated than it might seem at first glance is the fact that two of the few writers in Nashville to be identified as political liberals (through their support of George McGovern and Jimmy Carter) wrote the first songs defending American activities in Vietnam: Kris Kristofferson with "Vietnam Blues" (for Dave Dudley) and Tom T. Hall with "Hello Vietnam" (for Johnny Wright) and "Mama, Tell Them What We're Fighting For" (Dave Dudley). Both writers claimed, perhaps unconvincingly, that they merely defended American soldiers and not American policy.

A number of songs appeared, mostly in 1966, that can be described as "protesting the protestors." These included the Hall song mentioned above (built around a soldier's letter to his mother); a recitation by Johnny Seay, "Day of Decision," which catalogued the alleged rending of the social fabric by dissent and radicalism; Stonewall Jackson's "The Minute Men Are Turning in Their Graves," which attacked the alleged lack of patriotism shown by protestors; and at least three in 1970—Bobby Bare's "God Bless America Again," Bill Anderson's "Where Have All the Heroes Gone," and Merle Haggard's "The Fighting Side of Me"—which either complained about the polarization of American society or breathed threats against those who would "run down the country."

With songs like these, country music picked up support from Middle Americans everywhere and from grateful political administrations that appreciated such public displays of patriotism. The political realignments then taking place in the country—as people changed parties, joined George Wallace, or dropped out of politics altogether—were of course fed by much more than the debates over the war. Guy Drake's "Welfare Cadilac" [*sic*] in 1970 was clearly inspired by the Great Society's support of minority groups. The rise of the counterculture and the aggressive flaunting of alternative lifestyles alienated many people from their traditional political affiliations. Ernest Tubb, for example, a lifelong Democrat and ardent supporter of Adlai Stevenson, recorded a song called "Love It or Leave It." This attack upon hippies and Yippies was motivated by the same kind of suspicions that led to the most famous anti-protest song of the period: Merle Haggard's "Okie from Muskogee."

Recorded in 1969, and *Billboard*'s number one country song for four consecutive weeks at the end of the year, "Okie From Muskogee" was about an allegedly typical small-town Middle American with conventional ways and militant patriotism who was proud to be from a community where people didn't smoke marijuana, wear beads and sandals, burn their draft cards, or challenge authority. Written one day on the spur of the moment when Haggard's bus passed by the Muskogee city sign, and apparently first intended as a joke, the song's giant success must have greatly surprised the singer. It contributed to his selection as the CMA's Entertainer of the Year in 1970; it won him standing ovations in such cities as Philadelphia and Duluth; and it gained for him and for country music the endorsement of President Richard Nixon. Although Haggard may have stumbled into the commercial and popular success generated by "Okie," his next recording, "The Fighting Side of Me," was clearly calculated to capitalize on the "silent majority's" fear and disgust for hippies, peaceniks, and radicals. It deeply disappointed those fans who identified Haggard with the compassion and tenderness of "Hungry Eyes," but it was also his next big number one record.

When American involvement in the Vietnam War ended, and as the nation's polarization subsided, country songwriters began to lose their preoccupation with songs of anti-dissent. The obsession with politics had been out of character, just as had the unquestioning acceptance of national policies displayed in the war songs. Country music moved away from the endorsement of establishment values to a more comfortable, and traditional, absorption with the world of the working class. Country writers and singers became increasingly aware, however, that a message designed for plain, everyday people could also be appealing to suburban commuters and even to "hippies." While still trying to be all things to all people, country music nevertheless became more self-consciously working class in image and orientation at the end of the 1960s. Both Merle Haggard and Tom T. Hall were described as "poets of the working man," although Haggard's songs seemed more aggressively aimed at that constituency. Many of the "working men's songs," like Haggard's "Working Man's Blues" and Johnny Russell's "Rednecks, White Socks, and Blue Ribbon Beer," were more concerned with lifestyle than with work. Haggard's song describes a character who is hardworking, individualistic, patriotic, fatalistic, and opposed to welfare. Russell's song is a cliché-ridden paean to the working class and a not-so-subtle reminder of the social chasm that lies between workers and others. While problems inherent in the work process were frequently described in country songs, work itself was seldom extolled, and worker loyalty and competency were often emphasized. The main character of Haggard's "If We Make It through December" is laid off during the most critical season of the year, and "Oney," in a song written by Jerry Chesnut and recorded by Johnny Cash, patiently waits for his retirement day so that he can beat up his foreman. Johnny Paycheck's big hit, "Take This Job and Shove It" (written by David Allan Coe, and the basis for a movie), is unapologetically self-explanatory.

Truck-driving songs constituted the single-largest category of the era's work songs. The genre seems to have begun in 1939 when Ted Daffan wrote "Truck Driver's Blues," but it began to evolve into a full-fledged industry in 1963 when Dave Dudley (David Petruska) from Spencer, Wisconsin, recorded "Six Days on the Road." Dudley's confident, quasi-rockabilly performance effectively captured both the boredom and the excitement, as well as the swaggering masculinity, that often accompanied long-distance trucking. After 1965, a massive number of songs appeared that dealt with every aspect of trucker culture: truck stops, waitresses, billboards, citizen band radios (CBs), highway patrolmen (Smokies), mountain roads, "lady" truck drivers, pills, logbooks, convoys, overloads, and trucking folklore (about such topics as ghost truck drivers—as in "Phantom 309"—and tender-hearted truckers who help crippled children).

The songs multiplied in such profusion that their quality varied widely; nevertheless, a few will probably stand the test of time: "Truck Driving Man," "Give Me Forty Acres" (about an inept driver), "Tombstone Every Mile" (about a dangerous and icy stretch of road in the Maine woods), "Girl on the Billboard" (about a trucker's fantasy), and, most poignantly, "White Line Fever" (Merle Haggard's lament about a trucker who watches his life slip away as he rolls his truck down the white line of a thousand highways). While most country singers experimented with trucking songs at one time or another, only a few, such as Dudley, Dick Curless, Red Simpson, and Red Sovine, actually specialized in such material. Truck-driving songs remained largely confined to the country music world until the 1970s, when nationwide truckers' strikes and C. W. McCall's "Convoy," a major crossover hit and the inspiration for a movie of the same name, made Americans conscious of CBs, trucker lingo, and the whole culture that lay behind them. An indispensable ingredient of that culture was the late-night country music radio shows aimed at truckers and conducted by such eloquent personalities as Charlie Douglas on WWL in New Orleans and Bill Mack on WBAP in Fort Worth. These men's voices boomed out to thousands of truckers in virtually every state in the continental United States, and they played songs requested by their trucker buddies, advertised truck stops and trucking equipment, and gave valuable weather information. Douglas, who ran a popular show called the *Road Gang* on WWL in New Orleans before moving to Nashville in 1983, even served as a liaison to truckers during the crucial strike of independent owner-operators in 1972.

The popularity of truck-driving songs stood as merely one example of country music's renewed strength and vitality. Commercially, the music had reached the highest peak in its history, a tribute not only to the "Chet Atkins compromise" but also to the brilliant writing of people like Kris Kristofferson and Tom T. Hall and the singing of such hard country performers as Merle Haggard and Loretta Lynn. Stylistically, though, the music had reached a crossroads. Some routes led toward pop music and the blurring of identity; others beckoned those musicians who could combine tradition and innovation in an effective and commercially winning manner. One of these roads led toward bluegrass.

CHAPTER 10
Bluegrass

Bluegrass music has had a curious history.[1] Almost everyone has heard of it, but few people know what it is or where it came from. The name is sometimes used as a catch-all term to describe any form of country music, usually acoustic in nature, that suggests pre–World War II styles. But in fact it is *not* an old-time style at all; it did not begin to take shape as a distinct entity until the mid-1940s, and it was not named until a decade later, when fans, disc jockeys, and record merchandisers began using the term "bluegrass" to describe a sound associated with the music of Bill Monroe and his disciples. The music, of course, drew upon earlier string band and vocal styles and repertory (as most forms of country music did), but these inherited and borrowed styles were significantly modified. One need only compare the music of Bill Monroe, "the father of bluegrass music," with that of Charlie Poole—listen to their respective versions of "White House Blues," for example—or to Grayson and Whitter's and the Country Gentlemen's renditions of "Handsome Molly"[2] to understand the dynamic ways in which bluegrass musicians modified and updated the old-time styles. Much romanticism has grown up around bluegrass, as invariably happens when any musical form diverges from the commercial mainstream and gathers to it a host of true believers. Bluegrass, for example, is often equated with mountain

Bill Monroe. Bill Malone personal collection.

music or seen as its natural outgrowth. Many of the major performers did indeed come from the southeastern hill country, but some seminal bluegrass musicians—including Bill Monroe—came from other areas. Stylistically, bluegrass is indebted to musicians and styles from a variety of nonmountain *and* mountain sources, and its songs come from no one region.

Although bluegrass is not an old-time style and is instead a dynamic and ever-evolving form, it has nonetheless attracted a horde of fans and musicians with a traditional bent who have repaired to it as a refuge from the "progressive" and pop styles that have inundated mainstream country music. It is welcomed as one of the few areas of performance where acoustic instruments, high-lonesome singing, and down-to-earth songs can still be heard. As an increasingly popular phenomenon, however, and one that is marked by virtuoso styles of playing, bluegrass has also attracted many who have no commitment to tradition at all and who are instead charmed by the fresh and inventive musicianship that they find there. It has been the fate of bluegrass music to spawn the same kind of stylistic divergence, as well as debates concerning identity, that the larger country music field has experienced. "Traditional" bluegrass now competes with "progressive" bluegrass.

While the edifice of bluegrass was built by many hands and voices, the chief architect was that master musician from Kentucky, Bill Monroe.[3] William Smith Monroe was born on September 13, 1911, on a farm in western Kentucky, near Rosine and far from the aristocratic bluegrass region of the state. Eight years younger than his nearest brother, Charlie, and plagued by poor eyesight, Monroe became a reclusive child who made music his cherished retreat. Fortunately, he had several models and sources on whom to draw. His mother, Malissa Vandiver Monroe, who died when he was ten, bequeathed a love for music to all of her eight children through her ballad singing and skill on the harmonica, accordion, and fiddle. Her talented son, Bill, also received instruction in the shape-note singing schools that occasionally convened at the Baptist and Methodist churches in Rosine, but he seems to have absorbed even more from the congregational singing of the churches, and especially from the "Holiness" (Pentecostal) people who occasionally held revivals in the little town.

The powerful vocal inspiration exerted by the religious groups was complemented by the instrumental training he received from a black musician, Arnold Shultz, and an uncle, Pendleton Vandiver (sometimes spelled Vanderver). At about the age of twelve, Monroe began playing guitar accompaniment for Shultz at dances in western Kentucky. Until his death on April 14, 1931, Shultz—a coal miner by day and a musician at night—gained fame as both a hoedown fiddler and a thumb-and-finger-style guitarist. Shultz evidently played both "hillbilly" music and blues. The early indoctrination received from Shultz and other local black musicians, along with the sounds heard on the recordings of his favorite commercial performer, Jimmie Rodgers, gave Monroe a liking for the blues that remained with him throughout his performing career.

The greatest noncommercial influence in Monroe's musical life came from his Uncle Pen Vandiver. He lived with his uncle for several years, and as a teenager often accompanied the old fiddler with his guitar at country dances. Uncle Pen taught him timing and left him a large storehouse of tunes, such as "Jerusalem Ridge," which have endured in the bluegrass repertory. Monroe has memorialized his uncle in the songs he preserved but also more directly in an original composition, now a bluegrass standard, called "Uncle Pen."

Monroe played the guitar frequently as a young man, but he eventually settled on the mandolin largely because his older brothers, Birch and Charlie, had chosen the fiddle and guitar, respectively. Bill joined his brothers in Whiting, Indiana, in 1929, and soon began playing music with them. The famous Monroe Brothers duet (Charlie and Bill) came into existence in 1934 when Birch decided to forsake a full-time career in music. As a duet team, the Monroe Brothers set a standard of performing excellence that is still remembered by older country fans, particularly in the Carolinas, where they often played from 1935 to 1938 (under the sponsorship of Texas Crystals and Crazy Water Crystals). The harmony of their musical performances, however, was not consistently matched by a similar consonance in their brotherly relations. They fought both physically and verbally, and in 1938 they terminated their musical partnership.

Charlie soon organized a new band called the Kentucky Pardners; they made their first recordings for the Bluebird label in September 1938. Charlie tried to preserve some of the Monroe Brothers sound and therefore sought tenor singers of Bill's caliber as well as musicians who could play the mandolin. Several well-known mandolinists, such as Curly Sechler, Ira Louvin, Red Rector, and Clyde Baum, eventually played for Charlie, and even the famed guitarist and lead singer Lester Flatt put in a stint as mandolin player and tenor singer for the Kentucky Pardners in the early 1940s. The Kentucky Pardners always had the sound and flair of an old-time band—their two most famous songs were "Down in the Willow Garden" ("Rose Conley") and "Bringing in the Georgia Mail"—and Charlie's ebullient, outgoing personality always gave his performances an ambience far different from that of his serious and taciturn brother.

Bill had much to learn as he embarked upon an independent career. With the Monroe Brothers, he had never sung lead or solo (only high-tenor harmony), and he had never acted as a master of ceremonies. Although his mandolin playing had been rapid and dynamic, he had always kept it tied rather closely to the melodic line, marked by his attempt to emulate the continuous flowing notes of the fiddle. One finds little, then, of the jazzlike, improvisatory flair that later characterized his style. Monroe, however, was a man of rugged independence and intense, almost stubborn, pride. Coupled with brilliant musicianship, Bill's quiet resolve to be unique made him one of the most respected and influential performers in country music history.

Trying out his new independence, Monroe organized a band called the Kentuckians and played with them for three months on KARK in Little Rock, Arkansas. In that same year of 1938, he moved to the *Crossroad Follies* in Atlanta, where, in honor of his native state, he organized the Blue Grass Boys, totally unaware that, like Al Hopkins with the Hill Billies, he had coined a title that would one day become a generic term for a style of country music. The original group included Cleo Davis on guitar, Art Wooten on fiddle, and Monroe on mandolin. A few months later, John Miller joined them with his jug (one of several nonbluegrass instruments that Monroe used in the early years), but he was soon replaced by Amos Garin on the stand-up bass. In October 1939, the band auditioned successfully for a spot on the *Grand Ole Opry,* and Monroe delighted the show's founder, George D. Hay, with his high, clear tenor sound. Monroe remained a pillar of the show for over sixty years.

Until 1945, the Blue Grass Boys gave the surface appearance of being merely a string band in the mold of such groups as Mainer's Mountaineers and Roy Hall's Blue Ridge Entertainers. They were, however, a string band with a crucial difference: Bill Monroe. The listener was always aware that, despite the particular vocal or instrumental style conveyed, Monroe was the driving cog, and all other musicians revolved around him. With his mandolin setting the beat and rhythm for the band, Monroe also did most of the singing, taking most of the solo parts and then generally sweeping up to a high-tenor harmony on the choruses. Monroe's tenor singing—now often described as the "high lonesome sound"[4]—set a standard that most bluegrass musicians have

The Blue Grass Boys: left to right, *Birch Monroe, Lester Flatt, Bill Monroe, Earl Scruggs, Chubby Wise. Bill Malone personal collection; courtesy of Ralph Rinzler.*

strived to emulate. "Why, he can sing as high as Bill Monroe!" was one of the strongest compliments that a musician could receive.

On the strength of his Saturday-night broadcasts on powerful WSM, along with the Victor records that he began making on October 7, 1940, Monroe's fame began to spread throughout much of the nation. Few people at this time bothered to distinguish between Monroe's style and other forms of country music, and his extraordinary musicianship attracted a wide range of followers pursuing their own musical paths, such as the future honky-tonk ace George Jones and the rockabillies Sonny Curtis, Carl Perkins, and Elvis Presley. In his concerts, Monroe remained a man of few words, letting his music stand as "the only communication of his complex creative philosophy."[5] His Victor recordings of 1940 and 1941 included the mixture of styles that always characterized his performances: instrumental pieces (including the second known recording of "Orange Blossom Special"), solo songs by Monroe, traditional religious and secular numbers, contemporary songs both borrowed and original, and songs done by his lead singer (Clyde Moody, on the early sessions). Early on, Monroe began introducing songs like "New Muleskinner Blues" (his debut song on the *Grand Ole Opry*) and "Footprints in the Snow" that become standards in the bluegrass repertory.[6]

By 1945, much of the drive, dynamism, and timing of bluegrass music, as well as much of its repertory, had been integrated fully into Monroe's music. The Blue Grass Boys were already becoming famous for their fiddlers, such as Art Wooten, Tommy Magness, Howdy Forrester, and Jim Shumate, and Bill Monroe's distinctive mandolin chop rhythm gave the group an overall sound different from that of other country bands. But given the overriding importance assumed by the instrument in bluegrass music today, the most conspicuous omission from Monroe's band was the five-string banjo played in three-finger style.

Because of wartime restrictions, the Blue Grass Boys made no recordings between October 2, 1941, and February 13, 1945. When they resumed recording, this time on the Columbia label, their sound reflected the changes made in their performing style during the interim. Sally Forrester, wife of the fiddler Howdy Forrester, played the accordion and, most significantly, David "Stringbean" Akeman, who had joined the band in 1942, played the five-string banjo. By the mid-1940s, the banjo was perceived as a solo instrument, most often used by comic performers such as Uncle Dave Macon, Grandpa Jones, and Bashful Brother Oswald. When used in a band, it generally played only rhythmic, backup passages. Stringbean was much admired as a droll comedian, but when he quit the band in 1945 to team up with Lew Childre, his departure was not greatly mourned by the other Blue Grass Boys. Stringbean had contributed little to the overall sound of the band and had, in fact, hindered their drive by his tendency to drag the melody. But when Earl Scruggs joined the Blue Grass Boys in 1945, he revolutionized the band by bringing a sensational technique that rejuvenated the five-string banjo, making his own name preeminent among country and folk musicians and establishing bluegrass music as a national phenomenon.

Earl Scruggs was born on January 6, 1924, on a farm near Flint Hill, North Carolina (outside Shelby), in a region where banjo pickers thrived. His father and older brothers played the banjo in a style peculiar to their section of North Carolina—a three-finger style (thumb and index and middle fingers) that permitted the instrument to be played in a melodic, syncopated fashion. Besides learning it from these models, Scruggs was also exposed to the style through the playing of other western North Carolinians such as Mack Woolbright, Rex Brooks, Smith Hammett (a distant relative of Scruggs's), and Snuffy Jenkins. Jenkins, a product of Harris, North Carolina, had taken the technique to the largest audience through his performances on WBT in Charlotte in 1934 and on WIS in Columbia, South Carolina, after 1937. Many banjoists, including Don Reno and Ralph Stanley, credit Jenkins with having given them their first exposure to three-finger picking.

Earl Scruggs, therefore, did not invent the style that now bears his name, but he perfected it and carried it to greater technical proficiency than anyone before him. Above all, as a member of the Blue Grass Boys and later as a partner with Lester Flatt, he did the most to introduce "Scruggs picking" to the world. When he joined Bill Monroe in 1945 as an instrumentalist, the twenty-year-old musician already had several years of professional experience, including a short stint with Wiley and Zeke Morris in 1939 over WSPA in Spartanburg, South Carolina. He was part of Lost John Miller's band in Nashville when Monroe hired him as a Blue Grass Boy in August 1945. Scruggs added a new and dynamic ingredient to the Blue Grass Boys sound, and audiences were bowled over by the boy who, with a shower of syncopated notes, had made the banjo a lead instrument capable of playing the fastest of songs. Here was something new under the sun—a banjo player who acted as a serious musician and not as a figure of comic relief. Even Uncle Dave Macon, watching from the wings of the *Grand Ole Opry*, supposedly said of the poker-faced young man, "He ain't one damned bit funny."[7]

Scruggs joined a band of superb musicians that, to many bluegrass partisans, will always rank as both the first and the best in the bluegrass genre. This was classic bluegrass at its zenith. In addition to Monroe and Scruggs, this seminal band included Lester Flatt on guitar, Robert "Chubby" Wise on fiddle, and Cedric Rainwater (Howard Watts) on bass. Between 1945 and 1948, the modern bluegrass sound came into being. According to the bluegrass authority Pete Kuykendall, the first recorded numbers to bear all the elements of the new style were "Will You Be Loving Another Man," featuring the lead singing of its writer, Lester Flatt, and "Blue Yodel No. 4" (an old Jimmie Rodgers number), recorded for Columbia on September 16, 1946.[8] Well before the records came out, however, fans and musicians had ample time to be exposed to the exciting new sound through WSM broadcasts and the popular tent show tours hosted by Monroe. The Blue Grass Boys traveled in a nine-passenger Packard limousine with a rack on top for the bass fiddle, and with a complement of five trucks that transported the tent, bleachers, and chairs. Periodically, Monroe and the boys also challenged communities to sandlot baseball games, an effective way of breaking the monotony of constant travel and of advertising the night concerts.

In the three-year period from 1945 to 1948, the banjo assumed a prominence in Monroe's music that it had never enjoyed in any previous band, and an ensemble style of music, much like jazz in the improvised solo work of the individual instruments, came into existence. Throughout the nation, largely unnoticed by the more commercial world of country music, a veritable "bluegrass revolution" got under way as both fans and musicians became attracted to the music. Young musicians began copying the sounds they heard on Bill Monroe records: the mandolin, banjo, and fiddle passages of Monroe, Scruggs, and Wise; the guitar runs of Lester Flatt; and the high, hard harmony singing of Flatt and Monroe or of the trios and quartets featured on gospel numbers. It is no wonder that Bill Monroe felt bitterly disappointed, and even betrayed, when Flatt and Scruggs left the group in 1948. His greatest band now seemed a thing of the past, and he may not have realized that a host of great musicians were yearning to play for him.

The bluegrass "sound" did not become a "style" until other musical organizations began copying the instrumental and vocal traits first featured in Bill Monroe's performances. Neil Rosenberg believes that the Stanley Brothers' recording of "Molly and Tenbrooks," released in September 1948, provided "the first direct evidence" that musicians were copying the sound of the "original" bluegrass band.[9] The Stanley Brothers learned their version from a live performance by Monroe and actually recorded the song before Monroe's 1949 recording of the exciting racehorse song was released. In their recording, the Stanley Brothers featured the banjo played by Ralph in Scruggs's style and, in an obvious copy of Monroe's vocal performance, entrusted the vocal duties to the mandolin-playing, tenor-singing Pee Wee Lambert.

Ralph and Carter Stanley were part of a growing number of musicians in the mid- and late 1940s who either borrowed songs from

Ralph (left) and Carter (right) Stanley, 1966. Courtesy of Norman Carlson.

Monroe or copied the style of the Blue Grass Boys note for note. Like the Stanley Brothers, some of them recorded for a small record company in Johnson City, Tennessee, called Rich-R-Tone. Records by such performers as Wilma Lee and Stoney Cooper, Carl Sauceman, the Bailey Brothers, Buffalo Johnson, and Jim Eanes circulated extensively in

*Lester Flatt and Earl Scruggs. From the John Edwards Memorial
Foundation Records, #20001, 0641-01, Southern Folklife Collection,
Louis Round Wilson Special Collections Library, University of North
Carolina at Chapel Hill; photo courtesy Columbia Records.*

the southeastern hill country but received little exposure elsewhere.
Some of the fledgling bluegrass performers learned the music through
the performances of Monroe and the Blue Grass Boys; others, such as
Jim and Jesse McReynolds, the Lonesome Pine Fiddlers, Jim Eanes,
and Mac Wiseman (to name only a few), had already been pursuing

musical careers before Monroe's exciting Columbia records were released. In many cases, it was merely the addition of a Scruggs-style banjo player—such as Hoke Jenkins, who joined the McReynolds Brothers in 1949, or Allen Shelton, who teamed with Jim Eanes at about the same time—that marked the transition to bluegrass.

The Blue Grass Boys did more than inspire imitation. Beginning in 1939, the personnel of the Blue Grass Boys changed often, and the list of individuals who played with Monroe and then went on to found their own organizations or to play in other bands reads like a "Who's Who" of Bluegrass Music: Clyde Moody, Lester Flatt, Earl Scruggs, Don Reno, Gordon Terry, Carter Stanley, Mac Wiseman, Jimmy Martin, Vassar Clements, Peter Rowan, Roland White, Sonny Osborne, and James Monroe. The exodus began in 1948, when Flatt and Scruggs grew tired of the Blue Grass Boys' grinding road schedule and temporarily retired from the music business. Before the year was over, however, they had formed their own band, the Foggy Mountain Boys, named after a Carter Family song that they often performed. Joined by two other recent dropouts from the Blue Grass Boys, fiddler Jim Shumate and bass player Cedric Rainwater, along with another guitarist and featured singer, Mac Wiseman, Flatt and Scruggs began the independent professional career that would soon make them one of the most popular country acts in the nation.

After working for about three weeks in Hickory, North Carolina, Flatt and Scruggs moved in the spring of 1948 to WCYB in Bristol, Virginia, where they began receiving hundreds of cards and letters and requests for bookings too numerous to be filled. In that same busy year of 1948, they recorded the first of their songs for Mercury, a body of material that still stands as among the most exciting in the history of bluegrass music. Most bluegrass bands still include songs from Flatt and Scruggs's Mercury years (1948–1950) in their repertories: "My Little Girl in Tennessee," "Foggy Mountain Breakdown" (made doubly famous in 1967 as the theme for the movie *Bonnie and Clyde*), "My Cabin in Caroline," "We'll Meet Again, Sweetheart," "Old Salty Dog Blues," "Roll in My Sweet Baby's Arms." The popularity of the two last-named songs seems all the more remarkable in that they were recorded more or less as filler at the band's last Mercury recording session in October 1950, a session done in haste to fulfill a contractual obligation before moving to the Columbia label.

Flatt and Scruggs and the Foggy Mountain Boys also became one of the most active touring groups in country music, first in such "traditional" formats as store openings, drive-in movies, country schools, and county fairs, but eventually in the largest auditoriums in the nation, on college and university campuses, at folk festivals and clubs, at Carnegie Hall, and in Japan. A major breakthrough in their career came in 1953 when the Martha White Flour Mills hired them to do a fifteen-minute program on WSM each morning at 5:45. Fans came to know the Martha White jingle as well as they did other songs in the Flatt and Scruggs repertory, and the duo often received requests for the tune at their concerts. The association with Martha White Flour was mutually profitable for Flatt and Scruggs and the company. Their music was introduced to a steadily expanding public, even though the pace required to do personal appearances and then to return for the early-morning radio show was a killing one (WSM eventually, and mercifully, permitted the shows to be taped). On the strength of their mounting popularity and best-selling Columbia records, WSM added them to the regular cast of the *Grand Ole Opry* in 1955. This coveted forum further contributed to their growing fame, a recognition that not even the impending rock-and-roll invasion could diminish. The Martha White Company was not hesitant about expressing its gratitude to the Foggy Mountain Boys. Cohen T. Williams, president of the firm that advertised Hot Rize (a self-rising ingredient in the flour and meal), stated unequivocally that "Flatt and Scruggs and the Grand Ole Opry built the Martha White Mills."[10]

Flatt and Scruggs's music communicated beautifully via the radio microphone and phonograph recording, but to be fully appreciated it needed to be seen as well as heard. The physical interaction between the musicians, the smoothness of their performances, and the diversity of their material made the Flatt and Scruggs show both an auditory and a visual delight. Lester Flatt was responsible for much of the easygoing ambience of the show. Ever since his birth in Overton County, Tennessee, in 1914, he had been consumed with making music; but until he joined Charlie Monroe's Kentucky Pardners in 1943 as a mandolin player and tenor singer, the demands of an early marriage had never permitted him much respite from long periods of employment in textile mills. From the Kentucky Pardners he went directly to the Blue Grass Boys, where he gained invaluable experience as a master of ceremonies and as a lead singer. He was the only Blue Grass Boy in history to be identified on record labels along with

Bill Monroe. As co-leader of his own band, Flatt proved to be a genial and unassuming host, a singer with a relaxed and supple style, and a backup guitarist of considerable skill. When playing songs at breakneck speed with Bill Monroe, he devised a method of getting back on the beat before resuming singing after instrumental breaks. This was an ascending run that began on the bass E string and ended with a ringing note on the third, or G, string. Although this run was played most often in the key of G, the use of the capo permitted it to be used in other keys, such as A or B, both popular in bluegrass. The "Lester Flatt G-run," as it has come to be called, was widely copied by other guitarists. Bass runs of this type were among the most distinctive features of bluegrass music. Played on deep-toned acoustic guitars (usually Martin D28s) and coming at the end of fiddle, mandolin, or banjo sequences—sometimes at the end of vocal phrases, as in Monroe's "Uncle Pen" or Jimmy Martin's "Sunny Side of the Mountain"—the runs added a dramatic note of emphasis or finality to the overall mood of intensity created by the supercharged music.

Many people, of course, came to hear the Foggy Mountain Boys solely because of Earl Scruggs. His dazzling banjo style was made to seem even more remarkable by the seeming ease with which he did it. He usually stood poker-faced on the stage, his body appearing almost motionless as the three fingers of his right hand produced a torrent of notes. In October 1951, he introduced still another affecting technique that added further to his reputation as a master musician. On "Earl's Breakdown," he adjusted his tuning pegs at various intervals in the song to move from one chord to another and then back to the original. By the time he recorded "Flint Hill Special" in November 1952, he had devised a tuning mechanism that permitted quick retuning of the banjo's B and G strings. Scruggs was not content to be merely a banjo virtuoso; he occasionally picked up a guitar, especially on gospel numbers, and demonstrated a mastery of both fingerpicking and Carter Family thumb-style techniques.

Flatt and Scruggs were more than ably supported by the talented musicians who made up the Foggy Mountain Boys. Much of the verve and drive of the band came from its fiddlers, particularly Benny Martin (who also attempted a solo singing career in the 1950s) and Paul Warren. Martin had played on the great Mercury recording sessions, but Warren, an alumnus of Johnny and Jack's Tennessee Mountain Boys, performed with Flatt and Scruggs through all the important

years after 1954. A high point of each Flatt and Scruggs concert was
Warren's rendition of such hoedown tunes as "Sally Gooden" or his
showpiece, "Black Eyed Susan." Probably in an attempt to build a
sound different from Bill Monroe's, Flatt and Scruggs gave little
prominence to the mandolin; instead, their mandolin players were
best known for their harmony singing. Everett Lilly was a fine musician from Clear Creek, West Virginia, and he did take an occasional
instrumental break. Nevertheless, his real value to the Foggy Mountain Boys came through his high, crisp tenor singing. Curly Sechler
(also spelled Seckler) was even more important to the group because
he remained with them for many years, during both the Mercury and
Columbia periods, and after that was a mainstay of Lester Flatt's new
group, the Nashville Grass. Sechler's mandolin was almost never
heard—in his own words, he just "held the mandolin"[11]—but his tenor
harmony was unsurpassed in the whole field of bluegrass music. His
powerful, ringing voice complemented Lester Flatt's perfectly, and on
such songs as "Some Old Day" and "My Little Girl in Tennessee" they
gave echoes of the brother-duet style of singing while also defining
the essence of bluegrass harmony. Although the mandolin's relative
unimportance was a factor in establishing a unique identity for Flatt
and Scruggs, the addition of the Dobro in 1955 was much more significant. Some bluegrass purists lamented the use of an instrument
that had not been present in Bill Monroe's original band (forgetting
that the master himself had once employed an accordionist), but the
instrument immediately attracted the fancy of listeners and did much
to give Flatt and Scruggs an entree into the broader country and western field. The Dobro player was Burkett "Buck" Graves (also known in
his comedian's role as "Uncle Josh"). Graves may not have been the
first Dobro player in bluegrass music—Speedy Krise, for example, had
played the instrument on a Carl Butler recording in December 1950—
but he undoubtedly did most to revitalize it and to make it attractive
to younger musicians. During earlier periods with such performers
as Molly O'Day and Mac Wiseman, Graves had played the Dobro in a
style indebted to his hero, Cliff Carlisle, and to other musicians such as
Bashful Brother Oswald. Graves, though, was captivated by Scruggs's
rapid, multiple-noted banjo playing, and he became determined to
adapt that style, or something similar to it, to the Dobro. By the time
he became a Foggy Mountain Boy, Graves had perfected a rolling, syncopated style that enabled him to play galloping breakdowns as well

as slow love songs or ballads. With Graves leading the way, the Dobro made a major comeback in country music, and some of the old-time masters of the instrument—most notably Shot Jackson, who appeared on scores of records during the 1960s—began to reemerge from undeserved obscurity. A growing number of young musicians, such as Mike Auldridge, Rob Ickes, and Jerry Douglas, also began an experimentation with the instrument whose fruits would flower eloquently in the late 1960s and early 1970s.

The Foggy Mountain Boys did not merely play well; they also looked good while doing it. Since they used no electric instruments, they were heavily dependent on microphone amplification. Most of the places where they played had few microphones, so the musicians had to move in and out of the center stage in order to take their vocal and instrumental breaks, being careful not to bump into each other or to poke a fiddle bow into someone's eye. The Foggy Mountain Boys converted a technical necessity into an art, moving to and from the microphone with a smoothness and precision that seemed choreographed. The sight of Buck Graves weaving in and out of musicians in order to lift his Dobro to the microphone was something not soon forgotten. The dramatic stage presence exhibited by the group, along with the skillful blending of songs and instrumental pieces, sacred and secular numbers, and seriousness and comedy (usually performed by Graves and bassman Jake Tullock as "Uncle Josh" and "Cousin Jake"), all combined to make the Flatt and Scruggs show one of the legendary acts of country music history.

By the early 1950s, several major bands had emerged that exhibited a Monroe parentage or discipleship.[12] Some of these groups, such as those headed by Don Reno and Red Smiley, Mac Wiseman, and the Osborne Brothers, often had songs that appeared on country DJ shows and on jukeboxes—a phenomenon that is now extremely rare. Country music had not yet fragmented decisively into "hard country" and "pop country" categories, and the "old-time" country styles had not yet become casualties in Nashville's campaign to recoup its losses after the rock-and-roll assault. Furthermore, the word "bluegrass" had not yet come into complete and systematic usage, although an increasing number of people were beginning to attach the term to the proliferating number of bands that somehow seemed to be in the Bill Monroe mold. Why and when this happened are questions that will probably never be conclusively answered. At some undetermined point, probably in the late 1940s or early 1950s, fans, record sellers, and disc jockeys began using the term "bluegrass" as an identifying description. Neil Rosenberg suggests that the first usage of the word may have come about when fans of Flatt and Scruggs, who were aware that a feud existed between them and Bill Monroe, requested the "old blue grass songs you used to do" rather than mentioning their former boss by name.[13] Sometime in the early 1950s, Jimmie Skinner's Music Center in Cincinnati, founded by a deep-voiced singer and writer from Blue Lick, Kentucky (who wrote "Doing My Time," "You Don't Know My Mind," and other songs), began to advertise "bluegrass records" in its catalogues and newsletters. The music store had a large clientele of transplanted southern hillbillies who, like Skinner himself, still yearned for the music of home. The center also advertised on WCKY in Cincinnati, where such DJs as Wayne Raney, Nelson King, Marty Roberts, and Jimmie Logsdon labored to give the developing bluegrass genre a wider circulation. Over in Warrenton, Virginia, on WARL, Don Owens played a similar role while also helping to lay the groundwork for Washington, DC's, future reputation as a major bluegrass center. Bluegrass attracted supporters for a wide variety of reasons, but one powerful source of its appeal lay in its down-home ambience and the belief that it served as a refuge from both an overorganized, alienating society and an overstylized country music that was steadily forsaking its roots.

In those formative years before the urban folk revival introduced bluegrass to a new audience and a new repertory, at least six acts gave serious competition to Monroe and Flatt and Scruggs: Don Reno and Red Smiley, Mac Wiseman, the Osborne Brothers, Jimmy Martin, Jim and Jesse McReynolds, and the Stanley Brothers. Reno and Smiley headed a band called the Tennessee Cutups, even though neither of the two men hailed from that state. In a musical style in which versatility seemed to be the norm, Don Reno, from Spartanburg, South Carolina, possessed a range of talents that almost staggers the imagination. He was a good songwriter, an excellent tenor harmony singer, a comedian, and a master of several instruments, including the mandolin, guitar, and banjo. His guitar work has often been overlooked in the flood of praise that surrounds his seminal banjo contributions, but he was one of the first men in bluegrass to play the guitar as a lead instrument in flat-picking fashion. The stellar Doc Watson credits Reno as an influence on his own style. As a banjoist, Reno was surpassed by no one, not even Scruggs. He was a highly inventive banjo player, adept at both the three-finger and plectrum styles that were indebted to guitar and pedal steel playing. Reno learned the three-finger style from Snuffy Jenkins and employed it with such groups as the Morris Brothers in the 1940s. He played for Bill Monroe briefly in 1948, not long after Scruggs had resigned from the Blue Grass Boys, and then moved on to begin his own independent bluegrass career.

Reno organized the Tennessee Cutups in 1949 and was joined by Arthur Lee "Red" Smiley a few months later. The Asheville, North Carolina, native brought a warm and fluid baritone to the group that fit comfortably and closely with Reno's tenor. They performed on radio in Roanoke, Virginia, in 1949, and then moved to the *Wheeling Jamboree*, broadcast on powerful WWVA in Wheeling, West Virginia. Although they made a few records for the Federal label, the real burgeoning of their career came in 1952 when they recorded the first of their songs for King. "I'm Using My Bible for a Roadmap," written by Reno, contained the basic elements for which they became famous: his own ringing banjo playing, which combined both a three-finger roll and plectrum-style chords; Smiley's dramatic, run-filled guitar backup; and the two men's close, smooth harmony. Reno's tenor harmony singing was modeled on that of two markedly dissimilar stylists, Bill Monroe and Bill Bolick (of the Blue Sky Boys), and he could move alternately and easily from a high, almost falsetto, sound to a low and plaintive tenor.

Their most productive years in the 1950s and early 1960s found them ensconced on the *Old Dominion Barn Dance* in Richmond, Virginia, and on a daily television program in Roanoke. Their stage shows rivaled those of Flatt and Scruggs for diversity. In addition to Reno and Smiley's fine musicianship, the shows also featured Mack Magaha's acrobatic old-time fiddling and zany comedy skits in which all the band members dressed in costume and drag and played the roles of ridiculous characters. Reno and Smiley did hard-driving bluegrass and gospel numbers, as all bluegrass groups did, but they also performed honky-tonk style songs and other types that were close to mainstream country. Some of these songs, such as "Let's Live for Tonight," were written by Reno himself, or by members of the band (such as Magaha's "I Know You're Married, but I Love You Still"), or by outsiders, as in the case of Buck Owens's "Sweethearts in Heaven." Beginning in about 1954—partly through the requests of Syd Nathan at King Records—Reno began playing the guitar on many of their recorded numbers. Some of the group's most beautiful and compelling performances, such as "You Never Mentioned Him to Me," "East Bound Freight Train," and "Freight Train Boogie," were done with guitar accompaniment. In the midst of these busy years with the Tennessee Cutups, Reno made history in still another guise, as the banjoist on a recording of "Feudin' Banjos" with his old friend Arthur "Guitar Boogie" Smith. In this 1955 recording, Reno traded licks with Smith, who played the tenor banjo. Several years later the song reemerged in the soundtrack of the movie *Deliverance* as "Dueling Banjos." A successful lawsuit by Reno and Smith established conclusively that their version had been the model on which the movie tune was based.

Although Reno and Smiley had outstanding individual identities, it is nevertheless difficult to think of them apart. Mac Wiseman, on the other hand, hewed an independent course through most of his performing career and in the process became the best solo singer in bluegrass music. Wiseman is, in many ways, a man of paradox. He never considered himself solely a bluegrass musician; yet it is in that field of music that he established his reputation. No one knew more old songs than Wiseman, but no bluegrass singer was more receptive to new songs from other genres. Tradition lived strongly in Wiseman— in his style of singing and in his repertory of old songs—but he never resisted innovation and has even been a staunch defender of country-pop music.

Wiseman was born in 1925 in Crimora, in the Shenandoah Valley of Virginia, and reared in the Church of the Brethren faith. Although he was sometimes described as a descendant of the sturdy, pietistic German stock that had settled the area from Pennsylvania, Wiseman insists that his family was of English extraction. Growing up in an area where music was strongly valued and preserved, he gradually accumulated a huge repertory of songs, among the largest known by anyone in country music. He had a particularly large storehouse of material from the turn of the twentieth century, including such songs as "Just Tell Them That You Saw Me," "Preacher and the Bear," and "Letter Edged in Black." Many of these songs came from his mother, who heard them on radio broadcasts and transcribed them on school tablets, but others came from professional entertainers, and Wiseman's recorded repertory reflects this latter influence in songs chosen from Buddy Starcher, the Carter Family, Molly O'Day, Bradley Kincaid, and others.

It was with Molly O'Day that Wiseman broke into full-time professional music. In 1946, he joined this great singer as a bass player and
worked with her in Knoxville and Atlanta. He also played on many
of the recordings she made for Columbia and came away from the
experience with an additional collection of songs, such as "Six More
Miles to the Graveyard," which he performed throughout his career.
He organized his first band, the Country Boys, in 1947 and performed
with them for about a year on personal appearances and on the popular *Farm and Fun Time* in Bristol, Virginia. Like other musicians of
the time who had an old-time bent, Wiseman gravitated toward the
then-coalescing bluegrass style. He joined the first Flatt and Scruggs
band as a guitarist and featured singer—a role he played in all bands of
which he was a member—but then went with Bill Monroe to the *Grand
Ole Opry* in 1949.

From 1950 to 1957, when he ventured out on his own with a new version of the Country Boys, Wiseman experienced a commercial success
surpassed by no one in bluegrass music except Flatt and Scruggs (and
possibly Bill Monroe). Wiseman and his band averaged three hundred
personal appearances a year and recorded several songs that received
extensive airplay throughout the United States. His band had an exciting, surging sound, marked by the use of twin fiddles and Wiseman's
own inventive guitar runs, and he began building his reputation as "the
voice with a heart." That voice was a husky tenor with excellent range
and unusual expressiveness, and like Hank Snow's, his articulation
was precise and somewhat mannered. He could sing lead or harmony
and was equally adept at fast, rousing tunes or slow, serious numbers.
Whatever the style, Wiseman invested each song with a hard-to-resist
heartfelt sincerity. On such songs as "I Still Write Your Name in the
Sand," "Love Letters in the Sand," "I Wonder How the Old Folks Are
at Home," "Little White Church," and "Dreaming of a Little Cabin," he
demonstrated his knowledge of vintage material, both pop and country, while also bequeathing to country music some of its classic vocal
performances.

Mac Wiseman always maintained close ties with mainstream
country music, acting as Dot Records' country A&R man from 1957
to 1963 and recording an occasional song that employed standard
country instrumentation. The Osborne Brothers, however, did more
than any other group with bluegrass identification to fuse their music
with country and western styles. Bobby and Sonny Osborne were born

in the coal-mining town of Hyden, Kentucky, in 1931 and 1937 respectively, but they moved with their parents to Dayton, Ohio, in the early 1940s. The movement of country and incipient bluegrass musicians into and out of bands in the late 1940s and early 1950s was almost labyrinthine, and the Osbornes' affiliations are no exceptions. The Osbornes were born into a musical family—their father sang, yodeled, and played the banjo, fiddle, and guitar—and this home experience was augmented by the broadcasts of the *Grand Ole Opry*. As a small boy, Bobby was fascinated by Ernest Tubb, and he tried to emulate the sounds heard on the Texas Troubadour's records by singing in a low register and playing an electric guitar. By the time he was sixteen, though, his voice had changed to a high tenor, and he had heard the classic recordings of Monroe, Flatt, and Scruggs. He began performing locally in southern Ohio in 1949, and in July of that year he began the transition to bluegrass music in Middletown, Ohio, when he met Larry Richardson, a banjo player and tenor singer from Galax, Virginia. In November 1949, they joined a string band in Bluefield, West Virginia, called the Lonesome Pine Fiddlers. Richardson's three-finger banjo playing and Osborne's high tenor helped pull that old-time group into bluegrass music.

Between 1949 and 1951, or until Bobby was inducted into the US Marine Corps, he played for a shifting assemblage of musicians, but he began his fateful association with Jimmy Martin, with whom he made his first records for a major label (King), in August 1951. His younger brother, Sonny, began playing the banjo during this period, and Sonny, Bobby, their sister Louise, and Jimmy Martin made their first records for the small Kitty label in Miamisburg, Ohio, about 1951. By the summer of 1952, when he was barely fifteen, Sonny was appearing on the *Grand Ole Opry* with Bill Monroe and had made a series of recordings with the Blue Grass Boys. When Bobby returned to civilian life in 1953, he found that his brother was more than ready to join him in a professional music venture. They joined with Jimmy Martin again, played with him in Detroit for about a year, and in 1954 made a series of records in Nashville that are still highly prized by collectors of early bluegrass music. They spent much of 1955 at WWVA in Wheeling, West Virginia, working with Charlie Bailey (best known for his duet performances with his brother Danny), and then returned home to Dayton in 1956. In that year, they began another fateful association, this time with Kentucky-born Red Allen. Together, they produced some major innovations in the style of bluegrass singing, and the Osborne Brothers began their march toward becoming the most commercially successful act in the bluegrass field.

By the time they joined with Allen, Sonny had begun to take a more active role in singing, so they began to devise a trio style that in itself was rather rare for bluegrass music. Recording for MGM in 1956, they produced their first giant hit, "Ruby," which Bobby had been singing for years. Bobby had learned the song from his father, who in turn had picked it up from Cousin Emmy's 1947 recording. The song's instrumental backing was unusual—Bobby and Sonny both played banjos—but it was Bobby's piercing tenor singing that made the record so commercially appealing. Right at the end of the song the trio came in together and sang the last line with a slow, modulated, note-bending flourish that became one of their trademarks. In 1958, the trio made their most important innovations yet when they recorded a song called "Once More." Most bluegrass and country groups had typically put their harmony lines above the lead singer who sang the melody. In bluegrass trio singing, for example, someone usually sang a tenor just above the lead, and another voice either sang a baritone just below the lead or went up above the tenor into what was called a high baritone. The Osborne Brothers, on the other hand, put the two harmony voices below Bobby's high lead. They made this change in order to take advantage of Bobby's unusual tenor range and to make singing with him more comfortable for Sonny and Red Allen. Other bluegrass groups, though, were charmed by the sound's uniqueness and found that it permitted a wider range of vocal arrangements and choice of keys. The resulting style has been widely copied, but for the Osbornes, this was only the beginning of a series of departures from the bluegrass norm. Compared to most bluegrass groups, they weathered the rock-and-roll storm very well, and when the country music resurgence came in the early 1960s, the Osborne Brothers found themselves not only the most popular bluegrass band in America but a highly competitive group in mainstream country as well.

The Osborne Brothers' occasional partner, Jimmy Martin, clung steadfastly to the standards originally set by Bill Monroe. Through successive changes in bluegrass music, Martin adhered faithfully to the acoustic, hard-driving instrumental sound and high lonesome singing for which he became famous in the early 1950s. James Henry "Jimmy" Martin was born near Sneedville, Tennessee, in 1927, and almost from his birth, music became the all-consuming passion of his life. When he first heard Bill Monroe on WSM, the stylistic road he would follow became firmly fixed. Jimmy plowed corn one summer for his neighbors at fifty cents a day, and with the $7.50 accumulated, he bought his first Gene Autry guitar. He was working as a house painter and singing part-time on radio in Morristown, Tennessee, in late 1949, when he went to Nashville and successfully auditioned for a position as one of the Blue Grass Boys. In the opinion of many, he became the best lead singer and guitarist Bill Monroe ever had.

Martin's high, reedy voice and subtle intonations complemented Monroe's singing extremely well, and his strong rhythm guitar playing, punctuated frequently with dynamic bass runs, gave the Blue Grass Boys a surging, supercharged sound that not even the Lester Flatt years had witnessed. Martin's addition to the group coincided with Monroe's move to the Decca label, and during his two separate stints with the Blue Grass Boys, 1950–1951 and 1952–1954, he helped produce a sound that was every bit as "classic" as that made by Flatt and Scruggs in the 1940s. On such secular songs as "Uncle Pen" (first recorded during these years), "On the Old Kentucky Shore," and "The Little Girl and the Dreadful Snake," and on such religious pieces as "River of Death," "Lord Protect My Soul," and "Voice from on High," Martin and Monroe evoked images of that lonesome, rural life that had originally been the context for bluegrass music's emergence. It was truly "white soul singing" at its best.

During his periods of absence from the Blue Grass Boys, Martin began forging professional relations with other musicians, including the crucial one with the Osborne Brothers. In 1951, he and Bobby Osborne formed the Sunny Mountain Boys, the name that he continued to use for his band. As described earlier in this chapter, the Martin-Osborne association resulted in some memorable recordings—such as "20/20 Vision" for RCA—but they severed their partnership in August 1955, when the Osbornes left Detroit, where they had been working on WJR (they had also appeared on CKLW-TV in Windsor, Ontario). Martin remained in Detroit for a few months, but then moved to the *Louisiana Hayride* in about 1956. During this period, and on through his tenure on WWVA in the late 1950s, Martin attracted several excellent young musicians to the Sunny Mountain Boys, including mandolinists Earl Taylor and Paul Williams and banjoists Sam Hutchins, J. D. Crowe, and Bill Emerson. In Williams and Crowe, who accompanied him to

Shreveport, he found the musicians who came closest to matching him in timing, drive, and dynamism. Joined by Williams's high-tenor singing and Crowe's crisp and powerful banjo playing, Martin produced songs such as "Sophronie" and "Ocean of Diamonds" that became bluegrass standards.

Although Martin was often viewed as a controversial entertainer,[14] because of his outspokenness and his tendency to show his irritation with sidemen who could not match his very high standards, he was nevertheless a consistently loyal partisan of bluegrass music. And at his best (which was most of the time), he gave the music he loved some of its greatest moments both as a singer and as a guitarist.

Great moments also spiced the career of Carter and Ralph Stanley,[15] from Stratton, Virginia. The Stanleys were probably the most tradition-based act in bluegrass music, with a repertory heavily laced with old songs and a style of performance that often suggested the mountain string bands of the 1920s and 1930s. Growing up in the mountains of southwestern Virginia, Carter and Ralph were born early enough (in 1925 and 1927 respectively) to hear the radio broadcasts and recordings of such people as the Carter Family, Grayson and Whitter, Mainer's Mountaineers, and Roy Hall's Blue Ridge Entertainers. They also learned directly from their musical parents and from neighbors in their boyhood Baptist church near McClure, Virginia. Their father was a sawmill operator who sang old songs like "Man of Constant Sorrow" and "Wild Bill Jones," while their mother, the most musical of the two parents, played claw-hammer banjo style as did all of her brothers and sisters. The Stanleys often heard old hymns, such as "The Village Churchyard," lined out in the local church, usually by their father or an uncle, to a congregation that made no attempts to sing in parts. Much of the feeling, as well as a few of the songs, from that highly ornamented style insinuated itself into Carter and Ralph's music, although the boys' harmony obviously came from other sources.

When Carter and Ralph returned from military service in 1946, they began making attempts at a professional music career. By this time, Carter had fallen under the spell of Bill Monroe, and his admiration for the bluegrass master was second to no one's, not even Jimmy Martin's. He joined a band that included another Monroe disciple, mandolinist Pee Wee Lambert, and guitarist Roy Sykes. When Ralph received his military discharge, he also joined the group, but by December 1946, he and Carter had formed their own independent band

and were performing on WNVA in Norton, Virginia. Within about a month they moved to the king of bluegrass radio stations, WCYB in Bristol, Virginia, where the noontime *Farm and Fun Time* played host, at one time or another, to Flatt and Scruggs, Jim and Jesse, Mac Wiseman, Jimmy Martin, and Bobby Osborne. The sound of the early Stanleys is preserved in a small group of records that they made for Rich-R-Tone between September 1947 and June 1949. Their love for lonesome old songs is seen in their performance of items like "Little Glass of Wine," a murder-and-suicide ballad that was very popular with their hill country listeners. But even more discernible was the influence of Bill Monroe. Pee Wee Lambert, who played mandolin and sang tenor as Monroe did, sang the high harmony on most of their songs and performed the rousing "Molly and Tenbrooks" by himself. Ralph was a shy teenager when the Stanleys first organized, and his singing tended to be a bit hesitant. He usually sang a tenor just above Carter's lead, and Lambert sang a high baritone above him—a practice that endured on into their Columbia recording years. As a banjoist, though, Ralph was already excellent, possessing the ability to play the claw-hammer style learned from his mother, as well as the three-finger style picked up from Snuffy Jenkins.

The Columbia years, 1949–1953, are also distinguished by the maturing of Carter's songwriting abilities. He experimented with all the varieties of songs found in bluegrass, from gospel to secular, but he excelled in the writing of lonesome songs, full of pastoral imagery, that described personal loss or disappointment. Carter had a profound love for his mountain home and the beautiful rural landscape that defined its character. Like a true romanticist, he often wrote of the loss, or possible loss, of the people and places that he loved—parents, sweethearts, the old home place, the rural scenes of childhood. Bob Cantwell suggests that Carter was often singing about his own loneliness and private doubts, and about the growing distance between himself and his childhood home.[16] Like Will Hays and, above all, Albert Brumley, whose songs the Stanley Brothers eloquently performed ("Rank Stranger," "Nobody Answered Me," "If We Never Meet Again"), Carter often used nature or pastoral images as backdrops for his themes of parting, disappointment, and loneliness. In "The Lonesome River," one of the Stanleys' most haunting performances, "the lonesome wind blows and the water rolls high" as the narrator recalls his lover's betrayal. In "The Fields Have Turned Brown," nature seems to mirror the bleakness felt by a wayward son who returns to find his parents dead. And in "The White Dove," one of their most requested songs, the mourning dove, weeping willows, and deep rolling hills of old Virginia all combine to commiserate with the suffering child who recalls his departed parents and the peaceful mountain home they once shared.

By the time the Stanleys signed with Mercury in 1953, Ralph had overcome his early reticence and was using the assertive and penetrating tenor that had often been sublimated. His voice was unmistakably rural in phrasing and pronunciation, and he sang in the classic back-country pinched-throat style with a variety of affecting vocal turns and note embellishments. Over the years, his harmony singing became so powerful that it became, in effect, a lead voice, dominating the other voices and pulling them along in its sway. The Mercury years found the Stanley Brothers at the height of their performing powers, and their recordings were characterized by a sharp, bright sound, full of verve and energy. Ralph's blossoming tenor was, of course, responsible for much of this sound, but their band, the Clinch Mountain Boys, was pushed along to greater rhythmic drive by the pulsating bass of George Shuffler, one of the first great bass players in bluegrass music. Well before the urban folk revival made Americans conscious of traditional songs and styles, the Stanley Brothers were fusing their mountain sound with the dynamic bluegrass style. The results were what Alan Lomax would soon describe as "folk music with overdrive."[17]

The Stanley Brothers' neighbors from southwestern Virginia, Jim and Jesse McReynolds, who would also play crucial roles in introducing bluegrass music to the world, were nonetheless significantly different from the Stanleys and the other entertainers thus far discussed. Unlike all the others, who either played for Bill Monroe or were directly influenced by him, the McReynolds Brothers drew little direct inspiration from the bluegrass patriarch. Their roots lay in the brother-duet tradition of such singers as the Blue Sky Boys and the Delmore Brothers. Their principal inspirations, above all, were Ira and Charlie Louvin, whose style they suggest and whose songs they often sang. Jim and Jesse were born in a coal-mining region of Virginia in 1927 and 1929. Like the Stanley Brothers, they were heirs to a family musical tradition, and some forebears had even made a few records back in the late 1920s. When they began their first regular radio stint in 1947 on WNVA in Norton, Virginia, the McReynolds Brothers were closer to the mold of prewar hillbillies than they were to bluegrass. They sang country and old-time gospel songs, and Jesse played both the mandolin and the fiddle (the latter learned from old-time fiddler Marion Sumner). Their career took them to several radio stations in the mountain area and into the Midwest. While working in Waterloo, Iowa, and Wichita, Kansas, they even tried their luck with western-style singing and affected a style similar to that of the Sons of the Pioneers.

When Jesse McReynolds heard the exciting banjo style of Earl Scruggs, he set out to create a similar syncopated sound on his mandolin. He devised a cross-picking technique, marked by the rapid alternating of a flat-pick from string to string, that gave the illusion of multiple picks; it permitted him to play fast songs with a profusion of syncopated notes. He debuted with the style in 1951 when he, Jim, and Larry Roll recorded an album of gospel songs (such as "I'll Fly Away" and "God Put a Rainbow in the Clouds") for a small, and now defunct, Kentucky record label under the name of the Virginia Trio. In 1952, Jim and Jesse moved to the prestigious Capitol label, where they could introduce the style to a much larger audience, this time as the accompaniment of a Louvin Brothers song, "Are You Missing Me?"

The Capitol association also marked Jim and Jesse's transition to bluegrass. They were joined on the recordings by the three-finger banjo playing of Snuffy Jenkins's nephew, Hoke Jenkins, who had first played with them back in 1949. The Capitol years were artistically rewarding but commercially disappointing for the McReynolds Brothers, which made their tenure with the company relatively brief. They worked with some of Nashville's outstanding studio musicians, such as fiddlers Tommy Jackson and Tommy Vaden and bassist Bob Moore, and they recorded some of the classics of the bluegrass repertory, including "Airmail Special," "My Little Honeysuckle Rose," and, of course, "Are You Missing Me?"

Although Jim and Jesse's band, the Virginia Boys, always included great musicians—such as banjoist Allen Shelton and fiddler Vassar Clements—the group was most highly valued for its singing. Jesse McReynolds became the marvel of other mandolin players, admired for the remarkable dexterity and speed exhibited on songs like "Border Ride" and "El Cumbanchero" and for his cross-picking innovations. Nevertheless, instrumentation primarily provided support for the precise, high-harmony singing of the two brothers, and they chose keys to highlight their singing rather than for instrumental virtuosity. If Jesse was the instrumental mainstay of the duo, Jim was the key to their heralded vocal blend. His smooth and deceptively effortless tenor was sometimes reminiscent of Ira Louvin but without the latter's sharp edge. He was probably the least strident of bluegrass singers, and on some slow songs his voice assumed a plaintiveness that recalled the singing of Bill Bolick. Jim and Jesse brought a mellow, soft tone to bluegrass singing and a receptivity to songs from other genres that gave them an audience that extended well beyond the borders of their adopted musical field.

While bluegrass grew into a lush and fertile field, the man who had originally sown its seeds continued to evolve and improve as a musician. And, for a time, he also remained unaware of the revolution he had wrought. Bill Monroe was clearly embittered when Flatt and Scruggs left his band, and his irritation only grew as his own contributions were ignored in the avalanche of publicity that accompanied bluegrass music's rising popularity in the late 1950s. He did not speak to his two former colleagues for many years. Imitation may be the highest form of flattery, but Monroe did not recognize the truth of the aphorism, at least in the case of the Stanley Brothers. When the Stanleys signed with Columbia in 1949, Monroe severed his relations with the company, complaining that this competitive group played music too similar to his own. The Blue Grass Boys, though, continued to attract outstanding talent, and Monroe's long tenure with Decca (now MCA) saw no break in the outpouring of distinguished music that had long characterized the man.

As noted earlier, the Decca years were inaugurated by Monroe's performances with Jimmy Martin, the man whose voice so superbly complemented his own. In Rudy Lyle, Monroe also found a five-string banjoist who was almost as good as Earl Scruggs. With Martin and Lyle on board, he possessed a combination whose music more than held its own in competition with the sound of Flatt and Scruggs. Musicians came and departed from the Blue Grass Boys with such great rapidity in the years since 1950 that it would be cumbersome, if not impossible, to discuss them all. It is significant that Monroe clung to the concept of the five-string banjo after Scruggs's departure, and such outstanding banjoists as Lyle, Don Stover, Sonny Osborne, Bill Keith, Bobby Thompson, Vic Jordan, Alan Munde, and Bob Black spent some time as Blue Grass Boys. Of all instrumentalists, though, fiddlers were most highly prized by Monroe. Such men as Vassar Clements, Gordon Terry, Charlie Cline, Benny Martin, Bobby Hicks, and Benny Williams traveled and recorded with Monroe, but he did not find his consummate fiddler—the man he called "the best fiddler in bluegrass"—until Kenny Baker joined him in 1957. Baker was an ex–coal miner from eastern Kentucky who came to Monroe and bluegrass after earlier experience as a western swing and mainstream country performer. His smooth, flowing, jazz-inflected style made him popular with both Monroe and fans. Although his membership was not continuous, Baker served as a Blue Grass Boy longer than any other person. Joe Stuart, on the other hand, spent fewer years with Monroe but in some respects was the most remarkable musician ever employed as a Blue Grass Boy. After 1955, when he came to the Blue Grass Boys as a banjo player, Stuart played guitar, fiddle, bass, and banjo in the band. Only Monroe's monopolization of the mandolin kept Stuart from playing that instrument, too.

Over the years, Bill Monroe mellowed significantly, becoming more open with interviewers and accepting his role as the patriarch of bluegrass. The urban folk revival contributed greatly to Monroe's personal resurgence. Young folklorists or folk music enthusiasts, such as Mike Seeger, Jim Rooney, and Ralph Rinzler, praised Monroe's achievements and helped correct the critical imbalance that had arisen in the wake of the adulation given to Earl Scruggs. Rinzler also acted as Monroe's manager for a short period after 1962 and helped get him bookings at colleges, at folk clubs, and in other arenas of critical importance. Gradually, people began to understand that bluegrass was more than just a Scruggs-style banjo, and that Monroe had been the cog around which the bluegrass machine revolved. Monroe was particularly flattered, and humbled, by the adulation with which young people responded to him and his music. The interest evinced by some young northerners intrigued and gratified him, and a few of them became Blue Grass Boys: Richard Greene, Pete Rowan, Lamar Grier, Douglas B. Green, Roland White, and Bill Keith.

During the nine months that he worked for Monroe in 1963, William Bradford Keith (born in Boston in 1939) introduced the first great departure from Scruggs-style banjo. Designed to enhance the playing of fast and complicated fiddle tunes on the banjo, Keith's "chromatic" style (also fashioned independently by Bobby Thompson in about 1958) stresses the "exact and complete" melody of a tune.[18] Scruggs style, on the other hand, features a shower of syncopated notes, but not all of them fall directly into the melody. Keith's rendition of such tunes as "Sailor's Hornpipe" was widely admired, and his style became an ingredient of the developing "progressive bluegrass" movement.

Keith was only one of many young musicians outside the South who were drawn to the bluegrass medium. Even before the urban folk boom began, the bluegrass sounds were beginning to circulate nationally. The powerful broadcasts of WWVA, in Wheeling, West Virginia, introduced the music of such people as the Lilly Brothers, Bill Clifton, Wilma Lee and Stoney Cooper, Tex Logan, the Osborne Brothers, and Jimmy Martin to audiences in New England and the Northeast. Mac Martin, whose real name was William D. Colleran, grew up listening to WWVA at his home in Pittsburgh. He began his own music career in 1949, and after 1957, began a long tenure with his Dixie Travelers at Walsh's Lounge in Pittsburgh. His musical evolution was similar to that of Joe Valiante up in Boston. Valiante was introduced to bluegrass by the broadcasts of WWVA and other stations, and after listening to the Lilly Brothers at Boston's Hillbilly Ranch, he resolved to be a professional musician. Performing as Joe Val, with his New England Bluegrass Boys, he became famous for his high-tenor singing and dynamic mandolin playing. Like Mac Martin and many of the northern converts to bluegrass, Val adhered faithfully to the performance of traditional Monroe-style bluegrass.

Bluegrass bands played frequently at the country music parks that had flourished since the mid-1930s in the border areas contiguous to the Upper South. Southeastern Pennsylvania, Maryland, and Delaware was a particularly fruitful area for bluegrass expansion, and both local bands and touring musicians found enthusiastic audiences there. The New River Ranch at Rising Sun, Maryland, one of the most active of these parks, was established by the musicians Bud and Ola Belle Reed,[19] who played bluegrass and old-time music to the large mixture of transplanted hillbillies who had migrated to the region and to native northerners attracted to the music. Such parks as the New River Ranch and Sunset Park (in West Grove, Pennsylvania) became crucially important places of cultural exchange where tradition-based musicians, many of them southern-born, met northern fans who were just beginning to be awakened to the joys of folk music in the mid-1950s. The parks contributed to bluegrass music's national expansion and played a valuable role in the dawning urban folk revival.

Bluegrass musicians also found good receptions in many of the bars and honky-tonks where southern migrants gathered in cities such as

Baltimore; Washington, DC; Cincinnati; Dayton; Middletown, Ohio; and Detroit. Not only did Detroit attract professional musicians like Earl Taylor, Jimmy Martin, and the Osborne Brothers, it also spawned local bands among the large base of southern-born migrants there. Curly Dan and Wilma Ann (a husband-and-wife team) were fixtures on the local Detroit scene, as were Roy McGinnis and the Sunnysiders, and George and Mary Williamson, who performed as the Old Kentucky String Band. These musicians tended to gravitate toward old-time country and gospel sounds as a binding reminder of those southern hills of home; Fay McGinnis, for example, the wife of the musician Roy McGinnis, founded and led for many years the Stanley Brothers Fan Club, one of the most active country fan clubs in the nation.

One of the most fascinating cases of northern bluegrass interest was the phenomenon of Hillbilly Ranch. Located in a rough section of Boston, on the edge of the notorious center of bars and prostitution known as the "Combat Zone," the Hillbilly Ranch was home for several local and touring country music groups in the late 1940s and early 1950s. Boston was not without its own native-grown country talent. One of country music's greatest yodelers and cowboy-style singers, Kenny Roberts, worked out of Boston and the New England area in the late 1940s and early 1950s. Jerry and Sky (Gerald Howorth and Schuyler Snow), to cite still another example, were Portsmouth, New Hampshire, boys who generally performed over radio stations in Boston. They sang in brother-duet fashion and worked out a style of duet yodeling as good as anything done by southern hillbillies. Their version of "Sparkling Brown Eyes," recorded for the Sonora label in about 1945, is still the model for most performances of the song.

While the Lilly Brothers did not introduce country music to Boston or to Hillbilly Ranch, their music nevertheless had an impact on the local bluegrass scene that no other group equaled. Everett and Mitchell "Bea" Lilly were musicians from Clear Creek, West Virginia, who had grown up mesmerized by the music of the Monroe Brothers and the Blue Sky Boys. They began singing as teenagers and made appearances in the early 1940s on the *Old Farm Hour* at WCHS in Charleston, West Virginia. While playing on WWVA's *Wheeling Jamboree* in the late 1940s, they came to the attention of certain musicians who proved crucial to their later careers: the fiddler Tex Logan and Flatt and Scruggs. Flatt and Scruggs hired Everett Lilly in 1951 and considered him to be one of the best tenor singers and mandolin players they had ever had. Benjamin Franklin "Tex" Logan, the dapper and dynamic fiddler from Sweetwater, Texas, who had played with the Lillys and with Wilma Lee and Stoney Cooper in Wheeling, remembered the boys after he moved to Boston to attend graduate school at MIT. It was largely through Logan's encouragement that they also moved to Boston in 1952.

Everett and Mitchell worked briefly at the Plaza Bar and Mohawk Ranch, and then settled down for their long stint at Hillbilly Ranch, playing seven nights a week for truck drivers, sailors, working folk, "combat zone" denizens, and college students who were brave enough to venture into the place. It seems incongruous that the clear, high Appalachian sound of the Lillys should thrive so long in the frigid, working-class atmosphere of a New England honky-tonk, but many people were charmed by the hard-driving musicianship and vocal purity of the Lilly Brothers. The Lillys, for their part, capitalized on the romance associated with the South, styling themselves the Confederate Mountaineers (even though West Virginia had been a Union state). Many besotted customers probably paid no attention at all to the Lillys (a fate suffered by most honky-tonk musicians), but to many of the local, budding musicians, the music of the Lilly Brothers and their great banjoist, Don Stover, was like manna from heaven. Joe Val, Bill Keith, Jim Rooney, and the whole array of musicians who composed the Charles River Boys—one of the first northern bluegrass bands to spring into existence—were all directly inspired by these transplanted West Virginia musicians.

Although bluegrass demonstrated its appeal in places like Detroit and Boston, it found no urban reception stronger than that in the Washington, DC/Baltimore metropolitan area.[20] Country music had never been alien to the Washington music scene; Eddie Nesbitt had performed his brand of old-time music there for many years, but bluegrass attracted a heavy following in this southern-flavored city and in nearby Baltimore. The music's core audience probably lay among the people from the surrounding small towns and rural areas in Virginia and Maryland who had ventured into the metropolitan area to work at government jobs or in defense-related industries. Ernest "Pop" Stoneman, for example—the pioneer hillbilly artist of the 1920s—worked in a naval ordnance factory; his children organized one of the most sensational bluegrass bands of the 1960s, and Pop, playing with them, found a new audience for his old-time singing and autoharp playing.

Rural migrants, however, made up only part of the bluegrass audience. During the bluegrass heyday of the late 1950s and early 1960s, the full spectrum of Washington society, including US representatives and senators, could usually be found in attendance at bluegrass concerts, and at least one senator—Robert Byrd of West Virginia, an old-time fiddler—publicly performed the music. An abundance of outlets existed at the time for those who loved the music. Don Owens, for example, played the music on his radio shows long before it received the name of "bluegrass." Jimmy Dean's *Country Style* show on WTOP-TV included the banjoist Smitty Ervin and the fiddler Buck Ryan; Roy Clark, the son of Virginia migrants who had moved into the Washington area, played his banjo on Connie B. Gay's *Town and Country Time*; and a network of bars and clubs, such as the Shamrock in Georgetown and the Red Fox Inn in Bethesda, provided outlets for musicians in the greater Washington area. A profusion of musicians, such as Earl Taylor, Bill Harrell, Bill Clifton, Reno and Smiley, Benny and Vallie Cain, and Ola Belle and Bud Reed, played in clubs or parks in Baltimore, northwestern Maryland, and northern Virginia. In Washington itself, Buzz Busby served as a catalyst for bluegrass expansion. Born Bernarr Graham Busbice in West Monroe, Louisiana, the fiery mandolinist and high-tenor singer provided employment for budding bluegrass musicians in his Bayou Boys, while also contributing some of the finest examples of lonesome but hard-driving bluegrass songs: "Just Me and the Jukebox" and "I Stood on the Bridge at Midnight" (based on a Henry Wadsworth Longfellow poem).

Bluegrass really began to flourish in the Washington area, though, when the Country Gentlemen came into existence in 1957. The personnel of this great band changed radically through the years, but one of its founders, the singer-guitarist Charlie Waller, remained its leader for many years and gave it an enduring distinctiveness. Born in Joinerville, Texas, but reared near Monroe, Louisiana, Waller came to Washington as a member of Busby's Bayou Boys. When an automobile accident temporarily halted Busby's ability to perform, Waller joined with another mandolin player and tenor singer named John Duffey, banjoist Bill Emerson, and bass player Tom Gray to form the original version of the Country Gentlemen. Eddie Adcock replaced Emerson in 1959, and the band assumed the complexion that it would preserve until Duffey retired in 1969. The Country Gentlemen are now remembered as founding fathers of the progressive bluegrass style, but they did not always seem so in the early days of their existence. Although their avoidance of the fiddle may have been a calculated attempt to resist the harder and more rural sound associated with Bill Monroe, they nevertheless clung resolutely to the acoustic style. In some ways, they and many of the other young musicians of the time were "hyper-bluegrass,"[21] in that they often exaggerated the stereotyped features of the music: Charlie Waller's guitar runs occurred often and imaginatively; John Duffey's tenor soared to rarefied heights; and songs were performed at breakneck speed. The acceleration of tempos sometimes resulted in dynamic performances and permitted the musicians to exhibit their instrumental virtuosity, but in some cases speed only robbed a song of its pathos or sensitivity (as when the Country Gentlemen galloped through their version of the old parlor song "They Say It Is Sinful to Flirt"). These young musicians, however, played with an energy and excitement of discovery that was refreshingly contagious; above all, they restored the sense of vitality that had accompanied bluegrass music's first stirrings back in the mid-1940s.

The Country Gentlemen's support among both "classic" and "progressive" bluegrass fans was probably unmatched by any other group of musicians. Though they clung to acoustic instrumentation and used instruments that were identified with bluegrass music, the Country Gentlemen freely experimented with other musical forms. Duffey played jazz progressions on his mandolin, and Adcock was among the most versatile and inventive of banjoists, playing Scruggs-style, plectrum, and chromatic notes on his instrument. Like those of most bluegrass bands, they spiced their stage shows with comedy, but their humor tended to be more satirical and youth-oriented than that of most groups. Their style of comedy was sometimes zany in its manifestations, especially appealing to college students and urban folk enthusiasts. It was in their choice of songs, though, that the Country Gentlemen presaged the appearance of the progressive impulse in bluegrass music. They reached out for all kinds of music—folk, rock, pop, and vintage country—and converted them to bluegrass. Bob Dylan compositions such as "Baby Blue" and "Girl from the North Country," songs from Hollywood scores like "Theme from *Exodus*," Nashville tunes like Mel Tillis's "Matterhorn," pop standards like "Heartaches," hillbilly songs learned from old 78 rpm recordings such as Molly O'Day's "Poor Ellen Smith"—all appeared alongside songs from the days of classic bluegrass. This search for an eclectic repertory, inspired partly by the diversity of their Washington audiences, was further motivated by the emergence of the folk revival after 1958.[22]

When the urban folk craze arrived, it soon drew bluegrass into its orbit. Many fans who first became interested in folk or folklike music by hearing the Kingston Trio or Pete Seeger later began searching for more authentic manifestations. Some people dug back into early hillbilly music and discovered such old timers as Uncle Dave Macon, the Carter Family, or the Skillet Lickers, while others gravitated toward bluegrass, this dynamic sound that seemed to represent a vital updating and reinvigoration of traditional mountain string band and vocal styles. The linking of folk-song interest and bluegrass actually began as early as 1957, when the folklorist D.K. Wilgus began reviewing bluegrass records in the *Kentucky Folklore Record* and when Folkways released *American Banjo: Three-Finger and Scruggs Style* (produced by Mike Seeger and edited by Ralph Rinzler). The music really gained its first significant entree into the consciousness of America's literate but nonacademic urban middle class when Alan Lomax lent his support in 1959. In April of that year, Lomax sponsored a concert of folk music in New York at Carnegie Hall that included Earl Taylor and the Stoney Mountain Boys. In October, Lomax wrote a short article on bluegrass for *Esquire* magazine and called the form the "freshest sound" in American folk music. The journalist Robert Shelton probably reached a much larger readership when he began reviewing bluegrass as part of his folk music column in the *New York Times*; Shelton had nothing but enthusiastic praise for Earl Scruggs, calling him the Paganini of the five-string banjo.[23]

The participation of bluegrass musicians at folk-related affairs, probably inaugurated by Earl Taylor's Carnegie Hall performance, increased dramatically in late 1959 and in the early 1960s. Earl Scruggs's appearance at the Newport Folk Festival in 1959 (with Hylo Brown instead of Lester Flatt and the Foggy Mountain Boys) may have been the most prestigious of these events, but the Osborne Brothers' concert at Antioch College in February 1960 boded most favorably for the music's commercial expansion. Colleges proved important forums for bluegrass exposure up to the middle 1960s. Several bluegrass bands became active on the college circuit, but Flatt and Scruggs and the Stanley Brothers seemed to be the most popular attractions. Bluegrass groups everywhere began increasing the percentage of traditional music in their repertories, or in some cases performed songs they had learned from the urban folkies. The Stanley Brothers seemed to thrive artistically and commercially from their brush with the academic/ folk community. When the first stirrings of the folk revival came, the Stanleys were living in Live Oak, Florida, appearing daily on television for the Jim Walter Corporation (maker of prefabricated housing), but with their concert schedule greatly curtailed because of the rock-and-roll infestation of country music. Through the impetus of the folk revival, the Stanleys began resurrecting many of the old songs they had known since childhood (antiques or evergreens, as Carter Stanley called them), and Ralph began doing an occasional tune in the claw-hammer style learned from his mother. Recording now for the King label, and encouraged by Syd Nathan, who was forever seeking successors to the Delmore Brothers, the Stanley Brothers began featuring the sound of a lead guitar. Bill Napier, with his rapid notes and mandolin-style tremolo, was the first of their musicians to employ a flat-picking style. But George Shuffler did the most to popularize the fashion while also introducing a major innovation in country guitar picking: his cross-picking technique reproduced on the guitar a sound similar to what Jesse McReynolds achieved on the mandolin.

Flatt and Scruggs's association with the folk movement had more mixed results. The duo reached a huge audience through this relationship, and Earl Scruggs was lionized by urban folk enthusiasts. Flatt and Scruggs needed little encouragement to do old-time songs, for they had been performing such material all their lives. But they were also pressured—by their Columbia recording directors—to record contemporary material written by urban folk artists such as Bruce "Utah" Phillips and Bob Dylan, and with instrumental backing that sometimes smothered their fresh acoustic sound. This arrangement sometimes bore sweet melodic fruit, as in their popular performance of Phillips's "Rock Salt and Nails," but more often it resulted in listless, unimaginative renditions that seemed greatly out of character for the group. Earl Scruggs tolerated the material, partly through the influence of his musical sons, but Lester Flatt, who had to sing lyrics that he did not feel or, sometimes, understand, was uncomfortable in this role. Differences concerning musical direction eventually contributed to the breakup of the famous team in 1969.

Most bluegrass musicians were affected in one way or another by the folk revival. For example, Frank "Hylo" Brown (so called because of his great vocal range) recorded a host of songs taken from or inspired by the urban folkies. Bill Clifton, though, was country music's most important link to the movement as well as being a bridge to the international community. Born William Marburg in Riverdale, Maryland, in 1931, Clifton was a most unlikely apostle of old-time music.[24] The son of a wealthy investment banker, and himself the holder of a master's degree in business administration from the University of Virginia, Clifton was introduced to country music while visiting in the homes of the farmers who lived on his father's estate. Listening to the hillbilly songs that came over his hosts' radios, Clifton equated the music with the values and lifestyles of the farmers. That is, he felt that the music was decent, unaffected, and down-to-earth. Not even his attendance at prestigious prep schools (St. Paul's and Adirondack) could shake his affection for old-time country music. He listened faithfully to the radio barn dances, collected records, and even made pilgrimages to New York City to see Woody Guthrie. By the time he matriculated at the University of Virginia in 1949, he had learned the guitar and was ready to try his luck at radio singing. He performed on a local station in Charlottesville, Virginia, and began a singing partnership with fellow student Paul Clayton (who eventually became one of the mainstays of the folk revival). In 1954, performing with his Dixie Mountain Boys and recording for Blue Ridge, Clifton produced his first modest hit, "Flower Blooming in the Wildwood." This song came from the repertory of the Coon Creek Girls and was part of a large storehouse of old songs that Clifton brought to bluegrass music. Clifton printed one hundred and fifty of these songs in a large-format paperback edition that became indispensable for fledgling bluegrass singers and urban folk singers.[25] During the commercially bleak years of 1957 and 1958, when country music as a whole seemed in retreat from its traditional foundations, Clifton continued to record such melodic old-timers as "Little White Washed Chimney," "The Girl I Left in Sunny Tennessee," and "Mary Dear." Clifton, then, was already doing his part to preserve old-time music well before the folk revival exerted its influence. Furthermore, his contacts among both bluegrass people and urban folkies enabled him to work freely with both groups and to bring them together in common formats. He served as an adviser to the Newport Folk Festival and played a major role in the selection of country musicians for that affair.

Bluegrass definitely profited from the national preoccupation with folk music in the early 1960s. Reviving from the doldrums of the rock-and-roll period, bluegrass musicians found new places to play and new audiences to appreciate them. But, strangely, when the country music industry as a whole revived in the early 1960s, bluegrass found itself isolated from the country mainstream. Except when used as fillers, that is, to introduce commercials or to go into newsbreaks, bluegrass tunes virtually disappeared from radio disc jockey shows—casualties of the industry's reassessment of itself after the rock-and-roll siege and of the Top Forty format. Only rarely did a bluegrass song appear on a jukebox, and record buyers found it increasingly difficult to buy such items in retail outlets. Only those musicians who adopted country-and-western stylistic traits were able to achieve any kind of exposure in the country mainstream. Mac Wiseman, for example, received some airplay with songs like "Charlie's Pride and Johnny's Cash" that used country-style backing. He never complained about country music's drift toward pop or about the neglect from which bluegrass suffered; instead, he sought to succeed within the new formats that were coming into existence. Jim and Jesse McReynolds made a major attempt to thrive as country performers in the mid-1960s. Working from their base on the *Grand Ole Opry*, which they joined in 1964, Jim and Jesse built an act reminiscent of the Louvin Brothers, combining electric and acoustic instruments and singing songs that sounded much like those of their country-and-western contemporaries (e.g., "It's a Long Way to the Top of the World," "Stormy Horizons"). They traveled during this period with a group of musicians who could play drums and electric guitars as well as the conventional bluegrass instruments. Their biggest hit came in 1966 with a truck-driving song called "Diesel on My Tail," which was backed by electric guitar, pedal steel, drums, and piano. A 1965 album of Chuck Berry songs, called *Berry Pickin' in the Country*, was a delightful foray into another idiom, but as a departure from tradition, was probably an irritant to classic bluegrass fans.

The most successful band to adjust to country-and-western dominance was unquestionably that of the Osborne Brothers. Always innovative and never reluctant to experiment with musical forms, the Osborne Brothers enjoyed a wider exposure in American life than any other bluegrass group. They made a calculated attempt to overcome the resistance of country disc jockeys and promoters by using the modern material of Nashville songwriters (such as Felice and Boudleaux Bryant); by adopting drums, piano, and electric instruments; and, of course, by perfecting the unique, modulated style of harmony for which they were already famous. One of the biggest promoters of country music in the South, Carlton Haney, included the Osbornes in his big package shows along with such performers as Conway Twitty and Dottie West. The Osbornes more than held their own against such competition, but they became even more resolved to use electric instrumentation in order to attract country-and-western fans conditioned to accept such a sound. Their performance of "Rocky Top" (written by the Bryants) became one of the most-programmed bluegrass songs in the world, and by the early 1970s, they had begun winning awards in CMA polls as the best vocal group in country music. Tours with Merle Haggard's country show, also in the early 1970s, served as icing on the cake. Experiments with electric sounds, of course, provoked heated controversy within the bluegrass ranks, and purists accused the Osbornes and Jim and Jesse of selling the music out. The Osborne Brothers, though, stuck to their successful format and responded to their critics with angry, and sometimes ill-chosen, words of their own. Speaking in the heady atmosphere of success, Sonny Osborne charged that there had been no new ideas in bluegrass since 1948, and, he asserted, "Truly I don't care all that much for bluegrass."[26]

As bluegrass faded from the country mainstream, it found itself in the unusual position of being, in one sense, highly prominent in American popular culture, while at the same time thriving as a musical subculture. Bluegrass-style instrumentation appeared often as backing for radio and television commercials, and bluegrass songs cropped up frequently as themes for movies or television shows. Flatt and Scruggs's "The Ballad of Jed Clampett" became the number one country song for several months in 1962 and 1963 after it was introduced as the theme of the popular *Beverly Hillbillies* television show on CBS. Their "Foggy Mountain Breakdown," first recorded in 1949, gained renewed popularity in 1967 as part of the exciting sound track of the movie *Bonnie and Clyde*. Bluegrass gained additional exposure in still another widely circulated movie, *Deliverance*. Eric Weissberg played Scruggs-style banjo on a tune called "Dueling Banjos" (in this case, though, it was a "duel" between a guitar and a banjo). After the movie appeared, no banjoist could get through a concert without someone requesting this song, one of the few bluegrass tunes that most Americans know. (Incidentally, the movie also made Don Reno and Arthur Smith considerably richer as a result of their successful suit as the original "composers" of "Dueling Banjos.")

Although bluegrass musicians such as Bill Monroe, Flatt and

Scruggs, Jim and Jesse, and the Osborne Brothers did belong to the *Grand Ole Opry*, most other avenues of dissemination within country music were closed to the bluegrass folk. The major record labels showed little interest in bluegrass, and the genre therefore found its way to a host of smaller companies that often depended on mail-order or concert sales. Bluegrass musicians, thus, invariably hawked their records and tapes wherever a performance was given. In the early 1960s, Starday Records,[27] the Texas-born company founded by Jack Starnes and Pappy Daily, became the most active bluegrass distributor in the nation. Under Don Pierce, who became the firm's principal owner after its move to Nashville, Starday strove to fill the vacuum created by the major companies' preoccupations with modern and country-pop music. Although Starday concentrated on bluegrass performers, great and small, it also brought back to recording such old-time musicians as Sam and Kirk McGee, Lew Childre, and the Blue Sky Boys. When Starday declined, other labels such as County, Rebel, Rural Rhythm, Rounder, and Sugar Hill appeared to satisfy the needs of bluegrass and old-time music fans. Unfortunately, too many bluegrass fans were addicted to the taping of musical performances, whether at live concerts or festivals, or from someone else's records. To the great consternation of the musicians, and to the commercial detriment of the music as a whole, tape recorders abounded at festivals or anywhere that bluegrass was played. Uncle Jim O'Neal, the proprietor of Rural Rhythm and an active mail-order distributor, complained that "you can't sell bluegrass records to bluegrass fans. Nine out of ten of 'em want the records free. Either that or they go to a bluegrass festival and sit there on the stage to where most of the audience can't even see with their cassette recorders."[28]

The festivals to which Uncle Jim referred have constituted the core and salvation of bluegrass music. While his criticism of bluegrass fans had some merit, it did not tell the full story of devotion and loyalty shown by the thousands of supporters who traveled to festivals during the spring and summer months. Bill Clifton conceived one of the first festivals, a one-day event held at Luray, Virginia, in 1961. Although the event did not attract hordes of visitors, it contained the germ of the idea that characterized all later festivals—an outdoor meeting in which a wide variety of bands, amateur and professional, participated. The festivals got under way in earnest after Labor Day 1965, when Carlton Haney sponsored an affair at Cantrell's Horse Farm in

Roanoke, Virginia. Haney was a North Carolina–born promoter who became involved in bluegrass when he began booking Bill Monroe and Reno and Smiley in the mid-1950s. Haney brought a sense of drama and history to bluegrass through his presentation of little vignettes about the evolution of the music, tributes to individual musicians, and reunions in which former members of bands got back together on stage. Haney's own festival at Camp Springs, North Carolina, was long one of the most ambitious and best attended of these events, but it was certainly challenged by other festivals held at such places as Berryville, Virginia; McClure, Virginia (near Ralph Stanley's old home place); Cosby, Tennessee; Lavonia, Georgia; Kerrville, Texas; Hugo, Oklahoma; and Bean Blossom, Indiana. The Bean Blossom Festival became probably the biggest of the three hundred or more similar gatherings held all over the United States. Held for several days each June on property owned by Bill Monroe in the beautiful rolling hills of southern Indiana, the Bean Blossom Festival attracted the best bands in bluegrass music and thousands of fans who traveled there from all over the country.

The bluegrass festivals were reminiscent of the religious camp meetings held in rural America during the nineteenth century. As at the earlier camp meetings, the faithful attended in order to be revived, while the skeptics often went away converted. People camped out for days in tents or recreational vehicles (RVs), listened to the professional bands on stage, and participated in jam sessions that often lasted all night long. It was not uncommon to find musicians like Kenny Baker and Joe Stuart playing into the wee hours of the morning alongside earnest amateur banjo pickers, fiddlers, and other instrumentalists. Nowhere else in country music could one find such camaraderie among fans and musicians. Bluegrass fans could actually meet and shake the hands of their heroes, or have their photos taken with people like Bill Monroe, Ralph Stanley, or the Osborne Brothers. The festivals tapped a strong urge among Americans to return to the basics, to a simpler, more manageable, and allegedly more decent society. Most of the festivals banned drinking, drugs, and profanity, and attempted to create a wholesome, family atmosphere. Despite the best intentions, however, rowdy behavior and the freewheeling ambience of the rock festivals intruded into some of the bluegrass affairs, contributing to ugly confrontations between fans, musicians, and security guards.

On the whole, though, the bluegrass festivals were remarkable manifestations of good will. Their chief flaw, as it was with most country music gatherings, was the absence of African Americans, but among the folks who did attend the festivals one found a broad diversity of age, economic, and philosophical groupings. Hippies and rednecks, college students and truck drivers, government workers and farmers, and liberals and conservatives shared festival benches and often played in the same bands. During the 1972 presidential campaign, for example, automobiles and campers at bluegrass festivals often sported either George Wallace or George McGovern bumper stickers, a suggestion that many disaffected people on both the left and right saw in bluegrass music an antidote to a complex, overorganized society. No evidence exists that political attitudes changed as a result of this shared musical experience, but for a brief moment, generational, social, and ideological differences were narrowed, or forgotten, in the exhilaration of a bluegrass breakdown.

Those people who attended the festivals could hear music reminiscent of the "classic" period of the late 1940s and early 1950s, or they could hear sounds that were much influenced by rock, pop, or mainstream country stylings. Bluegrass, in short, had traveled many stylistic roads. While settling into his role as the bluegrass patriarch, Bill Monroe continued to produce exciting and dynamic music. Musicians came and went from the Blue Grass Boys with great frequency, but Kenny Baker remained as a bastion of tradition and excellence. Monroe's seminal work had now won universal acclaim, and he was named to the Country Music Hall of Fame in 1969. Perhaps most significant, Monroe now recognized his own relationship to other musicians who bore the bluegrass label. Reconciliations with the Stanley Brothers and Flatt and Scruggs had long ago been achieved, and he had begun to publicly perform with these and virtually every other bluegrass entertainer of stature. Monroe lent encouragement to all would-be bluegrass musicians, and one of the marvels of his Bean Blossom Festival was the giant jam session that included literally scores of banjoists, fiddlers, guitarists, and mandolin players.

Other "old-timers" also endured in bluegrass, although their ranks were increasingly thinned by death and retirement. The Flatt and Scruggs partnership dissolved in 1969, a victim of too many years together and of differences concerning future stylistic choices. Flatt returned to his real love—classic bluegrass—and he continued to produce good music with his new band, the Nashville Grass, until his death on May 11, 1979. Scruggs formed a band with his musical sons (Gary, Randy, and Steve) called the Earl Scruggs Revue. The Revue was only on the fringe of bluegrass, and Earl's banjo was generally smothered by the heavy cacophony of sound produced by his children's electric instruments. Earl, though, had the chance to exploit an opportunity presented to few fathers—the possibility of sharing his children's musical experiences—and in the person of Randy Scruggs, country music was introduced to one of its greatest guitarists.

Carter Stanley's death on December 1, 1966, brought an end to the career of bluegrass music's most traditional act, the Stanley Brothers. Ralph Stanley remained in professional music, however, and as the leader of the Clinch Mountain Boys, he became even more committed to old-time sounds and songs.[29] While maintaining the high, hard-driving sound of classic bluegrass, Stanley also added a broad sampling of a cappella material to his performances—songs that reflected the congregational singing of the Primitive Baptist Church and of mountain quartet singing. He also had the satisfaction and solace of having at his side two loyal musicians, the fiddler Curly Ray Cline and the bass player Jack Cooke, who were as deeply committed to traditional sounds as Ralph was. In his search for a replacement for his brother Carter, Ralph brought some excellent young talent into bluegrass music—Larry Sparks, an Ohio-born guitarist and singer with a lonesome, rural sound; Roy Lee Centers, a Kentuckian whose voice bore an uncanny resemblance to that of Carter Stanley, but whose promising career was cut short by his murder on May 2, 1974; and Keith Whitley and Ricky Skaggs, also Kentuckians, who had emulated the sound of the Stanley Brothers since they were teenagers. Ralph Stanley's disappointment must have been as keen as that of Bill Monroe upon Flatt and Scruggs's departure when Whitley and Skaggs eventually departed to pursue their own brilliant careers.

Illness and death also caused the dissolution of the great team of Reno and Smiley. Because of complications arising from wounds suffered during World War II, Smiley temporarily retired from full-time musicianship in 1964 but occasionally rejoined Reno on recordings and in concerts before his death in January 1972. Reno formed a partnership for several years with Bill Harrell, the Virginia singer and guitarist who had been a mainstay of the Washington, DC, bluegrass scene since the mid-1950s. Before Reno's death in 1984, though, Harrell had begun performing with his own band.

The other major bluegrass performers from the classic period, Mac Wiseman, Jimmy Martin, Jim and Jesse, and the Osborne Brothers, continued to be active participants of the festival scene until death— as in the case of Jimmy Martin and Jim McReynolds—brought an end to their careers. All of them returned to the older styles that they originally performed. With his body trimmed down from its once-rotund shape, and sporting a graying beard, Wiseman lent dignity to any stage where he performed. Performing solely with pickup bands, he could generally be depended upon to perform his familiar numbers, such as "Love Letters in the Sand" and "I Wonder How the Old Folks Are at Home," as well as more "modern" numbers such as "Catfish John" and "Me and Bobby McGee." Jimmy Martin clung tenaciously to hard-core bluegrass and employed a profusion of musicians, including some of his children. Jim and Jesse and the Osborne Brothers also utilized the services of family members, but, unlike Martin, they sometimes strayed far afield from traditional bluegrass. By the early 1980s, however, both of these groups had drawn back from their absorption with country and western and had moved closer to old-line bluegrass. Except for the electric bass, both groups abandoned the use of drums and electric guitars and returned to the performance of old or old-style material (although neither group stopped playing modern-composed songs).

While many of the original bluegrass musicians continued to perform, they were joined by a new generation of performers. Some of them hewed closely to the sounds of the 1940s and 1950s, while others took bluegrass far afield from the music originally heard on Monroe, Flatt and Scruggs, and Stanley recordings. No one label accurately described the new departures, because some groups, such as the Buck White Family, played music reflective of country and western, while others employed styles clearly derived from folk, rock, blues, jazz, and popular forms of music. It is also difficult to define them in terms of instrumentation. Some of the most innovative musicians, such as the Country Gentlemen and Seldom Scene, used only acoustic instruments, while others—including the traditional Jimmy Martin— experimented with electrification. The changes brought to bluegrass were the natural consequences of musicians' desires to be creative and experimental, and of the wishes of the performers—and their managers—to create a widely commercial product.

As we have seen, progressive bluegrass, or "newgrass," can be traced in part to experiments made by musicians within the "classic" bands. Don Reno, for example, always combined in his banjo playing innovative techniques borrowed from jazz and steel guitar playing with the more traditional mountain stylings. Bill Keith, during his brief tenure with Bill Monroe in 1963, popularized the chromatic style that constituted the first real departure from Scruggs, and Frank Wakefield, a dazzling mandolin player from Tennessee (with whom Keith played before his Monroe period), was already experimenting with complex chord progressions and unorthodox tunings while playing with the traditionalist Red Allen in the early 1960s. David Grisman, who was deeply impressed by Wakefield's inventiveness and flair, was only one of many "progressives" won over by the new sounds heard in bluegrass music in the early 1960s.

Several bands, both obscure and prominent, popularized new approaches to material and style in the early 1960s. A West Coast band, the Dillards (made up of Missouri transplants), introduced their Ozark humor and sophisticated musicianship to a national audience while performing on the Andy Griffith television show in the late 1950s and early 1960s. The Dillards and many of the other bluegrass bands of that period were influenced by the folk revival to perform songs that came not only from older sources but also from contemporary writers such as Bob Dylan, John Prine, Ian Tyson, and Gordon Lightfoot. Other California bands at the time, such as Clarence and Roland White and their Kentucky Colonels, and the Hillmen (which included Don Parmley, Chris Hillman, Rex Gosdin, and Vern Gosdin), also dabbled with folkie material.

The band, though, that really did most to inspire the innovations eventually known as "newgrass" was the Country Gentlemen. Through the inspired musicianship of banjoist Eddie Adcock and mandolinist John Duffey, and through their eclectic choice of material, the Country Gentlemen attracted new musicians to their style of playing and brought a whole new audience to bluegrass music. Not everyone admired their boldness, and Duffey was convinced that they were omitted from the first major festival in 1965 because of their departures from the norm. The Gentlemen continued to be a force for change at least through the 1970s, and when Duffey and Adcock left the band in 1969 and 1970, other experimental musicians (such as Jimmy Gaudreau, Doyle Lawson, and Ricky Skaggs) continued to contribute new ideas. In 1972, the Gentlemen's version of Crosby, Stills, and Nash's

"Teach Your Children" was selected in a *Muleskinner News* poll as the Song of the Year.

As the above song's popularity indicates, music continued to flow into the bluegrass repertory from other sources long after the folk revival subsided. Columbia record producers even persuaded Flatt and Scruggs to do such songs as Dylan's "Maggie's Farm" and "Wanted Man" (much to the disgust of Flatt, who disliked both the music and the liberal politics that surrounded it). Most younger musicians, however, probably had few reservations about performing nonbluegrass or noncountry songs, and so the songs of the Beatles, the Byrds, the First Edition, Creedence Clearwater Revival, and other contemporary musicians appeared frequently in newgrass performances. One of the first musicians to dip into such material with regularity was Cliff Waldron, a Jolo, West Virginia, native who moved to Washington, DC, in 1963. Beginning first with a band codirected with banjoist Bill Emerson in 1967, and later with his own group, the New Shades of Grass, Waldron built a repertory composed of classic material and contemporary songs such as "Proud Mary," "I Just Gotta Get a Message to You," and "Fox on the Run" (Waldron and Emerson's version of the last-named song remains the definitive version).

By the beginning of the 1970s, a number of groups had become well known for their receptivity to contemporary song material. A few of the bands, such as J. D. Crowe and the New South (formerly the Kentucky Mountain Boys), the Second Generation (organized by Eddie Adcock in 1971), and the Seldom Scene (created by John Duffey in the same year), were composed of experienced musicians whose careers dated back to the late 1950s. Other bands, such as Poor Richard's Almanac, the Bluegrass Alliance, Country Gazette, New Grass Revival, Spectrum (which included the remarkably versatile jazz-oriented banjoist Bela Fleck), and Hot Rize (a jazz-country-bluegrass fusion group led by Tim O'Brien and the scholar/musician Peter Wernick) were composed of younger performers whose musical sensibilities had been shaped by the post-Beatles rock revolution of the mid-1960s. Of the older groups, Adcock's Second Generation were the furthest removed from traditional bluegrass with their jazzlike experimentations and use of electric instrumentation. J. D. Crowe's New South never lost their identity as bluegrass musicians, nor their rapport with older fans, even though they roamed far and wide for material and pushed their instruments to limits generally not sought by other performers. Superb musicians, such as Larry Rice, Tony Rice, Doyle Lawson, and Ricky Skaggs, moved in and out of the New South, but all of them learned something from the timing, precision, and clarity exhibited by Crowe himself.

Seldom Scene not only was in the vanguard of the newgrass movement but was also the most popular of all modern bluegrass bands. The band, for the most part, was composed of all-star musicians who had seen service in other groups in the Washington, DC, area. In addition to Duffey, the group included banjoist Ben Eldridge and Dobroist Mike Auldridge (formerly of Waldron's New Shades of Grass), bass player Tom Gray (an early Country Gentleman), and John Starling (an army surgeon whose singing and guitar playing had been done mostly on an informal basis). Named Seldom Scene because of their infrequent concert appearances, the band settled down for a once-a-week gig at the Red Fox Inn in Bethesda, Maryland, and later for a weekly appearance at the Birchmere Restaurant in Alexandria, Virginia. Seldom Scene skillfully compiled a repertory of old and contemporary songs (some of them from country music's Top Forty) and performed them with mellow harmony and inventive instrumentation. A central, and almost defining, component of their sound was the Dobro playing of Mike Auldridge, one of the four or five great modern masters of the instrument. One of Auldridge's uncles, Ellsworth T. Cozzens, had played Hawaiian steel guitar on some of Jimmie Rodgers's records, but Mike seems not to have become impressed with the Dobro until he heard Buck Graves playing one with Wilma Lee and Stoney Cooper in about 1950. Building on the styles earlier featured by Graves, Shot Jackson, and Brother Oswald, Auldridge developed his own unique bell-like and melodious style. The results have been some of the prettiest and most soulful sounds heard in modern country music.

Some of the younger musicians seemed more closely aligned with rock music than with country, and a few of them, in dress and hairstyles, suggested the counterculture of the 1960s. The costuming and personal grooming habits of these musicians probably did more to alienate conservative bluegrass fans than did their music. Many people who heard the New Deal String Band (one of the first "hippie" bluegrass bands, from Chapel Hill, North Carolina), the Earl Scruggs Revue, or the New Grass Revival could scarcely listen to their music without thinking "Why doesn't somebody cut their hair?" The Country Gazette were usually much more circumspect in appearance (although they have also, on occasion, sported long hair and beards), but they had direct ties with California rock musicians through their founder and fiddler, Byron Berline. After leaving the University of Oklahoma in 1967, Berline worked with Bill Monroe briefly, spent some time in the army, and then went to California, where he worked as a session musician and played with the Dillard and Clark Expedition and Flying Burrito Brothers. In 1971, he founded the Country Gazette along with guitarist Kenny Wertz, bass player Roger Bush, and Berline's old friend from Oklahoma, Alan Munde. Berline's proficiency at old-time, Texas, and bluegrass styles of fiddling; Munde's note bending and precisely executed style of chromatic banjo; Bush's exuberant slapped-bass technique; and their intelligent use of both old-time and contemporary material made them one of the most appealing of the newgrass organizations. The Country Gazette, which later included the multitalented Roland White as guitarist and lead singer, became one of the most widely traveled bands, appearing often on college campuses, where band members combined music with lectures and seminars.

Another group that made important contributions to the shaping and popularization of the progressive sounds was the Bluegrass Alliance of Louisville, Kentucky. Centered originally around the traditional fiddling of Lonnie Peerce and the sensational flat-picking guitar work of Dan Crary, the band moved further and further away from classic bluegrass as new members joined. Crary was followed by two other superb guitarists and singers, Tony Rice and Curtis Burch. The musician, though, who really moved the Alliance into new territories of experimentation was Sam Bush, a fiddler and mandolin player whose chief inspiration was Jethro Burns. Bush came to the Alliance in 1970, along with the banjo player Courtney Johnson, from another experimental group, Poor Richard's Almanac. By the time he and Johnson left the Alliance to form yet another band, the New Grass Revival (in 1972), Bush had already become famous for his enthusiasm, his wild and extended improvisations, his perfectionism, and his tireless experimentations with other forms of music. For many people, the New Grass Revival became the quintessential progressive bluegrass band, playing a style of music that "borrowed heavily from the realms of rock, jazz and blues" without losing "the drive and melancholy that characterizes bluegrass music."[30]

While the progressives went about their business experimenting with musical fusions and breaking new stylistic ground, other musicians hewed closely to styles that they perceived to be grounded in the music of the "classic period" (circa 1945–1955). Many amateur and professional musicians throughout America still clung to the old repertory, and many of them adhered as closely as possible to the sounds first heard on Monroe, Stanley, or Flatt and Scruggs records. Among the "older" professional musicians, the Shenandoah Cutups (led by fiddler Clarence "Tater" Tate, mandolin player Hershel Sizemore, and banjoist Billy Edwards) and Vern Williams (an Arkansas-born mandolin player and tenor singer who led his own band in California) came closest to preserving the hard-driving energy and tangy, high lonesome style of harmony that had once characterized bluegrass music.

In an obvious reply to Eddie Adcock and his Second Generation, three veteran musicians—Red Rector, Don Stover, and Bill Clifton—organized themselves into a group called the First Generation and set out in 1978 on a tour of festivals and concerts in the United States and Europe. Clifton and Rector believed that bluegrass audiences needed a reintroduction to old-time duet singing. Gospel music continued to be a vital ingredient of bluegrass and a force in the preservation of traditional styles. Some groups performed nothing but the old-time style of rural gospel: these included the veteran Carl Story from North Carolina, the Marshall Family from Ohio by way of West Virginia, the Sullivan Family from St. Stephens, Alabama, and the Lewis Family from Lincolnton, Georgia. The Sullivans represented the Pentecostal tradition of soulful, emotional singing, with strong traces of the Bailes Brothers and Louvin Brothers. Margie Sullivan, an ordained minister (originally from Louisiana), reminded listeners of Molly O'Day with her southern rural phrasing and deep-felt, open-throated singing. The Lewis Family presented a joyous mixture of religion and tent-show comedy to their festival audiences. One heard little of the evangelism that sometimes surfaced in the Sullivans' concerts. Little Roy Lewis, the madcap banjoist of the group, was one of bluegrass music's finest natural, if sometimes aggravatingly manic, entertainers.

Other musicians who strived to preserve the feel, if not the exact form, of traditional bluegrass music included individuals old enough to have heard Monroe and his contemporaries in their heyday as well as those who were scarcely or not yet born when the "classic" style took shape. The discussion that follows is far from exhaustive, and it concentrates on those whose public performances, or whose entry into bluegrass, came since the late 1950s. Joe Wilson, from El Dorado, Arkansas, and the leader of a group called Bluegrass Kun-Tree, was one of the best singers in bluegrass music, with a soulful style that somehow suggested the phrasing and emotion of two great but dissimilar stylists: Ralph Stanley and George Jones. Wilson died from a heart attack at his home in El Dorado, Arkansas, on September 14, 1984.

The Pinnacle Boys were a force for revitalization in bluegrass through the twin fiddling of Randall Collins and Jerry Moore, and through their precise and smooth Louvin Brothers style of harmony. The Bluegrass Cardinals were a group founded in California by a Kentucky banjo player, Don Parmley, who had gone there in 1956 to work as a Trailways bus driver. Parmley founded one of the earliest bluegrass bands in California, the Golden State Boys, played with the Hillmen, and provided background banjo instrumentation for the *Beverly Hillbillies* television show for about nine years. Since making their first LP in 1975, the Bluegrass Cardinals—led by the singing of David Parmley, who was only fifteen when the group came into existence—became widely admired for their inventive syncopated harmonies. The Boys from Indiana, led by guitarist and singer Aubrey Holt, preserved the verve and drive of original bluegrass, while also becoming valued as one of the finest "show bands" in the music (presenting skits, history, impersonations). The late Charlie Moore was one of the greatest bluegrass singers to emerge in the postclassic era. His voice was smooth but soulful, and he had a sense of history and a storehouse of old songs that he had been picking up since his boyhood in Piedmont, South Carolina. From 1962 to 1966, he performed with flat-picking guitar ace Bill Napier and recorded some popularly received LPs with him for the King label. After 1966, Moore headed a band called the Dixie Partners, and in 1971 he introduced a song that became one of the most popular standards of bluegrass music, "The Legend of the Rebel Soldier," the tale of an imprisoned Confederate soldier whose dying prayer was that his soul might return to the Southland.

The Oklahomans Bill Grant and Delia Bell began singing together in about 1960 on KIHN's *Little Dixie Hayride* in Hugo, Oklahoma, but soon became fixtures on the festival circuit, especially at Grant's big festival each August in Hugo (one of the largest events west of the Mississippi River). Both were important musicians, and Grant became one of the few original writers in bluegrass (along with Hazel Dickens, Jake Landers, Aubrey Holt, Tom Uhr, and a few others). For a time,

Delia Bell became the rage of bluegrass, not simply because she was one of the few women at that time to win acceptance in the genre, but also because of the patronage that she received from Emmylou Harris. Harris was sufficiently impressed with Delia's singing, which she first heard on the LP *Bluer Than Midnight* (County 768), to sponsor and produce a major album of her singing in 1983 on the Warner Brothers label. Unfortunately, the public response to it suggested that Delia's singing may have been too pure, mournful, and rural for contemporary tastes.

One of the most interesting phenomena related to the preservation of traditional bluegrass music—and one to which students of southern migration should pay more attention—was the role played by musicians who had either migrated to the North or who had been born there of southern migrants. Three of the finest traditional singers in modern bluegrass, Larry Sparks, Dave Evans, and Del McCoury were northern-born children of southern migrants, while still another outstanding rural-tinged vocalist, Dudley Connell, was a southern-born boy who moved to a northern state with his parents. All sang in the high lonesome style with emotion-laden and rural-flavored phrasing, and each conveyed a strong sense of fundamentalist Protestant morality that lent intensity and conviction to their performances. Larry Sparks, born in Lebanon, Ohio, of Kentucky parents, spent an apprenticeship with Ralph Stanley before going on to lead his own organization. Dave Evans, from Portsmouth, Ohio, in turn spent some time with Sparks (1973–1974) and with other groups such as the Boys from Indiana, with whom he played banjo and took an occasional turn as guest soloist. In 1978, he formed his own group, River Bend, recorded a couple of LPs on the Vetco label, and immediately began impressing traditionalists with his emotional conviction and powerfully intense high-tenor singing.

The youngest person among these hard-core bluegrass singers, Dudley Connell, eventually gained fame as the lead singer of the progressive-minded Seldom Scene, but in the 1970s and 1980s, he headed a group that many people assumed would be the saviors of the old-time bluegrass style, the Johnson Mountain Boys. Connell was born in West Virginia but moved as a youngster with his family to Rockville, Maryland, in the suburbs of Washington, DC. He and his fellow band members, including the fiddler Eddie Stubbs, who later became a distinguished country radio announcer, resurrected old-time songs but supplemented them with numbers written by Connell. Known for their tight harmonies, brilliant musicianship, and commitment to tradition, this Washington, DC–based band was touted as the bluegrass band of the future and as the hope of traditionalists everywhere.

Delano Floyd "Del" McCoury was born in 1939 near York, Pennsylvania, in a family of southern migrants who had made the trip only a few years earlier from Bakersville, North Carolina. Of all the bluegrass musicians with southern roots, he has made the most impressive and enduring contributions to American music. Longtime residence in a northeastern state, as well as in Baltimore and even for a brief period in California, however, never diminished the essence of his southern-flavored speech nor the soulful intensity of his singing. His most crucial apprenticeship in bluegrass—before he met Bill Monroe—came in Baltimore in the early 1960s when he played with Jack Cooke's Virginia Mountain Boys. Although the banjo was then McCoury's instrument of choice, Bill Monroe hired him as a guitar player and lead singer in 1963. This one-year tenure with Monroe, in a band that also included Bill Keith and Kenny Baker, introduced him to the core repertory of traditional bluegrass music and cemented his reputation as a master of the high lonesome vocal style. Since that time, he has remained close to the Monroe mold. Along with his brother Jerry, he organized a band in 1969 called the Dixie Pals, but in recent times has become internationally famous while fronting a band that includes two of his sons, Ronnie and Robbie. While consistently using material of recent vintage (much of it from honky-tonk country or even rock sources), McCoury nevertheless preserved the sound and style of traditional bluegrass.

It is clear that the choices made by bluegrass musicians in the 1980s and the impulse to lean toward either tradition or innovation were not necessarily a matter of age. Young musicians like Connell and Evans often demonstrated a preference for that which was old or historically rooted. Indeed, many musicians moved easily back and forth between the classic and the progressive, either making no distinctions between the two or being at home in both. Buck White and his talented daughters, Sharon and Cheryl, filled their concerts with the western swing that Buck grew up with in Wichita Falls, Texas; the mainstream country that the girls harmonized so beautifully; and bluegrass that spanned the period from Bill Monroe to Seldom Scene. Doyle Lawson, the extraordinarily gifted musician from east

Tennessee, has played every style of bluegrass music since he started his professional career as a banjoist with Jimmy Martin in 1963. A stranger to no string instrument, he played guitar with J. D. Crowe in 1966 and mandolin with the Country Gentlemen after 1971 (while also demonstrating his expertise as a tenor harmony singer). In 1979, he organized his own band, Quicksilver, that became one of the prized progressive groups. Nevertheless, while the band was widely admired for its versatility and collective musicianship, Quicksilver's finest moments come when the musicians put down their instruments and did a cappella gospel songs that lay at the roots of country music's history. Lawson, J. D. Crowe, Tony Rice, Bobby Hicks, and Todd Phillips (each recognized as a premier progressive stylist) got together in 1982 to do an LP of material drawn from the 1940s and 1950s repertories of Bill Monroe, Flatt and Scruggs, and other seminal musicians. The album was so well received that they subsequently recorded two other LPs of such material and then went on a short tour at the end of 1983 as the Bluegrass Album Band. Ricky Skaggs, of course, who had been associated with all of these musicians at one time or another, played in bands that ranged from the old-timey mountain sound of Ralph Stanley to the jazz-related stylings of J. D. Crowe's New South (and for a short time he headed a band—Boone Creek—that tried to combine both impulses). Skaggs obviously has felt no incompatibility with any form of music.

By the end of the 1980s, no one could predict bluegrass music's future, but encouraging factors could be found at the festivals, or anywhere that bluegrass was played, by the prevalence of family bands and of very young musicians, some as young as six or seven, who played fiddles, banjos, mandolins, and guitars. Although young musicians moved in many directions after their initial explorations of the genre, they nevertheless continued to make some kind of music. The wellsprings of bluegrass, it seemed, would not soon dry up.

CHAPTER 11

Country Music, 1972–1984

Country music's history since the early 1970s has been one of unqualified commercial success. The music's ascent in mainstream American culture, however, has been accompanied by internal debates concerning definition and future direction. Musicians, industry leaders, and fans have been confused about what the music is or where it should go. The country music industry has discovered that its best interests lie in the distribution of a package with clouded identity, possessing no regional traits. The industry has strived to present a music that is all things to all people: middle-of-the-road and "American" but also southern, working-class, and occasionally youth-oriented and even rebellious in tone.

The *Grand Ole Opry*'s move in 1974 from the Ryman Auditorium to the spacious and modern accommodations of the new Opry House on the outskirts of Nashville was an event more than symbolic of country music's ambivalence about its rural past. The Ryman had been the site of the *Opry* since 1941, and many people had come to look on the historic old building—the "mother church of country music"—as almost sacrosanct. Reverence, however, was tempered by disquietude when one reflected upon the actual conditions of the building. Audiences dealt with excessive heat during the summer, draftiness during the winter, impaired vision much of the time because of the supportive columns that ran from the floor to the balcony, and limited parking facilities all of the time. While the acoustics were very good, performers had to contend with cramped and modestly furnished dressing rooms. The auditorium was located in a rundown section of downtown Nashville filled with souvenir shops, adult bookstores, and pornographic movie theaters. At the concluding show at the Ryman on March 16, 1974, Minnie Pearl cried unashamedly on stage as she reflected on the abandonment of the building where such hallowed figures as Uncle Dave Macon, Roy Acuff, Eddy Arnold, and Hank Williams had once held sway. Although most fans and musicians ultimately applauded the move to the spacious, comfortable, air-conditioned Opry House, and to the 110-acre Disneyland-like complex that surrounds it, the move nevertheless spawned much nostalgic regret while also inspiring the emergence of a powerful new cultural force in American life. After observing the closing ceremonies, Garrison Keillor wrote an affectionate and discerning article for the *New Yorker*, and then went back home to Minneapolis and founded the delightful radio show *A Prairie Home Companion*, designed to restore the flavor and ambience of old-time live broadcasting.[1]

Country music demonstrated its prominence in American life in a variety of ways. In 1973, Loretta Lynn appeared on the cover of *Newsweek* and was the central focus of the magazine's coverage of country music. One year later, Merle Haggard enjoyed similar exposure in *Time*,[2] and the sympathetic treatment that he and the music received probably reflected the nation's shift toward conservatism and the music's identification with white working-class culture (an ironic development in that the similar "discovery" of white folk music in the 1930s had been fueled by an awakening of liberal sentiment). In the proliferating published material that dealt with country music, the phenomenon was treated with a seriousness that had seldom before been witnessed. References to "corn," "hillbillies," "twang," and "nasal" that had dotted the usually condescending or hostile treatments of country music were missing, replaced by attempts to understand the origins and contemporary meaning of the music.

The producer/director Robert Altman may have had little affection for country music as an artistic medium, but he was sufficiently impressed with its influence to make it the centerpiece of the movie *Nashville* in 1975. The Nashville music world was depicted as a metaphor for modern American culture, and the movie garnered great critical acclaim and public response. Many country fans perceived the movie not as a fable of a society that had lost direction and purpose but as a frontal attack on their music and the culture that embodies it. The movie, though, probably won a new audience for country music, as many people went away intrigued by the ingenuous expression of feeling conveyed by the songs.

Although reactions to *Nashville* were mixed, few country fans had reservations about the movie depiction of Loretta Lynn's life, *Coal Miner's Daughter*, a critically acclaimed adaptation of her autobiography and a vehicle for Sissy Spacek's Academy Award–winning performance. The movie did not tell the full story of Loretta's life—it curiously omitted the crucial role played by the Wilburn Brothers in the furtherance of her career—but it did present a vivid account of life in the mountains that also provided glimpses of both the euphoria and the frustrations of the music business.

Loretta Lynn enjoyed enormous public visibility in the wake of the movie's success. Movies, in fact, became major vehicles for the mass exposure of country entertainers, if not always for country music itself. The fabulous guitarist Jerry Reed and singer/comedian Mel Tillis were among the most active of the entertainers who profited from the "good old boy" movies that began appearing in the 1970s, and, of course, from their association with such superstars as Burt Reynolds and Clint Eastwood. The enormously popular *Smokey and the Bandit* was the prototype for shows both in theaters and on television that featured hedonistic, simple-minded young men and their sexy girlfriends riding in fast cars or trucks with a backdrop of country music. Most country entertainers who ventured into the movie business rarely got beyond the status of supporting actor, but Dolly Parton became a household name throughout the world and exhibited a natural comic flair in such popular movies as *Nine to Five* and *Best Little Whorehouse in Texas*. Dolly's prominence as a "personality" was a major factor in her success as an actress. Though Willie Nelson profited from a similar aura, he also showed greater potential as a character actor than did Parton, first in a supporting role to Robert Redford in *The Electric Horseman*, and then in lead roles in *Honeysuckle Rose* and *Barbarosa*. *Honeysuckle Rose*'s thin story line was merely a device to highlight Nelson's singing and the honky-tonk atmosphere of Texas, but *Barbarosa*, which had almost no music at all, permitted Nelson to demonstrate a natural flair for acting in the role of a legendary western outlaw.

Most of these movies had no real impact on American popular culture, but *Tender Mercies* in 1984, probably the finest movie ever made about country music, garnered several Academy Award nominations, including one for Robert Duvall as best actor. *Urban Cowboy* in 1981 (based on an *Esquire* article about alienated oil workers in the Houston area) generated a boom for ersatz cowboy material—designer jeans, hats, boots, mechanical bulls, and western dance steps. Gilley's Club in Pasadena, Texas, self-styled "the biggest honky-tonk in the world" and the principal site of the movie's action, became known to the world, as did its singing proprietor, Mickey Gilley, and the house-band leader, Johnny Lee. The soundtrack, however, carried very little that was really native to the Texas honky-tonk scene and instead featured country-pop and rock material. Johnny Lee's "Looking for Love," for example—a lilting little pop song—became the featured song of the movie, and a huge commercial hit, mainly because the actor John Travolta expressed a liking for it.

Television continued to be a major vehicle for country music exposure, and country entertainers appeared in great profusion on commercial, public, and cable programming. The country awards shows, such as those produced by the CMA, the Academy of Country Music, and *Music City News*, elicited great audience response, as did occasional specials, such as HBO's *Dolly Parton Live from London*, or a popular series such as *Barbara Mandrell and the Mandrell Sisters*. Depictions of the lives of country musicians, fictional and real, sometimes appeared on commercial television but with mixed results. *Boone*, a series built around the life of an aspiring young country singer in the early 1950s, suffered from the romanticization of its subject and from a loose obeisance to historical fact—a not uncommon trait of television shows and movies devoted to country music. Occasionally a good biographical depiction of a country singer did appear on commercial television, as in the cases of Tammy Wynette (*Stand by Your Man*) and Hank Williams Jr. (*Living Proof*), but the most accurate and sensitive documentation of country music tended to appear on public radio and television. The long-running and immensely popular *A Prairie Home Companion*, hosted by the brilliant announcer and social critic Garrison Keillor, gave much exposure to country performers such as Chet Atkins, Johnny Gimble, Suzy Bogguss, and Emmylou Harris. This show presented country music to a large, literate, middle-class audience that would not otherwise have heard it. Public TV viewers also received the opportunity to see and hear excellent presentations of the life and music of such entertainers as Uncle Dave Macon, Prince Albert Hunt, Jimmie Rodgers, and Merle Haggard. Public TV also sponsored *Austin City Limits*, a marvelous showcase for all kinds of country music, along with impressive specials devoted to bluegrass, and the *Grand Ole Opry* was carried live and in its entirety on at least two different occasions. Nowhere else on television did country music receive such an honest and serious treatment, although the independent Nashville Network, a cable enterprise that debuted in 1983, gave promise of providing the coverage that the music had always lacked.

The Nashville Network, however, began its existence with a mishmash of mediocre game shows, musical variety presentations, outdoor sports and hunting functions, old movies, and a thoroughly silly western dance program that seemed little more than a weak imitation of *Soul Train*. The network was saved from total mediocrity by a few shows of superior caliber: *Nashville Now*, a variety/talk show hosted by Ralph Emery; *The Tommy Hunter Show*, a fast-paced variety program from Canada; *Yesteryear in Nashville*, a series of interviews with older performers conducted by Archie Campbell; *Fire on the Mountain*, a presentation of bluegrass and old-time music; and, preeminently, *Bobby Bare and Friends*, a tribute to songwriters featuring interviews and live music.

Although television exposure dramatically signaled the ubiquity of country music in American popular culture, nowhere was the music's newfound respectability more strongly displayed than in its identification with presidential politics. Since Lyndon B. Johnson's administration, the appearance of country entertainers at White House or presidential-related functions became almost routine, and musicians have sometimes been used to bolster administration positions. LBJ's famous Texas barbecues were often spiced with country music, and particularly with the antics of a comedy duo known as the Geezinslaw Brothers, a Texas act built around the mandolin playing and tenor singing of Sam Allred, a longtime Austin disc jockey, and his guitar-playing sidekick, Dewayne "Son" Smith. During the divisive period of the Vietnam War, Richard Nixon seized upon country music because a host of country songs criticized protestors and otherwise defended establishment values. Nixon consequently invited such singers as Merle Haggard and Johnny Cash to the White House. Cash's appearance sparked a minor controversy when the singer refused to do a couple of songs requested by Nixon's staff, "Okie from Muskogee" and "Welfare Cadilac" [*sic*]. His refusal, though, had nothing to do with political ideology; Cash simply did not know the songs, and he felt that they did not fit his style. It was not surprising that Nixon would journey to Nashville in 1974, in the midst of the Watergate crisis, to attend the official dedication of the new Grand Ole Opry House. The beleaguered president sought refuge in an institution that seemed solidly identified with Middle America. The Nixon–country music linkage seemed ominous to some liberal observers, and one writer was moved to describe the music as "the perfect musical extension of the Nixon administration."[3]

Jimmy Carter's well-known associations with country entertainers drew considerable inspiration from the political urge to cater to grassroots Americans, but a stronger motivation lay in his and the music's mutual southernness. Carter was the only president who seemed genuinely to love and understand country music. He had listened to country music since he was a boy, and the music had figured prominently in his campaigns for the Georgia governorship and for the presidency. As president, Carter often included country performers in government social functions, and he sometimes appeared on stage with them and even sang an occasional fragment of song. Singer James Talley, an Oklahoman who fused blues, country, and social comment in his songs, while eliciting some comparisons with Woody Guthrie, received extensive, though short-lived, publicity because First Lady Rosalynn Carter declared him to be her favorite singer. Such entertainers as Johnny Cash, Loretta Lynn, Tom T. Hall, Hank Snow, and Willie Nelson were prominent supporters of Carter and were active participants in presidential-related functions and in the 1980 reelection campaign. Country musicians, of course, were grateful for the support that Carter lent to their profession, and they and he profited, at least for a time, from the resurgence of the South in American life.

The Ronald Reagan administration continued the practice of bringing country entertainers to White House functions. The CMA's twenty-fifth anniversary celebration, in fact, was held in Washington in 1983 before a large audience including President and Mrs. Reagan and other government dignitaries. A parade of entertainers appeared in the lavish, flashily organized production, but the highest point, musically, came when Ricky Skaggs, Bill Monroe, Grandpa Jones, and Senator Robert Byrd, who combined old-time fiddling with his

Democratic leadership role, combined to do a version of "Lonesome Road Blues." Reagan's favorite country singer, though—judging by the frequency with which he appeared at presidentially sponsored affairs—was Merle Haggard. Haggard no doubt felt some loyalty to the man who had pardoned him during his earlier stint as governor of California, but his and Reagan's political presumptions did not seem incompatible. In the midst of the recession of 1982, Haggard endorsed Reagan's economic program,[4] but in songs like "Big City" he delivered a mixed message that commented on urban anonymity, wage inequities, and inadequate government support ("so-called social security"). Haggard's solution, though—a flight to the wilds of Montana—was a fantasy that working people may have shared but that only someone like a millionaire singer could realize.

Despite the identification of some country singers with political figures, country music's political stance remained difficult to categorize. Musicians voted both Democratic and Republican and stayed as free of ideological postures as did most Americans. Some performers leaned toward Reagan, but others supported the Democratic cause. Willie Nelson, Waylon Jennings, Jessi Colter, Dottie West, and Kris Kristofferson, among others, participated in a giant Democratic fundraising telethon of May 1983.

Just as there was no monolithic country music stance toward politics, neither was there a fixed position on the music's definition or future direction. Increasingly in the mid-1970s voices were raised among fans and entertainers alike protesting country music's dilution and the fusion with pop sounds. Traditionalists bemoaned the Top Forty formats and tight playlists favored by most "country" radio stations, and they denounced the crossover mania that lured a proliferating number of singers into the commercially fertile pastures of pop music. Above all, many partisans wept because of the difficulties faced by hard country and older musicians in getting their music recorded and distributed.

The CMA received considerable criticism because of its apparent complicity in the blurring of country music's identity. The rivals that occasionally arose, however, did not necessarily differ from the Nashville organization in their approaches to style. The California-based Academy of Country Music, for example, challenged Nashville's dominance and strove to give West Coast musicians greater exposure; it did not trouble itself with controversies concerning stylistic direction, and its awards went to performers whose sounds were as pop-flavored as those favored by the CMA. The boldest challenge to the CMA came from the short-lived Association of Country Entertainers (ACE), an organization that gave voice to the legitimate complaints of many fans and musicians but suffered from undigested priorities as well as the powerful opposition of the deeply entrenched CMA. ACE came into existence in November 1974, after Olivia Newton-John, an Australian pop singer who was briefly packaged as a country artist, won the CMA's Female Singer of the Year award. About fifty people met at George Jones and Tammy Wynette's home to create an organization that would "preserve the identity of country music"[5] and would be confined solely to entertainers (as opposed to promoters, record merchandisers, and other industry people). In the few years of its existence, ACE insisted that country music awards should go only to those people who considered themselves country, asserting that some musicians were merely opportunists who had hopped onto country music's burgeoning bandwagon and that many radio stations (such as New York City's WHN) adhered to a narrow selection of dubious country material. ACE encouraged radio stations everywhere to expand their playlists, and it sponsored concerts that were designed to give ignored performers opportunities to be heard.

Many people in the ACE leadership, such as Grandpa Jones and Vic Willis, were genuinely concerned about country music's growing fusion with pop. The organization as a whole, however, was timid about confronting the issue head-on, partly because it was fearful of alienating the Nashville commercial establishment, but largely because it included performers strongly attracted by pop sounds. An organization that included Tammy Wynette as a charter member and Barbara Mandrell as one of its presidents could hardly be described as traditional. It was easy for critics to argue, therefore, that ACE was primarily concerned with fostering a closed community among country musicians and that it was composed of jealous and parochial individuals who were trying to protect themselves from newcomers to the country field. Fans, of course, were excluded from membership in both CMA and ACE, and so the traditionalists among them stood by helplessly with no one to provide effective focus for their complaints.

Justin Tubb (Ernest's son) effectively summed up the feelings of many fans and musicians when he wrote and sang "What's Wrong with the Way That We're Doing It Now"—which, as one might expect, received very little airplay on the Top Forty stations. Tubb accurately described the difficulties that "hard country" musicians faced in getting their music recorded and played, but in discussing the "well-meaning people" changing the nature of the music,[6] he singled out only the "progressives," a term usually associated with such people as Willie Nelson and Waylon Jennings. He made no reference to the country-pop stylists and the crossover phenomenon that were contributing the most to the dilution and homogenization of country music. The crossover passion intensified in the late 1970s and early 1980s, and few singers, if their sound and style permitted it, could resist the temptation to go where the big money was.

Barbara Mandrell's career illustrated well the almost-irresistible allure of the pop sound. She won considerable commercial success with a song called "I Was Country When Country Wasn't Cool," but in a style that possessed no country flavor at all—and not even George Jones's cameo appearance on one verse of the song could save it from pop murkiness. Mandrell, then, was a good example of an entertainer who, while identifying with both Nashville and country music, was nevertheless drawn by pop sounds and styles. She was born in Houston in 1948 but grew up in California in a family that was associated with country music in both a business and a professional sense. Her father led a little family band while also working as the West Coast representative for Standel Amplifiers. The precocious Barbara had learned how to play piano, bass, guitar, five-string banjo, saxophone, and triple-neck steel guitar by the time she was a teenager, but it was her proficiency with the steel guitar that led her into a professional performing career. Joe Maphis and Chet Atkins heard the twelve-year-old girl playing the steel guitar at the annual trade convention in Chicago in 1960. Largely through Maphis's recommendation, she began playing the instrument on the *Town Hall Party* in Los Angeles. By the time she arrived in Nashville in early 1969, her versatility as a musician was being subordinated to her ambition to become a leading vocalist. Recording for Columbia, and working under the direction of the producer Billy Sherrill, Mandrell immediately began to create a middle-of-the-road sound closer to the Memphis and Motown soul singers than it was to country. Such songs as "Do Right Woman" and "If Loving You Is Wrong (Then I Don't Want to Be Right)" continued to be the most prominent types of material in her repertory. Whatever the sources of her style, Mandrell became one of the superstars of country music, twice voted the CMA's Entertainer of the Year.

Barbara Mandrell was only one among dozens of performers who proved that a huge audience existed for country-pop music. No one knew exactly who that audience was, or how long it had been attracted to country sounds—ersatz or real. Many country-pop fans, of course, had been with country music all along, and they either changed as the music did, or they had always leaned toward the smoother sounds ever since Eddy Arnold made his first tentative experiments back in the late 1940s. A large segment of listeners made no distinction between country singers and responded positively to anyone packaged as a country singer, whether a honky-tonk stylist like George Jones, a bluegrass-derived musician like Ricky Skaggs, or a pop-style vocalist like Larry Gatlin. An even larger number of fans probably made no distinctions between singers of any kind and did not trouble themselves with definition or categorization. They merely gravitated toward any singer, regardless of classification, who satisfied their musical cravings. Many at that time had been first lured to music by the rockabillies and, above all, by Elvis in the late 1950s. As the rockabilly fans grew older, they moved in a variety of musical directions, and some probably abandoned interest in any kind of rock-related music. Many men and women of this generation, though, never lost their fascination with performers who exuded energy, sexual appeal, charisma, and youthful good looks. These fans continued to find in the 1970s and 1980s a large number of entertainers in the country field who fulfilled these requirements.

Despite occasional experiments with other types of songs, Jerry Lee Lewis never strayed very far from his original rockabilly mold, and even the most conventional mainstream pop or country song received the special Lewis touch, a zestful, swaggering, and highly personal interpretation of the material. Among the younger performers, Billy Swan, Joe Stampley, and Gary Stewart seemed to hew most closely to the original rockabilly sound. With songs like "I Can Help," Swan recreated a fresh, gently rocking sound that suggested the early period of rock-and-roll music. Stampley and Stewart, on the other hand, wore several stylistic hats and were competent performers in any genre they chose. Temporarily miscast as a honky-tonk singer, Stampley was instead an all-purpose musician whose heart and musical preferences lay close to the rock and roll on which he was weaned. His rollicking, good-natured, good-old-boy duets with Moe Bandy in the early 1980s, however, were among the most commercially successful records that either had ever had. Stewart was one of the finest young honky-tonk singers of the modern period, when he chose to do that kind of material, but his driving piano style and hedonistic singing made him seem more reminiscent of Jerry Lee Lewis than of George Jones. Like many of the young singers of the South who came along during the 1970s, Stewart also revealed a strong kinship with such southern rock musicians as the Allman Brothers and the Marshall Tucker Band.

The rocking country singers were indeed influenced by a wide array of musicians who spanned the period from early Elvis right up to their own time. And in the case of Presley, it was generally the later Elvis, the superstar of Las Vegas fame, who exerted the strongest influence. Appearing in clubs all over America, a host of performers—many of them little more than pale imitations of Elvis—provided enduring testimony of "the King's" pervasive legacy. Usually dressed in skin-tight sequined suits, and sporting open shirts and necklaces, these singers tried to evoke the aura of aggressive energy and playful sexuality that their hero had created. Ronnie McDowell made his first vault to fame with a song of tribute to Presley and then settled into a predictable groove of dynamic, macho song performances. The most bizarre manifestation of the Elvis cult in country music came in the career of the singer Jimmy Ellis, from Pascagoula, Mississippi, who called himself Orion. Dressed in a mask and cape, Orion sang in a deep, sensual baritone filled with an exaggerated, throaty vibrato. No other singer came so close to re-creating the sound of the mature Presley.

The singers who profited most from the revolution that Presley had wrought, either as disciples or as spinoffs, were entertainers who built independent identities. Razzy Bailey, for example, shared the preference for high-voltage, sensual performance that other neo-rockabillies had, but his style seemed closer to soul music than any other form; his was the "blackest" sound in modern country music. Billy "Crash" Craddock, T. G. Sheppard, Ray Griff, Narvel Felts, T. Graham Brown, Eddie Rabbitt, Earl Thomas Conley, the Bellamy Brothers, and the Oak Ridge Boys were among those who exhibited obvious rock-and-roll traits while nonetheless creating distinctive styles that appealed to a broad spectrum of fans. Craddock bore the closest resemblance to hard-core rockabilly with such songs as "Knock Three Times" and the sexy "Rub It In," but by the beginning of the 1980s, like most of his rock-and-roll contemporaries, he had opted for a softer and less rollicking beat.

Country-pop won much of its audience among people who sought a middle-of-the-road, easily understood form of music—and one that did not reek too strongly of rural or working-class life. In short, they sought a replacement for the pop music that had died or gone underground when rock and roll achieved its hegemony in the late 1950s. If Perry Como and Doris Day were no longer available, then Glen Campbell, Steve Wariner, or Crystal Gayle would have to do. As country singers crossed over to the lucrative area of pop music, they encountered a swarm of pop singers of all descriptions—"old-timers" like Dean Martin, Patti Page, Teresa Brewer, Nat "King" Cole, and Ray Charles, and "newcomers" such as Anne Murray, John Denver, Kenny Rogers, and Olivia Newton-John who were trying to build or rebuild careers through an involvement in country music. Together, they plowed a common ground that increasingly defied definition, but one that in many respects constituted the new pop music of America. Glen Campbell, Roger Miller, and Eddy Arnold were already taking their music to Middle America when Olivia Newton-John made her fateful inroads into country music. In that same year, 1974, Charlie Rich recorded his giant hit "Behind Closed Doors," a dramatic departure from the blues and rockabilly tunes that had been the staples of his repertory ever since he began his career with Sun Records in the mid-1950s. The sensuous song was part of a growing list of such material, including Kristofferson's "Help Me Make It through the Night," Freddy Weller's "Sexy Lady," Conway Twitty's "You've Never Been This Far Before," the Bellamy Brothers' "If I Said You Had a Beautiful Body (Would You Hold It against Me)," and Freddie Hart's "Easy Loving," which ventured into the area of eroticism with a greater suggestiveness and openness than at any previous time of country music history. Many people applauded what they considered to be a broader vision in country music, but others expressed dismay at the alleged declining morality of the music. Grandpa Jones and Cindy Walker, for example, described such material as "skin songs,"[7] items cited as evidence of the harm that had come from country music's flirtation with other musical cultures.

In the years after 1974, a profusion of singers moved into country music from a wide variety of performing backgrounds. This occurred with such frequency that some critics described country music as a refuge for musicians with failed or quiescent careers. "Moving into country" often meant little more than adding a pedal steel guitar to one's accompanying instrumentation, or it might mean merely the use of Nashville recording studios and musicians. The country-pop impulse did not necessarily preclude the use of down-home country instruments such as fiddles or Dobros (or even the five-string banjo, which figured prominently in Nashville Brass performances), but being "country" was primarily a matter of being defined or packaged with that description. Pop-folk singer John Denver merely experimented with the idiom and seems never to have really sought full-scale country involvement; nevertheless, his ventures resulted in some major hits, such as "Back Home Again," "Thank God I'm a Country Boy," and the now classic "Country Roads," each of which was more "rural" than many of the songs then being recorded by mainstream country singers. Some singers, such as Olivia Newton-John, Charlie Rich, and Anne Murray, resisted country labeling even while prospering from the identification. None of them, of course, turned down either the rewards or the awards that emanated from the country music business, but they generally argued that their music was more broadly popular than a country categorization would suggest. The Canadian-born Anne Murray (from Spring Hill, Nova Scotia) grew up listening to every kind of music except country, which, according to her own admission, she hated: "I thought it was terrible, because at the time the only kind of thing I heard was Kitty Wells and to me it was more important that somebody could sing than what they were saying."[8] When she made her first tentative efforts at professional music in 1964, while pursuing a full-time job as a physical education teacher, she began to listen to country music seriously and to appreciate it. One of her first recordings in 1970 for Capitol's Canadian division was a folklike song called "Snowbird," a crossover tune that received extensive airplay on both country and pop music radio stations in the United States and Canada. Murray has ever since maintained that kind of broad appeal, partly through an intelligent selection of material that cuts across musical categories (such as "You Needed Me," "Cotton Jenny," and "Could I Have This Dance"), but also because of her relaxed, direct, and clearly articulated style of singing. Her appeal was much like that of Glen Campbell, who, in fact, contributed directly to her American acceptance by featuring her on his popular television show.

Murray's effective style of vocal communication and her preference for story songs were probably shaped by her involvement in the folk revival of the mid-1960s, as it would be in later years for other "coffee-house singers" such as Suzy Bogguss and Iris DeMent. Other singers who found a home in country music, such as Don Williams and Kenny Rogers, also profited from that experience. Don Williams began his professional career as lead singer for the pop-folk trio the Pozo Seco Singers, but then found a comfortable niche in country music. Born in a working-class home in Portland, Texas (near Corpus Christi), Williams had no difficulty relating to a type of music he had heard all his life. With his warm, rich, resonant baritone voice projected over spare string instrumentation, he won a large following here and in England that spilled across most musical boundaries. Like Jim Reeves, with whom he was often compared, Williams preserved the allegiance of hard-core country fans while fashioning a smooth and almost-crooning style of delivery. His failure to cross over into the pop charts with the frequency of someone like Kenny Rogers is probably attributable to the down-home ambience and rustic simplicity that his music conveyed. His version of "Amanda," written by Bob McDill, about the disappointed dreams of an aging hillbilly singer, should have been satisfying to anyone—a classic performance that somehow combined the flavor of old-time country music with a middle-of-the-road approach.

Williams's fellow Texan Kenny Rogers (from Houston) followed several stylistic paths before becoming one of America's pop super-stars. Although he garnered an acclaim that few singers in American history have received and certainly acquired a wealth that few can equal, he could still refer to himself as "basically a country singer who's capable of doing other things."[9] Rogers began recording and performing actively while still in high school, and in the ensuing years he performed rock and roll, modern jazz, and pop-folk (with the New Christy Minstrels) before settling down for six years in a successful commercial format with the First Edition. The First Edition was an eclectic trio that did pop, folk, and soft-rock music, but the group also performed pop versions of country songs, such as "Reuben James" and the very popular "Ruby, Don't Take Your Love to Town," in which Rogers gave hints of the personal, sensual style that later characterized his music.

After the 1976 demise of the First Edition, Rogers cast his lot with country music and devised a formula that gave him access to one of the largest audiences that any American singer has ever had. For three consecutive years in the late 1970s, he won the People's Choice Award as the top male singer (a survey conducted by the Gallup organization); from 1977 (when he recorded his first giant hit, "Lucille") to 1984, he sold an estimated $250 million worth of records; and he branched out into television network specials and movies (one TV movie was based on his popular hit recording "The Gambler"). While his songs were often country in theme and mood, the production behind them (as well as his concerts) was thoroughly Las Vegas in tone. The sophisticated arrangements and lavish orchestration, however, do not explain Rogers's appeal. His handsome looks, combining boyish facial features with graying hair and beard, along with an equally intriguing mixture of machismo and classiness, certainly contributed to his popularity. But his singing style, above all, was the chief source of his immense success. Rogers was a consummate storyteller, with an intimate and compelling style that almost demanded the listener's concentration. When his husky tenor voice slipped down into a raspy, gravelly register, as it often did, Rogers pulled the listener even further into his confidence.

Rogers's appeal to Middle America, though much stronger, was reminiscent of that of Conway Twitty. Twitty was born Harold Jenkins in Friars Point, Mississippi, about seventy miles south of Memphis and only forty miles from Elvis Presley's hometown of Tupelo. When he began his two-year army stint in 1953, he was still singing the country music that he grew up with, but when he returned to the United States in 1955, he heard Presley's recorded version of "Mystery Train" and was caught up in the excitement that was gripping young people everywhere. He formed a rock-and-roll band, changed his name to Conway Twitty (taken from small towns in Arkansas and Texas, respectively), and set out on a career that led him to stardom in two different fields of music. His 1957 MGM recording of "It's Only Make Believe" became number one in country, pop, and blues; he performed the song for the rest of his life.

Twitty returned in 1968 to country music—which he maintained he had always preferred to rock and roll—and immediately established credibility with fans and disc jockeys. His first number one country song was a pure honky-tonk weeper called "The Image of Me," but after that time he demonstrated a mastery of every kind of country material. His virtuosity was such that he became virtually uncategorizable. He was mainstream country, with a tinge of pop, but, unlike Kenny Rogers,

Conway Twitty and Loretta Lynn. Bill Malone personal collection.

there was scarcely a hint of crossover in his approach. His bestselling duets with Loretta Lynn and his relationship with the powerful MCA corporation helped give him access to a huge audience, but many of his fans had probably been with him since "It's Only Make Believe," having grown up with him and his music. An intense bond of loyalty existed between Twitty and his fans, many of whom were middle-aged women whose devotion to him began when he was a gyrating rock and roller. The sexuality of his lyrics was much more overt than that found in most other singers' material, and such songs as "You've Never Been

This Far Before," "Slow Hand," "I'd Love to Lay You Down," and "Tight Fittin' Jeans" raised eyebrows as they became major commercial hits. Twitty's performances, however, were physically restrained and contained none of the sensual body movements witnessed in the acts of many of the modern rockabillies. An affecting growl, similar to Kenny Rogers's, was about the only idiosyncratic element in his otherwise straight-ahead vocal style, but it was a highly effective communicator. Twitty's private life as a family man and successful businessman stood in striking contrast to the sexy world about which he often sang. His musical success enabled him to build one of country music's largest commercial empires. He owned a music promotion company, a minor league baseball team (the Nashville Sounds), much real estate, and a theme park, Twitty City, which contained his plantation-style house, homes for various relatives, a museum, gardens, and gift shops. In the first year after its opening in May 1982, Twitty City was host to a reported 200,000 tourists. The success garnered by Twitty City and other music-related theme parks, along with the profusion of mail-order programming on the Nashville Network, suggest that country music had still not traveled very far from the carnival and Mexican border atmosphere of its youth.

Larry Gatlin did not accumulate such an extensive portfolio of economic interests, but, like Twitty, he presented many faces to his listeners. He was, as one writer phrased it, "an arrogant young smartass to some, a prophetic truthseeker to others. A good-looking, sexual fantasy to one, yet a fine young Christian man to another."[10] Gatlin occasionally aroused anger by an aloofness to fans (such as a refusal to sign autographs) and by an air of supreme self-confidence. Politically, his views were aggressively right-wing. Interviews with him, however, as well as the evidence found in his song lyrics, suggest a man of considerable depth, sensitivity, intelligence, and compassion. His expressive tenor singing bore a strong resemblance to that of Glen Campbell, but it was definitely closer to the country mainstream than that of the Arkansas superstar. His style and sound were of broad appeal, but he never enjoyed a crossover success like many of his country contemporaries. The Odessa, Texas, native received his first musical experience singing in the Assembly of God church, but his entree to Nashville came as a songwriter when Dottie West heard some of his compositions and sponsored his move to the city. Gatlin always sang only his own songs, first as a soloist, but later with the backing of his brothers, Rudy and Steve, in a group called Larry Gatlin and the Gatlin Brothers Band. Beginning with "Sweet Becky Walker" in 1973, Gatlin recorded a succession of popular songs such as "Broken Lady," "I Just Wish You Were Someone I Loved," "Houston," and a controversial but compassionate song about derelicts in a rescue mission, "The Midnight Choir."

Steve Wariner, on the other hand, evoked no controversy, nor did he gain public exposure through outrageous political opinions or a flamboyant or bizarre lifestyle. He merely made some of the finest music available during the 1970s and early 1980s, and with an easy-listening but *country* vocal style. Born in Noblesville, Indiana, where he was introduced to hard country music by his father, Wariner came to Nashville and the *Grand Ole Opry* in 1971 as a bass player for Dottie West. From this invaluable experience, he moved on to a similar position with the dynamic rockabilly Bob Luman, but finally achieved his real dream in 1976 when he signed a recording contract with MCA. Over the course of the next twenty years and more, including stints with at least three other labels—RCA, Arista, and Capitol—Wariner produced an impressive body of music as a guitarist, songwriter, singer, and producer. Chet Atkins, who played a special role as a mentor to Wariner, described his "student" as one of the six best guitar players in the world (along with himself!). With his extraordinary vocal range and facility with a wide variety of song styles, Wariner begged comparison with Glen Campbell, another mentor with whom he often collaborated. In a career that included at least four Grammy nominations and admission to the *Grand Ole Opry* in 1998, Wariner wrote and recorded some of the era's finest songs, including "Life's Highway," "Lonely Women Make Good Lovers," and "All Roads Lead to You." In a beautiful duet performed with Glen Campbell—"The Hand That Rocks the Cradle"—he not only paid tribute to the mothers of the world, he also gave country music one of its superlative recorded moments.

Country duets, of course, had always been common, but the modern period saw a proliferation of major performers, such as Wariner and Campbell, Dolly Parton and Porter Wagoner, Conway Twitty and Loretta Lynn, and Merle Haggard and Willie Nelson, who combined their talents in duet performances. At least one father and daughter team, the Kendalls, won some success with songs like "Heaven's Just a Sin Away" and "The Pittsburgh Stealers" (about love thieves, not the famous football team). Brother duets were rare outside of bluegrass music, but at least one act, the Florida-born Bellamy Brothers (Howard and Dave) prospered with a mixture of rock and country sounds and a repertory of sexy songs such as "Do You Love as Good as You Look?" Trios were even rarer, but an occasional group such as Dave and Sugar (composed of Dave Rowland and a shifting duo of beautiful female singers) competed favorably with other country entertainers. Much more crucial to country music's commercial expansion than the duets and trios, however, were the quartets that thrived at the end of the 1970s.

Until the emergence of the Statler Brothers, the Oak Ridge Boys, and Alabama, quartets usually performed unobtrusively as backup voices for other singers. These singers, though, stepped out front to center stage and became some of country music's brightest superstars. The Statler Brothers were boyhood friends who began singing gospel music while still in high school in Staunton, Virginia. Brothers Don and Harold Reid and their friends, Lew DeWitt and Phil Balsley, first called themselves the Kingsmen and sang in a style suggestive of such major gospel quartets as the Statesmen Quartet and Blackwood Brothers. Eventually selecting the name Statler as a performing title (from the brand name of a local tissue product), the quartet became active throughout the Upper South singing a mixture of country, pop, and gospel material. They joined Johnny Cash's touring organization on March 9, 1964, and remained with the Cash troupe for eight and a half years. Although described as a gospel quartet, the Statlers continued to perform a diverse repertory. Johnny Cash negotiated a Columbia recording contract for them, and their third release in 1965 was a massive hit and Grammy Award winner named "Flowers on the Wall." Despite this auspicious beginning, the Statlers felt ill-served by Columbia, and they left the label in 1970. A new association with Mercury and producer Jerry Kennedy permitted them freedom of action as well as the promotion necessary to break through into a larger market. Beginning with "Bed of Rose's" in 1970, the Statlers built a popularity that led to their being named the CMA's Vocal Group of the Year for seven years in a row. Described by one journalist as "intelligent conservatives with a gift for communication and a respect for their conservative audience,"[11] the Statlers established a rapport with middle-class America that extended well beyond the borders of their native South. They reawakened memories of small-town radio for many Americans with their delightful spoof of amateur country bands, first heard in a 1973 recording called "The Saturday Morning Radio Show," and then followed up by an LP entitled *Live at Johnny Mack Brown High School.* Their mythical creations, Lester "Road-hog" Moran and the Cadillac Cowboys—sponsored by Burford's Barber Shop—were reminiscent of hundreds of similar earnest but plodding bands heard by Americans during radio's golden age. With their emphasis on traditional values, patriotism, and, above all, nostalgia, they struck responsive chords in 1970s America. Such songs as "The Class of '57" (about the failed dreams of a graduating class) and "Whatever Happened to Randolph Scott" (a tribute to the beloved cowboy movies of their youth) commercially satisfied the Statlers and even won the admiration of the novelist Kurt Vonnegut, who praised the "shrewd innocence" found in the lyrics.[12]

The Oak Ridge Boys also came to country music from a gospel background. Named in honor of the nearby atomic energy center, the quartet was founded by Wally Fowler in Knoxville, Tennessee. Down to the mid-1960s, the Oak Ridge Quartet remained part of the evangelistic singing movement and underwent numerous personnel changes, Long before they converted exclusively to country music, they had already become quite controversial in the gospel field by letting their hair grow long, by wearing modish and flashy apparel, by mixing secular and religious material, and by employing sexy and highly choreographed movements onstage. In other words, they entertained; they did not preach. Oak Ridge apologists saw them acquiring a new audience for gospel music; their detractors saw them as blasphemers who used the gospel format for opportunistically commercial purposes. The quartet that made the leap to country—first by including a few country songs in their Las Vegas concerts in the mid-1970s—included lead singers Duane Allen and Bill Golden from Texas and Alabama; tenor Joe Bonsall from Philadelphia; and bass Richard Sterban from New Jersey. Their first country record in 1977, "Y'all Come Back Saloon," was a huge success. Their "crossover" into country music, followed by other hits such as "Leaving Louisiana in the Broad Daylight" and "Trying to Love Two Women," merely served as the prelude to an even more lucrative intrusion into the broader area of pop music. That moment came in 1981 when they recorded "Elvira," a 1950s-style rockabilly tune that vaulted to the top of the country music charts, moved over into other fields of pop music, and won them a Grammy.

The Oak Ridge Boys talked openly of their desire to be the first group ever to win the CMA's Entertainer of the Year award. Despite their commercial viability and the dynamic showmanship for which they were known, they never attained this professed goal. It must have been a matter of some chagrin to the Oak Ridge Boys, then, that another vocal group with much less experience—Alabama—became not only the initial winner of this coveted award but continued to win it three years in succession (1982–1984). Alabama cultivated an audience among both young and old listeners with a style that reflected the musical crosscurrents of the 1970s—part country, part pop-rock (e.g., the Eagles, Jackson Browne), and with a tinge of southern rock. Unlike many of the entertainers who have thrived in country music's middle road, the musicians who composed Alabama did not come from other musical backgrounds. They succeeded commercially with the same sound and style with which they began as struggling teenagers playing in the clubs of Myrtle Beach, South Carolina, in the early 1970s. Composed of three cousins, Jeff Cook, Teddy Gentry, and Randy Owen (all from Fort Payne, Alabama), and a drummer friend named Mark Herndon, the group stressed close harmony and the mellow lead singing of Owen. As a group, they were also unique in that they provided their own instrumentation; Cook played the lead guitar, as well as the fiddle on occasion, while Gentry and Owen played the bass and rhythm guitar. Alabama discovered a winning commercial formula by judiciously mixing romantic ballads such as "Feels So Right" and "An Old Flame Burning in Your Heart" with rousing fast-tempo tunes like "Mountain Music" and "Tennessee River." The results were a balanced and fruitful mélange that brought Alabama an enthusiastic and broad audience of both mainstream country listeners and youthful devotees.

It is one of the givens of cultural history that youth the world over have fueled the revolution in popular music, shattering traditional forms and contributing to the rise of innovative styles. Their effect on country music, as we have seen, has been dramatic. Country music's recent history, then, has been all the more remarkable in that young people, both musicians and fans, have not only been in the vanguard of stylistic change but have also been forces for the preservation and revitalization of traditional elements. Admittedly, these have not been young adolescents but, instead, young adults who, for the most part, were originally won to music through rock and roll. The infusion of youthful styles and tastes into country music provided important and healthy alternatives to the "Nashville sound"; they were welcomed antidotes to the homogenization and mass production of country music.

The always-experimental Bob Dylan[13] was a powerful catalyst in breaking down the resistance to country music among young fans. He first came to Nashville in February 1966 and continued a fruitful relationship with the producer Bob Johnston that had begun earlier in New York City. With the assistance of some of Nashville's greatest session musicians, including the great harmonica player Charlie McCoy who superintended the sessions, Dylan produced a series of influential recordings, including *Blonde on Blonde, John Wesley Harding*, and *Nashville Skyline*. Dylan lent respectability to a musical form, and to a body of musicians, that had been perceived as "corny" or old-fashioned. Since the early 1970s, numerous young musicians identified with rock or pop-folk music have exhibited an interest in and facility for country music. John McEuen, of the Nitty Gritty Dirt Band, was one of the first musicians to play the five-string banjo in a folk-rock group. He and Jerry Garcia (the multitalented instrumentalist of the San Francisco rock group the Grateful Dead), John Fogerty (the marvelous lead singer of Creedence Clearwater Revival), Leon Russell (who recorded a few country albums under the name of Hank Wilson), Elvis Costello, Linda Ronstadt, Gram Parsons, and Chris Hillman were only a few of the major performers who experimented with country music. These musicians, some of whom had been identified with psychedelic and hard rock, exhibited an unexpected knowledge of country songs and harmonies and a talent for steel guitars, fiddles, mandolins, and five-string banjos.

A high point in the merger of youth and country music came in 1972 when the Nitty Gritty Dirt Band (best known for their recording of "Mr. Bojangles" in 1970) recorded a triple-disc album of country songs named for a Carter Family perennial called *Will the Circle Be Unbroken*. The group had started out as a jug band in Orange County, California, in the mid-1960s, and, like many of the young musicians of that era, they were ultraeclectic in repertory, playing everything from mountain music and bluegrass to hard rock. Largely through the inspiration of their manager and producer, William McEuen (the brother of banjo player John McEuen), the band did a marathon recording session with many of the great names of country music: Roy Acuff, Maybelle Carter, Merle Travis, Earl Scruggs, Doc Watson, Jimmy

Martin, Vassar Clements, Norman Blake, Bashful Brother Oswald, and Junior Huskey. Intended as a tribute to some of the sources of contemporary music, the finished product was critically acclaimed and commercially successful. Many people bought the collection solely on the strength of the Dirt Band's name and reputation, but in so doing they were inadvertently introduced to some of the giants of country music.

Although many young musicians experimented with country forms, no one converted the enterprise into a mission until Gram Parsons appeared. Parsons was born Cecil Ingram Connors in Winter Haven, Florida, and was the inheritor of great wealth from his mother's family, the Snivelys of Florida, and from her second marriage to Robert Parsons of New Orleans.[14] Despite his family connections and attendance at exclusive preparatory schools, Parsons developed a childhood affection for country music, although, as with most young people of his age, his first musical experience came through Elvis Presley. Parson's personal musical progression epitomizes that of many young people in the 1960s. While still in high school, 1963–1965, he organized an urban folk group called the Shilos. During a brief stay at Harvard in 1965, he moved toward the rock sound that the Beatles and other English groups had revitalized when he formed the International Submarine Band. This was a rock band, but with a difference: it featured the performance of modern country songs, and it included the pedal steel guitar playing of J. D. Maness, one of the pioneers of the instrument in rock music. The band's 1967 recordings of such songs as "Miller's Cave" and "Satisfied Mind" occurred well in advance of similar experiments made by the Nitty Gritty Dirt Band and other rock-oriented musicians.

In 1968, Parsons joined the pioneering folk-rock band the Byrds and began urging that group to combine country with rock. The chief result was a 1969 LP called *Sweetheart of the Rodeo*, an extremely influential and thoroughly country collection that included such vintage country songs as "I Am a Pilgrim" and "Blue Canadian Rockies," a Woody Guthrie song ("Pretty Boy Floyd"), a couple of Bob Dylan compositions, and some original numbers, including Parsons's beautiful, and now classic, "Hickory Wind." Although the songs were not consistently country in origin, the Byrds attempted, with erratic success, to render them in faithful country style, with the steel guitar work of J. D. Maness again playing a prominent role.

After leaving the Byrds, Parsons and another alumnus of the group, Chris Hillman, along with the steel guitarist Sneaky Pete Kleinow and bass player Chris Ethridge, founded a band that vividly illustrated the fusion of country music and youth-culture motifs. Choosing a self-mocking name, the Flying Burrito Brothers dressed in brightly arrayed and sequined Nudie suits that bore marijuana leaves instead of the traditional cactus plants and wagon wheels favored by country and western singers. Some of their songs, such as "Christine's Tune" and "Hot Burrito #1," were strongly rock flavored, but they also borrowed songs from the Louvin Brothers, George Jones, Merle Haggard, and other older hard-core country singers. Burrito instrumentation was similarly mixed, but the steel-guitar stylings of Sneaky Pete gave the group a distinctive honky-tonk flavor. The Burrito Brothers' most compelling songs were those written by Parsons and Hillman, especially the frequently performed "Sin City" and "Wheels," and they were rendered by these two singers in a sweet, clear duet harmony reminiscent of the Everly Brothers.

After he left the Burritos, Parsons continued to campaign for the fusion of country and rock audiences, but he won little success in his own lifetime. He made a few records on his own, including some excellent performances (such as "Hearts on Fire" and "Love Hurts") with Emmylou Harris, whom he met in Washington, DC, in 1972. Parsons died of a drug overdose on September 19, 1973, and was buried in a New Orleans suburb in a modestly marked grave. Although Parsons's final resting place is obscure, his contributions to country music are much more strongly marked. His influence is still heard in the music of many young musicians, both unknown and professional (as in the cases of groups like the Eagles and the New Riders of the Purple Sage), but his chief legacy is displayed in the career of his protégé Emmylou Harris, whom he converted to hard country music.

Gram Parsons came to "traditional" country music from rock; Charlie Daniels and Hank Williams Jr. moved in the other direction. And both found niches in a style generally described as "southern rock." Southern rock was essentially rock music performed by southern-born musicians, and hence little different from rock music elsewhere. These musicians nevertheless often demonstrated their southernness through their stylistic borrowings from blues and country music, but more often through an aggressive identification with the South, macho posturing, and good-old-boy imagery. The Marshall Tucker Band in

South Carolina, the Allman Brothers in Georgia, ZZ Top in Texas, and Lynyrd Skynyrd in Alabama were a few of the groups that combined cowboy and hippie attire while also occasionally using country riffs and songs in a basically hard-rock context.

Of all these musicians, Charlie Daniels bore the closest relationship to country music. Born in Wilmington, North Carolina, Daniels parlayed a talent for the fiddle and electric guitar into a job as a session musician in Nashville (he was on Dylan's *Nashville Skyline* album, for instance). Daniels's own group, the Charlie Daniels Band, was very much in the mold of the Allmans and the Marshall Tucker Band, and he acknowledged his kinship with the southern rockers in "The South's Gonna Do It Again." His fiddling, on the other hand, was strongly indebted to western swing, and his singing was redolently spiked with the flavor and accent of the rural South. This big, gruff, tobacco-chewing, outspoken musician embodied southern good-old-boy traits almost to the point of caricature. He was nationalistic, politically right wing, hedonistic, macho, . . . and lovable. He also made compelling music. His "Carolina, I Remember You" was an affectionate and poignant recollection of his state before the coming of the superhighways; "Still in Saigon" is one of the best songs yet written about the undying legacy of the Vietnam War; and his rousing "The Devil Went Down to Georgia" (a modern adaptation of the old theme of the devil as a fiddler) was the CMA's choice as Single of the Year in 1980.

Hank Williams Jr., of course, had one of the most famous pedigrees in country music.[15] He grew up, as one of his songs phrased it, "standing in the shadows" of his revered father and pushed into a mold by adoring fans and an overly ambitious mother. Hank Jr. was an enormously talented child with an affinity for most of the country string instruments. He was on the concert trail at the age of fourteen, singing an occasional blues tune or rock-and-roll song, but most often performing his daddy's songs and in his daddy's style. Neither fans nor promoters would permit him to stray very far from the path originally blazed by Hank Sr. During the early stages of his career, Hank Jr. was not unsuccessful, but his ascent to superstardom really did not come until he cast his lot with the southern rockers in the mid-1970s. With songs like "Dixie on My Mind," "Whiskey Bent and Hell Bound," and his high-powered, country-rock version of "Kawliga," Hank built enormous followings in both country and rock music. In his banner year of

1982, he had nine LPs on the charts at the same time, a feat unequaled by any other country entertainer.

Despite his unparalleled commercial success, Hank Jr. was not rewarded by the country music industry until 1987, when he was chosen as Entertainer of the Year. Some CMA voters may have questioned his authenticity as a country singer (although awards have been won often by performers less country than he), but his lifestyle and flaunting of the respectable conventions emphasized by the staid Nashville establishment alienated a much larger number of people. His songs consistently projected a mood of swaggering hedonism—a glorification of womanizing, hell raising, and drinking, with a stated preference for Jim Beam whiskey. In short, his music suggested a rowdiness that his father had only hinted at in his songs. Hank Jr. was not chastened by his head-first plunge from a mountaintop in Montana on August 8, 1975. Recovering from the near-fatal accident required massive plastic surgery, including the complete rebuilding of his face. After his return to health, his songs became even more aggressively hedonistic and macho, suggesting among other things that the old fundamentalist strain that had inhibited free expression while encouraging guilt was losing its force among rural southerners. If God looked disapprovingly at his conduct, Hank Jr. seemed not to care. He seemed similarly unconcerned about the responses made by northerners to his aggressive southern posture. "Dixie on My Mind" was one of several anti–New York City songs that appeared in country music in the 1970s and 1980s, and "A Country Boy Can Survive," while also taking potshots at that favorite scapegoat, was virtually a survivalist hymn with its emphasis on rural independence and its underlying hint of violence. With the appearance of such commercial songs, Hank Jr. made himself a force to be reckoned with in the broad realm of popular music. Still, the ghost of his father would not disappear, and largely because Hank Jr. seemed to feel a need to cling to the mystique, if not the reality, of Hank Williams. While complaining about having to live up to that myth, he nonetheless shamelessly exploited his famous family relationship by frequently alluding to his father in his songs, even up to the point of claiming Hank Sr. as one of country music's original "outlaws," a self-serving designation designed to lend historical legitimacy to his own rebellion.

Hank Jr. was not the only star who emerged from country music families. Lorrie Morgan, daughter of George; Pam Tillis, daughter of

Mel; Stella Parton, sister of Dolly; and, of course, Crystal Gayle, sister of Loretta Lynn, were only a few of the entertainers who could claim country lineage. In many respects, Rosanne Cash was the most interesting product of this tradition, and certainly the most cerebral. Born in Memphis, Tennessee, in 1955, just as her father's career with Sun Records was beginning, Rosanne lived for several years in Ventura, California, during her parents' brief sojourn in that state and after they divorced in 1967. Although she grew up immersed in her father's music and even worked with his road band for a few years in the early 1970s, she was drawn to all kinds of music, as well as to her own dreams of a writing or acting career. She actually spent short periods of time studying English and Drama at Vanderbilt University and at the Lee Strasberg Actors Studio in Hollywood. These varied aspirations informed the recordings that she made in the 1980s, beginning with "Seven Year Ache" and extending through that decade with other songs like "My Baby Thinks He's a Train," "Tennessee Flat Top Box," and "It's a Small World," recorded as a duet with her then-husband Rodney Crowell (who produced much of her early music). Collectively, these recordings yielded her at least thirteen Grammy nominations and the reputation of someone who could easily combine thoughtful lyrics with a variety of performing styles. As the writer of at least two books, numerous short stories, and tomes of social criticism, and as an active participant in various humanitarian campaigns, Rosanne Cash stood virtually alone in the country music world.

The mating of rock and country, so strongly displayed in the music of Hank Jr., Gram Parsons, and Rosanne Cash was most strongly effected in Austin, Texas. The Austin musicians also came close to accomplishing Parsons's other dream: that of bringing youth and adult audiences together in a commonly shared musical environment. The vigorous and eclectic music scene found in Austin in the 1970s was anticipated at Threadgill's bar in the previous decade. Threadgill's was the scene of a meeting, if not mating, of cultures in which college students and "rednecks" enjoyed musical communion with each other. Kenneth Threadgill, the proprietor and bartender of a honky-tonk housed in an abandoned gas station in North Austin (allegedly the recipient of the first beer license granted in Travis County after Prohibition repeal), was a singer and yodeler in the Jimmie Rodgers tradition. He made his establishment available to anyone who wanted to sit around his big round tables and pick and sing, and when time permitted, Threadgill would also sing and yodel, still wearing his apron and invariably clutching a bottle of beer in his hand. In the late 1950s, Threadgill's became a refuge, first, for graduate students and, later, for undergraduates from the University of Texas who were being won over to the emerging folk music revival. Janis Joplin was one of a small coterie of young musicians, many of them spillovers from the campus folk music club, who began frequenting Threadgill's in the early 1960s, both to perform and actually to rub shoulders with the real "folk" who constituted much of the bar's regular clientele. The listeners who packed into the tiny establishment—an unlikely assortment of students and working folk—could hear everything from hoary hillbilly material (like that of the Carter Family) to bluegrass, blues, traditional ballads, and Woody Guthrie and Bob Dylan songs.

The cultural/musical mix witnessed at Threadgill's bar was an acoustic-dominated phenomenon and one that drew upon grassroots musical material. Many of the musicians and fans who thronged to Threadgill's, however, were soon won away by the supercharged and electronic sounds of the British and San Francisco rock groups. Janis Joplin was not the only local musician who journeyed to the West Coast, and in Austin itself, a vigorous club scene emerged in the wake of the rock movement and the growth of the counterculture. The Armadillo World Headquarters, housed in a former national guard armory, was the center and symbol of this new musical culture. When it was established in August 1970, the club was intended as a forum for rock bands (such as the local Shiva's Headband) and as a refuge for Austin's hippie, or "freak," community. But the Armadillo also featured an occasional country band, and so cowboys and rednecks began to interact socially with the long-haired counterculture community. Gradually a music culture emerged that enveloped them all—one that reflected a curious combining of images and symbols: hippie, Texan, and, above all, cowboy (a usage that arose from the desire to find an indigenous and binding metaphor). The wearing of cowboy costumes, clubs with cowboy names (such as Split Rail, Broken Spoke, and Soap Creek Saloon), and the use of logos that suggested the Texas mystique (armadillos, Lone Star Beer, Longhorns) all became part of the rock/country music scene.

By the early 1970s, it had become apparent that Austin had become one of several interrelated colonies of musicians in Texas, not concentrated in one particular place, but all of whom were aware of and eager to use the cultural symbols of their home state. Although no form of music was alien to them, they found that country music was the most welcoming style available. Preeminent among these young musicians was Guy Clark, who grew up the son of a lawyer in Monahans, in the dusty south plains of West Texas, and in Rockport on the Texas Gulf Coast. Clark learned to love poetry at family gatherings around the dinner table, but he absorbed the basic ingredients of his early songs from the reminiscences of older relatives or from the characters seen and heard in the local barber shops, domino parlors, city cafes, and general stores. These vignettes of the old but vanishing Texas provided the basic story lines of songs like "Texas 1947" and "Desperados Waiting for a Train," both of which were introduced to a larger public in recordings made by Jerry Jeff Walker. Clark's art was also informed by the music of the folk revival, the music heard in scores of coffee houses or at gatherings like the Kerrville Folk Festival, or in the homes of guitar-picking buddies. Clark even sought musical satisfaction on the West Coast, and though he came away disillusioned from the experience, it did inspire one of his greatest songs: "L.A. Freeway."[16]

While playing in Houston at the Jester Club in 1965, Clark met one of his closest and most influential friends, the brilliant but troubled Townes Van Zandt. Van Zandt was born in Fort Worth, into a privileged and historic Texas family that traced its lineage back to the beginnings of the Texas Republic. An East Texas county, in fact, is named for the family. Van Zandt nevertheless abandoned this comfort to become a wandering minstrel, a journey that ultimately took him to Houston; Austin; Boulder, Colorado; and Nashville, and into a career that bequeathed to America some of its best songs. Van Zandt produced an extensive number of albums, with only limited success, but they included a few song gems that will stand the test of time, including "If I Needed You," "Tecumseh Valley," "White Freightliner Blues," "Snowing on Raton," and "Pancho and Lefty."

Van Zandt and Clark wound up in Nashville at about the same time in 1971. Both probably agreed with Clark, who said that though he preferred living in Austin, Nashville was where the music business was located. Van Zandt was at the height of his musical powers, but was already on the path to personal self-destruction, suffering from manic depression and addiction to alcohol and heroin. He lived with the Clarks for many months, and enjoyed the friendship and companionship of his soulmate, Guy Clark's wife, Susanna, an artist and accomplished songwriter in her own right. In the meantime, Guy Clark continued to serve as a mentor for fledgling songwriters while he perfected his craft, turning out a steady stream of personal songs that had the universal ring of truth, "Stuff That Works," "The Cape," "My Favorite Picture of You," and "The Randall Knife," a heart-searing tribute to his father.

Van Zandt wasn't the only musician who showed up often at the Clark home. Aspiring singers and songwriters came often for guidance, but on any given occasion, people like Ian Tyson, Jerry Jeff Walker, Emmylou Harris, John Prine, Jack Elliott, Steve Earle, and Rodney Crowell might show up to pick and sing or share a partially written song with the others. Rodney Crowell completed one of his greatest songs, "'Til I Gain Control Again," at one of these Clark song-sharing sessions. Crowell was born into a hardscrabble family in Houston that he chronicled in a fine book, *Chinaberry Sidewalks: A Memoir*.[17] Of all the people in the Guy Clark circle, Crowell was the most complete musician. He produced some of his wife Rosanne Cash's first albums; he led Emmylou Harris's Hot Band for a brief period; he was a member of the short-lived group, the Cherry Bombs, that also included Tony Brown and Vince Gill; he wrote some of the most literate lyrics found in the songs of the period (e.g., "Leaving Louisiana in the Broad Daylight," "Stars in the Water," "After All This Time," "'Til I Gain Control Again"); and he built a very successful career as a singer. In 1988, his Columbia album *Diamonds and Dirt* yielded five consecutive number one singles, a feat that no one else has accomplished.

While Nashville seduced some people like Crowell, Clark, and Van Zandt, other Texans were content to live out their playing days in Austin or elsewhere, arguing that living well was more important than making money. Bill and Bonnie Hearne, for example, built good and influential lives working the local club scene and the Kerrville Folk Festival in the nearby Texas Hill Country. The Hearnes demonstrated a thorough acquaintance with most forms of contemporary popular music, but their fine harmonies and Bonnie's piano playing most readily exhibited their debts to country and gospel styles. Jimmie Dale Gilmore was a roaming minstrel who included Austin as one of several stops in his quest for personal and musical fulfillment. Born in Amarillo, he had been part of a thriving musical culture in Lubbock that included Butch Hancock, Joe Ely, and the artist/musician Terry Allen. He had even spent some time in the 1970s in an ashram in Colorado, studying under an Indian guru, Prem Rawat. He cut a striking figure, with his graying shoulder-length hair, high cheekbones, and dark Native American physical features, and exhibited a gentle spirit that drew upon his Buddhist meditative resources. He arrived in Austin in the 1980s, playing at places like Threadgill's bar and contributing to the local music scene his appealing mixture of Zen Buddhism and gritty West Texas imagery. While Gilmore's compelling reedy tenor became his most valued asset, he was also an evocative songwriter. His musical portrait of Dallas, in a song of the same name, probably won him few fans in that supercapitalist city, but it became an oft-performed song in the Austin area and beyond.

Steve Fromholz and Michael Martin Murphey, on the other hand, had begun their musical careers in the Dallas/Denton urban folk music circuit. Marcia Ball was a blues pianist/singer from Louisiana before she became the vocalist for the Austin country-rock group Freda and the Firedogs. A young group of musicians from Berkeley, Asleep at the Wheel, had already begun combining rock and roll with western swing before they came to Austin, and Doug Sahm, a San Antonio native who was in and out of Austin, had long dabbled with Tex-Mex, country, and rhythm-and-blues forms before moving to hard rock in the mid-1960s. As the leader of the Sir Douglas Quintet, he was one of the first Americans to show the direct influence of the British rock invasion. The best-known musician to relocate in Austin, aside from Willie Nelson, was Jerry Jeff Walker. Born Ronald Clyde Crosby, a one-time folkie from Oneonta, New York, Walker perambulated around the country and did a stint in a New Orleans jail, and these experiences led to the writing of his most famous song, "Mr. Bojangles." This self-styled "gypsy songman" also became one of the first interpreters of Guy Clark's songs, with renditions of songs like "Desperados Waiting for a Train." Because of his loose, laid-back manner and free spirit (a reputation that sometimes found him compared to Jimmy Buffett), Walker seemed to epitomize, for many people, the atmosphere conveyed by Austin and the nearby Texas Hill Country. Austin had become a good place to play music, but it was an even greater place to live.

Although Austin audiences were diverse, the large and annually self-replenishing student body of the University of Texas provided a crucial core of support for the clubs that flourished in the city. A trio of key supporters contributed mightily to the publicizing of the music. Rod Kennedy, a local promoter and folk music patron, provided exposure for the Austin musicians at his popular festivals in the Hill Country town of Kerrville. Townsend Miller, a stockbroker by profession and a country music fan by avocation, euphorically touted the local musicians in a weekly newspaper column, and Darrell Royal, the popular coach of the University of Texas Longhorns football team, lent the Austin scene further publicity by his appearances at local music functions and through his friendship with many of the musicians who came to the city. He was actually known as the biggest groupie in Austin.

Most of the musicians who congregated in the city were young, eclectic in musical taste, and relatively new to the country music scene. A few veteran performers, though, such as Floyd Tillman and the fiddler Jesse Ashlock (a Texas Playboy alumnus) and, of course, Kenneth Threadgill, lived among them as patron saints. The Texas mystique clearly affected the imagery that Austin musicians used to describe themselves. The name and music of Bob Wills were often invoked because they supposedly embodied the spirit of liberation and innovation that Texas had contributed to music and on which the Austin musicians now drew. The folklorist Nicholas Spitzer referred to the Austin gestalt as "romantic regionalism,"[18] colorfully captured by Waylon Jennings's "Bob Wills Is Still the King,"[19] recorded live before an Austin audience that goes wild at certain catchwords such as "Red River," "Austin," and "Bob Wills." Even the listener gets caught up in the excitement.

Observers and musicians alike were hard pressed to find a label that sufficiently described the music coming out of Austin. Such terms as "country rock," "hip hillbilly," and "redneck rock" were occasionally used, but none of them gained much currency.[20] The singer Michael Martin Murphey coined a term that enjoyed a brief popularity when he recorded and performed "Cosmic Cowboy," a song that immediately conjured up visions of hippies in cowboy costumes with free lifestyles and unbounded musical tastes. Radio station KOKE-FM in Austin also introduced a label that was widely used, although not exclusively as a description of Austin music, through its popularization of a format known as "progressive country" (1973–1977). KOKE's publicists argued that they were presenting an alternative to the Top Forty concept by playing a wide assortment of music that ranged from Roy Acuff to the Nitty Gritty Dirt Band. KOKE's claim, however, was more hype than reality, for the recordings played on the station tended to come most often from rock or rock-influenced musicians. "Progressive" seemed to suggest those musicians who borrowed from other styles or who tried to appeal to rock-bred youth by taking country music far afield from its traditional roots.

When Willie Nelson moved to Austin in 1970,[21] the thriving music scene described above already existed. The way was already ripe for a fusion of youth and country music, as it was elsewhere in the country. Contrary to the mythology that has grown up around Nelson, his departure from Nashville was not occasioned by his rejection by the music establishment. He had been quite successful as a songwriter, and he was highly respected by other musicians in the city. On the other hand, his dream of acceptance as a singer had not been realized. He felt that RCA did not properly promote his records and that the Nashville area possessed few places in which to perform. Nelson had always maintained his contacts in Texas, and he was a fixture on the honky-tonk circuit to which he periodically returned. The collapse of his second marriage and the destruction of his house by fire confirmed his resolve to leave Nashville. He moved back to an audience that had always been with him, to a climate and ambience that were appealing, and to an already convergent music scene. Nelson could not have been unaware of Austin's youthful audience, but he became acutely more conscious of its receptivity to him when he performed at the counterculture-oriented Armadillo World Headquarters. In the months following his return to Austin, Nelson began making a calculated attempt to appeal to young people, and particularly to those who had grown up with rock music and who had been touched by counterculture values. Nelson let his hair grow long, sported a beard, began wearing a headband, an earring, jeans, and jogging shoes—quite a contrast to the earlier Willie Nelson, who, with short hair, turtleneck sweater, and a Nehru jacket, appeared on Nashville television in the 1960s. But Nelson claimed in an interview with Barbara Walters on June 15, 1982, that the Nashville attire had been atypical, and that he had always favored jeans and informal dress.

The most highly publicized examples of Nelson's efforts to bring attention to himself and to unite disparate audiences were his huge annual "picnics." The first of these outdoor festivals—a tentative experiment—convened at Dripping Springs, near Austin, in July 1971. The affair was an artistic success (it included old-timers like Roy Acuff, Tex Ritter, and Earl Scruggs, as well as a host of newer musicians like

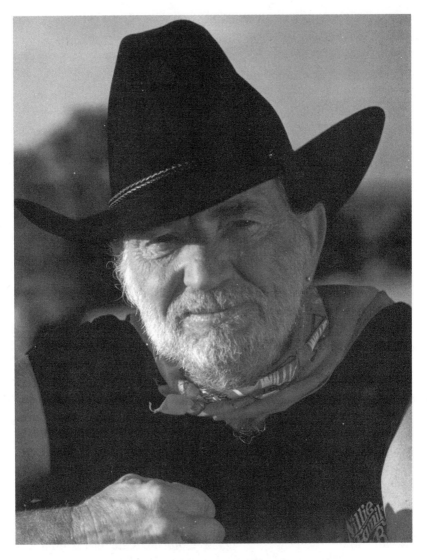

Willie Nelson. Courtesy of Becky Johnson.

Tom T. Hall and Billy Joe Shaver) but a financial disaster, as it was attended by a relatively sparse audience. Subsequent festivals, held usually on the Fourth of July and in various Texas communities, such as Dripping Springs, were massively attended, all the more remarkable because they were held under the broiling Texas sun. Widely touted as events that would bridge the gaps between young and old, hippies and rednecks, and country and rock fans, Willie's picnics, in actuality, soon lost much of their appeal to older people or to traditional country fans. The swirling dust, unrelenting heat, boogying fans, uninhibited youth in scanty or no clothing, marijuana fumes, and the proliferation of noncountry performers such as Leon Russell combined to give the events the aura of a Texas Woodstock. The sociologist William C. Martin had such concerns in mind when he spoke of "growing old at Willie's picnic."[22]

Willie's picnics, on the other hand, did attain the intended results: they made his name known far and wide (Nelson probably became better known than the Texas governor), and they cemented his relationship with the young, an association that brought him wealth and fame and assured him one of the longest careers in American music. After winning the youth, he then moved on to conquering Middle America and the adult market. In 1975 he and his wife, Connie, conceived an LP called *Red Headed Stranger*, a concept album (one which is built around a central theme or story) that dealt with stolen love, retribution, and murder in the Old West. The album became the biggest selling package he had ever put together, and one song from the LP, Fred Rose's gentle evocation of broken but undying love, "Blue Eyes Crying in the Rain," became the number one country song of the year. It is ironic that the first superhit recorded by this master songwriter was a song written by someone else. In the years following 1975, other songwriters continued to fuel Willie's ascent to stardom.

As Nelson became more popular and commercial, this most "progressive" of artists moved increasingly toward the performance of older songs and toward a style ever more explicitly basic and uncomplicated. Nelson never abandoned his jazz style of phrasing or his propensity to sing behind the beat, but his arrangements were built around a rather spare and uncluttered scheme of instrumentation dominated by his own clean, inventive, single-string style of guitar playing and the harmonica riffs of Mickey Raphael. His audience was so loyal that it responded enthusiastically to everything he chose to do, whether it was country rock or the gospel songs that he and his sister and pianist, Bobbie, had been singing since they were children. Nelson's fans also stayed with him when he reached back to record an album of vintage pop, *Stardust*, including such songs as "Stardust," "Georgia on My Mind," and "Blue Skies." These songs took him into another dimension of popular taste and won him another audience, that of the American middle class, which had little affinity for country music but had fond recollections of the pop songs that had largely disappeared.

Nelson's experimentations with songs, styles, and wearing apparel made him the hottest commercial property that country music had ever had, as well as one of the most visible figures in American popular culture. Awards and recognitions poured in, and he branched out into allied areas of entertainment: record production, dance hall management, and movie making. His commercial viability was so proven that he became one of the few country entertainers who was allowed to produce his own records and was permitted to take his road band into recording sessions. Nelson was voted the CMA's Entertainer of the Year in 1979, although many thought that the honor should have been his much earlier. He became a close friend of President Carter, and sang "The Star-Spangled Banner" at the Democratic National Convention in 1980. He has also exhibited a natural flair for character acting, a penchant magnified by the weathered face and graying beard and hair that he sported in the mid-1980s. His movie roles presented him to a larger audience than his musical performances could ever provide.

Although Willie Nelson did much to revive interest in older songs and performers while remaining stylistically close to the honky-tonk style of his native Texas, his ascent to national fame came through an identification with a group of musicians known as the Outlaws. The term "outlaw" is suggestive of lawless behavior, but if "rebellion" in any way marked the conduct of Waylon Jennings, Tompall Glaser, and their compadres, the rebellion was basically against the immobility and conservatism of the Nashville establishment. Like Willie Nelson, this loosely formed group of musicians sought artistic autonomy and the right to roam freely for material and style—objectives that ran counter to corporate Nashville's reluctance either to experiment or to offend.

The Outlaws were not a discrete, cohesive group; they really lived only in the fertile minds of publicists and press agents and in the fantasies of many listeners who wanted to believe that such a group existed. The Outlaws, of course, found it to be in their best commercial interests to promote such an image, and so they capitalized on the undying appeal of the cowboy—especially in the guise of the desperado or badman and of the rambler. They also profited, perhaps unconsciously, from a preoccupation with the antihero manifested in American popular culture since at least World War II.

Waylon Jennings. Bill Malone personal collection.

Standing at the center of the Outlaw group was a gifted singer from Littlefield, Texas, Waylon Jennings.[23] Although his song preferences and performing image sometimes roamed far afield from traditional country music, Jennings was an authentic son of the southern working class. His mother was a devout member of the Church of Christ, and his father was a failed cotton farmer, a truck driver, and a moderately successful produce distributor. One of the few pleasant memories that Jennings had of growing up on the wrong side of town in Littlefield was the hours spent listening to his dad sing and play the

COUNTRY MUSIC USA

guitar. Country music became an all-consuming passion for the young boy, and a means of escape from the cotton fields of West Texas. By the time he was thirteen, Jennings was fronting a little band called the Texas Longhorns and performing on a local station, KVOW, in Littlefield. During the next several years, while performing part-time and working as a disc jockey in Littlefield and in nearby Lubbock, Jennings remained close to the traditional country music of his parents, particularly to that of his first hero, Ernest Tubb. In 1958, Jennings came in contact with what was perhaps the most pivotal influence in his life, the music of Buddy Holly. Holly took a special interest in Jennings, arranged for his first recording session ("Jole Blon," in Clovis, New Mexico, October 1958), and hired him as his bass player at the end of the year. Holly's death in the plane crash of February 3, 1959, which also took the lives of the Big Bopper (J. P. Richardson) and Richie Valens, left Jennings demoralized for several months. It also left him permanently enveloped in the Holly mystique as the great rock-and-roll singer's protégé and as the man who had given up his plane seat to the Big Bopper before the fatal flight.

In the years following Holly's death, Jennings paid his musical dues playing in tough clubs throughout the Southwest and working as a disc jockey in Lubbock and in Phoenix, Arizona. The Phoenix years, 1961–1965, were crucial for the development of Jennings's career and for the shaping of his unique style. He signed his first major contract with Herb Alpert's A&M Records in 1963, and in the following year began singing six nights a week at a large country night club called J.D.'s. The audience there was a cultural mix that included businessmen, students from a nearby university, and cowboys—a prototype of the socially divergent audience found in Austin in the following decade. Jennings's already latitudinarian approach to music was accentuated further by the desire to please his heterogeneous listeners. He was singing at J.D.'s when Chet Atkins and RCA began showing an interest in him, a consequence of constant prodding by Jennings's friend, the comedian Don Bowman, and Bobby Bare, who repeatedly reminded Atkins of how good this Phoenix singer was. His first RCA records were released in May 1965.

Ironically, Waylon Jennings, the quintessential Outlaw of country music, was associated after 1965 with the great corporate giant RCA, and both the singer and the business prospered greatly because of the relationship. The association, however, was often a stormy one, with Jennings struggling to gain control over the choice of material and the manner in which it was recorded. Chet Atkins first groomed Jennings to be a "folk-country" performer (with songs like "Man of Constant Sorrow" and "Scarlet Ribbons"), periodically supplying him with pop-country material such as "Love of the Common People" and "MacArthur Park." Jennings could perform any type of song, but he resisted all efforts to push him into any type of mold. His ascent to superstardom came when he was given free rein to record anything he desired, and in the rock-influenced country style that gave him access to listeners far beyond the normal country audience. Jennings's voice was a richly textured and well-balanced mixture of masculinity, sensuality, and mournfulness—many people believe there has been no better singer in country music.[24]

Jennings's struggle for artistic independence contributed to his reputation for rebellion, but his lifestyle and personality did even more to fasten the label of Outlaw upon him. When he came to Nashville in 1965, his dress and grooming habits still reflected the 1950s rockabilly culture from which he emerged. With his swept-back unparted hair, high collars, and tight blue jeans, he looked like a hood hanging out on the corner or cruising around in his hotrod. His lead role in the Grade B movie *Nashville Rebel* (1966) only accentuated the image while also giving him a title. His dark good looks and natural shyness projected a kind of smoldering sexiness, and his experiments with drugs, drink, and high living (probably little different from those of many non-Outlaw musicians) did their part to evoke an aura of lawlessness.

Regardless of the personal mystique surrounding Jennings, it is clear that the Outlaw phenomenon was largely a product of promotional hype, most of it independent of Jennings himself. RCA nudged away from its conservative posture to endorse the concept of a bold highwayman who would ride away with the profits—for the corporation. In 1972, Jennings recorded a song called "Ladies Love Outlaws," and on the cover of a subsequent album of the same name, he was shown dressed in bad-man attire: black clothing and a six-gun, and facing an adoring young girl, actually posed for by his niece. From this point on, the word "outlaw" began to replace "rebel" as a descriptive label for Jennings and his music, and he began to dress the part— beard, black hat, vest, black trousers. Music publicists of all descriptions lost no time in attaching "outlaw" to Jennings, to other Nashville musicians who seemed at odds with the "establishment," and to the entire Austin community of musicians. Hazel Smith, the publicity chief at Glaser Music, for instance, recognized the commercial utility of outlawry and began using the word to describe the music produced by the Glaser Brothers and by the musicians who worked for them. The Glasers (Tompall, Jim, and Chuck) were a Nebraska-born trio who had long been admired for the smooth, soulful harmony that they developed as backup singers (most notably for Marty Robbins) and as an independent act. Tompall Glaser was also an excellent solo singer, writer, publisher, and free-thinking individualist whose establishment at 916 19th Avenue South in Nashville served as a kind of headquarters for other maverick musicians such as Bobby Bare, Billy Joe Shaver, and Waylon Jennings. The hard-living but multitalented Shaver, from Corsicana, Texas, whose first album of self-penned songs, *Old Five and Dimers Like Me*, had been released in 1973, came up with one of the best lines used by his rowdy confederates when he noted in a song that "the devil made me do it the first time; the second time I done it on my own."[25] This assertion of course has to be balanced with Shaver's well-known religious conviction, conveyed in songs like "Jesus Christ Is Still the King." He and the people who congregated around Tompall Glaser cultivated an air of laid-back informality, dressing generally in jeans, boots, and cowboy hats, and wearing long hair and beards. Their lifestyles were probably as scandalous to respectability-conscious Nashville as their music, but their "hedonism" was not at all unusual among country musicians. Even the establishment figure Johnny Cash, for example, had earlier been known for his zaniness, pill habits, and rowdy practical jokes.

A few musicians, such as David Allan Coe and Johnny Paycheck, sometimes went beyond fantasy to the borders of outlawry. However, Coe was the only one who seemed to delight in shocking audiences with his antisocial behavior. Originally billing himself as the Mysterious Rhinestone Cowboy, replete with mask and cape, Coe carried the outlaw tag beyond the confines of the Old West and suggested instead the lurid underworld of modern urban society. Coe was born in Akron, Ohio, and served several years in the Ohio State Penitentiary. He claimed to have killed a fellow inmate, although researchers have failed to find corroborating evidence of the act. After abandoning his cowboy attire, Coe generally opted for biker, or motorcycle gang, costuming, and his entourage often included similarly clad bikers. He made X-rated recordings that were advertised in "adult" magazines, and in concerts he often conveyed a threatening mood. This kind of behavior certainly got people's attention, but it is doubtful that he needed to do so. Coe was an excellent singer with a supple voice and a wonderful talent for mimicry and a distinctive stylist in his own right. His "You Never Even Call Me by My Name"—written by Steve Goodman and John Prine—was a delightfully outrageous spoof of country music, touting some of the basic clichés allegedly found in the music: trains, trucks, prisons, getting drunk, and mama.

Johnny Paycheck's destiny ultimately proved more pathetic than tragic. A man of almost-boundless musical talent, with an ability to interpret a song that was surpassed by no one, Paycheck could not resist occasional forays to the wild side of life. As he said in one of his songs, "I'm the only hell that Mama ever raised." Born Donald Lytle in Greenfield, Ohio, in 1938, Paycheck exhibited precocious skills as both an instrumentalist and a singer, and by the late 1950s was playing bass and steel guitar for George Jones. At the same time, he contributed some of the best harmony singing heard in country music. He toured with Ray Price's Cherokee Cowboys during their glory days, but also played and sang with performers like Faron Young. During the 1960s, he inaugurated his solo career and wrote and recorded such songs as "Apartment Number Nine" and "Touch My Heart," many of which were covered by other singers. Some of his most valued recordings, such as "She's All I Got" and "Take This Job and Shove It," came later, but were not enough to give him a sense of fulfillment or moral certitude. On December 19, 1985, he shot, but did not kill, a man at the North High Lounge in Hillsboro, Ohio. After lengthy appeals, he was eventually convicted and served about two years in the Chillicothe Correctional Institute.

The Nelson/Jennings/Glaser fraternity never really ventured into the dark zones inhabited by Coe and Paycheck. Of course, they did consume drugs and alcohol, but while they might sometimes flirt with errant forms of behavior—or at least give the impression of doing so—their rebellion was at base little more than an effort to assert their artistic independence within the confining context of a corporate musical structure. And, at least in the cases of Willie Nelson and Waylon Jennings, they found the maverick image to be tremendously valuable commercially. An album produced by RCA in 1976 entitled *Wanted! The Outlaws*, composed of older material done by Nelson, Jennings, Jessi Colter (Waylon's wife), and Tompall Glaser, became country music's first documented platinum record (one that sold one million copies). Despite the hype surrounding the Outlaws, they posed a healthy challenge to Nashville's homogenization. And while they drew freely from other forms of music, such as rock, they also remained respectful of their own and country music's roots. In fact, if they used any term in private to describe themselves it was "hillbilly" and not "outlaw." The ultimate irony of the Outlaws may be that, while drawing upon a diverse array of musical sources and reaching out to new audiences, they did more to preserve a distinct identity for country music than most of their contemporaries who wore the "country" label.

The so-called conflict in country music between traditionalists and country-pop or crossover advocates may exist primarily in the minds of disgruntled fans. But in the country music business itself, the "conflict" is seldom publicly aired. The country music fraternity tries to keep its problems private. Nevertheless, a growing concern about country music's clouded identity did manifest itself in the letters written to the trade journals, in the record reviews written by some critics, and in the comments made by occasional musicians on talk shows and in published articles (even Chet Atkins expressed some reservations about country music's growing fusion with other forms).[26] The subject of country music's identity was more openly discussed in the 1980s than at any previous time, and frequent rediscoveries have since been made that a market exists for the older sounds and styles. Television has provided some traditional acts, such as Grandpa Jones (on the *Hee Haw* show), and Slim Whitman and Boxcar Willie, with new formats in which to popularize themselves. The festivals, both here and in Europe, have lent further encouragement to individual musicians such as Doc Watson and to bluegrass music as a whole. Unfortunately, some of America's greatest hard-core singers, such as Dale Watson and Hazel Dickens, received very little public exposure. Dickens, for example, seldom appeared before country audiences, but instead sang in folk clubs, at colleges, and at events such as the Hardly Strictly Bluegrass festival in San Francisco. This festival was organized by Warren Hellmann in 2001, in large part, because he was such a strong champion of Hazel's music and wanted to guarantee a forum for its public expression. Her voice, though, was heard with compelling clarity on the sound track of the great documentary film *Harlan County, USA*.

Hazel Dickens represented one of the oldest traditions of singing in country music, that of the mountain South. Other revivalists found their inspiration in the music of the Southwest and Far West. The 1970s saw a strong revival of western swing. A few bands, of course, had never stopped playing this kind of music: Hank Thompson and his Brazos Valley Boys, Leon Rausch and his group in Fort Worth, and Hoyle Nix and the West Texas Cowboys, out of Big Spring, Texas. The patron saint of the style, Bob Wills, died on May 13, 1975, but was already becoming a cult figure long before that, especially in Austin. Two young bands, Ray Benson's Asleep at the Wheel[27] and Alvin Crow and the Pleasant Valley Boys, used Austin as their headquarters while combining western swing and rock and roll and otherwise project-ing an ambience palatable to their youthful, rock-weaned audiences. These young musicians made Wills's name known to new generations that had never actually heard his music.

Western swing and the Bob Wills legacy were further preserved and popularized through the patronage of mainstream country-and-western performers such as Willie Nelson, Ray Price, Merle Haggard, and Red Steagall. Nelson often spoke of his stylistic debt to Wills and performed such songs as "Stay All Night," while Price and Haggard both recorded tribute albums to Wills. Haggard's 1970 album, *A Trib-ute to the Best Damn Fiddle Player in the World (or, My Salute to Bob Wills)*, did most to usher in the western swing revival. Among other positive results, the album inspired Asleep at the Wheel to turn their attention full-time to the music of Wills. For his part, Haggard learned to play the fiddle like his hero; added a former member of the Texas Playboys, Tiny Moore, to his band; and began referring to his music as "country jazz." The Texas singer Red Steagall roamed all over the West with his Coleman County Cowboys, playing his brand of west-ern swing in dance halls and for rodeo dances. His popular version of "Lone Star Beer and Bob Wills Music" paid tribute to two cherished institutions of the Southwest.

The heightened interest in western swing inspired rediscovery of the veteran performers of the genre, including Eldon Shamblin and Johnny Gimble, who appeared on Haggard's tribute album. At least two musicians, the fiddler Jesse Ashlock (an alumnus of both Bob Wills's and Milton Brown's organizations) and Laura Lee McBride (Wills's first female singer) returned to Austin to perform with the young re-vivalists headquartered there. The Texas Playboys themselves were reconstituted under the leadership of Leon McAuliffe, while the Light

Crust Doughboys, led by Jim Boyd and Smokey Montgomery, became active once again. As might be expected, Austin was a popular market for such groups, and they found an enthusiastic reception on the syndicated television show *Austin City Limits* and at Rod Kennedy's festivals in Kerrville.

The western swing renascence was paralleled by a revival of cowboy music. As we have already seen, the cowboy myth manifested itself in a variety of ways, most notably in the vogue of the Outlaws but also in the brief flurry of interest in "urban cowboys" spawned by the movie of the same name. Real cowboy music—that is, songs about cowboys and the West—revived through the dedication of certain singers and songwriters who never abandoned their affection for this genre and the culture it represented. The grand masters of the romantic cowboy style, the Sons of the Pioneers, have never disbanded, although none of the original members remain. Through the years, and through successive personnel changes, the Pioneer sound, with its subtly nuanced vocal blend and rich harmonies, has remained remarkably intact. Marty Robbins maintained his commitment to cowboy songs until his death in 1983. Not only did he preserve such great old songs as "Streets of Laredo," he also contributed new and vital ones to the genre such as "El Paso City," a successor to his great hit of 1959, "El Paso." The ranks of the old movie cowboys gradually became thinned by death and retirement, but on occasion Roy Rogers and Rex Allen made special reappearances. Rex Allen Jr., whose deep, resonant voice was almost as good as his father's, did much to revive interest in the old-time cowboy singers when he sang about them in "Can You Hear Those Pioneers."

The most dedicated crusade to resurrect the cowboy style came from a trio of young, urban-born musicians who called themselves Riders in the Sky (Fred "Too Slim" LaBour, Woody Paul, and Douglas B. Green). Green is a country music scholar and diversely talented musician from Michigan who turned a childhood fascination with Grade B cowboy movies into a profession. Eventually joined by the accordion player Joey Miskulin, the group combined musical virtuosity—replete with close harmony, yodeling, and hot fiddling (done by Woody Paul)—and kooky stage humor to fill a niche that no one else was exploiting. Their experiment won them a multitude of fans, a position on the *Grand Ole Opry*, and selection as hosts of *Tumbleweed Theater* (a show featuring old western movies) on the Nashville Network.

Country musicians have not been concerned solely with the Old West or with the cowboys of yesteryear. They also write and sing about cowboys who ride the range in pickup trucks, or who follow the rodeo circuit, or whose lifestyles suggest the independence once associated with the men on horseback. Bill and Sharon Rice spoke for millions of people when they wrote "My Heroes Have Always Been Cowboys" (sung by Willie Nelson in the movie *The Electric Horseman*). Ed Bruce, a Memphis singer and songwriter, on the other hand, was referring more to a lifestyle than to an occupation when he wrote "Mamas, Don't Let Your Babies Grow Up to Be Cowboys," but he demonstrated the timeless appeal of the image. Rodeo life spawned a fairly large body of songs. A few of them—such as Ian Tyson's "Someday Soon," Doodle Owens's "Cowboys Ain't Supposed to Cry," and Terry Stafford and Paul Fraser's "Amarillo by Morning"—were quite poignant in their evocation of the loneliness and rootlessness that sometimes accompanied this unfettered but demanding existence. While wonderful versions of the modern cowboy songs were performed by mainline country singers—Jerry Jeff Walker, for example, recorded the first version of "Night Rider's Lament"—at least two singers, Moe Bandy and Red Steagall, both of whom had spent some time as bull riders, devoted major portions of their careers to performances at rodeos and rodeo dances.

The honky-tonk style survived into the 1980s, but not with the universal appeal it had once enjoyed. The sound that had once dominated country music seemed to run counter to the crossover impulse and threatened the respectability that the country industry was trying to attain. Honky-tonk music was deemed too "country" and too reflective of seamy barroom culture to attract that broad audience that the industry was trying to win. Gradually, many of the founders of the style were being taken by death or retirement. Ernest Tubb's career finally ground to a halt, a victim of emphysema, age, and endless miles; his death on September 6, 1984, brought to an end one of country music's longest and most respected careers. Floyd Tillman made infrequent appearances, mostly in the Austin area, where he was treated as an elder statesman by the young musicians. He was named to the Country Music Hall of Fame in October 1984. Lefty Frizzell had died in 1974, but in the early 1970s he had recorded some of his greatest performances (e.g., "That's the Way Love Goes," "I Never Go Around Mirrors") with a voice now richer, deeper, and more sensitive.

The most remarkable example of endurance shown by a honky-tonk singer was that of George Jones. Few singers achieved such artistic and commercial heights while descending to such personal depths of misery and self-abuse. From 1969 to 1975 he was married to Tammy Wynette, a dream pairing from the standpoint of fans, and once they began recording together, they were described as "the president and first lady" of country music. Their years together were commercially rewarding—their duet performances were popular, and Jones made some of his best solo recordings—but he could not control his urge to drink, nor the violent outbursts that sometimes accompanied his drinking bouts. Jones's marital difficulties and alcohol binges were the stuff of soap opera, especially when accompanied by the periodic announcements of his "reform" and rehabilitation. His problems only made him more attractive to fans, and they often equated the lyrics of his heart-wrenching songs with the distress of his life.

In the years following his divorce in 1975, Jones's personal life deteriorated even further, his acute alcoholism complicated by cocaine addiction. He became notorious for missing, arriving late, or showing up drunk for concerts, earning him the nickname "No Show Jones." But through it all, Jones remained intensely commercial and, in fact, began winning more music industry awards than at any previous time in his career. His resurgence was owed in large part to the skillful direction of Billy Sherrill, who became Jones's record producer in 1972. Jones, the traditionalist whose heart lay with the hard-core country music of his youth, and Sherrill, the sophisticated producer who seemed wedded to no particular style of music, constituted a highly unlikely but successful partnership. The son of an Alabama preacher, Sherrill served an apprenticeship with Sam Phillips in Memphis, but was working for Epic Records (a subsidiary of Columbia) in 1966 when he produced the first of a long string of hits, David Houston's "Almost Persuaded." Sherrill had a keen ear for commercial songs, many of which he wrote himself, and an acute perception of mass audience tastes. Many singers, including Charlie Rich, Tammy Wynette, Johnny Paycheck, Tanya Tucker, Johnny Duncan, and Janie Fricke, profited from his direction. George Jones was no exception. While many fans and critics complained about the elaborate and lush instrumental and vocal arrangements that sometimes threatened to smother the singer's individuality, the Jones-Sherrill team produced some of modern country music's biggest hits and some of Jones's finest performances: "The Grand Tour," "If Drinking Don't Kill Me," "The Same Old Me," "Shine On," and the 1980 Grammy Award winner "He Stopped Loving Her Today." Purportedly, Jones initially hated the last-named song because it too closely mirrored the emotional depths to which he had descended. But the song, written by Bobby Braddock and Curly Putman, and surrounded by the special Billy Sherrill instrumental touch, resurrected Jones's career. Many people liked to call "He Stopped Loving Her Today" the greatest country song of all time, when in fact, it was Jones's superb performance and not the lyrics that immortalized the song.[28]

Many singers were nurtured on honky-tonk music, or experimented with the style, but few remained with it consistently. Several singers, in fact, debuted or established country music identities with honky-tonk style performances and then moved quickly to more popular forms of music. Ronnie Milsap ("I Hate You"), Johnny Rodriguez ("Pass Me By"), John Conlee ("Rose Colored Glasses"), and Conway Twitty ("The Image of Me") began their country music careers with fine honky-tonk renditions, but then settled down into middle-of-the-road stylistic formats. Despite a noticeable but endearing stutter only when speaking, Mel Tillis made several superb honky-tonk recordings, such as "Heart over Mind," marked by the shuffle beat and twin fiddling borrowed from western swing instrumentation. He had also written many of the finest songs in the honky-tonk repertory, with Ray Price a principal beneficiary of his genius. By the beginning of the 1980s, though, Tillis had become an all-purpose entertainer—comedian, actor, singer, and songwriter—and his honky-tonk hits became rarer as his appearances on the Johnny Carson show became more frequent.

Quite a few young singers exhibited a flair for the hard honky-tonk style. Wayne Kemp, the singer and writer of "Who'll Turn Out the Lights," was heard all too rarely and was scarcely known outside the industry, where he was recognized as a great writer of other people's hits. A few singers of superior caliber, such as Norman Wade in Louisiana and Johnny Bush in Texas, unfortunately had only local followings. Other singers, including Vern Gosdin, Leon Everette, and Gary Stewart, wore several stylistic hats but seemed most comfortable and convincing in the hard country camp. Gary Stewart, born a coal miner's son in Payne Gap, Kentucky, but reared in Fort Pierce, Florida, never flirted with the country-pop sound, but instead veered between rockabilly and honky-tonk, combining the zest and bounce of the former with the tortured lament of the latter. He learned both styles singing and playing the piano in the rough, blood-bucket beer joints in the area around Fort Pierce. A stint as pianist with Charley Pride's band introduced him to a wider public, but his 1974 recording of "Drinking Thing" earned him critical praise as a worthy heir to George Jones and other honky-tonk greats. Hard-core country fans found Stewart's clear and pleading tenor voice, with its pronounced and breathy vibrato, immensely appealing. He was one of the few country entertainers to draw the approval of *Rolling Stone* reviewers. Their endorsement, however, was triggered by the rockabilly in him—by the hedonistic abandon and "let the good times roll" qualities that characterized much of his music. Regrettably, his wife's untimely death in November 2003 triggered a despondency that caused him to commit suicide before the end of the year.

The most consistent of the new generation of honky-tonk singers, and longtime holdouts against the pop impulse, were Mel Street, Moe Bandy, Gene Watson, John Anderson, and, sometimes, George Strait. Strait, though, was one of a kind, and the most enduring of them all. Strait was a genuine cowboy who grew up on a ranch near Pearsall, Texas. Although surrounded by country music during his youth, Strait did not sing publicly until his stint with the army in Hawaii in the late 1970s. Later, while pursuing a degree in agriculture and ranch management at Southwest Texas State University in San Marcos (now Texas State University), Strait organized his Ace in the Hole Band and began playing at a honky-tonk there on the edge of town, Kent Finley's Cheatham Street Warehouse. Located within a few feet of the railroad track, singers literally had to halt their act during the periodic passage of trains by the Warehouse. Combating this kind of noise and diversion, Strait could have asked for no better preparation for a honky-tonk career. From this apprenticeship in San Marcos, Strait moved on to honky-tonks throughout Central and East Texas, and from there to the biggest arenas in the United States.

Even though Austin was only thirty miles up the road, Strait never got caught up in the Outlaw mania. Instead, his music reflected the shuffle beat and Texas swing rhythms he had grown up with, as well as the singing of men like Ray Price, George Jones, and Merle Haggard. By 1982, music had become his full-time profession, and in the years that followed, he put songs like "The Fireman," "Let's Fall to Pieces Together," "Does Fort Worth Ever Cross Your Mind," and "Right or

George Strait. © 1984 by Scott Newton/Austin City Limits.

Wrong" (the Bob Wills standard) at the top of the country music charts. Some of Strait's finest songs came from the pen of Whitey Shafer, a pianist and singer from Waco, who earlier had built a very successful collaboration with Lefty Frizzell. A happy combination of boyish good looks, skillful song selection, and vocal suppleness eventually combined to make Strait one of country music's most outstanding and enduring superstars, a formidable position that he held until his retirement in June of 2014.[29]

Mel Street was a Virginia mountain boy who was drawn to the music of Texas—and particularly to the singing of his hero, George Jones. He was living in West Virginia and working in an automobile body shop when his "Borrowed Angel" appeared on an obscure label in 1970. The song was somewhat unusual in that it not only spoke of illicit love without guilt or apology but actually endorsed the practice. Listeners who responded positively to the record, however, did so because of its sound and not because of its content. Street's rich, melodic, and yet unadorned voice was beautifully complemented by the mournful strains of fiddle, Dobro, and pedal steel guitar. In an age of increasing pop-country fusion, the sound heard on "Borrowed Angel" was, to most hard-core country advocates, a much-welcomed respite.

Other big hits, such as "Smoky Mountain Memories," "I Met a Friend of Yours Today," and the intriguingly named "Lust Affair," followed in Street's brief career, but success did not compensate for whatever problems led him to suicide on his forty-fifth birthday, October 21, 1978. George Jones sang "Amazing Grace" at his funeral.

Moe Bandy was born in Meridian, Mississippi, and reared in San Antonio. Like Mel Street, and probably most young people who leaned toward honky-tonk, Bandy was a disciple of George Jones. While working eight hours a day in his father's sheet metal and gutter shop, Bandy also sang nightly in local clubs with a little group called the Mavericks, and they served as the opening act for most of the touring country groups who came to town. His first success at attracting attention outside of San Antonio came with "I Just Started Hating Cheating Songs." With that success, he became known for his "cheating and drinking songs," and he began a fruitful alliance with songwriter Whitey Shafer, who supplied him with other hits such as "Bandy the Rodeo Clown" and "The Biggest Airport in the World." Traditionalists waxed enthusiastic at the emergence of this hard country stylist who sang with remarkable clarity of tone, impeccable articulation, and emotional intensity. When he signed with his first big record company, Columbia, many people feared that the great corporation would tamper with his style and direct him toward the richer field of country-pop. His first Columbia release in 1975 was the cleverly written "Hank Williams, You Wrote My Life" (by Paul Craft). Despite fans' reservations, Bandy's performance remained thoroughly honky-tonk in style and content. Since that time, he has never strayed far afield from the honky-tonk mold.

Gene Watson was still another Texan who perfected his art in the dance halls of that state. Born in Palestine and reared in Paris, both in the northeastern part of Texas, Watson moved to Houston in 1963 when he was about twenty years old. Watson soon became a popular local favorite, singing in the many clubs of Houston and recording on a variety of labels. His first major chart hit was a sultry, sexy song about illicit passion in New Orleans, "Love in the Hot Afternoon," which in arrangement was wholly within the country-pop framework. Watson, though, consistently declared himself an outspoken advocate of "hard country" music, and his recordings since "Love in the Hot Afternoon" were generally spiced with a honky-tonk flavor. Watson fortunately possessed a strong, clear tenor voice, but with a hard-edged, slightly nasal sound that gave it a convincing country ring. Watson records also eschewed, for the most part, overarranged country-pop instrumentation and instead let Lloyd Green's pedal steel guitar set the dominant tone. "Farewell Party," a great hit for him in 1979, beautifully illustrated his basic approach and easily achieved the status of one of the classics of modern honky-tonk music. The song itself does nothing more than restate a very old theme, that of a self-pitying man who tries to make his cold lover feel guilty about his heartbreak. But Watson lifted the song above triteness with an utterly sincere and impassioned vocal that builds to a soaring finale.

John Anderson, from Apopka, Florida, was still another commercially successful singer of the 1980s. Rock and roll first attracted the young Anderson to music, but he was converted to country music at the age of fourteen when he first heard Merle Haggard. By 1973, Anderson had drifted to Nashville and was singing, largely unnoticed, in the bars downtown near the old Ryman Auditorium. George Jones somehow heard about the singer and soon became his champion. At the end of the 1970s, when his first records began to circulate, many people began to comment about the young man whose voice had an uncanny resemblance to that of Lefty Frizzell. The early 1980s saw him recording his first big hits, songs like "Your Lying Blue Eyes" and "I'm Just an Old Chunk of Coal," but even these were modest successes compared to his two blockbusters of 1983, "Swinging" and "Black Sheep." Anderson's repertory was somewhat analogous to that of Gary Stewart in that it veered from slow, melancholy honky-tonk songs to rollicking, rockabilly-style tunes like "Black Sheep." Anderson differed markedly from Stewart, though, in his homage to the singers of the past. He often resurrected older songs such as "The Waltz You Saved for Me" and Frizzell's "I Love You a Thousand Ways," and he was part of a small group of young musicians, including Emmylou Harris and Ricky Skaggs, who seemed genuinely respectful of older country music and dedicated to its preservation.

Musicians pursued several approaches to "tradition" in the 1980s. The neo-honky-tonk style favored by Anderson, Watson, and others was probably the most organic reflection of changes in country music and the culture that surrounds it, and therefore the most accurate representation of working-class values. The revivalists who consciously re-created older styles—such as the Hotmud Family and Red Clay Ramblers (old-timey string band music), Asleep at the

Emmylou Harris. Courtesy of C. Kuhl, www.chriskuhl.com;
Creative Commons Attribution-Share Alike 2.5,
www.creativecommons.org/licenses/by-sa/2.5/legalcode.

Wheel (western swing), and Riders in the Sky (made-for-movies cowboy music)—made exciting music but worked in obviously limited milieus. Bluegrass musicians pursued their independent course by building new forms within the framework of a basically acoustic approach to music. Still another group of musicians, represented by Emmylou Harris and Ricky Skaggs, made a virtue of the self-conscious employment of diversity, drawing upon many sources to create a music that was nevertheless "hard country" in its feel and ambience. Harris's and Skaggs's approaches seemed to augur well for country music's future: they were "traditional" in a modern and commercial context and immensely appealing to a vast audience of both older and younger listeners.

Emmylou Harris was born in Birmingham, Alabama, but was an "army brat" who traveled often and extensively with her parents. Her first venture into professional music came as an urban folk singer, singing in clubs in the Washington, DC, area such as the Red Fox Inn. Her orientation at that time was toward the music of Pete Seeger and Bob Dylan. Her introduction to hard country music came through Gram Parsons, whom she met in Washington in 1972. She became his protégé, began listening to the Louvin Brothers, George Jones, Merle Haggard, and Ralph Stanley, and performed with Parsons in concert and on recordings quite often during the last several months of his life. Their best duets, such as "Hearts on Fire," "Love Hurts," and "We'll Sweep Out the Ashes," have fortunately been preserved on recordings.

Harris began her independent country music career in 1975 with the recording of a little-known Louvin Brothers song, "If I Could Only Win Your Love." Her rise to superstardom since that time has come through cultivation of a basic, uncomplicated country approach and the revival of an extensive amount of older material. She accomplished this, ironically, while other women country singers, such as Dolly Parton and Barbara Mandrell, sought the pop-country middle ground. Harris's fresh, willowy beauty, of course, did not hurt her career, nor has her clear soprano voice that even yet shows a trace of Joan Baez and the other urban folksingers who influenced her early style. Like many young performers who have come to country music in more recent times, Harris has been a true eclectic, borrowing from many styles. Her concerts and LPs have continued to contain a mixture of contemporary and traditional material, rock-flavored songs and Appalachian-sounding ballads, and modern country-and-western numbers. Her supporting musicians, first called the Hot Band, and after 1991, the Nash Ramblers, showed themselves capable of playing both acoustic and electric music. One of Harris's greatest contributions to country music has been her encouragement, and employment, of other performers such as Delia Bell, Iris DeMent, the White Family, Rodney Crowell, Buddy Miller, Ricky Skaggs, and Sam Bush. Harris's vocal collaboration with Linda Ronstadt and Dolly Parton on a couple of albums, *Trio* and *Trio Two*, which consisted mostly of traditional country songs, endure as some of the finest recorded moments in modern country music.

Skaggs was born in Cordell, Kentucky, on July 18, 1954. The precocious youngster was playing the mandolin by the time he was five years old, and had appeared on radio (WTCR in Ashland, Kentucky) with his parents at about the same age. He and a friend, Keith Whitley (born in Sandy Hook, Kentucky, on July 1, 1954), played together often as teenagers and became skillful imitators of the Stanley Brothers. One night they went to hear Ralph Stanley at a small club in Louisa, Kentucky, and were asked to fill in until Stanley arrived. When Stanley walked into the club, he was both surprised and delighted to hear the young men doing Stanley Brothers songs and in Stanley Brothers style. Ricky and Keith joined Stanley's band in 1970 when they were only fifteen years old, and they remained with him long enough to be part of nine LPs. Stanley was greatly pleased with this band, and he sometimes talked of retiring and leaving his organization in the hands of these talented newcomers. Skaggs left Stanley, though, in 1972, and began playing in a succession of outstanding bluegrass bands such as Country Store, the Country Gentlemen, and the New South. He organized his own band, Boone Creek, in 1975 and became known in bluegrass circles for his proficiency with both traditional and progressive material. Beginning with an old-time/bluegrass perspective, Skaggs moved steadily toward progressive sounds and an eclectic repertory. His entree to a new and larger audience, however, came when he became a band member and front man for Emmylou Harris. In this first experience with an electric-based band, Skaggs played a variety of instruments and did some great duet singing with Harris, including "The Darkest Hour," which came from the repertory of his heroes, the Stanley Brothers. In his journey toward an independent performing career, Skaggs took time to record a superb album (*Skaggs and Rice*) that paid tribute to both his family and his musical roots. The album featured Skaggs's mandolin and Tony Rice's guitar and their soulful, close harmony. Skaggs and Rice beautifully recaptured the sound and mood of the brother duets on such songs as "Bury Me beneath the Willow" and "Will the Roses Bloom."

Skaggs made his first venture into mainstream country music in 1981. His new sound featured such electric instruments as the takeoff guitar, bass, and pedal steel with drums, piano, Dobro, and his own mandolin, fiddle, and acoustic guitar. He also selected songs from many sources, including western swing, contemporary country, pop-rock, and bluegrass. His LPs were skillfully marketed, and singles periodically chosen from them became successive hits: "I Don't Care," "Heartbroke," "I Wouldn't Change You If I Could," and "Highway 40 Blues," among others. Audiences who attended Skaggs's concerts were impressed more with his versatility than with his eclecticism. Skaggs was blessed with the clearest and most expressive tenor voice heard

Ricky Skaggs. © 1984 by Scott Newton/Austin City Limits.

in country music since Ira Louvin, and his instrumental virtuosity was breathtaking—he moved easily, and with mastery, from mandolin to fiddle to guitar. His selection as the CMA's Singer of the Year in 1982 and his nomination in several categories in the following years may or may not have been a recognition of his extraordinary talents, but they did suggest that tradition-based country music still had an ardent following in the United States.

Skaggs was hailed as a traditionalist, and he continued to refer to his music as "bluegrass" and openly spoke of building a repertory that would appeal to hard-core country fans. He seemed conscious, in fact, of filling a vacuum created by the country-pop impulse. But Skaggs, of course, was not purely a traditionalist, even though he did traditional material beautifully. His performances were informed by the wide range of music that he and other young people had heard and played in today's world—and by the experiences of living in a society vastly different from that of their parents.

Skaggs had a versatile band that could play bluegrass, honky-tonk, western swing, or rock. Like Emmylou Harris's band, they sometimes went on extended jams that could last for several minutes, a legacy probably of such country-rock bands as those of Marshall Tucker and Charlie Daniels. This was no doubt disconcerting to bluegrass or old-time fans who went to hear Skaggs, but it was a concession to the rock-weaned younger listeners who also went to his concerts.

Regardless of the strength shown by Skaggs and other neo-traditionalists, at the end of the 1980s it had become increasingly difficult to define country music or to assess its future. For every Ricky Skaggs there were a dozen pop-influenced performers who demonstrated great commercial appeal while also winning the country music industry's highest awards. Fans of traditional country music could easily identify with the musings of veteran country disc jockey Hugh Cherry when he warned about the music's seeming loss of history and identity: "Let us remember what happens when you kill the roots of a tree—it dies."[30] Country musicians might also recall the admonition that so many of them grew up with: "What shall it profit a man if he gains the whole world and loses his own soul?"

CHAPTER 12

Tradition and Change

Country Music, 1985–2000

I n the last decades of the twentieth century, the country music industry experienced, at varying times, both diminishing revenues and spectacular growth. In the decline that followed the urban cowboy craze, some commentators spoke ominously of the possible disappearance of the music. But by 1986, Randy Travis and other "neo-traditionalists," had generated a revitalization of hard country sounds and a new period of economic expansion. As exciting as the neo-traditionalist breakthrough had been, though, the early 1990s saw a virtual explosion that went far beyond anything ever before experienced in country music, when singers like Garth Brooks, Clint Black, and Reba McEntire established sales records for CDs and concert box-office receipts that often surpassed those attained by entertainers in any other field of music. Popular culture is a fickle mistress, however. When this chapter was originally written, some observers and even a few music industry leaders in Nashville were speaking balefully about the stagnation, and even the boring nature, of the products that they were marketing. Stylistically and artistically, contemporary country music continued to evoke debates concerning its identity and authenticity. The resentment held by most traditionalists about the changes that took place in country music in the 1990s was graphically described in a song that was selected in 2000 as the

International Bluegrass Music Association's (IBMA) Song of the Year and as the Country Music Association's Recorded Event of the Year (when recorded by George Strait and Alan Jackson). Entitled "Murder on Music Row," the song declared that "someone killed country music, cut out its heart and soul. They got away with murder down on music row."[1]

The word "country" endured as the description of a commercial genre of music, but the music that dominated the playlists of Top Forty radio at the turn of the century had little working-class feel to it, and bore little resemblance to the styles that once prevailed on country radio and jukeboxes. The Country Music Association (CMA) and its then director, Bill Ivey (who also served in the second Clinton administration as chairman of the National Endowment for the Arts), had long followed a practice of recognizing as "country" any artist or form of music marketed as such by radio and the recording companies. Consequently, partisans of "traditional" country styles had to seek emotional and artistic solace in venues that lay outside the Top Forty milieu, or they rejoiced when such "neo-traditionalists" as Randy Travis, Dwight Yoakam, Alan Jackson, Patty Loveless, Marty Stuart, and Brad Paisley won recognition within the country mainstream.

The occasional prophets who virtually predicted the commercial demise of country music did not reckon with the enduring American impulse to go back to basics; to live at least vicariously a simpler life; and to find a form of music, with singable and easily understood lyrics and melodies, that connotes a wholesome lifestyle. Certainly, no one could have anticipated the emergence of Garth Brooks and his remarkable ability to fuse the dynamics of rock stage culture with the traditional postures of country music, nor could one have easily forecast the country line dance craze of the 1990s, which brought thousands of people to the dance floor and reawakened an interest in "western" fashions. Astute producers such as Fred Foster, Jimmy Bowen, Tony Brown, Steve Buckingham, Emory Gordy Jr., Jim Ed Norman, Allen Reynolds, and Randy Scruggs also fueled country music's survival and commercial growth. They managed to create a musical product that simultaneously suggested a sense of tradition and incorporated the most advanced techniques available in modern popular culture. Music industry leaders, however, sometimes lag far behind the tastes or expectations of the public. In early 2001, the soundtrack from a popular movie called *O Brother, Where Art Thou?*, which included the

old-time singing of such people as Dan Tyminski, Alison Krauss, Emmylou Harris, Gillian Welch, and Ralph Stanley, was released on a CD
that quickly attained platinum status (the sale of one million copies).
Nonetheless, Top Forty country radio stations were still reluctant
to play selections from this very "hillbilly" sounding collection and
did not do so until fans made their desires known through telephone
calls and other communications. As a result, by mid-April 2001, Dan
Tyminski's version of "Man of Constant Sorrow" had entered the *Billboard* popularity charts. By March 2002, sales of the *O Brother, Where
Art Thou?* soundtrack were approaching three million, and the CD had
won five Grammy awards.

A traditionalist-modernist dialectic has animated country music
since at least the late 1950s in the wake of Elvis Presley's emergence
and the country-pop resolution made by Nashville producers. It has
only grown stronger as years have passed.[2] Since the late 1980s, a rash
of young and generally photogenic entertainers, described variously as
Young Country or New Country, have edged the older performers aside
and consequently have renewed anxieties concerning the music's
identity. Some musicians have attached themselves to country music
because it is in vogue or because they were advised to do so, mainly
as a marketing decision by promoters or recording executives who
believed that their clients could "fit" the market niche and profit from
country music's popularity with a "target" audience. Other performers had grown up in country households or otherwise had an intimate
awareness of its traditions. That is, they had heard country music at
home or were aware of their parents' interest in such music. Performing country music was an easy decision for musicians like Mark Chesnutt, who grew up as the son of a local musician in the working-class
musical environment of Beaumont, Texas; for Lee Ann Womack, who
always went to the radio station in Jacksonville, Texas, to hear the
records played by her disc jockey father; or for Sara Evans, who heard
her family play bluegrass music on the tobacco farm where she was
raised in New Franklin, Missouri; or for Dwight Yoakam, who equated
the music with the songs and stories learned from his coal-mining
grandfather in Pikeville, Kentucky. Most Young Country musicians,
though, like Suzy Bogguss and Trisha Yearwood, from Aledo, Illinois,
and Monticello, Georgia, respectively, had little reason to identify the
music with working-class culture, since their own lives and musical
choices had been shaped in a media-obsessed suburban culture. Their

"affluent," urbane origins, however, did not prevent them from becoming two of the most respected vocalists in country music.

Whether products of country music households or new "converts" to country, virtually all of the Young Country acts had grown up listening to all of the popular music styles available in America—rock, blues, soul, salsa, rap, pop. Country's new musicians typically cited such pop acts as the Eagles, the Allman Brothers, Bon Jovi, Led Zeppelin, or U2 as influences, an affinity evidenced by various country musicians' tributes to the Beatles, Lynyrd Skynyrd, and other pop or rock music bands. In 1993, one of these collections, *Common Thread: The Songs of the Eagles*, featuring the singing of such country musicians as Travis Tritt, Clint Black, Vince Gill, and Trisha Yearwood, yielded spectacular commercial success.

On the other hand, the cultural historian Curtis Ellison has noted the tendency shown by contemporary country entertainers to conform to the music's time-honored rituals and to pay proper deference to the music's pioneers.[3] Even though the venerable *Grand Ole Opry* no longer exerts the kind of influence that it once had, it still exhibits a powerful attraction for both fans and musicians. Hal Ketchum, Garth Brooks, Alison Krauss, and Vince Gill are only a few of country music's contemporary superstars who accepted membership in the show, and they have made periodic appearances on its Saturday-night programs. When a new performer is inducted into the *Opry*'s cast, a veteran entertainer makes the announcement in a solemn ceremony that stresses the enduring links between past and present.

The wearing of cowboy hats, jeans, and boots, of course, is well-nigh universal, even if the performers do not perform hard-core country music (and they seldom do). Travis Tritt, who alludes to southern rock as the chief musical influence in his life, apparently first used the term "hat acts" to describe these performers, suggesting that they were imitative singers who had no real distinctiveness and that they were just playing at being cowboys (or merely emulating George Strait). The hat acts have included such male singers as Garth Brooks, Clint Black, John Michael Montgomery, Wade Hayes, Tim McGraw, Trace Adkins, Kenny Chesney, Mark Chesnutt, Tracy Byrd, Collin Raye, Sammy Kershaw, Brad Paisley, and Alan Jackson, and at least one female, Terri Clark. The proliferation of such musicians, however different in style, musical competence, and commitment to tradition, made it quite clear that the music industry had become highly adept at co-opting trends and fashions. Singers were being groomed to fulfill symbolic expectations about cowboys while also being encouraged to perform contemporary styles appealing to a large audience with little or no experience with country music.

These new entertainers—"New Country"—fueled that tremendous commercial boom earlier described. Evidence of the music's popular appeal and commercial strength became available in May 1991 when *Billboard* magazine abandoned the imprecise practice of obtaining data on CD sales from salesclerks and began relying on reports gathered from a company named Soundscan. Through the scanning of bar codes on CDs made at the time of purchase, Soundscan provided a more accurate measurement of sales made in retail stores (including Walmart, Kmart, Target, and Blockbuster). The charts that utilized Soundscan data indicated a significantly higher performance scale for country singers than previously recognized. Country CD sales constituted 17 percent of the overall total for American music, a figure then second only to that of rock. Statistics concerning radio listenership were even more favorable to country music. The Simmons Market Research Bureau, in a 1995 survey compiled for the CMA, disclosed that over 37 percent of the American population (about 69,918,000 people) devoted some part of their time each week to listening to country music. The second-largest format, adult contemporary, claimed almost 19 million fewer listeners.

The musicians who contributed to country music's spectacular ascendance included some performers who had been paying their dues long before the New Country acts appeared. Between 1985 and 1989, for example, Earl Thomas Conley—a Portsmouth, Ohio, singer who is regrettably forgotten today—recorded a staggering list of number one hits, such as "Once in a Blue Moon." On the other hand, George Strait, the direct inspiration for most of the hat acts, and the singer who did so much to usher in the era of neo-traditionalism, endured as a major presence in country music. In a career that began in the late 1970s, the forever handsome Strait continued to make popular recordings that preserved the sound and flavor of western swing and other rhythms of his native state of Texas. The smooth and soulful blend of Alabama, a group whose career lasted nearly as long as George Strait's, could still be heard on country radio. The most obvious and enduring legacy of their career could be seen and heard in the music of scores of vocal groups such as Exile, Diamond Rio, Shenandoah, Sawyer Brown,

Confederate Railroad, Blackhawk, Little Texas, Highway 101, and the Mavericks (led by one of country music's finest singers, Raul Malo) who preserved the practice of good-time songs and close harmonies pioneered by Alabama in the early 1980s.

Some of the vocal groups were duets, including Foster and Lloyd (Radney Foster and Bill Lloyd), the O'Kanes (Jamie O'Hara and Kieran Kane), the Bellamy Brothers (Howard and David), and the Judds (mother Naomi and daughter Wynonna). With songs like "Crazy Over You," Foster and Lloyd exhibited a debt to the Buddy Holly rockabilly tradition, and, with their exuberant style of performance, meshed neatly with the line dance craze of the era. After hearing their good-time but often mindless music, some fans may have been surprised when Foster later built a solo career with serious, thoughtful lyrics, as in "Louisiana Blue," reminiscent of the songs fashioned by his Texas contemporary, Guy Clark. The O'Kanes, on the other hand, in their brief career as a duet, always seemed strongly grounded in country music. Blending sophisticated lyrics and tight soulful harmonies, they proved that country music could be both modern and tradition based. The O'Kanes performed love songs exclusively—like "Just Loving You," "Blue Love," and "When I Found You"—with a Louvin Brothers' vocal sound and flair and a mandolin-driven instrumental backing. Unfortunately, their career was short, ending in 1990, and included only three albums.

The Bellamy Brothers, in contrast, built a career that still endures. Growing up near Darby, Florida, on a small cattle ranch built by their great-great-grandfather, a Confederate veteran, the Bellamys had experienced their first giant hit in 1976, a mellow but gently rocking song called "Let Your Love Flow." The song won them a loyal following in both Europe and the United States, and was merely the first of a long string of hits, mostly on the Curb label, that followed during the next decade. Inspired by a line taken from Groucho Marx, they recorded in 1979 a sensuous song called "If I Said You Had a Beautiful Body (Would You Hold It against Me)." Following this with a cluster of well-written and beautifully performed songs, like "Do You Love as Good as You Look?," "Old Hippie," "You Ain't Just Whistlin' Dixie" (an affectionate and largely nonnationalistic recollection of the South), and "Kids of the Baby Boom," the Bellamys became, arguably, the most successful and critically praised duo in country music history.

In 1984, the Judds' number one recording of "Mama, He's Crazy" introduced their fresh harmonies and acoustic sound to a national country music public. But as is often the case with overnight sensations, the Judds had achieved this newfound success only after several years of hard work, sacrifice, and preparation (including several years in Hollywood and attempts at a movie career). With Naomi stressing their family orientation and Appalachian origins, the Judds were sometimes touted as traditionalists, particularly with songs like "Grandpa (Tell Me 'bout the Good Old Days)." Their down-home values meshed easily with their adroit embrace of sophisticated methods of marketing and showmanship. Between 1985 and 1991, the Judds dominated most of the awards given to vocal groups, whether by the CMA, the Academy of Country Music (ACM), or *Music City News*. Their audience was understandably saddened when Naomi disclosed in 1991 that she had hepatitis C, and the act was disbanded. The Judds' exhausting farewell tour covered 116 cities between February and October 1991. Wynonna, however, carried on with a solo career and was widely praised for her bluesy and soulful singing.

Reba McEntire was already an established star in 1985 when the new wave of neo-traditionalism represented by the Judds began in country music. She profited from this renewed interest in hard country styles but soon moved far beyond them. An album in 1984 called *My Kind of Country* (including such hit songs as "How Blue" and "Somebody Should Leave") had established her as a neo-traditionalist. Her affecting Oklahoma twang, the knowledge that she grew up in a ranching and rodeo family, and her now-dissolved marriage to the rodeo champ Charlie Battles inspired the mistaken belief that she was strongly wedded to hard country music. She began her public career as a child, singing with her sister and brother, but her entree into show business came in 1974 when Red Steagall heard her sing the national anthem at the National Rodeo Finals in Oklahoma City. The resulting Mercury recordings soon impressed listeners with her powerful vocal range and distinctive manner of bending and extending notes.

But McEntire's career really peaked later in the decade with vocal and instrumental sounds that were closer to country-pop. She had much going for her: good looks and a sparkling personality, a supple vocal style, a genius for recognizing good songs, and an astute business sense. These assets proved to be a great inspiration for women, not only because she stressed self-expression and identity but also because, like the earlier Oklahoma singer Gail Davies, she had taken firm control of the direction of her own career. Her assumption of the title role in Broadway's *Annie Get Your Gun,* presented in the year 2000, and the acquisition of a television sitcom series in which she starred from 2001 to 2007, introduced her to an even larger audience.

The mid- and late 1980s saw the emergence of so many new young country artists that one could almost view the phenomenon as the changing of the guard. Surveying the list of people who debuted in 1986, and in the years that immediately followed, it is hard to find an all-encompassing label that adequately defines their styles. To many fans, Randy Travis was the bright new hope of traditionalism, presenting an unadorned style that seemed reminiscent of Lefty Frizzell. Other singers, such as Steve Earle and Lyle Lovett, flavored their country music with sounds that had origins in rock, blues, or 1960s-style folk music. Although they were far from being traditional, they brought fresh ideas and a sense of experimentation to country music. Whatever the style, the young musicians of the mid-1980s soon edged veteran performers like Cash, Haggard, Jones, Parton, Lynn, and Nelson off the popularity charts and out of the playlists of Top Forty radio. George Jones's hit of 1985, "Who's Gonna Fill Their Shoes," was more poignant and prophetic than he probably realized.

Randy (Traywick) Travis, from Marshville, North Carolina, seemed the likeliest candidate to fill the shoes of the old-timers when his first records appeared in early 1986 (and this promise was finally rewarded in 2016 with his induction into the Country Music Hall of Fame). After a youthful brush with the law, Travis embraced country music and was singing in local clubs when he was only fourteen years old. With the support and management of Libby Hatcher, whom he later married, he moved to Nashville in 1981 and began making the rounds of the recording studios and publishing houses. Between May 1986, when "On the Other Hand" vaulted to the number one position on the *Billboard* country charts, and May 1990, when still another generation of country singers appeared, Travis enjoyed eleven number one songs and a couple that climbed to number two. His initial output garnered critical praise; the CMA's Horizon Award for 1986 (given to the most promising newcomer); and the award for Male Vocalist of the Year from the CMA, the ACM, and *Music City News* in 1987 and 1988.

Like that of his contemporary Keith Whitley, Travis's clearly enunciated and deeply resonant baritone vocal style exhibited a strong indebtedness to Lefty Frizzell. Although perceived as a bearer of the honky-tonk tradition, with a pedal-steel-guitar-driven sound that particularly suggested that influence, Travis actually sang few songs that carried the flavor of the barroom or bedroom. His songs sometimes conveyed sadness but almost never a suggestion of drinking or cheating. More often, they expressed messages like that of the Paul Overstreet composition "Forever and Ever, Amen," an upbeat, affirmative view of life and relationships.

Dwight Yoakam proved that neo-traditionalism could flourish with a strong admixture of rock and roll. He was born in Pikeville, Kentucky, but grew up in southern Ohio amid the throngs of expatriates from the Upper South who had traveled what Steve Earle described as "the hillbilly highway." By 1978, he had relocated to California, where he teamed with Pete Anderson, who became his guitarist and producer. There they found hospitable companionship among such West Coast cowpunks as Dave Alvin, Los Lobos, the Knitters, and Lone Justice. Yoakam and Anderson created a style that paid homage to traditional country music but brought to it the ambience and drive of rock. Above all, they incorporated the sound and sparkling electronic beat of Yoakam's heroes Buck Owens and the Buckaroos, a source to which they eventually paid tribute in a 1988 performance with Owens called "Streets of Bakersfield."

In the mid-1980s, Yoakam became well known, if not always listened to, because of his outspoken criticism of Nashville and his passionate defense of hillbilly music and values. At first, he was little more than a cult figure on the fringes of country music, but in 1986, two hit recordings, a remake of Johnny Horton's "Honky Tonk Man" and "Guitars, Cadillacs," carried him to the center. Yoakam's career has since been enhanced by his pouty good looks, sensuous stage movements (popularized through well-produced videos), appearances in movies, and charismatic presence.

The singer Keith Whitley exhibited not only a lifelong love of Lefty Frizzell and other classic honky-tonk stylists but also a long apprenticeship in bluegrass music. Consequently, one could always hear a touch of both Carter Stanley and Frizzell in Whitley's soulful vocal stylings. This Sandy Hook, Kentucky, native was in fact singing Stanley Brothers songs with Ricky Skaggs one night in 1970 when Ralph Stanley heard them for the first time. Whitley served two stints in Ralph's band but was playing with J. D. Crowe's great bluegrass unit when he made the transition to mainstream country music. He charted his first hit in 1986 with "Miami, My Amy," but the pinnacle of his career came in 1988 and 1989 with five number one recordings, including his most enduring song, "When You Say Nothing at All." Just when it seemed that Whitley had conquered every demon that blocked his path to success, he succumbed to the devil in the bottle that had plagued him since his teenage years. Neither the accolades of his fans nor his marriage to the beautiful singer Lorrie Morgan could save him. He died of alcohol poisoning on May 9, 1989, a few months after "I'm No Stranger to the Rain" first entered the popular charts. The recording became the CMA's Single of the Year.

Ricky Van Shelton seemed to have one foot in the country-pop field and the other in the realm of hard country. The Grit, Virginia, native sang with a smooth voice and "easy listening" style but peppered his repertory with rockabilly tunes, original numbers, and older country songs, some of which came from honky-tonk sources. His first number one recording, "Somebody Lied," was recorded in late 1986 and released in 1987. This and a string of similar successes that year, including his first album, *Wild-Eyed Dream,* won for him admission to the *Grand Ole Opry* and the CMA's Horizon award. In 1989, he was selected as the CMA's Male Vocalist of the Year. Shelton's boyish, handsome looks may have contributed to the efforts made by his producers to package him as a sex symbol. Early publicity photos sometimes showed him not only wearing the obligatory cowboy hat and jeans but attired in an undershirt along with a languorous, bedroom look (a photo image also used years later for the singer Tim McGraw). While his packaging and diverse repertory reflected efforts to make him broadly appealing, Shelton nevertheless took special pains to retain the affections of country music's traditional audience. He revived such classic songs as "From a Jack to a King," "Statue of a Fool," "Life Turned Her That Way," and "Somebody's Back in Town" that explicitly targeted older fans who needed reassurance that their brand of country music was still alive. By 1990, the emotional strain wrought by commercial insecurity, allegations of marital infidelity, and a problem with alcohol engendered a severe personal crisis. He made a religious renewal and in 1992 recorded a gospel album for his parents—*Don't Overlook Salvation*. The recording eventually won him a Grammy nomination and contributed to his popularity among Contemporary Christian fans (although he always insisted that he was first and foremost a country singer). Thereafter, Shelton recorded infrequently and expended much of his energy writing popular children's books. Asserting the desire to have complete freedom in what he produces, he refused to sign with a major company.

Neither k.d. lang (who spells her name without capital letters), Lyle Lovett, nor Steve Earle could be described as a traditional performer, even though one finds elements in their styles that were once highly prized in country music. They were valued not for their traditionalism but for their independence and cutting-edge styles. One of several Canadian performers (including Anne Murray, Terri Clark, and Shania Twain) who have attempted careers as country entertainers in the United States, and the first acknowledged lesbian in country music, k.d. lang (Katherine Dawn Lang) first came to country music through a fascination with the music of Patsy Cline. She promoted her first album, *A Truly Western Experience*, made in Canada in 1984, with a stage show that featured the singer and her entourage dressed in cowboy attire. Lang, however, was essentially a torch singer with a sound best suited to blues and soul music. Her American-made recordings, such as *Angel with a Lariat* (1987), generally received critical praise, and she won Grammy awards for her duet with Roy Orbison on "Crying" and for an album made in 1989, *Absolute Torch and Twang*. Lang nevertheless received little radio coverage in country music and eventually abandoned the field for a career in mainline pop music, a consequence of her musical experimentation and divergent lifestyle.

Lyle Lovett both impressed and confounded country listeners when his first album, *Lyle Lovett*, appeared in 1986. Folk revival fans, however, were familiar with his music because of his long tenure on the Texas club and festival scene, where he collaborated and communed with such local legends as Guy Clark, Butch Hancock, Robert Earl Keen, Townes Van Zandt, and Nanci Griffith. He first discovered that he could write songs while working on degrees in journalism and German at Texas A&M University, as a classmate and soulmate of still another clever Texas songwriter, Robert Earl Keen (whose "Merry Christmas from the Family" is simultaneously one of the funniest and most poignant songs in modern country music). Lovett first achieved acclaim as a winner at the Kerrville Folk Festival songwriters' contest (the venue that also introduced Nanci Griffith and Tish Hinojosa to music audiences). His angular looks and sky-high pompadour commanded attention, but his lyrics, delivered in a dry and droll, almost conversational manner, immediately captivated listeners and critics in fields far removed from country music. Four songs from his first CD, including the delightfully irreverent "God Will," moved onto the country charts. Since that promising debut CD, however, he has paid only occasional homage to traditional country music. His excellent double CD in 1998, *Step Inside This House*, honored Texas songwriters in particular. Lovett has remained a singular figure on the edge of mainstream country music, where he probably prefers to be.

Another talented Texan, Steve Earle, has similarly stayed on the fringes of country music but has profoundly impressed musicians both within that field and in bluegrass. He left his hometown of Schertz, just outside San Antonio, in 1973 to follow the rambling life of a folksinger popularized by his heroes Guy Clark and Townes Van Zandt. Unfortunately, he also shared Van Zandt's penchant for self-destruction, and the lure of drink and drugs almost permanently ruined his career in the mid-1990s. Earle arrived in Nashville in the mid-1970s, and by the time his first album appeared in 1986, he had crafted a body of songs that united the Texas tradition of storytelling[4] with the verve and aggressiveness of rock. *Guitar Town* was a critical success, and one of its featured songs, "Hillbilly Highway," effectively combined autobiography with vignettes about the migrations of southern rural folk to Detroit and other cities. To many people, Earle seemed to be the fulfillment of Gram Parsons's dream of fusing the styles and audiences of country and rock. That dream soon floundered, however, as Earle moved more insistently toward rock music and into an enslavement by cocaine and heroin. In 1994, he served a short jail term that was followed by a drug rehabilitation program. Earle happily turned his life around and recorded a series of CDs, including *El Corazón* and *Transcendental Blues*, that showcased his brilliant songwriting abilities and his fascination with bluegrass, blues, rock, Celtic, and country styles. His rough and sometimes profane concert style offended some listeners, including many of the bluegrass fans who attended his 1999 concerts with the Del McCoury Band, but no one has addressed contemporary issues with greater boldness, sensitivity, and compassion. Not only has he been an outspoken opponent of the death penalty, he was also one of the rare country singers in the age of affluence and complacency who could embrace the memory of the radical anarchist Emma Goldman and assert "Come back, Woody Guthrie" (as he did in one of the songs recorded on *El Corazón*).

The parade of talented newcomers accelerated during the rest of the decade and into the 1990s. With Clint Black and Garth Brooks in the vanguard, this assemblage of entertainers took country music to the highest commercial plateau it had ever reached. Indeed, their success often surpassed that won by musicians in other forms of music. Like the singers of the early 1980s, these musicians were also uncategorizable. Some of them were described as neo-traditional, but most were easily seduced by the allure of crossover success and were therefore more and more prone to dabble in the lucrative realm of pop. All the new singers played the game of being country, especially in their adoption of cowboy clothing. But they had also grown up in an era dominated by pop and rock, and, to a degree unprecedented in country music's history, their performances revealed those noncountry styles. Consequently, while winning great acclaim for themselves and for country music, they also provoked the strongest urge for alternative, and presumably more authentic, sounds yet evidenced in the field.

Clint Black was born in Long Branch, New Jersey, but grew up in Houston, where he absorbed the sounds of pop rock and honky-tonk country. Blessed with dark hair and a strong resemblance to the cowboy singer Roy Rogers, Black possessed a physical advantage that stood him in good stead in the unfolding age of music videos. Most important, he also had a powerful, wide-ranging voice that moved easily from romantic love songs to raucous barroom ditties. Black built an ardent following playing the clubs on the Houston-Galveston circuit, often with his songwriting partner Hayden Nicholas, but he did not win national visibility until Bill Ham became his manager. Ham, the former manager of the rock group ZZ Top, signed Black to a contract with RCA in 1988. The following year, Black recorded one of the most successful debut albums in country music history, *Killin' Time*, which sold over three million copies and yielded four number one singles. This collection and the one that followed in 1990, *Put Yourself in My Shoes*, marked Black as a traditionalist in the honky-tonk vein, an identification that he quickly overcame. In the years that followed his first two CDs, Black built the style and image of a pop-country performer.

If Clint Black's ascent seemed meteoric, that of Garth Brooks was even more dramatic. His first song to appear on the country charts, "Much Too Young (To Feel This Damn Old)" rose modestly in May 1989 to the number eight position. But during the next three years, he produced a string of number one songs and the best-selling country albums up to that time—*No Fences, Ropin' the Wind,* and *The Garth Brooks Collection.* By 1996, Brooks's accomplishment of over sixty million album sales had been surpassed only by the Beatles and Billy Joel, but he had achieved this spectacular figure more rapidly than any other artist in any field of music.

Although Brooks exuded the rough, if sometimes portly, good looks of an athlete, physical appearance cannot explain his success. He instead was a genius at merging musical styles and cultural symbols— rock and country, cowboy costuming, rock concert mannerisms and devices (including cordless microphones that permitted him to roam freely on large stages, and ropes and pulleys that enabled him to fly across the stage like Peter Pan)—and exhibited a mastery of marketing (his major at Oklahoma State). His penchant for self-promotion enabled him to embrace a populist stance against the recording industry by offering his albums directly to his audiences at below-market prices. His energy-driven and rock-derived stage style (inspired in large part by his hero Chris LeDoux, a former rodeo champion who became a country-rock performer) lured to his concerts thousands who had not previously listened to country music. In part because of an ego that sometimes translated into arrogance, but more especially because of the flamboyant trappings that surrounded his music, Brooks became the bane of, or even the whipping boy for, country traditionalists. Kinky Friedman, for example, called him the "anti-Hank." Even though they may not have been the kind of fare that Hank favored, such songs as "The Dance," "If Tomorrow Never Comes," "Unanswered Prayers," "Night Rider's Lament," and "Friends in Low Places" had memorable melodies and superb lyrics that spoke convincingly to a generation of suburban listeners who had few if any memories of, or ties to, working-class life. Abundant evidence proved the universal appeal of Brooks's music. His concert in New York's Central Park on August 7, 1997, played to an estimated 250,000 people and was seen and heard by additional multitudes that tuned in to HBO's *Garth Live from Central Park.*

Garth Brooks may have been the most commercially successful country singer of the late 1980s, but fellow Oklahoman Vince Gill was, arguably, the most talented of that generation. Endowed with athletic good looks, extraordinary musical gifts—including a sweet, soaring tenor—and an affable personality that any diplomat would envy, Gill accumulated more awards than any other country

Garth Brooks. Courtesy of Steve Juretson and CPacker; Creative Commons Attribution 2.0, www.creativecommons.org/licenses/by/2.0/legalcode.

entertainer, including, on two occasions, the CMA's most coveted award, Entertainer of the Year, and at least eighteen Grammies (for singing, instrumentation, and songwriting). Between 1989 and 1997, he virtually monopolized the Grammy award for Best Male Country Vocal Performance. Born in Norman, Oklahoma, in the household of a lawyer who became a federal appellate judge, Gill hardly fits the profile of the suffering working-class musician. He first won recognition as a guitarist and only slowly blossomed as a vocalist. In fact, for a time he was less well known as a singer than his first wife, Janis Oliver, who performed with her sister Kristine as part of the duo Sweethearts of the Rodeo.

Gill's professional career has been longer and more varied than those of most of his contemporaries, extending back to 1974, and included a lengthy stint in bluegrass with the Bluegrass Alliance, Boone Creek, and Byron Berline's Sundance band. He also played for a couple of years with the country-rock band Pure Prairie League and for an even shorter time with the Cherry Bombs, where he met and played with Rodney Crowell and future producer Tony Brown. Profiting from the experience of Ricky Skaggs, Gill entered mainstream country music in 1984, when he signed with RCA and eventually recorded three good but largely unrecognized albums. Superstardom came, though, when he joined MCA in 1989 and came under the direction of Tony Brown. *When I Call Your Name* (featuring a hit song with the same title) was the first of a series of CDs that illustrated his trademark mixture of pop-country, rock, bluegrass, and hard country material. Gill's professional generosity is exemplified by the numerous appearances he has made on other people's recordings,[5] while the mutual love affair between him and the country music industry was evidenced by his long service as the host of the CMA Awards show.

The emergence of young, good-looking entertainers like Vince Gill, who combined the energy and flair of rock music with the ambience of country, clearly contributed to country music's massive commercial growth in the late 1980s and early 1990s. This expansion also owed much to the dance craze of the early 1990s. The dance boom was, in part, a new phase of an interest that had been shown back in the urban cowboy era, when the Cotton-Eyed Joe and Texas Two-Step were prominently featured in new dance halls all across America. Country dancing's popularity peaked in the context of a more general enthusiasm for dancing of all kinds in the United States, particularly swing, ballroom, and Cajun dancing. The dance craze also coincided with, and was in large part a consequence of, the emergence and growth of the music video industry. Inspired by the precedent of MTV's rock music programming, the Oklahoma corporation Gaylord Enterprises introduced similar television venues for country music: The Nashville Network (TNN) and Country Music Television (CMT). Country music videos provided musicians instantaneous exposure among millions of viewers. The combining of young, good-looking entertainers and pulsating dance rhythms proved to be a potent and lucrative mixture.

The massive popularity of Billy Ray Cyrus's video and recording of "Achy Breaky Heart" in 1992 unleashed this new wave of dance interest. Within a year, a spate of similar videos and recordings appeared, each featuring a line dance as an accompaniment for the song. Dance clubs appeared all over the nation. At least two television shows appeared on TNN that featured recordings of new songs and throngs of average folks dancing to them; and instructional videos and columns touting the new dance steps appeared in country music magazines. Initially recorded but not immediately released in 1991 as part of a proposed Mercury CD, Cyrus's performance was first introduced as part of a video replete with line dance choreography provided by Melanie Greenwood. After receiving massive exposure on TNN and CMT, the song and the album were greeted by an enthusiastic public on a CD called *Some Gave All*, which sold over five million copies. In his T-shirt or tank top, Cyrus seemed far removed from the cowboy image conveyed by the hat acts. His performances displayed the sexual energy and masculine aggressiveness of a rockabilly. In the wake of his success, other country entertainers with a wide variety of styles introduced their own popular dance videos, including Mary Chapin Carpenter's "Down at the Twist and Shout," Tracy Byrd's "Watermelon Crawl," Tim McGraw's "Indian Outlaw" (the song that really inaugurated his career as a superstar), and Brooks & Dunn's "Boot Scootin' Boogie." Leon Eric "Kix" Brooks and Ronnie Dunn moved quickly beyond the line dance identification to become the most popular duo in country music. They had pursued independent careers until 1991, when they joined to make the album *Brand New Man*, which contained "Boot Scootin' Boogie" (written by Brooks) and at least three other songs that vaulted to the top of the country charts. With Dunn doing most of the lead singing and Brooks chiming in with occasional harmonies—but more often energizing audiences with his strutting stage presence—the duo brought thousands of people to the dance floor and secured a virtual monopoly in the award granted each year for Vocal Duo by the CMA and the ACM.

The country music made by Brooks & Dunn, Vince Gill, and others was recorded with state-of-the-art precision. Enhanced by digital recording techniques that permit the production of "perfect" recorded performances that can scarcely be re-created in live settings, the recordings were then pitched to radio stations but broadcast only if certain unnamed "consultants" recommended them. Such recordings appeared on increasingly automated formats, played by disc jockeys whose patter and vocal mannerisms suggested an apprenticeship in rock-and-roll radio. The handful of songs that managed to slip into these radio stations' "rotation" broadcasts each day were often described as Top Forty Country but actually were even fewer in number. The format did not differ substantially in any part of the United States. A listener traveling anywhere in America encountered the same body of recordings played by similar-sounding announcers who almost never gave the names of either songs or performers. Critics dismissed this music for its alleged suburban-mall lack of distinctiveness. But while the music that flowed out of Nashville in the 1990s may not have been "country" in any meaningful sense as identified by traditionalists, its sales indicate that it nevertheless filled the needs and expectations of millions of listeners who thought of themselves as fans of country music.

Bruce Feiler was the first observer to describe country music as "the music of suburbia."[6] He argued that a large audience of people like himself—well-educated, professional suburbanites who have a taste for sushi bars and computers—had become attracted to the music because singers like Garth Brooks had divested the music of its earlier "distasteful" trappings. No fan of traditional country music can read Feiler's analysis without being offended by some of his judgments and critiques—particularly his negative allusions to hay bales, overalls, and other "dusty old icons"—but he makes good sense in arguing that many people gravitated to country music because it conveys simple truths and values shorn of hayseed or redneck characteristics. Country music has profited commercially from the capitalistic-driven decision making and stylistic compromises made by producers such as Jimmy Bowen and artists who have created a product that successfully blends pop and country elements. And it has profited from the mood of social conservatism that has emerged in the United States since the late 1960s, and from the "new patriotism" that has flourished in the wake of the tragedies of September 11, 2001. Alan Jackson's Arista recording "Where Were You When the World Stopped Turning?"—a sensitive and deeply felt meditation about the disasters—was more than a masterpiece of compassion; it was also a highly commercial item.

Although produced by men and women with thoroughly urbane sensibilities, and in studios equipped with state-of-the-art techniques, country songs tout small towns and insist that the good life is pursued most often in southern or western locales. Traditional morality holds sway. Often performed by entertainers who flaunt their sex appeal, contemporary country lyrics nevertheless stress family values with little consciousness of irony. In keeping with the overall efforts to build a body of music that does not offend, partisan politics seldom intrudes into song lyrics, even though many country singers, like Travis Tritt, Larry Gatlin, Michael Martin Murphey, and Lee Greenwood, often played prominent roles at Republican Party conventions and have made their views known in interviews, onstage, and occasionally on recordings. Some listeners may gravitate toward country music because it is a "safe" and "white" alternative to hip-hop and other African American–derived styles, or because it still provides a musical forum where "good old boys" can trumpet their masculinity. But country music is popular, above all, not because of its politics, but because it speaks the language of millions of Americans in a simpler and more singable fashion than can be found in any other form of contemporary music. Its comprehensibility and its emphasis on traditional values have, in a sense, made it the nation's new "adult" pop music—even though in the late 1990s a horde of extremely young entertainers, such as Billy Gilman, Jessica Andrews, and LeAnn Rimes, won spectacular success as country singers.

One of the most positive developments of the 1980s and 1990s was the ascendance of women entertainers. These women came from a variety of backgrounds, sometimes exhibiting working-class origins and a close familiarity with country music's traditions, but more often from backgrounds that exhibited little or no intimacy with either blue-collar life or country music. Just like Emmylou Harris before her, Suzy Bogguss demonstrated that a conversion to country music could result in some of the best and most convincing singing that the genre had ever witnessed. Bogguss had hoped for some kind of music involvement all her life but had not taken her art in front of audiences until she earned a degree in jewelry making at Illinois State University. Wed to no particular style, she began singing in folk clubs and coffeehouses, but gradually became aware of the music of Merle Haggard and other hard country stylists. During a valuable apprenticeship singing daily in 1986 at Dolly Parton's theme park in Pigeon Forge, Tennessee, she built a large catalogue of country standards and became thoroughly familiar with the tastes of her listeners. Her conversion was complete when she learned to yodel, and put it on display in her breakthrough album in 1989, *Somewhere Between*, named for a Merle Haggard love song. Displaying a beautiful tone and a clearly enunciated vocal style as well as an astute skill at choosing songs, Bogguss gave flawless performances of such songs as "Drive South," "Someday Soon," and "Night Rider's Lament." The country music industry was not always as kind to her as it should have been, so Bogguss sought exposure in unconventional venues. She found a strong champion in Garrison Keillor, for example, who featured her often on his *A Prairie Home Companion* radio shows.

Women like Suzy Bogguss were not simply emerging as independent stylists and as architects of their own careers; they were also beginning to comment more freely on issues that were relevant to their lives and to the people around them. Equally important, their growing presence as singers and their large numbers of fans have encouraged men to be more conscious of women's concerns. Garth Brooks, for example, might not have become emboldened to record "The Thunder Rolls," his controversial song about domestic abuse, had it not been for the commercial power demonstrated by women consumers. Few of the women of country music were overt feminists, but they were clearly influenced in positive ways by the women's movement. They certainly had not attached themselves to the political arm of feminism. Instead, they lived out the precepts of feminism in their career moves and lifestyles, and increasingly even in their song lyrics. No longer could one find a woman entertainer who deferred to the authority of parents or husbands. Even LeAnn Rimes at age eighteen broke bitterly with her father over a contractual dispute. Above all, very few women now found their personalities subsumed by membership in a group. Women were assuming equality and independence as natural rights and were striking out boldly to assert control over their careers.

Although women speak out often on "women's issues," many have gone beyond private or gender concerns to address larger public problems. Rosanne Cash, for example, never abandoned her music in the 1990s, but her time and energy became increasingly concerned with questions of social justice, children's safety, and gun violence.[7] Reba McEntire spoke for many women when the protagonist of "Is There Life Out There?" voiced the need to pursue education and an independent life, and her message became even more universal when she warned about the danger of AIDS in "She Thinks His Name Was John." Several songs have commented on spousal abuse, such as Faith Hill's "A Man's Home Is His Castle," but none have been more graphic than Martina McBride's "Independence Day" and the Dixie Chicks' "Goodbye Earl." McBride's song spoke grimly of a fiery retribution, while the Dixie Chicks made a similar statement in a humorous song about an abused wife and her best friend who take the law into their own hands to deal with a cruel husband. A few songs, such as K. T. Oslin's "80's Ladies" and Deana Carter's "Did I Shave My Legs for This?," spoke about the frustrations that often accompany efforts to be free, sexy, and domestic. Faith Hill's "I Can't Do That Anymore" (written by Alan Jackson) and Mary Chapin Carpenter's "He Thinks He'll Keep Her" expressed the need to live one's own life, even if it meant defying other people's expectations or breaking the holy bonds of matrimony. The most positive message of that era, however, came in Lee Ann Womack's award-winning song of 2000, "You Can Fly," a statement made to young girls that they should feel free to take chances and pursue their own dreams.

Sexual equality and freedom are now taken for granted in the songs of women country singers. While one finds in country lyrics few bold statements concerning such matters as reproductive freedom, women do speak openly of their desire for sexual pleasure and fulfillment, and they are no longer reluctant to use their sexuality for commercial advantage. In the 1990s and early 2000s, such singers as Sara Evans, Faith Hill, and Shania Twain routinely appeared in videos that presented them in revealing costumes and suggestive poses. Faith Hill declared, in fact, that "sensuality is the most glorious gift a woman has,"[8] a conviction that animated her choice of wardrobe and the videos that she made. The sexuality displayed by Evans, Twain, Hill, and other contemporary women performers was not a new phenomenon in country music—Dolly Parton and Tanya Tucker, for example, often appeared in provocative clothing—but in our post-Madonna era, Twain and Hill asserted their sexuality much more aggressively.

Both women had classic country music and working-class biographies. Born Eilleen Edwards in Ontario, Canada, Shania Twain adopted the name of her stepfather, an Ojibwe Indian named Jerry Twain, who raised her after her father deserted the family. Jerry Twain and her mother were killed in an automobile accident, and Shania had to raise her younger siblings. As a child, she appeared often on Canadian country music television shows, singing the songs of Emmylou Harris and other leading country performers. Her career and style, though, revealed nothing of the blue-collar world that had nourished her, and instead conveyed the glitter and packaging of urban show business. Possessing the looks and self-assurance of a fashion model, Shania was ripe material for the physical packaging that her then-husband and producer, Mutt Lange, lent to her career. Her stage performances were marked by a playful and assertive sexiness, provocative songs, and costumes that took advantage of her physical attractiveness. She became famous, in fact, for her bare midriff. All these traits translated into one of the most commercially successful careers ever enjoyed by a woman performer. Shania's 1995 album, *The Woman in Me*, was said to be the best-selling album by a woman artist in country music history, selling nine million albums in the United States and twelve million worldwide.

Faith Hill grew up in the tiny town of Star, Mississippi, just south of Jackson, as the daughter of adoptive parents. She attended an all-white school but was fascinated with black gospel music, and she haunted black churches and soaked up as much of the music and style of Aretha Franklin as she could absorb. She relocated to Nashville when she was nineteen years old and worked at Opryland as a hostess and T-shirt salesperson until 1993, when her recording breakthrough came. Her first CD, *Take Me as I Am*, included the hit single "Wild One." Since that time, she has had immense commercial success, both as a solo artist and as a performer with her husband, Tim McGraw, as part of the Soul 2 Soul Tour. In the spring of 2000, her recording of "Breathe" (in an album of the same name) crossed over into pop music and won her a Grammy award.

Hill was country music's first true glamour queen, and her statuesque beauty attracted as much notice as her music. Although in interviews she occasionally expressed chagrin at the attention given such matters by the media, she nevertheless carefully cultivated an aura of sensuality with an avalanche of videos and photographs. The journalist Geoffrey Himes noted that "it may be a bit disingenuous to pose for thousands of photos and then claim that your looks have had nothing to do with your career."[9]

Country traditionalists might have been offended by the sexy personas projected by Twain and Hill, but one suspects that it was their vocal performance styles that inspired the strongest censure. Hard country fans would proclaim loudly that "they just ain't country." The Dixie Chicks, on the other hand, proved that overt sexual posturing and traditional music were not necessarily incompatible. When this trio of young women first emerged in the mid-1990s, their platinum blond hair, sassy personalities, and striking beauty seemed to mark them as country music's version of the Spice Girls. They soon proved, though, that they could sing fervently, write memorable songs, and play string instruments masterfully. In many ways, their emergence was the best news that modern country music had enjoyed in a long time. Not only did they inject much hard country material into their performances, they also attracted hosts of young women to their shows, presenting evidence that women can play country string instruments as well as any man.

The Chicks came to mainstream country after a lengthy experience in Texas as bluegrass musicians. The Erwin sisters (Emily on five-string banjo and Martie on fiddle) had played bluegrass in Dallas since 1984, when they were teenagers, and in 1989 they joined with Laura Lynch and Robin Macy to create the first version of the Dixie Chicks, named for a song performed by the rock band Little Feat. Between 1989 and 1993, they moved from street-corner concerts to stints as opening acts for such major stars as Garth Brooks and a performance at President Clinton's inaugural ball.

The present incarnation of the Dixie Chicks emerged in about 1995 after Lynch and Macy had left the band and Natalie Maines became lead vocalist. Natalie was the perky and strong-voiced daughter of Lloyd Maines, a well-known steel guitarist and record producer from Lubbock, Texas. The addition of Maines, a dropout from Boston's Berklee College of Music, gave the trio a modern mainstream sound and almost ensured a major broadening of their repertory. They also divested themselves of the big hair and cowgirl attire they had once sported and began dressing in contemporary clothing that accentuated their physical assets. Most important, they signed a contract in 1997 with Sony Records and in 1998 recorded an album, *Wide Open Spaces*, that sold over four million units within a year of its production. Their second Sony album, *Fly*, which contained the comic murder ballad "Goodbye Earl," rose to the top of *Billboard*'s charts after selling almost 350,000 copies within one week of the CD's release. No country group had ever had such an auspicious beginning.[10]

The Dixie Chicks' style and ambience were too broad-ranging to confine them to the neo-traditional category, but songs like "Goodbye Earl," "Tonight the Heartache's on Me" (a shuffle beat honky-tonk tune), and the heartrending "Am I the Only One (Who's Ever Felt This Way?)" satisfied a hunger that many people had for hard country material. The very characteristics that made contemporary country music broadly appealing to millions of Americans alienated many others. Narrow radio playlists and formulaic pop-rock sounds and arrangements may bring comfort to some listeners, but they have convinced others that the music is losing its soul, a quality that had reflected its working-class origins. In an effort to reach a larger public and to occupy that broad middle ground vacated by the disappearance of older forms of pop music, country music's producers created a body of songs that had little grit or down-home vitality. Moralists and patrons of respectability may have applauded the decline of cheating and drinking songs and the whole retinue of topics outlined by David Allan Coe in the Steve Goodman and John Prine composition "You Never Even Call Me by My Name." Similarly, although soothing songs of religious affirmation sometimes appeared in the repertories of country singers, the older passion-filled and doctrinaire gospel songs almost never surfaced on Top Forty country radio or in the performances of country entertainers. For example, if some of the songs earlier performed by the Bailes Brothers or Louvin Brothers ever appeared on modern radio shows, listeners would assume that the items came from another planet.

Sporadic manifestations of tradition, though, do sometimes appear within mainstream country music. Neo-traditionalism surfaces from time to time because corporate country music breeds boredom and dissent, and younger singers and writers long for the sense of rootedness and working-class flavor that once prevailed in the music. In the 1990s and early years of the twenty-first century, such singers as Suzy Bogguss, Sara Evans, Patty Loveless, Lee Ann Womack, Alan

Jackson, Mark Chesnutt, Marty Stuart, Wade Hayes, Joe Diffie, Toby Keith, and Brad Paisley gave renewed hope to those who like the old country sounds.

"Traditional," of course, is a highly relative or elastic term. None of the neo-traditionalists have been mere throwbacks to older styles of performance, and none of them could be described as "moldy figs," a term first used by jazz scholars to categorize musicians resistant to change. To cite only a couple of examples, Travis Tritt's and Marty Stuart's music suggests that rock and roll has exerted a strong, if ironic, influence among the neo-traditionalists. After all, rock and roll was the culprit that drove hard country music off the jukeboxes and radio playlists back in the late 1950s, and it perennially attracted the scorn of both moralists and traditional country music fans. Larry Cordle spoke of its enduring and harmful legacy in "Murder on Music Row," when he opined that "drums and rock-and-roll guitars" were "shoved right up in your face." Rock and roll, however, strongly colored the styles of people like Travis Tritt, the Marietta, Georgia, native who often spoke fondly of his reverence for the southern rock varieties of the genre; and Marty Stuart, the multitalented Mississippi musician who has been the most tireless champion of traditional country music. Stuart had joined the Sullivan Family bluegrass band when he was twelve and became part of Lester Flatt's Nashville Grass at the age of thirteen. After Flatt's death, Stuart became a member of Johnny Cash's band for a time and was married to one of Cash's daughters. A lifelong collector, historian, and photographer of country music,[11] he has passionately and eloquently defended traditional styles, illustrating his eclectic musical bent and willingness to combine seemingly disparate forms in such collections as *Hillbilly Rock* and *The Pilgrim*. Stuart was one of a small group in the 1980s that included Steve Earle and Dwight Yoakam, who proudly used the term "hillbilly" to describe their music. If versatility were not enough to ensure his fame in country music history, he was also married to the beautiful and talented Connie Smith, a singer described by her contemporaries as one of the greatest vocalists in country music. Eddie Stubbs, in fact, called her "the Rolls Royce of country singers.[12] About seventeen years younger than Smith, Stuart had had a crush on his future wife since he was a little boy.

Most other musicians have been wary of attaching themselves firmly to the neo-traditional camp. No one has a voice that is more

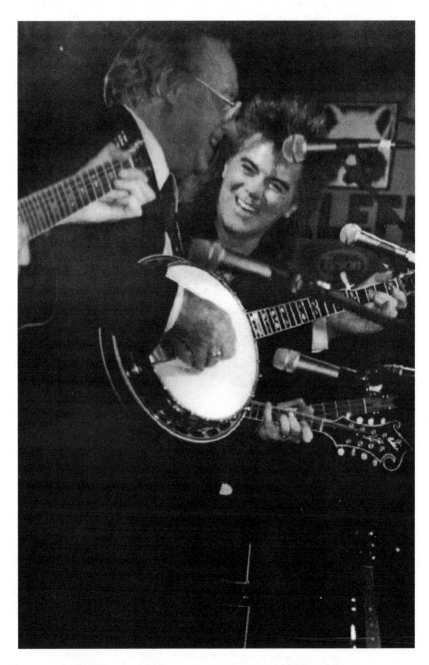

Earl Scruggs and Marty Stuart. Courtesy of Becky Johnson.

unmistakably country than Patty Loveless, a singer who communicates perfectly the inflections of her native Kentucky hills, but she has refused to identify with any specific stylistic label. A cousin of Loretta Lynn and Crystal Gayle, Loveless was born Patricia Ramey in Pikeville in eastern Kentucky, in the same hospital where Dwight Yoakam was born. Her father was a victim of black lung disease, the grim ailment that has taken the lives of many Appalachian coal miners. Country music has always been an integral and cherished part of her inheritance, but she has never hesitated to try her hand at other kinds of music. For instance, she sang rock and roll for a brief period and still injects songs with a rock flavor in her performances. Loveless first came to Nashville as a teenage employee of the Wilburn Brothers but did not figure prominently in that city's musical scene until 1987, when she joined MCA under the tutelage of producer Tony Brown. Brown directed her first album that year, which included her first chart single, "If My Heart Had Windows," a song learned from George Jones. Later recordings made for MCA and Epic, including the CMA's Album of the Year for 1995, *When Fallen Angels Fly*, often attained platinum status and won for her in 1996 the CMA's and ACM's prize as Female Vocalist of the Year. These recordings exhibited her eclectic tastes and only rarely ventured into the neo-traditional realm. If any question lingered, though, about her ability to sing traditional material, it was put to rest by her powerful performance (along with Ralph Stanley) of the great murder ballad "Pretty Polly" on Stanley's CD collection *Clinch Mountain Country*, and by her CD of 2001, *Mountain Soul*, a collection of hard country songs performed with acoustic backing.

Alan Jackson, in contrast, has proudly worn the mantle of neo-traditional country singer. Jackson grew up in Newnan, Georgia, as the son of an automobile mechanic whom he commemorated in a fine song called "Working Class Hero." In vocal style, Jackson exhibited neither a Hank Williams nor a Lefty Frizzell influence, but nevertheless had a believable and winning southern lilt and twang in his voice. Ever since his first major recordings for Arista in 1989, Jackson's advocacy of hard country music has been evidenced by his choice of songs and accompanying instrumentation. He knocked around Nashville for about four years, working in TNN's mailroom and making demos for other singers, before he recorded his first album, *Here in the Real World*. Since that time, Jackson has rarely strayed from his working-class roots or the hard country sound, with a long string of stellar recordings such as "Don't Rock the Jukebox," "Chattahoochee," "Mercury Blues," and "Midnight in Montgomery" (a tribute to Hank Williams). His music has often expressed a refreshing populist tinge and a reverence for his roots, a concern best heard in "Little Man" and "Working Class Hero." Jackson showed his disquietude about the nature of the music that was then being produced in Nashville in his decision to record, with George Strait, a cover version of "Murder on Music Row."

Other sometime country traditionalists, such as Mark Chesnutt, Travis Tritt, and Joe Diffie, spoke often of their reverence for traditional country music but have frequently veered from the hard country format. Chesnutt came from one of the citadels of working-class country music, the area surrounding Beaumont, Texas, where his father, Bob Chesnutt, had been a local country singer and a collector of country records. Mark often joined his old friend Tracy Byrd in gigs in the local bar and honky-tonk circuit that had nourished their hero George Jones. No one was surprised when Mark quit school in the tenth grade to play music. His first commercial hit came in 1990 with the recording "Too Cold at Home" (for MCA), which was followed soon thereafter by such songs as the beautifully crafted "Brother Jukebox" (written by Paul Craft) and "Bubba Shot the Jukebox."

Travis Tritt began his ascent to stardom in 1990 with his first Warner Brothers album, *Country Club*. Tritt never bothered with terms like neo-traditional but instead proudly identified with such southern rock luminaries as Charlie Daniels, Lynyrd Skynyrd, and Hank Williams Jr. Few country musicians, however, have been as gifted or as versatile. He sometimes exhibits his skill on the five-string banjo and can speak of experience as a bluegrass musician, and he has recorded some of the finest examples of modern honky-tonk material, including "Here's a Quarter (Call Someone Who Cares)," "Lord Have Mercy on the Working Man," "The Whiskey Ain't Working" (with Marty Stuart), and "Out of Control Raging Fire," a duet with Patty Loveless and one of the strongest moments on her CD *Mountain Soul*. A series of engagements with Stuart in 1992, called the "No Hats" tour, indicated the two musicians' suspicion of the numerous "hat acts" and revealed their affinity for both rock and roll and hard country.

Joe Diffie carried genuine blue-collar credentials, having worked in a foundry and at other wage jobs while pursuing his dream of country music. He grew up in an Oklahoma family where Haggard, Jones, and Frizzell were gods. He followed his dream to Nashville in 1986 and, prospering from the lucrative commercial scene that emerged that year, he became a much-sought-after singer on demo records. In 1990, he signed with Epic Records and recorded "Home," a song that immediately shot to the top of the charts. Widely heralded as a singer's singer and as a champion of hard country music, Diffie's music was, more accurately, an appealing synthesis of honky-tonk and rock, best exemplified in his CD of 1993, *Honky Tonk Attitude.*

The future of country neo-traditionalism has always been uncertain, but in the last years of the 1990s, Brad Paisley, a devoted disciple of Buck Owens, emerged as a chief torchbearer of hard country sounds. He was born in 1972 in Glen Dale, West Virginia, an Ohio River town. Growing up in a rural West Virginia environment, Paisley could hardly avoid hearing the sounds of genuine country music. His introduction came from his grandfather, who played Merle Travis–style guitar. He received further invaluable experience as a musician on the famous *Wheeling Jamboree,* where he played for eight years. Paisley moved to Nashville in the mid-1990s to enroll in Belmont University's music business program. Like Diffie, he soon began making music demos and writing songs. In 1999, he recorded his first Arista CD, *Who Needs Pictures,* on which he played all the guitar parts and for which he wrote all of the songs. Several of the album's songs received wide airplay, but the biggest hit of his early career was the cleverly worded "Me Neither." He was enrolled in the *Grand Ole Opry* in early 2001.

While the weaknesses of Top Forty country music were apparent, the most glaring deficiencies were the virtual abandonment of veteran performers and the reluctance to promote the music of unorthodox entertainers. George Jones did succeed in breaking through country music's youth curtain in 1996 with a song called "Choices" that somehow managed to make it onto the charts. In general, though, Jones and other classic country singers such as Johnny Cash, Willie Nelson, Merle Haggard, Loretta Lynn, Emmylou Harris, Dolly Parton, Charley Pride, Ray Price, Hank Thompson, Vern Gosdin, and Gene Watson had to seek new venues and audiences outside of mainstream country. A few of these musicians became icons of youth pop culture, admired for their honesty and endurance and, in some cases, because they had rebelled against the Top Forty establishment. Johnny Cash, for example, enjoyed the most remarkable career of any country musician. At least since his appearance at the Newport Folk Festival in 1964, Cash preserved a following among young fans that seemed only to be reinvigorated with each succeeding generation. Cultivating an air of mystery with his habit of dressing in black, exhibiting a receptivity to alternative styles and musicians, and clinging to a spare and almost austere acoustic sound, he impressed listeners as a man of rugged and uncompromising integrity. Totally exiled from Top Forty radio, Cash nevertheless maintained a commercial presence with a series of CDs (including the award-winning *American Recordings* in 1994) marketed to college and other independent radio stations. The aging Austin Outlaw, Willie Nelson, similarly preserved links to rock audiences through his well-publicized Farm Aid concerts, where he collaborated with such socially conscious rock singers as John Cougar Mellencamp and Neil Young and won admirers among adult Americans with his albums of vintage popular songs. Merle Haggard made fewer efforts to cultivate rock-culture youth and in fact had explicitly set himself apart from them in the early 1970s with his antihippie anthem, "Okie from Muskogee." He nevertheless won much support among counterculture youth who admired the man who "wore his own kind of hat." He became the subject of a fine tribute album, *Tulare Dust*, produced by the former cowpunk musician Dave Alvin and performed by a variety of alternative singers such as himself, Tom Russell, and Iris DeMent. This kind of patronage may have mellowed the outspoken country singer, because he did begin to offer some regrets about the political positions he took back in the early 1970s.[13]

To its credit, the *Grand Ole Opry* still made room each Saturday night for the music of such "old-timers" as Bill Anderson, Bill Carlisle, Little Jimmy Dickens, Jack Greene, Jimmy C. Newman, Jean Shepard, Connie Smith, Porter Wagoner, Billy Walker, and Charlie Walker. It was reassuring to traditionalists to see Porter Wagoner stride out on the stage still wearing his trademark Nudie costumes. Veteran musicians also found refuge in cities and venues outside of Nashville—in Branson, Missouri; in the clubs of Myrtle Beach, South Carolina; in the dance halls of Bandera, Texas; and in casinos and cruises that cater to Middle American tourists. The Statler Brothers, for example, may have been banished from Top Forty radio, but they were assured evenings of capacity crowds when they appeared at clubs like the Crystal Grand Music Theatre in the Wisconsin Dells resort town. Branson has long been a haven for entertainers who have either been ignored by Nashville or who do not want to stay on the road in order to make a living in the music business. Originating as an

Ozark tourist mecca built around the theme park Silver Dollar City and the outdoor pageant "Shepherd of the Hills" (both founded in 1960), the small city assumed country music overtones when a local hillbilly burlesque group called the Baldknobbers began playing old-time music in a local theater. Roy Clark was the first superstar who resettled in Branson, but he was soon followed by Mel Tillis, Boxcar Willie, Glen Campbell, Moe Bandy, and the most popular act of all, the Japanese fiddler Shoji Tabuchi, who had "converted" to country music in his native country after hearing Roy Acuff perform. The mile-long strip of road that runs through Branson became dotted with glittering music clubs, and thousands of slow-moving automobiles and tour buses bring tourists to this phenomenon often described as "Las Vegas without the gambling."

Texas continued to be a thriving area for working-class country music, even though the scene was sustained more often than not by college students and other urban listeners who longed to sample, at least for the moment, the laid-back life of Luckenbach along with "Willie, Waylon, and the Boys." Cowboy imagery and the Texas mystique—the conviction that the state has had a special legacy of freedom and innovation—continues to lure musicians to the region and to shape the kind of music they make. The popular television series *Austin City Limits* (PBS) has fed such perceptions to a large audience each week since its debut in 1976, becoming the "longest-running music program in television history," according to its website.[14] Visitors to the Hill Country cowboy towns of Helotes and Bandera could always hear good local country music, but if they were lucky, they might also have heard the soulful sounds of such visiting singers as Claude Gray, Johnny Bush, Darrell McCall, Justin Trevino, Hank Thompson, Ray Price, or Gene Watson, all of whom made frequent appearances in the local clubs. In Austin, fans could always be assured of hearing a wide variety of country styles. Much of it was rock inflected, but western swing and honky-tonk bands have also made the city their prime area of activity. The performers who have passed through Austin included some of the most distinctive singers and songwriters in country music. Most of them, however, like Pat Green, are seldom heard on Top Forty radio stations and regrettably remain unknown to most country music listeners outside Texas.

As noted in the previous chapter, Austin had briefly been the locus for the music of one of country music's most distinctive stylists,

Jimmie Dale Gilmore. In the early 1970s, though, he joined with a couple of talented friends from Lubbock, Butch Hancock and Joe Ely, to form a musical trio. As the Flatlanders, they won regional notoriety and enduring cult status, but little monetary reward. In 1971, they had recorded a body of songs that combined the flavor of old-time music with sophisticated New Age lyrics. The resulting album received almost no attention, but when released again in 1990 on the Rounder label, it was given the fitting title of *More a Legend Than a Band*.

Each Flatlander was a gifted entertainer in his own right, and each enjoyed his own solo career. Hancock had the lowest profile of the three but became famous for his songwriting, evoking the spirit of the Texas landscape and mirroring the dreams and anxieties of people everywhere with songs like "West Texas Waltz" and "Banks of the Guadalupe." Joe Ely, on the other hand, was a charismatic singer whose aggressive and high-energy style was best captured in songs like "Me and Billy the Kid" and Hancock's "She Never Spoke Spanish to Me." Jimmie Dale Gilmore, described in an earlier chapter, commanded the most widespread attention of the three Flatlanders. His clear, resonant tenor voice and precise diction were almost unique in country music, and his CD of 2000, *One Endless Night*, was a superb collection of songs written by his old friends Butch Hancock, Willis Alan Ramsey, John Hiatt, and other country poets. Gilmore's ironic suggestion that the CD was too country for Top Forty radio spoke volumes about the current state of country music, but for sheer lyric artistry and vocal interpretation, very little in that format could compete with it.

Junior Brown, who eventually moved to Tulsa, Oklahoma, was for many years the headliner at Austin's Continental Club. He was not totally unknown to the average country music listener because he made at least one award-winning video built around his song "My Wife Thinks You're Dead" that illustrated both his musicianship and his sense of humor. And he has certainly been highly regarded by his fellow musicians. Nevertheless, Brown has had to pursue his career in alternative venues outside Nashville and among largely rock-oriented fans. The Indiana-born entertainer sings in a deep baritone reminiscent of Ernest Tubb, whose television shows he had faithfully watched as a kid. Although that influence appears in his song "My Baby Don't Dance to Nothing but Ernest Tubb," Brown's masterful artistry defies labeling. His brilliant guitar playing borrows from country, jazz, and rock sources, most notably the style pioneered by Jimi Hendrix, but he has introduced his own individualistic and idiosyncratic innovations. Brown is a performer who actually has to be seen to be fully appreciated. Playing an instrument that he invented, the guit-steel (a double-necked instrument that permits both electric guitar and steel guitar stylings), Brown dazzles his audiences with his rapid and flawless ability to move quickly from one style to the other in the course of an individual song.

Don Walser, a gentle giant who was born in 1934 in Lamesa, Texas, also commanded physical attention from listeners with his size and bearing—he stood six foot six and weighed about 280 pounds. Most important, he performed country music the way that many people thought it should be sung. Walser had always sung country songs and had been particularly enamored of the music of Bob Wills and the yodeling of Elton Britt, but he made no attempt at a full-fledged professional career until the age of sixty, when he retired from forty-five years of service in the National Guard. He brought to his new career an encyclopedic knowledge of country song lyrics, a desire to preserve authentic country sounds, a clear and powerful tenor voice, and a hair-raising yodel. Someone described him as the "Pavarotti of the Plains." Walser became a fixture in the dance halls of Austin and Central Texas, but neither his songs nor his style of singing were classic honky-tonk in nature. He was instead highly diverse in his selection of songs, ranging from the soft pop-country tunes of Eddy Arnold to the hard country items of Ray Price and George Jones. Like Gilmore, Walser was considered alternative because his pure country style seemed anachronistic when measured against those that dominated Top Forty radio. He sang at the Summer Olympics in Atlanta in 1996 and participated in the Heritage tour along with Tish Hinojosa, but Walser was heard by too few people. The bulk of his concerts were confined to Texas, especially to the many clubs of Austin. Walser retired from performing in 2003 and passed away three years later.

If Don Walser's vocal style could not be defined by the clubs in which he played, that of Wayne Hancock, another fine Texas singer, is very much a product of honky-tonk culture. Hancock exhibits the marks of a youth spent listening to rock and roll and hard country, and vocally he comes about as close to a Hank Williams sound as anyone in country music. Communicating easily with a hard-edged, nasally punctuated tenor, and cultivating the air of a rambler, Hancock has tried hard to link his music to the honky-tonk tradition. In "Juke Joint Jumpin'," for example, he speaks of experiences that he could not have known but were probably learned about from his father—honky-tonking in the clubs that once lined the Gladewater highway in the East Texas oil fields. In songs like "Thunderstorms and Neon Signs," Hancock also mined the terrain of loneliness and despair that Hank Williams explored in his songs. But like most country musicians who ventured into the realm of honky-tonk music at the end of the 1990s, Hancock (and his chief disciple, Hank Williams III) seemed most comfortable belting out a good-time rock anthem or boogie tune.

The closest approximation of honky-tonk music, in all of its manifestations, could be found in the songs of Dale Watson. Born in Birmingham, Alabama; reared in Pasadena, Texas; and surviving a brief stint in California, Watson eventually became a fixture in the Austin musical scene. Watson's "Jack's Truck Stop and Cafe," an affectionate recollection of local music making in Tennessee, is not a literal account of a portion of the singer's life, but it evokes the kind of youthful experiences that shaped his music. Watson absorbed his values and music from his father, who was a truck driver and country singer, and he has remained passionately loyal to the culture that surrounded his father's life, preserving his fascination with trucking songs and with the music of that genre's greatest exponent, Dave Dudley. His concerts are essentially primers for his young fans, who are informed about the beauty found in the music of such "real" performers as Dudley, Merle Haggard, Wynn Stewart, and Conway Twitty. Watson has a strong, expressive baritone, and while he exhibits his debts to his honky-tonk mentors, he also infuses his concerts with the energy and drive of Memphis-style rockabilly. In many of his concerts, in fact, Watson performs solely with the spare, pared-down sound of the early rockabilly singers: lead electric guitar, rhythm guitar, and bass. Unlike other honky-tonk revivalists, such as Wayne Hancock, Watson also exhibits a fondness and affinity for slow, sad songs, such as "Blessed or Damned," "I Hate These Songs," and "Every Song I Write Is for You" (a song written as a tribute to his sweetheart, Teresa Herbert, who was killed in an automobile accident in April of 2002). Above all, he has been an uncompromising hillbilly nationalist and never hesitates to express his contempt for the music of Top Forty. In "Play Me a Real Country Song" he pays tribute to the radio stations of his youth that played authentic country music.

Although Watson and the other Austin musicians usually have been writers as well as singers, few of them can be identified with the singer-songwriter culture that emerged from the folk revival. Embracing a tradition that began with Woody Guthrie and flowered in the 1960s with Paul Simon, Joni Mitchell, and Bob Dylan, a contingent of musicians built a body of literate and often socially conscious music at festivals and in coffeehouses throughout America. These musical poets generally adhered to acoustic instruments, preferring intimate environments where their music could easily be absorbed and appreciated. The most successful, though, such as John Prine, Steve Earle, Mary Chapin Carpenter, Shelby Lynne, Lucinda Williams, and Gillian Welch, have adopted electric instruments and the aggressive tone of rock music. Their relationship with country music has been problematic, and few have received more than minimal acceptance in Nashville or on Top Forty radio.

Although few of the Austin musicians were identified with the culture that emerged from the folk revival, Texas singers have made vital contributions to the singer-songwriter genre. Nanci Griffith, for instance, grew up in a musical household in Austin but was swept away by the music of the folk revival, particularly when she heard a local performer, Carolyn Hester, and the songs of the star-crossed troubadour Townes Van Zandt. Van Zandt always remained on the periphery of country music even though he recorded at least fifteen albums and introduced such songs as "Pancho and Lefty," "If I Needed You," "White Freightliner Blues," and "Tecumseh Valley" to the permanent country music lexicon.

Griffith knew the songs of her colleagues in the folk movement, but she became highly regarded for the quality of her own songs, a talent first exhibited at the Kerrville Folk Festival in the Texas Hill Country. She found easy communion there with such festival regulars as Bill and Bonnie Hearne, the congenial and smooth-singing duo who also lent encouragement to Tish Hinojosa, Lyle Lovett, and other fledgling artists. Griffith had already had about eight years of music experience when she moved to Nashville in 1985 and made a critically praised album for Philo called *Once in a Very Blue Moon*. Although Kathy Mattea's 1986 version of Griffith's "Love at the Five and Dime" rose to number three on the *Billboard* charts, Griffith's tenure within the Nashville mainstream was neither happy nor commercially successful. Since that time she has kept the industry at arm's length but has

continued to make first-rate recordings, including two tributes to
other songwriters, *Other Voices, Other Rooms*, and *Other Voices, Too*,
and has cast her musical net more broadly by recording with the Nashville Symphony and the legendary Irish band the Chieftains. Along
with Tim O'Brien, Steve Earle, and Ricky Skaggs, Griffith has experimented often with presumed Celtic material and has won a large and
devoted following in Ireland.

Leticia "Tish" Hinojosa is still another Austin-based singer-
songwriter (now living in Germany) who can point to the experience
of the Kerrville Folk Festival as the stimulus for her career. Her sensibilities as a songwriter, however, grew out of her experiences in San
Antonio as the daughter of parents who had migrated from Mexico. As
the youngest of thirteen children, Hinojosa clung closely to her mother,
absorbing the lyrical love songs that she had transported across the
border. Tish also heard the Tejano and conjunto rhythms beloved by
her father and, of course, the pop and country songs that came to her
each day on the radio. Hinojosa spent two artistically productive but
commercially disappointing periods in New Mexico and Nashville
during the 1980s, performing a mixture of country, rock, and folk tunes.
Her first album, *Taos to Tennessee*, recalls that era. Her first major
recording, however, came in 1989, when she reached into the cultural
resources of her family and produced a CD called *Homeland*. There, in
songs like "West Side of Town" and "Joaquin," she documented and
paid tribute to the experiences of her family and other brave souls who
had made the perilous journey across the Rio Grande. She followed
these forays into family autobiography with powerfully honest and
sensitive songs, such as "Something in the Rain," that commented on
the abuses visited on migrant laborers, children, and women. Social
commentary has never vanished from her repertoire, but Hinojosa's
later recordings, which became increasingly bilingual, were intensely
introspective and mystical musings on her cultural heritage.

Iris DeMent was born in Paragould, Arkansas, on January 5, 1961,
but grew up in California surrounded by family and neighbors who still
bore the accents, values, and music of her birthplace and the working-
class South. With one of the most compelling, emotionally searing
voices heard in modern American music, she has memorialized those
origins in songs like "Mama's Opry" and "I'm Walking Home Tonight"
(about the death of her father). DeMent grew up hearing the sounds
of Jimmie Rodgers, the Carter Family, and Merle Haggard, but forged

her own personal and expressive style playing the coffeehouse circuit in Kansas City. After moving to Nashville in 1990 and coming under the tutelage of Emmylou Harris, she began singing backup vocals for other entertainers and in 1992 made her first solo record, *Infamous Angel*, for Philo. That album, and the two that followed (*My Life* in 1994, and *The Way I Should* in 1996), were critically acclaimed but seldom played on mainstream radio stations. She may have culled her intensely personal lyrics, in such songs as "Easy's Getting Harder" and "No Time to Cry," from autobiographical recollections, but she voiced the universal concerns of listeners with poignant lyrics and a penetrating emotional intimacy that few writers have achieved and few singers could deliver with such intensity. DeMent has made frequent guest appearances on other people's albums (such as John Prine's great tribute to hard country music, *In Spite of Ourselves*) or on anthologies such as *Songcatcher*, where she reprised the beautiful ballad, "Pretty Saro," which she had sung in the movie also called *Songcatcher*. She also collaborated briefly with Merle Haggard, as a cowriter and opening act. Haggard's response to her third CD, *The Way I Should*, which contains biting political commentary about some of the nation's social ills, has never been disclosed.

Unlike Hinojosa and DeMent, Lucinda Williams could not point to a working-class heritage. Born in Lake Charles, Louisiana, she grew up in a series of southern towns, the daughter of Miller Williams, a poet and university English professor (now a professor emeritus at the University of Arkansas) who read a poem at Bill Clinton's second inauguration. While she undoubtedly absorbed certain literary sensibilities from her father and a love for music from her mother, she probably learned more from Hank Williams and other southern musicians who populated the family's radio. It would be an imaginative leap indeed to assert that she learned from still another southern poet who bore the name of Williams, but her preoccupation with the dark underside of human existence and evocations of loneliness do bear some resemblance to the insights of Tennessee Williams. Her best-known collection, the Grammy-winning *Car Wheels on a Gravel Road*, makes constant references to such southern towns as Lafayette, Baton Rouge, Jackson, and Greenville, each serving as a backdrop or context for her tales of sensuous longing, disappointment, and death.

Tim O'Brien is country music's renaissance man. The West Virginia native had first won the allegiance of bluegrass fans through his versatile musicianship with the Colorado-based band Hot Rize. By the time this colorful and award-winning group disbanded in 1990, O'Brien had already achieved some success as a songwriter and had seen two of his songs, "Walk the Way the Wind Blows" and "Untold Stories," become major hits for fellow West Virginian Kathy Mattea. A duet with Mattea, "The Battle Hymn of Love," recorded in 1990, reached the Top Ten lists and won for him a contract with RCA. Even though no material from that proposed album was ever released, O'Brien's artistic production has never slowed down. In fact, he combined his incessant musical performance with the presidency of the IBMA, a post to which he was appointed in January 2002. Albums made for Sugar Hill and other labels reveal a staggering musicianship and a catholicity of taste that seems unending. He has made fine duet albums with his sister, Molly; has appeared as a singer and supporting musician on scores of recordings made by others; continues to write sensitive songs (such as the Nickel Creek hit "When You Come Back Down"); and, of course, produces and performs ably on his own CDs. His wide-ranging receptivity to songs and his ability to move freely and convincingly from traditional to modern material is documented in an album of Bob Dylan songs, *Red on Blonde*; an album of old-time fiddle tunes and ballads called *From the Mountain* (inspired by the novel *Cold Mountain*); and two albums called *The Crossing* and *Two Journeys* that explore the presumed, but tenuous, links between Appalachian music and Celtic culture.

O'Brien and the other musicians discussed above are, almost by definition, "alternative" entertainers. Either by choice or by necessity, they have had to pursue their careers outside the commercial channels controlled by Nashville. However, the term "alternative" or "alt-country" (originally "alt.country," a term that reveals the movement's origins in the first generation of Internet newsgroups) has been more often used to describe those musicians who have combined rock and country elements and who project an edge and vitality that seem absent from mainstream country music. In many cases, their accomplishments have centered on reviving styles and themes that once lay at the heart of country music. Gram Parsons, of course, provided a central source of inspiration for such musicians, while the punk country (or cowpunk) bands on the West Coast and elsewhere (such as Jason and the Scorchers) contributed still another. A key event in the shaping of the alternative country movement came in

Tim O'Brien. Courtesy of Tim O'Brien.

1990, when the Illinois country-rock band Uncle Tupelo recorded an album called *No Depression*, inspired by a 1930 Carter Family song of that name. Performed in acoustic country style and sung by Jay Farrar with his typically pained and clenched-throat vocal delivery, the title song and album inspired a website and magazine called *No Depression*. By 1994, Uncle Tupelo had splintered into two new bands, Wilco (headed by Jeff Tweedy) and Son Volt (led by Jay Farrar). Neither act has remained committed to the style or approach promised by Uncle Tupelo. In fact, they have moved more closely to the rock mainstream, but they did much to unleash a broad movement of rock and country fusion. Such bands as the Old 97's, the Bottle Rockets, the Jayhawks, Whiskeytown, and the Volebeats built styles that seemed derivative of, or analogous to, the music made by Uncle Tupelo.

The Bloodshot label in Chicago popularized still another term for alternative country groups when it described its own roster of talent as "insurgent" acts. Bloodshot musicians tended to be roots-oriented but iconoclastic in their choice of songs and styles. Most of the music on the Bloodshot label carried the aura, spirit, and sound of cowpunk music. That is, it was designed to shock, arouse, or even offend. Bloodshot's owners and directors, however, seemed genuinely respectful of hard country music's past and contemptuous of contemporary Nashville's offerings. On a subsidiary label, Bloodshot Revival, they reissued recordings of classic material performed by such people as Rex Allen, Johnny Bond, Spade Cooley, Jimmie Davis, Pee Wee King, Joe Maphis, Hank Penny, and Hank Thompson. The label also issued covers of older country material performed by Bloodshot acts on such anthologies as *For a Life of Sin* and *Straight Outta Boone County*.

Even though a roots emphasis defined the music produced by Bloodshot, the company marketed its product with an aggressiveness and swagger that seemed to come right out of rock culture. Furthermore, the "roots" that most appealed to Bloodshot's directors and artists were the presumed wild and hedonistic moments in country music's past (at best, the joys of drinking and dancing the night away and, at worst, recovering from a week-long binge). The Waco Brothers, who were virtually the Bloodshot house band, performed with an infectious abandon that was eminently suited for roadhouses and rock bars. Three members of the band—including its leader, the artist Jon Langford—came from England, and they tended to view and distill American country music into a dark brew filled with whiskey, sex, and violence. Bloodshot's best-known artist, Robbie Fulks, discovered hard country music after earlier flirtations with rock, bluegrass, and folk but became an ardent student of the genre. Although Fulks performs with the frenetic spirit of punk country (reminiscent of Jason Ringenberg, who fronts a band called the Scorchers), he has exhibited an informed knowledge of, and appreciation for, older and often-obscure country entertainers (examples of this interest can be heard in his Bloodshot CD, *13 Hillbilly Greats*). His own compositions, though, tend to take jabs at some of country music's sacred cows (romantic love with "Tell Her Lies," religion with "God Isn't Real," and Nashville in "Fuck This Town").

Rock-derived musicians may have been the first to be labeled as alternative country, but the description has since been so widely applied that it can no longer be defined in terms of style. The official journal of the movement, *No Depression*, often described itself as the "alternative country (whatever that is) bimonthly." As conceived at the turn of the twenty-first century, alternative country might best be understood as any form of music that lay outside of, and in opposition to, Top Forty country music. It has been inherently anti-Nashville, although a few musicians who have been identified as alternative artists, such as Tim O'Brien and Robbie Fulks, have tried and failed to make inroads into the city's corporate recording machine. Some musicians, of course, resisted being labeled as alternative and, in fact, fashioned styles that were far different from those of the rock-country performers. For example, Mike Ireland, a Kansas City musician who had played briefly with a rock-country group called the Starkweathers (named for a Midwestern mass murderer), went completely against the alternative grain with a CD called *Learning How to Live*, recorded for the Sub Pop label. The songs included in the album were unrelievedly somber in tone, reflecting the anguish and pain wrought by his then-recent marriage breakup, and in style were closer to the country-pop of Billy Sherrill's Nashville than anything done by the alternative country groups. In decided contrast, a young Chicago band called Freakwater often ventured into the realm of old-time country. Although they sometimes demonstrated that they could rock as hard as any alternative group, the principal singers in the band, Catherine Erwin and Janet Bean, sang songs like "Put My Little Shoes Away" with close, pristine harmonies that compared favorably with versions done earlier by pioneer hillbilly bands.

An assortment of swing and rockabilly groups, such as BR5-49, the Hot Club of Cowtown, and the Derailers, also flourished in the 1990s. This music had already been presaged in the 1970s by such musicians as the Austin bands Asleep at the Wheel and Commander Cody and His Lost Planet Airmen. (One of the newer swing-rockabilly musicians, Bill Kirchen, had in fact been the guitarist on Commander Cody's famous version of "Hot Rod Lincoln.") Sometimes described as retro-country, because they dressed in costumes that suggested the 1940s or 1950s and played music from those years, members of BR5–49 were fixtures for years at Robert's Western Wear in downtown Nashville. Taking their name from the "phone number" used by Junior Samples in his car-salesman skit on *Hee Haw*, they won a large following because of their campy clothes, relentless energy, immense storehouse of songs, and shows that could extend for four hours and more. Another young band, the Hot Club of Cowtown, inaugurated their musical dreams in New York City. After a short stint in San Diego, Elana James, Whit Smith, and Jake Erwin wound up in Austin, where they knew that an audience for their blend of western swing and cowboy music existed. Out on the West Coast, a band known as Big Sandy and his Fly-Rite Boys also capitalized on the national vogue for swing music that emerged in the early 1990s. Led by vocalist Robert Williams (Big Sandy), the Fly-Rite Boys played an infectious mixture of rockabilly, rhythm-and-blues, and western swing. Still another West Coast band, the Derailers, made Austin their home and popularized a style and repertory that owed as much to Buck Owens and the Buckaroos as it did to the rockabilly style with which they had begun.

Even though the Derailers and similar groups proudly acknowledged their debt to Owens and the Buckaroos, their sound and ambience were significantly different from the music made by their heroes and other honky-tonk pioneers. Honky-tonk country has been, in many ways, the most authentic expression of working-class country music culture, but it has been the least represented among young alternative musicians, even though such artists as the Derailers and BR5-49 are sometimes identified with the honky-tonk style, since their music is most often played in bars and dance halls. But with rare exceptions, such as Dale Watson, Jim Lauderdale, and Dallas Wayne, who have recorded some good cry-in-your-beer shuffle songs, alternative country musicians have not presented the full range of emotions heard in the classic performances of George Jones, Ray Price, or even Buck Owens. These alt-country musicians can boogie or rock, but they find it difficult to wear their hearts on their sleeves. One should not expect to hear most alternative musicians sing a heartbroken lament like "He Stopped Loving Her Today" and certainly not a sentimental weeper like "Flowers for Mama." At its worst, the No Depression or insurgent style could seem like a form of slumming in a poor-white-trash neighborhood, but at its best, alternative country paid homage to styles that had been abandoned by mainstream country and often succeeded in re-creating the gritty vitality and earthiness of working-class culture.

The most vital form of alternative country music, bluegrass, has flourished since 1984 with a paradoxical but complementary blend of tradition and innovation. On one hand, bluegrass has continued to be a refuge for tradition-minded fans and musicians. On the other, it has served also as a seedbed for artistic experimentation within an acoustic context. Romantic evocations of traditional rootedness and pastoral simplicity achieve expression through superb and innovative musicianship. Finding it almost impossible to build a niche on Top Forty radio, bluegrass musicians increasingly created their own infrastructure of promotion and exposure, including small record labels, radio shows, booking agencies, journals, festivals, and two promotional organizations, the IBMA and the Society for the Preservation of Bluegrass Music in America (SPBGMA). Founded in 1985, the IBMA functions essentially as a chamber of commerce, clearinghouse, and showcase for bluegrass musicians. Thousands of people assemble each October for the annual convention, to attend a trade show, awards ceremony, and dozens of concerts, or simply to jam night after night with fellow musicians. Since 1991, when Bill Monroe, Lester Flatt, and Earl Scruggs were selected, bluegrass immortals have been inducted into the IBMA's Hall of Honor. The music as a whole is commemorated in the International Bluegrass Music Museum and Hall of Fame located in Owensboro, Kentucky, not far from Bill Monroe's birthplace in Rosine.

Long before his death on September 9, 1996, Monroe had settled comfortably into the role of patriarch of bluegrass music and had established a mellow relationship with both fans and interviewers. After his demise, the venerable Ralph Stanley assumed the role of father figure (partly because Earl Scruggs remained less active). Joined in 1995 by his son Ralph II, Stanley stayed on the road with his

Bill Monroe and Doc Watson. Courtesy of Peter Feldmann, BlueGrass West!

Clinch Mountain Boys. But while he played the banjo less and less, he nevertheless clung to his traditional style and basked in such honors as a National Heritage Fellowship and an honorary doctorate from Lincoln Memorial University in Harrogate, Tennessee. "Dr. Ralph's" haunting voice and commitment to traditional values were introduced to audiences well outside the bluegrass community through his presence on the soundtrack of the movie *O Brother, Where Art Thou?* In 2002, his stark interpretation of a song from the movie's soundtrack, "O Death," won for him the Grammy award for the Best Country Vocal Performance.

Bluegrass offered a different kind of refuge for some singers who could find little exposure elsewhere. The renewed commitment to bluegrass sounds, of course, was easy for the veteran performer Ricky Skaggs, who took to the road in 1997 with a magnificent new band, Kentucky Thunder. Skaggs's marvelous versatility, clear tenor voice, and genuine devotion to traditional music immediately vaulted him into the front ranks of bluegrass musicians. Jim Lauderdale similarly was no stranger to bluegrass, since he had performed the music early in his career before he became a valued Nashville songwriter. But two CDs recorded with Ralph Stanley exhibited his ease and familiarity

Del McCoury Band. Courtesy of Nancy Cutlip.

with the genre. On the other hand, Dolly Parton and Steve Earle had almost no prior experience with the idiom when they ventured into their bluegrass experiments in the late 1990s. Backed by an array of bluegrass's finest young musicians, Parton paid tribute to her Appalachian origins in two critically praised CDs, the Grammy-winning *The Grass Is Blue* and *The Little Sparrow*. Steve Earle also garnered much attention in 1999 when he recorded an album called *The Mountain* with the Del McCoury Band. Touting this partnership between country-rock and bluegrass as an attempt to erase the borders between the two audiences, Earle then toured with the McCourys for several months.

Virtually all bluegrass musicians have adhered to the central canon of the style: the reliance on acoustic instruments. But in their experimentation with a wide array of styles and songs, they have moved their music far beyond the classic parameters originally established by Monroe, Flatt, and Scruggs. As a result, bluegrass's innovators have generated debates concerning authenticity and direction that are similar to those encountered in the larger realm of country music. Karl Shiflett, a musician from Longview, Texas, countered the work of the "progressives" with a delightful stage show that re-created the look and sound of Lester Flatt's classic bluegrass. Del McCoury, in contrast, demonstrated that classic bluegrass music could be popular and commercial without a mere recapitulation of older styles. He emerged as the leading heir of Bill Monroe's classic sound, with his own clear high tenor style and run-filled guitar playing, and with a band that included two of his sons, Ronnie and Robbie, the fiddler Jason Carter, and the bassist Mike Bub. The combination of veteran believability, youthful good looks, outstanding musicianship, and a talent for working around a single microphone with almost-choreographed precision made the Del McCoury Band the most popular bluegrass band at the beginning of the twenty-first century.

Like the Del McCoury Band, the groups that have won the highest accolades in bluegrass music are those that convey a traditional feel, or at least pay occasional homage to the music's roots and are able to communicate that feeling with powerful, inventive musicianship and soulful vocal harmonies. The Nashville Bluegrass Band has had significant personnel changes since it was founded in 1984, but the central trio that created the group's distinctive vocal and instrumental sound—banjoist Alan O'Bryant, guitarist Pat Enright, and fiddler Stuart Duncan—have been present almost from the beginning. Capable of playing hard-driving instrumental tunes (featuring the smooth, clear tones of Duncan's fiddle), re-creating sweet brother-style vocal harmonies, or rendering note-perfect a cappella versions of old gospel songs, the Nashville Bluegrass Band built a large following with a style that fused both traditional and progressive elements.

Other popular groups, such as IIIrd Tyme Out and the Lonesome River Band, have been similarly middle-of-the-road in their styles and selection of songs but became even more popular than the Nashville Bluegrass Band among young fans. IIIrd Tyme Out—so called because its founding members, Russell Moore, Ray Deaton, and Mike Hartgrove, played in two previous bands—brought their competitive sound to the bluegrass world in 1991. From 1994 to 2000 they owned the IBMA's Vocal Group of the Year award, and Moore (probably the finest singer in bluegrass) has won two awards as the Male Vocalist of the Year. The band has always featured bedrock bluegrass fare, including stellar a cappella performances of religious pieces (a universal convention in bluegrass since Ralph Stanley introduced the practice), but they have never been reluctant to venture into nontraditional territory. Russell Moore's virtuoso version of the Platters' song "Only You" has been one of their most popular numbers.

The Lonesome River Band, originally organized in Virginia in 1983, exhibits a similar mixture of tight, inventive vocal harmonies, dynamic instrumental patterns, and skillful retooling of old-time songs to fit contemporary tastes. The band is steeped in southern musical tradition. Their banjo player, Sammy Shelor, learned a variety of old-time styles from his grandfathers, and their mandolin player and tenor singer Don Rigsby inherited from his family a large repertory of lonesome religious pieces. The featured vocalist and bass player Ronnie Bowman brought to the band a lengthy prior experience as a gospel singer. Both individually and collectively, the Lonesome River Band has been one of the most commercially successful and critically rewarded groups in bluegrass music.

While the contributions made by these all-male bands have been immeasurable, the most important new trend in the music has been what Art Menius describes as the "feminization of bluegrass." Murphy Henry (who is herself a five-string banjo player as well as the chief historian of bluegrass women)[15] argues that women have been present in this vital genre since the days of Bill Monroe's pioneering band in the mid-1940s. She cites Sally Forrester, the accordion player and wife of fiddler Howard Forrester, and a member of Monroe's seminal mid-1940s band, as the first "bluegrass woman," although women had rarely played leading or distinctive roles in this quintessentially good-old-boys style. Since the mid-1980s, however, women in growing numbers have fronted their own bands, have achieved distinction as singers and songwriters, and have demonstrated that they can play instruments as well as or better than men.

Alison Krauss was the real groundbreaker and one of the first true female superstars to emerge in the bluegrass idiom. She began experimenting with bluegrass music in about 1983, when she was only twelve years old, playing the fiddle in and around her hometown of Champaign, Illinois. By 1986, she had joined the band headed by John Pennell called Union Station; had recorded her first album, *Too Late to Cry*, for the Rounder label; and was beginning to realize that she could sing as well as she could play. Despite the strengths of her musicianship, her singing has been her ticket to fame. With a sweet, supple, and clear voice that begs comparison with the young Dolly Parton, Krauss has won recognition far outside the bluegrass community. Although she has been richly rewarded by the IBMA and the Society for the Preservation of Bluegrass Music in America, she has also garnered

Alison Krauss. Courtesy of Becky Johnson.

Grammy awards, was inducted into the *Grand Ole Opry* in 1993 (as the youngest member ever chosen and the first bluegrass performer since 1964), has been a successful producer of other people's recordings, and was selected in 1995 as the CMA's Female Vocalist of the Year. Krauss achieved these goals without ever abandoning her acoustic-based style and without the benefit of major record label support. She almost single-handedly, in fact, converted the Rounder label into a major concern.

No other woman bluegrass performer has ranged quite as far as Krauss, nor been so richly rewarded, but many have nonetheless made crucial contributions to the music's development and popularity. Sara Watkins, the fine young singer and fiddler for Nickel Creek, whose singing bears a strong resemblance to that of Alison Krauss, has become widely known to multitudes of country music fans through the popular videos made by her group. Missy Raines has not yet attained a similar genre-bending status, but she has won the IBMA's award for best bass player many times and exhibits her talent through her far-flung tours with the sensational guitarist Jim Hurst. Lynn Morris organized her own band in 1988, but only after a lengthy apprenticeship with other bands in Colorado and Virginia. This Texas-born musician originally won plaudits as a five-string banjo player, but by 1996 had won the IBMA's Female Singer of the Year award and had recorded the poignant "Mama's Hand" (written by Hazel Dickens), which won the award for Best Song of the Year.

There has been no dearth of outstanding singers among the women of bluegrass. Some of them, like Dale Ann Bradley, Hazel Dickens, Carol Elizabeth Jones, Kathy Kallick, Katie Laur, Laurie Lewis, Claire Lynch, Kate MacKenzie, Valerie Smith, Stephanie Stevenson, Suzanne Thomas, Rhonda Vincent, and Linda Williams, have versatile voices that can successfully interpret any style of music. None of them, however, are solely vocalists. Hazel Dickens, above all, has long been recognized as one of country music's greatest songwriters. Carol Elizabeth Jones, best known for her performances with her onetime husband James Leva, is a consummate songwriter who skillfully attains a traditional feel with lyrics that address the most pressing and sometimes painful current issues. Her song "The Back of Your Hand," for example, is a sensitive and subtle comment on spousal abuse. Laurie Lewis has one of the sweetest voices in bluegrass music, as well as a soulful style of fiddle playing that easily compares with that of any

Rhonda Vincent. Courtesy of Becky Johnson.

other fiddler in the genre. Rhonda Vincent's musicianship is astonishing; she plays competently almost anything with strings on it. She won the Missouri State Fiddle Contest in 1973 when she was only eleven years old and for the next twelve years or so toured with her family's band, the Sally Mountain Show. During the late 1980s, Vincent occasionally made forays into mainstream country music and even toured with Jim Ed Brown for a brief period. But by the end of the 1990s, she had returned full-time to bluegrass. With a strong, passionate style of singing; a superb command of mandolin, fiddle, and guitar; and an intelligent selection of songs, Vincent had become one of the major artists in the field. A CD released in 2000, appropriately entitled *Back Home Again*, was universally praised as the best bluegrass album of the year. Such songs as "Jolene" (from the pen of Dolly Parton), "Lonesome Wind Blues," and "Little Angels," a powerful song about child abuse, dominated the bluegrass charts throughout the year.

Progressive bluegrass, or what has often been described as "newgrass," continued to compete with more traditional varieties of the style. Bluegrass, in fact, has incubated a large and thriving body of acoustic musicians whose stylistic experimentations have stretched the limitations of anyone's definition of the form. Such musicians as

Sam Bush, John Cowan, Bela Fleck, David Grisman, Paul Kowert, Edgar Meyer, Mark O'Connor, Noam Pikelny, Tony Rice, Andy Statman, Chris Thile, and Tony Trishka are as strongly identified with jazz, blues, and rock (and even classical music, as exhibited by recordings made by O'Connor and Fleck with the legendary cellist Yo-Yo Ma, and the Bach improvisations played by Chris Thile on mandolin) as with the bluegrass style that once commanded their loyalties. And even a musician like Tim O'Brien, whose affection for traditional rural styles has been apparent, is just as comfortable with the music of Bob Dylan, Stéphane Grappelli, or Miles Davis.

The defining progressive act, the New Grass Revival, reached its artistic peak after 1981, when Sam Bush, John Cowan, Bela Fleck, and Pat Flynn combined their talents in a reconstituted version of the group. They stayed together until 1989, always eliciting positive reviews for their jazz-inflected acoustic music but never winning the kind of commercial success for which they hoped. Bush continued to be one of the most highly sought-after musicians in country music, leading Emmylou Harris's band for a brief period and eventually playing with virtually every acoustic musician in the business. Bela Fleck took the five-string banjo to new stylistic dimensions with his Flecktones, never completely abandoning bluegrass but moving far beyond the parameters of that form.

At the beginning of the new century, the chief standard bearers of the newgrass style were an ensemble of California-born musicians known as Nickel Creek—a brother and sister team, Sean and Sara Watkins (on guitar and fiddle, respectively), their longtime friend Chris Thile (on mandolin), and varying individuals on string bass. What was truly remarkable about these accomplished musicians was that, although their ages ranged from eighteen to twenty-three, Thile and the Watkinses had already been playing together for over ten years. They first encountered bluegrass at a San Diego pizza parlor frequented by their parents, and by the time Sara and Chris were only eight years old, they were sitting in with adult musicians. They may have originally attracted attention as "cute kids holding instruments," but few musicians evolved as rapidly as these sophisticated master stylists. In 2000, they were selected by the IBMA as Emerging Artists of the Year, and in 2001 were chosen as the organization's Instrumental Group of the Year.

Recognition within the bluegrass community (which was met with

Chris Thile. Courtesy of Nancy Cutlip.

New Grass Revival: left to right, *Bela Fleck, Sam Bush, John Cowan,*
Pat Flynn. © *1984 by Scott Newton/Austin City Limits.*

the predictable skepticism of traditionalists) was only one facet of the
group's astounding ascent. Their first album, *Nickel Creek* (appropriately produced by Alison Krauss, and released by Sugar Hill in 2000),
generated more positive response in the country music world than
any bluegrass CD since Krauss's own recording of 1995, *Now That I've
Found You.* Nickel Creek appeared in two popular videos on CMT,
saw such songs as "Reasons Why" and "When You Come Back Down"
enter the *Billboard* country music popularity charts, and embarked
on a whirlwind period of personal appearances (topped off by enthusiastically received concerts in 2001 at MerleFest, the giant acoustic
celebration in Wilkesboro, North Carolina).

Nickel Creek's emergence marked a major departure in bluegrass
history and spoke volumes about the kinds of listeners who responded
to country music at the beginning of the twenty-first century. Theirs
was an almost wholly urban or suburban sound. Earlier newgrass
musicians, such as David Grisman, Sam Bush, and even Bela Fleck,
had sometimes exhibited the need to dip back into vintage bluegrass
music, but the Nickel Creek musicians paid little homage to Monroe,

Flatt, or Scruggs (they in fact had no banjo in their band). A few of their songs won acceptance in mainstream country music, but one finds no songs that carry either a rural or a working-class ambience. Nickel Creek's music instead conveyed the flavor and dynamics of a jazz string quartet, tempered by a New Age sensibility, and even a touch of Contemporary Christian aesthetics. In short, it seemed to be ultra California. Each musician demonstrated a mastery of his or her respective instrument. Traditionalists may blanch at the suggestion that Chris Thile is the best mandolin player in the world (he won the IBMA's mandolin award in 2001), but he will certainly do until the best comes along. Youth and charismatic stage presence enhance his appeal, but his mandolin playing is little short of astonishing, exhibiting a seemingly effortless ability to move from a high-powered fiddle tune to a soft and sweetly nuanced love song. The Nickel Creek musicians' harmonies on songs like "When You Come Back Down" are impeccable, and Thile's vocal performance of "The Fox" is a tour de force. This perfectly articulated performance of the old Burl Ives folk song served as a vehicle for an extended jam that synchs seamlessly into a rendition of Bob Dylan's "Subterranean Homesick Blues" and then back to the original song. It is no wonder that Thile was awarded a MacArthur Fellowship in 2012, or that he would be tapped by Garrison Keillor as his successor on the *A Prairie Home Companion* show when Keillor made his long-anticipated retirement in 2016.[16]

Nickel Creek's emergence reminds us that what we saw in the years leading up to the new century was a contest that not only questioned the meaning of country music, but also asked, To whom does this music belong? Nashville does not *own* country music, even though it shapes public perceptions of what that music is. It is a terrible condescension, however, for critics to dismiss out of hand the music that emanates from Nashville studios or the Top Forty format. That music is not simply the product of a handful of musicians and producers. It is sustained by millions of listeners. To cite only one example, Tim McGraw's album *Set This Circus Down*, which leaped to the number one position on the charts during the same week of its issuance, did not generate that meteoric rise through some kind of capitalistic conspiracy that imposed it upon thousands of unwilling fans. The hosts of fans who buy McGraw's CDs, or who faithfully attend Nashville's Fan Fair each June, find something to listen to in contemporary country music that many of us reject or simply cannot hear.

On the other hand, a big wide world of country music exists outside of Nashville that many listeners never experience. Ironically, one often has to search the "folk" or "country-rock" bins at record stores, listen to National Public Radio's *A Prairie Home Companion* or the occasional documentaries on NPR, or attend venues that usually cater to rock or alternative musicians to hear the music of such compelling and roots-based entertainers as Iris DeMent, Steve Earle, Rosie Flores, Jimmie Dale Gilmore, Jim Lauderdale, Buddy and Julie Miller, Allison Moorer, Jim Watson, Gillian Welch, Robin and Linda Williams, or Kelly Willis. A diligent search, however, will introduce the curious listener to vital forms of country music alive and even thriving throughout America. Cowboy music, for example, is obviously no longer available in the movies made by Hollywood or in radio serials such as those once made by Gene Autry and Roy Rogers, but such singers as Don Edwards, Red Steagall, Ian Tyson, Michael Martin Murphey, the Sons of the San Joaquin, KG and the Ranger, and the irrepressible Riders in the Sky still spin their romantic magic in the milieu of rodeo dances, cowboy poetry gatherings, and western music conventions. Eddie Stubbs is not the only disc jockey who still plays classic country records, even though his programs probably reach more people through the powerful broadcasts of WSM in Nashville. (Fans of traditional country music were alarmed in early 2002 by ominous reports that WSM might abandon its country music format, and were relieved when it did not.) The marvelous syndicated television show *Austin City Limits* provides a national showcase for all kinds of roots musicians who find little exposure elsewhere. Folk and bluegrass festivals not only present the music of talented professionals, they also provide a context in which devoted amateurs can commune and make music with each other. For example, the Kerrville Folk Festival, founded by Rod Kennedy in 1972, about fifty miles west of Austin, still brings musical enjoyment to thousands of people each summer and serves as a launching pad for new singers.

Visitors to such giant gatherings as San Francisco's Hardly Strictly Bluegrass Festival (funded by the investment banker Warren Hellmann and so named because its parameters extend far beyond the field of bluegrass) and MerleFest (founded in memory of Doc Watson's son and held each April in Wilkesboro, North Carolina), will typically hear the cream of America's acoustic musical crop. Regrettably, they will no longer be able to see and hear the music of the nation's greatest traditional musician, Doc Watson, who passed away on May 29, 2012. Watson had become virtually an icon in American popular culture, sustained not by the country music industry but by legions of youthful fans who admired his musicianship and integrity.

MerleFest, of course, is not free (in contrast to the Hardly Strictly Bluegrass Festival), and the entertainers who gather there are talented professionals. But we need to be reminded of an additional truth: country music does not belong solely to the professionals. It endures anywhere that music is made for enjoyment, self-fulfillment, or diversion—in people's homes, at festivals and workshops, in churches, in the jam sessions held in VFW and American Legion halls and other public settings, in small-town opries and jamborees, or in the dance halls and honky-tonks where part-time musicians seek refuge from their day jobs. In these local settings, we find earnest and enthusiastic amateurs trying hard to emulate what they saw and heard on a Shania Twain or Tim McGraw video, as well as musicians who can sing and play every song that Bill Monroe or Hank Williams ever made. If country music endures and preserves distinctiveness, it will do so through the devoted efforts of such loyal fans and local performers.

CHAPTER 13

A New Century

O f all the changes in country music as it entered the twenty-first century, at least one element remained constant: the question of what constitutes "real" country. The question may, in fact, be country music's single most enduring aspect, past or present. It emerged fully in the static over Bob Wills and His Texas Playboys using drums on the *Grand Ole Opry* during the 1940s. It gained traction with the rise of a full-fledged business industry in Nashville, even more particularly with the Nashville sound in the 1960s and its self-consciously crafted bid for post-rock-and-roll audiences. "What is real country music?" At issue is a question of balance between commercial viability and genuine expression, innovation and authenticity. These form a narrow passageway, a veritable Scylla and Charybdis, through which twenty-first-century country musicians must navigate. In so doing, each searches for ways to expand fan base and broaden appeal without seeming to kowtow to every fleeting fad. The extent to which a song or artist appears to push boundaries as an organic result of artistic exploration versus a deliberate bid for mass appeal can become a subtle distinction to clarify. Such efforts can be subject to harsh skepticism.

In the twenty-first century, the question of "what's real" in country hovers over general trends, like the one critics of contemporary stars

Luke Bryan on July 15, 2014. © Midwest Communications;
courtesy of Midwest Communications.

like Luke Bryan or Sam Hunt dub "bro country." It likewise frames debates over specific moments like the striking performance of "Daddy Lessons" by pop phenomenon Beyoncé ("Bey" to her fans) and the Dixie Chicks during the 2016 Country Music Association (CMA) Awards ceremony. Sparring about bro country and hand-wringing about "Daddy Lessons" are modern manifestations of a perennial contest. They enter the same cycle of vexation fueled by past media developments like format radio, industry organizations like the CMA or the Academy for Country Music (ACM), controversial award recipients like John Denver and Olivia Newton-John, and series of movements and subgenres: progressive country, the "outlaw movement," the "urban cowboy" trend, the neo-traditionalists, stadium country, roots country, alt-country. They all point to debate about the definition and boundaries of country music and tension over who guards its gates of access. While the question remains largely intact for the new millennium, the ground over which it plays out has shifted.

"Bro country" is a tag for music that sidesteps the potential human depth of country music's thematic bedrocks: family, home, nostalgia, simplicity, love, heartbreak, natural beauty, good-timing, drinking, hard work. Instead, bro country songs string together a formulaic subset of tropes about beer sipping, truck driving, sunglasses wearing, unpaved roads, and tanned girls in shorts, typically building to a predictable catchphrase singsong chorus. In short, it is the contemporary version of country music's recurrent consternation about "realness." Whether from a lack of sincerity or talent, "bro country" connotes a failure to successfully navigate the channel between sincerity and commercial appeal by caricaturing artists as less sophisticated or less capable than their more artistically accomplished peers. For critics, the issue with bro country is not its themes per se: beer drinking and country roads are at the heart of many classic country songs. Moreover, country music tradition depends on set themes, musical timbres, stylistic gestures, and wardrobe cues. Bro country, however, lingers at the shallow end of the pool, never venturing too deep. For its lack of depth, it draws detractors and parodists from both inside and outside the larger pool.

Maddie and Tae's "Girl in a Country Song" (2014), for example, makes fun of familiar bro country clichés. The duo sings, "We used to get a little respect, now we're lucky if we even get / to climb up in your truck, keep our mouth shut and ride along / and be the girl in a country song." They call out George Strait and Conway Twitty as icons of a musical past when men did know how to sing about the women in their lives. In the song's video, stereotypical images of young women in cutoffs, or *"Hee Haw* honey"–type outfits, switch to scenes of three somewhat homely men strutting around in ill-fitting clothes, preening and purring and washing cars in slow motion—all flip-flops of the stuff of bro country video. The millennial comedian Bo Burnham likely had some bro country hits in mind when he worked up his stand-up comedy spoof. Burnham takes biting aim at country stars he paints as out-of touch millionaires, quick to trade honesty for lists of pandering catchphrases. As he delivers in a convincing baritone lilt: "I write songs about riding tractors from the comfort of a private jet," and "I write songs for the people who do / jobs in the towns that I'd never move to."

The performance of "Daddy Lessons" at the 2016 CMA Awards became a more singular focal point for contemporary debate about country music. In this instance, the question centered as much on who was performing as it did on the content of the song itself. "Daddy

Lessons" features a steady, two-stepping beat driven by rhythm guitar and light rimshots. Its lyrical hook, "Oh, my Daddy said shoot," frames a vignette about a father coaching his daughter to be tough, to maintain personal wherewithal, and to defend herself when it comes to men: "Girl, it's your second amendment." The song is straightforward, set off by a simple electric guitar solo, which turns the verse midway through. The live CMA Awards performance with the Dixie Chicks fleshed out the relatively stripped-down sound of the original version with musicians sprawled across the stage: extra backup singers; a four-piece horn section punctuating with New Orleans–style licks; several percussionists, including a washboard player, a mandolin, and two additional guitar players to support the Chicks' trio of banjo, fiddle, and guitar. Hand claps drive the two-step groove, with vocals trading off between Beyoncé and the Dixie Chicks. A bluesy harmonica weaves its way in sonic bursts throughout, and the performance peaks as the baritone sax player dances his way through a solo. This builds to a horn section vamp, leading, in turn, to a fiddle transition into a quotation from the Dixie Chicks' song "Long Time Gone" (2002). "Daddy Lessons" spins out from this to close with a growling, energetic-unto-ecstatic finish.

"Daddy Lessons" first appeared earlier the same year on *Lemonade*, a singular concept album "dropped" via an hour-long video with no advance publicity in April 2016. Each song on *Lemonade* progresses through different stages of coping with spousal infidelity, presumably from Beyoncé's autobiographical perspective. Other voices contribute to the artistic whole as well, notably the poet Warsan Shire, whose words Beyoncé speaks between musical sections. A label precedes each section, progressing from intuition to resurrection—with denial, anger, apathy, and forgiveness in between—and each song explores a different musical style, ranging from rhythm and blues to reggae to hip-hop. "Daddy Lessons" is the album's country song, the chapter labeled "Accountability."

This CMA performance sparked a predictable buzz. Is "Daddy Lessons" a country song or not, and by what criteria do audiences decide: lyrical content, vocal delivery style, instrumental arrangement, structure, rhythm? Do the same criteria apply to other performers and other songs on the same showcase, or does personal identity have something to do with it? People took to the Internet to argue over whether or not the song belonged. Even before then, back in

Beyoncé and the Dixie Chicks performing at the CMA Awards on November 2,
2016. © Disney/ABC Television; Creative Commons Attribution-NoDerivs 2.0,
www.creativecommons.org/licenses/by-nd/2.0/legalcode.

mid-April when *Lemonade* first debuted, commentators weighed in
on CMT.com, the Country Music Television website, arguing one way
or the other: its acoustic guitar, rhythm, and emotional authenticity
qualified it as a solid country song; or, to the contrary, its yeehawin'
nods to Texas were only surface-level gestures and, quoting one *CMT*
writer, "This song is no more country than her 'Single Ladies (Put a
Ring on It).'" Fast-forward to the end of 2016 when, as the *No Depression* writer Brittney McKenna noted, the collaborative performance
reopened debate.

Vanderbilt professor Alice Randall wrote a web piece for *American
Songwriter* whose publication roughly coincided with the televised
performance. Randall is both a novelist (*The Wind Done Gone*) and
country songwriter (coauthor with Matraca Berg on Trisha Yearwood's hit "XXX's and OOO's (An American Girl)"), and a thoughtful
commentator on country music. In that piece, she affords full country
props to "Daddy Lessons" and compares the song to Miranda Lambert's "Gunpowder and Lead."[1] Randall places "Daddy Lessons" and
"Gunpowder and Lead" in the genre's highest echelon, contrasting

their emotional realness with the comparatively bland sounds and empty choruses of "bro country." As she writes it, "Everything's always alright in bro-country land. Never anything wrong a pretty girl and a drink can't fix. Like Haggard, Cash, and Jennings, Miranda and Bey know better."

The juxtaposition of artists from different genres was not new in 2016, on the CMA Awards or elsewhere. It is a common strategy to invigorate the ceremonial occasion, driven by television's inherent quest for yet another big event. Major award shows stage cross-genre collaborations so often it is no longer a surprise. On the previous year's CMA Awards, for instance, the pop sensation Justin Timberlake performed with Chris Stapleton, and "emo" rock band Fall Out Boy with Thomas Rhett. These performances often cross generations, too, as when Dolly Parton sang with pop singer Katy Perry during the ACM Awards. These performances can come across as artistically genuine, or they can seem wooden or forced. As a medium, television can be particularly challenging in this regard.

The show *Crossroads* is one ongoing example of television with musical cross-pollination as its raison d'être. Beginning in January 2002 on Country Music Television (CMT), *Crossroads* airs sporadically, meaning it avoids the dangers of mediocrity that a regular schedule might encourage. Notably, the idea originated outside the country music business, with the Manhattan-based entertainment executive and storied music journalist Bill Flanagan, already successful with programs for the VH1 channel. Each episode pairs a country artist with a performer from another genre. Its pilot featured Lucinda Williams performing with Elvis Costello. In 2016, *Crossroads* aired five episodes, including classic rockers Cheap Trick paired onstage with Jennifer Nettles, and R&B diva Alicia Keys performing with country music newcomer Maren Morris.

Television is not the only medium primed in the twenty-first century to explore what happens when artists mix it up in musical ways. It is not unusual to encounter audio and video recording projects by artists across genres, across generations, or both. The duet "Over and Over" (2004), for example, brought together the rapper Nelly and the country musician Tim McGraw. "Superman" (2012) was among the handful of joint efforts between the West Coast rapper and pop culture personality Snoop Dogg and Willie Nelson. Perhaps the most outstanding collaboration of this type was the Loretta Lynn album

Van Lear Rose (2004), produced in collaboration with rock's enfant terrible Jack White.

White exemplifies a twenty-first-century type of musician whose omnivorous musical imagination was shaped by digital access to stores of past American music.[2] He played guitar throughout the album, but the standout track is "Portland, Oregon," the duet he and Lynn sing together. The song sets Lynn's still-powerful country inflection against White's blues rock vocals and hard psychedelic rock musical setting. White's aesthetic vision bridged not only genres but technology as well. He recorded *Van Lear Rose* on only eight tracks to communicate a quality of authenticity shared across classic rock and traditional country. Furthermore, as he told CMT in an April 2004 interview, he aimed for single takes in order to keep the music "as real as possible, because that's what Loretta Lynn is."

Beyoncé and the Dixie Chicks together onstage, then, both typifies and exemplifies a twenty-first-century trend of musical cross-pollination and influences blending. On the level of aesthetics, it was an emotionally and artistically genuine performance. Yet, it's no contrived genre mash-up, but a powerful assertion that genre divisions are contrived in the first place. This assertion was deliberate and embodied: Beyoncé submitted "Daddy Lessons" to the Recording Academy as a candidate for Best Country Song that year, but her moment with the Dixie Chicks at the 2016 CMA Awards made that candidacy real. The song, the performers, the moment—all together, they invite a deeper exploration of the question "What is real country music?" in ways that intersect with race, politics, and gender in the twenty-first century.

What did it mean for the new century's most sensational pop music performer, an African American woman, to appear on the CMA Awards, a context still so closely associated with whiteness? Was the performance a juxtaposition of divergent musical worlds, an insertion (and not the first) of blackness into a white musical genre, or a timely acknowledgment of the deeply intertwined nature of white and black musical styles in the United States? Despite a handful of twenty-first-century exceptions, like Darius Rucker or Cowboy Troy or Valerie June, country music artists remain predominantly white, still locked in conceptually to the racialized framework established during the 1920s, at the start of the popular music record industry.

Despite historical, artistic evidence of the deeply tangled roots of "hillbilly" and "race" music, as it was christened in the beginning, whiteness continues to define country music. Still, black artists challenge that organically with their oeuvre and repertoire: performances by DeFord Bailey or Tina Turner, whose solo debut was a country record; more recent roots revival groups like the Carolina Chocolate Drops, who keep alive the long tradition of African American string band music; the black character Clay, introduced in 2016 on the CMT primetime drama *Nashville*: these and other examples push against the stubborn, racially bifurcated framework set in place nearly a century ago. Nevertheless, whiteness continues to remain a defining trait at the center of twenty-first-century country music identity.

Another question gets even more specific: What did it mean for Beyoncé to perform with the Dixie Chicks, whose status as political lightning rods shaped much of their twenty-first-century musical career? This performance at the CMAs was their first on a major mainstream country stage in more than a decade. The Dixie Chicks had been unofficially excluded from the industry after an off-the-cuff remark about President George W. Bush created a folderol far out of proportion to a twelve-word slapdash. At a March 2003 London concert, the group's lead singer, Natalie Maines, said, "Just so you know, we're on the good side with y'all. We do not want this war, this violence, and we're ashamed that the president of the United States is from Texas." The last part of the quip got reported in a UK newspaper. It was then picked up by US news sources and overblown in ways that mirror a more general downward spiral of substantive public discourse. The backlash took several forms: destroying Dixie Chicks CDs at protest-style rallies, banning the Dixie Chicks and deriding them on radio, and the group's contemporary Toby Keith admonishing them on Fox News.

In an age of 24/7 news and intense media scrutiny, sound-bite-sized fragments of information—decontextualized and underanalyzed—get circulated instantaneously. Like a flint ready to spark fire, these knee-jerk, emotion-infused sound bites fan flames of contention so that politics, including political discussion of music, has veered away from nuance and reasonable debate. "Us" versus "them" plays out in media discussions of country music as much as it does in politics. The result is a kind of hardening of ideological arteries, a political senility that threatens the processes of compromise that have grounded US democracy since its inception. Maines's remark and the fallout over it occupied journalists and scholars off and on for more than a decade, underscoring distinctive aspects of modern media, modern politics, and modern country music. There was little gray area in the controversy surrounding the Dixie Chicks in this context: they threatened the core American values of deference to the president from one point of view, or exercised the core American value of dissenting free expression from another.

It is not the engagement with politics that stands out in the Dixie Chicks incident. Country music mixed with civic affairs early on, for example, when Texas governor Pappy O'Daniel or two-time Louisiana governor Jimmie Davis, a country music legend in his own right, used music to further their campaigns. Political associations began to calcify, however, when Nixon conflated country music's characteristic themes of family, religious faith, and patriotism with the views of his so-called "silent majority." Reagan further cemented the relationship between right-wing politics and country music's typical nostalgia for home and celebration of ordinary, everyday life. Since then, partisan assumptions about country performers and audiences have obfuscated the music's more nuanced historical relationship to politics.

Even observers deeply familiar with country music's complex past can fall prey to generalizations about its politics being monolithic. The late music journalist Chet Flippo, writing early about the Dixie Chicks flap for his "Nashville Skyline" column in 2003, characterized country music fans as a "largely conservative and patriotic" cardboard stereotype.[3] The column brought him some respectful reminders, which he had the grace and good sense to post, that to oversimplify is to do injustice to the complexity of both country music audiences and patriotism alike. Three years later, the *New York Times* music critic Kelefa Sanneh looked for greater nuance in writing about their post-controversy album *Taking the Long Way*. Sanneh proposed that the Dixie Chicks had broken a "contract" with country fans that centered on a sustained "make-believe" connection to "mythical rural life."[4] It was less that Maines dismissed President Bush and more that she stepped outside the team-country-versus-team-city role of country music, forwarding an imagined southern rural ethos.

Offset by parentheses, Sanneh notes that "for female stars being outspoken carries particular risks." His punctuation glosses over what may well be the crux of the whole matter: the Dixie Chicks controversy was distinctively gendered in a way that illuminates larger issues for women in country music. Social and cultural analysts from a variety of perspectives noticed this as well. The political scientist Lesley Pruitt, for instance, compared the media coverage of the Dixie Chicks—often portraying them as immature, irrational, or worse—to the emphasis on Willie Nelson's courage to speak his mind via the antiwar song "Whatever Happened to Peace on Earth?" (2004). The philosopher Claire Katz examined a persistent social undercurrent that denies women agency to speak out regarding public affairs. CMT avoided airing Dixie Chicks while scheduling a special that featured Bruce Springsteen's protest songs.

Personal opinions from women regarding public affairs were subject to censure just at a time when artistic expression was more wide open than ever before. The Dixie Chicks mark a definite milestone in that history of country music women, whose range of expressive options were finally opening up to a broader acceptance early pioneers could not have fathomed. When Kitty Wells recorded the relatively polite "answer song" about male culpability ("It Wasn't God Who Made Honky-Tonk Angels," 1952), she was banned temporarily from NBC radio as well as the *Grand Ole Opry*.[5] Loretta Lynn's anthem of female reproductive agency ("The Pill," 1975), while nevertheless a chart success, inspired a similarly reactionary response.

These early precedents of songs about female empowerment cleared the way for women in country music, the Dixie Chicks included. The 1990s had seen the flourishing of what *Paste* magazine dubbed "country girl power songs." Published in April 2016, their list of twenty-one includes voices from both the center and the periphery of mainstream musical success. Songs range from party-anthem celebrations (Shania Twain's "Man! I Feel Like a Woman") to middle-aged musings on where different choices in youth might have led (Reba McEntire, "Is There Life Out There"). The list includes agonizing revelations of long-hidden sexual abuse (Iris DeMent, "Letter to Mom") and resolutions to leave an unfulfilling relationship (Chely Wright, "She Went Out for Cigarettes"). In its expression of vigilante justice toward spousal abusers, Martina McBride's "Independence Day" (1994) was a more direct precedent for "Goodbye Earl," the breakthrough hit for the Dixie Chicks.[6] "Goodbye Earl" was a cover of a song originally recorded by the all-male Sons of the Desert. Its lyrics, which lightheartedly describe two women resolving to kill an abusive spouse, sparked small *Thelma and Louise*–style flutters of reaction at the same time that it won the trio audiences even outside the normal

Miranda Lambert on July 15, 2014. © Midwest Communications;
courtesy of Midwest Communications.

country music crowd. Its success carried them from a decade playing
gigs like the Pillsbury Bakeoff to becoming the all-time best-selling
female musical ensemble.

The Dixie Chicks and other 1990s acts ushered in twenty-first-
century country music artists like Gretchen Wilson and Miranda Lambert, who furthered the musical claim for women to inhabit a full range
of human emotion. Wilson's "Homewrecker" (2004), for example,
recalls the spirit and sentiment of Loretta Lynn's "Fist City" (1968),
replacing Lynn's two-step feel with a 1970s southern rock vibe, colored
country by a prominent steel guitar. "One Bud Wiser" demonstrates a
similar kind of historic musical attunement. In this song, Wilson not
only veers topically into traditionally male territory of liquor-soaked
despair but places herself squarely in the middle of country music's
core lineage through musical inflection: When the song's protagonist
drops a quarter in the jukebox to play "Golden Ring," Wilson delivers
the next line ("placed my order with the guy") with a distinctively
George Jones inflection, particularly on the word "guy." This song and

others like it ("Here for the Party," for instance) push against gendered expectations with lyrics about depressed drinking, fighting for the fun of it, and rowdy partying—all the traditional purview of men. In addition to her song topics, Wilson's direct allusion to musical predecessors and her use of colloquialisms and swear words like "hell" and "damn," further stand out as practices more typical of male artists.[7]

In her album *Kerosene*, Miranda Lambert asserts a tough, self-reliant feminine voice: unwilling to sit at home and hope her man does the right thing, and equally unwilling to stand by her man if it turns out he doesn't deserve it. In the song "Hell on Heels," the protagonist swindles a no-good man out of his goods. Lambert's "Gunpowder and Lead" (2007) revisits the more serious framework of domestic violence with finality via lyrics that describe the female character of the song waiting for the perpetrator to return and her intent to "pull the trigger." Murder ballads and other dark-toned story songs enjoy a long history in country music. Yet twenty-first-century women were the first to avoid gendered static when singing edgier country material. In general, they enjoy more latitude to explore not only love, faithfulness, broken hearts, and weakness but also empowerment, autonomy, anger, and even revenge.

It may be a sign of progress that the contemporary superstar Carrie Underwood can sing lyrics about taking a baseball bat to a former lover's personal property in an act of outrage and not be subject to scorn. Perhaps women in country music enjoy greater receptivity for a broad range of emotional and lyrical content. Perhaps Underwood's publicity engine, in keeping with the history of country music women, takes pains to distinguish her from the song's persona. The scholar Kate Heidemann points out how Wells and other early country music women offset public pressure by emphasizing their "real selves" in contrast. Media support behind Underwood highlights her small-town roots and love of family. These elements not only contrast the cold-blooded character of the song but also offset the extent to which her pop diva sound and her pathway to success contrast with traditional notions of country music female stardom. Perhaps Underwood's repertoire balances out the vindictive sentiment of "Before He Cheats" with tearjerker vignettes like "Jesus, Take the Wheel" or "Temporary Home."

Regardless of its explanation, rising tides of acceptance for female wherewithal in country music do not cover the whole picture in the twenty-first century. Barriers based solely on their gender still exist for women in the business. The radio ratings consultant Keith Hill made that powerfully clear during a March 2015 interview for the industry rag *Country Aircheck Weekly*. In what came to be called "tomato-gate" during a stir he inspired, Hill asserted that a playlist database should include a sparse number of female artists—he named 19 percent as the maximum—if a radio station wants to succeed.[8] Women, then, were the tomatoes in his male lettuce-based salad. In a follow-up online interview with Alison Bonaguro for CMT, Hill clarified his position as hard-boiled: the clear-eyed perspective of country radio's goal to sell records, not to promote tradition or address social imbalance. Bonaguro offered up equally troubling statements the consultant made about the viability of female country music, such as "I don't know why people want to gargle glass and eat razor blades when there's donuts and salad."[9] Whether or not Hill truly meant that analogy as his industry opinion on the gender difference in music, he made it clear that impediments remain for country music women.

Those obstacles and barriers were not, however, in view during the 2016 CMA Awards performance by Beyoncé and the Dixie Chicks. Watching those six-plus minutes unfold felt like a momentary pause—a chance to glimpse musical possibilities that might be reframed or reimagined outside rigid associations of race, politics, or gender. Other aspects of the CMA Awards that year point to questions about style and the definition of mainstream for country music in the new century. For the ninth year in a row, Carrie Underwood and fellow superstar Brad Paisley hosted. These two strike a balance for their good-natured rapport and easy affability. Both are played over mainstream country radio, and both resonate broadly with audiences. If country music is a pool with a deep end and a shallow end, then it also has a middle. Underwood and Paisley dwell there together, despite conspicuous differences in their styles. Since winning the televised talent search contest *American Idol* in 2005, Underwood has scored consistent hits that typify "hot new country" Top Forty radio. Soaked in sentiment or dripping with attitude, her songs fit the new country framework of power pop anthems sometimes dressed with a touch of steel guitar or fiddle accent. Thus, they descend from the country-pop stylists of the previous century, the same thread of country music that some writers refer to as "soft-shell" country.

Brad Paisley was once named by the popular music critic Robert

Brad Paisley and Carrie Underwood hosting the 2016 CMA Awards on November 2, 2016. © Disney/ABC Television Group; Creative Commons Attribution-NoDerivs 2.0, www.creativecommons.org/licenses/by-nd/2.0/legalcode.

Christgau as one of Nashville's "most reliable" artists. His first release, *Who Needs Pictures* (1999), established him as a fresh voice, a perpetuator of country music traditions, and a descendant of hard-core predecessors. Paisley's albums demonstrate stylistic variety, mixing country dance numbers, shuffles, up-tempo love songs, a Bakersfield-inspired guitar boogie, and tunes of heartbreak—all carried along with fiddles, steel guitar, or barroom-style piano. He consistently includes an instrumental track and a gospel number. A song like "It Never Woulda Worked Out Anyway" (1999), off the debut album, features a short series of jazzlike solo guitar riffs. On the song "I've Been Better" (1999), Paisley takes in equal measures of Marty Robbins and Jimmy Buffet (who, in turn, internalized their own influences from Juan Vargas and Mighty Sparrow, mariachi and calypso, respectively). Legends like George Jones, Bill Anderson, Jimmy Dickens, and Dolly Parton join Paisley on musical tracks as well as on outtakes, hidden tracks, and humorous audio skits like the "Kung Pao Buckaroos" that call to mind old radio barn dance banter.

While respecting the past in overt musical ways, Paisley avoids coming across as stuck in it. Country music history is one relevant part of a larger and vital American cultural fabric. Thus, even as he collaborates with legends like Roger Miller or Charlie Daniels, he also records with contemporary country artists such as Dierks Bentley or Hunter Hayes (on *Wheelhouse* from 2013) or, more recently, with former Disney pop singer Demi Lovato on the song "Without a Fight" (2016). Alongside songs that establish his feel for older traditional styles, Paisley will also record a clever party anthem such as "Alcohol" (which includes the sing-out line "helps white people dance") or a sentimental rock-style ballad like "Waitin' on a Woman." Furthermore, one also hears influences in his music from other genres: a Joe Walsh/ Eagles guitar lick ("She's Everything"), a bit of Joni Mitchell's "Little Green" in "Out in the Parking Lot," and a touch of Jackson Browne falsetto in the sad tune "Rainin' You."

In general, Paisley's songwriting conveys appreciation for country music's typical emphasis on storyteller's detail: the story of a lost love captured in the image of an old camera with undeveloped film, or a stepfather's nurturing conveyed by way of his reflection in the neonatal ward window. He is willing to venture outside typical love-and-heartbreak-centered topics that dominate country and other popular music genres. *American Saturday Night* (2009), for example, includes a song expressing wonder and optimism over the election of Barack Obama, and joy over the motley and multicultural nature of US national identity and pastimes. The story song "Karate" from *Wheelhouse* (2013) manages to work humorous wordplay (she's secretly earning a "black belt to match her black eye") into an otherwise serious song about domestic abuse. "Accidental Racist" was a collaboration of questionable artistic success with rapper LL Cool J, noteworthy for attempting to directly address racism in the United States.

Paisley's reach extends outside music. For example, "Death of a Married Man"/"Harvey Bodine," again from *Wheelhouse*, takes gleeful delight in weaving in the comedic British voice of Monty Python's Eric Idle. A song about playing arcade video games in the 1980s incorporates Pac-Man-evoking audio. A hidden track features William Shatner's famous breathy voice telling listeners that the record is over. All in all, Paisley belongs to a generation of musicians maturing as artists just in an age when digital technology, beginning with the compact disc, made stores of pop culture's past freely and easily available. Alongside many of his contemporaries, Paisley takes elements of this musical and cultural pedigree—as much Eagles as George Jones, and as much old-school *Star Trek* as *Hee Haw*—and integrates, juxtaposes, mashes up. In this way he exemplifies one new-century type of country music artist.

Carrie Underwood represents contemporary country music trends less for the sound of her music than for her artistic persona and pathway to success. By emerging via television's *Idol*, Underwood bypassed established channels to country music stardom. In that alone, she shakes up prior-century assumptions about country music style as fundamentally an inheritance, a birthright of hard-luck station. The course of her *Idol* victory demanded that she cover wide stylistic ground, from McBride's "Independence Day" to a disco-infused cover of "MacArthur Park" à la Donna Summer; from Pat Benatar's rocker "Love Is a Battlefield" to "Hello, Young Lovers" from the Broadway musical *The King and I*. The idea that a performer could or should move effectively from an R&B crooner like "If You Don't Know Me By Now" to the 1980s power pop ballad "Making Love Out of Nothing at All" sets the stage to redefine what it means when that same singer becomes a country music superstar.

Underwood, then, stands for a twenty-first-century conception of style that can be called the *American Idol* proposition: that, like a mask, musical style is a set of characteristics or codes the most gifted performers can put on or take off at will. In its format and its expectations for contestants, *American Idol* asserts porous boundaries between one genre and the next. The competing TV talent contest *The Voice* assembles its panel of celebrity judges in a manner that similarly posits musical style as a fluid continuum. The country performer Blake Shelton presides with contemporaries from a breadth of genres—Adam Levine, Christina Aguilera, CeeLo Green, or producer Pharrell Williams. Country music becomes one set of features to employ or slough off at will. Thus, Taylor Swift can stake out country music as a marketable category for her early singer-songwriter style, then shake off these trappings for a more dance-oriented pop music persona. Cyndi Lauper can evolve from a 1980s pop music icon to write a Broadway-style musical and then record a country music album. Lady Gaga shifts from an electronic dance-pop hit with lyrics decrying rigid gender binaries to croon with nonagenarian jazz vocal stylist Tony Bennett on American songbook standards. She, too, turned out a country tune, then moved on.

These artists each demonstrate an unmooring of style. They meld their tastes, experiences, and influences into a unique sound and public persona, sometimes difficult to pinpoint in terms of genre, and sometimes temporary. Framing an artist within the bounds of "country music" might hinge on, say, verbal accent or attire, or that musician's associations within the music industry. Even within a given genre, country music included, style is increasingly syncretic, idiosyncratic, individual, and malleable in ways distinct from twentieth-century predecessors. What once may have been fluency across styles has morphed into something different: a fluidity between styles.

An iconic performer like Hank Williams, for example, absorbed broad influences to shape his individual artistry, from a 1920s vaudeville song to a Cajun tune like "Grand Texas." Ray Charles demonstrated fluency across styles when he recorded *Modern Sounds in Country and Western Music* in 1962. There he revealed close relationships between different streams of American music and the joys that can come from reimagining a classic from one genre in the style of another. An aging Johnny Cash recorded a devastatingly effective cover of "Hurt," a song by the rock group Nine Inch Nails. In these examples, the performer's individual style and the timbres and gestures that delineate that performer's genre transform and reinvent the outside material. This differs from the chameleonlike shifts displayed by some twenty-first-century performers, those who proceed according to the *American Idol* proposition.

Jason Aldean, for example, was already known for "hick-hop," a fusion *Rolling Stone* magazine traces back to the Bellamy Brothers' "Country Rap" (1987). Aldean had previously scored a hit with "Dirt Road Anthem" when he performed it with the hip-hop artist Ludacris during the 2011 CMT Awards. This was another example of cross-genre collaboration. In this case, the performance led them to rerelease the song as a remix and sparked ongoing collaborations for personal appearances and one another's recordings. When Aldean lent his voice for the chorus of "Burning Bridges" on the album *Ludaversal*, he embodied the *American Idol* proposition. Aldean actually shifts to a place in his singing voice that stretches the limits of recognition. It would be hard to imagine Hank Williams or Ray Charles taking so fluid or malleable an approach to style. If Paisley is a "reliable country artist," it may be because it is equally difficult to imagine his attempting a classic Broadway role in the way Underwood did for the December 2013 live televised version of *The Sound of Music*.

As revealing as it is to consider some of the artists on the CMA Awards stage in 2016, it is equally telling to consider who was not there. Sturgill Simpson was conspicuously absent despite the fact that he is among the best country singers of the early twenty-first century. Simpson's music orbits within the world of Americana and not in official country music industry circles. Simpson embodies the musical breadth of Americana, which attempts to draw new lines, new means for categorizing musicians and their work. His second album, *Metamodern Sounds in Country Music* (2014), a titular tip of the hat to Ray Charles's precedent, is a case in point. Intellectually and musically rich, the album journeys from country guitar boogie to two-steps, from up-tempo gospel to folk rock. The song "Turtles All the Way Down" sets out with a steel guitar–heavy setting and a straight-ahead country delivery in Simpson's deep, Waylon-esque baritone. The words pair Eastern philosophical and Western Judeo-Christian religious imagery, with reference to reptile aliens worked in for good measure. The song peaks at the bridge when the music takes a psychedelic turn and the lyrics drive home the message that only love matters in the end.

Lyrics for other songs take on topics like the vacuity of words in a media-saturated contemporary world. "Living the Dream" muses on God in expansive ways, making room for both "he" and "she" within God's magnitude, and doing so via a remarkable rhyme: "That old man upstairs, he wears a crooked smile / staring down at the chaos he created / He said 'son, if you ain't having fun just wait a little while / Momma's gonna wash it all away / and she thinks Mercy's overrated.'" Psychedelic sounds return later in the form of a backward loop extending the ending of "Just Let Go" and leading directly into "It Ain't All Flowers," the album's last song. Simpson's next album, *A Sailor's Guide to Earth*, continues to navigate wide pools of influence with a general spirit one writer dubbed "funky tonk" for its compelling preponderance of powerful soul horn licks.[10] Midway through, Simpson executes a highly original cover of "In Bloom," a song by the iconic 1990s grunge band Nirvana.

As much for his music, Simpson epitomizes Americana for his spirit. Generally distinguished from other categories by some aspect of sound, topical content, politics, or age, Americana artists share in common a quality of substance or sincerity more than musical

Sturgill Simpson in performance. © Vivian Wang; Creative Commons Attribution-NoDerivs 2.0, www.creativecommons.org/licenses/by-nd/2.0/legalcode.

specifics. The absence of overdetermined musical boundaries may be Americana's greatest conceptual strength, and this aspect has a historical beginning in the emergence of roots music during the 1990s. Roots music was a parent concept for any number of "alternative" ways to categorize music outside labels inherited from the 1920s. "Roots" connoted a sense of contrast to a perceived commercial mainstream and could freely append to other genres—among them, roots rock, roots blues, roots reggae, roots gospel. "Roots" communicated that the performing musicians were grounded to some degree in awareness of the music's history.

The parent concept brought forth a more differentiated offspring in alt-country, sometimes written "alt.country" in a technology-inflected nod to the early "listservs" that linked enthusiasts. Informal webs of communication led in 1995 to the beginning of a flagship publication, the magazine *No Depression*. This boosted the staying power of alt-country in ways missing from other types of roots music. *No Depression* was named for the debut album by the seminal alt-country band Uncle Tupelo, which was, in turn, named for the historical 1930s recording by the Carter Family. The magazine's tagline— "The Alternative Country (Whatever That Is) Bimonthly"—captured the genre's deliberate ambiguity and flexibility. In its elusive musical boundaries, alt-country was Americana's forebear. Its aural qualities became one musical subset contained within Americana: traditional country instrumentation, rock-influenced rhythms and tempos, an emphasis on virtuosity, and an adventurous aesthetic approach.

Alt-country conveyed discernment with regard to the question of what constitutes real country music versus dull pabulum pushed by people seated behind corporate desks at major labels. It also picked up, as the music scholars Barbara Ching and Pamela Fox point out, some conceptual baggage along the way. Alt-country could only engage country music's tradition of evangelical Christian gospel songs, for example, with an overt sense of irony. Furthermore, alt-country fascination with the past could easily devolve into "fetishization," or surface engagement with music of a few key figures—specifically Hank Williams, George Jones, and Merle Haggard. That its models and heroes were almost always men circumscribed (or re-circumscribed) alt-country as a hip, alternative space that, despite access granted to a handful of notable female performers like Iris Dement, Lucinda Williams, Emmylou Harris, and Gillian Welch, was strongly gendered male.[11]

Americana maintained the alt-country associations with artful craft, emotional authenticity, and historical awareness, minus its veneer of irony or its gendered and racialized hipsterism. Its widened musical scope mirrored the path of *No Depression*, which remained viable even after alt-country receded. Though its format changed more than once, including a period from 2009 to 2014 when it featured only online, fan-driven content, *No Depression* brought back a professional staff in the fall of 2015. It now uses the tagline "Quarterly Journal of Roots Music," the latter term synonymous with "Americana." While the word "Americana" avoids the confusion that potentially afflicts "roots," which can seem to refer only to old or historical music, roots music sidesteps the wariness that sometimes creeps in along with Americana's gradual institutionalization.

The Americana Music Association (AMA) first met and conferred its own awards in 2000. Granting awards helped the term gain parlance. It also delineates the aesthetic territory of Americana—its intersection of musical artists and tastes that appear to lack a home elsewhere. Recent top winners include Lucinda Williams, Dwight Yoakam, Patty Griffin, and Buddy Miller. The AMA gives awards for duo, instrumentalist, album, and song of the year, among others. These categories incorporate bluegrass performers, who, incidentally, also have their own awards-granting institution, the International Bluegrass Music Association (IBMA). As with Simpson, the exclusion of bluegrass from the CMA and other industry organizations is telling with regard to country music's present definitions in contrast with its past.

In addition to its current music awards, the AMA names a Trailblazer Award and a Spirit of Americana/Free Speech in Music Award, which seems directed at the repressive impulse to silence the Dixie Chicks for their disapproval of the Iraq War. The honor has gone to Johnny Cash, Mavis Staples, Buffy Sainte-Marie, and Billy Bragg, the first non-American to receive it. The Recording Academy conferred its outside sanction in 2010 when it created a separate Grammy category, splitting the former Folk/Americana award in two. Since identifying Americana as distinct, its Grammy winners have included Levon Helm, Mavis Staples, and William Bell, as well as Jason Isbell. *Billboard* magazine added a separate Americana chart in 2016.

Placing an artist within the boundaries of Americana versus country music is not necessarily a clear musical proposition. Within the commercial music industry, Sturgill Simpson and Brad Paisley operate in different spheres. Yet, setting aside a few of Paisley's more mundane songs like "Crushin' It," the two share more in common sonically than they differ. Certainly, Paisley overlaps more stylistically with Simpson than with Carrie Underwood or Keith Urban. Both are expert song crafters, and both partake in a musically ravenous manner from the spectrum of US popular music and culture. The extent to which their imaginations encompass a wide cross-section of influence is a matter of degree. Yet Paisley stands at the center of mainstream country music, hosting the CMA Awards for nearly a decade and rotating on new country radio lineups. Simpson stands at the outside edge of that world. In an age of media fragmentation and of radical upheavals in how a musician may reach an audience, it may no longer matter.

Wheeler Walker Jr., also known as Ben Hoffman, is another

artist missing entirely from either the 2016 CMA Awards or the AMA Awards. The success that same year of his album *Redneck Shit* illustrates how new-century media alter the playing field for musicians. Walker's recording partakes of an irony that connects further back than 1990s alt-country. He recalls the tongue-in-cheek persona adopted by Kinky Friedman during the mid-1970s. With his band the Texas Jewboys, Friedman sent up country music stereotypes in songs like "Asshole from El Paso," a contrafactum of Merle Haggard's "Okie from Muskogee." While creating very respectable country musical sounds, he penned songs like "They Ain't Making Jews Like Jesus Anymore" that were edgy enough for PBS to bar his episode during the first season of *Austin City Limits*. Walker shares Friedman's spirit but with a far more X-rated brand of country musical irony. In that, he also brings to mind David Allan Coe and his songs with titles not ready for primetime like "Fuck Aneta Briant" [*sic*]. Coe's lack of radio playability kept his music in an underground space.

Walker's album, by contrast, debuted at number nine on the *Billboard* country album charts, despite the fact that its content would keep it barred from ever airing on radio. His title track explodes the typical country music theme of celebrating life's simple pleasures— evoking but twisting the bawdy good-times spirit of Hank Williams Jr.'s "Family Tradition" or Garth Brooks's "Friends in Low Places." The black-and-white video shows Wheeler strutting around in front of a truck and a barnyard, pausing periodically to comically expose his chest hair. All the while, Wheeler cobbles together a list of outrageously lewd pastimes, interspersed with more printable ones like "eatin' tater tots," punctuated with the refrain "I love that redneck shit." He likewise amps up the typical heartbreak theme beyond the limits of broadcast playability with the tune "Fuck You Bitch." The lyrics dismiss a former lover in no uncertain terms, along with her friends and her dog, whom the narrator hopes she never finds. Walker's delivery is characterized by an over-the-top posture of wanton insolence. Writing a review of a Wheeler performance in Seattle during summer 2016 for *No Depression*, Mike Seely once again asks the implacable question: "What is 'real' country music? The question itself is worth mocking, and I actually think that's what Walker's doing."[12]

No fence posts marking the boundaries of twenty-first-century country music are set as provocatively as Walker's. More often, they delineate personal taste. There are listeners who jam to the latest "hot new country" (HNC) radio hit, and those who cringe over the way Cole Swindell's "Chillin' It" ham-fistedly iterates Brad Paisley's "Crushin' It" or Scott McCreery's "Feelin' It." Some listeners may find the hook for the Runaway June song "Lipstick" (2016)—she wants a man to ruin her lipstick and not her mascara—to be just catchy enough to hold their interest, while others hear a thin metaphor too weak to sustain an entire song. There are listeners who gravitate toward country music for its even quality—its ability to blend into the background, infusing life's mundane, everyday activities with a steady and distracting, but not disruptive, rhythm; then, there's anonymous YouTuber "Sir Mashalot," who's blended and even overlaid six contemporary country music hits, demonstrating their nearly identical musical content.[13]

Individual specifics of musical style, just as specific references to Chevys, Jack Daniels, or Stetsons, do not necessarily dictate whether a country artist dwells more in the shallow versus the deep end of the country music pool. The contemporary superstar Keith Urban, for instance, coiffed and dressed in 1990s grunge fashion, incorporates instrumentation and stylistic gestures of 1970s and 1980s rock. His sound moves some contemporary listeners, while others strain to hear a trace of aural continuity with the country music tradition. A relative newcomer to country music, Chris Stapleton likewise channels elements of earlier rock in his own way. Yet Stapleton conveys a more substantive engagement with country music tradition that won him widespread critical acclaim in 2016. This included awards from the CMA and ACM, but also from the AMA. In other words, he circulates in both worlds. To hold Urban and Stapleton side by side reveals diffuse and dispersed parameters for twenty-first-century country music. New and former genre distinctions overlap, spilling over the edges of older, twentieth-century media.

The new media environment, where Wheeler Walker Jr. can reach the *Billboard* Top Ten album charts with no support from old media like radio or TV, little resembles its twentieth-century forebears. Music as a physical product—album, cassette, CD—has become more of a novelty or a product aimed at the audio connoisseurs currently fueling a vinyl renaissance for the wider range of frequencies it can hold compared to digital formats. Listeners who once may have browsed the bins at a record store may now follow a trail, perhaps a hyperlink or a clue in a comment on YouTube. Or they depend on algorithms of personal taste, far more sophisticated than genre labels, to track music consumption on a personal digital device and suggest their next favorite song accordingly. New media enable people to craft personal media environments that only reflect the tastes, opinions, and interests they have already identified for themselves, or, should they wish, to draw from a sprawling range of material at the touch of a digit.

These shifts in how music reaches audiences topple long-established patterns of audience behavior and music industry business models. They shake up the definition of commercial success, a parameter once driven by radio and measured in the number of album sales. Record stores are rare enough that tracking physical album sales no longer makes sense. Furthermore, consumers no longer necessarily conceive of a song as part of an album; thus, the success of a track may or may not be tied to a larger whole. Sales figures for either might come in the form of download purchases, YouTube viewings, or Spotify streams, but validation also still occurs via airplay rotations or industry awards. Country music radio is still in this mix, in other words, but now merely as one among other potential drivers for success of a given recording or artist.

This has been in the works for a quarter century now. Old media models began collapsing in the early 1990s when cable television first threatened the dominance of the big three networks (ABC, CBS, and NBC). Individual cable stations typically contracted the range of programming, compared to the broad-interest network lineup. The early cable pioneer Country Music Television (CMT), for example, was typical. It compartmentalized country music into a specialized channel for increasingly narrow interest groups, alongside other channels for home improvement, outdoor sports, and old sitcoms.

During this same era, the concept of "branding" rose to the fore as a means to articulate the multifaceted nature of identity. Branding could apply to a media channel/outlet, a blue jeans company, a university, or a public figure. Contraction of programming on cable stations often presaged a strategic expansion guided by the logic of branding. CMT, for instance, shifted its content from country music videos toward an array of "lifestyle" shows aimed at the presumed demographic of its core audience. Early on, this comprised shows about fishing, cooking, and NASCAR. In the year 2016, CMT programming included competitions of physical strength or chainsaw carving, a sitcom starring the former country music star Billy Ray Cyrus, or a show titled *Dallas Cowboys Cheerleaders: Making the Team*, then in its eleventh season.

Branding operates according to multidimensional relationships of signs and meanings, not corresponding object to object, but with shifting points of connection, nearly always in flux. In the twenty-first century, branding gets even more complicated—or at least more calculated—including in ways that involve country music. Savvy media moguls or business entities sometimes forward country music to communicate a set of values or associations to target audiences. Thus, the National Football League opens games with country artists, most recently Carrie Underwood, to convey the televised sport as red-blooded, true-blue American entertainment, a middle-of-the-road good-time atmosphere for everyday people. Fox News, as a foreign-owned newcomer network trying to carve out potential audiences from the established "big three," strategically foregrounded country music to anchor its own brand.[14]

Fragmentation occurred for radio in similar ways to television. Back in 1993, the media journalist Eric Boehlert noted for *Billboard* that radio audiences were segregating toward "hot new country" versus "traditional country," categories mirroring the old soft-shell/hard-core dialectic. This separation disrupted the genre's long-held sense of historical continuity. In the age of XM satellite radio, beginning in 2001, Boehlert's two opposite dimensions explode in multiple directions at once. Out of 235 XM radio stations, 8 are devoted to country music, so that a twenty-first-century fan can narrow in on a particular niche far more finely and subtly tuned than "new" versus "traditional." In this radio soundscape, a phrase like "today's hits" means less than it once did because radio no longer so surely drives purchasing behavior for country music audiences.

Like their fan counterparts for other genres, country music lovers find and acquire new musical material via the World Wide Web, social media networks, and television shows like *Nashville*, which began in the fall of 2012. Following a model tested by its predecessor, *Glee*, new recording stars who are also actors introduce new songs or sometimes new versions of older songs as part of a music-driven plot. Viewings of the episode spark sales of the audio. While the airwaves are still relevant, multiple, proliferating platforms across the Internet or via digital satellite signals denote the most distinctive changes for country music in the twenty-first century: seismic shifts in media and multiplication of avenues by which musicians reach audiences.

The intellectual frameworks that made sense for the previous century no longer hold up. Mainstream versus the margins worked well to graft alt-country and other 1990s roots musics against a commercially dominant mainstream. Likewise, the framework productively structures analyses of everything from Tin Pan Alley to format radio. The twenty-first century, however, saw those predictable relationships between center and periphery explode. Another conceptual scaffold, the two-dimensional resonance of country-pop versus hard country—or "soft-shell/hard-core"—proved useful even into the 1990s when "new" versus "traditional" segregated on country radio. Conversations and debates about the music in the new century, now as dispersed as the sounds that get labeled country in the first place, need more dimensions. The fragmentation of media, the burgeoning pathways for artist success, the decreased centralization of industry gatekeeping, and the expansive dynamics of style send the question about country music's identity into multiple directions at once.

This century has seen the passing of many of country music's most central stylists, among them Waylon Jennings, June Carter and Johnny Cash, Eddy Arnold, Ray Price, Buck Owens, Ralph Stanley, Earl Scruggs, Kitty Wells and Johnny Wright, Hank Cochran, Jean Shepherd, Slim Whitman, George Jones, and Merle Haggard. In this age of immediate access and global economy, their sounds remain available at the click of an instant stream or in tangible formats released by overseas specialty labels like Bear Family Records. At the same time, traditional fans can find artists making new music that draws on country music's past in infinite ways. Sometimes this comes as a straightforward continuation of stylistic precedents like the "hard-core" neo-traditionalist Daryle Singletary. At other times, it takes form as inventive combinations of influences like the Texas-fiddling, close-harmonizing trio the Quebe Sisters.

Both examples perform music a discerning listener would recognize as traditional country, but neither gets attention within mainstream music industry circles. Both have been reviewed in *No Depression*. The Quebe Sisters span a musical range that encompasses covers of classic honky-tonk ("Cold, Cold Heart"), jazz standards ("How High the Moon"), and Appalachian folk song ("Wayfaring Stranger")—all within a western swing–inspired frame. They use the label Americana to describe their music making. Both Singletary and the Quebes earn a living as professionals, part of a sundry soundscape of twenty-first-century music making that occurs in small clubs, theaters, state park amphitheaters, and niche festivals. Country music likewise unfolds at weekly jam sessions in big cities and small communities alike, drawing music-loving amateurs who delight in revisiting and reinventing songs that traverse the breadth of the country genre's past.

Recent artists like Jason Isbell and Sturgill Simpson, or even Wheeler Walker Jr., all of whom achieved success outside traditional channels of country music promotion, allude to new realities beyond the simple emergence of a new genre of Americana. Genre is a fundamentally less powerful concept. On the one hand, it's a matter of proliferation: Ameripolitan, Bush band (Australian country music), country rap, punkabilly, Red Dirt are among the contemporary categories that come and go nearly as often as yet another cultural observer posts an online review. On the other hand, it's a practical matter. As Chet Flippo wrote for his blog in 2010, genre labels arose from the need to organize and categorize sounds in ways that make sense to audiences looking to purchase music.[15] They appear far less necessary in an age when listeners cross musical boundaries in unpredictable ways and cherry-pick artists from across industry categories.

All this leads to perhaps the most potent question of all: Who plays the role of gatekeeper at the doorway of musical success? The Internet has no gatekeepers: once upon a time, the *Grand Ole Opry* was the site for institutional sanctification of country musicians; format radio moved into the prime arbiter role during the early 1960s. Twenty-first-century gatekeepers are as diffuse, dispersed, and fragmented as audiences for music. Radio still can effectively promote music sales, but artists can also gain commercial success without it. For instance, despite all the controversy and negative media attention for the Dixie Chicks, *Taking the Long Way* (2006) sold well. The flap cost the Dixie Chicks some fans but won others. Shifting models for industry success and the decreased centrality of radio play out in other examples as well. Miranda Lambert's 2005 album *Kerosene*, for example, landed no Top Ten hits on the radio-determined country singles chart and, yet, reached the top of the country album chart.[16] Beyoncé can drop her album *Lemonade* without advance publicity, anticipating that the person-to-person social networks among her fans will fuel its success. She was correct.

While *Lemonade* broadly epitomizes new media shifts, its single "Daddy Lessons," in the end, illustrates country music's historical continuities and significant breaks with the past. Country music's persistent question remains alive in the new millennium, but its answers come from more dispersed fronts. The Recording Academy committee, for its part, excluded "Daddy Lessons" from consideration for Best Country Song in 2016. Yet neither the Recording Academy nor any other media entity gets to decide what is and what is not country music. Nor can anyone predict the means through which potential fans might find their way to country music in the twenty-first century. No gatekeeper guards the center because there is no center. A case in point turns up in the comments section beneath the YouTube video for the Dixie Chicks song "Long Time Gone." It saw a flutter of activity in early November 2016, just after the CMA Awards aired on television. A number of postings echoed the same sentiment: "Beyoncé brought me here."

Notes

PREFACE

1. *The Kentucky* (New York: Farrar & Rinehart, 1941), 128.

CHAPTER 1: THE FOLK BACKGROUND BEFORE COMMERCIALISM

1. I have explored Mike Seeger's theory more fully in *Music from the True Vine: Mike Seeger's Life and Musical Journey* (Chapel Hill: University of North Carolina Press, 2011). My emphasis on country music's southern origins has been challenged many times over the years, most recently in an entire issue of the *Journal of American Folklore* 127, no. 504 (Spring 2014). The issue editors, Thomas A. DuBois and James P. Leary, kindly permitted me to respond in a short essay, "'The Southern Thesis': Revisited and Reaffirmed," 226–229.

2. For an amplification of this view of southern abundance, see Frank Owsley, *Plain Folk of the Old South* (Baton Rouge: Louisiana State University Press, 1949). Grady McWhiney and Forrest McDonald make some of the same points, while also stressing the freedom promoted by the open and abundant southern range, in "The Antebellum Southern Herdsman: A Reinterpretation," *Journal of Southern History* 41, no. 2 (May 1975): 147–167. A brilliant exposition of the emergence of market capitalism among southern small farmers and the consequent spawning of rural radicalism is Steven Hahn, *The Roots of Southern Populism: Yeoman Farmers and the Transformation of the Georgia Upcountry, 1850–1890* (New York: Oxford University Press, 1983).

3. Arthur Palmer Hudson, "Folk Songs of the Southern Whites," in *Culture in the South*, ed. W. T. Couch (Chapel Hill: University of North Carolina Press, 1934), 520.

4. Richard A. Peterson and Russell Davis, "The Fertile Crescent of Country Music," *Journal of Country Music* 6, no. 1 (Spring 1975): 19–25.

5. McWhiney and McDonald, "The Antebellum Southern Herdsman."

6. The pioneer exploration of the interrelationship of southern black and white musical forms was Tony Russell, *Blacks, Whites, and Blues* (New York: Stein and Day, 1970). A more recent study that documents the existence of African American performers in early commercial country music is Diane Pecknold, ed., *Hidden in the Mix: The African American Presence in Country Music* (Durham, NC: Duke University Press, 2013). One of the contributors to that collection, Charles Hughes, has also written an impressive study, *Country Soul: Making Music and Making Race in the American South* (Chapel Hill: University of North Carolina Press, 2015).

7. Norm Cohen has compiled the definitive study of the railroad's impact on American music and musicians: *Long Steel Rail: The Railroad in American Folksong* (Urbana: University of Illinois Press, 1981).

8. For a perceptive view of the role played by cities in the post-Reconstruction South, see Edward L. Ayers, *The Promise of the New South: Life after Reconstruction* (New York: Oxford University Press, 1992).

9. This has been a much-discussed topic among historians, but I would suggest a start with John Boles, *The Great Revival: Beginnings of the Bible Belt* (Lexington: University Press of Kentucky, 1969).

10. Bernard Weisberger, *They Gathered at the River: The Story of the Great Revivalists and Their Impact upon Religion in America* (Boston: Little, Brown, 1958), 217.

11. W. J. Cash, *The Mind of the South* (New York: Alfred A. Knopf, 1941).

12. Augustus Baldwin Longstreet, *Georgia Scenes* (Atlanta: Cherokee Publishing, 1971; originally published in Augusta, Georgia, 1835), 12–22.

13. Alan Lomax, "Folk Song Style," *American Anthropologist* 61, no. 6 (December 1959): 929–930.

14. D. K. Wilgus, record reviews in various issues of *Kentucky Folklore Record* and *Journal of American Folklore*; Norm and Anne Cohen, "Folk and Hillbilly Music: Further Thoughts on Their Relation," *John Edwards Memorial Foundation Quarterly* 13, no. 46 (Summer 1977): 50–57.

15. Richard Nevins, notes to *Old-Time Fiddle Classics*, vol. 2: *1927–1934* (County 527).

CHAPTER 2: THE EARLY PERIOD OF COMMERCIAL HILLBILLY MUSIC

1. Richard K. Spottswood, *Ethnic Music on Records: A Discography of Ethnic Recordings Produced in the United States, 1893–1942*, 7 vols. (Urbana: University of Illinois Press, 1991).

2. Frederick Lewis Allen, *Only Yesterday* (New York: Harper and Brothers, 1931), 147–148.

3. President's Research Committee on Social Trends, *Recent Social Trends in the United States* (New York: McGraw-Hill Book Company, 1933), 211–212.

4. Letter to the author from Guthrie T. Meade, College Park, Maryland, February 21, 1967.

5. Barry Mazor has written a very good biography of this pioneering record talent scout: *Ralph Peer and the Making of Popular Roots Music* (Chicago Review Press, 2014).

6. Charles Wolfe, "Toward a Contextual Approach to Old-Time Music," *Journal of Country Music* 5, no. 2 (Summer 1974): 65–75.

7. Archie Green explored the origin of the term "hillbilly" and its identification with rural music (as popularized by Al Hopkins's string band), in "Hillbilly Music: Source and Symbol," *Journal of American Folklore* 78, no. 309 (July–September 1965): 204–228. Anthony Harkins has provided a good survey of the word's presence and influence in American culture, *Hillbilly: A Cultural History of an American Icon* (New York: Oxford University Press, 2004). Joe Wilson contributed most of what is known about Hopkins and the Hill Billies in his notes to *The Hill Billies*, County 405 (I am grateful to Mrs. Dot Wilson Moss, of Charlotte, North Carolina, for reminding me about this album and about the role played by her father, Frank Wilson, in the band). Wayne W. Daniel, the leading historian of Atlanta country music, has put forward another candidate for the band that did most to popularize "hillbilly": George Daniell's Hill Billies, who performed on powerful WSB as early as February 18, 1925. See his "George Daniell's Hill Billies: The Band That Named the Music?," *John Edwards Memorial Foundation Quarterly* 19, no. 70 (Summer 1983): 81–84.

8. Green, "Hillbilly Music: Source and Symbol," 223.

9. Anne and Norm Cohen, "Folk and Hillbilly Music: Further Thoughts on Their Relation," *John Edwards Memorial Foundation Quarterly* 13, no. 46 (Summer 1977): 50–57. Several scholars have explored the sources of country music, most notably Guthrie T. "Gus" Meade Jr., *Country Music Sources: A Biblio-Discography of Commercially Recorded Traditional Music* (Chapel Hill: University of North Carolina Press, 2002).

10. Tony Russell has compiled, by far, the single most important source for students of country music in the years before World War II: *Country Music Records: A Discography, 1921–1942* (New York: Oxford University Press, 2004). He has also written indispensable accounts of many lesser-known performers in *Country Music Originals: The Legends and the Lost* (New York: Oxford University Press, 2007).

11. Donald Knight Wilgus, *Anglo-American Folksong Scholarship since 1898* (New Brunswick, NJ: Rutgers University Press, 1959), 73.

12. Henry Sapoznik and Christopher King received Grammy nominations for an anthology of some of Stoneman's recordings: *Ernest V. Stoneman: The Unsung Father of Country Music, 1925–1934* (5-String Productions, 2008).

13. Outstanding evaluations of Poole and his music include Kinney Rorrer, *Rambling Blues: The Life and Songs of Charlie Poole* (London: OTM, 1982; reprint, Danville, VA: McCain Printing, 1992), and Patrick Huber, *Linthead Stomp: The Creation of Country Music in the Piedmont South* (Chapel Hill: University of North Carolina Press, 2008). Henry Sapoznik has produced and edited a fine collection of some of Poole's recordings: *You Ain't Talking to Me: Charlie Poole and the Roots of Country Music* (Columbia C3K 92780).

14. Loyal Jones tells us much about the early dissemination of "folk" music on radio in *Radio's "Kentucky Mountain Boy" Bradley Kincaid* (Berea, KY: Appalachian Center/Berea College, 1980).

15. Charles Wolfe contributed a good survey of country music in Kentucky in *Kentucky Country: Folk and Country Music of Kentucky* (Lexington: University Press of Kentucky, 1982).

16. Charles Wolfe, "George Reneau: A Biographical Sketch," *John Edwards Memorial Foundation Quarterly* 15, no. 56 (Winter 1979): 205.

17. Walter Darrell Haden, "Vernon Dalhart," in *Stars of Country Music*, ed. Bill C. Malone and Judith McCulloh (Urbana: University of Illinois Press, 1975), 69.

18. The recordings made in Bristol in 1927 and 1928 were reissued in 2011 by Bear Family: *The Bristol Sessions, 1927–1928: The Big Bang of Country Music*, 5 CDs (Bear BCD 16094 EK). Porterfield's quotation appeared in "Hey, Hey, Tell 'Em 'Bout Us: Jimmie Rodgers Visits the Carter Family," in *Country: The Music and the Musicians*, 2nd ed. (New York: Abbeville, 1994), 17.

19. The standard biographical treatment of the Carter Family is Mark Zwonitzer and Charles Hirshberg, *Will You Miss Me When I'm Gone? The Carter Family and Their Legacy in American Music* (New York: Simon and Schuster, 2002). The entire Carter Family recorded repertory is available in a box set, *In the Shadow of Clinch Mountain* (Bear), with excellent notes by Charles Wolfe.

20. Archie Green, "The Carter Family's 'Coal Miner's Blues,'" *Southern Folklore Quarterly* 25, no. 4 (December 1961): 231.

21. An impressive history of the Chicago radio show is Chad Berry, ed., *The Hayloft Gang: The Story of the National Barn Dance* (Urbana: University of Illinois Press, 2008).

22. George D. Hay, *A Story of the Grand Ole Opry* (Nashville: Privately published, 1953), 1.

23. Ibid.

24. Ralph Rinzler, notes to *Uncle Dave Macon*, Decca DL4760.

25. The best account of the early years of the Opry is Charles Wolfe, *A Good-Natured Riot: The Birth of the Grand Ole Opry* (Nashville: Country Music Foundation and Vanderbilt University Press, 1999).

26. Hay, *A Story of the Grand Ole Opry*, 9–10.

CHAPTER 3: THE FIRST COUNTRY SINGING STAR: JIMMIE RODGERS

1. The complete Jimmie Rodgers recorded repertory, along with meticulous notes by Nolan Porterfield, is available on the Bear Family anthology box set *The Singing Brakeman* (BCD 15540).

2. The comprehensive and still definitive biography of Jimmie Rodgers is Nolan Porterfield, *Jimmie Rodgers: The Life and Times of America's Blue Yodeler* (Urbana: University of Illinois Press, 1979). It can be usefully supplemented, however, by Barry Mazor, *Meeting Jimmie Rodgers: How America's Original Roots Music Hero Changed the Pop Sounds of a Century* (New York: Oxford University Press, 2009); and Jocelyn R. Neal, *The Songs of Jimmie Rodgers: A Legacy in Country Music* (Bloomington: Indiana University Press, 2009).

3. My knowledge of Rodgers's musical activities in New Orleans, and of his relationship with Goebel Reeves, is greatly indebted to the research of Fred Hoeptner, particularly in an unpublished paper he sent to me called "Goebel Reeves and Jimmie Rodgers: The 1925 Barnstorming Episode."

4. Ralph Peer, "Discovery of the First Hillbilly Great," *Billboard* 65, no. 20 (May 16, 1953): 20. For a fuller assessment of the recording entrepreneur, see Barry Mazor, *Ralph Peer and the Making of Popular Roots Music* (Chicago: Chicago Review Press, 2014).

5. William W. Sterling, *Trails and Trials of a Texas Ranger* (privately published, 1959), 189–191.

6. National Public Radio ran a segment on Chemirocha, "In a Kenyan Village, a 65-Year-Old Recording Comes Home" (June 28, 2015): http://www.npr.org /2015/06/28/417462792/in-a-kenyan-village-a-65-year-old-recording -comes-home.

7. Paul Oliver, "Jimmy Rodgers," *Recorded Folk Music* 2, no. 3 (May-June 1959): 6–10.

8. David Evans found some evidence of this indebtedness in interviews that he conducted in Mississippi: "Black Musicians Remember Jimmie Rodgers," *Old Time Music* 7 (1972–1973): 12–14.

9. For a fuller understanding of yodeling, see Timothy E. Wise, *Yodeling and Meaning in American Music* (Jackson: University Press of Mississippi, 2016); and Bart Plantenga, *Yodel-Ay-Ee-Oooo: The Secret History of Yodeling around the World* (New York: Routledge, 2004).

10. Alan Lomax, *The Folk Songs of North America* (New York: Doubleday, 1960), 281.

11. Roy Horton, notes to *Jimmie Rodgers: Country Music Hall of Fame*, RCA Victor LPM-2531.

CHAPTER 4: COUNTRY MUSIC DURING THE DEPRESSION

1. Lewis Atherton, *Main Street on the Middle Border* (Bloomington: Indiana University Press, 1954), 296.

2. The best treatment of the Mexican border stations is Gene Fowler and Bill Crawford, *Border Radio* (Austin: Texas Monthly Press, 1987).

3. The Chuck Wagon Gang and their music are the subject of a comprehensive box set produced by the Bear label in Germany. All of their recordings, from 1936 to 1955, are included.

4. Alton Delmore was one of the few early country performers who attempted an autobiography. Charles Wolfe edited the manuscript that became *Truth Is Stranger Than Publicity: Alton Delmore* (Nashville: Country Music Foundation Press, 1977).

5. Bear Family records issued a complete set of the Blue Sky Boys' RCA Victor material. The extensive liner notes that I wrote for the collection have been republished in Bill C. Malone, *Sing Me Back Home* (Norman: University of Oklahoma Press, 2017).

6. Although such songs are still performed today, particularly by bluegrass musicians in high-powered and often strident fashion, almost no one does such material in the gentle and subdued style favored by the Blue Sky Boys. A long-enduring link to the Bolicks, and to the mandolin-and-guitar tradition of the 1930s, were a wonderful husband-and-wife team, Ray and Ina Patterson, Texans who lived out their lives in Colorado. They made few public performances but left some excellent albums: *Old Time Ballads and Hymns*, County 708; *Old Time Songs, Vol. 2*, County 715; *Songs of Home and Childhood, Vol. 3*, County 737.

7. Bob Coltman, "Across the Chasm: How the Depression Changed Country Music," *Old Time Music*, no. 23 (Winter 1976–1977): 9–11.

8. Lily May Ledford wrote an autobiography, *Coon Creek Girl* (Berea, KY: Berea College Appalachian Center, 1977). She had an active second career during the folk revival of the 1960s.

9. Wade Mainer's story, and much else, has been told by Richard K. Spottswood in *Banjo on the Mountain: Wade Mainer's First Hundred Years* (Jackson: University Press of Mississippi, 2010).

10. Archie Green, notes to Sarah Ogan Gunning, *Girl of Constant Sorrow*, Folk-Legacy Records FSA-26.

11. I have written an essay on Albert Brumley that is included in Bill C. Malone, *Sing Me Back Home: Southern Roots and Country Music* (Norman: University of Oklahoma Press, 2017).

12. Woody Guthrie has inspired some fine biographies: Joe Klein, *Woody Guthrie: A Life* (New York: Delta, 1999); and Ed Cray, *Ramblin' Man: The Life and Times of Woody Guthrie* (New York: W. W. Norton, 2004).

13. Patrick Huber has contributed an outstanding study of the cotton mill songs and the culture that inspired them: *Linthead Stomp: The Creation of Country Music in the Piedmont South* (Chapel Hill: University of North Carolina Press, 2008).

14. Ivan Tribe, "John McGhee and Frank Welling: West Virginia's Most Recorded Old-Time Artists," *John Edwards Memorial Foundation Quarterly* 17, no. 62 (Summer 1981): 61.

CHAPTER 5: THE COWBOY IMAGE AND THE GROWTH OF WESTERN MUSIC

1. The great folklorist William A. Owens reminded people of this tradition in *Texas Folk Songs* (Austin: Texas Folklore Society, 1950).

2. Ball acknowledged that he learned the two songs from the Lomax book, and Columbia paid Lomax copyright fees of two cents per side for each record manufactured (John Lomax Family Papers, Eugene C. Barker Texas History Center, University of Texas at Austin).

3. The best discussion of Gene Autry is Holly George-Warren, *Public Cowboy No. 1: The Life and Times of Gene Autry* (New York: Oxford University Press, 2007).

4. *Sears Roebuck Catalogue*, Fall and Winter, 1933–1934, 535.

5. Ray White devoted much of his adult life to the study of his boyhood hero, Roy Rogers. The most important result was *King of the Cowboys, Queen of the West: Roy Rogers and Dale Evans* (Madison: University of Wisconsin Press, 2005). Much can also be learned from *My Brother Roy* (Ashland, KY: London Books, 2014), written by Rogers's sister, Cleda Slye Willoughby, with the assistance of John Roger Simon.

6. There is still no definitive history of the honky-tonk and its effects on country music. I have written a brief account, though, included in my anthology *Sing Me Back Home* (Norman: University of Oklahoma Press, 2017).

7. Ronnie Pugh's biography, *Ernest Tubb: The Texas Troubadour* (Durham, NC: Duke University Press, 1996), is one of the best books ever written on country music.

8. Tubb made at least two LPs in the late seventies for Pete Drake's First Generation label. One, called *The Legend and the Legacy*, was made up of duets with such singers as Willie Nelson, George Jones, and Loretta Lynn.

9. See Cary Ginell, *Milton Brown and the Founding of Western Swing* (Urbana: University of Illinois Press, 1994).

10. Interview with Bob Dunn, Houston, July 17, 1966.

11. Quoted by Gordon Baxter, "Pop Never Wanted Me to Be a Musician," *Music City News* 4, no. 8 (February 1967): 27.

12. The best discussion of Bob Wills is Charles Townsend's exhaustively researched *San Antonio Rose: The Life and Music of Bob Wills* (Urbana: University of Illinois Press, 1976).

13. *Billboard* 53, no. 34 (August 23, 1941): 13.

CHAPTER 6: THE WAR YEARS

1. The best account of the Renfro Valley Barn Dance's early years is Harry S. Rice, "Renfro Valley on the Radio, 1937–1941," *Journal of Country Music* 19, no. 2 (1997): 16–25.

2. Vance Randolph, *Ozark Folksongs* (Columbia: State Historical Society of Missouri, 1950), 4:59; W. J. Cash, *The Mind of the South* (New York: Alfred A. Knopf, 1941), 297.

3. The bulk of Acuff's enormous repertory can be found on *The King of Country Music, the Foundational Recordings Complete, 1936–1951* (Bear BCD 17300), 9 CDs and 1 DVD.

4. This remark has been attributed to the popular songwriter Frank Loesser: *Billboard* 55, no. 43 (October 23, 1943): 66.

5. Interview with Wesley Rose, Nashville, August 28, 1961.

6. *Life* 15, no. 11 (October 11, 1943): 55.

7. *Billboard* 55, no. 9 (February 27, 1943): 94.

CHAPTER 7: THE BOOM PERIOD

1. *Billboard* 59, no. 52 (December 27, 1947): 18.

2. Several fine studies of California country music now exist: James Gregory, *American Exodus: The Dust Bowl Migration and Okie Culture in California* (New York: Oxford University Press, 1989); Gerald Haslam, *Workin' Man Blues: Country Music in California* (Berkeley: University of California Press, 1999); Peter La Chapelle, *Proud to Be an Okie: Cultural Politics, Country Music, and Migration to Southern California* (Berkeley: University of California Press, 2007); and Robert E. Price, *The Bakersfield Sound: How a Generation of Displaced Okies Revolutionized American Music* (Bakersfield, CA: iUniverse, 2015).

3. The premier historian of the Louisiana show is Tracey E. W. Laird: *Louisiana Hayride: Radio and Roots Music along the Red River* (New York: Oxford University Press, 2004).

4. Stephen Ray Tucker, "The Louisiana Hayride, 1948–1954," *North Louisiana Historical Association Journal* 8, no. 5 (Fall 1977): 188.

5. The Nathan quotation came from Homer Bailes (author interview, Jennings, Louisiana, August 16, 1974).

6. At least one scholar has challenged the conventionally held ideas about early Nashville recording. Cary Ginell claims to have uncovered evidence in the Decca files at MCA in Los Angeles showing that Red Foley's records of 1945–1947 were actually made in Chicago and given New York matrix numbers (letter from Cary Ginell, Reseda, California, April 24, 1984).

7. A comprehensive collection of Louvin Brothers' songs, along with notes by Charles Wolfe, can be found in a Bear box collection: *Close Harmony* (Bear BCD 15561). Wolfe also wrote a book on the brothers, *In Close Harmony: The Story of the Louvin Brothers* (Jackson: University Press of Mississippi, 1996).

8. See Louis M. Jones, with Charles Wolfe, *Everybody's Grandpa: Fifty Years Behind the Mike* (Knoxville: University of Tennessee Press, 1984).

9. Author telephone conversation with Martha Carson, Nashville, August 16, 1973.

10. Author telephone conversation with Rose Maddox, Ashland, Oregon, January 23, 1982. For a fuller portrait of Rose and her brothers, see Jonny

Whiteside, *Ramblin' Rose: The Life and Career of Rose Maddox* (Nashville: Vanderbilt University Press, 1997).

11. Quoted in *The World of Country Music* (New York: Billboard, 1963), 61.

12. The best account of country music humor is Loyal Jones, *Country Music Humorists and Comedians* (Urbana: University of Illinois Press, 2008).

13. In the aftermath of Dickens's 1983 induction into the Country Music Hall of Fame, Columbia issued a welcomed anthology of his music, concentrating on the years 1949–1960: *Little Jimmy Dickens, Columbia Historic Edition,* FC 38905. Unfortunately, nine of the eleven songs are up-tempo novelties, and modern listeners will receive a mistaken impression of Dickens's range and stylistic versatility. None of his great heart songs are included in the collection.

14. Daniel Cooper has written a very good biography of Frizzell: *Lefty Frizzell: The Honky-Tonk Life of Country Music's Greatest Singer* (Boston: Little, Brown, 1995).

15. Author telephone conversation with Alice Frizzell, Dallas, March 2, 1982.

16. The standard biography of the Tennessee Plowboy is Michael Streissguth, *Eddy Arnold: Pioneer of the Nashville Sound* (New York: Schirmer, 1997).

17. Eddy Arnold, *It's a Long Way from Chester County* (New York: Pyramid Books, 1969), 85–86.

18. *Billboard* 60, no. 21 (May 22, 1948): 18.

19. Hank Snow wrote an autobiography, with Jack Ownbey and Robert Burris, *The Hank Snow Story* (Urbana: University of Illinois Press, 1994).

20. Hank Williams has been much written about, by such writers as Roger Williams, Chet Flippo, and Colin Escott. My favorite biography, though, is Paul Hemphill, *Lovesick Blues: The Life of Hank Williams* (New York: Viking, 2005).

21. *Billboard* 59, no. 14 (April 5, 1947): 123.

22. Quoted in Rufus Jarman, "Country Music Goes to Town," *Nation's Business* 41 (February 1953): 51.

23. Eli Waldron, "Country Music: The Death of Hank Williams," *The Reporter* 12, no. 10 (May 19, 1955): 35.

CHAPTER 8: THE DEVELOPMENT OF COUNTRY-POP MUSIC AND THE NASHVILLE SOUND

1. Michael Bertrand, *Race, Rock, and Elvis* (Urbana: University of Illinois Press, 2000).

2. Vance Packard's comment came in his testimony before a US Senate subcommittee: Hearings before the Subcommittee on Communications of the Committee on Interstate and Foreign Commerce, US 85th Congress, 2d session, on S. 2834 (A Bill to provide that a license for a radio or television broadcasting station shall not be granted to, or held by, any person or corporation engaged directly or indirectly in the business of publishing

music or of manufacturing or selling musical recordings), March 11–July 23, 1958. Lomax's statement is in *Esquire* 52, no. 4 (October 1959): 88.

3. The definitive chronicler of Presley is Peter Guralnick: *Last Train to Memphis: The Rise of Elvis Presley* (Boston: Little, Brown, 1994) and *Careless Love: The Unmaking of Elvis Presley* (Boston: Little, Brown, 1999). Also indispensable for its discussion of southern context is Joel Williamson, *Elvis Presley: A Southern Life* (New York: Oxford University Press, 2014).

4. See Greil Marcus, *Mystery Train: Images of America in Rock 'n' Roll* (New York: E. P. Dutton, 1975; 2d rev. ed., 1982).

5. Rick Bragg has written a masterful account of Lewis: *Jerry Lee Lewis: His Own Story* (New York: HarperCollins, 2014). Peter Guralnick rounds out the whole story of Sun Records and the rise of rockabilly in *Sam Phillips: The Man Who Invented Rock 'n' Roll* (Boston: Little, Brown, 2015).

6. Recorded in 1966 by the Lovin' Spoonful, *Hums of the Lovin' Spoonful* (Kama Sutra).

7. Maxine Brown wrote an autobiography, *Looking Back to See: A Country Music Memoir* (Fayetteville: University of Arkansas Press, 2005), that tells not only the story of the Browns but also much about the country scene of the 1950s and 1960s.

8. Used as the title of a Jim Reeves album (RCA Victor LPM 2487), composed exclusively of pop songs.

9. Important studies of Patsy Cline include Douglas Gomery, *Patsy Cline: The Making of an Icon* (Bloomington, IN: Trafford, 2011); Margaret Jones, *Patsy: The Life and Times of Patsy Cline* (New York: HarperCollins, 1994); Ellis Nassour, *Honky Tonk Angel: The Intimate Story of Patsy Cline* (Chicago Review Press, 2008); and Warren R. Hofstra, ed., *Sweet Dreams: The World of Patsy Cline* (Urbana: University of Illinois Press, 2013).

10. *Behind the Record of the Country Music Association* (Nashville, Country Music Association, n.d.), 4.

CHAPTER 9: THE REINVIGORATION OF MODERN COUNTRY MUSIC, 1960–1972

1. Johnny Cash has elicited a multitude of writings. Among the best are Johnny Cash, with Patrick Carr, *Cash: The Autobiography* (San Francisco: HarperSanFrancisco, 1997), and Robert Hilburn, *Johnny Cash: The Life* (Boston: Little, Brown, 2013).

2. John Fergus Ryan, "Press a Button and Out Comes 'Hee Haw,'" *Country Music* 2, no. 1 (September 1973): 28–34.

3. The sad incident inspired one of the great ballads of recent times, "The Ballad of Stringbean and Estelle," written by Guy Clark, Sam Bush, and Verlon Thompson. Thompson can be seen and heard telling the story, and singing the song, on YouTube in a dramatic and compelling rendition.

4. Omer Anderson, "Fifty Million Europeans Can't Be Wrong," *Billboard* 72, no. 28 (July 11, 1960): 1.

5. *Billboard Music Week* 73, no. 33 (September 25, 1961): 3.

6. Although Bear Family products can be ordered through various outlets, its website is the most direct source for them; see bear-family.com.

7. The BACM catalogue has been absorbed into a much larger operation, The Country Music Archive, which claims to contain over 600,000 recordings of varying descriptions. The Archive also offers a multitude of different CD titles for sale. Located in Dover, England, the archive can be contacted at http://country-music-archive.com/.

8. I (Bill C. Malone) have written a biography of Clifton: *Bill Clifton: America's Bluegrass Ambassador to the World* (Urbana: University of Illinois Press, 2016).

9. The best general account of the folk revival is Ronald D. Cohen, *Rainbow Quest: The Folk Music Revival, 1940–1970* (Boston: University of Massachusetts Press, 2002).

10. The Harry Smith collection was reissued by Smithsonian Folkways (SFW 40090) in 1997 as six CDs accompanied by a 96-page book. In his otherwise sympathetic liner notes, Greil Marcus regrettably used the phrase "weird old America" to describe the culture that had originally produced the music.

11. Ray Allen wrote the best account of the New Lost City Ramblers: *Gone to the Country: The New Lost City Ramblers and the Folk Music Revival* (Urbana: University of Illinois Press, 2010). While it is long out of print, the *New Lost City Ramblers Song Book* (New York: Oak Publications, 1964) remains an invaluable introduction to their repertory and to many of the classic hillbilly songs of the pre–World War II era.

12. Much more should be written on Watson and his legacy, but Kent Gustavson made a good start with *Blind but Now I See: The Biography of Music Legend Doc Watson* (Tulsa, OK: Sumach-Red Books, 2012).

13. In an interview for WWOZ-FM in New Orleans, Watson reemphasized his independence from bluegrass (interview conducted by Svare Forsland and Bill C. Malone, 1982).

14. John Roger Simon, *Cowboy Copas and the Golden Age of Country Music* (Ashland, KY: Jesse Stuart Foundation, 2008).

15. George Jones was refreshingly honest in the autobiography that he compiled with Tom Carter, *I Lived to Tell It All* (New York: Dell, 1975, 1996), but the best discussion of him has been provided by Rich Kienzle in his book *The Grand Tour: The Life and Music of George Jones* (New York: HarperCollins, 2016).

16. The photograph appears on the cover of an LP, *The Best of George Jones*, Epic KE33352, and in Dolly Carlisle, *Ragged but Right: The Life and Times of George Jones* (Chicago: Contemporary Books, 1984).

17. Nathan Gibson, *The Starday Story: The House That Country Music Built* (Jackson: University Press of Mississippi, 2011).

18. A major study of the shuffle beat style is needed, along with an exploration of the musicians who have kept the sound alive since Price's death.

19. Tom Ayres, "Ray Price Remembers Hank Williams," *Country Music* 5, no. 12 (September 1977): 56.

20. Robert E. Price wrote a lively and highly detailed account of the Bakersfield scene: *The Bakersfield Sound: How a Generation of Displaced Okies Revolutionized American Music* (Bakersfield, CA: iUniverse, 2015).

21. Owens's pledge was first carried in *Music City News* 2, no. 9 (March 1965): 5.

22. Written material on Merle Haggard can easily be found, but my suggested place to begin is David Cantwell, *Merle Haggard: The Running Kind* (Austin: University of Texas Press, 2013).

23. One of the best introductions to Haggard's recorded output (though not exhaustive, by any means) is *Down Every Road*, a four-cd box set of his Capitol releases from 1962 to 1994.

24. The phrase was used by William C. Martin in his essay "Tom T. Hall," in *Stars of Country Music,* edited by Bill C. Malone and Judith McCulloh (Urbana: University of Illinois Press, 1975), 399.

25. Loretta Lynn, "Coal Miner's Daughter," heard on the LP of the same name, MCA10.

26. One can easily get engulfed by the writings about Willie Nelson (much of it written by him), but my favorite synthesis is Joe Nick Patoski, *Willie Nelson: An Epic Life* (Boston: Little, Brown, 2008).

27. Hall also dabbled with fiction, poetry, and autobiography. A good example of his literary bent is *The Storyteller's Nashville* (Garden City, NY: Doubleday, 1979).

28. Martin, "Tom T. Hall," 398.

29. Readers interested in Nashville and the competitive world of country songwriting would profit greatly from Bobby Braddock, *A Life on Nashville's Music Row* (Nashville: Country Music Foundation and Vanderbilt University Press, 2015).

30. Loretta Lynn, with George Vecsey, *Loretta Lynn: Coal Miner's Daughter* (Chicago: Henry Regnery, 1976).

31. Joan Dew, *Singers and Sweethearts: The Women of Country Music* (Garden (City, NY: Doubleday, 1977), 8.

32. Tammy Wynette, with Joan Dew, *Stand by Your Man* (New York: Simon and Schuster, 1979). Important overviews of women country singers include Mary A. Bufwack and Robert K. Oermann, *Finding Her Voice: The Saga of Women in Country Music* (New York: Crown, 1993; reprint, Vanderbilt University Press and the Country Music Foundation Press 2003); and Charles K. Wolfe and James F. Akenson, eds., *The Women of Country Music: A Reader* (Lexington: University Press of Kentucky, 2003).

33. Tom Lamont conducted one of the most revealing interviews with Dolly Parton in *The Guardian* (London), December 6, 2014.

34. The "rediscovery" of DeFord Bailey happily inspired a biography by David C.

Morton and Charles K. Wolfe, *DeFord Bailey: A Black Star in Early Country Music* (Knoxville: University of Tennessee Press, 1991).

35. Ann Patton Malone provided a good outline of Pride's career, in "Charley Pride," *Stars of Country Music* (Urbana: University of Illinois Press, 1975).

36. In 1997, The Country Music Foundation and Warner Brothers produced the Grammy-nominated *From Where I Stand: The Black Experience in Country Music*. This boxed CD anthology surveyed the role played by black musicians since the 1920s.

37. Chris Willman compiled a good book-length examination of country music's politics: *Rednecks and Bluenecks: The Politics of Country Music* (New York: New Press, 2005).

CHAPTER 10: BLUEGRASS

1. Neil Rosenberg has written the most complete and accurate history of bluegrass music: *Bluegrass: A History* (Urbana: University of Illinois Press, 1985). Students and fans of the style, though, would also profit from a provocative study written by Robert Cantwell, *Bluegrass Breakdown: The Making of the Old Southern Sound* (Urbana: University of Illinois Press, 1984), and from the magazine *Bluegrass Unlimited*, founded in 1966 and published monthly in Warrenton, Virginia.

2. Each of these versions can be heard on YouTube recordings. Charlie Poole had recorded "White House Blues" for Columbia in 1926, and though Bill Monroe may have heard that recording, he could also have heard Poole's reissued version later in the Harry Smith Folkways Collection. Monroe first recorded the song for Decca in 1954. Grayson and Whitter recorded "Handsome Molly" for Victor in 1927, and the Country Gentlemen did their version on their first Folkways album, *Folk Songs and Bluegrass*, in 1961.

3. Richard Smith's *Can't You Hear Me Callin': The Life of Bill Monroe, Father of Bluegrass* (Boston: Little, Brown, 2000) is the best biography of the bluegrass patriarch, but it can be usefully supplemented by Tom Ewing, ed., *The Bill Monroe Reader* (Urbana: University of Illinois Press, 2000); and Bob Black, *Come Hither to Go Yonder: Playing Bluegrass with Bill Monroe* (Urbana: University of Illinois Press, 2005).

4. The term "high lonesome sound" is generally attributed to John Cohen, who had used it to describe the music of the mountain singer Roscoe Holcomb. I do not know how the term got from there to bluegrass.

5. Ralph Rinzler, "Bill Monroe," in *Stars of Country Music*, edited by Bill C. Malone and Judith McCulloh (Urbana: University of Illinois Press, 1975), 221.

6. Bill Monroe's complete repertory is available on Bear Family collections, but a very good representation of his style can be heard on a box collection, *The Music of Bill Monroe from 1936–1994* (MCA).

7. Although this quote is used by Charles Wolfe in his essay on Uncle Dave in

Stars of Country Music (53), neither Wolfe nor I know where it originated. It is just part of the large body of folklore that has circulated about Macon.

8. Pete Kuykendall, "Bill Monroe and His Bluegrass Boys," *Disc Collector*, no. 13 (no date): 19.

9. Neil Rosenberg, "From Sound to Style: The Emergence of Bluegrass," *Journal of American Folklore* 80, no. 316 (April–June 1967): 146.

10. Don Walker, "Music Built Mills: Martha White Head," *CMA Close Up*, February 1963, 3.

11. Sechler said this to me during a taping of Flatt and Scruggs's WSM radio shows (Nashville, August 23, 1961).

12. The music of the major founding bluegrass bands has been preserved and chronicled by the Bear Family label in Germany: These include Bill Monroe, Flatt and Scruggs, the Stanley Brothers, the Osborne Brothers, Jim and Jesse McReynolds, Reno and Smiley, Jimmy Martin, and the Country Gentlemen. Of all the Bear collections that have been produced, I think that Mac Wiseman's box set, *'Tis Sweet to Be Remembered* (Bear), merits special attention. Wiseman was a marvelous singer and, as this is being written, he continues to live as a fount of wisdom about bluegrass and old-time music.

13. Neil Rosenberg, Notes to *Flatt and Scruggs*, Country and Western Classics series (Time-Life Collection, 1982; TLCW-04), 12.

14. Tom Piazza has written one of the finest and most readable biographies of a bluegrass musician, *True Adventures with the King of Bluegrass: Jimmy Martin* (Nashville: Vanderbilt University Press, 1999).

15. The Stanley Brothers have fittingly inspired an extensive body of literature, including John Wright, *Traveling the High Way Home: Ralph Stanley and the World of Traditional Music* (Urbana: University of Illinois Press, 1993); David W. Johnson, *Lonesome Melodies: The Lives and Music of the Stanley Brothers* (Jackson: University Press of Mississippi, 2013); Ralph Stanley, with Eddie Dean, *Man of Constant Sorrow: My Life and Times* (New York: Gotham Books, 2009); and Gary B. Reid, *The Music of the Stanley Brothers* (Urbana: University of Illinois Press, 2014).

16. Bob Cantwell, "The Lonesome Sound of Carter Stanley," *Bluegrass Unlimited* 10, no. 12 (June 1976): 16.

17. Alan Lomax, "Bluegrass Background: Folk Music with Overdrive," *Esquire* 52, no. 4 (October 1959): 103–109.

18. Thomas Adler, "Manual Formulaic Composition: Innovation in Bluegrass Banjo Styles," *Journal of Country Music* 5, no. 2 (Summer 1974): 55–64.

19. Henry Glassie was responsible for the production of an extraordinary book, complete with two CDs, about Ola Belle Reed and her music: *Ola Belle Reed and Southern Mountain Music on the Mason-Dixon Line* (Atlanta: Dust to Digital, 2015).

20. See Tim Newby, *Bluegrass in Baltimore: The Hard Drivin' Sound and Its Legacy* (Jefferson, NC: McFarland, 2015).

21. I picked up this term from a friend, bluegrass fanatic, and mandolin player, Edward Mellon, in Austin, Texas, sometime back in the early 1960s.

22. As noted in an earlier chapter, Ronald D. Cohen has written the best general survey of this era of American folk music: *Rainbow Quest: The Folk Music Revival and American Society, 1940–1970* (Boston: University of Massachusetts Press, 2002). Robert Cantwell, though, has written the most provocative interpretation of the phenomenon: *When We Were Good: The Folk Revival* (Cambridge, MA: Harvard University Press, 1996).

23. Lomax, "Bluegrass Background," 108; Robert Shelton, *The Country Music Story* (New York: Bobbs-Merrill, 1966), 140.

24. See Bill C. Malone, *Bill Clifton: America's Bluegrass Ambassador to the World* (Urbana: University of Illinois, 2016).

25. Bill Clifton, *150 Old-Time Folk and Gospel Songs* (privately printed, 1955).

26. "Sonny Tells It Like It Is," *Bluegrass Unlimited* 3, no. 12 (June 1969): 12.

27. Starday is discussed in chapter 10 and by Nathan Gibson in his fine book *The Starday Story: The House That Country Music Built* (Jackson: University Press of Mississippi, 2011).

28. Unnamed article in *Music City News* 15, no. 8 (February 1978): 26.

29. Ralph Stanley, with Eddie Dean, *Man of Constant Sorrow*.

30. Ronni Lundy, "The New Grass Revival," *Bluegrass Unlimited* 13, no. 5 (November 1978): 10.

CHAPTER 11: COUNTRY MUSIC, 1972–1984

1. Garrison Keillor, "Onward and Upward with the Arts at the Opry," *New Yorker* 50, no. 11 (May 6, 1974): 46–70. See also Jon Bream, "A Prairie Home Companion," *Dallas Morning News*, July 1, 1984, 1C.

2. *Newsweek*, June 18, 1973; *Time*, May 5, 1974.

3. Richard Goldstein, "My Country Music Problem—and Yours," *Mademoiselle* 77, no. 2 (June 1973): 114–115, 185.

4. Bob Allen, "Haggard's a Working Man at Heart," *Music City News* 19, no. 12 (June 1982): 12.

5. *Music City News* 12, no. 6 (December 1974): 3.

6. Justin Tubb, "What's Wrong with the Way That We're Doing It Now," on *Justin Tubb*, First Generation Records, FGLP-GOOS-01.

7. Interview with Cindy Walker, Mexia, Texas, August 12, 1976.

8. John Gabree, "Anne Murray: The Girl Next Door Grows Up," *Country Music Beat* 1, no. 1 (January 1975): 43.

9. "Playboy Interview: Kenny Rogers," *Playboy* 30, no. 11 (November 1983): 69.

10. Dolly Carlisle, "Larry Gatlin: Straight Ahead," *Country Music* 8, no. 7 (April 1980): 21.

11. Patrick Carr, "The Statler Brothers: How the Class of '57 Buys a Schoolhouse, Wins Eight CMA Awards in an Air of Complete Calm," *Country Music* 9, no. 7 (March 1981): 40.

12. From Kurt Vonnegut's autobiography, *Palm Sunday*, quoted in ibid., 45.

13. Bob Dylan had shown an interest in country music all of his life. See his *Chronicles*, vol. 1 (New York: Simon and Schuster, 2004).

14. My favorite biography of Gram Parsons is Ben-Fong Torres, *Hickory Wind: The Life and Times of Gram Parsons* (New York: St. Martin's Press, 1991). Another book worth reading, because of his daughter's involvement, is Jessica Hundley, with Polly Parsons, *Grievous Angel: An Intimate Biography of Gram Parsons* (New York: Thunder's Mouth Press, 2005).

15. Hank Williams Jr. and Michael Bane wrote *Living Proof: An Autobiography* (New York: G. P. Putnam's, 1979), which in turn became the basis of a television movie in 1983.

16. Tamara Saviano's impressive biography of Clark is candid and sensitive: *Without Getting Killed or Caught: The Life and Music of Guy Clark* (College Station: Texas A&M University Press, 2016).

17. Rodney Crowell's autobiography is by far the best account written by a country musician. He is sensitive, brutally honest, and loving about his parents and their working-class country music culture: *Chinaberry Sidewalks* (New York: Alfred A. Knopf: 2011).

18. Nicholas Spitzer, "Bob Wills Is Still the King: Romantic Regionalism and Convergent Culture in Central Texas," *John Edwards Memorial Foundation Quarterly* 2, pt. 4, no. 4 (Winter 1975): 191–197.

19. Heard on Waylon Jennings, *Dreaming My Dreams*, RCA APL1-1062.

20. Jan Reid's *The Improbable Rise of Redneck Rock* (Austin: University of Texas Press, 2004) is still the best account of the Austin scene. Also perceptive and sophisticated in its analysis is Travis D. Stimeling, *Cosmic Cowboys and New Hicks: The Countercultural Sounds of Austin's Progressive Country Music Scene* (New York: Oxford University Press, 2011).

21. See Joe Nick Patoski, *Willie Nelson: An Epic Life* (Boston: Little, Brown, 2008).

22. William C. Martin, "Growing Old at Willie Nelson's Picnic," *Texas Monthly* 2 (October 1974): 94–98, 116–124.

23. Waylon Jennings, with Lenny Kaye, *Waylon: An Autobiography* (New York: Warner Books, 1996). Waylon gives a decidedly different picture of his early years—including a recollection that did not include Bob Wills—from the one mentioned in Spitzer's "Bob Wills Is Still the King."

24. Indeed, some people would extend this evaluation. I will never forget the night, a very long time ago, when Townsend Miller leaned across the table at the Station Inn in Nashville and said to me in almost-hushed tones: "There have been two great singers in American music, Ella Fitzgerald and Waylon Jennings."

25. The song was first recorded in 1987 in an album called *Salt of the Earth* (Columbia FC 40293).

26. Robert Windeler, "Bio—Chet Atkins," *People Weekly*, December 16, 1974, 62.

27. The brilliant singer and guitarist Ray Benson has told his story in *Comin'*

Right At Ya: How a Jewish Yankee Hippie Went Country, or, The Often Outrageous History of Asleep at the Wheel (Austin: University of Texas Press, 2015).

28. The books cited about George Jones in the previous chapter are still relevant here, but one other item presents some very provocative arguments about the relationship between Jones and Billy Sherrill: Jack Isenhour, *He Stopped Loving Her Today: George Jones, Billy Sherrill, and the Pretty-Much Totally True Story of the Making of the Greatest Country Record of All Time* (Jackson: University Press of Mississippi, 2011).

29. Retirements in country music do not always last. By the fall of 2016, Strait was back on the road again.

30. Hugh Cherry, "Country DJs Carry Music to People," *Music City News* 18, no. 4 (October 1980): 19.

CHAPTER 12: TRADITION AND CHANGE

1. The song "Murder on Music Row" was included in Larry Cordle and Lonesome Standard Time, *Murder on Music Row* (Shell Point 1001), and in George Strait, *Latest Greatest Straitest Hits* (MCA 088170 102-2).

2. For a discussion of the historical roots of this argument, see James C. Cobb, "Rednecks, White Socks, and Piña Coladas? Country Music Ain't What It Used to Be . . . And It Really Never Was," *Southern Cultures* 5, no. 4 (Winter 1999): 41–51.

3. Curtis W. Ellison, *Country Music Culture: From Hard Times to Heaven* (Jackson: University Press of Mississippi, 1995).

4. Earle also tried his hand at fiction, with a novel called *I'll Never Get Out of This World Alive* (New York: Houghton Mifflin Brace, 2011).

5. By late 2016, Gill was sitting in, without pay, at the Bluebird Inn as part of an outstanding group of all-star western swing musicians called the Time Jumpers. Including such stellar musicians as Larry Franklin and Doug Green, this group had played together informally since 1998 at a couple of Nashville clubs, Station Inn and Third and Lindsley. Their "amateurism," however, did not prevent them from recording a CD for Rounder that earned a Grammy award.

6. Bruce Feiler, *Dreaming Out Loud: Garth Brooks, Wynonna Judd, Wade Hayes, and the Changing Face of Nashville* (New York: Avon Books, 1998).

7. Rosanne Cash is a woman with eclectic interests. Among her several books is a brief autobiography, *Composed: A Memoir* (New York: Penguin, 2010).

8. Quoted in Tamara Saviano, Nick Krewen, and Michael McCall, "The Four Faces of Faith," *Country Music*, December–January 2001, 54.

9. Geoffrey Himes, "Faith Hill: Contradictions and Affirmations," *Country Music*, July–August 1996, 40.

10. These accolades came, of course, before the Chicks lost favor with much of the traditional country audience in 2003 when Natalie Maines denounced

President George W. Bush during a concert in London. Opposing America's impending entry into the war against Iraq, Maines said, "We're ashamed that the president of the United States is from Texas."

11. Marty Stuart has become one of the premier photographers of country music. His books of photos include *Pilgrims: Sinners, Saints, and Prophets* (Nashville, TN: Rutledge Hill, 2000); *Country Music: The Masters* (Naperville, IL: Sourcebooks Media Fusion, 2008); and *American Ballads: The Photographs of Marty Stuart* (Nashville, TN: Vanderbilt University Press, 2014).

12. Stubbs made this remark as the emcee on *The Marty Stuart Show*, RFD Television, episode 38, March 6, 2010.

13. Merle Haggard confounded both his conservative and liberal listeners when he endorsed, and wrote a song about, Hillary Clinton during the 2008 campaign. He defended the Dixie Chicks after they criticized President Bush, and opposed America's involvement in Iraq, while also calling for isolationism in "America First," recorded in *Chicago Wind* Capitol 7243).

14. The definitive study of the Austin show is Tracey E. W. Laird, *Austin City Limits: A History* (New York: Oxford University Press, 2014).

15. Murphy Hicks Henry, *Pretty Good for a Girl: Women in Bluegrass* (Urbana: University of Illinois Press, 2013).

16. For discerning portraits of Chris Thile and Garrison Keillor, see Abe Streep, "The Beauty of It Is That It Could Fail," *New York Times Magazine*, October 2, 2016, 32–35.

CHAPTER 13: A NEW CENTURY

1. Alice Randall, "Beyoncé's 'Daddy Lessons' Is Classic Country," *American Songwriter*, October 27, 2016, https://americansongwriter.com/2016/10 /beyonces-daddy-lessons-is-classic-country/.

2. I was influenced here by the idea I first encountered in Nadine Hubbs, *Rednecks, Queers, and Country Music* (Berkeley: University of California Press, 2014), 24. Hubbs draws on 1990s work by the sociologist Bethany Bryson, who suggests that middle-class consumers seek "cultural capital" less via high-culture pursuits, as was once common, and more in expansive, multicultural tastes. Hubbs explores reasons why this "cultural omnivore" approach often excludes country music.

3. Chet Flippo, "Nashville Skyline: Shut Up and Sing?," March 20, 2003, CMT website, http://www.cmt.com/news/1470672/nashville-skyline-shut-up -and-sing/.

4. Kelefa Sanneh, "It's Dixie Chicks vs. Country Fans, but Who's Dissing Whom?," *New York Times*, May 25, 2006, http://www.nytimes.com/2006/05 /25/arts/music/25sann.html.

5. See Mary Bufwack, "Kitty Wells: Don't Blame the 'Honky-Tonk,'" *All Things*

Considered, NPR broadcast, December 14, 2008, http://www.npr.org/2008 /12/14/98201349/kitty-wells-dont-blame-the-honky-tonk.

6. Writing for the *Journal of Country Music* in 2006, Craig Havighurst dismissively described McBride's hit as an example of "turn-of-the-millennium therapy songs"—"thera-pop," a term he coined as shorthand for songs "with themes of empowerment." See Havighurst, "Scenes from a Rose Garden," in *The Country Music Reader*, ed. Travis Stimeling (New York: Oxford University Press, 2015), 332, 337n.

7. The linguist Alena Horn analyzes thematic elements, past allusions, and vocabulary in "'Keepin' It Country': What Makes the Lyrics of Gretchen Wilson Hard?," *Popular Music and Society* 32, no. 4 (October 2009); 461–473.

8. Russ Penuell, "On Music and Scheduling," *Country Aircheck Weekly* 449 (May 26, 2015): 8, https://www.countryaircheck.com/pdfs/current052615.pdf.

9. Alison Bonaguro, "Men Are Lettuce, Women Are Tomatoes?," *CMT News*, May 27, 2015, http://www.cmt.com/news/1754800/men-are-lettuce-women -are-tomatoes/.

10. Neil Ferguson, "Sturgill Simpson Launches Spring Tour with Two Sold-Out Shows in Austin," *No Depression*, May 8, 2016, http://nodepression.com /live-review/sturgill-simpson-launches-spring-tour-two-sold-out-shows -austin.

11. For an overview on irony and "fetishization" in alt-country, see Pamela Fox and Barbara Ching's introduction to their edited collection *Old Roots, New Routes: The Cultural Politics of Alt.Country Music* (Ann Arbor: University of Michigan Press, 2008).

12. Mike Seely, "Wheeler Walker Jr. at the Tractor Tavern in Seattle, 7/8/16," live performance review, *No Depression*, July 9, 2016, http://nodepression .com/live-review/wheeler-walker-jr-tractor-tavern-seattle-7816.

13. "Sir Mashalot: Mind-Blowing SIX Song Country Mashup," YouTube, November 4, 2014, https://www.youtube.com/watch?v=FY8SwIvxj8o. As of April 8, 2017, the post had more than 6,300,000 viewings.

14. For analysis of Fox's use of country music, see Dave Robinson, "Country Crooners and FOX News: Country Music and the FOX Brand," in *Rock Brands: Selling Sound in a Media Saturated Culture*, ed. Elizabeth Barfoot Christian (Lanham, MD: Lexington Books, 2011).

15. Chet Flippo, "Why the Term 'Country Music' May Disappear," *Nashville Skyline*, originally published January 14, 2010; republished April 19, 2012, http://www.cmt.com/news/1683526/nashville-skyline-why-the-term -country-music-may-disappear/. It was also reprinted in Stimeling, *The Country Music Reader*, 354–356.

16. Skip Hollandsworth, "The Girl Who Played with Firearms," *Texas Monthly*, October 2011, http://www.texasmonthly.com/articles/the-girl-who-played -with-firearms/. The piece is also reprinted in Stimeling, *The Country Music Reader*, 363.

Bibliographical Essays

ABBREVIATIONS USED

BGU	*Bluegrass Unlimited*
CMA	Country Music Association
CMF	Country Music Foundation
CSR	*Country Song Roundup*
JAF	*Journal of American Folklore*
JCM	*Journal of Country Music*
JEMF	John Edwards Memorial Foundation
JEMFQ	*John Edwards Memorial Foundation Quarterly*
MCN	*Music City News*
OTM	*Old Time Music*
SFQ	*Southern Folklore Quarterly*

The following bibliographic information is presented for two purposes: to give the reader some idea about the sources of my information and ideas, and to suggest to potential country music scholars areas of research that they might find useful. The suggested items will not always be easily accessible, but most published books, scholarly essays, and popular articles can be found in public or school libraries. Much of the country music material, such as *Music City News*, *Country Music Magazine*, and the John Edwards Memorial Foundation (JEMF) newsletters, more than likely will be found only in such vernacular music repositories as the Center for Popular Music at Middle Tennessee State University in Murfreesboro, the Country Music Foundation Library and Media Center in Nashville, and the Southern Folklife Collection at the University of North Carolina in Chapel Hill. A remarkable number of items, however, can be referenced by a diligent search of the Internet, including in many cases major portions if not all of the contents of published books or articles. A special word should be said about the oral history involved in the telling of the story. Over the years, I talked to a very large number of people. Some of these encounters were formal taped interviews, some were discussions that were recorded in handwritten notes, and some were conversations that were not recorded at all. Although they all went into the making of my knowledge of country music, they unfortunately will not all be available to students. Many of these "discussions," along with most of the other items in my personal library, are now housed in "The Bill C. Malone Collection" in the Southern Folklife archives at Chapel Hill.

1. THE FOLK BACKGROUND BEFORE COMMERCIALISM

My approach to country music's history is predicated upon several assumptions. Among these are the belief that the phenomenon is, in one sense, very old, having drawn upon many cultural and ethnic sources, some of which long predate the colonization of the United States. Carl Bridenbaugh's wonderful book *Vexed and Troubled Englishmen, 1590–1642* (New York: Oxford University Press, 1968) suggests that many of the traits, such as restlessness and the ambivalent assertion of both hedonism and Puritanism, associated with the American character (and discussed in abundance in country lyrics) were part of the cultural baggage brought by the English and other "British" folk to American soil. In the American environment, British folk culture, which was already a composite of the shifting ethnic and racial strains of the British Isles, came into immediate contact with the cultural resources of other peoples. Above all, the close and often intimate relationship between Africans and poor white southerners gave "southern music" a distinctiveness that set it apart from music in other regions of the United States (see my *Southern Music/American Music* [Lexington: University Press of Kentucky, 1979]) and *Music from the True Vine: Mike Seeger's Life and Musical Journey* (Chapel Hill: University of North Carolina Press, 2011).

My contention that country music bears a special relationship to the South has been challenged by some scholars. The best account of such dissent is found in a special issue of the *Journal of American Folklore*, vol. 127, no. 504 (Spring 2014), edited by Thomas A. DuBois and James P. Leary. Exponents of the idea of "northern country music" include Simon J. Bronner, "Country Music Culture in Central New York State," *JEMFQ* 13, no. 47 (Winter 1977): 171–182; Peter Narváez, "Country Music in Diffusion: Juxtaposition and Syncretism in the Popular Music of Newfoundland," *JCM* 7, no. 2 (May 1978): 93–101; two works by Neil Rosenberg, "Folk and Country Music in the Canadian Maritimes: A Regional Model," *JCM* 5, no. 2 (Summer 1974): 76–83, and *Country Music in the Maritimes: Two Studies*, Memorial University of Newfoundland Reprint Series No. 2 (1974); an interesting account of non-British music that resembles its southern hillbilly counterpart by Robert Coltman, "Habitantbilly: French-Canadian Old Time Music," *OTM*, no. 11 (Winter 1973–1974): 9–12; and Clifford Murphy, *Yankee Twang: Country and Western Music in New England* (Urbana: University of Illinois Press, 2014).

While recognizing that commercial country music now has a following around the world and that rural-derived forms of music have always shown strength in various areas of the nation, I nonetheless remain convinced that *commercial* country music has always received its most fervent support—as well as the bulk of its performing personnel—in the region extending southwestward from Virginia to Texas (or in what Richard A. Peterson and Russell Davis called "The Fertile Crescent of Country Music," *JCM* 6, no. 1 [Spring 1975]: 19–25). Southern white plain folk culture—the seedbed of commercial country music—has drawn little attention from scholars, a neglect that seems even more striking when compared to the wealth of material dealing with black Americans since World War II. Nothing in the area of poor white scholarship compares to Lawrence A. Levine's masterful *Black Culture and Black Consciousness: Afro-American Folk Thought from Slavery to Freedom* (New York: Oxford University Press, 1977). Levine's recognition that folk culture is dynamic rather than static (adapting but not succumbing to change) and his assertion that folklore and oral history are useful tools for perceiving folk consciousness are insights that scholars of other folk cultures should find relevant to their own work. The idea that the South as a whole has been a folk culture has been most persuasively argued by David M. Potter in "The Enigma of the South," in his *The South and the Sectional Conflict* (Baton Rouge: Louisiana State University Press, 1968), 15. Cultural conservatism and an organic interrelationship with the land have been shared by both black and white southerners and, to a certain extent, by rich and poor alike. W. J. Cash's classic work *The Mind of the South* (New York: Alfred A. Knopf, 1941) implies the existence of a common folk culture (although he does not use the term) when he talks of the subtle ways in which blacks and whites have influenced each other. He also convincingly demonstrates that the rich diversity of the South did not prevent southerners from sharing a set of assumptions and cultural traits that would have been familiar from Virginia to Texas. Many factors contributed to the shaping of this commonality of thought and behavior, but its preservation and extension were insured by the tendency of southerners to migrate to areas where their familiar way of life and the cultivation of cotton could be continued. This migration tended to be southwestward in nature, as demonstrated by Frank L. Owsley in "The Pattern of Migration and Settlement on the Southern Frontier," *The Journal of Southern History* 11, no. 2 (1945): 147–176, and by Barnes F. Lathrop in *Migration into East Texas, 1835–1860: A Study from the United States Census* (Austin: University of Texas Press, 1949).

Frank Owsley and the students who studied under him at Vanderbilt long held a monopoly on the study of southern plain whites. His *Plain Folk of the Old South* (Baton Rouge: Louisiana State University Press, 1949) contained excellent social portraits of plain people but was somewhat marred by a tendency to romanticize its subjects and by a strained effort to show that the plain folk were neither poor nor class-conscious (most of them, argued Owsley, owned land or otherwise had access to the bountiful southern public domain). George Pullen Jackson, in the best work yet written on southern folk music, *White Spirituals in the Southern Uplands: The Story of the Fasola Folk, Their Songs, Singings, and "Buckwheat Notes"* (Chapel Hill: University of North Carolina Press, 1933), did not address himself to the question of class consciousness or conflict, but he did demonstrate that urban-rural antagonisms have affected cultural/musical preferences in the South. Thomas D. Clark, in his impressively researched and fact-filled *Pills, Petticoats, and Plows: The Southern Country Store* (Indianapolis: Bobbs-Merrill, 1944), comes closer than any other historian to re-creating the daily lives of nineteenth-century rural southerners. His study of the ubiquitous credit nexus, which governed southern economic relations throughout that century and much of the next, shows that an allegedly isolated rural South was in fact connected to the outside world in various insidious ways. Forrest McDonald and Grady McWhiney see unity in still another realm, and one that relates southerners not only to each other, but also to a dim and ancient historical past: Celticism. In a series of articles and public presentations, but most cogently in "The Antebellum Southern Herdsman: A Reinterpretation," *The Journal of Southern History* 41, no. 2 (May 1975): 147–167, McDonald and McWhiney reaffirm Owsley's assertions of an abundant and classless folk society, but go a step beyond him to argue that the most binding ingredient of the Old South was the common Celtic heritage shared by most white southerners. Preponderantly Scotch-Irish, white southerners according to this theory were clannish, fiercely independent, given to rash and impulsive action, and slovenly in their agricultural practices (because they preferred open-range stock raising to husbandry). Celticism has obvious implications for the understanding of southern folk music, but thus far, although McDonald and McWhiney promoted it often and with great passion, Celticism remains a theory in search of supportive data.

McDonald and McWhiney's Celtic theorizing is part of a reawakening of interest in the southern plain folk that gives promise of blossoming into a full-scale scholarly enterprise. Challenges have been made to the Owsley thesis, including Samuel C. Hyde Jr., ed., *Plain Folk of the South Revisited* (Baton Rouge: LSU Press, 1997). Steven Hahn's provocative *The Roots of Southern Populism: Yeoman Farmers and the Transformation of the Georgia Upcountry, 1850–1890* (New York: Oxford University Press, 1983) and J. Wayne Flynt's *Dixie's Forgotten People: The South's Poor Whites* (Bloomington: Indiana University Press, 1979) have been catalysts in the investigation of all realms of poor white life and culture. Unlike Owsley's conservative orientation, their books are informed by the liberal consciousness of our own time and by the belief that scholarship can promote the cause of social justice. Flynt believes, for example, that many southern whites have been and still are poor, but that their culture (religion, music, folkways) has been a sustaining force for them and a phenomenon worthy of the respect of others. Flynt and his wife, Dorothy S. Flynt, prepared a useful resource guide for students of plain folk culture: *Southern Poor Whites: A Selected, Annotated Bibliography of Published Sources* (New York: Garland Publishing, 1981).

Music has indeed been a constant presence in the lives of southern plain folk, or what we would now call the working class. A study of country music, then, should not begin in the 1920s when the first recordings were made, but instead should encompass the entire span of southern history. The precommercial and pre-twentieth-century manifestations of rural music should be studied with the same care devoted to other aspects of southern culture. Travel accounts can tell us something about revival singing, house parties, fiddle contests, or itinerant balladeers; country store ledgers, as Thomas Clark suggested, provide information on the purchase of songbooks and musical instruments; plantation records and diaries, although generally the property of the upper classes, sometime make mention of rural musicians; deeds, wills, and property settlements might itemize fiddles and banjos; and newspapers can give occasional hints about music among the common folk. Newspapers, it is true, usually gave most of their attention to the polite music of the gentry (balls, soirées, recitals), but on occasion music of a plainer sort received at least brief coverage; the earliest accounts of fiddle contests in America, for example, were carried in the *Virginia Gazette* in the 1730s. Since rowdy behavior sometimes accompanied public performances of music, court and police records might pay unexpected dividends to music historians. The literary fiction that dealt with poor whites in the nineteenth century—the southwestern humor of the antebellum period and the local color of the postwar years—should also be mined for the musical nuggets that might lie there. The most famous work in the genre, Augustus Baldwin Longstreet's *Georgia Scenes*, published in 1835 (but based upon earlier newspaper stories), describes a country dance in terms remarkably similar to accounts of such phenomena one hundred years later (reprinted, Atlanta: Cherokee Publishing Company, 1971). While fiction provides glimpses of rural/folk music, graphic representations may tell us even more. Archie Green reminded readers of the *JEMFQ* for several years, in his Music Graphics series, that placards, posters, handbills, and genre art like that of William Sidney Mount, Currier and Ives lithographs, magazine illustrations, and a host of other popular arts forms would enhance our understanding of American folk music (see, for example, the sketch of a rowdy dance in Denison, Texas, accompanied by a fiddle and guitar, in *Scribner's Monthly*, July 1873, and reprinted in *JEMFQ* 14, no. 30 [Summer 1978]: 84).

When delving into the pre-twentieth-century history of southern music, it is difficult to separate "rural" from "urban" music, chiefly because few people then made those kinds of distinctions. One also finds that the border between "popular" and "folk" music was often tenuous and that commercialization had never been a stranger to folk music. Talented folk musicians have always sought audiences (or audiences have sought them), and their performances have always been rewarded in some manner. Accounts of English medieval fairs, public hangings, or any large event where large groups congregated, as well as of wayfaring people, circuses, puppet shows, equestrian exhibitions, medicine shows, and taverns, abound with references to pipers, fiddlers, dancers, balladeers, and broadside vendors. This is a rich area of research that awaits music historians, and I will list only a few of the works that have been useful to me: Bridenbaugh's *Vexed and Troubled Englishmen*; W. Chappell, *Popular Music of the Olden Time* (London: Chappell, 1838); Charles Read Baskerville, *The Elizabethan Jig and Related Song Drama* (Chicago: University of Chicago Press, 1929); Gaston Vuillier, *A History of Dancing* (New York: D. Appleton, 1898); George Speaight, *The History of the English Puppet Theatre* (London: George G. Harrap, 1955); J. J. Jusserand, *English Wayfaring Life in the Middle Ages* (originally published in London: T. Fisher Unwin, 1889, and republished in New York: Barnes and Noble, 1950); Isaac J. Greenwood, *The Circus: Its Origin and Growth Prior to 1835* (New York: Dunlap Society, 1898); and Julian Mates, *The American Musical Stage before 1800* (New Brunswick, NJ: Rutgers University Press, 1962).

While some names are known to us, such as that of the great Philadelphia horn-pipe dancer of the late eighteenth century John Durang, or that of the famous English equestrian John Bill Ricketts, who danced hornpipes on the backs of galloping horses, most of the dancers and musicians who roamed through antebellum America will always remain anonymous. Whether urban professionals or rural folk, they both absorbed and disseminated music in the American hinterlands, so much so that much of the music emanating from the eighteenth and nineteenth centuries has no clear folk or popular identity. Indeed, some of the music and much of the dancing came from upper-class and even courtly sources. The student of old-time fiddling will reap a rich harvest of information by exploring John Playford's *English Dancing Master* (first published in 1651; reprint, Southwold, Binsted, UK: Dance Books, 2013), or Vuillier's *A History of Dancing*, or even such "high-art" music magazines as *The Etude* or *Musical America*. *Jacobs' Orchestra Monthly*, an unlikely source for country music, contains some of the best explications of such items as "hoedown," "hornpipe," and "breakdown" that I have yet found (I have seen the issues for 1910 and 1911).

The traveling shows of course contributed immeasurably to the dissemination of songs and dances among rural Americans. Little published work has appeared on the equestrian acts, circuses, and puppet shows that traveled through America during the colonial and early national periods, but all of them featured music in the form of fiddlers, hornpipe dancers, and singing clowns. The ubiquitous medicine shows, however, which traveled the length and breadth of rural America by wagon and by flatboat, have found a chronicler in Brooks McNamara, *Step Right Up: An Illustrated History of the Medicine Show* (Garden City, NY: Doubleday, 1976). Blackface minstrelsy, which contributed songs, dances, comedy, and instrumental styles to country music, has received extensive scholarly attention: an older work, Carl F. Wittke, *Tambo and Bones: A History of the American Minstrel Stage* (Durham, NC: Duke University Press, 1930), still has merit as a factual account of the phenomenon, but it has been superseded by Hans Nathan, *Dan Emmett and the Rise of Early Negro Minstrelsy* (Norman: University of Oklahoma Press, 1962); William W. Austin, *"Susanna," "Jeanie," and "The Old Folks at Home": The Songs of Stephen C. Foster from His Time to Ours* (New York: Macmillan, 1975); and Robert C. Toll, *Blacking Up: The Minstrel Show in Nineteenth-Century America* (New York: Oxford University Press, 1974). Rural Americans who ventured into town in the late nineteenth and early twentieth centuries had an opportunity to absorb the music of the vaudeville shows, discussed by Gilbert Douglas, *American Vaudeville: Its Life and Times* (New York: Dover Publications, 1963), and Albert F. McLean Jr., *American Vaudeville as Ritual* (Lexington: University of Kentucky Press, 1965), but they also encountered another approach to vaudeville in the traveling tent shows that came to rural America. The tent-repertory shows, or Toby shows (named after the red-wigged country boy character who appeared in many of them), have elicited much attention in the form of theses and dissertations, and at least two published works: Neil E. Schaffner, with Vance Johnson, *The Fabulous Toby and Me* (Englewood Cliffs, NJ: Prentice-Hall, 1968), and William L. Slout, *Theatre in a Tent: The Development of a Provincial Entertainment* (Bowling Green, OH: Popular Press, 1972).

Sheet music and pocket songsters were sources of much early country music (and in fact for many of the songs still heard today in bluegrass music). The collections of published music preserved in the Library of Congress and in other repositories, such as the Harris Collection of American Poetry and Plays in the John Hay Library at Brown University, the New York Public Library, and the William R. Hogan Jazz Archive at Tulane University, have been insufficiently utilized by scholars, but several published works suggest the utility of such research for the understanding of country music. Sigmund Spaeth often wrote with tongue in cheek when he discussed the sentimental songs of yesteryear, but in *Read 'Em and Weep: The Songs You Forgot to Remember* (New York: Doubleday, Page, 1927) and *Weep Some More, My Lady* (New York: Doubleday, Page, 1927), he compiled valuable lists of many songs that not only made Americans cry but in many cases were eventually preserved in the country music repertory. Edward B. Marks, the cowriter of "My Mother Was a Lady," provides further insight into the reasons why such songs were written and tells how they moved out into the hinterlands in his memoir, *They All Sang, from Tony Pastor to Rudy Vallee* (New York: Viking, 1934). Charles K. Harris, the New York composer of an extensive number of Tin Pan Alley tunes that eventually made their way into country music, tells a similar story in his memoir: *After the Ball: Forty Years of Melody* (New York: Frank-Maurice, 1926). A few scholars have begun to recognize the value of the "parlor songs" as a means of understanding the popular mind. Nicholas E. Tawa discusses the phenomenon for antebellum America in *Sweet Songs for Gentle Americans: The Parlor Song in America, 1790–1860* (Bowling Green, OH: Popular Press, 1980), but Norm Cohen has more clearly shown the relationship between nineteenth-century pop music and folk songs in "Tin Pan Alley's Contribution to Folk Music," *Western Folklore* 29, no. 1 (1970): 9–20. He and Anne Cohen also speculated on the way in which pop tunes were altered once they moved into the possession of the folk in "Tune Evolution as an Indicator of Traditional Musical Norms," *JAF* 86, no. 339 (January–March 1973): 37–47. Gene Wiggins conclusively demonstrated country fiddling's debt to turn-of-the-century pop music in "Popular Music and the Fiddler," *JEMFQ* 15, no. 55 (Fall 1979): 144–152, while William C. Ellis illustrated how one specific but powerful element of the sentimental tradition endured in country music: "The Sentimental Mother Song in American Country Music, 1923–1945" (PhD diss., Ohio State University, 1978). A vast literature of printed material—on sheet music, in song folios or songsters, in magazines and newspapers (such as the *Dallas Semi-Weekly Farm News*, where old songs were printed at the request of readers)—still awaits the researcher, as does the music distributed on piano rolls, in music boxes, and on early phonograph recordings. Norm Cohen has made a valuable contribution to our understanding of the link between pop and country music in a record collection that he produced and annotated: *Minstrels and Tunesmiths: The Commercial Roots of Early Country Music* (JEMF 109), an assemblage of songs recorded between 1902 and 1923.

Another powerful source of country music, and one that has affected both its style and content, is religion. Our venture into religion should properly begin with the dissenting Protestant sects who began populating the southern backcountry before the American Revolution. Much of their history—and particularly their song making—will forever be lost to us, but Donald G. Mathews, in *Religion in the Old South* (Chicago: University of Chicago Press, 1977), and Rhys Isaac, in *The Transformation of Virginia, 1740–1790* (Chapel Hill: University of North Carolina Press, 1982), tell us how they came to command the allegiance of most black and white southerners. The institution that most effectively evangelized the South, while also giving it over to the Baptists and Methodists and contributing to its staunch orthodoxy, was the camp meeting. Every student of the meetings comments on the powerful appeal of the music heard there—Charles A. Johnson, *The Frontier Camp Meeting: Religion's Harvest Time* (Dallas: Southern Methodist University Press, 1955); Bernard Weisberger, *They Gathered at the River: The Story of the Great Revivalists and Their Impact upon Religion in America* (Boston: Little, Brown, 1958); John Boles, *The Great Revival, 1787–1805: The Origins of the Southern Evangelical Mind* (Lexington: University Press of Kentucky, 1972); and Dickson D. Bruce Jr., *And They All Sang Hallelujah: Plain-Folk Camp-Meeting Religion, 1800–1845* (Knoxville: University of Tennessee Press, 1974)—but Bruce is the only historian who has tried to make music the central focus of his study. He argues that the choruses of the songs—improvised on the spot in order to encourage rapid learning and mass singing—are repositories of plain-folk theology.

The classic study of shape-note music and the singing schools that introduced the method to several generations of rural southerners is George Pullen Jackson's *White Spirituals in the Southern Uplands*. Every study of the shape-note style that has since been published is indebted to Jackson's pioneering work. Among the more significant of these works are Harry Eskew, "Shape-Note Hymnody in the Shenandoah Valley, 1816–1860" (PhD diss., Tulane University, 1966), and Rachel Augusta Harley, "Ananias Davisson: Southern Tunebook Compiler" (PhD diss., University of Michigan, 1972). The highly individualistic and conservative Sacred Harp tradition, named after one of the most famous of the shape-note songbooks, has been studied in Charles Linwood Ellington, "The Sacred Harp Tradition of the South: Its Origin and Evolution" (PhD diss., Florida State University, 1969), and in Buell E. Cobb Jr., *The Sacred Harp: A Tradition and Its Music* (Athens: University of Georgia Press, 1978).

Southern gospel music has been inadequately documented, but James R. Goff Jr. made a major contribution to our understanding with *Close Harmony: A History of Southern Gospel* (Chapel Hill: University of North Carolina Press, 2002). James C. Downey touched upon the subject in "The Music of American Revivalism" (PhD diss., Tulane University, 1968), and Jo Fleming wrote an excellent account of the Vaughan Publishing Company, the Lawrenceburg, Tennessee, concern that pioneered in the use of traveling quartets: "James D. Vaughan, Music Publisher" (SMD diss., Union Theological Seminary, 1972). The music of the Pentecostal movement has elicited little systematic study, a deficiency that progressively becomes more acute as the years pass and the founding fathers and mothers die. David Edwin Harrell Jr., *All Things Are Possible: The Healing and Charismatic Revivals in Modern America* (Bloomington: Indiana University Press, 1975), is a superior study of Pentecostalism's resurgence since World War II, while Robert Mapes Anderson, *Vision of the Disinherited: The Making of American Pentecostalism* (New York: Oxford University Press, 1979), is the best overall history of the phenomenon. Neither historian, though, says much about music. The deficiency has been rectified, in part, by an occasional academic article such as Larry T. Duncan's "Music among Early Pentecostals," *The Hymn* 38, no 1 (1987): 11–15. At least two short essays deal with the influence of Pentecostalism

on individual musicians: Van K. Brock, "Assemblies of God: Elvis and Pentecostalism," *Bulletin of the Center for the Study of Southern Culture and Religion* 3 (June
1979): 9–15; and Stephen R. Tucker, "Pentecostalism and Popular Culture in the
South: A Study of Four Musicians," *The Journal of Popular Culture* 16, no. 3 (Winter
1982): 68–80. (The four musicians discussed are James Blackwood, Tammy Wynette,
Johnny Cash, and Jerry Lee Lewis.) Although James Goff's previously mentioned
Close Harmony has competently covered the subject of gospel quartet singing, one
can find additional information in Lois S. Blackwell's brief overview of the subject,
The Wings of the Dove: The Story of Gospel Music in America (Norfolk, VA: Donning
Company, 1978), and in Stanley H. Brobston's thorough, but unpublished, "A Brief
History of White Southern Gospel Music and a Study of Selected Amateur Family
Gospel Singing Groups in Rural Georgia" (PhD diss., New York University, 1977).
A multitude of shape-note hymnals and revivalistic songbooks still await the investi-
gation of some scholar who would explore them for an understanding of southern folk
theology. My own extensive collection of such material is now housed at the Southern
Folklife Collection in Chapel Hill.

The most useful introduction to the sources of the songs that composed the early
country music repertory is Guthrie T. Meade Jr., *Country Music Sources: A Biblio-
Discography of Commercially Recorded Traditional Music* (Chapel Hill: University
of North Carolina Press, 2002). We can otherwise search the gospel hymnals, the
sheet music and songsters of the nineteenth century, the phonograph recordings that
became available at the turn of the century, and the vast panoply of folk resources
that surrounded rural singers (we should be aware, however, that rural musicians
sometimes learned songs from published folk music collections). In the realm of
traditional ballads, scholars have usually begun with the magisterial collection of
Francis James Child, *English and Scottish Popular Ballads*, 5 vols. (Boston: Houghton, Mifflin, 1882–1898), a work that has influenced all subsequent collectors. Leslie
Shepard, however, has probably come closest to explaining the type of British ballad
that actually made the transit of the Atlantic in *The Broadside Ballad: A Study in Origin and Meaning* (London: Herbert Jenkins, 1962). The best attempts to assess the
actual number of Child and broadside ballads that survived in America are Tristram
P. Coffin, *The British Traditional Ballad in North America*, rev. ed. (Philadelphia:
American Folklore Society, 1963), and G. Malcolm Laws Jr., *American Balladry from
British Broadsides* (Philadelphia: American Folklore Society, 1957). Although the
Child ballads are highly venerated by scholars, Norm Cohen and Guthrie Meade sug-
gest that few of them wound up on early hillbilly records: "The Sources of Old Time
Hillbilly Music, I: Child Ballads," *JEMFQ* 9, Part 2, no. 30 (Summer 1973): 56–61.

Printed folksong collections abound, but the two general compendiums that come
closest to reflecting the varied tastes of the folk (rather than that of the collector) are
The Frank C. Brown Collection of North Carolina Folklore, edited by Henry M. Belden
and Arthur Palmer Hudson, 7 vols. (Durham, NC: Duke University, 1952), and Vance
Randolph, *Ozark Folksongs*, 4 vols. (Columbia: State Historical Society of Missouri,
1946), revised by Norm Cohen in a one-volume edition (Urbana: University of Illinois Press, 1982). Arthur Palmer Hudson reminds us that preferences for folk songs
were pretty much the same throughout the rural South: "Folk-Songs of the Southern

Whites," in *Culture in the South*, edited by W. T. Couch (Chapel Hill: University of North Carolina Press, 1934). Alan Lomax, *The Folk Songs of North America* (New York: Doubleday, 1960), is still the best one-volume collection available, and is distinguished by the provocative theorizing and annotations of its compiler. The old songs come alive in the field recordings made for the Archive of Folk Song at the Library of Congress. This collection has been insufficiently utilized, even though many of the recordings are offered for public sale.

Old versions of songs can be reproduced, but our understanding of the ways in which they were originally performed can never be anything more than speculative. No sound recordings were made until the 1880s, and folk musicians were not recorded in any substantial numbers until the 1920s—approximately two hundred years after the first tentative settlements were made in the southern backcountry. We might assume that some of the old people living in the deep and sheltered recesses of the southern mountains or other rural regions, who were recorded in the decades after World War I, had preserved the singing styles of their ancestors, but we can never know conclusively. The researcher, though, should be aware of the arguments posed by the collectors Mark Wilson and Alan Jabbour, in interviews found on the web. They have argued persuasively that the styles and repertories of some noncommercial old-time fiddlers, such as the West Virginian Ed Haley and the Virginian Henry Reed, contain strong hints of the ways that fiddlers sounded in the nineteenth century.

Most hypothesizing about vocal and instrumental styles has been based upon twentieth-century observations. Alan Lomax has made the boldest assertions about style in *The Folk Songs of North America* and in "Folk Song Style," *American Anthropologist* 61, no. 6 (December 1959): 927–955, where he stresses the conservatism of style and contrasts the repressed, tight-throat style of the whites with the expressive, open-throated singing of the blacks. Roger Abrahams and George Foss concentrate on white singing exclusively in *Anglo-American Folksong Style* (Englewood Cliffs, NJ: Prentice-Hall, 1968), but none of these authorities, it seems to me, has sufficiently recognized that not one but many styles of folk singing existed. The best brief exposition of vocal and instrumental styles is a record anthology, *Going Down the Valley*, New World Records NW236 (edited and annotated by Norm Cohen).

D. K. Wilgus, in record reviews written for the *Kentucky Folklore Record* and *Journal of American Folklore*, and Norm and Anne Cohen, in "Folk and Hillbilly Music: Further Thoughts on Their Relation," *JEMFQ* 13, no. 46 (Summer 1977): 50–57, use the terms "domestic" and "assembly" to describe the two kinds of performance featured by folk musicians (home-centered and usually vocal music as opposed to the music performed instrumentally for a group of listeners or dancers). The assembly tradition, also called "display" by Richard Spottswood in vol. 14 of the record collection *Folk Music in America* (Library of Congress), has stimulated the interest of many scholars and enthusiasts. Charles Wolfe compiled a book on twentieth century fiddlers—*The Devil's Box: Masters of Southern Fiddling* (Nashville: Vanderbilt University Press, 2006)—that nevertheless may be suggestive of the older styles that undoubtedly influenced them. Fiddling is the central focus of a magazine also called *The Devil's Box*, published in Madison, Alabama, by the Tennessee Valley Old Time

Fiddlers Association, and is the subject of several good articles and academic theses: Linda C. Burman-Hall, "Southern American Folk Fiddle Styles," *Ethnomusicology* 19, no. 1 (January 1975): 47–65; Earl V. Spielman, "Traditional North American Fiddling: An Historical and Comparative Analytical Style Study of Instrumental Musical Traditions" (PhD diss., University of Wisconsin, 1975); Michael Mendelson, "A Bibliography of Fiddling in North America," which ran for several issues in *JEMFQ*, beginning with vol. 11, no. 38 (Summer 1975); John Burke, "Country Fiddling," *BGU* 6, no. 10 (April 1972): 17–20; and Barret E. Hansen, "The American Country Waltz," *JEMFQ* 5, Part 1, no. 13 (Spring 1969): 4–6. S. Foster Damon, "The History of Square-Dancing," *Proceedings of the American Antiquarian Society* 62, no. 1 (April 1952): 63–98, is not concerned with fiddling as such, but it does discuss one of the important milieus in which the fiddle held sway.

Other instruments and instrumental styles have not been quite as appealing to scholars as has the art of old-time fiddling. The mandolin, though, has been the subject of a doctoral dissertation by Scott Hambly, "Mandolins in the United States since 1880: An Industrial and Sociocultural History of Form" (PhD diss., University of Pennsylvania, 1977), and I have found some information on early Italian masters of the instrument in scattered music magazines such as *Etude* 61, no. 2 (February 1938): 127. The mandolin-banjo-guitar club craze early in the twentieth century inspired the formation of a few journals, such as *Gatcomb's Banjo and Guitar Gazette*, *Cadenza*, and *Crescendo*, which promoted the mandolin and other string instruments. Mail-order catalogues, like those from Sears-Roebuck and Montgomery Ward, made inexpensive brands available to the rural and small-town public.

Very little has been done on pre-twentieth-century string-band music as a whole, although Archie Green has made some interesting tentative observations in "String Bands," *JEMFQ* 15, no. 56 (Winter 1979): 215–224. The banjo has aroused the curiosity of Americans since at least 1784, when Thomas Jefferson referred to the "banjar" in *Notes on the State of Virginia*. Dena Epstein has documented the instrument's existence among American blacks, though, as early as 1754, in "The Folk Banjo: A Documentary History," *Ethnomusicology* 19, no. 3 (September 1975): 347–371, and in *Sinful Tunes and Spirituals: Black Folk Music to the Civil War* (Urbana: University of Illinois Press, 1977), 36. The addition of the fifth string and Joel Walker Sweeney's alleged contribution to the innovation are explored, and refuted, by Jay Bailey, in "Historical Origin and Stylistic Developments of the Five-String Banjo," *JAF* 85, no. 335 (January–March 1972): 58–65. Robert B. Winans sees a direct link between the banjo styles favored by blackface minstrels and the early frailing techniques of white country musicians: "The Folk, the Stage, and the Five-String Banjo in the Nineteenth Century," *JAF* 89, no. 354 (1976): 407–437. Cecelia Conway, on the other hand, sees African American playing as the source of southern rural styles in *African Banjo Echoes in Appalachia: A Study of Folk Traditions* (Knoxville: University of Tennessee Press, 1995).

The discovery of southern folk music came about in the late nineteenth and early twentieth centuries, first with the vogue for the spirituals in the 1870s, and later with the discovery of cowboy music and the romantic revelation of a still-surviving ballad and folk-song culture in the southern mountains. I have discussed these successive discoveries in *Southern Music/American Music*, 18–41, while Henry D. Shapiro, *Appalachia on Our Mind: The Southern Mountains and Mountaineers in the American Consciousness, 1870–1920* (Chapel Hill: University of North Carolina Press, 1978), and, preeminently, David Whisnant, *All That is Native and Fine: The Politics of Culture in an American Region* (Chapel Hill: University of North Carolina Press, 1983), have explored more comprehensively the roots of our romantic fascination with mountain culture. No book surpasses Whisnant's in its discussion of the role played by settlement workers in the shaping of public perceptions of mountain music. This essay should not be concluded without mentioning the names of three men who contributed immeasurably to a national awakening to the immense wealth of southern folk music: John Lomax, with his *Cowboy Songs and Other Frontier Ballads* (New York: Sturgis and Walton, 1910); Cecil Sharp, with Maud Karpeles, *English Folk Songs from the Southern Appalachians* (London: Oxford University Press, 1917); and Robert Winslow Gordon, whose early recording expeditions provided the nucleus for the Archive of Folk Song's great collection (a sampling of this material can be heard in Neil V. Rosenberg and Debora G. Kodish, eds., *Folk-Songs of America: The Robert Winslow Gordon Collection, 1922–1932*, Library of Congress, AFS L681 1978). Kodish has also written a biography, *Good Friends and Bad Enemies: Robert Winslow Gordon and the Study of American Folksong* (Urbana: University of Illinois Press, 1986).

2. THE EARLY PERIOD OF COMMERCIAL HILLBILLY MUSIC

The study of country music's early commercial period has been much enhanced by the establishment of two impressive repositories: The Country Music Library and Media Center at the Country Music Foundation (CMF) in Nashville, and the Southern Folklife Collection housed at the University of North Carolina in Chapel Hill. Both libraries contain enormous collections of phonograph recordings, tapes, videos, songbooks and folios, magazines, brochures, placards, assorted ephemera associated with the music industry, and interviews conducted with musicians and music industry people. The Southern Folklife Collection includes material originally accumulated by the Australian collector John Edwards, as well as numerous other holdings obtained from similar collectors in the United States and around the world. These depositories, however, do not contain complete runs of certain journals; the Country Music Library's collection of *Billboard*, for example, begins only in 1939. Other issues dating back to the early 1900s must be sought in other libraries, such as that of the University of Texas at Austin where I did my own study, or purchased on microfilm. Other important early journals, such as *Talking Machine World*, can be found at the Library of Congress. In any event, the Union List of Serials should be consulted by anyone who seeks to run down an early music or entertainment publication.

Except for occasional picture-songbooks printed at private expense (usually by radio stations or by the entertainers themselves), or song folios of the type sold by Bradley Kincaid on WLS, virtually no magazines devoted to country music were published during the twenties. The researcher, then, must look for tidbits wherever they can be found, in *Billboard* or *Variety* (where hillbilly musicians were rarely mentioned), in *Talking Machine World*, in *Radio Digest* and other short-lived broadcasting journals, in popular magazines and newspapers (where radio logs were often carried), in record company brochures and advertisements, and in mail-order catalogues where records and musical instruments were advertised.

The best published source for the music of the two decades before World War II is the invaluable book compiled by the English researcher Tony Russell: *Country Music Records: A Discography, 1921–1942* (New York: Oxford University Press, 2004). Supported by the encyclopedic knowledge of Bob Pinson, Russell provided a listing of *every* recording made in those years, complete with dates, places, and personnel. The old 78 rpm records themselves, however, need to be heard and felt. Many of them are on deposit at the CMF Library and Southern Folklife Collection, and an extensive number have been commercially reissued on a wide variety of CD and LP labels, by foundations or institutions such as the Smithsonian, or by private collectors. (See Willie Smyth, *Country Music Recorded Prior to 1943: A Discography of LP Reissues*, JEMF Special Series, no. 13.) Printed versions can be found in surviving songbooks from the period or in newly published versions transcribed directly from the old records. The New Lost City Ramblers, a folk revival band from New York City, reintroduced many of the songs in their concerts and also issued a fine collection of songs called *The New Lost City Ramblers Song Book*, edited by Mike Seeger and John Cohen (New York: Oak Publications, 1964).

When scholars made their first hesitant entries into the field of country music, they found their work seriously hampered by the lack of readily available source material. Many of the old-time performers had died, and very few had left any kind of papers or memoirs. The recording companies had maintained few files on their performing personnel and would disclose little information on the amount of record sales through the years. No reputable scholarly publication had considered country music worthy of attention. That the task of chronicling country music's significance and development has not been completely insurmountable is owed to a band of devoted hillbilly-music enthusiasts, unnoticed and unsung, who had been painstakingly gathering materials for decades. With little or no scholarly training, and with no motive other than a love for the music and a feeling that the older traditions should be preserved and memorialized, these individuals labored indefatigably to compile both discographical and biographical data on country performers. A veritable network of hillbilly-record collectors, not only in the United States but in countries such as England, Australia, Canada, and Japan, gathered the old records and songbooks and exchanged tapes and information with each other. Such people as Dave Barnes, Dave Wylie, Doug Jydstrup, Harlan Daniel, Joe Bussard, Gus Meade, Joe Hickerson, Will Roy Hearne, Peter Kuykendall, Joe Nicholas, Lou Deneumoustier, Eugene Earle, John Edwards, Garth Gibson, Fred Hoeptner, Bob Pinson, Richard K. Spottswood, and David Freeman, who were in no sense trained folklorists, used their private funds and all the available time at their disposal to search through radio stations, record shops, flea markets, junk stores, and private homes for the out-of-print records of earlier years. They conducted a similar kind of diligent, and often fruitless, search for information about the lives and careers of the old-time performers. They maintained contact with one another through newsletters and auction lists, and through such mimeographed journals as *Disc Collector*, *Country Directory*, *Blue Yodeler*, and

Country and Western Spotlight (a New Zealand publication). These magazines are treasure troves of recording data and biographical sketches.

Folk scholars had never totally ignored hillbilly music, but they had devoted most of their attention to uncommercialized folk music, not realizing that many of their collected items had begun life on hillbilly, blues, or other vernacular records, or had been picked up by hillbilly singers from folk sources. Although much more work needs to be done on this important subject, Ed Kahn, in an excellent exploratory article, "Hillbilly Music: Source and Resource," *JAF* 78, no. 309 (July–September 1965): 257–266, has pointed to the limited but pioneering scholarship done by such folklorists and scholars as Herbert Halpert, Guy B. Johnson, and Howard Odum on the relationship between traditional song and commercial recordings. Alan Lomax did similar work. As early as 1934 he and his father (John A. Lomax) began transcribing and publishing texts and tunes from commercial records, many of which were included in *American Ballads and Folk Songs* (New York: Macmillan Company, 1934). Not until 1947, however, did a discographical appendix appear in a standard folksong collection: John A. Lomax and Alan Lomax, eds., *Folk Song, U.S.A.* (New York: Duell, Sloan, and Pearce, 1947). Alan Lomax had earlier recognized the importance of commercial recordings and in 1940 had issued what was intended to be merely an introductory guide to the subject: *List of American Folk Songs on Commercial Records*, in *Report of the Committee of the Conference on Inter-American Relations in the Field of Music, William Berrien, Chairman* (Washington, DC: Department of State, September 1940). In 1948, Charles Seeger reviewed in the *Journal of American Folklore* a number of hillbilly and race recordings that had been released in previous years, marking the first time that the country's major scholarly folk publication had admitted the existence, or relevance, of commercial country music: "Reviews," *JAF* 61, no. 240 (April–June 1948): 215–218.

D. K. Wilgus was probably the first folklorist to make hillbilly records the subject of an academic thesis, "A Catalogue of American Folksongs on Commercial Records" (Master's thesis, Ohio State University, 1947). In the late fifties, Wilgus, as editor of the *Kentucky Folklore Record* at Western Kentucky State College, and later as director of the Center for the Study of Comparative Folklore and Mythology at UCLA, continued to stress the relationship between folk and hillbilly music. His record reviews in *Kentucky Folklore Record* and for the *JAF* made the study of phonograph records a legitimate aspect of folklore scholarship. John Greenway, an anthropologist and folklorist at the University of Colorado, made scattered comments about a few hillbillies like Jimmie Rodgers, Merle Travis, and the Carter Family in his *American Folk Songs of Protest* (Philadelphia: University of Pennsylvania Press, 1953), and in 1957 his essay on Jimmie Rodgers became the first article on hillbilly music to appear in a scholarly journal: "Jimmie Rodgers—a Folksong Catalyst," *JAF* 70, no. 277 (July–September 1957): 231–235. In the late fifties, Archie Green, who was then an associate professor of Labor and Industrial Relations at the University of Illinois and an authority on labor/protest music, also moved into the study of hillbilly music, recognizing that commercial recordings were valuable repositories of working-class life and lore. Since that time, the indefatigable and insatiably curious Green became America's most authoritative scholar of country music. Wilgus, Greenway, Green, and Ed Kahn (who was then preparing a doctoral thesis on the Carter Family at UCLA), consti-tuted the nucleus of a small but growing fraternity that recognized country music's distinctive position within American folk music, and one whose ranks were enlarged by the enthusiasm generated by the folk revival of the early sixties. One of the most impressive results of their intellectual labors, and for the student the most important introduction to the scholarly study of country music, is the "Hillbilly Issue" of the *Journal of American Folklore, JAF* 78, no. 309 (July–September 1965). This landmark issue, specially edited by John Greenway and D. K. Wilgus, was devoted exclusively to country music and included articles by each of the scholars previously mentioned along with two by new researchers to the field, Norm Cohen and L. Mayne Smith.

Country music scholarship has definitely blossomed since the early sixties, and has moved away from the domain of ephemeral and mimeographed journals. Three journals with scholarly orientation began to provide outlets for writers and histo-rians: the *JEMF Quarterly, Old Time Music* (edited by Tony Russell in England), and the *Journal of Country Music*, the organ of the CMF in Nashville. Each journal accepted articles from both popular and academic sources, but *JEMFQ* was most catholic in its receptivity to noncountry music scholarship (much to the dismay of some of its subscribers). *JCM* and *JEMFQ* accepted material on both old-time and modern country music, while *OTM* rarely moved past the World War II era.

When my formal research began in 1961 for the first edition of this book, no scholarly journal made country music its area of concern. Only a relative handful of works on country music had been published: Ruth Sheldon's biography of Bob Wills, *Hubbin' It: The Life of Bob Wills* (Tulsa, OK: Privately published, 1938); Carrie "Mrs. Jimmie" Rodgers, *My Husband, Jimmie Rodgers* (San Antonio: Southern Literary Institute, 1935); George D. Hay, *A Story of the Grand Ole Opry* (Nashville: Privately published, 1953); William R. McDaniel and Harold Seligman, *Grand Ole Opry* (New York: Greenberg, 1952); and Linnell Gentry, ed., *A History and Encyclopedia of Coun-try, Western, and Gospel Music* (Nashville: McQuiddy Press, 1961). Apart from the occasional articles that appeared in popular magazines and newspapers, as well as the rather light and journalistic accounts found in song magazines and fan journals (almost none of which dated back to the twenties), little reliable material was avail-able. I depended heavily on *Disc Collector, Country Directory, Country and Western Spotlight* (especially the articles written by John Edwards), and on the advice freely granted by Bob Pinson and Archie Green. The Sears-Roebuck and Montgomery Ward catalogues were useful compendiums of records, songbooks, and musical instru-ments. Record catalogues and brochures, records and liner notes, newspaper radio logs, *Billboard* magazines, publications that issued forth from the folk revival (such as *Sing Out* and *Little Sandy Review)*, and Gentry's assemblage of reprinted articles in *A History and Encyclopedia of Country, Western, and Gospel Music* constituted the bulk of my original research.

The discussion that follows reflects the scholarship that appeared both before and after the first edition of this book. If it is more extensive than some of the other chapter bibliographical essays, it is because the "folk-ness" of the early commercial music has generated more scholarship than the more recent manifestations of coun-try music.

The social context of the twenties, which encouraged both the exploitation and the rejection of rural culture, is discussed in a variety of works. Frederick Lewis Allen's *Only Yesterday* (New York: Harper and Brothers, 1931), though dated in some respects, is still a useful introduction to the period. A study that appeared in the early thirties, President's Research Committee on Social Trends, *Recent Social Trends in the United States* (New York: McGraw-Hill Book Company, 1933), documented some of the lasting innovations of the era. George B. Tindall, on the other hand, concentrated on the Ku Klux Klan and other negative factors that gave the South a bad reputation during the decade in "The Benighted South: Origins of a Modern Image," *Virginia Quarterly Review* 40 (Spring 1964): 281–294, and in *The Emergence of the New South, 1913–1945* (Baton Rouge: Louisiana State University Press, 1967). No one better epitomized the ambivalence of the era than Henry Ford, who propelled the nation into a new industrial age with his wonderful machine while simultaneously clinging to the values and prejudices of an earlier rural society. Ford, the fundamentalist and conservative farm boy, is discussed by Allan Nevins and Frank Ernest Hill in *Ford: Expansion and Challenge, 1915–1933*, vol. 2 (New York: Charles Scribner's Sons, 1957), 323, 492. His anti-Semitism and belief that jazz was an odious Jewish invention are reflected in his magazine the *Dearborn Independent* (see the issues of August 6 and 13, 1921, for examples). Ford's championship of fiddling and old-time dances was discussed quite often in the popular magazines of the twenties. "Fiddling to Henry Ford," *Literary Digest* 88, no. 1 (January 2, 1926), is a representative example. More recent discussions of the phenomenon include Estelle Schneider and Bob Norman, "The Henry Ford Dance Movement," *Sing Out* 25, no. 4 (November–December 1977): 24–27, and Don Robertson, "Uncle Bunt Stephens: Champion Fiddler," *OTM*, no. 5 (Summer 1972): 4–7.

Henry Ford's automobile was at the center of much of the social and technological change of the period, but the radio and phonograph contributed more to the discovery and expansion of hillbilly music. Leroy Hughbanks, *Talking Wax, or the Story of the Phonograph* (New York: Hobson Book Press, 1945), Roland Gelatt, *The Fabulous Phonograph* (New York: Lippincott, 1955), and Oliver Read and Walter L. Welch, *From Tin Foil to Stereo: The Evolution of the Phonograph* (New York: Bobbs-Merrill, 1959), are still the best discussions of that medium. Eric Barnouw was long considered to be the acknowledged authority on the radio, but one will learn nothing about country music programming from him. Much more pertinent to our purposes is William Mckinley Randle Jr., "History of Radio Broadcasting and Its Social and Economic Effects on the Entertainment Industry, 1920–1930" (PhD diss., Western Reserve University, 1966), vol. 1. Most of my statistics on radio stations in the twenties come from Frederick Lewis Allen, from *Recent Social Trends*, and from such contemporary magazines as *Literary Digest* 75, no. 6 (November 11, 1922): 29.

The recording of hillbilly music was, in part, a phase of the discovery and exploitation of racial and ethnic music in the twenties. Useful introductions to this material are Pekka Gronow, "A Preliminary Check-list of Foreign Language 78's," *JEMFQ* 9, Part 1, no. 29 (Spring 1973): 24–32, and Richard K. Spottswood, *Ethnic Music on Records: A Discography of Ethnic Recordings Produced in the United States, 1893–1942* (Urbana: University of Illinois Press, 1991).

Since phonograph records are relatively easy to find, catalogue, and preserve (in contrast to the extremely scarce material dealing with radio in the twenties), scholars have been much preoccupied with them. The relationship between the recording industry and early hillbilly music has been the central concern of Charles Wolfe in several fine essays: "Toward a Contextual Approach to Old-Time Music," *JCM* 5, no. 2 (Summer 1974): 65–75; "Ralph Peer at Work: The Victor 1927 Bristol Sessions," *OTM*, no. 5 (Summer 1972): 10–16; and "Columbia Records and Old-Time Music," *JEMFQ* 14, no. 51 (Autumn 1978): 118–125, 144. Wolfe's massive collection of country and gospel material is housed at the Center for Popular Music at Middle Tennessee State University.

Barry Mazor has given us the essential study of Ralph Peer: *Ralph Peer and the Making of Popular Roots Music* (Chicago Review Press, 2014). Earlier insights concerning Ralph Peer's role and methods are found in Nolan Porterfield, "Mr. Victor and Mr. Peer," *JCM* 7, no. 3 (December 1978): 3–21, and in Porterfield's *Jimmie Rodgers* (Urbana: University of Illinois Press, 1979), and Norm Cohen, in *Long Steel Rail: The Railroad in American Folksong* (Urbana: University of Illinois Press, 1981), tells us much about record sales in the twenties while demolishing a number of myths about alleged million sellers.

Tony Russell's book on country records is the indispensable guide to that subject. Before his book came along, my understanding of the early hillbilly repertory was enhanced by such record company catalogues as Brunswick's *Songs from Dixie* (1926–1928), *Catalog of Victor Records* (1925–1934), and *Columbia Record Catalogue* (1923–1941). The JEMF had also reprinted *Gennett Records of Old Time Tunes: A Catalog Reprint*, JEMF Special Series, no. 6. I of course have listened to as many of the old records as possible, both on the original 78s and on LPs and CDs of reissued material. One of the best discussions of the type of material found on the early records is Anne and Norm Cohen, "Folk and Hillbilly Music: Further Thoughts on Their Relation," *JEMFQ* 13, no. 46 (Summer 1977): 50–57, although Norm Cohen and Guthrie Meade, "The Sources of Old Time Hillbilly Music: Child Ballads," *JEMFQ* 9, no. 30 (Summer 1973): 56–62, is a useful corrective to some of the assumptions that many people once held about the hillbilly repertory.

The songwriters who began moving country music away from its traditional moorings in the twenties have not been properly studied or appreciated. Patrick Huber, though, has provided a useful discussion of Carson Robison in "The New York Sound: Citybilly Recording Artists and the Creation of Hillbilly Music, 1924–1932," *JAF* 127, no. 504 (Spring 2014): 140–158. Robison did receive some attention in articles devoted to his associate Vernon Dalhart, but only one article, and that in a popular magazine, concentrated on his writing: Hugh Leamy, "Now Come All You Good People," *Collier's* 84, no. 18 (November 2, 1929): 20–24, 58–59. Record reissues have also slighted Robison, but good selections of his music can be found on at least two albums: *Carson J. Robison: Just a Melody*, Old Homestead OHCS-134, which includes such self-penned songs as "Barnacle Bill the Sailor" and "Little Green Valley" and several duets with Frank Luther and Vernon Dalhart, and *The Immortal Carson Robison*, Glendale Records GL 6009, which includes such famous Robison compositions as "Carry Me Back to the Lone Prairie" and "I Left My Gal in the

Mountains." Charles Wolfe discussed Dick Burnett, the most traditional of the early songwriters, in successive issues of *OTM*, nos. 9 and 10 (Summer and Autumn 1973) and in *Kentucky Country: Folk and Country Music of Kentucky* (Lexington: University Press of Kentucky, 1982). D. K. Wilgus evaluated Blind Andy Jenkins in *A Good Tale and a Bonnie Tune*, edited by Mody C. Boatright, Wilson M. Hudson, and Allen Maxwell, Texas Folklore Society Publication 32 (Dallas: Southern Methodist University Press, 1964), 227–237. The blind tunesmith was also discussed by Charles Wolfe in "Frank Smith, Andrew Jenkins, and Early Commercial Gospel Music," *American Music* 1, no. 1 (Spring 1983): 49–60. Blind Alfred Reed was the subject of an article by certain unnamed members of the Rounder Record Company: "The Life of Blind Alfred Reed," *JEMFQ* 7, no. 23 (Autumn 1971): 113–115, and was the honoree of a commemorative CD, *Always Lift Him Up*, produced in 2007 by the West Virginia Music Hall of Fame. For information on the most sophisticated of the early hillbilly composers, Bob Miller, I am indebted to Joe Dan Boyd, who supplied me with information from the *Memphis Press-Scimitar*, May 5, 1939, and the *Memphis Commercial Appeal*, February 7, 1953. Like Carson Robison, Miller is deserving of much better scholarly treatment than he has received.

The literature on the singers and musicians of the early commercial period is large and growing. The logical place to begin is with Tony Russell, *Country Music Originals: The Legends and the Lost* (New York: Oxford University Press, 2007). Norm Cohen's essay "Early Pioneers" is also important. It is found in *Stars of Country Music*, edited by Bill C. Malone and Judith McCulloh (Urbana: University of Illinois Press, 1975), 3–42, and includes Eck Robertson, Henry Whitter, Fiddlin' John Carson, Ernest Stoneman, Charlie Poole, Gid Tanner, Riley Puckett, Clayton McMichen, and Carl T. Sprague. Tony Russell contributed some vital information that the early music was not lily white in *Blacks, Whites, and Blues* (New York: Stein and Day, 1970), an insight that has been augmented by the scholars found in Diane Pecknold, ed., *Hidden in the Mix: The African American Presence in Country Music* (Durham, NC: Duke University Press, 2013).

Early women performers have been too often neglected, but a good overview of them can be found in Mary Bufwack and Robert Oermann's *Finding Her Voice: The Saga of Women in Country Music* (New York: Crown, 1993). Robert Coltman has also done much to redress the problem in "Sweetheart of the Hills: Women in Early Country Music," *JEMFQ* 14, no. 52 (Winter 1978): 161–181. Three of the pioneer women performers (Roba Stanley, Zora Layman, and Sara Carter) are anthologized in the Time-Life collection *The Women*, but the best recorded introduction to the early women is *Banjo Pickin' Girl*, Rounder 1029 (notes by Charles Wolfe and Patricia A. Hall), which includes Eva Davis, Samantha Bumgarner, Roba Stanley, Louisiana Lou (Eva Conn), Billie Maxwell, Moonshine Kate (Rosa Lee Carson), and the Bowman Sisters (Jennie and Pauline).

The recognition of Eck Robertson's contributions began when Mike Keasler, a student in Roger Abrahams's folklore class at the University of Texas, interviewed the master fiddler in Amarillo on December 30, 1962. Other interviews followed, and that of John Cohen appeared in *Sing Out* 14, no. 2 (April–May 1964): 55–59. I found the reference to Robertson's early radio performance on WBAP in the *Fort Worth*

Star-Telegram, March 30, 1923. All of Robertson's recorded fiddle tunes have been reissued on Sonyatone Records STR 203, with extensive notes by Peter Feldmann.

Fiddlin' John Carson has received considerable attention from country music scholars. Gene Wiggins has contributed a full-scale biography, *Fiddlin' Georgia Crazy: Fiddlin' John Carson, His Real World, and the World of His Songs* (Urbana: University of Illinois Press, 1986), but the article that first publicized the account of Carson's pioneer recording was Kyle Crichton's "Thar's Gold in Them Hillbillies," *Collier's* 101 (April 30, 1938): 24–29. Archie Green corrected the errors in this original version and supplied missing data in his superb and oft-quoted "Hillbilly Music: Source and Symbol," *JAF* 78, no. 309 (July–September 1965): 204–228. Other biographical accounts include Bob Coltman, "Look Out! Here He Comes! Fiddlin' John Carson," *OTM* 9 (Summer 1973): 16–22; and Norm Cohen, "Fiddlin' John Carson: An Appreciation and a Discography," *JEMFQ* 10, no. 36 (Winter 1974): 138–157.

Ernest Stoneman, the patriarch of the Stoneman Family bluegrass band and a performer whose career spanned over forty years of country music history, received long overdue recognition in a Grammy-nominated CD collection edited by Henry Sapoznik: *Ernest V. Stoneman: The Unsung Father of Country Music, 1925–1934* (New York: 5-String Productions, 2008). He had been earlier discussed by Norm Cohen, Eugene Earle, and Graham Wickham in *The Early Recording Career of Ernest V. "Pop" Stoneman: A Bio-Discography*, JEMF Special Series, no. 1, 1968, and in Cohen and Earle, "An Ernest V. Stoneman Discography," *JEMFQ* 16, no. 57 (Spring 1980): 36–50.

Charlie Poole and the North Carolina Ramblers have been treated well by modern scholars and enthusiasts. His music was reintroduced to modern listeners in the Harry Smith Collection. Much of Poole's material has been reissued with great success by David Freeman on his County record label in Floyd, Virginia. Kinney Rorrer, a relative of both Poole and his first fiddler, Posey Rorer, has compiled two fine works on this wonderful North Carolina band: "Leaving Home: Charlie Poole's Early Years," *JCM* 9, no. 1 (1981): 82–86, and a book, *Rambling Blues: The Life and Songs of Charlie Poole* (London: OTM, 1982). Henry Sapoznik also received a Grammy nomination for his notes to a box set of some of Poole's recordings, *You Ain't Talkin' to Me: Charlie Poole and the Roots of Country Music* (Sony BMG 2005).

That other great, but dissimilar, band, the Skillet Lickers, has also received much attention, as have two of its stellar members, Clayton McMichen and Riley Puckett. Norm Cohen's essay "Early Pioneers" in *Stars of Country Music* is again the place to begin, but Cohen has also written on McMichen in "Clayton McMichen: His Life and Music," *JEMFQ* 11, no. 39 (Autumn 1975): 117–124. Both Cohen and Charles Wolfe, in "Clayton McMichen: Reluctant Hillbilly," *BGU* 13, no. 11 (May 1979): 56–63, stress the great fiddler's complexity and the conflict in his art between tradition and modernity. Norm Cohen's "Riley Puckett: King of the Hillbillies," *JEMFQ* 12, no. 44 (Winter 1976): 175–185, is probably the best capsule treatment of that influential guitarist and singer.

The man who took southern ballad and parlor singing to northern audiences—Bradley Kincaid—has had his story told well by Loyal Jones, an authority on the politics and culture of Appalachia. Jones first wrote on the "Kentucky Mountain Boy" in *JEMFQ* 12, no. 43 (Autumn 1976): 122–138, and again in a small book called *Radio's*

"Kentucky Mountain Boy" Bradley Kincaid (Berea, KY: Appalachian Center/Berea College, 1980). Kincaid's famous songbooks are also discussed in this work, as well as in Archie Green, "Bradley Kincaid's Folios," *JEMFQ* 13, no. 45 (Summer 1977): 21–28. The most complete collection of Kincaid's recordings is a box set produced by JSP records in England. Also good is a small collection, *Mountain Ballads and Old-Time Songs*, Old Homestead OHCS 107.

Some musicians clearly elicited research and publication because they were rediscovered during the folk revival of the sixties. Clarence Ashley, Dock Boggs, and Buell Kazee each enjoyed renewed careers; each was newly recorded; and each received written recognition. The great Kentucky ballad singer Buell Kazee told some of his story in an LP called *Buell Kazee Sings and Plays*, Folkways FS3810. Loyal Jones told more of it in his notes to a later album, *Buell Kazee*, June Appal 009. Kazee also told his story to me in Stillwater, Oklahoma, on April 7, 1972. Clarence Ashley was properly appreciated in Ralph and Richard Rinzler's notes to the album *Old-Time Music at Clarence Ashley's*, Folkways FA2355, and was the subject of an essay in *Tom Ashley, Sam McGee, Bukka White: Tennessee Traditional Singers*, edited by Thomas G. Burton (Knoxville: University of Tennessee Press, 1981). Dock Boggs was discussed briefly by Michael Seeger in the notes to the album *Dock Boggs*, Folkways FA 2351, and by himself in "I Always Loved the Lonesome Songs," *Sing Out* 14, no. 3 (July 1964): 32–37.

Boggs is not the only important musician who has received minimal attention, in some cases, one supposes, because they recorded only a few songs, or did not live long enough to be rediscovered during the folk revival. Charles Wolfe wrote a short but good account of George Reneau in "George Reneau: A Biographical Sketch," *JEMFQ* 15, no. 56 (Winter 1979): 205–208. Tony Russell did brief sketches on two others: "Frank Hutchison: The Pride of West Virginia," *OTM*, no. 1 (Summer 1971): 4–7, and "Kelly Harrell and the Virginia Ramblers," *OTM*, no. 2 (Autumn 1971): 8–11.

When the first edition of this book was prepared, my discussion of Vernon Dalhart relied principally on the research of the vaudeville music collector/historian Jim Walsh: "Favorite Pioneer Recording Artists: Vernon Dalhart," Part I, *Hobbies: The Magazine for Collectors* 65, no. 3 (May 1960): 33–35, 45; Part II, no. 5 (July 1960): 34, 36–37, 55; Part III, no. 6 (August 1960): 33–35; Part IV, no. 8 (October 1960): 34–36, 44; and "Death of Three Recording Artists," *Hobbies* 53, no. 10 (December 1948): 32. Although these articles still have great value, I have supplemented them with information garnered from Walter Darrell Haden, "Vernon Dalhart," in *Stars of Country Music*, 69–93. Norm Cohen, in *Long Steel Rail*, also clarifies much of the murky data dealing with the origins and sales figures of "The Prisoner's Song" and "The Wreck of the Old 97." After many years of neglect, Dalhart material began to reappear on recordings at the end of the 1970s. Representative LPs include *Old Time Songs*, Davis Unlimited DU 33030; *Ballads and Railroad Songs*, Old Homestead OHCS 129; and *Original Edison Recordings: First Recorded Railroad Songs*, Mark 56 Records 794.

The Carter Family has certainly not suffered from scholarly inattention. Mark Zwonitzer and Charles Hirshberg wrote a good biography of them, *Will You Miss Me When I'm Gone? The Carter Family and Their Legacy in American Music* (New York: Simon and Schuster, 2002), and Bear Family produced a comprehensive collection of their recordings, along with good biographical notes and song annotations by Charles Wolfe: *In the Shadow of Clinch Mountain*. During the research for *CMUSA*, I talked briefly with Maybelle Carter in Nashville on August 26, 1961, and with Joe Carter in Meridian, Mississippi, on March 24, 1978, but received little information that differed substantially from that found in the published works. Ed Kahn was the first person to do research on the Carter Family, but his dissertation, "The Carter Family: A Reflection of Changes in Society," UCLA, was not completed until 1970. I profited greatly, though, from his aid and encouragement. The closest thing to primary materials about the Family are the articles written by Maybelle's daughter, June Carter, "I Remember the Carter Family," *CSR* 17, no. 90 (October 1965): 16–17, and *CSR* 17, no. 91 (December 1965): 16–20—both reprinted in *Sing Out* 17, no. 3 (June–July 1967): 6–11. Another excellent record/biography collection is "The Carter Family on Border Radio," JEMF 101 (with extensive notes by Archie Green, Norm Cohen, and William H. Koon). Green's "The Carter Family's 'Coal Miner's Blues,'" *SFQ* 25, no. 4 (December 1961): 226–237, was a fine piece of work on a selected aspect of their career.

We now have a good history of the Chicago radio show *National Barn Dance*: Chad Berry, ed., *The Hayloft Gang: The Story of the National Barn Dance* (Urbana: University of Illinois Press, 2008). But I was grateful for the earlier support given to me by Dave Wylie and George Biggar on the WLS show. Wylie corresponded with me frequently in 1967, supplying me with the results of his research on the Barn Dance, and putting me in touch with Biggar, who also provided me with an extensive amount of material. It is regrettable that neither Wylie nor Biggar ever converted their research into a book. Biggar, who was also associated with other Midwestern barn dances, did write an article, "The WLS National Barn Dance Story: The Early Years," *JEMFQ* 7, no. 23 (Autumn 1971): 105–112. I learned much about the WLS performers from annually issued yearbooks and from a biweekly gossip magazine, *Stand By!*, both produced by the station. I also accumulated some information from Sears-Roebuck catalogues, and profited greatly from two books that dealt, at least indirectly, with WLS and the *National Barn Dance*: James F. Evans, *Prairie Farmer and WLS: The Burridge D. Butler Years* (Urbana: University of Illinois Press, 1969), and Boris Emmet and John E. Jeuck, *Catalogues and Counters: A History of Sears, Roebuck and Company* (Chicago: University of Chicago Press, 1950).

I learned about other barn dances and assorted hillbilly radio shows through newspaper research (as in the case of WBAP in 1923: *Fort Worth Star-Telegram*) and through a perusal of *Radio Digest* from 1929 to 1933. Information on the WSM *Barn Dance*, which ultimately became the *Grand Ole Opry*, came from a variety of published sources and interviews. I talked with Harry Stone in Nashville on August 28, 1961; Sam McGee in Franklin, Tennessee, on August 14, 1973; DeFord Bailey in Nashville on July 20, 1974 (Russell Stockard, a former student of mine at Tulane University, also talked with Bailey on October 6, 1973). George D. Hay wrote his own recollection of the show, *A Story of the Grand Ole Opry* (privately published in Nashville, 1953). Hay's daughter, Margaret Hay Daugherty, wrote a short account of her father, "George D. Hay: The Solemn Ole Judge—A Pioneer P-R Man," for *BGU* 17, no. 1 (July 1982): 28–34. William R. McDaniel and Harold Seligman wrote *Grand Ole Opry* (New York: Greenberg, 1952), and Jack Hurst compiled a large-format, lavishly illustrated account of the show, *Nashville's Grand Ole Opry* (New York: Abrams, 1975). Richard Peterson explained the interrelationship between the National Life and Accident Insurance Company, WSM, and the *Grand Ole Opry* in "Single Industry Firm to Conglomerate Synergistics: Alternative Strategies for Selling Insurance and Country Music," in *A Growing Metropolis: Aspects of Development in Nashville*, edited by James Blumstein and Benjamin Walter (Nashville: Vanderbilt University Press, 1975). Although all of these works were useful, the acknowledged authority on the early *Opry* was Charles Wolfe, who compiled *A Good-Natured Riot: The Birth of the Grand Ole Opry* (Nashville: Country Music Foundation and Vanderbilt University Press, 1999).

The most prominent of the early *Opry* performers have been discussed in various publications, including Wolfe's previously cited books on Tennessee music and the *Grand Ole Opry*. One of the *Opry* pioneers, the talented fiddler Sid Harkreader, wrote a memoir of his experiences, *Fiddlin' Sid's Memoirs: The Autobiography of Sidney J. Harkreader*, edited by Walter D. Haden, JEMF Special Series, no. 9; and Alton Delmore, who joined the show in 1933 with his brother Rabon, left an unfinished autobiography that was published in 1977 (to be discussed in the bibliographical essay for chapter 4). The story of Sam McGee has been told in a number of places: in Jon Pankake's notes to *The McGee Brothers and Arthur Smith*, Folkways FA2379; in Marvin Clemons, "Sam McGee from Tennessee," *BGU* 10, no. 4 (October 1975): 28–32; and by Charles Wolfe in *Tom Ashley, Sam McGee, Bukka White*. Wolfe and David C. Morton also wrote the much-needed *DeFord Bailey: A Black Star in Early Country Music* (Knoxville: University of Tennessee Press, 1991).

Finally, as might be expected, the irrepressible Uncle Dave Macon has drawn much attention from modern-day researchers. The best of this material includes Ralph Rinzler and Norm Cohen, eds., *Uncle Dave Macon: A Bio-Discography*, JEMF Special Series, no. 3; and Charles Wolfe's essay in *Stars of Country Music*, 43–69. Macon's complete recorded output has been issued by Bear Family: *Uncle Dave Macon: Keep My Skillet Good and Greasy*.

3. THE FIRST COUNTRY SINGING STAR: JIMMIE RODGERS

Although the definitive biography of Jimmie Rodgers is Nolan Porterfield, *Jimmie Rodgers: The Life and Times of America's Blue Yodeler* (Urbana: University of Illinois Press, 1979), it can be usefully supplemented by Barry Mazor, *Meeting Jimmie Rodgers: How America's Original Roots Music Hero Changed the Pop Sounds of a Century* (New York: Oxford University Press, 2009), and Jocelyn R. Neal, *The Songs of Jimmie Rodgers: A Legacy in Country Music* (Bloomington: Indiana University Press, 2009). Since these studies were not available when I wrote the first edition of this work, my original research on Jimmie Rodgers included a series of interviews with relatives and friends of the Blue Yodeler: Rodgers's sisters-in-law, Pearl Rodgers and Elsie McWilliams; his stepbrother, Jake Smith; a brother-in-law, Nate Williamson (all in Meridian, Mississippi, August 23–25, 1966); and his half sister, Lottie Mixon, in York, Alabama, on August 25, 1966. I also talked with a friend of Rodgers's, Claudia Rigby Vick, on August 23, 1966; and with the musician Bill Bruner, one of Rodgers's earliest singing disciples, on August 24, 1966 (also in Meridian).

Since these original interviews, I have also talked with a few musicians who either played with or had some association with Jimmie Rodgers. These include Billy Burkes in Meridian, May 26, 1978; Wilbur Ball in Meridian, May 24, 1978; Dwight Butcher in Meridian, May 25, 1978; Raymond Hall in Memphis, Tennessee, June 24, 1978 (I also had considerable correspondence with him); and Claude Grant (of the Tenneva Ramblers) in Bristol, Virginia, September 2, 1970.

I also explored *Billboard* carefully, from 1928 through Rodgers's death in May 1933, and found numerous accounts of his tent-rep and vaudeville appearances. Research in select newspapers, such as the *Houston Post-Dispatch*, December 1931–February 1932, and the *New Orleans Times-Picayune*, 1928–1929, also provided accounts of his theater performances and occasional radio appearances. Some of the most pertinent information on Rodgers's musical gigs in New Orleans and elsewhere came from an unpublished essay sent to me by Fred Hoeptner: "Goebel Reeves and Jimmie Rodgers: the 1925 Barnstorming Episode."

Few published accounts on Jimmie Rodgers existed in 1961 when I began my research. However, I did find Carrie "Mrs. Jimmie" Rodgers's remembrance of her husband, *My Husband, Jimmie Rodgers* (San Antonio: Southern Literary Institute, 1935), to be useful despite the romanticized and sanitized view presented of Rodgers. Especially helpful was John Greenway's pioneering article "Jimmie Rodgers— A Folksong Catalyst," *JAF* 70, no. 277 (July–September 1957): 231–235, even though I thought he placed too much emphasis on Rodgers's blues songs. Greenway's "Folk Song Discography," *Western Folklore* 21, no. 1 (January 1962): 71–76, was a much more satisfactory evaluation of the Blue Yodeler. Former Ranger William W. Sterling provided a few interesting glimpses of Rodgers's relationship to his adopted state of Texas in *Trails and Trials of a Texas Ranger* (privately published, 1959).

For my understanding of the blues tradition in which Jimmie Rodgers worked, I originally relied upon Samuel Charters, *The Country Blues* (New York: Rinehart and Company, 1959); Paul Oliver, *Blues Fell This Morning* (London: Cassell and Company, 1960); and Jerry Silverman, *Folk Blues: One Hundred and Ten American Folk Blues* (New York: Macmillan Company, 1958). Since the original publication of my book, there has been an explosion of scholarship in the blues field: Lawrence Levine, *Black Culture and Black Consciousness* (New York: Oxford University Press, 1977); Jeff Todd Titon, *Early Downhome Blues: A Musical and Cultural Analysis* (Urbana: University of Illinois Press, 1977); William Ferris Jr., *Blues from the Delta* (Garden City, NY: Doubleday, 1978); Robert Palmer, *Deep Blues* (New York: Viking Press, 1981); and David Evans, *Big Road Blues* (Berkeley: University of California Press, 1982).

One final mention might be made of the yodeling tradition, and of the role played by Rodgers in its popularity. Robert Coltman looked for the origins of the blue yodel in "Roots of the Country Yodel: Notes Toward a Life History," *JEMFQ* 12, no. 42 (Summer 1976): 91–94. Fuller treatments include Timothy E. Wise, *Yodeling and Meaning in American Music* (Jackson: University Press of Mississippi, 2016), and Bart Plantenga, *Yodel-Ay-Ee-Oooo: The Secret History of Yodeling around the World* (New York: Routledge, 2004).

4. COUNTRY MUSIC DURING THE DEPRESSION

An excellent place to begin the study of country music in the thirties is Bob Colt-man, "Across the Chasm: How the Depression Changed Country Music," *OTM*, no. 23 (Winter 1976–1977): 6–13. This is a thoughtful essay, concentrating on the years 1930–1934, that stresses the transitional nature of the period, when "amateurs gave way to professionals" and their music became more mellow and more geared toward novelty.

The reorganization of the record business inspired by hard times is illuminated somewhat by John Edwards, "The Old Labels—No. 2," *Country and Western Spotlight* (Special John Edwards Memorial Edition, September 1962): 14–15, but the indis-pensable work on record labels is Brian Rust, *The American Record Label Book* (New Rochelle, NY: Da Capo Press, 1978). Archie Green has compiled a useful chronology of the Okeh-Columbia relationship in Appendix III of "Hillbilly Music: Source and Sym-bol," *JAF* 78 (July–September 1965): 228. The crucial role played by the new Decca company in the thirties is described in "Platter War," *Business Week*, November 10, 1934, 14, and in *Time* 36, no. 10 (September 2, 1940): 45. Paul Cohen also provided me with information on this subject in an interview in Nashville, August 29, 1961. An almost complete listing of Decca's early hillbilly recordings made from 1934 to 1945 (the 5000 Series) is in *Record Research*, no. 23 (June–July 1959): 13–16, while a shorter listing is in *Country and Western Spotlight*, no. 42 (June 1963): 4–6. Although they are now extremely hard to obtain, the eleven LPs of Decca hillbilly material that were released in Japan under the general title of *From the Southeast to the Southwest: 1930's Decca Hillbilly Records* were compiled and annotated by a Japanese researcher, Toru Mitsui. The interested reader can probably find discographies on the web for virtually every record label in America.

Despite the extraordinary popularity of radio during the thirties, the medium has still not received the kind of study for which the country music researcher would hope. A few histories of individual radio stations, however, do exist: James F. Evans, *Prairie Farmer and WLS: The Burridge D. Butler Years* (Urbana: University of Illi-nois Press, 1969); C. Joseph Pusateri, *Enterprise in Radio: WWL and the Business of Broadcasting in America* (Washington, DC: University Press of America, 1980); and Lillian Jones Hall, "A Historical Study of Programming Techniques and Practices of Radio Station KWKH, Shreveport, Louisiana, 1922–1950" (PhD diss., Louisiana State University, 1959).

Information on the *Grand Ole Opry* during the thirties is available in Charles Wolfe's history of the radio show: *A Good Natured Riot: The Birth of the Grand Ole Opry* (Nashville: Country Music Foundation and Vanderbilt University Press, 1999); from Alton Delmore's autobiography, *Truth Is Stranger Than Publicity* (Nashville: Country Music Foundation Press, 1977); and from Elizabeth Schlappi, *Roy Acuff: The Smoky Mountain Boy* (Gretna, LA: Pelican Publishing, 1978). I also picked up some information on this subject from Harry Stone (interview, Nashville, August 28, 1961) and from Herald Goodman (interview, Carrollton, Texas, December 29, 1967).

As noted earlier, the bulk of my information on WLS and the *National Barn Dance* came from correspondence with Dave Wylie and George Biggar. James F. Evans's history of WLS was also very helpful, as was Lewis Atherton, *Main Street on the Middle Border* (Bloomington: Indiana University Press, 1954), which commented on the *Barn Dance*'s popularity among rural and small-town midwesterners. John Lair gave me some additional information in a conversation at Renfro Valley, Kentucky, August 18, 1973. *Billboard* issues provided some statistics concerning attendance and receipts at *Barn Dance* road shows. An interesting article on Bob Atcher in *Country Style* shed some light on the differences between the *National Barn Dance* and the *Grand Ole Opry*. According to Atcher, union scales hurt the Chicago show and contributed to its eventual demise (Matt Huff, "Smilin' Bob Atcher, Back on the Circuit," *Country Style*, no. 22 [July 28, 1977]: 35).

Other radio barn dances of the thirties have not been nearly so well documented as have the *Opry* and the *National Barn Dance*. A couple of good accounts of other shows, however, do exist: Willie J. Smyth, "Early Knoxville Radio (1921–41): WNOX and 'Mid-day Merry Go-Round,'" *JEMFQ* 18, nos. 67–68 (Fall–Winter 1982): 109–116; and Timothy A. Patterson, "Hillbilly Music among the Flatlanders: Early Midwestern Radio Barn Dances," *JCM* 6, no. 1 (Spring 1975): 12–18, which stresses the high percentage of nonsoutherners on these shows. Some information on radio shows can be gleaned from the studies of individual musicians (see Ivan and Deanna Tribe, "The Doc Williams Reunion," *BGU* 7, no. 9 (March 1983): 61–65, which also comments on WWVA, Wheeling, West Virginia). I found numerous references to radio barn dances in *Broadcasting and Broadcast Advertising* (Washington, DC), which I checked for the years 1934–1939. Such magazines as *Billboard* and *Radio Digest* also made occasional mention of such shows. The area of hillbilly radio research is clearly still wide open.

The alliance between advertising and country music became most strongly marked in the thirties. Pusateri, in *Enterprise in Radio*, talks about the "P.I. accounts" that accompanied hillbilly broadcasting all over the country and made the subject of his book, WWL (in New Orleans), known far and wide as the "aches and pills" station. I found *Broadcasting and Broadcast Advertising* to be an extremely fruitful source for references to Aladdin Mantle Lamps, Drug Trade Products, Alka-Seltzer, Garrett Snuff, and scores of other items that were intimately associated with country radio programming. Stewart H. Holbrook, *The Golden Age of Quackery* (New York: Macmillan Co., 1959), has a section on Black Draught and Wine of Cardui, products made by the Chattanooga Medicine Company, and long staples of the hillbilly radio trade. Don R. Jason, "WSM and Its 3,000 Salesmen," *The Advertiser* 5, no. 9 (October 1934): 23–24, gave an interesting account of how National Life and Accident Insurance salesmen sold premiums to working-class people by stressing the company's interrelationship with WSM and the *Grand Ole Opry*.

The largest advertiser of hillbilly music, Crazy Water Crystals, received much attention in the thirties because of its notoriety. It deserves similar attention from scholars today because of the role it played in making country music a national phenomenon. I am deeply indebted to Pat Ahrens, of Columbia, South Carolina, for information that she supplied, and also for her article "The Role of the Crazy Water Crystals Company in Promoting Hillbilly Music," *JEMFQ* 6, no. 19 (Autumn 1970): 107–109. I also interviewed the former president of the company, Carr P. Collins, in

Dallas, April 20, 1962, and Hubert Fincher, the son of the company's southeastern manager, J. W. Fincher, by phone from Columbia, South Carolina, October 17, 1970. Dorothy Neville, *Carr P. Collins: Man on the Move* (Dallas: Park Press, 1965), was also helpful, as were such contemporary accounts as Ruth DeForest Lamb, *American Chamber of Horrors* (New York: Farrar and Rinehart, 1936); Morris Fishbein, "Modern Medical Charlatans," *Hygeia* 16, no. 1 (January 1938): 21–25; and Richard Lee Strout, "The Radio Nostrum Racket," *Nation* 141 (July 17, 1935): 65–66.

One of the most notorious of the "medical charlatans," John R. Brinkley, played a crucial role in the emergence of the famous Mexican border stations. The most pertinent discussion for our purposes is by Gene Fowler and Bill Crawford: *Border Radio* (Austin: Texas Monthly Press, 1987). At least one doctoral dissertation has also concentrated on Brinkley's influence on American radio programming: Ansel Harlan Resler, "The Impact of John R. Brinkley on Broadcasting in the United States" (PhD diss., Northwestern University, 1958). Brinkley also received considerable published treatment in contemporary periodicals and by popular historians: Richard Hughes Bailey, "Dr. Brinkley of Kansas," *Nation* 135 (September 21, 1932): 254–255; J. C. Furnas, "Country Doctor Goes to Town," *Saturday Evening Post* 212, no. 43 (April 20, 1940): 12–13, 44ff; and Gerald Carson, *The Roguish World of Doctor Brinkley* (New York: Rinehart and Company, 1960). Discussions more pertinent to Brinkley's relationship to country music are Ed Kahn, "International Relations, Dr. Brinkley, and Hillbilly Music," *JEMFQ* 9, Part 2, no. 30 (Summer 1973): 47–55, and Mike Paris's account of a longtime performer on border radio, "The Jesse Rodgers Story," *OTM*, no. 13 (Winter 1974–75): 5–8. I obtained additional information on Mexican border programming from Carr P. Collins (April 20, 1962) and from the Rev. Sam Morris, who preached his temperance sermons on border stations for many years (interview, San Antonio, July 14, 1973).

When we turn to the country musicians of the thirties, we find a wealth of published material. The white blues singers of the period were merely the most recent manifestations of a very old fascination shown by white performers for black music and culture (see Tony Russell, *Blacks, Whites, and Blues* (New York: Stein and Day, 1970). One of the finest country-blues singers, Jimmie Tarlton, was rediscovered during the folk revival. He is discussed by Norm and Anne Cohen in "The Legendary Jimmie Tarlton," *Sing Out* 16, no. 4 (September 1966): 16–19, and by Graham Wickham, *Darby and Tarlton* (special edition of Doug Jydstrup's *Blue Yodeler*, 1967). The Allen Brothers were little known until Donald Lee Nelson found them in 1971: "The Great Allen Brothers Search," *JEMFQ* 7, Part 3, no. 23 (Autumn 1971): 126–129. Nelson followed that with "The Allen Brothers," *JEMFQ* 7, Part 4, no. 24 (Winter 1971): 147–151. Tony Russell soon thereafter discussed them in "Chattanooga Boys: The Allen Brothers," *OTM*, no. 4 (Spring 1972): 12–13, and in the notes to an LP, *The Allen Brothers: The Chattanooga Boys*, Old Timey LP-115. They also receive a brief mention in John P. Morgan and Thomas C. Tulloss, "The Jake Walk Blues," *JEMFQ* 13, no. 47 (Autumn 1977): 122–126. Cliff Carlisle has received scandalously little attention, even though he was one of the superb singer-yodelers of the period and a pioneer in the performance of the Dobro guitar. Charles Wolfe provides the best interpretation of his style and musical contributions in *Kentucky Country* (Lexington: University

Press of Kentucky, 1982), 62–65. Carlisle's clear, sparkling style can be sampled on at least two LPs of reissued material: Old Timey 103 and 104. Frank Hutchison is much less documented than Carlisle. Tony Russell did a short sketch on him called "Frank Hutchison: The Pride of West Virginia," *OTM*, no. 1 (Summer 1971): 4–7, and Mark Wilson provided the notes for Hutchison's reissue album, *The Train That Carried My Girl from Town*, Rounder 1007. In 1993, Columbia produced an impressive double-CD anthology of white performances of the blues: *White Country Blues, 1926–1938: A Lighter Shade of Blue* (Columbia 4722886).

Of all the entertainers who experimented with the blues idiom in the thirties, only two, Gene Autry (who will be discussed in the notes to chapter 5) and Jimmie Davis, went on to weather successive stylistic changes in the country music industry. I interviewed Davis in Baton Rouge, Louisiana, August 15, 1977, and Stephen Ray Tucker (Tulane University) interviewed him in Baton Rouge, February 12, 1980, and graciously provided me with some of the fruits of his research. I learned some additional information about Davis in an interview with one of his longtime musicians, Joe Shelton (Yantis, Texas, July 31, 1974), and from a little article by Floy Case, "Jimmie Davis," *Mountain Broadcast and Prairie Recorder*, no. 2 (December 1944): 3, 5, 6. Country music historians tend to be more interested in Davis's risqué-blues repertory than in his later and more varied offerings. Tony Russell (*Blacks, Whites, and Blues*) and Nick Tosches (*Country: The Biggest Music in America* [New York: Stein and Day, 1977], 118–128) concentrated on this phase of Davis's career.

For an introduction to the duet tradition in country music, one might begin with the Time-Life collection *Duets* (Time-Life Records, 1982), edited by Charles Wolfe. This collection surveys the style from 1927 (Mac and Bob) to 1972 (George Jones and Tammy Wynette). Wolfe also discusses "The Delmore Brothers" in *Pickin'* 2, no. 8 (September 1975): 4–12, and is the editor of Alton Delmore's autobiography, *Truth Is Stranger Than Publicity* (Nashville: Country Music Foundation Press, 1977). The latter is a rare autobiography by a country singer, and though it is sketchy for the post-1950 period, it evokes well the unsteady, barnstorming atmosphere of the thirties and forties. Delmore was candid in his remarks about other musicians and the music business and has some unflattering things to say about the *Grand Ole Opry*.

Interest in the music of the Dixon Brothers was revived during the urban folk period, when Dorsey Dixon enjoyed a brief second career. Archie Green was drawn toward the Dixons because they had worked in textile mills since childhood and had written songs about their factory experiences. Green wrote "Minstrel of the Mills" (about Dorsey) for *Sing Out* 16, no. 3 (July 1966): 10–13, and then produced and annotated Dorsey Dixon's fine LP, *Babies in the Mill*, Testament T-3301.

I have always had a warm spot in my heart for the Callahan Brothers, having grown up with their music, which I heard over KRLD in Dallas. Homer "Bill" Callahan was always extremely helpful to me and graciously supplied me with information and photographs on several occasions. I interviewed him twice, the first time with Bob Pinson in Dallas, August 23, 1963, and the second time alone in Dallas, July 10, 1978. I also talked to him frequently by telephone. Another interview with Paul Buskirk, the great mandolin player, provided additional information on the Callahans and Gus Foster (Houston, July 8, 1976). Of the printed material on the Callahan Brothers, two essays deserve special recognition: Bob Pinson, "The Callahan Brothers," *Country Directory* 2 (April 1961): 5–13, and Ivan Tribe, "Bill and Joe Callahan: A Great Brother Duet," *OTM*, no. 16 (Spring 1975): 15–22.

Lester McFarland and Robert A. Gardner (Mac and Bob) are sorely in need of a biographer. Their roles in popularizing the mandolin and in introducing such classic songs as "Twenty-one Years" should earn them much more than the slender documentation they have thus far received. Dave Wylie and George Biggar told me most of what I know about Mac and Bob, although John Edwards provided a skeleton outline of their career in "McFarland and Gardner," *Country and Western Spotlight* (September 1962): 15. Mac and Bob are also seldom anthologized in record reissues, although the Time-Life duet collection includes their version of "When the Roses Bloom Again." Dave Wylie did produce a good, but now out-of-print, LP of some of their most representative recordings: *Mac and Bob*, Birch Records 1944.

Charles Wolfe has pointed out that Karl Davis and Harty Taylor, another influential duet, has also suffered from historical neglect: "Whatever Happened to Karl and Harty," *BGU* 18, no. 4 (October 1983): 26–32. The Time-Life duet collection, though, did include three of their songs as well as a brief biographical sketch. My own knowledge of Karl and Harty had originally come from Dave Wylie, and particularly from a short account he supplied to me from *Stand By* magazine, November 2, 1935, 9.

The Blue Sky Boys and the Monroe Brothers, on the other hand, have been well anthologized and documented. Much of my information on the Blue Sky Boys (the Bolick Brothers) came from many interviews with Bill Bolick: the first in Greensboro, North Carolina, August 24, 1965, and the second by phone to Greensboro on September 3, 1970. While compiling information for the notes to the Bear Family anthology of the Blue Sky Boys RCA Victor years: *The Sunny Side of Life*, I spoke for many hours with Bill Bolick. Several published accounts of the Bolicks exist, including my liner notes to the Bear collection (which are also included in my anthology *Sing Me Back Home*). In the first edition of *CMUSA*, I made use of William A. Bolick, "Bill Bolick's Own Story of the Blue Sky Boys" (introduction and commentary by William A. Farr), *Sing Out* 17, no. 2 (April–May 1967): 18–21, and the notes to *The Blue Sky Boys*, Camden CAL797, by Archie Green. David Whisnant challenged some of the earlier conclusions about the Blue Sky Boys—particularly the idea that they retired from music because of stylistic inflexibility—in his notes to the LP *The Blue Sky Boys*, JEMF 104 (a reissue of *Presenting the Blue Sky Boys*, Capitol ST2483). Douglas B. Green supplied full and sensitive notes for the RCA reissue, RCA Bluebird AXM2–5525, and Wayne W. Daniel wrote a very good summary of the Blue Sky Boys' career in "Bill and Earl Bolick Remember the Blue Sky Boys," *BGU* 16, no. 3 (September 1981): 14–21. One of the most significant insights into the Bolicks' relationship with their fans is Douglas B. Green, ed., "The Blue Sky Boys on Radio, 1939–1940: A Newly Discovered Log of Their Daily Program, Kept by Ruth Walker," *JCM* 4, no. 4 (Winter 1973): 108–158. These notes, kept faithfully by this very loyal fan, tell us much about the Bolicks' repertory and remind us of the importance of radio to country entertainers.

The Monroe Brothers have received much attention, not only because of their vital and exciting performances but also because of their anticipation of bluegrass. Bill Monroe's story has been well told by several writers, and that bibliography will be discussed later in the notes to chapter 10. Particularly relevant, though, for the Monroe Brothers is Ralph Rinzler's essay on Bill in *Stars of Country Music*, edited by Bill C. Malone and Judith McCulloh (Urbana: University of Illinois Press, 1975), 221–243. Charlie Monroe has not been so fully treated, but Ivan Tribe's short essay "Charlie Monroe" in *BGU* 10, no. 4 (October 1975): 12–21, is a good place to begin. Douglas B. Green conducted a good and long interview with Charlie that is excerpted as "The Charlie Monroe Story" in *Muleskinner News* in three successive issues: 4, no. 1 (January 1973); 4, no. 2 (February 1973); and 4, no. 3 (March 1973). Green also organized and wrote the notes for the outstanding anthology of Monroe Brothers recordings, *Feast Here Tonight*, RCA Bluebird AXM2–5510 (thirty-two selections).

Women began to achieve a certain prominence in country music during the thirties, and in some cases even established independent identities. The Time-Life collection *The Women* (edited by several unnamed staff members), contains recordings by several entertainers who were active during the decade: Lulu Belle Wiseman, Zora Layman, Sara Carter, Patsy Montana, Girls of the Golden West, Coon Creek Girls, Dezurik Sisters, Louise Massey, Judy Canova, Texas Ruby, and Cousin Emmy. Published accounts of them, however, are still few and far between. All of my information on Grace Wilson came from Dave Wylie, particularly in a letter dated March 24, 1967. George Biggar supplied me with some material on Lulu Belle Wiseman, but I obtained more from Scott Wiseman in a telephone call to him in Spruce Pine, North Carolina, on August 19, 1973. Lulu Belle's performances and tours were also described frequently in *Billboard* and various radio-oriented magazines during the thirties. The best accounts of Cousin Emmy and the Coon Creek Girls are in Wolfe's *Kentucky Country*. The zestful performing style of Cousin Emmy is hinted at in the transcript of her performance given at the Ash Grove in Los Angeles in 1967: John Cohen, ed., "Cousin Emmy by Herself," *Sing Out* 18, nos. 2–3 (June–July 1968): 26–27, and fully displayed in recordings made with the New Lost City Ramblers. I obtained additional information on the Coon Creek Girls through a telephone interview with Lily May Ledford (Pennington), in Lexington, Kentucky, August 12, 1973, and from a short sketch in *Stand By!* magazine, April 3, 1937, 12. I visited with Millie Good McCluskey (in the early 1990s) in Cincinnati and also talked to her by phone (Cincinnati, August 11, 1973), and learned the basic details of the career of the Girls of the Golden West. I learned among other things that they came, not from Muleshoe, Texas, but from southern Illinois.

Individual musicians of the thirties have been discussed in a wide array of scattered sources. The extremely popular radio team of Asher Sizemore and Little Jimmy, whose songbooks appear frequently in antique barns, is discussed in Wolfe's *Kentucky Country*, 60–61. Lew Childre, an alumnus of the tent-rep vaudeville circuit and an itinerant radio performer during the decade, is discussed by Wolfe in "Doc Lew: The Life and Times of Lew Childre," *BGU* 13, no. 5 (November 1978): 26–30, and in the notes to *Lew Childre: On the Air, 1946*, an LP produced by Old Homestead (OHCS-132) and taken from radio transcriptions. The record captures some of the informality and ebullience that characterized his live performances. Two other performers who were best known for their radio work, Doc Williams and Buddy Starcher, have been poorly documented on recordings. Williams, however, is the subject of two articles that I have found useful: Barbara Kempf, "Meet Doc Williams, Country Music Star, Country Music Legend," *JEMFQ* 10, Part 1, no. 33 (Spring 1974): 1–7, and Rex Rutkoski, "Doc Williams," *BGU* 12, no. 11 (May 1978): 25–32. Buddy Starcher's life and career have been capsuled by Ivan Tribe in "Buddy Starcher—Mountain State Favorite," *BGU* 13, no. 9 (March 1979): 46–52.

Clyde Moody and Louis M. "Grandpa" Jones, on the other hand, made many recordings, but most of their work came after the thirties. During that decade they were also best known for their radio performances. I interviewed Moody on August 15, 1973, in Nashville, but also learned much from Ivan Tribe and John Morris, "Clyde Moody: Old-Time, Bluegrass and Country Musician," *BGU* 10, no. 1 (July 1975): 28–34. The versatile Grandpa Jones, whose career was one of the longest in country music, has been the subject of several good articles. With the assistance of Charles Wolfe, he also wrote his autobiography: *Everybody's Grandpa: Fifty Years Behind the Mike* (Knoxville: University of Tennessee Press, 1988).

Several fiddlers made names for themselves in the thirties independently of bands. Charles Wolfe has written short profiles of some of them in *The Devil's Box: Masters of Southern Fiddling* (Nashville: Vanderbilt University Press, 2006). Discussions of Clayton McMichen have already been cited in the notes to chapter 2. Curly Fox is described briefly in Mary Morgan, "Curly Fox: A Living Legend," *BGU* 11, no. 10 (April 1977): 12–16. The greatest fiddler of all, Arthur Smith, has received biographical treatment and stylistic evaluation from Charles Wolfe in two essays: "Fiddler's Dream: The Legend of Arthur Smith," *The Devil's Box* 11, no. 4 (December 1977), 26–67, and "The Odyssey of Arthur Smith," *BGU* 13, no. 2 (August 1978): 50–57. Twenty-eight of Smith's performances have been reissued on two LPs, *Fiddlin' Arthur Smith*, vols. 1 and 2, County 546 and 547 (taken from the period 1935–1940).

A few of the string bands from the southeastern states have elicited popular or scholarly treatment. The most "rural" of these bands, Mainer's Mountaineers, is discussed by Ivan Tribe and John Morris, in "J. E. and Wade Mainer," *BGU* 10, no. 5 (November 1975): 12–22, and by Brad McCuen, in "Mainer's Discography," *Disc Collector*, no. 24 (May 1973): 8–24. Richard Spottswood wrote a biography of Wade Mainer, *Banjo on the Mountain: Wade Mainer's First 100 Years* (Jackson: University Press of Mississippi, 2010). Two "graduates" of the Mainer band, Wiley and Zeke Morris, are discussed by Wayne Erbsen in "Wiley and Zeke, the Morris Brothers," *BGU* 15, no. 2 (August 1980): 40–50. Roy Hall's string band, the Blue Ridge Entertainers, possessed some of the raw, rustic vitality of Mainer's Mountaineers, but in other ways, such as their use of the Dobro, they anticipated the sound of the forties. The band's story is told by Ivan Tribe in "Roy Hall and His Blue Ridge Entertainers," *BGU* 13, no. 3 (September 1978): 44–50. The Prairie Ramblers, who began their existence as the Kentucky Ramblers, were even more transitional in their sound and choice of songs, sometimes sounding like an old-time band but more often reflecting the western swing sounds that were filtering in from the West. Bob Healy discusses the group in "The Prairie Ramblers," *Country Directory*, no. 3 (1962): 4–14, and Charles Wolfe evaluates their contributions to country music in *Kentucky Country*. Hank Penny did not identify with the rural musicians of the Southeast; his Radio Cowboys consequently were not transitional at all, but were strongly marked by the rhythms of western swing.

I interviewed Penny by phone at his home in Chatsworth, California (January 17, 1981), but also obtained relevant information from Rich Kienzle, "The Checkered Career of Hank Penny," *JCM* 8, no. 2 (1980): 43–78, and from Ken Griffis, "Hank Penny: The Original 'Outlaw'?," *JEMFQ* 18, nos. 65–66 (Spring–Summer 1982): 5–13.

The early history of the steel guitar has been one of the special research interests of Rich Kienzle (see his "Steel," *Country Music* 4, no. 4 [January 1976]: 35, 38, 61–62). Robert Gear discusses the pre-American origins of the style in "Hawaiian Music: Styles and Stylists of the Islands," *Frets* 3, no. 5 (May 1981): 34–36. Early recorded examples of the musicians who brought the instrument and style to the United States can be heard on *Hula Blues* (Rounder 1012). Early hillbilly exponents of the style are anthologized on an Old Timey LP, *Steel Guitar Classics* (Old Timey 133). The special contributions made by the Dopera Brothers with their famous Dobro are discussed in Duncan G. Robertson, "Dobro," *Guitar Player* 2, no. 5 (October 1968): 20–21, 50, and by Ed Dopera, as told to Michael Brooks, "The Story of the Dobro," *Guitar Player* 5, no. 8 (December 1971): 29–31, 39–40, 49. Jerry Byrd's seminal contributions to the art of steel guitar playing are explored in an interview with him conducted by Tom Bradshaw: "Jerry Byrd," *Guitar Player* 6, no. 2 (March 1972): 25, 45–48.

The rediscovery and romanticization of the folk in the context of the Great Depression have been touched upon by many writers, and several scholars have commented on the ways in which the government touched the lives of the plain folk, distributing relief, providing economic protection, and documenting and commemorating their culture. Although several government agencies, such as the Library of Congress, the Works Progress Administration (WPA) with its cultural projects, and the Farm Security Administration, strove to preserve folklore and folk music, no scholar has attempted to study all of these various campaigns in any comprehensive or systematic manner. Representative articles that discuss selected aspects of the government's approach to folk music include Harold Spivacke, "The Archive of American Folk Song in the Library of Congress," *SFQ* 2, no. 1 (March 1938): 31–35; Herbert Halpert, "Federal Theatre and Folksong," ibid., 81–85; and B. A. Botkin, "WPA and Folklore Research: Bread and Song," ibid. 3, no. 1 (March 1939): 7–14. A more extended discussion of the Archive of American Folk Song is provided by Debora Kodish, "'A National Project with Many Workers': Robert Winslow Gordon and the Archive of American Folk Song," *The Quarterly Journal of the Library of Congress* 35, no. 4 (October 1978): 218–233.

Southern labor unrest during the thirties is discussed in several fine works, including Thomas Tippett's contemporary treatment of the Piedmont textile strikes, *When Southern Labor Stirs* (New York: Jonathan Cape and Harrison Smith, 1931); Liston Pope's sociological study of the failure of unionism in North Carolina, *Millhands and Preachers: A Study of Gastonia* (New Haven: Yale University Press, 1942); John Hevener's study of the bloody struggle for economic justice in the Kentucky coal fields, *Which Side Are You On? The Harlan County Coal Miners, 1931–1939* (Urbana: University of Illinois Press, 1979); George B. Tindall's *The Emergence of the New South, 1913–1945* (Baton Rouge: Louisiana State University Press, 1967); and Irving Bernstein's superb general labor history, *The Lean Years: A History of the American Worker, 1920–1933* (Boston: Houghton Mifflin, 1960).

The music inspired by textile work is surveyed by Patrick Huber in *Linthead Stomp: The Creation of Country Music in the Piedmont South* (Chapel Hill: University of North Carolina Press, 2008), and by Archie Green in "Born on Picket Lines, Textile Workers' Songs Are Woven into History," *Textile Labor* 22, no. 4 (April 1961): 3–5, and in his notes to *Babies in the Mill*, Testament T-3301. David McCarn, the greatest of the textile-worker songwriters, is discussed by Huber and by William Henry Koon in "Dave McCarn," *JEMFQ* 11, Part 4, no. 40 (Winter 1975): 167–176. McCarn's songs can be heard on at least a couple of LPs: *Singers of the Piedmont*, Bear FV12505, and *Poor Man, Rich Man: American Country Songs of Protest*, Rounder 1026 (Mark Wilson, annotator).

Coal mining and balladry are the subjects of Archie Green's *Only a Miner: Studies in Recorded Coal-Mining Songs* (Urbana: University of Illinois Press, 1972), a work that is valuable not only for the subject it emphasizes but also for its understanding of the whole field of commercially recorded country music. Green addresses more directly the conflicts in the eastern Kentucky coal fields during the early thirties in his notes to Sarah Ogan Gunning, *Girl of Constant Sorrow*, Folk-Legacy FSA-26. Gunning was a labor union activist, as was her half-sister Aunt Molly Jackson, and both of them were protest singers who eventually took their songs north. Aunt Molly is the subject of a biography by Shelly Romalis, *Pistol Packin' Mama: Aunt Molly Jackson and the Politics of Folksong* (Urbana: University of Illinois Press, 1999). She was also memorialized in an entire issue of *Kentucky Folklore Record* 7, no. 4 (October–December 1961).

The Okie migration, which contributed greatly to the transplantation of hillbilly culture in California, has been well studied in both fiction and history. Walter J. Stein concentrated on California's reaction to the great horde of migrants in *California and the Dust Bowl Migration* (Westport, CT: Greenwood, 1973). Jacqueline Gordon Sherman, on the other hand, discussed the ways in which the Okies adjusted to their new home: "The Oklahomans in California during the Depression Decade, 1931–1941" (PhD diss., UCLA, 1970). Charles Todd and Robert Sonkin collected music among the Okies and deposited their research in the Archive of American Folk Song. They wrote of their experiences in "Ballads of the Okies," *New York Times Magazine*, November 17, 1940, 6–7, 18.

The great Okie balladeer and hillbilly singer Woody Guthrie has inspired an enormous amount of print, including his own self-justification, *Bound for Glory* (New York: E. P. Dutton, 1943). Richard Reuss compiled much of this material in *A Woody Guthrie Bibliography, 1912–1967* (New York: Guthrie Children's Trust Fund, 1968) and wrote his own assessment of the singer in "Woody Guthrie and His Folk Tradition," *JAF* 83, no. 329 (July–September 1970): 273–304. Guthrie has also inspired some fine biographies, such as Joe Klein, *Woody Guthrie: A Life* (New York: Alfred A. Knopf, 1980; reprint, New York: Delta, 1999), a superbly written and meticulously researched piece of scholarship, and Ed Cray, *Ramblin' Man: The Life and Times of Woody Guthrie* (New York: W. W. Norton, 2004). Guthrie's relationship to hillbilly music and culture is convincingly discussed in these books. Klein's book, for example, explores with great detail and deftness the role played by the Communist Party in promoting the idea of the folk song as a weapon in the class struggle. These biographies, along with John Greenway's *American Folk Songs of Protest* (Philadelphia: University of Pennsylvania Press, 1953) and R. Serge Denisoff's *Great Day Coming: Folk Music and the American Left* (Urbana: University of Illinois Press, 1971) should be utilized to understand the concept of "protest song" and the way in which music has been used to promote radical causes.

5. THE COWBOY IMAGE AND THE GROWTH OF WESTERN MUSIC

I have written an article, "Country Music in the Depression Southwest," for *The Depression in the Southwest*, edited by Donald W. Whisenhunt (Port Washington, NY: Kennikat, 1980), 58–75, stressing the innovative styles that emerged during the period, while also mindful that the region was an heir to the musical traditions of the older South. Texas's debt to southern folk tradition is discussed in Alan Lomax's notes to *Texas Folksongs*, Tradition Records, TLP 1929; by Norman L. McNeil, "The British Ballad West of the Appalachian Mountains" (PhD diss., University of Texas, 1956); and in William A. Owens, *Texas Folk Songs* (Austin: Texas Folklore Society, 1950; 2d ed., 1977) and his *Tell Me a Story, Sing Me a Song* (Austin: University of Texas Press, 1983). Francis E. Abernethy, folklorist and English professor at Stephen F. Austin State University in Nacogdoches, Texas, waged a lifelong campaign—as a singer and often as editor of *Publications of the Texas Folklore Society*—to remind us of Texas's rich folk traditions. A good example of his venture into this subject has been the excellent *Singin' Texas* (Dallas: E. Heart Press, 1983). Abernethy can recall, as can most Texans of rural origin, the "Young People's Page" of the *Dallas Semi-Weekly Farm News*, where old songs were printed on request, indicating that rural Texans' song preferences were no different from those in other rural southern areas (the Texas State Library has some scattered copies from the pre–World War I period). William W. Savage Jr., has written a useful survey of Oklahoma's folk and popular music traditions, *Singing Cowboys and All That Jazz: A Short History of Popular Music in Oklahoma* (Norman: University of Oklahoma Press, 1983). Similar studies of music in other states should be written.

The phenomenon that contributed greatly toward making Texas, Oklahoma, and Louisiana different from other southern states—oil—is discussed by Carl Coke Rister, *Oil! Titan of the Southwest* (Norman: University of Oklahoma Press, 1949). Too little has been done on the social consequences of the oil boom (particularly on the clash between rural folkways and this new industrial power), but a few writers have compiled some of the folklore that grew out of the oil discoveries: Alice Cashen, "Boom-Town Tales," in *Tales from the Big Thicket*, edited by Francis E. Abernethy (Austin: University of Texas Press, 1966), 137–154; Mody Boatright, *Folklore of the Oil Industry* (Dallas: Southern Methodist University Press, 1963); and Boatright and William A. Owens, *Tales from the Derrick Floor* (Lincoln: University of Nebraska Press, 1970). The reader, however, should not be expecting a collection of oil songs; very few emerged from the culture of oil work.

The other great phenomenon that set Texas and Oklahoma apart from the South—cowboy culture—has been subjected to massive and unending documentation. The Library of Congress's great exhibition in 1983, "The American Cowboy," was a dramatic visual reminder of the romantic appeal exerted by this universal American hero. A large library exists that discusses the effects of the western and cowboy image on American life, but among the more instructive works are George Bluestone, "The Changing Cowboy: From Dime Novel to Dollar Film," *Western Humanities Review* 14, no. 3 (Summer 1960): 331–337; David B. Davis, "Ten-Gallon Hero," *American Quarterly* 6, no. 2 (Summer 1954): 111–126; Kenneth Munden, "A Contribution to the Psychological Understanding of the Cowboy and His Myth," *American Imago* 15, no. 2 (Summer 1958): 103–147; and Joe B. Frantz and Julian Ernest Choate Jr., *The American Cowboy: The Myth and the Reality* (Norman: University of Oklahoma Press, 1955).

On the subject of singing cowboys and their relationship to country music, good places to begin one's research would be Stephen Ray Tucker, "The Western Image in Country Music" (Master's thesis, Southern Methodist University, 1976), and Douglas B. Green's lengthy survey, "The Singing Cowboy: An American Dream," *JCM* 7, no. 2 (May 1978): 4–62. Green continues to remind audiences of this tradition in another vital and entertaining way: as Ranger Doug, the singer-yodeler-guitarist of the revivalist-cowboy singing trio Riders in the Sky. Tucker and Green concentrate on the professionalization of cowboy music, but William R. Smith discusses music among real cowboys in "Hell among the Yearlings," *OTM*, no. 5 (Summer 1972): 16–19.

Several of the pioneer singing cowboys who made the first recordings in the twenties have been anthologized in *Authentic Cowboys and Their Western Folksongs*, RCA Victor Vintage Series LPV-522 (notes by Fred G. Hoeptner). The songs they sang had earlier been collected, for the most part, by the first two great compilers of cowboy songs: Nathan Howard Thorp, *Songs of the Cowboy* (Estancia, NM: New Print Shop, 1908), and John A. Lomax, *Cowboy Songs and Other Frontier Ballads* (New York: Sturgis and Walton, 1910). The John A. Lomax Family Papers, a massive collection housed at the Eugene C. Barker Texas History Center at the University of Texas at Austin, has been insufficiently utilized by country music scholars—except for Nolan Porterfield, *The Last Cavalier: The Life and Times of John A. Lomax, 1867–1948* (Urbana: University of Illinois Press, 1996)—but I have found much useful information relating to the early commercialization and artistic exploitation of cowboy and other kinds of folk music. At least two of the "original singing cowboys," Jules Verne Allen and John White, wrote their own recollections of cowboy life and song: Allen, *Cowboy Lore* (San Antonio: Naylor Company, 1933), and White, *Git Along, Little Dogies: Songs and Songmakers of the American West* (Urbana: University of Illinois Press, 1975). Both books brought a strong note of realism into the study of cowboy music by reminding us that (according to Allen) guitars and good voices were rare among cowboys, and (according to White) most cowboy songs began in the fertile minds of individuals—usually as poems in newspapers or magazines—and not in some romantically communal fashion.

When I was compiling information on the early singing cowboys, Archie Green reminded me of the early Charles Nabell recordings (letter, February 6, 1967). Long after this chapter was written, I came across an interview with Mark Wilson, who recalled having met Edward L. Crain in Oregon, and learning that this early cowboy singer was from Longview, Texas (see *The Old-Time Herald*, vol. 7, no. 6).

I interviewed Carl Sprague in Bryan, Texas, on August 4, 1963. Most of my scanty knowledge of Jules Verne Allen and the Cartwright Brothers came from the RCA Victor Vintage collection and from Allen's book. Since that time William Koon and Carol Collins have written "Jules Verne Allen, the Original Singing Cowboy," *OTM*, no. 10 (Autumn 1973): 17–19, and Bill Rattray (with the assistance of Jack Cartwright) has written "The Cartwright Brothers Story," *OTM*, no. 9 (Summer 1973): 10–14. Most of the extant knowledge of Goebel Reeves is possessed by Fred Hoeptner, whose findings were originally published in Robert Shelton, *The Country Music Story* (New York: Bobbs-Merrill, 1966), 149–151. More recently, Hoeptner has published "Goebel Reeves, the Texas Drifter," *OTM*, no. 18 (Autumn 1975): 10–17. Nolan Porterfield has also speculated on Reeves's alleged relationship with Jimmie Rodgers in *Jimmie Rodgers: The Life and Times of America's Blue Yodeler* (Urbana: University of Illinois Press, 1979), 43. John Edwards also briefly discussed Reeves in "The Mystery of the Texas Drifter," *Country and Western Spotlight*, September 1962, 31. The other Wobbly cowboy, Harry McClintock, told much of his story to Joe Nicholas in a long letter published in *Disc Collector*, no. 12, 1–2, and no. 13, 11–13.

The most professional of the original "singing cowboys," Otto Gray and Ken Maynard, have been better documented largely because they excelled in other realms: Gray as a businessman and Maynard as a Hollywood actor. Gray, of course, was not a singer at all, but as an effective organizer and promoter, he obtained recognition for his group in media that were usually hostile to any kind of country music. I found several references to Gray and his band in issues of *Billboard* dating from 1928 to 1932. Contemporary trade accounts can be well supplemented by Leslie A. McRill, "Music in Oklahoma by the Billy McGinty Cowboy Band," *Chronicles of Oklahoma* 38, no. 1 (Spring 1960): 66–74, and by William W. Savage, *Singing Cowboys and All That Jazz*. Ken Maynard, of course, appears in any history of Hollywood Westerns, but he has also been discussed by Ken Griffis in "The Ken Maynard Story," *JEMFQ* 9, Part 2, no. 30 (Summer 1973): 67–70. His songs are discussed by William H. Koon in the same issue, 70–76.

The greatest Hollywood singing cowboy, Gene Autry, was generally resistant to in-depth interviews, and his autobiography, *Back in the Saddle Again* (New York: Doubleday, 1978), written with the assistance of Mickey Herskowitz, is sketchy on many of the areas of musical performance in which historians are interested. He has found his biographer, however, in Holly George-Warren, *Public Cowboy No. 1: The Life and Times of Gene Autry* (New York: Oxford University Press, 2007). One of Autry's sidekicks, Johnny Bond, collected material on Autry for many years but did not convert it into a biography. Bond did, however, provide assistance to Douglas B. Green, who compiled a good short biography and evaluation of Autry that is available in *Stars of Country Music*, edited by Bill C. Malone and Judith McCulloh (Urbana: University of Illinois Press, 1975), 155–171. Green also did a short sketch, "Gene Autry: The Pre-Singing Cowboy Years," for *Pickin'* 2, no. 1 (December 1975): 22–26. The interview with Arthur Satherley, "'I'm a Record Man'—Uncle Art Satherley Reminisces," *JEMFQ* 8, Part 1, no. 25 (Spring 1972): 18–22, sheds some light on the early Autry years, as does Archie Green's "The Death of Mother Jones," *Labor History* 1, no. 1 (Winter 1960): 1–4. As in so many other areas, I found the Sears-Roebuck catalogues to be very helpful in building a profile of Autry's early commercial preferences. Douglas B. Green's article in *JCM*, "The Singing Cowboy: An American Dream," is the best introduction to the whole retinue of actors who followed in the wake of Autry's success. Johnny Bond is a good source for the cowboys who came to Hollywood as part of Autry's organization, and also for those who were hired by other studios to compete with Autry (see his *Reflections: The Autobiography of Johnny Bond*, JEMF Special Series, no. 8 [1976]). Bond's biography of Tex Ritter, *The Tex Ritter Story* (New York: Chappell, 1976), is the best account available on that singer. Douglas B. Green did a short appreciation of Ritter for *Frets* 1, no. 5 (July 1979): 10–12. Archie Green also came up with an interesting item about Ritter, a 1927 concert of cowboy songs that he performed with pianist Oscar Fox at the University of Texas: "Commercial Music Graphics," *JEMFQ* 12, no. 41 (September 1976): 29.

The prolific writer-researcher Ken Griffis has written about several of the Hollywood singing cowboys: "The Ray Whitley Story," *JEMFQ* 6, Part 2, no. 18 (Summer 1970): 65–68; and "I've Got So Many Million Years: The Story of Stuart Hamblen," *JEMFQ* 14, no. 49 (Spring 1978): 4–22. He has also given us the best account of the Sons of the Pioneers that has yet been written.

The Sons of the Pioneers' movie appearances, their popular radio transcriptions, and their many years of longevity in the music business made them known to a multitude of fans, and consequently has made them attractive to researchers. Their most famous alumnus, Roy Rogers, inspired an affectionate and authoritative biography by Ray White: *King of the Cowboys, Queen of the West: Roy Rogers and Dale Evans* (Madison: University of Wisconsin Press, 2005). I originally drew upon a biography of Roy Rogers by Elise Miller Davis, *The Answer Is God* (New York: McGraw-Hill, 1955), and a short sketch by John Edwards on the Sons of the Pioneers in *Country and Western Spotlight*, September 1962, 34. The best history now available is Ken Griffis, *Hear My Song: The Story of the Celebrated Sons of the Pioneers*, JEMF Special Series, no. 5, 1974. Griffis has also written shorter essays on individual members of the group, including "The Early Career of Tim Spencer," *JEMFQ* 8, Part 1, no. 25 (Spring 1972): 4–7; "The Hugh Farr Story," *JEMFQ* 7, Part 2, no. 22 (Summer 1971): 68–73; and "The Bob Nolan Story," *JEMFQ* 16, no. 58 (Summer 1980): 63–65. An extensive number of Sons of the Pioneers records have been reissued, and the JEMF issued an LP composed of material taken from radio transcriptions: *The Sons of the Pioneers*, JEMF LP102.

Several of the movie cowboys were also radio cowboys and, like Stuart Hamblen, had their own radio shows for many years, or, like the Sons of the Pioneers, were heard widely on transcriptions. Too little is known about the transcription business, but Linda Painter has enhanced our understanding with "The Rise and Decline of Standard Radio Transcription Company," *JEMFQ* 17, no. 64 (Winter 1981): 194–201. Douglas Green has also ventured into this area of research with his article "Foy Willing and the Riders of the Purple Sage: Teleways Transcriptions, 1946–1948," *JCM* 6, no. 1 (Spring 1975): 28–41. (The Riders of the Purple Sage were the chief competitors of the Sons of the Pioneers and were active in both radio and the movies.) The Beverly Hillbillies, who combined the cowboy and hillbilly images, were extremely popular radio personalities in California. Their story has been told by Bob Healy in *Country*

Directory, no. 23 (1962): 31, and by Ken Griffis in *JEMFQ* 16, no. 57 (Spring 1980): 3–17. For three of the most active cowboy/cowgirl radio acts of the thirties, I relied on interviews: Red River Dave McEnery, in San Antonio, Texas, June 19, 1973; Millie Good McCluskey (Girls of the Golden West), telephone interview in Cincinnati, August 11, 1973; and Patsy Montana, telephone interview in West Covina, California, August 20, 1973. Additional information on Patsy Montana can be found in Chris Comber, "Patsy Montana: The Cowboy's Sweetheart," *OTM*, no. 4 (Spring 1972): 10–11, and in Robert K. Oermann and Mary A. Bufwack, "Patsy Montana and the Development of the Cowgirl Image," *JCM* 7, no. 3 (1981): 18–33. I also visited with Millie Good McCluskey, sometime in the early 1990s, in her home in Cincinnati, but have been unable to find the precise date.

The New York cowboy singer phenomenon of the thirties is deserving of at least an article. Previously cited material on Tex Ritter and Ray Whitley would be good places to start, but additional pertinent sources would be the tapescript of Dwight Butcher in *JEMFQ* 5, no. 13 (Spring 1969): 10–22, and Jay Taylor, "Montana Slim: Canada's Legendary Wilf Carter," *JEMFQ* 13, no. 47 (Autumn 1977): 118–121. I picked up some information on the New York scene from Red River Dave and Bobby Gregory (interview in Nashville, August 30, 1971). Although she was not a cowgirl singer, Ethel Park Richardson collected folk songs and gave encouragement and exposure to the cowboys who came to New York. Her story is told by her grandson, Jon G. Smith, in "She Kept On A-Goin': Ethel Park Richardson," *JEMFQ* 13, no. 47 (Autumn 1977): 105–115.

One final word about the radio cowboys: their ranks were plentiful, and their performance territory was immense, ranging from New York to California and from California to the Mexican border. I heard many of them, such as Cowboy Slim Rinehart, J. R. Hall, and Texas Jim Robertson, as I was growing up. Other names like Tom Murray, Tex Owens, and Marc Williams have become familiar to me as I read through *Radio Digest* and old country music publications. I hope that students of country music will find some way of documenting their existence and evaluating their contributions.

Texas was characterized by more than cotton, cowboys, and oil; it was also a cosmopolitan mixture of racial and ethnic groups whose musical forms often intertwined while still maintaining some distinctiveness. One interesting example of this musical fusion is discussed by Clifton Machann in "Country-Western Music and the 'Now' Sound in Texas-Czech Polka Music," *JEMFQ* 19, no. 69 (Spring 1983): 3–7. No one, of course represents this hybridization better than the Czech-country musician Adolph Hofner, as I discovered in my interview with him in San Antonio, July 24, 1973. His musical eclecticism can be sampled on the LP *Adolph Hofner: South Texas Swing: His Early Recordings, 1935–55*, Arhoolie 5020 (notes by Tony Russell).

Texas's honky-tonk culture, which was nurtured by Prohibition repeal, the oil boom, electrical amplification, and the region's cosmopolitan musical mixture, is deserving of a major scholarly study. To my knowledge, I was the first writer to affix the term "honky-tonk" to a subgenre of country music (in the doctoral dissertation that preceded this book, 1965). The origin of the term has still not been tracked down, although Nick Tosches, in *Country: The Biggest Music in America*, has found a usage of it in Ardmore, Oklahoma, in 1894 (p. 24). I contributed to the selection of material and wrote the notes for a Time-Life collection called *Honky Tonkin'*, forty recordings including Al Dexter singing "Honky Tonk Blues"—the first country song to carry the term in its title—plus other singers, such as Ernest Tubb, Floyd Tillman, and Ted Daffan, who contributed to the shaping of the style. I wrote a short essay on the honky-tonk that has been anthologized in *Sing Me Back Home: Southern Roots and Country Music* (Norman: University of Oklahoma Press, 2017). Jukeboxes, which were constant accoutrements of the honky-tonk world, have not been properly documented or evaluated. *Billboard* issues provide some statistics on their numbers and circulation, and the popular press occasionally alludes to their significance (see, for example, Lewis Nichols, "The Ubiquitous Juke Box," *New York Times Magazine*, October 5, 1941, 22). More recently, John Morthland has commented on the music machine's significance for country music: "Jukebox Fever," *Country Music* 6, no. 8 (May 1978): 35–36.

Ernest Tubb, the first great singer to take his honky-tonk-nourished style to the stage of the *Grand Ole Opry*, has been the subject of an excellent book by Ronnie Pugh: *Ernest Tubb: The Texas Troubadour* (Durham, NC: Duke University Press, 1996). Townsend Miller wrote a good short sketch of Tubb in *Stars of Country Music*, 243–259. Of the many articles on Tubb in popular country music journals, the best include Townsend Miller, "Ernest Tubb's Early Recording Career," *JEMFQ* 8, Part 2, no. 26 (Summer 1972): 58–62; Peter Guralnick, "Ernest Tubb: Still the Texas Troubadour," *Country Music* 5, no. 8 (May 1977): 38ff; and Patrick Carr, "Ernest Tubb," ibid. 8, no. 8 (May 1980): 30–34. The story of Tubb's decision to add electric instrumentation to his recordings came from an interview that I had with him in Austin, March 24, 1962.

Electrification, an essential ingredient of the honky-tonk sound and a major force for change in country music, has only recently begun to attract much scholarship. My interview with Bob Dunn at his music store in Houston, July 17, 1966, marked the beginning of an understanding of the way that the electric guitar became a part of country instrumentation. Since that time, Rich Kienzle has done the most to clarify the process through which electrification became the norm in country music: "Steel," *Country Music* 4, no. 4 (January 1976): 37–38, 61–62, and "The Electric Guitar in Country Music: Its Evolution and Development," *Guitar Player* 13, no. 11 (November 1979): 30, 32–34, 36–37, 40–41. Alvino Rey's pioneering role in guitar electrification is mentioned in *Who Is Who in Music*, 5th ed. (1951), 346, and Lloyd Loar's contributions are described in Roger Siminoff, "Lloyd Loar," *Frets* 1, no. 5 (July 1979): 38–44. Ted Daffan's early experiments were described to me in various interviews: November 20, 1971; May 31, 1974; and July 7, 1976 (all in Houston, and the last two by telephone). The influence exerted by the black guitarists Eddie Durham and Charlie Christian is described in Leonard Feather, *The Book of Jazz* (New York: Meridian Books, 1960), 112–115, and in Joachim E. Berendt, *The New Jazz Book: A History and Guide* (New York: Hill and Wang, 1962), 190–193.

Since the early seventies, western swing has become one of the most active research areas in country music and a fertile field for record reissues, many of them coming out of California. Some of the earliest collectors and discographers of country music, such as Bob Pinson, Glenn Healy, Glenn White, and Fred Hoeptner, were avid western swing specialists. Their ranks have been joined in more recent years by such authorities as Rich Kienzle, Cary Ginell, Rod Moag—through his annotated recordings—Tony Russell, Chris Strachwitz, Charles Townsend, and Kevin Coffey, whose name appears in the byline of scores of record liner notes.

The early Texas fiddle bands have been much appreciated, but only rarely anthologized or historically documented. Charles Faurot and Bob Pinson probably knew more about Oscar and Doc Harper, Solomon (Ervin) and Hughes (Joe), and Prince Albert Hunt than any other researchers, but they have written very little about them (Charles Faurot, though, produced and wrote the notes for the important album *Texas Farewell*, County 517, an anthology covering the years from 1922 to 1930, and Pinson periodically shared some of his knowledge with me, particularly in Dallas, on August 23, 1963). I have since talked with Ona (Mrs. Doc) Harper in Terrell, Texas (by phone on July 11, 1978), but was not able to follow up with a more extended interview. My knowledge of the Humphries Brothers comes from interviews with Jess Humphries's daughter, Katherine Russell, in Burnet, Texas, July 6, 1976; Cecil Humphries's daughter, Mertice Pogue, in the same city on the same date; and the Humphries Brothers' sister, Velma Whitted, in Liberty Hill, Texas, July 6, 1976.

The East Texas Serenaders are the only early Texas fiddle band who had an entire album reissue devoted to them: County 410. They were also the subjects of an early sketch by Fred Hoeptner: "The Western Style—East Texas Serenaders," *Disc Collector*, no. 17 (May 1961): 8–11. I have since interviewed the band's guitarist, Cloet Hamman, in Lindale, Texas, July 5, 1978. Johnny Gimble told me that Huggins Williams was an early influence on his own style (interview in Kerrville, Texas, July 2, 1976).

My information on the Light Crust Doughboys and their controversial announcer, W. Lee O'Daniel, originally came from Bob Healy, "The Light Crust Doughboys," *Country Directory*, no. 3 (1962): 21–29; and "W. Lee O'Daniel and His Hillbilly Boys," ibid., no. 4 (1963): 6–11; and from Bob Pinson, "The Musical Brownies," ibid., 11–17. My knowledge has since been amplified by Charles Townsend, who wrote of the group in his essay on Bob Wills in *Stars of Country Music*, 171–195, and in his larger biography of Wills. I have also learned more about O'Daniel from Seth S. McKay, *W. Lee O'Daniel and Texas Politics, 1938–1942* (Lubbock: Texas Technological College Research Funds, 1944). Much more needs to be done on O'Daniel and his exploitation of country music for political purposes.

Cary Ginell has written an informative and well-researched biography of Milton Brown, *Milton Brown and the Founding of Western Swing* (Urbana: University of Illinois Press, 1994). Bob Pinson, though, was responsible for most of the information that country music specialists have on Milton Brown and his seminal band, the Musical Brownies. Pinson wrote a short sketch of the group in *Country Directory*, no. 4 (1963): 11–17, and then again for *OTM*, no. 1 (Summer 1971): 14–17. He later supplied a complete discography of the group for *OTM*, no. 5 (Summer 1972): 21–22. I also learned much about the Brownies in interviews with Roy Lee Brown (Milton's brother) and Fred "Papa" Calhoun, both in Fort Worth on May 24, 1963; Bob Dunn in Houston, July 17, 1966; and Cliff Bruner in League City, Texas, June 19, 1976, and Dickinson, Texas, January 31, 1989 (by phone).

Most of the western swing bands that appeared after 1935 were influenced by the Musical Brownies or were spin-offs from them (groups founded or led by former Brownies). The above-mentioned interviews with Dunn and Bruner provided information on some of the spin-off groups. Bob Healy wrote about Ocie Stockard in "Ocie Stockard and the Wanderers," in *Disc Collector*, no. 18 (no date given): 19–20, and he made brief mention of Dunn's Vagabonds in "The Ted Daffan Story," *Country Directory*, no. 4 (1963): 27–31.

Garna Christian provides a good survey of the western swing scene in Houston in "It Beats Picking Cotton: The Origins of Houston Country Music," *Red River Valley Historical Review* 7 (Summer 1982): 37–50. The Swift Jewel Cowboys are described in Tony Russell's notes to *Chuck Wagon Swing—Swift Jewel Cowboys*, String STR806. I learned some facts about Shelly Lee Alley in an interview with his widow in Houston, August 10, 1966. Bob Healy contributed a "Shelly Lee Alley Discography" to *JEMFQ* 9, Part 1, no. 29 (Spring 1973): 33–34. Other Houston musicians provided bits and pieces of information on Alley, and Nolan Porterfield added still more in his biography of Jimmie Rodgers. I learned about the Bar-X Cowboys from Garna Christian (cited above), and from interviews with Ted Daffan and Jerry Irby (in Houston, June 4, 1977). The extremely influential Blue Ridge Playboys (which included, at one time or another, Leon Selph, Ted Daffan, Floyd Tillman, and Moon Mullican) have not received the kind of academic or popular attention that their stellar membership should warrant. My knowledge of them has come mostly from interviews: Leon Selph, Houston, June 4, 1977; Ted Daffan, Houston, November 20, 1971; Floyd Tillman, Austin, October 21, 1971; and Gordon Baxter, Silsbee, Texas, June 27, 1978. The Baxter interview was particularly helpful on Moon Mullican as well as the East Texas honky-tonk scene of the forties and early fifties. Baxter also wrote an interesting article on Mullican called "Pop Never Wanted Me to Be a Musician," *MCN* 4, no. 8 (February 1967): 27.

The San Antonio western swing scene has received very little attention from country music specialists. My limited knowledge comes totally from the interview with Adolph Hofner (San Antonio, July 24, 1973) and from Tony Russell's notes on Hofner's Arhoolie LP (5020) and Cary Ginell's notes to *The Tune Wranglers, 1936–1938*, Texas Rose TXR2703.

The literature on the Dallas scene is a bit fuller, primarily because two very popular groups, Bill Boyd and the Cowboy Ramblers and the Shelton Brothers, worked in that environment. I talked to Jim Boyd in Dallas on April 20, 1962 (by phone), but the fullest account—biographically and musically—of the Cowboy Ramblers is supplied by Bob Pinson in his notes to the RCA Bluebird reissue, AXM2–5503. A complete discography of the Cowboy Ramblers, compiled by Brad McCuen, is in *Country Directory*, no. 3 (1962): 15–21. My understanding of the Shelton Brothers came from interviews with the three brothers: Merle, in Dallas, October 20, 1963; Bob, in Seven Points, Texas, July 3, 1971 (actually a short conversation between performances at a country festival); and Joe, in Yantis, Texas, late July, 1971.

The revival of interest in Bob Wills's music, and in the whole field of western swing, has been paralleled by a proliferation of published works on Wills and his music. Charles Townsend profited from the western swing revival, but he may have also contributed to its expansion in his biography of Wills. The first fruits of his research came in the essay on Wills that he wrote for *Stars of Country Music*, 171–194, but the crowning achievement was his highly praised biography, *San Antonio Rose: The Life and Music of Bob Wills* (Urbana: University of Illinois Press, 1976). The book was the product of several years of research and was bolstered with an impressively long list of interviews. One can quarrel with some of Townsend's interpretations, as I do—such as the assertion that Wills learned his music "directly" from blacks (and was the only country musician to do so), that he somehow derived his musical freedom and spontaneity from his exposure to the open Texas range country, and that he was essentially a jazz musician—and still recognize it as a major and impressive contribution to our understanding of one of the giant figures of both country and popular music.

In addition to Townsend's book, other significant contributions to the Bob Wills story include the Time-Life collection devoted to his music (with notes by Rich Kienzle); *The Bob Wills Anthology*, Columbia KG32416 (notes by Bill Ivey); Danny Hatcher's "Bob Wills: Discography of the Columbia Years, 1935–47," *JCM* 3, nos. 3–4 (Fall–Winter 1973): 114–134; a diary kept by some unknown fan, "Bob Wills and His Texas Playboys on Radio, 1942," *JCM* 5, no. 4 (Winter 1974): 135–193; Al Stricklin, with Jon McConal, *My Years with Bob Wills* (San Antonio: Naylor Company, 1976); and, of course, Ruth Sheldon's pioneering biography of Wills, *Hubbin' It: The Life of Bob Wills* (Tulsa: privately printed, 1938).

My own comprehension of Wills's music has been augmented by interviews with Johnny Gimble, Leon McAuliffe, and Al Stricklin (all in Kerrville, Texas, on July 2, 3, and 4, 1976), and with Cindy Walker (Mexia, Texas, August 12, 1976), Hoyle Nix (Kerrville, July 1, 1978), and Laura Lee McBride (Houston, November 2, 1978). Quite a few years later, I talked at length with Johnny Gimble while preparing an article on him for *No Depression* magazine.

Finally, a note about the recordings of western swing. The number of reissued LPs and CDs is too large to be listed comprehensively. Therefore, I will note only a few of the most important ones. In addition to the Bill Boyd and Bob Wills anthologies that have already been mentioned, *Okeh Western Swing*, Epic EG37324 (notes by John Morthland), is a collection well worth owning. The series produced by Chris Strachwitz includes a good sampling of virtually all of the western swing groups (Old Timey 105, 116, 117, 119, 120, 121). And because of their seminal importance, at least two collections devoted to Milton Brown and His Musical Brownies should be mentioned: *Milton Brown and His Brownies*, MCA 1509, and *Milton Brown and His Musical Brownies*, String STR804 (notes by Tony Russell). The Origin Jazz label actually reissued all of their recordings in a box set, but it went quickly out of print.

6. THE WAR YEARS: THE NATIONAL EXPANSION OF COUNTRY MUSIC

Historians are gradually beginning to explore the social and cultural consequences of World War II for America (see Geoffrey Perrett, *Days of Sadness, Years of Triumph: The American People, 1939–1945* (Baltimore: Penguin, 1973), but no one has yet concentrated on the revolutionary changes in southern society wrought by that conflict.

The war really gave a deathblow to farm tenantry, as poor southerners, white and black, moved by the millions into the cities and to the north and west. Chad Berry gave us much of this history in *Southern Migrants, Northern Exiles* (Urbana: University of Illinois Press, 2000). Jack Temple Kirby touched upon the overall dimensions of this migration in "The Southern Exodus, 1910–1960: A Primer for Historians," *The Journal of Southern History* 49, no. 4 (November 1983): 585–601. Scholars still need to examine the ways in which the migrants and their descendants were changed by the experience (and, indeed, the way in which their new homes were changed). Harriette Arnow's famous novel *The Dollmaker* (New York: Scribner, 1954) is a powerful fictional exposition of the effects wrought on a mountain family that moved to Detroit during the war years. Excellent preliminary sociological investigations of the phenomenon included Lewis M. Killian, *White Southerners* (New York: Random House, 1970) and "The Adjustment of Southern White Migrants to Northern Urban Norms," *Social Forces* 32, no. 1 (October 1953): 66–70; Harry Schwarzweller, James S. Brown, and J. J. Mangalam, *Mountain Families in Transition: A Case Study of Appalachian Migration* (University Park: Penn State University Press, 1971); and an unpublished paper by John Hevener, "Appalachians in Akron, 1914–1945: The Transfer of Southern Folk Culture" (delivered at the Northern Great Plains History Conference, October 1975). The effects that the migration had on the expansion of country music—the emergence of "hillbilly bars" and the growing appearance of hillbilly records on jukeboxes—is noted in *The Billboard Music Year Book* for 1944 and in various *Billboard* issues during the war years, as well as in Killian's article in *Social Forces*. Excellent descriptions of the movement of southern hillbilly music into northern border areas are found in Charles Camp and David Whisnant, "A Voice from Home: Southern Mountain Musicians on the Maryland-Pennsylvania Border," in *Long Journey Home: Folklife in the South* (Chapel Hill, NC: Southern Exposure), Summer–Fall 1977, 80–90, and Henry Glassie's outstanding account of Ola Belle Reed (previously cited). Although these studies are necessary and useful, scholars still need to explore the movement of southern rural people into *southern* cities. In what ways were the migrants, and the cities, changed—and what were the consequences for the style and popularity of country music?

Writers have often commented on the popularity of country music among American military personnel, and have noted the influence exerted by southern boys and girls who took their musical tastes into the barracks, service clubs, and military theaters. No one, though, has really examined such military magazines as *Yank* and *Stars and Stripes* to find documentation for such presumptions, nor have the dwindling number of ex-servicemen been interviewed in any kind of systematic way. Most of my information about servicemen's tastes (other than the impressionistic knowledge gained from relatives and friends who served in the military) comes from *The Billboard Music Year Book* for 1943 and 1944, and from *Movie-Radio Guide* 11, no. 1 (October 11–17, 1941): 1, and from selected issues of *Billboard*, such as 57, no. 10 (March 10, 1945), which quoted unnamed Army Special Service officers as saying that country music was "the most popular of all music with the services" (p. 29). My information on the Camel Caravan came from the above-mentioned issues of *Billboard* and *Movie-Radio Guide*, and from an interview with Minnie Pearl in Nashville, July 28,

1972, and from her autobiography, *Minnie Pearl*, written with Joan Dew (New York: Simon and Schuster, 1980).

The music industry controversies that affected country music's wartime growth—such as the BMI-ASCAP conflict, the American Federation of Musicians' strike, and shellac rationing—were discussed in *The Billboard Music Year Book*, 1943 and 1944 (and reviewed in the same publication in 1961); Roland Gelatt, *The Fabulous Phonograph* (New York: Lippincott, 1955); David Ewen, *Panorama of American Popular Music* (Englewood Cliffs, NJ: Prentice-Hall, 1957); Hazel Meyer, *The Gold in Tin Pan Alley* (New York: Lippincott, 1958); and Renfro Cole Norris, "The Ballad on the Air" (Master's thesis, University of Texas, 1951). A strong indication of country entertainers' resentment of ASCAP and their receptivity to BMI is found in the testimony that several of them (including Gene Autry, Jimmie Davis, and Roy Acuff) gave to a US Senate subcommittee in 1958: Hearings before the Subcommittee on Communications of the Committee on Interstate and Foreign Commerce, US Senate, 85th Congress, 2d Session, on S. 2834 (March 11–July 23, 1958).

In order to learn the extent of country music growth and expansion during the war—personal appearances, club appearances, record and jukebox activity, and radio barn dance activities—I combed through *Billboard and Billboard Year Book* issues for the years 1941–1945. Additional insights on the *Renfro Valley Barn Dance* were obtained from interviews with John Lair in Renfro Valley, Kentucky, August 18, 1973, and Harry Mullins (Little Clifford) in Mt. Vernon, Kentucky, August 18, 1973. Since that time I interviewed a large number of people associated with Renfro, with the intention of writing a history of the show. That desire was never consummated, and my material is now at the Southern Folklife Collection in Chapel Hill. The burgeoning western ballroom scene of California is discussed in Ken Griffis, "The Harold Hensley Story," *JEMFQ* 6, Part 4, no. 20 (Winter 1970): 146–151, and in Gerald F. Vaughan, "Foreman Phillips: Western Swing's Kingmaker," *JEMFQ* 15, no. 53 (Spring 1979): 27–28. *The Billboard Music Year Book*, 1944, gave statistics about attendance at Foreman Phillips's dances and concerts. Gene Autry's wartime popularity (before he volunteered for military service) was described in *Billboard* and in his autobiography and the Holly George-Warren biography.

The *Grand Ole Opry*'s rise to preeminence was described to me by Harry Stone (interview in Nashville, August 18, 1961) and Minnie Pearl (interview in Nashville, July 28, 1972). One of the most illuminating sources concerning the wartime *Grand Ole Opry* is "The Grand Ole Opry, 1944–45: A Radio Log Kept by Dick Hill, of Tecumseh, Nebraska," *JCM* 5, no. 3 (Fall 1974): 91–122. Hill corresponded with me frequently during the sixties and seventies and provided an early xeroxed copy of the log, along with other memorabilia dealing with midwestern barn dances and performers. Students of country music should be grateful to people like Hill who faithfully preserved such material, and we should be on the lookout for other data of this kind.

Before discussing the singers and songs of the war years, mention should first be made of a development that not only contributed to country music's commercial and national expansion but also adds a dimension to the historical understanding of the music: the appearance of journals devoted to country music. Only scattered copies of these magazines still remain, mostly in the possession of collectors or older musicians, but the Country Music Library and Media Center and the Southern Folklife Collection are gradually adding to their files. Archie Green did a preliminary study of these magazines, based upon those in the Joe Nicholas collection donated to the Country Music Library: "Early Country Music Journals," *JEMFQ* 16, no. 59 (Fall 1980): 141–147. His findings were amplified and clarified to a certain extent by Eddie Nesbitt, a veteran performer from the Washington, DC, area, in "A History of the Mountain Broadcast and Prairie Recorder," *JEMFQ* 13, nos. 65–66 (Spring–Summer 1982): 23–30. The earliest country music magazines (such as *Song Exchange News, The Jamboree, Cowboy Radio Guide*, and *The Mountain Broadcast and Prairie Recorder*) all seem to date from the early years of the war or from the immediate pre-war period. According to Nesbitt, *The Mountain Broadcast and Prairie Recorder* was the first to appear (in 1939), and one can easily agree with him that no better source exists for live country music radio programming of that era. Very few of the country music columnists from that era are still alive, but I was fortunate to get to know Floy Case (wife of local musician Bill Case, and an amateur historian) when she was still living in Fort Worth. If others can be found, they should be interviewed in order to deepen our understanding of both the personal qualities and the "nationalization" of country music.

Pertinent articles and books on several musicians who were prominent during the war (such as those on Gene Autry, Bob Wills, Ernest Tubb, Roy Hall, and Charlie Monroe) have been discussed in the bibliographical essays for chapters 4 and 5. My main concentration here will be on the dominant personality of the war period: Roy Acuff. Four discussions proved helpful in obtaining insights into Acuff's stylistic preferences and song sources: two with Acuff (Nashville, August 26, 1961, and Marthaville, Louisiana, 1981), one with Wesley Rose (Nashville, August 28, 1961), and one with Beecher Kirby (Nashville, July 27, 1972). Elizabeth Schlappi, however, has spent more time than anyone else researching the life and career of Acuff, and she has always freely provided assistance to me and to other historians. Her chief works are *Roy Acuff and His Smoky Mountain Boys Discography* (Country Research Series, *Disc Collector*, no. 23, 1966); the essay on Acuff in *Stars of Country Music*, edited by Bill C. Malone and Judith McCulloh (Urbana: University of Illinois Press, 1975), 195–221; and a book, *Roy Acuff, the Smoky Mountain Boy* (Gretna, LA: Pelican Publishing, 1978). Acuff was the subject of an excellent Time-Life collection, organized and annotated by John Rumble. Since this book was written, Bear Family has released a massive collection of Acuff's recordings: *The King of Country Music, the Foundational Recordings Complete, 1936–1951* (Bear BCD 17300).

Original stanzas of "The Wabash Cannonball" are printed in George Milburn, *The Hobo's Hornbook* (New York: Ives Washburn, 1930). The sources of Acuff's songs should be a good research project for someone, but at least one of the lesser-known writers who supplied songs for him has been the subject of a couple of short sketches: "Jim Anglin: I Wanted to Be a Novelist" (no author listed), *MCN* 5, no. 2 (August 1967): 17, and Ivan M. Tribe and John W. Morris, "The South's Favorite Trio: The Story of the Anglin Brothers," *BGU* 13, no. 5 (November 1978): 30–33. Another source, Fred Rose, is far from obscure. My original sketch of him came from *The ASCAP Biographical*

Dictionary of Composers, Authors, and Publishers, 3rd ed., 421, and from an interview with his son, Wesley Rose (Nashville, August 28, 1961). The definitive treatment of Rose now is John W. Rumble, "Fred Rose and the Development of the Nashville Music Industry, 1942–1954" (PhD diss., Vanderbilt University, 1980). Finally, the source of the famous quote "To hell with Roosevelt; to hell with Babe Ruth; to hell with Roy Acuff!" is still unknown. One of its earliest appearances in print is in Dickson Hartwell, "Caruso of Mountain Music," *Collier's* 123, no. 10 (March 5, 1949): 26. Acuff told me that the original source of the story was war correspondent Ernie Pyle (interview, August 26, 1961).

The songs of the World War II period have not been collected or anthologized in any systematic way. *Billboard* began making its first tentative listings of "hillbilly hits" (as judged by jukebox play) in 1940, when it included such songs with "foreign" numbers (ethnic recordings), and was still lumping hillbilly and "race" recordings together at the end of the war. Broadcast Music, Inc. (BMI), did not publish its lists of "country hits" until 1944, and only a few songs were mentioned (the BMI-licensed country songs that had "gained national acceptance as measured by consistent appearance in the music business trade press"): *BMI Country Hits, 1944–1968* (New York: Broadcast Music, Inc., 1968), 2. BMI, though, can supply author and publishing data for most of the songs that appeared during the earlier war years. Some of the songs from the forties have been anthologized in books published by various companies (for example, *Forty Country and Western Hits of Our Times* (New York: Leeds Music Corporation, 1955) and *One Hundred Great Country and Western Songs*, Vol. 2 (New York: Hill and Range Songs, 1964). Dorothy Horstman's *Sing Your Heart Out, Country Boy* (New York: Dutton, 1975), contains a large number of the songs that appeared between 1941 and 1945. Horstman's fine book (revised and enlarged in 1996) is unique in its attempt to explain the origins of songs in the composers' own words (as much as possible).

The country songs that commented on the war would compose a small volume by themselves. Horstman includes seven of the best in a section called "Songs of War and Patriotism," 232–251, and Jennie A. Chinn quoted several others in her article, "There's a Star-Spangled Banner Waving Somewhere: Country-Western Songs of World War II," *JEMFQ* 16, no. 58 (Summer 1980): 74–80. The article only scratches the surface, however, and much more work needs to be done on the subject. Charles Wolfe and James E. Akenson did include several World War II songs in a general and obviously preliminary study, *Country Music Goes to War* (Lexington: University Press of Kentucky, 2005).

The songs of the forties, of course, did not all deal with the war by any means. Except for an occasional patriotic song such as "There's a Star-Spangled Banner Waving Somewhere," the songs that really signaled country music's growing national acceptance dealt with lost love, nostalgia, self-pity, or romance—time-honored themes that harked back to country's folk roots. Rex Griffin, the writer of the perennial favorite "The Last Letter," still remains much less known than his great song. I learned a few things about him in interviews with musicians who knew or worked with him (Red River Dave, San Antonio, June 19, 1973; Hank Penny, January 17, 1981) and with his brother, Buddy Griffin (Dallas, July 6, 1973). Wiley Walker and Gene

Sullivan, whose recordings of the lonesome "Live and Let Live" and "When My Blue Moon Turns to Gold Again" remained on jukeboxes throughout the war period, have been largely forgotten in recent years. My knowledge of them comes from interviews with Mrs. Wiley Walker in Oklahoma City, January 25, 1982; Wiley Walker Jr., Oklahoma City, January 23, 1982; and Gene Sullivan, Oklahoma City, January 26, 1982 (all by phone). Several of their songs appeared on a reissue album, *Radio Favorites* (Old Homestead OHCD 4188).

Al Dexter, whose "Pistol Packin' Mama" took the country by storm in 1943 (particularly in a "cover" version by Bing Crosby and the Andrews Sisters), received a considerable amount of publicity during the war. A couple of contemporary articles that commented on Dexter and his song were an unsigned sketch in *Life* 15, no. 11 (October 11, 1943): 55, and Maurice Zolotow, "Hillbilly Boom," *Saturday Evening Post* 216 (February 12, 1944): 22–23. Dexter supplied me with biographical information in a letter dated September 21, 1973 (from Denton, Texas), and in a phone interview on August 26, 1973. He also sent me an article by John W. Moody called "Wine, Women, and Song," *Denton Record-Chronicle*, February 11, 1973. Nick Tosches tells the story of "Pistol Packin' Mama's" origins in *Country: The Biggest Music in America* (New York: Stein and Day, 1977), 192–195.

7. THE BOOM PERIOD: THE EMERGENCE OF A BIG BUSINESS, 1946–1953

When country music demonstrated its powerful commercial appeal after the war, the entertainment trade journals began to pay it a respect that had long been absent. Indeed, the whole world of show business began to take it into account. Consequently, *Billboard*'s "top ten" listings of country songs dates from 1948. The first summary listings of this material, covering the years from 1948 to 1963 and compiled by the Record Market Research Division of *Billboard*, appeared in *The World of Country Music* (New York: Billboard, 1963), 187, 189–199. *Country Song Roundup*, founded in Derby, Connecticut, in 1947, began its existence as the most enduring song-and-news magazine in country music history.

Information on record releases, country radio shows (both live and DJ-directed), and personal appearances fills the pages of *Billboard* during these years, as well as the occasional yearbooks and encyclopedias distributed by the journal (see, for example, *The Billboard Encyclopedia of Music*, 8th annual edition (1946–1947). I found additional information on record companies in Paul S. Carpenter, *Music: An Art and a Business* (Norman: University of Oklahoma Press, 1950), 72–73, and on radio barn dances in Linnell Gentry, ed., *A History and Encyclopedia of Country, Western, and Gospel Music* (Nashville: McQuiddy Press, 1961), 168–175 (unfortunately, this material was removed from Gentry's revised edition in 1969).

The exciting postwar California scene has been well covered by James Gregory, *American Exodus: The Dust Bowl Migration and Okie Culture in California* (New York: Oxford University Press, 1989); Gerald Haslam, *Workin' Man Blues: Country Music in California* (Berkeley: University of California Press, 1999); Peter La Chapelle, *Proud to Be an Okie: Cultural Politics, Country Music, and Migration to Southern California* (Berkeley: University of California Press, 2007); and Robert E. Price,

The Bakersfield Sound: How a Generation of Displaced Okies Revolutionized American Music (Bakersfield, CA: iUniverse, 2015). Several shorter articles have also been helpful to me. Gerald F. Vaughan comments on Foreman Phillips's active role in "Foreman Phillips: Western Swing's Kingmaker," *JEMFQ* 15, no. 53 (Spring 1979): 27–29, but Hank Penny presents a much more negative view of Phillips in Rich Kienzle, "The Checkered Career of Hank Penny," *JCM* 8, no. 2 (1980): 63 (this is the best survey of Penny's career, although Ken Griffis, "Hank Penny: The Original Outlaw," *JEMFQ* 18, nos. 65–66 [Spring–Summer 1982]: 5–13, is also useful). Vaughan also adds to our knowledge of California's western ballroom circuit with "That Ozark Playboy: Red Murrell," *JEMFQ* 17, no. 61 (Fall 1981): 119–122, while Ken Griffis reminds us that Ray Whitley was more than a singing cowboy; he was also a popular band leader: "The Ray Whitley Story," *JEMFQ* 6, Part 2, no. 18 (Summer 1970): 65–68.

The great impact made by Spade Cooley and Tex Williams is discussed by Griffis in "The Tex Williams Story," *JEMFQ* 15, no. 53 (Spring 1979): 5–19, and by Rich Kienzle, in "When a Country Star Turns Murderer: The Strange, Tragic Case of Spade Cooley," *Country Music* 5, no. 10 (July 1977): 34, 36, 38, 64. I also found a contemporary biographical sketch of Williams in the *National Hillbilly News* 3, no. 2 (December 1947). The best introduction to Cooley and Williams is in the exciting music they made, a good sampling of which is *Spade Cooley*, Columbia FC37467 (a reissue of selections recorded from 1944 to 1946).

Merle Travis, the all-purpose musician who performed as a solo act and as an accompanist for musicians throughout California, received his most serious treatment from Archie Green, in *Only a Miner: Studies in Recorded Coal-Mining Songs* (Urbana: University of Illinois Press, 1972). Here we find a discussion of how his classic "Sixteen Tons" and "Dark as a Dungeon" came to be written. The other and more prominent side of his performing nature—the good-natured, honky-tonk impulse—is portrayed in the Time-Life collection *Honky Tonkin'*. Two articles based on interviews demonstrate the man's versatility and intelligence: Dorothy Horstman, "Merle Travis," *Country Music* 4, no. 1 (October 1975): 31–34, and Bob Baxter, "Merle Travis: The Man, the Music," *Guitar Player* 10, no. 9 (September 1976): 20–21, 28–36. It is a shame that Travis never wrote his autobiography or a history of the California music scene. He was a walking library of country music history (see Merle Travis, "Recollections of Merle Travis, 1944–1955," *JEMFQ* 15, no. 54 [Summer 1979]: 107–114; and *JEMFQ* 15, no. 55 [Fall 1979]: 135–143).

Merle Travis and other California musicians played central roles in the development of the solid-body guitar and other electric instruments. In addition to the Rich Kienzle articles mentioned elsewhere, one should also read a couple of articles in *Guitar Player* that expound on the role played by Leo Fender: 5, no. 6 (September 1971): 9, 38; and 12, no. 5 (May 1978)—both based on interviews.

Nudie the Tailor's influence in country music was as pervasive as that of Leo Fender. Two short sketches of the man (aka Nudie Cohn) that were helpful are Bill A. Wheeler, "Nudie the Tailor," *Country Music Review* (March–April 1965): 40–41, and Jan Otteson, "Nudie Is the Original 'Rhinestone Cowboy,'" *MCN* 15, no. 8 (February 1978): 13.

Despite the dynamic influence exerted by California musicians and personalities, the *Grand Ole Opry* had become, at least symbolically, the most important country music institution in the world. A couple of magazine articles suggest the reverence that most fans had for the show: Rufus Jarman, "Country Music Goes to Town," *Nation's Business* 41 (February 1953): 44–51, and Don Eddy, "Hillbilly Heaven," *American Magazine* 153 (March 1952). The most illuminating material for me, however, was the transcripts of the *Prince Albert Shows* (the thirty-minute segments carried on NBC). The transcripts listed the songs as well as the dialogue between comedians Minnie Pearl and Rod Brasfield and host Red Foley. Regrettably, Foley has been almost forgotten since his glory days in the fifties. Record reissues have almost completely passed him by, and writers have seldom discussed him. Charles Wolfe, however, does discuss him in *Kentucky Country: Folk and Country Music of Kentucky* (Lexington: University Press of Kentucky, 1982), and at least one journal writer, John Pugh, has commemorated him: "The Late, Great Red Foley," *Country Music* 5, no. 9 (June 1976): 53–56.

The chief challenger of the *Grand Ole Opry*—the *Louisiana Hayride*—has found its historian in Tracey E. W. Laird: *Louisiana Hayride: Radio and Roots Music along the Red River* (New York: Oxford University Press, 2004). Stephen Ray Tucker, though, published a fine article, "The Louisiana Hayride, 1948–54," in the *North Louisiana Historical Journal* 8, no. 5 (Fall 1977): 187–201. I have obtained additional information on the show in interviews with Homer Bailes (Jennings, Louisiana, August 16, 1974), Paul Howard (Shreveport, Louisiana, August 26, 1974), and Pappy Covington (Shreveport, July 27, 1974).

The world of recording in the immediate postwar years has received scattered attention from writers, but no one has brought all the disparate threads together into one compact article or book. That crucial agent of country music dissemination, the disc jockey, has received only minimal historical treatment. Hugh Cherry, though, has written a good article, "Country DJs Carry Music to the People," *MCN* 18, no. 4 (October 1980): 18–19. The small record labels have not been much better documented, but Nathan Gibson has made a major contribution to the topic with *The Starday Story: The House That Country Music Built* (Jackson: University Press of Mississippi, 2011). I obtained some information on the Gold Star and Starday labels from Pappy Daily (interview, Houston, August 19, 1977). Syd Nathan and his King label are discussed in Richard L. Gordon, "The Man Who Is King," *Saga* (January 1951), reprinted in *JEMFQ* 4, no. 10, Part 2 (June 1968): 63–66, and the Bullet label's history is described by Martin Hawkins in "Bullet Records: A Shot in the Dark," *JCM* 8, no. 3 (1981): 33–41. And one must not overlook John Broven's enthusiastic and marvelously detailed *South to Louisiana* (Gretna, LA: Pelican Publishing, 1983), which discusses J. D. Miller and other Louisiana recording men who recorded an abundance of country, Cajun, and blues artists.

Nashville's rise to prominence as a recording center for country music should not cause one to forget that much recording went on in Louisiana, Dallas, Cincinnati, and other places. Jim Beck's Studio in Dallas, for example—where people like Lefty Frizzell, Ray Price, and Marty Robbins made some of their best recordings—has not been properly studied. The minimal amount of knowledge I have of Beck comes from an essay by Charles K. Wolfe, who regrettably dashes out a bit of hyperbole, "Honky Tonk

Starts Here: The Jim Beck Dallas Studio," *JCM* 11, no. 1 (1986): 25–30, and from Bill Callahan (interview, Dallas, February 8, 1982) and Buddy Griffin (interview, Dallas, July 6, 1973).

Nashville's early ventures into the recording field are well described in John Rumble, "The Emergence of Nashville as a Recording Center: Logbooks from the Castle Studios, 1952–53," *JCM* 7, no. 3 (December 1978): 22–42. The original Nashville sessions musicians are discussed in Time-Life's *Hank Williams* collection, and in Charles Wolfe, "Tommy Jackson: Nashville Fiddler," *BGU* 15, no. 3 (September 1980): 42–47. Chet Atkins's rise to prominence is discussed in Bill Ivey's "Chet Atkins," in *Stars of Country Music*, edited by Bill C. Malone and Judith McCulloh (Urbana: University of Illinois Press, 1975), 301–316, and in Atkins's autobiography (written with Bill Neely), *Country Gentleman* (Chicago: Henry Regnery, 1974).

My discussion of song writing and publishing in the early fifties owes much to interviews with Jim Denny (Nashville, August 25, 1961) and Cindy Walker (Mexia, Texas, August 12, 1976) and to a short article on songwriters in *The World of Country Music* (New York: *Billboard*, 1963), 146, 162–163. Sketches of individual songwriters that have been useful to me include (Author unnamed), "Jim Anglin: I Wanted to Be a Novelist," *MCN* 5, no. 2 (August 1967): 17; Ivan M. Tribe, "Mac Odell: The Ole Country Boy," *BGU* 11, no. 4 (October 1976): 30–34; and two on Felice and Boudleaux Bryant, "Country Music Is What You Make It" (by Boudleaux Bryant), *Nashville Sound* 1, no. 1 (September 1975): 8–10, and Lee Rector, "Writers Felice and Boudleaux Review Thirty Years," *MCN* 17, no. 8 (February 1980): 7. The intriguing Arthur Q. Smith (James Pritchett) is the subject of a Bear Family anthology, *Arthur Q. Smith: The Trouble with the Truth* (BCD 17426) that contains several songs, sung by Smith and others, that he allegedly wrote.

The brother duet and family tradition of singing lingered in the performances of such musicians as the Bailes Brothers, the Louvin Brothers, Johnny and Jack, the Maddox Brothers and Rose, and in bluegrass (which will be discussed in chapter 10). Most of my knowledge of the Bailes Brothers comes from a long interview with Homer Bailes (Jennings, Louisiana, August 16, 1974) and a shorter one with Clyde Baum (Pollock, Louisiana, October 19, 1974). Ivan Tribe also supplied me a tape of an interview he conducted with Johnnie Bailes (August 18, 1974). Tribe's two short essays on the group are indispensable: "The Bailes Brothers," *BGU* 9, no. 8 (February 1975): 8–13, and "West Virginia Homefolks: The Bailes Brothers," *OTM*, no. 19 (Winter 1975–1976): 17–20. Don Rhodes, "Remembering the Bailes Brothers," *Pickin'* 4, no. 2 (March 1977): 6–14, provides a good summary of their career, and *National Hillbilly News* 3, no. 3 (January–February 1948): 7, tells about them at the time they joined the *Louisiana Hayride*. The most interesting items of all on the Bailes Brothers, though, are the LPs composed of material taken from their transcribed radio shows on KWKH in the late forties. Complete with commercials, songbook pitches, and personal appearance announcements, the albums are wonderful introductions to the Bailes Brothers' style and to the era of live radio: *The Bailes Brothers*, Old Homestead OHCS 103 and 104.

The Louvin Brothers' repertory and style can be heard on *Close Harmony* (Bear BCD 15561), complete with a biography written by Charles Wolfe. Wolfe has also fashioned a larger biography, *In Close Harmony: The Story of the Louvin Brothers* (Jackson: University Press of Mississippi, 1996). The Brothers are also featured on an album composed of transcribed radio shows: *Songs That Tell a Story*, Rounder 1030 (notes by Douglas B. Green). Taken from programs presented on WZOB in Fort Payne, Alabama, in 1952, the LPs capture the Louvins at their best, when they were gospel singers performing with only mandolin and guitar. This is an important album to have, not only because it re-creates the atmosphere of old-time radio shows but also because it stresses a side of their performing approach that is neglected in other big reissue projects. Both the *Smithsonian Collection of Classic Country Music* and the Time-Life *Duet* project feature only the "secular" songs of the Louvins. I obtained some biographical information from Charlie Louvin (interview, Meridian, Mississippi, May 25, 1977), who later supplied me with tapes of most of the Louvin Brothers' recordings. Two of the better articles on the duo are Don Rhodes, "Looking Back on the Louvin Brothers," *Pickin'* 3, no. 2 (March 1976): 4–12, and Suzy Lowry Geno, "Charlie and Ira—The Louvin Brothers," *BGU* 17, no. 9 (March 1983): 12–18.

Johnny and Jack have been the subject of many scattered references and sketches, but they are seldom discussed in any extended fashion. Ivan Tribe and John Morris give some information about their origins (particularly Jack Anglin) in "The South's Favorite Trio: The Story of the Anglin Brothers," *BGU* 13, no. 5 (November 1978): 30–33, and Dixie Deen writes a very good summary of the two singers in "Johnny Wright: Again the Bugle Blows," *MCN* 5, no. 1 (July 1967): 3–6, 24.

Rose Maddox did much to clarify my understanding of her family in a telephone conversation on January 23, 1982 (to Ashland, Oregon), but the best introduction to the Maddox Brothers and Rose is the biography written by Jonny Whiteside, *Ramblin' Rose: The Life and Career of Rose Maddox* (Nashville: Vanderbilt University Press, 1997). Two albums on the Arhoolie label (5016 and 5017) convey the zest and vitality of their performances.

Rose Maddox was one of several women who began to compete favorably with men in the postwar years. She, Texas Ruby, Cousin Emmy, Molly O'Day, Wilma Lee Cooper, Kitty Wells, and Goldie Hill are anthologized in Time-Life's *Women* collection along with brief written biographies. I obtained some information about Martha Carson's career in a talk with her in Nashville, August 16, 1973. Information on her earlier career as part of the duet of James and Martha Carson is provided in Ivan Tribe, "James (Carson) Roberts," *BGU* 14, no. 11 (May 1980): 66–72. Wilma Lee Cooper has drawn the attention of researchers because of her unwavering commitment to tradition. Sue Thrasher conducted a good interview with her in *Long Journey Home: Folklife in the South* (Chapel Hill, NC: Southern Exposure), Summer–Fall 1977, 90–97, while Douglas B. Green, in "Wilma Lee and Stoney Cooper," *BGU* 8, no. 9 (March 1974): 25–27, and Wayne W. Daniel, "Wilma Lee Cooper: America's Most Authentic Mountain Singer," ibid. 16, no. 8 (February 1982): 12–17, present good summaries and evaluations of her career.

Molly O'Day's story has been well told by Ivan Tribe and John Morris: "Molly O'Day and Lynn Davis," *BGU* 9, no. 3 (September 1974): 10–15, and *Molly O'Day, Lynn Davis, and the Cumberland Mountain Folks: A Bio-Discography*, JEMF Special Series, no. 7 (1975). References to O'Day also show up in material devoted to Hank Williams, the Bailes Brothers, and Mac Wiseman, because she influenced these and other singers in dramatic ways.

As might be expected, published material on Kitty Wells has been extensive. Representative articles include Geoff Lane, "The Queen of Country Music," *Country Music* 3, no. 3 (December 1974): 40–45; Mary Ellen Moore, "Kitty Wells: The One and Only Queen of Country Music," *Country Music* 5, no. 6 (March 1977): 47–48; Douglas B. Green, "The Queen Still Reigns," *Country Music* 8, no. 9 (June 1980): 41–44; and an article that should put to rest any idea that Kitty was a woman's liberationist, "Woman Put on Earth for Man to Look After, Kitty Wells Says" (unsigned), *Country Style*, no. 3 (August 1976): 17. The previously mentioned article on Johnny Wright (by Dixie Deen) also contains interesting material on Kitty Wells. The best introduction to her quiet, soulful singing is in the music in her Bear Family collection.

There is a great need for a major article on the comedy-singing acts of country music, as well as an anthology of their recorded material. Loyal Jones fills much of the vacuum with *Country Music Humorists and Comedians* (Urbana: University of Illinois Press, 2008). Bill Carlisle is discussed by Dixie Deen in "Woman behind the Man," *MCN* 4, no. 1 (July 1966), and in Wolfe's *Kentucky Country*, 64–65. Lonzo and Oscar receive brief attention in Aline Miller, "Lonzo and Oscar," *Pickin'* 4, no. 4 (May 1977): 32–33, while Homer and Jethro are discussed by David Grisman in "Jethro Burns," *Frets* 1, no. 8 (October 1979): 38–41. Douglas B. Green has a section called "Comedy" in *Country Roots: The Origins of Country Music* (New York: Hawthorn Books, 1976), 65–87, in which Carlisle, Lonzo and Oscar, Homer and Jethro, and other comedians are briefly discussed. Brief biographical sketches of these men are also found in Gentry, *A History and Encyclopedia of Country, Western, and Gospel Music*, and of course in Paul Kingsbury, ed., *The Encyclopedia of Country Music: The Ultimate Guide to the Music* (New York: Oxford University Press, 1998).

The mainstream country singers of the early fifties—such as Carl Smith, Hank Locklin, and George Morgan—largely remain undocumented. Norm Cohen has suggested why: "The country music of the years immediately after the Second World War has fallen between the cracks of the reissue business. Too late to catch the interests of the old-timey enthusiasts, too old for contemporary country fans, too country for bluegrassers, it has been neglected by almost everyone" (*JEMFQ* 15, no. 56 [Winter 1979]: 244). Although sketches and occasional interviews with such musicians appear in *Country Song Roundup, Music City News*, and various short-lived country magazines, the reader is advised to consult Paul Kingsbury, *The Country Music Encyclopedia*, for basic biographical data, and available Bear Family CD box sets for their music.

Several of the honky-tonk stylists, however, have been justly appreciated. I participated in the organization and wrote the notes for Time-Life's *Honky Tonkin'*. Here one will hear the music of, and read sketches about, such performers as Floyd Tillman, Ernest Tubb, Hank Thompson, Webb Pierce, and Lefty Frizzell. These musicians and more are also in the *Smithsonian Collection of Classic Country Music*. Interviews have been helpful in obtaining knowledge about several of the honky-tonk performers. I interviewed Floyd Tillman in Austin, October 21, 1971; in Bacliff, Texas, May 31, 1974; and in Austin, February 15, 1982. As mentioned in the notes to chapter 5, my June 27, 1978, interview with Gordon Baxter in Silsbee, Texas, proved most helpful in understanding Moon Mullican. Special mention, though, should be made of an album devoted to Mullican: *Moon Mullican: Seven Nights to Rock*, Western 2001, an assemblage of several of his King recordings from 1946 to 1956, and with complete and discerning notes by Rich Kienzle. Ronnie Pugh tells us just about everything we need to know about Ernest Tubb in his biography, and readers can hear much of Tubb's music in his Bear Family box collection. A short talk with Hank Thompson in Kerrville, Texas, July 3, 1977, provided me with some insights about his long and important career. John Broven, in *South to Louisiana* (Gretna, LA: Pelican Publishing, 1983), has much to say that is good and enlightening about Harry Choates, particularly on pages 29–35. Mike Leadbitter had earlier discussed the singer-fiddler in "Harry Choates: Cajun Fiddle Ace," *OTM*, no. 6 (Autumn 1972): 20–22. I learned something about Choates's early performing years, and about the possible sources of his style, in an interview with Leo Soileau in Ville Platte, Louisiana, June 15, 1974.

A strong revival of interest in Lefty Frizzell occurred after his death, and particularly after his election to the Country Music Hall of Fame. One entire LP side (seven songs) of Time-Life's *Honky Tonkin'* collection album was devoted to Frizzell, and other reissues of his material have appeared frequently, the most important being his Bear Family box set. His biography has been written by Daniel Cooper, *Lefty Frizzell: The Honky-Tonk Life of Country Music's Greatest Singer* (Boston: Little, Brown, 1995). Bill Callahan and Alice Frizzell supplied me with information about Lefty's early life and career on February 18, 1982, and March 2, 1982 (both by telephone). Geoff Lane has written one of the best of the popular articles on Frizzell: "The Last of Lefty Frizzell," *Country Music* 4, no. 2 (November 1975): 38–42, 63.

The great gap between Webb Pierce's popularity in the early fifties and his later almost total neglect is hard to understand. His admission to the Country Music Hall of Fame in 2001 came ten years after his death. Gail Davies did her best to resurrect and commemorate him in an album she produced in 2002, *Caught in the Webb: A Tribute to the Legendary Webb Pierce*. A variety of singers like Dale Watson, Charley Pride, George Jones, and Emmylou Harris provided evidence of the infectious quality of Pierce's music. In the meantime, several articles gave glimpses of his personality, style, and contributions. These include Scott Cohen, "Webb," *Country Music* 3, no. 5 (February 1975): 34–37; "Pierce—a Leader Then, a Leader Now," *MCN* 13, no. 9 (March 1976): 16; Jack D. Johnson, "The Webb Pierce Story," *Country Music Review* 1, no. 6 (February 1964): 5; and a very favorable review of a Pierce concert in Austin, Texas, by John Bustin, "Pierce Has Solid Hold on Country Music Fans," *Austin American*, October 7, 1964. Pierce's role in popularizing the pedal steel guitar was discussed in Jean-Charles Costa, "The Country Guitar: The Mysterious Pedal Steel," *Country Music* 1, no. 1 (June 1973): 42–44, and by John Haggard, "Bud Isaacs," *Guitar Player* 10, no. 11 (November 1976): 31, 78, 80.

Eddy Arnold, the first great crossover stylist in country music, never suffered from media neglect. Michael Streissguth wrote his biography: *Eddy Arnold: Pioneer of the Nashville Sound* (New York: Schirmer, 1997). Dixie Deen had written an interesting and much earlier sketch of him called "Eddy Arnold: His World," *MCN* 3, no. 10 (April 1966): 1, 4, 23. Arnold's autobiography, *It's a Long Way from Chester County* (New

York: Pyramid Books, 1969), had given the basic facts of his life and career but said too little about the country music world that provided the context for his rise to fame. Arnold said nothing, for example, about Roy Wiggins, the steel guitarist who created the original Eddy Arnold instrumental sound. Douglas B. Green corrected that imbalance somewhat in "Roy Wiggins Stays 'In' with Ting-a-Ling Style," *MCN* 14, no. 4 (October 1976): 21. *Billboard* issues from the mid- and late forties provide all the evidence one needs of Arnold's powerful commercial appeal, and *The World of Country Music*, which summarized all the "top ten" listings from 1948 to 1963, showed that no other country singer equaled him in the recording of hit songs.

One of my greatest disappointments as a researcher was my inability to arrange an interview with Hank Snow, one of my all-time favorites. Snow's autobiography appeared well after the first versions of this book appeared: Hank Snow, with Jack Ownbey and Robert Burris, *The Hank Snow Story* (Urbana: University of Illinois Press, 1994). I instead relied on a handful of printed sources and, of course, his very large recorded output. *The Hank Snow Twenty-Fifth Anniversary Album* (Nashville: Privately printed, 1961) is a good compendium of biographical and discographical information. "Country Song Roundup Talks with Hank Snow," *CSR* 20, no. 112 (November 1968): 11–13, is a fairly substantial interview, and two *Country Music* essays provide good discussions of him: Marshall Fallwell, "Hank Snow Moves On in the Old Tradition," *Country Music* 2, no. 3 (November 1973): 66–71, and Peter Guralnick, "The Singing Ranger: Hank Snow," *Country Music* 7, no. 2 (November– December 1978): 28–32.

Another great stylist of the fifties, Slim Whitman, received extensive media attention in the years following the remarkable success of his "television special" records. Kenneth L. Gibble wrote an "inspirational" biography called *Mr. Songman: The Slim Whitman Story* (Elgin, IL: Brethren Press, 1982). Of the various popular accounts, Kelly Delaney, "Slim Whitman Is Loved around the World," *MCN* 17, no. 7 (January 1980): 13, is fair and objective, but Richard Sanders, "Slim Whitman," *Us* 5, no. 12 (June 9, 1981): 72–74, called him "the throaty thrush of the Moral Majority" and said that he "epitomizes all that is hokey and heartfelt in the American dream."

When writing on Hank Williams for the first edition of this book, I relied most heavily upon Eli Waldron, "Country Music: The Death of Hank Williams," *Reporter* 12, no. 10 (May 19, 1955): 35–37; Waldron, "Country Music: The Squaya Dansu from Nashville," *Reporter* 12, no. 11 (June 2, 1955): 39–41; *CSR* (Special Hank Williams Memorial Issue) 1, no. 24 (June 1953): 5–14; Rufus Jarman, "Country Music Goes to Town," *Nation's Business* 41 (February 1953): 44–51; Bernard Asbell, "Simple Songs of Sex, Sin, and Salvation," *Show: The Magazine of the Performing Arts* 2, no. 2 (February 1962): 88–91; various issues of *Billboard*; and conversations with Audrey Williams (Austin, July 2, 1962) and Wesley Rose (Nashville, August 28, 1961). Patrick Huber, Steve Goodson, and Dave Anderson have edited a compendium of such articles called *The Hank Williams Reader* (New York: Oxford University Press, 2014).

Since then, the story of Hank Williams has been broadened and clarified by the appearance of several biographies, at least one solid reminiscence by a Drifting Cowboy (Jerry Rivers), a wealth of reissued recordings, and a few fine articles. Roger Williams (no relation to Hank) wrote one of the best-balanced and most solidly researched biographies of Hank: *Sing a Sad Song: The Life of Hank Williams* (Garden City, NY: Doubleday, 1970; republished by University of Illinois Press, 1981). One of the great virtues of the University of Illinois Press edition is its inclusion of a Hank Williams discography compiled by Bob Pinson. Chet Flippo, in *Your Cheatin' Heart: A Biography of Hank Williams* (New York: Simon and Schuster, 1981), presented a less pleasing and more tragic picture of Hank than did Roger Williams. The book is troubling to many people because of its use of fictionalized dialogue and because of its assertion that Hank did not write some of the songs attributed to him. Jerry Rivers, on the other hand, gave an affectionate account of Williams in *Hank Williams: From Life to Legend* (Denver, CO: Heather Enterprises, 1976). My favorite biography is Paul Hemphill, *Lovesick Blues: The Life of Hank Williams* (New York: Viking, 2005). Among the best popular articles that touch upon Hank Williams are Ed Linn, "The Short Life of Hank Williams," *Saga* 13, no. 4 (January 1957): 8–11, 86–91; Tom Ayres, "Son, Can You Play That Thing," *Country Rambler*, no. 4 (November 4, 1976): 42–43 (about steel guitar player Felton Pruitt, but very good on Hank and the early *Louisiana Hayride*); and "Remembering Hank" (interviews with several people conducted by Hank Williams Jr.), *Country Music* 3, no. 6 (March 1975): 24–27. My understanding of Hank's second marriage and his last years on the *Louisiana Hayride* was enhanced by my interview with Paul Howard in Shreveport, July 26, 1974.

8. THE DEVELOPMENT OF COUNTRY-POP MUSIC AND THE NASHVILLE SOUND

A short sketch of Mitch Miller, the producer who did the most in the early fifties to move country songs into the repertories of pop singers—along with a list of such songs that made the transition—is in *The World of Country Music* (New York: *Billboard*, 1963), 145. But proof that "traditional" country singers such as Hank Snow were continuing to thrive on down to 1955 is in *Number One Country Singles* (New York: Billboard Publications, 1980). Further evidence of country music's burgeoning financial status was the appearance of two new country music journals, *Country and Western Jamboree* in 1955 and *Rustic Rhythm* in 1957, both with slick covers and attractive formats, and each boasting national circulation. Before long, though, each became filled with stories about the new rockabilly sensations, and neither survived long after the rock-and-roll explosion.

The books and articles that describe rock-and-roll's roots and its early development constitute a rather large library. A good place to begin is Michael Bertrand, *Race, Rock, and Elvis* (Urbana: University of Illinois Press, 2000). Arnold Shaw's *Honkers and Shouters: The Golden Years of Rhythm and Blues* (New York: Collier Books, 1978) is a detail-filled account that concentrates on the singers of the forties and fifties. Tony Glover, "R&B," *Sing Out* 15, no. 2 (May 1965): 7–13, is a good short survey that comments on the way rhythm-and-blues was watered down by rock-and-roll musicians. Nick Tosches, in *Country: The Biggest Music in America* (New York: Stein and Day, 1977), 29–33, talks about the hillbilly boogie exponents of the late forties and early fifties who may have influenced the early rockabillies. The most complete general histories of rock-and-roll are Carl Belz, *The Story of Rock* (New York, Oxford

University Press, 1969), and Charlie Gillett, *The Sound of the City: The Rise of Rock and Roll* (New York: Dell, 1972). Jim Miller, ed., *The Rolling Stone Illustrated History of Rock and Roll*, 2d rev. ed. (New York: Random House/Rolling Stone Press, 1981), is an anthology of articles dealing with all aspects of rock music, from Elvis to the 1980s. One of the best modern writer-critics of rock and popular music, Peter Guralnick, has written several provocative books of essays dealing with blues, rock-and-roll, and country musicians: These include *Feel like Going Home: Portraits in Blues and Rock 'n' Roll* (London: Omnibus Press, 1978), and *Lost Highway: Journeys and Arrivals of American Musicians* (Boston: David R. Godine, 1979). His greatest contributions, of course, were his biographies of Elvis Presley and Sam Phillips.

The most comprehensive account of the company that introduced the rockabilly sound to the world is Colin Escott and Martin Hawkins, *Sun Records: The Brief History of the Legendary Record Label*, 2d rev. ed. (New York: Quick Fox, 1980). John Pugh contributes a shorter chronicle of the famous label in "The Rise and Fall of Sun Records," *Country Music* 2, no. 3 (November 1973): 26–32, and Barbara Sims, a former publicist at the company, tells what it was like at the beginning in *The Next Elvis: Searching for Stardom at Sun Records* (Baton Rouge: LSU Press, 2014). Although Michael Bane touches on the subject in *White Boy Singin' the Blues: The Black Roots of White Rock* (New York: Penguin Books, 1982), the best compact account of rockabilly music is Nick Tosches, "Rockabilly," in *The Illustrated History of Country Music*, edited by Patrick Carr (New York: Country Music Magazine Press, 1979), 217–237.

Elvis Presley has inspired a vast and proliferating literature. Jerry Hopkins was one of the first to tackle the subject with *Elvis: A Biography* (New York: Warner Books, 1972; originally published in 1971). This reliable and objective book-length treatment of Presley was followed by *Elvis: The Final Years* (New York: St. Martin's Press, 1980), a balanced yet sobering account of his subject's tragic decline and demise. Albert Goldman's bestselling and widely publicized biography, *Elvis* (New York: McGraw-Hill, 1981), contains many fascinating vignettes, including the story of Colonel Parker's Dutch origins, but one can hardly escape the conclusion that Goldman despised Elvis, the South, and the hillbilly culture that gave the singer birth. The best interpretations of Presley, along with a study of Sam Phillips, are the books written by Guralnick: *Last Train to Memphis: The Rise of Elvis Presley* (Boston: Little, Brown, 1994); *Careless Love: The Unmaking of Elvis Presley* (Boston: Little, Brown, 1999); and *Sam Phillips: The Man Who Invented Rock 'n' Roll* (Boston: Little, Brown, 2015). Greil Marcus, though, presents a brilliant exposition of the tensions in southern culture that gave rise to both country music and rock and roll, in *Mystery Train: Images of America in Rock 'n' Roll Music*, 2d rev. ed. (New York: Dutton, 1982). A more extended effort to relate Presley to southern culture is Joel Williamson, *Elvis Presley: A Southern Life* (New York: Oxford University Press, 2014), and Jac Tharpe, ed., *Elvis: Images and Fancies* (Jackson: University Press of Mississippi, 1979), a series of essays by such writers as Stephen Ray Tucker, Linda Ray Pratt, Van K. Brock, Charles Wolfe, and myself.

The published accounts dealing with other rockabillies have become quite extensive. Among them, Rick Bragg's *Jerry Lee Lewis: His Own Story* (New York: HarperCollins, 2014) is unsurpassed. Women rockabillies have not been neglected, and Robert K. Oermann and Mary A. Bufwack have written a fine study, including a discography, of such singers as Wanda Jackson, Brenda Lee, and Janis Martin: "Rockabilly Women," *JCM* 8, no. 1 (May 1979): 65–94. Carl Perkins (with Ron Rendleman) wrote an autobiography, *Disciple in Blue Suede Shoes* (Grand Rapids, MI: Zondervan, 1978), which stressed his religious conversion. Further insight into Perkins's music, though, can be found in Michael Lydon, *Rock Folk: Portraits from the Rock 'n' Roll Pantheon* (New York: Dial Press, 1971), and in Patrick Carr, "Carl Perkins, Livin' Legend," *Country Music* 2, no. 1 (September 1973): 65–71. John Goldrosen, *The Buddy Holly Story*, 2d rev. ed. (New York: Quick Fox, 1979), is an excellent biography, but one can also learn much from William J. Bush, "Buddy Holly," *Guitar Player* 16, no. 6 (June 1982): 64–66, 74–82, 86, 90–108. Philip Norman discusses the Everly Brothers in *The Road Goes On Forever: Portraits from a Journey through Contemporary Music* (New York: Fireside Books, 1982), but their country background is best described in an essay written by their father: Ike Everly, "Father Calls Mother Secret of Amazing Success," *Country and Western Jamboree* 3, no. 5 (August 1957): 15, 34, and ibid. 4, no. 1 (Summer 1958): 10–16, 33, 38. Of course, no better example of their country roots can be cited than their album *Songs Our Daddy Taught Us* (Cadence CLP3016), which includes items like "I'm Just Here to Get My Baby Out of Jail," "The Lightning Express," and "Rocking Alone in an Old Rocking Chair."

Jerry Lee Lewis has been fascinating to writers. In addition to Rick Braggs's great book, Nick Tosches talks about Lewis at great length in *Country: The Biggest Music in America* and has written a biography of him with the provocative title *Hellfire: The Jerry Lee Lewis Story* (New York: Delacorte, 1982). The *New York Times* music critic Robert Palmer wrote a good article called "The Devil and Jerry Lee Lewis," *Rolling Stone* 13 (December 13, 1979), and later followed that up with a biography, *Jerry Lee Lewis Rocks* (New York: Delilah Books, 1981). A former wife, Myra Gail Lewis (with Murray Silver), wrote still another book on the controversial singer, *Great Balls of Fire: The Uncensored Story of Jerry Lee Lewis* (New York: Quill Books, 1982). When writing about Lewis, the subject of religion can hardly be avoided. One of the best short expositions of the impact made by Pentecostalism on Lewis is Stephen Ray Tucker, "Pentecostalism and Popular Culture in the South: A Study of Four Musicians," *The Journal of Popular Culture* 16, no. 3 (Winter 1982): 68–80.

Marty Robbins was the first mainstream country singer to jump on the rockabilly bandwagon. A couple of short articles give the main outlines of his story, "Marty Robbins," *Rustic Rhythm* 1, no. 1 (April 1957): 20–21, and "Alias Marty Robbins," *Hoedown* 1, no. 2 (June 1966): 8–12, but the best introduction to his life and music is the Time-Life collection *Marty Robbins* (with notes by Patricia Hall). These reissued recordings show just how versatile he was, but the fullest exposition of his rockabilly leanings is still another German reissue, *Rockin' Rollin' Robbins*, Bear Family BFX15045 (seventeen recordings made between 1954 and 1958).

Two other singers who adjusted to the new accent on youth generated by rock and roll were Sonny James and Johnny Cash. James certainly deserves more attention than he has received from writers. Two articles suggest why he has not been more appealing to publicists: Robert Adels, "Sonny James: At All Times, in All Ways, the Southern Gentleman," *Country Music* 2, no. 1 (September 1973): 46–49, and Michael

Bane, "Sonny James Sticks to Ice Cream," *Country Music* 5, no. 5 (February 1977): 42–46. Johnny Cash, on the other hand, has always demonstrated a superb mastery of media exploitation. He has been the subject of popular newsstand biographies, the best of which are Christopher Wren, *Winners Got Scars Too: The Life and Legends of Johnny Cash* (New York: Dial Press, 1971); Johnny Cash with Patrick Carr, *Cash: The Autobiography* (San Francisco: HarperSanFrancisco, 1997); and Robert Hilburn, *Johnny Cash: The Life* (Boston: Little, Brown, 2013). Cash also wrote an autobiography, *Man in Black* (Grand Rapids, MI: Zondervan, 1975), which was largely designed as an "inspirational" tract. John Grissim commented on Cash in *Country Music: White Man's Blues* (New York: Coronet Communications, 1970), and Tom Dearmore noted that Cash's protest and social activism tended to ignore contemporary questions of war, poverty, and racism: "First Angry Man of Country Singers," *New York Times Magazine*, September 21, 1969, 32–49, 54–58. Fred Danker was the most serious student of Cash, and he wrote about him in several forums: an essay in *Stars of Country Music*, edited by Bill C. Malone and Judith McCulloh (Urbana: University of Illinois Press, 1975), 317–337; articles such as "The Repertory and Style of a Country Singer: Johnny Cash," *JAF* 85 (October–December 1972): 309–329; and the notes to the Time-Life collection *Johnny Cash*. John L. Smith added further to our knowledge of Cash's recorded output with *Johnny Cash's Discography and Recording History, 1955–1968* (JEMF Special Series, no. 2 [1969]).

The country-pop impulse is well defined in Streissguth's biography of Eddy Arnold; in Arnold's autobiography, *It's a Long Way from Chester County* (New York: Pyramid Books, 1969); and in Chet Atkins's autobiography, *Country Gentleman* (Chicago: Henry Regnery, 1974). Charlie Lamb gave me his personal testimony as to how country music publicists adjusted to the desire for pop recognition (interview, Nashville, August 28, 1961). The forging of Chet Atkins's "compromise" is best described in Bill Ivey's essay on Atkins in *Stars of Country Music*, 301–316, and Atkins's reflections about what he had done are discussed in John Gabree, "Chet Atkins: Story of a Quiet Man," *Country Music* 2, no. 8 (April 1974): 24–31. Atkins expresses some regrets about the role he played in introducing sophisticated arrangements to country music in Robert Windeler, "Bio—Chet Atkins," *People Weekly*, December 16, 1974, 62.

The artists-and-repertory men who engineered the country-pop fusion are discussed in *The World of Country Music*, 58–72, and in several *Billboard* issues extending from 1957 to the early sixties—for example, 69, no. 46 (November 11, 1957): 42, and 72, no. 28 (July 11, 1960): 29. Popular articles that commented on the phenomenon and indicated its commercial fruits include Goddard Lieberson, "Country Sweeps the Country," *New York Times Magazine*, July 28, 1957, 153; Clarence B. Newman, "Homespun Harmony," *Wall Street Journal* 37, no. 141 (May 3, 1957): 1, 6; Bernard Asbell, "Simple Songs of Sex, Sin, and Salvation," *Show: The Magazine of the Performing Arts* 2, no. 2 (February 1962): 88–91; and Richard Warren Lewis, "Thar's Gold in Them Thar Hillbillies," *Show Business Illustrated* 2, no. 2 (February 1962): 32–38.

I do not know who coined the term "Nashville sound," but I first heard it used by the musician Tommy Hill, who was then a recording engineer for Starday Records, in a discussion in Nashville, August 23, 1961. The session musicians have often been mentioned in popular and trade magazines, but Rich Kienzle has written two of the most discerning articles about them: "Hank Garland: Country Jazz Pioneer," *Guitar Player* (January 1981): 76–86, and "The Piano Is a Stringed Instrument," *Country Music* 9, no. 7 (March 1981): 10, 12–13. Alice M. Gant wrote a heavily sociological article on the Nashville musicians that mentioned no one by name; however, in the midst of her long exposition (29–30), she did explain the "number system" used by the performers: "The Musicians in Nashville," *JCM* 3, no. 2 (Summer 1972): 24–44. Bill Ivey gave a twenty-five-year retrospective look at the Nashville sound in "Commercialization and Tradition in the Nashville Sound," in *Folk Music and Modern Sound*, edited by William Ferris and Mary Hart (Jackson: University Press of Mississippi, 1982), 129–141.

The literature on the country-pop singers of the late fifties is not extensive, but, again, *The Encyclopedia of Country Music* provides vignettes on most of them. Linnell Gentry, ed., did likewise in *A History and Encyclopedia of Country, Western, and Gospel Music* (Nashville: McQuiddy Press, 1961; rev. ed., 1969), and *BMI Country Hits, 1944–1968* (New York: Broadcast Music, 1968) and Billboard's *Number One Country Singles* gave evidence of their popularity (particularly in 1957 and 1958). Dixie Deen wrote a very good four-part article on Skeeter Davis: "Skeeter Davis: Born to Sing," *MCN* 4, no. 7 (January 1967): 3–4; no. 8 (February 1967): 6, 8–9; no. 9 (March 1967): 6, 9; no. 10 (April 1967): 30. Davis claimed in an interview with Archie Campbell, on the program *Yesteryear in Nashville*, that the 1953 recordings of the Davis Sisters influenced the style of harmony that came to prevail in country music (such as that of the Everly Brothers) while also popularizing the pedal-steel guitar (from a taped, syndicated presentation on the Nashville Television Network). Davis's colleague on RCA, Don Gibson, was discussed in an article whose title is a bit exaggerated: "Don Gibson: An Exclusive In-Depth Interview," *CSR* 21, no. 124 (November 1969): 12–13, 40. Ferlin Husky received brief treatment in Frieda Barter, "Ferlin Husky—What's in a Name," *Country and Western Jamboree* 1, no. 12 (February 1956): 8–9. Faron Young received more coverage than most, partly because of his enduring commercial appeal, but also because he was good copy with his humor and salty language. See Hubert Long, "Faron Young," *Rustic Rhythm* 1, no. 2 (May 1957): 16–20; Bob Allen, "Faron Young: Live Fast, Love Hard and Keep On Cussin'," *Country Music* 9, no. 1 (September 1980): 28–31; and Jerry Bailey, "The Singing Sheriff Shoots from the Hip," *Country Music* 3, no. 2 (November 1974): 58–66.

Three of the country-pop singers generated extensive written coverage while also being the subjects of numerous record reissues. Although each is deceased, Marty Robbins, Jim Reeves, and Patsy Cline continue to demonstrate enormous commercial appeal. Robbins has been discussed earlier. My knowledge of Jim Reeves comes mainly from visits with his mother, Beulah Reeves (DeBerry, Texas, September 7, 1966), and Tom Perryman (Henderson, Texas, September 7, 1966). Rich Kienzle wrote a good summary of Reeves in "Jim Reeves: The Undying Legacy," *Country Music* 7, no. 9 (July–August 1979): 19–21. Patsy Cline has been honored with a symposium and an anthology inspired by it: Warren Hofstra, ed., *Sweet Dreams: The World of Patsy Cline* (Urbana: University of Illinois Press, 2013). Three of her songs were included in the Time-Life collection *The Women* (more than any other performer), and she has been the subject of several books and numerous articles, such as Douglas Gomery,

Patsy Cline: The Making of an Icon (Bloomington, IN: Trafford, 2011); Margaret Jones, *Patsy: The Life and Times of Patsy Cline* (New York: HarperCollins, 1994); and Ellis Nassour, *Honky Tonk Angel: The Intimate Story of Patsy Cline* (Chicago Review Press, 2008).

The founding and purposes of the Country Music Association were discussed in *Billboard* 66, no. 46 (November 13, 1954): 14; and 70, no. 26 (June 30, 1958): 9; and by Harry Stone, "The Country Music Association," in *The Country Music's Who's Who* (first annual edition, 1960), 79. *CMA Close Up* (a monthly publication of the association) has since then been a continuing source of information on the active trade organization.

The establishment of the Country Music Hall of Fame and Museum was described in *Billboard Music Week*, November 6, 1961, 52, and November 17, 1962, 5; and in *MCN* 4, no. 10 (April 1967): 8, 15; and 5, no. 4 (November 1967): 32. Dixie Deen also provided a good history of the Hall of Fame and its official opening in "Country Music Hall of Fame Opens," *MCN* 4, no. 10 (April 1967): 4, 8, 15–16.

The phenomenon of the all-country-music radio stations was discussed in *CMA Close Up*, February 1967, 7, and in scholarly fashion in George Carney, "The Diffusion of the All-Country Music Radio Station in the United States, 1971–1974," *JEMFQ* 13, no. 46 (Summer 1977): 58–66, and in Richard P. Stockdell, "Early Country Radio: Dispelling a Myth," *JEMFQ* 15, no. 55 (Fall 1979): 152–156.

9. THE REINVIGORATION OF MODERN COUNTRY MUSIC, 1960–1972

Country music's commercial resurgence in the sixties was accompanied by a burgeoning of publicity and journalistic coverage. *Music City News*, originally owned by Faron Young, began its existence in July 1963 and endured as one of the chief publicists and sources of country music until it closed its doors in February 2000. This monthly newspaper was heavily fan-oriented and was rarely critical of any entertainer or any trend in country music. Its policy seemed to be, "If you can't say something good about somebody, then don't say anything." Nevertheless, the newspaper was an excellent source for the basic facts concerning country music, and its "Letters to the Editors" section sometimes contained evidence of the dissatisfaction felt by many fans about the growing pop emphasis in country music. Of the many writers who were associated with the publication, Dixie Deen (the wife of Tom T. Hall) was the most historically conscious. Her feature articles were very helpful to me.

I obtained some information about the appearance of country entertainers on early television experiments from interviews with Bobby Gregory (Nashville, August 30, 1971) and Red River Dave McEnery (San Antonio, June 19, 1973). At least two general articles concentrate on the subject: John Scott Colley, "The Sound Seen: Country Music on Television," *JCM* 3, nos. 3–4 (Fall–Winter 1973): 107–113; and Douglas B. Green, "Country Music's Big on the Tube Again," *Country Music* 5, no. 4 (January 1977): 42, 45–47. Two of the most popular hosts of syndicated television shows in the sixties—the Wilburn Brothers and Porter Wagoner—have received only minimal attention from writers (and both were overshadowed by their "girl singers," Loretta Lynn and Dolly Parton). Dixie Deen wrote good articles on both the Wilburns and

Wagoner: "The Woman behind the Man," *MCN* 3, no. 10 (April 1966): 5, 14, 19 (about Mom Wilburn and her sons); and "Purely Porter Wagoner," *MCN* 4, no. 9 (March 1967): 3–4. Paul Soelburg wrote a two-part article on Wagoner, "The Porter Wagoner Story," for *CSR* 24, nos. 23 and 24 (February and March 1972), but the best article on this singer was Dave Hickey, "Porter: The Last Great Hillbilly?" *Country Music* 3, no. 8 (May 1975): 22–27, 60–63.

The prime-time country television shows were described by Colley and Green (articles mentioned above). I found some description of Jimmy Dean's early shows in *Variety* 206, no. 3 (March 20, 1957): 35, and in *Billboard* 69, no. 21 (May 20, 1957): 146. Ellis Nassour's *Patsy Cline* also contains information on Dean's television interests and on Connie B. Gay. Glen Campbell and his popular television show evoked responses from all the popular magazines of the day, but one of the best articles that concentrated on his Arkansas origins was John Fergus Ryan, "They Knew Glen Campbell before He Was a Superstar," *Country Music* 2, no. 7 (March 1974): 68–73. Campbell's fellow Arkansas native Johnny Cash—still another of the major television personalities—was discussed in the bibliographical essay for chapter 8, but information more pertinent to his later career is in the *Sunday Showcase* of the *Nashville Tennessean*, April 20–26, 1969, 4–7 (by Kathy Sawyer) and in *Newsweek*, February 2, 1970, 84–85. One should not ignore Tom Dearmore, "First Angry Man of Country Singers," *New York Times Magazine*, September 21, 1969, 32–34, 36–39, 42, 49, 54–58; this is the best available critical analysis of Cash. My information about the computerized nature of *Hee Haw* comes from John Fergus Ryan, "Press a Button and Out Comes 'Hee Haw,'" *Country Music* 2, no. 1 (September 1973): 28–34. One of the gifted mainstays of the show, Roy Clark, has been much written about. The article that I found most useful was Jon Sievert, "Roy Clark: An Entertainer since Age Four, America's Most Visible Guitarist," *Guitar Player* 12, no. 11 (November 1978): 54–56, 120, 124, 126–136.

Country music's popularity and expansion abroad are subjects worthy of extended academic treatment. Ruth Ellen Gruber has written and lectured extensively about visions of America in Europe portrayed in country music. For example, see "Sturm, Twang and Sauerkraut Cowboys: The Imaginary Wild West in Europe," *Western Way* magazine (Summer 2009). Richard C. Helt has also made a good contribution in "A German Bluegrass Festival: The Country Boom and Some Notes on the History of American Popular Music in West Germany," *The Journal of Popular Culture* 10, no. 4 (Spring 1977): 821–832. Other sources that were helpful to me include Omer Anderson, "Fifty Million Europeans Can't Be Wrong," *Billboard* 72, no. 28 (July 11, 1960): 1; *Billboard Music Week* 73, no. 33 (September 25, 1961): 3; *Billboard Music Week* 73, no. 39 (October 2, 1961): 11; and "Country Music Goes International," in *The World of Country Music* (New York: Billboard, 1963), 165–167, 171–173. Extensive interviews with Bill Clifton, done in preparation for my biography of him—*Bill Clifton: America's Bluegrass Ambassador to the World*—provided me with considerable knowledge of foreign interest in country music. But I had interviewed Clifton much earlier in Baltimore, June 10, 1976. I also learned much from Martin Haerle, Nashville, August 23, 1961, and from Charlie Walker, Kerrville, Texas, July 1, 1977.

The urban folk revival still awaits a definitive treatment. But Ronald Cohen and

Robert Cantwell (discussed earlier) have made excellent beginnings. Oscar Brand's *The Ballad Mongers: Rise of the Modern Folk Song* (New York: Funk and Wagnalls, 1962) was a good early overview. R. Serge Denisoff explored the revival's identification with left-wing causes in *Great Day Coming: Folk Music and the American Left* (Urbana: University of Illinois Press, 1971). Contemporary magazines that documented the revival, while also printing many of its songs, included *Broadside, Little Sandy Review, Hootenanny,* and *Sing Out.* Articles on the urban folk movement appeared in prodigious numbers in other magazines. Among the best were Nat Hentoff, "Folk Finds a Voice," *Reporter* 26, no. 1 (January 4, 1962): 39–42; and "The Rise of Folkum Music," *The Commonweal* 75, no. 4 (October 20, 1961): 99–100; and John McPhee, "Folk Singing," *Time* 80, no. 21 (November 23, 1962): 54–60.

The best place to search for an understanding of the ways in which urban folk music and hillbilly music intersected are the albums of the New Lost City Ramblers (see, for example, *The New Lost City Ramblers,* Folkways FA2396). The indispensable account of this highly influential band is Ray Allen, *Gone to the Country: The New Lost City Ramblers and the Folk Music Revival* (Urbana: University of Illinois Press, 2010). Jon Pankake discussed the best-known member of the group in "Mike Seeger: The Style of Tradition," *Sing Out* 14, no. 3 (July 1964): 9–10. I have also written about him in *Music from the True Vine: Mike Seeger's Life and Musical Journey* (Chapel Hill: University of North Carolina Press, 2011). Many of the songs reintroduced by the Ramblers were collected in *The New Lost City Ramblers Song Book,* edited by Mike Seeger and John Cohen (New York: Oak Publications, 1964). This book is long out of print but is well worth having if a copy can be found. A powerful catalyst that contributed to the stimulation of interest in hillbilly music among urban folk fans was the *Anthology of American Folk Music,* produced by Folkways in 1952, and made up of hillbilly, blues, gospel, and Cajun material originally recorded between 1927 and 1933 (from the collection of Harry Smith). The greatest new discovery inspired by the folk revival, Doc Watson, has elicited a biography by Kent Gustavson, *Blind but Now I See: The Biography of Music Legend Doc Watson* (Tulsa, OK: Sumach-Red Books, 2012). Watson is also discussed in articles by Michael Bane, "A Chat with Doc Watson," *Country Music* 4, no. 11 (August 1976): 57, 59; Chet Flippo, "Doc Watson and His Tall Drink o' Water Merle," *Rolling Stone,* no. 137 (June 21, 1973): 24; H. Lloyd "Stretch" Whittaker, "Doc Watson," *BGU* 5, no. 5 (November 1970): 4–5; and, the best of the discussions, Don Rhodes, "Doc Watson," *BGU* 12, no. 7 (January 1978): 10–14). Svare Forsland and I also interviewed Watson for WWOZ-FM in New Orleans (1982).

As far as I can determine, my discussion of the saga song craze in the original edition of this book (*Country Music U.S.A.: A Fifty-Year History* (Austin: American Folklore Society/University of Texas Press, 1968], 300–303) is about the only published recognition of this phenomenon. I depended on *Billboard* issues extending from late 1958 through 1959, and on such LPs as *Jimmie Driftwood Sings Newly Discovered Early American Folk Songs* (RCA Victor RPM 1635); Johnny Cash, *Songs of Our Soil* (Columbia 1339); *Johnny Horton Makes History* (Columbia 1478); and Marty Robbins's *Gunfighter Ballads* (Columbia 1349).

The hard country resurgence of the sixties is documented in material dealing with such performers as George Jones, Ray Price, Buck Owens, and Merle Haggard—and above all in their recordings. Dolly Carlisle's biography *Ragged but Right: The Life and Times of George Jones* (Chicago: Contemporary Books, 1984) is an honest and sympathetic treatment of the singer, but the best introduction to the durable Jones is the Time-Life collection devoted to him. Pepi Plowman wrote a long biographical sketch of Jones in the inelegantly titled "A Singin' Fool," *Texas Monthly*, June 1982, 144–149, 232–239. One of the best older sketches of Jones is Dixie Deen, "The Crown Prince of C-W Music," *MCN* 4, no. 2 (August 1966): 1, 31. Conversations that were helpful to me included a short one with Jones in Austin, August 16, 1962, and a longer one with Pappy Daily in Houston, August 19, 1977.

I also talked with Ray Price in Austin on March 2, 1962, and learned a few biographical details about him from an unsigned article called "Hit Maker—Ray Price" in *Rustic Rhythm* 1, no. 2 (May 1957): 11–15. More recent articles that have been extremely helpful are "Cherokee Cowboys Reunion" (which lists many of his musicians over the years) in *Country Gazette* 1, no. 1 (February 1977): 4; Dave Hickey, "Hillbilly Heaven," *Country Music* 5, no. 6 (March 1976): 40–42, 61–64; and Tom Ayres, "Ray Price Remembers Hank Williams," *Country Music* 5, no. 12 (September 1977): 41–44, 56.

As noted earlier in this essay, the California country music scene is no longer neglected by writers. One of the father figures of Bakersfield country music, Bill Woods, is discussed by Lee Rector in "Bill Woods Helps Others to Stardom," *MCN* 15, no. 12 (June 1978): 34. However, we still need a comprehensive book on Buck Owens and his music. The Time-Life collection *Honky Tonkin'* includes one song by Owens and a very brief biographical blurb. Most of my original information came from sketches in the contemporary music magazines, such as Harris Martin, "Buck Owens Riding All Time Height of Popularity," *MCN* 2, no. 12 (June 1965): 1, 4.

Merle Haggard, on the other hand, has inspired so much writing that it is difficult to single out the very best. I believe you can't go wrong, though, with David Cantwell's *The Running Kind* (Austin: University of Texas Press, 2015). Other books include one of Merle's "autobiographies," written with Peggy Russell, *Sing Me Back Home: My Life* (New York: Quadrangle, 1981). Haggard is generally honest and candid about his life and career, almost to a fault, but he was long reluctant to say anything about "Okie from Muskogee," the most controversial song in his repertory and the one that really catapulted him to the top of the music business. A good example of the approval shown by some liberal critics for his music—before "Okie from Muskogee"—is Alfred G. Aronowitz, "New Country Twang Hits Town," *Life*, May 3, 1968, 12. Paul Hemphill also wrote from a liberal perspective in his essay on Haggard in *Stars of Country Music*, edited by Bill C. Malone and Judith McCulloh (Urbana: University of Illinois Press, 1975), 357–373. This was a good and sensitive assessment of Haggard (written after "Okie"), but was somewhat strained in its efforts to explain away his conservatism. Haggard did talk about "Okie" in an interview in *Penthouse* 8, no. 3 (November 1976): 126–128, 178–184. Another good short discussion of Haggard, stressing his eclectic musicianship, was Peter Guralnick, "Merle Haggard: In the Good Old Days (When Times Were Bad)," *JCM* 8, no. 1 (May 1979): 39–46, 63–64. Haggard's jazz inclinations were the subjects of Tim Schneckloth, "Merle Haggard: Country Jazz Messiah," *Down Beat* 47, no. 5 (May 1980): 16–19, 63 (one of the rare times that this magazine ventured an appreciation of a country artist), and John Morthland, "Merle Haggard's Country Jazz," *International Musician and Recording World*, November 1980, 38–39, 104.

The country writers who did so much to rejuvenate country music in the modern period were discussed singly and collectively in a variety of places; nevertheless, they still have not been given their proper due. The best overall discussion of country lyrics, which also includes material on the writers themselves, is Jimmie N. Rogers, *The Country Music Message* (Englewood Cliffs, NJ: Prentice-Hall, 1983). *Music City News* ran periodic "Songwriters Special" issues that included vignettes of leading writers. These include 16, no. 8 (February 1979); 17, no. 8 (February 1980); and 18, no. 8 (February 1981). I interviewed Bill Anderson in Nashville on August 22, 1961, and Harlan Howard in Nashville on August 24, 1961. Among the extensive number of sketches on writers found in various music journals, I have found the following to be of particular interest: "An Exclusive CSR Interview" (with Curley Putman), *CSR* 22, no. 129 (April 1970): 34–35; "Harlan Howard (in His Own Words)," *CSR* 22, no. 130 (May 1970): 30–32; Mira Smith and Margaret Lewis, "The Country Music Writer" (on Liz Anderson), *CSR* 27, no. 193 (August 1975): 27–29; and Fred Abdella, "John D. Loudermilk: From 'A Rose and a Baby Ruth' to a Grammy," *Acadiana Profile* 5, no. 4 (August–September 1976): 59–61.

The best place to begin for further insights into Tom T. Hall would be his autobiography, *The Storyteller's Nashville* (Garden City, NY: Doubleday, 1979). The book is much like Hall's songs; it is witty, sensitive, and conversational in tone. The most discerning portrait of Hall, as well as the most critical assessment of his songs, is William C. Martin's essay in *Stars of Country Music*, 391–415. I talked to Hall in Nashville on July 27, 1972, but also learned much from Dixie Deen, "Tom T. Hall's Touch of Greatness," *MCN* 5, no. 2 (August 1967): 3–4; Noel Coppage, "Tom T. Hall," *Stereo Review* 33, no. 2 (August 1974): 58–61; and Ken Stambaugh, "The Storyteller: Tom T. Hall," *Nashville West* 1, no. 3 (November 1975): 8–9, 26–28.

John Hartford, a man who did much to give country songwriting a new direction, is well treated in two good articles: Tom Hill, "John Hartford: Riverboats and Music," *Pickin'* 5, no. 4 (May 1978): 21–26, 64–67; and Barry Silver, "John Hartford," *BGU* 14, no. 4 (October 1979): 12–16. The most famous representative of country music's "new breed" of writers—Kris Kristofferson—has been much written about. Representative articles include David Rensin, "King Kristofferson," *Country Music* 2, no. 13 (September 1974): 25–32; Jack McClintock, "Just a Good Ole Rhodes Scholar," *Playboy* 22, no. 3 (March 1975): 120, 122, 170–175; Paul Hemphill, "Kris Kristofferson Is the New Nashville Sound," *New York Times Magazine*, December 6, 1970, 54–55, 137–142; and Tom Burke, "Kris Kristofferson's Talking Blues," *Rolling Stone*, no. 159 (April 25, 1974): 40–46.

Most academic treatments of women country singers concentrate on the period before Kitty Wells. Several popular writers, however, have presented overviews of the post-1960 generation of women singers. The best of these accounts is Joan Dew's *Singers and Sweethearts: The Women of Country Music* (Garden City, NY: Doubleday, 1977). Representative articles include Noel Coppage, "Country Music's Traipsin' Women," *Stereo Review* 33, no. 6 (December 1974): 84–89; Roy Blount, "Country's

Angels," *Esquire* 87, no. 3 (March 1977): 62–66, 124–126, 131–132; and Lynn Keller-
mann, "It Wasn't God Who Made Honky Tonk Angels," *Music Gig* 2, no. 11 (June
1976): 15–18. *Country Music* magazine also devoted a special issue to the subject—
"The Women in Country Music," 2, no. 11 (July 1974)—but only Dolly Parton received
any kind of extended treatment. The Time-Life collection devoted to women country
singers is oriented toward the pre–Kitty Wells era, but several modern performers
are included (Loretta Lynn, Tammy Wynette, Dolly Parton, Tanya Tucker, Lynn
Anderson, Jeanne Pruett, Barbara Mandrell, Jessi Colter, and Emmylou Harris).

Discussions and sketches of individual women singers filled the pages of *Music
City News* and *Country Music*, and on occasion a performer even drew the interest
of a rock-oriented magazine such as *Rolling Stone* or a men's magazine like *Playboy*.
Crystal Gayle, for example, received very approving treatment from Chet Flippo in
"The Problem with Crystal," *Playboy*, November 1981, 131–132, 156, 202–205, 209.
She was also discussed by Kelly Delaney in "Crystal Gayle Takes Time to Become a
Mother," *MCN* 20, no. 11 (May 1983): 8–9, and by Laura Eipper, in "Crystal," *Country
Music* 8, no. 6 (March 1980): 30–36, 68. Jeannie C. Riley's religion and regrets about
her early brazen image were discussed by Michael Bane in "Jeannie C. Riley Lowers
Her Hemline and Raises Her Hopes," *Country Music* 5, no. 3 (December 1976): 34–38,
71. Tanya Tucker has never suffered from neglect. *Country Music* magazine, for ex-
ample, devoted considerable attention to her: J. R. Young, "Tanya Tucker: Country's
Youngest Superstar," 1, no. 10 (June 1973): 32–36; Mary Ellen Moore, "Tanya: Ballad
of a Teenage Queen," 5, no. 10 (July 1977): 22–26; and Dolly Carlisle, "Tanya: Daddy's
Little Girl Grows Up," 7, no. 7 (May 1979): 34–37.

The three great women superstars, Loretta Lynn, Tammy Wynette, and Dolly
Parton, elicited extensive discussion and critical treatment. Lynn and Wynette wrote
autobiographies, and Parton was the subject of popular "newsstand biographies."
Lynn's autobiography, written with George Vecsey, is as charming and candid as the
singer: *Loretta Lynn: Coal Miner's Daughter* (Chicago: Henry Regnery, 1976). It is
especially good on her early Appalachian years, but predictable when it discusses the
problems that a simple country girl encounters once she finds show business success
(marital tension, illness, difficulties in balancing her career with home duties). She
was on the cover of *Newsweek* and was the centerpiece of that magazine's extensive
coverage of country music: Pete Axthelm, "Lookin' at Country with Loretta Lynn,"
Newsweek 81, no. 25 (June 18, 1973): 65–72. Sally Quinn wrote a good, brief sketch of
Loretta, "Country Girl," for the *New York Post*, August 16, 1975, 13, and Martha Hume
concentrated on the singer that the fans never see in "The Strange and Private World
of Loretta Lynn," *Country Music* 4, no. 4 (January 1976): 30–33, 54. Sharon Rowlett
wrote a profile of Loretta's husband in "Mooney Lynn," *Country Style*, no. 27 (January 1978): 25, 68, and Robert Windeler did a sketch of her most controversial song
in "Loretta Lynn's 'Pill' Is Hard for Some Fans to Swallow," *People Weekly* 3, no. 12
(March 31, 1975): 23–25.

Tammy Wynette was the only woman country singer who had a Time-Life
collection devoted to her. The writer of the collection's notes, Joan Dew, was also
Tammy's collaborator in her autobiography, *Stand by Your Man* (New York: Simon
and Schuster, 1979). Wynette was honest about her failed marriages and disappointed

loves and physical problems. Despite the heavy soap opera treatment, the book can still be read with profit as an introduction to southern lower-class life in the years following World War II and as a glimpse of the modern country music industry. The ever-dependable Dixie Deen wrote one of the best short articles on Wynette, not long after her career began, in "Tammy Finds Elusive Dream," *MCN* 5, no. 6 (December 1967): 3, 9. Tammy was one of the few country singers who was fascinating to rock journalists; consequently, her records were reviewed in *Rolling Stone*, and she was the subject of a lengthy article in that magazine—condescending, sarcastic, and generally contemptuous—by Michael Thomas: "Tammy Wynette: A Little Tear in Every Word," *Rolling Stone*, no. 108 (May 11, 1972): 44–47. Tammy was also interviewed in *Penthouse* 12, no. 1 (September 1980): 117–119, 172–176.

Dolly Parton has not only been written up in *Rolling Stone*, she has probably received more press coverage than any other country entertainer (with the possible exceptions of Willie Nelson, Johnny Cash, and Kenny Rogers). Her famous anatomy has certainly inspired more jokes than any other country entertainer has provoked. Alanna Nash's *Dolly* (Los Angeles: Reed Books, 1978) was one of the best of the popular biographies, but Chet Flippo wrote two admiring articles for *Rolling Stone*: "Dolly Parton: Tennessee Mountain Home-Grown," no. 198 (October 23, 1975): 24; and "Dolly Parton," no. 246 (August 15, 1977): 32–38. Chris Chase also did a good journalistic piece on Dolly called "The Country Girl," *New York Times Magazine*, May 9, 1976, 17, 60, 71–73. The most discerning insights into Dolly's personality can be found in the interview she did for *Playboy* 25, no. 10 (October 1978): 81–84, 88–91, 95–98, 101–110. The frankness and humor of her replies confirms the belief that she should write her autobiography.

The movement of non-Anglo, non-Protestant, and nonwhite performers into country music is a subject worthy of extended treatment. The vital tradition of Cajun music, which has maintained an independent identity while also often interrelating with country music, is best documented by Barry Jean Ancelet, with photographs by Elemore Morgan Jr., *The Makers of Cajun Music/Musiciens cadiens et créoles* (Austin: University of Texas Press, 1984). Other useful works include Tony Russell, *Blacks, Whites and Blues* (New York: Stein and Day, 1970); Nick Tosches, *Country: The Biggest Music in America* (New York: Stein and Day, 1977), esp. 167–229; Nicholas Spitzer, "Cajuns and Creoles: The French Gulf Coast," in *Long Journey Home: Folklife in the South,* edited by Allen Tullos (Chapel Hill, NC: Southern Exposure, 1977), 140–155; John Broven, *South to Louisiana: The Music of the Cajun Bayous* (Gretna, LA: Pelican Publishing, 1983); Dan Dickey, "The Development of *música tejana: Guitarreros, conjuntos* and *orquestas tejanas*" (unpublished paper presented at the annual meeting of the Texas State Historical Association, Austin, March 2, 1984); and Kay Council, "Exploratory Documentation of Texas *Norteño-Conjunto* Music" (Master's thesis, University of Texas at Austin, 1978).

Doug Kershaw, Jimmy C. Newman, Al Terry, and other Cajuns who have played country music are discussed in John Broven's book. Douglas B. Green wrote a good short sketch of Newman for *Country Music*: "Jimmy C. Newman and His Cajun Country Roots," 7, no. 7 (May 1979): 20, 66, 68. John Grissim devotes a chapter to Kershaw in *Country Music: White Man's Blues* (New York: Coronet Communications, 1970), but Kershaw's own short autobiography is the best introduction to the man: *Lou'siana Man* (New York: Collier Books, 1971). Since Freddy Fender was active in Louisiana, he draws some attention from John Broven. One of the best single essays on Fender, however, is Roxy Gordon, "Wasted Days, Wasted Nights?," *Country Music* 5, no. 6 (March 1976): 22–26, 64.

For information on African Americans who have sung or performed country music, see Diane Pecknold, ed., *Hidden in the Mix: The African American Presence in Country Music* (Durham, NC: Duke University Press, 2013) and Charles L. Hughes, *Country Soul: Making Music and Making Race in the American South* (Chapel Hill: University of North Carolina Press, 2015). Good examples of African Americans performing country music can be heard in *From Where I Stand*, a Grammy-nominated CD collection produced by Warner Brothers and the Country Music Foundation. I picked up some information from short sketches in the music magazines, but I also had an interview with Stoney Edwards in Nashville, October 15, 1971. Examples of the magazine sketches include Paula Becker, "Linda Martel: New Look, New Sound, New Star," *CSR* 22, no. 133 (August 1970): 12–13; "O. B. McClinton: The Black Country Irishman," *Soul* 6, no. 24 (March 27, 1972): 12; Mike Kosser, "Cotton Picker McClinton Walked Long Road to Stardom," *Country Style*, no. 7 (December 1976): 53; Mark Schwed, "Black Country Music Singer, Big Al Downing, Breaking the Industry's Color Barrier," *New Orleans Times-Picayune/States-Item*, December 16, 1982 (a UPI story); "Stoney Edwards: A Very Special Person," *CSR* 27, no. 189 (April 1975): 10–11, 44; and Peter Guralnick, "Stoney Edwards: Black Man Singing in a White Man's World," *Country Music* 7, no. 7 (May 1979): 42–44, 68.

A good synthesis of Charley Pride's early career is Ann Malone's essay in *Stars of Country Music*, 373–389. Examples of the rapport he established with white audiences, along with an introduction to his early style, can be heard in the LP recorded in 1969 at Fort Worth's Panther Hall: *Charley Pride in Person—Recorded Live*, RCA ANL1–0996. An appreciative evaluation of the man, and a critical review of several of his records, can be found in Charlie Burton, "Charley Pride," *Rolling Stone*, no. 83 (May 27, 1971): 52–53. Other representative articles included Melvin Shestack, "Charley Pride and the Chicken Ladies," *Esquire* 75, no. 3 (March 1971): 60, 66, 102–105; Patrick Carr, "What Now, Charley Pride," *Country Music* 3, no. 4 (January 1975): 58–59; and "No. 1 Country Singer," *Sepia* 21, no. 5 (May 1972): 35–42.

Chris Willman was chiefly concerned with a later period, but his book is the only one that tries to understand the political preoccupations of country entertainers: *Rednecks and Bluenecks: The Politics of Country Music* (New York: New Press, 2005). The political positions exhibited by some country singers and writers in the late sixties and early seventies, along with country music's identification with, first, George Wallace and then the "silent majority," inspired a rash of both good and poor writing. Paul Hemphill's *The Nashville Sound: Bright Lights and Country Music* (New York: Simon and Schuster, 1970) clearly profited from the music's political notoriety, and it received prominent reviews in such periodicals as *Life*. Hemphill alluded to the George Wallace identification but placed more stress on the music's working-class orientation. Two liberal writers saw only destructive consequences arising from country music's burgeoning commercial growth: Florence King, "Red

Necks, White Socks, and Blue Ribbon Fear," *Harper's* 249 (July 1974): 30–34; and Richard Goldstein, "My Country Music Problem—and Yours," *Mademoiselle* 77, no. 2 (June 1973): 114–115, 185. Radical writer Irwin Silber let the pro–Vietnam War songs speak for themselves, but he quoted their lyrics alongside reports of atrocities in the war: "A Study in Illusion and Reality," *Sing Out* 17, no. 4 (August–September 1967): 20–25. Selected contemporary articles that commented on country music's conservative politics include Paul Dickson, "Singing to Silent America," *Nation*, February 23, 1970, 211–213; Earl C. Gottschalk Jr., "Love It or Leave It: New Patriotic Music Wins Fans, Enemies," *Wall Street Journal*, August 18, 1970, 1, 12; and Neil Maxwell, "The Bigotry Business: Racist Records, Books Are Hits in the South," *Wall Street Journal*, April 20, 1967, 1, 12. At least one conservative song, "Welfare Cadilac," received extensive, and generally favorable, discussion in *Music City News*: "'Welfare Cadilac' Touches a Nerve," *MCN* 7, no. 11 (May 1970): 1, 25, 30. President Nixon's favorable response to the song and his request that Johnny Cash sing it at the White House are discussed in *Time* 95, no. 15 (April 13, 1970): 16. A good example of the rousing reception that northern audiences gave to "Okie from Muskogee" can be heard on Merle Haggard's LP, *The Fightin' Side of Me*, Capitol ST451, recorded live in Philadelphia. The scholar Patricia Averill, however, denies the ideological emphasis attributed to "Okie" and argues that Haggard's record company selected "the aspect of audience reaction that reinforced its own exoteric view of what the audience liked" (p. 36) in "Esoteric-Exoteric Expectations of Redneck Behavior and Country Music," *JCM* 4, no. 2 (Summer 1973): 34–38. Three other scholars also deny that country music was simply "right-wing know-nothingism": Paul DiMaggio, Richard A. Peterson, and Jack Esco Jr., "Country Music: Ballad of the Silent Majority," in *The Sounds of Social Change*, edited by R. Serge Denisoff and Richard A. Peterson (Chicago: Rand McNally, 1972), 38–55.

Country music's alleged working-class identification has often been commented on, but, except for my *Don't Get Above Your Raisin': Country Music and the Southern Working Class* (Urbana: University of Illinois Press, 2002), no study has fully explored the idea, either from the standpoint of the fans or from that of the musicians. Good collections and critiques of certain types of occupational songs exist (such as those done by Patrick Huber and Archie Green on cotton mill and coal-mining songs, and Norm Cohen's on railroad items—each of which has been previously discussed), but almost nothing exists on worker attitudes as expressed in songs. The one area of worker subculture that has attracted country singers—trucking—is actually a gray area, because many truck drivers (the independent owner-operators) think of themselves as small businesspeople rather than workers. Truck drivers, though, do like country music, and country singers have responded with a multitude of songs about their profession. Fred E. H. Schroeder made a good beginning in explaining the appeal of the truck driver in "A Bellyful of Coffee: The Truckdrivin' Man as Folk Hero," *The Journal of Popular Culture* 2, no. 4 (Spring 1969): 679–687, but Joyce Gibson Roach is superficial and condescending in "Diesel Smoke and Dangerous Curves: Folklore of the Trucking Industry," in *Hunters and Healers: Folklore Types and Topics*, edited by Wilson M. Hudson, Publications of the Texas Folklore Society, no. 35 (Austin: Encino Press, 1971), 45–53.

Robert Shelton was one of the first music critics to recognize the emergence of the truck-driving song genre: "Meet a New Folk Hero, the Truck Driver," *New York Times*, December 4, 1966. Neville Raymond does a good job in showing the interrelationship between trucking and country music in "Hitch Your Truck to a Country Star," *Country Music* 1, no. 1 (September 1972): 41–44, and the same magazine devoted several pages to the CB and trucking craze that accompanied C. W. McCall's big hit "Convoy" in 1976: 5, no. 3 (December 1976): 48–55, 71. Sketches of singers who have specialized in truck-driving songs appear in the various country music magazines. For example, the man who began the modern craze for such music is discussed by Dixie Deen in "'Six Days on the Road' Puts Ravin' Dave Dudley on Country Music Map," *MCN* 4, no. 1 (July 1966): 11, 20.

10. BLUEGRASS

Bluegrass is the best-documented genre of country music. It has drawn the loving attention of dedicated fans and the meticulous analysis of scholars (largely because it reached its commercial peak during the folk revival and the subsequent rediscovery of hillbilly music). The International Bluegrass Music Association (IBMA), founded in 1988, has been the prime force in the documentation of the music's history: through a museum, a hall of honor, and a major Video Oral Historical Project, designed for the videotaping of the music's "First Generation" (those whose careers preceded 1954).

The music's documentation, otherwise, resides primarily in short articles and discographies, many of which are not easily accessible to the general reader. Scott Hambly provided a good bibliographical survey of bluegrass material in the notes to his "San Francisco Bay Area Bluegrass and Bluegrass Musicians: A Study in Regional Characteristics," *JEMFQ* 16, no. 59 (Fall 1980): 118–120. When Hambly was writing, he found only three book-length historical surveys of bluegrass: Toru Mitsui, *Burugurasu Ongaku* [Bluegrass Music] (Toyohashi, Japan: Traditional-Song Society, 1967; rev. ed., 1975); Steven D. Price, *Old as the Hills: The Story of Bluegrass Music* (New York: Viking Press, 1975); and Bob Artis, *Bluegrass* (New York: Hawthorn Books, 1975). Mitsui's book, however, is unavailable to American readers; Price's is too superficial; and, while Artis's is good and reliable, it is far from being comprehensive. The neglect of bluegrass, though, has been fully remedied by Neil Rosenberg with his comprehensive treatment in *Bluegrass: A History* (Urbana: University of Illinois Press, 1985), and Robert Cantwell with a controversial and stimulating study called *Bluegrass Breakdown: The Making of the Old Southern Sound* (Urbana: University of Illinois Press, 1984).

The best short discussions of bluegrass, both in the *Journal of American Folklore*, concentrate on stylistic evolution: L. Mayne Smith, "An Introduction to Bluegrass," *JAF* 78, no. 309 (July–September 1965): 245–256; and Neil Rosenberg, "From Sound to Style: The Emergence of Bluegrass," *JAF* 80, no. 316 (April–June 1967): 143–150. Two academic studies of individual musicians also shed light on bluegrass's origins and development: Ralph Rinzler's essay on Bill Monroe, 221–243, and Rosenberg's essay on Flatt and Scruggs, 279–301, both in *Stars of Country Music*, edited by Bill C. Malone and Judith McCulloh (Urbana: University of Illinois Press, 1975). The music has attracted few of the contextual and cultural analyses that it needs, but Robert Cantwell has mapped out a fruitful route that might be followed in two thoughtful and provocative essays: "Believing in Bluegrass," *The Atlantic Monthly* 229, no. 3 (March 1972): 52–54, 58–60; and "The Lonesome Sound of Carter Stanley," *BGU* 10, no. 12 (June 1976): 10–16.

At least four magazines, *Frets, Muleskinner News, Pickin'*, and *Bluegrass Unlimited*, were devoted fully or in part to bluegrass music. *Frets* and *Pickin'* took all kinds of string instrumentation into their purview and provided technical information for musicians. *Muleskinner News*, founded by the promoter Carlton Haney in January 1970, and *Bluegrass Unlimited*, established in July 1966 by Peter Kuykendall and Richard Spottswood, were almost exclusively oriented toward bluegrass (except for occasional items on old-time musicians) and were aimed principally at fans. *Muleskinner News* is now defunct, but *Bluegrass Unlimited* has had a continuous existence since 1966 and is a gold mine of information on every phase of the music it promotes (biographical articles, discographies, record and book reviews, concert and festival dates, interviews, classified ads, and songs).

Although *Bluegrass Unlimited* prints song lyrics periodically, the best printed sources for bluegrass songs are Bill Clifton's *150 Old-Time, Folk, and Gospel Songs* (privately printed sometime in the 1950s), and Peter Wernick's *Bluegrass Songbook* (New York: Oak Publications, 1976). The Wernick book also contains excerpts from interviews with bluegrass singers giving advice on how to sing bluegrass music. The web, of course, is filled with sites devoted to song lyrics.

The recognition of Bill Monroe's seminal contributions to bluegrass music is largely a product of Ralph Rinzler's advocacy and scholarship. Rinzler wrote a short essay called "Bill Monroe: The Daddy of Blue Grass Music," in *Sing Out* 13, no. 1 (January 1963): 5–8, and the notes to some of Monroe's albums (such as *The High Lonesome Sound of Bill Monroe*, Decca DL4780). Rinzler presented a fuller portrait of Monroe in *Stars of Country Music*, 221–241. The best available biographies and analyses of Bill Monroe now include Richard Smith, *Can't You Hear Me Callin': The Life of Bill Monroe, Father of Bluegrass* (Boston: Little, Brown, 2000); Tom Ewing, ed., *The Bill Monroe Reader* (Urbana: University of Illinois Press, 2006); and Bob Black, *Come Hither to Go Yonder: Playing Bluegrass with Bill Monroe* (Urbana: University of Illinois Press, 2005).

Other useful works on Monroe include Alice Gerrard Foster, "Growing Up in Rosine, Kentucky: An Interview with Bill Monroe," *Sing Out* 19, no. 2 (July–August 1969): 6–11; Steve Rathe, "Bill Monroe," *Pickin'* 1, no. 1 (February 1974): 4–8; James Rooney, *Bossmen: Bill Monroe and Muddy Waters* (New York: Dial Press, 1971), and Neil Rosenberg, *Bill Monroe and His Blue Grass Boys: An Illustrated Discography* (Nashville: Country Music Foundation Press, 1974). Many of the classic Columbia recordings made by Monroe and the Blue Grass Boys between 1945 and 1949 have been reissued on the County label: vol. 1, CCS104, and vol. 2, CCS105 (with notes by Douglas B. Green) and, of course, massive compilations of Monroe's music can now be found on the Bear label.

The prolific Neil Rosenberg has also contributed the best summary and evaluation of Flatt and Scruggs, in his notes to the Time-Life collection *Flatt and Scruggs* and in his essay on the duo in *Stars of Country Music,* 279–299. The musician and songwriter Jake Lambert (with the assistance of Curly Sechler) wrote a biography of Lester Flatt that although anecdotal and sketchy is nonetheless informative and candid about the singer: *The Good Things Outweigh the Bad* (Hendersonville, TN: Jay-Lyn Publication, 1982). Conversations with Lester Flatt and Earl Scruggs in Nashville on August 23, 1961, and again with Scruggs in Austin on November 6, 1971, were extremely helpful. The Scruggs banjo style is described by Rinzler in the notes to *American Banjo: Tunes and Songs in Scruggs Style,* Folkways FA2314; by James D. Green Jr., "A Musical Analysis of the Banjo Style of Earl Scruggs: An Examination of *Country Music* (Mercury MG20358)," *JCM* 5, no. 1 (Spring 1974): 31–37; by Thomas Adler, "Manual Formulaic Composition: Innovation in Bluegrass Banjo Styles," *JCM* 5, no. 2 (Summer 1974): 55–64; and by Scruggs himself in *Earl Scruggs and the 5-String Banjo* (New York: Peer International, 1968). A vital and unique ingredient of the Flatt and Scruggs sound, Burkett "Uncle Josh" Graves is discussed in his memoir, *Bluegrass Blues Man: A Memoir,* edited by Fred Bartenstein (Urbana: University of Illinois Press, 2012). The postseparation careers of Flatt and Scruggs are discussed in Peter Kuykendall, "Lester Flatt and the Nashville Grass," *BGU* 5, no. 7 (January 1971): 3–6, and in Bill Littleton, "Earl Scruggs Still Wants to Break New Ground," *Country Music* 1, no. 2 (October 1972): 50–52. The best discography of Flatt and Scruggs is R. J. Ronald, "Lester Flatt and Earl Scruggs Discography," *BGU* 2, no. 7 (January 1968); and 2, no. 8 (February 1968): 5–9.

All of the old-timers have been well covered by the bluegrass magazines, although only a few—such as Monroe, Flatt and Scruggs, and the Osborne Brothers—have received additional exposure in other magazines or media journals. Most of the printed material on Reno and Smiley is centered around the versatile musician Don Reno; the best is Bill Vernon's long interview, "The Don Reno Story, Part 1: Early Years," *Muleskinner News* 4, no. 6 (June 1973): 8–11; "The Don Reno Story, Part 2: Bill Monroe and Beyond," ibid. 4, no. 8 (August 1973): 8–11; and "The Don Reno Story, Part 3: The Years with Red Smiley," ibid. 4, no. 9 (September 1973): 8–11. Reno's career is brought up to the beginning of the eighties in Linda Stanley's "Don Reno: A Bluegrass Family Tradition," *BGU* 15, no. 2 (August 1980): 17–23.

Much of my basic information on the Stanley Brothers came from discussions with Carter and Ralph in San Marcos, Texas, on February 6, 1964. The best critical analyses and appreciations of Carter Stanley are by Bob Cantwell, "The Lonesome Sound of Carter Stanley," *BGU* 10, no. 12 (June 1976): 10–16, and by Eddie Dean, "Carter Stanley: The Sibling That 'O Brother' Forgot," *Washington Post* (May 23, 2004). Dean also helped Ralph Stanley with his autobiography: *Man of Constant Sorrow: My Life and Times* (New York: Gotham Books, 2009). Because of his longevity as a performer and his commitment to tradition, Ralph Stanley inspired several good essays, including Fred Bartenstein, "The Ralph Stanley Story," *Muleskinner News* 3, no. 3 (March 1972): 6–18; Ralph Rinzler, "Ralph Stanley: The Tradition from the Mountains," *BGU* 8, no. 9 (March 1974): 7–11; Larry Mitchell, "'Dr.' Ralph Stanley," *Pickin'* 4, no. 7 (August 1977): 4–9, 12, 14; and Jack Tottle, "Ralph Stanley: The Stanley Sound," *BGU* 15, no. 11 (May 1981): 14–21. Other articles that shed some light on the Stanley Brothers are Joe Wilson, "Bristol's WCYB: Early Bluegrass Turf," *Muleskinner News* 3, no. 8

(October 1972): 8–12; Robert K. Oermann, "Rickey Skaggs Remembers the Stanley Brothers," *BGU* 15, no. 11 (May 1981): 26–29; and Peter Kuykendall, "Curly Ray Cline," *BGU* 15, no. 11 (May 1981): 32–37. The Stanley Brothers also inspired three full-length books: John Wright, *Traveling the High Way Home: Ralph Stanley and the World of Traditional Music* (Urbana: University of Illinois Press, 1993); David W. Johnson, *Lonesome Melodies: The Lives and Music of the Stanley Brothers* (Jackson: University Press of Mississippi, 2013); and Gary B. Reid's indispensable *The Music of the Stanley Brothers* (Urbana: University of Illinois Press, 2014).

Because of his ventures into other areas of country music, Mac Wiseman has generated a considerable amount of print in the journals devoted to the country field. The following articles concentrate on his bluegrass involvement: Douglas B. Green, "Mac Wiseman—Remembering" (based on interviews), *Muleskinner News* 3, no. 5 (July 1972): 2–8; Don Rhodes, "Mac Wiseman," *BGU* 16, no. 2 (August 1981): 16–22; and Tom Henderson, "Mac Wiseman," *Pickin'* 2, no. 7 (August 1975): 4–14.

Jimmy Martin is inevitably discussed in any work dealing with Bill Monroe, the Osborne Brothers, or any other entertainer with whom he has played. We get some inkling of his origins in Jimmy Martin, "My Childhood," *CSR* 17, no. 91 (December 1965) and in Peter Kuykendall, "Jimmy Martin: Super King of Bluegrass," *BGU* 14, no. 3 (September 1979): 10–18. The single-best discussion of Martin, however, is Tom Piazza, *True Adventures with the King of Bluegrass: Jimmy Martin* (Nashville: Vanderbilt University Press, 1999).

Jim and Jesse McReynolds are unique in being the first bluegrass musicians to have a book-length biography devoted to them: Nelson Sears, *Jim and Jesse: Appalachia to the Grand Ole Opry* (Lancaster, PA: Privately printed, 1976). Although this is an idealized portrait of the two men written by a faithful fan, one does get a good sense of both the problems and the joys inherent in the lives of professional performers. (Scott Hambly's evaluation of the book, "Jim and Jesse: A Review Essay on Fan Historiography," *JEMFQ* 13, no. 46 [Summer 1977]: 96–99, is strongly recommended.) I interviewed Jim McReynolds in Biloxi, Mississippi, on October 31, 1981, and obtained additional information from Dixie Deen, "'Diesel on My Tail'—Jim and Jesse," *MCN* 4, no. 11 (May 1967): 6, 8, 10; and Bill and Bonnie Smith, "100,000 Miles Away from Home: Jim and Jesse on the Road," *BGU* 10, no. 2 (August 1975): 8–18.

Since the Osborne Brothers experienced considerable success in mainstream country music, their names appeared often in *Music City News*, *Country Music*, and other journals that were usually only mildly receptive to bluegrass entertainers. The articles I have selected come from bluegrass-oriented periodicals: Neil Rosenberg, "The Osborne Brothers," *BGU* 6, no. 3 (September 1971): 5–10; and "The Osborne Brothers, Part 2," *BGU* 6, no. 8 (February 1972): 5–8; Peter Kuykendall, "The Osborne Brothers—From Rocky Top to Muddy Bottom," *BGU* 12, no. 6 (December 1977): 10–16; Don Rhodes, "The Osborne Brothers: Progressive, Innovative Bluegrass," *Pickin'* 6, no. 9 (October 1979): 20–28; and Bill Emerson, "The Osborne Brothers: Getting Started," *Muleskinner News* 2, no. 4 (July–August 1971): 2–11.

The Osborne Brothers won a larger following for themselves and for bluegrass with a progressive approach. The Lilly Brothers, on the other hand, took a very traditional sound into the north. Introductions to them, and to the Boston bluegrass scene, are found in Tom Heathwood, "The Lilly Brothers," *Muleskinner News* 1, no. 6 (November–December 1970): 4–5, 15, and Bill Vernon, "Tex Logan Remembers the Lilly Brothers," *Muleskinner News* 1, no. 6 (November–December 1970): 6–7. The most complete account of the Lillys, stressing their West Virginia experiences as well as their years in Boston, is Ivan M. Tribe, "Pros Long before Boston: The Entire Career of the Lilly Brothers," *BGU* 9, no. 1 (July 1974): 8–17. James J. McDonald gives some biographical information but concentrates more on musical style and repertory in what seems to be the only article on a bluegrass group ever written for a major folklore journal: "Principal Influences on the Music of the Lilly Brothers of Clear Creek, West Virginia," *JAF* 86, no. 342 (October–December 1973): 331–344.

If the Lilly Brothers carried the gospel of bluegrass and old-time country music north, Bill Clifton took it around the world. He also built bridges to the urban folk community that changed the nature and direction of bluegrass. I wrote a short biography of him called *Bill Clifton: America's Bluegrass Ambassador to the World* (Urbana: University of Illinois Press, 2016). My information came principally from interviews with Clifton, first in Lutherville, Maryland, June 9, 1976, and later by phone and at his home near Beckley, West Virginia. A short account of his influence in Great Britain (along with a discography of most of his recordings) was compiled by Ron Petronko, "Bill Clifton in Britain," *BGU* 6, no. 4 (October 1971): 10–15. Clifton's reemergence on the American bluegrass scene in 1978, as part of the First Generation (with Red Rector and Don Stover), is discussed in "A Bluegrass Experiment," *BGU* 13, no. 2 (August 1978): 22–27, and in John Atkins, "Bill Clifton and Red Rector," *Pickin'* 6, no. 4 (May 1979): 24–26. The bulk of Clifton's recorded repertory is available in a box set of eight CDs: *Around the World to Poor Valley* (Bear BCD-16425).

Bluegrass music's expansion to the north is touched upon in many of the previously mentioned articles dealing with Flatt and Scruggs, the Osbornes, Jimmy Martin, the Lillys, and Bill Clifton. The role played by lesser-known musicians is described by Henry Glassie in his fine article on Ola Belle Reed (Dust to Digital, 2015), and by Charles Camp and David Whisnant in "A Voice from Home: Southern Mountain Musicians on the Maryland-Pennsylvania Border," in *Long Journey Home: Folklife in the South*, edited by Allan Tullos (Chapel Hill, NC: Southern Exposure, 1977), 80–90. Studies of bluegrass music in such cities as Detroit and Cincinnati would profit greatly from what Tim Newby has done in *Bluegrass in Baltimore: The Hard Drivin' Sound and Its Legacy* (Jefferson, NC: McFarland, 2015). Ivan Tribe has provided us a glimpse of the way that records circulated among northern fans in "Jimmie Skinner: Country Singer, Bluegrass Composer, Record Retailer," *BGU* 11, no. 9 (March 1977): 34–38. My books on Hazel Dickens and Mike Seeger will provide additional information on bluegrass popularity in the north: *Working Girl Blues: The Life and Music of Hazel Dickens* (Urbana: University of Illinois Press, 2008), and *Music from the True Vine: Mike Seeger's Life and Musical Journey* (Chapel Hill: University of North Carolina Press, 2012).

The interrelationship between bluegrass and the urban folk revival, which was partly a product of the music's expansion north, is documented in a few books and several articles and in the liner notes of a few record albums that were marketed among urban folkies. I provided some information in the Dickens and Seeger biographies listed above. D. K. Wilgus introduced bluegrass to the academic audience through his record reviews in the *Kentucky Folklore Record* after 1957 and in the *Journal of American Folklore* after 1962. Folk fans learned about the music in a variety of magazines such as *Caravan: The Magazine of Folk Music, Hootenanny,* and *Little Sandy Review;* in Robert Shelton's folk music columns in the *New York Times;* and through the songs and notes of such LP's as Earl Taylor's *Folk Songs from the Blue Grass,* United Artists 3049 (notes by Alan Lomax), *American Banjo Scruggs Style,* Folkways FA2314 (notes by Ralph Rinzler), *Mountain Music Bluegrass Style,* Folkways FA2318 (notes by Mike Seeger), and *The Greenbriar Boys,* Vanguard VRS-9104 (notes by Rinzler). The larger world outside the folk-music scene learned about bluegrass through the popular television series *The Beverly Hillbillies,* the theme of which was Earl Scruggs's version of "The Ballad of Jed Clampett," and through brief articles in popular magazines: "Pickin' Scruggs," *Time* 77, no. 27 (June 30, 1961): 53; Peter Welding, "Music from the Bluegrass Roots," *Saturday Review* 44 (June 10, 1961): 48; and Alan Lomax, "Bluegrass Background: Folk Music with Overdrive," *Esquire* 52, no. 4 (October 1959): 103–109.

Baltimore bluegrass has been treated by the Newby book listed above, but the Washington, DC, bluegrass scene also deserves a comprehensive history and analysis. Part of the story is found in Peter Kuykendall, "Bluegrass on the Air," *BGU* 6, no. 4 (October 1971): 3–8 (concentrating on WKCW in Warrenton, Virginia). Other references to the Washington scene show up in articles or liner notes pertaining to people who have played there. Buzz Busby, for example, is discussed in the notes to *Honky Tonk Bluegrass,* Rounder 0031 (no author listed). Articles on the Stoneman Family generally tell of their role in popularizing bluegrass in the nation's capital; see, for example, Don Rhodes, "Roni Stoneman," *BGU* 11, no. 11 (May 1977): 13–17, and Ivan Tribe, "The Return of Donna Stoneman: First Lady of the Mandolin," *BGU* 17, no. 12 (June 1983): 16–26. Bob Artis devoted a chapter to the Washington sound and to the band the Country Gentlemen, which did most to create that sound (*Bluegrass,* 107–121). I gained some insights about the Gentlemen from a talk with Charlie Waller in Hugo, Oklahoma, on August 10, 1974, and from such articles as Bill Evans, "Good Music, Good Friends: The Country Gentlemen," *BGU* 12, no. 12 (June 1978): 18–25, and Roland Leiser, "Country Gentlemen: Tradition, Style, Humor," *Pickin'* 5, no. 11 (December 1978): 24–28.

Bluegrass's retreat to the festivals is treated at considerable length by me in the Bill Clifton biography and by Rosenberg. Carlton Haney, the man who did most to popularize the festival format, is discussed in Fred Bartenstein, "The Carlton Haney Story" (an interview), *Muleskinner News* 2, no. 4 (September 1971): 8–10, 18–21; and in "Carlton Haney: True Great," *BGU* 18, no. 3 (September 1983): 22–25. Festival schedules and advertisements are carried in *Bluegrass Unlimited.*

The "newgrass" phenomenon is documented in the lives and music of many musicians, including some, such as Don Reno, who are considered to be exponents of "classic" bluegrass. The chromatic-style banjo player Bill Keith is discussed in Tony Trischka, "Bill Keith," *BGU* 10, no. 6 (December 1975): 12–15, and Roger H. Siminoff, "Bill Keith: Yesterday, Today, and Tomorrow," *Pickin'* 4, no. 11 (December 1977): 4–17. The chromatic style is explained by Thomas Adler in "Manual Formulaic

Composition: Innovation in Bluegrass Banjo Styles," *JCM* 5, no. 2 (Summer 1974): 55–64. Frank Wakefield's contributions to "progressive" mandolin playing are discussed in Jack Tottle, "Bluegrass Mandolin, 1/3rd Century Later," *BGU* 6, no. 9 (March 1972): 5–9, and Dix Bruce, "Frank Wakefield," ibid. 18, no. 1 (July 1983): 14–22. The fiddler who moved furthest into the realms of jazz and rock, Vassar Clements, was discussed by Barry Silver in "Vassar Clements Out West," *BGU* 12, no. 11 (May 1978): 18–23. The marvelous musician Tony Rice, who was as much at home in jazz as he was in the traditional bluegrass in which he was reared, is discussed by Jack Tottle in "Tony Rice: East Meets West," ibid. 12, no. 4 (October 1977): 10–16. Mike Auldridge, the Dobroist who did much to define the sound of the Seldom Scene, drew extensive interest because of his session work in many areas of music. Two of the better articles on him and his music are Michael J. Weiss, "Mike Auldridge: Cruising on a Dobro," *Pickin'* 5, no. 3 (April 1978): 12–17, and Roger H. Siminoff, "Mike Auldridge," *Frets* 3, no. 5 (May 1981): 26–31.

The great band of which Auldridge was a part—the Seldom Scene—is discussed in several articles, including Bill Vernon, "Part-time Professionals: The Seldom Scene," *Muleskinner News* 4, no. 3 (March 1973): 6–8; Robert Kyle, "The Seldom Scene: Blue-grass Super Group," *Pickin'* 5, no. 10 (November 1978): 20–24, 30; Don Rhodes, "The Stability and Versatility of the Seldom Scene," *BGU* 15, no. 1 (July 1980): 14–19; and Jack Tottle, "Don't Wait for Them to Buy—Sell It: John Duffey and His Music," *BGU* 9, no. 5 (November 1974): 8–13.

Much scattered material exists on the newgrass, or progressive, bands. The fol-lowing is merely a sampling of articles that would be helpful to the interested fan or scholar: H. Lloyd Whittaker, "Cliff Waldron and the New Shades of Grass," *BGU* 5, no. 10 (April 1971): 51; Mary Jane Bolle, "Happy Medium—J. D. Crowe and the New South," *BGU* 8, no. 8 (February 1974): 7–9; Marty Godbey, "A Conversation with J. D. Crowe," *BGU* 16, no. 1 (July 1981): 14–21; Tom Henderson, "On the Cuttin' Edge . . . with Eddie Adcock," *Pickin'* 2, no. 9 (October 1975): 4–12; Peter Kuykendall, "II Gener-ation," *BGU* 9, no. 9 (March 1975): 10–15; Jack Tottle, "Doyle Lawson and Quicksilver," *BGU* 15, no. 5 (November 1980): 16–22; Jack Tottle, "The Country Gazette: Keep on Pushing," *Muleskinner News* 5, no. 7 (July 1974): 6–11, 16; Douglas B. Green, "Country Gazette: Alive and Well," *BGU* 14, no. 2 (August 1979): 12–15; Richard Smith, "Rodney Dillard: California Hillbilly," *Muleskinner News* 6, no. 1 (January–February 1975): 6–9; Marty Godbey, "Spectrum," *BGU* 15, no. 6 (December 1980): 14–21; and Ronni Lundy, "The New Grass Revival," *BGU* 13, no. 5 (November 1978): 10–15.

Gospel bluegrass is almost a genre by itself. Scores of bands, mostly in the South and Midwest, perform nothing but religious music. A full-scale study of such music, concentrating on the more obscure groups, would be very useful. Until such work is completed, an article by Howard Wight Marshall will serve as a good introduction to the field: "'Keep on the Sunny Side of Life': Pattern and Religious Expression in Blue-grass Gospel Music," *New York Folklore Quarterly* 30, no. 1 (March 1974), reprinted by the John Edwards Memorial Foundation, as Reprint No. 31. The pioneer of gospel bluegrass, Carl Story, is discussed by Don Rhodes in "Carl Story," *Pickin'* 4, no. 12 (January 1978): 6–13. Douglas B. Green discussed the Sullivan Family in "The Sul-livan Family—Goodwill Ambassadors of Bluegrass Gospel," *BGU* 15, no. 4 (October

1980): 11–15, and Don Rhodes concentrated on the Lewis Family in "On the Hallelujah Turnpike with the Lewis Family," *BGU* 14, no. 12 (June 1980): 18–24.

In earlier editions of this book, I referred to a group of musicians as "young traditionalists." They have obviously grown up, and some have died. I have had short conversations with four of these musicians: Charlie Moore in Reidsville, North Carolina, September 5, 1970; Del McCoury in Hugo, Oklahoma, August 10, 1974 (plus a much later radio interview on WORT in Madison, Wisconsin, whose date has been lost); Roy Lee Centers in McKinney, Texas, July 6, 1973; and Larry Sparks in McKinney, Texas, July 6, 1973. Charlie Moore received the attention of Peter Kuykendall in "Charlie Moore," *BGU* 7, no. 7 (January 1973): 5–9 (the article also includes a discography by Nick Barr), and of Kathy Kaplan in "Charlie Moore," *Pickin'* 2, no. 4 (May 1975): 4–6, 8, 10. Del McCoury's life and career up to 1973 is described by Gwen Taylor in "Del McCoury," *BGU* 7, no. 12 (June 1973): 17–19, and by Eugenia Snyder, in "Del McCoury, Low-Key but Powerful," *BGU* 16, no. 11 (May 1982): 17–24. As a master guitarist and soulful singer, Larry Sparks drew more attention than any of the other "young" musicians and graced the cover of *Pickin'* once and that of *Bluegrass Unlimited* at least three times: Terry Lickona, "Going to the Top with Larry Sparks," *Pickin'* 4, no. 4 (May 1977): 4–9; Douglas B. Green, "Larry Sparks," *BGU* 7, no. 6 (December 1972): 7–8; Thomas Cook, "Larry Sparks—I'm Giving It All I've Got," *BGU* 12, no. 2 (August 1977): 14–18; and Bill Vernon, "Larry Sparks," *BGU* 17, no. 10 (April 1983): 13–18.

Buck White and his daughters were really in a class by themselves—part bluegrass, part country, part folk—but they carried their version of bluegrass to an audience larger than that commanded by any other bluegrass musicians. Two good articles that assay different stages of their careers are Douglas Green, "Buck White and the Downhomers," *BGU* 7, no. 11 (May 1973): 7–10, and Boris Weintraub, "Buck White and the Down Home Folks," *BGU* 16, no. 5 (November 1981): 9–13.

11. COUNTRY MUSIC, 1972–1984

A new magazine appeared in late 1972—*Country Music*—contributing some of the most honest and objective criticism that the country field had ever received. The magazine attracted a number of excellent journalists, such as Dave Hickey, Nick Tosches, Rich Kienzle, Peter Carr, John Morthland, and Paul Hemphill, who were knowledgeable about most forms of popular music and who also had a thorough understanding of American popular culture. Some of the writers had experience in rock journalism, and a tinge of the *Rolling Stone* style (sarcastic, irreverent, salacious) intruded into their essays. Above all, several of the writers (such as Rich Kienzle in his "Retrospectives" column) had a genuine appreciation for and an understanding of older forms of country music. The magazine endured as an influential publication until it ceased operation in September 2003.

Rolling Stone itself occasionally ventured into the discussion of country music, although most of its applause went to musicians such as Gary Stewart, Johnny Cash, Waylon Jennings, and Willie Nelson who had an appeal to youthful and "hip" audiences. Chet Flippo was the magazine's most knowledgeable country music expert and one of its best writers. He later had a distinguished career in Nashville as an influential country music journalist. Other rock magazines, such as *Creem* and *Crawdaddy*, only rarely dealt with country music, but they did carry occasional stories on such country-rock musicians as Gram Parsons and the Nitty Gritty Dirt Band.

Newspaper columnists have played increasingly important roles in popularizing and documenting country music. Townsend Miller, for example, did much to make the Austin musicians known far and wide through his weekly columns in the *Austin American-Statesman* in the seventies. Jack Hurst, a *Chicago Tribune* columnist whose weekly articles were widely syndicated, was the most influential of all the newspaper country music specialists. Although he rarely said anything negative about the musicians whom he described and whose records he reviewed, he was always scrupulously fair and objective in his treatment of country music's varied styles. His personal preferences clearly leaned toward hard-core forms of country music.

The affairs of the country music industry itself, as well as occasional tidbits about performers and performances, were discussed in the official publication of the Country Music Association, *CMA Close Up* (published monthly in Nashville). The evidence of country music's commercial burgeoning is found in the pages of this little journal and in the rash of popular magazine articles that appeared in the last thirty years of the twentieth century (two of the most significant were *Newsweek*, June 18, 1973, and *Time*, May 5, 1974—both cover stories).

Another dramatic indication of country music's "arrival" in American popular culture was the success of the movie *Nashville* in 1975. The movie was widely and favorably reviewed, but the most important discussions of its relationship to country music (real and imagined) were Noel Coppage, "And Then There's 'Nashville,'" *Stereo Review*, October 1975, 55–56, and Patrick Anderson, "The Real Nashville," *New York Times Magazine*, August 31, 1975, 10–11, 36, 40–42. *Urban Cowboy*, the promoter of cowboy chic, was inspired by Aaron Latham's "The Ballad of the Urban Cowboy: America's Search for True Grit," *Esquire* 90 (September 12, 1978): 21–30. The singer who profited most from the movie's popularity, Mickey Gilley, was discussed in several articles, the most important of which were Peter Guralnick, "Mickey Gilley's Piano Roll Blues," *Country Music* 6, no. 6 (March 1978): 40–42, 63–66; Bob Claypool, "Just Ol' Mickey," ibid. 4, no. 7 (April 1976): 54–58; and Lee Rector, "Mickey Gilley," *MCN* 20, no. 7 (January 1983): 16–17. Michael Bane concentrated on another movie phenomenon that made heavy use of country music—and country musicians—in "Burt Reynolds: Smokey and His Country Music Bandits," *Country Music* 9, no. 2 (October 1980): 77–80. The politics of country music was discussed in the notes to chapter 9, but a couple of other articles deserve mention that commented on the music's relationship to presidential politics in the late seventies: Ed Kiersh, "What's Jimmy Carter Doing in This Magazine, Anyway?" *Country Music* 5, no. 3 (December 1976): 40–42; and Bob Allen, "Haggard's a Working Man at Heart," *MCN* 19, no. 12 (June 1982): 12.

Information on the Association of Country Entertainers (ACE) can be extracted from the music journals of the day, but the organization promoted its own cause in a plethora of mimeographed material that included a newsletter called "The Booster Bulletin."

The country-pop singers did not suffer from inattention. Barbara Mandrell was discussed approvingly by John Fergus Ryan, "A Visit with Barbara Mandrell," *Country Music* 2, no. 5 (January 1974): 32–34, 68–73; and by Genevieve Waddell, "Barbara Mandrell: Little Miss Versatility," *CSR* 26, no. 181 (August 1974): 8–9. The pop-rockabilly and sometimes-honky-tonk singer Joe Stampley was discussed by Neil Pond in "Joe Stampley Keeps Versatile," *MCN* 21, no. 4 (October 1983): 40, 49. Anne Murray was much discussed, as in John Gabree, "Anne Murray: The Girl Next Door Grows Up," *Country Music Beat* 1, no. 1 (January 1975): 43–45, and Lee Rector, "Canada's Anne Murray Brings Styles Together," *MCN* 17, no. 7 (January 1980): 16–17. John Lomax III conducted a very good interview with Don Williams in *JCM* 8, no. 1 (May 1979): 2–19, and Harry Morrow did a sympathetic portrait of Williams in "Whispering Thunder," *Country Music* 6, no. 6 (March 1978): 24–26, 65. Two of the best assessments of Larry Gatlin were in *Country Music*: Dolly Carlisle, "Larry Gatlin: Straight Ahead," 8, no. 7 (April 1980): 20–25, and Laura Eipper, "Larry Gatlin," 7, no. 4 (January–February 1977): 46–48, 95. Most articles on Gatlin stressed his sometimes troubled relationship with fans; material on Conway Twitty, on the other hand, concentrated on his close rapport with his intensely loyal audience: John Pugh, "Conway Twitty: Sexy Songs and Good Deeds Keep Him on Top," *Country Music* 5, no. 6 (March 1977): 39–40; Patrick Carr and Marshall Fallwell, "Introducing Harold Jenkins," *Country Music* 2, no. 9 (May 1974): 25–32; Charlie Burton, "Country Music Interviews: Conway Twitty," *Country Music* 1, no. 1 (September 1972): 47–52; Dixie Deen, "Conway Rocks Right into Country Success," *MCN* 4, no. 8 (February 1967): 3–4; and Sonia L. Nazario, "Country Music Fans Pay Tribute to Idols at Big Theme Parks," *Wall Street Journal*, December 12, 1983, 1. Kenny Rogers, of course, was a darling of the media, and was known to millions through his movies and television specials. Two magazine pieces that were particularly helpful were Bob Allen, "Kenny Rogers' Second Edition," *Country Music* 7, no. 1 (October 1977): 22–26, 58–59, and "Playboy Interview: Kenny Rogers," *Playboy* 30, no. 11 (November 1983): 65–69, 72–77, 80–82.

Country music's three great vocal groups, the Statler Brothers, the Oak Ridge Boys, and Alabama, have often been discussed. The Statlers had a Time-Life collection devoted to them (with notes by Charles Wolfe) and several articles, among which were Patrick Carr, "The Statler Brothers: How the Class of '57 Buys a Schoolhouse, Wins Eight CMA Awards in an Air of Complete Calm," *Country Music* 9, no. 7 (March 1981): 38–45, and Lee Rector, "The Statler Brothers Shore Themselves with Fans," *MCN* 20, no. 12 (June 1983): 32–33. As a group with a gospel past and an approach that appealed to a broad spectrum of fans, the Oak Ridge Boys showed up in a wide variety of periodicals, including an interview, "The Oaks: Acorns, Roots and Branches," in *Performance* 8, no. 38 (January 19, 1979): 50–56; Todd Everett, "The Oak Ridge Boys Go Secular," *High Fidelity and Musical America* 29, no. 4 (April 1979): 107–110; and Bob Anderson, "Crossing Over from Canaan: The Oak Ridge Boys Go Country," *Country Music* 6, no. 5 (February 1978): 34–38. The literature devoted to Alabama was enormous, but I depended primarily on Suzan Crane, "Alabama: Southern-bred and Stardom Bound," *Country Music* 9, no. 2 (October 1980): 30–33, and Barry Bronson, "Alabama: A Day in the Lives," *MCN* 21, no. 4 (October 1983): 28–29, 45.

The youth-country fusion of the seventies and the consequent emergence of country-rock are deserving of a lengthy study. Bud Scoppa did a preliminary survey of one aspect of the phenomenon in "The L.A. Turnaround," *Country Music* 2, no. 13 (September 1974): 58–65, and at least two writers have discussed the manifestations of country-rock in Austin: Jan Reid, with *The Improbable Rise of Redneck Rock* (Austin: Heidelberg, 1974), and Travis D. Stimeling, *Cosmic Cowboys and New Hicks: The Countercultural Sounds of Austin's Progressive Country Music Scene* (New York: Oxford University Press, 2011). Neil V. Rosenberg discussed Bob Dylan's contributions to the mating of country music and the youth audience in "Bob Dylan in Nashville," *JCM* 7, no. 3 (December 1978): 54–66. Dylan LPs like *John Wesley Harding* and *Nashville Skyline* are important documents of the youth/rock flirtation with country music, but the most significant milestones were the Nitty Gritty Dirt Band's *Will the Circle Be Unbroken*, United Artists UAS 9801; the Byrds' *Sweetheart of the Rodeo*, Columbia CS9670; the Flying Burrito Brothers' *The Gilded Palace of Sin*, A&M SP4175; and Gram Parsons's *GP*, Warner Brothers 0598. Noel Coppage wrote an excellent review of *Will the Circle Be Unbroken* for *Stereo Review* 30, no. 3 (March 1973): 104–105, and Jerry Leichtling conducted an insightful interview with the Nitty Gritty Dirt Band in *Modern Hi-Fi and Music* 5, no. 9 (November 1975): 23–26. Gram Parsons's crusade to fuse country and rock and his often bizarre lifestyle were discussed in such articles as Judson Klinger and Greg Mitchell, "Gram Finale," *Crawdaddy*, October 1976, 43–58; Patrick Sullivan, "Gram Parsons: The Mysterious Death—and Aftermath," *Rolling Stone*, no. 146 (October 25, 1973): 12, 14; Jimmy Cornelison, "Gram Parsons' Music Continues to Live On," *MCN* 21, no. 2 (August 1983): 12; and Ben Fong-Torres, "Gram Parsons: The Spirit of Country," *Esquire* 96, no. 6 (December 1981): 96–98. Two of the best books on Parsons are Ben-Fong Torres, *Hickory Wind: The Life and Times of Gram Parsons* (New York: St. Martin's Press, 1991), and Jessica Hundley with Polly Parsons, *Grievous Angel: An Intimate Biography of Gram Parsons* (New York: Thunder's Mouth Press, 2005).

The southern rock musicians were reviewed and discussed in such magazines as *Creem*, *Crawdaddy*, and *Rolling Stone*. The most country-oriented of the group, Charlie Daniels, also appeared frequently in country publications (for example, Stan Sucher, "Charlie Daniels Reacts to His Sound," *MCN* 14, no. 9 [March 1977]: 4; Russell Shaw, "Charlie Daniels: The Pride of Tennessee," *Country Music* 5, no. 6 [March 1977]: 42–43; and Bob Allen, "Charlie Daniels: Double Platinum Fiddle Player," *Country Music* 8, no. 7 [April 1980]: 28–30, 39–42).

The best introduction to Hank Williams Jr., aside from his music, is his autobiography (written with Michael Bane), *Living Proof: An Autobiography* (New York: G. P. Putnam's, 1979). Although one can question the reliability of the information concerning his father and mother, Hank Jr. was very frank about his own life. His account should be supplemented with John Eskow, "Oedipus Rocks: The Rise and Fall of Hank Williams Jr.," *New Times* 10, no. 11 (May 29, 1978): 38–43, 47–50, and Chet Flippo, "Hank Williams Jr's Hard Road," *Rolling Stone*, no. 266 (June 1, 1978): 8, 17.

The Austin musical scene was touted euphorically by Townsend Miller in his weekly columns for the *Austin American-Statesman*, and only slightly more dispassionately by such Southwest-based magazines as *Country Gazette* (published in Austin by Buster Doss), *Buddy Magazine* (named in honor of Buddy Holly and published in Dallas), *Austin Sun* (a counterculture organ), and *Picking Up the Tempo* (published in Albuquerque, but heavily oriented toward Austin). Travis Stimeling and Jan Reid wrote the above-mentioned books, but Reid followed that up with a eulogy for the phenomenon, "Who Killed Redneck Rock," *Texas Monthly* 4 (December 1976): 112–113, 209–216. Other scholarly assessments of Austin music, each of which concentrated on the symbols and images surrounding and shaping the musicians, are Archie Green, "Austin's Cosmic Cowboys: Words in Collision," in *And Other Neighborly Names: Social Process and Cultural Image in Texas Folklore*, edited by Richard Bauman and Roger D. Abrahams (Austin: University of Texas Press, 1981), 152–194; Archie Green, "Michael Adam's Honky-Tonk Paintings," *JEMFQ* 18, nos. 67–68 (Fall-Winter 1982): 155–165; David Perry, "Cosmic Cowboys and Cosmetic Politics," ibid. 15, no. 53 (Spring 1979): 38–43; and Nicholas Spitzer, "Bob Wills Is Still the King: Romantic Regionalism and Convergent Culture in Central Texas," *JEMFQ* 2, Part 4, no. 4 (Winter 1975): 191–197.

I had the good fortune to know Kenneth Threadgill, and to have been an active participant in the musical sessions held at his famous bar in the early sixties. I interviewed him in Austin on July 8, 1971, along with his older brother Frank, who had made a few records for Brunswick in the early 1930s. Among the more useful short articles on Kenneth Threadgill are Greg Olds, "Threadgill," *Austin American-Statesman Show World*, July 5, 1970, T26–T29; Prissy Mays, "Old Is Beautiful—in Music or on Threadgill," *Alcalde* (the magazine of the University of Texas Alumni Association), May 1973, 13–15; and Wayne Oakes, "Thousands Turn Out for Threadgill," *Texas Observer* 62 (August 7, 1970): 17–19.

My knowledge of the origins of the Armadillo World Headquarters came mostly from an interview with its founder and proprietor, Eddie Wilson, in Austin on June 5, 1974. Among the most helpful articles dealing with the club are Ed Ward, "There's a Little Bit of Everything in Texas," *Creem* 5, no. 4 (April 1974): 46–48, 76; and Henry Staten, "Armadillo World Headquarters," *Texas Observer* 63 (February 12, 1971): 18–19.

Articles on individual Austin musicians are plentiful. Although he became a musician of international acclaim, Guy Clark spent some of his formative musical years in Austin and Kerrville. Anyone interested in his music, or in him as a man, should read Tamara Saviano, *Without Getting Killed or Caught: The Life and Music of Guy Clark* (College Station: Texas A&M University Press, 2016). The man who coined the term "cosmic cowboy," Michael Murphey, is described by Lydia Dixon-Harden, "Michael Murphey Finally Gets Settled in Country Music," *MCN* 21, no. 4 (October 1983): 23, 45. Marcia Ball reveals that her heart was never really with country music in Bunny Matthews, "Irma's Still the Queen but Tall Texan Marcia Ball Is Heir Apparent to the New Orleans Musical Throne," *Wavelength*, no. 40 (February 1984): 18–20. The self-styled Texas Jewboy, Kinky Friedman, has been fascinating to writers as much for his irreverent humor as for his music: Kaye Northcott, "Kinky Friedman's First Roundup," *Texas Monthly* 1, no. 4 (May 1973): 95–96; Larry Sloman, "Kinky and the Money Changers," *Crawdaddy*, April 1975, 30–31; and Lester Bangs, review of *Sold American*, Vanguard VSD 97333, in *Rolling Stone*, no. 137 (June 21, 1973): 63. My undated interview with Kinky in Medina, Texas, in the late 1970s or early 1980s is now a part of my materials in the Southern Folklife Collection at the University of North Carolina-Chapel Hill. Except for Willie Nelson, Jerry Jeff Walker has inspired more print than any other Austin-based musician, including articles by Douglas Kent Hall, "Mr. Bojangles' Dance: The Odyssey and Oddities of Jerry Jeff Walker," *Rolling Stone*, no. 176 (December 19, 1974): 9, 20; John Moulder, "Jerry Jeff Walker, Hell-Raising Poet," *Country Rambler*, no. 2 (October 7, 1976): 8–10; and John Morthland, "Jerry Jeff Rides Again," *Country Music* 6, no. 6 (March 1978): 28–32. In addition to the above-mentioned articles, I also profited from interviews with Marcia Ball in Kerrville, Texas, July 2, 1978; Alvin Crow, Kerrville, July 4, 1977; and Steve Fromholz, Kerrville, July 4, 1977.

The articles and books on Willie Nelson cannot all be mentioned. The best place to begin would be Joe Nick Patoski, *Willie Nelson: An Epic Life* (Boston: Little, Brown, 2008). Of the many interviews with Nelson, among the best are Bob Allen's in *JCM* 8, no. 2 (1980): 3–14; David Breskin's in *Musician*, no. 45 (July 1982): 40–48, 84–85; and Alanna Nash's in *Stereo Review*, no. 5 (November 1979): 68–70. Other articles that are commendable in their summary or evaluation of Nelson's career are Chet Flippo, "Willie Nelson," *Rolling Stone*, no. 269 (July 13, 1978): 45–49; Roy Blount Jr., "Wrasslin' with This Thing Called Willie Nelson," *Esquire* (August 1981): 78–80, 83–87; and William C. Martin, "Growing Old at Willie Nelson's Picnic," *Texas Monthly* 2 (October 1974): 94–98, 116–124. Nelson's movie career is discussed by Bob Allen, "Willie Nelson: Being a Movie Star Sure Beats Working," *Country Music* 9, no. 2 (October 1980): 34–36, 45–47; Michael Bane, "Willie: The Gypsy Cowboy Goes Hollywood," *Country Music* 7, no. 7 (May 1979): 24–28; and John Pugh and Bill Oakey, "Willie Goes to the Movies," *Country Music* 8, no. 6 (March 1980): 56–58.

Willie's fellow "Outlaws" are discussed in a variety of places. Probably the best short summary of the group (and one which was influential in naming them) is Dave Hickey's "In Defense of the Telecaster Cowboy Outlaws," *Country Music* 2, no. 5 (January 1974): 90–95. The fullest history and critique is Michael Bane, *The Outlaws: Revolution in Country Music* (New York: Doubleday, 1978). Individual Outlaws receive attention in such essays as Mickey Lane, "Tompall—the Outlaw with Style and Flavor," *Nashville Sound* 2, no. 8 (November 1976): 18–21, 36; Kelly Delaney, "Billy Joe Shaver: Cowboy in His Soul," *Country Music* 9, no. 1 (September 1980): 76; Larry L. King, "David Allan Coe's Greatest Hits," *Esquire* 86 (July 1976): 71–73, 142–144; and Neil Pond, "David Allan Coe Polishes His Image," *MCN* 20, no. 12 (June 1983): 24–25.

Waylon: An Autobiography (New York: Warner Books, 1996), written by Waylon Jennings with the help of Lenny Kaye, is strongly recommended for its candor and detail. R. Serge Denisoff, *Waylon* (Knoxville: University of Tennessee Press, 1983), has received mixed reviews, but it does present the basic facts (and discography) of Jennings's life and career. It should be supplemented with John L. Smith, "I Ain't No Ordinary Dude—a Bio-Discography of Waylon Jennings," *JCM* 6, no. 2 (Summer 1975): 45–95; Bob Campbell, "Waylon: An Interview," *Country Music* 7, no. 4 (January–February 1979): 50–55; and Lee Rector, "An Inside Look at the Real Waylon Jennings," *MCN* 20, no. 6 (December 1982): 16–17.

The hard country revivalists have received scattered attention. The western swing and rodeo singer Red Steagall is discussed by Cindy Kent, "Red Steagall Attests to Bob Wills Music," *MCN* 14, no. 3 (September 1976): 8. I also talked to Steagall in Kerrville on July 3, 1977. Lee Rector did a short sketch of Riders in the Sky, "Western Music Comes Alive with Riders," in *MCN* 18, no. 4 (October 1980): 42. The honky-tonk–rockabilly singer Gary Stewart received extensive press coverage in 1976 (his peak year) because of his expertise in two different styles of expression. The best of these articles are Patrick Carr, "Goodtime Gary," *Country Music* 5, no. 9 (June 1976): 34–41, and Kit Rachlis, "Honky-Tonkin' Blues in Rock-and-Roll Shoes," *Rolling Stone*, no. 209 (March 25, 1976): 56, 58. A glimpse of the obscure honky-tonk singer Vernon Oxford and of his remarkable popularity abroad is provided by John Pugh in "The Vernon Oxford Conspiracy," *Country Music* 9, no. 2 (October 1980): 59–62.

Although George Strait deserves a full-scale biography, two writers have attempted to tell his story: Mark Bego, *George Strait: The Story of Country's Living Legend* (New York: Kensington, 1997), and Austin Teutsch, *King George: The Triumphs and Tragedies in the Life of George Strait* (Austin: Golden Touch Press, 2010). Gene Watson also deserves more coverage than he has received, but two of the better sketches on him are Bill Oakey, "Gene Watson," *Country Music* 9, no. 3 (November 1980): 60–61, and Tom Robinson, "Gene Watson: A New Look, but the Same Sound," *MCN* 20, no. 7 (January 1983): 10, 20. I interviewed Moe Bandy in Kerrville on July 3, 1977, and learned additional information about him from Bob Allen, "Moe Bandy: Honky Tonk Hero, Hardcore Country Survivor," *Country Music* 7, no. 4 (January–February 1979): 42–44, and from Nick Tosches, "Honky Tonk Lives," *Country Music* 3, no. 7 (April 1975): 35–38. The most commercially successful of the young honky-tonk singers in the late 1970s—John Anderson—did not attain the kind of magazine exposure that seemed commensurate with his widespread public popularity. One brief article, though, that I found helpful was Bob Allen, "Country John," *US* 5, no. 5 (March 3, 1981): pages not numbered.

Material dealing with George Jones was described in the notes for chapter 9, but two additional articles that shed light on his remarkable endurance in the seventies are Bob Allen, "The Decline and Fall of George Jones," *Country Music* 7, no. 4 (January–February 1979): 28–30, 32–34, and Richard Nusser and Patrick Carr, "George Jones: Problems, Problems, Problems," *Country Music* 4, no. 3 (December 1975): 30–34, 59.

As might be expected of someone with both beauty and talent, Emmylou Harris has been a favorite of magazine writers. The following list of articles is certainly not exhaustive but will give you a good overview of her life and career: Bill Littleton, "Emmylou Gives 'Piece of the Sky,'" *MCN* 13, no. 2 (August 1975): 9; Bud Scoppa, "Emmylou Harris's Quiet Country Sky," *Rolling Stone*, no. 184 (April 10, 1975): 60, 62; Dave Hickey, "Emmylou Harris: Stardom Hasn't Gone to Her Head," *Country Music* 4, no. 12 (September 1976): 23–26, 59; Ben Fong-Torres, "Emmylou Harris: Whole-Wheat Honky Tonk," *Rolling Stone*, no. 259 (February 23, 1978): 8, 10, 18, 21; Joyce Maynard Bethel, "Emmylou Harris—Heart Is Still in Country Music," *New York Times*, March 12, 1978, 241; Jas Obrecht, "Pro's Reply: Emmylou Harris," *Guitar Player* 12, no. 11 (November 1978): 8, 152, 154, 158–159; Lee Rector, "Emmylou Harris,

Doing the Music She Likes," *MCN* 17, no. 11 (May 1980): 16–17; and Rip Kirby, "Emmylou," *Country Music* 9, no. 1 (September 1980): 36–44.

Harris's one-time partner and fellow neo-traditionalist Ricky Skaggs has not been so well publicized. His accelerating commercial success, though, will inevitably be documented in a rash of books and magazine articles. I originally relied on such articles as Jack Tottle, "Ricky Skaggs: Clinch Mountain to Boone Creek," *BGU* 11, no. 7 (January 1977): 8–16; Robert K. Oermann, "Ricky Skaggs Remembers the Stanley Brothers," *BGU* 15, no. 11 (May 1981): 26–29; and Robert Kyle, "Ricky Skaggs: Moving beyond Bluegrass," *Pickin'* 6, no. 1 (February 1979): 51–54.

Charles Hughes, *Country Soul: Making Music and Making Race in the American South* (Chapel Hill: University of North Carolina Press, 2016) is one of the indispensable books on modern American music. An earlier piece that commented on the interchange between soul and country music is Lee May, "Blacks Join the Country Music Surge," *Los Angeles Times*, August 30, 1983, 1, 11. The concern about country music losing its own "soul" was voiced by Hugh Cherry in "Country DJs Carry Music to People," *MCN* 18, no. 4 (October 1980): 18–19; and by Bobby Bare in Lydia Dixon's "Bobby Bare: The Songwriter Speaks Up for the Soul of Country Music," *MCN* 20, no. 11 (May 1983): 10A.

12. TRADITION AND CHANGE: COUNTRY MUSIC, 1985–2000

Anyone who wishes to explore the state of country music during these years and after will find copious detail on the Internet. Every performer has an "official" website and, usually, several unofficial ones conducted by fans or followers of country music. Reams of history abound on the Internet, and YouTube sources of recordings, old and new, can easily captivate the attention of browsers for hours. One cannot depend on the endurance of popular magazines, but some supermarket shelf items, such as *Country Weekly*, provide a steady diet of gossip about country entertainers along with news about the latest CD or video releases. *CMA Close Up* conveys information from a Nashville music industry perspective. Virtually any current performer can also be seen and heard on music videos shown by Country Music Television or the Nashville Network (later named the National Network). Furthermore, many of the entertainers who work outside of Nashville's orbit can be seen on the syndicated television shows carried on RFD-TV or on *Austin City Limits*. *The Marty Stuart Show*, seen each Saturday evening on RFD-TV, is filled with both entertainment and history. The Austin show has been documented by Tracey E. W. Laird, along with wonderful photographs by Scott Newton, in *Austin City Limits: A History* (New York: Oxford University Press, 2014).

A variety of encyclopedias also provide basic information. These include Kurt Wolff, ed., *Country Music: The Rough Guide* (London: Rough Guides, 2000); David Goodman, ed., *Modern Twang: An Alternative Country Music Guide and Directory* (Nashville: Dowling Press, 1999); Barry McCloud, ed., *Definitive Country: The Ultimate Encyclopedia of Country Music and Its Performers* (New York: Berkley, 1995); and Paul Kingsbury, ed., *The Encyclopedia of Country Music: The Ultimate Guide to the Music* (New York: Oxford University Press, 1998; rev. 2012). The Kingsbury volume, sponsored by the Country Music Foundation, and greatly enlarged in 2012, is the most authoritative and includes articles and biographical vignettes written by an assortment of academicians, journalists, and freelance writers.

Country music journals have too often been short-lived. *Country Music* magazine limped along until September of 2003. The *Journal of Country Music* had a similarly brief existence, from 1971 to 2007, but it presented lengthy, well-researched articles and reviews on both historical and contemporary issues. Many of the journal's best essays and reviews have been excerpted in Paul Kingsbury, ed., *The Country Reader* (Nashville: Country Music Foundation Press and Vanderbilt University Press, 1996). *Bluegrass Unlimited* has always been a thorough compendium of material on both bluegrass and old-time music. *Old-Time Herald*, however, is the best source of information on traditional styles of country music, particularly the string bands and other acts that sprang from the folk revival. The best current journal devoted to country music and other roots expressions is *No Depression* (published in Seattle, Washington), and issued in both magazine and online formats. It is exhaustive in its coverage of classic country, bluegrass, country-rock, and other "alternative" forms. The *Oxford American*, a bimonthly magazine published in Oxford, Mississippi, runs a special issue each year dealing with the various styles of southern music.

A body of interpretive and specialized studies now exists that should help clarify the modern period of country music while providing some contextual history. The previously mentioned book edited by Diane Pecknold, *Hidden in the Mix: The African American Presence in Country Music* (Durham, NC: Duke University Press, 2013), uses the insights and research of such scholars as Patrick Huber and Charles Hughes to redress an imbalance that has too long existed in country music historiography. My *Singing Cowboys and Musical Mountaineers* (Athens: University of Georgia Press, 1993) grew out of a series of lectures presented at Mercer University in Macon, Georgia, and is composed of essays dealing with country music's precommercial origins, its indebtedness to nineteenth-century popular music, and the influence of romantic symbols on its development. My *Don't Get Above Your Raisin': Country Music and the Southern Working Class* (Urbana: University of Illinois Press, 1997) is an interpretive study that addresses many of the basic issues found in country songs. Richard A. Peterson challenges the idea of country music's evolution as a working-class phenomenon in a much-quoted book called *Creating Country Music: Fabricating Authenticity* (Chicago: University of Chicago Press, 1997). Cecelia M. Tichi, in *High Lonesome: The American Culture of Country Music* (Chapel Hill: University of North Carolina Press, 1994), argues that country musicians explore the same themes, such as home, the lure of the open road, and spirituality, that our greatest poets have addressed. Laurence Leamer and Bruce Feiler have written the best broad interpretive surveys of contemporary Top Forty country music. Leamer's *Three Chords and the Truth: Hope, Heartbreak, and Changing Fortunes in Nashville* (New York: HarperCollins, 1997) is a nonsentimental but perceptive and sympathetic study, and it contains good biographical portraits of such people as Shania Twain and Mary Chapin Carpenter. Feiler's *Dreaming Out Loud: Garth Brooks, Wynonna Judd, Wade Hayes, and the Changing Face of Nashville* (New York: Avon Books, 1998) also has perceptive studies of the musicians named in its title and is the best available critique and defense of the music that now emanates from Nashville.

Nicholas Dawidoff's beautifully written *In the Country of Country: People and Places in American Music* (New York: Pantheon Books, 1997) is my favorite book among the "recent" interpretive studies of country music (probably because he and I tend to like the same kind of country singers). Dawidoff presents a jaundiced view of contemporary Nashville and sympathetic portraits of such "roots performers" as Iris DeMent, Doc Watson, Ralph Stanley, and Merle Haggard.

Between November 1991 and August 1993, Curtis W. Ellison traveled over five thousand miles, including trips to Nashville's Fan Fair and every other conceivable type of performing venue, to write *Country Music Culture: From Hard Times to Heaven* (Jackson: University Press of Mississippi, 1995). It is the best account of country music as a community or "family" consisting of fans and musicians. Alanna Nash, *Behind Closed Doors: Talking with the Legends of Country Music* (New York: Knopf, 1988), presents an insider's view of her subject based on twenty-seven interviews with stars ranging from Roy Acuff to Hank Williams Jr.

Murphy Henry edits a quarterly newsletter, *Women in Bluegrass* (published in Winchester, Virginia), and has written *Pretty Good for a Girl: Women in Bluegrass* (Urbana: University of Illinois Press, 2013). Her 1999 master's thesis at George Mason University in Fairfax, Virginia, "The Story of Sally Ann Forrester: The Original Bluegrass Girl" (1999), has been reprinted with the same title in Charles K. Wolfe and James E. Akenson, eds., *Country Music Annual, 2001* (Lexington: University Press of Kentucky, 2001). The *Country Music Annual*, which has appeared in two volumes (2000 and 2001), grew out of the International Country Music Conference, held each year at Belmont University in Nashville.

13. A NEW CENTURY: AN ADDITIONAL BIBLIOGRAPHIC SAMPLING

The twenty-first century has been a rich time for scholarship on country music, and its explosion spread in disciplinary directions that range from music to politics, from religion to cultural studies. Work on country music appears both in print and online in the form of books, edited collections, and peer-reviewed journals, as well as popular publications like *Paste, Billboard, Salon, Slate, CMT.com, American Songwriter, Vanity Fair*, and *No Depression*, as well as the *New York Times*. I highlight works that were especially helpful in preparing this chapter.

Edited collections continue to emerge that address country music through a wide range of lenses. Two useful projects overseen by the musicologist Travis Stimeling include one for primary readings, *The Country Music Reader* (New York: Oxford University Press, 2015), and the set of topical scholarly essays *The Oxford Handbook of Country Music* (New York: Oxford University Press, 2017), to which I contributed the essay on country music and television. Others slice off a particular subset of the topic: compilations edited by the late Charles K. Wolfe and James E. Akenson, for example, include *The Women of Country Music: A Reader* (Lexington: University Press of Kentucky, 2003) and *Country Music Goes to War* (Lexington: University Press of Kentucky, 2005). Another strong example is the collection edited by Pamela

Fox and Barbara Ching exploring the alt-country subculture: *Old Roots, New Routes: The Cultural Politics of Alt.Country Music* (Ann Arbor: University of Michigan Press, 2008). Two recent monographs offer particularly useful ways to reexamine oft-trodden modes of thinking about country music: Nadine Hubbs explores shifting dynamics of class and politics in *Rednecks, Queers, and Country Music* (Berkeley: University of California Press, 2014); and, more broadly, Karl Hagstrom Miller digs deeply into questions that first stirred my curiosity in work on the *Louisiana Hayride*, particularly early recordings of Jimmie Davis, about how race shaped the music industry from its inception; see Miller's book *Segregating Sound: Inventing Folk and Pop Music in the Age of Jim Crow* (Durham, NC: Duke University Press, 2010).

Still other work on country music appears as a topic framed within a larger inquiry. For example, Trent Hill brings a cultural studies point of view in his chapter "Why Isn't Country Music 'Youth' Culture?" in the work edited by Roger Beebe, Denise Fulbrook, and Ben Saunders, *Rock Over the Edge: Transformations in Popular Music Culture* (Durham, NC: Duke University Press, 2002), 161–190. The linguist Alena Horn reflects specifically on the gendered implications of the artist's language in "'Keepin' It Country': What Makes the Lyrics of Gretchen Wilson Hard?," *Popular Music and Society* 32, no. 4 (October 2009); 461–473. Media itself comes to the fore in online scholarly pieces like Molly Brost's "Negotiating Authenticity: *Coal Miner's Daughter*, the Biopic, and Country Music," *Americana: The Journal of American Popular Culture (1900 to Present)* 7, no. 2 (Fall 2008); or Max Fraser's comparison of the contemporary TV series *Nashville* with the 1975 Robert Altman film of the same title in "Country Music Capital," *Dissent* (Winter 2016): 15–19. Dave Robinson addresses the use of country music to brand Fox News in "Country Crooners and FOX News: Country Music and the FOX Brand," in *Rock Brands: Selling Sound in a Media Saturated Culture*, ed. Elizabeth Barfoot Christian (Lanham, MD: Lexington Books, 2011), 213–232.

The controversy over Dixie Chicks member Natalie Maines's infamous offhand remark drew numerous scholarly perspectives. Some examples I found useful include another by Brost titled "Post–Dixie Chicks Country: Carrie Underwood and the Negotiation of Feminist Country Identity" in a broader collection edited by Joseph P. Fisher and Brian Flota, *The Politics of Post-9/11 Music: Sound, Trauma, and the Music Industry in the Time of Terror* (Burlington, VT: Ashgate, 2011), 161–172. Others include Claire Katz, "'The Eternal Irony of the Community': Prophecy, Patriotism, and the Dixie Chicks," *Shofar* 26, no. 4, Special Issue: Emmanuel Levinas and Jewish Thought: Translating Hebrew into Greek (Summer 2008): 139–160; Lesley Pruitt, "Real Men Kill and a Lady Never Talks Back: Gender Goes to War in Country Music," *International Journal on World Peace* 24, no. 4 (December 2007): 85–106; and Gabriel Rossman, "Elites, Masses, and Media Blacklists: The Dixie Chicks Controversy," *Social Forces* 83, no. 1 (September 2004): 61–79.

Once a marginal topic of inquiry, country music gets explored in scholarly conferences from the most narrowly focused, like the International Country Music Conference (ICMC), to broad interdisciplinary groups like the collective Post45. My own work has benefited from colleagues affiliated with the Society for Ethnomusicology and the Society for American Music. Modern technology brings a new dimension to the potential benefits of these gatherings. For example, though unable to attend in person, I benefited from Anthony Cosar's unpublished overview on recent Brad Paisley releases at ICMC in 2015, among other presentations, because they were available via the efforts of Martin Fisher at Middle Tennessee State University. Online primary resources are another modern wonder. The *Critical Past* website, for instance, makes available a video of Richard Nixon speaking at the *Grand Ole Opry* in 1974. The boon of Internet accessibility will assuredly continue to fuel the passions of country music scholars and enthusiasts for decades to come.

LOCAL AND REGIONAL STUDIES

A fairly extensive list of publications provides reminders that country music exists outside of Nashville. The most impressive of these studies is one that not only demonstrates the importance of the music in a local setting but also provides insight as to why it appeals to a broad swath of working Americans everywhere: Aaron Fox, *Real Country: Music and Language in Working-Class Culture* (Durham, NC: Duke University Press, 2004). Fox immersed himself in the lives of his informants in Lockhart, Texas, a little town south of Austin, and found how music provided both identity and protection in an elite-dominated society. Joe Carr and Alan Munde, musicians and instructors in the Commercial Music Program at South Plains College in Levelland, Texas, discuss West Texas as an incubus of many important musicians: *Prairie Nights to Neon Lights: The Story of Country Music in West Texas* (Lubbock: Texas Tech University Press, 1995). Wayne W. Daniel contributes a fine account of a city that once rivaled Nashville as a country music center: *Pickin' on Peachtree: A History of Country Music in Atlanta, Georgia* (Urbana: University of Illinois Press, 1990). With Bill Sloan's help, Horace Logan talks about his own important career as a radio announcer and promoter, while also discussing the once-thriving country music scene in Shreveport, Louisiana, in *Elvis, Hank, and Me: Making Musical History on the Louisiana Hayride* (New York: St. Martin's Press, 1998). Johnny Horton's bass player and confidant, Tillman Franks, also talks about the *Louisiana Hayride* and more in *Tillman Franks: "I Was There When It Happened"* (Many, LA: Sweet Dreams Publishing, 2000). The popular comedian Pete Stamper similarly entwines his own story with that of an important radio show in *It All Happened in Renfro Valley* (Lexington: University Press of Kentucky, 1999). Reta Spears-Stewart talks about Red Foley and the regional show he hosted in *Remembering the Ozark Jubilee* (Springfield, MO: Stewart, Dillbeck, and White Productions, 1993). One of my favorite country music historians, the prolific Ivan Tribe, discusses the Wheeling radio scene and much more in *Mountaineer Jamboree: Country Music in West Virginia* (Lexington: University Press of Kentucky, 1984).

I will conclude with a note about recordings but will resist the temptation to give a comprehensive list of available material. Readers might want to consult my discography in *Don't Get Above Your Raisin'*, but no assurance can be given that items listed there will still be in print by the time this book is published, or that they will not have become outmoded by more relevant items. Serious researchers in old-time, or pre–World War II, country music will need to visit the major repositories for such material in Nashville, Chapel Hill, and Murfreesboro, where they will be permitted to hear "listening copies" of relevant recordings.

Since 1985, the major recording labels have reissued much older country material, either as anthologies or as boxed collections devoted to single performers. Most of these recordings come from the decades after 1960 and tend to be repetitious in nature. Pre-1960 items more often show up as leased recordings on such labels as Time-Life, Rounder, County, Sugar Hill, Shanachie, Old Hat, Yazoo, JSP, Proper, Living Era, Razor and Tie, Rhino, Bloodshot Revival, CMF (Country Music Foundation), Document, Trikont, Dust to Digital, Bear Family, and Smithsonian Folkways. Bear Family, located in Hambergen, Germany, has the most impressive library of reissued vintage country music. Interested purchasers can obtain the "complete" recordings of a staggering list of such musicians as Roy Acuff, Cliff Bruner, the Carter Family, Johnny Cash, Bill Clifton, Jimmie Davis, Lefty Frizzell, Ray Price, Marty Robbins, Jimmie Rodgers, Hank Snow, Ernest Tubb, and Bob Wills in box sets that include full biographical and discographical notes and reams of photographs. The Smithsonian Institution now owns Moe Asch's massive Folkways catalogue and has gradually been re-releasing these items as CDs under the Smithsonian Folkways imprint. The most epochal consequence of this merger has been the reissuance in 1997 of Harry Smith's *Anthology of American Folk Music* on compact discs. Originally released in 1952, this collection is my choice as the most significant body of roots recordings made in the twentieth century. Pirated material, of course, also appears frequently on labels located in the United States, Europe, and Japan. A large market for older recordings definitely exists. Some of the Time-Life anthologies, for example, have experienced vigorous sales and have appeared on *Billboard*'s popularity charts. The availability of this material, along with ordering information, can easily be ascertained by consulting the websites of County Sales in Floyd, Virginia; Old Homestead in Brighton, Michigan; or Downhome Music in El Cerrito, California.

Finally, fans of contemporary country music can easily find information on desired recordings by going to the web, or by checking the pages of *No Depression, Bluegrass Unlimited,* or *Old-Time Herald* (for alternative, bluegrass, and traditional music), or by consulting *Billboard, Country Weekly,* or Amazon.com (for mainstream country items).

Index

Note: Italic page numbers refer to
   photographs.

A&M Records, 470
A&R (artists-and-repertoire) representatives,
   46, 226, 246, 247, 399
Abbott Records, 305
ABC, 315, 317
Aberbach, Gene, 212
Aberbach, Julian, 212
Abernathy, Will, 69
Absolute Torch and Twang (album), 499
Academy of Country Music (ACM), 436,
   439–440, 495, 496, 506, 515, 545, 550, 567
accordions, 51, 171, 181, 386, 394
Ace in the Hole Band, 480
Ace of Clubs, Big Spring, Texas, 271
Acuff, Mildred, 227
Acuff, Neill, 222–223
Acuff, Roy Claxton: and Tom Ashley, 69; and
   baseball, 223, 279; and Country Music Hall
   of Fame, 313; and Dixon Brothers, 130; and
   Dobro steel guitars, 150; and electrical
   amplification, 225; and J. L. Frank, 218,
   224; and *Grand Ole Opry*, 85, 115, 150, 217,
   218, 223, 224–225, 227, 228, 241, 335, 434;
   health of, 223; and hillbilly music, 223;
   identity as individual singer, 146; income
   of, 227; and instrumental accompaniment,
   222, 225; with Louvin Brothers, 222;
   and Tommy Magness, 147; and medicine
   shows, 7; and Willie Nelson's picnics,
   465; and Nitty Gritty Dirt Band, 454; and
   Foreman Phillips, 219; and political songs,
   159; recordings of, 224, 225, 229, 232, 324,
   464; repertory of, 224–225, 226, 254; and
   Fred Rose, 212, 226, 227–228; and Smoky
   Mountain Boys, 149; as songwriter, 213,
   375; style of, 206, 221–222, 226–227; and
   Shoji Tabuchi, 519; and Rachel Veach, 141;
   vocal style of, 146, 215, 220, 221–222, 223,
   224–227, 258, 268, 283, 302, 334, 335; and
   Hank Williams, 282, 283, 285
Acuff-Rose Publishing House, 212, 227, 228,
   240, 248, 283, 303, 310
Adcock, Eddie, 412, 413, 424, 425, 428
Adkins, Trace, 492
Adolph Hofner's Texans, 199
advertising: and fiddlers, 21; and hillbilly
   music, 112, 119–121, 125; and Mexican
   border stations, 119; and P.I. (per inquiry)
   account, 120–121
agriculture, 2, 3, 9, 13, 35, 48, 152, 208
Aguilera, Christina, 560
Air Transport Command, Special Services
   unit, 219
Akeman, David "Stringbean," 148, 320, 386,
   582n3
Alabama (band), 451, 453, 493–494
Alabama Boys, 204

Aladdin Laddies, 190–191, 202

Aladdin Mantle Lamp Company, 191

Aldean, Jason, 561

Alderman, Tony, *36*

Alexander, Charles, 14

Alka-Seltzer, 112, 116, 119–120

all-country radio stations, 311–312, 314

Allen, Austin, 123–125, 159, 290

Allen, Duane, 452

Allen, Jules Verne, 165

Allen, Lee, 123–125, 159, 290

Allen, Red, 400–401, 424

Allen, Rex, 172, 476, 528

Allen, Rex, Jr., 476

Allen, Rosalie, 244

Allen, Steve, 294

Allen, Terry, 462

Allen Brothers, 123–125, 159, 290

Alley, Alvin, 196

Alley, Shelly Lee, 107, 196

Alley Cats, 196, 197

Allman Brothers Band, 443, 457, 492

Allred, Sam, 437

Almanac Singers, 326

Alpert, Herb, 470

alternative country (alt-country), 520–526, 528–531, 546, 563–564, 566, 570

Altman, Robert, 434–435

Alvin, Dave, 497, 518

Americana, 562–565, 566, 567, 570, 571

Americana Music Association (AMA), 564–565, 566, 567

American Bandstand (television show), 294

American Banjo: Three-Finger and Scruggs Style (album), 414

American Corporation, 240

American Federation of Musicians (AFM), 210–212, 240

American Folklife Center, 151

American Idol (television show), 557, 560, 561

American Record Company (ARC): and Roy Acuff, 224; and Alley Cats, 196; and Gene Autry, 168; and Brunswick, 112; and Callahan Brothers, 130; and Carter Family, 79; and Lew Childre, 141; and Mac and Bob, 132–133; and Tex Ritter, 179; and Arthur Satherley, 46, 168

American Recordings (album), 518

American Saturday Night (album), 559

American Society of Composers, Authors and Publishers (ASCAP), 209–210, 212, 228, 240

American Songwriter, 549–550

American West, 107, 162–163. *See also* western image in country music

Ameripolitan, 571

Anderson, Bill, 340, 352–353, 355, 359, 376, 518, 558

Anderson, John, 271, 333, 480, 483

Anderson, Liz, 345

Anderson, Lynn, 361

Anderson, Pete, 497

Andrews, Jessica, 507

Andrews Sisters, 212, 232, 269

Angel with a Lariat (album), 499

Anglin, Jack, 243, 254–255. *See also* Anglin Brothers; Johnny and Jack

Anglin, Jim, 226, 230, 249–250

Anglin Brothers, 128, 226

Anglo-Celtic immigrants, 1

Anita Kerr Singers, 301, 340

Annie Get Your Gun (Broadway musical), 496

Anthology of American Folk Music, 55, 67, 70, 327–328

anti-Semitism, 49

Appalachian Mountains, 4, 12, 33, 152

Archive of American Folk Song, 151

Arista Records, 450, 507, 515, 517

Arizona Wranglers, 174

Arkansas, 3, 152, 162

Arkie the Woodchopper, 83

Armadillo World Headquarters, Austin, Texas, 460, 465F

Armed Forces Network (AFN), 215, 227, 256, 321–322

Armstrong, Lillian, 104

Armstrong, Louis, 104, 213, 319

Armstrong Twins (Lloyd and Floyd), 238

Arnold, Eddy: and Camel Caravan, 215, 276; and country-pop, 299, 310, 442, 444; death of, 570; and *Grand Ole Opry*, 217, 276, 277, 434; and radio, 264, 277; recordings of, 276–278, 333; repertory of, 277; and Marty Robbins, 308; vocal style of, 275, 276–277, 288, 299; and Don Walser, 521

Arnspiger, Herman, 190–191, *191*, 202, *203*, 205

Arthur, Charline, 293

Arthur, Emry, 55

Arthur Godfrey Show (television show), 307, 309

Arthur Godfrey's Talent Scouts (television show), 309

Artists' Service Bureau, 114

Ashley, Clarence "Tom," 7, 69–70, 328

Ashlock, Jesse, 194, 200, 203, 464, 475

Asia, 320

Asleep at the Wheel, 203, 463, 475, 483–484, 530

Association of Country Entertainers (ACE), 276, 440

Atcher, Bob, 215–216

Atchison, Shelby "Tex," 143, *175*

Atherton, Lewis, 115

Atkins, Chester "Chet": and definition of country music, 474; and *Grand Ole Opry*, 301; guitar style of, 301; and Homer and Jethro, 264; and Waylon Jennings, 470, 471; and Barbara Mandrell, 441; and Charley Pride, 372; and radio, 223, 436; and Jim Reeves, 305; as session musician, 247, 254, 279, 300–302, 309, 313; and Connie Smith, 359; and Merle Travis, 236, 301; and Steven Wariner, 450

Atkins, Jim, 300–301

Atlanta, Georgia: bibliographic resources on country music in, 677; and fiddle contests, 22, 62; and Ralph Peer, 44; radio stations in, 39–40. *See also* WGST (Atlanta); WSB (Atlanta)

Atlanta Old-Time Fiddlers' Contest, 62

atomic energy, 374–375

Attlesey, Bob, Joe, and Merle. *See* Shelton Brothers (Bob, Joe, and Merle)

Auldridge, Mike, 395, 426

Aunt Idy, 216

Austin, Gene, 68, 106

Austin, Lonnie, 61

Austin, Texas: and country-rock, 459–465; music scene of, 367, 472, 480, 519–523, 530; and western swing, 475–476, 530. *See also* KOKE-FM (Austin); KUT (Austin)

Austin City Limits (television show), 437, 476, 519, 543, 566

Australia, 101, 167, 321, 571

Austria, 322

autoharps, 32, 51, 58, 79, 411

Autry, Gene: and Eddy Arnold, 276; and Carl Cotner, 143; and Country Music Hall of Fame, 313; and country-pop, 274; and cowboy music, 168–173, 177; films of, 170–171, 177, 219, 274; and J. L. Frank, 218; and hillbilly music, 170, 171; international popularity of, 321; and medicine shows, 6; and *National Barn Dance*, 115, 168;

photograph of, *169*; radio stations owned by, 240; recordings of, 168–169, 170, 171, 206, 207, 219, 220, 232, 375, 543; repertory of, 226; and risqué songs, 125–126, 127; and Marty Robbins, 308; and Jimmie Rodgers, 108–109, 126, 168, 170; and Fred Rose, 228; in World War II, 219–220; and yodeling, 168

Aycock, Clint, 201

Bacharach, Burt, 299

Back Home Again (album), 538

Back to the Country (radio show), xi

Baez, Joan, 328, 333, 361, 374, 485

Bailes, Homer, *253*

Bailes, Johnnie, *253*, 263

Bailes Brothers (Walter, Johnnie, Homer, and Kyle): and *Louisiana Hayride*, 243, 252; photograph of, *253*; recordings of, 230, 245–246, 389, 512; repertory of, 252, 262, 296; style of, xvi, 251–252, 334, 428

Bailey, Charlie, 251, 400–401

Bailey, Danny, 251, 400–401

Bailey, Deford, 89, 370, 552

Bailey, Razzy, 443

Bailey Brothers (Charlie and Danny), 251, 400–401

Baker, James Britt. *See* Britt, Elton

Baker, Kenny, 408, 420, 421, 431

Baker, Norman, 118

Bakers, 25

Bakersfield, California, 214, 341–345

Bakersfield Brass, 343

Bakunin, Mikhail, 152

Baldknobbers, 519

Balfa Brothers, 331

Ball, Bentley, 38, 163, 579n2

Ball, Marcia, 173, 463

Ball, Wilbur, 126

ballads: and Alabama, 453; Americanization of British ballads, 4–5, 17, 18, 253; banjos in instrumentation of, 148; and Blue Sky Boys, 136; and Dock Boggs, 71; and Callahan Brothers, 130, 131; and country-pop, 560; and cowboy music, 17, 166, 188; and Vernon Dalhart, 73–74, 75; and dulcimers, 31; and Tommy Duncan, 204; event ballads, 54, 57, 331, 349–350; and folksingers, 19; and Great Depression, 152–153; and Woodie Guthrie, 156; and Emmylou Harris, 485; hawkers of, 16, 18, 21; and hillbilly music, 1, 37, 123–124; and Al Hopkins, 115; and Buell Kazee, 67;

and Bradley Kincaid, 66, 121; and Kingston Trio, 326; and Mary Klick, 317; and Louvin Brothers, 253; and Bascom Lunsford, 68; and Mainer's Mountaineers, 144; murder ballads, 17, 56, 137, 253, 258, 326, 404, 512, 515, 556; and *National Barn Dance*, 82; and Molly O'Day, 258; and Luther Ossenbrink, 83; and Brad Paisley, 559; and Jimmie Rodgers, 107; and saga songs, 331–334; sentimental songs compared to, 12, 18–19; and B. F. Shelton, 77; and Shelton Brothers, 128; and Skillet Lickers, 62; and social class, 3; and Stanley Brothers, 404; and *Sunday Morning Gathering*, 216; and Jimmie Tarlton, 123; and textile workers as country singers, 157; and traditional ballads, 3, 17–18, 111, 161; and Doc Watson, 329

Balsley, Phil, 451

Baltimore, Maryland, and bluegrass, 410, 411, 431

Bandera, Texas, 518, 519

Bandy, Moe, 443, 477, 480, 482, 519

banjos: and blackface minstrel shows, 29, 30; and bluegrass, 144, 386, 388, 413; and Dock Boggs's style, 71; chromatic style, 408, 413, 424, 427; claw-hammer style, 404, 415; and country dances, 21, 26, 34; and country-pop, 445; and electrical amplification, 317; and jazz music, 30, 425; and Bill Keith's style, 408–409; and Uncle Dave Macon's style, 30, 86, 148, 386; men as banjo players, 26; plectrum style, 397, 413; role of, 30–31, 148; and Earl Scruggs, 386–387, 388, 391, 393, 394, 397, 406, 407, 408, 413, 414, 422, 424; and string bands, 29, 30, 31, 50, 58; three-finger roll style, 145, 148, 386–387, 393, 396, 400, 404, 406; and Doc Watson, 329

Banner records, 112

Barbara Mandrell and the Mandrell Sisters (television series), 436

Barbarosa (film), 435

Bare, Bobby, 331, 334–335, 357, 376, 470, 472

Barfield, Johnny, 264

Barnard, Junior, 204

Barn Dance Fiddlers, 83

Barn Dance Sweethearts (Martha and James Carson), 251

Barnes, Dave, 323

Barnyard Frolics (radio show), 302

Barrel House, Bakersfield, 344

Bar-X Cowboys, 196, 197

basses: and bluegrass, 393; and Johnny Bond, 171; and electrical amplification, 239–240, 339, 423; and honky-tonk music, 183; slapped bass, 255, 290, 298, 427; string basses, 144, 148–149, 183, 239; walking bass, 339

Bate, Alcyone, 85

Bate, Dr. Humphrey, 85, 89

Battles, Charlie, 495

Baum, Clyde, 252, 255, 383

Baxter, Don, 119

Bayou Boys, 412

Bean, Janet, 529

Bean Blossom Festival, 420

Bear Family Records, 322, 570, 586n12

Beasler, Norma Jean, 316

Beatles, 280, 425, 455, 492, 502

Beaulieu, Johnny, 278

Beck, Jim, 246

Bedell, Cora, 100

Behrens, Jerry, 108, 122

Belafonte, Harry, 326, 329

Belgium, 322

Bell, Delia, 429–430, 485

Bell, William, 565

Bellamy Brothers (Howard and Dave), 443, 444, 451, 494, 561

Benatar, Pat, 560

Bennett, Sheldon, 144

Bennett, Tony, 560

Benson, Ray, 475

Benson, Willie, xiv

Bentley, Dierks, 559

Berea College, Kentucky, 66

Berg, Matraca, 549

Bergen, Dick, 218

Berkeley, Busby, 154

Berline, Byron, 427, 504

Bernard, Al, 205

Berry, Chuck, 289, 290, 417

Berry Pickin' in the Country (album), 417

The Best Little Whorehouse in Texas (film), 360, 435

Beverly Hillbillies (band), 174–175

The Beverly Hillbillies (television show), 334, 418, 429

Beyoncé, 546, 547–550, *549*, 551, 552, 557, 571–572

Big D Jamboree (radio show), 234, 243, 278, 293, 296, 339

Biggar, George, 116

Big Sandy and his Fly-Rite Boys, 530

Bigsby, Paul, 239

Bigsby guitars, 239

Big Slim, 142

Billboard: Americana chart of, 565; and Eddie Arnold's appearances, 277; country charts of, 229, 261, 268, 272, 278, 288, 302, 303, 334, 337, 342, 351, 353, 355, 376–377, 491, 493, 496, 512, 523, 541, 566, 569; coverage of country music in, 167, 213, 232, 234; and Tennessee Ernie Ford, 295; on hillbilly music, 219; pop music chart of, 309; reviews of country music, 207, 283; and Soundscan, 493

Bill Woods Band, 342

Birchmere Restaurant, Alexandria, Virginia, 426

Black, Bob, 407

Black, Clint, 489, 492, 501

Blackboard, Bakersfield, 344

Blackboard Jungle (film), 290

Black Draught, 120, 316

blackface minstrel shows: and Roy Acuff, 223; and banjos, 29, 30; and Al Bernard, 205; and dialect, 127; and fiddlers, 21, 22, 27, 29; and folk music, 10; and *Grand Ole Opry*, 218; hillbilly music compared to, 115; and hillbilly songs, 52; instrumentation of, 29; and Uncle Dave Macon, 86; marketing of minstrel tunes, 37; and medicine shows, 7; popular songs of, 9–10; and professional song-and-dance men, 20, 30; and Jimmie Rodgers, 95; and singing groups, 25; and southern music, 36; and yodeling, 105

Blackhawk, 494

black influence: on barrelhouse style of piano playing, 198; on country music, 5, 6, 23, 80, 87, 123–124, 127–128, 180, 264, 290; and dialect, 73, 127; on gospel music, 154–155, 510; on guitar style, 204; on hillbilly music, 71, 122; in Louisiana, 160–161; on rock-and-roll music, 289–290, 292; and steel guitar, 150; and western swing, 188, 205; on white folk music, 1, 14, 34

black music: and cultural transmission, 5–6, 11, 551; and Jimmie Davis, 127; early recordings, 6, 41–42; and fiddles, 20; and Red Foley, 243; and folk culture, 2; market for, 42; and Syd Nathan, 245, 246; and Ralph Peer, 41–42, 44, 45; and race records,

44, 112, 124, 211, 213, 289, 551–552; and Jimmie Rodgers, 6, 91, 93, 94, 104–105, 124, 125; and shape-note singing, 26; and soul, 123; and Hank Williams, 6, 282; and youth culture, 293

black musicians in country music: and banjo playing style, 30; and Beyoncé, 551; and Jimmie Davis, 127; and Delmore Brothers, 128; and fiddlers, 22; guitar styles of, 30, 32; and Bill Monroe, 382–383; and Charley Pride, 358, 369, 370–374; recognition of, 6

Black Shirts, 224

Blackwood Brothers, 292, 451

Blake, Norman, 329, 455

Blake, Randy, 244

Blanchard, Lowell, 223

Blevins, Rubye. *See* Montana, Patsy

Bliss, P. P., 14

Blonde on Blonde (album), 454

Bloodshot Records, 528–529

Bloodshot Revival Records, 528

Bluebird Records: and Blue Ridge Entertainers (Bolick Brothers), 136; and Delmore Brothers, 128; and Kentucky Pardners, 383; and Mainer's Mountaineers, 145; and Monroe Brothers, 137; and Musical Brownies, 194; and patriotic songs, 229; and George Puckett, 63; and Tennessee Ramblers, 143; and Victor Records, 112

bluegrass: and Americana, 565; bibliographic essay on, 659–666; and country music parks, 409; and Dixie Chicks, 511; and Dobro steel guitars, 150; and Steve Earle, 500, 533; and ensemble style, 388, 395; and Flatt and Scruggs, 391–392, 396, 399, 402, 407, 414, 418–419, 423; and gospel music, 250, 388, 397, 410, 428, 432; history of, 380–382, 390–391, 395–396, 420; instrumentation of, 144, 387, 388, 394, 401, 413, 417, 418, 423, 425, 432, 533; and international popularity of country music, 324; and Louvin Brothers, 254; and Mainer's Mountaineers, 144, 145; and Bill Monroe, 221, 380, 381, 382–391, 394, 395, 396, 399, 401, 403, 405, 407–408, 409, 413, 418, 421, 423, 424, 428, 431, 531, 533, 534, 541; as musical subculture, 418; and Tim O'Brien, 525–526; and Dolly Parton, 533; and recording companies, 419; repertory of, 380, 383, 386, 388, 391, 396, 403, 406, 414–415, 416, 418, 423, 424–431; as roots music, 313; and shifts in band personnel, 400, 407–408, 412, 421, 424, 426; and Carl Smith, 268; and songwriters, 250, 251, 357; and Ernest Stoneman, 59; and Marty Stuart, 513; styles of, 214, 381, 382, 423, 484, 491, 531, 533–534; and television, 334, 424, 437; traditional bluegrass, 382, 423, 425, 428, 429–431, 531, 533–535, 541, 542; and urban folk revival, 328, 396, 405, 408–409, 413, 414–417, 424–425; and vocal styles, 137, 144, 380, 382, 384–385, 388, 394, 401, 414, 428, 429, 430, 451, 533, 534, 537–538; and Doc Watson, 329; and women, 430, 535, 537–538; and youth culture, 413, 539, 541–542. *See also* newgrass; progressive bluegrass

Bluegrass Album Band, 432

Bluegrass Alliance, 425, 427, 504

Blue Grass Boys, 221, 384, *385*, 386–392, 397, 400, 402, 407–408

Bluegrass Cardinals, 429

Bluegrass Kun-Tree, 429

Blue Ridge Entertainers (Bolick Brothers), 136

Blue Ridge Entertainers (Roy Hall), 146, 149, 221, 384, 403

Blue Ridge Mountain Entertainers, 69

Blue Ridge Mountain Folk, 140

Blue Ridge Playboys, 196, 197–198

Blue Ridge Records, 416

Bluer Than Midnight (album), 430

Blue Sky Boys (Bill and Earl Bolick): instrumentation of, 134, 136, 251; and Lilly Brothers, 410; photograph of, *135*; recordings of, 111, 137, 419; repertory of, 133, 134–137, 251, 252, 262, 296, 578n6; style of, xvi, 206, 251; vocal style of, 136–137, 397, 405; and World War II, 221

blues music: black cultural origins of, 5, 33–34, 122, 123–124, 125; and bluegrass, 427, 539; and Cajun music, 180; and Delmore Brothers, 128–129; and duet singing, 128; and hillbilly music, 71, 122, 123–124, 126; as influence on country music, 180; as influence on folk style, 27; and Maddox Brothers and Rose, 255; and Bill Monroe, 383; and Prohibition, 124–125; recording of, 42; and Jimmie Rodgers, 95, 104–105, 106, 122; and rural areas, 11; and southern rock, 456; and urban folk revival, 327, 328; and Bob Wills, 205. *See also* country blues; rhythm-and-blues music

Bobby Bare and Friends (television show), 437

Bob Miller Publishing Company, 57

Boehlert, Eric, 569

Bogan, Henry, 190

Boggs, Moran Lee "Dock," 6, 51, 71, 205, 327, 328

Boggs, Noel, 144, 151, 188

Bogguss, Suzy, 436, 446, 491–492, 507–508, 512

"Bohemian" music: as influence on country music, 180–181; and Willie Nelson, 354; and western swing, 188. *See also* Czech-country music

Bolick, Bill, 134–137, 252, 397, 407. *See also* Blue Sky Boys (Bill and Earl Bolick)

Bolick, Earl, 134–137, 252. *See also* Blue Sky Boys (Bill and Earl Bolick)

Bonaguro, Alison, 557

Bond, Johnny, 146, 171, 238, 250, 274, 353, 528

bones, as instruments, 29

Bon Jovi, 492

Bonner, M. J., 40

Bonnie and Clyde (film), 391, 418

Bonsall, Joe, 452

Bonus Bill for World War I veterans, 158

Bonus March (1932), 158

boogie tunes: and Delmore Brothers, 128, 246, 265, 290; and Red Foley, 242–243, 265, 290; and Moon Mullican, 195, 198, 246, 265, 269, 290; in postwar era, 264–265

booking agents: and bluegrass, 531; in Nashville, 310; in postwar era, 240–241, 247, 300

Boone (television series), 436

Boone County Jamboree (radio show), 116, 216

Boone Creek (band), 432, 486, 504

Booth, Tony, 340

Boston, Massachusetts, 410–411. *See also* WBZ (Boston)

Bottle Rockets, 528

Bowen, Jimmy, 490, 506

Bowers, Bryan, 32

Bowman, Don, 470

Bowman, Ronnie, 535

Boxcar Willie, 324, 474, 519

Boyd, Bill, 199–200

Boyd, Jim, 199–200, 204, 476

Boys from Indiana, 429

BR5-49, 530

Braddock, Robert Valentine "Bobby," 349, 355, 356, 479

Bradford, Perry, 42

Bradley, Dale Ann, 537

Bradley, Owen, 247, 309

Brady, Buddy, 190

Bragg, Billy, 565

branding, 568–569

Brand New Man (album), 505

Branson, Missouri, 518–519

Brasfield, Rod, 217, 242

Brasfield, Uncle Cyp and Aunt Sap, 315

Brazos Valley Boys, 266, 475

breakdowns, 62, 148, 188, 203, 204, 393

Breakfast Club (radio show), 277

Brewer, Teresa, 444

Briley, Beverly, 312

Brinkley, John R., 117–118

Bristol, Tennessee, 76, 79, 96

British Academy of Country Music (BACM), 323

British immigrants and migrants, 4, 5, 31

British Isles, popularity of country music in, 321–325

British tradition: and folk culture, 1–2, 4–5, 17, 18, 20, 22, 23, 27, 33, 123, 161, 267; and hillbilly songs, 51–52, 54, 66, 137. *See also* ballads; Celticism

Britt, Elton, 155, 175, 178–179, 229, 375, 521

Broadcast Music, Inc. (BMI), 209–210, 212, 220, 240, 248, 289, 311, 353

Broady, Joseph A. (Steve), 73

Brockman, Polk, 44–46, 56–57

bro country, 546–547, 550

Broken Spoke, Austin, Texas, 460

Brooks, Garth: and Dixie Chicks, 511; and *Grand Ole Opry*, 492; and neo-traditionalism, 490; photograph of, *503*; popularity of, 501–502, 506; recordings of, 489, 508, 566

Brooks, Leon Eric "Kix," 505–506

Brooks, Rex, 387

Brooks & Dunn (Kix Brooks and Ronnie Dunn), 505–506

Broonzy, Big Bill, 325

brother duets: and Bellamy Brothers, 451; and Delmore Brothers, 129; and Everly Brothers, 295; and Jerry and Sky, 410; and Johnny and Jack, 254; and Mac and Bob, 132; and McReynolds Brothers, 405; and Nashville Bluegrass Band, 534; and Nashville Grass, 394; and Shelton Brothers, 200–201; and Ricky Skaggs and Tony Rice, 486; and Wilburn Brothers, 315

Brothers Four, 326

Brower, Cecil, *192*, 194–195, 199–200, 202

Brown, Bonnie, 302

Brown, Durwood, 191, *192*, 194–195

Brown, Frank "Hylo," 329, 414–415

Brown, George, 108

Brown, Greg, 100

Brown, Jim Ed, 302, 538

Brown, Johnny Mack, 172

Brown, Junior, 520–521

Brown, Maxine, 302

Brown, Milton: and Aladdin Laddies, 190–191, 202; and hot dance style, 196; and Light Crust Doughboys, 193, 204; and Musical Brownies, 144, 187, *192*, 193, 194–195; and music from cities' "sin streets," 11; and western swing, 189, 202, 235, 475

Brown, Roy, 289

Brown, T. Graham, 443

Brown, Tony, 462, 490, 504, 515

Browne, Harry, 38

Browne, Jackson, 453, 559

Browns, 302

Brown's Ferry Four, 256, 262–263, 320

Bruce, Ed, 477

Brumley, Albert E., 155, 342, 404

Brumley, Tom, 341, 342

Bruner, Bill, 108

Bruner, Cliff, 127, 187, 194–196, 198, 206

Brunswick Record Company, 46, 47, 67, 112, 132, 166, 190, 205

brush arbor meetings, 13–14

Bryan, Luke, 546, *546*

Bryan, William Jennings, 55

Bryant, Boudleaux, 144, 228, 249, 250–251, 296, 417–418

Bryant, Felice, 228, 249, 250–251, 296, 417–418

Bryant, Hoyt "Slim," 143, 149

Bryant, Jimmy, 239, 341

Bub, Mike, 534

Buchanan, Roy, 239

Buckaroos, 342, 343, 497, 531

Buckingham, Steve, 490

Buck Lake Ranch, Angola, Indiana, 218

Buck Owens Ranch (television show), 343

Buck White Family, 423

Buffett, Jimmy, 463, 558

Bullet Records, 245, 339

Bumgarner, Samantha, 26, 58

Burch, Curtis, 427

Burnett, Richard "Dick," 18, 50, 54–55, 66

Burnette, Lester Alvin "Smiley," 170–171

Burnham, Bo, 547

Burns, "Happy" Hal, 218–219, 231

Burns, Ken, xi

Burns, Kenneth "Jethro," 148, 263–264, 279, 427

Burns, Walter Noble, 56–57

Burr, Henry, 82

Burrus Mills, 191–192, 193

Burton, James, 239, 341

Busby, Buzz, 412

Bush, George W., 552, 553, 589–590n10, 590n13

Bush, Johnny, 340, 479, 519

Bush, Roger, 427

Bush, Sam, 427, 485, 539, 541, *541*

Bush band (Australian country music), 571

Buskirk, Paul, 132, 148

Butcher, Dwight, 108, 109, 179

Butler, Carl, 334, 394

Butler, Pearl, 334

Byrd, Billy, 186

Byrd, Jerry, 151, 247

Byrd, Robert, 412, 438–439

Byrd, Tracy, 492, 505, 516

Byrds, 425, 455–456

Cackle Sisters, 141

Cain, Benny, 412

Cain, Vallie, 412

Cain's Academy, Tulsa, 202

Cajun music: and blues music, 180; and Harry Choates, 270; and guitars, 29; as influence in country music, 180, 505; and Doug Kershaw, 319, 367, 369; and Moon Mullican, 270; and Jimmy Newman, 330–331; in Texas, 162; and urban folk revival, 327; and western swing, 188

Calaway, William R., 224

Calhoun, Fred "Papa," *192*, 194–195, 198, 204

California: and cowboy music, 160, 173–178; and electrical amplification, 239; and honky-tonk music, 236, 268, 341–345, 347; Okies' migration to, 152, 156, 208, 214, 235, 255, 341, 346; in postwar era, 234–239; recording companies in, 113. *See also specific cities*

California sound, 341–342

Callahan, Bill, 172

Callahan Brothers (Homer "Bill" and Walter

"Joe"), xiii, 122, 128, 130–132, *131*, 140, 147, 221

Camel Caravan, 215, 276

Campbell, Archie, 320, 437

Campbell, Cecil, 143

Campbell, Glen, 183, 318–319, 444, 445, 449, 450, 519

Campbell, Muryel "Zeke," 187, 193, 204

camp meetings, 12–13, 420

Canada, 109, 117, 278, 437, 445, 499, 510

Cannon, Ellen, 190

Cantrell's Horse Farm, Roanoke, 419–420

Cantwell, Bob, 404

Capitol Records: and American Federation of Musicians, 211; and California sound, 341; and Stoney Edwards, 373; and Merle Haggard, 345; and Ferlin Husky, 306–307; and Louvin Brothers, 253; and Bob Luman, 450; and Jim and Jesse McReynolds, 406; and Anne Murray, 445; and Buck Owens, 342; and Wynn Stewart, 345; and Hank Thompson, 266; and Merle Travis, 236; and Tex Williams, 236; and Faron Young, 307

Cardwell, Jack, 286

Carlisle, Bill, 126, 223, 263, 518

Carlisle, Clifford Raymond "Cliff," 104, 108, 126, 127–128, 150, 263, 394

Carnegie Hall, 234, 269, 392, 414

carnivals, 21

Carolina Chocolate Drops, xvi, 552

Carolina Tar Heels, 69

Carousel Club, Nashville, 301

Carpenter, Mary Chapin, 505, 509, 523

Carson, Fiddlin' John: and Roy Acuff, 223; bands of, 61; and Brockman, 44, 56; at old-time fiddlers' convention, *36*; and political songs, 159; recordings of, 43, 44–46, 111; and string bands, 58; vocal style of, 45, 50, 51, 63; WSB radio appearances, 40, 44

Carson, James, 221, 251, 257

Carson, Jenny Lou, 242, 250

Carson, Johnny, 318, 479

Carson, Martha (Irene Amburgey), 221, 251, 257, 262, 263

Carter, Alvin Pleasant, 52, *77*, 78–81, 225. *See also* Carter Family

Carter, Anita, 257

Carter, Anna, 126

Carter, Deana, 509

Carter, Ezra, 78

Carter, Helen, 257

Carter, Jason, 534

Carter, Jimmy, 376, 438, 468

Carter, June, 257, 319, 570

Carter, Maybelle Addington: and autoharp, 32, 78; guitar style of, 149, 156; instruments played by, 78, 79; and Mother Maybelle and the Carter Sisters, 247, 257; and Nitty Gritty Dirt Band, 454; photograph of, *77*; recordings of, 247; and television, 319; vocal style of, 79. *See also* Carter Family

Carter, Rosalynn, 438

Carter, Sara Dougherty, *77*, 78–79, 81, 108

Carter, Wilf. *See* Montana Slim (Wilf Carter)

Carter Family: and Roy Acuff, 223, 225; and Iris DeMent, 524; disbanding of, 257; and Foggy Mountain Boys, 391; and Great Depression, 154; and Woodie Guthrie, 156; instrumental sound of, 79; and Mexican border stations, 119; music of, xiii; photograph of, *77*; public appearances of, 79–80; and radio, 78, 80, 111; recordings of, 44, 76, 77, 78–80, 111, 528, 564; repertory of, 80–81; and Jimmie Rodgers, 108; and Stanley Brothers, 403; and urban folk revival, 327, 414; and veneration of home and family, 78, 81; vocal style of, 70, 76, 79; and Mac Wiseman, 398

Carter Sisters, 247

Cartwright Brothers (Bernard and Jack), 165, 188

Carver, Bill, 261

Carver, Cynthia May. *See* Cousin Emmy

Car Wheels on a Gravel Road (album), 525

Cash, Johnny: alleged prison record of, 345; and Americana, 565; and black music, 292; and country-pop, 299; death of, 570; and Bob Dylan, 330; and *Grand Ole Opry*, 244; and Merle Haggard, 345, 346; and Doug Kershaw, 369; and Kris Kristofferson, 357; and Newport Folk Festival, 329–330; photograph of, *297*; and politics, 437–438; practical jokes of, 472; and radio, 496; recordings of, 357, 378, 459, 561; and rockabilly music, 296–297, 298; and saga songs, 332; as songwriter, 297, 298, 319, 330, 349, 351, 550; and Statler Brothers, 451; and Marty Stuart, 513; and television, 318, 319, 369; vocal style of, 298; and youth culture, 517–518

Cash, June Carter, 319, 570

Cash, Rosanne, 459, 462, 509

Cash, W. J., 20, 224

Cassell, Pete, 275

Castle Recording Company, 246–247

Catholics, 367

CBS, 232, 309, 317

Cedarwood Publishing Company, 310

Cellar Full of Folk (radio show), 323

cellos, 51, 149, 190

Celticism: and fiddling, 27; in southern folk culture, 4, 20, 23; and urban folk revival, 524, 526

Centers, Roy Lee, 422

Chad Mitchell Trio, 326

Chappelear, Leon, 201, 202

Charles, Ray, 289, 370, 444, 561, 562

Charles River Boys, 411

Charlie Daniels Band, 457

Chattanooga Medicine Company, 120, 316

Chatwell, J. R., 195

chautauquas, 7, 32, 150

Cheap Trick, 550

Cheatham Street Warehouse, San Marcos, Texas, 480

cheating songs, 171, 269, 274, 349, 360, 482, 512

Chenoweth, William B., 58–59

Chenoweth's Cornfield Symphony Orchestra, 59

Cherokee Cowboys, 325, 338, 339, 340, 473

Cherry, Hugh, 245, 488

Cherry Bombs, 462, 504

Chesney, Kenny, 492

Chesnut, Jerry, 378

Chesnutt, Bob, 516

Chesnutt, Mark, 271, 491, 492, 513, 516

Chet Atkins compromise, 300–302, 313, 379

Chieftains, 524

Childre, Lew, 7, 121–122, 141–142, 201, 231, 386, 419

Chinaberry Sidewalks: A Memoir (Crowell), 462, 588n17

Ching, Barbara, 564

CHNS (Halifax, Nova Scotia), 278

Choates, Harry, 270–271, 374

Christgau, Robert, 557–558

Christian, Ben, 196

Christian, Charlie, 149, 204

Christian, Elmer, 196

Christian, Tom, 105

Chuck Wagon Gang, xiii, 121, 126, 188, 262

Church of England, 12

circuses, 7, 21

cities: black migration to, 41; ethnic subcultures in, 38; growth of, 2; interaction with rural areas, 7–9; and religious music, 14–15; "sin streets" of, 10–11; and southern migrants, 213–214; and urban-middle-class audience, 11, 19, 98, 171, 249, 269, 274, 317, 370, 414, 436; and urban-oriented popular entertainment, 37; and urban revivals, 14. *See also specific cities*

civil rights movement, 326, 372, 375–376

Civil War, 15, 19, 153, 216, 349, 350, 429

CKLW-TV (Windsor, Ontario), 402

clarinets, 51

Clark, Dick, 294

Clark, Guy, 327, 331, 461–462, 463, 494, 499, 500

Clark, Roy, 308, 320, 323, 353, 412, 519

Clark, Susanna, 461–462

Clark, Terri, 492, 499

Clark, Thomas D., xv

Clay, Henry, 21, 243

Clayton, Paul, 416

Clement, Jack, 372

Clements, Vassar, 391, 406, 407, 455

Clements, Zeke, 116, 229, 275

Clifton, Bill, 323–324, 409, 412, 416, 419, 428, 525

Clinch Mountain Boys, 405, 422, 532

Clinch Mountain Clan, 261

Clinch Mountain Country (album), 515

Cline, Charlie, 407

Cline, Curly Ray, 422

Cline, Patsy, 308–309, 310, 353–354, 358, 362, 499

Clinton, Bill, 490, 511, 525

Clodhoppers, 84

Clooney, Rosemary, 263

Clower, Jerry, 320

CMA Awards: Album of the Year, 515; and Beyoncé's performance of "Daddy Lessons," 546, 547–551, 549, 552, 557, 572; Entertainer of the Year, 362, 373, 377, 442, 453, 458, 468, 504; and exposure of country music, 436; Female Vocalist of the Year, 367, 440, 515, 537; Vince Gill as host of, 504; Horizon Award, 496, 498; hosting of, 558, 565; Male Vocalist of the Year, 496; Recorded Event of the Year, 490; Single of the Year, 457, 487, 498; Song of the Year, 357; Vocal Duo of the Year, 506; Vocal Group of the Year, 418, 451, 495

CMA Music Festival, 542

CMT (Country Music Television), 505, 541, 549, 550, 552, 554, 557, 568–569

Coal Miner's Daughter (film), 362, 435

Coal Miner's Daughter (Lynn), 362

coal-mining songs, 87, 152–153, 238, 333, 349, 356, 361–362

Coben, Cy, 250

Cochran, Hank, 309, 340, 353–354, 355, 356, 570

Coe, David Allan, 378, 472–473, 512, 566

Coffman, Wanna, 192, 194

Cohan, George M., 50

Cohen, Anne, 24, 51–52

Cohen, John, 328

Cohen, Norm, 24, 51–52

Cohen, Paul, 113, 246, 261, 312

Cohn, Nudie "the Tailor," 172, 238–239, 273, 317, 456, 518

Cole, Grady, 155, 258

Cole, Hazel, 155, 258

Cole, M. M., 112, 210

Cole, Nat "King," 444

Coleman, Keith, 235

Coleman County Cowboys, 475

Colleran, William D., 409

Colley, Sarah Ophelia. *See* Minnie Pearl

Collie, Biff, 245

Collins, Carr P., 118

Collins, Larry, 238

Collins, Lorrie, 238

Collins, Randall, 429

Collins, Tommy, 341, 342, 347

Collins Kids, 238

Colter, Jessi, 439, 473–474

Coltman, Bob, 138–139

Columbia films, 170

Columbia Record Company: and Allen Brothers, 124; and American Federation of Musicians, 211; and Bentley Ball, 38, 163, 579n2; and Moe Bandy, 482; and Blue Grass Boys, 386; and Carter Family, 79; and Chuck Wagon Gang, 121; and Spade Cooley, 236; and Wilma Lee Cooper, 260; and country music as old familiar tunes, 16; and Rodney Crowell, 462; and Vernon Dalhart, 57; and Delmore Brothers, 128; and Flatt and Scruggs, 391, 392, 394, 415, 425; and Lefty Frizzell, 272; and hillbilly music, 46; and Don Law, 246; and Barbara Mandrell, 441; and Bill Monroe, 391, 407; and George

Morgan, 276; and Molly O'Day, 259, 399; and Okeh Records, 112; and Ralph Peer, 44; and Ray Price, 339; and George Puckett, 63; and Marty Robbins, 307–308; and Jimmie Rodgers, 387; and saga songs, 331–332; and Skillet Lickers, 62; and Stanley Brothers, 404, 407; and Statler Brothers, 451; and Jimmie Tarlton, 123; and Taylor-Griggs Louisiana Melody Makers, 190

comb and paper, as instrument, 32

comedians in country music: and banjo players, 386, 387; and bass players, 149; and bluegrass, 413; and Callahan Brothers, 132; and Jimmy Dickens, 268; and Geezinslaw Brothers, 437; and *Grand Ole Opry*, 242; and *Hee Haw*, 319–320; and Hoosier Hot Shots, 216; and Ferlin Husky, 306, 307; and Grandpa Jones, 69, 256; and Beecher Kirby, 225; and Lewis Family, 428; and Lulu Belle and Scotty, 139; and Mack Magaha, 397; and rural skits, 62, 114; and Shelton Brothers, 201; and James Clell Summey, 225; and television, 315, 316; and women, 358

Comets, 290

comic songs, 69, 75, 216, 263–264, 268, 307

Commander Cody and His Lost Planet Airmen, 530

commercialization of country music: and all-country radio stations, 311–312, 314; ballad makers' transition to, 18; bibliographic essays on, 637–645, 650–659, 666–673; and black musicians, 6; and branding, 568–569; and Chet Atkins compromise, 301; and Country Music Association, 312; and country-pop, 287–288; and cowboy music, 165, 167; and folk cultural expressions, 2; and harmony singing, 25; and hat acts, 492, 493, 505; and hillbilly music, 31, 42, 44–48, 49, 50, 58, 59, 69, 70–71, 73–75, 96, 111, 113–114, 118–119, 189, 211–213, 219, 327, 328; and identity and definition of country music, 324, 417, 433, 439–441, 444–445, 474, 488, 489–493, 506–507, 512, 520, 522, 542–543, 545–549–554, 557, 560–561, 564, 565–567, 568, 569, 570, 571–572; and management, 240–241; men's monopolization of, 26–27; and Ralph Peer, 44, 45; in postwar era, 233, 234, 240–242, 245, 248, 264; and preservation of southern origins, 1; and radio barn dances, 90; and recording companies, ix, 16–17, 36, 111;

and songwriters, 248–249, 355, 356, 379; and urban areas, 38; and western swing, 189; and Hank Williams's death, 287; and women as instrumentalists, 26; and World War II, 209

Common Thread: The Songs of the Eagles (album), 492

communism, 375

Como, Perry, 277, 444

Confederate Mountaineers, 411

Confederate nostalgia, 349

Confederate Railroad, 494

Confederate reunions, 21

conjunto music, 524

Conlee, John, 479

Conley, Earl Thomas, 443, 493

Connell, Dudley, 430–431

Connors, Cecil Ingram. *See* Parsons, Gram

Conqueror Record Time (radio show), 168

conservatism: country music's identification with, 374, 375–376, 434, 468, 507, 553; and gender roles, 360–361, 362, 363; in South, 2, 3, 6, 11, 35, 48–49, 153, 350

Constitution Hall, Washington, DC, 227

Contemporary Christian music, 498, 542

Continental Club, Austin, Texas, 520

Cook, Jeff, 453

Cooke, Jack, 422, 431

Cooley, Donnell Clyde "Spade," 235–236, 528

Coolidge, Calvin, 47

Coon Creek Girls, 139–140, *140*, 216, 416

coon songs, 22–23

Cooper, I. W., 100

Cooper, James Fenimore, 162

Cooper, Myrtle Eleanor, 68, 115, 139, 216, 242, 375

Cooper, Stoney, 117, 260–261, 325, 389, 409, 411, 426

Cooper, Wilma Lee: and bluegrass, 409, 411, 426; and *Grand Ole Opry*, 325; independent identity of, 257; and Leary Family Singers, 259–260; recordings of, 260, 389; and religious music, 250, 258, 261; and Fred Rose, 260–261; vocal style of, 261, 268; and *Wheeling Jamboree*, 117, 261

Copas, Lloyd "Cowboy": death of, 309; and *Grand Ole Opry*, 217; and Clayton McMichen, 143; recordings of, 245, 248, 250, 263, 334; repertory of, 266–267

Copland, Aaron, 33

Cordle, Larry, 513

Cornbread Matinee (radio show), 266
Cornfield Symphony Orchestra, 59
Costello, Elvis, 338, 454, 550
Cotner, Carl, 143, 147, 171
Cotton-Eyed Joe (dance step), 504
counterculture of 1960s, 356, 376–377, 426,
    460, 465, 518
Country Aircheck Weekly, 557
Country and Western Music Academy, 345
country blues, 42, 122–124, 127–131, 264, 289
Country Boys, 399
Country Gazette, 425, 426–427
Country Gentlemen: and progressive
    bluegrass, 325, 380, 412–413, 423, 424–425,
    426, 432; recordings of, 333; and Ricky
    Skaggs, 486
country jazz: and Callahan Brothers, 132;
    and Carl Cotner, 147; and Merle Haggard,
    347; and Homer and Jethro, 264, 475; and
    mandolin style, 148; and Musical Brownies,
    194; and Radio Cowboys, 144; and Jimmie
    Rodgers, 104; and Roy Newman and His
    Boys, 199–200
Country Music Association (CMA): and
    bluegrass, 565; establishment of, 310–312;
    expansion of, xvi; and identity of country
    music, 439–440, 490; and Simmons Market
    Research Bureau survey, 493; and tributes,
    306; twenty-fifth anniversary celebration,
    438–439. *See also* CMA Awards; CMA
    Music Festival
Country Music Foundation, xiv
Country Music Hall of Fame and Museum:
    establishment of, 312; honorees of, 198, 218,
    227, 278, 280, 306, 313, 359, 421, 477, 496;
    Library and Media Center, 313; omissions
    from, 44, 313; Walkway of the Stars,
    312–313
country music parks, 409
Country Music Reporter, 299
Country Music Television (CMT), 505, 541,
    549, 550, 552, 554, 557, 568–569
countrypolitan music, 308, 313, 319, 361
country-pop: and Eddie Arnold, 299, 310,
    442, 444; bibliographic essay on, 645–650;
    and Clint Black, 501; and Patsy Cline,
    308–309, 310; and Skeeter Davis, 302–303;
    and definition of country music, 440–441,
    444–445, 474, 488, 506; development of,
    287–288, 298–299, 300, 302–303, 309–310,
    313, 314, 316, 491; and Crystal Gayle, 362;

and hard country, 395; and Faith Hill,
    510; and Ferlin Husky, 306–307; instru-
    mentation of, 299, 445; and international
    popularity of country music, 324; and
    Sonny James, 296, 299; and Waylon
    Jennings, 471; and Reba McEntire, 495;
    and Barbara Mandrell, 440, 441–442, 485;
    and Jimmy Newman, 330; and Oak Ridge
    Boys, 452; and Dolly Parton, 367, 485; and
    Ray Price, 338, 340–341; and Jim Reeves,
    302, 303–306, 310, 324; and Marty Robbins,
    288, 299, 307–308, 310; and Connie Smith,
    359; and songwriters, 303; and television,
    317, 319; and Carrie Underwood, 556, 557,
    560; and *Urban Cowboy* soundtrack, 436;
    and urban folk revival, 326, 330; and vocal
    style, 274–277, 302, 442; and Gene Watson,
    482–483; and Slim Whitman, 279; and
    Mac Wiseman, 398, 399, 417; and Faron
    Young, 307
country rap, 571
country-rock: in Austin, Texas, 459–465; and
    Garth Brooks, 502; ethnic diversity in,
    367; and Mike Ireland, 529; and Waylon
    Jennings, 471; and Patty Loveless, 515;
    and Marshall Tucker Band, 488; and Gram
    Parsons, 455–456, 459, 500; and Uncle
    Tupelo, 528
Country Store (band), 486
Country Style (television show), 412
county-line taverns, 182
County Records, 419
Coursey, Farris, 247
Cousin Emmy, 139, 148, 401
Covington, Pappy, 243
Cowan, John, 539, *541*
Coward, Buster, 199, 273
cowboy influence on modern country music,
    321, 324
cowboy music: affectation of performers,
    122, 179; and Gene Autry, 168–173, 177;
    bibliographic essay on, 624–632; and
    films, 170–172, 177, 179, 476; and Great
    Depression, 154; and Hawaiian musicians,
    104; and Hot Club of Cowtown, 530; and
    international popularity of country music,
    324; and lonesome cowboy wail, 105; and
    Mexican border stations, 119; and Prairie
    Ramblers, 143; and recording companies,
    38, 113, 173, 543; and Goebel Reeves,
    165–166; revival in 1970s, 476–477, 484;

and Marty Robbins, 308, 333, 476; and
  Jimmie Rodgers, 107, 167, 168, 170; and
  song collections, 163; and western cowgirls,
  141, 173, 193, 258; and western swing, 188;
  and Slim Whitman, 279, 280, 325
Cowboy Ramblers, 173, 200
Cowboy Songs and Other Frontier Ballads
  (Lomax), 163, 579n2
Cowboy Troy, 551
cowpunk music, 526, 528, 529
Cox, Billy, 108, 159, 273
Cozzens, Ellsworth T., 104, 150, 426
Craddock, Billy "Crash," 443–444
Craft, Paul, 331, 482, 516
Cramer, Floyd, 301–302, 307
Crary, Dan, 329, 427
Crazy Barn Dance (radio show), 116, 120, 130,
  143
Crazy Hickory Nuts, 120, 136
Crazy Mountaineers, 120, 144–145
Crazy Tennesseans, 223
Crazy Water Crystals Company, 116, 118, 120,
  136, 138, 145, 383
Creedence Clearwater Revival, 425, 454
Crissman, Maxine, 156
Crockett, John H. "Dad," 173
Crockett Family, 173
Crook Brothers, 85
Crosby, Bing: films of, 250; recordings of,
  113, 188, 206, 207, 212, 232, 234; Jimmie
  Rodgers compared to, 100; and Cindy
  Walker, 250
Crosby, Fanny, 14
Crosby, Ronald Clyde. *See* Walker, Jerry Jeff
Crosby, Stills, and Nash, 424–425
Cross, Hugh, 115, 225
cross-genre collaborations, 549–551, 560–561,
  571
The Crossing (album), 526
crossover songs: and country-pop, 287, 296,
  298, 303, 439, 441, 444, 445, 446, 474, 501;
  and Bing Crosby, 234; and Faith Hill, 510;
  and Johnny Rodriguez, 370; and songwrit-
  ers, 348; and truck-driving songs, 378
Crossroad Follies (radio show), 144, 384
Crossroads (television show), 550
Crouch, Tom, xiv
Crow, Alvin, 475
Crowe, J. D., 402–403, 425–426, 432, 497
Crowell, Rodney, 356, 357, 459, 462, 485, 504,
  588n17

Crudup, Arthur, 291
Crystal Grand Music Theatre, Wisconsin
  Dells, 518
Crystal Springs Ballroom, Fort Worth, 191,
  194
Cumberland Ridge Runners, 115, 116, 133,
  134, 242
Cumberland Trio, 326
Curb Records, 494
Curless, Dick, 322, 378
Curly Dan and Wilma Ann, 410
Curtis, Sonny, 385
cylinder recordings, 10, 58
Cyrus, Billy Ray, 505, 568
Czech-country music, 180–181. *See also*
  "Bohemian" music; Hofner, Adolph

Dacus, Smokey, *203*, 204
Daffan, Theron Eugene "Ted": in California,
  236; and electrical amplification, 188, 195,
  197; and Foreman Phillips, 235; recordings
  of, 206, 220, 232; as songwriter, 197, 213,
  230, 378; and western swing, 197
Daily, Harold W. "Pappy," 337, 419
Dalhart, Vernon: and cowboy music, 163; as
  full-time show business performer, 50;
  photograph of, 72; recordings of, 54, 57,
  73–75, 163, 229; and Carson Robison, 52,
  54; and Hank Snow, 278; vocal style of, 51,
  71, 73–76, 274
Dallas, Texas: and Deep Ellum, 11; Elm Street
  in, 10; and radio barn dances, 234, 243; and
  recording companies, 246; and urban folk
  revival, 463; and western swing, 199–200.
  See also Big D Jamboree (radio show);
  KRLD (Dallas); WFAA (Dallas); WRR
  (Dallas)
Dalton, Lacy J., 361
Damrosch, Walter, 89
dances and dancing: black influence on, 5; and
  Cajun dancing, 505; and Camel Caravan,
  215; and Czech-country music, 181; and
  electrical amplification, 188; and hot dance
  music, 63, 113, 136, 188, 194, 196; line dance
  craze of 1990s, 490, 494, 504–506; and
  Musical Brownies, 194; in postwar era,
  234–235; and radio barn dances, 40–41, 58,
  81–82, 89–90, 114, 115–117, 121, 215–217,
  219, 221, 234, 238, 243, 338, 416, 558; and
  southern music, 20–21, 26, 34; in Texas,
  162, 181–182; and traditional country

music, 518; Virginia reel, 20; and western swing, 154, 188, 196, 202, 206. *See also* honky-tonk music

Dandurand, Tommy, 82–83

Daniels, Charlie, 456, 457, 488, 516, 559

Daniels, Tom, 322

Darby, Tom, 123

Dave and Sugar, 451

David, Hal, 299

Davidson, Joel, 86

Davies, Gail, 358, 495

Davis, Art, 199, 200

Davis, Betty Jack, 302–303

Davis, Cleo, 384

Davis, Eva, 26, 58

Davis, Gussie, 19, 75

Davis, James Houston "Jimmie": and films, 172; as hillbilly politician, 118, 126–127, 193, 201, 207, 553; and radio, 126; recordings of, 127, 206, 207, 214, 232, 263, 528; and Jimmie Rodgers, 108, 126; and Shelton Brothers, 201; stylistic preferences of, 126, 127–128, 290

Davis, Karl, 115, 133, *134*

Davis, Lynn, 258, *259*

Davis, Miles, 539

Davis, Oscar, 218–219, 241

Davis, Skeeter, 302–303

Davis, Walter, 69

Davis Sisters, 302–303

Dawson, Bart (Fred Rose), 228

Day, Doris, 444

Day, J. W., 18

Day, Lazy Jim, 217–218

Dean, Carl, 366

Dean, Eddie, 238, 275

Dean, Jimmy, 308, 317–318, 333, 412

DeArman, Raymond, 191

Deason, Muriel. *See* Wells, Kitty

Deaton, Ray, 534

Decca Records: and American Federation of Musicians, 211; and Carter Family, 79; and Patsy Cline, 309; and Paul Cohen, 246; and Bing Crosby, 113, 212; and Jimmie Davis, 127; and Red Foley, 246, 269; and Gennett Records, 112; and Stuart Hamblen, 176; and Lone Star Cowboys, 201; and Loretta Lynn, 362; and Bill Monroe, 402, 407; and Musical Brownies, 194, 195; and Webb Pierce, 199, 246; and George Puckett, 63; and Taylor-Griggs Louisiana Melody Makers,

190; and Ernest Tubb, 184, 186, 220, 246, 269; and Kitty Wells, 261, 269; and Wilburn Brothers, 315

Decker, Peter, 45

Deen, Dixie, 323

Deliverance (film), 398, 418

Del McCoury Band, 500, 533–534, *533*

Delmore Brothers (Alton and Rabon): and black music, 290; and Brown's Ferry Four, 256, 263; and country blues, 128–129; and duet singing, 122, 128, 129, 252; and duet yodeling, 122; and *Grand Ole Opry*, 114, 115; instrumental work of, 128–129; and Uncle Dave Macon, 88; and Jim and Jesse McReynolds, 405; and music from cities' "sin streets," 11; recordings of, 128, 245, 246, 265, 415; and Jimmie Rodgers, 128; and Arthur Smith, 147; and Doc Watson, 128, 129, 329; and World War II, 221

DeMent, Iris, 327, 446, 485, 518, 524–525, 543, 554, 564

Democratic Party, 159, 439, 468

Denman, Josh, 38

Denny, Jim, 241, 309, 310

Denton, Texas, 463

Denver, John, 444, 445, 546

Derailers, 530

Desmond, Holly, 99

Dessau Hall, 265–266

Detroit, Michigan, 410, 411

DeWitt, Lew, 451

Dexter, Al (Albert Poindexter): and electrical amplification, 187; and honky-tonk music, 182–183; recordings of, 206, 220; as songwriter, 212, 231–232; and Cindy Walker, 250

Dezurik, Maryjane and Caroline, 141

Diamond Rio, 493

Diamonds and Dirt (album), 462

Dickens, Hazel, 429, 474–475, 537

Dickens, "Little" Jimmy, 117, 250, 263, 266, 268, 308, 518, 558, 581n13

Dickerson, Patricia Gail. *See* Davies, Gail

Dickey, Tom, 199

Diddley, Bo, 296

Diffie, Joe, 513, 516–517

digital downloading, 567–568

digital recording techniques, 506, 507, 559, 567

Dill, Danny, 333

Dillard and Clark Expedition, 427

Dillards, 424

Dinner Bell Roundup (radio show), 234, 237, 238

disc jockeys: and all-country radio stations, 311–312; and bluegrass, 380, 395, 396, 417; and military personnel, 322; in postwar era, 244–245, 299; and Charley Pride, 372; and Jim Reeves, 305; and rock-and-roll music, 291, 506; and traditional country music, 543

Disc Jockeys Convention, 310

Dixie Chicks: and CMA Awards of 2016, 546, 548, *549*, 551, 552, 557, 572; and politics, 552–554, 565, 571, 589–590n10, 590n13; stage persona of, 511–512, 555; and women's rights, 509, 554

Dixie Entertainers, 61

Dixieland music, 30

Dixieliners, 147

Dixie Mountain Boys, 416

Dixie Mountaineers, 59

Dixie Pals, 431

Dixie Partners, 429

Dixie Serenaders, 196

Dixie Travelers, 409

Dixon Brothers (Howard and Dorsey), 129–130, 157

Dobro steel guitars, 126, 150–151, 225, 261, 330, 394–395, 426, 445. *See also* steel guitars

Doc Hauer's medicine show, 223

Dolly Parton Live from London (HBO special), 436

domestic tradition, 24

Domino, Fats, 290

Don't Overlook Salvation (album), 498

Doolittle, Jesse, 82

Dopyera Brothers (Ed, Robert, and Rudy), 150

Dorsey, Thomas A., 154–155, 243

Dorsey Brothers, 284

Dot Records, 245, 330, 399

Douglas, Charlie, 378–379

Douglas, Jerry, 395

Downing, Big Al, 373

Drake, Guy, 376

Dresser, Paul, 19

Drifting Cowboys, 282, 339

Driftwood, Jimmie, 332, 333

drugs, and hillbilly music, 125

drums: and bluegrass, 423; and Smokey Dacus, 204; and Bob Wills, 220, 545

Dudley, Dave, 376, 378, 522

duet singing: and Gene Autry, 170; and Bellamy Brothers, 494; and bluegrass, 428; of Blue Sky Boys, 136–137; of Carl and Pearl Butler, 334; and Martha and James Carson, 251; of Carter Family, 79; and comic songs, 263–264; and Delmore Brothers, 122, 128, 129, 252; and Emmylou Harris and Ricky Skaggs, 486; and Flying Burrito Brothers, 456; and Girls of the Golden West, 173; and Merle Haggard, 345, 450; harmony style of, 122, 129; and Emmylou Harris and Gram Parsons, 485; and Karl and Harty, 133; and Louvin Brothers, 128, 251, 252–254, 428, 429; Loretta Lynn and Conway Twitty, 334, 448, 450; and Mac and Bob, 132–133; and Mainer's Mountaineers, 145; and mandolin-and-guitar duets, 132; and Mexican border stations, 119; and Monroe Brothers, 137, 138, 221, 383, 384; and Dolly Parton and Porter Wagoner, 316, 334, 366, 367, 450; and Ray Price, 339; and World War II, 221; and Tammy Wynette and George Jones, 364, 478; and yodeling, 122, 130, 410. *See also* brother duets

Duff, Arlie [Arleigh], 337

Duffey, John, 412, 413, 424, 425, 426

Duke of Paducah, 217

dulcimers, 31

Dumont, Louis, 144

Duncan, Eddie, 144, 199

Duncan, Johnny, 478

Duncan, Stuart, 534

Duncan, Tommy, 108, 168, 193, *203*, 204–206, 265, 347, 373

Dunn, Bob, 187–188, *192*, 194–195, 199, 204

Dunn, Ronnie, 505–506

Durham, Eddie, 149

Duvall, Robert, 436

Dylan, Bob: and Johnny Cash, 330; ideology of, 374; as influence on country music, 454; and Tim O'Brien, 526, 539; recordings of, 454, 542; as songwriter, 348, 413, 415, 424, 425, 455, 460, 485, 523; and television, 319; and urban folk revival, 326, 327

Eagles, 453, 456, 492, 559, 560

E and E Tavern, San Antonio, 185

Eanes, Jim, 389–391

Earle, Steve: and bluegrass, 500, 533; and Guy Clark, 462; and hillbilly as term, 48, 513;

on hillbilly highway, 497; repertory of, 496, 499, 500, 543; as songwriter, 327, 523, 524
Earle Theatre, Washington, DC, 97–98
Earl Scruggs Revue, 422, 426
East Hickory String Band, 136
East Texas Serenaders, 190
Eastwood, Clint, 435
Edenton, Ray, 247, 301
Edison Male Quartet, 38
Edison records, 73, 74, 75
Ed Sullivan Show (television show), 307
Edwards, Billy, 428
Edwards, Don, 543
Edwards, Eilleen. *See* Twain, Shania
Edwards, Stoney, 271, 373–374
Eighth Street Theatre, 115–116
El Corazón (album), 500
Eldridge, Ben, 426
electrical amplification: and Roy Acuff, 225; and banjos, 317; and basses, 239–240, 339, 423; and bluegrass, 417–418, 425; in California, 239; and Callahan Brothers, 130; and Ted Daffan, 188, 195, 197; and Bob Dunn, 187; and fiddles, 339; and guitars, 149, 150, 183, 186–187, 188, 204, 239, 265, 301, 317, 341; and hillbilly music, 183; and Johnny and Jack, 255; and mandolins, 148, 187, 195; and Shelton Brothers, 202; and steel guitars, 122, 150–151, 187–188, 195, 204, 239, 265; and Floyd Tillman, 197; and Ernest Tubb, 186–187, 220; and western swing, 207
The Electric Horseman (film), 435, 477
Ellington, Buford, 312
Elliott, Jack, 462
Ellis, Jimmy, 443
Ellison, Curtis, 492
Ely, Joe, 462, 520
Emerson, Bill, 402, 412, 425
Emerson, Ralph Waldo, 82
Emery, Ralph, 437
Emmett, Dan, 52
Emmons, Buddy, 340
Empire Theatre, Montgomery, Alabama, 282
English, Paul, 98
Enright, Pat, 534
Epic Records, 364, 478, 515, 517
Ervin, Smitty, 317, 412
Erwin, Catherine, 529
Erwin, Emily, 511
Erwin, Jake, 530

Erwin, Martie, 511
Eskew, Mary Lee, 56
Esquire magazine, 414, 436
ethnic recordings, 367, 369–374
Ethridge, Chris, 456
Europe, popularity of country music in, 306, 320, 321, 322, 323, 324, 474, 494
European immigration, 2
European Theater of Operations, Special Services Division, 215
Evans, Dave, 430, 431
Evans, Jim, 110
Evans, Sara, 491, 509, 512
Everette, Leon, 479
Everly, Ike, 295
Everly Brothers (Don and Phil), 133, 137, 292, 295–296, 456
Exile, 493

Fairburn, Werly, 292
Fairchild, Barbara, 361
Fall Out Boy, 550
Fan Fair, 542
Fargo, Donna, 361
Farm and Fun Time (radio show), 234, 243, 399, 404
Farmer, James, 308
Farm Hour (radio show), 317
Farm Security Administration (FSA), 151
Farr, Hugh, 176–177
Farr, Karl, 176–177
Farrar, Jay, 528
Father Kemp's Old Folks, 25
Faulkner, William, 348
Federal Radio Commission, 118
Federal Records, 397
Feiler, Bruce, 506
Felts, Narvel, 443
feminism, 360, 362, 508–509
Fender, Freddy (Baldemar Huerta), 369
Fender, Leo, 239
Fender guitars, 239
Ferera, Frank, 75
Ferguson, Ernest, 252
Ferguson, George, 218
Ferguson, Joe, *203*
festivals: bluegrass festivals, 329, 419–421, 424, 428, 429, 432, 474, 531, 541, 543; folk festivals, 259–260, 329, 331, 392, 523, 543; niche festivals, 571
fiddle-and-guitar bands, 189

fiddle contests: and Atlanta, 22, 62; and Fiddlin' John Carson, 40, 44–45; and Delmore Brothers, 128; and Henry Ford, 49; and Curly Fox, 147; and George Hay, 84; and Clayton McMichen, 143; and Mainer's Mountaineers, 144; men participating in, 26; and Eck Robertson, 27, 42; social setting of, 21–22, 37; and southern music, 4; and western swing, 188, 189; and Bob Wills, 202, 206

fiddlers: and blackface minstrel shows, 21, 22, 27, 29; black musicians as, 22; and Blue Grass Boys, 386; and breakdown fiddling, 58, 62, 188, 203, 204; conservatism of, 27; and country dances, 21, 26, 34; and cowboy music, 165, 177, 476; and folk melodies, 22; and hornpipes, 20; individual identities of, 146–147; men as, 26; and political events, 20, 21, 22, 40, 45, 58; professionalism of, 21; and puppet shows, 7; and radio, 40; recordings of, 58–59; repertory of, 23; and Roy Newman and His Boys, 200; and southern rock, 457; styles of, 27, 29, 84, 122, 143, 146–148, 195, 339, 427; and western swing, 188, 195, 199, 203, 206; women as, 535, 537, 538

fiddles: and bluegrass, 144, 386, 388, 427; and country-pop, 299, 445; and electrical amplification, 339; and folk music, 20; and rural house parties, 20–21, 27, 58, 188, 189, 202; and string bands, 29, 30, 31, 50, 58; and Texas fiddle music, 143–144; and western swing, 190, 457

fiddle tunes, 22–23, 82, 147, 148, 190, 204, 329

15,000-D series (Columbia hillbilly recordings), 47

films: and American Federation of Musicians, 211; and American West, 162; of Gene Autry, 170–171, 177, 219, 274; and cowboy music, 170–172, 177, 179, 476; and hillbilly music, 47, 112, 171, 172; and mass exposure of country music, 434–436; of Willie Nelson, 435, 468, 477; of Dolly Parton, 360, 435; of Tex Ritter, 172, 179; of Bob Wills, 172, 177, 205, 250; and World War II, 209. *See also specific films*

Fincher, J. W., 116, 120, 130

Finley, Kent, 480

Fire on the Mountain (television show), 437

First Edition, 425, 446

First Generation, 428

First Generation Records, 579n8

Fischer, Johann Christian, 23

Fisk Jubilee Singers, 34

Fitzgerald, Ella, 213

Five Easy Pieces (film), 364

Flanagan, Bill, 550

Flatlanders (Butch Hancock, Joe Ely, and Jimmie Dale Gilmore), 520

Flatt, Lester: and Blue Grass Boys, 221, *385*, 387–388, 391, 392–393, 402; death of, 422, 513; and IBMA's Hall of Honor, 531; and Kentucky Pardners, 383, 392; and Monroe Brothers, 137; and Nashville Grass, 394, 421–422, 513; performing style of, 392, 393; photograph of, *390*; as songwriter, 387; and textile-mill environment, 129, 392; and traditional bluegrass, 533, 542; and urban folk revival, 415, 425; vocal style of, 388

Flatt and Scruggs: and bluegrass, 391–392, 396, 399, 402, 407, 414, 418–419, 423; breakup of, 415, 421; and Davis Sisters, 302; and *Grand Ole Opry*, 392; independent career of, 391; and instrumentation, 394–395, 397; and Lilly Brothers, 410–411; and Bill Monroe, 421, 422; photograph of, *390*; and radio, 404; recordings of, 391, 392, 418, 423, 425, 428, 432; and Scruggs's picking, 387; and television shows, 315, 334; and urban folk revival, 415; vocal style of, 400, 410; and Mac Wiseman, 399

Fleck, Bela, 425, 539, 541, *541*

Flecktones, 539

Fleming, Reese, 122

Fletcher, Carmen William "Curley," 165, 178

Flippo, Chet, 553, 571

Flores, Bobby, 340

Flores, Rosie, 543

Fly (album), 512

Flying Burrito Brothers, 427, 456

Flynn, Pat, 539, *541*

Fogerty, John, 454

Foggy Mountain Boys, 391–395, 414

Foley, Clyde Julian "Red": and Brown's Ferry Four, 256, 263; and Jerry Byrd, 151; and Cumberland Ridge Runners, 115, *134*; and *Grand Ole Opry*, 242–243; guitar style of, 278; and Lulu Belle, 139; and *Ozark Jubilee*, 315; and Elvis Presley, 291; and Charley Pride, 372; recordings of, 246, 265, 269, 288, 290, 580n6; session musicians of, 247; and vaudeville, 131; vocal style of, 242, 275,

276; and Hank Williams, 285; and World War II, 229

folk music: of Australian Bush, 321; bibliographic essay on, 593–603; and blackface minstrel shows, 10; black influence on, 1, 14, 34; and Blue Sky Boys, 134–136; and fiddles, 20; folk music parks, 218; and Great Depression, 151–153, 156, 325, 326, 327, 434; and hillbilly music, 1, 34–36, 49–50, 153; and hillbilly songs, 51, 54, 55; instrumentation of, 27–33; and Mainer's Mountaineers, 144; and Mexican border stations, 119; and myth of "folk isolation," 6; oral sources of, 35; and phonograph industry, 41; professionalization of, 24; recording of, 43, 46, 151; and religious music, 15–16; revival of 1950s, 31; Jimmie Rodgers's influence on, 100–101; and southern folk culture, 4–5, 6, 11, 16–18, 23, 33–34; in Texas, 4, 162; and typical southern folk musician, 34–36; urban performances of, 38; variations in, 4, 5, 33–34; and western swing, 189; and WSB, 40. *See also* folk style; urban folk revival

Folk Songs of the Hills (album), 295

folk style: and domestic tradition, 24, 34; and harmony embellishments, 25; influences on, 27; southern folk styles, 23–24. *See also* urban folk revival

Folkways anthologies, 55, 67, 70, 327

Folkways Records, 327–328, 414

For a Life of Sin (album), 528

Ford, Benny, 217

Ford, Henry, 49, 87, 214

Ford, Tennessee Ernie, 238, 265, 290, 295, 323

Ford and Glenn, 82

Forrester, Howard "Howdy," 147, 225, 386, 535

Forrester, Sally, 386, 535

Fort Worth, Texas, 246. *See also* KFJZ (Fort Worth); KGKO (Fort Worth); KTAT (Fort Worth); WBAP (Fort Worth)

Fort Worth Doughboys, 191

Foster, Fred, 366, 490

Foster, Gus, 131

Foster, Gwen, 69

Foster, Radney, 494

Foster, Stephen, 216

Foster and Lloyd, 494

Four Star Records, 245, 308

Fowler, Wally, 452

Fox, Arnim Leroy "Curly," 121, 147, 201, 218

Fox, Oscar, 163, 179

Fox, Pamela, 564

Fox News, 552, 569

Frank, J. L., 218, 224, 241

Franklin, Al, *203*

Franklin, Aretha, 510

Franks, Tillman, 332

Frantz, Joe B., xiv

Fraser, Paul, 477

Frazier, Dallas, 349, 355, 359

Freakwater, 529

Freda and the Firedogs, 463

Freed, Alan, 289

French culture, 5, 20

French harps, 21, 31–32, 51, 75, 329

Fricke, Janie, 478

Friedman, Kinky, 367, *368*, 502, 566

Frisby, Lou, 197

Frizzell, Alice, 271

Frizzell, David, 334

Frizzell, William Orville "Lefty": and John Anderson, 483; in California, 236, 238; and Bill Callahan, 132; death of, 477; and Joe Diffie, 516; and honky-tonk music, 271–272, 477; photograph of, *272*; and radio, 238; recordings, of, 246, 272–273, 333–334, 353; and Jimmie Rodgers, 110, 168, 271, 273; and Whitey Shafer, 481; and Randy Travis, 496; vocal style of, 273, 345, 347, 477, 496; and Keith Whitley, 497

frolic music, 20

Fromholz, Steve, 463

From the Mountain (album), 526

Frontier Ranch Park, Columbus, Ohio, 359

Fruit Jar Drinkers, 84–85

The Fugitive (television show), 345

Fulks, Robbie, 529

Fulton, Richard, 312

Funk, Joseph, 26

Gabriel, Charles, 14

Gannaway, Al, 315

Garcia, Jerry, 454

Gardner, Robert, 51, 68, 132–133

Garin, Amos, 384

Garland, Hank, 247, 301

Garland, Jim, 152–153

Garroway, Dave, 317

The Garth Brooks Collection (album), 502

Garth Live from Central Park (HBO special), 502

Gaslight Era, 75

Gatlin, Larry, 442, 449–450, 507

Gatlin, Rudy, 450

Gatlin, Steve, 450

Gatlin Brothers Band (Larry, Steve, and Rudy), 450

Gaudreau, Jimmy, 424

Gay, Connie B., 241, 309, 317, 412

Gayle, Crystal, 106, 361–362, 444, 459, 515

Gaylord Enterprises, 505

Geezinslaw Brothers, 437

General Phonograph Corporation, 42, 43, 44, 112

Gennett Records, 46, 66, 112, 126, 141

Gentry, Bobbie, 355

Gentry, Teddy, 453

George, David Graves, 74

George Daniell's Hill Billies, 575n7

Georgia, 3, 4. *See also* Atlanta, Georgia

Georgia Old-Time Fiddlers' Association, 45

Georgia Potlickers, 61

Georgia Wildcats, 63, 143, 145

Georgia Yellow Hammers, 61

German culture, 5, 12, 23, 31, 34, 180, 188, 196

Germany, popularity of country music in, 322–323

Gibson, Don, 302, 303

Gibson Company, 33, 172, 187, 188

Gill, Cecil, 189

Gill, Vince, 462, 492, 502, 504, 506, 589n5

Gilley, Mickey, 293, 436

Gilley's Club, Pasadena, Texas, 436

Gilliland, Henry, 42

Gilman, Billy, 507

Gilmore, Jimmie Dale, 462–463, 520, 521, 543

Gimble, Johnny, 190, 203, 235, 246, 436, 475

Girls of the Golden West, 122, 141, 173, *174*

Glaser, Tompall, 301, 468, 472, 473–474

Glaser Brothers (Tompall, Jim, and Chuck), 301, 472

Glaser Music, 472

Glee (television show), 569

The Glen Campbell Goodtime Hour (television show), 318–319

glossolalia, 16

Goldband Records, 366

Golden, Bill, 452

Golden, Billy, 38

Golden State Boys, 429

Golden West Cowboys, 215, 276

Goldman, Emma, 500

Gold Star Records, 245, 270

Good, Millie and Dolly, 122, 141, 173, *174*. *See also* Girls of the Golden West

Good Coffee Boys, 136

Goodman, Benny, 143

Goodman, Herald, 115, 147

Goodman, Steve, 473, 512

Gordon, Robert Winslow, 151

Gordy, Emory, Jr., 490

Gore, Lesley, 361

Gosdin, Rex, 424

Gosdin, Vern, 424, 479, 517

gospel music: and Roy Acuff, 225–226; and alternative country, 564; black influence on, 154–155, 510; and bluegrass, 250, 388, 397, 410, 428, 432; and Blue Sky Boys, 136, 252, 262; and boogie tunes, 265; and Ronnie Bowman, 535; and Callahan Brothers, 130, 131; and camp meeting music, 14, 15; and Coon Creek Girls, 140; and Jimmie Davis, 126; and Delmore Brothers, 129; and duet singing, 128, 251; family gospel groups, 34; and Flatt and Scruggs, 393; and Red Foley, 243; and folk fatalism, 15; and Great Depression, 154; and harmony singing, 25, 26; and Faith Hill, 510; and hillbilly music, 122, 188; as influence on country music, 180, 512; and Jenkins Family, 56; and Johnny and Jack, 254; and Grandpa Jones, 256; and Louvin Brothers, 253, 262; and Uncle Dave Macon, 87; and Jim and Jesse McReynolds, 406; and Maddox Brothers and Rose, 255; and Mexican border stations, 119; and Nashville Bluegrass Band, 534; and Willie Nelson, 354; and Oak Ridge Boys, 452; and Molly O'Day, 258; and Mac Odell, 249–250, 262; and Brad Paisley, 558; and Elvis Presley, 292; and quartets, 25, 26, 451; and sheet music, 118; and singing conventions, 25–26; and Carl Smith, 268; and television shows, 315; and urban folk revival, 327, 328; and Hank Williams, 280, 282, 283. *See also* religious music

Graham, Billy, 263

Grammer, Billy, 317

Grand Ole Opry (radio show): and Roy Acuff, 85, 115, 150, 217, 218, 223, 224–225, 227, 228, 241, 335, 434; and Eddy Arnold, 217, 276, 277, 434; and Chet Atkins, 301; and Bailes Brothers, 252; and Deford Bailey, 370; and Camel Caravan, 215, 276; and Zeke Clements, 275; and Patsy Cline, 309;

and Delmore Brothers, 128; and Flatt and Scruggs, 392, 419; and Red Foley, 242–243; and Great Depression, 114; and hillbilly music, 116; influence of, 492, 571; and George Jones, 244, 335, 337; and Grandpa Jones, 256; and Alison Krauss, 537; and Louvin Brothers, 252, 253; and Uncle Dave Macon, 37, 85, 86–87, 88, 89, 387, 434, 585–586n7; and Jim and Jesse McReynolds, 417, 419; and Bill Monroe, 115, 217–218, 221, 335, 384, 386, 399, 400, 418–419; as national institution, 90, 217–218, 241, 244; old-timers featured on, 518; origins of, 83, 88–89; and Sonny Osborne, 400; and Osborne Brothers, 419; and Brad Paisley, 517; performers of, xiii, 85, 88–89, 114–115, 217–218, 241–243, 300; and personal appearances, 215; in postwar era, 234, 241; and Ray Price, 339; and Jim Reeves, 305; and Riders of the Sky, 476; segments of, 242; and Ricky Van Shelton, 498; and Connie Smith, 359; and Hank Snow, 279; sponsors of, 114; and string bands, 85–86; and television, 315, 437; tent shows of, xi, 10, 218; in Tokyo, 322; and Ernest Tubb, 186, 187, 217–218, 220, 234; and Porter Wagoner, 316, 317, 518; and Steve Wariner, 450; and Kitty Wells, 554; and Hank Williams, 244, 284, 285, 434; and Bob Wills, 220, 545; and Mac Wiseman, 399

Grant, Bill, 429

Grant, Marshall, 298

Grant Brothers (Jack and Claude), 96

Grappelli, Stéphane, 27, 142, 539

The Grass Is Blue (album), 533

Grateful Dead, 454

Graves, Burkett "Buck" (Uncle Josh), 261, 394–395, 426

Gray, Claude, 354, 519

Gray, Momie, 167

Gray, Otto, 10, 166–167

Gray, Tom, 412, 426

Grayson, Gilliam Banmon, 43, 380, 403

Grayzell, Rudy, 292

Great Depression: bibliographic essay on, 615–624; and escapism, 154; and folk music, 151–153, 156, 325, 326, 327, 434; and Harrell, 70, 71; and hillbilly music, 112, 153–154; and honky-tonk music, 181; and Uncle Dave Macon, 87; and oil industry, 181; and phonograph industry, 41; and

politics and country music, 152–159; and radio, 112, 113–117; and recording companies, 112–113; and religion, 153, 154–155; and Jimmie Rodgers, 94, 104, 110, 154

Great Revival of early 1800s, 12

Greek immigrants, 38

Green, Archie, xvi, 47, 48, 80, 152

Green, CeeLo, 560

Green, Douglas B., 408, 476

Green, Lloyd, 483

Green, Pat, 519

Greenbriar Boys, 328

Greene, Clarence, 69

Greene, Jack, 220, 518

Greene, Richard, 408

Green Grow the Lilacs (play), 179

Greenway, John, xiv, 101

Greenwood, Lee, 507

Greenwood, Melanie, 505

Gregory, Bobby, 314

Grier, Lamar, 408

Griff, Ray, 443

Griffin, Patty, 565

Griffin, Rex, 108, 128, 230–231, 284

Griffith, Andy, 424

Griffith, Nanci, 327, 499, 523–524

Grisman, David, 424, 539, 541

Gross, Clifford, 147, *191*, 193

Guard, Dave, 326

Guion, David, 163

guitars: Chet Atkins's three-finger style, 301; and Gene Autry, 168–169, 171; and bass runs, 149; and bluegrass, 144, 534; and bottleneck style, 123; and Carter Family, 79, 393; claw-hammer style, 149; and country dances, 21; cross-picking technique, 415; electrical amplification of, 149, 150, 183, 186–187, 188, 204, 239, 265, 301, 317, 341; fingerpicking style technique, 85, 123, 129, 130; flat-picking style, 278, 296, 329, 334, 415, 427, 429; Gene Autry "Roundup" Guitar, 168–169, 402; Gibson SJ-200, 172; and hound-dog guitar, 64, 83; and Lester Flatt G-run, 393; open-chord backup style, 149; and religious music, 16; Jimmie Rodgers's style of, 101; role of, 148, 149; and single-string style, 143, 177, 186, 187, 197, 204, 298, 341, 467; and "sock" rhythm, 143, 183; and string bands, 29–30, 31, 50; takeoff guitar, 220, 265; tenor guitars, 51; thumb-brush technique, 79; thumb-style technique, 143, 326, 393; and Floyd Till-man, 197; Merle Travis's style of, 143, 149, 236, 295, 301, 517; and Doc Watson's style, 329. *See also* steel guitars

Guitar Town (album), 500

Gully Jumpers, 85

Gunning, Sarah Ogan, 152

Gunter, Hardrock, 265, 290

Gus's Palm Garden, San Antonio, 197

Guthrie, Jeff, 156

Guthrie, Leon "Jack," 156, 233, 255, 265

Guthrie, Woodrow Wilson "Woody": as bard of Okies, 153, 156; and Bill Clifton, 416; guitar style of, 156; and Merle Haggard, 346; and hillbilly music, 156–157; omitted from Country Music Hall of Fame, 313; and Gram Parsons, 455; repertory of, 255; role in country and folk music, 155–157; as songwriter, 156–157, 523; James Talley compared to, 438; and Kenneth Threadgill, 460; and urban folk revival, 326

Gutter, Karl August, 32

Haden, Walter, 71, 73

Haerle, Martin C., 323

Hagar, Fred, 41, 44

Hager Twins, 343

Haggard, Merle: and alternative country, 564; and John Anderson, 483; and Bakersfield music scene, 343–345; and Suzy Bogguss, 508; conservative songs of, 153–154; death of, 570; and Iris DeMent, 524, 525; and Joe Diffie, 516; duets with Willie Nelson, 450; and Flying Burrito Brothers, 456; and Lefty Frizzell, 271, 272; and Emmylou Harris, 485; and instrumentation, 347; and George Jones, 338; and Osborne Brothers, 418; photograph of, *344*; and politics, 437, 439, 518, 525, 590n13; and radio, 496; recordings of, 345–347; and Jimmie Rodgers, 110, 347; and Johnny Rodriguez, 369; as songwriter, 343, 346–348, 366, 376–378, 550, 566; style of, xvi, 475, 517; and television, 437; in *Time*, 434; vocal style of, 344–345, 347, 379, 480; and Dale Watson, 522; and Bob Wills, 347, 475; and youth culture, 518

Hale, Monte, 177

Haley, Bill, 290

Hall, Hillman, 369

Hall, Jay Hugh, 145, 146

Hall, J. R. (the Utah Cowboy), 119, 173

Hall, Raymond, 107

Hall, Roy, 146–147, 149, 221, 226, 294, 384, 403

Hall, Tom T.: and Dixie Deen, 323; and Willie Nelson's picnics, 466; and politics, 438; and Johnny Rodriguez, 369; as songwriter, 331, 355–356, 376, 377, 379

Hall, Wendell, 52

Hall Brothers, 146

Halsey, Jim, 241

Ham, Bill, 501

Hamblen, Stuart, 173, 175–176, 263

Hamilton, George, IV, 299, 308, 323, 330

Hamlett, Norman, 347

Hamman, Cloet, 190

Hammett, Smith, 387

Hancock, Butch, 462, 499, 520

Hancock, Wayne, 521–522

Handcox, John, 152–153

Haney, Carlton, 418–420

Haney's Big House, Mississippi, 294

Happy Chappies, 177

Happy-Go-Lucky Boys, 145

Happy Shahan's Alamo Village, Brackettville, Texas, 369

hard country: and Moe Bandy, 482; and Blood-shot Records, 528; and Suzy Bogguss, 508; and Carl Butler, 334; and country-pop, 395; and Joe Diffie, 517; and Dixie Chicks, 511, 512; and Flying Burrito Brothers, 456; and Robbie Fulks, 529; and Don Gibson, 303; and Merle Haggard, 347, 379; and Emmylou Harris, 456, 483, 484–485, 487; and Alan Jackson, 515; and George Jones, 295, 338, 478; and Patty Loveless, 515; and Loretta Lynn, 379; and Reba McEntire, 495; and Roger Miller, 318; and Buck Owens, 343; and Brad Paisley, 517; and Ray Price, 300, 325, 338, 339; and recording companies, 439, 441; revival of 1980s, 489; revival of mid-1960s, 341, 401, 417; and Ricky Skaggs, 483, 484, 487; and songwriters, 359; and Mel Street, 481–482; and Porter Wagoner, 316, 317; and Dale Watson, 474; and Gene Watson, 482; and women, 361

Hardly Strictly Bluegrass Festival, 474, 543, 544

Hargrove, Linda, 360

Harkreader, Sid, 88

Harlan County, USA (film), 474

Harman, Buddy, 247, 301

harmonicas, 21, 31–32, 43, 51, 467

Harper, Oscar and Doc, 189

Harrell, Bill, 412, 422

Harrell, Kelly, 50, 70–71, 97, 107, 129

Harris, Charles, 52

Harris, Emmylou: and alternative country, 564; and Delia Bell, 430; and Sam Bush, 539; and Guy Clark, 462; and Iris DeMent, 485, 525; duets of, 334, 485, 486; and hard country, 456, 483, 484–485, 487; and George Jones, 338, 485; and Louvin Brothers, 254, 485; and mainstream country, 517; and Gram Parsons, 456, 485; photograph of, *484*; recordings of, 485, 491; and Ricky Skaggs, 485, 486; and television, 436; and Shania Twain, 510; and urban folk revival, 361, 484–485; vocal style of, 507

Harris, Wynonie, 289

Hart, Freddie, 238, 444

Harte, Bret, 162

Hartford, John, 318, 356, 357

Hartford Company (publishing house), 25

Hartford Music Company, 25

Hartgrove, Mike, 534

Hartman, Dick, 143

Harvey, Carey D., 107

Harvey, Roy, *60*, 61, 149

Hat, Connie Tex, 322

Hatcher, Dynamite, 225

Hatcher, Libby, 496

Hawaiian guitars. *See* steel guitars

Hawaiian music: and steel guitars, 32, 51, 75, 104, 105, 123, 126, 150, 151, 181, 187, 195, 276, 277, 426; and string bands, 7, 11, 32, 40

Hawaiian Music Foundation, 151

Hawkins, Harold "Hawkshaw," 117, 220, 245, 309, 333, 334

Hawkins, Ted, 63, 132

Hay, George D., 83–84, 89–90, 241, 384

Hayes, Hunter, 559

Hayes, Red, 322

Hayes, Wade, 492, 513

Hayloft Hoedown (radio show), 277

Haynes, Henry "Homer." *See* Homer and Jethro

Hays, William S. "Will," 19, 404

Heap, Jimmy, 265–266

Hearne, Bill and Bonnie, 462, 523

Hearst, Patricia, 350

Hee Haw (television show), 256, 318, 319–320, 343, 474, 530, 547, 560

Hee Haw Gospel Quartet, 320

Heidemann, Kate, 556

Hellmann, Warren, 474, 543

Hello World Coffee, 201

Helm, Levon, 565

Helms, Bill, 61

Helms, Bobby, 299–300

Helotes, Texas, 519

Hemingway, Ernest, 355

Henderson, W. K., 201

Hendrix, Jimi, 521

Henry, Murphy, 535

Hensley, Harold, 238

Hensley, Virginia Patterson. *See* Cline, Patsy

Herald, John, 328

Herbert, Teresa, 522

Here in the Real World (album), 515

Herman the Hermit, 238

Herndon, Mark, 453

Hester, Carolyn, 523

Heywood, Eddy, 45

Hiatt, John, 520

Hibbard, Charles, 45

hick-hop, 561

Hickory Records, 227, 260–261

Hicks, Bobby, 407, 432

Hidden Guns (film), 307

High Pockets, Bakersfield, 344

Highway 101, 494

Hill, Eddie, 245, 311

Hill, Faith, 509–511

Hill, Joe, 153

Hill, Keith, 557

Hill, William J. "Billy," 108, 178

Hill and Range publishing firm, 212

Hill Billies, 47–48, 59, 384

hillbilly bars, in northern cities, 214

Hillbilly Boys, 193

Hillbilly Flour, 193

Hillbilly Hit Parade (radio show), 278

Hillbilly Jamboree (radio show), 227

hillbilly music: and advertising, 112, 119–121, 125; and Gene Autry, 170, 171; bibliographic essay on, 603–613; and BMI, 210; commercial recordings of, 31, 42, 44–48, 49, 50, 58, 59, 69, 70–71, 73–75, 96, 111, 113–114, 118–119, 189, 211–213, 219, 327, 328; country music as, 1, 47–48; and cowboy songs, 163, 230; and early musicians, 49–51, 167–168; and electric guitars, 183; and films, 47, 112, 171, 172; folk music compared to, 1, 34–36, 49–50, 153; and Great Depression, 112,

153–154; and Jim and Jesse McReynolds, 405–406; Bill Malone's early experiences with, x, xiv; and Pappy O'Daniel, 193; origins of, 551–552; and Ralph Peer, 44; and personal appearances, 113, 114, 115, 119, 121, 141, 215–216; and political events, 49, 118, 119, 201, 207; promoters of, 218–219; and publishing, 112; and radio, xv, 40–41, 48, 50, 59, 64, 81, 112, 113–114, 118–119, 121, 131, 218, 219, 221, 234; and Jim Reeves, 305–306; and scouting activity, 42, 46; and Shelton Brothers, 201–202; and shifts in band personnel, 145–146; stereotypes of, 59, 62–63, 64, 66; and television, 319–320; as term, 47, 48–49, 59, 269, 474, 513, 575n7; and urban folk revival, 328, 414; and western image, 172, 179–180; and Hank Williams, 280, 281–282, 284–285; and World War II, 207, 212–213, 229–230; and Dwight Yoakam, 497, 513

Hillbilly Ranch, Boston, 409, 410, 411

Hillbilly Reveille (radio show), 322

Hillbilly Rock (album), 513

hillbilly songs: arrangements of, 52; and BMI, 210; and Vernon Dalhart, 73; event songs, 54, 55, 57, 73, 349; and Woodie Guthrie, 156–157; and Uncle Dave Macon, 88; and moralism, 55–56, 66, 81, 134–136, 154; in northern cities, 214; origins of, 51–52, 57; and songwriters, 52, 54–58, 70–71, 156, 170, 178, 240

Hillman, Chris, 424, 454, 456

Hillmen, 424, 429

Hillsboro Theatre, 89

Hilo Five Hawaiian Orchestra, 40

Himes, Geoffrey, 511

Hinojosa, Leticia "Tish," 499, 521, 523, 524, 525

hip hillbilly music, 464

hip-hop, 5, 507

hoboes, 152, 166, 324, 346

hobo songs, 155, 166, 225, 350

Hoeptner, Fred, 165

Hoffman, Ben, 565–566, 567, 568, 571

Hofner, Adolph, 180–181, 197–199, 236

Hofner, Emil, 181, 197–199

Hofner Brothers, 198–199

Holiness movement: and Roy Acuff, 224; and Bailes Brothers, 252; and Martha Carson, 257–258; and Blind Andy Jenkins, 56; and Jerry Lee Lewis, 293; and Bill Monroe, 382;

and Ernest Phipps, 76; and Elvis Presley, 291–292; and religious music, 15–16, 55; and Sullivan Family, 428

hollering, 105, 255

Holley, Doyle, 343

Holley, Joe, 203

Holly, Buddy, 292, 470, 494

Hollywood Follies (tent show), 98

Holmes, Floyd "Salty," 143, *175*

Holt, Aubrey, 429

Homeland (album), 524

Homeland Harmony Quartet, 265

Homer and Jethro, 148, 263–264

Hometown Boys, 62

Hometown Jamboree (radio show), 234, 238, 306, 332

Honeysuckle Rose (film), 435

Honky Tonk Attitude (album), 517

honky-tonk music: and John Anderson, 333; and Moe Bandy, 480, 482; and bluegrass, 411; in California, 236, 268, 341–345, 347; and electrical amplification, 186, 188, 220; and Flying Burrito Brothers, 456; and Lefty Frizzell, 271–272, 477; and Wayne Hancock, 521–522; and hillbilly music, 219; as influence on country music, 182–183, 196, 206, 230–231, 255, 341; and international popularity of country music, 324; and George Jones, 335, 337, 339, 442, 478, 480, 482, 516; and Loretta Lynn, 362; and Maddox Brothers and Rose, 255; and Melody Masters, 266; and Moon Mullican, 198, 269, 270; and Willie Nelson, 354, 465, 468; and Jimmy Newman, 330; and Buck Owens, 342; and Leon Payne, 275; and Webb Pierce, 271, 274; in postwar era, 265, 268–271; and Ray Price, 325, 338, 339, 340, 479; and Jim Reeves, 305; and Dick Reinhart, 171; and Don Reno, 397; and Johnny Rodriguez, 369, 479; and Shelton Brothers, 201; and Gary Stewart, 479–480, 483; in Texas, 181–182, 436, 519; and Ernest Tubb, 184, 185, 220, 230, 269, 477; and Conway Twitty, 314, 479; and T. Texas Tyler, 267–268; and Dale Watson, 522–523, 530; and Gene Watson, 480, 482–483; and Kitty Wells, 262, 362; and Hank Williams, 282, 283; and World War II, 183

Hoosier Hot Shots, 216

Hooten, David, 264

Hoover, Herbert, 154, 158

Hopkins, Al, 10, *36*, 47–48, 59, 384
Hopkins, Howard "Doc," 115, 121, 133
Hopkins, John, *36*
hornpipes, 20
horns: and Gene Autry, 171; and Merle
    Haggard, 347; and hillbilly music, 51; and
    religious music, 16; and Texas Playboys,
    202, 204, 235; and western swing, 144, 196
Hornsby, Dan, 46
Horton, Hal, 266, 278, 311
Horton, Holly, 200
Horton, Johnny, 331–333, 497
Horton, Roy, 312
Horton, Vaughn, 250
Hot Band, 462, 485
Hot Club of Cowtown, 530
Hot Club of France, 27, 142
Hotmud Family, 483
Hot Rize, 425, 526
Hotshots, 69
house parties, 4, 20–21, 27, 58, 188, 189, 202
Houston, Cisco, 153, 326
Houston, David, 332, 364, 478
Houston, Texas, 196–198. *See also* KLEE
    (Houston); KPRC (Houston); KTRH
    (Houston); KXYZ (Houston)
Howard, Clint, 328
Howard, Fred, 165, 177–178
Howard, Harlan, 309, 340, 342, 352, 353–355
Howorth, Gerald, 410
Hubbard, Carroll, 200
Hubbs, Nadine, 590n2
Hudson, Arthur Palmer, 3
Huerta, Baldemar. *See* Fender, Freddy
    (Baldemar Huerta)
Huff, Leon, 108, 109, *191*, 193
Hughes, Jay, 189
Hughes, Marvin, 247
Humphries, Cynthia, 190
Humphries Brothers (Jess and Cecil),
    189–190
Hundley, R. D., 70
Hunt, Prince Albert, 189, 437
Hunt, Sam, 546
Huntington's Chorea, 156
Hurst, Jim, 537
Hurt, Charles "Chuck," 143, *175*
Hurt, Mississippi John, 328
Huskey, Junior, 247, 455
Husky, Ferlin, 299, 306–307, 341
Hutchins, Sam, 402

Hutchinson Family Singers of New
    Hampshire, 25
Hutchison, Frank, 6, 71, 123, 149–150, 205, 334
Hutchison, Virginia, 6

Ickes, Rob, 395
Idle, Eric, 559
Idlewild Orchestra, 57
Imperial Records, 245, 279
Indian culture, 5, 34, 105, 351
Industrial Workers of the World (Wobblies),
    155, 165, 166
Infamous Angel (album), 525
Inman, Autry, 375
Innis, Louis, 247
In Old Santa Fe (film), 170
In Spite of Ourselves (album), 525
insurgent country, 528, 531
International Bluegrass Music Association
    (IBMA): and awards, 565; founding of, 531;
    Hall of Honor, 531; and Alison Krauss, 535;
    and Nickel Creek, 539; and Tim O'Brien,
    526; and Missy Raines, 537; Song of the
    Year, 490; and Chris Thile, 542; Vocal
    Group of the Year, 534
International Bluegrass Music Museum and
    Hall of Fame, Owensboro, Kentucky, 531
International Country Music Conference
    (ICMC), xv
international popularity of country music:
    and bluegrass, 416; and commercial vi-
    ability, 320–325; and country-pop, 324; and
    Jim Reeves, 306; and World War II, 321
International Submarine Band, 455
Internet, 526, 548, 569, 571
Iowa Barn Dance Frolic (radio show), 116
Iraq War, 565, 589–590n10
Irby, Jerry, 230
Ireland, Mike, 529
Ireland, 524
Irving Berlin Company, 57
Isaacs, Bud, 274
Isbell, Jason, xvi, 565, 571
Italian immigrants, 32–33, 38
Ives, Burl, 325, 354, 542
Ivey, Bill, 490

Jackson, Alan, 490, 492, 507, 509, 512–513,
    515–516
Jackson, Andrew, 22, 152, 332
Jackson, Aunt Molly, 152–153

Jackson, Shot, 252, 255, 395, 426
Jackson, Stonewall, 376
Jackson, Tommy, 247, 299, 340, 406
Jackson, Wanda, 292–293
James, Elana, 530
James, Sonny, 296, 299, 315
James K. Polk, Inc., 44
Jamup and Honey (Lee Roy "Lasses" White and Lee David Wilds), 10, 218
Japan, 322, 324, 392
Jason and the Scorchers (Jason Ringenberg), 526, 529
Jayhawks, 528
jazz music: and banjos, 30, 425; and bluegrass, 413, 424, 425, 427, 539, 542; and Cajun music, 180; and cities, 10–11; and fiddlers, 27; and Henry Ford, 49; and improvisation, 388; as influence on country music, 5, 11; and Light Crust Doughboys, 193–194; and Clayton McMichen, 63; and Willie Nelson, 467; and Okie jazz, 188; popularity of, 33–34; and radio, 40; and religious music, 16; and Fred Rose, 57; and steel guitars, 150, 151, 194; and string bands, 122; and string basses, 149. *See also* country jazz; western swing
J.D.'s, Phoenix, 470
Jefferson, Thomas, 21, 30
Jenkins, Andrew "Blind Andy," 54, 55, 56–57, 107
Jenkins, Carl, 246
Jenkins, Dewitt "Snuffy," 145, 148, 387, 397, 404, 406
Jenkins, Floyd (Fred Rose), 228
Jenkins, Harold. *See* Twitty, Conway
Jenkins, Hoke, 391, 406
Jenkins, Homer, 100
Jenkins Family, 56
Jennings, Waylon: and country-rock, 471; death of, 570; and definition of country music, 441; as disc jockey, 470; and hillbilly as term, 48; and George Jones, 338; and Willie Nelson, 468; and Outlaw musicians, 468, 469–474; photograph of, *469*; and politics, 439; as songwriter, 550; and Wynn Stewart, 342; and Ernest Tubb, 470; and urban folk revival, 330; vocal style of, 471, 562, 588n24; and Bob Wills, 464, 588n23
Jerry and Sky, 273, 410
Jester Club, Houston, 461
Jewel Oil and Shortening, 196

Jews: in country music, 367, 566; as ethnic buying population, 38
Jew's harps, 32, 51
JFG Coffee, 130, 136
Jimmie Rodgers Entertainers, 96
Jimmie Rodgers Society, 110
Jimmy Wakely Trio, 171, 235
Jim Walter Corporation, 415
Joel, Billy, 502
Johnny and Jack, 244, 249, 254–255, 261, 286, 393
The Johnny Cash Show (television show), 318, 319
Johnny Fair Syrup Hour (radio show), 284
Johnson, Buffalo, 389
Johnson, Charles, 149
Johnson, Courtney, 427
Johnson, Earl, 58, 61
Johnson, Gene, 240
Johnson, Jack, 372
Johnson, Lyndon B., 193, 437
Johnson, Paul, 149
Johnson, Sleepy, 191, *191, 203*
Johnson Brothers, 149
Johnson Family, 262
Johnson Mountain Boys, 430, 431
Johnston, Bob, 454
John Wesley Harding (album), 454
Jolson, Al, 50, 61, 93, 100
Jones, Carol Elizabeth, 537
Jones, Eva Thompson, 84
Jones, George: and alternative country, 564; and John Anderson, 483; and Association of Country Entertainers, 440; death of, 570; and Joe Diffie, 516; and Flying Burrito Brothers, 456; and *Grand Ole Opry*, 244, 335, 337; and Emmylou Harris, 338, 485; and honky-tonk music, 335, 337, 339, 442, 478, 480, 482, 516; and Patty Loveless, 515; and Barbara Mandrell, 441; and Bill Monroe, 385; and Brad Paisley, 558, 560; and Johnny Paycheck, 473; photograph of, *336*; and radio, 337, 496; recordings of, 335, 337–338, 478–479, 496, 517; and Mel Street, 481, 482; style of, xvi, 271, 295, 442, 531; and Ernest Tubb, 579n8; vocal style of, 335, 337, 338, 339, 429, 443, 480, 481, 555; and Don Walser, 521; and Hank Williams, 288, 337; and Tammy Wynette, 364, 478
Jones, Isham, 82
Jones, Jesse, 196

Jones, Joe, 198

Jones, Kennedy, 236

Jones, Louis Marshall "Grandpa": and banjo playing style, 386; and Brown's Ferry Four, 256, 263; and CMA's twenty-fifth anniversary celebration, 438–439; and comic songs, 69, 256; and definition of country music, 440; and electric amplification, 256; and *Grand Ole Opry*, 256; and *Hee Haw*, 319, 320, 474; international popularity of, 256, 322; and Bradley Kincaid, 65–66, 256; and radio, 141, 256; recordings of, 245–246; repertory of, 256–257; on skin songs, 444; style of, 206, 251; and Merle Travis, 236

Jones, Ramona Riggins, 257

Jones, Sam, 14, 89

Joplin, Janis, 327, 460

Jordan, Louis, 289

Jordan, Luke, 125

Jordan, Vic, 407

Jordanaires, 301

Joyce, Jolly, 240

Judd, Naomi, 494, 495

Judd, Wynonna, 494, 495

Judds, 494–495

jug bands, 454

jugs, as instruments, 384

jukeboxes: and American Federation of Musicians, 211; and bluegrass, 395, 417; and Jimmy Dickens, 268; and Lefty Frizzell, 272; and hillbilly music, 213, 214, 220; and honky-tonk music, 182, 186; and Kitty Wells, 262; and western swing, 206; and Hank Williams, 286; and World War II, 209, 214–215

juke joints, 5, 11, 182, 198, 290

June, Valerie, 551

Justice, Dick, 6, 71, 123, 125, 149

Kaipo, Joe, 104, 150

Kallick, Kathy, 537

Kallinger, Paul, 311

Kane, Kieran, 494

Kapp, David, 113, 186

KARK (Little Rock), 384

Karl and Harty, 115, 133, 135, 296

Karnes, Alfred, 76

Katz, Claire, 554

Kazee, Buell, 66–67, 69, 133, 328

kazoos, 32, 51, 124

KDAV (Lubbock), 311

KDKA (Pittsburgh), 64

Keen, Robert Earl, 499

Keeshan, Chuck, 197

Keillor, Garrison, 434, 436, 508, 542

Keith, Toby, 513, 552

Keith, William Bradford "Bill," 407, 408–409, 411, 424, 431

Keith-Orpheum Theater, 10

Kekuku, Joseph, 32

Kell, Leslie E., 99

Kell Company (tent show), 99

Kemble, Will Ed, 194

Kemp, Wayne, 479

Kendalls (Royce and Jeanie), 450–451

Kennedy, Jerry, 451

Kennedy, John F., 333, 349

Kennedy, Rod, 463–464, 476, 543

Kentuckians, 384, 422

Kentucky, 12–13, 66–67

Kentucky Barn Dance (radio show), 302

Kentucky Colonels, 424

Kentucky Folklore Record, 414

Kentucky Mountain Boys, 425

Kentucky Pardners, 221, 383, 392

Kentucky Ramblers, 143

Kentucky School for the Blind, 132

Kentucky Thunder, 532

Kenya, 101

Kerosene (album), 556, 571

Kerrville Folk Festival, 420, 461–462, 464, 476, 499, 523–524, 543

Kershaw, Doug, 319, 331, 367, 369

Kershaw, Rusty, 367, 369

Kershaw, Sammy, 492

Ketchum, Hal, 492

Key, Jimmy, 355

Keys, Alicia, 550

KFI (Compton, California), 238

KFJZ (Fort Worth), 191

KFKB (Milford, Kansas), 117–118

KFRC (San Francisco), 166

KFVD (Los Angeles), 156

KFWB (Hollywood), 174, 177

KG and the Ranger, 543

KGKB (Tyler, Texas), 201

KGKO (Fort Worth), 185, 186

KGRI (Henderson, Texas), 305

KIHN (Hugo, Oklahoma), 429

Killers Three (film), 346

Killin' Time (album), 501

Kimberley Jim (film), 306

Kincaid, Bradley: and Grandpa Jones, 65–66, 256; and *National Barn Dance*, 83; omitted from Country Music Hall of Fame, 313; photograph of, *65*; recordings of, 111; repertory of, 66, 121, 134, 135, 188–189; and Jimmie Rodgers, 109; show business career of, 64–66; vocal style of, 51, 64; and Mac Wiseman, 398

King, B. B., 291

King, Claude, 332, 333

King, Nelson, 244, 311, 396

King, Pee Wee, 215, 218, 223, 230, 248, 276, 528

The King and I (Broadway musical), 560

King Records: and Bailes Brothers, 246; and Delmore Brothers, 128, 245, 265, 290, 415; and Red Foley, 247; and Charlie Moore, 429; and Moon Mullican, 269, 270; and Sydney Nathan, 245–246, 290; and Bobby Osborne, 400; and Stanley Brothers, 295, 415; and Tennessee Cutups, 397–398

Kingsmen, 451

Kingston Trio, 326, 327, 331, 414

Kipsigis tribe, 101

Kirby, Beecher (Bashful Brother Oswald), 141, 150, 225, 386, 394, 426, 455

Kirby, Fred, 126, 374–375

Kirchen, Bill, 530

Kirk, Eddie, 238, 274

Kirkes, Walter, 199, 200

Kitty Records, 400

KLEE (Houston), 245

Kleinow, Sneaky Pete, 456

Klick, Mary, 308–309, 317

KLRA (Little Rock), 302

KMA (Shenandoah, Iowa), 81

KMAC (San Antonio), 99

KMBC (Kansas City), 83

KMPC (Los Angeles), 175

Knight, Joe, 246

Knitters, 497

Koehler, Esther "Violet," 140, *140*

KOKE-FM (Austin), 464–465

Kolomoku, Walter, 187

KONO (San Antonio), 184

Korea, 322

Korean War, 306, 374–375

Kotlyarenko, Nuta. *See* Cohn, Nudie "the Tailor"

Kowert, Paul, 539

KPRC (Houston), 179, 191

Kraft Television Theatre (television show), 307

Krauss, Alison, 491, 492, 535, *536*, 537, 541

Krise, Speedy, 394

Kristofferson, Kris: and Bobby Bare, 331; and politics, 439; as songwriter, 331, 340, 353, 356–357, 360, 376, 379, 444

KRLD (Dallas), 131, 221, 278

KSIJ (Gladewater, Texas), 245

KTAT (Fort Worth), 193, 194

KTRH (Houston), 196

KTTV-TV, 238

Ku Klux Klan, 48, 375

Kurtze, Earl, 218

KUT (Austin), 189

Kuykendall, Pete, 387

KVOO (Tulsa), 121, 168, 202, *203*, 220

KVOW (Littlefield, Texas), 470

KWFT (Wichita Falls), 131

KWKH (Shreveport), 127, 147, 201, 243–244, 252, 284, 307

KWTO (Springfield, Missouri), 316

KXLA (Pasadena), 238, 245, 311

KXLW (St. Louis), 306

KXYZ (Houston), 196

LaBeef, Sleepy, 292

labor songs, 166, 170

labor unions: and American Federation of Musicians, 210–211; and folk music, 325; and Great Depression, 152–153, 157–158, 170; and trucker strikes, 378–379

LaBour, Fred "Too Slim," 476

Lady Gaga, 560

La Farge, Peter, 330, 351

Laine, Frankie, 298

Lair, John, 115, 116, 133, *134*, 139, 140, 216, 242, 313

Laird, Tracey, xiii

Lamb, Charles, 299

Lambert, Miranda, 549–550, 555, *555*, 556, 571

Lambert, Pee Wee, 388, 403–404

Landers, Jake, 429

Lane, Robert William, 167

Lang, Eddie, 284

lang, k. d., 499

Lange, Evelyn "Daisy," 140, *140*

Lange, Mutt, 510

Langford, Jon, 528

Lansford, Son, *203*

Larkin, Don "Barkin'," 245

Larkin, Uncle Bob, 118

Las Vegas, Nevada: and country singers, 360; and Oak Ridge Boys, 452; and Elvis Presley, 443

Lauder, Harry, 50, 93

Lauderdale, Jim, 530, 532–533, 543

Laugh-In (television show), 319

Lauper, Cyndi, 560

Laur, Katie, 537

Law, Don, 246, 259

Lawson, Doyle, 424, 426, 431–432

Learning How to Live (album), 529

Leary Family Singers, 259–260

Ledbetter, Huddie "Leadbelly," 325, 330

Ledford, Lily May, 139–140, *140*, 148, 578n8

Ledford, Rosie, 140, *140*

Ledford, Steve, 145

Ledford, Susie, 140

LeDoux, Chris, 502

Led Zeppelin, 492

Lee, Brenda, 293, 315

Lee, Dixie. *See* O'Day, Molly

Lee, Johnny, 436

Lefty Frizzell Sings the Songs of Jimmie Rodgers (album), 273

Lefty Lou, 156

The Legend and the Legacy (album), 579n8

Legion Stadium, El Monte, California, 238

Lemonade (album), 548, 549, 571–572

Lester Flatt G-run, 393

Leva, James, 537

Levine, Adam, 560

Lewey, Fred, 73–74

Lewis, Furry, 328

Lewis, Jerry Lee, 292, 293–294, 314, 442, 443

Lewis, Laurie, 537–538

Lewis, Little Roy, 428

Lewis Family, 428

liberalism, 56, 356–357, 374, 375–376, 425, 434, 438

Library of Congress, 58, 68, 151, 325

licensing rights, 209–210

Lick the Skillet Band, 62

Life magazine, 232

Light Crust Doughboys: and Cowboy Ramblers, 200; and electrical amplification, 187; and films, 171; and Great Depression, 154; and Pappy O'Daniel, 191–193; photograph of, *191*; recordings of, 191, 192, 193; repertory of, 193–194; revival of, 475–476; and

Jimmie Rodgers, 109; and Bob Wills, 193, 202, 204

Light Crust Flour, 191

Lightfoot, Gordon, 424

Lillie, Margaret, 216

Lilly, Everett, 137, 394, 410–411

Lilly, Mitchell "Bea," 137, 410–411

Lilly Brothers (Everett and Mitchell), 137, 158, 409, 410–411

Lincoln, Abraham, 152

Little Clifford, 216

Little Dixie Hayride (radio show), 429

Little Feat, 511

Little Red Songbook (IWW), 166

The Little Sparrow (album), 533

Little Texas, 494

Live at Johnny Mack Brown High School (album), 452

Living Proof (television show), 436

LL Cool J, 559

Lloyd, Bill, 494

Loar, Lloyd, 33, 187

Locklin, Hank, 275–276, 301, 308

Loesser, Frank, 211, 229–230

Loew's Theatre Circuit, 10, 86

Logan, Benjamin Franklin "Tex," 409, 410, 411

Logan, Horace, 243

Logsdon, Jimmie, 396

Lomax, Alan, 24, 29, 105–106, 107, 151, 289, 405, 414

Lomax, John A., 33, 151, 163, 165

London Palladium, 280

Lone Justice, 497

Lonesome Pine Fiddlers, 390–391, 400

Lonesome River Band, 534–535

Lone Star Café, New York City, 367

Lone Star Cowboys, 173, 201

The Lone Star Rangers (radio show), 179

Long, Hubert, 241, 310

Long, Huey, 57

Long, Jimmie, 170

Longfellow, Henry Wadsworth, 412

Longhorn Luke, 165

Longstreet, A. B., 20–21

Lonzo and Oscar, 263–264

Los Angeles, California: and California sound, 341; and hillbilly music, 214, 219; and session musicians, 318. *See also* KFVD (Los Angeles); KMPC (Los Angeles)

Los Angeles County Barn Dance (radio show), 219

Los Lobos, 497

Loudermilk, Ira and Charles. *See* Louvin Brothers (Ira and Charlie)

Loudermilk, John D., 355

Louisiana: black influence in, 160–161; and cowboy music, 160; oil industry in, 162; radio stations in, 121; recording companies in, 113; and southern music, 3; and western swing, 190. *See also* Cajun music; *and specific cities*

Louisiana Hayride (radio show): and Bailes Brothers, 243, 252; and Johnny Horton, 332; and Sonny James, 296; and Johnny and Jack, 254; and George Jones, 337; and Jimmy Martin, 402; and Webb Pierce, 273; in postwar era, 234, 243–244; and Jim Reeves, 305; and Slim Whitman, 279; and Hank Williams, 244, 283–284, 285; and Faron Young, 307

Louvin, Charlie, 137, 261, 405

Louvin, Ira, 137, 261, 383, 405, 407, 487

Louvin Brothers (Ira and Charlie): with Roy Acuff, 222; and duet singing, 128, 251, 252–254, 428, 429; and Flying Burrito Brothers, 456; and *Grand Ole Opry*, 252, 253; and Emmylou Harris, 254, 485; and Jim and Jesse McReynolds, 405, 406, 417; and Monroe Brothers, 137; and O'Kanes, 494; and radio, 252–253; recordings of, 253–254, 512; repertory of, 253, 262; songwriting of, 261, 302, 374

Lovato, Demi, 559

Love, Daddy John, 122, 144–145

Loveless, Patty, 490, 512, 515–516

Lovett, Lyle, 496, 499–500, 523

Lovullo, Sam, 319

lower-middle class, 9

Loyola University, 121

Luckenbach, Texas, 519

Lucky Spot, Bakersfield, 344

Lucky Strike Hit Parade (radio show), 232

Ludacris, 561

Ludaversal (album), 561

Luke the Drifter, 284

Lulu Belle and Scotty, 68, 115, 139, 216, 242, 375

Luman, Bob, 292, 450

Luncheon at Sardi's (radio shows), 277

Lunsford, Bascom Lamar, 68

Luther, Frank, 51, 75, 178

Lyle, Rudy, 407

Lyle Lovett (album), 499–500

Lynch, Claire, 537

Lynch, Laura, 511

Lynn, Doolittle, 362

Lynn, Loretta: autobiography of, 362, 435; duets with Conway Twitty, 334, 448, 450; and Patty Loveless, 515; and mainstream country, 517; in *Newsweek*, 434; photograph of, *448*; and politics, 438; and radio, 362, 496; recordings of, 362; as songwriter, 349, 362, 555; stage persona of, 361, 379; and television shows, 316, 362; and Ernest Tubb, 220, 579n8; and Jack White, 550–551; on women's rights, 360, 362, 554

Lynne, Shelby, 523

Lynyrd Skynyrd, 457, 492, 516

Lytle, Donald. *See* Paycheck, Johnny

Ma, Yo Yo, 539

Mac and Bob, 51, 68, 132–133

MacArthur Fellowship, 542

McAuliffe, Harry (Big Slim, the Lone Cowboy), 117, 142

McAuliffe, Leon, 188, *191*, 193, *203*, 204, 475

McBride, Dickie, 196, 198, 235

McBride, Laura Lee, 235, 475

McBride, Martina, 509, 554, 560, 591n6

McBurney, Albert, 187

McCall, C. W., 378

McCall, Darrell, 340, 519

McCarn, David, 125, 158

McCarty, Mac, 230

McClintock, Harry "Haywire Mac," 165, 166, 173

McClinton, O. B., 373

McCoury, Delano Floyd "Del," 430, 431, 500, 533–534

McCoury, Jerry, 431

McCoury, Robbie, 431, 534

McCoury, Ronnie, 431, 534

McCoy, Charlie, 454

McCravy Brothers (Frank and James), 133

McCreath, Ray, 98

McCreery, Scott, 567

McCurry, Clarence Earl. *See* Ashley, Clarence "Tom"

McDonald, Skeets, 238

McDowell, Ronnie, 443

McEnery, Red River Dave, 173, 230, 314–315, 349–350

McEntire, Reba, 361, 489, 495–496, 509, 554

McEuen, John, 454

McEuen, William, 454

McFarland, Lester, 51, 68, 132–133

McGee, Kirk, 85, 88, 147, 419

McGee, Sam, 85, 88, 147, 149, 205, 419

McGhee, John, 157–158

McGinnis, Fay, 410

McGinnis, Roy, 410

McGinty, Billy, 167

McGinty Cowboys, 167

McGovern, George, 376, 421

McGraw, Tim, 492, 498, 505, 510, 542, 544, 550

McGuire Sisters, 302

Mack, Bill, 378–379

McKenna, Brittney, 549

MacKenzie, Kate, 537

McLeod, Odell, 249–250, 262

McMichen, Clayton, 62–63, 107, 143, 146

McNally, Zeb, *203*

McNatt, Speedy, 276

Macon, Dorris, *87*, 88

Macon, Mathilda Richardson, 86

Macon, Uncle Dave: and banjo playing style, 30, 88, 148, 386; in *Grand Ole Opry*, 37, 85, 86–87, 88, 89, 387, 434, 585–586n7; in *Grand Ole Opry* tent show, xi, 218; and John Hartford, 356; and Sam McGee, 85, 88; and medicine shows, 7, 50; photograph of, *87*; protest songs of, 158; and radio, 88; recordings of, 87–88, 158; repertory of, 86–87; and southern music, 50; and southern theater circuits, 10; and television, 437; and urban folk revival, 327, 414; and vaudeville shows, 37, 86, 88; vocal style of, 51, 85

Macon Midway Mule and Wagon Transportation Company, 86

McReynolds, Jesse, 406, 415

McReynolds, Jim, 406–407, 423

McReynolds, Jim and Jesse: and bluegrass, 390–391, 396, 405–407, 417, 418, 419; and bluegrass festivals, 423; and hillbilly music, 405–406; in Japan, 324; and mandolin-and-guitar duets, 251; and Newport Folk Festival, 329; and radio, 404, 406; vocal style of, 406–407

McWilliams, Elsie, 95, 106–107

Macy, Robin, 511

Macy Records, 305

Maddie and Tae, 547

Maddox, Rose, 239, 255–258, 309

Maddox Brothers and Rose, 239, 255, 265, 290

Madison, Wisconsin, xi

Madison Square Garden Rodeo, 179

Magaha, Mack, 316–317, 397

Magness, Tommy, 147, 225, 386

Mainer, J. E., 10, 111, 144–145, 147

Mainer, Wade, 144–145, 148

Mainer's Mountaineers, 10, 111, 144–146, 207, 220–221, 384, 403

Maines, Lloyd, 511

Maines, Natalie, 511, 552–553, 589–590n10

Malin, Don, 64

Malo, Raul, 494

Malone, Bill C., ix–xii, xvii–xviii, *368*

Malone, Bobbie, xi–xii, xvii

Malone, Cleburne, xvii

Malone, Kelly, xiv

Malone, Maude Owens, ix, xvii

Malone, Wylie, xiv

mandolin-and-guitar duets: and Armstrong Twins, 238; and banjos, 148; and Blue Sky Boys, 134, 136, 251; emergence of, 122; and Karl and Harty, 133; and Louvin Brothers, 253; and Mac and Bob, 132–133; and Monroe Brothers, 134, 137–138; and Wiley and Zeke Morris, 146, 221; and Shelton Brothers, 200–201

mandolins: and bluegrass, 144, 148, 383, 384, 386, 388, 406; cross-picking technique, 406; electrical amplification of, 148, 187, 195; in hillbilly music, 51, 132; and Italian immigrants, 32–33; and Bill Monroe, 137, 148, 383, 384, 386, 394, 408; and Joe Shelton, 201; tunings of, 424

Mandrell, Barbara, 360, 436, 440, 441–442, 485

Maness, J. D., 455

Manners, Zeke, 175, 178

Mannes, Leo, 175

Maphis, Joe, 238, 341, 441, 528

Maphis, Rose, 238

Maple City Four Quartet, 82

Marburg, William. *See* Clifton, Bill

Maritime Provinces, Canada, 2

Marks, Edward B., 19, 210

Marshall, Charlie, 174

Marshall Family, 428

Marshall Tucker Band, 443, 456–457, 488

Martel, Linda, 373

Martha White Flour, 252, 392

Martin, Asa, 10

Martin, Benny, 393, 407

Martin, Dean, 291, 298, 444

Martin, Grady, 247, 301, 329

Martin, James Henry "Jimmy": and bluegrass, 396, 401–403, 409, 410; and Blue Grass Boys, 391, 402; and instrumentation, 423; and Doyle Lawson, 432; and Nitty Gritty Dirt Band, 454–455; and Bobby Osborne, 400; and radio, 404; as songwriter, 393; vocal style of, 402, 407

Martin, Janis, 292

Martin, Lecil Travis. *See* Boxcar Willie

Martin, Mac, 409

Martin, William C., 467

Martin Brothers, 157

Marvin, Frankie, 108, 168

Marvin, Johnny, 168

Marvin, Ken (Lonzo), 264

Marvin Brothers, 168

Marx, Groucho, 494

Marx, Karl, 152

Mascot films, 170

Massey, Guy, 74

Masters, Johnny, 263

Masters Family (Johnny and Lucille), 262

Mattea, Kathy, 523, 526

Mavericks (Charlie Marshall's), 174

Mavericks (Moe Bandy), 482

Mavericks (Raul Malo), 494

Maynard, Ken, 170

Mayo, O. W., 250

MCA Records: and Mark Chesnutt, 516; and Decca Records, 186, 407; and Vince Gill, 504; and Patty Loveless, 515; and Conway Twitty, 448; and Steve Wariner, 450

Meade, Guthrie T. (Gus), 23, 40

Meador, Constance June. *See* Smith, Connie

medicine shows: and Roy Acuff, 223; and advertising, 119; and Tom Ashley, 69; and fiddlers, 21; and Uncle Dave Macon, 7, 50; and Jimmie Rodgers, 7, 93, 95–96; in rural areas, 7, 34; and Bob Wills, 202

Mellencamp, John Cougar, 518

Melody Masters, 265–266

Melody Ranch (radio show), 171, 322

Melotone records, 112

Memorial Auditorium, Shreveport, 243

Memphis, Tennessee, 10. *See also* WHBQ (Memphis); WMPS (Memphis)

men: as folk musicians, 34–36; monopolization of early commercial country music, 26–27

Mencken, H. L., 151

Menius, Art, 535

Mercer, Johnny, 211

Mercury Records: and Billy Ray Cyrus, 505; and Flatt and Scruggs, 391, 393, 394; and George Jones, 337; and Reba McEntire, 495; and Johnny Rodriguez, 369; and Stanley Brothers, 405; and Statler Brothers, 451

MerleFest, 541, 543–544

Metamodern Sounds in Country Music (album), 562

Mexican American performers in country music, 367, 369

Mexican border stations, 80, 117–119, 130, 209

Mexican culture, 5, 180

Mexican *grito*, 105

Meyer, Edgar, 539

MGM Records, 283, 401, 447

Mid-Day Merry-Go-Round (radio show), 223, 243, 303

middle-class audiences: and Gene Autry, 171, 274; and Jimmie Dean, 317; ethic of, 312, 346, 348; and mandolins, 32–33; and Willie Nelson, 467–468; and parlor songs, 18–19; and Charley Pride, 370; and professional songwriters, 11; and radio, 436; and sentimental songs, 19; and Statler Brothers, 451; and traditional country music, 518; and urban folk revival, 414

Midnight Jamboree (radio show), 359

Midwest, 113, 115

Midwestern Hayride (television show), 315

Mighty Sparrow, 558

migration: black migration to cities, 41; of Okies, 152, 156, 208, 214, 235, 255, 341, 346; southern migrants, 3, 208, 213–214, 245, 334, 411, 412, 430, 431; and World War II, 208–209, 213–214

military personnel and country music, 321–322, 348, 355

Miller, Bob, 54, 57–58, 132, 229

Miller, Buddy, 485, 543, 565

Miller, Emmett, 203, 204, 205, 284, 347

Miller, John, 384

Miller, Julie, 543

Miller, Lost John, 387

Miller, Roger, 305, 318, 340, 352, 355, 357, 444, 559

Miller, Slim, 115, *134*

Miller, Townsend, 464

Milsap, Ronnie, 479

Mineral Wells, Texas, 116, 118, 120

Minnie Pearl, 215, 217, 242, 320, 434

Miskulin, Joey, 476

Mississippi, 39

Mitchell, Chad, Trio, 326

Mitchell, Joni, 327, 523, 559

Mize, Billy, 341

Moc-A-Tan Compound, 223

modal scale, 5

Modern Mountaineers, 196

Modern Sounds in Country and Western Music (album), 370, 561

Mohawk Ranch, Boston, 411

Monkey Trial of 1925, 54

Monroe, Bill: and Bean Blossom Festival, 420, 421; and Byron Berline, 427; and bluegrass, 221, 380, 381, 382–391, 394, 395, 396, 399, 401, 403, 405, 407–408, 409, 413, 418, 421, 423, 424, 428, 431, 531, 533, 534, 541; Blue Grass Boys, 221, 384, *385*, 386, 387–393, 397, 400, 407–408, 421; and CMA's twenty-fifth anniversary celebration, 438–439; and Flatt and Scruggs, 391, 396, 407, 422; and *Grand Ole Opry*, 115, 217–218, 221, 335, 384, 386, 399, 400, 418–419; and Carlton Haney, 420; and IBMA's Hall of Honor, 531; and George Jones, 335, 337; and Del McCoury, 431; and McReynolds Brothers, 405; and Tommy Magness, 147; and mandolin style, 137, 148, 383, 384, 386, 394, 408; and Jimmy Martin, 401–402, 407; and Monroe Brothers, 137–138, *138*, 383–384; musical training of, 382–383; and Newport Folk Festival, 329; photograph of, *381*; and Elvis Presley, 291, 295; recordings of, 248, 374, 385–386, 388, 391, 402, 423; repertory of, 385–386, 428, 432, 544; as songwriter, 383, 393; and Stanley Brothers, 404; vocal style of, 221, 254, 302, 383, 384–385, 388, 397, 400, 402, 404; with Doc Watson, *532*; women in bands of, 535

Monroe, Birch, 137, 383, *385*

Monroe, Charlie, 137–138, *138*, 221, 382, 383–384, 392

Monroe, James, 391

Monroe, Malissa Vandiver, 382

Monroe Brothers (Charlie and Bill): and duet singing, 137, 138, 221, 383, 384; and Lilly Brothers, 410; and mandolin-and-guitar duets, 134, 137–138; and Byron Parker, 138, *138*, 145; recordings of, 158, 252; repertory of, 111

Montana, Patsy, 122, 173, *175*, 258

Montana Slim (Wilf Carter), 109, 122, 179, 278

Montgomery, John Michael, 492

Montgomery, Marvin, 194, 200

Montgomery, Melba, 335, 361

Montgomery, Smokey, 476

Montgomery Ward, 33, 112–113

Monty Python, 559

Monument Records, 357, 366

Moody, Clyde, 145, 245, 386, 391

Moody, Dwight L., 14

Mooney, Ralph, 339, 341, 342

Moonshine Kate, 58

Moore, Bob, 301, 406

Moore, Byrd, 69

Moore, Charlie, 429

Moore, Jerry, 429

Moore, Lee, 244

Moore, Russell, 534

Moore, Squeakin' Deacon, 245

Moore, Tiny, 475

Moorer, Allison, 543

More a Legend Than a Band (album), 520

Moreland, Arnot Jackson "Peg," 67–68, 188, 202

Morgan, George, 275, 276, 458

Morgan, J. Doug, 99

Morgan, Lorrie, 458, 497

morphine, 125

Morris, Claude "Zeke," 144–145, 146, 221, 329, 387

Morris, George, 145

Morris, James, 332

Morris, Lynn, 537

Morris, Maren, 550

Morris, Wiley, 145, 146, 221, 329, 387

Morris Brothers, 397

Morton, Tex, 108, 167

Mother Maybelle and the Carter Sisters, 247, 257

Motown, 441

Mott, Tiny, *203*

The Mountain (album), 533

Mountain Soul (album), 515

MTV, 505

Muenich, Jeanne, 115

Muleskinner News, 425

Mullican, Aubrey "Moon": and barrelhouse style of piano playing, 198, 270; and boogie tunes, 195, 198, 246, 265, 269, 290; and Cliff Bruner, 195; and Jimmie Davis, 127; recordings of, 245, 246, 265, 269, 271; and

Jim Reeves, 305; vocal style of, 269–270; and western swing, 197

Mullins, Harry, 216

Munde, Alan, 407, 427

Munich Morning Report (radio show), 227

Munich Mountaineers, 256, 322

Munnerlyn, John, 190

Murphey, Michael Martin, 463, 464, 507, 543

Murphy, Joaquin, 235

Murray, Anne, 444, 445–446, 499

Murrell, Red, 235, 238

Musical Brownies, 144, 187–188, *192*, 193, 194–195, 196, 197, 199

Music Center, Cincinnati, 396

Music City News, 323, 436, 495, 496

Music Hall, Cincinnati, 227

music videos: and Beyoncé, 548; and Clint Black, 501; and Junior Brown, 520; and CMT, 568; and Billy Ray Cyrus, 505; and Faith Hill, 509, 511; and Nickel Creek, 537, 541; and Shania Twain, 509, 544; and Wheeler Walker Jr., 566; and Dwight Yoakam, 497

Mutual Broadcasting System, 277

My Kind of Country (album), 495

My Life (album), 525

Myrick, David. *See* Tyler, T. Texas

Myrick, Weldon, 359

Myrtle Beach, South Carolina, 518

Nabell, Charles, 163

Napier, Bill, 415, 429

NASCAR, 568

Nash, Len, 173–174

Nash Ramblers, 485

Nashville, Tennessee: and Acuff-Rose Publishing House, 212, 228, 248; as music center, 151, 212, 228, 241, 246–248, 300, 310, 395, 439–440, 529, 542, 545; publishing in, 212, 228, 247–248, 300, 310; recording companies in, 246–247, 269, 310, 580n6; songwriters of, 300, 303, 310, 352–353. *See also* WDAD (Nashville); WKDA (Nashville); WSM (Nashville)

Nashville (film), 434–435

Nashville (television show), 552, 569

Nashville Bluegrass Band, 100, 534

Nashville Brass, 445

Nashville Grass, 394, 421–422, 513

Nashville Network (TNN), 437, 449, 476, 505, 515

Nashville Nevada Club, Las Vegas, 345

Nashville Now (television show), 437

Nashville Rebel (film), 471

Nashville Skyline (album), 454, 457

Nashville Songwriters Association Hall of Fame, 197

Nashville sound, 300–301, 310, 454, 545

Natchee the Indian, 143

Nathan, Sydney, 245–246, 290, 295, 397–398, 415

National Association of Broadcasters, 209

National Barn Dance (radio show): and Gene Autry, 115, 168; and Red Foley, 242; and George Hay, 83; and hillbilly music, 83; and Karl and Harty, 133; and Lily May Ledford, 140; and Lulu Belle and Scotty, 139; and Mac and Bob, 132, 133; performers of, xiii, 64, 68, 82–83, 115; and personal appearances, 215–216; and Prairie Ramblers, 143; sponsors of, 116, 120; and WLS, 40, 81–82, 115–116; and women entertainers, 139–140, 141

National Endowment for the Arts, 490

National Folk Festival, Washington, DC, 259–260

National Football League, 569

National Life and Accident Insurance Company, 83–84, 217

National Musical Instrument Company, 150

National Public Radio, 543

National Recovery Administration (NRA), 159

National Rodeo Finals, 495

nativism, 49

NBC: and Country Music Hall of Fame and Museum opening, 312; and dramatizations, 178; and *Grand Ole Opry*, 114, 116, 217, 224, 241, 242; and *Midwestern Hayride*, 315; *Music Appreciation Hour*, 89; and *National Barn Dance*, 116

Neal, Bob, 291

Neal, Thurman, 200

Negro American League, 371

Nelly, 550

Nelson, Bobbie, 354, 467

Nelson, Connie, 467

Nelson, Willie: in Austin, Texas, 463, 465–468; and black music, 6; and definition of country music, 441; duets with Merle Haggard, 450; and Farm Aid concerts, 518; films of, 435, 468, 477; and Outlaw musicians, 468, 473–474, 518; photograph of, *466*; picnics

of, 465–467; and Webb Pierce, 273; and
politics, 438, 439, 468; and Ray Price, 340;
and radio, 496; repertory of, 354, 517, 518;
and Fred Rose, 228; and Snoop Dogg, 550;
as songwriter, 307, 309, 340, 354–355, 465,
554; and television shows, 315; vocal style
of, 354; and Bob Wills, 354, 475
Nennstiel, G. A., 68
neo-traditionalism: and Alan Jackson,
490, 515; and Reba McIntyre, 495–496;
and Daryle Singletary, 570; and Ricky
Skaggs, 488; and Randy Travis, 490,
496–497; trends in, 483–484, 489, 490–491,
493–494, 501, 512–513, 515–517, 546; and
Dwight Yoakam, 490, 497
Nesbitt, Eddie, 411
Nettles, Jennifer, 550
Nevins, Richard, 27
New Age, 520, 542
Newbury, Mickey, 356
New Christy Minstrels, 446
New Country, 491, 493
New Deal, 158–159, 296
New Deal String Band, 426
New England, 2, 117
New England Bluegrass Boys, 409
newgrass, 423–427, 538–539, 541–542
New Grass Revival, 425, 426–427, 539, *541*
Newkeys Music, 355
New Lost City Ramblers, 328
Newman, Jimmy C., 330–331, 355, 518
Newman, Roy, 199–200, 231
New Orleans, Louisiana, 10, 199. *See also*
WWL (New Orleans)
Newport Folk Festival, 329, 414, 416, 517
New Riders of the Purple Sage, 456
New River Ranch, Rising Sun, Maryland, 409
New Shades of Grass, 425, 426
New South, 425–426, 432, 486
Newsweek, 434
Newton, Ernie, 247
Newton-John, Olivia, 440, 444, 445, 546
New York City: and country music, 178–179,
180; and Kinky Friedman, 367; and Tin Pan
Alley songwriters, 7. *See also* WHN (New
York City); WMCA (New York City); WOR
(New York City)
New Yorker, 434
New York Times, 414, 553
New Zealand, 321
Nicholas, Hayden, 501

Nichols, Joe Paul, 340
Nichols, Roy, 239, 255, 341, 347
Nickel Creek, 526, 537, 539, 541–542
Nickel Creek (album), 541
Nine Inch Nails, 561
Nine to Five (film), 435
Nirvana, 562
Nitty Gritty Dirt Band, 454–455, 464
Nix, Hoyle, 206, 475
Nixon, Richard, 377, 437–438, 553
Nobles, Robert Clarence, 176
No Depression (album), 528, 564
No Depression (magazine), 528, 529, 531, 549,
563–564, 566, 570
Noell, Charlie, 73–74
No Fences (album), 502
Nolan, Bob, 176
Noontime Varieties (radio show), 199
Norman, Jim Ed, 490
Norris, Fate, 62
North Africa, 321
North Carolina Ramblers, 59–61, *60*, 70, 125
Now That I've Found You (album), 541
Nudie the Tailor. See Cohn, Nudie "the Tailor"
numbering system of Nashville musicians,
300

Oak Ridge Boys, 443, 451, 452–453
Oak Ridge Quartet, 452
Oaks, Charlie, 18, 50, 54, 55, 66, 68
Obama, Barack, 559
Oberstein, Eli, 46, 136
O'Brien, Molly, 526
O'Brien, Tim, 425, 524, 525–526, *527*, 529, 539
O Brother, Where Art Thou? soundtrack (film),
490–491, 532
O'Bryant, Alan, 534
Ochs, Phil, 326, 374
O'Connor, Bill, 82
O'Connor, Mark, 539
O'Daniel, Mike, 193
O'Daniel, Pat, 193
O'Daniel, W. Lee "Pappy," 109, 118, 154,
191–193, *191*, 553
O'Day, Molly: and Carl Butler, 394; with
Lynn Davis, *259*; recordings of, 230, 283,
399, 413; style of, xvi, 251, 257; vocal style
of, 258–259, 261, 268, 309, 428; and Mac
Wiseman, 398, 399
Odell, Mac, 249–250, 262
Oh, Susanna! (film), 171

O'Hara, Jamie, 494

oil industry: in California, 341; and *Louisiana Hayride*, 244; and songwriters, 231; in southwest, 160; in Texas, 162, 181, 436

O'Kanes, 494

O'Keefe, James, 46

Okeh records: and Polk Brockman, 44; and Fiddlin' John Carson, 45, 111; and Columbia Records, 112; and cowboy music, 163; and Kelly Harrell, 70; and Hill Billies, 47; and Humphries Brothers, 189; and Radio Cowboys, 144; and recording tactics, 43, 46; and Goebel Reeves, 166; and Mamie Smith, 41–42; and Ernest Stoneman, 58; and Wiley Walker, 231; and Henry Whitter, 70, 74, 123; and Bob Wills, 202

Okie jazz, 188

Okies: and Woodie Guthrie, 153; migration of, 152, 156, 208, 214, 235, 255, 341, 346

Okinawa, 227

Oklahoma: cowboy music in, 160; oil industry in, 162; recording companies in, 113

Oklahoma (musical), 179

Oklahoma Cowboys, 167, 283

Oklahoma Playboys, 198–199

Old 97's, 528

Old Dominion Barn Dance (radio show), 397

Old Farm Hour (radio show), 410

Old Five and Dimers Like Me (album), 472

Old Kentucky String Band, 410

Old Settlers' Days, 21

Old Settlers' Reunion, Round Rock, Texas, 189

Oliver, Janis, 504

Oliver, Kristine, 504

Oliver, Paul, 103

Once in a Very Blue Moon (album), 523

O'Neal, Uncle Jim, 419

O'Neal, Waldo, 107

One Endless Night (album), 520

Opry House, 433–434, 438

Opryland Park, 89, 434, 510

Orbison, Roy, 250, 292, 499

Ordway's Aeolians, 25

organized labor. *See* labor unions

organs: in hillbilly music, 51; parlor organs, 21, 31

Original Country Boys, 174

Oriole records, 112

Orion, 443

Osborne, Bobby, 220, 399–402, 404

Osborne, Jimmie, 245

Osborne, Louise, 400

Osborne, Sonny, 391, 399–401, 407, 418

Osborne Brothers: and bluegrass, 395, 396, 399–401, 409, 410, 414, 417–419; and bluegrass festivals, 420, 423; and Jimmy Martin, 401, 402; recordings of, 401, 402; repertory of, 139; vocal style of, 417

Oslin, K. T., 509

Ossenbrink, Luther, 83

Oswald, Bashful Brother (Beecher Kirby), 141, 150, 225, 386, 394, 426, 455

Other Voices, Other Rooms (album), 524

Other Voices, Too (album), 524

Outlaw musicians, 468–474, 476, 480, 546

Overstake, Eva, 242

Overstreet, Paul, 497

Owen, Randy, 453

Owens, Alvis Edgar "Buck": and Bakersfield music scene, 342–343; death of, 570; and Derailers, 530; and Fender guitars, 239; as guitarist, 341; and Harlan Howard, 353; and Brad Paisley, 517; and radio, 238, 343; recordings of, 342–343, 353; as songwriter, 397; style of, 531; and television shows, 315, 320, 343; and Dwight Yoakam, 497

Owens, Bonnie, 345

Owens, Buddy Alan, 343

Owens, Don, 245, 396, 412

Owens, Doodle, 477

Owens, Ruby Agnes "Texas Ruby," 116, 147, 218, 235, 257–258

Owens, Tex, 235, 277, 314

Owens, Tom, 82

Oxford, Vernon, 324

Oxydol Cowboys, 321

Ozark Jubilee (television show), 315, 316

Ozark Mountains, 4

Packard, Vance, 289, 581n2

Page, Patti, 248, 444

Paisley, Brad, 490, 492, 513, 517, 557–562, *558*, 565, 567

Paley, Tom, 328

Pamper publishing company, 310, 353, 354

Panama Pacific World Exposition, San Francisco, 32, 75, 104

Panhandle Cowboys and Indians, 187

Paramount Record Company, 46, 157

Parker, Byron, 138, *138*, 145

Parker, Chubby, 83

Parker, Colonel Tom, 218, 241

Parker, John W. "Knocky," 194, 200

Parker, Linda, 115, *134*

Parks, Lucien "Piggy," 95

parlor organs, 21, 31

parlor songs: and Delmore Brothers, 128, 129; and Great Depression, 154; and Bradley Kincaid, 66; and Mainer's Mountaineers, 145; and middle-class audiences, 18–19; and Obed Pickard, 85

Parmley, Don, 424, 429

Parsons, Gram, 254, 327, 454, 455–456, 459, 485, 500, 526

Parsons, Robert, 455

Parton, Dolly: and bluegrass, 533; films of, 360, 435; and Emmylou Harris, 485; and mainstream country, 517; mountain folk beginnings of, 364, 366; and Brad Paisley, 558; and Katy Perry, 550; photograph of, *365*; and radio, 496; recordings of, 365–366; as songwriter, 349, 365, 366, 538; stage persona of, 360, 361, 509–510; as superstar, 359, 362, 364, 366; and television shows, 316, 365, 367; theme park in Pigeon Forge, Tennessee, 508; vocal style of, 366, 535; and Porter Wagoner, 316, 334, 366, 367, 450; on women's rights, 360

Parton, Stella, 459

Paste magazine, 554

patent medicines, 7, 118, 119, 125

patriotic songs, 163, 229, 230, 376–377, 452, 507

Paul, Woody, 476

Paul English Players, 98, 108

Paul Whiteman Club (radio show), 277

Paycheck, Johnny, 340, 378, 472, 473, 478

Payne, Leon, 275

Payne, Myrtie, 275

Payne, Rufus "Tee-Tot," 282

Peacock Fiddle Band, 41

Pearl Harbor attack, 208

peddlers, 6

Peer, Ralph: and black music, 41–42, 44, 45; and Carter Family, 78–79, 80, 108; and Harrell, 71; and hillbilly band names, 59, 69; as music publisher, 80, 96, 111, 210; recording career of, 41–44, 46, 47, 52, 76, 78–79, 96, 246; and Eck Robertson, 43; and Jimmie Rodgers, 80, 96, 97, 98

Peerce, Lonnie, 427

Pellettieri, Vito, 114, 242

Penick, Mary Frances, 302–303

Pennell, John, 535

Penny, Herbert Clayton "Hank," 121, 143–144, 195, 235, 251, 290, 528

Pentecostalism, 15–16, 55, 56, 76, 382

People's Choice Award, 447

Pep Records, 342

Perfect Records, 112

Perkins, Carl, 292, 385

Perkins, Lefty, 188, 200

Perkins, Luther, 298

Perry, Katy, 550

Perryman, Lloyd, 177

Perryman, Tom, 245, 305

personal appearances: and hillbilly music, 113, 114, 115, 119, 121, 141, 215–216; in postwar era, 234, 240

Peter, Paul and Mary, 327

Petrillo, James C., 210–211

Petruska, David. *See* Dudley, Dave

The Phantom Empire (cowboy/science fiction serial), 170

Phillips, Bruce "Utah," 415

Phillips, Dewey, 291

Phillips, Foreman, 219, 227, 235, 238

Phillips, Sam, 291, 294, 298, 478

Phillips, Todd, 432

Philo Records, 523, 525

Phipps, Ernest, 76

phonograph industry, 37, 38, 41, 55, 113, 182, 211, 212

piano rolls, 10

pianos: and barrelhouse style, 198, 270; and country dances, 21; and Floyd Cramer's "slip-note" technique, 301–302; in hillbilly music, 51; and honky-tonk music, 183; and Jerry Lee Lewis, 293, 443; and sheet music, 19, 31; and Gary Stewart, 443; and western swing, 195, 199, 204

Pickard, Obed "Dad," 85

Pickard Family, 85, 119, 121

Pierce, Don, 323, 419

Pierce, Jack, 96

Pierce, Webb: and Cedarwood Publishing Company, 310; and *Grand Ole Opry*, 244; and honky-tonk music, 271, 274; and Willie Nelson, 273; recordings of, 199, 246, 273, 274, 288, 337; vocal style of, 274; and Wilburn Brothers, 315; and Faron Young, 307

Pikelny, Noam, 539

The Pilgrim (album), 513

Pillsbury Bakeoff, 555

Pinnacle Boys, 429

Pinson, Bob, xvi

Pioneer Trio, 176

Pitts, Kenneth, 200

Platters, 290, 534

Plaza Bar, Boston, 411

Pleasant Valley Boys, 475

politics and country music: and Jimmie Davis, 118, 126–127, 193, 201, 207, 553; and Dixie Chicks, 552–554, 565, 571, 589–590n10, 590n13; and fiddlers, 20, 21, 22, 40, 45, 58; and Great Depression, 152–159; and Merle Haggard, 437, 439, 518, 525, 590n13; and hillbilly music, 49, 118, 119, 201, 207; and Korean War, 374–375; and labor unions, 325; and Pappy O'Daniel, 192, 193, 553; and presidential support, 437–439, 553; and repertory, 254; and songwriters, 350, 374–376, 377, 507; and southern music, 23–24; and urban folk revival, 326, 374; and Vietnam War, 437–438; and Watergate crisis, 350, 438; and women, 360, 362, 508–509, 552–554

Poole, Charlie: and medicine shows, 50; with North Carolina Ramblers, 59–61, *60*; recordings of, 61, 380, 585n2; repertory of, 59–61, 125, 380; and southern music, 50; and string bands, 124, 146; and urban folk revival, 327; vocal style of, 51, 60–61, 63, 70

Poor Richard's Almanac (band), 425, 427

Porterfield, Nolan, 76, 94, 102

Porter Wagoner Show (television show), 316

Possum Hunters, 84–85

Poulton, Curt, 115

Powell, Stewart, 374

Powers, Fiddlin', 58

Pozo Seco Singers, 446

A Prairie Home Companion (radio show), xi, 434, 436, 508, 542, 543

Prairie Ramblers, 143, 173, *175*

Prem Rawat, 463

Presley, Elvis: and Red Foley, 242; legacy of, 443; and Jerry Lee Lewis, 294; and *Louisiana Hayride*, 244; and Bill Monroe, 385; and Tom Parker, 218; and Gram Parsons, 455; popularity of, 292, 294–295, 325, 442, 491; recordings of, 275, 292, 295, 301; and rhythm-and-blues music, 291, 292; and Marty Robbins, 308; and rock-and-roll music, 291, 292, 294, 443; style of, 291–292; and Conway Twitty, 447

Preston, Frances, 311

Preston, Terry, 306

Price, Bill, 304

Price, Fred, 328

Price, Kenny, 320

Price, Lloyd, 289

Price, Ray: appearances in Texas, 519; and Cherokee Cowboys, 325, 338, 339, 340, 473; death of, 570; recordings of, 246, 294, 339–341, 352, 353, 354, 357, 479; style of, 271, 338, 339, 340–341, 475, 480, 517, 531; and Don Walser, 521; and Hank Williams, 271, 288, 300, 338, 339

Pride, Charley, 279, 358, 369, 370–374, *371*, 480, 517

Prince Albert Tobacco, 217, 242

Prine, John, 424, 462, 473, 512, 523, 525

Prins, Kitty, 322

Pritchett, James Arthur, 249, 418

progressive bluegrass: and Bluegrass Alliance, 427; and Country Gentlemen, 325, 380, 412–413, 423, 424–425, 426, 432; and David Grisman, 424; and Bill Keith, 409, 424; and New Grass Revival, 425, 426–427, 539, *541*; and Nickel Creek, 526, 537, 539, 541–542; origins of, 423–424; repertory of, 413–414, 425–427, 533, 538–539; and Seldom Scene, 423, 425, 426, 430, 431; and Ricky Skaggs, 424, 426, 432, 442, 486, 532; and traditional bluegrass, 382, 428, 431

progressive country, 464–465, 546

Prohibition: and hillbilly music, 124–125; repeal of, 158, 181, 182; in rural areas, 20, 48

protest music: and Harry McClintock, 166; and Bruce Springsteen, 554; and urban folk revival, 326; and Vietnam War, 374

Pruett, Jeanne, 361

Pruitt, Jack, 320

Pruitt, Lesley, 554

publishing: and Hartford Company, 25; and hillbilly music, 112; and Bob Miller, 57; in Nashville, 212, 228, 247–248, 300, 310; and Buck Owens, 343; and Ralph Peer, 80, 96, 111, 210

Puckett, George Riley: and drugs, 125; and fiddle-and-banjo duo, 58; recordings of, 63, 132; repertory of, 63–64, 135; songwriting of, 97; and southern music, 50; and Tanner, 62; vocal style of, 51, 63, 105

Pugh, Virginia Wynette. *See* Wynette, Tammy

Punch and Judy shows, 21

punkabilly, 571
punk country, 526, 528, 529
puppet shows, 7
Pure Prairie League, 504
Purina Mills, 277
Putman, Curley, 355, 366, 479
Put Yourself in My Shoes (album), 501

quartets: and gospel music, 25, 26, 451; late
    1970s, 451–452; and Nashville sound, 301;
    and Ralph Stanley, 422
Quebe Sisters, xvi, 570
Quicksilver, 432

Rabbitt, Eddie, 443
race relations, 349, 375, 551, 559
radio: all-country stations, 311–312, 314;
    and AM broadcast band, 117; and ASCAP,
    209–210; and ballads, 188; and barn dances,
    40–41, 58, 81–82, 89–90, 114, 115–117, 121,
    215–217, 219, 221, 234, 238, 243, 338, 416,
    558; and cowboy music, 165, 166, 170, 171,
    173–177; and cross-fertilization of styles,
    138–139, 142–143, 440; and disc-jockey
    programs, 39–40; early programming of,
    40–41; entertainers' reputations based
    in, 141–142; and fifty-thousand-watt clear
    channel stations, 114, 120–121, 209, 217,
    219, 244; format radio, 546, 570, 571; growth
    of, 39, 41; and hillbilly music, xv, 40–41, 48,
    50, 59, 64, 81, 112, 113–114, 118–119, 121, 131,
    218, 219, 221, 234; independent stations,
    518; listener statistics, 493; and market
    fragmentation, 569, 570, 571; and Mexican
    border stations, 80, 117–119, 130; and Buck
    Owens, 238, 343; and P.I. (per inquiry)
    account, 120–121; and politics, 192; in
    postwar era, 234; public radio, 436; and
    rotation broadcasts, 506; in South, 39–40;
    and tight playlist concept, 311, 512, 513; and
    urban folk revival, 325–326; urbanizing
    influence of, 38; and western swing, 191,
    199; and women artists, 557; XM satellite
    radio, 569; and youth culture, 294. *See also*
    disc jockeys; Top-Forty radio; *and specific*
    radio programs and stations
Radio Cowboys, 143, 144, 145, 173, 195
Radio Luxembourg, 321
Rager, Mose, 236
ragtime music, 5, 11, 16, 27, 33, 49, 61, 128, 132,
    190, 334

railroads: and Roy Acuff, 225; and Gene Autry,
    168; and ballads, 73–74, 75; and Boxcar
    Willie, 324; and interaction of urban and
    rural areas, 9; and Jimmie Rodgers, 93–94,
    95, 96, 100, 103, 104, 105, 106; and train
    songs, 89
Raines, Missy, 537
Rainwater, Cedric, 387, 391
Raley, Leo, 148, 187, 195
rambling man image in country music: and
    Boxcar Willie, 324; and Wayne Hancock,
    521–522; and Jimmie Rodgers, 78, 93, 94,
    102, 103, 106, 125, 155; and songwriters, 351
Ramey, Patricia. *See* Loveless, Patty
Ramsey, Willis Alan, 520
Randall, Alice, 549–550
Randolph, Boots, 301
Randolph, Vance, 224
Raney, Wayne, 245, 256, 263, 265, 311, 396
Raphael, Mickey, 467
Rausch, Leon, 265, 475
Ravine Park, Blairsville, Pennsylvania, 218
Raye, Collin, 492
RCA Victor: and Clint Black, 501; and Davis
    Sisters, 302–303; and Don Gibson, 302,
    303; and Vince Gill, 504; and Waylon
    Jennings, 330, 470–471, 473; and Montana
    Slim, 109; and Willie Nelson, 465, 473; and
    Tim O'Brien, 526; and Osborne Brothers,
    402; and Dolly Parton and Porter Wagoner
    duets, 316, 366; and Elvis Presley, 301; and
    Charley Pride, 370, 372, 373; recording
    studios of, 247, 301–302; and Jim Reeves,
    305–306; and Jimmie Rodgers, 109, 110;
    and Connie Smith, 359; and Porter Wag-
    oner, 316; and Steven Wariner, 450; and
    Kitty Wells, 261; and Slim Whitman, 279
RCA Victor Show (radio show), 277
Reagan, Nancy, 438
Reagan, Ronald, 438–439, 553
Rebel Records, 419
Recording Academy, 551, 565, 572
recording companies: and American Federa-
    tion of Musicians, 210–212; and barbershop
    quartets, 25; bibliographic resources on,
    677–678; of black music, 6; and bluegrass,
    419; and commercialization of country
    music, ix, 16–17, 36, 111; and cowboy music,
    38, 113, 173, 543; cylinder recordings, 10,
    58; digital recording techniques, 506, 507;
    and electrical amplification, 187; field

recordings, 23, 44, 46, 151, 246, 325, 327; and Great Depression, 112–113; and hillbilly music, 31, 42, 44–48, 49, 50, 59, 73–75, 96, 111, 113–114, 212–213; in Nashville, 246–247, 300, 310, 580n6; in postwar era, 233, 234, 245; and price of records, 113; and race records, 44, 112, 124, 211, 213, 289; and rural areas, 37–38; and string band music, 27; and western swing, 189; and youth culture, 294. *See also specific companies*

Rector, John, *36*

Rector, Red, 148, 221, 383, 428

Red Clay Ramblers, 483

Red Dirt, 571

Redford, Robert, 435

Red Fox Inn, Bethesda, 412, 426, 485

Red Hot and Blue (radio show), 291

redneck rock, 459, 460, 464

Redneck Shit (album), 566

Red on Blonde (album), 526

Reece, Florence, 152–153

Reed, Blind Alfred, 50, 54–56, 77

Reed, Bud, 409, 412

Reed, Jerry, 435

Reed, Ola Belle, 409, 412

reeds, 202, 204

Reeves, Beulah, 304

Reeves, Goebel, 95, 165–166

Reeves, James Travis "Jim," 244, 288, 302, 303–306, *304*, 310, 324, 446, 582n8

Reeves, Tom, 303

Reid, Don, 451

Reid, Harold, 451

Reinhardt, Django, 27, 142

Reinhart, Dick, 171

religion: bigotry in, 48; and brush arbor meetings, 13–14; and camp meetings, 12–13, 420; and evangelical Protestantism, 3, 12, 13, 14, 15–16, 17, 35, 124, 161, 183, 224, 252, 257–258, 430; and Great Depression, 153, 154–155; and Holiness-Pentecostal revival, 15–16, 55, 56, 76, 224, 252, 257–258, 291–292, 293, 382, 428; as influence on country music, 12, 18; and Methodist circuit riders, 6; and tradition of British religious dissent, 12; and urban revivals, 14

religious music: and Roy Acuff, 223, 224, 225–226; and Bailes Brothers, 252; and Blue Sky Boys, 137; and camp meetings, 12–13, 14, 15, 35; and Martha Carson, 257; and contest between hedonism and Puritanism, 20, 35; and Wilma Lee Cooper, 250, 258, 261; and Red Foley, 243, 263; "folkness" of, 15–16; and Great Depression, 158; and harmony singing, 25; and *Hee Haw*, 320; and hillbilly songs, 56, 66, 71; as influence on country music, 12–13, 16, 36, 119, 262, 512; and George Jones, 335; and Lonesome River Band, 535; and Maddox Brothers and Rose, 255; and Mainer's Mountaineers, 145; and Bill Monroe, 385, 402; and Elvis Presley, 292; and Ray Price, 340; and radio, 40; and Jimmie Rodgers, 91; and Connie Smith, 359; and Ralph Stanley, 422, 534; and Stanley Brothers, 403; and *Sunday Morning Gathering*, 216; and Merle Travis, 237–238; and vocal style, 51; and Hank Williams, 280, 284. *See also* gospel music

Reneau, George, 68–69

Renfro Valley, Kentucky, 216

Renfro Valley Barn Dance (radio show), 115, 116, 133, 140, 151, 215, 216, 242

Reno, Don: banjo playing style of, 387, 396–397, 398, 424; and bluegrass, 395, 396, 412; and Blue Grass Boys, 391, 397; death of, 422; and *Deliverance*, 398, 418; guitar style of, 396, 398; and Carlton Haney, 420; and Bill Harrell, 422; and Snuffy Jenkins, 145, 397; and Mack Magaha, 316; and Zeke Morris, 146; as songwriter, 396, 397; and Doc Watson, 329, 396

Reno and Smiley, 316–317, 396, 397–398, 412, 420, 422

Reo Palm Isle, Longview, Texas, 305

Republican Party, 439, 507

Republic Studios, 170, 172, 177

retro-country, 530

Revard, Jimmie, 198–199

Rey, Alvino, 187

Reynolds, Allen, 490

Reynolds, Burt, 435

Reynolds, Malvina, 326

Reynolds, Nick, 326

Rhett, Thomas, 550

Rhodes, Speck, 316

Rhododendron Festival, Asheville, North Carolina, 130

rhythm-and-blues music: as black music, 5, 289; and cross-genre collaborations, 550; and Elvis Presley, 291, 292; and Marty Robbins, 295

Rice, Bill, 477

Rice, Glen, 174–175

Rice, Larry, 426

Rice, Sharon, 477

Rice, Tony, 329, 426, 427, 432, 486, 539

Rice Brothers (Paul and Hoke), 207

Rice Brothers Gang, 243

Rich, Charlie, 6, 292, 444, 445, 478

Rich, Don, 342

Richardson, Ethel Park, 178

Richardson, J. P., 470

Richardson, Larry, 400

Rich-R-Tone Records, 245, 260, 389, 404

Rickenbacker guitars, 239

Riddle, Jimmie, 320

Riddles, Lesley, 80

Riders in the Sky, 476, 484, 543

Riders of the Purple Sage, 173, 177

Rigsby, Don, 535

Riley, Jeannie C., 355, 359, 361

Rimes, LeAnn, 507, 508

Rinehart, Nolan "Cowboy Slim," xiii, 119

Ringenberg, Jason, 526, 529

Rinzler, Ralph, 86, 328, 408, 414

risqué songs, 106, 124, 125, 127, 128

Ritchie, Jean, 31, 325

Ritter, Woodward Maurice "Tex": and cowboy music, 178, 179; and films, 172, 179; and Willie Nelson's picnics, 465; and radio, 238; recordings of, 211, 213, 220, 230; and Hank Thompson, 266

River Bend, 430

Riverside Ramblers, 273

Riverside Rancho Ballroom, California, 235

R. J. Reynolds Tobacco Company, 114, 215

RKO Interstate, 98

RKO-Pathe Theater, 10

Road Gang (radio show), 379

Robbins, Hargus "Pig," 247, 301

Robbins, Marty: and country-pop, 288, 299, 307–308, 310; and cowboy music, 308, 333, 476; and Glaser Brothers, 472; and Brad Paisley, 558; recordings of, 246, 295; and saga songs, 333

Roberts, Kenny, 410

Roberts, Marty, 396

Robertson, Alexander Campbell "Eck," 27, *28*, 42–43, 46

Robertson, Don, 301–302

Robertson, Texas Jim, 178

Robert's Western Wear, Nashville, 530

Robison, Carson, 51–52, *53*, 54, 75, 178, 229, 313, 321

rockabilly music: ascendency of, 339, 442; and black music, 293; and Johnny Cash, 296–297, 298; and Derailers, 530; and Foster and Lloyd, 494; and Don Gibson, 303; and Johnny Horton, 332; and Waylon Jennings, 471; and Doug Kershaw, 367; and Jerry Lee Lewis, 292, 293–294, 314, 442, 443; and Maddox Brothers and Rose, 255–256, 290; and neo-rockabilly, 443; and Oak Ridge Boys, 452; and Buck Owens, 342; revival in 1990s, 530; and Marty Robbins, 308; and Gary Stewart, 480; and Dale Watson, 522; and Faron Young, 307; and youth culture, 294, 307, 314

rock-and-roll music: black influence on, 289–290, 292; and bluegrass, 401, 426–427, 539; emergence of, 289–290; influence on country music, 295–296, 298–299, 309–310, 311, 325, 395, 415, 416, 417, 443, 454–455, 545, 551, 561, 564, 567; and neo-traditionalism, 497, 513; and Elvis Presley, 291, 292, 294, 443; and Telecaster guitars, 239; and *Urban Cowboy* soundtrack, 436; and urban folk revival, 327; and western swing, 475; and youth culture, 288–289, 293, 294–295, 330, 454. *See also* country-rock; rockabilly music; Southern rock

Rodeheaver, Homer, 14

rodeos, 477

Rodgers, Aaron W., 93–94

Rodgers, Anita, 99

Rodgers, Carrie, 94, 96, 99, 109, 184

Rodgers, Eliza Bozeman, 93

Rodgers, Jesse, 119

Rodgers, Jimmie: and Louis Armstrong, 319; bibliographic essay on, 613–614; and black music, 6, 91, 93, 94, 104–105, 124, 125; and Callahan Brothers, 130; concerts of, 97–98; and Country Music Hall of Fame, 280, 313; and cowboy music, 107, 167, 168, 170; and Ellsworth T. Cozzens, 426; death of, 100, 111; and Delmore Brothers, 128; and Iris DeMent, 524; and Tommy Duncan, 204; and Lefty Frizzell, 110, 168, 271, 273; and Great Depression, 94, 104, 110, 154; and Woodie Guthrie, 156; and Merle Haggard, 110, 347; health of, 94, 97, 99, 100, 102; and hillbilly music, 75, 76, 93, 95, 110; influence on country music, 100–110, 122, 126, 179;

instruments played by, 94, 95, 103; international following of, 321; and Grandpa Jones, 256; lifestyle of, 102; and medicine shows, 7, 93, 95–96; and Bill Monroe, 383; and music from cities' "sin streets," 11; myths concerning, 102–103; and Ralph Peer, 80, 96, 97, 98; performing style of, 103–104, 108; photograph of, *92*; and Webb Pierce, 273–274; and radio, 96, 97, 99; and rambling man tradition, 78, 93, 94, 102, 103, 106, 125, 155; recordings of, 44, 56, 71, 75, 76, 77, 91, 97, 98, 99, 100, 101–104, 106–107, 109–110, 196, 200, 205, 324, 387; as "singing brakeman," 94, 98; and Hank Snow, 109, 278; and steel guitar, 150; and television, 437; and Ernest Tubb, 101, 109–110, 168, 184; and vaudeville circuits, 10, 97, 98; and Bob Wills, 203, 205; yodeling of, 51, 63, 91, 95, 97, 98, 101, 102, 104, 105–108, 109, 110, 122, 126, 159, 166, 168, 184, 273, 278, 459

Rodriguez, Juan Raul Davis "Johnny," 369–370, 479

Rogers, Kenny, 361, 444, 446–447, 448, 449

Rogers, Roy, 108, 172, 176–177, 220, 476, 501, 543

Rogers, Will, 99, 168, 177

Roll, Larry, 406

Rolling Stone, 480, 561

Romeo Records, 112

Ronstadt, Linda, 454, 485

Rooney, Jim, 408, 411

Roosevelt, Franklin D., 158–159, 163

Root, George F., 14

roots music, 313, 528–529, 543, 546, 551–552, 563, 564, 570

Ropin' the Wind (album), 502

Rorer, Posey, *60*, 61, 70

Rosas, Juventino, 23

Rose, Fred: and Roy Acuff, 212, 226, 227–228; and Wilma Lee Cooper, 260–261; and Country Music Hall of Fame, 280, 313; and cowboy music, 177; and Molly O'Day, 258, 283; as songwriter, 57, 177, 212, 226, 227–228; and Hank Williams, 228, 283

Rose, Wesley, 228, 283

Rosemary Clooney Show (television show), 307

Rosenberg, Neil, 388, 396

Rounder Records, 419, 535, 537

Rowan, Peter, 391, 408

Rowell, Glenn, 82

Rowland, Dave, 451

Royal, Darrell, 464

Royal Chemical Corporation, 119

Roy Newman and His Boys, 199–200

Rozell, Slim, 95

Rucker, Darius, 551

Runaway June, 567

rural areas: and agriculture, 2, 3; and banjo music, 30–31; and contest between hedonism and Puritanism, 20, 35; and gospel music, 155; and guitar music, 29–30; and mandolins, 33; musical trends introduced to, 7–11, 33, 34, 38, 162; and nostalgia for rural past, 15, 19, 22, 37, 48, 78, 81, 103, 106, 127, 216, 349, 355, 452, 553; and parlor songs, 19; performers from, 38; and phonograph industry, 41; and radio, 38–39, 41, 114, 119–120; and railroads, 9; and religion, 13–14; and World War II, 208–209, 215

Rural Rhythm Records, 419

Rush, Ford, 82

Russell, Johnny, 377

Russell, Leon, 454, 467

Russell, Tom, 518

Russell, Tony, 51–52

Rutherford, Leonard, 54

Rutland, Georgia Slim, 132, 147

Ryan, Buck, 317, 412

Ryman, Thomas, 89

Ryman Auditorium, Nashville, 89, 227, 241, 433–434

Sacred Harp (White), 26

Sacred Harp conventions, 4

Sadler, Harley, 231

saga songs, 331–334

Sahm, Doug, 463

A Sailor's Guide to Earth (album), 562

Sainte-Marie, Buffy, 565

Sally Mountain Show, 538

Salvation Army, 14

"Sambo and Liza" skit, 10

Samples, Junior, 320

San Antonio, Texas, 181, 198–199. *See also* KMAC (San Antonio); KONO (San Antonio); WOAI (San Antonio)

Sankey, Ira, 14

Sanneh, Kelefa, 553

Santa Monica Ballroom, California, 235

Satherley, Arthur, 46, 144, 168–169, 226, 259

Saturday Night Roundup (radio show), 243
Saturday Night Shindig (radio show), 296
Sauceman, Carl, 389
Sawyer Brown, 493
Sayers, Peter, 322
Scandinavia, 306
Schaffer, Ed, 127
Schwarz, Tracy, 328
Scott, "Doc" Tommy, 7
Scribner's Monthly, 29
Scruggs, Earl: and banjo playing style,
    386–387, 388, 391, 393, 394, 397, 406, 407,
    408, 413, 414, 422, 424; and Blue Grass
    Boys, 221, *385*, 386, 387, 388, 391; death
    of, 570; and *Earl's Breakdown*, 393; Earl
    Scruggs Revue, 422; and IBMA's Hall of
    Honor, 531; and Snuffy Jenkins, 145; and
    Zeke Morris, 146; and Willie Nelson's
    picnics, 465; and Newport Folk Festival,
    329; and Nitty Gritty Dirt Band, 454;
    photograph of, *390*; recordings of, 393;
    with Marty Stuart, *514*; and traditional
    bluegrass, 533, 542; and urban folk revival,
    415. *See also* Flatt and Scruggs
Scruggs, Gary, 422
Scruggs, Randy, 422, 490
Scruggs, Steve, 422
Sears Conqueror Records, 168
Sears-Roebuck: and Gene Autry, 168–169; and
    mandolins, 33; and records, 112–113; and
    WLS, 82
Sears-Roebuck Farm, Home, and Musical
    Programs, 116
Seay, Johnny, 376
Sebastian, John, 300
Sechler, Curly, 221, 383, 394
Second Generation (bluegrass), 425, 428
Seeger, Mike, 2, 328, 408, 414
Seeger, Pete, 153, 326, 414, 485
Seely, Mike, 566
Seldom Scene, 423, 425, 426, 430, 431
Selected Editions of Standard American
    Catalogues (SESAC), 210
Sellers transcription service, 119
Selph, Leon "Pappy," 196–197
sentimental songs: and Roy Acuff, 226; ballads
    compared to, 12, 18–19; and Blue Sky Boys,
    137, 252; and Coon Creek Girls, 140; and
    Cowboy Copas, 267; and cowboy music,
    167; and Jimmie Davis, 127; and duet
    singing, 128; families' singing of, xiii–xiv;

and Red Foley, 242; and Great Depression,
    155, 157–158; and Johnny and Jack, 254;
    and Grandpa Jones, 256; and Bradley
    Kincaid, 66; and Lulu Belle and Scotty,
    139; and Maddox Brothers and Rose, 255;
    and Mainer's Mountaineers, 145; and
    Moon Mullican, 270; and *National Barn
    Dance*, 82; and Obed Pickard, 85; and Jim
    Reeves, 305; and Marty Robbins, 308; and
    Jimmie Rodgers, 93, 97, 106, 107; and Slim
    Whitman, 279
September 11, 2001 attacks, 507
Service, Robert Stewart, 331–332
session musicians: and Chet Atkins, 247, 254,
    279, 300–302, 309, 313; and Byron Berline,
    427; Jerry Byrd as, 151; and Glen Campbell,
    318; Charlie Daniels as, 457; and Bob Dylan,
    454; and Jim and Jesse McReynolds, 406;
    in Nashville, 247, 300–301; numbering
    system of, 300
Setters, Jilson, 18
Set This Circus Down (album), 542
settlement-school teachers, 66
Sewell Production Company, 217
sexy songs, 125–126, 127, 359, 444, 451, 482
Shafer, Whitey, 481, 482
Shamblin, Eldon, 204, 475
Shamrock, Georgetown, 412
Shane, Bob, 326
shape-note music, 4, 6, 15, 25, 26, 35, 162,
    262–263, 382
Sharp, Cecil, 5, 33
Shatner, William, 559
Shaver, Billy Joe, 331, 466, 472
Shea, Jack, 284
sheet music: and bluegrass, 416; and
    Richard Burnett, 50, 55; and A. P. Carter,
    80; and cowboy music, 165, 168; and
    hillbilly music, 112, 114, 118, 121, 229; and
    Bradley Kincaid's songbooks, 64; and
    music industry, 37, 247, 310; and pianos,
    19, 31; and songsheet hawkers, 18, 34; and
    vaudeville, 10
Shelor, Sammy, 535
Shelton, Aaron, 246
Shelton, Allen, 391, 406
Shelton, B. F., 77
Shelton, Blake, 560
Shelton, Bob, 201
Shelton, Joe, 148, 201
Shelton, Merle, 202

Shelton, Ricky Van, 498–499

Shelton, Robert, 414

Shelton Brothers (Bob, Joe, and Merle): and Jimmie Davis, 127; and Curly Fox, 147; and radio, 243; recordings of, 206; and Arthur Smith, 147; style of, xiii, 128, 199, 200–202; and Wiley Walker, 231; and WWL, 121

Shenandoah, 493

Shenandoah Cutups, 428

Shepard, Jean, 306, 309, 361, 518, 570

Sheppard, T. G., 443

Sheppard Brothers, 245

Sherrill, Billy, 364, 441, 478–479, 529

Sherrill, Homer, 136, 145–146

Shiflett, Karl, 533

Shilkret, Nathaniel, 74

Shilos, 455

Shire, Warsan, 548

Shiva's Headband, 460

Sholes, Steven, 247, 301, 312

Short, Jimmie, 186

Short Brothers (Jimmie and Leon), 186

showboats, 21

Show Boys, 199

Shreveport, Louisiana, 10, 677. *See also* KWKH (Shreveport)

shuffle beat style, 339, 340, 341, 479, 480, 512, 530, 558

Shuffler, George, 405, 415

Shuler, Eddie, 366

Shultz, Arnold, 382–383

Shumate, Jim, 386, 391

silent majority, country music's identification with, 374, 377, 553

Silver Dollar City theme park, 519

Silverstein, Shel, 331, 356

Simmons Market Research Bureau, 493

Simon, Paul, 327, 348, 523

Simons, Bobby, 187

Simpson, Red, 378

Simpson, Sturgill, xvi, 562–563, *563*, 565, 571

Sinatra, Frank, 100, 215, 227, 232

Singer's Glen, 26

singer-songwriter culture, 327, 523–526

singing conventions, 25, 292

singing cowboys, 107, 167, 169, 170–172, 177–178, 220, 274, 476

singing-school masters, 26, 35, 162

Singletary, Daryle, 570

Sipes, Leonard Raymond. *See* Collins, Tommy

Sir Douglas Quintet, 463

Sir Mashalot, 567

Sizemore, Asher and Little Jimmie, 141

Sizemore, Hershel, 428

Skaggs, Ricky: and CMA's twenty-fifth anniversary celebration, 438–439; and hard country, 483, 484, 487; and Emmylou Harris, 485, 486; photograph of, *487*; and progressive bluegrass, 424, 426, 432, 442, 486, 532; and radio, 485; recordings of, 486; repertory of, 432, 483, 484, 485–488, 504, 524; songwriting of, xvii; and Ralph Stanley, 422, 432, 486, 497; vocal style of, 486–487

Skaggs and Rice (album), 486

Skillet Lickers, 59, 61–63, 67, 125, 143, 145, 327, 414

Skinner, Jimmie, 286, 396

"skin songs," 444

Skyline Club, Austin, Texas, 265

Slaughter, Marion Try. *See* Dalhart, Vernon

slavery, 2–3, 5, 22, 30, 161

slip-note style, 301–302

Sloan, Jerry, 133

Sloan and Threadgill, 133

Slye, Leonard. *See* Rogers, Roy

Slye Brothers, 176

Smik, Andrew J. *See* Williams, Doc

Smiley, Arthur Lee "Red," 316–317, 395–398, 412, 418, 420, 422

Smith, Al, 158

Smith, Arthur (fiddler), 147–148, 224

Smith, Arthur "Guitar Boogie" (guitarist), 233, 239, 265, 290, 398

Smith, Arthur Q. (songwriter), 249

Smith, Bessie, 203, 205

Smith, Carl, 266, 268, 285, 288, 333

Smith, Connie, 353, 358–359, 513, 518

Smith, Dewayne "Son," 437

Smith, Fay "Smitty," 186

Smith, Guy, 224

Smith, Gypsy, 14

Smith, Hal, 247, 310, 353

Smith, Harmie, 243

Smith, Harry, 55, 327

Smith, Hazel, 472

Smith, Hobart, 29

Smith, Mamie, 41–42

Smith, Margo, 361

Smith, Sammi, 357, 360

Smith, Slim, 159

Smith, Valerie, 537

Smith, Warren, 292

Smith, Whit, 530

Smithsonian Folklife Festival, 331

Smokey and the Bandit (film), 435

Smoky Mountain Boys, 149, 224, 225–226

Smoky Mountain Glenn, 88

Smothers Brothers, 318

snakehandlers, 16

Snoop Dogg, 550

Snow, Clarence Eugene "Hank": and civil
rights movement, 375; costumes of, 317;
and cowboy music, 167, 278; guitar style of,
278; and politics, 438; and Elvis Presley,
291; and radio, 278; recordings of, 278–279,
288; repertory of, 278; and Jimmie Rodgers,
109, 278; vocal style of, 167, 278, 399; and
Wheeling Jamboree, 117

Snow, Kilby, 32

Snow, Schuyler, 410

Snow White and the Seven Dwarfs (film), 275

Soap Creek Saloon, Austin, Texas, 460

social class: and dances, 20; and middle-class
ethic, 312, 346, 348; and sentimental songs,
19; in South, 2–3; and textile mill songs,
158; and urban folk revival, 326. *See also*
middle-class audiences; working-class
audiences

social media networks, 569

Society for the Preservation of Bluegrass
Music in America (SPBGMA), 531, 535

Soileau, Leo, 270

Solomon, Ervin, 189

Some Gave All (album), 505

Somewhere Between (album), 508

Songcatcher (album), 525

Songcatcher (film), 525

Song of the Gringo (film), 179

Songs of the Cowboys (Thorp), 163

Songs Our Daddy Taught Us (album), 296

songwriters: and Roy Acuff, 213; and Shelly
Lee Alley, 196; and BMI, 210; and Johnny
Bond, 171–172, 250; and broadsides, 18, 55;
and commercialization of country music,
248–249, 355, 356, 379; and compassion,
350–351; and conservatism, 374–375; and
cowboy music, 171–172, 176, 177–178; and
credits, 249; and Ted Daffan, 197, 213; and
Al Dexter, 212, 231–232; and Bob Dylan,
348, 413, 415, 424, 425, 455, 460, 485, 523;
emergence of vaudeville songwriters, 7,
10; and event songs, 349–350; and Tom T.
Hall, 331, 355–356, 376, 377, 379; and Stuart

Hamblen, 176; and hard country, 359; and
hillbilly songs, 52, 54–58, 70–71, 156, 170,
178, 240; and Kris Kristofferson, 331, 340,
353, 356–357, 360, 376, 379, 444; Nashville
as base of, 300, 303, 310, 352–353; and
Willie Nelson, 307, 309, 340, 354–355, 465,
554; and nostalgia, 349, 352, 355; and Pappy
O'Daniel, 192; and parlor songs, 19; and
poetic expression, 357–358; and politics,
350, 374–376, 377, 507; and rambling man
image, 351; and religious music, 14–15; and
Fred Rose, 57, 177, 212, 226, 227–228; and
storytelling tradition, 355–356, 446, 559;
and television, 437; and Texas Playboys,
205; and Floyd Tillman, 197–198, 213,
230, 250; and Tin Pan Alley, 7, 11, 210;
and Ernest Tubb, 220, 230; and urban folk
revival, 327, 523–526; and Vietnam War,
355, 374, 375, 377, 457; and Hank Williams,
282, 283, 339; women as, 358, 360, 362, 537;
and World War II, 228–232, 348

Sonora Records, 410

Sons of the Desert, 554

Sons of the Mountaineers, 145

Sons of the Pioneers, 122, 172, 176–177, 308,
375, 406, 476

Sons of the San Joaquin, 543

Son Volt, 528

Sony Records, 512

Soul 2 Soul Tour, 510

soul music, 123, 441, 443, 492, 499

The Sound of Music (televised version), 562

Soundscan, 493

South: and Civil War defeat, 15; and commercialization of country music, 113; and fiddle
contests, 4, 22, 62; folk culture of, 2, 3–5, 6,
11, 23–24, 34–36, 151–152, 153, 162, 180; and
Great Depression, 151–153; migration from,
3, 208, 213–214, 245, 334, 411, 412, 430, 431;
New South, 22, 157; racial hierarchy in, 3;
and radio, 39–40; rural nature of, 2, 3, 11;
social conservatism in, 2, 3, 6, 11, 35, 48–49,
153, 350

South Africa, 306, 320

Southern Folklife Collection, University of
North Carolina in Chapel Hill, xiv

Southern Harmony (Walker), 26

Southern Historical Association, xv

southern music: and country dances, 20–21,
26, 34; and folk culture, 2, 4–5, 6, 23–24,
34–36; and grassroots music, 38, 325,

438; and origins of country music, 1, 3, 5, 11–12, 39, 46–48, 50; and Ralph Peer, 44, 46; recording of, 46; and singing-school masters, 26; and songwriters, 57; and vocal styles, 5, 23, 27, 68

Southern Music Company, 80, 96, 111, 210

southern novelists, 348

southern rock: and Alabama, 453; and Charlie Daniels, 456, 457; and Travis Tritt, 492, 513; and Hank Williams Jr., 456, 457–458; and Gretchen Wilson, 555

Southern Tenant Farmers' Union, 152

Soviet bloc nations, 321

Soviet Union, 323, 374

Sovine, Red, 307, 337, 372, 378

Spacek, Sissy, 435

Spade Cooley and His Orchestra, 235

Spain, Irene, 56–57

Spanish-American War, 35, 97

Spanish culture, 5

Sparks, Larry, 422, 430

Spectrum, 425

Spencer, Tim, 176

Spice Girls, 511

Spike Jones Show (radio show), 277

spirituals, 5, 34. *See also* gospel music

Spitzer, Nicholas, 464

Split Rail, Austin, Texas, 460

Spotify, 568

Sprague, Carl T., 67, 75, 163, *164*, 165, 188

Springsteen, Bruce, 374, 554

square dances, 20

S. S. Stewart Company, 30

stadium country, 546

Stafford, Terry, 477

Stampley, Joe, 442–443

Stamps-Baxter Company, 25

Stamps-Baxter Music Company, 25

Stamps Quartet, xiii, 292

Stand by Your Man (television show), 436

Stanley, Carter: and bluegrass, 403–404; and Blue Grass Boys, 391; death of, 422; and George Jones, 338; and Bill Monroe, 403; and Monroe Brothers, 137; photograph of, *389*; and repertory, 415; songwriting of, 404–405; vocal style of, 404; and Keith Whitley, 497

Stanley, Ralph: banjo playing style of, 387, 388, 404, 415; and bluegrass, 403–404, 531–532, 534; and bluegrass festivals, 420; Clinch Mountain Boys, 422, 532; death of, 570; and

Emmylou Harris, 485; honorary doctorate of, 532; and Patty Loveless, 515; and Monroe Brothers, 137; photograph of, *389*; recordings of, 532–533; and Ricky Skaggs, 422, 432, 486, 497; style of, xvi; vocal style of, 404, 405, 422, 429, 430, 491

Stanley, Ralph, II, 531–532

Stanley Brothers: and bluegrass, 388–389, 396, 403–405, 414–415, 423; and death of Carter Stanley, 422; and Bill Monroe, 404, 407, 421; and Monroe Brothers, 137; photograph of, *389*; and radio, 403–404; recordings of, 388, 404–405, 423, 428; and rhythm-and-blues music, 295; and Ricky Skaggs, 486, 497; and urban folk revival, 414–415; vocal style of, 403, 404

Stanley Brothers Fan Club, 410

Staples, Mavis, 565

Stapleton, Chris, 550, 567

Starcher, Buddy, 142, 158, 398

Starday Records, 245, 323, 334, 337, 419

Stardust (album), 467

Starkweathers, 529

Starling, John, 426

Starnes, Jack, 337, 419

Starr, Thomas, xiv

Starrett, Charles, 172

Starr Piano Company, 66, 112

Star Trek (television show), 560

state-line taverns, 182

Statesmen Quartet, 285, 451

Statler Brothers, 451, 452, 518

Statman, Andy, 539

Steagall, Alfred, 70

Steagall, Red, 475, 477, 495, 543

steel guitars: and Roy Acuff, 225; and Gene Autry, 171; and bluegrass, 424, 426; and bottleneck style, 150; and Carter Family, 79; and Ted Daffan, 197; as defining feature of country music, 149–150, 445; and Dixon Brothers, 130; Dobro steel guitars, 126, 150–151, 225, 261, 330, 394–395, 426, 445; and Bob Dunn, 187–188, 194, 195, 204; and electric amplification, 122, 150–151, 187–188, 195, 204, 239, 265; and Flying Burrito Brothers, 456; and Hawaiian music, 32, 51, 75, 104, 105, 123, 126, 150, 151, 181, 187, 195, 276, 277, 426; and hillbilly music, 122; and Shot Jackson, 252, 255; and knife style, 149; and Barbara Mandrell, 441; and Syd Nathan, 246; National steel guitars,

150; pedal steel guitars, 239, 274, 339, 341, 347, 455; and Jimmie Rodgers, 104; and Jimmie Tarlton, 123; and Ernest Tubb, 220; and western swing, 199

Steinbarth, Henry, *191*

Stephens, Uncle Bunt, 49

Step Inside This House (album), 500

Sterban, Richard, 452

Sterchi Brothers, 68

stereopticon slide shows, 10

Sterling, William W., 99

Sterling Records, 283

Steve Allen Show (television show), 307

Stevenson, Adlai, 376

Stevenson, Stephanie, 537

Stewart, Cal, 38

Stewart, Gary, 442, 443, 479–480, 483

Stewart, Henry "Redd," 230, 248

Stewart, Wynn, 341, 342, 345, 353, 522

Stickbuddy Jamboree (radio show), 322

Stockard, Ocie, *192*, 194–195

Stoker, Gordon, 247

Stokes, Lowe, 61–62

Stone, Cliffie, 238

Stone, Harry, 88, 114

Stoneman, Ernest V. "Pop," 32, 48, 59, 63, 70, 76, 411

Stoneman, Hattie, 76

Stoney Mountain Boys, 414

Story, Carl, 428

Stover, Don, 407, 411, 428

Stover, Everett, *203*

Straight Outta Boone County (album), 528

Strait, George, 480–481, *481*, 490, 492, 493, 516, 547

Strangers, 345, 347

Street, Mel, 480, 481–482

street cries, 105

street musicians, 11, 21

Streisand, Barbra, 361

Stricklin, Al, 198, *203*, 204

strikes, 152, 153, 210–212, 378–379

string bands: and audience expectations, 59; and black music, 552; and bluegrass, 380, 384, 403, 414; and cowboy music, 167, 200; and electrical amplification, 188; growth of interest in, xvi, 76; and Hawaiian music, 7, 11, 32, 40; instrumentation of, 29–31, 32, 33, 50–51, 58, 61, 122; lack of "stars," 146; as male-dominated, 27; and Mexican border stations, 119; military servicemen forming,

322; and Musical Brownies, 195; origins of, 29, 34, 58; and radio, 40, 84, 85–86, 89; recordings of, 58–59, 88; repertory of, 144; and Jimmie Rodgers, 96; and urban folk revival, 328; and vocal styles, 63; and western swing, 188, 196, 199

Stuart, Joe, 408, 420

Stuart, Marty, 490, 513, *514*, 516

Stuart, Uncle Am, *36*

Stubbs, Eddie, 430, 513, 543

Sub Pop Records, 529

Suffolk Marketing Company, 325

Sugar Hill Records, 419, 526, 541

Sullivan, Gene, 230–231

Sullivan, John, 264

Sullivan, Margie, 428

Sullivan, Rollin (Oscar), 264

Sullivan Family, 428, 513

Summer, Donna, 560

Summey, James Clell (Cousin Jody), 150, 225

Sumner, Marion, 406

Sunbrock, Larry, 143, 218

Sundance (band), 504

Sunday, Billy, 14

Sunday Down South (radio show), 277

Sunday Morning Gathering (radio show), 216

Sunday School Union, 14

Sunny Mountain Boys, 402

Sunnysiders, 410

Sun Records, 245, 291, 292, 295, 296, 444, 459

Sunset Park, West Grove, Pennsylvania, 409

Sunshine Boys, 201

Sure-Fire publishing company, 310

Swaggart, Jimmy, 293

Swain, Charlie, 224

Swain, W. I., 98–99

Swan, Billy, 442

Sweeney, Joel Walker, 30

Sweetheart of the Rodeo (album), 455

Sweethearts of the Rodeo (Janis and Kristine Oliver), 504

Swift, Taylor, 560

Swift Jewel Cowboys, 173, 196

Swindell, Cole, 567

Sykes, Roy, 403

Sylvia, 361

Tabuchi, Shoji, 519

Take Me as I Am (album), 510

Taking the Long Way (album), 553, 571

Talley, James, 438

Tally Records, 345

tambourines, 16, 29

Tanner, Gid, 51, 58, 61–62, 223

Taos to Tennessee (album), 524

Tarlton, Johnny James Rimbert "Jimmie," 123, 129–130, 149–150, 328

Tate, Clarence "Tater," 428

Taylor, Earl, 402, 410, 412, 414

Taylor, "Happy" Jack, *175*

Taylor, Hartford Connecticut, 115, 133, *134*. *See also* Karl and Harty

Taylor, James, 338

Taylor Brothers (Bob and Alf), 21

Taylor-Christian Hat Company, 76

Taylor-Griggs Louisiana Melody Makers, 190

Taylor "Happy" Jack, 143

Ted Fio Rito's Orchestra, 194

Tejano music, 369, 524

Telecaster guitars, 239, 341

television: and American West, 162; and Eddie Arnold, 277; and awards shows, 550; and barn dance format, 315; and bluegrass, 334, 424, 437; country music featured on, 314–319, 334, 343, 435, 436–437, 474, 505; and Tennessee Ernie Ford, 295; and *Grand Ole Opry*, 315, 437; and Ferlin Husky, 307; market fragmentation of, 568, 570; and Kenny Rogers, 447; and Roy Rogers, 172; and Ernest Tubb, 315, 522. *See also specific television shows*

Tender Mercies (film), 436

Tennessee: and Great Depression, 152; and hillbilly music, 68–70. *See also* Nashville, Tennessee

Tennessee Crackerjacks, 223

Tennessee Cutups, 317, 396, 397–398

Tennessee Mountain Boys, 254, 261, 393

Tennessee Ramblers, 143

Tennessee Valley Boys, 147

Tenneva Ramblers, 76, 96–97

tent-repertory shows: and barn dances, 58, 216; and Lew Childre, 142; of *Grand Ole Opry*, xi, 10, 218; and Hawaiian steel guitars, 150; and Lewis Family, 428; and Uncle Dave Macon, 88; and Bill Monroe, 388; and Jimmie Rodgers, 94, 97, 98, 99–100, 108; in rural communities, 7–8; and television, 315; as traveling shows, 7–8, 10, 58; and Wiley Walker, 231

Terrell's Comedians, 94

Terry, Al, 288

Terry, Gordon, 391, 407

Texas: bibliographic resources on country music in, 677; and cowboy music, 160, 163, 167–168; cross-cultural matrix of music from, 180–181; culture of, 162; folk music in, 4, 162; and hillbilly music, 67–68, 159; honky-tonk music in, 181–182; oil industry in, 162, 181, 436; radio in, 39; recording companies in, 113; Jimmie Rodgers associated with, 97, 99–100, 102, 107–108, 167, 168; southern migrants in, 3; and working-class music, 519. *See also specific cities*

Texas Centennial, 177

Texas Crystals, 137, 383

Texas Jewboys, 367, 566

Texas Longhorns (band), 470

Texas Playboys: and films, 172; instrumentation of, 202, 204, 235, 545; and Leon McAuliffe, 475; and Bob Wills, 193, 202–206, *203*, 220, 373, 464, 545

Texas Ramblers, 189

Texas Rose, 193

Texas Rotary Club, 99

Texas Two-Step (dance step), 504

Texas Wanderers, 187, 195, 198

Tex-Mex music, 188, 327, 463

textile mill songs, 130, 157–158

textile workers as country singers: and Dixon Brothers, 129–130, 157; and Lester Flatt, 129, 392; and Great Depression, 152–153, 157–158; and Roy Hall, 146; and Kelly Harrell, 70; and hillbilly music, 35; and Charlie Poole, 50, 61; and Jimmie Tarlton, 123; and Henry Whitter, 43

Thall, Willie, 247

Thelma and Louise (film), 554

Thibodeaux, Rufus, 330

Thigpen's Log Cabin, Alabama, 282

Thile, Chris, 539, *540*, 542

IIIrd Tyme Out, 534

13 Hillbilly Greats (album), 529

Thomas, Dick, 234

Thomas, Jean, 18

Thomas, Suzanne, 537

Thompson, Bobby, 407, 408

Thompson, Hank, 236, 261, 266, *267*, 475, 517, 519, 528

Thompson, Uncle Jimmy, 84

Thorp, Nathan Howard, 163

Threadgill, Frank, 133

Threadgill, Kenneth, 459–460, 464

Threadgill's, Austin, Texas, xiv, 459, 463

Three Little Maids, 242

Throckmorton, Sonny, 355

Tierney, Louis, 203

Tillis, Mel, 331, 340, 354–355, 413, 435, 459, 479, 519

Tillis, Pam, 458–459

Tillman, Floyd: in Austin, Texas, 464, 477; as guitarist, 197, 204; and Willie Nelson, 354; photograph of, *161*; recordings of, 206, 220, 269, 271; and Jimmie Rodgers, 168; as songwriter, 197–198, 213, 230, 250, 413; vocal style of, 197, 198, 269; and western swing, 197

Timberlake, Justin, 550

Timberliners, 329

Time, 434

Time Jumpers, 203

Tindley, Charles, 154

Tin Pan Alley: and Blue Sky Boys, 137; and cowboy themes, 108, 163, 177, 266–267; and hillbilly music, 36, 51; and Uncle Dave Macon, 87; and George Puckett, 63–64; and sentimental songs, 12; as show-business model, 91; and Skillet Lickers, 62; and songwriters, 7, 11, 210; and Hank Williams, 284

"Toby Shows," 7

Todd, Mazy, 88

The Tommy Hunter Show (television show), 437

Tonight Show (television show), 307, 318, 479

Too Late to Cry (album), 535

Tootsie's Orchid Lounge, Nashville, 354

Top-Forty radio: and alternative country, 529; alternative formats to, 464; and Austin musical scene, 519; and bluegrass, 531; and Johnny Cash, 517, 518; and Jimmie Dale Gilmore, 520; and gospel music, 512; and hillbilly music, 491; and hot new country, 557, 566–567, 569; and identity of country music, 324, 417, 439, 441, 490, 506, 542, 569; and Seldom Scene, 426; and Don Walser, 521; and Dale Watson, 522; and women musicians, 361; and youth culture, 496

Town and Country Time (radio show), 308–309, 412

Town Hall Party (radio show), 234, 237, 238, 273, 441

Townsend, Respers, 122

Townsend Plan movement, 159

Tragic Songs of Life (album), 253

Transcendental Blues (album), 500

traveling shows: and folk style, 27; musical ideas transported by, 7; tent shows, 7–8, 10, 58. *See also* medicine shows

Travis, Merle: and Chet Atkins, 236, 301; and Brown's Ferry Four, 256, 263; guitars of, 239; guitar style of, 143, 149, 236, 295, 301, 517; and Newport Folk Festival, 329; and Nitty Gritty Dirt Band, 454; photograph of, *237*; and radio, 238; recordings of, 233–234, 236, 245; as songwriter, 237, 295; and Doc Watson, 329

Travis, Randy, 271, 489–490, 496–497

Travolta, John, 436

Tree Publishing Company, 310, 354

Trent, Buck, 317

Trevino, Justin, 340, 519

Tribe, Ivan, 158

A Tribute to the Best Damn Fiddle Player in the World (or, My Salute to Bob Wills) (album), 475

Trio (album), 485

Trio Music Company, 25

Trio Two (album), 485

Trishka, Tony, 539

Tritt, Travis, 492, 507, 513, 516

truck-driving songs: and Merle Haggard, 346–347, 378; and Jim and Jesse McReynolds, 417; popularity of, 197, 351–352, 378–379; and Dale Watson, 522

A Truly Western Experience (album), 499

trumpets, 51, 236

Tubb, Ernest: and Roy Acuff, 227; and cowboy music, 167–168; death of, 477; and electric amplification, 186–187, 220; and films, 172; and J. L. Frank, 218; and *Grand Ole Opry*, 186, 187, 217–218, 220, 234; and honky-tonk music, 184, 185, 220, 230, 269, 477; and Harlan Howard, 353; and instrumental accompaniment, 186–187; and Waylon Jennings, 470; and Willie Nelson, 354, 579n8; and Bobby Osborne, 400; photograph of, *185*; and radio, 184, 185, 359; recordings of, 184, 186, 206, 214, 220, 232, 271, 275, 286, 288, 376, 579n8; on Jimmie Rodgers, 101, 109–110, 168, 184; and Hank Snow, 279; as songwriter, 220, 230; style of, xvi, 184; television show of, 315, 522; vocal style of, 109, 184, 302, 520; and Cindy Walker, 250; and Hank Williams, 220, 282, 285, 286

Tubb, Justin, 440–441
Tubb, Roger Dale, 220
Tucker, Sophie, 228
Tucker, Stephen Ray, 243–244
Tucker, Tanya, 359–360, 370, 478, 509–510
Tulare Dust (album), 518
Tulloch, Jake, 395
Tumbleweed Theater (television show), 476
Tumbling Tumbleweeds (film), 170
Tune Wranglers, 199
Turner, Big Joe, 289
Turner, Tina, 552
Turner, Zeke, 247
Tuttle, Wesley, 233, 238, 274
Twain, Jerry, 510
Twain, Shania, 499, 509–510, 511, 544, 554
Tweedy, Jeff, 528
Twitty, Conway: duets with Loretta Lynn, 334, 448, 450; and honky-tonk music, 314, 479; and Osborne Brothers, 418; photograph of, *448*; and rockabilly music, 314, 449; and rock-and-roll music, 292, 447, 448; as songwriter, 444, 547; vocal style of, 449; and Dale Watson, 522
Twitty City, 449
Two Journeys (album), 526
Tyler, T. Texas, 235, 266, 267–268
Tyminski, Dan, 491
Tyrolese Rainer Family, 25
Tyson, Ian, 424, 462, 477, 543

U2, 492
Uhr, Tom, 429
ukuleles, 32, 51
Uncle Tupelo, 528, 564
Underwood, Carrie, 556–557, *558*, 560, 562, 565, 569
Underwood, Sheriff Loyal, 174
unions. *See* labor unions
Union Station (Alison Krauss), 535
Universal Mills, 186
Upson, Dean, 115, 243, 252
Upson County Band, 61
Urban, Keith, 565, 567
urban areas. *See* cities
Urban Cowboy (film), 436, 476
urban cowboy trend, 22, 436, 476, 489, 504, 546
urban folk revival: and Tom Ashley, 69–70, 328; and Austin, Texas, 460; and bluegrass, 328, 396, 405, 408–409, 413, 414–417,

424–425; and Guy Clark, 461; and Dallas, 463; and Dorsey Dixon, 129, 130; and Emmylou Harris, 361, 484–485; and Lyle Lovett, 499; and mainstream country music, 329–330, 331, 334–335; and Bill Monroe, 408; and Anne Murray, 446; and Jimmy Newman, 330–331; origins of, 153, 325–326; politics of, 326, 374; and saga songs, 331–333; and singer-songwriter culture, 327, 523–526; and youth culture, 325, 326, 327, 328, 330
Utah Cowboy (J. R. Hall), 119, 173

Vaden, Tommy, 406
Vagabonds, 114–115, 195, 243
Val, Joe (Joe Valiante), 409, 411
Valens, Richie, 470
Valiante, Joe, 409
Vandiver, Pendleton, 382–383
Van Dyke, Leroy, 312, 315
Van Eps, Fred, 30
Van Lear Rose (album), 551
Van Zandt, Townes, 327, 461–462, 499, 500, 523
Vargas, Juan, 558
vaudeville: and Callahan Brothers, 131; and cowboy music, 187; entertainers' musical success in, 50; and fiddle tunes, 10, 23; and folk music, 38; and Hawaiian steel guitars, 150; and hillbilly music, 36, 63, 75; and instruments, 32; and Lester McFarland, 132; and songwriters, 7, 10; and urban areas, 37; vocal style in, 25, 61, 105
Vaughan, James D., 25
Veach, Rachel, 141, 225
Venice Pier Ballroom, California, 219, 227, 235
Vetco Records, 430
VH1, 550
Victor Records: and Allen Brothers, 124; and American Federation of Musicians, 211; and Eddy Arnold, 276–277; and Gene Autry, 168; and Bluebird Records, 112; and Carter Family, 76, 79; and Cowboy Ramblers, 200; and Vernon Dalhart, 52, 73, 74; and Jimmie Davis, 127; and Dixon Brothers, 130; and field recordings, 46; and Henry Gilliland, 42–43; and Kerry Harrell, 70; and Light Crust Doughboys, 191; and David McCarn, 158; and Harry McClintock, 166; and Bill Monroe, 385–386; and Fiddlin' Power, 58; and Alfred Reed, 55; and Eck Robertson,

42–43; and Jimmie Rodgers, 76, 91, 94, 97,
98, 100, 101; and Hank Snow, 109, 278; and
Carl Sprague, 163; and Ernest Tubb, 184
Vietnam War: and politics, 437–438; and
songwriters, 355, 374, 375, 377, 457
Village Boys, 196
Vincent, Gene, 292
Vincent, Nat, 165, 177–178
Vincent, Rhonda, 537, 538, *538*
Virginia, 3, 5, 70–71
Virginia Boys, 406
Virginia Breakdowners, 58
Virginia Mountain Boys, 431
Virginia reel, 20
Virginia Reelers, 58, 61
Virginia Trio, 406
Vocalion Records, 68, 88, 124
vocal styles: and bluegrass, 137, 144, 380, 382,
384–385, 388, 394, 401, 414, 428, 429, 430,
451, 533, 534, 537–538; of Fiddlin' John
Carson, 45, 50, 51, 63; of Carter Family, 70,
76, 79; diversity of, 51; and falsetto, 51, 62,
105; and fiddlers, 29; and folk music, 34;
of Lefty Frizzell, 273, 345, 347, 477, 496;
of Merle Haggard, 344–345, 347, 379, 480;
and identities of individual singers, 146; of
George Jones, 335, 337, 338, 339, 429, 443,
480, 481, 555; of Buell Kazee, 67; of Bill
Monroe, 221, 254, 302, 383, 384–385, 388,
397, 400, 402, 404; pinched-throat style,
51, 405, 528; of Charlie Poole, 51, 60–61, 63,
70; of Jimmie Rodgers, 104; and southern
music, 5, 23, 27, 68; and string bands, 63;
of Jimmie Tarlton, 123; and vaudeville, 25,
61, 105; of Kitty Wells, 257–258, 309, 445;
and western swing, 195, 204; and women's
home singing, 24, 34. *See also* duet singing;
quartets; yodeling
The Voice (television show), 560
Volebeats, 528
Volu-Tone amplifiers, 187, 197
Vonnegut, Kurt, 452

WAAT (Newark, New Jersey), 245
Waco Brothers, 528
Wade, Norman, 479
WAGM (Presque Isle, Maine), 219
Wagner, Fred, 40
Wagner, J. H., 23
Wagoner, Porter, 315–317, 334, 366–367, 450,
518

Wakefield, Frank, 424
Wakely, Jimmy, 147, 171, 235, 269, 274–275
Waldron, Cliff, 425, 426
Walker, Aaron "T-Bone," 149, 204
Walker, Billy, 354, 518
Walker, Charlie, 300, 322, 353, 518
Walker, Cindy, 177, 205, 228, 250–251, 444
Walker, Frank, 46, 57, 246, 283
Walker, Jerry Jeff, 461, 462, 463, 477
Walker, Wheeler, Jr., 565–566, 567, 568, 571
Walker, Wiley, 231
Walker, William, 26
Walker-Meador, Jo, xvi, 311
Wallace, George, 375, 376, 421
Waller, Charlie, 412–413
Walser, Don, 521
Walsh, Dock, 69
Walsh, Joe, 559
Walsh's Lounge, Pittsburgh, 409
Walters, Barbara, 465
Wanderers Three, 326
Wanted! The Outlaws (album), 473–474
Wariner, Steve, 444, 450
WARL (Arlington, Virginia), 245, 396
War Memorial Auditorium, 89
Warner Brothers: and Delia Bell, 430; and Gail
Davies, 358; and Al Hopkins, 47; and Nudie
the Tailor, 238; and Travis Tritt, 516
Warner's Seven Aces, 45
Warren, Paul, 255, 393–394
Washington, DC: and bluegrass, 214, 325, 396,
410, 411–414, 422, 425, 426, 430–431; folk
festivals in, 259–260; and radio, 308, 317;
southern migration to, 208, 213, 214
Watergate crisis, 350, 438
Watkins, Sara, 537, 539
Watkins, Sean, 539
Watson, Arthel "Doc": death of, 544; and Del-
more Brothers, 128, 129, 329; and festivals,
474, 543; with Bill Monroe, *532*; and Nitty
Gritty Dirt Band, 454; and Don Reno, 329,
396; repertory of, 329, 333, 583n13; and
urban folk revival, 328–329
Watson, Dale, xvi, 474, 522–523
Watson, Gene, 480, 482–483, 517, 519
Watson, Jim, 543
Watson, Merle, 329, 543
Watson, Tom, 21
Watts, Howard. *See* Rainwater, Cedric
Watts, Isaac, 13
Watts, Wilmer, 158

The Way I Should (album), 525

Waylors, 342

Wayne, Dallas, 530

WBAP (Fort Worth), 40–41, 43, 81, 121, 191, 379

WBIG (Greensboro, North Carolina), 254

WBT (Charlotte), 116, 120, 144, 387

WBZ (Boston), 64

WCHS (Charleston, West Virginia), 410

WCKY (Cincinnati), 244, 396

WCYB (Bristol, Virginia), 391, 404

WDAD (Nashville), 85

WDOD (Chattanooga), 95

WEAF (New York), 64

Weaver, Sylvester, 204

Weaver Brothers and Elviry, 10, 131

Webb, Brenda Gail. *See* Gayle, Crystal

Webb, Jim, 318

Weber-Simon Agency, 167

Weems, Mason "Parson," 21

Weisberger, Bernard, 19

Weissberg, Eric, 328, 418

Weize, Richard, 322

Welch, Gillian, 491, 523, 543, 564

Weller, Freddy, 444

Welling, Frank, 157–158

Wells, Kitty: death of, 570; and Johnny and Jack, 254; and *Louisiana Hayride*, 243; photograph of, *260*; as "Queen of Country Music," 261, 362; and radio, 223, 243; recordings of, 246, 261–262, 269, 274, 288, 353, 554; stage persona of, 361, 556; vocal style of, 257–258, 309, 445

Wembley Festival, 322

Werner, Joe, 273

Wernick, Peter, 425

Wertz, Kenny, 427

West, Dottie, 361, 418, 439, 449, 450

West, Shelly, 334, 361

West, Speedy, 236, 341

Westbrook, John, 104, 150

Western Caravan, 236

western image in country music, 160, 167–173, 176–180, 206, 226, 230, 238–239, 268. *See also* cowboy music

western swing: and banjos, 30; and bluegrass, 431; circles of musicians in bands, 195–196, 197, 199, 200; decline in popularity of, 265, 266; and Great Depression, 154; and Adolph Hofner, 181; instrumentation of, 479; and Clayton McMichen, 143; origins of, 188–191; and Hank Penny, 144; and Foreman Phillips, 235; and Prairie Ramblers, 143; revival in 1970s, 475–476, 484; revival in 1990s, 530; and George Strait, 493; and vocal styles, 195, 204; and Bob Wills, 143, 189, 190–191, 199, 202–206, 214, 235, 475

Western Theatre (radio show), 277

Weston, Dick. *See* Rogers, Roy

West Texas Cowboys, 206, 475

We the People (radio show), 277

WFAA (Dallas), 67–68, 196, 199, 201

WFBR (Baltimore), 142

WGN (Chicago), 82

WGST (Atlanta), 136

WGY (Schenectady), 64

Whalen, Kermit, 188, 193

WHBQ (Memphis), 291

Wheeler, Billy Edd, 355

Wheelhouse (album), 559

Wheeling Jamboree (radio show): and Wilma Lee and Stoney Cooper, 117, 261; and Davis Sisters, 302; emergence of, 117, 234; and Lilly Brothers, 410; and Brad Paisley, 517; and personal appearances, 215; and Reno and Smiley, 397

When Fallen Angels Fly (album), 515

When I Call Your Name (album), 504

Whiskeytown, 528

whistles, 51

White, Benjamin F., 26

White, Bob, 45

White, Buck, 431

White, Cheryl, 431

White, Clarence, 329, 424

White, Jack, 550–551

White, John, 166

White, Josh, 325

White, Lee Roy "Lasses," 10, 218

White, Roland, 391, 408, 424, 427

White, Sharon, 431

White Family, 485

white supremacy, 2

Whiting, Margaret, 275

Whitley, Eddie, 199

Whitley, Keith, 271, 422, 485–486, 496, 497–498

Whitley, Ray, 172, 179, 235

Whitman, Otis Dewey "Slim," 278, 279–280, 321, 324–325, 474, 570

Whitter, Henry, 43, 46, 58, 70, 74, 123, 129, 380, 403

WHN (New York City), 314, 440
WHN Barn Dance (radio show), 179
WHO (Des Moines), 116
Who Needs Pictures (album), 517, 558
Wide Open Spaces (album), 512
Wiggins, Ella May, 152
Wiggins, Roy, 277
Wilburn Brothers (Teddy and Doyle), 244, 315–316, 340, 362, 375, 435, 515
Wilburn Brothers Show (television show), 315–316, 362
Wilco, 528
Wild-Eyed Dream (album), 498
Wilds, Lee David, 10, 218
Wilgus, D. K., 24, 414
Wilgus, Donald Knight, 58
Wilkin, Marijohn, 333, 357
Will Ed Kemble's furniture store, 194
William Jacobs Agency, 167
Williams, Ann, 169
Williams, Audrey Sheppard, 283, 285
Williams, Benny, 407
Williams, Billie Jones, 285, 333
Williams, Cohen T., 392
Williams, Curley, 235
Williams, Daniel Huggins "Lefty," 190
Williams, Doc, 117, 142
Williams, Don, 324, 334, 446
Williams, Hank, Jr., 436, 456, 457–458, 459, 516, 566
Williams, Hank, III, 522
Williams, King Hiram "Hank": and alternative country, 564; and black music, 6, 282; and Country Music Hall of Fame, 313; death of, 280, 284, 285–286, 287, 288, 333; and films, 284; and *Grand Ole Opry*, 244, 284, 285, 434; and Merle Haggard, 272; and Wayne Hancock, 521, 522; and hillbilly music, 280, 281–282, 284–285; and Alan Jackson, 515, 516; and George Jones, 288, 337; and Kris Kristofferson, 357; and *Louisiana Hayride*, 244, 283–284, 285; and medicine shows, 7; and music from cities' "sin streets," 11; and Molly O'Day, 258; photograph of, *281*; popularity of, 273, 280, 284, 285, 298; and Ray Price, 271, 288, 300, 338, 339; and Charley Pride, 372; recordings of, 275, 283, 284, 285, 310, 324; repertory of, 282, 544, 561; and Fred Rose, 228, 283; and session musicians, 247; as songwriter, 282, 283, 339; and Ernest Tubb, 220, 282, 285, 286; vocal style

of, 283, 284–285; and Hank Williams Jr., 457, 458; and Lucinda Williams, 525
Williams, Lawton, 299
Williams, Lilly, 280, 282
Williams, Linda, 537, 543
Williams, Lonnie, 280
Williams, Lucinda, 523, 525, 550, 564, 565
Williams, Miller, 525
Williams, Paul, 402–403
Williams, Perk, 266
Williams, Pharrell, 560
Williams, Robert, 530
Williams, Robin, 543
Williams, Sollie Paul "Tex," 233, 235–236, 238
Williams, Tennessee, 525
Williams, Vern, 428
Williamson, George, 410
Williamson, Kitty, 193
Williamson, LaVerne. *See* O'Day, Molly
Williamson, Mary, 410
William Wade Agency, 119
Willing, Foy, 177
Willis, Kelly, 543
Willis, Vic, 283, 440
Willis Brothers (Vic, Guy, and Skeeter), 283
Wills, Bob (James Robert): and Austin, Texas, 464; and black music, 6; in California, 214, 234–235; death of, 475; and Stoney Edwards, 373; as fiddler, 203; and films, 172, 177, 205, 250; and Merle Haggard, 347, 475; hot dance style, 63, 196; legacy of, 475; and Light Crust Doughboys, 193, 202, 204; and Light Crust Flour, 191; and Roger Miller, 318; and Willie Nelson, 354, 475; and Foreman Phillips, 219; and Ray Price, 339; and radio barn dances, 121; and Leon Rausch, 265; recordings of, 205–206, 230, 231, 232; repertory of, 204–206, 226, 266; and Jimmie Rodgers, 168; songs identified with, 146; and George Strait, 481; and Al Stricklin, 198; and Texas Playboys, 193, 202–206, *203*, 220, 373, 464, 545; and Cindy Walker, 250; and Don Walser, 521; and western swing, 143, 189, 190–191, 199, 202–206, 214, 235, 475; and World War II, 220, 230
Wills, John, 202
Wills Point, Sacramento, 235
Wills's Fiddle Band, 190, 202
Will the Circle Be Unbroken (album), 454–455
Wilson, Frank, 47

Wilson, Grace, 82–83

Wilson, Gretchen, 555–556

Wilson, Hank, 454

Wilson, Joe, 429

WINC (Winchester, Virginia), 308

The Wind Done Gone (Randall), 549

Wine of Cardui, 120, 316

WIS (Columbia, South Carolina), 145, 387

Wise, Robert "Chubby," *385*, 387–388

Wiseman, Lulu Belle, 139, 258

Wiseman, Mac: and bluegrass, 390–391, 395, 396, 398, 399, 417; and Blue Grass Boys, 391; and bluegrass festivals, 423; and Carl Butler, 394; and *Grand Ole Opry*, 399; and Newport Folk Festival, 329; and Molly O'Day, 398, 399; and radio, 404; repertory of, 398, 399; vocal style of, 398, 399

Wiseman, Scott, 68, 115, 139, 216, 242, 375

WIS Hillbillies, 145, 146

Wister, Owen, 162

W. I. Swain (tent show), 98–99

WJJD (Chicago), 244

WJR (Detroit), 85, 402

WKDA (Nashville), 245

WKY (Oklahoma City), 231

WLS (Chicago), 40, 41, 64, 81, 115–116, 168–170, 216, 240. *See also National Barn Dance* (radio show)

WLS Artists' Bureau, 218

WLW (Cincinnati), 64, 116, 151, 215, 216

WLW Barn Dance (radio show), 215

WMCA (New York City), 179

WMPS (Memphis), 276

WNAX (Yankton), 81

WNOX (Knoxville), 132, 223

WNVA (Norton, Virginia), 404, 405

WOAI (San Antonio), 165, 191

Wolfe, Charles, 46, 69

Womack, Lee Ann, 491, 509, 512

The Woman in Me (album), 510

women: and alternative country, 564; and bluegrass, 430, 535, 537–538; and cowboy music, 141, 173, 193; cultivation of women entertainers, 139–141; as executives in country music business, 311; and folk style of home singing, 24, 34; and gender roles, 360–361, 362, 363, 509, 553–557; and honky-tonk music, 183; independent identity of, 257, 358–367, 508, 509–511; as instrumentalists, 26, 34, 139, 140; modern era of women country singers, 308–309,

507–509; and musical contests, 26; and politics, 360, 362, 508–509, 552–554; recognition in country music, 257–262, 554–557; and rockabilly music, 292–293; songs about suffrage, 69; as songwriters, 358, 360, 362, 537; stage personas of, 359–363; and television, 316; as western cowgirls, 141, 173, 193, 258, 309, 358

women's rights, 360, 362, 508–509

Woodlieff, Norman, 61

Woods, Bill, 341–342, 347

Woods, Oscar, 127

Woolbright, Mack, 387

Wooley, Sheb, 320

Wooten, Art, 384, 386

WOR (New York City), 178, 179

Work, Henry Clay, 19

working-class audiences: and alternative country, 531; in California, 214; and civil rights movement, 375–376; and conservatism, 434; and disc jockeys, 244; and Great Depression, 159; and honky-tonk music, 182, 341, 483; and Charley Pride, 372–373; and radio, 40, 41, 84, 490, 491; and Jimmie Rodgers, 98; and songwriters, 348, 377–378; and Floyd Tillman, 269

working-class songs, xvi, 348–349, 362, 377–378

World's Fair of 1939 (New York), 315

World War I, 35, 105, 123, 162, 187

World War II: and Almanac Singers, 326; bibliographic essay on country music during, 632–637; and Carter Family retirement, 78; and folk music, 326; and hillbilly music, 207, 212–213, 229–230; and honky-tonk music, 183; and identification of country music, 37; industrialization during, 162, 214; and international popularity of country music, 321; and migration, 208–209, 213–214; and rationing, 221; and rural areas, 208–209, 215; and shellac rationing, 212–213; and songwriters, 228–232, 348; and western swing, 195

World Wide Web, 569

WORT (Madison), xi

WOV (New York), 244

WPA, 151, 184, 325

Wright, Chely, 554

Wright, J. B. F., 15

Wright, Johnny, 243, 254–255, 261–262, 376, 570. *See also* Johnny and Jack

WROL (Knoxville), 223

WRR (Dallas), 199, 200

WSAZ (Huntington, West Virginia), 141

WSB (Atlanta), 39–41, 44, 56, 62–63, 81, 144, 147, 251, 275

WSB Barn Dance (radio show), 221, 234

WSFA (Montgomery), 282

WSM (Nashville): and barn dances, 40, 84, 88–89, 147; and Blue Grass Boys, 388; booking agency of, 310; disc jockeys of, 245, 543; as fifty-thousand-watt clear channel station, 114, 217, 219; and Flatt and Scruggs, 392; and Hay, 83–84, 89; and Bradley Kincaid, 64; and Bill Monroe, 385, 388, 402; programming of, 41, 85–86; and recording studio, 246; and Fred Rose, 228; and Asher Sizemore, 141; talent bureau of, 240. *See also Grand Ole Opry* (radio show)

WSPA (Spartanburg, South Carolina), 387

WTAS (Elgin, Illinois), 83

WTCR (Ashland, Kentucky), 485

WTFF (Washington, DC), 97–98

WTJS (Jackson, Tennessee), 264, 276

WTOP (Washington, DC), 317

WTOP-TV (Washington, DC), 412

W. T. Smith Lumber Company, 280

Wurlitzer Company, 182

WWL (New Orleans), 121, 144, 201, 378–379

WWNC (Asheville), 96, 97, 136

WWVA (Wheeling), 117, 142, 234, 244, 278, 397, 400, 402, 409

Wynette, Tammy, 362–363, *363*, 364, 366, 436, 440, 478

XEAW (Reynosa, Mexico), 118

XENT (Nuevo Laredo, Mexico), 118

XEPN, 118, 187

XERA (Villa Acuña, Mexico), 117–118

XERF (Del Rio, Texas), 80

XM satellite radio, 569

X stations, 117

Yandell, Paul, 254

Yearwood, Trisha, 491–492, 549

Yellin, Bob, 328

Yesteryear in Nashville (television show), 437

YMCA, 14, 64

Yoakam, Dwight, 48, 490, 491, 497, 513, 515, 565

yodeling: and Eddie Arnold, 277; and Gene Autry, 168; blue yodels, 63, 91, 95, 97, 98, 101, 102, 104, 105, 106, 108, 109, 110, 126; and Suzy Bogguss, 508; and Elton Britt, 175, 229, 521; and Callahan Brothers, 130; and Cliff Carlisle, 126; and Sara Carter, 79; and Jimmie Davis, 127; and duet singing, 122, 130, 410; and Tommy Duncan, 204; and Lefty Frizzell, 273; and Girls of the Golden West, 173; and Leon Huff, 193; and international popularity of country music, 324; and Mainer's Mountaineers, 145; and Mexican border stations, 119; and Patsy Montana, 173; and Tex Morton, 167; and Dolly Parton, 366; and George Puckett, 63, 105; and Goebel Reeves, 166; and Riders of the Sky, 476; and Kenny Roberts, 410; and Jimmie Rodgers, 51, 63, 91, 95, 97, 98, 101, 102, 104, 105–108, 109, 110, 122, 126, 159, 166, 168, 184, 273, 278, 459; and Roy Rogers, 177; and Margo Smith, 361; and Hank Snow, 167, 278; and Songs of the Pioneers, 176; Swiss yodelers, 7, 11, 105, 122, 126; and Kenneth Threadgill, 459–460; and Ernest Tubb, 109, 184; and Don Walser, 521; and Slim Whitman, 279, 325; and Hank Williams, 284

York Brothers (George and Leslie), 245

Young, Donnie. *See* Paycheck, Johnny

Young, Faron, 244, 288, 307, 315, 323, 354, 473

Young, Neil, 518

Young Country, 491–492

youth culture: and bluegrass, 413, 539, 541–542; and Johnny Cash, 517–518; and country-pop, 299; and country-rock, 456, 459, 465; as influence on country music, 453–454, 517; and Willie Nelson, 467; and rhythm-and-blues music, 289; and rockabilly music, 294, 307, 314; and rock-and-roll music, 288–289, 290, 293, 294–295, 330, 454; and Ricky Skaggs, 488; and urban folk revival, 325, 326, 327, 328, 330

YouTube, 567, 568, 572

Zero Records, 362

zithers, 51

Zucker, Stan, 240

ZZ Top, 457, 501

Index of Song Titles

"Abilene," 330

"Above and Beyond," 342, 353

"Accidental Racist," 559

"Achy Breaky Heart," 505

"Act Naturally," 342

"After All This Time," 462

"Airmail Special," 406

"Alabam," 334

"Alcohol," 559

"Allá en el rancho grande," 180, 195

"All for the Love of a Girl," 332

"All I Have to Do Is Dream," 296

"All In and Down and Out Blues," 87, 158

"All I've Got's Gone," 158

"All My Friends Are Gonna Be Strangers," 345

"All Roads Lead to You," 450

"All the World Is Lonely Now," 226

"Almost," 276

"Almost Persuaded," 351, 478

"Amanda," 446

"Amarillo by Morning," 477

"Amateur in Love," 279

"Amazing Grace," 482

"Am I the Only One (Who's Ever Felt This Way?)," 512

"Another Place, Another Time," 294

"Apartment Number Nine," 364, 473

"Are You from Dixie?," 136

"Are You Missing Me?," 254, 406

"Are You Waiting Just for Me," 229

"Arkansas Traveler," 23, 43

"Ashes of Love," 249, 254

"As Long as I Live," 226

"As Long as the Wind Blows," 355

"Asshole from El Paso," 566

"Atlantic Coastal Line," 372

"At Mail Call Today," 229

"At the End of a Long Lonely Day," 308

"At the Rainbow's End," 176

"Away Out on the Mountain," 70–71, 97, 107

"Babies in the Mill," 130

"Baby Blue," 413

"Back Home Again," 445

"Back in the Saddle Again," 171–172

"The Back of Your Hand," 537

"Back Street Affair," 274

"Back to the Barrooms," 346

"The Baggage Coach Ahead," 19

"Ballad of a Teenage Queen," 299

"The Ballad of Boot Hill," 332

"The Ballad of Charles Guiteau"/"Charles Guiteau," 17, 70

"Ballad of Forty Dollars," 356

"The Ballad of Ira Hayes," 351

"The Ballad of Jed Clampett," 334, 418

"The Ballad of Rodger Young," 230

"Ballad of the Green Berets," 349

"Bandera Waltz," 279

"Bandy the Rodeo Clown," 482

"Banks of the Guadalupe," 520

"Banks of the Ohio," 130, 137

"Barbara Allen," 3, 52, 66, 296

"Basin Street Blues," 205

"The Battle Hymn of Love," 526

"The Battle of Bull Run," 332

"The Battle of New Orleans," 332–333

"Bay Rum Blues," 125

"Beaumont Rag," 190, 204

"Beautiful Brown Eyes," 148

"Beautiful Texas," 192

"Bed of Rose's," 450

"Before He Cheats," 556

"Before the Next Teardrop Falls," 369

"Behind Closed Doors," 444

"Be Honest with Me," 228

"Ben Dewberry's Final Run," 56, 107

"Bessie the Heifer," 263

"The Bible's True," 87

"Big Beaver," 205

"Big City," 439

"Biggest Airport in the World," 482

"Big John," 333

"Big River Blues" ("Deep River Blues"), 128

"Big Rock Candy Mountain," 166

"Bill Woods of Bakersfield," 347

"Billy Bayou," 305

"Billy in the Lowground," 62

"Billy the Kid," 56

"Bimbo," 305

"Bird Dog," 296

"Birmingham Bounce," 242

"Birmingham Jail," 123, 279

"Black and White Rag," 190, 195

"Blackberry Blossom," 148

"Black Eyed Susan," 394

"Black Jack David," 34, 126, 267

"Blackland Farmer," 8

"Black Mountain Rag," 329

"Black Sheep," 483

"Blessed or Damned," 522

"The Blind Boy's Dog," 230

"Blue Blue Day," 303

"Blue Canadian Rockies," 455

"Blue Eyed Elaine," 220

"Blue Eyes Crying in the Rain," 228, 467

"Blue Love," 494

"Blue Moon of Kentucky," 291, 295

"Blue Railroad Train," 128

"Blue Skies," 467

"Blue-Tailed Fly," 10

"Blue Yodel No. 1," 71, 97, 102, 205

"Blue Yodel No. 4," 387

"Blue Yodel No 9," 104

"Bob Wills Is Still the King," 464

"Boil Them Cabbage Down," 62, 143

"Bonaparte's Retreat," 22

"Bonus Blues," 158

"Boogie Woogie," 264

"Boot Scootin' Boogie," 505

"Border Ride," 406

"Born to Lose," 183, 197, 213, 230, 370

"Borrowed Angel," 481

"The Bottle Let Me Down," 346

"Bouquet of Roses," 277

"Branded Man," 346

"Branded Wherever I Go," 226, 249

"Brand on My Heart," 278

"Breadline Blues," 159

"Break My Mind," 330

"Breathe," 510

"Bright Sherman Valley," 166

"Bringing Home the Bacon," 83

"Bringing in the Georgia Mail," 383

"Broken Lady," 450

"Brother Jukebox," 516

"Brown's Ferry Blues," 128

"Bubba Shot the Jukebox," 516

"Bubbles in My Beer," 250

"Buck Dancer's Choice," 85

"Budded on Earth," 251

"Buddy, Won't You Roll Down the Line," 87

"Building on the Sand," 252

"Bully of the Town," 22

"Burning Bridges," 561

"Burning Memories," 340

"Burning the Midnight Oil," 360

"Bury Me beneath the Willow," 486

"Bury Me Not on the Lone Prairie," 85

"Bury Me Under the Weeping Willow," 79

"The Butcher's Boy," 67, 137

"Bye Bye Love," 296

"By the Time I Get to Phoenix," 318

"California Cotton Fields," 349

"Call of the Canyon," 178

"Candy Kisses," 276

"Cannonball Blues," 80

"Can't Yo' Heah Me Callin', Caroline," 73

"Can You Forgive," 146

"The Cape," 462

"Carolina, I Remember You," 457

"The Carroll County Accident," 316
"Carry Me Back to the Lone Prairie," 54
"Casting My Lasso to the Sky," 279
"Catfish John," 350–351, 423
"Cattle Call," 277, 325
"Chained to a Memory," 277
"Charles Guiteau"/"The Ballad of Charles
    Guiteau," 17, 70
"Charlie's Pride and Johnny's Cash," 417
"Chattahoochee," 516
"Chattanooga Shoe Shine Boy," 242, 265
"Cherokee Boogie," 265
"Cherokee Maiden," 205, 250
"Chicken Reel," 23
"Childish Love," 254
"Chillin' It," 567
"Choices," 517
"Christine's Tune," 456
"Cielito lindo," 195
"Cimarron," 171–172
"Cincinnati, Ohio," 359
"Cindy," 136
"City Lights," 300, 339, 353
"The Class of '57," 452
"Coal Miner's Daughter," 361
"Coat of Many Colors," 366
"Cocaine," 125
"Cocaine Blues," 125
"Cold, Cold Heart," 570
"Color of the Blues," 338
"Columbus Stockade Blues," 123
"Come Back Little Pal," 146, 226
"Come Sundown," 357
"Coney Isle," 334
"Conversation with Death" ("Oh Death"), 15
"Convoy," 378
"The Coo Coo Bird," 70
"Cool Water," 176
"Corn Licker Rag," 130
"Corrine, Corrina," 205
"Cosmic Cowboy," 464
"Cotton-Eyed Joe," 22, 180–181, 204
"Cotton Jenny," 445
"Cotton Mill Blues," 158
"Cotton Mill Colic," 158
"Could I Have This Dance," 445
"Country Blues," 71
"Country Boy," 250, 263
"A Country Boy Can Survive," 458
"Country Girl," 307
"Country Rap," 561

"Country Roads," 445
"Cowards over Pearl Harbor," 229
"Cowboys Ain't Supposed to Cry," 477
"The Cowboy's Prayer," 166
"Crazy," 309, 354
"Crazy Arms," 294, 300, 339
"Crazy Blues," 42
"Crazy Over You," 494
"Cripple Creek," 22
"Crushin' It," 565, 567
"Cry, Cry, Cry," 298
"Cry, Cry Darling," 330
"Crying," 499
"Cumberland Gap," 22

"Daddy and Home," 93, 106
"Daddy Lessons," 546–549, 551, 571–572
"The Dance," 502
"Danny Boy," 340
"Dark as a Dungeon," 238
"The Darkest Hour," 486
"Darling Cory," 77
"Day of Decision," 376
"A Dear John Letter," 306
"Death of a Married Man," 559
"The Death of Floyd Collins," 57, 58, 75, 107
"The Death of Hank Williams," 286
"The Death of Mother Jones," 170
"Deck of Cards," 267
"Deed I Do," 228
"Deep Elem Blues," 201
"Deep River Blues," 128, 329
"Delta Dawn," 350
"The Democratic Donkey Is in His Stall Again,"
    159
"Desperados Waiting for a Train," 461
"Detour," 233
"Detroit City," 331, 334–335
"The Devil Went Down to Georgia," 457
"Dickson County Blues," 148
"Did I Shave My Legs for This?," 509
"Did You Ever Go Sailing? (Down the River of
    Memories)," 155
"Diesel On My Tail," 417
"Dill Pickle Rag," 23
"Dim Lights, Thick Smoke, and Loud, Loud
    Music," 341
"Dirt Road Anthem," 561
"D-I-V-O-R-C-E," 356, 363
"Divorce Me C.O.D.," 233–234, 236
"Dixie on My Mind," 457, 458

"DJ for a Day," 355

"Do-Do-Daddling Thing," 127

"Does Fort Worth Ever Cross Your Mind," 480

"Doing My Time," 396

"Don't Come Home a-Drinkin' (with Lovin' on Your Mind)," 362

"Don't It Make My Brown Eyes Blue," 361

"Don't Just Stand There," 268

"Don't Let Me Cross Over," 334

"Don't Let Them Take the Bible Out of Our Schoolrooms," 253

"Don't Let Your Deal Go Down," 61

"Don't Let Your Sweet Love Die," 146, 221

"Don't Make Me Go to Bed and I'll Be Good," 228

"Don't Rock the Jukebox," 516

"Don't Sell Daddy Any More Whiskey," 258

"Don't Stop the Music," 338

"Don't Take Your Guns to Town," 332

"Don't Touch Me," 354, 356

"Don't You Ever Get Tired of Hurting Me," 354

"Do-Re-Mi," 156

"Do Right Daddy Blues," 125–126

"Do Right Woman," 441

"Doug MacArthur," 375

"Down at the Old Country Church," 127

"Down at the Twist and Shout," 505

"Down by the Old Mill Stream," 82

"Down from Dover," 366

"Down in the Willow Garden," 296, 383

"Down South Blues," 71

"Down South in New Orleans," 254

"Down the Old Road to Home," 107

"Down Where the River Bends," 229

"Do You Love as Good as You Look?," 451, 494

"Dream Baby," 250

"Dreaming of a Little Cabin," 155, 399

"Dreamland Waltz," 181

"Driftwood on the River," 351

"Drinking Thing," 480

"Drive South," 508

"Driving Nails in My Coffin," 183, 230

"A Drunkard's Child," 107

"Drunken Driver," 258

"Dueling Banjos," 398, 418

"Dumb Blonde," 366

"Dust on the Bible," 252

"Dusty Skies," 205, 250

"The Dying Cowboy," 38, 163

"The Dying Girl's Message," 75

"Each Night at Nine," 197, 229

"Earl's Breakdown," 393

"East Bound Freight Train," 398

"The Eastbound Train," xiii, 133

"The Eastern Gate," 254

"Easy Loving," 444

"Easy's Getting Harder," 525

"80's Ladies," 509

"Eighth of January," 22, 332

"Eight More Miles to Louisville," 256

"El Cumbanchero," 406

"Election Day in Kentucky," 67

"Eleven Cent Cotton and Forty Cent Meat," 57

"El Paso," 308, 333

"El Paso City," 476

"Elvira," 452

"Empty Cot in the Bunkhouse," 171

"The End of the World," 303

"Engine 143," 81

"Everybody Does It in Hawaii," 107

"Everybody's Gonna Have a Wonderful Time Up There," 265

"Every Song I Write Is for You," 522

"Excuse Me, I Think I've Got a Heartache," 342, 353

"Faded Coat of Blue," 67

"Faded Love," 205

"Fallen Leaves," 256

"A Fallen Star," 330

"Family Bible," 354

"Family Tradition," 566

"The Family Who Prays," 253, 254

"Farewell Blues," 143

"Farewell Party," 483

"Farewell Song"/"Man of Constant Sorrow," 55, 330, 403, 471, 491

"The Farmer Is the Man," 8

"Farm Relief," 87

"Farther Along," xiv, 15, 154, 315

"Fatal Derby Day," 66

"Fatal Flower Garden," 18

"The Fatal Wedding," 19, 66, 75, 111

"Father, Dear Father, Come Home," 19

"Feast Here Tonight," 138

"Feelin' It," 567

"Feels So Right," 453

"Feudin' Banjos," 398

"The Fields Have Turned Brown," 404–405

"The Fighting Side of Me," 376, 377

"Filipino Baby," 159, 266–267

"Finger Poppin' Time," 295

"The Fireman," 480

"Fire on the Mountain," 22

"Fisher's Hornpipe," 23

"Fist City," 362, 555

"500 Miles," 331

"Five Feet High and Rising," 297, 349

"Flint Hill Special," 393

"Flop-Eared Mule," 22

"Flowers for Mama," 531

"Flowers on the Wall," 451

"Fly Around My Pretty Little Miss," 52

"Flying South to Dixie," 250

"Foggy Mountain Breakdown," 391, 418

"Folsom Prison Blues," 319

"Foolin' Around," 353

"Footprints in the Snow," 221, 386

"Forever and Ever, Amen," 497

"The Forgotten Soldier Boy," 158

"For the Good Times," 341, 357

"Fort Worth Jail," 171

"Four or Five Times," 202

"Four Strong Winds," 330, 331

"Four Walls," 305

"The Fox," 542

"Fox on the Run," 425

"Frankie and Johnny," 106

"Franklin Roosevelt's Back Again," 159

"Fraulein," 299

"Freight Train Boogie," 265, 398

"Friends in Low Places," 502, 566

"Froggie Went a-Courtin'," 18

"From a Jack to a King," 498

"From Earth to Heaven," 86

"From Mother's Arms to Korea," 374

"From the Manger to the Cross," 249

"Fruit Jar Blues," 125

"Fuck Aneta Briant" [*sic*], 566

"Fuck This Town," 529

"Fuck You Bitch," 566

"Fujiyama Mama," 293

"Funny How Time Slips Away," 354

"Galveston," 318

"The Gambler," 447

"Gambling Barroom Blues," 196

"Gambling Polka Dot Blues," 107, 205

"A Gangster's Warning," 170

"Gathering Flowers for the Master's Bouquet," 255

"Gentle on My Mind," 318, 330, 356

"Georgia on My Mind," 467

"Get Along Home, Cindy," 194

"Girl from the North Country," 413

"The Girl I Left in Sunny Tennessee," 416

"The Girl I Loved in Sunny Tennessee," 156

"Girl in a Country Song," 547

"A Girl I Used to Know," 338

"The Girl Most Likely," 359

"Girl of My Dreams," 194

"Girl on the Billboard," 378

"Give Me Forty Acres," 378

"Give Mother My Crown," 252

"The Glory of Love," 178

"God Bless America Again," 376

"God Isn't Real," 529

"God Put a Rainbow in the Clouds," 56, 406

"God Will," 500

"Going Steady," 307

"Golden Ring," 555

"Golden River," 176

"Gold Mine in the Sky," 177

"Gold Star in the Window," 230

"Gone," 299, 306

"Gonna Quit My Rowdy Ways," 130

"Goodbye Earl," 509, 512, 554

"Goodbye Sweet Liza Jane," 61

"Goodnight, Irene," 326

"Good Old Mountain Dew," 68

"Good Rockin' Tonight," 289

"A Good Woman's Love," 351

"Goo Goo Dada," 302

"Gosh, I Miss You All the Time," 170

"Gospel Boogie," 265

"Governor Al Smith," 87

"Grandfather's Clock," 19

"Grandma Harp," 346

"Grandma's Song," 358

"Grandpa (Tell Me 'bout the Good Old Days)," 495

"Grand Texas," 561

"The Grand Tour," 479

"Great Balls of Fire," 294

"The Great Judgment Morning," 226

"The Great Speckled Bird," 16, 213, 224–225

"The Great Speckled Bird No. 2," 224

"Green, Green Grass of Home," 316, 348, 355

"Groundhog Rootin' in My Backyard," 125

"Guitar Boogie," 233, 239, 265

"Guitar Rag," 204

"Guitars, Cadillacs," 497

"Gulf Coast Blues," 205

"Gunpowder and Lead," 549, 556
"The Gypsy Laddie," 126

"Hallelujah, I'm a Bum," 166
"Handsome Molly," 43, 380
"The Hands You're Holding Now," 308
"The Hand That Rocks the Cradle," 450
"Hangover Blues," 255, 290
"Hank, It Will Never Be the Same without You," 286
"Hank and Lefty Raised My Country Soul," 373–374
"Hank Williams, You Wrote My Life," 482
"Hank Williams Will Live Forever," 286
"Harper Valley PTA," 348, 351, 355, 359, 361
"Haunted Hungry Heart," 279
"Have I Stayed Away Too Long?," 230
"Have I Told You Lately That I Love You?," 139, 305
"Hawaiian Honeymoon," 199
"Headin' Down the Wrong Highway," 183, 197, 230
"Heartaches," 413
"Heartaches by the Number," 300, 353
"Heartbreak Hotel," 301
"Heartbreak U.S.A.," 261
"Heartbroke," 486
"Heart over Mind," 340, 479
"Hearts of Stone," 242
"Hearts on Fire," 456, 485
"Heaven's Just a Sin Away," 450
"He'll Have to Go," 306
"Hello, Central, Give Me Heaven," 52
"Hello, Young Lovers," 560
"Hell on Heels," 556
"Hello Vietnam," 355, 376
"Hello Walls," 307, 354
"Help Me Make It through the Night," 357, 360, 444
"Henry Clay Beattie," 70
"Here for the Party," 556
"Here's a Quarter (Call Someone Who Cares)," 516
"Here Today and Gone Tomorrow," 302
"Herr Schmidt," 180
"Hesitation Blues," 144, 194
"He Stopped Loving Her Today," 479, 531
"He Thinks He'll Keep Her," 509
"Hey, Porter," 298
"Hey Joe," 251, 268
"Hickory Wind," 455

"High Behind Blues," 127
"High on a Hilltop," 342
"High Powered Mama," 103
"High School Confidential," 294
"Highway 40 Blues," 486
"Hill Billie Blues," 88
"Hillbilly Boogie," 128, 265, 290
"Hillbilly Highway," 500
"A Hillbilly Wedding in June," 170
"The Hills of Roane County," 226
"The Hobo and the Cop," 166
"Hobo Bill's Last Ride," 106, 107, 155
"Hobo's Lullaby," 166
"Hobo's Meditation," 155
"Hole in the Bottom of the Sea," 264
"Home," 517
"Homecoming," 356
"Home on the Range," 163
"The Homestead on the Farm," 81
"Homewrecker," 555
"Honest and Truly," 228
"Honky Tonk Blues," 182–183
"Honky Tonk Mama," 183
"Honky Tonk Man," 332, 497
"Hoover Blues," 158
"Hot Burrito #1," 456
"Hot Rod Lincoln," 530
"Hot Time Mama," 144
"The House Carpenter," 17, 70
"The House of the Rising Sun," 131, 330
"House of the Rising Sun"/"Rounders Luck," 131
"The House Where We Were Wed," 133
"Houston," 450
"How Blue," 495
"How Can a Poor Man Stand Such Times and Live?," 56
"How Great Thou Art," 359
"How High the Moon," 570
"How Many Biscuits Can You Eat?," 140
"How Much Is That Doggie in the Window," 264
"How Much Is That Hound Dog in the Winder," 264
"Humpty Dumpty Heart," 266
"Hungry Eyes," 343, 346, 377
"Hurrah for Roosevelt," 159
"Hurt," 561

"I Ain't Goin' Honky Tonkin' Anymore," 183
"I Ain't Got No Home in This World Anymore," 156

"I Am a Pilgrim," 237, 455

"I Believe It for My Mother Told Me So," 19, 137

"I Believe the South's Gonna Rise Again," 349

"I Can Help," 442

"I Can't Do That Anymore," 509

"I Can't Stop Loving You," 303, 370

"I Couldn't Keep from Crying," 308

"Ida Red," 204

"I Didn't Hear Nobody Pray," 130

"I'd Love to Lay You Down," 449

"I'd Love to Live in Loveland with a Girl Like You," 83

"I Don't Believe You've Met My Baby," 254

"I Don't Care," 274, 486

"I Don't Care If Tomorrow Never Comes," 258, 283

"I Don't Claim to Be an Angel," 262

"I Don't Hurt Anymore," 288

"I Don't Love Nobody," 205

"I'd Rather Have Jesus," 255

"I Fall to Pieces," 309, 354

"If Drinkin Don't Kill Me," 479

"If I Could Hear My Mother Pray Again," 56

"If I Could Only Win Your Love," 485

"If I Needed You," 461, 523

"If I Said You Had a Beautiful Body (Would You Hold It against Me)," 444, 494

"If Loving You Is Wrong (Then I Don't Want to Be Right)," 441

"If My Heart Had Windows," 515

"I Forgot More Than You'll Ever Know," 302

"I Found You among the Roses," 79

"If Tomorrow Never Comes," 502

"If We Make It through December," 346, 377–378

"If We Never Meet Again," 404

"If You Don't Know Me by Now," 560

"If You Got the Money," 271

"I Got a Woman," 289

"I Guess I'm Crazy," 306

"I Had but Fifty Cents," 67

"I Hate These Songs," 522

"I Hate You," 479

"I Heard You Crying in Your Sleep," 283

"I Just Gotta Get a Message to You," 425

"I Just Started Hating Cheating Songs," 482

"I Just Wish You Were Someone I Loved," 450

"I Know You're Married, but I Love You Still," 397

"I'll Be All Smiles Tonight," 11, 66, 75, 80, 115

"I'll Be Back in a Year, Little Darlin'," 229

"I'll Be True While You're Gone," 229

"I'll Fly Away," 155, 406

"I'll Get Over You," 361

"I'll Keep on Loving You," 197

"I'll Never Pass This Way Again," 279

"I'll Never Slip Around Again," 269

"I'll Remember You, Love, in My Prayers," 19

"I'll Sail My Ship Alone," 270

"I'll Step Aside," 172

"I'll Still Write Your Name in the Sand," 142

"I'll Wait for You," 229

"I Love You a Thousand Ways," 271, 483

"I Love You Because," 275

"I Love You So Much It Hurts," 198, 269

"The Image of Me," 447, 479

"I'm a Honky Tonk Girl," 362

"I'm a Lonesome Fugitive," 345

"I'm an Old Cowhand," 177

"I'm Changing the Words to My Love Song," 254

"I Met a Friend of Yours Today," 482

"I'm Forever Blowing Bubbles," 133

"I'm Going to Georgia," 63

"I'm Just an Old Chunk of Coal," 483

"I'm Just Here to Get My Baby Out of Jail," 115, 133

"I'm Lonely and Blue," 107

"I'm Moving On," 278–279

"I'm My Own Grandpa," 264

"I'm No Communist," 375

"I'm No Stranger to the Rain," 498

"I'm Thinking Tonight of My Blue Eyes," 80, 215–216, 224

"I'm Using My Bible for a Roadmap," 397

"I'm Walking Home Tonight," 524

"In Bloom," 562

"Independence Day," 509, 554, 560

"Indian Love Call," 279

"Indian Outlaw," 505

"I Never Go Around Mirrors," 477

"In the Good Old Days When Times Were Bad," 349, 366

"In the Jailhouse Now," 184, 273–274

"In the Pines," 97

"In the Shade of the Old Apple Tree," 83

"In the Shadow of the Pines," 70

"Intoxicated Rat," 130

"Invitation to the Blues," 339

"I Overlooked an Orchid," 249

"I Really Don't Want to Know," 277, 299

"Irish Washerwoman," 22

"Is There Life Out There," 509, 554

"I Still Write Your Name in the Sand," 399

"I Stood on the Bridge at Midnight," 412

"It Ain't All Flowers," 562

"I Take the Chance," 302

"I Threw Away the Rose," 346

"It Is No Secret," 263

"It Makes No Difference Now," xiv, 183, 197–198, 230

"It Never Woulda Worked Out Anyway," 558

"It's a Long Way to the Top of the World," 417

"It's a Sin," 277

"It's a Small World," 459

"It's Only Make Believe," 447–448

"It Wasn't God Who Make Honky Tonk Angels," 261–262, 554

"I've Been Better," 558

"I've Got a New Heartache," 339

"I've Got Spurs That Jingle, Jangle, Jingle," 211

"I've Got the Kansas City Blues," 128

"I've Ranged, I've Roamed and I've Travelled," 102

"I Walk the Line," 298

"I Want to Be a Cowboy's Sweetheart," 173

"I Want to Be Loved," 252

"I Was Country When Country Wasn't Cool," 441

"I Was Sorta Wonderin'," 270

"I Wish I'd Stayed in the Wagon Yard," 67

"I Wonder How the Old Folks Are at Home," 399, 423

"I Wonder Where You Are Tonight," 146, 172, 274

"I Wouldn't Change You If I Could," 249, 486

"Jack's Truck Stop and Cafe," 522

"Jake Walk Blues," 125

"Jambalaya," 285

"Jealous Heart," 370

"The Jealous Lover," 156

"Jerusalem Ridge," 383

"Jesse James," 163, 166

"Jesus, Take the Wheel," 556

"Jesus Christ Is Still the King," 472

"Jesus Hits Like an Atom Bomb," 254

"Jimmie Brown the Newsboy," 80

"Joaquin," 524

"Joe Turner Blues," 194

"John Henry," 145

"Johnny Reb," 332

"Johnson's Old Grey Mule," 145, 147

"The John T. Scopes Trial," 54

"Jole Blon," 180, 270, 470

"Jolene," 538

"Jordan Is a Hard Road to Travel," 52

"Joshua," 366

"Juke Joint Jumpin'," 522

"Just a Closer Walk with Thee," 243, 263

"Just a Friend," 226

"Just Because," 201

"Just Because I'm a Woman," 366

"Just between You and Me," 373

"Just Get Up and Close the Door," 360

"Just Let Go," 562

"Just Loving You," 494

"Just Me and the Jukebox," 412

"Just One More," 338

"Just Tell Them That You Saw Me," 19, 398

"Just When I Needed You," 268

"Kansas City Star," 318

"Karate," 559

"Katie Dear," 130

"Kawliga," 457

"Keeper of the Key," 345

"Keep My Skillet Good and Greasy," 88

"Keep on the Firing Line," 14

"Keep on the Sunny Side," 80

"Kentucky," 133, 251

"Kentucky Means Paradise," 236

"Kentucky Waltz," 248

"Kids of the Baby Boom," 494

"King of the Road," 318

"Kinnie Wagner," 56

"Kisses Sweeter Than Wine," 326, 330

"Kitty Wells," 85

"Knock Three Times," 443

"Knot Hole Blues," 202

"The Knoxville Girl," 253

"Korea, Here We Come," 374

"Ladies Love Outlaws," 471

"The Lady Gay," 67

"L.A. Freeway," 461

"The Lass of Roch Royal," 17

"Last Date," 302

"The Last Letter," xiv, 80, 183, 230–231

"The Last Roundup," 178

"Lawdy Miss Clawdy," 289

"Leather Breeches," 22

"Leave It There," xiv, 154

"Leaving Home," 61

"Leaving Louisiana in the Broad Daylight,"
    452, 462
"Lee Highway Blues," 43
"Legend in My Time," 303
"Legend of Bonnie and Clyde," 346
"The Legend of John Henry's Hammer,"
    329–330
"Legend of the Dogwood Tree," 261
"The Legend of the Rebel Soldier," 429
"The Legend of the Robin Red Breast," 66
"Leonard," 347
"Let Me Be the One," 275
"Let Me Be Your Salty Dog" ("Salty Dog
    Blues"), 146
"Let Me Call You Sweetheart," 63
"Let Me Go, Lover," 264
"Let Me Go Blubber," 264
"Let Old Mother Nature Have Her Way," 268
"Let's Fall to Pieces Together," 480
"Let's Live a Little," 268
"Let's Live for Tonight," 397
"Letter Edged in Black," 11, 66, 398
"Letter to Mom," 554
"Let Your Love Flow," 494
"Life's Elevator," 250
"Life's Highway," 450
"Life's Railway to Heaven," 68
"Life Turned Her That Way," 268, 498
"Lightning Express," 296
"Lipstick," 567
"Listen to the Mockingbird," 22, 27, 147, 190
"Little Angels," 538
"Little Betty Brown," 194
"A Little Bitty Tear," 354
"The Little Black Mustache," 75
"Little Darling Pal of Mine," 80, 156
"The Little Girl and the Dreadful Snake," 402
"Little Glass of Wine," 404
"Little Green," 559
"Little Green Valley," 54
"Little Maggie," 43
"Little Man," 516
"Little Marian Parker," 56
"Little Matty Groves," 17
"The Little Old Log Cabin in the Lane," 19, 45,
    63
"The Little Paper Boy," 254
"Little Poplar Log House on the Hill," 81
"Little Rosewood Casket," 11
"Little Stream of Whiskey," 55, 66
"Little Village Churchyard," 81

"Little White Church," 399
"Little White Washed Chimney," 416
"Live and Let Live," 231
"Living the Dream," 562
"The Log Train," 280
"Lonely Mound of Clay," 226
"Lonely Women Make Good Lovers," 450
"Lonesome 7-7203," 334
"Lonesome Blue Yodel," 109
"The Lonesome River," 404
"Lonesome Road Blues," 43, 439
"Lonesome Wind Blues," 538
"Lone Star Beer and Bob Wills Music," 475
"Lone Star Rag," 204
"Lone Star Trail," 250
"The Long Black Veil," 333
"The Longest Train," 97
"Long Tall Sally," 295
"Long Time Gone," 296, 548, 572
"Looking Back to See," 302
"Looking for Love," 436
"Loose Talk," 268
"Lord Have Mercy on the Working Man,"
    516
"Lord Lovel," 3
"Lord Protect My Soul," 402
"Lord Randall," 17
"Lost Highway," 275, 351
"Louisiana Blue," 494
"Louisiana Man," 367, 369
"Love at the Five and Dime," 523
"Love Hurts," 456, 485
"Love in the Hot Afternoon," 482
"Love Is a Battlefield," 560
"Love It or Leave It," 376
"Love Letters in the Sand," 399, 423
"Love of the Common People," 471
"Lovesick Blues," 244, 284
"Lowe Bonnie," 123
"Lucille," 447
"Luckenbach, Texas," 352
"Lullaby Yodel," 102
"Lust Affair," 482

"MacArthur Park," 471, 560
"Maggie's Farm," 425
"Making Believe," 262
"Making Love Out of Nothing at All," 560
"Mama, He's Crazy," 494
"Mama, Tell Them What We're Fighting For,"
    355, 376

"Mamas, Don't Let Your Babies Grow Up to Be Cowboys," 477

"Mama Sang a Song," 352

"Mama's Hand," 537

"Mama's Opry," 524

"Mama Tried," 343, 346

"Man! I Feel Like a Woman," 554

"Man of Constant Sorrow"/"Farewell Song," 55, 330, 403, 471, 491

"Man of Galilee," 251

"A Man's Home Is His Castle," 509

"Maple on the Hill," 19, 145

"María Elena," 181

"Marie Laveau," 331

"The Marion Massacre," 157

"Marriage Vow," 278

"Mary Dear," 416

"Match Box Blues," 202

"Mathew 24," 258, 261

"Matterhorn," 413

"Matty Groves," 329

"Maybelline," 295

"Me and Billy the Kid," 520

"Me and Bobby McGee," 357, 423

"Mellow Mountain Moon," 177

"Me Neither," 517

"Mercury Blues," 516

"Merry Christmas from the Family," 499

"Mexican Joe," 305

"Mexican Love Songs," 360

"Miami, My Amy," 498

"The Midnight Choir," 450

"Midnight in Montgomery," 516

"Midnight on the Stormy Deep," 133

"Miller's Cave," 331, 455

"Milwaukee Blues," 61

"The Minutemen Are Turning in Their Graves," 376

"Mississippi, You're on My Mind," 373

"Mississippi Delta Blues," 205

"Mississippi Moon," 107

"Mississippi Sawyer," 22

"Miss the Mississippi and You," 106

"Mistreated Mama Blues," 71

"Molly, Put the Kettle On," 22

"Molly and Tenbrooks," 388, 404

"Molly Darling," 19

"Mommy, Please Stay Home with Me," 277

"Mommy for a Day," 353

"Moonlight and Skies," 107, 109

"More and More," 274

"Mother, I Thank You for the Bible You Gave," 229

"A Mountain Boy Makes His First Record," 67

"Mountain Dew," 256

"Mountain Music," 453

"Move It On Over," 283

"Moving Day," 61

"Movin' On," 347

"Mr. Bojangles," 454, 463

"Much Too Young (To Feel This Damn Old)," 501

"Muleskinner Blues," 94, 221, 366

"Murder on Music Row," 490, 513, 516

"My Baby Don't Dance to Nothing but Ernest Tubb," 520

"My Baby Thinks He's a Train," 459

"My Blue Heaven," 68

"My Brown-Eyed Texas Rose," 176

"My Bucket's Got a Hole in It," 282

"My Cabin in Caroline," 391

"My Carolina Sunshine Girl," 106

"My Confession," 205

"My Elusive Dreams," 364, 366

"My Favorite Picture of You," 462

"My God Is Real," 293

"My Heroes Have Always Been Cowboys," 477

"My Little Girl in Tennessee," 391, 394

"My Little Home in Tennessee," 315

"My Little Honeysuckle Rose," 406

"My Little Lady," 106, 107

"My Little Old Sod Shanty on My Claim," 83

"My Long Journey Home," 138

"My Mary," 176, 194

"My Million Dollar Smile," 154

"My Mother Was a Lady," 19

"My Old Pal of Yesterday," 170

"My Pretty Quadroon," 178

"My Rough and Rowdy Ways," 106

"My Shoes Keep Walking Back to You," 300, 339

"My Special Angel," 299–300

"Mystery Train," 447

"My Wife Thinks You're Dead," 520

"Nancy Rollin," 62

"Natchez Under the Hill," 22

"Never No Mo' Blues," 106

"New Deal Blues," 159

"New London Texas School Tragedy," 155

"New Muleskinner Blues," 386

"A New Salty Dog," 124

"New San Antonio Rose," 146

"Night Life," 354

"Night Rider's Lament," 477, 502, 508

"Nine Pound Hammer," 138

"Ninety-Nine Year Blues," 107

"Nobody Answered Me," 404

"Nobody's Darling on Earth," 19, 70

"No Hard Times," 154

"No Help Wanted," 263

"No Money in This Deal," 337

"No One Will Ever Know," 228

"The North Carolina Textile Strike," 157

"No Time to Cry," 525

"NRA Blues," 159

"The Object of My Affection," 194

"Ocean of Diamonds," 403

"O Death," 532

"Ode to Billie Joe," 355

"Ode to the Little Brown Shack Out Back," 355

"Oh Lonesome Me," 303

"Oh So Many Years," 252

"Okie from Muskogee," 376–377, 438, 518, 566

"Oklahoma Hills," 156–157, 233

"Old Age Pension Check," 159

"Old Apache Squaw," 332

"The Old Country Church," 182

"Old Dan Tucker," 10, 22

"Old Dogs, Children, and Watermelon Wine," 356

"An Old Flame Burning in Your Heart," 453

"The Old Hen Cackled and the Rooster's Going to Crow," 45, 49

"Old Hippie," 494

"Old Love Letters," 172

"Old Molly Hare," 22

"Old Pal of My Heart," 106

"Old Rattler," 69, 256

"Old Reuben," 133

"The Old Rugged Cross," 15

"Old Salty Dog Blues," 391

"Old Shep," 242

"Old Soldiers Never Die," 375

"The Old Spinning Wheel," 178

"Old Zip Coon," 10, 22

"Ole Man Atom," 375

"Ole Slew Foot," 332

"Omie Wise," 17, 43, 329

"Once a Day," 353, 359

"Once in a Blue Moon," 493

"Once More," 401

"One Bud Wiser," 555

"One Day at a Time," 352

"One Has My Name (The Other Has My Heart)," 171, 275

"One Mint Julep," 289

"The One Rose," 106

"One's on the Way," 362

"Oney," 378

"On Jordan's Stormy Banks," 13

"Only One Step More," 137

"Only You," 534

"On the Dixie Bee Line," 87

"On the Old Kentucky Shore," 402

"On the Other Hand," 496

"On the Wings of a Dove," 306

"Onward Christian Soldiers," 14

"Optimistic," 303

"Orange Blossom Special," 147, 385

"The Other Woman," 351

"Our Baby's Book," 220

"Out Behind the Barn," 263

"Out in the Parking Lot," 559

"Out of Control," 351

"Out of Control Raging Fire," 516

"Over and Over," 550

"Over the Waves"/"Sobre las olas," 23

"Pan American Blues," 89

"Pan American Man," 126

"Pancho and Lefty," 461, 523

"Pass Me By," 369, 479

"Pastures of Plenty," 156

"Patty on the Turnpike," 22

"Paying for That Back Street Affair," 261–262, 274

"Peace in the Valley," 243, 263

"Peach Picking Time in Georgia," 107

"Pearl Bryan," 55

"Phantom 309," 378

"The Philadelphia Lawyer," 156–157, 255

"Pickin' Time," 297

"Pick Me Up on Your Way Down," 300, 353

"The Pill," 362, 554

"Pinball Boogie," 242–243

"Pins and Needles in My Heart," 228

"Pistol Packin' Mama," 106, 212, 231

"The Pittsburg Stealers," 450–451

"Play Me a Real Country Song," 522

"Please Help Me, I'm Falling," 301

"Please Paint a Rose on the Garden Wall," 279

"Poison Love," 254

"Poor Ellen Smith," 258, 413

"Poor Man, Rich Man," 158

"Prairie Lullaby," 108

"Preacher and the Bear," 398

"Preach the Gospel," 253

"The Precious Jewel," 226

"Precious Lord, Take My Hand," 154–155

"Precious Memories," 15

"Pretty Boy Floyd," 455

"Pretty Polly," 77, 140, 515

"Pretty Saro," 525

"Prisoned Cowboy," 109, 278

"Prisoner at the Bar," xiii–xiv, 67

"Prisoner's Dream," 133

"The Prisoner's Song," 73, 74, 75

"Prosperity Special," 204

"Proud Mary," 425

"PT 109," 333, 349

"Puppy Love," 366

"Purple People Eater," 320

"Purple Robe," 250

"Put Me in Your Pocket," 192

"Put My Little Shoes Away," 529

"The Race Is On," 337

"Ragged but Right," 63, 132

"Ragtime Annie," 23, 190

"Railroad Blues," 85

"Railroad Boomer," 166

"Rainbow, My Pretty Rainbow," 23

"Rainin' You," 559

"The Randall Knife," 462

"Rank Stranger," 404

"Rattlesnake Daddy," 131

"Reasons Why," 541

"Red Apple Rag," 148

"Red Hot Mama," 228

"Rednecks, White Socks, and Blue Ribbon Beer," 376

"Red Nightgown Blues," 127

"Red Sails in the Sunset," 63–64

"The Red We Want Is the Red We've Got (in the Old Red, White, and Blue)," 375

"Red Wing," 23

"Release Me," 266

"Remember Me When the Candle Lights Are Gleaming," 139, 267

"Reno Blues," 255

"Reuben James," 446

"Ridin' Down the Canyon," 171

"Right or Wrong," 205, 480–481

"River of Death," 402

"Rock All Our Babies to Sleep," 63, 105

"Rock Around the Clock," 290

"Rocking Alone in an Old Rocking Chair," 57

"The Rock Island Line," 330

"Rock It," 295

"Rock Salt and Nails," 415

"Rocky Top," 251, 352, 418

"Roll in My Sweet Baby's Arms," 138, 391

"Roll the Union On," 153

"Roly Poly," 205

"The Roots of My Raising," 346

"A Rose and a Baby Ruth," 299

"Rosebuds and You," 7

"Rose Colored Glasses," 479

"Rose Conley," 383

"Rose Marie," 279–280

"Rose of Old Pawnee," 205

"Rotation Blues," 374

"Rounder's Luck"/"House of the Rising Sun," 131

"The Round-up in Cheyenne," 171

"Rowan County Troubles," 18

"Rub It In," 443

"Ruby," 401

"Ruby, Don't Take Your Love to Town," 446

"Ruby"/"Ruby, Are You Mad at Your Man?," 139

"Rudolph the Red-Nosed Reindeer," 108, 220

"Run Mountain," 145

"Saginaw, Michigan," 333, 353

"Sailor's Hornpipe," 409

"Sailor's Plea," 107

"St. Louis Blues," 130, 195, 205

"St. Louis Tickle," 190

"Sallie Gooden," 27, 42, 43

"Sally Gooden," 394

"Salty Dog Blues," 146, 221

"Sam Bass," 166

"The Same Old Me," 339, 479

"Same Sweet Girl," 275

"San Antonio Rose," 181, 188, 205–206

"Satan and the Saint," 253

"Satan Lied to Me," 253

"Satin Sheets," 361

"Satisfied," 257

"A Satisfied Mind," 316, 322, 455

"Scarlet Ribbons," 471

"Searching for a Soldier's Grave," 230

"Second Fiddle," 342

"Secret Love," 279

"Send Me the Pillow That You Dream On," 275

"Serves 'Em Fine," 158

"Set Him Free," 303

"Seven Year Ache," 459

"Sexy Lady," 444

"Shame on You," 233, 236

"Shanghai Rooster Yodel," 126

"She Never Spoke Spanish to Me," 520

"She's All I Got," 473

"She's Everything," 559

"She's My Curly Headed Baby," 131

"She Thinks His Name Was John," 509

"She Thinks I Still Care," 338

"She Went Out for Cigarettes," 554

"Shine On," 479

"The Ship That Never Returned," 19

"Short Life of Trouble," 55

"Shotgun Boogie," 265

"Signed, Sealed and Delivered," 267

"Silver Dew on the Blue Grass Tonight," 229

"Silver Threads among the Gold," 82

"Sin City," 456

"Sing a Sad Song," 345, 347

"Singing Teacher in Heaven," 286

"Singing the Blues," 295

"The Singing Waterfall," 258

"Single Ladies (Put a Ring on It)," 549

"Sing Me Back Home," 346, 350

"Sink the Bismarck," 332

"Sioux City Sue," 234

"Sir Hugh, or the Jew's Daughter," 18

"Sittin' on Top of the World," 202, 205

"Six Days on the Road," 378

"Six More Miles to the Graveyard," 258, 283

"Sixteen Tons," 238, 295

"Skip a Rope," 351

"Sleep, Baby, Sleep," 97, 106

"Sleeping at the Foot of the Bed," 263

"Slipping Around," 198, 269, 275

"Slow Hand," 449

"Slowly," 274

"Slow Wicked Blues," 123

"Smoke on the Water," 229

"Smoke! Smoke! Smoke!," 236

"Smoky Mountain Memories," 482

"Snakes Crawl at Night," 372

"Snowbird," 445

"Snow Deer," 23

"Snowing on Raton," 461

"So Blue," 295

"Sobre las olas"/"Over the Waves," 23

"Soldier's Joy," 22, 125, 333

"Soldier's Last Letter," 230

"The Soldier's Sweetheart," 97

"Somebody Lied," 498

"Somebody's Back in Town," 498

"Somebody Should Leave," 495

"Someday Soon," 477, 508

"Some Old Day," 394

"Someone Is Looking for Someone Like You," 358

"Something Got a Hold of Me," 16

"Something in the Rain," 524

"Something to Brag About," 356

"The Son of Hickory Holler's Tramp," 350

"Sophronie," 403

"So Round, So Firm, So Fully Packed," 236–237

"Sourwood Mountain," 22

"The Southern Cannonball," 106, 107

"Southern Moon," 129

"The South's Gonna Do It Again," 457

"Sparkling Brown Eyes," 159, 273, 410

"Stand By Me," 154

"Stand by Your Man," 363, 364

"Standing on the Corner," 104

"Stardust," 467

"Stars and Stripes on Iwo Jima," 230

"Stars in the Water," 462

"The Star-Spangled Banner," 468

"Statue of a Fool," 498

"Stay All Night," 475

"Stay in the Wagon Yard," 8, 202

"Steal Away," 243, 263

"Steel Guitar Rag," 204

"Steel Rail Blues," 330

"Step It Up and Go," 131, 255

"Stern Old Bachelor," 83

"Still," 352

"Still in Saigon," 457

"Stompin' at the Honky Tonk," 183

"The Stone Was Rolled Away," 250

"Stormy Horizons," 417

"The Story of My Life," 299, 308

"The Strawberry Roan," 165

"Strawberry Roan," 178

"Streets of Bakersfield," 497

"Streets of Laredo," 476

"Stuck Up Blues," 226, 249

"Stuff That Works," 462

"Subterranean Homesick Blues," 542

"Sunday Morning Coming Down," 357

"Sunny Side of the Mountain," 142, 393

"Sunrise," 279

"Superman," 550

"Sweet Becky Walker," 450

"Sweeter Than the Flowers," 270

"The Sweetest Gift," 251

"Sweethearts in Heaven," 397

"Sweet Temptation," 237

"Sweet Thing," 142

"Swinging," 483

"Swinging Doors," 346

"Sydney Allen," 75

"Take an Old Cold Tater and Wait," 263

"Take a Whiff on Me" ("Take a Drink on Me"), 125

"Take Me as I Am," 251, 268

"Take Me Back and Try Me One More Time," 220

"Take Me Back to Tulsa," 204, 231

"Take Me in the Lifeboat," 145

"Take This Job and Shove It," 378, 473

"Talking Dust Bowl Blues," 156

"TB Blues," 102, 107

"Teach Your Children," 425

"Teardrops Falling in the Snow," 230, 258

"Tears Can Never Drown the Flame," 279

"Tecumseh Valley," 461, 523

"Tell Her Lies," 529

"Temporary Home," 556

"Tender Years," 338

"Tennessee Flat Top Box," 459

"Tennessee Mountain Home," 366

"Tennessee River," 453

"Tennessee Saturday Night," 242

"Tennessee Stud," 333

"Tennessee Wagoner," 22

"The Tennessee Waltz," 248, 287, 298, 310

"Ten Thousand Drums," 333

"Texas 1947," 461

"Texas Plains," 176

"Texas Rangers," 165, 166

"Texas Sand," 199, 273

"T for Texas," 256

"Thank God I'm a Country Boy," 8, 445

"Thank You for Calling," 250

"That Heart Belongs to Me," 274

"That Little Boy of Mine," 133, 242

"That Old-Time Religion," 16

"That's All Right, Mama," 291, 295, 308

"That Silver Haired Daddy of Mine," 170

"That's the Way Love Goes," 477

"Theme from Exodus," 413

"Then and Only Then," 359

"There'll Be No Distinction There," 56

"There'll Come a Time," 137

"There's a Home in Wyoming," 177

"There's a Star-Spangled Banner Waving Somewhere," 229, 232

"There's More Pretty Girls Than One," 148

"There Stands the Glass," 274

"They Ain't Makin' Jews Like Jesus Anymore," 566

"They Can Only Fill One Grave," 226

"They Cut Down the Old Pine Tree," 178

"They'll Never Take Her Love from Me," 275

"They're All Going Home but One," 133

"They're Tearing the Labor Camps Down," 346

"They Say It Is Sinful to Flirt," 413

"They Took the Stars Out of Heaven," 197, 213, 230, 269

"Thirty Pieces of Silver," 250, 261

"This Cold War with You," 197

"This Land Is Your Land," 156

"This Old House," 263

"This World Can't Stand Long," 254

"This World Is Not My Home," 15, 16

"Those Brown Eyes," 142

"The Three Bells," 302

"Three Times Seven," 236–237

"The Thunder Rolls," 508

"Thunderstorms and Neon Signs," 522

"Tight Fittin' Jeans," 449

"Till I Get It Right," 363

"'Til I Gain Control Again," 562

"Time Changes Everything," 205

"The Tip of My Fingers," 353

"'Tis Sweet to Be Remembered," 133

"The Titanic," 59

"Tobacco Road," 355

"To Daddy," 366

"Today I Started Loving You Again," 346

"Together Again," 343

"Tombstone Every Mile," 378

"Tom Cat and Pussy Blues," 127

"Tom Cat Blues," 126

"Tom Dooley," 43, 326, 331

"Tonight the Heartache's on Me," 512

"Too Cold at Home," 516

"Too Late," 274

"Too Old to Cut the Mustard," 263

"Touch My Heart," 473

"The Tragic Romance," 256, 267
"The Train Carrying Jimmie Rodgers Home," 100
"Tramp on the Street," 16, 155, 258, 261
"Traveling Blues," 107, 196, 273
"Traveling Man," 366
"Treasures Untold," 104
"Trip to Hyden," 356
"Trouble in Mind," 205
"Truck Driver's Blues," 197, 378
"Truck Driver's Coffee Stop," 171
"Truck Driving Man," 378
"Trying to Love Two Women," 452
"Tumbling Tumbleweeds," 176
"Turkey in the Straw," 22, 229
"Turtles All the Way Down," 562
"20/20 Vision," 402
"Twenty-One Years," 57, 133

"Unanswered Prayers," 502
"Uncle Pen," 383, 393, 402
"Under the Double Eagle," 23, 200
"Unloved and Unclaimed," 226
"Untold Stories," 526

"Vietnam Blues," 376
"Vigilante Man," 156
"The Village Churchyard," 403
"Voice from on High," 402

"The Wabash Cannonball," 80, 225
"The Wagoner's Lad," 67
"Waiting for a Train," 102, 106
"Waitin' on a Woman," 559
"Wake Up, Little Susie," 296
"Walking after Midnight," 309
"Walking My Lord Up Calvary's Hill," 261
"Walking the Floor over You," 184, 186, 220, 230
"Walk the Way the Wind Blows," 526
"Walk through This World with Me," 338
"Waltz of the Angels," 345
"The Waltz You Saved for Me," 194, 483
"Wanted Man," 425
"Warm Red Wine," 250, 351
"Wasted Days and Wasted Nights," 369
"Watermelon Crawl," 505
"Way Down the Old Plank Road," 87
"Wayfaring Stranger," 570
"The Way It Was in '51," 272
"Way Out West in Kansas," 54

"Wealth Won't Save Your Soul," 283
"Weary Blues," 339
"Weave Room Blues," 130, 157
"We Could," 251, 268
"Wedding Bells," 249
"A Week in a Country Jail," 356
"Welfare Cadilac" [*sic*], 238, 376
"We'll Meet Again, Sweetheart," 229, 391
"We'll Sweep Out the Ashes," 485
"We'll Understand It Better By and By," 154
"We Must Have Been Out of Our Minds," 335
"We Parted by the Riverside," 19, 59
"West Side of Town," 524
"West Texas Waltz," 520
"The West Virginia Polka," 261
"What about You," 249, 254, 268
"Whatever Happened to Peace on Earth?," 554
"Whatever Happened to Randolph Scott," 452
"What's Made Milwaukee Famous," 294
"What's Wrong with the Way That We're Doing It Now," 440–441
"What Would You Give in Exchange for Your Soul?," 15, 137
"Wheels," 456
"When God Comes and Gathers His Jewels," 258, 283
"When Heaven Comes Down," 252
"When I Call Your Name," 502
"When I Found You," 494
"When I Grow Too Old to Dream," 279
"When I Stop Dreaming," 253
"When It's Springtime in Alaska," 331–332
"When It's Time for the Whippoorwill to Sing," 129
"When My Blue Moon Turns to Gold Again," 229, 230–231
"When My Sugar Walks Down the Street," 213
"When That Hell Bomb Falls," 374–375
"When the Bloom Is on the Sage," 177
"When the Cactus Is in Bloom," 106, 108
"When the Roses Bloom Again," 132–133
"When the Saints Go Marching In," 16
"When the White Azaleas Start Blooming," 57
"When the Work's All Done This Fall," 163
"When the World Has Turned You Down," 220
"When Two Worlds Collide," 352
"When You Come Back Down," 526, 541–542
"When You Say Nothing at All," 498
"When You Wore a Tulip," 82
"Where Have All the Heroes Gone," 376

"Where the Old Red River Flows," 127

"Where the River Shannon Flows," 123

"Where the Roses Never Fade," 15

"Where We'll Never Grow Old," 15

"Where Were You When the World Stopped Turning?," 507

"Which One Is to Blame," 340

"Which Side Are You On?," 153

"Whipping That Old TB," 102

"The Whiskey Ain't Working," 516

"Whiskey Bent and Hell Bound," 457

"Whiskey Is the Devil," 252

"Whistling Rufus," 22

"White Cross on Okinawa," 230

"The White Dove," 405

"White Freightliner Blues," 461, 523

"White House Blues," 380

"White Lightning," 337

"White Line Fever," 347, 378

"A White Sport Coat," 299, 308

"Whoa Sailor," 266

"Whole Lotta Shakin' Goin' On," 294

"Who'll Turn Out the Lights," 479

"Whose Heart Are You Breaking Now," 205

"Whose Shoulder Will You Cry On," 262

"Who's Gonna Fill Their Shoes," 496

"Who's Gonna Mow Your Grass," 342–343

"Who Shot Sam," 337

"Who Wouldn't Be Lonely," 202

"Why Baby Why," 337

"Why Do You Bob Your Hair, Girls," 49, 55

"Why Not Confess," 137

"Wichita Lineman," 318

"The Wife of Usher's Well," 67

"Wild Bill Jones," 403

"Wild One," 510

"The Wild Side of Life," 261, 266

"Wildwood Flower," 11, 79, 80, 200

"Willie Moore," 55

"Wills Breakdown," 205

"Will the Circle Be Unbroken," 81

"Will the Roses Bloom," 486

"Will You Be Loving Another Man," 387

"The Window Up Above," 338

"Wishful Thinking," 345

"Without a Fight," 559

"Wolverton Mountain," 333

"Woman's Suffrage," 69

"Wondering," 273

"Won't You Ride in My Little Red Wagon," 144

"Working Class Hero," 515, 516

"Working Man's Blues," 377

"Worried Blues," 149

"Worried Man Blues," 81

"Worried Mind," 197, 230

"Would You Lay with Me (in a Field of Stone)," 360

"The WPA Blues," 282

"Wreck of the Number Nine," 54

"The Wreck of the Old 97," 17, 43, 73–74, 75

"Wreck of the Tennessee Gravy Train," 87

"The Wreck of the Virginian," 55

"Wreck on the Highway," 130

"XXX's and OOO's (An American Girl)," 549

"Y'all Come," 337

"Y'all Come Back Saloon," 452

"The Year That Clayton Delaney Died," 356

"Yellow Rose of Texas," 10

"Yes Sir, That's My Baby," 226

"The Yodeling Ranger," 99, 107

"You Ain't Just Whistlin' Dixie," 494

"You Ain't Woman Enough (to Take My Man)," 362

"You Are My Sunshine," 126, 207

"You Better Not Do That," 342

"You Can Fly," 509

"You Don't Know Me," 250

"You Don't Know My Mind," 396

"You Gotta Have a License," 342

"You'll Still Have a Place in My Heart," 275

"You Needed Me," 445

"You Never Even Call Me by My Name," 473, 512

"You Never Mentioned Him to Me," 398

"Young Love," 296, 299

"Your Cheatin' Heart," 283

"You're in My Heart," 337

"You're the Only Star in My Blue Heaven," 274

"Your Good Girl's Gonna Go Bad," 362–363, 364

"Your Lying Blue Eyes," 483

"You've Never Been This Far Before," 444, 449

"You Will Never Miss Your Mother Until She Is Gone," 68

"Zeb Turney's Girl," 54